The
Encyclopaedia of
**FORMS
AND
PRECEDENTS**

Fifth Edition
2004 Reissue

Volume 22(2)A

The
Encyclopaedia of
FORMS
AND
PRECEDENTS

Fifth Edition
2004 Reissue

The Rt. Hon. Lord Millett, P.C.

A Lord of Appeal in Ordinary

Editor–in–Chief

Volume 22(2)A

Landlord and Tenant (Business Tenancies)

Whole Leases

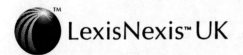
LexisNexis™ UK

Members of the LexisNexis Group worldwide

United Kingdom	LexisNexis UK, a Division of Reed Elsevier (UK) Ltd, Halsbury House, 35 Chancery Lane, LONDON, WC2A 1EL, and 4 Hill Street, EDINBURGH EH2 3JZ
Argentina	LexisNexis Argentina, BUENOS AIRES
Australia	LexisNexis Butterworths, CHATSWOOD, New South Wales
Austria	LexisNexis Verlag ARD Orac GmbH & Co KG, VIENNA
Canada	LexisNexis Butterworths, MARKHAM, Ontario
Chile	LexisNexis Chile Ltda, SANTIAGO DE CHILE
Czech Republic	Nakladatelství Orac sro, PRAGUE
France	Editions du Juris-Classeur SA, PARIS
Germany	LexisNexis Deutschland GmbH, FRANKFURT, MUNSTER
Hong Kong	LexisNexis Butterworths, HONG KONG
Hungary	HVG-Orac, BUDAPEST
India	LexisNexis Butterworths, NEW DELHI
Ireland	LexisNexis, DUBLIN
Italy	Giuffrè Editore, MILAN
Malaysia	Malayan Law Journal Sdn Bhd, KUALA LUMPUR
New Zealand	LexisNexis Butterworths, WELLINGTON
Poland	Wydawnictwo Prawnicze LexisNexis, WARSAW
Singapore	LexisNexis Butterworths, SINGAPORE
South Africa	LexisNexis Butterworths, DURBAN
Switzerland	Stämpfli Verlag AG, BERNE
USA	LexisNexis, DAYTON, Ohio

© Reed Elsevier (UK) Ltd 1997, 2004
Published by LexisNexis UK

A CIP Catalogue record for this book is available from the British Library.

First Edition: Published between 1902 and 1909

Second Edition: Published in 1925 and 1926

Third Edition: Published between 1939 and 1950

Fourth Edition: Published between 1964 and 1983

Fifth Edition: Published from 1985 with selective reissues between 1993 and 2004

ISBN *for complete set of volumes:* 0 406 02360 3
ISBN for this volume: 0 406 97606 6

ISBN 0-406-97606-6

9 780406 976062

Set in 10 on 11 pt Bembo.
Printed and bound in Great Britain by Antony Rowe Ltd, Chippenham, Wiltshire

Visit LexisNexis UK at www.lexisnexis.co.uk

Editor–in–Chief

THE RT. HON. LORD MILLETT, P.C.

A Lord of Appeal in Ordinary

Consulting Editors

For Land Registry matters:

RICHARD FEARNLEY, B.A., Solicitor

Land Registrar,
Her Majesty's Land Registry

For Direct Taxation matters:

JOHN JEFFREY-COOK, C.T.A. (Fellow), F.C.A., F.C.I.S.

Contributor

LANDLORD AND TENANT (BUSINESS TENANCIES)

ANDREW WHITTAKER, LL.B., Solicitor

Volume 22(2)A

2004 Reissue

No volume should be discarded on receipt of this volume. Please retain volume 22(2) (1997 Reissue) until publication of volume 22(2)B LANDLORD AND TENANT (BUSINESS TENANCIES) in November 2004.

> For current information on the titles published in the Encyclopaedia, subscribers should refer to the *List of Titles*, in the Information Binder of the looseleaf Service, which will always represent the most recent position of titles.

This volume will be kept up to date by material in the Fifth Edition Service which is issued quarterly and which should be filed in the appropriate Fifth Edition Service Binders.

Summary of Titles

(For full details of the contents of the volume see the Table of Contents to the title and the index to the volume)

reference no

LANDLORD AND TENANT (BUSINESS TENANCIES) . . . . [1]

Volume 22(2)A LANDLORD AND TENANT (BUSINESS TENANCIES) contains revised and updated precedents reflecting the legislative and judicial developments and changes in practice that have taken place since the publication of volume 22(2) (1997 Reissue) in connection with the letting and occupation of business premises.

The volume contains forms of licence and tenancy at will. It also contains whole leases of the most commonly encountered types of business property – industrial and warehouse buildings, shops and offices – in a wide variety of situations from stand-alone units with and without ancillary rights to premises forming part of multi-occupied buildings. In addition, specimen leases of a hotel and a commercial car park are included. The forms are drafted so as to strike a reasonably fair balance between the interests of the landlord and of the tenant, although issues that may be of particular concern to one party or the other are highlighted where appropriate with practical guidance as to how they may best be resolved. Practical guidance is also provided in relation to the impact of issues such as land registration and 1954 Act exclusion.

The legislative changes covered include:
- the Contracts (Rights of Third Parties) Act 1999;
- the Enterprise Act 2002;
- the Land Registration Act 2002;
- the Land Registration Rules 2003; and
- the Regulatory Reform (Business Tenancies) (England and Wales) Order 2003.

Changes in practice are also dealt with and current trends in relation to alienation and the allocation of uninsured risk are reflected. The terms and impact of The Code of Practice for Commercial Leases in England and Wales (2nd edition) in these and other respects are comprehensively covered.

A new feature of this reissue is the inclusion of an integral contents table with each precedent to enable the user to navigate around the clauses.

Volume 22(2)B will be published in November 2004 and contains precedent variations for status or interest of the parties and also leases by way of reference. A major new section is added containing a number of whole subleases. Until publication of volume 22(2)B, subscribers should **retain** volume 22(2) (1997 Reissue) as Form 46 onwards may still be used.

INDEX. . . . . **[2996]**

TABLE OF STATUTES

References are to the numbers in square brackets which appear
on the right-hand side of the text

reference no

Arbitration Act 1996 . . . . 257, 436,
626, 826, 1035, 1196,
1426, 1707, 1906, 2195
Clean Air Act 1993 . .322, 505, 674, 884, 2218
Contracts (Rights of Third Parties) Act
1999 . . . . . . 311, 491, 653,
873, 1059, 1233, 1471,
1739, 1951, 2212, 2368
Defective Premises Act 1972 . . 237, 419, 612,
806, 1018, 1176, 1406,
1689, 1878, 2180, 2350
s 4 (4) 201, 401, 593,
759, 989, 1140, 1370,
1650, 1853, 2152, 2339
Environmental Protection Act 1990 . . .324,
506, 675, 886
Finance Act 1985
s 93 . . . . . . 232, 414,
607, 801, 1013, 1171,
1401, 1684, 1873, 2175
Insolvency Act 1986 . . . 301, 467, 651,
871, 1057, 1231, 1457,
1737, 1937, 2210, 2366
Pt I, Pt II 302, 468, 652,
872, 1058, 1232, 1458,
1738, 1938, 2211, 2367
s 286 . . . . . . 302, 468, 652,
872, 1058, 1232, 1458,
1738, 1938, 2211, 2367
Pt IV–VI 302, 468, 652,
872, 1058, 1232, 1458,
1738, 1938, 2211, 2367
Pt VIII, Pt IX 302, 468,
652, 872, 1058, 1232, 1458,
1738, 1938, 2211, 2367
Sch 1B
para 43 (4), (6) . . . 302, 468, 652,
872, 1058, 1232, 1458,
1738, 1938, 2211, 2367
Interpretation Act 1978
s 17, 23 (3) 169, 377, 569,
735, 967, 1121, 1327,
1618, 1821, 2117, 2314
Land Registration Act 2002 . . 155, 355, 555,
705, 954, 1106, 1305,
1605, 1806, 2105, 2305
s 4 (1) (c) 157, 357, 557,
707, 956, 1108, 1307,
1607, 1808, 2107, 2307
s 6 . . . . . . 159, 359, 559,
709, 957, 1110, 1310,
1609, 1810, 2108, 2308
27 (2) (b) (i) 157, 357, 557,
707, 956, 1108, 1307,
1607, 1808, 2107, 2307

reference no

Landlord and Tenant Act 1927 . . 216, 407, 600,
786, 1006, 1155, 1386,
1677, 1859, 2168, 2346
Pt I (ss 1–17) 197, 398,
590, 757, 987, 1138,
1368, 1648, 1849, 2149
s 9 . . . . 197, 398,
590, 757, 987, 1138,
1368, 1648, 1849, 2149
19 (1) 212, 402, 594, 1151, 1382,
1672, 1854, 2162, 2341
(1A) 212, 213, 214, 402,
403, 404, 405, 406, 594,
595, 596, 598, 599, 782,
783, 784, 785, 1002, 1003,
1004, 1005, 1151, 1152,
1153, 1154, 1382, 1383,
1384, 1385, 1672, 1673,
1675, 1676, 1854, 1855,
1856, 1858, 1859, 2162,
2163, 2164, 2166, 2167,
2341, 2342, 2344, 2345
(2) 197, 398, 590, 757, 987,
1368, 1648, 1849, 2149
Landlord and Tenant Act 1954 166,
261, 321, 374, 440,
503, 566, 609, 629, 673,
732, 830, 882, 964, 1039,
1064, 1117, 1173, 1200,
1241, 1324, 1430, 1493,
1615, 1711, 1761, 1817,
1872, 1911, 1973, 2115,
2177, 2199, 2216, 2313
Pt II (ss 23–46) . . . 4, 54, 61, 104, 218,
409, 602, 788, 1008,
1157, 1388, 1679, 1861
s 24–28 . . . .4, 159, 172, 217, 219, 235,
284, 285, 315, 359, 379,
408, 410, 417, 464, 465,
495, 496, 559, 571, 601,
603, 610, 644, 645, 657,
659, 707, 737, 787, 789,
804, 854, 855, 877, 878,
957, 969, 1007, 1009,
1016, 1054, 1055, 1063,
1110, 1123, 1156, 1158,
1174, 1224, 1225, 1237,
1238, 1310, 1343, 1387,
1389, 1404, 1454, 1455,
1475, 1476, 1609, 1620,
1678, 1680, 1687, 1734,
1735, 1743, 1810, 1823,
1860, 1862, 1876, 1934,

reference no

Landlord and Tenant Act 1954—*cont*
s 24–28—*cont.* . . 1935, 1956, 1957, 2108,
2120, 2169, 2170, 2171,
2178, 2207, 2208, 2215,
2308, 2315, 2348, 2371
25 . . . . 231, 413,
606, 792, 1012, 1161,
1392, 1683, 2174, 2347
37 . . . . 312, 492, 654,
874, 1060, 1234, 1472,
1740, 1952, 2213, 2369
38A 219, 410,
603, 789, 1009, 1158,
1389, 1680, 1862, 2171
(1) 159, 172,
315, 359, 379, 496, 559,
571, 659, 709, 737, 957,
969, 1063, 1110, 1123,
1238, 1310, 1343, 1476,
1609, 1620, 1743, 1810,
1823, 1957, 2108, 2120,
2215, 2308, 2315, 2371
(3) 315, 496, 659,
878, 1063, 1238, 1476,
1743, 1957, 2215, 2371
42 . . . . . 171, 212, 221, 358, 379,
403, 412, 558, 570, 595,
604, 708, 737, 782, 791,
969, 1002, 1010, 1109,
1123, 1151, 1159, 1308,
1309, 1342, 1382, 1391,
1619, 1672, 1682, 1809,
1822, 1855, 1863, 2119,
2163, 2172, 2341, 2346
43 (3) 4, 104
49 . . . 197, 757, 987, 1368, 1849, 2149
Landlord and Tenant Act 1988 . 216, 407, 600,
786, 1006, 1155, 1386,
1677, 1859, 2168, 2346
s 4 . . . . 239, 421, 614,
807, 1019, 1178, 1408,
1691, 1880, 2182, 2351
Landlord and Tenant (Covenants) Act
1995 . . . . . 165, 166, 213, 219,
373, 374, 404, 410, 565,
566, 597, 603, 731, 732,
783, 789, 822, 963, 964,
1003, 1009, 1116, 1117,
1152, 1158, 1323, 1324,
1383, 1389, 1422, 1456,
1614, 1615, 1674, 1680,
1816, 1817, 1857, 1862,
1902, 2114, 2115, 2165,
2171, 2312, 2313, 2343
1 (4) 314, 495, 658,
877, 1062, 1238, 1476,
1743, 1957, 2215, 2371
3 . . . . 281, 461,
641, 851, 1051, 1221,
1451, 1731, 1931, 2204

reference no

Landlord and Tenant (Covenants) Act 1995—*cont*
s 8 . . . . 239, 421, 614,
807, 1019, 1178, 1408,
1691, 1880, 2182, 2351
11 . . . . . . 214, 405, 598,
784, 1004, 1153, 1384,
1675, 1858, 2166, 2344
(2) 215, 406, 599,
785, 1005, 1154, 1385,
1676, 1859, 2167, 2345
16 (3) (a) 218, 409,
602, 788, 1008, 1157,
1388, 1679, 1861, 2170
(6) 215, 406, 599,
785, 1005, 1154, 1385,
1676, 1859, 2167, 2345
18 . . . . . . 283, 463,
643, 853, 1053, 1223,
1453, 1733, 1933, 2206
19 . . . . . . 314, 495,
658, 877, 1062, 1238,
1743, 1957, 2215, 2371
20 (1), (2) 314, 495, 658,
877, 1062, 1238, 1476,
1743, 1957, 2215, 2371
25 . . . . . 239, 286, 421, 466,
614, 646, 807, 856, 1019,
1056, 1178, 1226, 1408,
1456, 1691, 1736, 1880,
1936, 2182, 2209, 2351
26 (1) (a) 239, 421, 614,
807, 1019, 1178, 1408,
1691, 1880, 2182, 2351
27 . . . . . . 286, 466,
646, 856, 1056, 1226,
1456, 1736, 1936, 2209
28 (1) 172, 379, 571,
737, 969, 1123, 1343,
1620, 1823, 2120, 2315
Law of Property Act 1925
s 38 . . 495, 658, 877, 1237, 1475, 1956
61 . . . . . . 160, 360, 560,
710, 958, 1111, 1311,
1610, 1811, 2109, 2309
62 . . 494, 656, 876, 1236, 1474, 1955
140 . . . . . . 282, 462,
642, 852, 1052, 1222,
1452, 1732, 1932, 2205
141 (1) 281, 461,
641, 851, 1051, 1221,
1451, 1731, 1931, 2204
146 . . . . 54, 231,
282, 413, 462, 606,
642, 792, 852, 1012,
1052, 1161, 1222, 1392,
1452, 1683, 1732, 1872,
1932, 2174, 2205, 2347
147 . . . . . . 231, 413, 606,
792, 1012, 1161, 1392,
1683, 1872, 2174, 2347

reference no

Leasehold Property (Repairs) Act
1938 . . . . . . 201, 401, 593,
759, 989, 1140, 1370,
1650, 1853, 2152, 2339
Mental Health Act 1983 . . . . 238, 419,
612, 806, 1018, 1176,
1406, 1689, 1879, 2180
Planning and Compensation
Act 1991 . . . . . 168, 375, 567,
733, 965, 1119, 1325,
1616, 1819, 2115, 2313
Planning (Consequential Provisions)
Act 1990 . . . . . . 168, 375, 567,
733, 965, 1119, 1325,
1616, 1819, 2115, 2313
Planning (Hazardous Substances)
Act 1990 . . . . . 168, 375, 567,
733, 965, 1119, 1325,
1616, 1819, 2115, 2313

reference no

Planning (Listed Buildings and Conservation Areas)
Act 1990 . . . . . . 168, 375, 567,
733, 965, 1119, 1325,
1616, 1819, 2115, 2313
Radioactive Substances Act 1993
s 18 . . . . . . 324, 506, 675, 886
Sunday Trading Act 1994
s 3 . . . . 1066, 1246, 1497
Town and Country Planning
Act 1990 . . . . . . 168, 375, 567,
733, 965, 1119, 1325,
1616, 1819, 2115, 2313
s 55 . . . . 160, 360, 560,
710, 958, 1111, 1311,
1610, 1811, 2109, 2309
Unfair Contract Terms Act 1977 . . . 283,
463, 643, 822, 853,
1053, 1223, 1422, 1453,
1733, 1902, 1933, 2206

TABLE OF
STATUTORY INSTRUMENTS

*References are to the numbers in square brackets which appear
on the right-hand side of the text*

reference no

Construction (Design and Management) Regulations
    1994, SI 1994/3140   .   . 199, 214, 399, 405,
            591, 598, 758, 784,
           988, 1004, 1139, 1153,
           1369, 1384, 1649, 1675,
           1851, 1858, 2151, 2166

Fire Precautions (Factories, Offices, Shops
  and Railway Premises) Order 1989,
  SI 1989/76   .   .   .   . . 63, 113

Land Registration Rules 2003, SI 2003/1417
  r 6 (2) 211, 402, 593,
           781, 1001, 1141, 1381,
           1671, 1853, 2161, 2340

  181 .   .   .   . 157, 357, 557,
           707, 956, 1108, 1307,
           1607, 1808, 2107, 2307

  203 .   .   .   . 221, 412, 604,
           791, 1010, 1159, 1390,
           1681, 1863, 2172, 2346

reference no

Regulatory Reform (Business Tenancies)
  (England and Wales) Order 2003,
  SI 2003/3096
  Sch 2   .   .   .   . 315, 496, 659,
           878, 1063, 1238, 1476,
           1743, 1957, 2215, 2371

Town and Country Planning (Control of
  Advertisements) Regulations 1992,
  SI 1992/666.   .   .   . 198, 398, 590,
           757, 987, 1138, 1368,
           1648, 1850, 2149, 2336

Town and Country Planning (Use Classes)
  Order 1987, SI 1987/764
  Schedule   .   .   . 167, 374, 567,
           733, 965, 1118, 1325

TABLE OF CASES

*References are to the numbers in square brackets which appear
on the right-hand side of the text*

reference no

A

Addiscombe Garden Estates Ltd v Crabbe [1958] 1 QB 513, [1957] 3 All ER 563,
  [1957] 3 WLR 980, 101 Sol Jo 959, 170 Estates Gazette 704, CA 11
Allied Dunbar Assurance plc v Homebase Ltd [2002] EWCA Civ 666,
  [2003] 1 P & CR 75, [2002] 2 EGLR 23, [2002] 27 EG 144, [2002] L & TR 27,
  [2002] 24 LS Gaz R 38 . . . . 218, 409, 602, 788,
                                                1008, 1157, 1388, 1679, 2170

B

Barton v Reed [1932] 1 Ch 362, 101 LJ Ch 219, [1931] All ER Rep 425, 146 LT 501 . . 56, 106, 166,
                                                374, 566, 732, 964, 1117,
                                                1324, 1615, 1817, 2115, 2313
Baxendale v North Lambeth Liberal and Radical Club Ltd [1902] 2 Ch 427, 71 LJ Ch 806,
  50 WR 650, 46 Sol Jo 616, 87 LT 161, 18 TLR 700 . . . . . . 501, 504, 671, 678,
                                                879, 887, 1239, 1491, 1971
Beacon Carpets Ltd v Kirby [1985] QB 755, [1984] 2 All ER 726, [1984] 3 WLR 489,
  48 P & CR 445, 128 Sol Jo 549, [1984] LS Gaz R 1603, CA 261, 440, 630, 830, 1039,
                                                1200, 1430, 1711, 1911, 2199
Berrycroft Management Co Ltd v Sinclair Gardens Investments (Kensington) Ltd
  (1996) 75 P & CR 210, 29 HLR 444, [1997] 1 EGLR 47, [1997] 22 EG 141,
  [1996] EGCS 143, CA 253, 433, 623, 824, 1033,
                                                1194, 1424, 1703, 1904, 2192
Bovis Group Pension Fund Ltd v GC Flooring & Furnishing Ltd [1984] 1 EGLR 123,
  269 Estates Gazette 1252, CA 311, 491, 653, 873, 1059, 1233,
                                                1471, 1739, 1951, 2212, 2368
Brett v Brett Essex Golf Club Ltd (1986) 52 P & CR 330, [1986] 1 EGLR 154,
  278 Estates Gazette 1476, CA 166, 374, 566, 732, 964, 1117,
                                                1324, 1615, 1817, 2115, 2313
British Anzani (Felixstowe) Ltd v International Marine Management (UK) Ltd
  [1980] QB 137, [1979] 2 All ER 1063, [1979] 3 WLR 451, 39 P & CR 189,
  123 Sol Jo 64, 250 Estates Gazette 1183 . . . . .191, 391, 583, 752, 982, 1132,
                                                1362, 1642, 1843, 2143, 2332
Bulstrode v Lambert [1953] 2 All ER 728, [1953] 1 WLR 1064, 97 Sol Jo 557 . . 501, 671, 879, 1239

C

Callard v Beeney [1930] 1 KB 353, 99 LJKB 133, 142 LT 45 . . . . . 501, 671, 879, 1239
Cellulose Acetate Silk Co Ltd v Widnes Foundry (1925) Ltd [1933] AC 20,
  101 LJKB 694, 38 Com Cas 61, [1932] All ER Rep 567, 147 LT 401,
  48 TLR 595, HL 162, 362, 562, 712, 960, 1113,
                                                1313, 1612, 1813, 2111, 2310
Celsteel Ltd v Alton House Holdings Ltd (No 2) [1987] 2 All ER 240,
  [1987] 1 WLR 291, 54 P & CR 171, 131 Sol Jo 166, [1987] 1 EGLR 48,
  [1987] LS Gaz R 741, 281 Estates Gazette 1446, CA 251, 431, 621, 821, 1031, 1191,
                                                1421, 1701, 1901, 2183, 2361
Clapman v Edwards [1938] 2 All ER 507, 82 Sol Jo 295 . . . . . . 398, 590, 757, 987,
                                                1138, 1648, 1850, 2149, 2336
Cohen v Tannar [1900] 2 QB 609, 69 LJQB 904, 48 WR 642,
  83 LT 64, CA 251, 431, 621, 821, 1031, 1191,
                                                1421, 1701, 1901, 2183, 2361

reference no

Collins v Howell-Jones [1981] 2 EGLR 108, 259 Estates Gazette 331,
  [1981] EGD 207, CA 311, 491, 653, 873, 1059, 1233,
  1471, 1739, 1951, 2212, 2368
Commercial General Administration Ltd v Thomsett [1979] 1 EGLR 62,
  250 Estates Gazette 547, CA 222, 412, 605, 791, 1011, 1160,
  1391, 1682, 1871, 2173, 2337

D

Dawson v Dyer (1833) 5 B & Ad 584, 2 Nev & MKB 559 . . . 251, 431, 621, 821, 1031, 1191,
  1421, 1701, 1901, 2183, 2361
Dennett v Atherton (1872) LR 7 QB 316, 41 LJQB 165, 20 WR 442, Ex Ch 251, 431,
  621, 821, 1031, 1191,
  1421, 1701, 1901, 2183, 2361
Dunlop Pneumatic Tyre Co Ltd v New Garage and Motor Co Ltd
  [1915] AC 79, 83 LJKB 1574, [1914-15] All ER Rep 739, 111 LT 862, 30 TLR 625, HL . . 162,
  362, 562, 712, 960, 1113,
  1313, 1612, 1813, 2111, 2310
Dunraven Securities Ltd v Holloway [1982] 2 EGLR 47,
  264 Estates Gazette 709, CA 222, 413, 605, 792, 1011, 1160,
  1391, 1682, 1871, 2173, 2337

E

Edge v Boileau (1885) 16 QBD 117, 55 LJQB 90, 34 WR 103,
  [1881-5] All ER Rep 510, 53 LT 907, 2 TLR 100, DC . . . 251, 431, 621, 821, 1031, 1191,
  1421, 1701, 1901, 2183, 2361

F

Facchini v Bryson (1952) 96 Sol Jo 395, [1952] 1 TLR 1386, CA 11

G

Graysim Holdings Ltd v P & O Property Holdings Ltd [1996] AC 329,
  [1995] 4 All ER 831, [1995] 3 WLR 854, [1996] 02 LS Gaz R 28,
  [1995] NLJR 1813, [1996] 03 EG 124, 140 Sol Jo LB 23, HL 5

H

Hagee (London) Ltd v AB Erikson and Larson [1976] QB 209, [1975] 3 All ER 234,
  [1975] 3 WLR 272, 29 P & CR 512, 119 Sol Jo 354, CA 54
Halifax Building Society v Keighley [1931] 2 KB 248, 100 LJKB 390, 145 LT 142 . 263, 632, 832, 1039,
  1202, 1432, 1714, 1913, 2201
Hammersmith London Borough Council v Creska (No 2) [2000] L & TR 288 . . . . 201, 401,
  593, 759, 989, 1140,
  1370, 1650, 1853, 2152, 2339
Hammond v Prentice Bros Ltd [1920] 1 Ch 201, 18 LGR 73, 84 JP 25, 89 LJ Ch 91,
  64 Sol Jo 131, 122 LT 307, 36 TLR 98 . . . . 501, 504, 671, 678,
  879, 887, 1239, 1491, 1971
Hampstead and Suburban Properties Ltd v Diomedous [1969] 1 Ch 248,
  [1968] 3 All ER 545, [1968] 3 WLR 990, 19 P & CR 880, 112 Sol Jo 656 222,
  412, 605, 791, 1011, 1160,
  1391, 1682, 1871, 2173, 2337
Harrison, Ainslie & Co v Muncaster [1891] 2 QB 680, 56 JP 69, 61 LJQB 102,
  40 WR 102, 65 LT 481, 7 TLR 688, CA 251, 431, 621, 821, 1031, 1191,
  1421, 1701, 1901, 2183, 2361

reference no

Hastie and Jenkerson (a firm) v McMahon [1991] 1 All ER 255, [1990] 1 WLR 1575,
    134 Sol Jo 725, [1990] 22 LS Gaz R 35, [1990] RVR 172, CA . . 313, 493, 655, 875, 1061, 1235,
                                              1473, 1741, 1953, 2214, 2370
Hindcastle Ltd v Barbara Attenborough Associates Ltd [1997] AC 70, [1996] 1 All ER 737,
    [1996] 2 WLR 262, [1996] 2 BCLC 234, [1996] 12 LS Gaz R 29, [1996] NLJR 281,
    [1996] 15 EG 103, 140 Sol Jo LB 84, HL 284, 464, 644, 854, 1054,
                                            1224, 1454, 1734, 1934, 2207
Holme v Brunskill (1878) 3 QBD 495, 42 JP 757, 47 LJQB 610, 38 LT 838, CA . . . 283, 463,
                                                 643, 853, 1053,
                                        1223, 1453, 1733, 1933, 2206

I

IBM United Kingdom Ltd v Rockware Glass Ltd [1980] FSR 335, CA . . . 258, 260, 437, 439, 627,
                                             629, 827, 829, 1036, 1038,
                                        1197, 1199, 1427, 1429, 1708,
                                        1710, 1908, 1910, 2196, 2198

J

Jervis v Harris [1996] Ch 195, [1996] 1 All ER 303, [1996] 2 WLR 220, [1995] NPC 171,
    [1996] 1 EGLR 78, [1995] 10 EG 159, 140 Sol Jo LB 13, CA . . .201, 401, 593, 759, 989, 1140,
                                          1370, 1650, 1853, 2152, 2339
Joel v International Circus and Christmas Fair (1920) 65 Sol Jo 293, 124 LT 459, CA 5

K

King, Re, Robinson v Gray [1963] Ch 459, [1963] 1 All ER 781, [1963] 2 WLR 629,
    107 Sol Jo 134, [1963] RVR 245, CA 261, 440, 630, 830,
                                        1039, 1430, 1711, 1911, 2199
Koumoundouros and Marathon Realty Co Ltd, Re (1978) 89 DLR (3d) 551 . . . . 222, 413,
                                           605, 792, 1011, 1160,
                                        1391, 1682, 1871, 2173, 2337

L

Laurence v Lexcourt Holdings Ltd [1978] 2 All ER 810, [1978] 1 WLR 1128,
    122 Sol Jo 681 . . . . 311, 491, 653, 873, 1059, 1233,
                                          1471, 1739, 1951, 2212, 2368
Law Society v United Service Bureau Ltd [1934] 1 KB 343, 31 LGR 436, 98 JP 33,
    103 LJKB 81, 30 Cox CC 37, 77 Sol Jo 815, 150 LT 159, 50 TLR 77,
    DC 158, 358, 558, 708, 957, 1109,
                                          1308, 1608, 1809, 2108, 2308
Lee-Parker v Izzet [1971] 3 All ER 1099, [1971] 1 WLR 1688, 22 P & CR 1098,
    115 Sol Jo 641 . . . . .191, 391, 583, 752, 982, 1132,
                                          1362, 1642, 1843, 2143, 2332
Lonsdale & Thompson Ltd v Black Arrow Group plc [1993] Ch 361, [1993] 3 All ER 648,
    [1993] 2 WLR 815, 65 P & CR 392, [1993] 2 Lloyd's Rep 428, [1993] 1 EGLR 87,
    [1993] 11 LS Gaz R 46, [1993] 25 EG 145 . . . . . . .258, 437, 627, 827, 1036,
                                          1197, 1427, 1708, 1908, 2196

M

McAuley v Bristol City Council [1992] QB 134, [1992] 1 All ER 749, [1991] 3 WLR 968,
    89 LGR 931, 23 HLR 586, [1991] NPC 81, [1991] 2 EGLR 64, [1991] 46 EG 155,
    CA 201, 401, 593, 759, 989, 1140,
                                          1370, 1650, 1853, 2152, 2339

reference no

McIlraith v Grady [1968] 1 QB 468, [1967] 3 All ER 625, [1967] 3 WLR 1331,
  111 Sol Jo 583, 203 Estates Gazette 687, CA 501, 671, 879, 1239
Manchester City Council v National Car Parks Ltd [1982] 1 EGLR 94,
  262 Estates Gazette 1297, CA 5
Manfield & Sons Ltd v Botchin [1970] 2 QB 612, [1970] 3 All ER 143,
  [1970] 3 WLR 120, 21 P & CR 587, 114 Sol Jo 338, 215 Estates Gazette 163 . . . . 54, 104
Matania v National Provincial Bank Ltd and Elevenist Syndicate Ltd [1936] 2 All ER 633,
  106 LJKB 113, 80 Sol Jo 532, 155 LT 74, CA 251, 431, 621, 821, 1031, 1191,
  1421, 1701, 1901, 2183, 2361
Meux v Jacobs (1875) LR 7 HL 481, 39 JP 324, 44 LJ Ch 481, 23 WR 526, 32 LT 171,
  [1874–80] All ER Rep Ext 2167, HL 158, 358, 558, 708, 957, 1109,
  1308, 1608, 1809, 2108, 2308
Miller v Emcer Products Ltd [1956] Ch 304, [1956] 1 All ER 237, [1956] 2 WLR 267,
  100 Sol Jo 74, CA 251, 431, 621, 821, 1031, 1191,
  1421, 1701, 1901, 2183, 2361
Monkland v Jack Barclay Ltd [1951] 2 KB 252, [1951] 1 All ER 714, 95 Sol Jo 236,
  [1951] 1 TLR 763, CA 258, 260, 437, 439, 627,
  629, 827, 829, 1036, 1038,
  1197, 1199, 1427, 1429, 1708,
  1710, 1908, 1910, 2196, 2198
Mumford Hotels Ltd v Wheler [1964] Ch 117, [1963] 3 All ER 250, [1963] 3 WLR 735,
  107 Sol Jo 810 . . . . 258, 259, 437, 438, 627,
  628, 827, 828, 1036, 1037,
  1197, 1198, 1427, 1428, 1708,
  1709, 1908, 1909, 2196, 2197

N

NW Investments (Erdington) Ltd v Swani (1970) 214 Estates Gazette 1115 . . 258, 260, 437, 439, 627,
  629, 827, 829, 1036, 1038,
  1197, 1199, 1427, 1429, 1708,
  1710, 1908, 1910, 2196, 2198
Nussey v Provincial Bill Posting Co and Eddison [1909] 1 Ch 734, 78 LJ Ch 539,
  53 Sol Jo 418, 100 LT 687, 25 TLR 489, CA 222, 413, 605, 792, 1011, 1160,
  1391, 1682, 1871, 2173, 2337

O

Oceanic Village Ltd v United Attractions Ltd [2000] Ch 234, [2000] 1 All ER 975,
  [2000] 2 WLR 476, 79 P & CR D42, [1999] NPC 156, [1999] EGCS 152 . . . 56, 106, 166,
  374, 566, 732, 964, 1117,
  1324, 1615, 1817, 2115, 2313
Owen v Gadd [1956] 2 QB 99, [1956] 2 All ER 28, 100 Sol Jo 301, CA . . 883, 1242, 1494, 1974

P

Penniall v Harborne (1848) 11 QB 368, 17 LJQB 94, 12 Jur 159, 10 LTOS 305 . 432, 623, 1032, 2192

R

Rowlands (Mark) Ltd v Berni Inns Ltd [1986] QB 211, [1985] 3 All ER 473,
  [1985] 3 WLR 964, [1985] 2 Lloyd's Rep 437, 129 Sol Jo 811, [1986] LS Gaz R 35,
  [1985] NLJ Rep 962, 276 Estates Gazette 191, CA 258, 265, 437, 445, 627,
  634, 827, 834, 1036, 1043,
  1197, 1204, 1427, 1434, 1708,
  1716, 1908, 1915, 2196, 2203

reference no

S

Sanderson v Berwick-upon-Tweed Corpn (1884) 13 QBD 547, 49 JP 6, 53 LJQB 559,
   33 WR 67, 51 LT 495, CA 251, 431, 621, 821, 1031, 1191,
   1421, 1701, 1901, 2183, 2361
Shell-Mex and BP Ltd v Manchester Garages Ltd [1971] 1 All ER 841, [1971] 1 WLR 612,
   115 Sol Jo 111, 218 Estates Gazette 285, CA 14
Shiloh Spinners Ltd v Harding [1973] AC 691, [1973] 1 All ER 90, [1973] 2 WLR 28,
   25 P & CR 48, 117 Sol Jo 34, HL 15
Spencer v Marriott (1823) 1 B & C 457, 1 LJOSKB 134, 2 Dow & Ry KB 665 . . . 251, 431,
   621, 821, 1031, 1191,
   1421, 1701, 1901, 2183, 2361
Stevenson and Rush (Holdings) Ltd v Langdon (1978) 38 P & CR 208, 122 Sol Jo 827,
   249 Estates Gazette 743, CA 231, 413, 606, 792, 1012, 1161,
   1392, 1683, 1872, 2174, 2347
Swift (P & A) Investments (a firm) v Combined English Stores Group plc [1989] AC 632,
   [1988] 2 All ER 885, [1988] 3 WLR 313, 57 P & CR 42, [1988] 2 EGLR 67,
   [1988] 43 EG 73, HL 281, 461, 641, 851, 1051,
   1221, 1451, 1731, 1931, 2204
Swire v Redman (1876) 1 QBD 536, 24 WR 1069, [1874-80] All ER Rep 1255,
   35 LT 470 . . . . 283, 463, 643, 853, 1053,
   1223, 1453, 1733, 1933, 2206

T

Terrell v Mabie Todd & Co Ltd (1952) 69 RPC 234, 96 Sol Jo 596, [1952] 2 TLR 574;
   affd (1953) 70 RPC 97, CA 258, 260, 437, 439, 627,
   629, 827, 829, 1036, 1038,
   1197, 1199, 1427, 1429, 1708,
   1710, 1908, 1910, 2196, 2198

V

VT Engineering Ltd v Richard Barland & Co Ltd (1968) 19 P & CR 890,
   207 Estates Gazette 247 . . . . 501, 671, 879, 1239
Vyvyan v Arthur (1823) 1 B & C 410, 2 Dow & Ry KB 760, [1814-23] All ER Rep 349,
   sub nom Vivyan v Arthur 1 LJOSKB 138 . . . . 182, 380, 582, 751, 981,
   1131, 1641, 1842, 2142, 2331

W

Walji v Mount Cook Land Ltd [2002] 1 P & CR 163, [2000] NPC 148, 81 P & CR D24, CA . . 104
Walter v Selfe (1851) 4 De G & Sm 315, 20 LJ Ch 433, 15 Jur 416, 64 ER 849,
   17 LTOS 103; on appeal (1852) 19 LTOS 308 . . . . 222, 412, 605, 791, 1011, 1160,
   1391, 1682, 1871, 2173, 2337
Westminster City Council v Southern Rly Co, Rly Assessment Authority and
   W H Smith & Son Ltd [1936] AC 511, [1936] 2 All ER 322, 34 LGR 313,
   24 Ry & Can Tr Cas 189, 105 LJKB 537, 80 Sol Jo 671, 52 TLR 541, sub nom Southern Rly Co's
   Appeals, Re 100 JP 327, 155 LT 33, HL. 5
Wettern Electric Ltd v Welsh Development Agency [1983] QB 796,
   [1983] 2 All ER 629, [1983] 2 WLR 897, 47 P & CR 113, 127 Sol Jo 286 16
Wheeler v Mercer [1957] AC 416, [1956] 3 All ER 631, [1956] 3 WLR 841,
   100 Sol Jo 836, 168 Estates Gazette 520, HL 54
Williams v Gabriel [1906] 1 KB 155, 75 LJKB 149, 54 WR 379, 94 LT 17,
   22 TLR 217 . . . . 251, 431, 621, 821, 1031, 1191,
   1421, 1701, 1901, 2183, 2361

Y

Yorkbrook Investments Ltd v Batten (1985) 52 P & CR 51, 18 HLR 25,
   [1985] 2 EGLR 100, 276 Estates Gazette 545, CA 431, 621, 821, 1031, 1191,
   1421, 1701, 1901, 2183, 2361

LANDLORD AND TENANT (BUSINESS TENANCIES)

References are to the numbers in square brackets which appear
on the right hand side of the pages of text

reference no

Forms and Precedents

A: LICENCES AND TENANCIES AT WILL
    1   *Licence to occupy* . . . . [1]
    2   *Tenancy at will* . . . . [51]
    3   *Tenancy at will for use on termination of an excluded lease* . . . . [101]

B: WHOLE LEASES
1:   INDUSTRIAL AND WAREHOUSE PREMISES
    4   *Lease of a light industrial building or warehouse where the*
         landlord does not own adjoining property . . . . [151]
    5   *Lease of a light industrial building or warehouse with access via*
         a private road across the landlord's adjoining property . . . . [351]
    6   *Lease of a light industrial building or warehouse on a small estate* . . . . [551]
    7   *Lease of a light industrial or warehouse unit forming part of*
         a building on an estate . . . . [701]

2:   SHOPS
    8   *Lease of a shop, with or without a yard, where the landlord*
         does not own adjoining property . . . . [951]
    9   *Lease of a shop and maisonette forming part of a parade* . . . . [1101]
    10   *Lease of a shop in a shopping centre* . . . . [1301]

3:   OFFICES
    11   *Lease of the whole of an office building, with or without land,*
         where the landlord does not own adjoining property . . . . [1601]
    12   *Lease of a suite of offices forming part of a building, with parking*
         bays and additional parking rights . . . . [1801]

4:   HOTELS
    13   *Lease of a hotel* . . . . [2101]

5:   CAR PARKS
    14   *Lease of land for use as a commercial car park* . . . . [2301]

Forms and Precedents

A: LICENCES AND TENANCIES AT WILL

1

Licence to occupy[1]

CONTENTS

(NB: numbers in [ ] below refer to this volume and should be altered to suit the page or reference numbers actually used)

1 DEFINITIONS AND INTERPRETATION

1.1 'The Accessways' . . . . [5]
1.2 'The Building' . . . . [5]
1.3 'The Car Park' . . . . [5]
1.4 'The Designated Hours' . . . . [5]
1.5 'The Designated Parking Space' . . . . [6]
1.6 'The Designated Space' . . . . [6]
1.7 Headings . . . . [6]
1.8 'The Licence Fee' . . . . [7]
1.9 'The Licence Period' . . . . [7]
1.10 'The Premises' . . . . [7]
1.11 References to clauses . . . . [7]
1.12 'VAT' . . . . [7]
[1]

2 THE LICENCE . . . . [11]

3 LICENSEE'S UNDERTAKINGS

3.1 Licence fee and outgoings . . . . [11]
3.2 Deposit . . . . [12]
3.3 Consent for chattels . . . . [12]
3.4 Condition of property . . . . [12]
[3.5 Display of goods . . . . [12]]
3.6 Accessways . . . . [12]
[3.7 Signs and notices . . . . [13]]
3.8 Nuisance . . . . [13]
3.9 Statutory requirements and insurance . . . . [13]
[3.10 Registration numbers . . . . [13]]
3.11 Indemnity . . . . [13]

3.12 Rules and regulations . . . . [13]
[3.13 Observation of restrictions of Owner's lease . . . . [14]]
3.14 Owner's costs . . . . [14]
3.15 Owner's rights . . . . [14]

4 GENERAL

4.1 Determination . . . . [15]
4.2 Assignment prohibited . . . . [15]
4.3 Warranty excluded . . . . [16]
4.4 Liability excluded . . . . [16]
4.5 Notices . . . . [16]
                                                                                                [2]

AGREEMENT

THIS AGREEMENT is made the ...... day of .... BETWEEN:

(1)   *(name of owner)* [of *(address)* *(or as appropriate)* the registered office of which is at *(address)*] [Company Registration no ...][2] ('the Owner') and

(2)   *(name of licensee)* [of *(address)* *(or as appropriate)* the registered office of which is at *(address)*] [Company Registration no ...] ('the Licensee')

                                                                                                [3]

1   As to stamp duty land tax see the Information Binder: Stamp Duty Land Tax [1].
        As to licences generally and the distinction between leases and licences see vol 22(1) (2003 Reissue) LANDLORD AND TENANT (BUSINESS TENANCIES) Paragraph 1 [1] et seq.
        In *Street v Mountford* [1985] AC 809, [1985] 2 All ER 289, HL it was held that, generally, an agreement granting an occupier of land exclusive possession creates a tenancy: see vol 22(1) (2003 Reissue) LANDLORD AND TENANT (BUSINESS TENANCIES) Paragraph 1 [1] et seq. For circumstances in which the courts have held that an agreement to occupy land did not grant exclusive possession see vol 22(1) (2003 Reissue) LANDLORD AND TENANT (BUSINESS TENANCIES) Paragraph 6 [11].
        This licence is for use where the owner of land proposes to allow some other party to occupy part of it, but wants to retain the right to move that other party to another part of the land on notice. The licence extends to the use of a car parking space or spaces. If no car parking facilities are to be provided the Form should be amended appropriately.
        The grant of a lease is inappropriate as there are, in effect, no specific premises to be let, and the owner simply gives the other party a right, or licence, to use designated parts of his land. It is submitted that a provision entitling the owner to relocate the occupier is inconsistent with the grant of exclusive possession. The point is not, however, covered by direct authority, and the draftsman should be aware that, if exclusive possession *is* in fact granted, or if the provision is inserted merely in an attempt to prevent a tenancy from arising, the occupier will almost certainly be a tenant and not a licensee.
        If an owner of land wants to ensure that an occupier does not obtain the protection of the Landlord and Tenant Act 1954 Pt II (ss 23–46) (23 Halsbury's Statutes (4th Edn) LANDLORD AND TENANT), then, if there is a possibility that the occupier will have exclusive possession of a particular parcel of land, a tenancy at will, or a tenancy for less than six months falling within the Landlord and Tenant Act 1954 s 43(3), or a tenancy in respect of which the parties have agreed to exclude the provisions of the Landlord and Tenant Act 1954 ss 24–28 would be safer than a licence.
2   If any party is a company it is desirable to include the company registration number. This avoids any problems arising when a company has been wound up and a new company formed with the same name, or when the name of a company is changed, or if companies swap names, eg on a reconstruction of a group of companies.

                                                                                                [4]

NOW IT IS AGREED as follows:

1   DEFINITIONS AND INTERPRETATION

In this agreement the following expressions have the meanings given in this clause.

1.1   'The Accessways'

'The Accessways' means the roads, paths, entrance halls, corridors, lifts and staircases of the Premises the use of which is necessary to obtain access to and egress from the Designated Space and the Designated Parking Space, or those of them that afford reasonable access and egress thereto and therefrom and that the Owner from time to time in his absolute discretion designates on *(state period, eg 28 days')* notice to the Licensee.

1.2   'The Building'

'The Building' means the part of the Premises shown [for the purpose of identification only] edged *(state colour, eg blue)* on the plan annexed to this agreement.

1.3   'The Car Park'

'The Car Park' means the part of the Premises shown [for the purpose of identification only] edged *(state colour, eg green)* on the plan annexed to this agreement.

1.4   'The Designated Hours'[3]

'The Designated Hours' means *(specify hours)* on [Mondays to Fridays inclusive, bank and other public holidays excepted, [or such other hours as the Owner from time to time in his absolute discretion determines on *(state period, eg 28 days')* notice to the Licensee] *(or as the case may be)*].

---

3   In *Manchester City Council v National Car Parks Ltd* [1982] 1 EGLR 94, CA it was stated by Lawton LJ that a clause in an agreement giving a licensee the right to use a site between specified hours 'did not grant, and was not intended to grant, ... exclusive possession'. The fact that the owner did not enforce this restriction was not material, because the circumstances were such that it was obvious that the owner intended from the beginning to enforce the right, and thus not to grant exclusive possession. However, see *Joel v International Circus and Christmas Fair* (1920) 124 LT 459, CA; *Westminster City Council v Southern Rly Co* [1936] AC 511, [1936] 2 All ER 322, HL; *Graysim Holdings Ltd v P & O Property Holdings Ltd* [1996] AC 329, [1995] 4 All ER 831, HL. These were all cases where an occupier was treated as having exclusive possession and, therefore, a tenancy despite restrictions on the hours of access. It thus appears that restricting access to certain times of the day does not always preclude the grant of exclusive possession. Other factors, notably the need to maintain security in shopping centres and office buildings in multiple occupation, may well lead to the conclusion that, despite the restriction, the occupier has exclusive possession and is a tenant.

In appropriate cases the licensee may want to leave items in the premises outside the designated hours. In *Manchester City Council v National Car Parks Ltd* [1982] 1 EGLR 94, CA the fact that the agreement envisaged that some kind of portable kiosk could be left on the land did not affect the court's decision.

[5]

1.5   'The Designated Parking Space'

'The Designated Parking Space' means the [space *(or as appropriate)* spaces] shown [for the purpose of identification only] edged *(state colour, eg brown)* on the plan annexed to this agreement or such other [space *(or as appropriate)* spaces] within the Car Park, being suitable and of a sufficient size for the parking of *(number)* private motor [car *(or as appropriate)* cars], as the Owner may from time to time in his absolute discretion designate on *(state period, eg 28 days')* notice to the Licensee.

1.6   'The Designated Space'

'The Designated Space' means the area shown [for the purpose of identification only] edged *(state colour, eg yellow)* on the plan annexed to this agreement or such other [office *(or as appropriate)* storage *(or as appropriate)* retail] space, comprising a single area of not less than *(number)* square metres, [within *(or as required)* outside] the Building as the Owner may from time to time in his absolute discretion designate on *(state period, eg 28 days')* notice to the Licensee.

1.7   Headings[4]

The clause headings and the table of contents do not form part of this agreement and must not be taken into account in its construction or interpretation. *(amend if marginal notes are used instead of headings)*

4   Headings and marginal notes require the draftsman to provide a word or two to describe every clause in the document. This is not always easy and there are times when the draftsman will have to settle for something less than perfection, the only alternative being a heading or note that would be inappropriately long. It would be quite wrong for that title, which its author might admit was not totally apposite but was the best that he could do in a few words, to be used in construing the clause in question.

[6]

1.8   'The Licence Fee'

'The Licence Fee' means £... a month [or such other amount as the Owner may from time to time determine in his absolute discretion on *(state period, eg 28 days')*[5] notice to the Licensee].

5   The licensee should ensure that the period of notice specified in this clause is the same as that specified in clause 4.1 [15] DETERMINATION.

1.9   'The Licence Period'

'The Licence Period' means the period from the date of this agreement until the date on which the Licensee's rights under clause 2 THE LICENCE are determined in accordance with clause 4.1 DETERMINATION.

1.10   'The Premises'

'The Premises' means the land and buildings shown [for the purpose of identification only] edged *(state colour, eg red)* on the plan annexed to this agreement.

1.11   References to clauses

Any reference in this agreement to a clause without further designation is to be construed as a reference to the clause of this agreement so numbered.

1.12   'VAT'

'VAT' means value added tax or any other tax of a similar nature[6].

6   As to VAT generally see the Information Binder: Property [1]: VAT and Property.

[7]–[10]

2   THE LICENCE

Subject to clause 3 LICENSEE'S UNDERTAKINGS and clause 4 GENERAL, the Owner gives the Licensee the right, for the Licence Period and during the Designated Hours, in common with the Owner and all others authorised by the Owner so far as is not inconsistent with the rights given, to use the Designated Space for *(specify purpose)*, to use the Designated Parking Space for parking *(number)* private motor [car *(or as appropriate)* cars], and to use the Accessways for access to and egress from the Designated Space and the Designated Parking Space.

3   LICENSEE'S UNDERTAKINGS[7]

The Licensee agrees and undertakes as set out in this clause 3.

7   A tenant, as a general rule, is able to exercise all the rights of an owner of the land, subject to any rights reserved to the landlord and restrictions contained in the lease. A licence, on the other hand, only gives the licensee permission to do something that would otherwise be unlawful. For this reason it is unnecessary to include in a licence the sort of restrictions found in a lease, except where required to exclude rights that might be implied because of the nature of the rights specifically given. The inclusion of reservations and restrictions usually found in a lease in fact renders it more likely that the court would hold the agreement to be a tenancy: see *Facchini v Bryson* [1952] 1 TLR 1386, CA; *Addiscombe Garden Estates Ltd v Crabbe* [1958] 1 QB 513, [1957] 3 All ER 563, CA.

3.1   Licence fee and outgoings

The Licensee must pay the Licence Fee, together with any VAT, to the Owner in advance on the first day of each month, the first payment, or a due proportion of it apportioned on a day-to-day basis to be made on the date of this agreement, and must pay on demand a fair and reasonable proportion, apportioned in respect of the Licence Period, of all rates and other outgoings of a periodically recurring nature incurred in respect of the Premises, together with any VAT.

[11]

3.2   Deposit

The Licensee must deposit £... with the Owner as security for the performance and observance of the undertakings contained in this clause 3, to be repayable to the Licensee— less any amount due to the Owner in respect of any non-performance or non-observance by the Licensee — within *(state period, eg 14 days)* of the determination of the Licence Period or such longer period as may be necessary to ascertain any amount due to the Owner.

3.3   Consent for chattels

The Licensee must not bring any furniture, equipment, goods or chattels onto the Premises without the consent of the Owner, except as is necessary for the exercise of the rights given in clause 2 THE LICENCE.

3.4   Condition of property

The Licensee must keep the Designated Space and the Designated Parking Space clean and tidy and clear of rubbish and leave them in a clean and tidy condition and free of the Licensee's furniture, equipment, goods and chattels at the end of the Licence Period.

[3.5   Display of goods

The Licensee must maintain at the Designated Space an attractive display of goods in keeping with the standards maintained elsewhere in the Building.]

3.6   Accessways

The Licensee must not obstruct the Accessways, or make them dirty or untidy, or leave any rubbish on them.

[3.7   Signs and notices

The Licensee must not display any signs or notices at the Designated Space without the prior written consent of the Owner.]

[12]

3.8   Nuisance

The Licensee must not use the Designated Space, the Designated Parking Space or the Accessways in such a way as to cause any nuisance, damage, disturbance, annoyance, inconvenience or interference to the Premises or adjoining or neighbouring property or to the owners, occupiers or users of any adjoining or neighbouring property.

3.9   Statutory requirements and insurance

The Licensee must not do anything that will or might constitute a breach of any statutory requirement affecting the Premises or that will or might wholly or partly vitiate any insurance effected in respect of the Premises from time to time.

[3.10   Registration numbers

The Licensee must immediately give to the Owner details of the registration number of the motor [car *(or as appropriate)* cars], that will be parked on the Designated Parking Space, and the name of the owner and driver of the motor [car *(or as appropriate)* cars], and must notify the Owner of any change in those details before the change is made.]

3.11   Indemnity

The Licensee must indemnify the Owner, and keep the Owner indemnified, against all losses, claims, demands, actions, proceedings, damages, costs or expenses or other liability arising in any way from this agreement, any breach of any of the Licensee's undertakings contained in this clause, or the exercise or purported exercise of any of the rights given in clause 2 THE LICENCE[8].

8   An obligation may be imposed on the licensee to insure against third party liability.

3.12   Rules and regulations

The Licensee must observe any [reasonable] rules and regulations the Owner makes and notifies to the Licensee from time to time, governing the Licensee's use of the Designated Space, the Designated Parking Space, or the Accessways.

[13]

[3.13 Observation of restrictions of Owner's lease[9]

The Licensee must not do, or permit or suffer any person exercising or purporting to exercise the rights given in clause 2 THE LICENCE to do, anything on or in relation to the Premises that would or might cause the Owner to be in breach of the tenant's covenants and the conditions contained in a lease dated *(date)* and made between (1) *(name of landlord)* and (2) [the Owner], or that, if done by the Owner, would or might constitute a breach of that lease.]

9   This clause is applicable only if the owner is himself a tenant. In such a case the owner should consider the alienation provisions in the lease. The grant of a genuine licence may not be a breach of a covenant against parting with possession but is a breach of a covenant against parting with or sharing occupation. The licensee should consider the effect of such a breach on the indemnity given in clause 3.11 [13] INDEMNITY.

3.14 Owner's costs

The Licensee must pay to the Owner on demand, and indemnify the Owner against, all costs and expenses of professional advisers and agents, including any VAT, incurred by the Owner in connection with the preparation, negotiation and completion of this agreement.

3.15 Owner's rights

The Licensee must not in any way impede the Owner, or his [officers,] servants or agents, in the exercise of his rights of possession and control of the Premises and every part of the Premises[10].

10   See *Shell-Mex and BP Ltd v Manchester Garages Ltd* [1971] 1 All ER 841, [1971] 1 WLR 841, CA.

[14]

4   GENERAL

4.1   Determination

The rights granted in clause 2 THE LICENCE are to determine — without prejudice to the Owner's rights in respect of any breach of the undertakings contained in clause 3 LICENSEE'S UNDERTAKINGS —

4.1.1   immediately on notice given by the Owner at any time following any breach by the Licensee of his undertakings contained in clause 3 LICENSEE'S UNDERTAKINGS[11], and

4.1.2   on not less than *(state period, eg 28 days')* notice given by the Owner or the Licensee to the other party to expire on the last day of a month.

11   For the possibility that a licensee may be able to take advantage of the courts' general equitable jurisdiction to grant relief against forfeiture see *Shiloh Spinners Ltd v Harding* [1973] AC 691, [1973] 1 All ER 90, HL.

4.2   Assignment prohibited

The benefit of this licence is personal to the Licensee and not assignable, and the rights given in clause 2 THE LICENCE may only be exercised by the Licensee [and his employees [and customers]][12].

12   It has long been the practice to provide in licences that the parties do not intend to create a tenancy, but the professed intention of the parties cannot alter the effect of the agreement: see vol 22(1) (2003 Reissue) LANDLORD AND TENANT (BUSINESS TENANCIES) Paragraph 3 [5].

[15]

4.3   Warranty excluded

The Owner gives no warranty that the Premises are legally or physically fit for the purposes specified in clause 2 THE LICENCE[13].

13   In *Wettern Electric Ltd v Welsh Development Agency* [1983] QB 796 at 808, [1983] 2 All ER 629 at 637, it was stated that it was possible for terms as to fitness for purpose to be implied in licences. In that case a warranty was implied that the premises were of sound construction and reasonably suitable for the purposes required by the licensee. It is considered that this exclusion will be effective.

4.4   Liability excluded

The Owner is not to be liable for the death of, or injury to the Licensee or his employees [and customers], or for damage to any property of theirs, or for any losses, claims, demands, actions, proceedings, damages, costs or expenses or other liability incurred by them in the exercise or purported exercise of the rights granted by clause 2 THE LICENCE.

4.5   Notices

All notices given by either party pursuant to the provisions of this agreement must be in writing, and are to be sufficiently served if delivered by hand or sent by registered post or recorded delivery, or sent by fax provided that a confirmatory copy is delivered by hand or sent by registered post or recorded delivery on the same day, to the other party at his [registered office *(or as required)* last known address].

AS WITNESS etc *(see vol 12(2) (2003 Reissue) DEEDS, AGREEMENTS ETC)*

(signatures of both parties)
[16]–[50]

2

Tenancy at will[1]

CONTENTS

(NB: numbers in [ ] below refer to this volume and should be altered to suit the page or reference numbers actually used)

1 DEFINITIONS AND INTERPRETATION

1.1 Gender and number . . . . [55]
1.2 Headings . . . . [55]
1.3 'The Interior' . . . . [55]
1.4 Interpretation of 'the Landlord' and 'the Tenant' . . . . [55]
1.5 Joint and several liability . . . . [56]
1.6 Obligation not to permit or suffer . . . . [56]
1.7 'The Permitted Use' . . . . [56]
1.8 'The Premises' . . . . [56]
1.9 References to clauses . . . . [56]
1.10 'The Rent' . . . . [56]
1.11 'The Tenancy' . . . . [56]
1.12 'VAT' . . . . [56]

2 RECITALS . . . . [61]

3 TENANCY AT WILL . . . . [61]

4 RENT
4.1 Payment of rent . . . . [62]
4.2 Refund on termination . . . . [62]
4.3 Periodic tenancy excluded . . . . [62]

5 THE TENANT'S OBLIGATIONS
5.1 Payment of the Rent . . . . [62]
5.2 Outgoings . . . . [62]
5.3 Interest . . . . [62]
5.4 Repair . . . . [63]
5.5 Alterations . . . . [63]
5.6 Return of the Premises . . . . [63]
5.7 Use . . . . [63]
5.8 Nuisance . . . . [63]
5.9 Disposal . . . . [63]
5.10 Occupation . . . . [63]
5.11 Entry . . . . [63]

6 INDEMNITY . . . . [64]

7 DECLARATIONS
7.1 Determination . . . . [64]
7.2 Exclusion of warranty as to use . . . . [64]

[8 COSTS . . . . [64]]
                                                                                        [52]

AGREEMENT

THIS TENANCY AGREEMENT is made the ...... day of .... BETWEEN:

(1)   *(name of landlord)* [of *(address)* *(or as appropriate)* the registered office of which is
        at *(address)*] [Company Registration no ...][2] ('the Landlord') and

(2)   *(name of tenant)* [of *(address)* *(or as appropriate)* the registered office of which is at
        (address)] [Company Registration no ...] ('the Tenant')

                                                                                        [53]

1   As to stamp duty land tax see the Information Binder: Stamp Duty Land Tax [1].
            As to tenancies at will generally see vol 22(1) (2003 Reissue) LANDLORD AND TENANT
        (BUSINESS TENANCIES) Paragraph 9 [31] et seq.
            A tenancy at will may arise by implication of law or be created by express agreement. If, during an
        implied tenancy at will, rent is paid by reference to a period the tenancy is generally converted into a
        periodic tenancy at law. An *express* tenancy at will may remain a tenancy at will notwithstanding that
        a periodic rent is payable (see *Manfield & Sons Ltd v Botchin* [1970] 2 QB 612, [1970] 3 All ER 143;
        Hagee (London) Ltd v AB Erikson and Larson [1976] QB 209, [1975] 3 All ER 234, CA), but the courts
        will look closely at the tenancy to ensure that it is not in reality a periodic tenancy (see *Hagee (London)
        Ltd v AB Erikson and Larson* [1976] QB 209, [1975] 3 All ER 234, CA).

A tenancy at will is a tenancy determinable at any time at the will of either party. This applies even if, in the case of an express tenancy at will, it is expressed to be at the will of one party only. Note that a tenancy at will is not protected by the Landlord and Tenant Act 1954 Part II (ss 23–46) (23 Halsbury's Statutes (4th Edn) LANDLORD AND TENANT): see *Wheeler v Mercer* [1957] AC 416, [1956] 3 All ER 631, HL as regards implied tenancies at will; *Hagee (London) Ltd v AB Erikson and Larson* [1976] QB 209, [1975] 3 All ER 234, CA as regards express tenancies at will. It should also be noted that, because a tenancy at will can be determined at any time by the landlord the provisions of the Law of Property Act 1925 s 146 (37 Halsbury's Statutes (4th Edn) REAL PROPERTY) do not apply in relation to the determination of a tenancy at will on breach by the tenant.

This is a general form of express tenancy at will. The draftsman of a tenancy at will must bear in mind that the relationship between landlord and tenant at will may be brought to an end at any time, and for any, or no, reason, by either party. It is, therefore, inappropriate to include provisions such as a proviso for re-entry, an option to determine, or a rent-abatement clause. Given the nature of a tenancy at will, it is also unlikely that the tenant will be prepared to take on any particularly onerous obligations.

For a form of express tenancy at will suitable for use in circumstances where a tenant who does not enjoy security of tenure under the Landlord and Tenant Act 1954 is holding over following the expiry of his lease see Form 3 [101].

2   If any party is a company it is desirable to include the company registration number. This avoids any problems arising when a company has been wound up and a new company formed with the same name, or when the name of a company is changed, or if companies swap names, eg on a reconstruction of a group of companies.

[54]

NOW IT IS AGREED as follows:

1   DEFINITIONS AND INTERPRETATION

In this agreement the following expressions have the meanings given in this clause.

1.1   Gender and number

Words importing one gender are to be construed as importing any other gender; words importing the singular are to be construed as importing the plural and vice versa.

1.2   Headings[3]

The clause headings and the table of contents do not form part of this agreement and must not be taken into account in its construction or interpretation. *(amend if marginal notes are used instead of headings)*

3   Headings and marginal notes require the draftsman to provide a word or two to describe every clause in the document. This is not always easy and there are times when the draftsman has to settle for something less than perfection, the only alternative being a heading or note that would be inappropriately long. It would be quite wrong for that title, which its author might admit was not totally apposite but was the best that he could do in a few words, to be used in construing the clause in question.

1.3   'The Interior'

'The Interior' means the internal coverings of the walls of the Premises, the floor and ceiling finishes of the Premises, and the doors, door-frames, windows and window-frames of the Premises.

1.4   Interpretation of 'the Landlord' and 'the Tenant'

The expressions 'the Landlord' and 'the Tenant' shall not include any successors in title or assigns of either party.

[55]

1.5   Joint and several liability

Where any party comprises more than one person, the obligations and liabilities of that party under this agreement are to be joint and several obligations and liabilities of those persons.

1.6   Obligation not to permit or suffer

Any covenant by the Tenant not to do anything includes an obligation not to permit or suffer[4] that thing to be done by another person.

4   'Permit' may have a different meaning from 'suffer': see *Barton v Reed* [1932] 1 Ch 362 at 375 per Luxmore J. A covenant not to 'permit' activity is broken if the covenantor himself carries it on: see *Oceanic Village Ltd v United Attractions Ltd* [2000] Ch 234, [2000] 1 All ER 975.

1.7   'The Permitted Use'

'The Permitted Use' means *(specify permitted use)*.

1.8   'The Premises'

'The Premises' means all that *(describe the premises)*.

1.9   References to clauses

Any reference in this agreement to any clause without further designation is to be construed as a reference to the clause of this agreement so numbered.

1.10   'The Rent'

'The Rent' means the rent of £... a month [together with VAT].

1.11   'The Tenancy'

'The Tenancy' means the tenancy granted by this agreement.

1.12   'VAT'

'VAT' means value added tax or any other tax of a similar nature[5].

5   As to VAT generally see the Information Binder: Property [1]: VAT and Property.

[56]–[60]

2   RECITALS[6]

(insert as required)

6   The court looks closely at any tenancy at will created by express agreement under which rent is paid by reference to a period to ensure that it is not in substance a periodic tenancy. The main difference is that a periodic tenancy is, but a tenancy at will is not, within the Landlord and Tenant Act 1954 Pt II (ss 23–46): see vol 22(1) (2003 Reissue) LANDLORD AND TENANT (BUSINESS TENANCIES) Paragraphs 14.2 [46], 430 [2033]. It is desirable to incorporate recitals to document the background to and the purpose of the agreement and to explain the reasons why the parties wish to able to determine the arrangement with little or no notice. This is all with a view to providing evidence in support of the creation of a tenancy at will. The terms of any recitals will vary according to the circumstances involved. For examples of recitals for use in a tenancy at will created on the termination of an excluded lease see Form 3 clause 2 [111] RECITALS.

3   TENANCY AT WILL

The Landlord lets and the Tenant takes the Premises on a tenancy at will commencing on the date of this agreement the Tenant yielding and paying to the Landlord the Rent.

[61]

4   RENT

4.1   Payment of rent

The Rent is to be paid in advance without deduction on the first day in each month, the first payment, or a proportionate part in respect of the period from and including the date of this agreement to and including the last day of the month now current, to be made on the date of this agreement.

4.2   Refund on termination

On termination of the Tenancy, any rent previously paid in respect of any period falling after the date of termination must be repaid to the Tenant immediately.

4.3   Periodic tenancy excluded

Neither the payment of any rent, nor any demand for payment of it, nor the fact that the amount of the Rent is calculated by reference to a period, is to create, or cause the Tenancy to become, a periodic tenancy.

5   THE TENANT'S OBLIGATIONS

The Tenant agrees with the Landlord to observe and perform the requirements of this clause 5.

5.1   Payment of the Rent

The Tenant must pay the Rent in accordance with clause 4.1 PAYMENT OF RENT.

5.2   Outgoings

The Tenant must pay, and indemnify the Landlord against, all existing and future rates, taxes, assessments, duties, charges, impositions and outgoings of an annual or other periodically recurring nature and insurance premiums paid by the Landlord in respect of the Premises during the currency of the Tenancy apportioned on a time basis if necessary by the Landlord's surveyor for the time being.

5.3   Interest

If and whenever the Tenant fails to pay the Rent or any other money due under this agreement on the due date, the Tenant must pay to the Landlord interest on the Rent or other money as the case may be at the rate of ...% per year above the base rate from time to time of *(specify bank)* from the date on which the payment is due to the date of payment, both before and after any judgment.

[62]

5.4   Repair

The Tenant must keep the Interior in repair and in good decorative order[7].

7   The tenant is unlikely to agree to more than this: see note 1 [54] above.

5.5   Alterations

The Tenant must not make any alteration or addition whatsoever either to the exterior or the interior of the Premises.

5.6   Return of the Premises

The Tenant must return the Premises in the state required by this agreement on determination of this agreement, and immediately thereafter (and notwithstanding termination of this agreement) clear away all rubbish and make good any damage to the Premises caused by the Tenant, his agents and invitees.

5.7   Use

The Tenant must not use the Premises or any part of them otherwise than for the Permitted Use.

5.8   Nuisance

The Tenant must not cause any nuisance or annoyance to the Landlord or to any adjoining owners or occupiers.

5.9   Disposal

The Tenant must not hold the Premises on trust for another and must not assign, sublet, charge, part with the possession of, or otherwise dispose of the Premises or any part of the Premises.

5.10   Occupation

The Tenant must not permit the Premises or any part of the Premises to be occupied or used by any person other than the Tenant and the Tenant's employees [and must not permit the Premises to be occupied by more than ... persons][8].

8   See eg the Fire Precautions (Factories, Offices, Shops and Railway Premises) Order 1989, SI 1989/76.

5.11   Entry

The Tenant must allow the Landlord, and all persons authorised by the Landlord, to enter the Premises at any [reasonable] time to ascertain whether the terms of this agreement have been complied with.

[63]

6   INDEMNITY

The Tenant agrees at all times to indemnify the Landlord against all losses, claims, demands, actions, proceedings, damages, costs or expenses or other liability arising through any default in compliance with this agreement or arising from any other act or default of the Tenant its agents or invitees.

7   DECLARATIONS

The parties agree and declare as set out in this clause 7.

7.1   Determination

This agreement is to be determined[9] immediately:

7.1.1   by any demand for possession of the Premises made by or on behalf of the Landlord[10], or

7.1.2   (without prejudice to any subsisting obligation of the Tenant imposed by this agreement) by any delivery of possession by the Tenant to the Landlord[11], or

7.1.3   the Tenancy being personal to the parties, by the death or dissolution of either party or by any disposition or purported disposition of the interest of either party whether voluntary or otherwise[12].

9   A right of re-entry is inappropriate for a tenancy at will as the landlord can demand possession at any time.

10   It is an inherent feature of a tenancy at will that it is determinable at any time at the will of either party: see note 1 above.

11   It is an inherent feature of a tenancy at will that it is determinable at any time at the will of either party: see note 1 above.

12   A tenancy at will is a personal relationship between the original landlord and tenant, and so has traditionally been held to be determined by, eg, the death of either party, the tenant's bankruptcy, or voluntary alienation of the premises by either party with notice to the other. The authorities for these propositions are, however, somewhat old, and the agreement should deal expressly with them.

7.2   Exclusion of warranty as to use

The Landlord does not imply or warrant that the Premises may be used for the purpose authorised by this agreement or any other purpose.

[8   COSTS

The Tenant will on exchange of this agreement pay the costs of the Landlord's solicitors in respect of the preparation of this agreement amounting to £... together with VAT.]

AS WITNESS etc *(see vol 12(2) (2003 Reissue) DEEDS, AGREEMENTS ETC)*

(signatures of both parties)
[64]–[100]

3

Tenancy at will for use on termination of an excluded lease[1]

CONTENTS

(NB: numbers in [ ] below refer to this volume and should be altered to suit the page or reference numbers actually used)

1 DEFINITIONS AND INTERPRETATION

1.1 Gender and number .... [105]
1.2 Headings .... [105]
1.3 Interpretation of 'the Landlord' and 'the Tenant' .... [105]
1.4 Interpretation of 'the Premises' .... [106]
1.5 Joint and several liability .... [106]
1.6 'The Lease' .... [106]
1.7 Obligation not to permit or suffer .... [106]
1.8 References to clauses .... [106]
1.9 'The Rent' .... [106]
1.10 'The Tenancy' .... [106]
1.11 'VAT' .... [106]
[101]

2 RECITALS

2.1 Past occupation . . . . [111]
2.2 Negotiations . . . . [111]
2.3 Continued occupation . . . . [111]

3 TENANCY AT WILL . . . . [111]

4 RENT

4.1 Payment of rent . . . . [112]
4.2 Refund on termination . . . . [112]
4.3 Periodic tenancy excluded . . . . [112]

5 THE TENANT'S OBLIGATIONS

5.1 Compliance with terms of Lease . . . . [112]
5.2 Payment of the Rent . . . . [112]
5.3 Outgoings . . . . [113]
5.4 Interest . . . . [113]
5.5 Alterations . . . . [113]
5.6 Return of the Premises . . . . [113]
5.7 Nuisance . . . . [113]
5.8 Disposal . . . . [113]
5.9 Occupation . . . . [113]
5.10 Entry . . . . [113]

6 INDEMNITY . . . . [114]

7 DECLARATIONS

7.1 Determination . . . . [114]
7.2 Exclusion of warranty as to use . . . . [115]

[8 COSTS . . . . [115]]
                                                                            [102]

AGREEMENT

THIS TENANCY AGREEMENT is made on the ...... day of ...... BETWEEN:

(1)   *(name of landlord)* [of *(address) (or as appropriate)* the registered office of which is
       at *(address)*] [Company Registration no ...][2] ('the Landlord') and

(2)   *(name of tenant)* [of *(address) (or as appropriate)* the registered office of which is at
       (address)] [Company Registration no ...] ('the Tenant)

                                                                            [103]

---

1   As to stamp duty land tax see the Information Binder: Stamp Duty Land Tax [1].
        As to tenancies at will generally see vol 22(1) (2003 Reissue) LANDLORD AND TENANT
     (BUSINESS TENANCIES) Paragraph 9 [31] et seq.
        One of the situations where an implied tenancy at will can arise is where a tenant is holding over
     following the expiry of a lease that does not enjoy the protection of the Landlord and Tenant Act 1954
     Part II (ss 23–46) (23 Halsbury's Statutes (4th Edn) LANDLORD AND TENANT). This precedent
     assumes the parties intend that a new lease will be entered into and creates an express tenancy at will
     documenting the terms of the continued occupancy pending completion of that new lease. Its purpose
     is to try to avoid a tenant subsequently arguing that the interim occupation is under a periodic (or other)
     form of tenancy that attracts security of tenure as was successfully done in *Walji v Mount Cook Land Ltd*
     [2002] 1 P & CR 163, CA. It should be noted that the Landlord and Tenant Act 1954 s 43(3) prevents

a landlord from using a lease for a term of less than six months as a way of avoiding the security of tenure provisions of the Landlord and Tenant Act 1954 where the tenant has been in occupation for more than twelve months. This precedent has been drafted on the basis that it is completed upon expiry of the lease concerned and should be viewed as nothing more than a short-term measure pending completion of the proposed new lease. In *Manfield & Sons Ltd v Botchin* [1970] 2 QB 612, [1970] 3 All ER 143 the tenant remained in occupation for over four and a half years and it was held that this was not inconsistent with a tenancy at will. However, the passage of time is likely to increase the prospects of the tenant being able to successfully argue that a new form of protected tenancy has arisen by virtue of the acts of the parties. This being so, if the proposed new lease is not completed quickly, the tenant should be required to vacate.

For a general form of tenancy of will see Form 2 [51].

2   If any party is a company it is desirable to include the company registration number. This avoids any problems arising when a company has been wound up and a new company formed with the same name, or when the name of a company is changed, or if companies swap names, eg on a reconstruction of a group of companies.

[104]

NOW IT IS AGREED as follows:

1   DEFINITIONS AND INTERPRETATION

1.1   Gender and number

Words importing one gender are to be construed as importing any other gender; words importing the singular are to be construed as importing the plural and vice versa.

1.2   Headings[3]

The clause headings and the table of contents do not form part of this agreement and must not be taken into account in its construction or interpretation. *(amend if marginal notes are used instead of headings)*

3   Headings and marginal notes require the draftsman to provide a word or two to describe every clause in the document. This is not always easy and there are times when the draftsman has to settle for something less than perfection, the only alternative being a heading or note that would be inappropriately long. It would be quite wrong for that title, which its author might admit was not totally apposite but was the best that he could do in a few words, to be used in construing the clause in question.

1.3   Interpretation of 'the Landlord' and 'the Tenant'

The expressions 'the Landlord' and 'the Tenant' shall not include any successors in title or assigns of either party.

[105]

1.4   Interpretation of 'the Premises'

'The Premises' means *(describe the premises)* as comprised in the Lease and reference to the Premises includes reference to any part of the Premises.

1.5   Joint and several liability

Where any party comprises more than one person, the obligations and liabilities of that party under this agreement are to be joint and several obligations and liabilities of those persons.

1.6   'The Lease'

'The Lease' means a lease dated *(date)* and made between (1) [the Landlord] *(or as the case may be)* and (2) [the Tenant] *(or as the case may be)*.

1.7   Obligation not to permit or suffer

Any covenant by the Tenant not to do anything includes an obligation not to permit or suffer[4] that thing to be done by another person.

4   'Permit' may have a different meaning from 'suffer': see *Barton v Reed* [1932] 1 Ch 362 at 375 per Luxmore J. A covenant not to 'permit' activity is broken if the covenantor himself carries it on: see *Oceanic Village Ltd v United Attractions Ltd* [2000] Ch 234, [2000] 1 All ER 975.

1.8   References to clauses

Any reference in this agreement to any clause without further designation is to be construed as a reference to the clause of this agreement so numbered.

1.9   'The Rent'

'The Rent' means the rent of £... a day [together with VAT].

1.10   'The Tenancy'

'The Tenancy' means the tenancy granted by this agreement.

1.11   'VAT'

'VAT' means value added tax or any other tax of a similar nature[5].

5   As to VAT generally see the Information Binder: Property [1]: VAT and Property.

[106]–[110]

2   RECITALS

(adapt to suit the circumstances concerned)

2.1   Past occupation

The Tenant has been in occupation of the Premises in accordance with the terms of the Lease.

2.2   Negotiations

At the date of this agreement the Landlord and the Tenant are negotiating (subject to contract) the grant by the Landlord to the Tenant of a new lease of the Premises.

2.3   Continued occupation

The Tenant has asked the Landlord not to require the Tenant to yield up possession of the Premises in accordance with the Lease and instead to allow the Tenant to continue in occupation of the Premises on the basis of this agreement whilst the negotiations are in progress on the express condition that either the Landlord or the Tenant may without giving any reason immediately determine this agreement on written notice to the other and the Tenant will be bound immediately to vacate the Premises.

3   TENANCY AT WILL

At the Tenant's request the Landlord allows the Tenant to occupy the Premises as a tenant at will commencing on and from the end of the term of the Lease the Tenant yielding and paying to the Landlord the Rent.

[111]

4   RENT

4.1   Payment of rent

The Rent is to be paid on demand and in advance at such time or times as the Landlord thinks fit.

4.2   Refund on termination

On termination of the Tenancy, any rent previously paid in respect of any period falling after the date of termination must be repaid to the Tenant immediately.

4.3   Periodic tenancy excluded

Neither the payment of any rent, nor any demand for payment of it, nor the fact that the amount of the Rent is calculated by reference to a period, is to create, or to cause the Tenancy to become, a periodic tenancy.

5   THE TENANT'S OBLIGATIONS

The Tenant agrees with the Landlord to observe and perform the requirements of this clause 5.

5.1   Compliance with terms of Lease

The Tenant must comply with the terms of the Lease in so far as they are not varied by this agreement and are not inconsistent with a tenancy at will.

5.2   Payment of the Rent

The Tenant must pay the Rent in accordance with clause 4.1 PAYMENT OF RENT.

[112]

5.3   Outgoings

The Tenant must pay, and indemnify the Landlord against, all existing and future rates, taxes, assessments, service charges, and outgoings of an annual or other periodically recurring nature, and insurance premiums paid by the Landlord in respect of the Premises during the currency of the Tenancy apportioned on a time basis if necessary by the Landlord's surveyor for the time being.

5.4   Interest

If and whenever the Tenant fails to pay the Rent or any other money due under this agreement on the due date, the Tenant must pay to the Landlord interest on the Rent or other money as the case may be at the rate of ...% per year above the base rate from time to time of *(specify bank)* from the date on which the payment is due to the date of payment, both before and after any judgment.

5.5   Alterations

The Tenant must not make any alteration or addition whatsoever either to the exterior or the interior of the Premises.

5.6 Return of the Premises

The Tenant must return the Premises in the state required by the Lease on determination of this agreement, and immediately thereafter (and notwithstanding termination of this agreement) clear away all rubbish and make good any damage to the Premises caused by the Tenant, his agents and invitees.

5.7 Nuisance

The Tenant must not cause any nuisance or annoyance to the Landlord or to any adjoining owners or occupiers.

5.8 Disposal

The Tenant must not hold the Premises on trust for another and must not assign, sublet, charge, part with the possession of, or otherwise dispose of the Premises.

5.9 Occupation

The Tenant must not permit the Premises to be occupied or used by any person other than the Tenant and the Tenant's employees [and must not permit the Premises to be occupied by more than ... persons][6].

6   See eg the Fire Precautions (Factories, Offices, Shops and Railway Premises) Order 1989, SI 1989/76.

5.10 Entry

The Tenant must allow the Landlord, and all persons authorised by the Landlord, to enter the Premises at any [reasonable] time to ascertain whether the terms of this agreement have been complied with.

[113]

6 INDEMNITY

The Tenant agrees at all times to indemnify the Landlord against all losses, claims, demands, actions, proceedings, damages, costs or expenses or other liability arising through any default in compliance with this agreement or arising from any other act or default of the Tenant its agents or invitees.

7 DECLARATIONS

The parties agree and declare as set out in this clause 7.

7.1 Determination

This agreement is to be determined[7] immediately:

7.1.1   by any demand for possession of the Premises made by or on behalf of the Landlord[8], or

7.1.2   (without prejudice to any subsisting obligation of the Tenant imposed by this agreement) by any delivery of possession by the Tenant to the Landlord[9], or

7.1.3   the Tenancy being personal to the parties, by the death or dissolution of either party or by any disposition or purported disposition of the interest of either party whether voluntary or otherwise[10].

[114]

7   A right of re-entry is inappropriate for a tenancy at will as the landlord can demand possession at any time.

8   It is an inherent feature of a tenancy at will that it is determinable at any time at the will of either party: see Form 2 note 1 [54].

9   It is an inherent feature of a tenancy at will that it is determinable at any time at the will of either party: see Form 2 note 1 [54].

10   A tenancy at will is a personal relationship between the original landlord and tenant, and so has traditionally been held to be determined by, eg, the death of either party, the tenant's bankruptcy, or voluntary alienation of the premises by either party with notice to the other. The authorities for these propositions are, however, somewhat old, and the agreement should deal expressly with them.

7.2   Exclusion of warranty as to use

The Landlord does not imply or warrant that the Premises may be used for the purpose authorised by this agreement or any other purpose.

[8   COSTS

The Tenant will on exchange of this agreement pay the costs of the Landlord's solicitors in respect of the preparation of this agreement amounting to £... together with VAT.]

AS WITNESS etc *(see vol 12(2) (2003 Reissue) DEEDS, AGREEMENTS ETC)*

(signatures of both parties)
[115]–[150]

B: WHOLE LEASES

1: INDUSTRIAL AND WAREHOUSE PREMISES

4

Lease of a light industrial building or warehouse where the landlord does not own adjoining property[1]

CONTENTS

(NB: numbers in [ ] below refer to this volume and should be altered to suit the page or reference numbers actually used)

1 DEFINITIONS AND INTERPRETATION

1.1 'The Conduits' . . . . [158]
1.2 'The [Contractual] Term' . . . . [159]
1.3 'Development' . . . . [160]
[1.4 'The Exterior Decorating Years' . . . . [160]]
1.5 Gender and number . . . . [160]
1.6 Headings . . . . [160]
1.7 'The Industrial Covenants' . . . . [161]
[151]

[1.8 'The Initial Rent' .... [161]]
1.9 'The Insurance Rent' .... [161]
1.10 'The Insured Risks' .... [161]
1.11 'Interest' .... [162]
1.12 'The Interest Rate' .... [162]
[1.13 'The Interior Decorating Years' .... [163]]
1.14 Interpretation of 'consent' and 'approved' .... [163]
1.15 Interpretation of 'the Guarantor' .... [164]
1.16 Interpretation of 'the Landlord' .... [164]
1.17 Interpretation of 'the last year of the Term' and 'the end of the Term' .... [164]
1.18 Interpretation of 'the Tenant' .... [164]
1.19 Interpretation of 'this Lease' .... [164]
1.20 Joint and several liability .... [165]
1.21 'The Liability Period' .... [165]
1.22 'Losses' .... [166]
1.23 'The 1954 Act' .... [166]
1.24 'The 1995 Act' .... [166]
1.25 Obligation not to permit or suffer .... [166]
1.26 'The Permitted Use' .... [167]
1.27 'The Plan' .... [167]
1.28 'The Planning Acts' .... [168]
1.29 'The Premises' .... [168]
1.30 References to clauses and schedules .... [169]
1.31 References to rights of access .... [169]
1.32 References to statutes .... [169]
1.33 'The Rent' .... [170]
1.34 'The Rent Commencement Date' .... [170]
[1.35 'The Review Dates' .... [171]]
1.36 'The Surveyor' .... [171]
[1.37 'The Term' .... [172]]
1.38 Terms from the 1995 Act .... [172]
1.39 'VAT' .... [172]

2 DEMISE .... [181]
                                                              [152]

3 THE TENANT'S COVENANTS

3.1 Rent .... [191]
3.2 Outgoings and VAT .... [192]
[3.3 Cost of services consumed .... [192]]
3.4 Repair, cleaning and decoration .... [193]
3.5 Waste and alterations .... [196]
3.6 Aerials, signs and advertisements .... [198]
3.7 Statutory obligations .... [198]
3.8 Entry to inspect and notice to repair .... [200]
3.9 Alienation .... [211]
3.10 Nuisance and residential restrictions .... [222]
3.11 Costs of applications, notices and recovery of arrears .. [231]
3.12 Planning and development .... [232]
3.13 Plans, documents and information .... [234]

3.14 Indemnities . . . . [235]
3.15 Reletting boards and viewing . . . . [235]
3.16 Obstruction and encroachment . . . . [236]
3.17 Yielding up . . . . [236]
3.18 Interest on arrears . . . . [237]
3.19 Statutory notices . . . . [237]
3.20 Keyholders . . . . [237]
3.21 Viewing on sale of reversion . . . . [237]
3.22 Defective premises . . . . [237]
3.23 Replacement guarantor . . . . [238]
3.24 Exercise of the Landlord's rights . . . . [238]
3.25 The Industrial Covenants . . . . [239]
3.26 Costs of grant of this Lease . . . . [239]
3.27 Consent to the Landlord's release . . . . [239]

4 QUIET ENJOYMENT . . . . [251]
[153]

5 INSURANCE
5.1 Warranty as to convictions . . . . [252]
5.2 Covenant to insure . . . . [253]
5.3 Details of the insurance . . . . [253]
5.4 Payment of the Insurance Rent . . . . [255]
5.5 Suspension of the Rent . . . . [256]
5.6 Reinstatement and termination . . . . [257]
5.7 Tenant's further insurance covenants . . . . [262]
[5.8 Landlord's further insurance covenants . . . . [264]]

6 GUARANTEE PROVISIONS
6.1 The Guarantor's covenants . . . . [281]
[6.2 The Landlord's covenant . . . . [286]]

7 FORFEITURE . . . . [301]

8 MISCELLANEOUS
8.1 Exclusion of warranty as to use . . . . [311]
8.2 Exclusion of third party rights . . . . [311]
8.3 Representations . . . . [311]
8.4 Documents under hand . . . . [312]
8.5 Tenant's property . . . . [312]
8.6 Compensation on vacating excluded . . . . [312]
8.7 Notices . . . . [313]
8.8 [New (or) Old] lease . . . . [314]
[8.9 Capacity of tenants . . . . [315]]
[8.10 Exclusion of the 1954 Act Sections 24–28 . . . . [315]]

SCHEDULE 1: THE RIGHTS RESERVED
1-1 Right of entry to inspect . . . . [321]
1-2 Access on renewal or rent review . . . . [321]

SCHEDULE 2: THE RENT AND RENT REVIEW

SCHEDULE 3: THE INDUSTRIAL COVENANTS

3-1 Use . . . . [322]
3-2 Smoke abatement . . . . [322]
3-3 Environmental protection . . . . [323]
3-4 Roof and floor loading . . . . [325]
3-5 Machinery . . . . [325]
3-6 Signs . . . . [325]

SCHEDULE 4: THE SUBJECTIONS

SCHEDULE 5: THE AUTHORISED GUARANTEE AGREEMENT

[154]

AGREEMENT

[HM LAND REGISTRY

LAND REGISTRATION ACT 2002

Administrative area	*(insert details)*
Title number out of which lease is granted	*(title number)*
Property let	*(postal address or description)*]

[155]

THIS LEASE is made the .... day of .... BETWEEN:

(1)   *(name of landlord)* [of *(address)* *(or as appropriate)* the registered office of which is at *(address)*] [Company Registration no ...][2] ('the Landlord') [and]

(2)   *(name of tenant)* [of *(address)* *(or as appropriate)* being a company registered in [England and Wales *(or)* Scotland][3] the registered office of which is at *(address)*] [Company Registration no ...] ('the Tenant') [and

(3)   *(name of guarantor)* [of *(address)* *(or as appropriate)* the registered office of which is at *(address)*] [Company Registration no ...] ('the Guarantor')]

[156]

---

1   As to stamp duty land tax see the Information Binder: Stamp Duty Land Tax [1].

As to Land Registry Fees see the Information Binder: Property [1]: Property Fees.

On the grant out of an unregistered freehold estate in land of a lease for a term of more than seven years from the date of the grant, application must be made to register the title to the leasehold interest granted: see the Land Registration Act 2002 s 4(1)(c) (37 Halsbury's Statutes (4th Edn) REAL PROPERTY). The tenant must obtain an epitome of title to the freehold reversion, investigate it, and mark it as examined, otherwise he will not be able to be registered with an absolute title: see vol 25(1) (2003 Reissue) LAND REGISTRATION Paragraph 21.1 [132].

If the freehold reversion is registered, the grant of a lease for a term of more than seven years from the date of the grant must be completed by registration: see the Land Registration Act 2002 s 27(2)(b)(i).

As to the form and contents of leases see vol 22(1) (2003 Reissue) LANDLORD AND TENANT (BUSINESS TENANCIES) Paragraph 104 [601] et seq. As to registered land generally see vol 25(1) (2003 Reissue) LAND REGISTRATION. As to registration of title to leases see vol 25(1) (2003 Reissue) LAND REGISTRATION Paragraph 143 [601] et seq.

This is a lease of land on a part of which a light industrial building or warehouse has been erected. The landlord owns no adjoining premises and no rights are granted or services provided. The tenant is responsible for repair of the premises and the decoration of both the exterior and the interior. The landlord insures the premises and the tenant refunds the cost of the premiums. There is provision for rent review, and also for a guarantor.

2   If any party is a company it is desirable to include the company registration number. This avoids any problems arising when a company has been wound up and a new company formed with the same name, or when the name of a company is changed, or if companies swap names, eg on a reconstruction of a group of companies. In addition, where a company applies to be registered as proprietor of a registered estate or registered charge, the application must state the company's registration number: see the Land Registration Rules 2003, SI 2003/1417 r 181.

3   Where the tenant is a company registered in England and Wales or Scotland, and the lease is registrable, an application for first registration of the lease (where the landlord's title is unregistered), or registration of the lease as a registrable disposition (where the landlord's title is registered), and the tenant as proprietor of the leasehold title, must state the company's registered number: see SI 2003/1417 r 181(1). There seems to be no reason why the certificate and statement should not be contained in the disposition in favour of the proprietor, where convenient.

[157]

NOW THIS DEED WITNESSES as follows:

1   DEFINITIONS AND INTERPRETATION

For all purposes of this Lease[4] the terms defined in this clause have the meanings specified.

4   One view would add 'unless the context otherwise requires' or 'where the context so admits' and in fact this may be implied (see *Meux v Jacobs* (1875) LR 7 HL 481 at 493; *Law Society v United Service Bureau Ltd* [1934] 1 KB 343, DC) but the better course is to use defined terms in such a way that there are no circumstances where the defined meaning does not apply.

1.1   'The Conduits'

'The Conduits' means the pipes, sewers, drains, mains, ducts, conduits, gutters, watercourses, wires, cables, [laser optical fibres, data or impulse transmission, communication or reception systems,] channels, flues and all other conducting media — including any fixings, louvres, cowls, covers and any other ancillary apparatus — that are in, on, over or under the Premises.

[158]

1.2   'The [Contractual] Term'[5]

'The [Contractual][6] Term' means *(insert number)* years commencing on and including *(date of commencement of term)*[7].

5   As to the commencement of the term see vol 22(1) (2003 Reissue) LANDLORD AND TENANT (BUSINESS TENANCIES) Paragraph 135 [670].

As to registration see note 1 above. Where the landlord's title is unregistered, the grantee must apply for registration within a period of two months from the date of the disposition if the lease is granted for a term of more than seven years. If no such application is made the disposition becomes void as regards any transfer, grant or creation of a legal estate: see the Land Registration Act 2002 s 6. Where the landlord's title is registered and the lease is for a term of more than seven years, the tenant should protect the intended lease by applying for an official search, and an application to register the lease should be made before expiry of the search, otherwise the lease will be susceptible to loss of priority: see the Land Registration Act 2002 s 27.

6   The demise in this lease is for 'the Contractual Term', which is defined as a fixed term of years. The expression 'the Term', as defined in clause 1.37 [172] 'THE TERM', is used in covenants so that they continue to apply during any period of holding over or continuance or extension of the contractual term. Some difficulties arise if this structure is used in a draft lease where security of tenure is to be excluded under the Landlord and Tenant Act 1954 s 38A(1) as inserted by SI 2003/3096 (23 Halsbury's Statutes (4th Edn) LANDLORD AND TENANT). The demise is for the contractual term and the inclusion of the definition of 'the Term' does not prevent the lease being 'for a term of years certain' as required by the Landlord and Tenant Act 1954 s 38A(1). However, reference to continuance of the contractual term by statute is inappropriate where the operation of the security of tenure provisions in the Landlord and Tenant Act 1954 ss 24–28 is to be excluded. If a lease is contracted out of the Landlord and Tenant Act 1954 there can be no statutory extension, and if the tenant remains in occupation at the end of the contractual term he is holding over unlawfully unless there is an express agreement to extend the contractual term operating as a surrender and re-grant so that the original lease — and the agreement under the Landlord and Tenant Act 1954 s 38A(1) — has no further effect. It is suggested that in these circumstances the drafting should be simplified to include a single term (defined simply as 'the Term') by reference to the period of the contractual term. This can be achieved by amending this clause in the manner suggested and substituting it for clause 1.37 [172] 'THE TERM'.

7   For estate management reasons it is usually desirable to insert a quarter day here — or a rent day when rent is due on days other than quarter days — ie generally the one preceding the earlier of the date of possession and the date of execution.

[159]

1.3   'Development'

References to 'development' are references to development as defined by the Town and Country Planning Act 1990 Section 55.

[1.4   'The Exterior Decorating Years'

'The Exterior Decorating Years' means *(specify years).*] *(omit if not required, eg if the first alternative in clause 3.4.6 [195] DECORATION is used)*

1.5   Gender and number

Words importing one gender include all other genders; words importing the singular include the plural and vice versa[8].

8   See the Law of Property Act 1925 s 61 (37 Halsbury's Statutes (4th Edn) REAL PROPERTY).

1.6   Headings[9]

The clause, paragraph and schedule headings and the table of contents do not form part of this document and are not to be taken into account in its construction or interpretation. *(amend if marginal notes are used instead of headings)*

9   Headings and marginal notes require the draftsman to provide a word or two to describe every clause in the lease. This is not always easy and there are times when the draftsman will have to settle for something less than perfection, the only alternative being a heading or note that would be inappropriately long. It would be quite wrong for that title, which its author might admit was not totally apposite but was the best that he could do in a few words, to be used in construing the clause in question.

[160]

1.7   'The Industrial Covenants'

'The Industrial Covenants' mean the covenants set out in schedule 3 THE INDUSTRIAL COVENANTS.

[1.8   'The Initial Rent'

'The Initial Rent' means [the sum of £... a year *(or as required by the rent and review provisions to be used)*].] *(this definition is not required if the rent is not reviewable)*

1.9   'The Insurance Rent'[10]

'The Insurance Rent' means the [gross sums including any commission *(or as required)* sums net of any commission] that the Landlord from time to time pays —

1.9.1   by way of premium for insuring the Premises, including insuring for loss of rent, in accordance with his obligations contained in this Lease,

1.9.2   by way of premium for insuring in such amount and on such terms as [the Landlord acting reasonably considers appropriate *(or as required)* is reasonable] against all liability of the Landlord to third parties arising out of or in connection with any matter including or relating to the Premises, and

1.9.3   for insurance valuations.

10   As to reimbursement of insurance premiums see vol 22(1) (2003 Reissue) LANDLORD AND TENANT (BUSINESS TENANCIES) Paragraph 230 [1026].

1.10   'The Insured Risks'

'The Insured Risks' means the risks of loss or damage by fire[, storm, tempest, earthquake, lightning, explosion, riot, civil commotion, malicious damage, [terrorism,] impact by vehicles and by aircraft and articles dropped from aircraft — other than war risks — flood damage and bursting and overflowing of water pipes and tanks,] and such other risks, whether or not in the nature of the foregoing, as the Landlord [acting reasonably] from time to time decides to insure against[11].

11   As to the risks to be insured and the tenant's concerns see vol 22(1) (2003 Reissue) LANDLORD AND TENANT (BUSINESS TENANCIES) Paragraph 235 [1033].

[161]

1.11   'Interest'

References to 'interest' are references to interest payable during the period from the date on which the payment is due to the date of payment, both before and after any judgment, at the Interest Rate then prevailing [*(where the interest rate is defined by reference to a bank base rate)* or, should the base rate referred to in clause 1.12 'THE INTEREST RATE' cease to exist[12], at another rate of interest closely comparable with the Interest Rate [to be agreed between the parties or in default of agreement to be determined by [the Surveyor, acting as an expert and not as an arbitrator *(or as required)* a chartered accountant appointed by agreement between the parties or in default of agreement nominated by the President of the Institute of Chartered Accountants in England and Wales, acting as an expert and not as an arbitrator][13] *(or as required)* decided on by the Landlord acting reasonably]].

12   If base rates are referred to, the possibility of their ceasing to exist should be provided for. Alternatively, the Law Society's interest rate may be specified.
13   This provision may be expanded to provide for deeming the parties to have disagreed after a certain time, deputy appointors etc.

1.12   'The Interest Rate'

'The Interest Rate'[14] means the rate of ...% a year[15] above [the base lending rate of *(specify bank)* or such other bank [being a member of the British Bankers Association] as the Landlord may from time to time nominate in writing[16] *(or as required)* the Law Society's interest rate[17]].

14   As to the covenant to pay interest see vol 22(1) (2003 Reissue) LANDLORD AND TENANT (BUSINESS TENANCIES) Paragraph 154 [767].
15   Words such as 'with a minimum of ...%' should not be used because, if interest rates drop during the term to such an extent that the minimum rate specified represents significantly more than a few percent over the basic borrowing rate, the provision might be void as a penalty. As to what amounts to a penalty see *Dunlop Pneumatic Tyre Co Ltd v New Garage and Motor Co Ltd* [1915] AC 79, HL; *Cellulose Acetate Silk Co Ltd v Widnes Foundry (1925) Ltd* [1933] AC 20, HL. In view of this, landlords would be unwise to provide for a rate of more than a few percent over base rate, and even this is in fact a penalty rate and should be resisted by the tenant.
16   The chance to change the bank may be useful, especially on a sale of the reversion, so that the landlord can always provide for his bank for the time being to be specified, but the tenant should try to limit the choice to major clearing banks.
17   The Law Society's interest rate is published weekly in the Law Society's Gazette.

[162]

[1.13   'The Interior Decorating Years'

'The Interior Decorating Years' means *(specify years.] (omit if not required, eg if the first alternative in clause 3.4.6 [195] DECORATION is used)*

1.14   Interpretation of 'consent' and 'approved'

1.14.1   *Prior written consent or approval*

References to 'consent of the Landlord' or words to similar effect are references to a prior written consent signed by or on behalf of the Landlord and references to the need for anything to be 'approved by the Landlord' or words to similar effect are references to the need for a prior written approval by or on behalf of the Landlord.

1.14.2   *Consent or approval of mortgagee or head landlord*

Any provisions in this Lease referring to the consent or approval of the Landlord are to be construed as also requiring the consent or approval of any mortgagee of the Premises and any head landlord where that consent is required [under a mortgage or headlease in existence at the date of this document][18]. Nothing in this Lease is to be construed as imposing any obligation on a mortgagee or head landlord not to refuse any such consent or approval unreasonably.

18   The tenant should include these words so that the clause applies *only* where the consent of the mortgagee or head landlord is in fact required under the terms of an *existing* mortgage or headlease. The tenant should request a copy of the document concerned to establish the rights of the mortgagee or head landlord in relation to any consents that he may seek. The risk to the tenant of the clause without these words is that, by subsequently creating a mortgage or headlease, the landlord could, innocently or deliberately, bring about a situation where his consent may be refused in circumstances in which it would otherwise have been unreasonable to do so. In particular, the effect on the tenant's ability to assign or sublet could be serious.

[163]

1.15   Interpretation of 'the Guarantor'[19]

The expression 'the Guarantor' includes [*(where there is a guarantor for the original tenant)* not only the person named above as the Guarantor, but also][20] any person who enters into covenants with the Landlord pursuant to clause 3.9.5.2 CONDITIONS or clause 3.23 REPLACEMENT GUARANTOR.

19   As to guarantors see vol 22(1) (2003 Reissue) LANDLORD AND TENANT (BUSINESS TENANCIES) Paragraphs 40 [201], 71 [278] et seq.
20   Where there is no guarantor for the original tenant, if it is felt undesirable to have covenants in a lease and no party, at least initially, to enter into them, the guarantor's covenants could be included in a schedule.

1.16   Interpretation of 'the Landlord'

The expression 'the Landlord' includes the person or persons from time to time entitled to possession of the Premises when this Lease comes to an end.

1.17   Interpretation of 'the last year of the Term' and 'the end of the Term'

References to 'the last year of the Term' are references to the actual last year of the Term howsoever it determines, and references to the 'end of the Term' are references to the end of the Term whensoever and howsoever it determines.

1.18   Interpretation of 'the Tenant'

'The Tenant' includes any person who is for the time being bound by the tenant covenants of this Lease except where the name of *(name of original tenant)* appears.

1.19   Interpretation of 'this Lease'

Unless expressly stated to the contrary, the expression 'this Lease' includes any document supplemental to or collateral with this document or entered into in accordance with this document.

[164]

1.20   Joint and several liability

Where any party to this Lease for the time being comprises two or more persons, obligations expressed or implied to be made by or with that party are deemed to be made by or with the persons comprising that party jointly and severally.

1.21   'The Liability Period'[21]

'The Liability Period' means —

[1.21.1   in the case of *(name of guarantor for the original tenant)*, the period during which *(name of original tenant)* is bound by the tenant covenants of this Lease together with any additional period during which *(name of original tenant)* is liable under an authorised guarantee agreement,] *(omit if there is no guarantor for the original tenant)*

1.21.2   in the case of any guarantor required pursuant to clause 3.9.5.2 CONDITIONS, the period during which the relevant assignee is bound by the tenant covenants of this Lease together with any additional period during which that assignee is liable under an authorised guarantee agreement,

1.21.3   in the case of any guarantor under an authorised guarantee agreement, the period during which the relevant assignee is bound by the tenant covenants of this Lease, and

1.21.4   in the case of any guarantor required pursuant to clause 3.9.8.7 TERMS OF A PERMITTED SUBLEASE, the period during which the relevant assignee of the sublease is bound by the tenant covenants of that sublease.

21   The liability of the guarantor should be expressed to last while the original tenant, or as the case may be the assignee, is bound by the tenant covenants in the lease — or in the case of clause 1.21.4 the sublease — rather than while the lease is vested in that person, to take account of the possibility of an excluded assignment being made and the tenant — or subtenant — remaining liable. An excluded assignment means that the tenant — or subtenant — is precluded from tenant release under the Landlord and Tenant (Covenants) Act 1995 (23 Halsbury's Statutes (4th Edn) LANDLORD AND TENANT).
     The Landlord and Tenant (Covenants) Act 1995 does not clearly indicate whether the liability of a contractual guarantor can be expressed to extend to any period during which the tenant is bound by an authorised guarantee agreement, but the better view is that it is possible. The policy of the Act certainly suggests that this should be the case.

[165]

1.22   'Losses'

References to 'losses' are references to liabilities, damages or losses, awards of damages or compensation, penalties, costs, disbursements and expenses arising from any claim, demand, action or proceedings.

1.23   'The 1954 Act'

'The 1954 Act' means the Landlord and Tenant Act 1954 [and all statutes, regulations and orders included by virtue of clause 1.32 REFERENCES TO STATUTES][22].

22   The words in square brackets are strictly speaking not required because they merely state what would be the case anyway by virtue of clause 1.32 [169] REFERENCES TO STATUTES. Nevertheless, as much could turn on the point (see *Brett v Brett Essex Golf Club Ltd* (1986) 52 P & CR 330, [1986] 1 EGLR 154, CA), the parties may prefer to deal expressly with the point.

1.24   'The 1995 Act'

'The 1995 Act' means the Landlord and Tenant (Covenants) Act 1995 [and all statutes, regulations and orders included by virtue of clause 1.32 REFERENCES TO STATUTES][23].

23   See note 22 to clause 1.23 [166] 'THE 1954 ACT'.

1.25   Obligation not to permit or suffer

Any covenant by the Tenant not to do anything includes an obligation [to use reasonable endeavours] not to permit or suffer[24] that thing to be done by another person [where the Tenant is aware that the thing is being done].

24   'Permit' may have a different meaning from 'suffer': see *Barton v Reed* [1932] 1 Ch 362 at 375 per Luxmore J. A covenant not to 'permit' activity is broken if the covenantor himself carries it on: see *Oceanic Village Ltd v United Attractions Ltd* [2000] Ch 234, [2000] 1 All ER 975.

[166]

1.26   'The Permitted Use'[25]

'The Permitted Use' means [*(specify use)* or such other use falling within Classes *(state classes, eg B1, B2 or B8)* of the Schedule to the Town and Country Planning (Use Classes) Order 1987, notwithstanding any amendment or revocation of that Order[26], as the Landlord from time to time approves[, such approval not to be unreasonably withheld [or delayed]] *(or if the landlord does not require control over the specific trade)* any use that falls within Classes *(state classes, eg B1, B2 or B8)* of the Schedule to the Town and Country Planning (Use Classes) Order 1987, notwithstanding any amendment or revocation of that Order].

25   As to use see vol 22(1) (2003 Reissue) LANDLORD AND TENANT (BUSINESS TENANCIES) Paragraph 170 [861] et seq.

26   As use classes orders change frequently, it is important to make clear which class is intended to apply, the class in existence at the date of the lease or the class as amended during the term of the lease.

1.27   'The Plan'[27]

'The Plan' means the plan annexed to this Lease.

27   As to the use and role of plans see vol 22(1) (2003 Reissue) LANDLORD AND TENANT (BUSINESS TENANCIES) Paragraphs 117 [636], 118 [638]. A plan may not always be required, eg a demise of all the land within a registered title. If the lease is registrable, a plan 'for identification purposes only' or where there is some other disclaimer as to the extent to which it can be relied on for conveyancing purposes is not sufficient if part of the land in a registered title is being dealt with.

[167]

1.28   'The Planning Acts'

'The Planning Acts' means the Town and Country Planning Act 1990, the Planning (Listed Buildings and Conservation Areas) Act 1990, the Planning (Consequential Provisions) Act 1990, the Planning (Hazardous Substances) Act 1990, the Planning and Compensation Act 1991, the Planning and Compulsory Purchase Act 2004 [and all statutes, regulations and orders included by virtue of clause 1.32 REFERENCES TO STATUTES][28].

28   See note 22 to clause 1.23 [166] 'THE 1954 ACT'.

1.29   'The Premises'[29]

1.29.1   *Definition of 'the Premises'*

'The Premises' means the land and building known as *(insert postal address)* [shown [for the purpose of identification only] edged *(state colour, eg red)* on the Plan].

29   As to parcels generally see vol 22(1) (2003 Reissue) LANDLORD AND TENANT (BUSINESS TENANCIES) Paragraph 116 [634].

1.29.2   *Interpretation of 'the Premises'[30]*

The expression 'the Premises' includes —

1.29.2.1   all buildings, erections, structures, fixtures[31], fittings and appurtenances on the Premises from time to time,

1.29.2.2   all additions, alterations and improvements carried out during the Term, and

1.29.2.3   the Conduits,

but excludes [the air space above[32] and] any fixtures installed by the Tenant [or any predecessors in title] that can be removed from the Premises without defacing the Premises. Unless the contrary is expressly stated, 'the Premises' includes any part or parts of the Premises.

30   As to implied grants and reservations see vol 22(1) (2003 Reissue) LANDLORD AND TENANT (BUSINESS TENANCIES) Paragraph 125 [650].
31   As to fixtures see vol 22(1) (2003 Reissue) LANDLORD AND TENANT (BUSINESS TENANCIES) Paragraph 121 [644].
32   As to air space, subsoil, cellars and footings see vol 22(1) (2003 Reissue) LANDLORD AND TENANT (BUSINESS TENANCIES) Paragraph 119 [640]. Strictly speaking, this exclusion means that the tenant may not go onto the roof to inspect or repair it unless he is held to have an easement of necessity to do so. As to easements of necessity generally see 13 Halsbury's Laws (4th Edn Reissue) EASEMENTS AND PROFITS À PRENDRE. If the landlord requires the upper limit of the demised premises to be defined, the tenant, in the case of a full repairing lease, should require a right to enter the landlord's air space above the demised premises to inspect or repair the upper limit of the premises. For a form that may be modified for this purpose see vol 22(3) (1997 Reissue) LANDLORD AND TENANT (BUSINESS TENANCIES) Form 77 [6451].

[168]

1.30   References to clauses and schedules

Any reference in this document to a clause, paragraph or schedule without further designation is to be construed as a reference to the clause, paragraph or schedule of this document so numbered.

1.31   References to rights of access

References to any right of the Landlord to have access to the Premises are to be construed as extending to any head landlord and any mortgagee of the Premises [— where the headlease or mortgage grants such rights of access to the head landlord or mortgagee —] and to all persons authorised in writing by the Landlord and any head landlord or mortgagee, including agents, professional advisers, contractors, workmen and others.

1.32   References to statutes

Unless expressly stated to the contrary, any reference to a specific statute includes any statutory extension or modification, amendment or re-enactment of that statute and any regulations or orders made under it, and any general reference to a statute includes any regulations or orders made under that statute[33].

33   Unfortunately the Interpretation Act 1978 ss 17, 23(3) (41 Halsbury's Statutes (4th Edn) STATUTES) does not quite go far enough to enable this clause to be dispensed with altogether, particularly where a statute is modified.

[169]

1.33   'The Rent'[34]

[Until the First Review Date 'the Rent' means the Initial Rent. Thereafter 'the Rent' means the sum ascertained in accordance with schedule 2 THE RENT AND RENT REVIEW. 'The Rent' does not include the Insurance Rent[35], but the term 'the Lease Rents' means both the Rent and the Insurance Rent. *(or as required by the rent and review provisions used)*]

34   This clause assumes that the rent is reviewable. If the rent is not reviewable clause 1.8 [161] 'THE INITIAL RENT' should be omitted and this clause amended as appropriate.
35   Because of this exclusion the insurance rent is not suspended under clause 5.5 [256] SUSPENSION OF THE RENT.

1.34 'The Rent Commencement Date'

'The Rent Commencement Date' means *(insert the date on which payment of rent is to start)*[36].

36   This provision may be used to provide for a rent-free period, or for the situation where the tenant had possession before the execution of the lease on the basis that rent should be paid from the date of possession. If either the date of execution of the lease or the date of commencement of the term is to be the date for commencement of rent, that date should be inserted here.

[1.35 'The Review Dates'[37]

'The First Review Date' means *(date)*. 'The Review Dates' means the First Review Date and every *(insert ordinal, eg 3rd)* anniversary of that date during the [Contractual] Term [*(if appropriate for the review provisions used)* — and any other date from time to time specified under *(insert the relevant provision: see eg vol 22(3) (1997 Reissue) LANDLORD AND TENANT (BUSINESS TENANCIES) Form 180 paragraph {2}-4 [6728] EFFECT OF COUNTER-INFLATION PROVISIONS)*]. References to 'a review date' are references to any one of the Review Dates.] *(omit if not required by the review provisions to be used, or if the rent is not reviewable)*

37   As to rent review dates and intervals see vol 22(1) (2003 Reissue) LANDLORD AND TENANT (BUSINESS TENANCIES) Paragraph 302 [1333] et seq. Where there might be a statutory continuation of the lease, the landlord may wish to ensure that there is a review date shortly before the end of the contractual term to obviate the need to apply for an interim rent. The tenant may wish to insist on the word 'contractual' remaining so that the rent review provisions do not apply during any period of lawful holding over or extension or continuance of the contractual term. In circumstances where there is no prospect of statutory continuation the word 'contractual' should be omitted in any event: see note 6 to clause 1.2 [159] 'THE [CONTRACTUAL] TERM'.

1.36 'The Surveyor'[38]

'The Surveyor' means *(name)* or any person or firm appointed by the Landlord in his place. The Surveyor may be an employee of the Landlord or a company that is a member of the same group as the Landlord within the meaning of the 1954 Act Section 42. The expression 'the Surveyor' includes the person or firm appointed by the Landlord to collect the Lease Rents[39].

38   For a provision that the landlord's surveyor must be a member of a relevant professional body see vol 22(3) (1997 Reissue) LANDLORD AND TENANT (BUSINESS TENANCIES) Form 152 [6648].
39   As to the definition of 'the Lease Rents' see clause 1.33 [170] 'THE RENT'.

[1.37 'The Term'

'The Term' means the Contractual Term and any period of holding-over or extension or continuance of the Contractual Term by statute or common law[40].] *(omit if the lease is to be contracted out of the Landlord and Tenant Act 1954)*[41]

40   The demise in this lease is for 'the Contractual Term', which is defined as a fixed term of years. The expression 'the Term' is used in covenants so that they continue to apply during any period of holding-over or continuance or extension of the contractual term. As to the liability of a guarantor during a period of statutory continuation see vol 22(1) (2003 Reissue) LANDLORD AND TENANT (BUSINESS TENANCIES) Paragraph 73 [282].
41   Some difficulties arise if the structure referred to in note 40 above is used in a draft lease where security of tenure is to be excluded under the Landlord and Tenant Act 1954 s 38A(1) as inserted by SI 2003/3096. The demise is for the contractual term and the inclusion of the definition of 'the Term' does not prevent the lease being 'for a term of years certain' as required by the Landlord and

Tenant Act 1954 s 38A(1). However, reference to continuance of the contractual term by statute is inappropriate where the operation of the security of tenure provisions in the Landlord and Tenant Act 1954 ss 24–28 is to be excluded. If a lease is contracted out of the Landlord and Tenant Act 1954 there can be no statutory extension, and if the tenant remains in occupation at the end of the contractual term he is holding over unlawfully unless there is an express agreement to extend the contractual term operating as a surrender and re-grant so that the original lease — and the agreement under the Landlord and Tenant Act 1954 s 38A(1) — has no further effect. It is suggested that in these circumstances the drafting should be simplified to include a single term (defined simply as 'the Term') by reference to the period of the contractual term. This can be achieved by amending clause 1.2 [159] 'THE [CONTRACTUAL] TERM' as suggested and substituting it for this clause.

1.38   Terms from the 1995 Act

Where the expressions 'landlord covenants', 'tenant covenants', or 'authorised guarantee agreement' are used in this Lease they are to have the same meaning as is given by the 1995 Act Section 28(1).

1.39   'VAT'[42]

'VAT' means value added tax or any other tax of a similar nature and unless otherwise expressly stated all references to rents or other sums payable by the Tenant are exclusive of VAT.

42   As to VAT generally see the Information Binder: Property [1]: VAT and Property.

[172]–[180]

2   DEMISE

The Landlord lets[43] the Premises to the Tenant [with [full *(or)* limited] title guarantee], excepting and reserving to the Landlord the rights specified in schedule 1 THE RIGHTS RESERVED, to hold the Premises to the Tenant for the [Contractual][44] Term, subject to [all rights, easements, privileges, restrictions, covenants and stipulations of whatever nature affecting the Premises including any matters contained or referred to in schedule 4 THE SUBJECTIONS *(or as required)* the rights, easements, privileges, restrictions, covenants and stipulations affecting the Premises contained or referred to in schedule 4 THE SUBJECTIONS][45], yielding and paying[46] to the Landlord —

2.1   the Rent, without any deduction or set-off[47], by equal quarterly payments in advance[48] on the usual quarter days[49] in every year and proportionately for any period of less than a year, the first such payment, being a proportionate sum in respect of the period from and including the Rent Commencement Date to and including the day before the quarter day next after the Rent Commencement Date, to be paid on the date of this document[50], and

2.2   by way of further rent, the Insurance Rent[51], payable on demand in accordance with clause 5.4 PAYMENT OF THE INSURANCE RENT.

[181]

43   Traditionally, the operative word in a lease executed as a deed was 'demises' but any words sufficient to show the parties' intention may be used.
44   See note 41 to clause 1.37 [172] 'THE TERM'.
45   The tenant should argue for the second version, making the schedule comprehensive rather than illustrative.
46   The words 'yielding and paying' imply a covenant to pay rent: see *Vyvyan v Arthur* (1823) 1 B & C 410. An express covenant is now invariably included, because further procedural matters are contained in it.
47   As to deductions and set off see vol 22(1) (2003 Reissue) LANDLORD AND TENANT (BUSINESS TENANCIES) Paragraph 147 [753].
48   In the absence of an express provision, rent is payable in arrears.

49   The usual quarter days are 25 March, 24 June, 29 September and 25 December. A reference to 'the usual quarter days' is all that is necessary when rent is to be paid on these days.

50   If the first payment is not a complete instalment, the lease must provide for the date on which it is to be paid, the amount, and the period it is to cover.

51   As to the advantages of reserving the insurance rent as rent see vol 22(1) (2003 Reissue) LANDLORD AND TENANT (BUSINESS TENANCIES) Paragraph 151 [761].

[182]–[190]

3   THE TENANT'S COVENANTS

The Tenant covenants with the Landlord to observe and perform the requirements of this clause 3.

3.1   Rent

3.1.1   *Payment of the Lease Rents*

The Tenant must pay the Lease Rents[52] on the days and in the manner set out in this Lease, and must not exercise or seek to exercise any right or claim to withhold rent, or any right or claim to legal or equitable set-off[53] [except that referred to in *(give details of any provisions granting an express right of set-off)*][54].

52   As to the definition of 'the Lease Rents' see clause 1.33 [170] 'THE RENT'.

53   See, eg, *British Anzani (Felixstowe) Ltd v International Marine Management (UK) Ltd* [1980] QB 137, [1979] 2 All ER 1063; *Lee-Parker v Izzet* [1971] 3 All ER 1099, [1971] 1 WLR 1688. As to deductions and set-off see vol 22(1) (2003 Reissue) LANDLORD AND TENANT (BUSINESS TENANCIES) Paragraphs 147 [753], 148 [755].

54   If any express right of set-off is granted to the tenant, reference to the provision concerned should be included here to avoid inconsistency.

3.1.2   *Payment by banker's order*[55]

If so required in writing by the Landlord, the Tenant must pay the Lease Rents[56] by banker's order or credit transfer to any bank and account [in the United Kingdom] that the Landlord nominates from time to time.

55   This is a clause with dangers for both parties. If the existence of a breach of covenant is known to the landlord he must instruct his bank to refuse to accept the rent, otherwise his right of forfeiture is lost. As to implied waiver of the right of forfeiture see vol 22(1) (2003 Reissue) LANDLORD AND TENANT (BUSINESS TENANCIES) Paragraph 284 [1173]. The tenant may feel that he requires more control over the payment of rent. In any event, the financial systems operated by many companies prevent payments being made in this way.

56   As to the definition of 'the Lease Rents' see clause 1.33 [170] 'THE RENT'.

[191]

3.2   Outgoings and VAT

The Tenant must pay, and must indemnify the Landlord against —

3.2.1   all rates, taxes[57], assessments, duties, charges, impositions and outgoings that are now or may at any time during the Term be charged, assessed or imposed upon the Premises or on the owner or occupier of them[, excluding any payable by the Landlord occasioned by receipt of the Lease Rents[58] or by any disposition of or dealing with this Lease or ownership of any interest reversionary to the interest created by it][59] [— provided that if the Landlord suffers any loss of rating relief that may be applicable to empty premises after the end of the Term because the relief has been allowed to the Tenant in respect of any period before the end of the Term then the Tenant must make good such loss to the Landlord],

3.2.2   all VAT that may from time to time be charged on the Lease Rents or other sums payable by the Tenant under this Lease[60], and

3.2.3   all VAT incurred in relation to any costs that the Tenant is obliged to pay or in respect of which he is required to indemnify the Landlord under the terms of this Lease, save where such VAT is recoverable or available for set-off by the Landlord as input tax[61].

57   As to covenants to pay rates and taxes see vol 22(1) (2003 Reissue) LANDLORD AND TENANT (BUSINESS TENANCIES) Paragraph 153 [765].
58   As to the definition of 'the Lease Rents' see clause 1.33 [170] 'THE RENT'.
59   The tenant should add the words in square brackets to make it clear that he is not paying the landlord's taxes.
60   As to VAT on rent, service charges and insurance premiums see the Information Binder: Property [1]: VAT and Property.
61   As to payment of VAT on legal costs paid by a person other than the solicitor's own client see the Information Binder: Property [1]: VAT and Property.

[3.3   Cost of services consumed[62]

The Tenant must pay to the suppliers, and indemnify the Landlord against, all charges for electricity, water, gas, telecommunications and other services consumed or used at or in relation to the Premises, including meter rents and standing charges, and must comply with the lawful requirements and regulations of their respective suppliers.] *(omit if the premises have independent supplies of all services)*

62   Where the premises comprise a separate building, a separate supply is usually provided and the tenant makes his own arrangements with the suppliers. In that case this clause is unnecessary.

[192]

3.4   Repair, cleaning and decoration

3.4.1   *Repair of the Premises*[63]

The Tenant must repair the Premises and keep them in good condition and repair, except for damage caused by one or more of the Insured Risks save to the extent that the insurance money is irrecoverable due to any act or default of the Tenant or anyone at the Premises expressly or by implication[64] with his authority [and under his control][65].

63   As to repair see vol 22(1) (2003 Reissue) LANDLORD AND TENANT (BUSINESS TENANCIES) Paragraph 196 [931] et seq. For a covenant to repair, rebuild and renew see vol 22(3) (1997 Reissue) LANDLORD AND TENANT (BUSINESS TENANCIES) Form 85 [6460]. For provisos excluding, eg, work that is prevented etc see vol 22(3) (1997 Reissue) LANDLORD AND TENANT (BUSINESS TENANCIES) Forms 87 [6462], 88 [6463].
       If a landlord is unable to obtain full insurance cover without excess, it should be made clear whether the tenant is to be liable to pay the excess where damage is caused by an insured risk. For a covenant limiting the tenant's repairing obligations by reference to uninsurable as well as insured risks see vol 22(3) (1997 Reissue) LANDLORD AND TENANT (BUSINESS TENANCIES) Form 90 [6465]. It should be noted that it is now recommended 'best practice' that if the premises are so damaged by an uninsured risk as to prevent occupation, the tenant should be allowed to terminate the lease unless the landlord agrees to reinstate at his own cost: see vol 22(1) (2003 Reissue) LANDLORD AND TENANT (BUSINESS TENANCIES) Paragraph 85 [402]. If adopted, this recommendation involves damage preventing occupation caused by uninsured or uninsurable risks being excluded from the ambit of the tenant's repairing covenant.
64   The expression 'by implication' is intended to include a caller on the premises, such as a tradesman, where there has been no express invitation but the person cannot be classed as a trespasser.
65   The tenant should add the words in square brackets.

[193]

3.4.2   *Replacement of landlord's fixtures*

The Tenant must replace from time to time any landlord's fixtures and fittings in the Premises that are beyond repair at any time during or at the end of the Term.

3.4.3   *Cleaning and tidying*

The Tenant must keep the Premises clean and tidy and clear of all rubbish and, without prejudice to the generality of the above, must clean both sides of all windows in the Premises [at least *(state frequency, eg once every month) (or as required)* as is reasonably necessary].

[3.4.4   *The Open Land*

3.4.4.1   **Care of the Open Land**

The Tenant must keep any part of the Premises that is not built on ('the Open Land') adequately surfaced, in good condition and free from weeds [and must keep all landscaped areas properly cultivated].

3.4.4.2   **Storage on the Open Land**

The Tenant must not store anything on the Open Land [or bring anything onto it] [that is or might become untidy, unclean, unsightly or in any way detrimental to the Premises or the area generally].

3.4.4.3   **Rubbish on the Open Land**

The Tenant must not deposit any waste, rubbish or refuse on the Open Land[, or place any receptacle for them, on it].

3.4.4.4   **Vehicles on the Open Land**

The Tenant must not keep or store any [*(if the land cannot be used for parking)* vehicle,] caravan or movable dwelling on the Open Land.] *(adapt clause 3.4.4 as required in the circumstances, or omit if no open land is included)*

[194]

3.4.5   *Care of abutting land*

The Tenant must not cause any land, roads or pavements abutting the Premises to be untidy or dirty and in particular, but without prejudice to the generality of the foregoing, must not deposit refuse or other materials on them.

3.4.6   *Decoration*

[The Tenant must redecorate the outside and inside of the Premises, as often as is necessary in the [reasonable] opinion of the Surveyor in order to maintain a high standard of decorative finish and attractiveness and to preserve the Premises and in the last year of the Term, *(or as required)* The Tenant must redecorate the outside of the Premises in each of the External Decorating Years and the last year of the Term and must redecorate the inside of the Premises in each of the Interior Decorating Years and the last year of the Term, in all instances][66] in a good and workmanlike manner, with appropriate materials of good quality[, to the [reasonable] satisfaction of the Surveyor], any change in the tints, colours and patterns of the decoration to be approved by the Landlord[67][, whose approval may not be unreasonably withheld [or delayed]] [, provided that the covenants relating to the last year of the Term are not to apply where the Tenant has performed the obligation in question less than *(state period, eg 18 months)* before the end of the Term].

66   The draftsman should discuss with the landlord and his property advisers whether he wishes to have the flexibility of the first option or the certainty of the second.
67   The tenant may amend to provide for the landlord's approval to tints etc to apply only in the last year of the term.

3.4.7   *Shared facilities*

Where the use of any of the Conduits or any boundary structures or other things is common to the Premises and other property, the Tenant must be responsible for, and indemnify the Landlord against, all sums due from the owner, tenant or occupier of the Premises in relation to those Conduits, boundary structures or other things and must undertake all work in relation to them that is his responsibility.

[195]

3.5   Waste and alterations

3.5.1   *Waste, additions and alterations*[68]

The Tenant must not commit any waste, make any addition to the Premises, unite the Premises with any adjoining premises, or make any alteration to the Premises except as permitted by the provisions of this clause 3.5.

68   As to alterations see vol 22(1) (2003 Reissue) LANDLORD AND TENANT (BUSINESS TENANCIES) Paragraph 186 [911] et seq.

3.5.2   *Pre-conditions for alterations*

The Tenant must not make any [internal non-structural] alterations to the Premises unless he first —

3.5.2.1   obtains and complies with the necessary consents of the competent authorities and pays their charges for them,

3.5.2.2   makes an application to the Landlord for consent, supported by drawings and where appropriate a specification in duplicate [prepared by an architect[, or a member of some other appropriate profession,] who must supervise the work throughout to completion],

3.5.2.3   pays the fees of the Landlord, any head landlord, any mortgagee and their respective professional advisers,

3.5.2.4   enters into any covenants the Landlord requires as to the execution and reinstatement of the alterations, and

3.5.2.5   obtains the consent of the Landlord, whose consent may not be unreasonably withheld [or delayed].

[In the case of any works of a substantial nature, the Landlord may require the Tenant to provide, before starting the works, adequate security in the form of a deposit of money or the provision of a bond, as assurance to the Landlord that any works he permits from time to time will be fully completed].

[196]

3.5.3 *Removal of alterations*[69]

At the end of the Term, if so requested by the Landlord, the Tenant must remove any additional buildings, additions, alterations or improvements made to the Premises and must make good any part of the Premises that is damaged by their removal.

69   This clause has probably come to be inserted because landlords hope that it will defeat the effect of the compensation provisions of the Landlord and Tenant Act 1927 Pt I (ss 1–17) (23 Halsbury's Statutes (4th Edn) LANDLORD AND TENANT) — as to which see vol 22(1) (2003 Reissue) LANDLORD AND TENANT (BUSINESS TENANCIES) Paragraph 192 [923] et seq — because, if the improvement has been removed, it will not be an improvement to the holding at the time of quitting the premises. In fact, the clause might not achieve this effect, because the Landlord and Tenant Act 1927 s 9 as amended by the Landlord and Tenant Act 1954 s 49 prohibits contracting out. Also, the clause may be void under the Landlord and Tenant Act 1927 s 19(2), so far as that applies to improvements, on the grounds that it purports to fetter the court in deciding what is reasonable. The tenant should not, however, rely on the application of these statutory provisions and should seek to strike out the clause.

3.5.4 *Connection to the Conduits*

The Tenant must not make any connection with the Conduits except in accordance with plans and specifications approved by the Landlord[, whose approval may not be unreasonably withheld [or delayed]], and subject to consent to make the connection having previously been obtained from the competent authority, undertaker or supplier.

[197]

3.6   Aerials, signs and advertisements

3.6.1 *Masts and wires*

The Tenant must not erect any pole or mast [or install any cable or wire] on the Premises, whether in connection with telecommunications or otherwise.

3.6.2 *Advertisements*[70]

The Tenant must not, without the consent of the Landlord, fix to or exhibit on the outside of the Premises, or fix to or exhibit through any window of the Premises, or display anywhere on the Premises, any placard, sign, notice, fascia board or advertisement.

70   See the Town and Country Planning (Control of Advertisements) Regulations 1992, SI 1992/666 as amended. In the absence of a covenant such as this and subject to those Regulations, the tenant may exhibit advertisements etc on the premises, whether or not they are connected with his business: see *Clapman v Edwards* [1938] 2 All ER 507.

3.7   Statutory obligations

3.7.1 *General provision*[71]

The Tenant must comply in all respects with the requirements of any statutes, and any other obligations so applicable imposed by law or by any byelaws, applicable to the Premises or the trade or business for the time being carried on there.

71   As to the covenant to comply with statutes see vol 22(1) (2003 Reissue) LANDLORD AND TENANT (BUSINESS TENANCIES) Paragraph 182 [905]. For a provision requiring the landlord to pay compensation for works above a certain value see vol 22(3) (1997 Reissue) LANDLORD AND TENANT (BUSINESS TENANCIES) Form 169 [6693].

[198]

3.7.2   *Particular obligations*

3.7.2.1   **Works required by statute, department or authority**

Without prejudice to the generality of clause 3.7.1, the Tenant must execute all works and provide and maintain all arrangements on or in respect of the Premises or the use to which they are being put that are required in order to comply with the requirements of any statute already or in the future to be passed, or the requirements of any government department, local authority or other public or competent authority or court of competent jurisdiction, regardless of whether the requirements are imposed on the owner, the occupier, or any other person.

3.7.2.2   **Acts causing losses**

Without prejudice to the generality of clause 3.7.1, the Tenant must not do in or near the Premises anything by reason of which the Landlord may incur any losses under any statute.

3.7.2.3   **Construction (Design and Management) Regulations**

Without prejudice to the generality of clause 3.7.1, the Tenant must comply with the provisions of the Construction (Design and Management) Regulations 1994 ('the CDM Regulations'), be the only client, as defined in the provisions of the CDM Regulations, fulfil, in relation to all and any works, all the obligations of the client as set out in or reasonably to be inferred from the CDM Regulations, and make a declaration to that effect[72] to the Health and Safety Executive in accordance with the Approved Code of Practice published from time to time by the Health and Safety Executive in relation to the CDM Regulations. The provisions of clause 5.7.3 FIRE-FIGHTING EQUIPMENT are to have effect in any circumstances to which these obligations apply.

3.7.2.4   **Delivery of health and safety files**

At the end of the Term, the Tenant must forthwith deliver to the Landlord any and all health and safety files relating to the Premises in accordance with the CDM Regulations.

---

72   If works are being carried out for the tenant, the landlord will not want to accept the liabilities that are placed on a client under the Construction (Design and Management) Regulations 1994, SI 1994/3140 and the Health and Safety Executive Approved Code of Practice. The landlord will need to ensure that the tenant actually makes the declaration required, and that he obtains the notification served on the tenant by the Health and Safety Executive.

[199]

3.8   **Entry to inspect and notice to repair**

3.8.1   *Entry and notice*

The Tenant must permit the Landlord[73] [on reasonable notice during normal business hours except in emergency][74] —

3.8.1.1   to enter the Premises to ascertain whether or not the covenants and conditions of this Lease have been observed and performed,

3.8.1.2   to view the state of repair and condition of the Premises, and to open up floors and other parts of the Premises where that is necessary in order to do so, and

3.8.1.3   to give to the Tenant, or notwithstanding clause 8.7 NOTICES leave on the Premises, a notice ('a notice to repair') specifying the works required to remedy any breach of the Tenant's obligations in this Lease as to the repair and condition of the Premises,

provided that any opening-up must be made good by and at the cost of the Landlord if it reveals no breach of the terms of this Lease.

73   The provisions of clause 1.31 [169] REFERENCES TO RIGHTS OF ACCESS should be noted.
74   The tenant should add the words in square brackets.

3.8.2   *Works to be carried out*

The Tenant must carry out the works specified in a notice to repair immediately, including making good any opening up that revealed a breach of the terms of this Lease.

[200]

[3.8.3   *Landlord's power in default*[75]

If within *(state period, eg 1 month)* of the service of a notice to repair the Tenant has not started to execute the work referred to in that notice, or is not proceeding diligently with it, or if the Tenant fails to finish the work within *(state period, eg 2 months)*[76][, or if in the [Landlord's *(or as required)* Surveyor's] [reasonable] opinion the Tenant is unlikely to finish the work within that period], the Tenant must permit the Landlord to enter the Premises to execute the outstanding work, and must within *(state period, eg 14 days)* of a written demand pay to the Landlord the cost of so doing and all expenses incurred by the Landlord, including legal costs and surveyor's fees.]

75   The advantages of this clause for the landlord must be weighed against the potential liability that it creates under the Defective Premises Act 1972 s 4(4) (31 Halsbury's Statutes (4th Edn) NEGLIGENCE): see *McAuley v Bristol City Council* [1992] QB 134, [1992] 1 All ER 749, CA.
       It has been held that a claim by the landlord for recovery of costs under such a clause is a claim for recovery of a debt, and can therefore be enforced without requiring leave of the court under the Leasehold Property (Repairs) Act 1938 (23 Halsbury's Statutes (4th Edn) LANDLORD AND TENANT): see *Jervis v Harris* [1996] Ch 195, [1996] 1 All ER 303, CA.
       However, even where a landlord has been granted a right of this nature the court does not compel the tenant to allow the landlord the right to enter and carry out repairs where these would be of no benefit and where no loss is being caused to the landlord: see *Hammersmith London Borough Council v Creska (No 2)* [2000] L & TR 288.
76   The tenant would prefer to be given 'a reasonable period' to do the work required to remedy the breaches because it may take longer than the specified number of months.

[201]–[210]

3.9   Alienation[77]

3.9.1   *Alienation prohibited*

The Tenant must not hold the Premises on trust for another. The Tenant must not part with possession of the Premises or any part of the Premises or permit another to occupy them or any part of them except pursuant to a transaction permitted by and effected in accordance with the provisions of this Lease.

77   As to alienation see vol 22(1) (2003 Reissue) LANDLORD AND TENANT (BUSINESS TENANCIES) Paragraph 156 [801] et seq. Where the lease is registrable, this prohibition or restriction on dealings will be reflected in an entry on the register excepting from the effects of registration all estates, rights, interests, powers and remedies arising on or by reason of any dealing made in breach of the prohibition or restriction: see the Land Registration Rules 2003, SI 2003/1417 r 6(2).

3.9.2   *Assignment, subletting and charging of part*[78]

(version 1)

[The Tenant must not assign, sublet or charge part only of the Premises.] *(where assignment, subletting or charging of the whole is allowed)*

(version 2)

[The Tenant must not assign or charge part only of the Premises and must not sublet the whole or any part of the Premises.] *(where assignment or charging of the whole is permitted, but subletting is not allowed at all)*

78   Whether subletting should be permitted is a commercial matter. Some landlords consider that the fact that they cannot unreasonably refuse consent to an assignment gives the tenant all the protection he requires and are not prepared to permit subletting. An advantage to the tenant of the ability to sublet is that he has an element of control over a subtenant but not over an assignee, for whom he may retain liability under an authorised guarantee agreement. Further, with stringent assignment tests or in a bad market, subletting may be the only option open to the tenant.

[211]

3.9.3   *Assignment of the whole*

Subject to clauses 3.9.4 CIRCUMSTANCES and 3.9.5 CONDITIONS, the Tenant must not assign the whole of the Premises without the consent of the Landlord, whose consent may not be unreasonably withheld [or delayed][79].

79   This residual discretion is the old test of reasonableness under the Landlord and Tenant Act 1927 s 19(1). Thus the tenant and the proposed assignee may satisfy the circumstances and conditions specified for the purposes of the Landlord and Tenant Act 1927 s 19(1A) as inserted by the Landlord and Tenant (Covenants) Act 1995 s 22 (as to which see clause 3.9.4 [212] CIRCUMSTANCES and clause 3.9.5 [214] CONDITIONS), but the landlord may still refuse consent on reasonable grounds: see vol 22(1) (2003 Reissue) LANDLORD AND TENANT (BUSINESS TENANCIES) Paragraph 159 [812] et seq.

3.9.4   *Circumstances*

If any of the following circumstances[80] — which are specified for the purposes of the Landlord and Tenant Act 1927 Section 19(1A)[81] — applies either at the date when application for consent to assign is made to the Landlord, or after that date but before the Landlord's consent is given, the Landlord may withhold his consent and if, after the Landlord's consent has been given but before the assignment has taken place, any such circumstances apply, the Landlord may revoke his consent[82], whether his consent is expressly subject to a condition as referred to in clause 3.9.5.4 CONDITIONS or not. The circumstances are —

3.9.4.1   that any sum due from the Tenant under this Lease remains unpaid[83],

3.9.4.2   that in the Landlord's reasonable[84] opinion the assignee is not a person who is likely to be able to comply with the tenant covenants of this Lease and to continue to be able to comply with them following the assignment,

[3.9.4.3   that without prejudice to clause 3.9.4.2, in the case of an assignment to a company in the same group as the Tenant[85] within the meaning of the 1954 Act Section 42 in the Landlord's reasonable opinion the assignee is a person who is, or may become, less likely to be able to comply with the tenant covenants of this Lease than the Tenant requesting consent to assign, which likelihood is adjudged by reference in particular to the financial strength of that Tenant aggregated with that of any guarantor of the obligations of that

Tenant and the value of any other security for the performance of the tenant covenants of this Lease when assessed at the date of grant or — where that Tenant is not *(name of original tenant)* — the date of the assignment of this Lease to that Tenant[86],] or

3.9.4.4   that the assignee or any guarantor for the assignee, other than any guarantor under an authorised guarantee agreement, is a corporation registered — or otherwise resident — in a jurisdiction in which the order of a court obtained in England and Wales will not necessarily be enforced against the assignee or guarantor without any consideration of the merits of the case.

(for examples of circumstances for use in unusual cases, see vol 22(3) (1997 Reissue) LANDLORD AND TENANT (BUSINESS TENANCIES) *Form 117 [6501])*

[212]

80   The Landlord and Tenant Act 1927 s 19(1A) as inserted by the Landlord and Tenant (Covenants) Act 1995 s 22 enables the landlord and tenant to a post-1995 lease to agree in advance the terms upon which an assignment may be permitted. It distinguishes between on the one hand circumstances, the existence of which entitles the landlord to refuse consent to assignment, and on the other hand conditions that may be imposed on the grant of his consent. This clause and clause 3.9.5 [214] CONDITIONS are drafted on the assumption that this is a valid approach and seek to draw a clear distinction between circumstances and conditions.

It should be noted that provisions that are overly restrictive may have an adverse impact at any rent review. It should also be noted that it is recommended 'best practice' that unless the particular circumstances of the letting justify greater control, the only restriction on assignment of the whole should be obtaining the landlord's consent, which is not to be unreasonably withheld: see vol 22(1) (2003 Reissue) LANDLORD AND TENANT (BUSINESS TENANCIES) Paragraph 85 [401] and 'A code of practice for commercial leases in England and Wales (2nd edition)' which can be found in vol 22(1) (2003 Reissue) LANDLORD AND TENANT (BUSINESS TENANCIES) as Form 1 [4501].

Each letting must be looked at in the light of its own particular facts and circumstances but it is considered that the provisions of this clause do, in the ordinary course, strike a reasonable balance between the landlord's desire for control and the tenant's ability to dispose of his interest without undue restriction. For a less restrictive approach see vol 22(1) (2003 Reissue) LANDLORD AND TENANT (BUSINESS TENANCIES) Form 7 clause 5.2 [5538].

81   The Landlord and Tenant Act 1927 s 19(1A) as inserted by the Landlord and Tenant (Covenants) Act 1995 s 22 seems to require the alienation clause to state that the circumstances it mentions are specified for the purposes of that subsection.

82   The landlord may require that certain circumstances are absent not only before consent has been given to the assignment, but also up to the date on which the assignment takes place — when the die is cast and the lease covenants bind the assignee. For example, the landlord may require the rent to be paid up to date not only before the application for consent is made, but also at the date when consent is given and the possibly later date when the lease is actually assigned.

83   The tenant may want to limit this to the rent, as it may be thought that a dispute is more likely to arise over the insurance rent or other payments. If the tenant has retained any right of set-off, it should also be referred to here.

84   Circumstances and conditions must either be factual or, if they contain an element of discretion, require that discretion to be exercised reasonably (see the Landlord and Tenant Act 1927 s 19(1C)(a) as inserted by the Landlord and Tenant (Covenants) Act 1995 s 22), or must give the tenant a right of appeal to an expert (see the Landlord and Tenant Act 1927 s 19(1C)(b) as inserted by the Landlord and Tenant (Covenants) Act 1995 s 22). If the discretion is to be exercised reasonably, as suggested by this provision, the tenant can take any dispute about its exercise to the court. The court will consider whether *this* landlord has acted within the range of reasonable decisions, not whether a reasonable landlord would have reached the same decision or whether the test is itself reasonable. For a clause where an expert is used see vol 22(3) (1997 Reissue) LANDLORD AND TENANT (BUSINESS TENANCIES) Form 117 [6501].

85   There have been suggestions that intra-group assignments should be banned completely. However, this is considered to be too draconian and would prevent legitimate corporate restructuring needed for reasons other than avoidance of liability under the Landlord and Tenant (Covenants) Act 1995. The landlord's concern is that a strong tenant may assign to a weak group company; the assignment is acceptable because the assignor gives an authorised guarantee agreement for the assignee. The second group company may then itself assign outside the group; the landlord will lose the authorised guarantee agreement of the strong first group company and have only the possibly worthless authorised guarantee

agreement of the second group company. The possibilities for exploitation of this scenario are obvious and it is therefore felt that this is the one situation in which measuring the financial strength of the assignee in relation to that of the assignor is justified. Equivalence tests are not generally thought to be appropriate, because a strong first covenant may make the lease almost unassignable, adversely affecting the rent at review.

86   Consider whether the time at which the tenant's financial status is measured should be when he acquired the lease, when his status was acceptable to the landlord, or at the date of the application for consent to assign, when it may have deteriorated sharply. On the other hand, the outgoing tenant may be a better covenant now than when he acquired the lease: the wily landlord may wish to leave himself free to pick whichever of the two dates gives the better picture.

[213]

3.9.5   *Conditions*

The Landlord may impose any or all of the following conditions[87] — which are specified for the purposes of the Landlord and Tenant Act 1927 Section 19(1A)[88] — on giving any consent for an assignment by the Tenant, and any such consent is to be treated as being subject to each of the following conditions —

3.9.5.1   a condition that on or before any assignment and before giving occupation to the assignee, the Tenant requesting consent to assign, together with any former tenant who by virtue of the 1995 Act Section 11 was not released on an earlier assignment of this Lease[89], must enter into an authorised guarantee agreement[90] in favour of the Landlord in the terms set out in schedule 5 THE AUTHORISED GUARANTEE AGREEMENT,

3.9.5.2   a condition that if reasonably so required by the Landlord on an assignment to a limited company, the assignee must ensure that at least *(state number, eg 2)* directors of the company, or some other guarantor or guarantors [reasonably] acceptable to the Landlord, enter into direct covenants with the Landlord in the form of the guarantor's covenants contained in clause 6 GUARANTEE PROVISIONS with 'the Assignee' substituted for 'the Tenant',

3.9.5.3   a condition that on or before any assignment, the Tenant making the request for consent to assign must give to the Landlord a copy of the health and safety file required to be maintained under the Construction (Design and Management) Regulations 1994 containing full details of all works undertaken to the Premises by that Tenant, and

3.9.5.4   a condition that if, at any time before the assignment, the circumstances specified in clause 3.9.4 CIRCUMSTANCES, or any of them, apply, the Landlord may revoke the consent by written notice to the Tenant.

[214]

87   The Landlord and Tenant Act 1927 s 19(1A) as inserted by the Landlord and Tenant (Covenants) Act 1995 s 22 enables the landlord and tenant to a post-1995 lease to agree in advance the terms upon which an assignment may be permitted. It distinguishes between on the one hand circumstances, the existence of which entitles the landlord to refuse consent to assignment, and on the other hand conditions that may be imposed on the grant of his consent. This clause and clause 3.9.4 [212] CIRCUMSTANCES are drafted on the assumption that this a valid approach and seek to draw a clear distinction between circumstances and conditions.

It should be noted that provisions that are overly restrictive may have an adverse impact at any rent review. It should also be noted that it is recommended 'best practice' that unless the particular circumstances of the letting justify greater control, the only restriction on assignment of the whole should be obtaining the landlord's consent, which is not to be unreasonably withheld: see vol 22(1) (2003 Reissue) LANDLORD AND TENANT (BUSINESS TENANCIES) Paragraph 85 [401] and 'A code of practice for commercial leases in England and Wales (2nd edition)' which can be found in vol 22(1) (2003 Reissue) LANDLORD AND TENANT (BUSINESS TENANCIES) as Form 1 [4501].

Each letting must be looked at in the light of its own particular facts and circumstances but it is considered that the provisions of this clause do, in the ordinary course, strike a reasonable balance between the landlord's desire for control and the tenant's ability to dispose of his interest without undue restriction.

88   The Landlord and Tenant Act 1927 s 19(1A) as inserted by the Landlord and Tenant (Covenants) Act 1995 s 22 seems to require the alienation clause to state that the conditions it mentions are specified for the purposes of that subsection.

89   See the Landlord and Tenant (Covenants) Act 1995 ss 11(2), 16(6).

90   As to authorised guarantee agreements see vol 22(1) (2003 Reissue) LANDLORD AND TENANT (BUSINESS TENANCIES) Paragraph 54 [247]. It should be noted that 'A code of practice for commercial leases in England and Wales (2nd edition)' urges landlords to consider requiring authorised guarantee agreements only where the assignee is of lower financial standing than the assignor at the date of the assignment.

[215]

3.9.6   *Charging of the whole*

The Tenant must not charge the whole of the Premises without the consent of the Landlord, whose consent may not be unreasonably withheld [or delayed][91].

91   As to unreasonable withholding of consent under the Landlord and Tenant Act 1927 see vol 22(1) (2003 Reissue) LANDLORD AND TENANT (BUSINESS TENANCIES) Paragraph 158.2 [806] and as to unreasonable delay under the Landlord and Tenant Act 1988 (23 Halsbury's Statutes (4th Edn) LANDLORD AND TENANT) see vol 22(1) (2003 Reissue) LANDLORD AND TENANT (BUSINESS TENANCIES) Paragraph 158.3 [808].

[3.9.7   *Subletting*

The Tenant must not sublet[92] the whole of the Premises without the consent of the Landlord, whose consent may not be unreasonably withheld [or delayed]][93]. *(omit if subletting is prohibited)*

92   See note 78 to clause 3.9.2 [211] ASSIGNMENT, SUBLETTING AND CHARGING OF PART.

93   As to unreasonable withholding of consent under the Landlord and Tenant Act 1927 see vol 22(1) (2003 Reissue) LANDLORD AND TENANT (BUSINESS TENANCIES) Paragraph 158.2 [806] and as to unreasonable delay under the Landlord and Tenant Act 1988 see vol 22(1) (2003 Reissue) LANDLORD AND TENANT (BUSINESS TENANCIES) Paragraph 158.3 [808].

[216]

[3.9.8   *Terms of a permitted sublease*[94]

Every permitted sublease must be granted, without a fine or premium, at a rent not less than whichever is the greater of the then open market rent payable in respect of the Premises [— to be approved by the Landlord before the sublease is granted [and to be determined by the Surveyor, acting as an expert and not as an arbitrator]—] and the Rent[95], to be payable in advance on the days on which the Rent is payable under this Lease. Every permitted sublease must contain provisions approved by the Landlord —

3.9.8.1   for the upwards only review of the rent reserved by it, on the basis set out in schedule 2 THE RENT AND RENT REVIEW and on the Review Dates[96],

3.9.8.2   prohibiting the subtenant from doing or allowing anything in relation to the Premises inconsistent with or in breach of the provisions of this Lease,

3.9.8.3   for re-entry by the sublandlord on breach of any covenant by the subtenant,

3.9.8.4   imposing an absolute prohibition against all dealings with the Premises other than assignment[, subletting] [or charging] of the whole,

3.9.8.5   prohibiting assignment[, subletting][97] [or charging] of the whole of the Premises without the consent of the Landlord under this Lease,

3.9.8.6   requiring the assignee on any assignment of the sublease to enter into direct covenants with the Landlord to the same effect as those contained in clause 3.9.9 SUBTENANT'S DIRECT COVENANTS,

3.9.8.7   requiring on each assignment of the sublease that the assignor enters into an authorised guarantee agreement[98] in favour of the Landlord in the terms set out in schedule 5 THE AUTHORISED GUARANTEE AGREEMENT but adapted to suit the circumstances in which the guarantee is given,

3.9.8.8   prohibiting the subtenant from holding on trust for another or permitting another to share or occupy the whole or any part of the Premises,

3.9.8.9   imposing in relation to any permitted assignment[, subletting] [or charge] the same obligations for registration with the Landlord as are contained in this Lease in relation to dispositions by the Tenant,

[3.9.8.10   imposing in relation to any permitted subletting the same obligations as are contained in this clause 3.9.8 and in clause 3.9.9 SUBTENANT'S DIRECT COVENANTS[, clause 3.9.11 ENFORCEMENT OF THE SUBLEASE and clause 3.9.12 SUBLEASE RENT REVIEW],] and

3.9.8.11   excluding the provisions of Sections 24–28 of the 1954 Act from the letting created by the sublease.] *(omit if subletting is prohibited)*

[217]

94   As to the validity of provisions of this nature see vol 22(1) (2003 Reissue) LANDLORD AND TENANT (BUSINESS TENANCIES) Paragraph 161 [817].
95   It will not be in the landlord's interest for the premises to be sublet at a rent less than that payable under the headlease, because it could allow into the premises a subtenant of doubtful financial status, with whom the landlord may in the future have to deal direct, eg on the grant of a new lease under the Landlord and Tenant Act 1954 Pt II (ss 23–46). Also a low rent could be used as a 'comparable' in arriving at the open market rent on rent reviews or lease renewals. On the other hand following the decision in *Allied Dunbar Assurance plc v Homebase Ltd* [2002] EWCA Civ 666, [2003] 1 P & CR 75, [2002] 2 EGLR 23 a provision of this kind may effectively render the lease inalienable and being a potentially onerous restriction on disposition (as to which see vol 22(1) (2003 Reissue) LANDLORD AND TENANT (BUSINESS TENANCIES) Paragraph 348.2 [1440]) have an adverse impact at rent review from a landlord's perspective.
96   Alternatively the landlord might prefer the sublease rents to be reviewed just before the review dates in the headlease. As to recommended 'best practice' in relation to the basis of rent review in leases of business premises see vol 22(1) (2003 Reissue) LANDLORD AND TENANT (BUSINESS TENANCIES) Paragraph 85 [401] and 'A code of practice for commercial leases in England and Wales (2nd edition)' which can be found in vol 22(1) (2003 Reissue) LANDLORD AND TENANT (BUSINESS TENANCIES) as Form 1 [4501].
97   The landlord may well wish to prohibit any further subletting by requiring an absolute covenant against subletting to be inserted in any sublease.
98   By virtue of the Landlord and Tenant (Covenants) Act 1995 s 16(3)(a), where a head landlord's consent is needed to the assignment of a sublease, the head landlord can require the assignor of the sublease to enter into an authorised guarantee agreement. It should be noted that 'A code of practice for commercial leases in England and Wales (2nd edition)' urges landlords to consider requiring authorised guarantee agreements only where the assignee is of lower financial standing than the assignor at the date of the assignment.

[218]

[3.9.9   *Subtenant's direct covenants*[99]

Before any permitted subletting, the Tenant must ensure that the subtenant enters into a direct covenant with the Landlord that while he is bound by the tenant covenants of the sublease[100] and while the subtenant is bound by an authorised guarantee agreement the subtenant will observe and perform the tenant covenants contained in this Lease — except the covenant to pay the rent reserved by this Lease — and in that sublease.] *(omit if subletting is prohibited)*

99   See note 94 to clause 3.9.8 [218] TERMS OF A PERMITTED SUBLEASE.
100   The liability of the subtenant should be expressed to last while he is bound by the tenant covenants of the sublease, rather than while the sublease is vested in him, to take account of the possibility of an excluded assignment being made and the subtenant remaining liable. An excluded assignment means that the subtenant is precluded from tenant release under the Landlord and Tenant (Covenants) Act 1995.

[3.9.10   *Requirement for 1954 Act exclusion*[101]

The Tenant must not grant a sublease or permit a subtenant to occupy the Premises unless an effective agreement has been made to exclude the operation of Sections 24 to 28 of the 1954 Act pursuant to Section 38A of the 1954 Act.] *(omit if subletting is prohibited)*

101   As to contracting out of the security of tenure provisions of the Landlord and Tenant Act 1954 see vol 22(1) (2003 Reissue) LANDLORD AND TENANT (BUSINESS TENANCIES) Paragraph 431 [2035].

[219]

[3.9.11   *Enforcement, waiver and variation of subleases*

In relation to any permitted sublease, the Tenant must enforce the performance and observance by every subtenant of the provisions of the sublease, and must not at any time either expressly or by implication waive any breach of the covenants or conditions on the part of any subtenant or assignee of any sublease, or — without the consent of the Landlord, whose consent may not be unreasonably withheld or delayed — vary the terms or accept a surrender of any permitted sublease.] *(omit if subletting is prohibited)*

[3.9.12   *Sublease rent review*

In relation to any permitted sublease —

3.9.12.1   the Tenant must ensure that the rent is reviewed in accordance with the terms of the sublease,

3.9.12.2   the Tenant must not agree the reviewed rent with the subtenant without the approval of the Landlord,

3.9.12.3   where the sublease provides such an option, the Tenant must not, without the approval of the Landlord, agree whether the third party determining the revised rent in default of agreement should act as an arbitrator or as an expert,

3.9.12.4   the Tenant must not, without the approval of the Landlord, agree any appointment of a person to act as the third party determining the revised rent,

3.9.12.5   the Tenant must incorporate as part of his representations to that third party representations [reasonably] required[102] by the Landlord, and

3.9.12.6   the Tenant must give notice to the Landlord of the details of the determination of every rent review within *(state period, eg 28 days)*,

provided that the Landlord's approvals specified above may not be unreasonably withheld [or delayed].] *(omit if subletting is prohibited)*

102   This seems preferable to providing, as is sometimes done, that the head landlord's representations have to be brought to the attention of the expert or arbitrator because it would appear that he can refuse to have regard to them, the head landlord not being a party to the lease with which he is concerned.

[220]

3.9.13   *Registration of permitted dealings*

Within *(state period, eg 28 days)* of any assignment, charge, [sublease, or subunderlease,] or any transmission or other devolution relating to the Premises, the Tenant must produce a certified copy[103] of any relevant document for registration with the Landlord's solicitor, and must pay the Landlord's solicitor's [reasonable] charges for registration of at least £...

103   There seems to be no reason why the tenant should part with the original. However, under the Land Registration Rules 2003, SI 2003/1417 r 203, it is open to the applicant for registration to ask for the transfer, charge, sublease or subunderlease giving effect to the disposition to be returned for retention by the applicant, provided a certified copy of the instrument is lodged with the application. Accordingly, in such cases, applicants should use this facility if they wish to be able to lodge the lease with the landlord after its return by the registrar. If there is a time limit specified in the lease, then the registrar should be told about this, so that he is aware of the need to return the instrument within the required period.

[3.9.14   *Sharing with a group company*

Notwithstanding clause 3.9.1 ALIENATION PROHIBITED, the Tenant may share the occupation of the whole or any part of the Premises with a company that is a member of the same group as the Tenant within the meaning of the 1954 Act Section 42, for so long as both companies remain members of that group and otherwise than in a manner that transfers or creates a legal estate.] *(omit if sharing with a group company is not to be permitted)*

[221]

3.10   Nuisance and residential restrictions

3.10.1   *Nuisance*[104]

The Tenant must not do anything on the Premises, or allow anything to remain on them that may be or become or cause a nuisance, or annoyance, disturbance, inconvenience, injury or damage to the Landlord or his tenants or the owners or occupiers of adjacent or neighbouring premises.

104   'Nuisance' is a term to be construed according to 'plain and sober and simple notions among the English people': *Walter v Selfe* (1851) 4 De G & Sm 315 at 322 per Knight-Bruce V-C. 'I have no doubt that what is a nuisance or annoyance will continue to be determined by the courts according to robust and commonsense standards': *Hampstead and Suburban Properties Ltd v Diomedous* [1969] 1 Ch 248 at 258, [1968] 3 All ER 545 at 550 per Megarry J. But a tenant can only be said to have permitted a nuisance if the landlord can show that the tenant has failed to take reasonable steps to prevent the nuisance: see *Commercial General Administration Ltd v Thomsett* [1979] 1 EGLR 62, CA.

3.10.2   *Auctions, trades and immoral purposes*

The Tenant must not use the Premises for any auction sale, any dangerous, noxious, noisy or offensive[105] trade, business, manufacture or occupation, or any illegal or immoral act or purpose.

105   As to the meaning of 'offensive' see *Re Koumoudouros and Marathon Realty Co Ltd* (1978) 89 DLR (3d) 551 where it was held that the word did not have a definite legal meaning and should be read in the context of the lease. Surrounding circumstances can affect whether a particular trade is offensive: see *Nussey v Provincial Bill Posting Co and Eddison* [1909] 1 Ch 734, CA; *Dunraven Securities Ltd v Holloway* [1982] 2 EGLR 47, CA.

[222]–[230]

3.10.3   *Residential use, sleeping and animals*

The Tenant must not use the Premises as sleeping accommodation or for residential purposes, or keep any animal, bird or reptile on them.

3.11   Costs of applications, notices and recovery of arrears[106]

The Tenant must pay to the Landlord on an indemnity basis all costs, fees, charges, disbursements and expenses — including, without prejudice to the generality of the above, those payable to counsel, solicitors, surveyors and bailiffs — [properly and reasonably] incurred by the Landlord in relation to or incidental to —

3.11.1   every application made by the Tenant for a consent or licence required by the provisions of this Lease, whether it is granted, refused or offered subject to any [lawful] qualification or condition, or the application is withdrawn[, unless the refusal, qualification or condition is unlawful, whether because it is unreasonable or otherwise],

3.11.2   the contemplation, preparation and service of a notice under the Law of Property Act 1925 Section 146, or by reason or the contemplation of proceedings under Sections 146 or 147 of that Act, even if forfeiture is avoided otherwise than by relief granted by the court[107],

3.11.3   the recovery or attempted recovery of arrears of rent or other sums due under this Lease, and

3.11.4   any steps taken in [contemplation of or in] [direct] connection with the preparation and service of a schedule of dilapidations during or after the end of the Term[108].

106   As to payment of VAT on legal costs by a person other than the solicitor's own client see the Information Binder: Property [1]: VAT and Property.
107   As to forfeiture see vol 22(1) (2003 Reissue) LANDLORD AND TENANT (BUSINESS TENANCIES) Paragraph 283 [1171] et seq.
108   The landlord should not be tempted to extend this provision to costs etc incurred by him in consequence of serving a notice under the Landlord and Tenant Act 1954 s 25 because that is void: see *Stevenson and Rush (Holdings) Ltd v Langdon* (1978) 38 P & CR 208, CA.

[231]

3.12   Planning and development

3.12.1   *Compliance with the Planning Acts*

The Tenant must observe and comply with the provisions and requirements of the Planning Acts affecting the Premises and their use, and must indemnify the Landlord, and keep him indemnified, both during the Term and following the end of it, against all losses in respect of any contravention of those Acts.

3.12.2   *Consent for applications*

The Tenant must not make any application for planning permission without the consent of the Landlord[, whose consent may not be unreasonably withheld [or delayed] [in any case where application for and implementation of the planning permission will not create or give rise to any tax liability for the Landlord or where the Tenant indemnifies the Landlord against such liability][109].

109   These words were devised when development land tax — abolished by the Finance Act 1985 s 93 — applied. The provision may, however, still be relevant should similar taxation be introduced in the future.

3.12.3   *Permissions and notices*

The Tenant must at his expense obtain any planning permissions and serve any notices that may be required to carry out any development on or at the Premises.

3.12.4   *Charges and levies*

Subject only to any statutory direction to the contrary, the Tenant must pay and satisfy any charge or levy that may subsequently be imposed under the Planning Acts in respect of the carrying out or maintenance of any development on or at the Premises.

[232]

3.12.5   *Pre-conditions for development*

Notwithstanding any consent that may be granted by the Landlord under this Lease, the Tenant must not carry out any development on or at the Premises until all necessary notices under the Planning Acts have been served and copies produced to the Landlord, all necessary permissions under the Planning Acts have been obtained and produced to the Landlord, and the Landlord has acknowledged that every necessary planning permission is acceptable to him[, such acknowledgement not to be unreasonably withheld]. The Landlord may refuse to acknowledge his acceptance of a planning permission on the grounds that any condition contained in it or anything omitted from it or the period referred to in it would[, in the [reasonable] opinion of the Surveyor,] be, or be likely to be, prejudicial to the Landlord or to his reversionary interest in the Premises whether during or following the end of the Term.

3.12.6   *Completion of development*

Where a condition of any planning permission granted for development begun before the end of the Term[110] requires works to be carried out to the Premises by a date after the end of the Term, the Tenant must, unless the Landlord directs otherwise, finish those works before the end of the Term.

110   The provisions of clause 1.17 [164] INTERPRETATION OF 'THE LAST YEAR OF THE TERM' AND 'THE END OF THE TERM' should be noted.

3.12.7   *Security for compliance with conditions*

In any case where a planning permission is granted subject to conditions, and if the Landlord [reasonably] so requires, the Tenant must provide sufficient security for his compliance with the conditions and must not implement the planning permission until the security has been provided.

[233]

[3.12.8   *Appeal against refusal or conditions*[111]

If [reasonably] required by the Landlord to do so, but[, where reasonable,] at his own cost, the Tenant must appeal against any refusal of planning permission or the imposition of any conditions on a planning permission relating to the Premises following an application for planning permission by the Tenant.]

111   The tenant should not accept this clause because it could impose on him the cost of a planning appeal. He should strike it out, leaving planning appeals to be a matter for discussion as and when the situation arises during the term, or at least insist that he should bear the cost only where reasonable.

3.13   Plans, documents and information

3.13.1   *Evidence of compliance with this Lease*

If so requested, the Tenant must produce to the Landlord or the Surveyor any plans, documents and other evidence the Landlord [reasonably] requires to satisfy himself that the provisions of this Lease have been complied with.

3.13.2   *Information for renewal or rent review*

If so requested, the Tenant must produce to the Landlord, the Surveyor, or any person acting as the third party determining the Rent in default of agreement between the Landlord and the Tenant under any provisions for rent review contained in this Lease, any information [reasonably] requested in writing in relation to any pending or intended step under the 1954 Act or the implementation of any provisions for rent review.

[234]

3.14   Indemnities[112]

The Tenant must keep the Landlord fully indemnified against all losses arising directly or indirectly out of any act, omission or negligence of the Tenant, or any persons at the Premises expressly or impliedly[113] with his authority [and under his control][114], or any breach or non-observance by the Tenant of the covenants, conditions or other provisions of this Lease or any of the matters to which this demise is subject.

112   The tenant should seek to delete all *general* indemnity provisions on the basis that his remedies for breach of covenant and in tort adequately protect the landlord. The tenant should argue that an indemnity unreasonably extends his liability. If this clause is omitted, however, it should be replaced by a covenant to observe and perform the restrictions etc to which the demise is subject, possibly coupled with a *specific* indemnity in respect of any breach.
113   The expression 'impliedly' is intended to include a caller on the premises, such as a tradesman, where there has been no express invitation but the person cannot be classed as a trespasser.
114   The tenant should add the words in square brackets.

3.15   Reletting boards and viewing

[Unless [a valid court application under the 1954 Act Section 24 has been made or][115] the Tenant is [otherwise] entitled to remain in occupation or to a new tenancy of the Premises, at any time during *(or as required)* At any time during] the *(state period, eg last 6 months)* of the [Contractual] Term[116] and at any time thereafter, [and whenever the Lease Rents or any part of them are in arrear and unpaid for longer than *(state period, eg 14 days)*,] the Tenant must permit the Landlord to enter the Premises and fix and retain anywhere on them a board advertising them for reletting. While any such board is on the Premises the Tenant must permit viewing of the Premises at reasonable times of the day.

115   This phrase and the word 'otherwise' should be omitted if the operation of the security of tenure provisions in the Landlord and Tenant Act 1954 ss 24–28 is to be excluded in relation to the lease.
116   This defined term will require amendment where the operation of the security of tenure provisions in the Landlord and Tenant Act 1954 ss 24–28 is to be excluded in relation to the lease: see note 6 to clause 1.2 [159] 'THE [CONTRACTUAL] TERM'.

[235]

3.16   Obstruction and encroachment

3.16.1   *Obstruction of windows*

The Tenant must not stop up, darken or obstruct any window or light belonging to the Premises.

3.16.2   *Encroachments*

The Tenant must take all [reasonable] steps to prevent the construction of any new window, light, opening, doorway, path, passage, pipe or the making of any encroachment or the acquisition of any easement in relation to the Premises and must notify the Landlord immediately if any such thing is constructed, encroachment is made or easement acquired, or if any attempt is made to construct such a thing, encroach or acquire an easement. At the request of the Landlord the Tenant must adopt such means as are [reasonably] required to prevent the construction of such a thing, the making of any encroachment or the acquisition of any easement[117].

117   For a shorter clause see vol 22(3) (1997 Reissue) LANDLORD AND TENANT (BUSINESS TENANCIES) Form 172 [6696].

3.17   Yielding up

At the end of the Term[118] the Tenant must yield up the Premises with vacant possession, decorated and repaired in accordance with and in the condition required by the provisions of this Lease, give up all keys of the Premises to the Landlord, remove tenant's fixtures and fittings [if requested to do so by the Landlord], and remove all signs erected by the Tenant or any of his predecessors in title in, on or near the Premises, immediately making good any damage caused by their removal.

118   The provisions of clause 1.17 [164] INTERPRETATION OF 'THE LAST YEAR OF THE TERM' AND 'THE END OF THE TERM' should be noted.

[236]

3.18   Interest on arrears[119]

The Tenant must pay interest on any of the Lease Rents[120] or other sums due under this Lease that are not paid [within *(state period, eg 14 days)* of the date due], whether formally demanded or not[, the interest to be recoverable as rent][121]. Nothing in this clause entitles the Tenant to withhold or delay any payment of the Lease Rents or any other sum due under this Lease or affects the rights of the Landlord in relation to any non-payment.

119   As to the covenant to pay interest see vol 22(1) (2003 Reissue) LANDLORD AND TENANT (BUSINESS TENANCIES) Paragraph 154 [767].
120   As to the definition of 'the Lease Rents' see clause 1.33 [170] 'THE RENT'.
121   These words seek to attach to interest the rights associated with rent. As to the reasons for this see vol 22(1) (2003 Reissue) LANDLORD AND TENANT (BUSINESS TENANCIES) Paragraph 151 [761]. However, this clause applies to interest on arrears of other sums payable under the lease that are not rent as well as to rent itself, and it might be felt inappropriate for interest to be deemed to be rent where the payment on which the interest is due is not itself rent.

3.19   Statutory notices

The Tenant must give full particulars to the Landlord of any notice, direction, order or proposal relating to the Premises made, given or issued to the Tenant by any government department or local, public, regulatory or other authority or court within *(state period, eg 7 days)* of receipt, and if so requested by the Landlord must produce it to the Landlord. The Tenant must without delay take all necessary steps to comply with the notice, direction or order. At the request of the Landlord, but at his own cost, the Tenant must make or join with the Landlord in making any objection or representation the Landlord deems expedient against or in respect of any notice, direction, order or proposal.

3.20   Keyholders

The Tenant must ensure that at all times [the Landlord has *(or as required)* the Landlord and the local police force have] written notice of the name, home address and home telephone number of at least *(state number, eg 2)* keyholders of the Premises.

3.21   Viewing on sale of reversion

The Tenant must[, on reasonable notice,] at any time during the Term, permit prospective purchasers of the Landlord's reversion or any other interest superior to the Term, or agents instructed in connection with the sale of the reversion or such an interest, to view the Premises without interruption provided they have the prior written authority of the Landlord or his agents.

3.22   Defective premises

The Tenant must give notice to the Landlord of any defect in the Premises that might give rise to an obligation on the Landlord to do or refrain from doing anything in order to comply with the provisions of this Lease or the duty of care imposed on the Landlord, whether pursuant to the Defective Premises Act 1972 or otherwise, and must at all times display and maintain any notices the Landlord from time to time [reasonably] requires him to display at the Premises.

[237]

3.23   Replacement guarantor[122]

3.23.1   *Guarantor replacement events*

In this clause 3.23 references to a 'guarantor replacement event' are references, in the case of an individual, to death, bankruptcy, having a receiving order made against him, having a receiver appointed under the Mental Health Act 1983 or entering into a voluntary arrangement and, in the case of a company, to passing a resolution to wind up, entering into liquidation, a voluntary arrangement or administration or having a receiver appointed.

---

122   As to guarantors see vol 22(1) (2003 Reissue) LANDLORD AND TENANT (BUSINESS TENANCIES) Paragraph 71 [278] et seq. The tenant should propose that, on the execution of a guarantee by a new guarantor, the original guarantor or his estate should be released.

3.23.2 *Action on occurrence of a guarantor replacement event*

Where during the relevant Liability Period a guarantor replacement event occurs to the Guarantor or any person who has entered into an authorised guarantee agreement, the Tenant must give notice of the event to the Landlord within *(state period, eg 14 days)* of his becoming aware of it. If so required by the Landlord, the Tenant must within *(state period, eg 28 days)* obtain some other person [reasonably] acceptable to the Landlord to execute a guarantee in the form of the Guarantor's covenants in clause 6 GUARANTEE PROVISIONS or the authorised guarantee agreement in schedule 5 THE AUTHORISED GUARANTEE AGREEMENT, as the case may be, for the residue of the relevant Liability Period.

3.24   Exercise of the Landlord's rights[123]

The Tenant must permit the Landlord to exercise any of the rights granted to him by virtue of the provisions of this Lease at all times during the Term without interruption or interference.

123   The provisions of clause 1.31 [169] REFERENCES TO RIGHTS OF ACCESS should be noted.

[238]

3.25   The Industrial Covenants

The Tenant must observe and perform the Industrial Covenants.

3.26   Costs of grant of this Lease[124]

[The Tenant must pay the fees and disbursements of the Landlord's solicitors, agents and surveyors and all other costs and expenses incurred by the Landlord in relation to the negotiation, preparation, execution and grant of this Lease. *(or as required)* On the grant of this Lease, the Tenant must pay the sum of £... as a contribution to the Landlord's solicitors' charges for the negotiation, execution and completion of this Lease.]

124   As to covenants to pay the landlord's legal fees see vol 22(1) (2003 Reissue) LANDLORD AND TENANT (BUSINESS TENANCIES) Paragraph 155 [769]. As to payment of VAT on legal costs by a person other than the solicitor's own client see the Information Binder: Property [1]: VAT and Property.

3.27   Consent to the Landlord's release[125]

The Tenant must not unreasonably withhold consent to a request made by the Landlord under the 1995 Act Section 8 for a release from all or any of the landlord covenants of this Lease.

125   By virtue of the Landlord and Tenant (Covenants) Act 1995 each successive landlord remains bound by the landlord covenants of the lease unless released under the machinery provided in the Act — as to which see vol 22(1) (2003 Reissue) LANDLORD AND TENANT (BUSINESS TENANCIES) Paragraph 57 [252] et seq — or by a specific release given otherwise (see the Landlord and Tenant (Covenants) Act 1995 s 26(1)(a)). Bald statements limiting the landlord's liability, such as those in use before the commencement of the Act, will not withstand the wide anti-avoidance provisions of the Landlord and Tenant (Covenants) Act 1995 s 25, and covenants by the tenant to give consent to release are unlikely to fall within the exception of s 26. None of the ingenious schemes for limiting the landlord's liability, eg making all covenants personal, suggested in the early days of the 1995 Act has stood up to critical scrutiny, although none has yet been tested by the courts. Thus landlords look instead to the alternative of a right of redress if the tenant makes an unreasonable objection to release. This covenant is modelled on the provisions of the Landlord and Tenant Act 1988, which gives tenants a right of action for loss caused by landlords who unreasonably withhold or delay consent to assignment (see the Landlord and Tenant Act 1988 s 4). In view of the strict time limits under the Landlord and Tenant (Covenants) Act 1995 and the fact that failure to respond to the landlord's request for release is deemed to be consent, it is not thought necessary to extend this covenant to unreasonable delay in replying to such a request.

[239]–[250]

4   QUIET ENJOYMENT[126]

The Landlord covenants with the Tenant to permit the Tenant peaceably and quietly to hold and enjoy the Premises without any interruption or disturbance from or by the Landlord or any person claiming under or in trust for him[127] [or by title paramount][128].

126   As to the landlord's covenant for quiet enjoyment see vol 22(1) (2003 Reissue) LANDLORD AND TENANT (BUSINESS TENANCIES) Paragraph 168 [856]. As to covenants for quiet enjoyment generally see 23 Halsbury's Laws (4th Edn Reissue) LANDLORD AND TENANT.
          The words 'the Tenant paying the rents reserved by and observing and performing the covenants on his part and the conditions contained in this lease' are frequently included in a covenant for quiet enjoyment, but they have no practical effect and do not make payment of the rent and performance of the covenants into conditions precedent to the operation of the covenant for quiet enjoyment: see *Edge v Boileau* (1885) 16 QBD 117; *Dawson v Dyer* (1833) 5 B & Ad 584; *Yorkbrook Investments Ltd v Batten* (1985) 52 P & CR 51, [1985] 2 EGLR 100, CA.
127   The covenant is frequently expressed to apply to 'lawful' interruption by persons 'rightfully' claiming under the landlord, but it seems that the addition of these words has no practical effect: see *Williams v Gabriel* [1906] 1 KB 155 at 157.
128   Without the reference to title paramount the landlord is liable only for the acts of persons so far as they are his successors in title or have authority from him to do the acts complained of: *Harrison Ainslie & Co v Muncaster* [1891] 2 QB 680, CA; *Matania v National Provincial Bank Ltd and Elevenist Syndicate Ltd* [1936] 2 All ER 633, CA; *Miller v Emcer Products Ltd* [1956] Ch 304, [1956] 1 All ER 237, CA. If a subtenant holds under a lease containing a qualified covenant on the part of his landlord — ie one where there is no reference to title paramount — and the head landlord evicts the subtenant because the head rent has not been paid, this is not a breach of the covenant for quiet enjoyment (see *Spencer v Marriott* (1823) 1 B & C 457; *Dennett v Atherton* (1872) LR 7 QB 316, Ex Ch), but it is a breach if the sublandlord submits to judgment in an action by a person with no title to sue, and the subtenant is in consequence evicted (*Cohen v Tannar* [1900] 2 QB 609, CA). Actionable interruptions under this covenant are not confined to interference with title or possession, but may extend to interference with the ordinary and lawful enjoyment of the premises: *Sanderson v Berwick-upon-Tweed Corpn* (1884) 13 QBD 547 at 551, CA. As to persons claiming 'under' the landlord see *Celsteel Ltd v Alton House Holdings Ltd (No 2)* [1987] 2 All ER 240, [1987] 1 WLR 291, CA.

[251]

5   INSURANCE[129]

5.1   Warranty as to convictions[130]

The Tenant warrants that before the execution of this document he has disclosed to the Landlord in writing any conviction, judgment or finding of any court or tribunal relating to the Tenant[, or any director, other officer or major shareholder of the Tenant,] of such a nature as to be likely to affect the decision of any insurer or underwriter to grant or to continue insurance of any of the Insured Risks.

129   As to insurance see vol 22(1) (2003 Reissue) LANDLORD AND TENANT (BUSINESS TENANCIES) Paragraph 227 [1021] et seq.
130   A contract of insurance is one uberrimae fidei. The insured must disclose to the insurers all material facts that are within his actual or presumed knowledge, whether there is a formal proposal form or not. A fact is material if non-disclosure of it would influence a prudent and reasonable insurer. This warranty is designed to rebut any suggestion by the landlord's insurers that the landlord had knowledge of the matters concerned. By inserting this clause in the lease, and thus specifically bringing the point to the tenant's attention, the landlord can argue that he has done all that is practical to establish the existence of any such matters. The absence of any written disclosure pursuant to this clause is strong evidence that the landlord has no actual or presumed knowledge of such matters. Further, the landlord has a right of action against the tenant for any breach of the warranty. As to non-disclosure and misrepresentation in contracts of non-marine insurance see 22 Halsbury's Laws (4th Edn Reissue) INSURANCE.

[252]

5.2   Covenant to insure

The Landlord covenants with the Tenant to insure the Premises [in the joint names of the Landlord and the Tenant[131] [and any other person the Landlord [reasonably] requires][132]] unless the insurance is vitiated by any act of the Tenant or by anyone at the Premises expressly or by implication[133] with his authority [and under his control][134].

131   As to insurance in joint names see vol 22(1) (2003 Reissue) LANDLORD AND TENANT (BUSINESS TENANCIES) Paragraph 229 [1024].

132   Unless some expression such as this is included, a covenant to insure in specified names is broken by insurance in those and other names: see *Penniall v Harborne* (1848) 11 QB 368.

133   The expression 'by implication' is intended to include a caller on the premises, such as a tradesman, where there has been no express invitation but the person cannot be classed as a trespasser.

134   The tenant should add the words in square brackets.

5.3   Details of the insurance

5.3.1   *Office, underwriters and agency*

Insurance is to be effected in such [substantial and reputable] insurance office, or with such underwriters[135], and through such agency as the Landlord from time to time decides[136].

135   The expression 'insurance office' would probably not include Lloyd's underwriters. The landlord's right to nominate the office and agency is absolute, with no implied restrictions: *Berrycroft Management Co Ltd v Sinclair Gardens Investments (Kensington) Ltd* (1996) 75 P & CR 210, [1997] 1 EGLR 47, CA.

136   It should be noted that it is recommended 'best practice' in circumstances where the building is let to one tenant and the landlord insures that, in appropriate cases, the tenant should be given the opportunity to influence the choice of insurer: see vol 22(1) (2003 Reissue) LANDLORD AND TENANT (BUSINESS TENANCIES) Paragraph 85 [401] and 'A code of practice for commercial leases in England and Wales (2nd edition)' which can be found in vol 22(1) (2003 Reissue) LANDLORD AND TENANT (BUSINESS TENANCIES) at Form 1 [4501].

[253]

5.3.2   *Insurance cover*[137]

Insurance must be effected for the following amounts —

5.3.2.1   the sum that the Landlord is from time to time advised [by the Surveyor] is the full cost of rebuilding and reinstating the Premises, including [VAT[138],] architects', surveyors', engineers', solicitors' and all other professional persons' fees, the fees payable on any applications for planning permission or other permits or consents that may be required in relation to rebuilding or reinstating the Premises, the cost of preparation of the site including shoring-up, debris removal, demolition, site clearance and any works that may be required by statute, and incidental expenses, and

5.3.2.2   loss of the Rent, taking account of any rent review that may be due, for *(state period, eg 3 years)* or such longer period as the Landlord from time to time [reasonably] requires for planning and carrying out the rebuilding or reinstatement.

137   As to the sum insured see vol 22(1) (2003 Reissue) LANDLORD AND TENANT (BUSINESS TENANCIES) Paragraph 231 [1028] et seq.

It should be noted that it is recommended 'best practice' that, where the landlord has arranged insurance, the terms should be made known to the tenant and any material change in the insurance should be notified to the tenant: see Recommendation 14 of 'A code of practice for commercial leases in England and Wales (2nd edition)' which can be found in vol 22(1) (2003 Reissue) LANDLORD AND TENANT (BUSINESS TENANCIES) at Form 1 [4501].

138   As to VAT and the level of insurance cover see the Information Binder: Property [1]: VAT and
      Property. The expense of insuring against the VAT payable on reinstatement costs is not justified where
      the landlord has opted to tax and will be able to recover the VAT. There is a theoretical possibility that
      a future landlord may not opt to tax and that the sum insured may then be too low. It is also possible
      that a landlord may wish to preserve the 'exempt' status of a property. Normally, however, the cost of
      reinstatement need not expressly mention VAT, although the cashflow implications of having to pay
      VAT on construction works need to be remembered.

[254]

5.3.3   *Risks insured*[139]

Insurance must be effected against damage or destruction by any of the Insured Risks to
the extent that such insurance may ordinarily be arranged [with a substantial and
reputable insurer] for properties such as the Premises, subject to such excesses, exclusions
or limitations as the insurer requires.

139   As to the risks to be insured against see vol 22(1) (2003 Reissue) LANDLORD AND TENANT
      (BUSINESS TENANCIES) Paragraph 235 [1033].
          It should be noted that it is recommended 'best practice' that, where the landlord has arranged
      insurance, the terms should be made known to the tenant and any material change in the insurance
      should be notified to the tenant: see Recommendation 14 of 'A code of practice for commercial leases
      in England and Wales (2nd edition)' which can be found in vol 22(1) (2003 Reissue) LANDLORD AND
      TENANT (BUSINESS TENANCIES) at Form 1 [4501].

5.4   Payment of the Insurance Rent

The Tenant covenants to pay the Insurance Rent for the period starting on the Rent
Commencement Date and ending on the day before the next policy renewal date on the
date of this document, and subsequently to pay the Insurance Rent on demand and, if
so demanded, in advance of the policy renewal date[, but not more than *(state period, eg
… months)* in advance].

[255]

5.5   Suspension of the Rent[140]

5.5.1   *Events giving rise to suspension*

If and whenever the Premises or any part of them are damaged or destroyed by one or
more of the Insured Risks[141] [— except one against which insurance may not ordinarily
be arranged [with a substantial and reputable insurer] for properties such as the Premises
unless the Landlord has in fact insured against that risk —] so that the Premises or any
part of them are unfit for occupation or use, and payment of the insurance money is not
wholly or partly refused because of any act or default of the Tenant or anyone at the
Premises expressly or by implication[142] with his authority [and under his control][143], then
the provisions of clause 5.5.2 SUSPENDING THE RENT are to have effect.

140   As to suspension of rent see vol 22(1) (2003 Reissue) LANDLORD AND TENANT (BUSINESS
      TENANCIES) Paragraph 241 [1044] et seq.
141   It should be noted that it is recommended 'best practice' that if premises are so damaged by an
      uninsured risk as to prevent occupation, the tenant should be allowed to terminate the lease unless the
      landlord agrees to reinstate at his own cost: see vol 22(1) (2003 Reissue) LANDLORD AND TENANT
      (BUSINESS TENANCIES) Paragraph 85 [402] and 'A code of practice for commercial leases in England
      and Wales (2nd edition)' which can be found in vol 22(1) (2003 Reissue) LANDLORD AND TENANT
      (BUSINESS TENANCIES) at Form 1 [4501]. If adopted, this recommendation involves rent suspension
      also becoming operative in the event of the premises becoming unusable because of uninsured risks.
142   The expression 'by implication' is intended to include a caller on the premises, such as a tradesman,
      where there has been no express invitation but the person cannot be classed as a trespasser.
143   The tenant should add the words in square brackets.

[256]

5.5.2   *Suspending the Rent*

In the circumstances mentioned in clause 5.5.1 EVENTS GIVING RISE TO SUSPENSION the Rent, or a fair proportion of it according to the nature and the extent of the damage sustained, is to cease to be payable until the Premises, or the affected part, have been rebuilt or reinstated so as to render the Premises, or the affected part, fit for occupation and use, [or until the end of *(state period, eg 3 years)* from the destruction or damage, whichever period is the shorter,][144] [the proportion of the Rent suspended and the period of the suspension to be determined by the Surveyor acting as an expert and not as an arbitrator *(or as required)* any dispute as to the proportion of the Rent suspended or the period of the suspension to be determined in accordance with the Arbitration Act 1996 by an arbitrator to be appointed by agreement between the Landlord and the Tenant or in default by the President or other proper officer for the time being of the Royal Institution of Chartered Surveyors on the application of either the Landlord or the Tenant].

144   As to the length of the suspension and the tenant's concerns see vol 22(1) (2003 Reissue) LANDLORD AND TENANT (BUSINESS TENANCIES) Paragraph 244 [1048]. For a provision extending suspension of the rent where reinstatement is delayed see vol 22(3) (1997 Reissue) LANDLORD AND TENANT (BUSINESS TENANCIES) Form 111 [6495].

5.6   **Reinstatement and termination**[145]

5.6.1   *Obligation to obtain permissions*

If and whenever the Premises or any part of them are damaged or destroyed by one or more of the Insured Risks [— except one against which insurance may not ordinarily be arranged [with a substantial and reputable insurer] for properties such as the Premises, unless the Landlord has in fact insured against that risk —] and payment of the insurance money is not wholly or partly refused because of any act or default of the Tenant or anyone at the Premises expressly or by implication[146] with his authority [and under his control][147], the Landlord must use his best endeavours[148] to obtain the planning permissions or other permits and consents ('permissions') that are required under the Planning Acts or otherwise to enable him to rebuild and reinstate the Premises.

[257]

145   It has been held that, in the absence of an express covenant to reinstate, where the landlord must keep the premises adequately insured against comprehensive risks and the insurance is effected at the tenant's expense, the obligation is one intended to enure for the benefit of both parties: *Mumford Hotels Ltd v Wheler* [1964] Ch 117, [1963] 3 All ER 250; see also *Mark Rowlands Ltd v Berni Inns Ltd* [1986] QB 211, [1985] 3 All ER 473, CA; *Lonsdale & Thompson Ltd v Black Arrow Group plc* [1993] Ch 361, [1993] 3 All ER 648. This is not, however, a general principle of law and the tenant should therefore always require a specific covenant to reinstate.

These provisions are restricted to circumstances where damage or destruction is caused by an insured risk. It should be noted that it is recommended 'best practice' that if premises are so damaged by an uninsured risk as to prevent occupation, the tenant should be allowed to terminate the lease unless the landlord agrees to reinstate at his own cost: see vol 22(1) (2003 Reissue) LANDLORD AND TENANT (BUSINESS TENANCIES) Paragraph 85 [401] and 'A code of practice for commercial leases in England and Wales (2nd edition)' which can be found in vol 22(1) (2003 Reissue) LANDLORD AND TENANT (BUSINESS TENANCIES) at Form 1 [4501].

As to reinstatement and termination where reinstatement is not possible see vol 22(1) (2003 Reissue) LANDLORD AND TENANT (BUSINESS TENANCIES) Paragraph 237 [1037] et seq. For a provision for termination or surrender on destruction or substantial damage see vol 22(3) (1997 Reissue) LANDLORD AND TENANT (BUSINESS TENANCIES) Form 107 [6483].

146   The expression 'by implication' is intended to include a caller on the premises, such as a tradesman, where there has been no express invitation but the person cannot be classed as a trespasser.

147   The tenant should add the words in square brackets.
148   The extent of the duty to use best endeavours depends upon the facts in each case: see *Monkland v Jack Barclay Ltd* [1951] 2 KB 252, [1951] 1 All ER 714, CA; *Terrell v Mabie Todd & Co Ltd* [1952] 2 TLR 574; *NW Investments (Erdington) Ltd v Swani* (1970) 214 Estates Gazette 1115. In the light of *IBM United Kingdom Ltd v Rockware Glass Ltd* [1980] FSR 335, CA, it may be that there is little practical difference between a covenant to use best endeavours, a covenant to use reasonable endeavours and a covenant to take all reasonable steps.

[258]

5.6.2   *Obligation to reinstate*

Subject to the provisions of clause 5.6.3 RELIEF FROM THE OBLIGATION TO REINSTATE, and, if any permissions are required, after they have been obtained, the Landlord must as soon as reasonably practicable apply all money received in respect of the insurance effected by the Landlord pursuant to this Lease, except sums in respect of loss of the Rent, in rebuilding or reinstating the Premises[, making up any difference between the cost of rebuilding and reinstating and the money received out of his own money][149].

149   Where the landlord's covenant is 'to apply all money received in respect of the insurance in rebuilding or reinstating' rather than simply 'to reinstate', it seems that the landlord does not have to complete the work out of his own money if the insurance money is insufficient because he has complied with his covenant by laying out all the insurance money received. The situation is different if the tenant can establish that the landlord was in breach of his covenant to insure for the full cost of reinstatement and that this has caused the shortfall: see *Mumford Hotels Ltd v Wheler* [1964] Ch 117, [1963] 3 All ER 250. The tenant should, therefore, require a specific covenant from the landlord to make up any shortfall, to prevent a situation in which the landlord refuses to complete the rebuilding. This is of particular concern if the suspension of rent proviso is expressed to operate for a limited period, because on the expiry of that period the tenant becomes liable for rent unless he can satisfy the court that the lease has been frustrated.
      It should be noted that it is recommended 'best practice' that if premises are so damaged by an uninsured risk as to prevent occupation, the tenant should be allowed to terminate the lease unless the landlord agrees to reinstate at his own cost: see vol 22(1) (2003 Reissue) LANDLORD AND TENANT (BUSINESS TENANCIES) Paragraph 85 [401] and 'A code of practice for commercial leases in England and Wales (2nd edition)'which can be found in vol 22(1) (2003 Reissue) LANDLORD AND TENANT (BUSINESS TENANCIES) at Form 1 [4501]. If this recommendation is adopted and the landlord merely covenants to apply insurance money received, the principle should be extended to damage or destruction resulting from insured risks in circumstances where the insurance money is insufficient to enable reinstatement to be completed.
      For a proviso relieving the landlord from the obligation to reinstate the premises in the same form see vol 22(3) (1997 Reissue) LANDLORD AND TENANT (BUSINESS TENANCIES) Form 106 [6482].

[259]

5.6.3   *Relief from the obligation to reinstate*[150]

The Landlord need not rebuild or reinstate the Premises if and for so long as rebuilding or reinstatement is prevented because —

5.6.3.1   the Landlord, despite using his best endeavours[151], cannot obtain any necessary permission,

5.6.3.2   any permission is granted subject to a lawful condition with which [it is impossible for *(or as required)* in all the circumstances it is unreasonable to expect] the Landlord to comply,

5.6.3.3   there is some defect or deficiency in the site on which the rebuilding or reinstatement is to take place that [renders it impossible *(or as required)* means it can only be undertaken at a cost that is unreasonable in all the circumstances],

5.6.3.4   the Landlord is unable to obtain access to the site to rebuild or reinstate,

5.6.3.5   the rebuilding or reinstating is prevented by war, act of God, government action[, strike or lock-out], or

because of the occurrence of any other circumstances beyond the Landlord's control.

150   As to the need for a right to terminate where reinstatement is not possible see vol 22(1) (2003 Reissue) LANDLORD AND TENANT (BUSINESS TENANCIES) Paragraph 226 [998].

151   The extent of the duty to use best endeavours depends upon the facts in each case: see *Monkland v Jack Barclay Ltd* [1951] 2 KB 252, [1951] 1 All ER 714, CA; *Terrell v Mabie Todd & Co Ltd* [1952] 2 TLR 574; *NW Investments (Erdington) Ltd v Swani* (1970) 214 Estates Gazette 1115. In the light of *IBM United Kingdom Ltd v Rockware Glass Ltd* [1980] FSR 335, CA, it may be that there is little practical difference between a covenant to use best endeavours, a covenant to use reasonable endeavours and a covenant to take all reasonable steps.

[260]

5.6.4   *Notice to terminate*[152]

If, at the end of a period[153] of *(state period, eg 3 years)* starting on the date of the damage or destruction, the Premises are still not fit for the Tenant's occupation and use, either the Landlord or the Tenant may by notice served at any time within *(state period, eg 6 months)* of the end of that period ('a notice to terminate following failure to reinstate') implement the provisions of clause 5.6.5 TERMINATION FOLLOWING FAILURE TO REINSTATE[154].

152   For alternative provisions where the landlord's right to terminate is limited to specified circumstances see vol 22(3) (1997 Reissue) LANDLORD AND TENANT (BUSINESS TENANCIES) Form 109 [6492].

153   The period to be inserted must be carefully considered. Particular regard should be had to the terms of any rent suspension provision and the extent of insurance cover for loss of rent.

154   As to the effect of the Landlord and Tenant Act 1954 see vol 22(1) (2003 Reissue) LANDLORD AND TENANT (BUSINESS TENANCIES) Paragraph 226 [998].

5.6.5   *Termination following failure to reinstate*

On service of a notice to terminate following failure to reinstate, the Term is to cease absolutely — but without prejudice to any rights or remedies that may have accrued[155]— and all money received in respect of the insurance effected by the Landlord pursuant to this Lease is to belong to the Landlord absolutely[156].

155   The effect of this clause is that the right to terminate arises after the end of the appropriate period, whatever the reason for the delay, but the tenant still has a right of action against the landlord if the landlord is in breach of his covenant to reinstate.

156   In the absence of provision for ownership of the insurance money the position is uncertain. In *Re King, Robinson v Gary* [1963] Ch 459, [1963] 1 All ER 781, CA it was held that the insurance money belongs to the party who paid the premiums even if the insurance was placed in the joint names of the landlord and the tenant. The dissenting view of Denning MR that insurance in joint names envisages that each party should be insured as to his insurable interest and that the insurance money should therefore be divided in proportion to their interests in the property should, however, be noted. In *Beacon Carpets Ltd v Kirby* [1985] QB 755, [1984] 2 All ER 726, CA the court adhered to this view and held that the proportion payable depended on the parties' interests in the premises at the time of the destruction. The landlord will prefer an express provision in the lease for the insurance money to be retained by him in full if reinstatement proves impossible. The tenant ought perhaps to accept that it would be unrealistic to amend this to provide for the insurance money to belong to the tenant, but should suggest that a provision be inserted under which the money is to be divided in accordance with their respective interests in the premises at the time when the insurance money became due. For an alternative provision for ownership of the insurance money etc see vol 22(3) (1997 Reissue) LANDLORD AND TENANT (BUSINESS TENANCIES) Form 108 [6491].

[261]

5.7   Tenant's further insurance covenants[157]

The Tenant covenants with the Landlord to observe and perform the requirements of this clause 5.7.

157   In order to comply with many of these covenants, the tenant will need to be supplied with details of the landlord's insurance policy. In any event, it should be noted that it is recommended 'best practice' that where the landlord has arranged insurance, the terms should be made known to the tenant and any material change in the insurance should be notified to the tenant: see Recommendation 14 of 'A code of practice for commercial leases in England and Wales (2nd edition)' which can be found in vol 22(1) (2003 Reissue) LANDLORD AND TENANT (BUSINESS TENANCIES) at Form 1 [4501].

5.7.1   *Requirements of insurers*

The Tenant must comply with all the requirements and recommendations of the insurers.

5.7.2   *Policy avoidance and additional premiums*

The Tenant must not do or omit anything that could cause any insurance policy on or in relation to the Premises to become wholly or partly void or voidable, or do or omit anything by which additional insurance premiums may become payable unless he has previously notified the Landlord and has agreed to pay the increased premium.

5.7.3   *Fire-fighting equipment*

The Tenant must keep the Premises supplied with such fire fighting equipment [as the insurers and the fire authority require and must maintain the equipment to their satisfaction *(or as required)* as the Landlord reasonably requires and must maintain the equipment to the reasonable satisfaction of the insurers and the fire authority] and in efficient working order. At least once in every *(state period, eg 6 months)* the Tenant must cause any sprinkler system and other fire fighting equipment to be inspected by a competent person.

5.7.4   *Combustible materials*

The Tenant must not store on the Premises or bring onto them anything of a specially combustible, inflammable or explosive nature, and must comply with the requirements and recommendations of the fire authority [and the [reasonable] requirements of the Landlord] as to fire precautions relating to the Premises.

5.7.5   *Fire escapes, equipment and doors*

The Tenant must not obstruct the access to any fire equipment or the means of escape from the Premises or lock any fire door while the Premises are occupied.

5.7.6   *Notice of events affecting the policy*

The Tenant must give immediate notice to the Landlord of any event that might affect any insurance policy on or relating to the Premises, and any event against which the Landlord may have insured under this Lease.

5.7.7   *Notice of convictions*

The Tenant must give immediate notice to the Landlord of any conviction, judgment or finding of any court or tribunal relating to the Tenant, or any director other officer or major shareholder of the Tenant, of such a nature as to be likely to affect the decision of any insurer or underwriter to grant or to continue any such insurance[158].

158   This clause provides a continuation of the warranty given by the tenant in clause 5.1 [252] WARRANTY AS TO CONVICTIONS. As to non-disclosure and misrepresentation in contracts of non-marine insurance see 22 Halsbury's Laws (4th Edn Reissue) INSURANCE.

5.7.8   *Other insurance*

If at any time the Tenant is entitled to the benefit of any insurance of the Premises that is not effected or maintained in pursuance of any obligation contained in this Lease, the Tenant must apply all money received by virtue of that insurance in making good the loss or damage in respect of which the money is received[159].

159   An insurance policy frequently provides that if there is any other insurance effected by or on behalf of the insured, covering the premises that are the subject of the policy, the insurers are liable only for a rateable proportion of the damage. Such provisions extend to a case where one of the policies is in the joint names of the persons interested in the premises and the other is in the name of one only of those persons: *Halifax Building Society v Keighley* [1931] 2 KB 248. Therefore, at least when the insurance is in joint names, the landlord must ensure that the tenant will use all money received under any policy he has effected to reinstate the premises.

[5.7.9   *Reinstatement on refusal of money through default*

If at any time the Premises or any part of them are damaged or destroyed by one or more of the Insured Risks and the insurance money under the policy of insurance effected by the Landlord pursuant to his obligations contained in this Lease is wholly or partly irrecoverable because of any act or default of the Tenant or of anyone at the Premises expressly or by implication[160] with his authority [and under his control][161], the Tenant must immediately, at the option of the Landlord, either rebuild and reinstate the Premises or the part of them destroyed or damaged, to the reasonable satisfaction and under the supervision of the Surveyor — in which case, on completion of the rebuilding and refurbishment, the Landlord must pay to the Tenant the amount that the Landlord has actually received under the insurance policy in respect of the destruction or damage— or pay to the Landlord on demand [with interest] the amount of the insurance money so irrecoverable—in which case the provisions of clauses 5.5 SUSPENSION OF THE RENT and 5.6 REINSTATEMENT AND TERMINATION are to apply.]

160   The expression 'by implication' is intended to include a caller on the premises, such as a tradesman, where there has been no express invitation but the person cannot be classed as a trespasser.
161   The tenant should add the words in square brackets.

[5.8   **Landlord's further insurance covenants**[162]

The Landlord covenants with the Tenant to observe and perform the requirements set out in this clause 5.8 in relation to the insurance policy effected by the Landlord pursuant to his obligations contained in this Lease.

162   Unless insurance is to be in the joint names of the landlord and the tenant, the tenant should seek covenants such as these from the landlord.

5.8.1   *Copy policy*

The Landlord must produce to the Tenant on demand [a copy of the policy and the last premium renewal receipt *(or as required)* reasonable evidence of the terms of the policy and the fact that the last premium has been paid][163].

163   The landlord can reasonably insist on the second alternative in square brackets. If the premises are insured under a block policy, it would be inappropriate for him to have to disclose to the tenant information about his other properties.

It should be noted that it is recommended 'best practice' that where the landlord has arranged insurance, the terms should be made known to the tenant and any material change in the insurance should be notified to the tenant: see Recommendation 14 of 'A code of practice for commercial leases in England and Wales (2nd edition)' which can be found in vol 22(1) (2003 Reissue) LANDLORD AND TENANT (BUSINESS TENANCIES) at Form 1 [4501].

5.8.2   *Noting of the Tenant's interest*

The Landlord must ensure that the interest of the Tenant is noted or endorsed on the policy[164].

164   Where insurance in the joint names of the landlord and the tenant is not practical, the tenant should insist that a note of his interest is endorsed on the policy. This protects the tenant because the insurers should give notice to him of any lapse in the policy and, where it can be shown that the tenant is responsible for the insurance premium under the terms of the lease, it is likely — but not certain — that the insurers would not exercise subrogation rights against the tenant.

It is recommended 'best practice' that where the landlord has arranged insurance, any interest of the tenant should be covered by the policy: see Recommendation 14 of 'A code of practice for commercial leases in England and Wales (2nd edition)' which can be found in vol 22(1) (2003 Reissue) LANDLORD AND TENANT (BUSINESS TENANCIES) at Form 1 [4501].

[264]

5.8.3   *Change of risks*

The Landlord must notify the Tenant of any [material] change in the risks covered by the policy from time to time[165].

165   It should be noted that it is recommended 'best practice' that where the landlord has arranged insurance, the terms should be made known to the tenant and any material change in the insurance should be notified to the tenant: see Recommendation 14 of 'A code of practice for commercial leases in England and Wales (2nd edition)' which can be found in vol 22(1) (2003 Reissue) LANDLORD AND TENANT (BUSINESS TENANCIES) at Form 1 [4501].

[5.8.4   *Waiver of subrogation*[166]

The Landlord must produce to the Tenant on demand written confirmation from the insurers that they have agreed to waive all rights of subrogation against the Tenant.]]

166   Generally an insurer who has paid out under a policy stands in the shoes of the insured with regard to any claim the latter may have had against any third party. If the insurance is in joint names, the tenant is an insured party and there can be no subrogation against him. It would seem, also, that where the tenant covenants to reimburse the landlord for sums expended by the landlord in insuring the premises, the landlord's insurers cannot make a subrogated claim against the tenant where the premises are destroyed by the tenant's negligence: *Mark Rowlands Ltd v Berni Inns Ltd* [1986] QB 211, [1985] 3 All ER 473, CA. The tenant may still, however, wish to obtain a specific waiver of subrogation if possible.

[265]–[280]

6   GUARANTEE PROVISIONS

6.1   The Guarantor's covenants[167]

6.1.1   *Nature and duration*

The Guarantor's covenants with the Landlord are given as sole or principal debtor or covenantor, with the landlord for the time being and with all his successors in title[168] without the need for any express assignment, and the Guarantor's obligations to the Landlord will last throughout the Liability Period.

167   The covenants in this clause should *not* be omitted where no guarantor is a party to the lease, because they may be required under clause 3.9.5.2 [214] CONDITIONS. If it is felt undesirable to have covenants in a lease and no party, at least initially, to enter into them, ie where there is no guarantor for the original tenant, the contents of this clause could alternatively be included in a schedule.

168   The new provisions governing the transmission of the benefit and burden of covenants (see the Landlord and Tenant (Covenants) Act 1995 s 3) only apply to landlord and tenant covenants. The law in force before 1 January 1996 remains unchanged for guarantor covenants, so that the benefit passes with the landlord's reversion. This occurs, not under the Law of Property Act 1925 s 141(1), which has been repealed for post-1995 tenancies by the 1995 Act, but under common law. The guarantee covenant touches and concerns the legal estate vested in the new reversioner: see *P & A Swift Investments v Combined English Stores Group plc* [1989] AC 632, [1988] 2 All ER 885, HL.

[281]

6.1.2   *The covenants*

The Guarantor covenants with the Landlord to observe and perform the requirements of this clause 6.1.2.

6.1.2.1   Payment of rent and performance of the Lease

The Tenant must pay the Lease Rents[169] and VAT charged on them punctually and observe and perform the covenants and other terms of this Lease, and if, at any time during the Liability Period while the Tenant is bound by the tenant covenants of this Lease[170], the Tenant defaults in paying the Lease Rents or in observing or performing any of the covenants or other terms of this Lease, then the Guarantor must pay the Lease Rents and observe or perform the covenants or terms in respect of which the Tenant is in default and make good to the Landlord on demand, and indemnify the Landlord against, all losses resulting from such non-payment, non-performance or non-observance notwithstanding —

(a)   any time or indulgence granted by the Landlord to the Tenant, any neglect or forbearance of the Landlord in enforcing the payment of the Lease Rents or the observance or performance of the covenants or other terms of this Lease, or any refusal by the Landlord to accept rent tendered by or on behalf of the Tenant at a time when the Landlord is entitled — or will after the service of a notice under the Law of Property Act 1925 Section 146 be entitled — to re-enter the Premises[171],

(b)   that the terms of this Lease may have been varied by agreement between the Landlord and the Tenant[, provided that no variation is to bind the Guarantor to the extent that it is materially prejudicial to him][172],

(c)   that the Tenant has surrendered part of the Premises — in which event the liability of the Guarantor under this Lease is to continue in respect of the part of the Premises not surrendered after making any necessary apportionments under the Law of Property Act 1925 Section 140[173], and

(d)   anything else (other than a release by deed) by which, but for this clause 6.1.2.1, the Guarantor would be released.

[282]

169   As to the definition of 'the Lease Rents' see clause 1.33 [170] 'THE RENT'.

170   This obligation lasts while the lease is vested in the tenant and for any period of extended liability following an excluded assignment. It is not appropriate once the tenant has entered into an authorised guarantee agreement, when the contractual guarantor's obligations are at one remove. As to the guaranteeing of obligations under an authorised guarantee agreement: see vol 22(1) (2003 Reissue) LANDLORD AND TENANT (BUSINESS TENANCIES) Paragraph 74 [284] and clause 6.1.2.4 [285] GUARANTEE OF THE TENANT'S LIABILITIES UNDER AN AUTHORISED GUARANTEE AGREEMENT.

171   If a creditor 'gives time' to the debtor in a binding manner, this releases the guarantor: see *Swire v Redman* (1876) 1 QBD 536; *Holme v Brunskill* (1877) 3 QBD 495, CA. The guarantee should, therefore, be expressed to apply notwithstanding any time or indulgence granted by the landlord to the tenant, or neglect or forbearance on the part of the landlord in enforcing the payment of rent and the other covenants in the lease. It has been suggested, however, that such wording does not protect a landlord who refuses to accept rent so as not to waive a breach of covenant by the tenant. This is unresolved but to avoid any doubt the point should be expressly dealt with. It appears that any provision in a guarantor's covenant that purports to exonerate the landlord from the consequences of his own negligence must satisfy the reasonableness test of the Unfair Contract Terms Act 1977 (11 Halsbury's Statutes (4th Edn) CONTRACT).

172   Any variation of the terms of the contract between the creditor and the debtor will discharge the guarantor (*Holme v Brunskill* (1877) 3 QBD 495, CA), unless the guarantor consents, although it has been suggested that an immaterial variation that was not prejudicial to the guarantor might not release him. No guarantor should accept a provision by which the guarantee is to continue notwithstanding any variation, but on the other hand it seems unfair on the landlord for the guarantor to escape his liability merely because a minor change has been agreed between the landlord and the tenant. A provision that the guarantee is to continue to apply notwithstanding an immaterial variation not prejudicial to the guarantor seems a fair compromise. It should be noted that the Landlord and Tenant (Covenants) Act 1995 s 18 does not apply to the guarantor of the current tenant.

      It should also be noted that it is recommended 'best practice' that landlords and tenants should seek the agreement of any guarantors to proposed material changes to the terms of the lease, or even minor changes which could increase the guarantor's liability: see Recommendation 15 of 'A code of practice for commercial leases in England and Wales (2nd edition)' which can be found in vol 22(1) (2003 Reissue) LANDLORD AND TENANT (BUSINESS TENANCIES) at Form 1 [4501].

173   In the light of *Holme v Brunskill* (1877) 3 QBD 495, CA, the position on surrender of part of the premises should be dealt with expressly.

[283]

6.1.2.2   New lease following disclaimer[174]

If, at any time during the Liability Period while the Tenant is bound by the tenant covenants of this Lease[175], any trustee in bankruptcy or liquidator of the Tenant disclaims this Lease, the Guarantor must, if so required by notice served by the Landlord within *(state period, eg 60 days)* of the Landlord's becoming aware of the disclaimer, take from the Landlord forthwith a lease of the Premises for the residue of the [Contractual][176] Term as at the date of the disclaimer, at the Rent then payable under this Lease and subject to the same covenants and terms as in this Lease — except that the Guarantor need not ensure that any other person is made a party to that lease as guarantor — the new lease to commence on the date of the disclaimer. The Guarantor must pay the costs of the new lease and VAT charged thereon, except where such VAT is recoverable or available for set-off by the Landlord as input tax[177], and execute and deliver to the Landlord a counterpart of the new lease.

174   This put option should be included because on disclaimer of a lease the lease ceases to exist, although it is deemed to continue for the purpose of determining the liability to the landlord of persons, including guarantors, other than the tenant whose liquidator or trustee has disclaimed: see *Hindcastle Ltd v Barbara Attenborough Associates Ltd* [1997] AC 70, [1996] 1 All ER 737, HL.

175   This obligation lasts while the lease is vested in the tenant and for any period of extended liability following an excluded assignment. It is not appropriate once the tenant has entered into an authorised guarantee agreement when the tenant's — ie the former tenant's — liquidator or trustee in bankruptcy will not be in a position to disclaim the lease because it will no longer be vested in the former tenant.

176   This defined term will require amendment where the operation of the security of tenure provisions in the Landlord and Tenant Act 1954 ss 24–28 is to be excluded in relation to the lease: see note 6 to clause 1.2 [159] 'THE [CONTRACTUAL] TERM'.

177   As to payment of VAT on legal costs by a person other than the solicitor's own client see the Information Binder: Property [1]: VAT and Property.

[284]

6.1.2.3   Payments following disclaimer[178]

If this Lease is disclaimed and the Landlord does not require the Guarantor to accept a new lease of the Premises in accordance with clause 6.1.2.2 NEW LEASE FOLLOWING DISCLAIMER, the Guarantor must pay to the Landlord on demand an amount equal to [the difference between any money received by the Landlord for the use or occupation of the Premises and] the Lease Rents [in both cases] for the period commencing with the date of the disclaimer and ending on whichever is the earlier of the date *(state period, eg 6 months)* after the disclaimer, the date, if any, upon which the Premises are relet, and the end of the [Contractual][179] Term.

178   This clause could be a useful alternative for a landlord who may not be unhappy to regain possession of the premises but would like some rental income before reletting etc. For a covenant by the tenant to assign to the guarantor see vol 22(3) (1997 Reissue) LANDLORD AND TENANT (BUSINESS TENANCIES) Form 159 [6666].

179   This defined term will require amendment where the operation of the security of tenure provisions in the Landlord and Tenant Act 1954 ss 24–28 is to be excluded in relation to the lease: see note 6 to clause 1.2 [159] 'THE [CONTRACTUAL] TERM'.

6.1.2.4   Guarantee of the Tenant's liabilities under an authorised guarantee agreement

If, at any time during the Liability Period while the Tenant is bound by an authorised guarantee agreement, the Tenant defaults in his obligations under that agreement, the Guarantor must make good to the Landlord on demand, and indemnify the Landlord against, all losses resulting from that default notwithstanding —

(a)   any time or indulgence granted by the Landlord to the Tenant, or neglect or forbearance of the Landlord in enforcing the payment of any sum or the observance or performance of the covenants of the authorised guarantee agreement[180],

(b)   that the terms of the authorised guarantee agreement may have been varied by agreement between the Landlord and the Tenant [provided that no variation is to bind the Guarantor to the extent that it is materially prejudicial to him][181], or

(c)   anything else (other than a release by deed) by which, but for this clause 6.1.2.4, the Guarantor would be released.

180   See note 171 to clause 6.1.2.1 [283] PAYMENT OF RENT AND PERFORMANCE OF THE LEASE.

181   See note 172 to clause 6.1.2.1 [283] PAYMENT OF RENT AND PERFORMANCE OF THE LEASE.

[285]

6.1.3   *Severance*

6.1.3.1   Severance of void provisions

Any provision of this clause 6 rendered void by virtue of the 1995 Act Section 25 is to be severed from all remaining provisions, and the remaining provisions are to be preserved.

6.1.3.2   Limitation of provisions

If any provision in this clause 6 extends beyond the limits permitted by the 1995 Act Section 25, that provision is to be varied so as not to extend beyond those limits.

[6.2 The Landlord's covenant[182]

The Landlord covenants with the Guarantor that he will not attempt to recover from the Guarantor payment of any amount, determined by a court or in binding arbitration or agreed between the Landlord and the Tenant, payable in respect of a breach of covenant by the Tenant, unless he has served on the Guarantor, within 6 months of the payment being determined or agreed, a notice in the form prescribed by Section 27 of the 1995 Act as if the payment were a fixed charge under that Act.]

182 This clause is a tenant's amendment. It provides for a notice equivalent to a default notice under the Landlord and Tenant (Covenants) Act 1995 to be served. It protects the interests of existing and future contractual guarantors. As to service of default notices see vol 22(1) (2003 Reissue) LANDLORD AND TENANT (BUSINESS TENANCIES) Paragraph 61 [260].

[286]–[300]

7 FORFEITURE[183]

If and whenever during the Term —

7.1 the Lease Rents[184], or any of them or any part of them, or any VAT payable on them, are outstanding for *(state period, eg 14 days)* after becoming due, whether formally demanded or not[185], or

7.2 the Tenant [or the Guarantor] breaches any covenant or other term of this Lease, or

7.3 the Tenant [or the Guarantor][186], being an individual, becomes subject to a bankruptcy order[187] [or has an interim receiver appointed to his property][188], or

7.4 the Tenant [or the Guarantor][189], being a company, enters into liquidation[190] whether compulsory or voluntary — but not if the liquidation is for amalgamation or reconstruction of a solvent company — [or enters into administration][191] [or has a receiver appointed over all or any part of its assets][192], or

7.5 the Tenant [or the Guarantor][193] enters into or makes a proposal to enter into any voluntary arrangement pursuant to the Insolvency Act 1986[194] or any other arrangement or composition for the benefit of his creditors, or

7.6 the Tenant has any distress, sequestration or execution levied on his goods

and, where the Tenant [or the Guarantor] is more than one person, if and whenever any of the events referred to in this clause happens to any one or more of them, the Landlord may at any time re-enter the Premises or any part of them in the name of the whole — even if any previous right of re-entry has been waived[195] — and thereupon the Term is to cease absolutely but without prejudice to any rights or remedies that may have accrued to the Landlord against the Tenant or the Guarantor [or to the Tenant against the Landlord] in respect of any breach of covenant or other term of this Lease, including the breach in respect of which the re-entry is made.

[301]

183 As to forfeiture generally see vol 22(1) (2003 Reissue) LANDLORD AND TENANT (BUSINESS TENANCIES) Paragraph 283 [1171] et seq.
　　The precise range of insolvency-related circumstances that will trigger the proviso should be carefully considered. Tenants should note that their inclusion, in practice, means that the lease cannot be used as security for a loan. Landlords generally seek to have the ability to forfeit in the widest range of circumstances. It should, however, be noted that, in certain circumstances, leave of the court or of the insolvency practitioner administering the procedure may be required before any contractual right can be exercised: see eg, in respect of administration, the Insolvency Act 1986 Sch 1B para 43(4), (6) as inserted by the Enterprise Act 2002 s 248 (4 Halsbury's Statutes (4th Edn) BANKRUPTCY AND INSOLVENCY).

184 As to the definition of 'the Lease Rents' see clause 1.33 [170] 'THE RENT'.

185   The words 'whether formally demanded or not' should be used to avoid the common law requirement that an actual demand has to be made.

186   The lease may provide for a right of re-entry on insolvency of the guarantor or a tenant's covenant to find an acceptable replacement (see clause 3.23 [238] REPLACEMENT GUARANTOR) or both.

187   As to bankruptcy generally see the Insolvency Act 1986 Pt IX (ss 264–371).

188   As to interim receivers see the Insolvency Act 1986 s 286.

189   See note 186 above.

190   As to liquidation generally see the Insolvency Act 1986 Pts IV–VI (ss 73–246).

191   As to administration generally see the Insolvency Act 1986 Pt II as substituted by the Enterprise Act 2002 s 248. The tenant may seek to argue that if the administrator pays rent and if there are no other material breaches of the lease the landlord should not be entitled to forfeit the lease on this ground.

192   The tenant may seek to argue that if the receiver pays rent and if there are no other material breaches of the lease the landlord should not be entitled to forfeit the lease on this ground.

193   See note 186 above.

194   As to company voluntary arrangements see the Insolvency Act 1986 Pt I (ss 1–7B) as amended by the Insolvency Act 2000. As to individual voluntary arrangements see the Insolvency Act 1986 Pt VIII (ss 252–263G) as amended by the Enterprise Act 2002 s 264.

195   The landlord has the option whether to take advantage of a right of forfeiture or not. If he elects not to do so, the forfeiture is waived. The election may be express or implied, eg if the landlord does any act by which he recognises that the relationship of landlord and tenant is still continuing after the event of forfeiture has come to his knowledge.

[302]–[310]

8   MISCELLANEOUS

8.1   Exclusion of warranty as to use

Nothing in this Lease or in any consent granted by the Landlord under this Lease is to imply or warrant that the Premises may lawfully be used under the Planning Acts for the Permitted Use[196].

196   See *Laurence v Lexcourt Holdings Ltd* [1978] 2 All ER 810, [1978] 1 WLR 1128; *Collins v Howell-Jones* [1981] 2 EGLR 108, 259 Estates Gazette 331, CA; and the comments of Eveleigh LJ on estate agents' particulars relating to use in *Bovis Group Pension Fund Ltd v GC Flooring & Furnishing Ltd* (1984) 269 Estates Gazette 1252 at 1253, CA.

8.2   Exclusion of third party rights

Nothing in this Lease is intended to confer any benefit on any person who is not a party to it[197].

197   By virtue of the Contracts (Rights of Third Parties) Act 1999 (11 Halsbury's Statutes (4th Edn) CONTRACT) third-party rights may be conferred where they are not clearly excluded. This being so, it is advisable to incorporate a specific exclusion except where the parties actually intend to confer rights of action on a third party. In the standard letting situation it is unlikely that the parties will wish to extend liability in this manner. As to the Contracts (Rights of Third Parties) Act 1999 generally see vol 4(3) (2001 Reissue) BOILERPLATE CLAUSES.

8.3   Representations

The Tenant acknowledges that this Lease has not been entered into in reliance wholly or partly on any statement or representation made by or on behalf of the Landlord, except any such statement or representation expressly set out in this Lease[198] [or made by the Landlord's solicitors in any written response to enquiries raised by the Tenant's solicitors in connection with the grant of this Lease].

195   See the comments of Eveleigh LJ on estate agents' particulars relating to use in *Bovis Group Pension Fund Ltd v GC Flooring & Furnishing Ltd* (1984) 269 Estates Gazette 1252 at 1253, CA. For an alternative provision see vol 22(4) (1997 Reissue) LANDLORD AND TENANT (BUSINESS TENANCIES) Form 400 clauses 7.1 [7520], 7.2 [7521].

[311]

8.4   Documents under hand

While the Landlord is a limited company or other corporation, any licence, consent, approval or notice required to be given by the Landlord is to be sufficiently given if given under the hand of a director, the secretary or other duly authorised officer of the Landlord [or by the Surveyor on behalf of the Landlord].

8.5   Tenant's property

If, after the Tenant has vacated the Premises at the end of the Term, any property of his remains in or on the Premises and he fails to remove it within *(state period, eg 7 days)* after a written request from the Landlord to do so, or, if the Landlord is unable to make such a request to the Tenant, within *(state period, eg 14 days)* from the first attempt to make it, then the Landlord may, as the agent of the Tenant, sell that property. The Tenant must indemnify the Landlord against any liability incurred by the Landlord to any third party whose property is sold by him in the mistaken belief held in good faith — which is to be presumed unless the contrary is proved — that the property belonged to the Tenant. If, having made reasonable efforts to do so, the Landlord is unable to locate the Tenant, then the Landlord may retain the proceeds of sale absolutely unless the Tenant claims them within *(state period, eg 6 months)* of the date upon which he vacated the Premises. The Tenant must indemnify the Landlord against any damage occasioned to the Premises and any losses caused by or related to the presence of the property in or on the Premises.

8.6   Compensation on vacating excluded

Any statutory right of the Tenant to claim compensation from the Landlord on vacating the Premises is excluded to the extent that the law allows[199].

199   As to compensation where an order for a new tenancy is precluded on certain grounds see the Landlord and Tenant Act 1954 s 37 as amended by the Local Government and Housing Act 1989 s 149, Sch 7 and by SI 2003/3096.
　　　　As to the effectiveness of provisions of this nature see vol 22(1) (2003 Reissue) LANDLORD AND TENANT (BUSINESS TENANCIES) Paragraph 468 [3079].

[312]

8.7   Notices

8.7.1   *Form and service of notices*

A notice under this Lease must be in writing and, unless the receiving party or his authorised agent acknowledges receipt, is valid if, and only if[200] —

8.7.1.1   it is given by hand, sent by registered post or recorded delivery, or sent by fax[201] provided that a confirmatory copy is given by hand or sent by registered post or recorded delivery on the same day, and

8.7.1.2   it is served —

　　(a)   where the receiving party is a company incorporated within Great Britain, at the registered office,

　　(b)   where the receiving party is the Tenant and the Tenant is not such a company, at the Premises, and

　　(c)   where the receiving party is the Landlord [or the Guarantor] and [the Landlord *(or as required)* that party] is not such a company, at [the Landlord's *(or as required)* that party's] address shown in this Lease or at any address specified in a notice given by [the Landlord to the Tenant *(or as required)* that party to the other parties].

200   Notice clauses are either mandatory or permissive. The words 'and only if' are inserted to make it clear that this clause is mandatory.
201   As to service by fax see *Hastie and Jenkerson v McMahon* [1991] 1 All ER 255, [1990] 1 WLR 1575, CA.

[313]

8.7.2   *Deemed delivery*[202]

8.7.2.1   By registered post or recorded delivery

Unless it is returned through the Royal Mail undelivered, a notice sent by registered post or recorded delivery is to be treated as served on the third working day after posting whenever and whether or not it is received.

8.7.2.2   By fax

A notice sent by fax is to be treated as served on the day upon which it is sent, or the next working day where the fax is sent after 1600 hours or on a day that is not a working day, whenever and whether or not it or the confirmatory copy is received unless the confirmatory copy is returned through the Royal Mail undelivered.

8.7.2.3   'A working day'

References to 'a working day' are references to a day when the United Kingdom clearing banks are open for business in the City of London.

202   It is a fundamental aspect of any notice clause to specify the circumstances in which the server, provided he has complied with the requirements of the clause, has for the purposes of the document served a notice, even if the recipient claims that he never received it.

8.7.3   *Joint recipients*

If the receiving party consists of more than one person, a notice to one of them is notice to all.

8.8   [New *(or)* Old] lease

[This Lease [is *(or as appropriate)* is not] a new tenancy for the purposes of the 1995 Act Section 1. *(or as appropriate)* This Lease is granted under the 1995 Act Section 19 and [is *(or as appropriate)* is not] a new tenancy for the purposes of Section 1 of that Act][203].

203   A tenancy granted on or after 1 January 1996 that is an overriding lease is not a 'new' tenancy where the tenancy being overridden is one granted before that date: see the Landlord and Tenant (Covenants) Act 1995 ss 1(4), 20(1). Where the lease being granted is an overriding lease, the lease must include a statement that it is an overriding lease and indicate whether the overriding lease is or is not a 'new' tenancy: see the Landlord and Tenant (Covenants) Act 1995 s 20(2). In these circumstances the second alternative should be used.

[314]

[8.9   Capacity of tenants

It is declared that the persons comprising the Tenant hold the Premises as [joint tenants *(or as required)* tenants in common].]

[8.10   Exclusion of the 1954 Act Sections 24–28[204]

8.10.1   *Notice and declaration*

On *(date)* the Landlord served notice on the Tenant pursuant to the provisions of the 1954 Act Section 38A(3) as inserted by the Regulatory Reform (Business Tenancies) (England and Wales) Order 2003 and on *(date)* the Tenant made a [simple *(or as appropriate)* statutory] declaration pursuant to schedule 2 of the Regulatory Reform (Business Tenancies) (England and Wales) Order 2003.

8.10.2   *Agreement to exclude*

Pursuant to the provisions of the 1954 Act Section 38A(1) as inserted by the Regulatory Reform (Business Tenancies) (England and Wales) Order 2003, the parties agree that the provisions of the 1954 Act Sections 24–28 inclusive are to be excluded in relation to the tenancy created by this Lease.]

204   As to contracting out of the Landlord and Tenant Act 1954 and the requirements that need to be complied with see vol 22(1) (2003 Reissue) LANDLORD AND TENANT (BUSINESS TENANCIES) Paragraph 431 [2035].

(include other clauses as required: eg, break clauses and options (see vol 22(3) (1997 Reissue) LANDLORD AND TENANT (BUSINESS TENANCIES) Forms 136 [6544]–142 [6569]) or a proviso as to termination on rent review (see vol 22(3) (1997 Reissue) LANDLORD AND TENANT (BUSINESS TENANCIES) Form 143 [6570]))

IN WITNESS etc *(see vol 12(2) (2003 Reissue) DEEDS, AGREEMENTS ETC)*

[315]–[320]

SCHEDULE 1: THE RIGHTS RESERVED[205]

1-1   **Right of entry to inspect**

The right to enter[206], or in emergency to break into and enter, the Premises at any time during the Term [at reasonable times and upon reasonable notice except in emergency] to inspect them, to take schedules or inventories of fixtures and other items to be yielded up at the end of the Term, and to exercise any of the rights granted to the Landlord elsewhere in this Lease.

205   As to rights reserved see vol 22(1) (2003 Reissue) LANDLORD AND TENANT (BUSINESS TENANCIES) Paragraph 124 [648] et seq.
206   For a covenant by the landlord to make good damage so caused see vol 22(3) (1997 Reissue) LANDLORD AND TENANT (BUSINESS TENANCIES) Form 79 [6453].

1-2   **Access on renewal or rent review**

[The right to enter the Premises with the Surveyor and the third party determining the Rent under any provisions for rent review contained in this Lease at [any time *(or as required)* convenient hours and on reasonable prior notice] to inspect [and measure] the Premises for all purposes connected with any pending or intended step under the 1954 Act or the implementation of the provisions for rent review. *(or as required in view of the rent review provisions used: see vol 22(3) (1997 Reissue) LANDLORD AND TENANT (BUSINESS TENANCIES) Forms 180 [6711]–194 [6987]))*]

SCHEDULE 2: THE RENT AND RENT REVIEW

(insert rent review provisions as required: see vol 22(3) (1997 Reissue) LANDLORD AND TENANT (BUSINESS TENANCIES) Forms 180 [6711]–194 [6987])

[321]

SCHEDULE 3: THE INDUSTRIAL COVENANTS

3-1   Use

3-1.1   *Permitted Use only*

The Tenant must use the Premises for the Permitted Use only.

3-1.2   *Cesser of business*

The Tenant must not [cease carrying on business in the Premises or] leave the Premises [continuously] unoccupied for more than *(state period, eg 1 month)* [without notifying the Landlord, and providing such caretaking or security arrangements for the protection of the Premises as the Landlord [reasonably] requires and the insurers or underwriters require].

3-2   Smoke abatement

3-2.1   *Furnace construction*

The Tenant must ensure that every furnace, boiler or heater at the Premises is constructed and used so as substantially to consume or burn the smoke arising from it.

3-2.2   *Noxious emissions*

The Tenant must not cause or permit any gritty, noxious or offensive emissions from any engine, furnace, chimney or other apparatus on the Premises without using [the best possible *(or as required)* all reasonable] means for preventing or counteracting the emissions.

3-2.3   *Statutory controls*

The Tenant must comply with the provisions of the Clean Air Act 1993 and with the requirements of any notice served under it by the relevant authority or body.

[322]

3-3   Environmental protection[207]

3-3.1   *Discharge of dangerous substances*

3-3.1.1   **Damage to the Conduits and environment**

The Tenant must not permit any oil or grease or any deleterious, objectionable, dangerous, poisonous or explosive matter or substance to be discharged into any of the Conduits, and must take all [reasonable] measures to ensure that any effluent discharged into the Conduits does not harm the environment, or corrode or otherwise harm the Conduits or cause obstruction or deposit in them.

3-3.1.2   **Poisons and pollutants**

The Tenant must not permit the discharge into any of the Conduits of any fluid of a poisonous or noxious nature or of a kind likely to sicken or injure the fish, or that does in fact destroy them, or likely to contaminate or pollute the water, of any stream or river.

---

207   It may be advisable for the landlord and tenant to commission a soil survey before the lease is entered into. The results could be annexed to the lease. A further survey could then be carried out towards the end of the term ascertaining whether or not contamination has in fact occurred. The tenant's obligations regarding restriction or clean-up or both will then be clear. If the original soil survey reveals contamination, then thought should be given to including provisions in the lease making it clear whose responsibility the contamination is and whether or not the tenant is obliged to resolve it or clean it up.

[323]

3-3.2   *Spillages and contamination*

The Tenant must take all practicable precautions to ensure that no noxious substances are spilled or deposited on the Premises and that contamination does not occur.

3-3.3   *Controlled, special or radioactive waste*

The Tenant must not deposit on the Premises any controlled or special waste as defined in the Environmental Protection Act 1990, or radioactive waste as defined in the Radioactive Substances Act 1993 Section 18, or any other substance that may produce concentrations or accumulations of noxious gasses or noxious liquids that may cause pollution of the environment or harm to human health.

3-3.4   *Notice of spillages and inspection*

Within 14 days of the spilling or deposit on the Premises of any noxious substance in a quantity that may cause serious damage to or pollution of the environment or serious damage to property or serious harm to human health, the Tenant must inform the Landlord of this and permit him to enter and inspect the Premises.

3-3.5   *Indemnity for damage and pollution*

The Tenant must indemnify the Landlord, and keep him indemnified, against any losses in respect of damage to, or pollution of, the environment or damage to property or harm to human health caused by the Premises or any substance on them whether in liquid or solid form or in the form of gas or vapour.

[324]

3-4   Roof and floor loading

3-4.1   *Heavy items*

The Tenant must not bring into or permit to remain in any building on the Premises any safes, machinery, goods or other articles that will or may strain or damage the building or any part of it.

3-4.2   *Protection of the roof*

The Tenant must not, without the consent of the Landlord, suspend any weight from the [portal frames, stanchions or roof purlins *(or as the case may be)*] of any building on the Premises or use them for the storage of goods or place any weight on them.

3-4.3   *Expert advice*

If the Tenant applies for the Landlord's consent under paragraph 3-4.2 PROTECTION OF THE ROOF, the Landlord may consult any engineer or other person in relation to the roof or floor loading proposed by the Tenant, and the Tenant must repay the fees of the engineer or other person to the Landlord on demand.

3-5   Machinery

3-5.1   *Maintenance of machinery*

The Tenant must keep all plant, apparatus and machinery, including any boilers and furnaces, on the Premises ('the Machinery') properly maintained and in good working order, and for that purpose must employ reputable contractors [to be approved in writing by the Landlord[, whose approval may not be unreasonably withheld [or delayed],]] ('the Contractors') to carry out regular periodic inspection and maintenance of the Machinery.

3-5.2   *Renewal of parts*

The Tenant must renew all working and other parts of the Machinery as and when necessary or when recommended by the Contractors.

3-5.3   *Operation*

The Tenant must ensure, by directions to his staff and otherwise, that the Machinery is properly operated.

3-5.4   *Damage from the Machinery*

The Tenant must avoid damage to the Premises by vibration or otherwise.

3-6   **Signs**

The Tenant must at all times display and maintain, at a point on the outside of the Premises or elsewhere on the Premises to be specified in writing by the Landlord, a suitable sign, of a size and kind first approved by the Landlord, showing the Tenant's trading name and business.

[325]

SCHEDULE 4: THE SUBJECTIONS

(insert details)

SCHEDULE 5: THE AUTHORISED GUARANTEE AGREEMENT

(insert the form of authorised guarantee agreement: see, eg vol 22(3) (1997 Reissue) LANDLORD AND TENANT (BUSINESS TENANCIES) *Form 217 [7053])*

(signature (or common seal) of landlord: lease)
(signature (or common seal) of tenant (and guarantor): counterpart)
(signatures of witnesses)
[326]–[350]

5

Lease of a light industrial building or warehouse with access via a private road across the landlord's adjoining property[1]

CONTENTS

(NB: numbers in [ ] below refer to this volume and should be altered to suit the page or reference numbers actually used)

1 DEFINITIONS AND INTERPRETATION

1.1 'The Adjoining Conduits' .... [358]
1.2 'Adjoining property of the Landlord' .... [358]
1.3 'The Conduits' .... [358]
1.4 'The [Contractual] Term' .... [359]
1.5 'Development' .... [360]
[1.6 'The Exterior Decorating Years' .... [360]]
1.7 Gender and number .... [360]
1.8 Headings .... [360]
1.9 'The Industrial Covenants' .... [360]
[1.10 'The Initial Rent' .... [360]]
1.11 'The Insurance Rent' .... [361]
1.12 'The Insured Risks' .... [361]
1.13 'Interest' .... [362]

[351]

1.14 'The Interest Rate' .... [362]
[1.15 'The Interior Decorating Years' .... [371]]
1.16 Interpretation of 'consent' and 'approved' .... [371]
1.17 Interpretation of 'the Guarantor' .... [372]
1.18 Interpretation of 'the Landlord' .... [372]
1.19 Interpretation of 'the last year of the Term' and 'the end of the Term' .... [372]
1.20 Interpretation of 'the Tenant' .... [372]
1.21 Interpretation of 'this Lease' .... [372]
1.22 Joint and several liability .... [373]
1.23 'The Liability Period' .... [373]
1.24 'Losses' .... [374]
1.25 'The 1954 Act' .... [374]
1.26 'The 1995 Act' .... [374]
1.27 Obligation not to permit or suffer .... [374]
1.28 'Other buildings' .... [374]
1.29 'The Permitted Use' .... [374]
1.30 'The Plan' .... [375]
1.31 'The Planning Acts' .... [375]
1.32 'The Premises' .... [375]
1.33 References to clauses and schedules .... [377]
1.34 References to rights of access .... [377]
1.35 References to statutes .... [377]
1.36 'The Rent' .... [377]
1.37 'The Rent Commencement Date' .... [378]
[1.38 'The Review Dates' .... [378]]

1.39 'The Road' .... [378]
1.40 'The Surveyor' .... [379]
[1.41 'The Term' .... [379]]
1.42 Terms from the 1995 Act .... [379]
1.43 'VAT' .... [379]

2 DEMISE .... [380]
                                                      [352]

3 THE TENANT'S COVENANTS
3.1 Rent .... [391]
3.2 Outgoings and VAT .... [392]
[3.3 Cost of services consumed .... [393]]
3.4 Repair, cleaning and decoration .... [394]
3.5 Waste and alterations .... [397]
3.6 Aerials, signs and advertisements .... [398]
3.7 Statutory obligations .... [399]
3.8 Entry to inspect and notice to repair .... [400]
3.9 Alienation .... [402]
3.10 Nuisance and residential restrictions .... [412]
3.11 Costs of applications, notices and recovery of arrears .... [413]
3.12 Planning and development .... [414]
3.13 Plans, documents and information .... [416]
3.14 Indemnities .... [416]
3.15 Reletting boards and viewing .... [417]
3.16 Obstruction and encroachment .... [417]
3.17 Yielding up .... [418]
3.18 Interest on arrears .... [418]
3.19 Statutory notices .... [419]
3.20 Keyholders .... [419]
3.21 Viewing on sale of reversion .... [419]
3.22 Defective premises .... [419]
3.23 Replacement guarantor .... [419]
3.24 Exercise of the Landlord's rights .... [420]
3.25 The Industrial Covenants .... [420]
3.26 Costs of grant of this Lease .... [420]
3.27 Consent to the Landlord's release .... [421]

4 THE LANDLORD'S COVENANTS
4.1 Quiet enjoyment .... [431]
[4.2 Repairs .... [431]]

5 INSURANCE
5.1 Warranty as to convictions .... [432]
5.2 Covenant to insure .... [432]
5.3 Details of the insurance .... [433]
5.4 Payment of the Insurance Rent .... [434]
5.5 Suspension of the Rent .... [435]
5.6 Reinstatement and termination .... [437]
5.7 Tenant's further insurance covenants .... [441]
[5.8 Landlord's further insurance covenants .... [443]]
                                                      [353]

6 GUARANTEE PROVISIONS

6.1 The Guarantor's covenants . . . . [461]
[6.2 The Landlord's covenant . . . . [466]]

7 FORFEITURE . . . . [467]

8 MISCELLANEOUS

8.1 Exclusion of warranty as to use . . . . [491]
8.2 Exclusion of third party rights . . . . [491]
8.3 Representations . . . . [491]
8.4 Documents under hand . . . . [492]
8.5 Tenant's property . . . . [492]
8.6 Compensation on vacating excluded . . . . [492]
8.7 Notices . . . . [493]
8.8 Rights and easements . . . . [494]
[8.9 The perpetuity period . . . . [495]]
[8.10 Party walls . . . . [495]]
8.11 [New (or) Old] lease . . . . [495]
[8.12 Capacity of tenants . . . . [496]]
[8.13 Exclusion of the 1954 Act Sections 24–28 . . . . [496]]

SCHEDULE 1: THE RIGHTS GRANTED

1-1 Right of way . . . . [501]
1-2 Passage and running through Adjoining Conduits . . . . [501]

SCHEDULE 2: THE RIGHTS RESERVED

2-1 Passage and running through the Conduits . . . . [502]
2-2 Right to construct conduits . . . . [502]
2-3 Access . . . . [503]
2-4 Right to erect new buildings . . . . [503]

SCHEDULE 3: THE RENT AND RENT REVIEW

SCHEDULE 4: THE INDUSTRIAL COVENANTS

4-1 Use of the Road and the Adjoining Conduits . . . . [504]
4-2 Use . . . . [505]
4-3 Smoke abatement . . . . [505]
4-4 Environmental protection . . . . [506]
4-5 Roof and floor loading . . . . [507]
4-6 Machinery . . . . [507]
4-7 Signs . . . . [507]

SCHEDULE 5: THE SUBJECTIONS

SCHEDULE 6: THE AUTHORISED GUARANTEE AGREEMENT

[354]

AGREEMENT

[HM LAND REGISTRY

LAND REGISTRATION ACT 2002

Administrative area   *(insert details)*

Title number out of which lease is granted   *(title number)*

Property let   *(postal address or description)]*

[355]

THIS LEASE is made the .... day of .... BETWEEN:

(1)   *(name of landlord)* [of *(address)* *(or as appropriate)* the registered office of which is at *(address)*] [Company Registration no ...][2] ('the Landlord') [and]

(2)   *(name of tenant)* [of *(address)* *(or as appropriate)* being a company registered in [England and Wales *(or)* Scotland][3] the registered office of which is at *(address)*] [Company Registration no ...] ('the Tenant') [and

(3)   *(name of guarantor)* [of *(address)* *(or as appropriate)* the registered office of which is at *(address)*] [Company Registration no ...] ('the Guarantor')]

[356]

1   As to stamp duty land tax see the Information Binder: Stamp Duty Land Tax [1].
        As to Land Registry Fees see the Information Binder: Property [1]: Property Fees.
        On the grant out of an unregistered freehold estate in land of a lease for a term of more than seven years from the date of the grant, application must be made to register the title to the leasehold interest granted: see the Land Registration Act 2002 s 4(1)(c) (37 Halsbury's Statutes (4th Edn) REAL PROPERTY). The tenant must obtain an epitome of title to the freehold reversion, investigate it, and mark it as examined, otherwise he will not be able to be registered with an absolute title: see vol 25(1) (2003 Reissue) LAND REGISTRATION Paragraph 21.1 [132].
        If the freehold reversion is registered, the grant of a lease for a term of more than seven years from the date of the grant must be completed by registration: see the Land Registration Act 2002 s 27(2)(b)(i).
        As to the form and contents of leases see vol 22(1) (2003 Reissue) LANDLORD AND TENANT (BUSINESS TENANCIES) Paragraph 104 [601] et seq. As to registered land generally see vol 25(1) (2003 Reissue) LAND REGISTRATION. As to registration of title to leases see vol 25(1) (2003 Reissue) LAND REGISTRATION Paragraph 143 [601] et seq.
        This is a lease of a light industrial building or warehouse premises where the landlord owns adjoining property. The tenant is granted a right of way over a road forming part of the landlord's property to gain access to the premises and the right to use conducting media running through that property. The tenant covenants to pay a fair proportion of the cost of maintaining the road and conducting media. The tenant is responsible for repair of the premises and the decoration of both the exterior and the interior. The landlord insures the premises and the tenant refunds the cost of the premiums. There is provision for the rent to be reviewed. There is also provision for a guarantor.
        This Form could be adapted for an office building by substituting the covenants in Form 11 schedule 3 [1762] THE OFFICE COVENANTS for the covenants contained in schedule 4 [504] THE INDUSTRIAL COVENANTS, and by amending clause 3 [391] THE TENANT'S COVENANTS to correspond with Form 11 clause 3 [1642] THE TENANT'S COVENANTS.
        Whatever the nature of the building, this lease is not appropriate where the landlord may in the future let all or part of his retained land. In that case the concept of the small estate, as illustrated by Form 6 [551], would be preferable. If a lease such as this is used, and then parts of the retained land are let to different tenants at a later stage, it is difficult to introduce appropriate arrangements for maintenance of items the use of which is then common to several tenants.
        The question of the boundary between the retained land and the demised land needs to be considered. There will no doubt be a fence or wall to divide the two plots, and ownership of this must be dealt with, eg by making it part of the demised premises by referring to it in clause 1.32.2 [376]

'INTERPRETATION OF 'THE PREMISES'. If a single building is involved, part being retained by the landlord and part being let, the boundary between the retained and demised land, or at least part of it, will be a wall through the building. It is suggested that this should be made a party wall.

The tenant should ensure that the landlord deduces title to the adjoining land affected by the rights he is granted, especially where the lease is registrable, because if title is not shown and any consents, eg of any chargee or landlord of the adjoining land, obtained, the rights may be excluded from the title.

2   If any party is a company it is desirable to include the company registration number. This avoids any problems arising when a company has been wound up and a new company formed with the same name, or when the name of a company is changed, or if companies swap names, eg on a reconstruction of a group of companies. In addition, where a company applies to be registered as proprietor of a registered estate or registered charge, the application must state the company's registration number: see the Land Registration Rules 2003, SI 2003/1417 r 181.

3   Where the tenant is a company registered in England and Wales or Scotland, and the lease is registrable, an application for first registration of the lease (where the landlord's title is unregistered), or registration of the lease as a registrable disposition (where the landlord's title is registered), and the tenant as proprietor of the leasehold title, must state the company's registered number: see SI 2003/1417 r 181(1). There seems to be no reason why the certificate and statement should not be contained in the disposition in favour of the proprietor, where convenient.

[357]

NOW THIS DEED WITNESSES as follows:

1   DEFINITIONS AND INTERPRETATION

For all purposes of this Lease[4] the terms defined in this clause have the meanings specified.

4   One view would add 'unless the context otherwise requires' or 'where the context so admits' and in fact this may be implied (see *Meux v Jacobs* (1875) LR 7 HL 481 at 493; *Law Society v United Service Bureau Ltd* [1934] 1 KB 343, DC) but the better course is to use defined terms in such a way that there are no circumstances where the defined meaning does not apply.

1.1   'The Adjoining Conduits'

'The Adjoining Conduits' means the pipes, sewers, drains, mains, ducts, conduits, gutters, watercourses, wires, cables, [laser optical fibres, data or impulse transmission, communication or reception systems,] channels, flues and all other conducting media — including any fixings, louvres, cowls, covers and other ancillary apparatus — that are in, on, over or under any adjoining property of the Landlord that serve the Premises.

1.2   'Adjoining property of the Landlord'

References to 'adjoining property of the Landlord' are references to each and every part of the land neighbouring or adjoining the Premises in which the Landlord, or a company that is a member of the same group as the Landlord within the meaning of the 1954 Act Section 42, has or during the Term acquires an interest or estate.

1.3   'The Conduits'

'The Conduits' means the pipes, sewers, drains, mains, ducts, conduits, gutters, watercourses, wires, cables, [laser optical fibres, data or impulse transmission, communication or reception systems,] channels, flues and all other conducting media — including any fixings, louvres, cowls, covers and any other ancillary apparatus — that are in, on, over or under the Premises.

[358]

1.4   'The [Contractual] Term'[5]

'The [Contractual][6] Term' means *(insert number)* years commencing on and including *(date of commencement of term)*[7].

5   As to the commencement of the term see vol 22(1) (2003 Reissue) LANDLORD AND TENANT (BUSINESS TENANCIES) Paragraph 135 [670].
       As to registration see note 1 above. Where the landlord's title is unregistered, the grantee must apply for registration within a period of two months from the date of the disposition if the lease is granted for a term of more than seven years. If no such application is made the disposition becomes void as regards any transfer, grant or creation of a legal estate: see the Land Registration Act 2002 s 6 (37 Halsbury's Statutes (4th Edn) REAL PROPERTY). Where the landlord's title is registered and the lease is for a term of more than seven years, the tenant should protect the intended lease by applying for an official search, and an application to register the lease should be made before expiry of the search, otherwise the lease will be susceptible to loss of priority: see the Land Registration Act 2002 s 27.

6   The demise in this lease is for 'the Contractual Term', which is defined as a fixed term of years. The expression 'the Term', as defined in clause 1.41 [379] 'THE TERM', is used in covenants so that they continue to apply during any period of holding over or continuance or extension of the contractual term. Some difficulties arise if this structure is used in a draft lease where security of tenure is to be excluded under the Landlord and Tenant Act 1954 s 38A(1) as inserted by SI 2003/3096 (23 Halsbury's Statutes (4th Edn) LANDLORD AND TENANT). The demise is for the contractual term and the inclusion of the definition of 'the Term' does not prevent the lease being 'for a term of years certain' as required by the Landlord and Tenant Act 1954 s 38A(1). However, reference to continuance of the contractual term by statute is inappropriate where the operation of the security of tenure provisions in the Landlord and Tenant Act 1954 ss 24–28 is to be excluded. If a lease is contracted out of the Landlord and Tenant Act 1954 there can be no statutory extension, and if the tenant remains in occupation at the end of the contractual term he is holding over unlawfully unless there is an express agreement to extend the contractual term operating as a surrender and re-grant so that the original lease— and the agreement under the Landlord and Tenant Act 1954 s 38A(1) — has no further effect. It is suggested that in these circumstances the drafting should be simplified to include a single term (defined simply as 'the Term') by reference to the period of the contractual term. This can be achieved by amending this clause in the manner suggested and substituting it for clause 1.41 [379] 'THE TERM'.

7   For estate management reasons it is usually desirable to insert a quarter day here — or a rent day when rent is due on days other than quarter days — ie generally the one preceding the earlier of the date of possession and the date of execution.

[359]

1.5   'Development'

References to 'development' are references to development as defined by the Town and Country Planning Act 1990 Section 55.

[1.6   'The Exterior Decorating Years'

'The Exterior Decorating Years' means *(specify years).*] *(omit if not required, eg if the first alternative in clause 3.4.6 [396] DECORATION is used)*

1.7   Gender and number

Words importing one gender include all other genders; words importing the singular include the plural and vice versa[8].

8   See the Law of Property Act 1925 s 61 (37 Halsbury's Statutes (4th Edn) REAL PROPERTY).

1.8   Headings[9]

The clause, paragraph and schedule headings and the table of contents do not form part of this document and are not be taken into account in its construction or interpretation. *(amend if marginal notes used instead of headings)*

9   Headings and marginal notes require the draftsman to provide a word or two to describe every clause in the lease. This is not always easy and there are times when the draftsman will have to settle for something less than perfection, the only alternative being a heading or note that would be inappropriately long. It would be quite wrong for that title, which its author might admit was not totally apposite but was the best that he could do in a few words, to be used in construing the clause in question.

1.9 'The Industrial Covenants'

'The Industrial Covenants' means the covenants set out in schedule 4 THE INDUSTRIAL COVENANTS.

[1.10 'The Initial Rent'

'The Initial Rent' means [the sum of £... a year *(or as required by the rent and the review provisions used)*].] *(this definition is not required if the rent is not reviewable)*

[360]

1.11 'The Insurance Rent'[10]

'The Insurance Rent' means the [gross sums including any commission *(or as required)* sums net of any commission] that the Landlord from time to time pays —

1.11.1   by way of premium for insuring the Premises, including insuring for loss of rent, in accordance with his obligations contained in this Lease,

1.11.2   by way of premium for insuring in such amount and on such terms as [the Landlord acting reasonably considers appropriate *(or as required)* is reasonable] against all liability of the Landlord to third parties arising out of or in connection with any matter including or relating to the Premises, and

1.11.3   for insurance valuations,

provided that where the insurance includes other premises[11] the Tenant is only to be obliged to pay the proportion of those sums reasonably attributable to the Premises. That proportion is to be determined from time to time by the Surveyor acting as an expert and not as arbitrator.

10   As to reimbursement of insurance premiums see vol 22(1) (2003 Reissue) LANDLORD AND TENANT (BUSINESS TENANCIES) Paragraph 230 [1026].
11   The landlord may insure his retained premises under the same policy.

1.12 'The Insured Risks'

'The Insured Risks' means the risks of loss or damage by fire[, storm, tempest, earthquake, lightning, explosion, riot, civil commotion, malicious damage, [terrorism,] impact by vehicles and by aircraft and articles dropped from aircraft — other than war risks — flood damage and bursting and overflowing of water pipes and tanks,] and such other risks, whether or not in the nature of the foregoing, as the Landlord [acting reasonably] from time to time decides to insure against[12].

12   As to the risks to be insured and the tenant's concerns see vol 22(1) (2003 Reissue) LANDLORD AND TENANT (BUSINESS TENANCIES) Paragraph 235 [1033].

[361]

1.13 'Interest'

References to 'interest' are references to interest payable during the period from the date on which the payment is due to the date of payment, both before and after any judgment, at the Interest Rate then prevailing [*(where the interest rate is defined by reference to a bank base rate)* or, should the base rate referred to in clause 1.14 'THE INTEREST RATE' cease to exist[13], at another rate of interest closely comparable with the Interest Rate [to be agreed between the parties or in default of agreement to be determined by [the Surveyor, acting as an expert and not as an arbitrator *(or as required)* a chartered accountant appointed by agreement between the parties or in default of agreement nominated by the President of the Institute of Chartered Accountants in England and Wales, acting as an expert and not as an arbitrator][14] *(or as required)* decided on by the Landlord acting reasonably]].

13   If base rates are referred to, the possibility of their ceasing to exist should be provided for. Alternatively, the Law Society's interest rate may be specified.

14   This provision may be expanded to provide for deeming the parties to have disagreed after a certain time, deputy appointors etc.

1.14   'The Interest Rate'

'The Interest Rate'[15] means the rate of ...% a year[16] above [the base lending rate of *(specify bank)* or such other bank [being a member of the British Bankers Association] as the Landlord may from time to time nominate in writing[17] *(or as required)* the Law Society's interest rate[18]].

15   As to the covenant to pay interest see vol 22(1) (2003 Reissue) LANDLORD AND TENANT (BUSINESS TENANCIES) Paragraph 154 [767].

16   Words such as 'with a minimum of ...%' should not be used because, if interest rates drop during the term to such an extent that the minimum rate specified represents significantly more than a few percent over the basic borrowing rate, the provision might be void as a penalty. As to what amounts to a penalty see *Dunlop Pneumatic Tyre Co Ltd v New Garage and Motor Co Ltd* [1915] AC 79, HL; *Cellulose Acetate Silk Co Ltd v Widnes Foundry (1925) Ltd* [1933] AC 20, HL. In view of this landlords would be unwise to provide for a rate of more than a few percent over base rate, and even this is in fact a penalty and should be resisted by the tenant.

17   The chance to change the bank may be useful, especially on a sale of the reversion, so that the landlord can always provide for his bank for the time being to be specified. The tenant should try to limit the choice to major clearing banks.

18   The Law Society's interest rate is published weekly in the Law Society's Gazette.

[362]–[370]

[1.15   'The Interior Decorating Years'

'The Interior Decorating Years' means *(specify years).*] *(omit if not required, eg if the first alternative in clause 3.4.6 [396] DECORATION is used)*

1.16   Interpretation of 'consent' and 'approved'

1.16.1   *Prior written consent or approval*

References to 'consent of the Landlord' or words to similar effect are references to a prior written consent signed by or on behalf of the Landlord and references to the need for anything to be 'approved by the Landlord' or words to similar effect are references to the need for a prior written approval by or on behalf of the Landlord.

1.16.2   *Consent or approval of mortgagee or head landlord*

Any provisions in this Lease referring to the consent or approval of the Landlord are to be construed as also requiring the consent or approval of any mortgagee of the Premises and any head landlord where that consent is required [under a mortgage or headlease in existence at the date of this document][19]. Nothing in this Lease is to be construed as imposing any obligation on a mortgagee or head landlord not to refuse any such consent or approval unreasonably.

19   The tenant should include these words so that the clause applies *only* where the consent of the mortgagee or head landlord is in fact required under the terms of an *existing* mortgage or headlease. The tenant should request a copy of the document concerned to establish the rights of the mortgagee or head landlord in relation to any consents that he may seek. The risk to the tenant of the clause without these words is that, by subsequently creating a mortgage or headlease, the landlord could, innocently or deliberately, bring about a situation where his consent may be refused in circumstances in which it would otherwise have been unreasonable to do so. In particular, the effect on the tenant's ability to assign or sublet could be serious.

[371]

1.17   Interpretation of 'the Guarantor'[20]

The expression 'the Guarantor' includes [*(where there is a guarantor for the original tenant)* not only the person named above as the Guarantor, but also][21] any person who enters into covenants with the Landlord pursuant to clause 3.9.5.2 CONDITIONS or clause 3.23 REPLACEMENT GUARANTOR.

20   As to guarantors see vol 22(1) (2003 Reissue) LANDLORD AND TENANT (BUSINESS TENANCIES) Paragraphs 40 [201], 71 [278] et seq.
21   Where there is no guarantor for the original tenant, if it is felt undesirable to have covenants in a lease and no party, at least initially, to enter into them, the guarantor's covenants could be included in a schedule.

1.18   Interpretation of 'the Landlord'

The expression 'the Landlord' includes the person or persons from time to time entitled to possession of the Premises when this Lease comes to an end.

1.19   Interpretation of 'the last year of the Term' and 'the end of the Term'

References to 'the last year of the Term' are references to the actual last year of the Term howsoever it determines, and references to 'the end of the Term' are references to the end of the Term whensover and howsoever it determines.

1.20   Interpretation of 'the Tenant'

'The Tenant' includes any person who is for the time being bound by the tenant covenants of this Lease except where the name of *(name of original tenant)* appears.

1.21   Interpretation of 'this Lease'

Unless expressly stated to the contrary, the expression 'this Lease' includes any document supplemental to or collateral with this document or entered into in accordance with this document.

[372]

1.22   Joint and several liability

Where any party to this Lease for the time being comprises two or more persons, obligations expressed or implied to be made by or with that party are deemed to be made by or with the persons comprising that party jointly and severally.

1.23   'The Liability Period'[22]

'The Liability Period' means —

[1.23.1   in the case of *(name of guarantor for the original tenant)*, the period during which *(name of original tenant)* is bound by the tenant covenants of this Lease together with any additional period during which *(name of original tenant)* is liable under an authorised guarantee agreement,] *(omit where there is no guarantor for the original tenant)*

1.23.2   in the case of any guarantor required pursuant to clause 3.9.5.2 CONDITIONS, the period during which the relevant assignee is bound by the tenant covenants of this Lease together with any additional period during which that assignee is liable under an authorised guarantee agreement,

1.23.3   in the case of any guarantor under an authorised guarantee agreement, the period during which the relevant assignee is bound by the tenant covenants of this Lease, and

1.23.4   in the case of any guarantor required pursuant to clause 3.9.8.7 TERMS OF A PERMITTED SUBLEASE, the period during which the relevant assignee of the sublease is bound by the tenant covenants of that sublease.

22   The liability of the guarantor should be expressed to last while the original tenant, or as the case may be the assignee, is bound by the tenant covenants in the lease — or in the case of clause 1.23.4 the sublease — rather than while the lease is vested in that person, to take account of the possibility of an excluded assignment being made and the tenant — or subtenant — remaining liable. An excluded assignment means that the tenant — or subtenant — is precluded from tenant release under the Landlord and Tenant (Covenants) Act 1995 (23 Halsbury's Statutes (4th Edn) LANDLORD AND TENANT).

   The Landlord and Tenant (Covenants) Act 1995 does not clearly indicate whether the liability of a contractual guarantor can be expressed to extend to any period during which the tenant is bound by an authorised guarantee agreement, but the better view is that it is possible. The policy of the Act certainly suggests that this should be the case.

[373]

1.24   'Losses'

References to 'losses' are references to liabilities, damages or losses, awards of damages or compensation, penalties, costs, disbursements or expenses arising from any claim, demand, action or proceedings.

1.25   'The 1954 Act'

'The 1954 Act' means the Landlord and Tenant Act 1954 [and all statutes, regulations and orders included by virtue of clause 1.35 REFERENCES TO STATUTES][23].

23   The words in square brackets are strictly speaking not required because they merely state what would be the case anyway by virtue of clause 1.35 [377] REFERENCES TO STATUTES. Nevertheless, as much could turn on the point (see *Brett v Brett Essex Golf Club Ltd* (1986) 52 P & CR 330, [1986] 1 EGLR 154, CA), the parties may prefer to deal expressly with the point.

1.26   'The 1995 Act'

'The 1995 Act' means the Landlord and Tenant (Covenants) Act 1995 [and all statutes, regulations and orders included by virtue of clause 1.35 REFERENCES TO STATUTES][24].

24   See note 23 to clause 1.25 [374] 'THE 1954 ACT'.

1.27   Obligation not to permit or suffer

Any covenant by the Tenant not to do anything includes an obligation [to use reasonable endeavours] not to permit or suffer[25] that thing to be done by another person [where the Tenant is aware that the thing is being done].

25   'Permit' may have a different meaning from 'suffer': see *Barton v Reed* [1932] 1 Ch 362 at 375 per Luxmore J. A covenant not to 'permit' activity is broken if the covenantor himself carries it on: see *Oceanic Village Ltd v United Attractions Ltd* [2000] Ch 234, [2000] 1 All ER 975.

1.28   'Other buildings'

References to 'other buildings' are references to any buildings now or at any time during the Term erected on any adjoining property of the Landlord.

1.29   'The Permitted Use'[26]

'The Permitted Use' means [*(specify use)* or such other use falling within Classes *(state classes, eg B1, B2 or B8)* of the Schedule to the Town and Country Planning (Use Classes) Order 1987, notwithstanding any amendment or revocation of that Order[27], as the Landlord from time to time approves[, such approval not to be unreasonably withheld [or delayed]] *(or if the landlord does not require control over the specific trade)* any use that falls within Classes *(state classes, eg B1, B2 or B8)* of the Schedule to the Town and Country Planning (Use Classes) Order 1987, notwithstanding any amendment or revocation of that Order].

26   As to use see vol 22(1) (2003 Reissue) LANDLORD AND TENANT (BUSINESS TENANCIES) Paragraph 170 [861] et seq.

27   As use classes orders change frequently, it is important to make clear which class is intended to apply, the class in existence at the date of the lease or the class as amended during the term of the lease.

[374]

1.30   'The Plan'[28]

'The Plan' means the plan annexed to this Lease.

28   As to the use and role of plans see vol 22(1) (2003 Reissue) LANDLORD AND TENANT (BUSINESS TENANCIES) Paragraphs 117 [636], 118 [638]. A plan may not always be required, eg a demise of all the land within a registered title. If the lease is registrable, a plan 'for identification purposes only' or where there is some other disclaimer as to the extent to which it can be relied on for conveyancing purposes is not sufficient if part of the land in a registered title is being dealt with.

1.31   'The Planning Acts'

'The Planning Acts' means the Town and Country Planning Act 1990, the Planning (Listed Buildings and Conservation Areas) Act 1990, the Planning (Consequential Provisions) Act 1990, the Planning (Hazardous Substances) Act 1990, the Planning and Compensation Act 1991, the Planning and Compulsory Purchase Act 2004 [and all statutes, regulations and orders included by virtue of clause 1.35 REFERENCES TO STATUTES][29].

29   See note 23 to clause 1.25 [374] 'THE 1954 ACT'.

1.32   'The Premises'[30]

1.32.1   *Definition of 'the Premises'*

'The Premises' means the land and building known as *(insert postal address)* shown [for the purpose of identification only] edged *(state colour, eg red)* on the Plan.

30   As to parcels generally see vol 22(1) (2003 Reissue) LANDLORD AND TENANT (BUSINESS TENANCIES) Paragraph 116 [634].

[375]

1.32.2   *Interpretation of 'the Premises'*[31]

The expression 'the Premises' includes —

1.32.2.1   all buildings, erections, structures, fixtures[32], fittings and appurtenances on the Premises from time to time,

[1.32.2.2   the [fence *(or as appropriate)* wall] dividing the Premises from any adjoining property of the Landlord,]

1.32.2.3   all additions, alterations and improvements carried out during the Term, and

1.32.2.4   the Conduits,

but excludes [the air space above[33] and] any fixtures installed by the Tenant [or any predecessors in title] that can be removed from the Premises without defacing the Premises. Unless the contrary is expressly stated 'the Premises' includes any part or parts of the Premises.

31   As to implied grants and reservations see vol 22(1) (2003 Reissue) LANDLORD AND TENANT (BUSINESS TENANCIES) Paragraph 125 [650].
32   As to fixtures see vol 22(1) (2003 Reissue) LANDLORD AND TENANT (BUSINESS TENANCIES) Paragraph 121 [644].
33   As to air space, subsoil, cellars and footings see vol 22(1) (2003 Reissue) LANDLORD AND TENANT (BUSINESS TENANCIES) Paragraph 119 [640]. Strictly speaking, this exclusion means that the tenant would not be permitted to go on to the roof to inspect or repair it, unless he is held to have an easement of necessity to do so. As to easements of necessity generally see 13 Halsbury's Laws (4th Edn Reissue) EASEMENTS AND PROFITS À PRENDRE. If the landlord requires the upper limit of the demised premises to be defined, the tenant, in the case of a full repairing lease, should require a right to enter the landlord's air space above the demised premises to inspect or repair the upper limit of the premises. For a form that may be modified for this purpose see vol 22(3) (1997 Reissue) LANDLORD AND TENANT (BUSINESS TENANCIES) Form 77 [6451].

[376]

1.33   References to clauses and schedules

Any reference in this document to a clause, paragraph or schedule without further designation is to be construed as a reference to the clause, paragraph or schedule of this document so numbered.

1.34   References to rights of access

References to any right of the Landlord to have access to the Premises are to be construed as extending to any head landlord and any mortgagee of the Premises [— where the headlease or mortgage grants such rights of access to the head landlord or mortgagee —] and to all persons authorised in writing by the Landlord and any head landlord or mortgagee, including agents, professional advisers, contractors, workmen and others.

1.35   References to statutes

Unless expressly stated to the contrary, any reference to a specific statute includes any statutory extension or modification, amendment or re-enactment of that statute and any regulations or orders made under it, and any general reference to a statute includes any regulations or orders made under that statute[34].

34   Unfortunately the Interpretation Act 1978 ss 17, 23(3) (41 Halsbury's Statutes (4th Edn) STATUTES) does not quite go far enough to enable this clause to be dispensed with altogether, particularly where a statute is modified.

1.36   'The Rent'[35]

[Until the First Review Date 'the Rent' means the Initial Rent. Thereafter 'the Rent' means the sum ascertained in accordance with schedule 3 THE RENT AND RENT REVIEW. 'The Rent' does not include the Insurance Rent[36], but the term 'the Lease Rents' means both the Rent and the Insurance Rent. *(or as required by the rent and review provisions used)*]

35   This clause assumes that the rent is reviewable. If the rent is not reviewable clause 1.10 [360] 'THE INITIAL RENT' should be omitted and this clause amended as appropriate.
36   Because of this exclusion the insurance rent is not suspended under clause 5.5 [435] SUSPENSION OF THE RENT.

[377]

1.37   'The Rent Commencement Date'

'The Rent Commencement Date' means *(insert date on which payment of the rent is to start)*[37].

37   This provision may be used to provide for a rent-free period, or for the situation where the tenant had possession before the execution of the lease on the basis that rent should be paid from the date of possession. If either the date of execution of the lease or the date of commencement of the term is to be the date for commencement of rent, that date should be inserted here.

[1.38   'The Review Dates'[38]

'The First Review Date' means *(date)*. 'The Review Dates' means the First Review Date and every *(insert ordinal, eg 3rd)* anniversary of it during the [Contractual] Term [*(if appropriate for the review provisions used)* — and any other date from time to time specified under *(insert the relevant provision: see eg vol 22(3) (1997 Reissue) LANDLORD AND TENANT (BUSINESS TENANCIES) Form 180 paragraph {2}-4 [6728] EFFECT OF COUNTER-INFLATION PROVISIONS)*]. References to 'a review date' are references to any one of the Review Dates.] *(omit if not required by the review provisions to be used, or if the rent is not reviewable)*

38   As to rent review dates and intervals see vol 22(1) (2003 Reissue) LANDLORD AND TENANT (BUSINESS TENANCIES) Paragraph 302 [1333] et seq. Where there might be a statutory continuation of the lease, the landlord may wish to ensure that there is a review date shortly before the end of the contractual term to obviate the need to apply for an interim rent. The tenant may wish to insist on the word 'contractual' remaining so that the rent review provisions do not apply during any period of lawful holding-over or extension or continuance of the contractual term.

1.39   'The Road'

'The Road' means the road shown coloured *(state colour, eg brown)* on the Plan.

[378]

1.40   'The Surveyor'[39]

'The Surveyor' means *(name)* or any person or firm appointed by the Landlord in his place. The Surveyor may be an employee of the landlord or a company that is a member of the same group as the Landlord within the meaning of the 1954 Act Section 42. The expression 'the Surveyor' includes the person or firm appointed by the Landlord to collect the Lease Rents.

39   For a provision that the landlord's surveyor must be a member of a relevant professional body see vol 22(3) (1997 Reissue) LANDLORD AND TENANT (BUSINESS TENANCIES) Form 152 [6648].

[1.41 'The Term'

'The Term' means the Contractual Term and any period of holding-over or extension or continuance of the Contractual Term whether by statute or common law[40].] *(omit if the lease is to be contracted out of the Landlord and Tenant Act 1954)*[41]

40   The demise in this lease is for 'the Contractual Term', which is defined as a fixed term of years. The expression 'the Term' is used in covenants so that they continue to apply during any period of holding-over or continuance or extension of the contractual term. As to the liability of a guarantor during a period of statutory continuation see vol 22(1) (2003 Reissue) LANDLORD AND TENANT (BUSINESS TENANCIES) Paragraph 73 [282].

41   Some difficulties arise if the structure referred to in note 40 above is used in a draft lease where security of tenure is to be excluded under the Landlord and Tenant Act 1954 s 38A(1) as inserted by SI 2003/3096. The demise is for the contractual term and the inclusion of the definition of 'the Term' does not prevent the lease being 'for a term of years certain' as required by the Landlord and Tenant Act 1954 s 38A(1). However, reference to continuance of the contractual term by statute is inappropriate where the operation of the security of tenure provisions in the Landlord and Tenant Act 1954 ss 24–28 is to be excluded. If a lease is contracted out of the Landlord and Tenant Act 1954 there can be no statutory extension, and if the tenant remains in occupation at the end of the contractual term he is holding over unlawfully unless there is an express agreement to extend the contractual term operating as a surrender and re-grant so that the original lease — and the agreement under the Landlord and Tenant Act 1954 s 38A(1) — has no further effect. It is suggested that in these circumstances the drafting should be simplified to include a single term (defined simply as 'the Term') by reference to the period of the contractual term. This can be achieved by amending clause 1.4 [359] 'THE [CONTRACTUAL] TERM' as suggested and substituting it for this clause.

1.42   Terms from the 1995 Act

Where the expressions 'landlord covenants', 'tenant covenants', or 'authorised guarantee agreement' are used in this Lease they are to have the same meaning as is given by the 1995 Act Section 28(1).

1.43   'VAT'[42]

'VAT' means value added tax or any other tax of a similar nature and unless otherwise expressly stated all references to rents or other sums payable by the Tenant are exclusive of VAT.

42   As to VAT generally, see the Information Binder: Property [1]: VAT and Property.

[379]

2   DEMISE

The Landlord lets[43] the Premises to the Tenant [with [full *(or)* limited] title guarantee], together with the rights specified in schedule 1 THE RIGHTS GRANTED, but excepting and reserving to the Landlord the rights specified in schedule 2 THE RIGHTS RESERVED, to hold the Premises to the Tenant for the [Contractual][44] Term, subject to [all rights, easements, privileges, restrictions, covenants and stipulations of whatever nature affecting the Premises including any matters contained or referred to in schedule 5 THE SUBJECTIONS *(or as required)* the rights, easements, privileges, restrictions, covenants and stipulations affecting the Premises contained or referred to in schedule 5 THE SUBJECTIONS][45], yielding and paying[46] to the Landlord —

2.1   the Rent, without any deduction or set-off[47], by equal quarterly payments in advance[48] on the usual quarter days[49] in every year and proportionately for any period of less than a year, the first such payment, being a proportionate sum in respect of the period from and including the Rent Commencement Date to and including the day before the quarter day next after the Rent Commencement Date, to be paid on the date of this document[50], and

2.2   by way of further rent the Insurance Rent[51] payable on demand in accordance with clause 5.4 PAYMENT OF THE INSURANCE RENT.

43   Traditionally, the operative word in a lease executed as a deed was 'demises' but any words sufficient to show the parties' intention may be used.

44   See note 41 to clause 1.41 [379] 'THE TERM'.

45   The tenant should argue for the second version, making the schedule comprehensive rather than illustrative.

46   The words 'yielding and paying' imply a covenant to pay rent: see *Vyvyan v Arthur* (1823) 1 B & C 410. An express covenant is now invariably included because further procedural matters are contained in it.

47   As to deductions and set off see vol 22(1) (2003 Reissue) LANDLORD AND TENANT (BUSINESS TENANCIES) Paragraph 147 [753].

48   In the absence of an express provision, rent is payable in arrears.

49   The usual quarter days are 25 March, 24 June, 29 September and 25 December. A reference to 'the usual quarter days' is all that is necessary when rent is to be paid on these days.

50   If the first payment is not a complete instalment, the lease must provide for the date on which it is to be paid, the amount, and the period it is to cover.

51   As to the advantages of reserving the insurance rent as rent see vol 22(1) (2003 Reissue) LANDLORD AND TENANT (BUSINESS TENANCIES) Paragraph 151 [761].

[380]–[390]

3   THE TENANT'S COVENANTS

The Tenant covenants with the Landlord to observe and perform the requirements of this clause 3.

3.1   Rent

3.1.1   *Payment of the Lease Rents*

The Tenant must pay the Lease Rents[52] on the days and in the manner set out in this Lease and must not exercise or seek to exercise any right or claim to withhold rent or any right or claim to legal or equitable set-off[53] [except that referred to in *(give details of any provisions granting an express right of set-off)*][54].

52   As to the definition of 'the Lease Rents' see clause 1.36 [377] 'THE RENT'.

53   See, eg, *British Anzani (Felixstowe) Ltd v International Marine Management (UK) Ltd* [1980] QB 137, [1979] 2 All ER 1063; *Lee-Parker v Izzet* [1971] 3 All ER 1099, [1971] 1 WLR 1688. As to deductions and set-off see vol 22(1) (2003 Reissue) LANDLORD AND TENANT (BUSINESS TENANCIES) Paragraphs 147 [753], 148 [755].

54   If any express right of set-off is granted to the tenant, reference to the provision concerned should be included here to avoid inconsistency.

3.1.2   *Payment by banker's order*[55]

If so required in writing by the Landlord, the Tenant must pay the Lease Rents[56] by banker's order or credit transfer to any bank and account [in the United Kingdom] that the Landlord nominates from time to time.

55   This is a clause with dangers for both parties. If the existence of a breach of covenant is known to the landlord he must instruct his bank to refuse to accept the rent, otherwise his right of forfeiture is lost. As to implied waiver of the right of forfeiture see vol 22(1) (2003 Reissue) LANDLORD AND TENANT (BUSINESS TENANCIES) Paragraph 284 [1173]. The tenant may feel that he requires more control over the payment of rent. In any event, the financial systems operated by many companies prevent payments being made in this way.

56   As to the definition of 'the Lease Rents' see clause 1.36 [377] 'THE RENT'.

[391]

3.2 Outgoings and VAT

3.2.1 *Outgoings exclusive to the Premises*

The Tenant must pay, and must indemnify the Landlord against —

3.2.1.1 all rates, taxes[57], assessments, duties, charges, impositions and outgoings that are now or may at any time during the Term be charged, assessed or imposed upon the Premises or upon the owner or occupier of them[, excluding any payable by the Landlord occasioned by receipt of the Lease Rents[58] or by any disposition of or dealing with this Lease or ownership of any interest reversionary to the interest created by it][59] [— provided that if the Landlord suffers any loss of rating relief that may be applicable to empty premises after the end of the Term because the relief has been allowed to the Tenant in respect of any period before the end of the Term then the Tenant must make good such loss to the Landlord],

3.2.1.2 all VAT that may from time to time be charged on the Lease Rents or other sums payable by the Tenant under this Lease[60], and

3.2.1.3 all VAT incurred in relation to any costs that the Tenant is obliged to pay or in respect of which he is required to indemnify the Landlord under the terms of this Lease, save where such VAT is recoverable or available for set-off by the Landlord as input tax[61].

57 As to covenants to pay rates and taxes see vol 22(1) (2003 Reissue) LANDLORD AND TENANT (BUSINESS TENANCIES) Paragraph 153 [765].
58 As to the definition of 'the Lease Rents' see clause 1.36 [377] 'THE RENT'.
59 The tenant should add the words in square brackets to make it clear that he is not paying the landlord's taxes.
60 As to VAT on rent, service charges and insurance premiums see the Information Binder: Property [1]: VAT and Property.
61 As to payment of VAT on legal costs paid by a person other than the solicitor's own client see the Information Binder: Property [1]: VAT and Property.

[392]

3.2.2 *Outgoings assessed on the Premises and other property*

The Tenant must pay, and must indemnify the Landlord against, the proportion reasonably attributable to the Premises — to be determined from time to time by the Surveyor, acting as an expert and not as an arbitrator[62] — of all rates, taxes, assessments, duties, charges, impositions and outgoings that are now or at any time during the Term may be charged, assessed or imposed on the Premises and any other property, including any adjoining property of the Landlord, or on their owners or occupiers.

62 As to the distinction between an expert and an arbitrator see vol 22(1) (2003 Reissue) LANDLORD AND TENANT (BUSINESS TENANCIES) Paragraph 364 [1523].

[3.3 Cost of services consumed[63]

The Tenant must pay to the suppliers, and indemnify the Landlord against, all charges for electricity, water, gas, telecommunications and other services consumed or used at or in relation to the Premises, including meter rents and standing charges, and must comply with the lawful requirements and regulations of the respective suppliers.] *(omit if the premises have independent supplies of all services)*

63 Where the premises comprise a separate building, a separate supply is usually provided and the tenant makes his own arrangements with the suppliers. In that case this clause is unnecessary.

[393]

3.4   Repair, cleaning and decoration

3.4.1   *Repair of the Premises*[64]

The Tenant must repair the Premises and keep them in good condition and repair, except for damage caused by one or more of the Insured Risks save to the extent that the insurance money is irrecoverable due to any act or default of the Tenant or anyone at the Premises expressly or by implication[65] with his authority [and under his control][66].

---

64   As to repair see vol 22(1) (2003 Reissue) LANDLORD AND TENANT (BUSINESS TENANCIES) Paragraph 196 [931] et seq. For a covenant to repair, rebuild and renew see vol 22(3) (1997 Reissue) LANDLORD AND TENANT (BUSINESS TENANCIES) Form 85 [6460]. For provisos excluding, eg, work that is prevented etc see vol 22(3) (1997 Reissue) LANDLORD AND TENANT (BUSINESS TENANCIES) Forms 87 [6462], 88 [6463].

        If a landlord is unable to obtain full insurance cover without excess, it should be made clear whether the tenant is to be liable to pay the excess where damage is caused by an insured risk. For a covenant limiting the tenant's repairing obligations by reference to uninsurable as well as insured risks see vol 22(3) (1997 Reissue) LANDLORD AND TENANT (BUSINESS TENANCIES) Form 90 [6465]. It should be noted that it is now recommended 'best practice' that if the premises are so damaged by an uninsured risk as to prevent occupation, the tenant should be allowed to terminate the lease unless the landlord agrees to reinstate at his own cost: see vol 22(1) (2003 Reissue) LANDLORD AND TENANT (BUSINESS TENANCIES) Paragraph 85 [402]. If adopted, this recommendation involves damage preventing occupation caused by uninsured or uninsurable risks being excluded from the ambit of the tenant's repairing covenant.

65   The expression 'by implication' is intended to include a caller on the premises, such as a tradesman, where there has been no express invitation but the person cannot be classed as a trespasser.

66   The tenant should add the words in square brackets.

                                                                                [394]

3.4.2   *Replacement of landlord's fixtures*

The Tenant must replace from time to time any landlord's fixtures and fittings in the Premises that are beyond repair at any time during or at the end of the Term.

3.4.3   *Cleaning and tidying*

The Tenant must keep the Premises clean and tidy and clear of all rubbish and, without prejudice to the generality of the above, must clean both sides of all windows in the Premises [at least *(state frequency, eg once every month) (or as required)* as is reasonably necessary].

[3.4.4   *The Open Land*

3.4.4.1   Care of the Open Land

The Tenant must keep that part of the Premises that is not built on ('the Open Land') adequately surfaced, in good condition and free from weeds [and must keep all landscaped areas properly cultivated].

3.4.4.2   Storage on the Open Land

The Tenant must not store anything on the Open Land [or bring anything onto it] [that is or might become untidy, unclean, unsightly or in any way detrimental to the Premises or any adjoining property of the Landlord or the area generally].

                                                                                [395]

3.4.4.3   Rubbish on the Open Land

The Tenant must not deposit any waste, rubbish or refuse on the Open Land [or place any receptacle for them on it].

3.4.4.4   Vehicles on the Open Land

The Tenant must not keep or store any [*(if the land cannot be used for parking)* vehicle,] caravan or movable dwelling on the Open Land.] *(adapt clause 3.4.4 as required in the circumstances, or omit if no open land is included)*

3.4.5   *Care of adjoining property and abutting land*

The Tenant must not cause any adjoining property of the Landlord or any other land, roads or pavements abutting the Premises to be untidy or dirty and in particular, but without prejudice to the generality of the foregoing, must not deposit refuse or other materials on them.

3.4.6   *Decoration*

[The Tenant must redecorate the outside and inside of the Premises, as often as is necessary in the [reasonable] opinion of the Surveyor in order to maintain a high standard of decorative finish and attractiveness and to preserve the Premises and in the last year of the Term, *(or as required)* The Tenant must redecorate the outside of the Premises in each of the External Decorating Years and the last year of the Term and must redecorate the inside of the Premises in each of the Interior Decorating Years and the last year of the Term, in all instances][67] in a good and workmanlike manner and with appropriate materials of good quality[, to the [reasonable] satisfaction of the Surveyor], any change in the tints, colours and patterns of the decoration to be approved by the Landlord[68][, whose approval may not be unreasonably withheld [or delayed]]] [, provided that the covenants relating to the last year of the Term are not to apply where the Tenant has performed the obligation in question less than *(state period, eg 18 months)* before the end of the Term].

[67]   The draftsman should discuss with the landlord and his property advisers whether he wishes to have the flexibility of the first option or the certainty of the second.
[68]   The tenant may amend to provide for the landlord's approval to tints etc to apply only in the last year of the term.

3.4.7   *Shared facilities*

Where the use of any of the Conduits or any boundary structures or other things is common to the Premises and any adjoining or neighbouring premises, other than any adjoining property of the Landlord, the Tenant must be responsible for, and indemnify the Landlord against, all sums due from the owner, tenant or occupier of the Premises in relation to those Conduits, boundary structures or other things, and must undertake all work in relation to them that is his responsibility[69].

[69]   This covenant applies to items common to the demised premises and property other than that retained by the landlord. Its effect is to impose on the tenant all liability attaching to the owner or occupier of the demised premises in relation to such items.

3.5   Waste and alterations

3.5.1   *Waste, additions and alterations*[70]

The Tenant must not commit any waste, make any addition to the Premises, unite the Premises with any adjoining premises, or make any alteration to the Premises save as permitted by the provisions of this clause 3.5.

70   As to control of alterations see vol 22(1) (2003 Reissue) LANDLORD AND TENANT (BUSINESS TENANCIES) Paragraph 186 [911] et seq.

3.5.2   *Pre-conditions for alterations*

The Tenant must not make any [internal non-structural] alterations to the Premises unless he first —

3.5.2.1   obtains and complies with the necessary consents of the competent authorities and pays their charges for them,

3.5.2.2   makes an application to the Landlord for consent, supported by drawings and where appropriate a specification in duplicate [prepared by an architect[, or a member of some other appropriate profession,] who must supervise the work throughout to completion],

3.5.2.3   pays the fees of the Landlord, any head landlord, any mortgagee and their respective professional advisers,

3.5.2.4   enters into any covenants the Landlord requires as to the execution and reinstatement of the alterations, and

3.5.2.5   obtains the consent of the Landlord, whose consent may not be unreasonably withheld [or delayed].

[In the case of any works of a substantial nature, the Landlord may require the Tenant to provide, before starting the works, adequate security in the form of a deposit of money or the provision of a bond, as assurance to the Landlord that any works he permits from time to time will be fully completed].

[397]

3.5.3   *Removal of alterations*[71]

At the end of the Term, if so requested by the Landlord, the Tenant must remove any additional buildings, additions, alterations or improvements made to the Premises and must make good any part or parts of the Premises that may be damaged by their removal.

71   This clause has probably come to be inserted because landlords hope that it will defeat the effect of the compensation provisions of the Landlord and Tenant Act 1927 Pt I (ss 1–17) (23 Halsbury's Statutes (4th Edn) LANDLORD AND TENANT) — as to which see vol 22(1) (2003 Reissue) LANDLORD AND TENANT (BUSINESS TENANCIES) Paragraph 192 [923] et seq — ie because, if the improvement has been removed, it will not be an improvement to the holding at the time of quitting the premises. In fact, the clause might not achieve this effect, because the Landlord and Tenant Act 1927 s 9 as amended by the Landlord and Tenant Act 1954 s 49 prohibits contracting out. Also, the clause may be void under the Landlord and Tenant Act 1927 s 19(2) so far as it applies to improvements on the grounds that it purports to fetter the court in deciding what is reasonable. The tenant should not, however, rely on the application of these statutory provisions and should seek to strike out the clause.

3.5.4   *Connection to the Conduits*

The Tenant must not make any connection with the Conduits except in accordance with plans and specifications approved by the Landlord[, whose approval may not be unreasonably withheld [or delayed]], and subject to consent to make the connection having previously been obtained from the competent authority, undertaker or supplier.

3.6   Aerials, signs and advertisements

3.6.1   *Masts and wires*

The Tenant must not erect any pole or mast [or install any cable or wire] on the Premises, whether in connection with telecommunications or otherwise.

3.6.2   *Advertisements*[72]

The Tenant must not, without the consent of the Landlord, fix to or exhibit on the outside of the Premises, or fix to or exhibit through any window of the Premises, or display anywhere on the Premises, any placard, sign, notice, fascia board or advertisement.

72   See the Town and Country Planning (Control of Advertisements) Regulations 1992, SI 1992/666 as amended. In the absence of a covenant such as this and subject to those Regulations, the tenant may exhibit advertisements etc on the premises whether or not they are connected with his business: see *Clapman v Edwards* [1938] 2 All ER 507.

[398]

3.7   Statutory obligations

3.7.1   *General provision*[73]

The Tenant must comply in all respects with the requirements of any statutes, and any other obligations so applicable imposed by law or by any byelaws, applicable to the Premises or the trade or business for the time being carried on there.

73   As to the covenant to comply with statutes see vol 22(1) (2003 Reissue) LANDLORD AND TENANT (BUSINESS TENANCIES) Paragraph 182 [905]. For a provision requiring the landlord to pay compensation for works above a certain value see vol 22(3) (1997 Reissue) LANDLORD AND TENANT (BUSINESS TENANCIES) Form 169 [6693].

3.7.2   *Particular obligations*

3.7.2.1   Works required by statute, department or authority

Without prejudice to the generality of clause 3.7.1, the Tenant must execute all works and provide and maintain all arrangements on or in respect of the Premises or the use to which they are being put that are required in order to comply with the requirements of any statute already or in the future to be passed, or the requirements of any government department, local authority or other public or competent authority or court of competent jurisdiction, regardless of whether the requirements are imposed on the owner, the occupier, or any other person.

3.7.2.2   Acts causing losses

Without prejudice to the generality of clause 3.7.1, the Tenant must not do anything in or near the Premises by reason of which the Landlord may incur any losses under any statute.

3.7.2.3   Construction (Design and Management) Regulations

Without prejudice to the generality of clause 3.7.1, the Tenant must comply with the provisions of the Construction (Design and Management) Regulations 1994 ('the CDM Regulations'), be the only client, as defined in the provisions of the CDM Regulations, fulfil, in relation to all and any works, all the obligations of the client as set out in or reasonably to be inferred from the CDM Regulations, and make a declaration to that effect[74] to the Health and Safety Executive in accordance with the Approved Code of Practice published from time to time by the Health and Safety Executive in relation to the CDM Regulations. The provisions of clause 5.7.3 FIRE-FIGHTING EQUIPMENT are to have effect in any circumstances to which these obligations apply.

3.7.2.4   Delivery of health and safety files

At the end of the Term, the Tenant must forthwith deliver to the Landlord any and all health and safety files relating to the premises in accordance with the CDM Regulations.

74   If works are being carried out for the tenant, the landlord will not want to accept the liabilities that are placed on a client under the Construction (Design and Management) Regulations 1994, SI 1994/3140 and the Health and Safety Executive Approved Code of Practice. The landlord will need to ensure that the tenant actually makes the declaration required, and that he obtains the notification served on the tenant by the Health and Safety Executive.

[399]

3.8   Entry to inspect and notice to repair

3.8.1   *Entry and notice*

The Tenant must permit the Landlord[75] [on reasonable notice during normal business hours except in emergency][76] —

3.8.1.1   to enter the Premises to ascertain whether or not the covenants and conditions of this Lease have been observed and performed,

3.8.1.2   to view the state of repair and condition of the Premises, and to open up floors and other parts of the Premises where that is necessary in order to do so, and

3.8.1.3   to give to the Tenant, or notwithstanding clause 8.7 NOTICES leave on the Premises, a notice ('a notice to repair') specifying the works required to remedy any breach of the Tenant's obligations as to the repair and condition of the Premises in this Lease,

provided that any opening-up must be made good by and at the cost of the Landlord if it reveals no breach of the terms of this Lease.

75   The provisions of clause 1.34 [377] REFERENCES TO RIGHTS OF ACCESS should be noted.
76   The tenant should add the words in square brackets.

3.8.2   *Works to be carried out*

The Tenant must carry out the works specified in a notice to repair immediately, including making good any opening up that revealed a breach of the terms of this Lease.

[400]

[3.8.3   *Landlord's power in default*[77]

If within *(state period, eg 1 month)* of the service of a notice to repair the Tenant has not started to execute the work referred to in that notice, or is not proceeding diligently with it, or if the Tenant fails to finish the work within *(state period, eg 2 months)*[78][, or if in the [Landlord's *(or as required)* Surveyor's] [reasonable] opinion the Tenant is unlikely to finish the work within that period], the Tenant must permit the Landlord to enter the Premises to execute the outstanding work, and must within *(state period, eg 14 days)* of a written demand pay to the Landlord the cost of so doing and all expenses incurred by the Landlord, including legal costs and surveyor's fees.]

77   The advantages for the landlord of this clause must be weighed against the potential liability that it creates under the Defective Premises Act 1972 s 4(4) (31 Halsbury's Statutes (4th Edn) NEGLIGENCE): see *McAuley v Bristol City Council* [1992] QB 134, [1992] 1 All ER 749, CA.
      It has been held that a claim by the landlord for recovery of costs under such a clause is a claim for recovery of a debt, and can therefore be enforced without requiring leave of the court under the Leasehold Property (Repairs) Act 1938 (23 Halsbury's Statutes (4th Edn) LANDLORD AND TENANT): see *Jervis v Harris* [1996] Ch 195, [1996] 1 All ER 303, CA.
      However, even where a landlord has been granted a right of this nature the court does not compel the tenant to allow the landlord the right to enter and carry out repairs where these would be of no benefit and where no loss is being caused to the landlord: see *Hammersmith London Borough Council v Creska (No 2)* [2000] L & TR 288.
78   The tenant would prefer to be given 'a reasonable period' to do the work required to remedy the breaches because it may take longer than the specified number of months.

                                                                                                    [401]

3.9   Alienation[79]

3.9.1   *Alienation prohibited*

The Tenant must not hold the Premises on trust for another. The Tenant must not part with possession of the Premises or any part of the Premises or permit another to occupy them or any part of them except pursuant to a transaction permitted by and effected in accordance with the provisions of this Lease.

79   As to alienation see vol 22(1) (2003 Reissue) LANDLORD AND TENANT (BUSINESS TENANCIES) Paragraph 156 [801] et seq. Where the lease is registrable, this prohibition or restriction on dealings will be reflected in an entry on the register excepting from the effects of registration all estates, rights, interests, powers and remedies arising on or by reason of any dealing made in breach of the prohibition or restriction: see the Land Registration Rules 2003, SI 2003/1417 r 6(2).

3.9.2   *Assignment, subletting and charging of part*[80]

(version 1)

[The Tenant must not assign, sublet or charge part only of the Premises.] *(where assignment, subletting or charging of the whole is allowed)*

(version 2)

[The Tenant must not assign or charge part only of the Premises and must not sublet the whole or any part of the Premises.] *(where assignment or charging of the whole is permitted, but subletting is not allowed at all)*

80   Whether subletting should be permitted is a commercial matter. Some landlords consider that the fact that they cannot unreasonably refuse consent to an assignment gives the tenant all the protection he requires and are not prepared to permit subletting. An advantage to the tenant of the ability to sublet is that he has an element of control over a subtenant but not over an assignee, for whom he may retain liability under an authorised guarantee agreement. Further, with stringent assignment tests or in a bad market, subletting may be the only option open to the tenant.

3.9.3   *Assignment of the whole*

Subject to clauses 3.9.4 CIRCUMSTANCES and 3.9.5 CONDITIONS, the Tenant must not assign the whole of the Premises without the consent of the Landlord, whose consent may not be unreasonably withheld [or delayed][81].

81   This residual discretion is the old test of reasonableness under the Landlord and Tenant Act 1927 s 19(1). Thus the tenant and the proposed assignee may satisfy the circumstances and conditions specified for the purposes of the Landlord and Tenant Act 1927 s 19(1A) as inserted by the Landlord and Tenant (Covenants) Act 1995 s 22 (as to which see clause 3.9.4 [403] CIRCUMSTANCES and clause 3.9.5 [405] CONDITIONS), but the landlord may still refuse consent on reasonable grounds: see vol 22(1) (2003 Reissue) LANDLORD AND TENANT (BUSINESS TENANCIES) Paragraph 159 [812] et seq.

[402]

3.9.4   *Circumstances*

If any of the following circumstances[82] — which are specified for the purposes of the Landlord and Tenant Act 1927 Section 19(1A)[83] — applies either at the date when application for consent to assign is made to the Landlord, or after that date but before the Landlord's consent is given, the Landlord may withhold his consent and if, after the Landlord's consent has been given but before the assignment has taken place, any such circumstances apply, the Landlord may revoke his consent[84], whether his consent is expressly subject to a condition as referred to in clause 3.9.5.4 CONDITIONS or not. The circumstances are —

3.9.4.1   that any sum due from the Tenant under this Lease remains unpaid[85],

3.9.4.2   that in the Landlord's reasonable[86] opinion the assignee is not a person who is likely to be able to comply with the tenant covenants of this Lease and to continue to be able to comply with them following the assignment,

[3.9.4.3   that without prejudice to clause 3.9.4.2, in the case of an assignment to a company in the same group as the Tenant[87] within the meaning of the 1954 Act Section 42 in the Landlord's reasonable opinion the assignee is a person who is, or may become, less likely to be able to comply with the tenant covenants of this Lease than the Tenant requesting consent to assign, which likelihood is adjudged by reference in particular to the financial strength of that Tenant aggregated with that of any guarantor of the obligations of that Tenant and the value of any other security for the performance of the tenant covenants of this Lease when assessed at the date of grant or — where that Tenant is not *(name of original tenant)* — the date of the assignment of this Lease to that Tenant[88],] or

3.9.4.4   that the assignee or any guarantor for the assignee, other than any guarantor under an authorised guarantee agreement, is a corporation registered — or otherwise resident — in a jurisdiction in which the order of a court obtained in England and Wales will not necessarily be enforced against the assignee or guarantor without any consideration of the merits of the case.

(for examples of circumstances for use in unusual cases, see vol 22(3) (1997 Reissue) LANDLORD AND TENANT (BUSINESS TENANCIES) Form 117 [6501])

[403]

82   The Landlord and Tenant Act 1927 s 19(1A) as inserted by the Landlord and Tenant (Covenants) Act 1995 s 22 enables the landlord and tenant to a post-1995 lease to agree in advance the terms upon which an assignment may be permitted. It distinguishes between on the one hand circumstances, the existence of which entitles the landlord to refuse consent to assignment, and on the other hand conditions that may be imposed on the grant of his consent. This clause and clause 3.9.5 [405] CONDITIONS are drafted on the assumption that this is a valid approach and seek to draw a clear distinction between circumstances and conditions.

It should be noted that provisions that are overly restrictive may have an adverse impact at any rent review. It should also be noted that it is recommended 'best practice' that unless the particular circumstances of the letting justify greater control, the only restriction on assignment of the whole should be obtaining the landlord's consent, which is not to be unreasonably withheld: see vol 22(1) (2003 Reissue) LANDLORD AND TENANT (BUSINESS TENANCIES) Paragraph 85 [401] and 'A code of practice for commercial leases in England and Wales (2nd edition)' which can be found in vol 22(1) (2003 Reissue) LANDLORD AND TENANT (BUSINESS TENANCIES) as Form 1 [4501].

Each letting must be looked at in the light of its own particular facts and circumstances but it is considered that the provisions of this clause do, in the ordinary course, strike a reasonable balance between the landlord's desire for control and the tenant's ability to dispose of his interest without undue restriction. For a less restrictive approach see vol 22(1) (2003 Reissue) LANDLORD AND TENANT (BUSINESS TENANCIES) Form 7 clause 5.2 [5538].

83   The Landlord and Tenant Act 1927 s 19(1A) as inserted by the Landlord and Tenant (Covenants) Act 1995 s 22 seems to require the alienation clause to state that the circumstances it mentions are specified for the purposes of that subsection.

84   The landlord may require that certain circumstances are absent not only before consent has been given to the assignment, but also up to the date on which the assignment takes place — when the die is cast and the lease covenants bind the assignee. For example, the landlord may require the rent to be paid up to date not only before the application for consent is made, but also at the date when consent is given and the possibly later date when the lease is actually assigned.

85   The tenant may want to limit this to the rent, as it may be thought that a dispute is more likely to arise over the insurance rent or other payments. If the tenant has retained any right of set-off, it should also be referred to here.

86   Circumstances and conditions must either be factual or, if they contain an element of discretion, require that discretion to be exercised reasonably (see the Landlord and Tenant Act 1927 s 19(1C)(a) as inserted by the Landlord and Tenant (Covenants) Act 1995 s 22), or must give the tenant a right of appeal to an expert (see the Landlord and Tenant Act 1927 s 19(1C)(b) as inserted by the Landlord and Tenant (Covenants) Act 1995 s 22). If the discretion is to be exercised reasonably, as suggested by this provision, the tenant can take any dispute about its exercise to the court. The court will consider whether *this* landlord has acted within the range of reasonable decisions, not whether a reasonable landlord would have reached the same decision or whether the test is itself reasonable. For a clause where an expert is used see vol 22(3) (1997 Reissue) LANDLORD AND TENANT (BUSINESS TENANCIES) Form 117 [6501].

87   There have been suggestions that intra-group assignments should be banned completely. However, this is considered to be too draconian and would prevent legitimate corporate restructuring needed for reasons other than avoidance of liability under the Landlord and Tenant (Covenants) Act 1995. The landlord's concern is that a strong tenant may assign to a weak group company; the assignment is acceptable because the assignor gives an authorised guarantee agreement for the assignee. The second group company may then itself assign outside the group; the landlord will lose the authorised guarantee agreement of the strong first group company and have only the possibly worthless authorised guarantee agreement of the second group company. The possibilities for exploitation of this scenario are obvious and it is therefore felt that this is the one situation in which measuring the financial strength of the assignee in relation to that of the assignor is justified. Equivalence tests are not generally thought to be appropriate, because a strong first covenant may make the lease almost unassignable, adversely affecting the rent at review.

88   Consider whether the time at which the tenant's financial status is measured should be when he acquired the lease, when his status was acceptable to the landlord, or at the date of the application for consent to assign, when it may have deteriorated sharply. On the other hand, the outgoing tenant may be a better covenant now than when he acquired the lease: the wily landlord may wish to leave himself free to pick whichever of the two dates gives the better picture.

[404]

3.9.5   *Conditions*

The Landlord may impose any or all of the following conditions[89] — which are specified for the purposes of the Landlord and Tenant Act 1927 Section 19(1A)[90] — on giving any consent for an assignment by the Tenant, and any such consent is to be treated as being subject to each of the following conditions —

3.9.5.1   a condition that on or before any assignment and before giving occupation to the assignee, the Tenant requesting consent to assign, together with any former tenant who by virtue of the 1995 Act Section 11 was not released on an earlier assignment of this Lease[91], must enter into an authorised guarantee agreement[92] in favour of the Landlord in the terms set out in schedule 6 THE AUTHORISED GUARANTEE AGREEMENT,

3.9.5.2   a condition that if reasonably so required by the Landlord on an assignment
            to a limited company, the assignee must ensure that at least *(state number, eg 2)*
            directors of the company, or some other guarantor or guarantors [reasonably]
            acceptable to the Landlord, enter into direct covenants with the Landlord in
            the form of the Guarantor's covenants contained in clause 6 GUARANTEE
            PROVISIONS with 'the Assignee' substituted for 'the Tenant',

3.9.5.3   a condition that on or before any assignment, the Tenant making the request
            for consent to assign must give to the Landlord a copy of the health and safety
            file required to be maintained under the Construction (Design and
            Management) Regulations 1994 containing full details of all works
            undertaken to the Premises by that Tenant, and

3.9.5.4   a condition that if, at any time before the assignment, the circumstances
            specified in clause 3.9.4 CIRCUMSTANCES, or any of them, apply, the Landlord
            may revoke the consent by written notice to the Tenant.

                                                                        [405]

89   The Landlord and Tenant Act 1927 s 19(1A) as inserted by the Landlord and Tenant (Covenants) Act
      1995 s 22 enables the landlord and tenant to a post-1995 lease to agree in advance the terms upon which
      an assignment may be permitted. It distinguishes between on the one hand circumstances, the existence
      of which entitles the landlord to refuse consent to assignment, and on the other hand conditions that
      may be imposed on the grant of his consent. This clause and clause 3.9.4 [403] CIRCUMSTANCES are
      drafted on the assumption that this a valid approach and seek to draw a clear distinction between
      circumstances and conditions.
          It should be noted that provisions that are overly restrictive may have an adverse impact at any rent
      review. It should also be noted that it is recommended 'best practice' that unless the particular
      circumstances of the letting justify greater control, the only restriction on assignment of the whole
      should be obtaining the landlord's consent, which is not to be unreasonably withheld: see vol 22(1)
      (2003 Reissue) LANDLORD AND TENANT (BUSINESS TENANCIES) Paragraph 85 [401] and 'A code
      of practice for commercial leases in England and Wales (2nd edition)' which can be found in vol 22(1)
      (2003 Reissue) LANDLORD AND TENANT (BUSINESS TENANCIES) as Form 1 [4501].
          Each letting must be looked at in the light of its own particular facts and circumstances but it is
      considered that the provisions of this clause do, in the ordinary course, strike a reasonable balance
      between the landlord's desire for control and the tenant's ability to dispose of his interest without undue
      restriction.
90   The Landlord and Tenant Act 1927 s 19(1A) as inserted by the Landlord and Tenant (Covenants) Act
      1995 s 22 seems to require the alienation clause to state that the conditions it mentions are specified for
      the purposes of that subsection.
91   See the Landlord and Tenant (Covenants) Act 1995 ss 11(2), 16(6).
92   As to authorised guarantee agreements see vol 22(1) (2003 Reissue) LANDLORD AND TENANT
      (BUSINESS TENANCIES) Paragraph 54 [247]. It should be noted that 'A code of practice for
      commercial leases in England and Wales (2nd edition)' urges landlords to consider requiring authorised
      guarantee agreements only where the assignee is of lower financial standing than the assignor at the date
      of the assignment.

                                                                        [406]

3.9.6   *Charging of the whole*

The Tenant must not charge the whole of the Premises without the consent of the
Landlord, whose consent may not be unreasonably withheld [or delayed][93].

93   As to unreasonable withholding of consent under the Landlord and Tenant Act 1927 see vol 22(1)
      (2003 Reissue) LANDLORD AND TENANT (BUSINESS TENANCIES) Paragraph 158.2 [806] and as to
      unreasonable delay under the Landlord and Tenant Act 1988 (23 Halsbury's Statutes (4th Edn)
      LANDLORD AND TENANT) see vol 22(1) (2003 Reissue) LANDLORD AND TENANT (BUSINESS
      TENANCIES) Paragraph 158.3 [808].

[3.9.7   *Subletting*

The Tenant must not sublet[94] the whole of the Premises without the consent of the Landlord, whose consent may not be unreasonably withheld [or delayed]][95]. *(omit if subletting is prohibited)*

94   See note 80 to clause 3.9.2 [402] ASSIGNMENT, SUBLETTING AND CHARGING OF PART.
95   As to unreasonable withholding of consent under the Landlord and Tenant Act 1927 see vol 22(1) (2003 Reissue) LANDLORD AND TENANT (BUSINESS TENANCIES) Paragraph 158.2 [806] and as to unreasonable delay under the Landlord and Tenant Act 1988 see vol 22(1) (2003 Reissue) LANDLORD AND TENANT (BUSINESS TENANCIES) Paragraph 158.3 [808].

[407]

[3.9.8   *Terms of a permitted sublease*[96]

Every permitted sublease must be granted, without a fine or premium, at a rent not less than whichever is the greater of the then open market rent payable in respect of the Premises [— to be approved by the Landlord before the sublease is granted [and to be determined by the Surveyor, acting as an expert and not as an arbitrator] —] and the Rent[97], to be payable in advance on the days on which the Rent is payable under this Lease. Every permitted sublease must contain provisions approved by the Landlord —

3.9.8.1   for the upwards only review of the rent reserved by it, on the basis set out in schedule 3 THE RENT AND RENT REVIEW and on the Review Dates[98],

3.9.8.2   prohibiting the subtenant from doing or allowing anything in relation to the Premises inconsistent with or in breach of the provisions of this Lease,

3.9.8.3   for re-entry by the sublandlord on breach of any covenant by the subtenant,

3.9.8.4   imposing an absolute prohibition against all dealings with the Premises other than assignment[, subletting] [or charging] of the whole,

3.9.8.5   prohibiting assignment[, subletting][99] [or charging] of the whole of the Premises without the consent of the Landlord under this Lease,

3.9.8.6   requiring the assignee on any assignment of the sublease to enter into direct covenants with the Landlord to the same effect as those contained in clause 3.9.9 SUBTENANT'S DIRECT COVENANTS,

3.9.8.7   requiring on each assignment of the sublease that the assignor enters into an authorised guarantee agreement[100] in favour of the Landlord in the terms set out in schedule 6 THE AUTHORISED GUARANTEE AGREEMENT but adapted to suit the circumstances in which the guarantee is given,

3.9.8.8   prohibiting the subtenant from holding on trust for another or permitting another to share or occupy the whole or any part of the Premises,

3.9.8.9   imposing in relation to any permitted assignment[, subletting] [or charge] the same obligations for registration with the Landlord as are contained in this Lease in relation to dispositions by the Tenant,

[3.9.8.10   imposing in relation to any permitted subletting the same obligations as contained in this clause 3.9.8 and in clause 3.9.9 SUBTENANT'S DIRECT COVENANTS[, clause 3.9.11 ENFORCEMENT OF THE SUBLEASE and clause 3.9.12 SUBLEASE RENT REVIEW],] and

3.9.8.11   excluding the provisions of Sections 24–28 of the 1954 Act from the letting created by the sublease.] *(omit if subletting is prohibited)*

[408]

96   As to the validity of provisions of this nature see vol 22(1) (2003 Reissue) LANDLORD AND TENANT (BUSINESS TENANCIES) Paragraph 161 [817].

97   It will not be in the landlord's interest for the premises to be sublet at a rent less than that payable under the headlease, because it could allow into the premises a subtenant of doubtful financial status, with whom the landlord may in the future have to deal direct, eg on the grant of a new lease under the Landlord and Tenant Act 1954 Pt II (ss 23–46). Also a low rent could be used as a 'comparable' in arriving at the open market rent on rent reviews or lease renewals. On the other hand following the decision in *Allied Dunbar Assurance plc v Homebase Ltd* [2002] EWCA Civ 666, [2003] 1 P & CR 75, [2002] 2 EGLR 23 a provision of this kind may effectively render the lease inalienable and being a potentially onerous restriction on disposition (as to which see vol 22(1) (2003 Reissue) LANDLORD AND TENANT (BUSINESS TENANCIES) Paragraph 348.2 [1440]) have an adverse impact at rent review from a landlord's perspective.

98   Alternatively the landlord might prefer the sublease rents to be reviewed just before the review dates in the headlease. As to recommended 'best practice' in relation to the basis of rent review in leases of business premises see vol 22(1) (2003 Reissue) LANDLORD AND TENANT (BUSINESS TENANCIES) Paragraph 85 [401] and 'A code of practice for commercial leases in England and Wales (2nd edition)' which can be found in vol 22(1) (2003 Reissue) LANDLORD AND TENANT (BUSINESS TENANCIES) as Form 1 [4501].

99   The landlord may well wish to prohibit any further subletting by requiring an absolute covenant against subletting to be inserted in any sublease.

100   By virtue of the Landlord and Tenant (Covenants) Act 1995 s 16(3)(a), where a head landlord's consent is needed to the assignment of a sublease, the head landlord can require the assignor of the sublease to enter into an authorised guarantee agreement. It should be noted that 'A code of practice for commercial leases in England and Wales (2nd edition)' urges landlords to consider requiring authorised guarantee agreements only where the assignee is of lower financial standing than the assignor at the date of the assignment.

[409]

[3.9.9   *Subtenant's direct covenants*[101]

Before any permitted subletting, the Tenant must ensure that the subtenant enters into a direct covenant with the Landlord that while the subtenant is bound by the tenant covenants of the sublease[102] and while the subtenant is bound by an authorised guarantee agreement the subtenant will observe and perform the tenant covenants contained in this Lease — except the covenant to pay the rent reserved by this Lease — and in that sublease.] *(omit if subletting is prohibited)*

101   See note 96 to clause 3.9.8 [409] TERMS OF A PERMITTED SUBLEASE.

102   The liability of the subtenant should be expressed to last while he is bound by the tenant covenants of the sublease, rather than while the sublease is vested in him, to take account of the possibility of an excluded assignment being made and the subtenant remaining liable. An excluded assignment means that the subtenant is precluded from tenant release under the Landlord and Tenant (Covenants) Act 1995.

[3.9.10   *Requirement for 1954 Act exclusion*[103]

The Tenant must not grant a sublease or permit a subtenant to occupy the Premises unless an effective agreement has been made to exclude the operation of Sections 24 to 28 of the 1954 Act pursuant to Section 38A of the 1954 Act.] *(omit if subletting is prohibited)*

103   As to contracting out of the security of tenure provisions of the Landlord and Tenant Act 1954 see vol 22(1) (2003 Reissue) LANDLORD AND TENANT (BUSINESS TENANCIES) Paragraph 431 [2035].

[3.9.11   *Enforcement, waiver and variation of subleases*

In relation to any permitted sublease, the Tenant must enforce the performance and observance by every subtenant of the provisions of the sublease, and must not at any time either expressly or by implication waive any breach of the covenants or conditions on the part of any subtenant or assignee of any sublease, or — without the consent of the Landlord, whose consent may not be unreasonably withheld or delayed — vary the terms or accept a surrender of any permitted sublease.] *(omit if subletting is prohibited)*

[410]

[3.9.12   *Sublease rent review*

In relation to any permitted sublease —

3.9.12.1   the Tenant must ensure that the rent is reviewed in accordance with the terms of the sublease,

3.9.12.2   the Tenant must not agree the reviewed rent with the subtenant without the approval of the Landlord,

3.9.12.3   where the sublease provides such an option, the Tenant must not, without the approval of the Landlord, agree whether the third party determining the revised rent in default of agreement should act as an arbitrator or as an expert,

3.9.12.4   the Tenant must not, without the approval of the Landlord, agree any appointment of a person to act as the third party determining the revised rent,

3.9.12.5   the Tenant must incorporate as part of his representations to that third party representations [reasonably] required[104] by the Landlord, and

3.9.12.6   the Tenant must give notice to the Landlord of the details of the determination of every rent review within *(state period, eg 28 days)*,

provided that the Landlord's approvals specified above may not be unreasonably withheld [or delayed].] *(omit if subletting is prohibited)*

---

104   This seems preferable to providing, as is sometimes done, that the head landlord's representations have to be brought to the attention of the expert or arbitrator because it would appear that he can refuse to have regard to them, the head landlord not being a party to the lease with which he is concerned.

[411]

3.9.13   *Registration of permitted dealings*

Within *(state period, eg 28 days)* of any assignment, charge, [sublease, or subunderlease,] or any transmission or other devolution relating to the Premises, the Tenant must produce a certified copy[105] of any relevant document for registration with the Landlord's solicitor, and must pay the Landlord's solicitor's [reasonable] charges for registration of at least £...

---

105   There seems to be no reason why the tenant should part with the original. However, under the Land Registration Rules 2003, SI 2003/1417 r 203, it is open to the applicant for registration to ask for the transfer, charge, sublease or subunderlease giving effect to the disposition to be returned for retention by the applicant, provided a certified copy of the instrument is lodged with the application. Accordingly, in such cases, applicants should use this facility if they wish to be able to lodge the lease with the landlord after its return by the registrar. If there is a time limit specified in the lease, then the registrar should be told about this, so that he is aware of the need to return the instrument within the required period.

[3.9.14   *Sharing with a group company*

Notwithstanding clause 3.9.1 ALIENATION PROHIBITED, the Tenant may share the occupation of the whole or any part of the Premises with a company that is a member of the same group as the Tenant within the meaning of the 1954 Act Section 42, for so long as both companies remain members of that group and otherwise than in a manner that transfers or creates a legal estate.] *(omit if sharing with a group company is not to be permitted)*

3.10   Nuisance and residential restrictions

3.10.1   *Nuisance*[106]

The Tenant must not do anything on the Premises, or allow anything to remain on them, that may be or become or cause a nuisance, or annoyance, disturbance, inconvenience, injury or damage to the Landlord or his tenants or the owners or occupiers of any adjoining property of the Landlord or any other adjacent or neighbouring premises.

106   'Nuisance' is a term to be construed according to 'plain and sober and simple notions among the English people': *Walter v Selfe* (1851) 4 De G & Sm 315 at 322 per Knight-Bruce V-C. 'I have no doubt that what is a nuisance or annoyance will continue to be determined by the courts according to robust and commonsense standards': *Hampstead and Suburban Properties Ltd v Diomedous* [1969] 1 Ch 248 at 258, [1968] 3 All ER 545 at 550 per Megarry J. But a tenant can only be said to have permitted a nuisance if the landlord can show that the tenant has failed to take reasonable steps to prevent the nuisance: see *Commercial General Administration Ltd v Thomsett* [1979] 1 EGLR 62, CA.

[412]

3.10.2   *Auctions, trades and immoral purposes*

The Tenant must not use the Premises for any auction sale, any dangerous, noxious, noisy or offensive[107] trade, business, manufacture or occupation, or for any illegal or immoral act or purpose.

107   As to the meaning of 'offensive' see *Re Koumoudouros and Marathon Realty Co Ltd* (1978) 89 DLR (3d) 551 where it was held that the word did not have a definite legal meaning and should be read in the context of the lease. Surrounding circumstances can affect whether a particular trade is offensive: see *Nussey v Provincial Bill Posting Co and Eddison* [1909] 1 Ch 734, CA; *Dunraven Securities Ltd v Holloway* [1982] 2 EGLR 47, CA.

3.10.3   *Residential use, sleeping and animals*

The Tenant must not use the Premises as sleeping accommodation or for residential purposes, or keep any animal, bird or reptile on them.

3.11   Costs of applications, notices and recovery of arrears[108]

The Tenant must pay to the Landlord on an indemnity basis all costs, fees, charges, disbursements and expenses — including without prejudice to the generality of the above those payable to counsel, solicitors, surveyors and bailiffs — [properly and reasonably] incurred by the Landlord in relation to or incidental to —

3.11.1   every application made by the Tenant for a consent or licence required by the provisions of this Lease, whether it is granted, refused or offered subject to any [lawful] qualification or condition, or the application is withdrawn[, unless the refusal, qualification or condition is unlawful, whether because it is unreasonable or otherwise],

3.11.2   the contemplation, preparation and service of a notice under the Law of Property Act 1925 Section 146, or by reason or the contemplation of proceedings under Sections 146 or 147 of that Act, even if forfeiture is avoided otherwise than by relief granted by the court[109],

3.11.3   the recovery or attempted recovery of arrears of rent or other sums due under this Lease, and

3.11.4   any steps taken in [contemplation of or in] [direct] connection with the preparation and service of a schedule of dilapidations during or after the end of the Term[110].

108   As to payment of VAT on legal costs by a person other than the solicitor's own client see the
      Information Binder: Property [1]: VAT and Property.
109   As to forfeiture see vol 22(1) (2003 Reissue) LANDLORD AND TENANT (BUSINESS TENANCIES)
      Paragraph 283 [1171] et seq.
110   The landlord should not be tempted to extend this provision to costs etc incurred by him in
      consequence of serving a notice under the Landlord and Tenant Act 1954 s 25 because that is void: see
      Stevenson and Rush (Holdings) Ltd v Langdon (1978) 38 P & CR 208, CA.

[413]

3.12   Planning and development

3.12.1   *Compliance with the Planning Acts*

The Tenant must observe and comply with the provisions and requirements of the
Planning Acts affecting the Premises and their use and must indemnify the Landlord, and
keep him indemnified, both during the Term and following the end of it, against all
losses in respect of any contravention of those Acts.

3.12.2   *Consent for application*

The Tenant must not make any application for planning permission without the consent
of the Landlord[, whose consent may not be unreasonably withheld [or delayed] [in any
case where application for and implementation of the planning permission will not create
or give rise to any tax liability for the Landlord or where the Tenant indemnifies the
Landlord against such liability][111]].

111   These words were devised when development land tax — abolished by the Finance Act 1985 s 93 —
      applied. The provision may, however, still be relevant should similar taxation be introduced in the
      future.

3.12.3   *Permissions and notices*

The Tenant must at his expense obtain any planning permissions and serve any notices
that may be required to carry out any development on or at the Premises.

3.12.4   *Charges and levies*

Subject only to any statutory direction to the contrary, the Tenant must pay and satisfy
any charge or levy that may subsequently be imposed under the Planning Acts in respect
of the carrying out or maintenance of any development on or at the Premises.

[414]

3.12.5   *Pre-conditions for development*

Notwithstanding any consent that may be granted by the Landlord under this Lease, the
Tenant must not carry out any development on or at the Premises until all necessary
notices under the Planning Acts have been served and copies produced to the Landlord,
all necessary permissions under the Planning Acts have been obtained and produced to
the Landlord, and the Landlord has acknowledged that every necessary planning
permission is acceptable to him[, such acknowledgement not to be unreasonably
withheld]. The Landlord may refuse to acknowledge his acceptance of a planning
permission on the grounds that any condition contained in it or anything omitted from
it or the period referred to in it would[, in the [reasonable] opinion of the Surveyor,]
be, or be likely to be, prejudicial to the Landlord or to his reversionary interest in the
Premises or any adjoining property of the Landlord whether during or following the end
of the Term.

3.12.6   *Completion of development*

Where a condition of any planning permission granted for development begun before the end of the Term[112] requires works to be carried out to the Premises by a date after the end of the Term, the Tenant must, unless the Landlord directs otherwise, finish those works before the end of the Term.

112   The provisions of clause 1.19 [372] INTERPRETATION OF 'THE LAST YEAR OF THE TERM' AND 'THE END OF THE TERM' should be noted.

3.12.7   *Security for compliance with conditions*

In any case where a planning permission is granted subject to conditions, and if the Landlord [reasonably] so requires, the Tenant must provide sufficient security for his compliance with the conditions and must not implement the planning permission until that security has been provided.

[3.12.8   *Appeal against refusal or conditions*[113]

If [reasonably] required by the Landlord to do so, but[, where reasonable,] at his own cost, the Tenant must appeal against any refusal of planning permission or the imposition of any conditions on a planning permission relating to the Premises following an application for planning permission by the Tenant.]

113   The tenant should not accept this clause because it could impose on him the cost of a planning appeal. He should strike it out, leaving planning appeals to be a matter for discussion as and when the situation arises during the term, or at least insist that he should bear the cost only where reasonable.

[415]

3.13   Plans, documents and information

3.13.1   *Evidence of compliance with this Lease*

If so requested, the Tenant must produce to the Landlord or the Surveyor any plans, documents and other evidence the Landlord [reasonably] requires in order to satisfy himself that the provisions of this Lease have been complied with.

3.13.2   *Information for renewal or rent review*

If so requested, the Tenant must produce to the Landlord, the Surveyor, or any person acting as the third party determining the Rent in default of agreement between the Landlord and the Tenant under any provisions for rent review contained in this Lease, any information [reasonably] requested in writing in relation to any pending or intended step under the 1954 Act or the implementation of any provisions for rent review.

3.14   Indemnities[114]

The Tenant must keep the Landlord fully indemnified against all losses arising directly or indirectly out of any act, omission or negligence of the Tenant or any persons at the Premises expressly or impliedly[115] with his authority [and under his control][116], or any breach or non-observance by the Tenant of the covenants, conditions or other provisions of this Lease or any of the matters to which this demise is subject.

114   The tenant should seek to delete all *general* indemnity provisions on the basis that his remedies for breach of covenant and in tort adequately protect the landlord. The tenant should argue that an indemnity unreasonably extends his liability. If, however, this clause is omitted, it should be replaced by a covenant to observe and perform restrictions etc to which the demise is subject, possibly coupled with a *specific* indemnity in respect of any breach.

115   The expression 'impliedly' is intended to include a caller on the premises, such as a tradesman, where there has been no express invitation but the person cannot be classed as a trespasser.

116   The tenant should add the words in square brackets.

[416]

3.15   Reletting boards and viewing

[Unless [a valid court application under the 1954 Act Section 24 has been made or][117] the Tenant is [otherwise] entitled to remain in occupation or to a new tenancy of the Premises, at any time during *(or as required)* At any time during] the *(state period, eg last 6 months)* of the [Contractual][118] Term and at any time thereafter, [and whenever the Lease Rents or any part of them are in arrear and unpaid for longer than *(state period, eg 14 days)*,] the Tenant must permit the Landlord to enter the Premises and fix and retain anywhere on them a board advertising them for reletting. While any such board is on the Premises the Tenant must permit viewing of the Premises at reasonable times of the day.

117   This phrase and the word 'otherwise' should be omitted if the operation of the security of tenure provisions in the Landlord and Tenant Act 1954 ss 24–28 is to be excluded in relation to the lease.

118   This defined term will require amendment where the operation of the security of tenure provisions in the Landlord and Tenant Act 1954 ss 24–28 is to be excluded in relation to the lease: see note 6 to clause 1.4 [359] 'THE [CONTRACTUAL] TERM'.

3.16   Obstruction and encroachment

3.16.1   *Obstruction of windows*

The Tenant must not stop up, darken or obstruct any windows or light belonging to the Premises.

3.16.2   *Encroachments*

The Tenant must take all [reasonable] steps to prevent the construction of any new window, light, opening, doorway, path, passage, pipe or the making of any encroachment or the acquisition of any easement in relation to the Premises and must notify the Landlord immediately if any such thing is constructed, encroachment is made or easement acquired, or any attempt is made to construct such a thing, to encroach or acquire an easement. At the request of the Landlord the Tenant must adopt such means as are [reasonably] required to prevent the construction of such a thing, the making of any encroachment or the acquisition of any easement[119].

119   For a shorter clause see vol 22(3) (1997 Reissue) LANDLORD AND TENANT (BUSINESS TENANCIES) Form 172 [6696].

[417]

3.17   Yielding up

At the end of the Term[120] the Tenant must yield up the Premises with vacant possession, decorated and repaired in accordance with and in the condition required by the provisions of this Lease, give up all keys of the Premises to the Landlord, remove tenant's fixtures and fittings [if requested to do so by the Landlord], and remove all signs erected by the Tenant or any of his predecessors in title in upon or near the Premises, immediately making good any damage caused by their removal.

120   The provisions of clause 1.19 [372] INTERPRETATION OF 'THE LAST YEAR OF THE TERM' AND 'THE END OF THE TERM' should be noted.

3.18 Interest on arrears[121]

The Tenant must pay interest on any of the Lease Rents[122] or other sums due under this Lease that are not paid [within *(state period, eg 14 days)* of the date due] whether formally demanded or not[, the interest to be recoverable as rent][123]. Nothing in this clause entitles the Tenant to withhold or delay any payment of the Lease Rents or any other sum due under this Lease or affects the rights of the Landlord in relation to any non-payment.

121 As to the covenant to pay interest see vol 22(1) (2003 Reissue) LANDLORD AND TENANT (BUSINESS TENANCIES) Paragraph 154 [767].
122 As to the definition of 'the Lease Rents' see clause 1.36 [377] 'THE RENT'.
123 These words seek to attach to interest the rights associated with rent. As to the reasons for this see vol 22(1) (2003 Reissue) LANDLORD AND TENANT (BUSINESS TENANCIES) Paragraph 151 [761]. However, this clause applies to interest on arrears of other sums payable under the lease that are not rent as well as to rent itself, and it might be felt inappropriate for interest to be deemed to be rent where the payment on which the interest is due is not itself rent.

[418]

3.19 Statutory notices

The Tenant must give full particulars to the Landlord of any notice, direction, order or proposal relating to the Premises made, given or issued to the Tenant by any government department or local, public, regulatory or other authority or court within *(state period, eg 7 days)* of receipt, and if so requested by the Landlord must produce it to the Landlord. The Tenant must without delay take all necessary steps to comply with the notice, direction or order. At the request of the Landlord, but at his own cost, the Tenant must make or join with the Landlord in making any objection or representation the Landlord deems expedient against or in respect of any notice, direction, order or proposal.

3.20 Keyholders

The Tenant must ensure that at all times [the Landlord has *(or as required)* the Landlord and the local police force have] written notice of the name, home address and home telephone number of at least *(state number, eg 2)* keyholders of the Premises.

3.21 Viewing on sale of reversion

The Tenant must[, on reasonable notice,] at any time during the Term, permit prospective purchasers of the Landlord's reversion or any other interest superior to the Term, or agents instructed in connection with the sale of the reversion or such an interest, to view the Premises without interruption provided they have the prior written authority of the Landlord or his agents.

3.22 Defective premises

The Tenant must give notice to the Landlord of any defect in the Premises that might give rise to an obligation on the Landlord to do or refrain from doing anything in order to comply with the provisions of this Lease or the duty of care imposed on the Landlord, whether pursuant to the Defective Premises Act 1972 or otherwise, and must at all times display and maintain any notices the Landlord from time to time [reasonably] requires him to display at the Premises.

3.23   Replacement guarantor[124]

3.23.1   *Guarantor replacement events*

In this clause 3.23 references to a 'guarantor replacement event' are references, in the case of an individual, to death, bankruptcy, having a receiving order made against him or having a receiver appointed under the Mental Health Act 1983 or entering into a voluntary arrangement and, in the case of a company, to passing a resolution to wind up, entering into liquidation, a voluntary arrangement or administration or having a receiver appointed.

124   As to guarantors see vol 22(1) (2003 Reissue) LANDLORD AND TENANT (BUSINESS TENANCIES) Paragraph 71 [278] et seq. The tenant should propose that, on the execution of a guarantee by a new guarantor, the original guarantor or his estate should be released.

[419]

3.23.2   *Action on occurrence of a guarantor replacement event*

Where during the relevant Liability Period a guarantor replacement event occurs to the Guarantor or any person who has entered into an authorised guarantee agreement, the Tenant must give notice of the event to the Landlord within *(state period, eg 14 days)* of his becoming aware of it. If so required by the Landlord, the Tenant must within *(state period, eg 28 days)* obtain some other person [reasonably] acceptable to the Landlord to execute a guarantee in the form of the Guarantor's covenants in clause 6 GUARANTEE PROVISIONS or the authorised guarantee agreement in schedule 6 THE AUTHORISED GUARANTEE AGREEMENT, as the case may be, for the residue of the relevant Liability Period.

3.24   Exercise of the Landlord's rights[125]

The Tenant must permit the Landlord to exercise any of the rights granted to him by virtue of the provisions of this Lease at all times during the Term without interruption or interference.

125   The provisions of clause 1.34 [377] REFERENCES TO RIGHTS OF ACCESS should be noted.

3.25   The Industrial Covenants

The Tenant must observe and perform the Industrial Covenants.

3.26   Costs of grant of this Lease[126]

[The Tenant must pay the fees and disbursements of the Landlord's solicitors, agents and surveyors and all other costs and expenses incurred by the Landlord in relation to the negotiation, preparation, execution and grant of this Lease. *(or as required)* On the grant of this Lease the Tenant must pay the sum of £... as a contribution to the Landlord's solicitors' charges for the negotiation, execution and completion of this Lease.]

126   As to covenants to pay the landlord's legal fees see vol 22(1) (2003 Reissue) LANDLORD AND TENANT (BUSINESS TENANCIES) Paragraph 155 [769]. As to payment of VAT on legal costs by a person other than the solicitor's own client see the Information Binder: Property [1]: VAT and Property.

[420]

3.27   Consent to the Landlord's release[127]

The Tenant must not unreasonably withhold consent to a request made by the Landlord under the 1995 Act Section 8 for a release from all or any of the landlord covenants of this Lease.

127   By virtue of the Landlord and Tenant (Covenants) Act 1995 each successive landlord remains bound by the landlord covenants of the lease unless released under the machinery provided in the Act — as to which see vol 22(1) (2003 Reissue) LANDLORD AND TENANT (BUSINESS TENANCIES) Paragraph 57 [252] et seq — or by a specific release given otherwise (see the Landlord and Tenant (Covenants) Act 1995 s 26(1)(a)). Bald statements limiting the landlord's liability, such as those in use before the commencement of the Act, will not withstand the wide anti-avoidance provisions of the Landlord and Tenant (Covenants) Act 1995 s 25, and covenants by the tenant to give consent to release are unlikely to fall within the exception of s 26. None of the ingenious schemes for limiting the landlord's liability, eg making all covenants personal, suggested in the early days of the 1995 Act has stood up to critical scrutiny, although none has yet been tested by the courts. Thus landlords look instead to the alternative of a right of redress if the tenant makes an unreasonable objection to release. This covenant is modelled on the provisions of the Landlord and Tenant Act 1988, which gives tenants a right of action for loss caused by landlords who unreasonably withhold or delay consent to assignment (see the Landlord and Tenant Act 1988 s 4). In view of the strict time limits under the Landlord and Tenant (Covenants) Act 1995 and the fact that failure to respond to the landlord's request for release is deemed to be consent, it is not thought necessary to extend this covenant to unreasonable delay in replying to such a request.

[421]–[430]

4   THE LANDLORD'S COVENANTS

The Landlord covenants with the Tenant to observe and perform the requirements of this clause 4.

4.1   Quiet enjoyment[128]

The Landlord must permit the Tenant peaceably and quietly to hold and enjoy the Premises without any interruption or disturbance from or by the Landlord or any person claiming under or in trust for him[129] [or by title paramount][130].

128   As to the landlord's covenant for quiet enjoyment see vol 22(1) (2003 Reissue) LANDLORD AND TENANT (BUSINESS TENANCIES) Paragraph 168 [856]. As to covenants for quiet enjoyment generally see 23 Halsbury's Laws (4th Edn Reissue) LANDLORD AND TENANT.
        The words 'the Tenant paying the rents reserved by and observing and performing the covenants on its part and the conditions contained in this lease' are frequently included in a covenant for quiet enjoyment, but they have no practical effect and do not make payment of the rent and performance of the covenants into conditions precedent to the operation of the covenant for quiet enjoyment: see *Edge v Boileau* (1885) 16 QBD 117; *Dawson v Dyer* (1833) 5 B & Ad 584; *Yorkbrook Investments Ltd v Batten* (1985) 52 P & CR 51, [1985] 2 EGLR 100, CA.
129   The covenant is frequently expressed to apply to 'lawful' interruption or by persons 'rightfully' claiming under the landlord, but it seems that the addition of these words has no practical effect: see *Williams v Gabriel* [1906] 1 KB 155 at 157.
130   Without the reference to title paramount the landlord is liable only for the acts of persons so far as they are his successors in title or have authority from him to do the acts complained of: *Harrison Ainslie & Co v Muncaster* [1891] 2 QB 680, CA; *Matania v National Provincial Bank Ltd and Elevenist Syndicate Ltd* [1936] 2 All ER 633, CA; *Miller v Emcer Products Ltd* [1956] Ch 304, [1956] 1 All ER 237, CA. If a subtenant holds under a lease containing a qualified covenant on the part of his landlord — ie one where there is no reference to title paramount — and the head landlord evicts the subtenant because the head rent has not been paid, this will not be a breach of the covenant for quiet enjoyment (see *Spencer v Marriott* (1823) 1 B & C 457; *Dennett v Atherton* (1872) LR 7 QB 316, Ex Ch), but it is a breach if the sublandlord submits to judgment in an action by a person with no title to sue, and the subtenant is in consequence evicted (*Cohen v Tannar* [1900] 2 QB 609, CA). Actionable interruptions under this covenant are not confined to interference with title or possession, but may extend to interference with the ordinary and lawful enjoyment of the premises: *Sanderson v Berwick-upon-Tweed Corpn* (1884) 13 QBD 547 at 551, CA. As to persons claiming 'under' the landlord see *Celsteel Ltd v Alton House Holdings Ltd (No 2)* [1987] 2 All ER 240, [1987] 1 WLR 291, CA.

[4.2   Repairs

The Landlord must maintain the Road — unless it is adopted as a highway maintainable at the public expense — and the Adjoining Conduits, and keep it and them in good and substantial repair and condition.]

[431]

5   INSURANCE[131]

5.1   Warranty as to convictions[132]

The Tenant warrants that before the execution of this document he has disclosed to the Landlord in writing any conviction, judgment or finding of any court or tribunal relating to the Tenant[, or any director, other officer or major shareholder of the Tenant,] of such a nature as to be likely to affect the decision of any insurer or underwriter to grant or to continue insurance of any of the Insured Risks.

131   As to insurance see vol 22(1) (2003 Reissue) LANDLORD AND TENANT (BUSINESS TENANCIES) Paragraph 227 [1021] et seq.

132   A contract of insurance is one uberrimae fidei. The insured must disclose to the insurers all material facts that are within his actual or presumed knowledge, whether there is a formal proposal form or not. A fact is material if non-disclosure of it would influence a prudent and reasonable insurer. This warranty is designed to rebut any suggestion by the landlord's insurers that the landlord had knowledge of the matters concerned. By inserting this clause in the lease, and thus specifically bringing the point to the tenant's attention, the landlord can argue that he has done all that is practical to establish the existence of any such matters. The absence of any written disclosure pursuant to this clause is strong evidence that the landlord has no actual or presumed knowledge of such matters. Further, the landlord has a right of action against the tenant for any breach of the warranty. As to non-disclosure and misrepresentation in contracts of non-marine insurance see 22 Halsbury's Laws (4th Edn Reissue) INSURANCE.

5.2   Covenant to insure

The Landlord covenants with the Tenant to insure the Premises [in the joint names of the Landlord and the Tenant[133] [and any other person the Landlord [reasonably] requires][134]] unless the insurance is vitiated by any act of the Tenant or by anyone at the Premises expressly or by implication[135] with the his authority [and under his control][136].

133   As to insurance in joint names see vol 22(1) (2003 Reissue) LANDLORD AND TENANT (BUSINESS TENANCIES) Paragraph 229 [1024].

134   Unless some expression such as this is included, a covenant to insure in specified names is broken by insurance in those names and other names: see *Penniall v Harborne* (1848) 11 QB 368.

135   The expression 'by implication' is intended to include a caller on the premises, such as a tradesman, where there has been no express invitation but the person cannot be classed as a trespasser.

136   The tenant should add the words in square brackets.

[432]

5.3   Details of the insurance

5.3.1   *Office, underwriters and agency*

Insurance is to be effected in such [substantial and reputable] insurance office, or with such underwriters[137], and through such agency as the Landlord from time to time decides[138].

137   The expression 'insurance office' would probably not include Lloyd's underwriters. The landlord's right to nominate the office and agency is absolute, with no implied restrictions: *Berrycroft Management Co Ltd v Sinclair Gardens Investments (Kensington) Ltd* (1996) 75 P & CR 210, [1997] 1 EGLR 47, CA.

138   It should be noted that it is recommended 'best practice' in circumstances where the building is let to one tenant and the landlord insures that, in appropriate cases, the tenant should be given the opportunity to influence the choice of insurer: see vol 22(1) (2003 Reissue) LANDLORD AND TENANT (BUSINESS TENANCIES) Paragraph 85 [401] and 'A code of practice for commercial leases in England and Wales (2nd edition)' which can be found in vol 22(1) (2003 Reissue) LANDLORD AND TENANT (BUSINESS TENANCIES) at Form 1 [4501].

5.3.2 *Insurance cover*[139]

Insurance must be effected for the following amounts —

5.3.2.1   the sum that the Landlord is from time to time advised [by the Surveyor] is the full cost of rebuilding and reinstating the Premises, including [VAT[140],] architects', surveyors', engineers', solicitors' and all other professional persons' fees, the fees payable on any applications for planning permission or other permits or consents that may be required in relation to rebuilding or reinstating the Premises, the cost of preparation of the site including shoring-up, debris removal, demolition, site clearance and any works that may be required by statute, and incidental expenses, and

5.3.2.2   loss of the Rent, taking account of any rent review that may be due, for *(state period, eg 3 years)* or such longer period as the Landlord from time to time [reasonably] requires for planning and carrying out the rebuilding or reinstatement.

139   As to the sum insured see vol 22(1) (2003 Reissue) LANDLORD AND TENANT (BUSINESS TENANCIES) Paragraph 231 [1028] et seq.

      It should be noted that it is recommended 'best practice' that, where the landlord has arranged insurance, the terms should be made known to the tenant and any material change in the insurance should be notified to the tenant: see Recommendation 14 of 'A code of practice for commercial leases in England and Wales (2nd edition)' which can be found in vol 22(1) (2003 Reissue) LANDLORD AND TENANT (BUSINESS TENANCIES) at Form 1 [4501].

140   As to VAT and the level of insurance cover see the Information Binder: Property [1]: VAT and Property. The expense of insuring against the VAT payable on reinstatement costs is not justified where the landlord has opted to tax and will be able to recover the VAT. There is a theoretical possibility that a future landlord may not opt to tax and that the sum insured may then be too low. It is also possible that a landlord may wish to preserve the 'exempt' status of a property. Normally, however, the cost of reinstatement need not expressly mention VAT, although the cashflow implications of having to pay VAT on construction works need to be remembered.

[433]

5.3.3   *Risks insured*[141]

Insurance must be effected against damage or destruction by any of the Insured Risks to the extent that such insurance may ordinarily be arranged [with a substantial and reputable insurer] for properties such as the Premises, subject to such excesses, exclusions or limitations as the insurer requires.

141   As to the risks to be insured against see vol 22(1) (2003 Reissue) LANDLORD AND TENANT (BUSINESS TENANCIES) Paragraph 235 [1033].

      It should be noted that it is recommended 'best practice' that, where the landlord has arranged insurance, the terms should be made known to the tenant and any material change in the insurance should be notified to the tenant: see Recommendation 14 of 'A code of practice for commercial leases in England and Wales (2nd edition)' which can be found in vol 22(1) (2003 Reissue) LANDLORD AND TENANT (BUSINESS TENANCIES) at Form 1 [4501].

5.4   Payment of the Insurance Rent

The Tenant covenants to pay the Insurance Rent for the period starting on the Rent Commencement Date and ending on the day before the next policy renewal date on the date of this Lease, and subsequently to pay the Insurance Rent on demand and, if so demanded, in advance of the policy renewal date[, but not more than *(state period, eg ... months)* in advance].

[434]

5.5   Suspension of the Rent[142]

5.5.1   *Events giving rise to suspension*

If and whenever the Premises or any part of them are damaged or destroyed by one or more of the Insured Risks[143] [—except one against which insurance may not ordinarily be arranged [with a substantial and reputable insurer] for properties such as the Premises unless the Landlord has in fact insured against that risk —] so that the Premises or any part of them are unfit for occupation or use, or the Road or the Adjoining Conduits are damaged or destroyed so that the Premises or any part of them are unfit for occupation or use[144], and payment of the insurance money is not wholly or partly refused because of any act or default of the Tenant or anyone at the Premises expressly or by implication[145] with his authority [and under his control][146] then the provisions of clause 5.5.2 SUSPENDING THE RENT are to have effect.

142   As to suspension of rent see vol 22(1) (2003 Reissue) LANDLORD AND TENANT (BUSINESS TENANCIES) Paragraph 241 [1044] et seq.
143   It should be noted that it is recommended 'best practice' that if premises are so damaged by an uninsured risk as to prevent occupation, the tenant should be allowed to terminate the lease unless the landlord agrees to reinstate at his own cost: see vol 22(1) (2003 Reissue) LANDLORD AND TENANT (BUSINESS TENANCIES) Paragraph 85 [402] and 'A code of practice for commercial leases in England and Wales (2nd edition)' which can be found in vol 22(1) (2003 Reissue) LANDLORD AND TENANT (BUSINESS TENANCIES) at Form 1 [4501]. If adopted, this recommendation involves rent suspension also becoming operative in the event of the premises becoming unusable because of uninsured risks.
144   The premises may be rendered unfit for use because the tenant is unable to gain access to them or because the supply of services is interrupted. In a letting such as this, the road over the adjoining premises and the adjoining conduits may not be insured and so the point must be dealt with expressly. Adding the road and conduits into the general provision protects the tenant only if the landlord insures them.
145   The expression 'by implication' is intended to include a caller on the premises, such as a tradesman, where there has been no express invitation but the person cannot be classed as a trespasser.
146   The tenant should add the words in square brackets.

[435]

5.5.2   *Suspending the Rent*

In the circumstances mentioned in clause 5.5.1 EVENTS GIVING RISE TO SUSPENSION the Rent, or a fair proportion of it according to the nature and the extent of the damage sustained, is to cease to be payable until the Premises, or the affected part, or the Road or the Adjoining Conduits have been rebuilt or reinstated so as to render the Premises, or the affected part, fit for occupation and use, [or until the end of *(state period, eg 3 years)* from the destruction or damage, whichever period is the shorter,][147] [the proportion of the Rent suspended and the period of the suspension to be determined by the Surveyor acting as an expert and not as an arbitrator *(or as required)* any dispute as to the proportion of the Rent suspended or the period of the suspension to be determined in accordance with the Arbitration Act 1996 by an arbitrator to be appointed by agreement between the Landlord and the Tenant or in default by the President or other proper officer for the time being of the Royal Institution of Chartered Surveyors upon the application of either the Landlord or the Tenant].

147   As to the length of the suspension and the tenant's concerns see vol 22(1) (2003 Reissue) LANDLORD AND TENANT (BUSINESS TENANCIES) Paragraph 244 [1048]. For a provision extending suspension of the rent where reinstatement is delayed see vol 22(3) (1997 Reissue) LANDLORD AND TENANT (BUSINESS TENANCIES) Form 111 [6495].

[436]

5.6   Reinstatement and termination[148]

5.6.1   *Obligation to obtain permissions*

If and whenever the Premises or any part of them are damaged or destroyed by one or more of the Insured Risks [— except one against which insurance may not ordinarily be arranged [with a substantial and reputable insurer] for properties such as the Premises, unless the Landlord has in fact insured against that risk —], or the Road or the Adjoining Conduits are damaged or destroyed so that the Premises or any part of them are unfit for occupation or use, and payment of the insurance money is not wholly or partly refused because of any act or default of the Tenant or anyone at the Premises expressly or by implication[149] with his authority [and under his control][150], the Landlord must use his best endeavours[151] to obtain the planning permissions and other permits and consents ('permissions') that are required under the Planning Acts or otherwise to enable him to rebuild and reinstate the Premises, the Road or the Adjoining Conduits.

148   It has been held that, in the absence of an express covenant to reinstate, where the landlord must keep the premises adequately insured against comprehensive risks and the insurance is effected at the tenant's expense, the obligation is one intended to enure for the benefit of both parties: *Mumford Hotels Ltd v Wheler* [1964] Ch 117, [1963] 3 All ER 250; see also *Mark Rowlands Ltd v Berni Inns Ltd* [1986] QB 211, [1985] 3 All ER 473, CA; *Lonsdale & Thompson Ltd v Black Arrow Group plc* [1993] Ch 361, [1993] 3 All ER 648. This is not, however, a general principle of law and the tenant should therefore always require a specific covenant to reinstate.

    These provisions are restricted to circumstances where damage or destruction is caused by an insured risk. It should be noted that it is recommended 'best practice' that if premises are so damaged by an uninsured risk as to prevent occupation, the tenant should be allowed to terminate the lease unless the landlord agrees to reinstate at his own cost: see vol 22(1) (2003 Reissue) LANDLORD AND TENANT (BUSINESS TENANCIES) Paragraph 85 [401] and 'A code of practice for commercial leases in England and Wales (2nd edition)' which can be found in vol 22(1) (2003 Reissue) LANDLORD AND TENANT (BUSINESS TENANCIES) at Form 1 [4501].

    As to termination where reinstatement is not possible, see vol 22(1) (2003 Reissue) LANDLORD AND TENANT (BUSINESS TENANCIES) Paragraph 237 [1037]. et seq. For a provision for termination or surrender on destruction or substantial damage see vol 22(3) (1997 Reissue) LANDLORD AND TENANT (BUSINESS TENANCIES) Form 107 [6483].

149   The expression 'by implication' is intended to include a caller on the premises, such as a tradesman, where there has been no express invitation but the person cannot be classed as a trespasser.

150   The tenant should add the words in square brackets.

151   The extent of the duty to use best endeavours depends upon the facts in each case: see *Monkland v Jack Barclay Ltd* [1951] 2 KB 252, [1951] 1 All ER 714, CA; *Terrell v Mabie Todd & Co Ltd* [1952] 2 TLR 574; *NW Investments (Erdington) Ltd v Swani* (1970) 214 Estates Gazette 1115. In the light of *IBM United Kingdom Ltd v Rockware Glass Ltd* [1980] FSR 335, CA, it may be that there is little practical difference between a covenant to use best endeavours, a covenant to use reasonable endeavours and a covenant to take all reasonable steps.

[437]

5.6.2   *Obligation to reinstate*

Subject to the provisions of clause 5.6.3 RELIEF FROM THE OBLIGATION TO REINSTATE, and, if any permissions are required, after they have been obtained, the Landlord must as soon as reasonably practicable apply all money received in respect of the insurance effected by the Landlord pursuant to this Lease, except sums in respect of loss of the Rent, in rebuilding or reinstating the Premises, or as the case may be in rebuilding or reinstating the Road or the Adjoining Conduits[, making up any difference between the cost of rebuilding and reinstating and the money received out of his own money][152].

152   Where the landlord's covenant is 'to apply all money received in respect of the insurance in rebuilding or reinstating' rather than simply 'to reinstate', it seems that the landlord does not have to complete the work out of his own money if the insurance money is insufficient because he has complied with his covenant by laying out all the insurance money received. The situation is different if the tenant can

establish that the landlord was in breach of his covenant to insure for the full cost of reinstatement and that this has caused the shortfall: see *Mumford Hotels Ltd v Wheler* [1964] Ch 117, [1963] 3 All ER 250. The tenant should, therefore, require a specific covenant from the landlord to make up any shortfall, to prevent a situation in which the landlord refuses to complete the rebuilding. This is of particular concern if the suspension of rent proviso is expressed to operate for a limited period, because on the expiry of that period the tenant becomes liable for rent unless he can satisfy the court that the lease has been frustrated.

It should be noted that it is recommended 'best practice' that if premises are so damaged by an uninsured risk as to prevent occupation, the tenant should be allowed to terminate the lease unless the landlord agrees to reinstate at his own cost: see vol 22(1) (2003 Reissue) LANDLORD AND TENANT (BUSINESS TENANCIES) Paragraph 85 [401] and 'A code of practice for commercial leases in England and Wales (2nd edition)'which can be found in vol 22(1) (2003 Reissue) LANDLORD AND TENANT (BUSINESS TENANCIES) at Form 1 [4501]. If this recommendation is adopted and the landlord merely covenants to apply insurance money received, the principle should be extended to damage or destruction resulting from insured risks in circumstances where the insurance money is insufficient to enable reinstatement to be completed.

For a proviso relieving from the obligation to reinstate in the same form see vol 22(3) (1997 Reissue) LANDLORD AND TENANT (BUSINESS TENANCIES) Form 106 [6482].

[438]

5.6.3   *Relief from the obligation to reinstate*[153]

The Landlord need not rebuild or reinstate the Premises, the Road or the Adjoining Conduits if and for so long as rebuilding or reinstating is prevented because —

5.6.3.1   the Landlord, despite using his best endeavours[154], cannot obtain any necessary permission,

5.6.3.2   any permission is granted subject to a lawful condition with which [it is impossible for *(or as required)* in all the circumstances it is unreasonable to expect] the Landlord to comply,

5.6.3.3   there is some defect or deficiency in the site on which the rebuilding or reinstatement is to take place that [renders it impossible *(or as required)* means it can only be undertaken at a cost that is unreasonable in all the circumstances],

5.6.3.4   the Landlord is unable to obtain access to the site to rebuild or reinstate,

5.6.3.5   the rebuilding or reinstating is prevented by war, act of God, government action[, strike or lock-out], or

because of the occurrence of any other circumstances beyond the Landlord's control.

153   As to the need for a right to terminate where reinstatement is not possible see vol 22(1) (2003 Reissue) LANDLORD AND TENANT (BUSINESS TENANCIES) Paragraph 226 [998].

154   The extent of the duty to use best endeavours depends upon the facts in each case: see *Monkland v Jack Barclay Ltd* [1951] 2 KB 252, [1951] 1 All ER 714, CA; *Terrell v Mabie Todd & Co Ltd* [1952] 2 TLR 574; *NW Investments (Erdington) Ltd v Swani* (1970) 214 Estates Gazette 1115. In the light of *IBM United Kingdom Ltd v Rockware Glass Ltd* [1980] FSR 335, CA, it may be that there is little practical difference between a covenant to use best endeavours, a covenant to use reasonable endeavours and a covenant to take all reasonable steps.

[439]

5.6.4   *Notice to terminate*[155]

If at the end of a period[156] of *(state period, eg 3 years)* starting on the date of the damage or destruction the Premises, the Road, or the Adjoining Conduits have not been rebuilt or reinstated so that the Premises are fit for the Tenant's occupation and use, either the Landlord or the Tenant may by notice served at any time within *(state period, eg 6 months)* of the end of that period ('a notice to terminate following failure to reinstate') implement the provisions of clause 5.6.5 TERMINATION FOLLOWING FAILURE TO REINSTATE[157].

155   For alternative provisions where the landlord's right to terminate is limited to specified circumstances see vol 22(3) (1997 Reissue) LANDLORD AND TENANT (BUSINESS TENANCIES) Form 109 [6492].

156   The period to be inserted must be carefully considered. Particular regard should be had to the terms of any rent suspension provision and the extent of insurance cover for loss of rent.

157   As to the effect of the Landlord and Tenant Act 1954 see vol 22(1) (2003 Reissue) LANDLORD AND TENANT (BUSINESS TENANCIES) Paragraph 226 [998].

5.6.5   *Termination following failure to reinstate*

On service of a notice to terminate following failure to reinstate, the Term is to cease absolutely — but without prejudice to any rights or remedies that may have accrued[158]— and all money received in respect of the insurance effected by the Landlord pursuant to this Lease is to belong to the Landlord absolutely[159].

158   The effect of this clause is that the right to terminate arises after the end of the appropriate period, whatever the reason for the delay, but the tenant still has a right of action against the landlord where the landlord is in breach of his covenant to reinstate.

159   In the absence of provision for ownership of the insurance money the position is uncertain. In *Re King, Robinson v Gray* [1963] Ch 459, [1963] 1 All ER 781, CA it was held that the insurance money belongs to the party who paid the premiums even if the insurance was placed in the joint names of the landlord and the tenant. The dissenting view of Denning MR that insurance in joint names envisages that each party should be insured as to his insurable interest and that the insurance money should therefore be divided in proportion to their interests in the property should, however, be noted. In *Beacon Carpets Ltd v Kirby* [1985] QB 755, [1984] 2 All ER 726, CA the court adhered to this view and held that the proportion payable depended on the parties' interests in the premises at the time of the destruction. The landlord will prefer an express provision in the lease for the insurance money to be retained by him in full if reinstatement proves impossible. The tenant ought perhaps to accept that it would be unrealistic to amend this to provide for the insurance money to belong to the tenant, but should suggest that a provision be inserted under which the money is to be divided in accordance with their respective interests in the premises at the time when the insurance money became due. For an alternative provision for ownership of the insurance money etc, see vol 22(3) (1997 Reissue) LANDLORD AND TENANT (BUSINESS TENANCIES) Form 108 [6484].

[440]

5.7   **Tenant's further insurance covenants**[160]

The Tenant covenants with the Landlord to observe and perform the requirements of this clause 5.7.

160   In order to comply with many of these covenants, the tenant will need to be supplied with details of the landlord's insurance policy. In any event, it should be noted that it is recommended 'best practice' that where the landlord has arranged insurance, the terms should be made known to the tenant and any material change in the insurance should be notified to the tenant: see Recommendation 14 of 'A code of practice for commercial leases in England and Wales (2nd edition)' which can be found in vol 22(1) (2003 Reissue) LANDLORD AND TENANT (BUSINESS TENANCIES) at Form 1 [4501].

5.7.1   *Requirements of insurers*

The Tenant must comply with all the requirements and recommendations of the insurers.

5.7.2   *Policy avoidance and additional premiums*

The Tenant must not do or omit anything that could cause any insurance policy on or in relation to the Premises to become wholly or partly void or voidable, or do or omit anything by which additional insurance premiums may become payable unless he has previously notified the Landlord and has agreed to pay the increased premium.

5.7.3   *Fire-fighting equipment*

The Tenant must keep the Premises supplied with such fire fighting equipment [as the insurers and the fire authority require and must maintain the equipment to their satisfaction *(or as required)* as the Landlord reasonably requires and must maintain the equipment to the reasonable satisfaction of the insurers and the fire authority] and in efficient working order. At least once in every *(state period, eg 6 months)* the Tenant must cause any sprinkler system and other fire fighting equipment to be inspected by a competent person.

[441]

5.7.4   *Combustible materials*

The Tenant must not store on the Premises or bring onto them anything of a specially combustible, inflammable or explosive nature, and must comply with the requirements and recommendations of the fire authority [and the [reasonable] requirements of the Landlord] as to fire precautions relating to the Premises.

5.7.5   *Fire escapes, equipment and doors*

The Tenant must not obstruct the access to any fire equipment or the means of escape from the Premises, or lock any fire door while the Premises are occupied.

5.7.6   *Notice of events affecting the policy*

The Tenant must give immediate notice to the Landlord of any event that might affect any insurance policy on or relating to the Premises and any event against which the Landlord may have insured under this Lease.

5.7.7   *Notice of convictions*

The Tenant must give immediate notice to the Landlord of any conviction, judgment or finding of any court or tribunal relating to the Tenant, or any director other officer or major shareholder of the Tenant, of such a nature as to be likely to affect the decision of any insurer or underwriter to grant or to continue any insurance[161].

161   This clause provides a continuation of the warranty given by the tenant in clause 5.1 [432] WARRANTY AS TO CONVICTIONS. As to non-disclosure and misrepresentation in contracts of non-marine insurance see 22 Halsbury's Laws (4th Edn Reissue) INSURANCE.

5.7.8   *Other insurance*

If at any time the Tenant is entitled to the benefit of any insurance of the Premises that is not effected or maintained in pursuance of any obligation contained in this Lease, the Tenant must apply all money received by virtue of that insurance in making good the loss or damage in respect of which the money is received[162].

162   An insurance policy frequently provides that, if there is any other insurance effected by or on behalf of the insured covering the premises that are the subject of the policy, the insurers are liable only for a rateable proportion of the damage. Such provisions extend to a case where one of the policies is in the joint names of the persons interested in the premises and the other is in the name of one only of those persons: *Halifax Building Society v Keighley* [1931] 2 KB 248. Therefore, at least when the insurance is in joint names, the landlord needs to ensure that the tenant will use all money received under any policy he has effected to reinstate the premises.

[442]

[5.7.9   *Reinstatement on refusal of money through default*

If at any time the Premises or any part of them are damaged or destroyed by one or more of the Insured Risks and the insurance money under the policy of insurance effected by the Landlord pursuant to his obligations contained in this Lease is wholly or partly irrecoverable because of any act or default of the Tenant or of anyone at the Premises expressly or by implication[163] with his authority [and under his control][164], the Tenant must immediately, at the option of the Landlord, either rebuild and reinstate the Premises or the part of them destroyed or damaged, to the reasonable satisfaction and under the supervision of the Surveyor — in which case, on completion of the rebuilding and refurbishment, the Landlord must pay to the Tenant the amount that the Landlord has actually received under the insurance policy in respect of the destruction or damage — or pay to the Landlord on demand [with interest] the amount of the insurance money so irrecoverable — in which case the provisions of clauses 5.5 SUSPENSION OF THE RENT and 5.6 REINSTATEMENT AND TERMINATION are to apply.]

163   The expression 'by implication' is intended to include a caller on the premises, such as a tradesman, where there has been no express invitation but the person cannot be classed as a trespasser.
164   The tenant should add the words in square brackets.

[5.8   Landlord's further insurance covenants[165]

The Landlord covenants with the Tenant to observe and perform the requirements set out in this clause 5.8 in relation to the insurance policy effected by the Landlord pursuant to his obligations contained in this Lease.

165   Unless insurance is to be in the joint names of the landlord and the tenant, the tenant should seek such covenants from the landlord.

[443]

5.8.1   *Copy policy*

The Landlord must produce to the Tenant on demand [a copy of the policy and the last premium renewal receipt *(or as required)* reasonable evidence of the terms of the policy and the fact that the last premium has been paid][166].

166   The landlord can reasonably insist on the second alternative in square brackets. If the premises are insured under a block policy, it would be inappropriate for the landlord to have to disclose to the tenant information about his other properties.
        It should be noted that it is recommended 'best practice' that where the landlord has arranged insurance, the terms should be made known to the tenant and any material change in the insurance should be notified to the tenant: see Recommendation 14 of 'A code of practice for commercial leases in England and Wales (2nd edition)' which can be found in vol 22(1) (2003 Reissue) LANDLORD AND TENANT (BUSINESS TENANCIES) at Form 1 [4501].

5.8.2   *Noting of the Tenant's interest*

The Landlord must ensure that the interest of the Tenant is noted or endorsed on the policy[167].

167   Where insurance in the joint names of the landlord and the tenant is not practical, the tenant should insist that a note of his interest is endorsed on the policy. This protects the tenant because the insurers should give notice to him of any lapse in the policy and, where it can be shown that the tenant is responsible for the insurance premium under the terms of the lease, it is likely — but not certain — that the insurers would not exercise subrogation rights against the tenant.
        It is recommended 'best practice' that where the landlord has arranged insurance, any interest of the tenant should be covered by the policy: see Recommendation 14 of 'A code of practice for commercial leases in England and Wales (2nd edition)' which can be found in vol 22(1) (2003 Reissue) LANDLORD AND TENANT (BUSINESS TENANCIES) at Form 1 [4501].

[444]

5.8.3 *Change of risks*

The Landlord must notify the Tenant of any [material] change in the risks covered by the policy from time to time[168].

168   It should be noted that it is recommended 'best practice' that where the landlord has arranged insurance, the terms should be made known to the tenant and any material change in the insurance should be notified to the tenant: see Recommendation 14 of 'A code of practice for commercial leases in England and Wales (2nd edition)' which can be found in vol 22(1) (2003 Reissue) LANDLORD AND TENANT (BUSINESS TENANCIES) at Form 1 [4501].

[5.8.4 *Waiver of subrogation*[169]

The Landlord must produce to the Tenant on demand written confirmation from the insurers that they have agreed to waive all rights of subrogation against the Tenant.]]

169   Generally an insurer who has paid out under a policy stands in the shoes of the insured with regard to any claim the latter may have had against any third party. If the insurance is in joint names, the tenant is an insured party and there can be no subrogation against him. It would seem, also, that where the tenant covenants to reimburse the landlord for sums expended by the landlord in insuring the premises, the landlord's insurers cannot make a subrogated claim against the tenant where the premises are destroyed by the tenant's negligence: *Mark Rowlands Ltd v Berni Inns Ltd* [1986] QB 211, [1985] 3 All ER 473, CA. The tenant may still, however, wish to obtain a specific waiver of subrogation if possible.

[445]–[460]

6   GUARANTEE PROVISIONS

6.1   The Guarantor's covenants[170]

6.1.1   *Nature and duration*

The Guarantor's covenants with the Landlord are given as sole or principal debtor or covenantor, with the landlord for the time being and with all his successors in title[171] without the need for any express assignment, and the Guarantor's obligations to the Landlord will last throughout the Liability Period.

170   The covenants in this clause should *not* be omitted where no guarantor is a party to the lease, because they may be required under clause 3.9.5.2 [405] CONDITIONS. If it is felt undesirable to have covenants in a lease and no party, at least initially, to enter into them, ie where there is no guarantor for the original tenant, the contents of this clause could alternatively be included in a schedule.
171   The new provisions governing the transmission of the benefit and burden of covenants (see the Landlord and Tenant (Covenants) Act 1995 s 3) only apply to landlord and tenant covenants. The law in force before 1 January 1996 remains unchanged for guarantor covenants, so that the benefit passes with the landlord's reversion. This occurs, not under the Law of Property Act 1925 s 141(1), which has been repealed for post-1995 tenancies by the 1995 Act, but under common law. The guarantee covenant touches and concerns the legal estate vested in the new reversioner: see *P & A Swift Investments v Combined English Stores Group plc* [1989] AC 632, [1988] 2 All ER 885, HL.

[461]

6.1.2   *The covenants*

The Guarantor covenants with the Landlord to observe and perform the requirements of this clause 6.1.2.

6.1.2.1   Payment of rent and performance of the Lease

The Tenant must pay the Lease Rents[172] and VAT charged on them punctually and observe and perform the covenants and other terms of this Lease, and if, at any time during the Liability Period while the Tenant is bound by the tenant covenants of this Lease[173], the Tenant defaults in paying the Lease Rents or in observing or performing any of the covenants or other terms of this Lease, then the Guarantor must pay the Lease

Rents and observe or perform the covenants or terms in respect of which the Tenant is in default and make good to the Landlord on demand, and indemnify the Landlord against, all losses resulting from such non-payment, non-performance or non-observance notwithstanding —

(a)   any time or indulgence granted by the Landlord to the Tenant, any neglect or forbearance of the Landlord in enforcing the payment of the Lease Rents or the observance or performance of the covenants or other terms of this Lease, or any refusal by the Landlord to accept rent tendered by or on behalf of the Tenant at a time when the Landlord is entitled — or will after the service of a notice under the Law of Property Act 1925 Section 146 be entitled — to re-enter the Premises[174],

(b)   that the terms of this Lease may have been varied by agreement between the Landlord and the Tenant[, provided that no variation is to bind the Guarantor to the extent that it is materially prejudicial to him][175],

(c)   that the Tenant has surrendered part of the Premises — in which event the liability of the Guarantor under this Lease is to continue in respect of the part of the Premises not surrendered after making any necessary apportionments under the Law of Property Act 1925 Section 140[176], and

(d)   anything else (other than a release by deed) by which, but for this clause 6.1.2.1, the Guarantor would be released.

[462]

172   As to the definition of 'the Lease Rents' see clause 1.36 [377] 'THE RENT'.
173   This obligation lasts while the lease is vested in the tenant and for any period of extended liability following an excluded assignment. It is not appropriate once the tenant has entered into an authorised guarantee agreement, when the contractual guarantor's obligations are at one remove: see vol 22(1) (2003 Reissue) LANDLORD AND TENANT (BUSINESS TENANCIES) Paragraph 74 [284] and clause 6.1.2.4 [465] GUARANTEE OF THE TENANT'S LIABILITIES UNDER AN AUTHORISED GUARANTEE AGREEMENT.
174   If a creditor 'gives time' to the debtor in a binding manner, this releases the guarantor: see *Swire v Redman* (1876) 1 QBD 536; *Holme v Brunskill* (1877) 3 QBD 495, CA. The guarantee should, therefore, be expressed to apply notwithstanding any time or indulgence granted by the landlord to the tenant, or neglect or forbearance on the part of the landlord in enforcing the payment of rent and the other covenants in the lease. It has been suggested, however, that such wording does not protect a landlord who refuses to accept rent so as not to waive a breach of covenant by the tenant. This is unresolved but to avoid any doubt the point should be expressly dealt with. It appears that any provision in a guarantor's covenant that purports to exonerate the landlord from the consequences of his own negligence must satisfy the reasonableness test of the Unfair Contract Terms Act 1977 (11 Halsbury's Statutes (4th Edn) CONTRACT).
175   Any variation of the terms of the contract between the creditor and the debtor will discharge the guarantor (*Holme v Brunskill* (1877) 3 QBD 495, CA), unless the guarantor consents, although it has been suggested that an immaterial variation that was not prejudicial to the guarantor might not release him. No guarantor should accept a provision by which the guarantee is to continue notwithstanding any variation, but on the other hand it seems unfair on the landlord for the guarantor to escape his liability merely because a minor change has been agreed between the landlord and the tenant. A provision that the guarantee is to continue to apply notwithstanding an immaterial variation not prejudicial to the guarantor seems a fair compromise. It should be noted that the Landlord and Tenant (Covenants) Act 1995 s 18 does not apply to the guarantor of the current tenant.
       It should also be noted that it is recommended 'best practice' that landlords and tenants should seek the agreement of any guarantors to proposed material changes to the terms of the lease, or even minor changes which could increase the guarantor's liability: see Recommendation 15 of 'A code of practice for commercial leases in England and Wales (2nd edition)' which can be found in vol 22(1) (2003 Reissue) LANDLORD AND TENANT (BUSINESS TENANCIES) at Form 1 [4501].
176   In the light of *Holme v Brunskill* (1877) 3 QBD 495, CA, the position on surrender of part of the premises should be dealt with expressly.

[463]

6.1.2.2   New lease following disclaimer[177]

If, at any time during the Liability Period while the Tenant is bound by the tenant covenants of this Lease[178], any trustee in bankruptcy or liquidator of the Tenant disclaims this Lease, the Guarantor must, if so required by notice served by the Landlord within *(state period, eg 60 days)* of the Landlord's becoming aware of the disclaimer, take from the Landlord forthwith a lease of the Premises for the residue of the [Contractual][179] Term as at the date of the disclaimer, at the Rent then payable under this Lease and subject to the same covenants and terms as in this Lease — except that the Guarantor need not ensure that any other person is made a party to that lease as guarantor — the new lease to commence on the date of the disclaimer. The Guarantor must pay the costs of the new lease and VAT charged thereon, except where such VAT is recoverable or available for set-off by the Landlord as input tax[180], and execute and deliver to the Landlord a counterpart of the new lease.

177   This put option should be included because on disclaimer of a lease the lease ceases to exist, although it is deemed to continue for the purpose of determining the liability to the landlord of persons, including guarantors, other than the tenant whose liquidator or trustee has disclaimed: see *Hindcastle Ltd v Barbara Attenborough Associates Ltd* [1997] AC 70, [1996] 1 All ER 737, HL.

178   This obligation lasts while the lease is vested in the tenant and for any period of extended liability following an excluded assignment. It is not appropriate once the tenant has entered into an authorised guarantee agreement when the tenant's — ie the former tenant's — liquidator or trustee in bankruptcy will not be in a position to disclaim the lease because it will no longer be vested in the former tenant.

179   This defined term will require amendment where the operation of the security of tenure provisions in the Landlord and Tenant Act 1954 ss 24–28 is to be excluded in relation to the lease: see note 6 to clause 1.4 [359] 'THE [CONTRACTUAL] TERM'.

180   As to payment of VAT on legal costs by a person other than the solicitor's own client see the Information Binder: Property [1]: VAT and Property.

[464]

6.1.2.3   Payments following disclaimer[181]

If this Lease is disclaimed and the Landlord does not require the Guarantor to accept a new lease of the Premises in accordance with clause 6.1.2.2 NEW LEASE FOLLOWING DISCLAIMER, the Guarantor must pay to the Landlord on demand an amount equal to [the difference between any money received by the Landlord for the use or occupation of the Premises and] the Lease Rents [in both cases] for the period commencing with the date of the disclaimer and ending on whichever is the earlier of the date *(state period, eg 6 months)* after the disclaimer, the date, if any, upon which the Premises are relet, and the end of the [Contractual][182] Term.

181   This clause could be a useful alternative for a landlord who may not be unhappy to regain possession of the premises but would like some rental income before reletting etc. For a covenant by the tenant to assign to the guarantor see vol 22(3) (1997 Reissue) LANDLORD AND TENANT (BUSINESS TENANCIES) Form 159 [6666].

182   This defined term will require amendment where the operation of the security of tenure provisions in the Landlord and Tenant Act 1954 ss 24–28 is to be excluded in relation to the lease: see note 6 to clause 1.4 [359] 'THE [CONTRACTUAL] TERM'.

6.1.2.4   Guarantee of the Tenant's liabilities under an authorised guarantee agreement

If, at any time during the Liability Period while the Tenant is bound by an authorised guarantee agreement, the Tenant defaults in his obligations under that agreement, the Guarantor must make good to the Landlord on demand, and indemnify the Landlord against, all losses resulting from that default notwithstanding —

(a)   any time or indulgence granted by the Landlord to the Tenant, or neglect or forbearance of the Landlord in enforcing the payment of any sum or the observance or performance of the covenants of the authorised guarantee agreement[183],

(b)   that the terms of the authorised guarantee agreement may have been varied by agreement between the Landlord and the Tenant [provided that no variation is to bind the Guarantor to the extent that it is materially prejudicial to him][184], or

(c)   anything else (other than a release by deed) by which, but for this clause 6.1.2.4, the Guarantor would be released.

183   See note 174 to clause 6.1.2.1 [463] PAYMENT OF RENT AND PERFORMANCE OF THE LEASE.
184   See note 175 to clause 6.1.2.1 [462] PAYMENT OF RENT AND PERFORMANCE OF THE LEASE.

[465]

6.1.3   *Severance*

6.1.3.1   Severance of void provisions

Any provision of this clause 6 rendered void by virtue of the 1995 Act Section 25 is to be severed from all remaining provisions, and the remaining provisions are to be preserved.

6.1.3.2   Limitation of provisions

If any provision in this clause 6 extends beyond the limits permitted by the 1995 Act Section 25, that provision is to be varied so as not to extend beyond those limits.

[6.2   The Landlord's covenant[185]

The Landlord covenants with the Guarantor that he will not attempt to recover from the Guarantor payment of any amount, determined by a court or in binding arbitration or agreed between the Landlord and the Tenant, payable in respect of a breach of covenant by the Tenant, unless he has served on the Guarantor, within 6 months of the payment being determined or agreed, a notice in the form prescribed by Section 27 of the 1995 Act as if the payment were a fixed charge under that Act.]

185   This clause is a tenant's amendment. It provides for a notice equivalent to a default notice under the Landlord and Tenant (Covenants) Act 1995 to be served. It protects the interests of existing and future contractual guarantors. As to service of default notices see vol 22(1) (2003 Reissue) LANDLORD AND TENANT (BUSINESS TENANCIES) Paragraph 61 [260].

[466]

7   FORFEITURE[186]

If and whenever during the Term —

7.1   the Lease Rents[187], or any of them or any part of them, or any VAT payable on them, are outstanding for *(state period, eg 14 days)* after becoming due, whether formally demanded or not[188], or

7.2   the Tenant [or the Guarantor] breaches any covenant or other term of this Lease, or

7.3   the Tenant [or the Guarantor][189], being an individual, becomes subject to a bankruptcy order[190] [or has an interim receiver appointed to his property][191], or

7.4   the Tenant [or the Guarantor][192], being a company, enters into liquidation[193] whether compulsory or voluntary — but not if the liquidation is for amalgamation or reconstruction of a solvent company — [or enters into administration][194] [or has a receiver appointed over all or any part of its assets][195], or

7.5   the Tenant [or the Guarantor][196] enters into or makes a proposal to enter into any voluntary arrangement pursuant to the Insolvency Act 1986[197] or any other arrangement or composition for the benefit of his creditors, or

7.6   the Tenant has any distress, sequestration or execution levied on his goods

and, where the Tenant [or the Guarantor] is more than one person, if and whenever any of the events referred to in this clause happens to any one or more of them, the Landlord may at any time re-enter the Premises or any part of them in the name of the whole — even if any previous right of re-entry has been waived[198] — and thereupon the Term is to cease absolutely but without prejudice to any rights or remedies that may have accrued to the Landlord against the Tenant or the Guarantor [or to the Tenant against the Landlord] in respect of any breach of covenant or other term of this Lease, including the breach in respect of which the re-entry is made.

[467]

---

186   As to forfeiture generally see vol 22(1) (2003 Reissue) LANDLORD AND TENANT (BUSINESS TENANCIES) Paragraph 283 [1171] et seq.
        The precise range of insolvency-related circumstances that will trigger the proviso should be carefully considered. Tenants should note that their inclusion, in practice, means that the lease cannot be used as security for a loan. Landlords generally seek to have the ability to forfeit in the widest range of circumstances. It should, however, be noted that, in certain circumstances, leave of the court or of the insolvency practitioner administering the procedure may be required before any contractual right can be exercised: see eg, in respect of administration, the Insolvency Act 1986 Sch 1B para 43(4), (6) as inserted by the Enterprise Act 2002 s 248 (4 Halsbury's Statutes (4th Edn) BANKRUPTCY AND INSOLVENCY).

187   As to the definition of 'the Lease Rents' see clause 1.36 [377] 'THE RENT'.

188   The words 'whether formally demanded or not' should be used to avoid the common law requirement that an actual demand has to be made.

189   The lease may provide for a right of re-entry on insolvency of the guarantor or a tenant's covenant to find an acceptable replacement (see clause 3.23 [419] REPLACEMENT GUARANTOR) or both.

190   As to bankruptcy generally see the Insolvency Act 1986 Pt IX (ss 264–371).

191   As to interim receivers see the Insolvency Act 1986 s 286.

192   See note 189 above.

193   As to liquidation generally see the Insolvency Act 1986 Pts IV–VI (ss 73–246).

194   As to administration generally see the Insolvency Act 1986 Pt II as substituted by the Enterprise Act 2002 s 248. The tenant may seek to argue that if rent is paid by the administrator and if there are no other material breaches of the lease the landlord should not be entitled to forfeit the lease on this ground.

195   The tenant may seek to argue that if the receiver pays rent and if there are no other material breaches of the lease the landlord should not be entitled to forfeit the lease on this ground.

196   See note 189 above.

197   As to company voluntary arrangements see the Insolvency Act 1986 Pt I (ss 1–7B) as amended by the Insolvency Act 2000. As to individual voluntary arrangements see the Insolvency Act 1986 Pt VIII (ss 252–263G) as amended by the Enterprise Act 2002 s 264.

198   The landlord has the option whether to take advantage of a right of forfeiture or not. If he elects not to do so, the forfeiture is waived. The election may be express or implied, eg if the landlord does any act by which he recognises that the relationship of landlord and tenant is still continuing after the cause of forfeiture has come to his knowledge.

[468]–[490]

8   MISCELLANEOUS

8.1   Exclusion of warranty as to use

Nothing in this Lease or in any consent granted by the Landlord under this Lease is to imply or warrant that the Premises may lawfully be used under the Planning Acts for the Permitted Use[199].

199   See *Laurence v Lexcourt Holdings Ltd* [1978] 2 All ER 810, [1978] 1 WLR 1128; *Collins v Howell-Jones* [1981] 2 EGLR 108, 259 Estates Gazette 331, CA and the comments of Eveleigh LJ on estate agents' particulars relating to use in *Bovis Group Pension Fund Ltd v GC Flooring & Furnishing Ltd* (1984) 269 Estates Gazette 1252 at 1253, CA.

8.2   Exclusion of third party rights

Nothing in this Lease is intended to confer any benefit on any person who is not a party to it[200].

200   By virtue of the Contracts (Rights of Third Parties) Act 1999 (11 Halsbury's Statutes (4th Edn) CONTRACT) third-party rights may be conferred where they are not clearly excluded. This being so, it is advisable to incorporate a specific exclusion except where the parties actually intend to confer rights of action on a third party. In the standard letting situation it is unlikely that the parties will wish to extend liability in this manner. As to the Contracts (Rights of Third Parties) Act 1999 generally see vol 4(3) (2001 Reissue) BOILERPLATE CLAUSES.

8.3   Representations

The Tenant acknowledges that this Lease has not been entered into in reliance wholly or partly on any statement or representation made by or on behalf of the Landlord, except any such statement or representation expressly set out in this Lease[201] [or made by the Landlord's solicitors in any written response to enquiries raised by the Tenant's solicitors in connection with the grant of this Lease].

201   See the comments of Eveleigh LJ on estate agents' particulars relating to use in *Bovis Group Pension Fund Ltd v GC Flooring & Furnishing Ltd* (1984) 269 Estates Gazette 1252 at 1253, CA. For an alternative provision see vol 22(4) (1997 Reissue) LANDLORD AND TENANT (BUSINESS TENANCIES) Form 400 clauses 7.1 [7520], 7.2 [7521].

[491]

8.4   Documents under hand

While the Landlord is a limited company or other corporation, any licence, consent, approval or notice required to be given by the Landlord is to be sufficiently given if given under the hand of a director, the secretary or other duly authorised officer of the Landlord [or by the Surveyor on behalf of the Landlord].

8.5   Tenant's property

If, after the Tenant has vacated the Premises at the end of the Term, any property of his remains in or on the Premises and he fails to remove it within *(state period, eg 7 days)* after a written request from the Landlord to do so, or, if the Landlord is unable to make such a request to the Tenant, within *(state period, eg 14 days)* from the first attempt to make it, then the Landlord may, as the agent of the Tenant, sell that property. The Tenant must indemnify the Landlord against any liability incurred by the Landlord to any third party whose property is sold by him in the mistaken belief held in good faith — which is to be presumed unless the contrary is proved — that the property belonged to the Tenant. If, having made reasonable efforts to do so, the Landlord is unable to locate the Tenant, then the Landlord may retain the proceeds of sale absolutely unless the Tenant claims them within *(state period, eg 6 months)* of the date upon which he vacated the Premises. The Tenant must indemnify the Landlord against any damage occasioned to the Premises and any losses caused by or related to the presence of the property in or on the Premises.

8.6   Compensation on vacating excluded

Any statutory right of the Tenant to claim compensation from the Landlord on vacating the Premises is excluded to the extent that the law allows[202].

202   As to compensation where an order for a new tenancy is precluded on certain grounds see the Landlord and Tenant Act 1954 s 37 as amended by the Local Government and Housing Act 1989 s 149, Sch 7 and by SI 2003/3096.
        As to the effectiveness of provisions of this nature see vol 22(1) (2003 Reissue) LANDLORD AND TENANT (BUSINESS TENANCIES) Paragraph 468 [3079].

[492]

8.7   Notices

8.7.1   *Form and service of notices*

A notice under this Lease must be in writing and, unless the receiving party or his authorised agent acknowledges receipt, is valid if, and only if[203] —

8.7.1.1   it is given by hand, sent by registered post or recorded delivery, or sent by fax[204] provided that a confirmatory copy is given by hand or sent by registered post or recorded delivery on the same day, and

8.7.1.2   it is served —

    (a)   where the receiving party is a company incorporated within Great Britain, at the registered office,

    (b)   where the receiving party is the Tenant and the Tenant is not such a company, at the Premises, and

    (c)   where the receiving party is the Landlord [or the Guarantor] and [the Landlord *(or as required)* that party] is not such a company, at [the Landlord's *(or as required)* that party's] address shown in this Lease or at any address specified in a notice given by [the Landlord to the Tenant *(or as required)* that party to the other parties].

203   Notice clauses are either mandatory or permissive. The words 'and only if' are inserted to make it clear that this clause is mandatory.
204   As to service by fax see *Hastie and Jenkerson v McMahon* [1991] 1 All ER 255, [1990] 1 WLR 1575, CA.

[493]

8.7.2   *Deemed delivery*[205]

8.7.2.1   By registered post or recorded delivery

Unless it is returned through the Royal Mail undelivered, a notice sent by registered post or recorded delivery is to be treated as served on the third working day after posting whenever, and whether or not, it is received.

8.7.2.2   By fax

A notice sent by fax is to be treated as served on the day on which it is sent, or the next working day where the fax is sent after 1600 hours or on a day that is not a working day, whenever and whether or not it or the confirmatory copy is received unless the confirmatory copy is returned through the Royal Mail undelivered.

8.7.2.3   'A working day'

References to 'a working day' are references to a day when the United Kingdom clearing banks are open for business in the City of London.

205   It is a fundamental aspect of any notice clause to specify the circumstances in which the server, provided he has complied with the requirements of the clause, has for the purposes of the document served a notice, even if the recipient claims that he never received it.

8.7.3   *Joint recipients*

If the receiving party consists of more than one person, a notice to one of them is notice to all.

8.8   Rights and easements[206]

The operation of the Law of Property Act 1925 Section 62 is excluded from this Lease. The only rights granted to the Tenant are those expressly set out in this Lease and the Tenant is not to be entitled to any other rights affecting any adjoining property of the Landlord.

206   Where the Law of Property Act 1925 s 62 may operate, it is sensible to define in the lease those rights that are included, and then specifically exclude the operation of that section.

[494]

[8.9   The perpetuity period[207]

The perpetuity period applicable to this Lease is *(state period, eg 80 years)* from the commencement of the [Contractual][208] Term, and whenever in this Lease any party is granted a future interest it must vest within that period or be void for remoteness.]

207   As to the rule against perpetuities see vol 22(1) (2003 Reissue) LANDLORD AND TENANT (BUSINESS TENANCIES) Paragraph 132 [664]. This clause should be included if the term exceeds 21 years because this lease contains grants of future interests.
208   This defined term will require amendment where the operation of the security of tenure provisions in the Landlord and Tenant Act 1954 ss 24–28 is to be excluded in relation to the lease (see note 6 to clause 1.4 [359] 'THE [CONTRACTUAL] TERM') although this is probably unlikely in connection with the grant of such a long lease.

[8.10   Party walls[209]

Any walls dividing the buildings on the Premises from any other buildings are to be party walls within the meaning of the Law of Property Act 1925 Section 38 and must be maintained at the equally shared expense of the Tenant and the Landlord.]

209   This clause should be included where a single building is involved, part being retained by the landlord and part being let: see note 1 above.

8.11 [New *(or)* Old] lease

[This Lease [is *(or as appropriate)* is not] a new tenancy for the purposes of the 1995 Act Section 1. *(or as appropriate)* This Lease is granted under the 1995 Act Section 19 and [is *(or as appropriate)* is not] a new tenancy for the purposes of Section 1 of that Act][210].

210   A tenancy granted on or after 1 January 1996 that is an overriding lease is not a 'new' tenancy where the tenancy being overridden is one granted before that date: see the Landlord and Tenant (Covenants) Act 1995 ss 1(4), 20(1). Where the lease being granted is an overriding lease, the lease must include a statement that it is an overriding lease and indicate whether the overriding lease is or is not a 'new' tenancy: see the Landlord and Tenant (Covenants) Act 1995 s 20(2). In these circumstances the second alternative should be used.

[495]

[8.12   Capacity of tenants

It is declared that the persons comprising the Tenant hold the Premises as [joint tenants *(or as required)* tenants in common].]

[8.13   Exclusion of the 1954 Act Sections 24–28[211]

8.13.1   *Notice and declaration*

On *(date)* the Landlord served notice on the Tenant pursuant to the provisions of the 1954 Act Section 38A(3) as inserted by the Regulatory Reform (Business Tenancies) (England and Wales) Order 2003 and on *(date)* the Tenant made a [simple *(or as appropriate)* statutory] declaration pursuant to schedule 2 of the Regulatory Reform (Business Tenancies) (England and Wales) Order 2003.

8.13.2   *Agreement to exclude*

Pursuant to the provisions of the 1954 Act section 38A(1) as inserted by the Regulatory Reform (Business Tenancies) (England and Wales) Order 2003, the parties agree that the provisions of the 1954 Act Sections 24–28 inclusive are to be excluded in relation to the tenancy created by this Lease.]

211   As to contracting out of the Landlord and Tenant Act 1954 and the requirements that need to be complied with see vol 22(1) (2003 Reissue) LANDLORD AND TENANT (BUSINESS TENANCIES) Paragraph 431 [2035].

(include other clauses as required: eg, break clauses and options (see vol 22(3) (1997 Reissue) LANDLORD AND TENANT (BUSINESS TENANCIES) *Forms 136 [6544]–142 [6569]) or a proviso as to termination on rent review (see vol 22(3) (1997 Reissue)* LANDLORD AND TENANT (BUSINESS TENANCIES) *Form 143 [6570]))*

IN WITNESS etc *(see vol 12(2) (2003 Reissue) DEEDS, AGREEMENTS ETC)*

[496]–[500]

SCHEDULE 1: THE RIGHTS GRANTED[212]

1-1   Right of way

The right, subject to [temporary] interruption for repair, alteration, rebuilding or replacement, for the Tenant and all persons expressly or by implication authorised by him[213] — in common with the Landlord and all other persons having a like right — to pass and repass[214] to and from the Premises over and along the Road [at all times *(or as required)* at any time between *(state time, eg 0700 hours)* on Monday and *(state time, eg 1800 hours)* on Friday in each week, except public holidays][215], for all purposes connected with the use and enjoyment of the Premises but not otherwise[216], [with or without vehicles of any description *(or as required)* with vehicles not exceeding ... metres in length or ... kilograms unladen weight][217].

212   As to rights granted see vol 22(1) (2003 Reissue) LANDLORD AND TENANT (BUSINESS TENANCIES) Paragraph 123 [647] et seq.
213   The term 'the Tenant and all persons expressly or by implication authorised by him' is an updated version of 'the Tenant and his successors in title the owners and occupiers for the time being of the Premises and his or their respective servants and licensees': see *Baxendale v North Lambeth Liberal and Radical Club Ltd* [1902] 2 Ch 427 at 429 per Swinfen Eady J; *Hammond v Prentice Bros Ltd* [1920] 1 Ch 201.
214   There is an implied right to stop for a reasonable time for loading and unloading, but there is no right to park unless one is specifically granted: see *Bulstrode v Lambert* [1953] 2 All ER 728, [1953] 1 WLR 1064; *McIlraith v Grady* [1968] 1 QB 468, [1967] 3 All ER 625, CA; *VT Engineering Ltd v Richard Barland & Co Ltd* (1968) 19 P & CR 890.
215   Limitation of the right of way to specified hours is justifiable only where there are problems of access, security or services.
216   See *Callard v Beeney* [1930] 1 KB 353 at 357 per Talbot J.
217   The landlord may reasonably wish to limit the size and weight of vehicles using his road.

1-2   Passage and running through the Adjoining Conduits

The right, subject to temporary interruption for repair, alteration or replacement, to the free passage and running of all services to and from the Premises through the appropriate Adjoining Conduits, in common with the Landlord and all other persons having a like right.

[501]

SCHEDULE 2: THE RIGHTS RESERVED[218]

2-1   Passage and running through the Conduits

The right to the free and uninterrupted passage and running of all appropriate services and supplies from and to any adjoining property of the Landlord in and through the appropriate Conduits and through any structures of a similar use or nature that may at any time be constructed in, on, over or under the Premises as permitted by. paragraph 2-2 RIGHT TO CONSTRUCT CONDUITS.

218   As to rights reserved see vol 22(1) (2003 Reissue) LANDLORD AND TENANT (BUSINESS TENANCIES) Paragraph 124 [648] et seq.

2-2   Right to construct conduits[219]

The right to construct[220] and to maintain at any time during the Term any pipes, sewers, drains, mains, ducts, conduits, gutters, watercourses, wires, cables, [laser optical fibres, data or impulse transmission, communication or reception systems,] channels, flues and other necessary conducting media for the provision of services or supplies — including any fixings, louvres, cowls and any other ancillary apparatus — for the benefit of any adjoining property of the Landlord[, making good any damage caused by the exercise of the right].

219   If the term of the lease exceeds 21 years a perpetuity provision — see clause 8.9 [495] THE PERPETUITY PERIOD — is required in the lease because this is a grant of a future interest.
220   For a covenant to make good after exercising rights of access see vol 22(3) (1997 Reissue) LANDLORD AND TENANT (BUSINESS TENANCIES) Form 79 [6453].

[502]

2-3   Access

2-3.1   *Access to inspect* etc[221]

The right to enter, or in emergency to break into and enter, the Premises [at any time during the Term *(or as required)* at reasonable times and on reasonable notice except in emergency] —

2-3.1.1   to inspect the condition and state of repair of the Premises,

2-3.1.2   to inspect, clean, connect to, repair, remove, replace with others, alter or execute any works whatever to or in connection with the conduits, easements, services or supplies referred to in paragraphs 2-1 PASSAGE AND RUNNING THROUGH THE CONDUITS and 2-2 RIGHT TO CONSTRUCT CONDUITS,

2-3.1.3   to carry out work of any kind to any adjoining property of the Landlord or any other buildings [that cannot [conveniently] be carried out without access to the Premises],

2-3.1.4   to carry out work or do anything whatever that the Landlord is obliged to do under this Lease,

2-3.1.5   to take schedules or inventories of fixtures and other items to be yielded up at the end of the Term, and

2-3.1.6   to exercise any of the rights granted to the Landlord in this Lease.

221   For a covenant to make good after exercising rights of access see vol 22(3) (1997 Reissue) LANDLORD AND TENANT (BUSINESS TENANCIES) Form 79 [6453].

2-3.2   *Access on renewal or rent review*

[The right to enter the Premises with the Surveyor and the third party determining the Rent under any provisions for rent review contained in this Lease at [any time *(or as required)* convenient hours and on reasonable prior notice] to inspect [and measure] the Premises for all purposes connected with any pending or intended step under the 1954 Act or the implementation of the provisions for rent review. *(or as required in view of the rent review provisions used: see, eg, vol 22(3) (1997 Reissue)* LANDLORD AND TENANT (BUSINESS TENANCIES) *Forms 180 [6711]–194 [6987])*]

2-4   **Right to erect new buildings**[222]

Full right and liberty at any time to build, rebuild, alter or raise the height of any building on any adjoining property of the Landlord in such manner as the Landlord thinks fit, even if doing so obstructs, affects or interferes with the amenity of or the access to the Premises or the passage of light and air to the Premises[and even if it materially affects *(or as required)* but provided it does not materially affect] the Premises or the use and enjoyment of the Premises.

222   As to reservation of the right to develop other land see vol 22(1) (2003 Reissue) LANDLORD AND TENANT (BUSINESS TENANCIES) Paragraphs 130 [660], 131 [662].

SCHEDULE 3: THE RENT AND RENT REVIEW

(insert rent review provisions as required: see vol 22(3) (1997 Reissue) LANDLORD AND TENANT (BUSINESS TENANCIES) *Forms 180 [6711]–194 [6987])*

SCHEDULE 4: THE INDUSTRIAL COVENANTS

4-1   Use of the Road and the Adjoining Conduits

4-1.1   *Contribution to costs*[223]

The Tenant must pay the Landlord on demand a fair proportion[, to be determined by the Surveyor, acting as an expert and not as an arbitrator,] of any sums that may be incurred by the Landlord in or incidentally to [*(where the landlord covenants to maintain road and conduits)* the performance of his obligations under clause 4.2 REPAIRS *(or where the landlord does not covenant to maintain road and conduits)* maintaining the Road — unless it is adopted as a highway maintainable at the public expense — and the Adjoining Conduits, and keeping it and them in good and substantial repair and condition].

---

223   A covenant to reimburse a 'fair proportion' of infrequent expenditure allows for flexibility, so that, eg, changes in the number of properties using the road, or expense caused by misuse by one occupier, can be taken into account. Provision for determination of the proportion due must be made.

4-1.2   *Parking*

The Tenant must not permit any vehicles belonging to him or to any persons calling on the Premises expressly or by implication with his authority[224] to stand on the Road [so as to cause an obstruction][225] or on the pavements and must use his best endeavours to ensure that any such persons do not permit any vehicle so to stand on the Road or pavements.

---

224   The reference to persons calling 'expressly or by implication with his authority' is an updated version of 'the Tenant and his successors in title the owners and occupiers for the time being of the Premises and his or their respective servants and licensees': see *Baxendale v North Lambeth Liberal and Radical Club Ltd* [1902] 2 Ch 427 at 429 per Swinfen Eady J; *Hammond v Prentice Bros Ltd* [1920] 1 Ch 201.

225   If these words are included, the inference is that cars may be parked on the road provided they do not cause an obstruction. Without specific provision, parking rights are not included in a right of way.

[504]

4-2   Use

4-2.1   *Permitted Use only*

The Tenant must use the Premises for the Permitted Use only.

4-2.2   *Cesser of business*

The Tenant must not [cease carrying on business in the Premises or] leave the Premises [continuously] unoccupied for more than *(state period, eg 1 month)* [without notifying the Landlord, and providing such caretaking or security arrangements for the protection of the Premises as the Landlord [reasonably] requires and the insurers or underwriters require].

4-3   Smoke abatement

4-3.1   *Furnace construction*

The Tenant must ensure that every furnace boiler or heater at the Premises is constructed and used so as substantially to consume or burn the smoke arising from it.

4-3.2   *Noxious emissions*

The Tenant must not cause or permit any gritty, noxious or offensive emissions from any engine, furnace, chimney or other apparatus on the Premises without using [the best possible *(or as required)* all reasonable] means for preventing or counteracting the emissions.

4-3.3   *Statutory controls*

The Tenant must comply with the provisions of the Clean Air Act 1993 and with the requirements of any notice served under it by the relevant authority or body.

[505]

4-4   Environmental protection[226]

4-4.1   *Discharge of dangerous substances*

4-4.1.1   Damage to the Conduits and environment

The Tenant must not permit any oil or grease or any deleterious, objectionable, dangerous, poisonous or explosive matter or substance to be discharged into any of the Conduits, and must take all [reasonable] measures to ensure that any effluent discharged into the Conduits does not harm the environment, or corrode or otherwise harm the Conduits or cause obstruction or deposit in them.

4-4.1.2   Poisons and pollutants

The Tenant must not permit the discharge into any of the Conduits of any fluid of a poisonous or noxious nature or of a kind likely to sicken or injure the fish, or that does in fact destroy them, or likely to contaminate or pollute the water of any stream or river.

226   It may be advisable for the landlord and tenant to commission a soil survey before the lease is entered into. The results could be annexed to the lease. A further survey could then be carried out towards the end of the term ascertaining whether or not contamination has in fact occurred. The tenant's obligations regarding restriction or clean-up or both will then be clear. If the original soil survey reveals contamination, then thought should be given to including provisions in the lease making it clear whose responsibility the contamination is and whether or not the tenant is obliged to resolve it or clean it up.

4-4.2   *Spillages and contamination*

The Tenant must take all practicable precautions to ensure that no noxious substances are spilled or deposited on the Premises and that contamination does not occur.

4-4.3   *Controlled, special or radioactive waste*

The Tenant must not deposit on the Premises any controlled or special waste as defined in the Environmental Protection Act 1990, or radioactive waste as defined in the Radioactive Substances Act 1993 Section 18, or any other substance that may produce concentrations or accumulations of noxious gasses or noxious liquids that may cause pollution of the environment or harm to human health.

4-4.4   *Notice of spillages and inspection*

Within 14 days of the spilling or deposit on the Premises of any noxious substance in a quantity that may cause serious damage to or pollution of the environment or serious damage to property or serious harm to human health, the Tenant must inform the Landlord of this and permit him to enter and inspect the Premises.

4-4.5   *Indemnity for damage and pollution*

The Tenant must indemnify the Landlord, and keep him indemnified, against any losses in respect of damage to, or pollution of, the environment or damage to property or harm to human health caused by the Premises or any substance on them whether in liquid or solid form or in the form of gas or vapour.

[506]

4-5   Roof and floor loading

4-5.1   *Heavy items*

The Tenant must not bring into or permit to remain in any building on the Premises any safes, machinery, goods or other articles that will or may strain or damage the building or any part of it.

4-5.2   *Protection of the roof*

The Tenant must not, without the consent of the Landlord, suspend any weight from the [portal frames, stanchions or roof purlins *(or as the case may be)*] of any building on the Premises or use them for the storage of goods or place any weight on them.

4-5.3   *Expert advice*

If the Tenant applies for the Landlord's consent under paragraph 4-5.2 PROTECTION OF THE ROOF the Landlord may consult any engineer or other person in relation to the roof or floor loading proposed by the Tenant, and the Tenant must repay the fees of the engineer or other person to the Landlord on demand.

4-6   Machinery

4-6.1   *Maintenance of machinery*

The Tenant must keep all plant, apparatus and machinery, including any boilers and furnaces, on the Premises, ('the Machinery') properly maintained and in good working order, and for that purpose must employ reputable contractors [to be approved in writing by the Landlord[, whose approval may not be unreasonably withheld [or delayed],]] ('the Contractors') to carry out regular periodic inspection and maintenance of the Machinery.

4-6.2   *Renewal of parts*

The Tenant must renew all working and other parts of the Machinery as and when necessary or when recommended by the Contractors.

4-6.3   *Operation*

The Tenant must ensure by directions to his staff and otherwise that the Machinery is properly operated.

4-6.4 *Damage from the Machinery*

The Tenant must avoid damage to the Premises by vibration or otherwise.

4-7   Signs

The Tenant must at all times display and maintain, at a point on the Premises to be specified in writing by the Landlord, a suitable sign, of a size and kind first approved by the Landlord, showing the Tenant's trading name and business.

[507]

SCHEDULE 5: THE SUBJECTIONS

(insert details)

SCHEDULE 6: THE AUTHORISED GUARANTEE AGREEMENT

(insert the form of authorised guarantee agreement: see, eg, vol 22(3) (1997 Reissue) LANDLORD AND TENANT (BUSINESS TENANCIES) *Form 217 [7053])*

(signature (or common seal) of landlord: lease)
(signature (or common seal) of tenant (and guarantor): counterpart)
(signatures of witnesses)
[508]–[550]

6

Lease of a light industrial building or warehouse on a small estate[1]

CONTENTS

(NB: numbers in [ ] below refer to this volume and should be altered to suit the page or reference numbers actually used)

1 DEFINITIONS AND INTERPRETATION

1.1 'The Adjoining Conduits' . . . . [558]
1.2 'Adjoining property of the Landlord' . . . . [558]
1.3 'The Conduits' . . . . [558]
1.4 'The [Contractual] Term' . . . . [559]
1.5 'Development' . . . . [560]
1.6 'The Estate' . . . . [560]
1.7 'The Estate Roads' . . . . [560]
[1.8 'The Exterior Decorating Years' . . . . [560]]
1.9 Gender and number . . . . [560]
1.10 Headings . . . . [560]
1.11 'The Industrial Covenants' . . . . [561]
[1.12 'The Initial Rent' . . . . [561]]

[551]

1.13 'The Insurance Rent' . . . . [561]
1.14 'The Insured Risks' . . . . [561]
1.15 'Interest' . . . . [562]
1.16 'The Interest Rate' . . . . [562]
[1.17 'The Interior Decorating Years' . . . . [563]]
1.18 Interpretation of 'consent' and 'approved' . . . . [563]
1.19 Interpretation of 'the Guarantor' . . . . [564]
1.20 Interpretation of 'the Landlord' . . . . [564]
1.21 Interpretation of 'the last year of the Term' and 'the end of the Term' . . . . [564]
1.22 Interpretation of 'the Tenant' . . . . [564]
1.23 Interpretation of 'this Lease' . . . . [564]
1.24 Joint and several liability . . . . [564]
1.25 'The Liability Period' . . . . [565]
1.26 'Losses' . . . . [566]
1.27 'The 1954 Act' . . . . [566]
1.28 'The 1995 Act' . . . . [566]
1.29 Obligation not to permit or suffer . . . . [566]
1.30 'Other buildings' . . . . [566]
1.31 'The Permitted Use' . . . . [567]
1.32 'The Plan' . . . . [567]
1.33 'The Planning Acts' . . . . [567]
1.34 'The Premises' . . . . [568]
1.35 References to clauses and schedules . . . . [569]
1.36 References to rights of access . . . . [569]
1.37 References to statutes . . . . [569]
1.38 'The Rent' . . . . [569]
1.39 'The Rent Commencement Date' . . . . [570]
[1.40 'The Review Dates' . . . . [570]]
1.41 'The Surveyor' . . . . [570]
[1.42 'The Term' . . . . [571]]
1.43 Terms from the 1995 Act . . . . [571]
1.44 'VAT' . . . . [571]

2 DEMISE . . . . [581]
                                                                        [552]

3 THE TENANT'S COVENANTS
3.1 Rent . . . . [583]
3.2 Outgoings and VAT . . . . [584]
[3.3 Cost of services consumed . . . . [585]]
3.4 Repair, cleaning and decoration . . . . [586]
3.5 Waste and alterations . . . . [589]
3.6 Aerials, signs and advertisements . . . . [590]
3.7 Statutory obligations . . . . [591]
3.8 Entry to inspect and notice to repair . . . . [592]
3.9 Alienation . . . . [593]
3.10 Nuisance and residential restrictions . . . . [605]
3.11 Costs of applications, notices and recovery of arrears . . . . [606]
3.12 Planning and development . . . . [607]
3.13 Plans, documents and information . . . . [609]
3.14 Indemnities . . . . [609]
3.15 Reletting boards and viewing . . . . [610]

3.16 Obstruction and encroachment . . . . [610]
3.17 Yielding up . . . . [611]
3.18 Interest on arrears . . . . [611]
3.19 Statutory notices . . . . [611]
3.20 Keyholders . . . . [612]
3.21 Viewing on sale of reversion . . . . [612]
3.22 Defective premises . . . . [612]
3.23 Replacement guarantor . . . . [612]
3.24 Exercise of the Landlord's rights . . . . [613]
3.25 The Industrial Covenants . . . . [613]
3.26 Costs of grant of this Lease . . . . [613]
3.27 Consent to the Landlord's release . . . . [614]

4 THE LANDLORD'S COVENANTS

4.1 Quiet enjoyment . . . . [621]
4.2 Repairs . . . . [621]

5 INSURANCE

5.1 Warranty as to convictions . . . . [622]
5.2 Covenant to insure . . . . [623]
5.3 Details of the insurance . . . . [623]
5.4 Payment of the Insurance Rent . . . . [625]
5.5 Suspension of the Rent . . . . [625]
5.6 Reinstatement and termination . . . . [626]
5.7 Tenant's further insurance covenants . . . . [631]
[5.8 Landlord's further insurance covenants . . . . [633]]
[553]

6 GUARANTEE PROVISIONS

6.1 The Guarantor's covenants . . . . [641]
[6.2 The Landlord's covenant . . . . [646]]

7 FORFEITURE . . . . [651]

8 MISCELLANEOUS

8.1 Exclusion of warranty as to use . . . . [653]
8.2 Exclusion of third party rights . . . . [653]
8.3 Representations . . . . [653]
8.4 Documents under hand . . . . [654]
8.5 Tenant's property . . . . [654]
8.6 Compensation on vacating excluded . . . . [654]
8.7 Notices . . . . [655]
8.8 Rights and easements . . . . [656]
8.9 Covenants relating to adjoining property . . . . [657]
8.10 Disputes with adjoining occupiers . . . . [657]
8.11 Effect of waiver . . . . [657]
[8.12 The perpetuity period . . . . [657]]
[8.13 Party walls . . . . [658]]
8.14 [New (or) Old] lease . . . . [658]
[8.15 Capacity of tenants . . . . [658]]
[8.16 Exclusion of the 1954 Act Sections 24–28 . . . . [659]]

SCHEDULE 1: THE RIGHTS GRANTED

1-1 Rights of way . . . . [671]
1-2 Passage and running through Adjoining Conduits . . . . [671]

SCHEDULE 2: THE RIGHTS RESERVED

2-1 Passage and running through the Conduits . . . . [672]
2-2 Right to construct conduits . . . . [672]
2-3 Access . . . . [673]
2-4 Right to erect new buildings . . . . [673]

SCHEDULE 3: THE RENT AND RENT REVIEW

SCHEDULE 4: THE INDUSTRIAL COVENANTS

4-1 Use . . . . [674]
4-2 Smoke abatement . . . . [674]
4-3 Environmental protection . . . . [675]
4-4 Roof and floor loading . . . . [676]
4-5 Machinery . . . . [677]
4-6 Signs . . . . [677]
4-7 Service charge . . . . [677]
4-8 Parking . . . . [678]
4-9 Regulations . . . . [678]

SCHEDULE 5: THE SUBJECTIONS

SCHEDULE 6: THE AUTHORISED GUARANTEE AGREEMENT

[554]

AGREEMENT

[HM LAND REGISTRY

LAND REGISTRATION ACT 2002

Administrative area	*(insert details)*
Title number out of which lease is granted	*(title number)*
Property let	*(postal address or description)*]

[555]

THIS LEASE is made the . . . . day of . . . . BETWEEN:

(1)   *(name of landlord)* [of *(address)* *(or as appropriate)* the registered office of which is at *(address)*] [Company Registration no ...][2] ('the Landlord') [and]

(2)   *(name of tenant)* [of *(address)* *(or as appropriate)* being a company registered in [England and Wales *(or)* Scotland][3] the registered office of which is at *(address)*] [Company Registration no ...] ('the Tenant') [and

(3)   *(name of guarantor)* [of *(address)* *(or as appropriate)* the registered office of which is at *(address)*] [Company Registration no ...] ('the Guarantor')]

[556]

1   As to stamp duty land tax see the Information Binder: Stamp Duty Land Tax [1].

As to Land Registry Fees see the Information Binder: Property [1]: Property Fees.

On the grant out of an unregistered freehold estate in land of a lease for a term of more than seven years from the date of the grant, application must be made to register the title to the leasehold interest granted: see the Land Registration Act 2002 s 4(1)(c) (37 Halsbury's Statutes (4th Edn) REAL PROPERTY). The tenant must obtain an epitome of title to the freehold reversion, investigate it, and mark it as examined, otherwise he will not be able to be registered with an absolute title: see vol 25(1) (2003 Reissue) LAND REGISTRATION Paragraph 21.1 [132].

If the freehold reversion is registered, the grant of a lease for a term of more than seven years from the date of the grant must be completed by registration: see the Land Registration Act 2002 s 27(2)(b)(i).

As to the form and contents of leases see vol 22(1) (2003 Reissue) LANDLORD AND TENANT (BUSINESS TENANCIES) Paragraph 104 [601] et seq. As to registered land generally see vol 25(1) (2003 Reissue) LAND REGISTRATION. As to registration of title to leases see vol 25(1) (2003 Reissue) LAND REGISTRATION Paragraph 143 [601] et seq.

This is a lease of light industrial or warehouse premises comprising the whole of a building on a small industrial estate. The tenant is granted the right to use the estate roads and the conducting media through other parts of the estate. The tenant is responsible for the repair of the premises and the decoration of both the exterior and the interior. The landlord covenants to maintain the estate roads and conducting media and to cultivate any landscaped areas forming part of the estate. The tenant covenants to reimburse the landlord a specific percentage of all expenditure so incurred by the landlord or alternatively a share that is not fixed but expressed to be a fair proportion to be determined by the landlord's surveyor. The landlord insures the premises and the tenant refunds the costs of the premiums. There is provision for the rent to be reviewed and for a guarantor.

It is assumed that, where the buildings on the estate are detached, the fences and walls between each property are included within the premises demised by the various leases so that each tenant is responsible for all or some of his boundary structures. Where, however, buildings are split into two or more units that are let separately, it is suggested that such dividing walls should be party structures.

The tenant should ensure that the landlord deduces title to the land affected by the rights he is granted, especially where the lease is registrable, because if title is not shown and any consents, eg of any chargee or landlord of the land, obtained, the rights may be excluded from the title.

2   If any party is a company it is desirable to include the company registration number. This avoids any problems arising when a company has been wound up and a new company formed with the same name, or when the name of a company is changed, or if companies swap names, eg on a reconstruction of a group of companies. In addition, where a company applies to be registered as proprietor of a registered estate or registered charge, the application must state the company's registration number: see the Land Registration Rules 2003, SI 2003/1417 r 181.

3   Where the tenant is a company registered in England and Wales or Scotland, and the lease is registrable, an application for first registration of the lease (where the landlord's title is unregistered), or registration of the lease as a registrable disposition (where the landlord's title is registered), and the tenant as proprietor of the leasehold title, must state the company's registered number: see SI 2003/1417 r 181(1). There seems to be no reason why the certificate and statement should not be contained in the disposition in favour of the proprietor, where convenient.

[557]

NOW THIS DEED WITNESSES as follows:

1   DEFINITIONS AND INTERPRETATION

For all purposes of this Lease[4] the terms defined in this clause have the meanings specified.

4   One view would add 'unless the context otherwise requires' or 'where the context so admits' and in fact this may be implied (see *Meux v Jacobs* (1875) LR 7 HL 481 at 493; *Law Society v United Service Bureau Ltd* [1934] 1 KB 343, DC) but the better course is to use defined terms in such a way that there are no circumstances where the defined meaning does not apply.

1.1   'The Adjoining Conduits'

'The Adjoining Conduits' means the pipes, sewers, drains, mains, ducts, conduits, gutters, watercourses, wires, cables, [laser optical fibres, data or impulse transmission, communication or reception systems,] channels, flues and all other conducting media — including any fixings, louvres, cowls, covers and other ancillary apparatus —that are in, on, over or under the Estate that serve the Premises.

1.2 'Adjoining property of the Landlord'

References to 'adjoining property of the Landlord' are references to each and every part of the land neighbouring or adjoining the Premises, including the rest of the Estate, in which the Landlord, or a company that is a member of the same group as the Landlord within the meaning of the 1954 Act Section 42, has or during the Term acquires an interest or estate.

1.3 'The Conduits'

'The Conduits' means the pipes, sewers, drains, mains, ducts, conduits, gutters, watercourses, wires, cables, [laser optical fibres, data or impulse transmission, communication or reception systems,] channels, flues and all other conducting media — including any fixings, louvres, cowls, covers and any other ancillary apparatus — that are in, on, over or under the Premises.

[558]

1.4 'The [Contractual] Term'[5]

'The [Contractual][6] Term' means *(insert number)* years commencing on and including *(insert date of commencement of the term)*[7].

5   As to the commencement of the term see vol 22(1) (2003 Reissue) LANDLORD AND TENANT (BUSINESS TENANCIES) Paragraph 135 [670].
     As to registration see note 1 above. Where the landlord's title is unregistered, the grantee must apply for registration within a period of two months from the date of the disposition if the lease is granted for a term of more than seven years. If no such application is made the disposition becomes void as regards any transfer, grant or creation of a legal estate: see the Land Registration Act 2002 s 6 (37 Halsbury's Statutes (4th Edn) REAL PROPERTY). Where the landlord's title is registered and the lease is for a term of more than seven years, the tenant should protect the intended lease by applying for an official search, and an application to register the lease should be made before expiry of the search, otherwise the lease will be susceptible to loss of priority: see the Land Registration Act 2002 s 27.
6   The demise in this lease is for 'the Contractual Term', which is defined as a fixed term of years. The expression 'the Term', as defined in clause 1.42 [571] 'THE TERM', is used in covenants so that they continue to apply during any period of holding over or continuance or extension of the contractual term. Some difficulties arise if this structure is used in a draft lease where security of tenure is to be excluded under the Landlord and Tenant Act 1954 s 38A(1) as inserted by SI 2003/3096 (23 Halsbury's Statutes (4th Edn) LANDLORD AND TENANT). The demise is for the contractual term and the inclusion of the definition of 'the Term' does not prevent the lease being 'for a term of years certain' as required by the Landlord and Tenant Act 1954 s 38A(1). However, reference to continuance of the contractual term by statute is inappropriate where the operation of the security of tenure provisions in the Landlord and Tenant Act 1954 ss 24–28 is to be excluded. If a lease is contracted out of the Landlord and Tenant Act 1954 there can be no statutory extension, and if the tenant remains in occupation at the end of the contractual term he is holding over unlawfully unless there is an express agreement to extend the contractual term operating as a surrender and re-grant so that the original lease— and the agreement under the Landlord and Tenant Act 1954 s 38A(1) — has no further effect. It is suggested that in these circumstances the drafting should be simplified to include a single term (defined simply as 'the Term') by reference to the period of the contractual term. This can be achieved by amending this clause in the manner suggested and substituting it for clause 1.42 [571] 'THE TERM'.
7   For estate management reasons it is usually desirable to insert a quarter day here — or a rent day when rent is due on days other than quarter days — ie generally the one preceding the earlier of the date of possession and the date of execution.

[559]

1.5 'Development'

References to 'development' are references to development as defined by the Town and Country Planning Act 1990 Section 55.

1.6 'The Estate'

'The Estate' means the land and buildings known as *(name)* Industrial Estate shown [for the purpose of identification only] edged *(state colour, eg blue)* on the Plan.

1.7 'The Estate Roads'

'The Estate Roads' means the roads coloured *(state colour, eg brown)* on the Plan.

[1.8   'The Exterior Decorating Years'

'The Exterior Decorating Years' means *(specify years).*] *(omit if not required, eg if the first alternative in clause 3.4.6 [588] DECORATION is used)*

1.9   Gender and number

Words importing one gender include all other genders; words importing the singular include the plural and vice versa[8].

8   See the Law of Property Act 1925 s 61 (37 Halsbury's Statutes (4th Edn) REAL PROPERTY).

1.10   Headings[9]

The clause, paragraph and schedule headings and the table of contents do not form part of this document and must not be taken into account in its construction or interpretation. *(amend if marginal notes are used instead of headings)*

9   Headings and marginal notes require the draftsman to provide a word or two to describe every clause in the lease. This is not always easy and there are times when the draftsman will have to settle for something less than perfection, the only alternative being a heading or note that would be inappropriately long. It would be quite wrong for that title, which its author might admit was not totally apposite but was the best that he could do in a few words, to be used in construing the clause in question.

[560]

1.11   'The Industrial Covenants'

'The Industrial Covenants' means the covenants set out in schedule 4 THE INDUSTRIAL COVENANTS.

[1.12   'The Initial Rent'

'The Initial Rent' means [the sum of £... a year *(or as required by the rent and review provisions to be used)*].] *(this definition is not required if the rent is not reviewable)*

1.13   'The Insurance Rent'[10]

'The Insurance Rent' means a fair proportion reasonably attributable to the Premises of the [gross sums including any commission *(or as required)* sums net of any commission] that the Landlord is from time to time liable to pay —

1.13.1   by way of premium for insuring the Estate, including insuring for loss of rent, in accordance with his obligations contained in this Lease[— or, where the insurance includes the Estate and other property[11], the proportion of those sums [reasonably] attributable to the Estate, such proportion to be determined from time to time by the Surveyor acting as an expert and not as an arbitrator],

1.13.2   by way of premium for insuring in such a manner and on such terms as [the Landlord acting reasonably considers appropriate *(or as required)* is reasonable] against all liability of the Landlord to third parties arising out of or in connection with any matter including or relating to the Estate, and

1.13.3   for insurance valuations.

and all of any increased premium payable because of any act or omission of the Tenant.

10   As to reimbursement of insurance premiums see vol 22(1) (2003 Reissue) LANDLORD AND TENANT (BUSINESS TENANCIES) Paragraph 230 [1026]. If each property on the estate is insured separately see Form 4 clause 1.9 [161] 'THE INSURANCE RENT'.

11   The estate may be insured with other property under a block policy.

1.14 'The Insured Risks'

'The Insured Risks' means the risks of loss or damage by fire[, storm, tempest, earthquake, lightning, explosion, riot, civil commotion, malicious damage, [terrorism,] impact by vehicles and by aircraft and articles dropped from aircraft — other than war risks — flood damage and bursting and overflowing of water pipes and tanks,] and such other risks, whether or not in the nature of the foregoing, as the Landlord [acting reasonably] from time to time decides to insure against[12].

12   As to the risks to be insured and the tenant's concerns see vol 22(1) (2003 Reissue) LANDLORD AND
      TENANT (BUSINESS TENANCIES) Paragraph 235 [1033].

[561]

1.15 'Interest'

References to 'interest' are references to interest payable during the period from the date on which the payment is due to the date of payment, both before and after any judgment, at the Interest Rate then prevailing [*(where the interest rate is defined by reference to a bank base rate)* or, should the base rate referred to in clause 1.16 'THE INTEREST RATE' cease to exist[13], at another rate of interest closely comparable with the Interest Rate [to be agreed between the parties or in default of agreement to be determined by [the Surveyor, acting as an expert and not as an arbitrator *(or as required)* a chartered accountant appointed by agreement between the parties or in default of agreement nominated by the President of the Institute of Chartered Accountants in England and Wales, acting as an expert and not as an arbitrator][14] *(or as required)* decided on by the Landlord acting reasonably]].

13   If base rates are referred to, the possibility of their ceasing to exist should be provided for. Alternatively,
      the Law Society's interest rate may be specified.
14   This provision may be expanded to provide for deeming the parties to have disagreed after a certain
      time, deputy appointors etc.

1.16 'The Interest Rate'

'The Interest Rate'[15] means the rate of ...% a year[16] above [the base lending rate of *(specify bank)* or such other bank [being a member of the British Bankers Association] as the Landlord may from time to time nominate in writing[17] *(or as required)* the Law Society's interest rate[18]].

15   As to the covenant to pay interest see vol 22(1) (2003 Reissue) LANDLORD AND TENANT (BUSINESS
      TENANCIES) Paragraph 154 [767].
16   Words such as 'with a minimum of ...%' should not be used because, if interest rates drop during the
      term to such an extent that the minimum rate specified represents significantly more than a few percent
      over the basic borrowing rate, the provision might be void as a penalty. As to what amounts to a penalty
      see *Dunlop Pneumatic Tyre Co Ltd v New Garage and Motor Co Ltd* [1915] AC 79, HL; *Cellulose Acetate
      Silk Co Ltd v Widnes Foundry (1925) Ltd* [1933] AC 20, HL. In view of this, landlords would be unwise
      to provide for more than a few percent over base rate, and even this is in fact a penalty and should be
      resisted by the tenant.
17   The chance to change the bank may be useful, especially on a sale of the reversion, so that the landlord
      can always provide for his bank for the time being to be specified. The tenant should try to limit the
      choice to major clearing banks.
18   The Law Society's interest rate is published weekly in the Law Society's Gazette.

[562]

[1.17 'The Interior Decorating Years'

'The Interior Decorating Years' means *(specify years).*] *(omit if not required, eg if the first alternative in clause 3.4.6 [588] DECORATION is used)*

1.18   Interpretation of 'consent' and 'approved'

1.18.1   *Prior written consent or approval*

References to 'consent of the Landlord' or words to similar effect are references to a prior written consent signed by or on behalf of the Landlord and references to the need for anything to be 'approved by the Landlord' or words to similar effect are references to the need for a prior written approval by or on behalf of the Landlord.

1.18.2   *Consent or approval of mortgagee or head landlord*

Any provisions in this Lease referring to the consent or approval of the Landlord are to be construed as also requiring the consent or approval of any mortgagee of the Premises and any head landlord where that consent is required [under a mortgage or headlease in existence at the date of this document][19]. Nothing in this Lease is to be construed as imposing any obligation on a mortgagee or head landlord not to refuse any such consent or approval unreasonably.

19   The tenant should include these words so that the clause applies *only* where the consent of the mortgagee or head landlord is in fact required under the terms of an *existing* mortgage or headlease. The tenant should request a copy of the document concerned to establish the rights of the mortgagee or head landlord in relation to any consents that he may seek. The risk to the tenant of the clause without these words is that, by subsequently creating a mortgage or headlease, the landlord could, innocently or deliberately, bring about a situation where his consent may be refused in circumstances in which it would otherwise have been unreasonable to do so. In particular, the effect on the tenant's ability to assign or sublet could be serious.

[563]

1.19   Interpretation of 'the Guarantor'[20]

The expression 'the Guarantor' includes [*(where there is a guarantor for the original tenant)* not only the person named above as the Guarantor, but also][21] any person who enters into covenants with the Landlord pursuant to clause 3.9.5.2 CONDITIONS or clause 3.23 REPLACEMENT GUARANTOR.

20   As to guarantors see vol 22(1) (2003 Reissue) LANDLORD AND TENANT (BUSINESS TENANCIES) Paragraphs 40 [201], 71 [278] et seq.
21   Where there is no guarantor for the original tenant, if it is felt undesirable to have covenants in a lease and no party, at least initially, to enter into them, the guarantor's covenants could be included in a schedule.

1.20   Interpretation of 'the Landlord'

The expression 'the Landlord' includes the person or persons from time to time entitled to possession of the Premises when this Lease comes to an end.

1.21   Interpretation of 'the last year of the Term' and 'the end of the Term'

References to 'the last year of the Term' are references to the actual last year of the Term howsoever it determines, and references to the 'end of the Term' are references to the end of the Term whensoever and howsoever it determines.

1.22   Interpretation of 'the Tenant'

'The Tenant' includes any person who is for the time being bound by the tenant covenants of this Lease except where the name of *(name of original tenant)* appears.

1.23   Interpretation of 'this Lease'

Unless expressly stated to the contrary, the expression 'this Lease' includes, any document supplemental to or collateral with this document or entered into in accordance with this document.

1.24   Joint and several liability

Where any party to this Lease for the time being comprises two or more persons, obligations expressed or implied to be made by or with that party are deemed to be made by or with the persons comprising that party jointly and severally.

[564]

1.25   'The Liability Period'[22]

'The Liability Period' means —

[1.25.1   in the case of *(name of guarantor for the original tenant)*, the period during which *(name of original tenant)* is bound by the tenant covenants of this Lease together with any additional period during which *(name of original tenant)* is liable under an authorised guarantee agreement,] *(omit where there is no guarantor for the original tenant)*

1.25.2   in the case of any guarantor required pursuant to clause 3.9.5.2 CONDITIONS, the period during which the relevant assignee is bound by the tenant covenants of this Lease together with any additional period during which that assignee is liable under an authorised guarantee agreement,

1.25.3   in the case of any guarantor under an authorised guarantee agreement, the period during which the relevant assignee is bound by the tenant covenants of this Lease, and

1.25.4   in the case of any guarantor required pursuant to clause 3.9.8.7 TERMS OF A PERMITTED SUBLEASE, the period during which the relevant assignee of the sublease is bound by the tenant covenants of that sublease.

---

22   The liability of the guarantor should be expressed to last while the original tenant, or as the case may be the assignee, is bound by the tenant covenants in the lease — or in the case of clause 1.25.4 the sublease — rather than while the lease is vested in that person, to take account of the possibility of an excluded assignment being made and the tenant — or subtenant — remaining liable. An excluded assignment means that the tenant — or subtenant — is precluded from tenant release under the Landlord and Tenant (Covenants) Act 1995 (23 Halsbury's Statutes (4th Edn) LANDLORD AND TENANT).

The Landlord and Tenant (Covenants) Act 1995 does not clearly indicate whether the liability of a contractual guarantor can be expressed to extend to any period during which the tenant is bound by an authorised guarantee agreement, but the better view is that it is possible. The policy of the Act certainly suggests that this should be the case.

[565]

1.26 'Losses'

References to 'losses' are references to liabilities, damages or losses, awards of damages or compensation, penalties, costs, disbursements or expenses arising from any claim, demand, action or proceedings.

1.27 'The 1954 Act'

'The 1954 Act' means the Landlord and Tenant Act 1954 [and all statutes, regulations and orders included by virtue of clause 1.37 REFERENCES TO STATUTES][23].

23   The words in square brackets are strictly speaking not required because they merely state what would be the case anyway by virtue of clause 1.37 [569] REFERENCES TO STATUTES. Nevertheless, as much could turn on the point (see *Brett v Brett Essex Golf Club Ltd* (1986) 52 P & CR 330, [1986] 1 EGLR 154, CA), the parties may prefer to deal expressly with the point.

1.28 'The 1995 Act'

'The 1995 Act' means the Landlord and Tenant (Covenants) Act 1995 [and all statutes, regulations and orders included by virtue of clause 1.37 REFERENCES TO STATUTES][24].

24   See note 23 to clause 1.27 [566] 'THE 1954 ACT'.

1.29 Obligation not to permit or suffer

Any covenant by the Tenant not to do anything includes an obligation [to use reasonable endeavours] not to permit or suffer[25] that thing to be done by another person [where the Tenant is aware that the thing is being done].

25   'Permit' may have a different meaning from 'suffer': see *Barton v Reed* [1932] 1 Ch 362 at 375 per Luxmore J. A covenant not to 'permit' activity is broken if the covenantor himself carries it on: see *Oceanic Village Ltd v United Attractions Ltd* [2000] Ch 234, [2000] 1 All ER 975.

1.30 'Other buildings'

References to 'other buildings' are references to any buildings now or at any time during the Term erected on any adjoining property of the Landlord.

[566]

1.31 'The Permitted Use'[26]

'The Permitted Use' means [*(specify use)* or any other use falling within Classes *(state classes, eg B1, B2 or B8)* of the Schedule to the Town and Country Planning (Use Classes) Order 1987, notwithstanding any amendment or revocation of that Order[27], as the Landlord from time to time approves[, such approval not to be unreasonably withheld [or delayed]] *(or where the landlord does not require control over the specific trade)* any use that falls within Classes *(state classes, eg B1, B2 or B8)* of the Schedule to the Town and Country Planning (Use Classes) Order 1987, notwithstanding any amendment or revocation of that Order].

26   As to use see vol 22(1) (2003 Reissue) LANDLORD AND TENANT (BUSINESS TENANCIES) Paragraph 170 [861] et seq.

27   As use classes orders change frequently, it is important to make clear which class is intended to apply, the class in existence at the date of the lease or the class as amended during the term of the lease.

1.32   'The Plan'[28]

'The Plan' means the plan annexed to this Lease.

28   As to the use and role of plans see vol 22(1) (2003 Reissue) LANDLORD AND TENANT (BUSINESS
      TENANCIES) Paragraphs 117 [636], 118 [638]. Although a plan is necessary in the circumstances
      assumed by this lease, a plan may not always be required, eg a demise of all the land within a registered
      title. If the lease is registrable, a plan 'for identification purposes only' or where there is some other
      disclaimer as to the extent to which it can be relied on for conveyancing purposes is not sufficient if
      part of the land in a registered title is being dealt with.

1.33   'The Planning Acts'

'The Planning Acts' means the Town and Country Planning Act 1990, the Planning
(Listed Buildings and Conservation Areas) Act 1990, the Planning (Consequential
Provisions) Act 1990, the Planning (Hazardous Substances) Act 1990, the Planning and
Compensation Act 1991, the Planning and Compulsory Purchase Act 2004 [and all
statutes, regulations and orders included by virtue of clause 1.37 REFERENCES TO
STATUTES][29].

29   See note 23 to clause 1.27 [566] 'THE 1954 ACT'.

[567]

1.34   'The Premises'[30]

1.34.1   *Definition of 'the Premises'*

'The Premises' means all that land and building known as Block *(identify block, eg by name
or number)* on the Estate shown [for the purpose of identification only] edged *(state colour,
eg red)* on the Plan.

30   As to parcels generally see vol 22(1) (2003 Reissue) LANDLORD AND TENANT (BUSINESS
      TENANCIES) Paragraph 116 [634].

1.34.2   *Interpretation of 'the Premises'*[31]

The expression 'the Premises' includes —

1.34.2.1   all buildings, erections, structures, fixtures[32], fittings and appurtenances on
            the Premises from time to time,

[1.34.2.2   the boundary structures on the *(identify boundaries)* of the Premises,]

1.34.2.3   all additions, alterations and improvements carried out during the Term, and

1.34.2.4   the Conduits,

but excludes [the air space above[33] and] any fixtures installed by the Tenant [or any
predecessors in title] that can be removed from the Premises without defacing the
Premises. Unless the contrary is expressly stated 'the Premises' includes any part or parts
of the Premises.

31   As to implied grants and reservations see vol 22(1) (2003 Reissue) LANDLORD AND TENANT
      (BUSINESS TENANCIES) Paragraph 125 [650].
32   As to fixtures see vol 22(1) (2003 Reissue) LANDLORD AND TENANT (BUSINESS TENANCIES)
      Paragraph 121 [644].
33   As to air space, subsoil, cellars and footings see vol 22(1) (2003 Reissue) LANDLORD AND TENANT
      (BUSINESS TENANCIES) Paragraph 119 [640]. Strictly speaking, this exclusion means that the tenant
      would not be permitted go onto the roof to inspect or repair it, unless he is held to have an easement
      of necessity to do so. As to easements of necessity generally see 13 Halsbury's Laws (4th Edn Reissue)
      EASEMENTS AND PROFITS À PRENDRE. If the landlord requires the upper limit of the demised
      premises to be defined, the tenant, in the case of a full repairing lease, should require a right to enter
      the landlord's air space above the demised premises to inspect or repair the upper limit of the premises.
      For a form that may be modified for this purpose see vol 22(3) (1997 Reissue) LANDLORD AND
      TENANT (BUSINESS TENANCIES) Form 77 [6451].

[568]

1.35 References to clauses and schedules

Any reference in this document to a clause, paragraph or schedule without further designation is to be construed as a reference to the clause, paragraph or schedule of this document so numbered.

1.36 References to rights of access

References to any right of the Landlord to have access to the Premises are to be construed as extending to any head landlord and any mortgagee of the Premises [— where the headlease or mortgage grants such rights of access to the head landlord or mortgagee —] and to all persons authorised in writing by the Landlord and any head landlord or mortgagee, including agents, professional advisers, contractors, workmen and others.

1.37 References to statutes

Unless expressly stated to the contrary, any reference to a specific statute includes any statutory extension or modification, amendment or re-enactment of that statute and any regulations or orders made under it, and any general reference to a statute includes any regulations or orders made under that statute[34].

34   Unfortunately the Interpretation Act 1978 ss 17, 23(3) (41 Halsbury's Statutes (4th Edn) STATUTES) does not quite go far enough to enable this clause to be dispensed with altogether, particularly where a statute is modified.

1.38 'The Rent'[35]

[Until the First Review Date 'the Rent' means the Initial Rent. Thereafter 'the Rent' means the sum ascertained in accordance with schedule 3 THE RENT AND RENT REVIEW. 'The Rent' does not include the Insurance Rent[36] but the term 'the Lease Rents' means both the Rent and the Insurance Rent[37]. *(or as required by the rent and review provisions used)*]

35   This clause assumes that the rent is reviewable. If the rent is not reviewable clause 1.12 [561] 'THE INITIAL RENT' should be omitted and this clause amended as appropriate.
36   Because of this exclusion the insurance rent is not suspended under clause 5.5 [625] SUSPENSION OF THE RENT.
37   The tenant's obligation to contribute to the landlord's expenditure in relation to estate roads, conducting media and any landscaped areas forming part of the estate could also be incorporated in the definition of 'Lease Rents'. However, unless regular substantial expenditure is anticipated, this is probably not necessary.

[569]

1.39 'The Rent Commencement Date'

'The Rent Commencement Date' means *(insert the date on which payment of the rent is to start)*[38].

38   This provision may be used to provide for a rent-free period, or for the situation where the tenant had possession before the execution of the lease on the basis that rent should be paid from the date of possession. If the date of execution of the lease or the date of commencement of the term is to be the date for commencement of rent, that date should be inserted here.

[1.40 'The Review Dates'[39]

'The First Review Date' means *(date)*. 'The Review Dates' means the First Review Date and every *(insert ordinal, eg 3rd)* anniversary during the [Contractual] Term [*(if appropriate for the review provisions used)* — and any other date from time to time specified under *(insert the relevant provision: see eg vol 22(3) (1997 Reissue)* LANDLORD AND TENANT *(BUSINESS* TENANCIES) *Form 180 paragraph {2}-4 [6728]* EFFECT OF COUNTER-INFLATION PROVISIONS)]. References to 'a review date' are references to any one of the Review Dates.] *(omit if not required by the review provisions to be used, or if the rent is not reviewable)*

39   As to rent review dates and intervals see vol 22(1) (2003 Reissue) LANDLORD AND TENANT (BUSINESS TENANCIES) Paragraph 302 [1333] et seq. Where there might be a statutory continuation of the lease, the landlord may wish to ensure that there is a review date shortly before the end of the contractual term to obviate the need to apply for an interim rent. The tenant may wish to insist on the word 'contractual' remaining so that the rent review provisions do not apply during any period of lawful holding-over or extension or continuance of the contractual term.

1.41 'The Surveyor'[40]

'The Surveyor' means *(name)* or any person or firm appointed by the Landlord in his place. The Surveyor may be an employee of the Landlord or a company that is a member of the same group as the Landlord within the meaning of the 1954 Act Section 42. The expression 'the Surveyor' includes the person or firm appointed by the Landlord to collect the Lease Rents.

40   For a provision that the landlord's surveyor must be a member of a relevant professional body see vol 22(3) (1997 Reissue) LANDLORD AND TENANT (BUSINESS TENANCIES) Form 152 [6648].

[570]

[1.42 'The Term'

'The Term' means the Contractual Term and any period of holding-over or extension or continuance of the Contractual Term by statute or common law[41].] *(omit if the lease is to be contracted out of the Landlord and Tenant Act 1954)[42]*

41   The demise in this lease is for 'the Contractual Term', which is defined as a fixed term of years. The expression 'the Term' is used in covenants so that they continue to apply during any period of holding-over or continuance or extension of the contractual term. As to the liability of a guarantor during a period of statutory continuation see vol 22(1) (2003 Reissue) LANDLORD AND TENANT (BUSINESS TENANCIES) Paragraph 73 [282].
42   Some difficulties arise if the structure referred to in note 41 above is used in a draft lease where security of tenure is to be excluded under the Landlord and Tenant Act 1954 s 38A(1) as inserted by SI 2003/3096. The demise is for the contractual term and the inclusion of the definition of 'the Term' does not prevent the lease being 'for a term of years certain' as required by the Landlord and Tenant Act 1954 s 38A(1). However, reference to continuance of the contractual term by statute is inappropriate where the operation of the security of tenure provisions in the Landlord and Tenant Act 1954 ss 24–28 is to be excluded. If a lease is contracted out of the Landlord and Tenant Act 1954 there can be no statutory extension, and if the tenant remains in occupation at the end of the contractual term he is holding over unlawfully unless there is an express agreement to extend the contractual term operating as a surrender and re-grant so that the original lease — and the agreement under the Landlord and Tenant Act 1954 s 38A(1) — has no further effect. It is suggested that in these circumstances the drafting should be simplified to include a single term defined by reference to the period of the contractual term. This can be achieved by amending clause 1.4 [559] 'THE [CONTRACTUAL] TERM' as suggested and substituting it for this clause.

1.43   Terms from the 1995 Act

Where the expressions 'landlord covenants', 'tenant covenants', or 'authorised guarantee agreement' are used in this Lease they are to have the same meaning as is given by the 1995 Act Section 28(1).

1.44 'VAT'[43]

'VAT' means value added tax or any other tax of a similar nature and unless otherwise expressly stated all references to rents or other sums payable by the Tenant are exclusive of VAT.

43   As to VAT generally see the Information Binder: Property [1]: VAT and Property.

[571]–[580]

2   DEMISE

The Landlord lets[44] the Premises to the Tenant [with [full (or) limited] title guarantee], together with the rights specified in schedule 1 THE RIGHTS GRANTED, but excepting and reserving to the Landlord the rights specified in schedule 2 THE RIGHTS RESERVED, to hold the Premises to the Tenant for the [Contractual][45] Term, subject to [all rights, easements, privileges, restrictions, covenants and stipulations of whatever nature affecting the Premises including any matters contained or referred to in schedule 5 THE SUBJECTIONS (or as required) the rights, easements, privileges, restrictions, covenants and stipulations affecting the Premises contained or referred to in schedule 5 THE SUBJECTIONS][46], yielding and paying[47] to the Landlord —

2.1   the Rent, without any deduction or set off[48], by equal quarterly payments in advance[49] on the usual quarter days[50] in every year and proportionately for any period of less than a year, the first such payment, being a proportionate sum in respect of the period from and including the Rent Commencement Date to and including the day before the quarter day next after the Rent Commencement Date, to be paid on the date of this document[51], and

2.2   by way of further rent the Insurance Rent[52] payable on demand in accordance with clause 5.4 PAYMENT OF THE INSURANCE RENT.

[581]

44   Traditionally, the operative word in a lease executed as a deed was 'demises' but any words sufficient to show the parties' intention may be used.

45   See note 42 to clause 1.42 [571] 'THE TERM'.

46   The tenant should argue for the second version, making the schedule comprehensive rather than illustrative.

47   The words 'yielding and paying' imply a covenant to pay rent: see *Vyvyan v Arthur* (1823) 1 B & C 410. An express covenant is now invariably included because further procedural matters are contained in it.

48   As to deductions and set off see vol 22(1) (2003 Reissue) LANDLORD AND TENANT (BUSINESS TENANCIES) Paragraph 147 [753].

49   In the absence of an express provision, rent is payable in arrears.

50   The usual quarter days are 25 March, 24 June, 29 September and 25 December. A reference to 'the usual quarter days' is all that is necessary when rent is to be paid on these days.

51   If the first payment is not a complete instalment, the lease must provide for the date on which it is to be paid, the amount, and the period it is to cover.

52   As to the advantages of reserving the insurance rent as rent see vol 22(1) (2003 Reissue) LANDLORD AND TENANT (BUSINESS TENANCIES) Paragraph 151 [761]. The tenant's obligation to contribute to the landlord's expenditure in relation to estate roads, conducting media and any landscaped areas forming part of the estate could also be incorporated in this clause. However, unless regular expenditure of substance is anticipated, it is considered to be more appropriate, if required, simply to refer to the payment as 'additional rent' in the operative provision: see paragraph 4-7 [677] SERVICE CHARGE.

[582]

3   THE TENANT'S COVENANTS

The Tenant covenants with the Landlord to observe and perform the requirements of this clause 3.

3.1   Rent

3.1.1   *Payment of the Lease Rents*

The Tenant must pay the Lease Rents[53] on the days and in the manner set out in this Lease, and must not exercise or seek to exercise any right or claim to withhold rent, or any right or claim to legal or equitable set-off[54] [except that referred to in *(give details of any provisions granting an express right of set-off)*][55].

---

53   As to the definition of 'the Lease Rents' see clause 1.38 [569] 'THE RENT'.
54   See, eg, *British Anzani (Felixstowe) Ltd v International Marine Management (UK) Ltd* [1980] QB 137, [1979] 2 All ER 1063; *Lee-Parker v Izzet* [1971] 3 All ER 1099, [1971] 1 WLR 1688. As to deductions and set-off see vol 22(1) (2003 Reissue) LANDLORD AND TENANT (BUSINESS TENANCIES) Paragraphs 147 [753], 148 [755].
55   If any express right of set-off is granted to the tenant, reference to the provision concerned should be included here to avoid inconsistency.

3.1.2   *Payment by banker's order*[56]

If so required in writing by the Landlord, the Tenant must pay the Lease Rents[57] by banker's order or credit transfer to any bank and account [in the United Kingdom] that the Landlord nominates from time to time.

---

56   This is a clause with dangers for both parties. If the existence of a breach of covenant is known to the landlord he must instruct his bank to refuse to accept the rent, otherwise his right of forfeiture is lost. As to implied waiver of the right of forfeiture see vol 22(1) (2003 Reissue) LANDLORD AND TENANT (BUSINESS TENANCIES) Paragraph 284 [1173]. The tenant may feel that he requires more control over the payment of rent. In any event, the financial systems operated by many companies prevent payments being made in this way.
57   As to the definition of 'the Lease Rents' see clause 1.38 [569] 'THE RENT'.

[583]

3.2   Outgoings and VAT

3.2.1   *Outgoings exclusive to the Premises*

The Tenant must pay, and must indemnify the Landlord against —

3.2.1.1   all rates, taxes[58], assessments, duties, charges, impositions and outgoings that are now or may at any time during the Term be charged, assessed or imposed upon the Premises or upon the owner or occupier of them[, excluding any payable by the Landlord occasioned by receipt of the Lease Rents[59] or by any disposition of or dealing with this Lease or ownership of any interest reversionary to the interest created by it][60] [— provided that if the Landlord suffers any loss of rating relief that may be applicable to empty premises after the end of the Term because the relief has been allowed to the Tenant in respect of any period before the end of the Term then the Tenant must make good such loss to the Landlord],

3.2.1.2   all VAT that may from time to time be charged on the Lease Rents or other sums payable by the Tenant under this Lease[61], and

3.2.1.3   all VAT incurred in relation to any costs that the Tenant is obliged to pay or in respect of which he is required to indemnify the Landlord under the terms of this Lease, save where such VAT is recoverable or available for set-off by the Landlord as input tax[62].

58   As to covenants to pay rates and taxes see vol 22(1) (2003 Reissue) LANDLORD AND TENANT
        (BUSINESS TENANCIES) Paragraph 153 [765].
59   As to the definition of 'the Lease Rents' see clause 1.38 [569] 'THE RENT'.
60   The tenant should add the words in square brackets to make it clear that he is not paying the landlord's
        taxes.
61   As to VAT on rent, service charges and insurance premiums see the Information Binder: Property [1]:
        VAT and Property.
62   As to payment of VAT on legal costs paid by a person other than the solicitor's own client see the
        Information Binder: Property [1]: VAT and Property.

[584]

3.2.2   *Outgoings assessed on the Premises and other property*

The Tenant must pay, and must indemnify the Landlord against, the proportion
reasonably attributable to the Premises — to be determined from time to time by the
Surveyor, acting as an expert and not as an arbitrator[63] — of all rates, taxes, assessments,
duties, charges, impositions and outgoings that are now or at any time during the Term
may be charged, assessed or imposed on the Premises and any other property, including
any adjoining property of the Landlord, or on their owners or occupiers.

63   As to the distinction between an expert and an arbitrator see vol 22(1) (2003 Reissue) LANDLORD
        AND TENANT (BUSINESS TENANCIES) Paragraph 364 [1523].

[3.3   Cost of services consumed[64]

The Tenant must pay to the suppliers, and indemnify the Landlord against, all charges
for electricity, water, gas, telecommunications and other services consumed or used at or
in relation to the Premises, including meter rents and standing charges, and must comply
with the lawful requirements and regulations of the respective suppliers.] *(omit if the
premises have independent supplies of all services)*

64   Where the premises comprise a separate building, a separate supply is usually provided and the tenant
        makes his own arrangements with the suppliers. In that case this clause is unnecessary.

[585]

3.4   Repair, cleaning and decoration

3.4.1   *Repair of the Premises[65]*

The Tenant must repair the Premises and keep them in good condition and repair,
except for damage caused by one or more of the Insured Risks save to the extent that
the insurance money is irrecoverable due to any act or default of the Tenant or anyone
at the Premises expressly or by implication[66] with his authority [and under his control][67].

65   As to repair see vol 22(1) (2003 Reissue) LANDLORD AND TENANT (BUSINESS TENANCIES)
        Paragraph 196 [931] et seq. For a covenant to repair, rebuild and renew, see vol 22(3) (1997 Reissue)
        LANDLORD AND TENANT (BUSINESS TENANCIES) Form 85 [6460]. For provisos excluding, eg,
        work that is prevented etc see vol 22(3) (1997 Reissue) LANDLORD AND TENANT (BUSINESS
        TENANCIES) Forms 87 [6462], 88 [6463].
            If a landlord is unable to obtain full insurance cover without excess, it should be made clear whether
        the tenant is to be liable to pay the excess where damage is caused by an insured risk. For a covenant
        limiting the tenant's repairing obligations by reference to uninsurable as well as insured risks see vol
        22(3) (1997 Reissue) LANDLORD AND TENANT (BUSINESS TENANCIES) Form 90 [6465]. It should
        be noted that it is now recommended 'best practice' that if the premises are so damaged by an uninsured
        risk as to prevent occupation, the tenant should be allowed to terminate the lease unless the landlord
        agrees to reinstate at his own cost: see vol 22(1) (2003 Reissue) LANDLORD AND TENANT (BUSINESS
        TENANCIES) Paragraph 85 [402]. If adopted, this recommendation involves damage preventing
        occupation caused by uninsured or uninsurable risks being excluded from the ambit of the tenant's
        repairing covenant.
66   The expression 'by implication' is intended to include a caller on the premises, such as a tradesman,
        where there has been no express invitation but the person cannot be classed as a trespasser.
67   The tenant should add the words in square brackets.

[586]

3.4.2   *Replacement of landlord's fixtures*

The Tenant must replace from time to time any landlord's fixtures and fittings in the Premises that are beyond repair at any time during or at the end of the Term.

3.4.3   *Cleaning and tidying*

The Tenant must keep the Premises clean and tidy and clear of all rubbish and, without prejudice to the generality of the above, must clean both sides of all windows in the Premises [at least *(state frequency, eg once every month) (or as required)* as is reasonably necessary].

[3.4.4   *The Open Land*

3.4.4.1   Care of the Open Land

The Tenant must keep that part of the Premises that is not built on ('the Open Land') adequately surfaced, in good condition and free from weeds [and must keep all landscaped areas properly cultivated].

3.4.4.2   Storage on the Open Land

The Tenant must not store anything on the Open Land [or bring anything onto it] [that is or might become untidy, unclean, unsightly or in any way detrimental to the Premises or any adjoining property of the Landlord or the area generally].

3.4.4.3   Rubbish on the Open Land

The Tenant must not deposit any waste, rubbish or refuse on the Open Land [or receptacle for them on it].

3.4.4.4   Vehicles on the Open Land

The Tenant must not keep or store any [*(if the land cannot be used for parking)* vehicle,] caravan or movable dwelling on the Open Land.] *(adapt clause 3.4.4 as required in the circumstances or omit if no open land is included)*

3.4.5   *Care of adjoining property and abutting land*

The Tenant must not cause any adjoining property of the Landlord or any other land, roads or pavements abutting the Premises to be untidy or dirty and in particular, but without prejudice to the generality of the foregoing, must not deposit refuse or other materials on them.

[587]

3.4.6   *Decoration*

[The Tenant must redecorate the outside and inside of the Premises, as often as is necessary in the [reasonable] opinion of the Surveyor in order to maintain a high standard of decorative finish and attractiveness and to preserve the Premises and in the last year of the Term, *(or as required)* The Tenant must redecorate the outside of the Premises in each of the External Decorating Years and the last year of the Term and must redecorate the inside of the Premises in each of the Interior Decorating Years and the last year of the Term, in all instances][68] in a good and workmanlike manner and with appropriate materials of good quality[, to the [reasonable] satisfaction of the Surveyor], any change in the tints, colours and patterns of the decoration to be approved by the

Landlord[69][, whose approval may not be unreasonably withheld [or delayed]] [, provided that the covenants relating to the last year of the Term are not to apply where the Tenant has performed the obligation in question less than *(state period, eg 18 months)* before the end of the Term].

68   The draftsman should discuss with the landlord and his property advisers whether he wishes to have the flexibility of the first option or the certainty of the second.

69   The tenant may amend to provide for the landlord's approval to tints etc to apply only in the last year of the term.

3.4.7   *Shared facilities*

Where the use of any the Conduits or any boundary structures or other things is common to the Premises and any adjoining or neighbouring premises, other than any adjoining property of the Landlord, the Tenant must be responsible for, and indemnify the Landlord against, all sums due from the owner, tenant or occupier of the Premises in relation to those Conduits, boundary structures or other things, and must undertake all work in relation to them that is his responsibility[70].

70   This covenant applies to items common to the demised premises and property other than that retained by the landlord. Its effect is to impose on the tenant all liability attaching to the owner or occupier of the demised premises in relation to such items.

[588]

3.5   **Waste and alterations**

3.5.1   *Waste, additions and alterations*[71]

The Tenant must not commit any waste, make any addition to the Premises, unite the Premises with any adjoining premises, or make any alteration to the Premises save as permitted by the provisions of this clause 3.5.

71   As to control of alterations see vol 22(1) (2003 Reissue) LANDLORD AND TENANT (BUSINESS TENANCIES) Paragraph 186 [911] et seq.

3.5.2   *Pre-conditions for alterations*

The Tenant must not make any [internal non-structural] alterations to the Premises unless he first —

3.5.2.1   obtains and complies with the necessary consents of the competent authorities and pays their charges for them,

3.5.2.2   makes an application to the Landlord for consent, supported by drawings and where appropriate a specification in duplicate [prepared by an architect[, or a member of some other appropriate profession,] who must supervise the work throughout to completion],

3.5.2.3   pays the fees of the Landlord, any head landlord, any mortgagee and their respective professional advisers,

3.5.2.4   enters into any covenants the Landlord requires as to the execution and reinstatement of the alterations, and

3.5.2.5   obtains the consent of the Landlord, whose consent may not be unreasonably withheld [or delayed].

[In the case of any works of a substantial nature, the Landlord may require the Tenant to provide, before starting the works, adequate security in the form of a deposit of money or the provision of a bond, as assurance to the Landlord that any works he permits from time to time will be fully completed].

[589]

3.5.3   *Removal of alterations*[72]

At the end of the Term, if so requested by the Landlord, the Tenant must remove any additional buildings, additions, alterations or improvements made to the Premises and must make good any part or parts of the Premises that may be damaged by their removal.

72   This clause has probably come to be inserted because landlords hope that it will defeat the effect of the compensation provisions of the Landlord and Tenant Act 1927 Pt I (ss 1–17) (23 Halsbury's Statutes (4th Edn) LANDLORD AND TENANT) — as to which see vol 22(1) (2003 Reissue) LANDLORD AND TENANT (BUSINESS TENANCIES) Paragraph 192 [923] et seq — ie because, if the improvement has been removed, it will not be an improvement to the holding at the time of quitting the premises. In fact, the clause might not achieve this effect, because the Landlord and Tenant Act 1927 s 9 as amended by the Landlord and Tenant Act 1954 s 49 prohibits contracting out. Also, the clause may be void under the Landlord and Tenant Act 1927 s 19(2) so far as it applies to improvements on the grounds that it purports to fetter the court in deciding what is reasonable. The tenant should not, however, rely on the application of these statutory provisions and should seek to strike out the clause.

3.5.4   *Connection to the Conduits*

The Tenant must not make any connection with the Conduits except in accordance with plans and specifications approved by the Landlord[, whose approval may not be unreasonably withheld [or delayed]], and subject to consent to make the connection having previously been obtained from the competent authority, undertaker or supplier.

3.6   Aerials, signs and advertisements

3.6.1   *Masts and wires*

The Tenant must not erect any pole or mast on the Premises [or install any cable or wire on them], whether in connection with telecommunications or otherwise.

3.6.2   *Advertisements*[73]

The Tenant must not, without the consent of the Landlord, fix to or exhibit on the outside of the Premises, or fix to or exhibit through any window of the Premises, or display anywhere on the Premises, any placard, sign, notice, fascia board or advertisement.

73   See the Town and Country Planning (Control of Advertisements) Regulations 1992, SI 1992/666 as amended. In the absence of a covenant such as this and subject to those Regulations, the tenant may exhibit advertisements etc on the premises whether or not they are connected with his business: see *Clapman v Edwards* [1938] 2 All ER 507.

[590]

3.7   Statutory obligations

3.7.1   *General provision*[74]

The Tenant must comply in all respects with the requirements of any statutes, and any other obligations imposed by law or by any byelaws, applicable to the Premises or the trade or business for the time being carried on there.

74   As to the covenant to comply with statutes see vol 22(1) (2003 Reissue) LANDLORD AND TENANT (BUSINESS TENANCIES) Paragraph 182 [905]. For a provision requiring the landlord to pay compensation for works above a certain value see vol 22(3) (1997 Reissue) LANDLORD AND TENANT (BUSINESS TENANCIES) Form 169 [6693].

3.7.2   *Particular obligations*

3.7.2.1   Works required by statute, department or authority

Without prejudice to the generality of clause 3.7.1, the Tenant must execute all works and provide and maintain all arrangements on or in respect of the Premises or the use to which they are being put that are required in order to comply with the requirements of any statute already or in the future to be passed, or the requirements of any government department, local authority or other public or competent authority or court of competent jurisdiction, regardless of whether the requirements are imposed on the owner, the occupier, or any other person.

3.7.2.2   Acts causing losses

Without prejudice to the generality of clause 3.7.1, the Tenant must not do anything in or near the Premises by reason of which the Landlord may incur any losses under any statute.

3.7.2.3   Construction (Design and Management) Regulations

Without prejudice to the generality of clause 3.7.1, the Tenant must comply with the provisions of the Construction (Design and Management) Regulations 1994 ('the CDM Regulations'), be the only client, as defined in the provisions of the CDM Regulations, fulfil, in relation to all and any works, all the obligations of the client as set out in or reasonably to be inferred from the CDM Regulations, and make a declaration to that effect[75] to the Health and Safety Executive in accordance with the Approved Code of Practice published from time to time by the Health and Safety Executive in relation to the CDM Regulations. The provisions of clause 5.7.3 FIRE-FIGHTING EQUIPMENT are to have effect in any circumstances to which these obligations apply.

3.7.2.4   Delivery of health and safety files

At the end of the Term, the Tenant must forthwith deliver to the Landlord any and all health and safety files relating to the premises in accordance with the CDM Regulations.

75   If works are being carried out for the tenant, the landlord will not want to accept the liabilities that are placed on a client under the Construction (Design and Management) Regulations 1994, SI 1994/3140 and the Health and Safety Executive Approved Code of Practice. The landlord will need to ensure that the tenant actually makes the declaration required, and that he obtains the notification served on the tenant by the Health and Safety Executive.

[591]

3.8   Entry to inspect and notice to repair

3.8.1   *Entry and notice*

The Tenant must permit the Landlord[76] [on reasonable notice during normal business hours except in emergency][77] —

3.8.1.1   to enter the Premises to ascertain whether or not the covenants and conditions of this Lease have been observed and performed,

3.8.1.2   to view the state of repair and condition of the Premises, and to open up floors and other parts of the Premises where that is necessary in order to do so, and

3.8.1.3   to give to the Tenant, or notwithstanding clause 8.7 NOTICES leave on the Premises, a notice ('a notice to repair') specifying the works required to remedy any breach of the Tenant's obligations as to the repair and condition of the Premises in this Lease,

provided that any opening-up must be made good by and at the cost of the Landlord if it reveals no breach of the terms of this Lease.

76   The provisions of clause 1.36 [569] REFERENCES TO RIGHTS OF ACCESS should be noted.
77   The tenant should add the words in square brackets.

3.8.2   *Works to be carried out*

The Tenant must carry out the works specified in a notice to repair immediately, including making good any opening up that revealed a breach of the terms of this Lease.

[592]

[3.8.3   *Landlord's power in default*[78]

If within *(state period, eg 1 month)* of the service of a notice to repair the Tenant has not started to execute the work referred to in that notice, or is not proceeding diligently with it, or if the Tenant fails to finish the work within *(state period, eg 2 months)*[79][, or if in the [Landlord's *(or as required)* Surveyor's] [reasonable] opinion the Tenant is unlikely to finish the work within that period], the Tenant must permit the Landlord to enter the Premises to execute the outstanding work, and must within *(state period, eg 14 days)* of a written demand pay to the Landlord the cost of so doing and all expenses incurred by the Landlord, including legal costs and surveyor's fees.]

78   The advantages for the landlord of this clause must be weighed against the potential liability that it creates under the Defective Premises Act 1972 s 4(4) (31 Halsbury's Statutes (4th Edn) NEGLIGENCE): see *McAuley v Bristol City Council* [1992] QB 134, [1992] 1 All ER 749, CA.
        It has been held that a claim by the landlord for recovery of costs under such a clause is a claim for recovery of a debt, and can therefore be enforced without requiring leave of the court under the Leasehold Property (Repairs) Act 1938 (23 Halsbury's Statutes (4th Edn) LANDLORD AND TENANT): see *Jervis v Harris* [1996] Ch 195, [1996] 1 All ER 303, CA.
        However, even where a landlord has been granted a right of this nature the court does not compel the tenant to allow the landlord the right to enter and carry out repairs where these would be of no benefit and where no loss is being caused to the landlord: see *Hammersmith London Borough Council v Creska (No 2)* [2000] L & TR 288.
79   The tenant would prefer to be given 'a reasonable period' to do the work required to remedy the breaches because it may take longer than the specified number of months.

3.9   Alienation[80]

3.9.1   *Alienation prohibited*

The Tenant must not hold the Premises on trust for another. The Tenant must not part with the possession of the Premises or any part of the Premises or permit another to occupy them or any part of them except pursuant to a transaction permitted by and effected in accordance with the provisions of this Lease.

80   As to alienation see vol 22(1) (2003 Reissue) LANDLORD AND TENANT (BUSINESS TENANCIES) Paragraph 156 [801] et seq. Where the lease is registrable, this prohibition or restriction on dealings will be reflected in an entry on the register excepting from the effects of registration all estates, rights, interests, powers and remedies arising on or by reason of any dealing made in breach of the prohibition or restriction: see the Land Registration Rules 2003, SI 2003/1417 r 6(2).

[593]

3.9.2 *Assignment, subletting and charging of part*[81]

(version 1)

[The Tenant must not assign, sublet or charge part only of the Premises.] *(where assignment, subletting or charging of the whole is allowed)*

(version 2)

[The Tenant must not assign or charge part only of the Premises and must not sublet the whole or any part of the Premises.] *(where assignment or charging of the whole is permitted, but subletting is not allowed at all)*

81   Whether subletting should be permitted is a commercial matter. Some landlords consider that the fact that they cannot unreasonably refuse consent to an assignment gives the tenant all the protection he requires and are not prepared to permit subletting. An advantage to the tenant of the ability to sublet is that he has an element of control over a subtenant but not over an assignee, for whom he may retain liability under an authorised guarantee agreement. Further, with stringent assignment tests or in a bad market, subletting may be the only option open to the tenant.

3.9.3 *Assignment of the whole*

Subject to clauses 3.9.4 CIRCUMSTANCES and 3.9.5 CONDITIONS, the Tenant must not assign the whole of the Premises without the consent of the Landlord, whose consent may not be unreasonably withheld [or delayed][82].

82   This residual discretion is the old test of reasonableness under the Landlord and Tenant Act 1927 s 19(1). Thus the tenant and the proposed assignee may satisfy the circumstances and conditions specified for the purposes of the Landlord and Tenant Act 1927 s 19(1A) as inserted by the Landlord and Tenant (Covenants) Act 1995 s 22 (as to which see clause 3.9.4 [595] CIRCUMSTANCES and clause 3.9.5 [598] CONDITIONS), but the landlord may still refuse consent on reasonable grounds: see vol 22(1) (2003 Reissue) LANDLORD AND TENANT (BUSINESS TENANCIES) Paragraph 159 [812] et seq.

[594]

3.9.4 *Circumstances*

If any of the following circumstances[83] — which are specified for the purposes of the Landlord and Tenant Act 1927 Section 19(1A)[84] — applies either at the date when application for consent to assign is made to the Landlord, or after that date but before the Landlord's consent is given, the Landlord may withhold his consent and if, after the Landlord's consent has been given but before the assignment has taken place, any such circumstances apply, the Landlord may revoke his consent[85], whether his consent is expressly subject to a condition as referred to in clause 3.9.5.4 CONDITIONS or not. The circumstances are —

3.9.4.1   that any sum due from the Tenant under this Lease remains unpaid[86],

3.9.4.2   that in the Landlord's reasonable[87] opinion the assignee is not a person who is likely to be able to comply with the tenant covenants of this Lease and to continue to be able to comply with them following the assignment,

[3.9.4.3   that without prejudice to clause 3.9.4.2, in the case of an assignment to a company in the same group as the Tenant[88] within the meaning of the 1954 Act Section 42 in the Landlord's reasonable opinion the assignee is a person who is, or may become, less likely to be able to comply with the tenant covenants of this Lease than the Tenant requesting consent to assign, which likelihood is adjudged by reference in particular to the financial strength of that Tenant aggregated with that of any guarantor of the obligations of that Tenant and the value of any other security for the performance of the tenant covenants of this Lease when assessed at the date of grant or — where that Tenant is not *(name of original tenant)* — the date of the assignment of this Lease to that Tenant[89],] or

3.9.4.4   that the assignee or any guarantor for the assignee, other than any guarantor under an authorised guarantee agreement, is a corporation registered — or otherwise resident — in a jurisdiction in which the order of a court obtained in England and Wales will not necessarily be enforced against the assignee or guarantor without any consideration of the merits of the case.

(for examples of circumstances for use in unusual cases, see vol 22(3) (1997 Reissue) LANDLORD AND TENANT (BUSINESS TENANCIES) *Form 117 [6501])*

[595]

83   The Landlord and Tenant Act 1927 s 19(1A) as inserted by the Landlord and Tenant (Covenants) Act 1995 s 22 enables the landlord and tenant to a post-1995 lease to agree in advance the terms upon which an assignment may be permitted. It distinguishes between on the one hand circumstances, the existence of which entitles the landlord to refuse consent to assignment, and on the other hand conditions that may be imposed on his consent. This clause and clause 3.9.5 [598] CONDITIONS are drafted on the assumption that this is a valid approach and seek to draw a clear distinction between circumstances and conditions.

It should be noted that provisions that are overly restrictive may have an adverse impact at any rent review. It should also be noted that it is recommended 'best practice' that unless the particular circumstances of the letting justify greater control, the only restriction on assignment of the whole should be obtaining the landlord's consent, which is not to be unreasonably withheld: see vol 22(1) (2003 Reissue) LANDLORD AND TENANT (BUSINESS TENANCIES) Paragraph 85 [401] and 'A code of practice for commercial leases in England and Wales (2nd edition)' which can be found in vol 22(1) (2003 Reissue) LANDLORD AND TENANT (BUSINESS TENANCIES) as Form 1 [4501].

Each letting must be looked at in the light of its own particular facts and circumstances but it is considered that the provisions of this clause do, in the ordinary course, strike a reasonable balance between the landlord's desire for control and the tenant's ability to dispose of his interest without undue restriction. For a less restrictive approach see vol 22(1) (2003 Reissue) LANDLORD AND TENANT (BUSINESS TENANCIES) Form 7 clause 5.2 [5538].

84   The Landlord and Tenant Act 1927 s 19(1A) as inserted by the Landlord and Tenant (Covenants) Act 1995 s 22 seems to require the alienation clause to state that the circumstances it mentions are specified for the purposes of that subsection.

[596]

85   The landlord may require that certain circumstances are absent not only before consent has been given to the assignment, but also up to the date on which the assignment takes place — when the die is cast and the lease covenants bind the assignee. For example, the landlord may require the rent to be paid up to date not only before the application for consent is made, but also at the date when consent is given and the possibly later date when the lease is actually assigned.

86   The tenant may want to limit this to the rent, as it may be thought that a dispute is more likely to arise over the insurance rent or other payments. If the tenant has retained any right of set-off, it should also be referred to here.

87   Circumstances and conditions must either be factual or, if they contain an element of discretion, require that discretion to be exercised reasonably (see the Landlord and Tenant Act 1927 s 19(1C)(a) as inserted by the Landlord and Tenant (Covenants) Act 1995 s 22), or must give the tenant a right of appeal to an expert (see the Landlord and Tenant Act 1927 s 19(1C)(b) as inserted by the Landlord and Tenant (Covenants) Act 1995 s 22). If the discretion is to be exercised reasonably, as suggested by this provision, the tenant can take any dispute about its exercise to the court. The court will consider whether *this* landlord has acted within the range of reasonable decisions, not whether a reasonable landlord would have reached the same decision or whether the test is itself reasonable. For a clause where an expert is used see vol 22(3) (1997 Reissue) LANDLORD AND TENANT (BUSINESS TENANCIES) Form 117 [6501].

88   There have been suggestions that intra-group assignments should be banned completely. However, this is considered to be too draconian and would prevent legitimate corporate restructuring needed for reasons other than avoidance of liability under the Landlord and Tenant (Covenants) Act 1995. The landlord's concern is that a strong tenant may assign to a weak group company; the assignment is acceptable because the assignor gives an authorised guarantee agreement for the assignee. The second group company may then itself assign outside the group; the landlord will lose the authorised guarantee agreement of the strong first group company and have only the possibly worthless authorised guarantee agreement of the second group company. The possibilities for exploitation of this scenario are obvious and it is therefore felt that this is the one situation in which measuring the financial strength of the assignee in relation to that of the assignor is justified. Equivalence tests are not generally thought to be appropriate, because a strong first covenant may make the lease almost unassignable, adversely affecting the rent at review.

89   Consider whether the time at which the tenant's financial status is measured should be when he acquired the lease, when his status was acceptable to the landlord, or at the date of the application for consent to assign, when it may have deteriorated sharply. On the other hand, the outgoing tenant may be a better covenant now than when he acquired the lease: the wily landlord may wish to leave himself free to pick whichever of the two dates gives the better picture.

[597]

3.9.5   *Conditions*

The Landlord may impose any or all of the following conditions[90] — which are specified for the purposes of the Landlord and Tenant Act 1927 Section 19(1A)[91] — on giving any consent for an assignment by the Tenant, and any such consent is to be treated as being subject to each of the following conditions —

3.9.5.1   a condition that upon or before any assignment and before giving occupation to the assignee, the Tenant requesting consent to assign, together with any former tenant who by virtue of the 1995 Act Section 11 was not released on an earlier assignment of this Lease[92], must enter into an authorised guarantee agreement[93] in favour of the Landlord in the terms set out in schedule 6 THE AUTHORISED GUARANTEE AGREEMENT,

3.9.5.2   a condition that if reasonably so required by the Landlord on an assignment to a limited company, the assignee must ensure that at least *(state number, eg 2)* directors of the company, or some other guarantor or guarantors [reasonably] acceptable to the Landlord, enter into direct covenants with the Landlord in the form of the Guarantor's covenants contained in clause 6 GUARANTEE PROVISIONS with 'the Assignee' substituted for 'the Tenant',

3.9.5.3   a condition that upon or before any assignment, the Tenant making the request for consent to assign must give to the Landlord a copy of the health and safety file required to be maintained under the Construction (Design and Management) Regulations 1994 containing full details of all works undertaken to the Premises by that Tenant, and

3.9.5.4   a condition that if, at any time before the assignment, the circumstances specified in clause 3.9.4 CIRCUMSTANCES, or any of them, apply, the Landlord may revoke the consent by written notice to the Tenant.

[598]

90   The Landlord and Tenant Act 1927 s 19(1A) as inserted by the Landlord and Tenant (Covenants) Act 1995 s 22 enables the landlord and tenant to a post-1995 lease to agree in advance the terms upon which an assignment may be permitted. It distinguishes between on the one hand circumstances, the existence of which entitles the landlord to refuse consent to assignment, and on the other hand conditions that may be imposed on his consent. This clause and clause 3.9.4 [595] CIRCUMSTANCES are drafted on the assumption that this a valid approach and seek to draw a clear distinction between circumstances and conditions.

It should be noted that provisions that are overly restrictive may have an adverse impact at any rent review. It should also be noted that it is recommended 'best practice' that unless the particular circumstances of the letting justify greater control, the only restriction on assignment of the whole should be obtaining the landlord's consent, which is not to be unreasonably withheld: see vol 22(1) (2003 Reissue) LANDLORD AND TENANT (BUSINESS TENANCIES) Paragraph 85 [401] and 'A code of practice for commercial leases in England and Wales (2nd edition)' which can be found in vol 22(1) (2003 Reissue) LANDLORD AND TENANT (BUSINESS TENANCIES) as Form 1 [4501].

Each letting must be looked at in the light of its own particular facts and circumstances but it is considered that the provisions of this clause do, in the ordinary course, strike a reasonable balance between the landlord's desire for control and the tenant's ability to dispose of his interest without undue restriction.

91 The Landlord and Tenant Act 1927 s 19(1A) as inserted by the Landlord and Tenant (Covenants) Act 1995 s 22 seems to require the alienation clause to state that the conditions it mentions are specified for the purposes of that subsection.

92 See the Landlord and Tenant (Covenants) Act 1995 ss 11(2), 16(6).

93 As to authorised guarantee agreements see vol 22(1) (2003 Reissue) LANDLORD AND TENANT (BUSINESS TENANCIES) Paragraph 54 [247]. It should be noted that 'A code of practice for commercial leases in England and Wales (2nd edition)' urges landlords to consider requiring authorised guarantee agreements only where the assignee is of lower financial standing than the assignor at the date of the assignment.

[599]

3.9.6   *Charging of the whole*

The Tenant must not charge the whole of the Premises without the consent of the Landlord, whose consent may not be unreasonably withheld [or delayed][94].

94 As to unreasonable withholding of consent under the Landlord and Tenant Act 1927 see vol 22(1) (2003 Reissue) LANDLORD AND TENANT (BUSINESS TENANCIES) Paragraph 158.2 [806] and as to unreasonable delay under the Landlord and Tenant Act 1988 (23 Halsbury's Statutes (4th Edn) LANDLORD AND TENANT) see vol 22(1) (2003 Reissue) LANDLORD AND TENANT (BUSINESS TENANCIES) Paragraph 158.3 [808].

[3.9.7   *Subletting*

The Tenant must not sublet[95] the whole of the Premises without the consent of the Landlord, whose consent may not be unreasonably withheld [or delayed]][96]. *(omit if subletting is prohibited)*

95 See note 81 to clause 3.9.2 [594] ASSIGNMENT, SUBLETTING AND CHARGING OF PART.

96 As to unreasonable withholding of consent under the Landlord and Tenant Act 1927 see vol 22(1) (2003 Reissue) LANDLORD AND TENANT (BUSINESS TENANCIES) Paragraph 158.2 [806] and as to unreasonable delay under the Landlord and Tenant Act 1988 see vol 22(1) (2003 Reissue) LANDLORD AND TENANT (BUSINESS TENANCIES) Paragraph 158.3 [808].

[600]

[3.9.8   *Terms of a permitted sublease*[97]

Every permitted sublease must be granted, without a fine or premium, at a rent not less than whichever is the greater of the then open market rent payable in respect of the Premises [— to be approved by the Landlord before the sublease is granted [and to be determined by the Surveyor, acting as an expert and not as an arbitrator]—] and the Rent[98], to be payable in advance on the days on which the Rent is payable under this Lease. Every permitted sublease must contain provisions approved by the Landlord —

3.9.8.1   for the upwards only review of the rent reserved by it, on the basis set out in schedule 3 THE RENT AND RENT REVIEW and on the Review Dates[99],

3.9.8.2   prohibiting the subtenant from doing or allowing anything in relation to the Premises inconsistent with or in breach of the provisions of this Lease,

3.9.8.3   for re-entry by the sublandlord on breach of any covenant by the subtenant,

3.9.8.4   imposing an absolute prohibition against all dealings with the Premises other than assignment[, subletting] [or charging] of the whole,

3.9.8.5   prohibiting assignment[, subletting][100] [or charging] of the whole of the Premises without the consent of the Landlord under this Lease,

3.9.8.6   requiring the assignee on any assignment of the sublease to enter into direct covenants with the Landlord to the same effect as those contained in clause 3.9.9 SUBTENANT'S DIRECT COVENANTS,

3.9.8.7   requiring on each assignment of the sublease that the assignor enters into an authorised guarantee agreement[101] in favour of the Landlord in the terms set out in schedule 6 THE AUTHORISED GUARANTEE AGREEMENT but adapted to suit the circumstances in which the guarantee is given,

3.9.8.8   prohibiting the subtenant from holding on trust for another or permitting another to share or occupy the whole or any part of the Premises,

3.9.8.9   imposing in relation to any permitted assignment[, subletting] [or charge] the same obligations for registration with the Landlord as are contained in this Lease in relation to dispositions by the Tenant,

[3.9.8.10   imposing in relation to any permitted subletting the same obligations as are contained in this clause 3.9.8 and in clause 3.9.9 SUBTENANT'S DIRECT COVENANTS[, clause 3.9.11 ENFORCEMENT OF THE SUBLEASE and clause 3.9.12 SUBLEASE RENT REVIEW],] and

3.9.8.11   excluding the provisions of Sections 24–28 of the 1954 Act from the letting created by the sublease.] *(omit if subletting is prohibited)*

[601]

97   As to the validity of provisions of this nature see vol 22(1) (2003 Reissue) LANDLORD AND TENANT (BUSINESS TENANCIES) Paragraph 161 [817].

98   It will not be in the landlord's interest for the premises to be sublet at a rent less than that payable under the headlease, because it could allow into the premises a subtenant of doubtful financial status, with whom the landlord may in the future have to deal direct, eg on the grant of a new lease under the Landlord and Tenant Act 1954 Pt II (ss 23–46). Also a low rent could be used as a 'comparable' in arriving at the open market rent on rent reviews or lease renewals. On the other hand following the decision in *Allied Dunbar Assurance plc v Homebase Ltd* [2002] EWCA Civ 666, [2003] 1 P & CR 75, [2002] 2 EGLR 23 a provision of this kind may effectively render the lease inalienable and being a potentially onerous restriction on disposition (as to which see vol 22(1) (2003 Reissue) LANDLORD AND TENANT (BUSINESS TENANCIES) Paragraph 348.2 [1440]) have an adverse impact at rent review from a landlord's perspective.

99   Alternatively the landlord might prefer the sublease rents to be reviewed just before the review dates in the headlease. As to recommended 'best practice' in relation to the basis of rent review in leases of business premises see vol 22(1) (2003 Reissue) LANDLORD AND TENANT (BUSINESS TENANCIES) Paragraph 85 [401] and 'A code of practice for commercial leases in England and Wales (2nd edition)' which can be found in vol 22(1) (2003 Reissue) LANDLORD AND TENANT (BUSINESS TENANCIES) as Form 1 [4501].

100   The landlord may well wish to prohibit any further subletting by requiring an absolute covenant against subletting to be inserted in any sublease.

101   By virtue of the Landlord and Tenant (Covenants) Act 1995 s 16(3)(a), where a head landlord's consent is needed to the assignment of a sublease, the head landlord can require the assignor of the sublease to enter into an authorised guarantee agreement. It should be noted that 'A code of practice for commercial leases in England and Wales (2nd edition)' urges landlords to consider requiring authorised guarantee agreements only where the assignee is of lower financial standing than the assignor at the date of the assignment.

[602]

[3.9.9   *Subtenant's direct covenants*[102]

Before any permitted subletting, the Tenant must ensure that the subtenant enters into a direct covenant with the Landlord that while he is bound by the tenant covenants of the sublease[103] and while the subtenant is bound by an authorised guarantee agreement the subtenant will observe and perform the tenant covenants contained in this Lease — except the covenant to pay the rent reserved by this Lease — and in that sublease.] *(omit if subletting is prohibited)*

102   See note 97 to clause 3.9.8 [602] TERMS OF A PERMITTED SUBLEASE.
103   The liability of the subtenant should be expressed to last while he is bound by the tenant covenants of the sublease, rather than while the sublease is vested in him, to take account of the possibility of an excluded assignment being made and the subtenant remaining liable. An excluded assignment means that the subtenant is precluded from tenant release under the Landlord and Tenant (Covenants) Act 1995.

[3.9.10   *Requirement for 1954 Act exclusion*[104]

The Tenant must not grant a sublease or permit a subtenant to occupy the Premises unless an effective agreement has been made to exclude the operation of Sections 24 to 28 of the 1954 Act pursuant to Section 38A of the 1954 Act.] *(omit if subletting is prohibited)*

104   As to contracting out of the security of tenure provisions of the Landlord and Tenant Act 1954 see vol 22(1) (2003 Reissue) LANDLORD AND TENANT (BUSINESS TENANCIES) Paragraph 431 [2035].

[3.9.11   *Enforcement, waiver and variation of subleases*

In relation to any permitted sublease, the Tenant must enforce the performance and observance by every subtenant of the provisions of the sublease, and must not at any time either expressly or by implication waive any breach of the covenants or conditions on the part of any subtenant or assignee of any sublease, or — without the consent of the Landlord, whose consent may not be unreasonably withheld or delayed — vary the terms or accept a surrender of any permitted sublease.] *(omit if subletting is prohibited)*

[603]

[3.9.12   *Sublease rent review*

In relation to any permitted sublease —

3.9.12.1   the Tenant must ensure that the rent is reviewed in accordance with the terms of the sublease,

3.9.12.2   the Tenant must not agree the reviewed rent with the subtenant without the approval of the Landlord,

3.9.12.3   where the sublease provides such an option, the Tenant must not, without the approval of the Landlord, agree whether the third party determining the revised rent in default of agreement should act as an arbitrator or as an expert,

3.9.12.4   the Tenant must not, without the approval of the Landlord, agree any appointment of a person to act as the third party determining the revised rent,

3.9.12.5   the Tenant must incorporate as part of his representations to that third party representations [reasonably] required[105] by the Landlord, and

3.9.12.6   the Tenant must give notice to the Landlord of the details of the determination of every rent review within *(state period, eg 28 days)*,

provided that the Landlord's approvals specified above may not be unreasonably withheld [or delayed].] *(omit if subletting is prohibited)*

105   This seems preferable to providing, as is sometimes done, that the head landlord's representations have to be brought to the attention of the expert or arbitrator because it would appear that he can refuse to have regard to them, the head landlord not being a party to the lease with which he is concerned.

3.9.13   *Registration of permitted dealings*

Within *(state period, eg 28 days)* of any assignment, charge, [sublease, or subunderlease,] or any transmission or other devolution relating to the Premises, the Tenant must produce a certified copy[106] of any relevant document for registration with the Landlord's solicitor, and must pay the Landlord's solicitor's [reasonable] charges for registration of at least £...

106   There seems to be no reason why the tenant should part with the original. However, under the Land Registration Rules 2003, SI 2003/1417 r 203, it is open to the applicant for registration to ask for the transfer, charge, sublease or subunderlease giving effect to the disposition to be returned for retention by the applicant, provided a certified copy of the instrument is lodged with the application. Accordingly, in such cases, applicants should use this facility if they wish to be able to lodge the lease with the landlord after its return by the registrar. If there is a time limit specified in the lease, then the registrar should be told about this, so that he is aware of the need to return the instrument within the required period.

[3.9.14   *Sharing with a group company*

Notwithstanding clause 3.9.1 ALIENATION PROHIBITED, the Tenant may share the occupation of the whole or any part of the Premises with a company that is a member of the same group as the Tenant within the meaning of the 1954 Act Section 42, for so long as both companies remain members of that group and otherwise than in a manner that transfers or creates a legal estate.] *(omit if sharing with a group company is not to be permitted)*

[604]

3.10   Nuisance and residential restrictions

3.10.1   *Nuisance*[107]

The Tenant must not do anything on the Premises, or allow anything to remain on them, that may be or become a nuisance, or cause annoyance, disturbance, inconvenience, injury or damage to the Landlord or his tenants or the owners or occupiers of any adjoining property of the Landlord or any other adjacent or neighbouring premises.

107   'Nuisance' is a term to be construed according to 'plain and sober and simple notions among the English people': *Walter v Selfe* (1851) 4 De G & Sm 315 at 322 per Knight-Bruce V-C. 'I have no doubt that what is a nuisance or annoyance will continue to be determined by the courts according to robust and commonsense standards': *Hampstead and Suburban Properties Ltd v Diomedous* [1969] 1 Ch 248 at 258, [1968] 3 All ER 545 at 550 per Megarry J. But a tenant can only be said to have permitted a nuisance if the landlord can show that the tenant has failed to take reasonable steps to prevent the nuisance: see *Commercial General Administration Ltd v Thomsett* [1979] 1 EGLR 62, CA.

3.10.2   *Auctions, trades and immoral purposes*

The Tenant must not use the Premises for any auction sale, any dangerous, noxious, noisy or offensive[108] trade, business, manufacture or occupation, or for any illegal or immoral act or purpose.

108   As to the meaning of 'offensive' see *Re Koumoudouros and Marathon Realty Co Ltd* (1978) 89 DLR (3d) 551 where it was held that the word 'offensive' did not have a definite legal meaning and that it should be read in the context of the lease. Surrounding circumstances can affect whether a particular trade is offensive: see *Nussey v Provincial Bill Posting Co and Eddison* [1909] 1 Ch 734, CA; *Dunraven Securities Ltd v Holloway* [1982] 2 EGLR 47, CA.

3.10.3   *Residential use, sleeping and animals*

The Tenant must not use the Premises as sleeping accommodation or for residential purposes, or keep any animal, bird or reptile on them.

[605]

3.11   Costs of applications, notices and recovery of arrears[109]

The Tenant must pay to the Landlord on an indemnity basis all costs, fees, charges, disbursements and expenses — including without prejudice to the generality of the above those payable to counsel, solicitors, surveyors and bailiffs — [properly and reasonably] incurred by the Landlord in relation to or incidental to —

3.11.1   every application made by the Tenant for a consent or licence required by the provisions of this Lease, whether it is granted, refused or offered subject to any [lawful] qualification or condition, or the application is withdrawn[, unless the refusal, qualification or condition is unlawful whether because it is unreasonable or otherwise],

3.11.2   the contemplation, preparation and service of a notice under the Law of Property Act 1925 Section 146, or by reason or the contemplation of proceedings under Sections 146 or 147 of that Act, even if forfeiture is avoided otherwise than by relief granted by the court[110],

3.11.3   the recovery or attempted recovery of arrears of rent or other sums due under this Lease, and

3.11.4   any steps taken in [contemplation of or in] [direct] connection with the preparation and service of a schedule of dilapidations during or after the end of the Term[111].

109   As to payment of VAT on legal costs by a person other than the solicitor's own client see the Information Binder: Property [1]: VAT and Property.
110   As to forfeiture see vol 22(1) (2003 Reissue) LANDLORD AND TENANT (BUSINESS TENANCIES) Paragraph 283 [1171] et seq.
111   The landlord should not be tempted to extend this provision to costs etc incurred by him in consequence of serving a notice under the Landlord and Tenant Act 1954 s 25 because that is void: see *Stevenson and Rush (Holdings) Ltd v Langdon* (1978) 38 P & CR 208, CA.

[606]

3.12   Planning and development

3.12.1   *Compliance with the Planning Acts*

The Tenant must observe and comply with the provisions and requirements of the Planning Acts affecting the Premises and their use and must indemnify the Landlord, and keep him indemnified, both during the Term and following the end of it, against all losses in respect of any contravention of those Acts.

3.12.2   *Consent for applications*

The Tenant must not make any application for planning permission without the consent of the Landlord[, whose consent may not be unreasonably withheld [or delayed] [in any case where application for and implementation of the planning permission will not create or give rise to any tax liability for the Landlord or where the Tenant indemnifies the Landlord against such liability][112]].

112   These words were devised when development land tax — abolished by the Finance Act 1985 s 93 — applied. The provision may, however, still be relevant should similar taxation be introduced in the future.

3.12.3   *Permissions and notices*

The Tenant must at his expense obtain any planning permissions and serve any notices that may be required for the carrying out of any development on or at the Premises.

[607]

3.12.4   *Charges and levies*

Subject only to any statutory direction to the contrary, the Tenant must pay and satisfy any charge or levy that may subsequently be imposed under the Planning Acts in respect of the carrying out or maintenance of any development on or at the Premises.

3.12.5   *Pre-conditions for development*

Notwithstanding any consent that may be granted by the Landlord under this Lease, the Tenant must not carry out any development on or at the Premises until all necessary notices under the Planning Acts have been served and copies produced to the Landlord, all necessary permissions under the Planning Acts have been obtained and produced to the Landlord, and the Landlord has acknowledged that every necessary planning permission is acceptable to him[, such acknowledgement not to be unreasonably withheld]. The Landlord may refuse to acknowledge his acceptance of a planning permission on the grounds that any condition contained in it or anything omitted from it or the period referred to in it would[, in the [reasonable] opinion of the Surveyor,] be, or be likely to be, prejudicial to the Landlord or to his reversionary interest in the Premises or any of adjoining property of the Landlord whether during the Term or following the end of it.

3.12.6   *Completion of development*

Where a condition of any planning permission granted for development begun before the end of the Term[113] requires works to be carried out to the Premises by a date after the end of the Term, the Tenant must, unless the Landlord directs otherwise, finish those works before the end of the Term.

113   The provisions of clause 1.21 [564] INTERPRETATION OF 'THE LAST YEAR OF THE TERM' AND 'THE END OF THE TERM' should be noted.

3.12.7   *Security for compliance with conditions*

In any case where a planning permission is granted subject to conditions, and if the Landlord [reasonably] so requires, the Tenant must provide sufficient security for his compliance with the conditions and must not implement the planning permission until that security has been provided.

[3.12.8   *Appeal against refusal or conditions*[114]

If [reasonably] required by the Landlord to do so, but[, where reasonable,] at his own cost, the Tenant must appeal against any refusal of planning permission or the imposition of any conditions on a planning permission relating to the Premises following an application for planning permission by the Tenant.]

114   The tenant should not accept this clause because it could impose on him the cost of a planning appeal. He should strike it out, leaving planning appeals to be a matter for discussion as and when the situation arises during the term, or at least insist that he should bear the cost only where reasonable.

[608]

3.13   Plans, documents and information

3.13.1   *Evidence of compliance with this Lease*

If so requested, the Tenant must produce to the Landlord or the Surveyor any plans, documents and other evidence the Landlord [reasonably] requires in order to satisfy himself that the provisions of this Lease have been complied with.

3.13.2   *Information for renewal or rent review*

If so requested, the Tenant must produce to the Landlord, the Surveyor, or any person acting as the third party determining the Rent in default of agreement between the Landlord and the Tenant under any provisions for rent review contained in this Lease, any information [reasonably] requested in writing in relation to any pending or intended step under the 1954 Act or the implementation of any provisions for rent review.

3.14   Indemnities[115]

The Tenant must keep the Landlord fully indemnified against all losses arising directly or indirectly out of any act, omission or negligence of the Tenant or any persons at the Estate expressly or impliedly[116] with his authority [and under his control][117], or any breach or non-observance by the Tenant of the covenants, conditions or other provisions of this Lease or any of the matters to which this demise is subject.

115   The tenant should seek to delete all *general* indemnity provisions on the basis that his remedies for breach of covenant and in tort adequately protect the landlord. The tenant should argue that an indemnity unreasonably extends his liability. If, however, this clause is omitted, it should be replaced by a covenant to observe and perform restrictions etc to which the demise is subject, possibly coupled with a *specific* indemnity in respect of any breach.
116   The expression 'impliedly' is intended to include a caller, such as a tradesman, where there has been no express invitation but the person cannot be classed as a trespasser.
117   The tenant should add the words in square brackets.

[609]

3.15   Reletting boards and viewing

[Unless [a valid court application under the 1954 Act Section 24 has been made or][118] the Tenant is [otherwise] entitled to remain in occupation or to a new tenancy of the Premises, at any time during *(or as required)* At any time during] the *(state period, eg last 6 months)* of the [Contractual][119] Term and at any time thereafter, [and whenever the Lease Rents or any part of them are in arrear and unpaid for longer than *(state period, eg 14 days)*,] the Tenant must permit the Landlord to enter the Premises and fix and retain anywhere on them a board advertising them for reletting. While any such board is on the Premises the Tenant must permit viewing of the Premises at reasonable times of the day.

118   This phrase and the word 'otherwise' should be omitted if the operation of the security of tenure provisions in the Landlord and Tenant Act 1954 ss 24–28 is to be excluded in relation to the lease.
119   This defined term will require amendment where the operation of the security of tenure provisions in the Landlord and Tenant Act 1954 ss 24–28 is to be excluded in relation to the lease: see note 6 to clause 1.4 [559] 'THE [CONTRACTUAL] TERM'.

3.16   Obstruction and encroachment

3.16.1   *Obstruction of windows*

The Tenant must not stop up, darken or obstruct any windows or light belonging to the Premises.

3.16.2   *Encroachments*

The Tenant must take all [reasonable] steps to prevent the construction of any new window, light, opening, doorway, path, passage, pipe or the making of any encroachment or the acquisition of any easement in relation to the Premises and must notify the Landlord immediately if any such thing is constructed, encroachment is made or easement acquired, or any attempt is made to construct such a thing, to encroach or acquire an easement. At the request of the Landlord the Tenant must adopt such means as are [reasonably] required to prevent the construction of such a thing, the making of any encroachment or the acquisition of any easement[120].

120   For a shorter clause see vol 22(3) (1997 Reissue) LANDLORD AND TENANT (BUSINESS TENANCIES) Form 172 [6696].

[610]

3.17   Yielding up

At the end of the Term[121] the Tenant must yield up the Premises with vacant possession, decorated and repaired in accordance with and in the condition required by the provisions of this Lease, give up all keys of the Premises to the Landlord, remove tenant's fixtures and fittings [if requested to do so by the Landlord], and remove any signs erected by the Tenant or any of his predecessors in title in, upon or near the Premises, immediately making good any damage caused by their removal.

121   The provisions of clause 1.21 [564] INTERPRETATION OF 'THE LAST YEAR OF THE TERM' AND 'THE END OF THE TERM' should be noted.

3.18   Interest on arrears[122]

The Tenant must pay interest on any of the Lease Rents[123] or other sums due under this Lease that are not paid [within *(state period, eg 14 days)* of the date due] whether formally demanded or not[, the interest to be recoverable as rent][124]. Nothing in this clause entitles the Tenant to withhold or delay any payment of the Rent or any other sum due under this Lease or affects the rights of the Landlord in relation to any non-payment.

122   As to the covenant to pay interest see vol 22(1) (2003 Reissue) LANDLORD AND TENANT (BUSINESS TENANCIES) Paragraph 154 [767].

123   As to the definition of 'the Lease Rents' see clause 1.38 [569] 'THE RENT'.

124   These words seek to attach to interest the rights associated with rent. As to the reasons for this see vol 22(1) (2003 Reissue) LANDLORD AND TENANT (BUSINESS TENANCIES) Paragraph 151 [761]. However, this clause applies to interest on arrears of other sums payable under the lease that are not rent as well as to rent itself, and it might be felt inappropriate for interest to be deemed to be rent where the payment on which the interest is due is not itself rent.

3.19   Statutory notices

The Tenant must give full particulars to the Landlord of any notice, direction, order or proposal relating to the Premises made, given or issued to the Tenant by any government department or local, public, regulatory or other authority or court within *(state period, eg 7 days)* of receipt, and if so requested by the Landlord must produce it to the Landlord. The Tenant must without delay take all necessary steps to comply with the notice, direction or order. At the request of the Landlord, but at his own cost, the Tenant must make or join with the Landlord in making any objection or representation the Landlord deems expedient against or in respect of any notice, direction, order or proposal.

[611]

3.20   Keyholders

The Tenant must ensure that at all times [the Landlord has *(or as required)* the Landlord and the local police force have] written notice of the name, home address and home telephone number of at least *(state number, eg 2)* keyholders of the Premises.

3.21   Viewing on sale of reversion

The Tenant must[, on reasonable notice,] at any time during the Term, permit prospective purchasers of the Landlord's reversion or any other interest superior to the Term, or agents instructed in connection with the sale of the reversion or such an interest, to view the Premises without interruption provided they have the prior written authority of the Landlord or his agents.

3.22   Defective premises

The Tenant must give notice to the Landlord of any defect in the Premises that might give rise to an obligation on the Landlord to do or refrain from doing anything in order to comply with the provisions of this Lease or the duty of care imposed on the Landlord, whether pursuant to the Defective Premises Act 1972 or otherwise, and must at all times display and maintain any notices the Landlord from time to time [reasonably] requires him to display at the Premises.

3.23   Replacement guarantor[125]

3.23.1   *Guarantor replacement events*

In this clause 3.23 references to a 'guarantor replacement event' are references, in the case of an individual, to death, bankruptcy, having a receiving order made against him or having a receiver appointed under the Mental Health Act 1983 or entering into a voluntary arrangement and, in the case of a company, to passing a resolution to wind up, entering into liquidation, a voluntary arrangement or administration or having a receiver appointed.

125   As to guarantors see vol 22(1) (2003 Reissue) LANDLORD AND TENANT (BUSINESS TENANCIES) Paragraph 71 [278] et seq. The tenant should propose that, on the execution of a guarantee by a new guarantor, the original guarantor or his estate should be released.

[612]

3.23.2   *Action on occurrence of a guarantor replacement event*

Where during the relevant Liability Period a guarantor replacement event occurs to the Guarantor or any person who has entered into an authorised guarantee agreement, the Tenant must give notice of the event to the Landlord within *(state period, eg 14 days)* of his becoming aware of it. If so required by the Landlord, the Tenant must within *(state period, eg 28 days)* obtain some other person [reasonably] acceptable to the Landlord to execute a guarantee in the form of the Guarantor's covenants in clause 6 GUARANTEE PROVISIONS or the authorised guarantee agreement in schedule 6 THE AUTHORISED GUARANTEE AGREEMENT, as the case may be, for the residue of the relevant Liability Period.

3.24   **Exercise of the Landlord's rights**[126]

The Tenant must permit the Landlord to exercise any of the rights granted to him by virtue of the provisions of this Lease at all times during the Term without interruption or interference.

126   The provisions of clause 1.36 [569] REFERENCES TO RIGHTS OF ACCESS should be noted.

3.25   **The Industrial Covenants**

The Tenant must observe and perform the Industrial Covenants.

3.26   **Costs of grant of this Lease**[127]

[The Tenant must pay the fees and disbursements of the Landlord's solicitors, agents and surveyors and all other costs and expenses incurred by the Landlord in relation to the negotiation, preparation, execution and grant of this Lease. *(or as required)* On the grant of this Lease the Tenant must pay the sum of £... as a contribution to the Landlord's solicitors' charges for the negotiation, execution and completion of this Lease].

127   As to covenants to pay the landlord's legal fees see vol 22(1) (2003 Reissue) LANDLORD AND TENANT (BUSINESS TENANCIES) Paragraph 155 [769]. As to payment of VAT on legal costs by a person other than the solicitor's own client see the Information Binder: Property [1]: VAT and Property.

[613]

3.27   **Consent to the Landlord's release**[128]

The Tenant must not unreasonably withhold consent to a request made by the Landlord under the 1995 Act Section 8 for a release from all or any of the landlord covenants of this Lease.

128   By virtue of the Landlord and Tenant (Covenants) Act 1995 each successive landlord remains bound by the landlord covenants of the lease unless released under the machinery provided in the Act — as to which see vol 22(1) (2003 Reissue) LANDLORD AND TENANT (BUSINESS TENANCIES) Paragraph 57 [252] et seq — or by a specific release given otherwise (see the Landlord and Tenant (Covenants) Act 1995 s 26(1)(a)). Bald statements limiting the landlord's liability, such as those in use before the commencement of the Act, will not withstand the wide anti-avoidance provisions of the Landlord and Tenant (Covenants) Act 1995 s 25, and covenants by the tenant to give consent to release are unlikely to fall within the exception of s 26. None of the ingenious schemes for limiting the landlord's liability, eg making all covenants personal, suggested in the early days of the 1995 Act has stood up to critical scrutiny, although none has yet been tested by the courts. Thus landlords look instead to the alternative of a right of redress if the tenant makes an unreasonable objection to release. This covenant is modelled on the provisions of the Landlord and Tenant Act 1988, which gives tenants a right of action for loss caused by landlords who unreasonably withhold or delay consent to assignment (see the Landlord and Tenant Act 1988 s 4). In view of the strict time limits under the Landlord and Tenant (Covenants) Act 1995 and the fact that failure to respond to the landlord's request for release is deemed to be consent, it is not thought necessary to extend this covenant to unreasonable delay in replying to such a request.

[614]–[620]

4   THE LANDLORD'S COVENANTS

The Landlord covenants with the Tenant to observe and perform the requirements of this clause 4.

4.1   Quiet enjoyment[129]

The Landlord must permit the Tenant peaceably and quietly to hold and enjoy the Premises without any interruption or disturbance from or by the Landlord or any person claiming under or in trust for him[130] [or by title paramount][131].

129   As to the landlord's covenant for quiet enjoyment see vol 22(1) (2003 Reissue) LANDLORD AND TENANT (BUSINESS TENANCIES) Paragraph 168 [856]. As to covenants for quiet enjoyment generally see 23 Halsbury's Laws (4th Edn Reissue) LANDLORD AND TENANT.
        The words 'the Tenant paying the rents reserved by and observing and performing the covenants on its part and the conditions contained in this lease' are frequently included in a covenant for quiet enjoyment, but they have no practical effect and do not make payment of the rent and performance of the covenants into conditions precedent to the operation of the covenant for quiet enjoyment: see *Edge v Boileau* (1885) 16 QBD 117; *Dawson v Dyer* (1833) 5 B & Ad 584; *Yorkbrook Investments Ltd v Batten* (1985) 52 P & CR 51, [1985] 2 EGLR 100, CA.
130   The covenant is frequently expressed to apply to 'lawful' interruption or by persons 'rightfully' claiming under the landlord, but it seems that the addition of these words has no practical effect: see *Williams v Gabriel* [1906] 1 KB 155 at 157.
131   Without the reference to title paramount the landlord is liable only for the acts of persons so far as they are his successors in title or have authority from him to do the acts complained of: *Harrison Ainslie & Co v Muncaster* [1891] 2 QB 680, CA; *Matania v National Provincial Bank Ltd and Elevenist Syndicate Ltd* [1936] 2 All ER 633, CA; *Miller v Emcer Products Ltd* [1956] Ch 304, [1956] 1 All ER 237, CA. If a subtenant holds under a lease containing a qualified covenant on the part of his landlord — ie one where there is no reference to title paramount — and the head landlord evicts the subtenant because the head rent has not been paid, this is not a breach of the covenant for quiet enjoyment (see *Spencer v Marriott* (1823) 1 B & C 457; *Dennett v Atherton* (1872) LR 7 QB 316, Ex Ch), but it is a breach if the sublandlord submits to judgment in an action by a person with no title to sue, and the subtenant is in consequence evicted (*Cohen v Tannar* [1900] 2 QB 609, CA). Actionable interruptions under this covenant are not confined to interference with title or possession, but may extend to interference with the ordinary and lawful enjoyment of the premises: *Sanderson v Berwick-upon-Tweed Corpn* (1884) 13 QBD 547 at 551, CA. As to persons claiming 'under' the landlord see *Celsteel Ltd v Alton House Holdings Ltd (No 2)* [1987] 2 All ER 240, [1987] 1 WLR 291, CA.

4.2   Repairs

4.2.1   *The Estate Roads*

The Landlord must repair the Estate Roads, maintain them and keep them reasonably clean.

4.2.2   *The Adjoining Conduits*

The Landlord must repair the Adjoining Conduits, maintain them and where necessary replace them.

4.2.3   *Street lighting*

The Landlord must light the Estate Roads to such standard and during such hours as the Landlord [acting reasonably *(or as required)* in his absolute discretion] deems appropriate.

4.2.4   *Planted areas*

The Landlord must cultivate any planted or grassed parts of the Estate and keep them [reasonably] neat and tidy.

[621]

5   INSURANCE[132]

5.1   Warranty as to convictions[133]

The Tenant warrants that before the execution of this document he has disclosed to the Landlord in writing any conviction, judgment or finding of any court or tribunal relating to the Tenant[, or any director, other officer or major shareholder of the Tenant,] of such a nature as to be likely to affect the decision of any insurer or underwriter to grant or to continue insurance of any of the Insured Risks.

132   As to insurance see vol 22(1) (2003 Reissue) LANDLORD AND TENANT (BUSINESS TENANCIES) Paragraph 227 [1021] et seq.
133   A contract of insurance is one uberrimae fidei. The insured must disclose to the insurers all material facts that are within his actual or presumed knowledge, whether there is a formal proposal form or not. A fact is material if non-disclosure of it would influence a prudent and reasonable insurer. This warranty is designed to rebut any suggestion by the landlord's insurers that the landlord had knowledge of the matters concerned. By inserting this clause in the lease, and thus specifically bringing the point to the tenant's attention, the landlord can argue that he has done all that is practical to establish the existence of any such matters. The absence of any written disclosure pursuant to this clause is strong evidence that the landlord has no actual or presumed knowledge of such matters. Further, the landlord has a right of action against the tenant for any breach of the warranty. As to non-disclosure and misrepresentation in contracts of non-marine insurance see 22 Halsbury's Laws (4th Edn Reissue) INSURANCE.

[622]

5.2   Covenant to insure

The Landlord covenants with the Tenant to insure the Premises [in the joint names of the Landlord and the Tenant[134] [and any other person the Landlord [reasonably] requires][135]] unless the insurance is vitiated by any act of the Tenant or by anyone at the Premises expressly or by implication[136] with the Tenant's authority [and under his control][137].

134   As to insurance in joint names see vol 22(1) (2003 Reissue) LANDLORD AND TENANT (BUSINESS TENANCIES) Paragraph 229 [1024].
135   Unless some expression such as this is included, a covenant to insure in specified names is broken by insurance in those names and other names: see *Penniall v Harborne* (1848) 11 QB 368.
136   The expression 'by implication' is intended to include a caller on the premises, such as a tradesman, where there has been no express invitation but the person cannot be classed as a trespasser.
137   The tenant should add the words in square brackets.

5.3   Details of the insurance

5.3.1   *Office, underwriters and agency*

Insurance is to be effected in such [substantial and reputable] insurance office, or with such underwriters[138], and through such agency as the Landlord from time to time decides[139].

138   The expression 'insurance office' would probably not include Lloyd's underwriters. The landlord's right to nominate the office and agency is absolute, with no implied restrictions: *Berrycroft Management Co Ltd v Sinclair Gardens Investments (Kensington) Ltd* (1996) 75 P & CR 210, [1997] 1 EGLR 47, CA.
139   It should be noted that it is recommended 'best practice' in circumstances where the building is let to one tenant and the landlord insures that, in appropriate cases, the tenant should be given the opportunity to influence the choice of insurer: see vol 22(1) (2003 Reissue) LANDLORD AND TENANT (BUSINESS TENANCIES) Paragraph 85 [401] and 'A code of practice for commercial leases in England and Wales (2nd edition)' which can be found in vol 22(1) (2003 Reissue) LANDLORD AND TENANT (BUSINESS TENANCIES) at Form 1 [4501].

[623]

5.3.2 *Insurance cover*[140]

Insurance must be effected for the following amounts —

5.3.2.1   the sum that the Landlord is from time to time advised [by the Surveyor] is the full cost of rebuilding and reinstating the Premises, including [VAT[141],] architects', surveyors', engineers', solicitors' and all other professional persons' fees, the fees payable on any applications for planning permission or other permits or consents that may be required in relation to rebuilding or reinstating the Premises, the cost of preparation of the site including shoring-up, debris removal, demolition, site clearance and any works that may be required by statute, and incidental expenses, and

5.3.2.2   loss of the Rent, taking account of any rent review that may be due, for *(state period, eg 3 years)* or such longer period as the Landlord from time to time [reasonably] requires for planning and carrying out the rebuilding or reinstatement.

140   As to the sum insured see vol 22(1) (2003 Reissue) LANDLORD AND TENANT (BUSINESS TENANCIES) Paragraph 231 [1028] et seq.
        It should be noted that it is recommended 'best practice' that, where the landlord has arranged insurance, the terms should be made known to the tenant and any material change in the insurance should be notified to the tenant: see Recommendation 14 of 'A code of practice for commercial leases in England and Wales (2nd edition)' which can be found in vol 22(1) (2003 Reissue) LANDLORD AND TENANT (BUSINESS TENANCIES) at Form 1 [4501].

141   As to VAT and the level of insurance cover see the Information Binder: Property [1]: VAT and Property. The expense of insuring against the VAT payable on reinstatement costs is not justified where the landlord has opted to tax and is able to recover the VAT. There is a theoretical possibility that a future landlord may not opt to tax and that the sum insured may then be too low. It is also possible that a landlord may wish to preserve the 'exempt' status of a property. Normally, however, the cost of reinstatement need not expressly mention VAT, although the cashflow implications of having to pay VAT on construction works need to be remembered.

5.3.3 *Risks insured*[142]

Insurance must be effected against damage or destruction by any of the Insured Risks to the extent that such insurance may ordinarily be arranged [with a substantial and reputable insurer] for properties such as the Premises, subject to such excesses, exclusions or limitations as the insurer requires.

142   As to risks to be insured against see vol 22(1) (2003 Reissue) LANDLORD AND TENANT (BUSINESS TENANCIES) Paragraph 235 [1033].
        It should be noted that it is recommended 'best practice' that, where the landlord has arranged insurance, the terms should be made known to the tenant and any material change in the insurance should be notified to the tenant: see Recommendation 14 of 'A code of practice for commercial leases in England and Wales (2nd edition)' which can be found in vol 22(1) (2003 Reissue) LANDLORD AND TENANT (BUSINESS TENANCIES) at Form 1 [4501].

[624]

5.4   Payment of the Insurance Rent

The Tenant covenants to pay the Insurance Rent for the period starting on the Rent Commencement Date and ending on the day before the next policy renewal date on the date of this Lease, and subsequently to pay the Insurance Rent on demand and, if so demanded, in advance of the policy renewal date[, but not more than *(state period, eg … months)* in advance].

5.5   Suspension of the Rent[143]

5.5.1   *Events giving rise to suspension*

If and whenever the Premises or any part of them are damaged or destroyed by one or more of the Insured Risks[144] [— except one against which insurance may not ordinarily be arranged [with a substantial and reputable insurer] for properties such as the Premises unless the Landlord has in fact insured against that risk —] so that the Premises or any part of them are unfit for occupation or use, or the Estate Roads or the Adjoining Conduits are damaged or destroyed so that the Premises or any part of them are unfit for occupation or use[145], and payment of the insurance money is not wholly or partly refused because of any act or default of the Tenant or anyone at the Premises expressly or by implication[146] with his authority [and under his control][147], then the provisions of clause 5.5.2 SUSPENDING THE RENT are to have effect.

143   As to suspension of rent see vol 22(1) (2003 Reissue) LANDLORD AND TENANT (BUSINESS TENANCIES) Paragraph 241 [1044] et seq.

144   It should be noted that it is recommended 'best practice' that if premises are so damaged by an uninsured risk as to prevent occupation, the tenant should be allowed to terminate the lease unless the landlord agrees to reinstate at his own cost: see vol 22(1) (2003 Reissue) LANDLORD AND TENANT (BUSINESS TENANCIES) Paragraph 85 [402] and 'A code of practice for commercial leases in England and Wales (2nd edition)' which can be found in vol 22(1) (2003 Reissue) LANDLORD AND TENANT (BUSINESS TENANCIES) at Form 1 [4501]. If adopted, this recommendation involves rent suspension also becoming operative in the event of the premises becoming unusable because of uninsured risks.

145   The premises may be rendered unfit for use because the tenant is unable to gain access to them or because the supply of services is interrupted. In a letting such as this, the estate roads and the adjoining conduits may not be insured and so the point must be dealt with expressly. Adding the roads and conduits into the general provision protects the tenant only if the landlord insures them.

146   The expression 'by implication' is intended to include a caller on the premises, such as a tradesman, where there has been no express invitation but the person cannot be classed as a trespasser.

147   The tenant should add the words in square brackets.

[625]

5.5.2   *Suspending the Rent*

In the circumstances mentioned in clause 5.5.1 EVENTS GIVING RISE TO SUSPENSION the Rent, or a fair proportion of it according to the nature and the extent of the damage sustained, is to cease to be payable until the Premises, or the affected part, or the Estate Roads or the Adjoining Conduits have been rebuilt or reinstated so as to render the Premises, or the affected part, fit for occupation and use, [or until the end of *(state period, eg 3 years)* from the destruction or damage, whichever period is the shorter,][148] [the proportion of the Rent suspended and the period of the suspension to be determined by the Surveyor acting as an expert and not as an arbitrator *(or as required)* any dispute as to the proportion of the Rent suspended or the period of the suspension to be determined in accordance with the Arbitration Act 1996 by an arbitrator to be appointed by agreement between the Landlord and the Tenant or in default by the President or other proper officer for the time being of the Royal Institution of Chartered Surveyors on the application of either the Landlord or the Tenant].

148   As to the length of the suspension and the tenant's concerns see vol 22(1) (2003 Reissue) LANDLORD AND TENANT (BUSINESS TENANCIES) Paragraph 244 [1048]. For a provision extending suspension of the rent where reinstatement is delayed see vol 22(3) (1997 Reissue) LANDLORD AND TENANT (BUSINESS TENANCIES) Form 111 [6495].

5.6   Reinstatement and termination[149]

5.6.1   *Obligation to obtain permissions*

If and whenever the Premises or any part of them are damaged or destroyed by one or more of the Insured Risks [— except one against which insurance may not ordinarily be arranged [with a substantial and reputable insurer] for properties such as the Premises, unless the Landlord has in fact insured against that risk —], or the Estate Roads or the Adjoining Conduits are damaged or destroyed so that the Premises or any part of them are unfit for occupation or use, and payment of the insurance money is not wholly or partly refused because of any act or default of the Tenant or anyone at the Premises expressly or by implication[150] with his authority [and under his control][151], the Landlord must use his best endeavours[152] to obtain the planning permissions and other permits and consents ('permissions') that may be required under the Planning Acts or otherwise to enable him to rebuild and reinstate the Premises, the Estate Roads or the Adjoining Conduits.

[626]

---

149   It has been held that, in the absence of an express covenant to reinstate, where the landlord must keep the premises adequately insured against comprehensive risks and the insurance is effected at the tenant's expense, the obligation is one intended to enure for the benefit of both parties: *Mumford Hotels Ltd v Wheler* [1964] Ch 117, [1963] 3 All ER 250; see also *Mark Rowlands Ltd v Berni Inns Ltd* [1986] QB 211, [1985] 3 All ER 473, CA; *Lonsdale & Thompson Ltd v Black Arrow Group plc* [1993] Ch 361, [1993] 3 All ER 648. This is not, however, a general principle of law and the tenant should therefore always require a specific covenant to reinstate.

These provisions are restricted to circumstances where damage or destruction is caused by an insured risk. It should be noted that it is recommended 'best practice' that if premises are so damaged by an uninsured risk as to prevent occupation, the tenant should be allowed to terminate the lease unless the landlord agrees to reinstate at his own cost: see vol 22(1) (2003 Reissue) LANDLORD AND TENANT (BUSINESS TENANCIES) Paragraph 85 [401] and 'A code of practice for commercial leases in England and Wales (2nd edition)' which can be found in vol 22(1) (2003 Reissue) LANDLORD AND TENANT (BUSINESS TENANCIES) at Form 1 [4501].

As to termination where reinstatement is not possible see vol 22(1) (2003 Reissue) LANDLORD AND TENANT (BUSINESS TENANCIES) Paragraph 237 [1037]. For a provision for termination or surrender on destruction or substantial damage see vol 22(3) (1997 Reissue) LANDLORD AND TENANT (BUSINESS TENANCIES) Form 107 [6483].

150   The expression 'by implication' is intended to include a caller on the premises, such as a tradesman, where there has been no express invitation but the person cannot be classed as a trespasser.

151   The tenant should add the words in square brackets.

152   The extent of the duty to use best endeavours depends upon the facts in each case: see *Monkland v Jack Barclay Ltd* [1951] 2 KB 252, [1951] 1 All ER 714, CA; *Terrell v Mabie Todd & Co Ltd* [1952] 2 TLR 574; *NW Investments (Erdington) Ltd v Swani* (1970) 214 Estates Gazette 1115. In the light of *IBM United Kingdom Ltd v Rockware Glass Ltd* [1980] FSR 335, CA, it may be that there is little practical difference between a covenant to use best endeavours, a covenant to use reasonable endeavours and a covenant to take all reasonable steps.

[627]

5.6.2   *Obligation to reinstate*

Subject to the provisions of clause 5.6.3 RELIEF FROM THE OBLIGATION TO REINSTATE, and, if any permissions are required, after they have been obtained, the Landlord must as soon as reasonably practicable apply all money received in respect of the insurance effected by the Landlord pursuant to this Lease, except sums in respect of loss of the Rent, in rebuilding or reinstating the Premises, or as the case may be in rebuilding or reinstating the Estate Roads or the Adjoining Conduits[, making up any difference between the cost of rebuilding and reinstating and the money received out of his own money][153].

153   Where the landlord's covenant is 'to apply all money received in respect of the insurance in rebuilding or reinstating' rather than simply 'to reinstate', it seems that the landlord does not have to complete the work out of his own money if the insurance money is insufficient because he has complied with his covenant by laying out all the insurance money received. The situation is different if the tenant can establish that the landlord was in breach of his covenant to insure for the full cost of reinstatement and that this has caused the shortfall: see *Mumford Hotels Ltd v Wheler* [1964] Ch 117, [1963] 3 All ER 250. The tenant should, therefore, require a specific covenant from the landlord to make up any shortfall, to prevent a situation in which the landlord refuses to complete the rebuilding. This is of particular concern if the suspension of rent proviso is expressed to operate for a limited period, because on the expiry of that period the tenant becomes liable for rent unless he can satisfy the court that the lease has been frustrated.

It should be noted that it is recommended 'best practice' that if premises are so damaged by an uninsured risk as to prevent occupation, the tenant should be allowed to terminate the lease unless the landlord agrees to reinstate at his own cost: see vol 22(1) (2003 Reissue) LANDLORD AND TENANT (BUSINESS TENANCIES) Paragraph 85 [401] and 'A code of practice for commercial leases in England and Wales (2nd edition)'which can be found in vol 22(1) (2003 Reissue) LANDLORD AND TENANT (BUSINESS TENANCIES) at Form 1 [4501]. If this recommendation is adopted and the landlord merely covenants to apply insurance money received, the principle should be extended to damage or destruction resulting from insured risks in circumstances where the insurance money is insufficient to enable reinstatement to be completed.

For a proviso relieving from the obligation to reinstate in the same form see vol 22(3) (1997 Reissue) LANDLORD AND TENANT (BUSINESS TENANCIES) Form 106 [6482].

[628]

5.6.3   *Relief from the obligation to reinstate*[154]

The Landlord need not rebuild or reinstate the Premises, the Estate Roads or the Adjoining Conduits if and for so long as rebuilding or reinstating is prevented because —

5.6.3.1   the Landlord, despite using his best endeavours[155], cannot obtain any necessary permission,

5.6.3.2   any permission is granted subject to a lawful condition with which [it is impossible for *(or as required)* in all the circumstances it is unreasonable to expect] the Landlord to comply,

5.6.3.3   there is some defect or deficiency in the site on which the rebuilding or reinstatement is to take place that [renders it impossible *(or as required)* means it can only be undertaken at a cost that is unreasonable in all the circumstances],

5.6.3.4   the Landlord is unable to obtain access to the site to rebuild or reinstate,

5.6.3.5   the rebuilding or reinstating is prevented by war, act of God, government action[, strike or lock-out], or

because of the occurrence of any other circumstances beyond the Landlord's control.

154   As to the need for a right to terminate where reinstatement is not possible see vol 22(1) (2003 Reissue) LANDLORD AND TENANT (BUSINESS TENANCIES) Paragraph 226 [998].

155   The extent of the duty to use best endeavours depends upon the facts in each case: see *Monkland v Jack Barclay Ltd* [1951] 2 KB 252, [1951] 1 All ER 714, CA; *Terrell v Mabie Todd & Co Ltd* [1952] 2 TLR 574; *NW Investments (Erdington) Ltd v Swani* (1970) 214 Estates Gazette 1115. In the light of *IBM United Kingdom Ltd v Rockware Glass Ltd* [1980] FSR 335, CA, it may be that there is little practical difference between a covenant to use best endeavours, a covenant to use reasonable endeavours and a covenant to take all reasonable steps.

5.6.4 *Notice to terminate*[156]

If at the end of a period[157] of *(state period, eg 3 years)* starting on the date of the damage or destruction the Premises, the Estate Roads, or the Adjoining Conduits have not been rebuilt or reinstated so that the Premises are fit for the Tenant's occupation and use, either the Landlord or the Tenant may by notice served at any time within *(state period, eg 6 months)* of the end of that period ('a notice to terminate following failure to reinstate') implement the provisions of clause 5.6.5 TERMINATION FOLLOWING FAILURE TO REINSTATE[158].

156   For alternative provisions where the landlord's right to terminate is limited to specified circumstances see vol 22(3) (1997 Reissue) LANDLORD AND TENANT (BUSINESS TENANCIES) Form 109 [6492].
157   The period to be inserted must be carefully considered. Particular regard should be had to the terms of any rent suspension provision and the extent of insurance cover for loss of rent.
158   As to the effect of the Landlord and Tenant Act 1954 see vol 22(1) (2003 Reissue) LANDLORD AND TENANT (BUSINESS TENANCIES) Paragraph 226 [998].

[629]

5.6.5 *Termination following failure to reinstate*

On service of a notice to terminate following failure to reinstate, the Term is to cease absolutely — but without prejudice to any rights or remedies that may have accrued[159]— and all money received in respect of the insurance effected by the Landlord pursuant to this Lease is to belong to the Landlord absolutely[160].

159   The effect of this clause is that the right to terminate arises after the end of the appropriate period, whatever the reason for the delay, but the tenant still has a right of action against the landlord where the landlord is in breach of his covenant to reinstate.
160   In the absence of provision for ownership of the insurance money the position is uncertain. In *Re King, Robinson v Gray* [1963] Ch 459, [1963] 1 All ER 781, CA it was held that the insurance money belongs to the party who paid the premiums even if the insurance was placed in the joint names of the landlord and the tenant. The dissenting view of Denning MR that insurance in joint names envisages that each party should be insured as to his insurable interest and that the insurance money should therefore be divided in proportion to their interests in the property should, however, be noted. In *Beacon Carpets Ltd v Kirby* [1985] QB 755, [1984] 2 All ER 726, CA the court adhered to this view and held that the proportion payable depended on the parties' interests in the premises at the time of the destruction. The landlord will prefer an express provision in the lease for the insurance money to be retained by him in full if reinstatement proves impossible. The tenant ought perhaps to accept that it would be unrealistic to amend this to provide for the insurance money to belong to the tenant, but should suggest that a provision be inserted under which the money is to be divided in accordance with their respective interests in the premises at the time when the insurance money became due. For an alternative provision for ownership of the insurance money etc see vol 22(3) (1997 Reissue) LANDLORD AND TENANT (BUSINESS TENANCIES) Form 108 [6491].

[630]

5.7   Tenant's further insurance covenants[161]

The Tenant covenants with the Landlord to observe and perform the requirements of this clause 5.7.

161   In order to comply with many of these covenants, the tenant will need to be supplied with details of the landlord's insurance policy. In any event, it should be noted that it is recommended 'best practice' that where the landlord has arranged insurance, the terms should be made known to the tenant and any material change in the insurance should be notified to the tenant: see Recommendation 14 of 'A code of practice for commercial leases in England and Wales (2nd edition)' which can be found in vol 22(1) (2003 Reissue) LANDLORD AND TENANT (BUSINESS TENANCIES) at Form 1 [4501].

5.7.1 *Requirements of insurers*

The Tenant must comply with all the requirements and recommendations of the insurers.

5.7.2   *Policy avoidance and additional premiums*

The Tenant must not do or omit anything that could cause any insurance policy on or in relation to the Premises to become wholly or partly void or voidable, or do or omit anything by which additional insurance premiums may become payable unless he has previously notified the Landlord and has agreed to pay the increased premium.

5.7.3   *Fire-fighting equipment*

The Tenant must keep the Premises supplied with such fire fighting equipment [as the insurers and the fire authority require and must maintain the equipment to their satisfaction *(or as required)* as the Landlord reasonably requires and must maintain the equipment to the reasonable satisfaction of the insurers and the fire authority] and in efficient working order. At least once in every *(state period, eg 6 months)* the Tenant must cause any sprinkler system and other fire fighting equipment to be inspected by a competent person.

5.7.4   *Combustible materials*

The Tenant must not store on the Premises or bring onto them anything of a specially combustible, inflammable or explosive nature, and must comply with the requirements and recommendations of the fire authority [and the [reasonable] requirements of the Landlord] as to fire precautions relating to the Premises.

5.7.5   *Fire escapes, equipment and doors*

The Tenant must not obstruct the access to any fire equipment or the means of escape from the Premises or lock any fire door while the Premises are occupied.

[631]

5.7.6   *Notice of events affecting the policy*

The Tenant must give immediate notice to the Landlord of any event that might affect any insurance policy on or relating to the Premises and any event against which the Landlord may have insured under this Lease.

5.7.7   *Notice of convictions*

The Tenant must give immediate notice to the Landlord of any conviction, judgment or finding of any court or tribunal relating to the Tenant, or any director other officer or major shareholder of the Tenant, of such a nature as to be likely to affect the decision of any insurer or underwriter to grant or to continue any insurance[162].

162   This clause provides a continuation of the warranty given by the tenant in clause 5.1 [622] WARRANTY AS TO CONVICTIONS. As to non-disclosure and misrepresentation in contracts of non-marine insurance see 22 Halsbury's Laws (4th Edn Reissue) INSURANCE.

5.7.8   *Other insurance*

If at any time the Tenant is entitled to the benefit of any insurance of the Premises that is not effected or maintained in pursuance of any obligation contained in this Lease, the Tenant must apply all money received by virtue of that insurance in making good the loss or damage in respect of which the money is received[163].

163   An insurance policy frequently provides that, if there is any other insurance effected by or on behalf of the insured covering the premises that are the subject of the policy, the insurers are liable only for a rateable proportion of the damage. Such provisions extend to a case where one of the policies is in the joint names of the persons interested in the premises and the other is in the name of one only of those persons: *Halifax Building Society v Keighley* [1931] 2 KB 248. Therefore, at least when the insurance is in joint names, the landlord needs to ensure that the tenant will use all money received under any policy he has effected to reinstate the premises.

[5.7.9   *Reinstatement on refusal of money through default*

If at any time the Premises or any part of them are damaged or destroyed by one or more of the Insured Risks and the insurance money under the policy of insurance effected by the Landlord pursuant to his obligations contained in this Lease is wholly or partly irrecoverable because of any act or default of the Tenant or of anyone at the Premises expressly or by implication[164] with his authority [and under his control][165], the Tenant must immediately, at the option of the Landlord, either rebuild and reinstate the Premises or the part of them destroyed or damaged, to the reasonable satisfaction and under the supervision of the Surveyor — in which case, on completion of the rebuilding and refurbishment, the Landlord must pay to the Tenant the amount that the Landlord has actually received under the insurance policy in respect of the destruction or damage — or pay to the Landlord on demand [with interest] the amount of the insurance money so irrecoverable — in which case the provisions of clauses 5.5 SUSPENSION OF THE RENT and 5.6 REINSTATEMENT AND TERMINATION are to apply.]

164   The expression 'by implication' is intended to include a caller on the premises, such as a tradesman, where there has been no express invitation but the person cannot be classed as a trespasser.
165   The tenant should add the words in square brackets.

[632]

[5.8   Landlord's further insurance covenants[166]

The Landlord covenants with the Tenant to observe and perform the requirements set out in this clause 5.8 in relation to the insurance policy effected by the Landlord pursuant to his obligations contained in this Lease.

166   Unless insurance is to be in the joint names of the landlord and the tenant, the tenant should seek such covenants from the landlord.

5.8.1   *Copy policy*

The Landlord must produce to the Tenant on demand [a copy of the policy and the last premium renewal receipt *(or as required)* reasonable evidence of the terms of the policy and the fact that the last premium has been paid][167].

167   The landlord can reasonably insist on the second alternative. If the premises are insured under a block policy, it would be inappropriate for the landlord to have to disclose to the tenant information about his other properties.
       It should be noted that it is recommended 'best practice' that where the landlord has arranged insurance, the terms should be made known to the tenant and any material change in the insurance should be notified to the tenant: see Recommendation 14 of 'A code of practice for commercial leases in England and Wales (2nd edition)' which can be found in vol 22(1) (2003 Reissue) LANDLORD AND TENANT (BUSINESS TENANCIES) at Form 1 [4501].

5.8.2   *Noting of the Tenant's interest*

The Landlord must ensure that the interest of the Tenant is noted or endorsed on the policy[168].

168   Where insurance in the joint names of the landlord and the tenant is not practical, the tenant should insist that a note of his interest is endorsed on the policy. This protects the tenant because the insurers should give notice to him of any lapse in the policy and, where it can be shown that the tenant is responsible for the insurance premium under the terms of the lease, it is likely — but not certain — that the insurers would not exercise subrogation rights against the tenant.
       It is recommended 'best practice' that where the landlord has arranged insurance, any interest of the tenant should be covered by the policy: see Recommendation 14 of 'A code of practice for commercial leases in England and Wales (2nd edition)' which can be found in vol 22(1) (2003 Reissue) LANDLORD AND TENANT (BUSINESS TENANCIES) at Form 1 [4501].

[633]

5.8.3   *Change of risks*

The Landlord must notify the Tenant of any [material] change in the risks covered by the policy from time to time[169].

169   It should be noted that it is recommended 'best practice' that where the landlord has arranged insurance, the terms should be made known to the tenant and any material change in the insurance should be notified to the tenant: see Recommendation 14 of 'A code of practice for commercial leases in England and Wales (2nd edition)' which can be found in vol 22(1) (2003 Reissue) LANDLORD AND TENANT (BUSINESS TENANCIES) at Form 1 [4501].

[5.8.4   *Waiver of subrogation*[170]

The Landlord must produce to the Tenant on demand written confirmation from the insurers that they have agreed to waive all rights of subrogation against the Tenant.]]

170   Generally an insurer who has paid out under a policy stands in the shoes of the insured with regard to any claim the latter may have had against any third party. If the insurance is in joint names, the tenant is an insured party and there can be no subrogation against him. It would seem, also, that where the tenant covenants to reimburse the landlord for sums expended by the landlord in insuring the premises, the landlord's insurers cannot make a subrogated claim against the tenant where the premises are destroyed by the tenant's negligence: *Mark Rowlands Ltd v Berni Inns Ltd* [1986] QB 211, [1985] 3 All ER 473, CA. The tenant may still, however, wish to obtain a specific waiver of subrogation if possible.

[634]–[640]

6   GUARANTEE PROVISIONS

6.1   The Guarantor's covenants[171]

6.1.1   *Nature and duration*

The Guarantor's covenants with the Landlord are given as sole or principal debtor or covenantor, with the landlord for the time being and with all his successors in title[172] without the need for any express assignment, and the Guarantor's obligations to the Landlord will last throughout the Liability Period.

171   The covenants in this clause should *not* be omitted where no guarantor is a party to the lease, because they may be required under clause 3.9.5.2 [598] CONDITIONS. If it is felt undesirable to have covenants in a lease and no party, at least initially, to enter into them, ie where there is no guarantor for the original tenant, the contents of this clause could alternatively be included in a schedule.

172   The new provisions governing the transmission of the benefit and burden of covenants (see the Landlord and Tenant (Covenants) Act 1995 s 3) only apply to landlord and tenant covenants. The law in force before 1 January 1996 remains unchanged for guarantor covenants, so that the benefit passes with the landlord's reversion. This occurs, not under the Law of Property Act 1925 s 141(1), which has been repealed for post-1995 tenancies by the 1995 Act, but under common law. The guarantee covenant touches and concerns the legal estate vested in the new reversioner: see *P & A Swift Investments v Combined English Stores Group plc* [1989] AC 632, [1988] 2 All ER 885, HL.

[641]

6.1.2   *The covenants*

The Guarantor covenants with the Landlord to observe and perform the requirements of this clause 6.1.2.

6.1.2.1   Payment of rent and performance of the Lease

The Tenant must pay the Lease Rents[173] and VAT charged on them punctually and observe and perform the covenants and other terms of this Lease, and if, at any time during the Liability Period while the Tenant is bound by the tenant covenants of this Lease[174], the Tenant defaults in paying the Lease Rents or in observing or performing any of the covenants or other terms of this Lease, then the Guarantor must pay the Lease

Rents and observe or perform the covenants or terms in respect of which the Tenant is in default and make good to the Landlord on demand, and indemnify the Landlord against, all losses resulting from such non-payment, non-performance or non-observance notwithstanding —

(a)   any time or indulgence granted by the Landlord to the Tenant, any neglect or forbearance of the Landlord in enforcing the payment of the Lease Rents or the observance or performance of the covenants or other terms of this Lease, or any refusal by the Landlord to accept rent tendered by or on behalf of the Tenant at a time when the Landlord is entitled — or will after the service of a notice under the Law of Property Act 1925 Section 146 be entitled — to re-enter the Premises[175],

(b)   that the terms of this Lease may have been varied by agreement between the Landlord and the Tenant[, provided that no variation is to bind the Guarantor to the extent that it is materially prejudicial to him][176],

(c)   that the Tenant has surrendered part of the Premises — in which event the liability of the Guarantor under this Lease is to continue in respect of the part of the Premises not surrendered after making any necessary apportionments under the Law of Property Act 1925 Section 140[177], and

(d)   anything else (other than a release by deed) by which, but for this clause 6.1.2.1, the Guarantor would be released.

[642]

173   As to the definition of 'the Lease Rents' see clause 1.38 [569] 'THE RENT'.
174   This obligation lasts while the lease is vested in the tenant and for any period of extended liability following an excluded assignment. It is not appropriate once the tenant has entered into an authorised guarantee agreement, when the contractual guarantor's obligations are at one remove: see vol 22(1) (2003 Reissue) LANDLORD AND TENANT (BUSINESS TENANCIES) Paragraph 74 [284] and clause 6.1.2.4 [645] GUARANTEE OF THE TENANT'S LIABILITIES UNDER AN AUTHORISED GUARANTEE AGREEMENT.
175   If a creditor 'gives time' to the debtor in a binding manner, this releases the guarantor: see *Swire v Redman* (1876) 1 QBD 536; *Holme v Brunskill* (1877) 3 QBD 495, CA. The guarantee should, therefore, be expressed to apply notwithstanding any time or indulgence granted by the landlord to the tenant, or neglect or forbearance on the part of the landlord in enforcing the payment of rent and the other covenants in the lease. It has been suggested, however, that such wording does not protect a landlord who refuses to accept rent so as not to waive a breach of covenant by the tenant. This is unresolved but to avoid any doubt the point should be expressly dealt with. It appears that any provision in a guarantor's covenant that purports to exonerate the landlord from the consequences of his own negligence must satisfy the reasonableness test of the Unfair Contract Terms Act 1977 (11 Halsbury's Statutes (4th Edn) CONTRACT).
176   Any variation of the terms of the contract between the creditor and the debtor will discharge the guarantor (*Holme v Brunskill* (1877) 3 QBD 495, CA), unless the guarantor consents, although it has been suggested that an immaterial variation that was not prejudicial to the guarantor might not release him. No guarantor should accept a provision by which the guarantee is to continue notwithstanding any variation, but on the other hand it seems unfair on the landlord for the guarantor to escape his liability merely because a minor change has been agreed between the landlord and the tenant. A provision that the guarantee is to continue to apply notwithstanding an immaterial variation not prejudicial to the guarantor seems a fair compromise. It should be noted that the Landlord and Tenant (Covenants) Act 1995 s 18 does not apply to the guarantor of the current tenant.
        It should also be noted that it is recommended 'best practice' that landlords and tenants should seek the agreement of any guarantors to proposed material changes to the terms of the lease, or even minor changes which could increase the guarantor's liability: see Recommendation 15 of 'A code of practice for commercial leases in England and Wales (2nd edition)' which can be found in vol 22(1) (2003 Reissue) LANDLORD AND TENANT (BUSINESS TENANCIES) at Form 1 [4501].
177   In the light of *Holme v Brunskill* (1877) 3 QBD 495, CA, the position on surrender of part of the premises should be dealt with expressly.

[643]

6.1.2.2   New lease following disclaimer[178]

If, at any time during the Liability Period while the Tenant is bound by the tenant covenants of this Lease[179], any trustee in bankruptcy or liquidator of the Tenant disclaims this Lease, the Guarantor must, if so required by notice served by the Landlord within *(state period, eg 60 days)* of the Landlord's becoming aware of the disclaimer, take from the Landlord forthwith a lease of the Premises for the residue of the [Contractual][180] Term as at the date of the disclaimer, at the Rent then payable under this Lease and subject to the same covenants and terms as in this Lease — except that the Guarantor need not ensure that any other person is made a party to that lease as guarantor — the new lease to commence on the date of the disclaimer. The Guarantor must pay the costs of the new lease and VAT charged thereon, except where such VAT is recoverable or available for set-off by the Landlord as input tax[181], and execute and deliver to the Landlord a counterpart of the new lease.

178   This put option should be included because on disclaimer of a lease the lease ceases to exist, although it is deemed to continue for the purpose of determining the liability to the landlord of persons, including guarantors, other than the tenant whose liquidator or trustee has disclaimed: see *Hindcastle Ltd v Barbara Attenborough Associates Ltd* [1997] AC 70, [1996] 1 All ER 737, HL.

179   This obligation lasts while the lease is vested in the tenant and for any period of extended liability following an excluded assignment. It is not appropriate once the tenant has entered into an authorised guarantee agreement when the tenant's — ie the former tenant's — liquidator or trustee in bankruptcy will not be in a position to disclaim the lease because it is no longer be vested in the former tenant.

180   This defined term will require amendment where the operation of the security of tenure provisions in the Landlord and Tenant Act 1954 ss 24–28 is to be excluded in relation to the lease: see note 6 to clause 1.4 [559] 'THE [CONTRACTUAL] TERM'.

181   As to payment of VAT on legal costs by a person other than the solicitor's own client see the Information Binder: Property [1]: VAT and Property.

[644]

6.1.2.3   Payments following disclaimer[182]

If this Lease is disclaimed and the Landlord does not require the Guarantor to accept a new lease of the Premises in accordance with clause 6.1.2.2 NEW LEASE FOLLOWING DISCLAIMER, the Guarantor must pay to the Landlord on demand an amount equal to [the difference between any money received by the Landlord for the use or occupation of the Premises and] the Lease Rents [in both cases] for the period commencing with the date of the disclaimer and ending on whichever is the earlier of the date *(state period, eg 6 months)* after the disclaimer, the date, if any, upon which the Premises are relet, and the end of the [Contractual][183] Term.

182   This clause could be a useful alternative for a landlord who may not be unhappy to regain possession of the premises but would like some rental income before reletting etc. For a covenant by the tenant to assign to the guarantor see vol 22(3) (1997 Reissue) LANDLORD AND TENANT (BUSINESS TENANCIES) Form 159 [6666].

183   This defined term will require amendment where the operation of the security of tenure provisions in the Landlord and Tenant Act 1954 ss 24–28 is to be excluded in relation to the lease: see note 6 to clause 1.4 [559] 'THE [CONTRACTUAL] TERM'.

6.1.2.4   Guarantee of the Tenant's liabilities under an authorised guarantee agreement

If, at any time during the Liability Period while the Tenant is bound by an authorised guarantee agreement, the Tenant defaults in his obligations under that agreement, the Guarantor must make good to the Landlord on demand, and indemnify the Landlord against, all losses resulting from that default notwithstanding —

(a)   any time or indulgence granted by the Landlord to the Tenant, or neglect or forbearance of the Landlord in enforcing the payment of any sum or the observance or performance of the covenants of the authorised guarantee agreement[184],

(b)   that the terms of the authorised guarantee agreement may have been varied by agreement between the Landlord and the Tenant [provided that no variation is to bind the Guarantor to the extent that it is materially prejudicial to him][185], or

(c)   anything else (other than a release by deed) by which, but for this clause 6.1.2.4, the Guarantor would be released.

184   See note 175 to clause 6.1.2.1 [642] PAYMENT OF RENT AND PERFORMANCE OF THE LEASE.
185   See note 176 to clause 6.1.2.1 [642] PAYMENT OF RENT AND PERFORMANCE OF THE LEASE.

[645]

6.1.3 *Severance*

6.1.3.1   Severance of void provisions

Any provision of this clause 6 rendered void by virtue of the 1995 Act Section 25 is to be severed from all remaining provisions, and the remaining provisions are to be preserved.

6.1.3.2   Limitation of provisions

If any provision in this clause 6 extends beyond the limits permitted by the 1995 Act Section 25, that provision is to be varied so as not to extend beyond those limits.

[6.2   The Landlord's covenant[186]

The Landlord covenants with the Guarantor that he will not attempt to recover from the Guarantor payment of any amount, determined by a court or in binding arbitration or agreed between the Landlord and the Tenant, payable in respect of a breach of covenant by the Tenant, unless he has served on the Guarantor, within 6 months of the payment being determined or agreed, a notice in the form prescribed by Section 27 of the 1995 Act as if the payment were a fixed charge under that Act.]

186   This clause is a tenant's amendment. It provides for a notice equivalent to a default notice under the Landlord and Tenant (Covenants) Act 1995 to be served. It protects the interests of existing and future contractual guarantors. As to service of default notices see vol 22(1) (2003 Reissue) LANDLORD AND TENANT (BUSINESS TENANCIES) Paragraph 61 [260].

[646]–[650]

7   FORFEITURE[187]

If and whenever during the Term —

7.1   the Lease Rents[188], or any of them or any part of them, or any VAT payable on them, are outstanding for *(state period, eg 14 days)* after becoming due, whether formally demanded or not[189], or

7.2   the Tenant [or the Guarantor] breaches any covenant or other term of this Lease, or

7.3   the Tenant [or the Guarantor][190], being an individual, becomes subject to a bankruptcy order[191] [or has an interim receiver appointed to his property][192], or

7.4   the Tenant [or the Guarantor][193], being a company, enters into liquidation[194] whether compulsory or voluntary — but not if the liquidation is for amalgamation or reconstruction of a solvent company — [or enters into administration][195] [or has a receiver appointed over all or any part of its assets][196], or

7.5   the Tenant [or the Guarantor][197] enters into or makes a proposal to enter into any voluntary arrangement pursuant to the Insolvency Act 1986[198] or any other arrangement or composition for the benefit of his creditors, or

7.6   the Tenant has any distress, sequestration or execution levied on his goods

and, where the Tenant [or the Guarantor] is more than one person, if and whenever any of the events referred to in this clause happens to any one or more of them, the Landlord may at any time re-enter the Premises, or any part of them in the name of the whole — even if any previous right of re-entry has been waived[199] — and thereupon the Term is to cease absolutely but without prejudice to any rights or remedies that may have accrued to the Landlord against the Tenant or the Guarantor [or to the Tenant against the Landlord] in respect of any breach of covenant or other term of this Lease, including the breach in respect of which the re-entry is made.

[651]

187   As to forfeiture generally see vol 22(1) (2003 Reissue) LANDLORD AND TENANT (BUSINESS TENANCIES) Paragraph 283 [1171] et seq.
        The precise range of insolvency-related circumstances that will trigger the proviso should be carefully considered. Tenants should note that their inclusion, in practice, means that the lease cannot be used as security for a loan. Landlords generally seek to have the ability to forfeit in the widest range of circumstances. It should, however, be noted that, in certain circumstances, leave of the court or of the insolvency practitioner administering the procedure may be required before any contractual right can be exercised: see eg, in respect of administration, the Insolvency Act 1986 Sch 1B para 43(4), (6) as inserted by the Enterprise Act 2002 s 248 (4 Halsbury's Statutes (4th Edn) BANKRUPTCY AND INSOLVENCY).
188   As to the definition of 'the Lease Rents' see clause 1.38 [569] 'THE RENT'.
189   The words 'whether formally demanded or not' should be used to avoid the common law requirement that an actual demand has to be made.
190   The lease may provide for a right of re-entry on insolvency of the guarantor or a tenant's covenant to find an acceptable replacement (see clause 3.23 [612] REPLACEMENT GUARANTOR) or both.
191   As to bankruptcy generally see the Insolvency Act 1986 Pt IX (ss 264–371).
192   As to interim receivers see the Insolvency Act 1986 s 286.
193   See note 190 above.
194   As to liquidation generally see the Insolvency Act 1986 Pts IV–VI (ss 73–246).
195   As to administration generally see the Insolvency Act 1986 Pt II as substituted by the Enterprise Act 2002 s 248. The tenant may seek to argue that if the administrator pays rent and if there are no other material breaches of the lease the landlord should not be entitled to forfeit the lease on this ground.
196   The tenant may seek to argue that if the receiver pays rent and if there are no other material breaches of the lease the landlord should not be entitled to forfeit the lease on this ground.
197   See note 190 above.
198   As to company voluntary arrangements see the Insolvency Act 1986 Pt I (ss 1–7B) as amended by the Insolvency Act 2000. As to individual voluntary arrangements see the Insolvency Act 1986 Pt VIII (ss 252–263G) as amended by the Enterprise Act 2002 s 264.
199   The landlord has the option whether to take advantage of a right of forfeiture or not. If he elects not to do so, the forfeiture is waived. The election may be express or implied, eg if the landlord does any act by which he recognises that the relationship of landlord and tenant is still continuing after the cause of forfeiture has come to his knowledge.

[652]

8   MISCELLANEOUS

8.1   Exclusion of warranty as to use

Nothing in this Lease or in any consent granted by the Landlord under this Lease is to imply or warrant that the Premises may lawfully be used under the Planning Acts for the Permitted Use[200].

200   See *Laurence v Lexcourt Holdings Ltd* [1978] 2 All ER 810, [1978] 1 WLR 1128; *Collins v Howell-Jones* [1981] 2 EGLR 108, 259 Estates Gazette 331, CA and the comments of Eveleigh LJ on estate agents' particulars relating to use in *Bovis Group Pension Fund Ltd v GC Flooring & Furnishing Ltd* (1984) 269 Estates Gazette 1252 at 1253, CA.

8.2   Exclusion of third party rights

Nothing in this Lease is intended to confer any benefit on any person who is not a party to it[201].

201   By virtue of the Contracts (Rights of Third Parties) Act 1999 (11 Halsbury's Statutes (4th Edn) CONTRACT) third-party rights may be conferred where they are not clearly excluded. This being so, it is advisable to incorporate a specific exclusion except where the parties actually intend to confer rights of action on a third party. In the standard letting situation it is unlikely that the parties will wish to extend liability in this manner. As to the Contracts (Rights of Third Parties) Act 1999 generally see vol 4(3) (2001 Reissue) BOILERPLATE CLAUSES.

8.3   Representations

The Tenant acknowledges that this Lease has not been entered into in reliance wholly or partly on any statement or representation made by or on behalf of the Landlord, except any such statement or representation expressly set out in this Lease[202] [or made by the Landlord's solicitors in any written response to enquiries raised by the Tenant's solicitors in connection with the grant of this Lease].

202   See the comments of Eveleigh LJ on estate agents' particulars relating to use in *Bovis Group Pension Fund Ltd v GC Flooring & Furnishing Ltd* (1984) 269 Estates Gazette 1252 at 1253, CA. For an alternative provision see vol 22(4) (1997 Reissue) LANDLORD AND TENANT (BUSINESS TENANCIES) Form 400 clauses 7.1 [7520], 7.2 [7521].

[653]

8.4   Documents under hand

While the Landlord is a limited company or other corporation, any licence, consent, approval or notice required to be given by the Landlord is to be sufficiently given if given under the hand of a director, the secretary or other duly authorised officer of the Landlord [or by the Surveyor on behalf of the Landlord].

8.5   Tenant's property

If, after the Tenant has vacated the Premises at the end of the Term any property of his remains in or on the Premises and he fails to remove it within *(state period, eg 7 days)* after a written request from the Landlord to do so, or, if the Landlord is unable to make such a request to the Tenant, within *(state period, eg 14 days)* from the first attempt to make it, then the Landlord may, as the agent of the Tenant, sell that property. The Tenant must indemnify the Landlord against any liability incurred by the Landlord to any third party whose property is sold by him in the mistaken belief held in good faith — which is to be presumed unless the contrary is proved — that the property belonged to the Tenant.

If, having made reasonable efforts to do so, the Landlord is unable to locate the Tenant, then the Landlord may retain the proceeds of sale absolutely unless the Tenant claims them within *(state period, eg 6 months)* of the date upon which he vacated the Premises. The Tenant must indemnify the Landlord against any damage occasioned to the Premises and any losses caused by or related to the presence of the property in or on the Premises.

8.6   Compensation on vacating excluded

Any statutory right of the Tenant to claim compensation from the Landlord on vacating the Premises is excluded to the extent that the law allows[203].

203   As to compensation where an order for a new tenancy is precluded on certain grounds see the Landlord and Tenant Act 1954 s 37 as amended by the Local Government and Housing Act 1989 s 149, Sch 7 and by SI 2003/3096.
        As to the effectiveness of provisions of this nature see vol 22(1) (2003 Reissue) LANDLORD AND TENANT (BUSINESS TENANCIES) Paragraph 468 [3079].

[654]

8.7   Notices

8.7.1   *Form and service of notices*

A notice under this Lease must be in writing and, unless the receiving party or his authorised agent acknowledges receipt, is valid if, and only if[204] —

8.7.1.1   it is given by hand, sent by registered post or recorded delivery, or sent by fax[205] provided that a confirmatory copy is given by hand or sent by registered post or recorded delivery on the same day, and

8.7.1.2   it is served —

    (a)   where the receiving party is a company incorporated within Great Britain, at the registered office,

    (b)   where the receiving party is the Tenant and the Tenant is not such a company, at the Premises, and

    (c)   where the receiving party is the Landlord [or the Guarantor] and [the Landlord *(or as required)* that party] is not such a company, at [the Landlord's *(or as required)* that party's] address shown in this Lease or at any address specified in a notice given by [the Landlord to the Tenant *(or as required)* that party to the other parties].

204   Notice clauses are either mandatory or permissive. The words 'and only if' are inserted to make it clear that this clause is mandatory.
205   As to service by fax see *Hastie and Jenkerson v McMahon* [1991] 1 All ER 255, [1990] 1 WLR 1575, CA.

[655]

8.7.2   *Deemed delivery*[206]

8.7.2.1   By registered post or recorded delivery

Unless it is returned through the Royal Mail undelivered, a notice sent by registered post or recorded delivery is to be treated as served on the third working day after posting whenever, and whether or not, it is received.

8.7.2.2   By fax

A notice sent by fax is to be treated as served on the day upon which it is sent, or the next working day where the fax is sent after 1600 hours or on a day that is not a working day, whenever and whether or not it or the confirmatory copy is received unless the confirmatory copy is returned through the Royal Mail undelivered.

8.7.2.3 'A working day'

References to 'a working day' are references to a day when the United Kingdom clearing banks are open for business in the City of London.

206   It is a fundamental aspect of any notice clause to specify the circumstances in which the server, provided he has complied with the requirements of the clause, has for the purposes of the document served a notice, even if the recipient claims that he never received it.

8.7.3 *Joint recipients*

If the receiving party consists of more than one person, a notice to one of them is notice to all.

8.8 Rights and easements[207]

The operation of the Law of Property Act 1925 Section 62 is excluded from this Lease. The only rights granted to the Tenant are those expressly set out in this Lease and the Tenant is not to be entitled to any other rights affecting any adjoining property of the Landlord.

207   Where the Law of Property Act 1925 s 62 may operate, it is sensible to define in the lease those rights that are included, and then specifically exclude the operation of that section.

[656]

8.9 Covenants relating to adjoining property

The Tenant is not to be entitled to the benefit of or the right [to enforce or][208] to prevent the release or modification of any covenant agreement or condition entered into by any tenant of the Landlord in respect of any adjoining property of the Landlord.

208   As to when tenants would be able to enforce covenants against each other see vol 22(1) (2003 Reissue) LANDLORD AND TENANT (BUSINESS TENANCIES) Paragraph 48 [235]. Where this might arise, 'to enforce or' should be deleted by the tenant.

8.10 Disputes with adjoining occupiers

If any dispute arises between the Tenant and the tenants or occupiers of any adjoining property of the Landlord in connection with the Premises and any of that adjoining property, it is to be decided [by the Landlord or in such manner as the Landlord directs *(or as required)* by the Surveyor acting as an expert and not as an arbitrator][209].

209   Such a provision is binding on the landlord and the tenant, but binds a tenant of the landlord's adjoining property only if there is a similar provision in his lease.

8.11 Effect of waiver

Each of the Tenant's covenants is to remain in full force both at law and in equity even if the Landlord has waived or released that covenant, or waived or released any similar covenant affecting any adjoining property of the Landlord[210].

210   But as to waiver of a right of forfeiture see vol 22(1) (2003 Reissue) LANDLORD AND TENANT (BUSINESS TENANCIES) Paragraph 284 [1173].

[8.12   The perpetuity period[211]

The perpetuity period applicable to this Lease is *(state period, eg 80 years)* from the commencement of the [Contractual][212] Term, and whenever in this Lease any party is granted a future interest it must vest within that period or be void for remoteness.]

211   As to the rule against perpetuities see vol 22(1) (2003 Reissue) LANDLORD AND TENANT (BUSINESS TENANCIES) Paragraph 132 [664]. This clause should be included if the term exceeds 21 years because this lease contains grants of future interests.
212   This defined term will require amendment where the operation of the security of tenure provisions in the Landlord and Tenant Act 1954 ss 24–28 is to be excluded in relation to the lease (see note 6 to clause 1.4 [559] 'THE [CONTRACTUAL] TERM') although this is probably unlikely in connection with the grant of such a long lease.

[657]

[8.13   Party walls[213]

Any walls dividing the buildings on the Premises from any other buildings are to be party walls within the meaning of the Law of Property Act 1925 Section 38 and must be maintained at the equally shared expense of the Tenant and the other party.]

213   It is assumed that, where the buildings on the estate are detached, the fences and walls between each property are included within the premises demised by the various leases so that each tenant is responsible for all or some of his boundary structures. Where, however, buildings are split into two or more units that are let separately, such dividing walls ought probably to be party structures.

8.14   [New *(or)* Old] lease

[This Lease [is *(or as appropriate)* is not] a new tenancy for the purposes of the 1995 Act Section 1. *(or as appropriate)* This Lease is granted under the 1995 Act Section 19 and [is *(or as appropriate)* is not] a new tenancy for the purposes of Section 1 of that Act][214].

214   A tenancy granted on or after 1 January 1996 that is an overriding lease is not a 'new' tenancy where the tenancy being overridden is one granted before that date: see the Landlord and Tenant (Covenants) Act 1995 ss 1(4), 20(1). Where the lease being granted is an overriding lease, the lease must include a statement that it is an overriding lease and indicate whether the overriding lease is or is not a 'new' tenancy: see the Landlord and Tenant (Covenants) Act 1995 s 20(2). In these circumstances the second alternative should be used.

[8.15   Capacity of tenants

It is declared that the persons comprising the Tenant hold the Premises as [joint tenants *(or as required)* tenants in common].]

[658]

[8.16   Exclusion of the 1954 Act Sections 24–28[215]

8.16.1   *Notice and declaration*

On *(date)* the Landlord served notice on the Tenant pursuant to the provisions of the 1954 Act Section 38A(3) as inserted by the Regulatory Reform (Business Tenancies) (England and Wales) Order 2003 and on *(date)* the Tenant made a [simple *(or as appropriate)* statutory] declaration pursuant to schedule 2 of the Regulatory Reform (Business Tenancies) (England and Wales) Order 2003.

8.16.2   *Agreement to exclude*

Pursuant to the provisions of the 1954 Act Section 38A(1) as inserted by the Regulatory Reform (Business Tenancies) (England and Wales) Order 2003, the parties agree that the provisions of the 1954 Act Sections 24–28 inclusive are to be excluded in relation to the tenancy created by this Lease.]

215   As to contracting out of the Landlord and Tenant Act 1954 and the requirements that need to be complied with see vol 22(1) (2003 Reissue) LANDLORD AND TENANT (BUSINESS TENANCIES) Paragraph 431 [2035].

(include other clauses as required: eg, break clauses and options (see vol 22(3) (1997 Reissue) LANDLORD AND TENANT *(BUSINESS TENANCIES) Forms 136 [6544]–142 [6569]) or a proviso as to termination on rent review (see vol 22(3) (1997 Reissue)* LANDLORD AND TENANT *(BUSINESS TENANCIES) Form 143 [6570]))*

IN WITNESS etc *(see vol 12(2) (2003 Reissue) DEEDS, AGREEMENTS ETC)*

[659]–[670]

SCHEDULE 1: THE RIGHTS GRANTED[216]

1-1   Rights of way

The right, subject to [temporary] interruption for repair, alteration, rebuilding or replacement, for the Tenant and all persons expressly or by implication authorised by him[217] — in common with the Landlord and all other persons having a like right — to pass and repass[218] to and from the Premises over and along the Estate Roads [at all times *(or as required)* at any time between *(state time, eg 0700 hours)* on Monday and *(state time, eg 1800 hours)* on Friday in each week, except public holidays][219] for all purposes connected with the use and enjoyment of the Premises but not otherwise[220], [with or without vehicles of any description *(or as required)* with vehicles not exceeding ... metres in length or ... kilograms unladen weight][221].

216   As to rights granted see vol 22(1) (2003 Reissue) LANDLORD AND TENANT (BUSINESS TENANCIES) Paragraph 123 [647] et seq.
217   The term 'the Tenant and all persons expressly or by implication authorised by him' is an updated version of 'the Tenant and his successors in title the owners and occupiers for the time being of the Premises and his or their respective servants and licensees': see *Baxendale v North Lambeth Liberal and Radical Club Ltd* [1902] 2 Ch 427 at 429 per Swinfen Eady J; *Hammond v Prentice Bros Ltd* [1920] 1 Ch 201.
218   There is an implied right to stop for a reasonable time for loading and unloading, but there is no right to park unless one is specifically granted: see *Bulstrode v Lambert* [1953] 2 All ER 728, [1953] 1 WLR 1064; *McIlraith v Grady* [1968] 1 QB 468, [1967] 3 All ER 625, CA; *VT Engineering Ltd v Richard Barland & Co Ltd* (1968) 19 P & CR 890.
219   Limitation of the right of way to specified hours is justifiable only where there are problems of access, security or services.
220   See *Callard v Beeney* [1930] 1 KB 353 at 357 per Talbot J.
221   The landlord may reasonably wish to limit the size and weight of vehicles using the estate roads.

1-2   Passage and running through Adjoining Conduits

The right, subject to temporary interruption for repair, alteration or replacement, to the free passage and running of all services to and from the Premises through the appropriate Adjoining Conduits, in common with the Landlord and all other persons having a like right.

[671]

SCHEDULE 2: THE RIGHTS RESERVED[222]

2-1   Passage and running through the Conduits

The right to the free and uninterrupted passage and running of all services and supplies from and to other parts of the Estate or any adjoining property of the Landlord through the appropriate Conduits and through any structures of a similar use or nature that may at any time be constructed in, on, over or under the Premises as permitted by paragraph 2-2 RIGHT TO CONSTRUCT CONDUITS.

222   As to rights reserved see vol 22(1) (2003 Reissue) LANDLORD AND TENANT (BUSINESS TENANCIES) Paragraph 124 [648] et seq.

2-2   Right to construct conduits[223]

The right to construct[224] and to maintain at any time during the Term any pipes, sewers, drains, mains, ducts, conduits, gutters, watercourses, wires, cables, [laser optical fibres, data or impulse transmission, communication or reception systems,] channels, flues and other necessary conducting media for the provision of services or supplies — including any fixings, louvres, cowls and any other ancillary apparatus — for the benefit of any part of the Estate or any other adjoining property of the Landlord[, making good any damage caused by the exercise of the right].

223   If the term of the lease exceeds 21 years a perpetuity provision — see clause 8.12 [657] THE PERPETUITY PERIOD — is required in the lease because this is a grant of a future interest.
224   For a covenant to make good after exercising rights of access see vol 22(3) (1997 Reissue) LANDLORD AND TENANT (BUSINESS TENANCIES) Form 79 [6453].

[672]

2-3   Access

2-3.1   *Access to inspect etc*[225]

The right to enter, or in emergency to break into and enter, the Premises [at any time during the Term *(or as required)* at reasonable times and on reasonable notice except in emergency] —

2-3.1.1   to inspect the condition and state of repair of the Premises,

2-3.1.2   to inspect, clean, connect to, repair, remove, replace with others, alter or execute any works whatever to or in connection with the conduits, easements, services or supplies referred to in paragraphs 2-1 PASSAGE AND RUNNING THROUGH THE CONDUITS and 2-2 RIGHT TO CONSTRUCT CONDUITS,

2-3.1.3   to carry out work of any kind to any adjoining property of the Landlord or any other buildings [that cannot [conveniently] be carried out without access to the Premises],

2-3.1.4   to carry out work or do anything whatever that the Landlord is obliged to do under this Lease,

2-3.1.5   to take schedules or inventories of fixtures and other items to be yielded up at the end of the Term, and

2-3.1.6   to exercise any of the rights granted to the Landlord in this Lease.

225   For a covenant to make good after exercising rights of access see vol 22(3) (1997 Reissue) LANDLORD AND TENANT (BUSINESS TENANCIES) Form 79 [6453].

2-3.2   *Access on renewal or rent review*

[The right to enter the Premises with the Surveyor and the third party determining the Rent under any provisions for rent review contained in this Lease, at [any time *(or as required)* convenient hours and on reasonable prior notice], to inspect [and measure] the Premises for all purposes connected with any pending or intended step under the 1954 Act or the implementation of the provisions for rent review. *(or as required in view of the rent review provisions used: see, eg, vol 22(3) (1997 Reissue)* LANDLORD AND TENANT *(BUSINESS* TENANCIES) Forms 180 [6711]–194 [6987])]

2-4   Right to erect new buildings[226]

Full right and liberty at any time to build, rebuild, alter or raise the height of any building on any adjoining property of the Landlord in such manner as the Landlord thinks fit, even if doing so obstructs, affects or interferes with the amenity of or the access to the Premises or the passage of light and air to the Premises[and even if it materially affects *(or as required)* but provided it does not materially affect] the Premises or the use and enjoyment of the Premises.

---

226   As to reservation of the right to develop other land see vol 22(1) (2003 Reissue) LANDLORD AND TENANT (BUSINESS TENANCIES) Paragraphs 130 [660], 131 [662].

SCHEDULE 3: THE RENT AND RENT REVIEW

(insert rent review provisions as required: see vol 22(3) (1997 Reissue) LANDLORD AND TENANT *(BUSINESS* TENANCIES) Forms 180 [6711]–194 [6987])

[673]

SCHEDULE 4: THE INDUSTRIAL COVENANTS

4-1   Use

4-1.1   *Permitted Use*

The Tenant must use the Premises for the Permitted Use only.

4-1.2   *Cesser of business*

The Tenant must not [cease carrying on business in the Premises or] leave the Premises [continuously] unoccupied for more than *(state period, eg 1 month)* [without notifying the Landlord, and providing such caretaking or security arrangements for the protection of the Premises as the Landlord [reasonably] requires and the insurers or underwriters require].

4-2   Smoke abatement

4-2.1   *Furnace construction*

The Tenant must ensure that every furnace boiler or heater at the Premises is constructed and used so as substantially to consume or burn the smoke arising from it.

4-2.2   *Noxious emissions*

The Tenant must not cause or permit any gritty, noxious or offensive emissions from any engine, furnace, chimney or other apparatus on the Premises without using [the best possible *(or as required)* all reasonable] means for preventing or counteracting the emissions.

4-2.3   *Statutory controls*

The Tenant must comply with the provisions of the Clean Air Act 1993 and with the requirements of any notice served under it by the relevant authority or body.

[674]

4-3   Environmental protection[227]

4-3.1   *Discharge of dangerous substances*

4-3.1.1   Damage to the Conduits and environment

The Tenant must not permit any oil or grease or any deleterious, objectionable, dangerous, poisonous or explosive matter or substance to be discharged into any of the Conduits, and must take all [reasonable] measures to ensure that any effluent discharged into the Conduits does not harm the environment, or corrode or otherwise harm the Conduits or cause any obstruction or deposit in them.

4-3.1.2   Poisons and pollutants

The Tenant must not permit the discharge into any of the Conduits of any fluid of a poisonous or noxious nature or of a kind likely to sicken or injure the fish, or that does in fact destroy them, or likely to contaminate or pollute the water of any stream or river.

227   It may be advisable for the landlord and tenant to commission a soil survey before the lease is entered into. The results could be annexed to the lease. A further survey could then be carried out towards the end of the term ascertaining whether or not contamination has in fact occurred. The tenant's obligations regarding restriction or clean-up or both will then be clear. If the original soil survey reveals contamination, then thought should be given to including provisions in the lease making it clear whose responsibility the contamination is and whether or not the tenant is obliged to resolve it or clean it up.

4-3.2   *Spillages and contamination*

The Tenant must take all practicable precautions to ensure that no noxious substances are spilled or deposited on the Premises and that contamination does not occur.

4-3.3   *Controlled, special or radioactive waste*

The Tenant must not deposit on the Premises any controlled or special waste as defined in the Environmental Protection Act 1990, or radioactive waste as defined in the Radioactive Substances Act 1993 Section 18, or any other substance that may produce concentrations or accumulations of noxious gasses or noxious liquids that may cause pollution of the environment or harm to human health.

[675]

4-3.4   *Notice of spillages and inspection*

Within 14 days of the spilling or deposit on the Premises of any noxious substance in a quantity that may cause serious damage to or pollution of the environment or serious damage to property or serious harm to human health, the Tenant must inform the Landlord of this and permit him to enter and inspect the Premises.

4-3.5   *Indemnity for damage and pollution*

The Tenant must indemnify the Landlord, and keep him indemnified, against any losses in respect of damage to, or pollution of, the environment or damage to property or harm to human health caused by the Premises or any substance on them whether in liquid or solid form or in the form of gas or vapour.

4-4   Roof and floor loading

4-4.1   *Heavy items*

The Tenant must not bring into or permit to remain in any building on the Premises any safes, machinery, goods or other articles that will or may strain or damage the building or any part of it.

4-4.2   *Protection of the roof*

The Tenant must not, without the consent of the Landlord, suspend any weight from the [portal frames, stanchions or roof purlins *(or as the case may be)*] of any building on the Premises or use them for the storage of goods or place any weight on them.

4-4.3   *Expert advice*

If the Tenant applies for the Landlord's consent under paragraph 4-4.2 PROTECTION OF THE ROOF the Landlord may consult any engineer or other person in relation to the roof or floor loading proposed by the Tenant, and the Tenant must repay the fees of the engineer or other person to the Landlord on demand.

[676]

4-5   Machinery

4-5.1   *Maintenance of machinery*

The Tenant must keep all plant, apparatus and machinery, including any boilers and furnaces on the Premises, ('the Machinery') properly maintained and in good working order, and for that purpose must employ reputable contractors [to be approved by the Landlord[, whose approval may not be unreasonably withheld [or delayed],]] ('the Contractors') to carry out regular periodic inspection and maintenance of the Machinery.

4-5.2   *Renewal of parts*

The Tenant must renew all working and other parts of the Machinery as and when necessary or when recommended by the Contractors.

4-5.3   *Operation*

The Tenant must ensure by directions to his staff and otherwise that the Machinery is properly operated.

4-5.4   *Damage from the Machinery*

The Tenant must avoid damage to the Premises by vibration or otherwise.

4-6   Signs

The Tenant must at all times display and maintain, at a point on the Premises to be specified in writing by the Landlord, a suitable sign, of a size and kind first approved by the Landlord, showing the Tenant's trading name and business.

4-7   Service charge[228]

The Tenant must pay to the Landlord on demand as additional rent[229] [an amount equal to ...% — or such other percentage as the Surveyor, acting as an expert and not as an arbitrator, from time to time determines is appropriate to the Premises — *(or as required)* a fair proportion to be determined by the Surveyor, acting as an expert and not as an arbitrator,][230] of all sums the Landlord may be liable to pay in connection with the performance of the covenants set out in clause 4.2 REPAIRS.

---

228   If regular substantial expenditure is anticipated, this obligation should be included in the definition of 'Lease Rents': see note 37 to clause 1.38 [569] 'THE RENT'.
229   See note 52 to clause 2 [581] DEMISE.
230   As to the question of fixed or flexible shares see vol 22(1) (2003 Reissue) LANDLORD AND TENANT (BUSINESS TENANCIES) Paragraph 268 [1115] et seq.

[677]

4-8   Parking

The Tenant must not permit any vehicles belonging to him or to any persons calling on the Premises expressly or by implication with his authority[231] to stand on the Estate Roads [so as to cause an obstruction][232] or on the pavements, and must use his best endeavours to ensure that such persons do not permit any vehicle so to stand on any of the Estate Roads or pavements.

231   The reference to persons calling 'expressly or by implication with his authority' is an updated version of 'the Tenant and his successors in title the owners and occupiers for the time being of the Premises and his or their respective servants and licensees': see *Baxendale v North Lambeth Liberal and Radical Club Ltd* [1902] 2 Ch 427 at 429 per Swinfen Eady J; *Hammond v Prentice Bros Ltd* [1920] 1 Ch 201.
232   If these words are included, the inference is that cars may be parked on the road provided they do not cause an obstruction. Without specific provision, parking rights are not included in a right of way.

4-9   Regulations

The Tenant must comply with all [reasonable] regulations made by the Landlord from time to time for the management of the Estate [and notified to the Tenant in writing][, provided that nothing in the regulations may purport to amend the terms of this Lease, and, in the event of any inconsistency between the terms of this Lease and the regulations, that the terms of this Lease are to prevail][233].

233   Almost every lease of premises on an estate includes this provision but only rarely are any regulations made. The tenant should strike out the provision on the basis that he is being asked to accept some unknown commitment. Failing this the tenant should —
     (i)   where applicable strike out 'and restrictions' if the expression 'regulations and restrictions', which seems to be wider than 'regulations', is used,
     (ii)   insist that he is formally notified in writing of any regulations that may be made, and
     (iii)   provide that the regulations must always remain subservient to the lease.

[678]

SCHEDULE 5: THE SUBJECTIONS

(insert details)

SCHEDULE 6: THE AUTHORISED GUARANTEE AGREEMENT

(insert the form of authorised guarantee agreement: see, eg, vol 22(3) (1997 Reissue) LANDLORD AND TENANT (BUSINESS TENANCIES) *Form 217 [7053])*

(signature (or common seal) of landlord: lease)
(signature (or common seal) of tenant (and guarantor): counterpart)
(signatures of witnesses)
[679]–[700]

7

Lease of a light industrial or warehouse unit forming part of a building on an estate[1]

CONTENTS

(NB: numbers in [ ] below refer to this volume and should be altered to suit the page or reference numbers actually used)

1 DEFINITIONS AND INTERPRETATION

1.1 'The Accountant' .... [708]
1.2 'The Adjoining Conduits' .... [708]
1.3 'Adjoining property of the Landlord' .... [708]
1.4 'The Building' .... [708]
1.5 'The Common Parts' .... [708]
1.6 'The Conduits' .... [709]
1.7 'The [Contractual] Term' .... [709]
[1.8 'The Decorating Years' .... [710]]
1.9 'Development' .... [710]
1.10 'The Estate' .... [710]

[701]

1.11 'The Estate Roads' .... [710]
1.12 Gender and number .... [710]
1.13 Headings .... [710]
1.14 'The Industrial Covenants' .... [710]
[1.15 'The Initial Rent' .... [711]]
1.16 'The Insurance Rent' .... [711]
1.17 'The Insurance Rent Percentage' .... [711]
1.18 'The Insured Risks' .... [711]
1.19 'Interest' .... [712]
1.20 'The Interest Rate' .... [712]
1.21 Interpretation of 'consent' and 'approved' .... [713]
1.22 Interpretation of 'the Estate' .... [713]
1.23 Interpretation of 'the Guarantor' .... [713]
1.24 Interpretation of 'the Landlord' .... [714]
1.25 Interpretation of 'the last year of the Term' and 'the end of the Term' .... [714]
1.26 Interpretation of 'the Tenant' .... [714]
1.27 Interpretation of 'this Lease' .... [714]
1.28 Joint and several liability .... [714]
1.29 'The Landlord's Expenses' .... [714]
1.30 'The Liability Period' .... [731]
1.31 'Losses' .... [732]
1.32 'The 1954 Act' .... [732]
1.33 'The 1995 Act' .... [732]
1.34 Obligation not to permit or suffer .... [732]
1.35 'Other buildings' .... [732]
1.36 'The Parking Bays' .... [732]
1.37 'The Permitted Use' .... [733]
1.38 'The Plan' .... [733]

1.39 'The Planning Acts' . . . . [733]
1.40 'The Premises' . . . . [733]
1.41 References to clauses and schedules . . . . [735]
1.42 References to rights of access . . . . [735]
1.43 References to statutes . . . . [735]
1.44 'The Rent' . . . . [735]
1.45 'The Rent Commencement Date' . . . . [735]
[1.46 'The Review Dates' . . . . [736]]
1.47 'The Service Charge' . . . . [736]
1.48 'The Service Charge Percentage' . . . . [736]
1.49 'The Services' . . . . [736]
1.50 'The Surveyor' . . . . [737]
[1.51 'The Term' . . . . [737]]
1.52 Terms from the 1995 Act . . . . [737]
1.53 'VAT' . . . . [737]

2 DEMISE . . . . [751]

[702]

3 THE TENANT'S COVENANTS

3.1 Rent . . . . [752]
3.2 Outgoings and VAT . . . . [753]
[3.3 Cost of services consumed . . . . [754]]
3.4 Repair, cleaning and decoration . . . . [754]
3.5 Waste and alterations . . . . [756]
3.6 Aerials, signs and advertisements . . . . [757]
3.7 Statutory obligations . . . . [758]
3.8 Entry to inspect and notice to repair . . . . [759]
3.9 Alienation . . . . [781]
3.10 Nuisance and residential restrictions . . . . [791]
3.11 Costs of applications, notices and recovery of arrears . . . . [792]
3.12 Planning and development . . . . [801]
3.13 Plans, documents and information . . . . [803]
3.14 Indemnities . . . . [803]
3.15 Reletting boards and viewing . . . . [804]
3.16 Obstruction and encroachment . . . . [804]
3.17 Yielding up . . . . [805]
3.18 Interest on arrears . . . . [805]
3.19 Statutory notices . . . . [805]
3.20 Keyholders . . . . [806]
3.21 Viewing on sale of reversion . . . . [806]
3.22 Defective premises . . . . [806]
3.23 Replacement guarantor . . . . [806]
3.24 Exercise of the Landlord's rights . . . . [806]
3.25 The Industrial Covenants . . . . [807]
3.26 The Services . . . . [807]
3.27 Costs of grant of this Lease . . . . [807]
3.28 Consent to the Landlord's release . . . . [807]

4 THE LANDLORD'S COVENANTS

4.1 Quiet enjoyment . . . . [821]
4.2 The Services . . . . [822]

5 INSURANCE

5.1 Warranty as to convictions . . . . [823]
5.2 Covenant to insure . . . . [823]
5.3 Details of the insurance . . . . [824]
5.4 Payment of the Insurance Rent . . . . [825]
5.5 Suspension of the Rent . . . . [825]
5.6 Reinstatement and termination . . . . [826]
5.7 Tenant's further insurance covenants . . . . [831]
5.8 Increase or decrease of the Estate . . . . [833]
[5.9 Landlord's further insurance covenants . . . . [833]]

6 GUARANTEE PROVISIONS

6.1 The Guarantor's covenants . . . . [851]
[6.2 The Landlord's covenant . . . . [856]]

7 FORFEITURE . . . . [871]

[703]

8 MISCELLANEOUS

8.1 Exclusion of warranty as to use . . . . [873]
8.2 Exclusion of third party rights . . . . [873]
8.3 Representations . . . . [873]
8.4 Documents under hand . . . . [874]
8.5 Tenant's property . . . . [874]
8.6 Compensation on vacating excluded . . . . [874]
8.7 Notices . . . . [875]
8.8 Rights and easements . . . . [876]
8.9 Covenants relating to adjoining property . . . . [876]
8.10 Disputes with adjoining occupiers . . . . [876]
8.11 Effect of waiver . . . . [876]
[8.12 The perpetuity period . . . . [877]]
[8.13 Party walls . . . . [877]]
8.14 Exclusion of liability . . . . [877]
8.15 [New (or) Old] lease . . . . [877]
[8.16 Capacity of tenants . . . . [878]]
[8.17 Exclusion of the 1954 Act Sections 24–28 . . . . [878]]

SCHEDULE 1: THE RIGHTS GRANTED

1-1 Rights of way . . . . [879]
1-2 Right to use the Common Parts . . . . [880]
1-3 Passage and running through Adjoining Conduits . . . . [880]
1-4 Support and protection . . . . [880]

SCHEDULE 2: THE RIGHTS RESERVED

2-1 Passage and running through the Conduits . . . . [881]
2-2 Right to construct conduits . . . . [881]
2-3 Access . . . . [882]

2-4 Right to erect scaffolding . . . . [883]
2-5 Rights of support and shelter . . . . [883]
2-6 Right to erect new buildings . . . . [883]

SCHEDULE 3: THE RENT AND RENT REVIEW

SCHEDULE 4: THE INDUSTRIAL COVENANTS

4-1 Use . . . . [884]
4-2 Smoke abatement . . . . [884]
4-3 Environmental protection . . . . [885]
4-4 Roof and floor loading . . . . [886]
4-5 Machinery . . . . [887]
4-6 Signs . . . . [887]
4-7 Unloading and parking . . . . [887]
4-8 Selling in the Common Parts . . . . [888]
4-9 Regulations . . . . [888]

SCHEDULE 5: THE SUBJECTIONS

SCHEDULE 6: THE SERVICE CHARGE

6-1 Definitions . . . . [889]
6-2 Service charge provisions . . . . [890]
6-3 The Services . . . . [892]

SCHEDULE 7: THE AUTHORISED GUARANTEE AGREEMENT

[704]

AGREEMENT

[HM LAND REGISTRY

LAND REGISTRATION ACT 2002

Administrative area	*(insert details)*
Title number out of which lease is granted	*(title number)*
Property let	*(postal address or description)*]

[705]

THIS LEASE is made the . . . . day of . . . . BETWEEN:

(1)   *(name of landlord)* [of *(address)* *(or as appropriate)* the registered office of which is at *(address)*] [Company Registration no ...][2] ('the Landlord') [and]

(2)   *(name of tenant)* [of *(address)* *(or as appropriate)* being a company registered in [England and Wales *(or)* Scotland][3] the registered office of which is at *(address)*] [Company Registration no ...] ('the Tenant') [and

(3)   *(name of guarantor)* [of *(address)* *(or as appropriate)* the registered office of which is at *(address)*] [Company Registration no ...] ('the Guarantor')]

[706]

1   As to stamp duty land tax see the Information Binder: Stamp Duty Land Tax [1].

As to Land Registry Fees see the Information Binder: Property [1]: Property Fees.

On the grant out of an unregistered freehold estate in land of a lease for a term of more than seven years from the date of the grant, application must be made to register the title to the leasehold interest granted: see the Land Registration Act 2002 s 4(1)(c) (37 Halsbury's Statutes (4th Edn) REAL PROPERTY). The tenant must obtain an epitome of title to the freehold reversion, investigate it, and mark it as examined, otherwise he will not be able to be registered with an absolute title: see vol 25(1) (2003 Reissue) LAND REGISTRATION Paragraph 21.1 [132].

If the freehold reversion is registered, the grant of a lease for a term of more than seven years from the date of the grant must be completed by registration: see the Land Registration Act 2002 s 27(2)(b)(i).

As to the form and contents of leases see vol 22(1) (2003 Reissue) LANDLORD AND TENANT (BUSINESS TENANCIES) Paragraph 104 [601] et seq. As to registered land generally see vol 25(1) (2003 Reissue) LAND REGISTRATION. As to registration of title to leases see vol 25(1) (2003 Reissue) LAND REGISTRATION Paragraph 143 [601] et seq.

This is a lease of light industrial or warehouse premises, comprising part of a building on an industrial estate that includes only the interior of the unit and the inner half of the non-structural walls dividing it from the adjoining unit(s). The tenant's repairing covenant is similarly limited. Rights are granted over land adjoining the premises. The landlord covenants to provide services that include the repair and maintenance of those parts of the estate not intended for letting, such as the common parts and the structure, roof and foundations of the buildings. The landlord is to be fully reimbursed by means of a service charge, the tenant paying a fixed percentage of the costs of providing the services and any other sums incurred by the landlord in relation to the estate. The landlord insures and the tenant refunds a proportion of the premium. There is provision for the rent to be reviewed and for a guarantor.

The tenant should ensure that the landlord deduces title to the land affected by the rights he is granted, especially where the lease is registrable, because if title is not shown and any consents, eg of any chargee or landlord of the adjoining land, obtained, the rights may be excluded from the title.

2   If any party is a company it is desirable to include the company registration number. This avoids any problems arising when a company has been wound up and a new company formed with the same name, or when the name of a company is changed, or if companies swap names, eg on a reconstruction of a group of companies. In addition, where a company applies to be registered as proprietor of a registered estate or registered charge, the application must state the company's registration number: see the Land Registration Rules 2003, SI 2003/1417 r 181.

3   Where the tenant is a company registered in England and Wales or Scotland, and the lease is registrable, an application for first registration of the lease (where the landlord's title is unregistered), or registration of the lease as a registrable disposition (where the landlord's title is registered), and the tenant as proprietor of the leasehold title, must state the company's registered number: see SI 2003/1417 r 181(1). There seems to be no reason why the certificate and statement should not be contained in the disposition in favour of the proprietor, where convenient.

[707]

NOW THIS DEED WITNESSES as follows:

1   DEFINITIONS AND INTERPRETATION

For all purposes of this Lease[4] the terms defined in this clause have the meanings specified.

4   One view would add 'unless the context otherwise requires' or 'where the context so admits' and in fact this may be implied (see *Meux v Jacobs* (1875) LR 7 HL 481 at 493; *Law Society v United Service Bureau Ltd* [1934] 1 KB 343, DC) but the better course is to use defined terms in such a way that there are no circumstances where the defined meaning does not apply.

1.1   'The Accountant'[5]

'The Accountant' means *(name)* or any qualified accountant or firm of accountants appointed by the Landlord in his place. The Accountant may be an employee of the Landlord or a company that is a member of the same group of the Landlord within the meaning of the 1954 Act Section 42.

5   For a provision that a surveyor or accountant must be a member of a relevant professional body see vol 22(3) (1997 Reissue) LANDLORD AND TENANT (BUSINESS TENANCIES) Form 152 [6648].

1.2   'The Adjoining Conduits'

'The Adjoining Conduits' means all the pipes, sewers, drains, mains, ducts, conduits, gutters, watercourses, wires, cables, [laser optical fibres, data or impulse transmission, communication or reception systems,] channels, flues and all other conducting media— including any fixings, louvres, cowls, covers and other ancillary apparatus — that are in, on, over or under the Estate that serve the Premises.

1.3   'Adjoining property of the Landlord'

References to 'adjoining property of the Landlord' are references to each and every part of any neighbouring or adjoining land, including the rest of the Estate, in which the Landlord, or a company that is a member of the same group as the Landlord within the meaning of the 1954 Act Section 42, has or during the Term acquires an interest or estate.

1.4   'The Building'

'The Building' means *(describe the building, eg by name or number)* on the Estate shown [for the purpose of identification only] edged *(state colour, eg green)* on the Plan.

1.5   'The Common Parts'

'The Common Parts' means the areas and amenities on the Estate made available from time to time by the Landlord for use in common by the tenants and occupiers of the Estate and visitors to the Estate, or any of them, including the pedestrian ways, forecourts, landscaped areas and roads but not limited to them.

[708]

1.6   'The Conduits'

'The Conduits' means the pipes, sewers, drains, mains, ducts, conduits, gutters, watercourses, wires, cables, [laser optical fibres, data or impulse transmission, communication or reception systems,] channels, flues and all other conducting media — including any fixings, louvres, cowls, covers and any other ancillary apparatus — that are in, on, over or under the Premises.

1.7   'The [Contractual] Term'[6]

'The [Contractual][7] Term' means *(insert number)* years commencing on and including *(date of commencement of term)*[8].

---

6   As to the commencement of the term see vol 22(1) (2003 Reissue) LANDLORD AND TENANT (BUSINESS TENANCIES) Paragraph 135 [670].
        As to registration see note 1 above. Where the landlord's title is unregistered, the grantee must apply for registration within a period of two months from the date of the disposition if the lease is granted for a term of more than seven years. If no such application is made the disposition becomes void as regards any transfer, grant or creation of a legal estate: see the Land Registration Act 2002 s 6 (37 Halsbury's Statutes (4th Edn) REAL PROPERTY). Where the landlord's title is registered and the lease is for a term of more than seven years, the tenant should protect the intended lease by applying for an official search, and an application to register the lease should be made before expiry of the search, otherwise the lease will be susceptible to loss of priority: see the Land Registration Act 2002 s 27.

7   The demise in this lease is for 'the Contractual Term', which is defined as a fixed term of years. The expression 'the Term', as defined in clause 1.51 [737] 'THE TERM', is used in covenants so that they continue to apply during any period of holding over or continuance or extension of the contractual term. Some difficulties arise if this structure is used in a draft lease where security of tenure is to be excluded under the Landlord and Tenant Act 1954 s 38A(1) as inserted by SI 2003/3096 (23 Halsbury's Statutes (4th Edn) LANDLORD AND TENANT). The demise is for the contractual term and the

inclusion of the definition of 'the Term' does not prevent the lease being 'for a term of years certain' as required by the Landlord and Tenant Act 1954 s 38A(1). However, reference to continuance of the contractual term by statute is inappropriate where the operation of the security of tenure provisions in the Landlord and Tenant Act 1954 ss 24–28 is to be excluded. If a lease is contracted out of the Landlord and Tenant Act 1954 there can be no statutory extension, and if the tenant remains in occupation at the end of the contractual term he is holding over unlawfully unless there is an express agreement to extend the contractual term operating as a surrender and re-grant so that the original lease— and the agreement under the Landlord and Tenant Act 1954 s 38A(1) — has no further effect. It is suggested that in these circumstances the drafting should be simplified to include a single term (defined simply as 'the Term') by reference to the period of the contractual term. This can be achieved by amending this clause in the manner suggested and substituting it for clause 1.51 [737] 'THE TERM'.

8   For estate management reasons it is usually desirable to insert a quarter day here — or a rent day when rent is due on days other than quarter days — ie generally the one preceding the earlier of the date of possession and the date of execution.

[709]

[1.8   'The Decorating Years'

'The Decorating Years' means *(specify years).*] *(omit if not required, eg if the first alternative in clause 3.4.6 [755] DECORATION is used)*

1.9   'Development'

References to 'development' are references to development as defined by the Town and Country Planning Act 1990 Section 55.

1.10   'The Estate'

'The Estate' means all the land and buildings known as the *(name)* Industrial Estate shown [for the purpose of identification only] edged *(state colour, eg blue)* on the Plan.

1.11   'The Estate Roads'

'The Estate Roads' means the roads within the Estate that are neither let to any tenant nor maintainable at the public expense.

1.12   Gender and number

Words importing one gender include all other genders; words importing the singular include the plural and vice versa[9].

9   See the Law of Property Act 1925 s 61 (37 Halsbury's Statutes (4th Edn) REAL PROPERTY).

1.13   Headings[10]

The clause, paragraph and schedule headings and the table of contents do not form part of this document and are not to be taken into account in its construction or interpretation. *(amend if marginal notes are used instead of headings)*

10   Headings and marginal notes require the draftsman to provide a word or two to describe every clause in the lease. This is not always easy and there are times when the draftsman will have to settle for something less than perfection, the only alternative being a heading or note that would be inappropriately long. It would be quite wrong for that title, which its author might admit was not totally apposite but was the best that he could do in a few words, to be used in construing the clause in question.

1.14   'The Industrial Covenants'

'The Industrial Covenants' means the covenants set out in schedule 4 THE INDUSTRIAL COVENANTS.

[710]

[1.15 'The Initial Rent'

'The Initial Rent' means [the sum of £... a year *(or as required by the rent and review provisions to be used)*].] *(this definition is not required if the rent is not reviewable)*

1.16 'The Insurance Rent'[11]

'The Insurance Rent' means the Insurance Rent Percentage of the [gross sums including any commission *(or as required)* sums net of any commission] that the Landlord is from time to time liable to pay —

1.16.1   by way of premium for insuring the Estate, including insuring for loss of rent, in accordance with his obligations contained in this Lease[— or, where the insurance includes the Estate and other property[12], the proportion of such sums [reasonably] attributable to the Estate, such proportion to be determined from time to time by the Surveyor acting as an expert and not as an arbitrator],

1.16.2   by way of premium for insuring in such amount and on such terms as [the Landlord acting reasonably considers appropriate *(or as required)* is reasonable] against all liability of the Landlord to third parties arising out of or in connection with any matter involving or relating to the Estate, and

1.16.3   for insurance valuations,

and all of any increased premium payable because of any act or omission of the Tenant.

11   As to reimbursement of insurance premiums see vol 22(1) (2003 Reissue) LANDLORD AND TENANT (BUSINESS TENANCIES) Paragraph 230 [1026].
12   The estate may be insured with other property under a block policy.

1.17 'The Insurance Rent Percentage'

'The Insurance Rent Percentage' means ...%.

1.18 'The Insured Risks'

'The Insured Risks' means the risks of loss or damage by fire[, storm, tempest, earthquake, lightning, explosion, riot, civil commotion, malicious damage, [terrorism,] impact by vehicles and by aircraft and articles dropped from aircraft — other than war risks — flood damage and bursting and overflowing of water pipes and tanks,] and such other risks, whether or not in the nature of the foregoing, as the Landlord [acting reasonably] from time to time decides to insure against[13].

13   As to the risks to be insured and the tenant's concerns see vol 22(1) (2003 Reissue) LANDLORD AND TENANT (BUSINESS TENANCIES) Paragraph 235 [1033].

[711]

1.19 'Interest'

References to 'interest' are references to interest payable during the period from the date on which the payment is due to the date of payment, both before and after any judgment, at the Interest Rate then prevailing [*(where the interest rate is defined by reference to a bank base rate)* or, should the base rate referred to in clause 1.20 'THE INTEREST RATE' cease to exist[14], at another rate of interest closely comparable with the Interest Rate [to be agreed between the parties or in default of agreement to be determined by the Accountant[15], acting as an expert and not as an arbitrator *(or as required)* decided upon by the Landlord acting reasonably]].

14   If base rates are referred to, the possibility of their ceasing to exist should be provided for. Alternatively, the Law Society's interest rate may be specified.
15   Where the structure of the lease is such that an accountant is required in the operation of its terms he is a more appropriate person than the surveyor to determine this issue.

1.20 'The Interest Rate'

'The Interest Rate'[16] means the rate of ...% a year[17] above [the base lending rate of *(specify bank)* or such other bank [being a member of the British Bankers Association] as the Landlord may from time to time nominate in writing[18]*(or as required)* the Law Society's interest rate[19]].

16   As to the covenant to pay interest see vol 22(1) (2003 Reissue) LANDLORD AND TENANT (BUSINESS TENANCIES) Paragraph 154 [767].

17   Words such as 'with a minimum of ...%' should not be used because, if interest rates drop during the term to such an extent that the minimum rate specified represents significantly more than a few percent over the basic borrowing rate, the provision might be void as a penalty. As to what amounts to a penalty see *Dunlop Pneumatic Tyre Co Ltd v New Garage and Motor Co Ltd* [1915] AC 79, HL; *Cellulose Acetate Silk Co Ltd v Widnes Foundry (1925) Ltd* [1933] AC 20, HL. In view of this, landlords would be unwise to provide for more than a few percent over base rate, and even this is in fact a penalty and should be resisted by the tenant.

18   The chance to change the bank may be useful, especially on a sale of the reversion, so that the landlord can always provide for his bank for the time being to be specified. The tenant should try to limit the choice to major clearing banks.

19   The Law Society's interest rate is published weekly in the Law Society's Gazette.

[712]

1.21 Interpretation of 'consent' and 'approved'

1.21.1 *Prior written consent or approval*

References to 'consent of the Landlord' or words to similar effect are references to a prior written consent signed by or on behalf of the Landlord and references to the need for anything to be 'approved by the Landlord' or words to similar effect are references to the need for a prior written approval by or on behalf of the Landlord.

1.21.2 *Consent or approval of mortgagee or head landlord*

Any provisions in this Lease referring to the consent or approval of the Landlord are to be construed as also requiring the consent or approval of any mortgagee of the Premises and any head landlord, where that consent is required [under a mortgage or headlease in existence at the date of this document][20]. Nothing in this Lease is to be construed as imposing any obligation on a mortgagee or head landlord not to refuse any such consent or approval unreasonably.

20   The tenant should include these words so that the clause applies *only* where the consent of the mortgagee or head landlord is in fact required under the terms of an *existing* mortgage or headlease. The tenant should request a copy of the document concerned to establish the rights of the mortgagee or head landlord in relation to any consents that he may seek. The risk to the tenant of the clause without these words is that, by subsequently creating a mortgage or headlease, the landlord could, innocently or deliberately, bring about a situation where his consent may be refused in circumstances in which it would otherwise have been unreasonable to do so. In particular, the effect on the tenant's ability to assign or sublet could be serious.

1.22 Interpretation of 'the Estate'

The expression 'the Estate', where the context so admits, includes any other adjoining property of the Landlord that is constructed or acquired to form [an integral] part of the Estate[21].

21   As to problems in connection with the service charge caused by expansion of the estate see vol 22(1) (2003 Reissue) LANDLORD AND TENANT (BUSINESS TENANCIES) Paragraph 269.1 [1117].

1.23   Interpretation of 'the Guarantor'[22]

The expression 'the Guarantor' includes [*(where there is a guarantor for the original tenant)* not only the person named above as the Guarantor, but also][23] any person who enters into covenants with the Landlord pursuant to clause 3.9.5.2 CONDITIONS or clause 3.23 REPLACEMENT GUARANTOR.

22   As to guarantors see vol 22(1) (2003 Reissue) LANDLORD AND TENANT (BUSINESS TENANCIES) Paragraphs 40 [201], 71 [278] et seq.
23   Where there is no guarantor for the original tenant, if it is felt undesirable to have covenants in a lease and no party, at least initially, to enter into them, the guarantor's covenants could be included in a schedule.

[713]

1.24   Interpretation of 'the Landlord'

The expression 'the Landlord' includes the person or persons from time to time entitled to possession of the Premises when this Lease comes to an end.

1.25   Interpretation of 'the last year of the Term' and 'the end of the Term'

References to 'the last year of the Term' are references to the actual last year of the Term howsoever it determines, and references to the 'end of the Term' are references to the end of the Term whensoever and howsoever it determines.

1.26   Interpretation of 'the Tenant'

'The Tenant' includes any person who is for the time being bound by the tenant covenants of this Lease except where the name of *(name of original tenant)* appears.

1.27   Interpretation of 'this Lease'

Unless expressly stated to the contrary, the expression 'this Lease' includes any document supplemental to or collateral with this document or entered into in accordance with this document.

1.28   Joint and several liability

Where any party to this Lease for the time being comprises two or more persons, obligations expressed or implied to be made by or with that party are deemed to be made by or with the persons comprising that party jointly and severally.

1.29   'The Landlord's Expenses'

'The Landlord's Expenses' means the costs and expenditure — including all charges, commissions, premiums, fees and interest — paid or incurred, or deemed in accordance with the provisions of paragraph 6-2.3 DEEMED LANDLORD'S EXPENSES to be paid or incurred, by the Landlord in respect of or incidental to all or any of the Services or otherwise required to be taken into account for the purpose of calculating the Service Charge, except those recovered from any insurance policy effected by the Landlord pursuant to clause 5.2 COVENANT TO INSURE.

[714]–[730]

1.30 'The Liability Period'[24]

'The Liability Period' means —

[1.30.1 in the case of *(name of guarantor for the original tenant)*, the period during which *(name of original tenant)* is bound by the tenant covenants of this Lease together with any additional period during which *(name of original tenant)* is liable under an authorised guarantee agreement,] *(omit where there is no guarantor for the original tenant)*

1.30.2 in the case of any guarantor required pursuant to clause 3.9.5.2 CONDITIONS, the period during which the relevant assignee is bound by the tenant covenants of this Lease together with any additional period during which that assignee is liable under an authorised guarantee agreement,

1.30.3 in the case of any guarantor under an authorised guarantee agreement, the period during which the relevant assignee is bound by the tenant covenants of this Lease, and

1.30.4 in the case of any guarantor required pursuant to clause 3.9.8.7 TERMS OF A PERMITTED SUBLEASE, the period during which the relevant assignee of the sublease is bound by the tenant covenants of that sublease.

---

24   The liability of the guarantor should be expressed to last while the original tenant, or as the case may be the assignee, is bound by the tenant covenants in the lease — or in the case of clause 1.30.4 the sublease — rather than while the lease is vested in that person, to take account of the possibility of an excluded assignment being made and the tenant — or subtenant — remaining liable. An excluded assignment means that the tenant — or subtenant — is precluded from tenant release under the Landlord and Tenant (Covenants) Act 1995 (23 Halsbury's Statutes (4th Edn) LANDLORD AND TENANT).

The Landlord and Tenant (Covenants) Act 1995 does not clearly indicate whether the liability of a contractual guarantor can be expressed to extend to any period during which the tenant is bound by an authorised guarantee agreement, but the better view is that it is possible. The policy of the Act certainly suggests that this should be the case.

[731]

1.31 'Losses'

References to 'losses' are references to liabilities, damages or losses, awards of damages or compensation, penalties, costs, disbursements or expenses arising from any claim, demand, action or proceedings.

1.32 'The 1954 Act'

'The 1954 Act' means the Landlord and Tenant Act 1954 [and all statutes, regulations and orders included by virtue of clause 1.43 REFERENCES TO STATUTES][25].

---

25   The words in square brackets are strictly speaking not required because they merely state what would be the case anyway by virtue of clause 1.43 [735] REFERENCES TO STATUTES. Nevertheless, as much could turn on the point (see *Brett v Brett Essex Golf Club Ltd* (1986) 52 P & CR 330, [1986] 1 EGLR 154, CA), the parties may prefer to deal expressly with the point.

1.33 'The 1995 Act'

'The 1995 Act' means the Landlord and Tenant (Covenants) Act 1995 [and all statutes, regulations and orders included by virtue of clause 1.47 REFERENCES TO STATUTES][26].

---

26   See note 25 to clause 1.32 [732] 'THE 1954 ACT'.

1.34   Obligation not to permit or suffer

Any covenant by the Tenant not to do anything includes an obligation [to use reasonable endeavours] not to permit or suffer[27] that thing to be done by another person [where the Tenant is aware that the thing is being done].

27   'Permit' may have a different meaning from 'suffer': see *Barton v Reed* [1932] 1 Ch 362 at 375 per Luxmore J. A covenant not to 'permit' activity is broken if the covenantor himself carries it on: see *Oceanic Village Ltd v United Attractions Ltd* [2000] Ch 234, [2000] 1 All ER 975.

1.35   'Other buildings'

References to 'other buildings' are references to any buildings — excluding the Building — now or at any time during the Term erected on any adjoining property of the Landlord.

1.36   'The Parking Bays'

'The Parking Bays' means the car parking bays and loading area shown *(state colour, eg red hatched black)* on the Plan.

[732]

1.37   'The Permitted Use'[28]

'The Permitted Use' means [*(specify use)* or any other use falling within Classes *(state classes, eg B1, B2 or B8)* of the Schedule to the Town and Country Planning (Use Classes) Order 1987, notwithstanding any amendment or revocation of that Order[29], as the Landlord from time to time approves[, such approval not to be unreasonably withheld [or delayed]] *(or where the landlord does not require control over the specific trade)* any use that falls within Classes *(state classes, eg B1, B2 or B8)* of the Schedule to the Town and Country Planning (Use Classes) Order 1987, notwithstanding any amendment or revocation of that Order].

28   As to use see vol 22(1) (2003 Reissue) LANDLORD AND TENANT (BUSINESS TENANCIES) Paragraph 170 [861] et seq.
29   As use classes orders change frequently, it is important to make clear which class is intended to apply, the class in existence at the date of the lease or the class as amended during the term of the lease.

1.38   'The Plan'[30]

'The Plan' means the plan annexed to this Lease.

30   As to the use and role of plans see vol 22(1) (2003 Reissue) LANDLORD AND TENANT (BUSINESS TENANCIES) Paragraphs 117 [636], 118 [638]. Although a plan is necessary in the circumstances assumed by this lease, a plan may not always be required, eg a demise of all the land within a registered title. If the lease is registrable, a plan 'for identification purposes only' or where there is some other disclaimer as to the extent to which it can be relied on for conveyancing purposes is not sufficient if part of the land in a registered title is being dealt with.

1.39   'The Planning Acts'

'The Planning Acts' means the Town and Country Planning Act 1990, the Planning (Listed Buildings and Conservation Areas) Act 1990, the Planning (Consequential Provisions) Act 1990, the Planning (Hazardous Substances) Act 1990, the Planning and Compensation Act 1991, the Planning and Compulsory Purchase Act 2004 [and all statutes, regulations and orders included by virtue of clause 1.43 REFERENCE TO STATUTES][31].

31   See note 25 to clause 1.32 [732] 'THE 1954 ACT'.

1.40   'The Premises'[32]

1.40.1   *Definition of 'the Premises'*

'The Premises' means Unit *(number of unit)* of the Building shown [for the purpose of identification only] edged *(state colour, eg red)* on the Plan.

---

32   As to parcels generally see vol 22(1) (2003 Reissue) LANDLORD AND TENANT (BUSINESS TENANCIES) Paragraph 116 [634]. As to the property definition in leases of part of a building see vol 22(1) (2003 Reissue) LANDLORD AND TENANT (BUSINESS TENANCIES) Paragraph 120 [642].

[733]

1.40.2   *Interpretation of 'the Premises'[33]*

The expression 'the Premises' includes —

[1.40.2.1   the floor and ceiling finishes, but not any other part of the floor slabs and ceiling slabs that bound the Premises,

1.40.2.2   the inner half served medially of the internal non-loadbearing walls that divide the Premises from any other premises,

1.40.2.3   the interior plaster and decorative finishes of all walls bounding the Premises,

1.40.2.4   the doors and windows and door and window frames at the Premises,

1.40.2.5   all additions and improvements to the Premises,

1.40.2.6   all the Landlord's fixtures and fittings, and fixtures of every kind that are from time to time in or on the Premises, whether originally fixed or fastened to or on the Premises or otherwise, except any fixtures installed by the Tenant [or any predecessors in title] that can be removed from the Premises without defacing them[34],

1.40.2.7   the Conduits exclusively serving the Premises, and

1.40.2.8   the Parking Bays,

but excludes the roof and the roof space, the foundations, all external, structural or loadbearing walls, columns, beams and supports, and any of the Conduits that do not exclusively serve the Premises *(or as required in the circumstances, according to the construction methods used)*][35]. Unless the contrary is expressly stated 'the Premises' includes any part or parts of the Premises.

---

33   As to implied grants and reservations see vol 22(1) (2003 Reissue) LANDLORD AND TENANT (BUSINESS TENANCIES) Paragraph 125 [650].

34   As to fixtures see vol 22(1) (2003 Reissue) LANDLORD AND TENANT (BUSINESS TENANCIES) Paragraph 121 [644].

35   It is very dangerous for the draftsman to rely on one set of general words that he hopes will apply to the division of all buildings. These 'standard words' may prove totally unsuitable for a particular building having regard to its nature, configuration and the methods of construction used and also having regard to the nature and extent of any surrounding land included within the demise. Surveyors and engineers must be involved and each building must be looked at individually. There can be no uniform answer as to who should repair which parts of the premises. This clause may need amendment according to the view taken. As to the allocation of legal and financial responsibility for repairs see vol 22(1) (2003 Reissue) LANDLORD AND TENANT (BUSINESS TENANCIES) Paragraph 199 [936].

[734]

1.41   References to clauses and schedules

Any reference in this document to a clause, paragraph or schedule without further designation is to be construed as a reference to the clause, paragraph or schedule to this document so numbered.

1.42   References to rights of access

References to any right of the Landlord to have access to the Premises are to be construed as extending to any head landlord and any mortgagee of the Premises [— where the headlease or mortgage grants such rights of access to the head landlord or mortgagee —] and to all persons authorised in writing by the Landlord and any head landlord or mortgagee, including agents, professional advisers, contractors, workmen and others.

1.43   References to statutes

Unless expressly stated to the contrary any references to a specific statute include any statutory extension or modification amendment or re-enactment of that statute and any regulations or orders made under it and any general reference to a statute includes any regulations or orders made under that statute[36].

36   Unfortunately the Interpretation Act 1978 ss 17, 23(3) (41 Halsbury's Statutes (4th Edn) STATUTES) does not quite go far enough to enable this clause to be dispensed with altogether, particularly where a statute is modified.

1.44   'The Rent'[37]

[Until the First Review Date 'the Rent' means the Initial Rent. Thereafter 'the Rent' means the sum ascertained in accordance with schedule 3 THE RENT AND RENT REVIEW. 'The Rent' does not include the Insurance Rent and the Service Charge[38], but the term 'the Lease Rents' means both the Rent and the Insurance Rent and the Service Charge. *(or as required by the rent and review provisions used)*]

37   This clause assumes that the rent is reviewable. If the rent is not reviewable clause 1.15 [711] 'THE INITIAL RENT' should be omitted and this clause amended as appropriate.
38   Because of this exclusion the insurance rent and service charge are not suspended under clause 5.5 [825] SUSPENSION OF THE RENT.

1.45   'The Rent Commencement Date'

'The Rent Commencement Date' means *(insert date on which payment of the rent is to start)*[39].

39   This provision may be inserted to provide for a rent-free period, or for the situation where the tenant has had possession before the execution of the lease on the basis that rent should be paid from the date of possession. If either the date of execution of the lease, or the date of commencement of the term, is to be the date of commencement of rent, that date should be inserted here.

[735]

[1.46   'The Review Dates'[40]

'The First Review Date' means *(date)*. 'The Review Dates' means the First Review Date and every *(insert ordinal, eg 3rd)* anniversary of that date during the [Contractual] Term [*(if appropriate for the review provisions used)* — and any other date from time to time specified under *(insert the relevant provision: see eg vol 22(3) (1997 Reissue) LANDLORD AND TENANT (BUSINESS TENANCIES) Form 180 paragraph {2}-4 [6728] EFFECT OF COUNTER-INFLATION PROVISIONS)*]. References to 'a review date' are references to any one of the Review Dates.] *(omit if not required by the review provisions to be used, or if the rent is not reviewable)*

40   As to rent review dates and intervals see vol 22(1) (2003 Reissue) LANDLORD AND TENANT (BUSINESS TENANCIES) Paragraph 302 [1333] et seq. Where there might be a statutory continuation of the lease, the landlord may wish to ensure that there is a review date shortly before the end of the contractual term to obviate the need to apply for an interim rent. The tenant may wish to insist on the word 'contractual' remaining so that the rent review provisions do not apply during any period of lawful holding over or extension or continuance of the contractual term.

1.47   'The Service Charge'

'The Service Charge' means the Service Charge Percentage of the Landlord's Expenses.

1.48   'The Service Charge Percentage'

'The Service Charge Percentage' means ...% subject to the provisions for variation contained in paragraph 6-2.6 VARIATION OF THE SERVICE CHARGE PERCENTAGE. *(this definition may not be required where the tenant's proportion is determined by reference to net internal areas: see vol 22(3) (1997 Reissue) LANDLORD AND TENANT (BUSINESS TENANCIES) Form 150 [6626])*

1.49   'The Services'

'The Services' means the services, facilities and amenities specified in paragraph 6-3 THE SERVICES.

[736]

1.50   'The Surveyor'[41]

'The Surveyor' means *(name)* or any person or firm appointed by the Landlord in his place. The Surveyor may be an employee of the Landlord or a company that is a member of the same group as the Landlord within the meaning of the 1954 Act Section 42. The expression 'the Surveyor' includes the person or firm appointed by the Landlord to collect the Lease Rents.

41   For a provision that the landlord's surveyor must be a member of a relevant professional body see vol 22(3) (1997 Reissue) LANDLORD AND TENANT (BUSINESS TENANCIES) Form 152 [6648].

[1.51   'The Term'

'The Term' means the Contractual Term and any period of holding-over or extension or continuance of the Contractual Term by statute or common law[42].] *(omit if the lease is to be contracted out of the Landlord and Tenant Act 1954)*[43]

42   The demise in this lease is for 'the Contractual Term', which is defined as a fixed term of years. The expression 'the Term' is used in covenants so that they continue to apply during any period of holding over or continuance or extension of the contractual term. As to the liability of a guarantor during a period of statutory continuation see vol 22(1) (2003 Reissue) LANDLORD AND TENANT (BUSINESS TENANCIES) Paragraph 73 [282].

43   Some difficulties arise if the structure referred to in note 42 above is used in a draft lease where security of tenure is to be excluded under the Landlord and Tenant Act 1954 s 38A(1) as inserted by SI 2003/3096. The demise is for the contractual term and the inclusion of the definition of 'the Term' does not prevent the lease being 'for a term of years certain' as required by the Landlord and Tenant Act 1954 s 38A(1). However, reference to continuance of the contractual term by statute is inappropriate where the operation of the security of tenure provisions in the Landlord and Tenant Act 1954 ss 24–28 is to be excluded. If a lease is contracted out of the Landlord and Tenant Act 1954 there can be no statutory extension, and if the tenant remains in occupation at the end of the contractual term he is holding over unlawfully unless there is an express agreement to extend the contractual term operating as a surrender and re-grant so that the original lease — and the agreement under the Landlord and Tenant Act 1954 s 38A(1) — has no further effect. It is suggested that in these circumstances the drafting should be simplified to include a single term defined by reference to the period of the contractual term. This can be achieved by amending clause 1.7 [709] 'THE [CONTRACTUAL] TERM' as suggested and substituting it for this clause.

1.52 Terms from the 1995 Act

Where the expressions 'landlord covenants', 'tenant covenants', or 'authorised guarantee agreement' are used in this Lease they are to have the same meaning as is given by the 1995 Act Section 28(1).

1.53 'VAT'[44]

'VAT' means value added tax or any other tax of a similar nature and unless otherwise expressly stated all references to rents or other sums payable by the Tenant are exclusive of VAT.

44   As to VAT generally see the Information Binder: Property [1]: VAT and Property.

[737]–[750]

2   DEMISE

The Landlord lets[45] the Premises to the Tenant [with [full *(or)* limited] title guarantee], together with the rights specified in schedule 1 THE RIGHTS GRANTED, but excepting and reserving to the Landlord the rights specified in schedule 2 THE RIGHTS RESERVED, to hold the Premises to the Tenant for the [Contractual][46] Term, subject to [all rights, easements, privileges, restrictions, covenants and stipulations of whatever nature affecting the Premises including any matters contained or referred to in schedule 5 THE SUBJECTIONS *(or as required)* the rights, easements, privileges, restrictions, covenants and stipulations affecting the Premises contained or referred to in schedule 5 THE SUBJECTIONS][47], yielding and paying[48] to the Landlord —

2.1   the Rent, without any deduction or set off[49], by equal quarterly payments in advance[50] on the usual quarter days[51] in every year and proportionately for any period of less than a year, the first such payment, being a proportionate sum in respect of the period from and including the Rent Commencement Date to and including the day before the quarter day next after the Rent Commencement Date, to be paid on the date of this document[52], and

2.2   by way of further rent the Insurance Rent[53] payable on demand in accordance with clause 5.4 PAYMENT OF THE INSURANCE RENT, and

2.3   by way of further rent the Service Charge[54] payable in accordance with schedule 6 THE SERVICE CHARGE.

45   Traditionally, the operative word in a lease executed as a deed was 'demises' but any words sufficient to show the parties' intention may be used.
46   See note 43 to clause 1.51 [737] 'THE TERM'.
47   The tenant should argue for the second version, making the schedule comprehensive rather than illustrative.
48   The words 'yielding and paying' imply a covenant to pay rent: see *Vyvyan v Arthur* (1823) 1 B & C 410. An express covenant is now invariably included because further procedural matters are contained in it.
49   As to deductions and set off see vol 22(1) (2003 Reissue) LANDLORD AND TENANT (BUSINESS TENANCIES) Paragraph 147 [753].
50   In the absence of an express provision, rent is payable in arrears.
51   The usual quarter days are 25 March, 24 June, 29 September and 25 December. A reference to 'the usual quarter days' is all that is necessary when rent is to be paid on these days.
52   If the first payment is not a complete instalment, the lease must provide for the date on which it is to be paid, the amount, and the period it is to cover.
53   As to the advantages of reserving the insurance rent as rent see vol 22(1) (2003 Reissue) LANDLORD AND TENANT (BUSINESS TENANCIES) Paragraph 151 [761].
54   As to the advantages of reserving the service charge as rent see vol 22(1) (2003 Reissue) LANDLORD AND TENANT (BUSINESS TENANCIES) Paragraph 151 [761].

[751]

3   THE TENANT'S COVENANTS

The Tenant covenants with the Landlord to observe and perform the requirements of this clause 3.

3.1   Rent

3.1.1   *Payment of the Lease Rents*

The Tenant must pay the Lease Rents[55] on the days and in the manner set out in this Lease and must not exercise or seek to exercise any right or claim to withhold rent or any right or claim to legal or equitable set-off[56] [except that referred to in *(give details of any provisions granting an express right of set-off)*][57].

55   As to the definition of 'the Lease Rents' see clause 1.44 [735] 'THE RENT'.
56   See, eg, *British Anzani (Felixstowe) Ltd v International Marine Management (UK) Ltd* [1980] QB 137, [1979] 2 All ER 1063; *Lee-Parker v Izzet* [1971] 3 All ER 1099, [1971] 1 WLR 1688. As to deductions and set-off see vol 22(1) (2003 Reissue) LANDLORD AND TENANT (BUSINESS TENANCIES) Paragraphs 147 [753], 148 [755].
57   If any express right of set-off is granted to the tenant, reference to the provision concerned should be included here to avoid inconsistency.

3.1.2   *Payment by banker's order*[58]

If so required in writing by the Landlord, the Tenant must pay the Lease Rents[59] by banker's order or credit transfer to any bank and account [in the United Kingdom] that the Landlord nominates from time to time.

58   This is a clause with dangers for both parties. If the existence of a breach of covenant is known to the landlord he must instruct his bank to refuse to accept the rent, otherwise his right of forfeiture is lost. As to implied waiver of the right of forfeiture see vol 22(1) (2003 Reissue) LANDLORD AND TENANT (BUSINESS TENANCIES) Paragraph 284 [1173]. The tenant may feel that he requires more control over the payment of rent. In any event, the financial systems operated by many companies prevent payments being made in this way.
59   As to the definition of 'the Lease Rents' see clause 1.44 [735] 'THE RENT'.

[752]

3.2   Outgoings and VAT

3.2.1   *Outgoings exclusive to the Premises*

The Tenant must pay, and must indemnify the Landlord against —

3.2.1.1   all rates, taxes[60], assessments, duties, charges, impositions and outgoings that are now or may at any time during the Term be charged, assessed or imposed upon the Premises or upon the owner or occupier of them[, excluding any payable by the Landlord occasioned by receipt of the Lease Rents[61] or by any disposition of or dealing with this Lease or ownership of any interest reversionary to the interest created by it][62] [— provided that if the Landlord suffers any loss of rating relief that may be applicable to empty premises after the end of the Term because the relief has been allowed to the Tenant in respect of any period before the end of the Term then the Tenant must make good such loss to the Landlord],

3.2.1.2   all VAT that may from time to time be charged on the Lease Rents or other sums payable by the Tenant under this Lease[63], and

3.2.1.3   all VAT incurred in relation to any costs that the Tenant is obliged to pay or in respect of which he is required to indemnify the Landlord under the terms of this Lease, save where such VAT is recoverable or available for set-off by the Landlord as input tax[64].

60   As to covenants to pay rates and taxes see vol 22(1) (2003 Reissue) LANDLORD AND TENANT
      (BUSINESS TENANCIES) Paragraph 153 [765].
61   As to the definition of 'the Lease Rents' see clause 1.44 [735] 'THE RENT'.
62   The tenant should add the words in square brackets to make it clear that he is not paying the landlord's
      taxes.
63   As to VAT on rent, service charges and insurance premiums see the Information Binder: Property [1]:
      VAT and Property.
64   As to payment of VAT on legal costs paid by a person other than the solicitor's own client see the
      Information Binder: Property [1]: VAT and Property.

3.2.2   *Outgoings assessed on the Premises and other property*

The Tenant must pay, and must indemnify the Landlord against, the proportion
reasonably attributable to the Premises — to be determined from time to time by the
Surveyor, acting as an expert and not as an arbitrator[65] — of all rates, taxes, assessments,
duties, charges, impositions and outgoings that are now or at any time during the Term
may be charged, assessed or imposed on the Premises and any other premises, including
any adjoining property of the Landlord, or on their owners or occupiers.

65   As to the distinction between an expert and an arbitrator see vol 22(1) (2003 Reissue) LANDLORD
      AND TENANT (BUSINESS TENANCIES) Paragraph 364 [1523].

[753]

[3.3   Cost of services consumed[66]

The Tenant must pay to the suppliers, and indemnify the Landlord against, all charges
for electricity, water, gas, telecommunications and other services consumed or used at or
in relation to the Premises, including meter rents and standing charges, and must comply
with the lawful requirements and regulations of the respective suppliers.] *(omit if the
premises have independent supplies of all services)*

66   Premises comprising only part of a building may well not have separate supplies of all services and, in
      these circumstances, this clause should be included.

3.4   Repair, cleaning and decoration

3.4.1   *Repair of the Premises*[67]

The Tenant must repair the Premises and keep them in good condition and repair,
except for damage caused by one or more of the Insured Risks save to the extent that
the insurance money is irrecoverable due to any act or default of the Tenant or anyone
at the Premises expressly or by implication[68] with his authority [and under his control][69].

67   As to repair see vol 22(1) (2003 Reissue) LANDLORD AND TENANT (BUSINESS TENANCIES)
      Paragraph 196 [931] et seq. For a covenant to repair, rebuild and renew see vol 22(3) (1997 Reissue)
      LANDLORD AND TENANT (BUSINESS TENANCIES) Form 85 [6460]. For provisos excluding, eg,
      work that is prevented etc see vol 22(3) (1997 Reissue) LANDLORD AND TENANT (BUSINESS
      TENANCIES) Forms 87 [6462], 88 [6463].
          If a landlord is unable to obtain full insurance cover without excess, it should be made clear whether
      the tenant is to be liable to pay the excess where damage is caused by an insured risk. For a covenant
      limiting the tenant's repairing obligations by reference to uninsurable as well as insured risks see vol
      22(3) (1997 Reissue) LANDLORD AND TENANT (BUSINESS TENANCIES) Form 90 [6465]. It should
      be noted that it is now recommended 'best practice' that if the premises are so damaged by an uninsured
      risk as to prevent occupation, the tenant should be allowed to terminate the lease unless the landlord
      agrees to reinstate at his own cost: see vol 22(1) (2003 Reissue) LANDLORD AND TENANT (BUSINESS
      TENANCIES) Paragraph 85 [402]. If adopted, this recommendation involves damage preventing
      occupation caused by uninsured or uninsurable risks being excluded from the ambit of the tenant's
      repairing covenant.
68   The expression 'by implication' is intended to include a caller on the premises, such as a tradesman,
      where there has been no express invitation but the person cannot be classed as a trespasser.
69   The tenant should add the words in square brackets.

[754]

3.4.2   *Replacement of landlord's fixtures*

The Tenant must replace from time to time any landlord's fixtures and fittings in the Premises that may be or become beyond repair at any time during or at the end of the Term.

3.4.3   *Cleaning and tidying*

The Tenant must keep the Premises clean and tidy and clear of all rubbish and, without prejudice to the generality of the above, must clean both sides of all windows in the Premises [at least *(state frequency, eg once every month) (or as required)* as is reasonably necessary].

3.4.4   *The Parking Bays*

3.4.4.1   **Care of the Parking Bays**

The Tenant must keep the Parking Bays adequately surfaced, in good condition and free from weeds and use them for car parking only.

3.4.4.2   **Storage on the Parking Bays**

The Tenant must not store anything on the Parking Bays [or bring anything onto them] [that is or might become untidy, unclean, unsightly or in any way detrimental to the Premises, any adjoining property of the Landlord or the area generally].

3.4.4.3   **Rubbish on the Parking Bays**

The Tenant must not deposit any waste, rubbish or refuse on the Parking Bays or place any receptacle for waste, rubbish or refuse on them.

3.4.4.4   **Vehicles on the Parking Bays**

The Tenant must not keep or store any caravan or movable dwelling on the Parking Bays.

3.4.5   *Care of adjoining property*

The Tenant must not cause any adjoining property of the Landlord or any other land, roads or pavements abutting the Premises to be untidy or dirty and in particular, but without prejudice to the generality of the foregoing, must not deposit refuse or other materials on them.

3.4.6   *Decoration*

[As often as may in the [reasonable] opinion of the Surveyor be necessary in order to maintain a high standard of decorative finish and attractiveness and to preserve the Premises *(or as required)* In each of the Decorating Years][70] and in the last year of the Term the Tenant must redecorate the Premises[71] in a good and workmanlike manner, with appropriate materials of good quality[, to the [reasonable] satisfaction of the Surveyor], any change in the tints, colours and patterns of the decoration to be approved by the Landlord [, whose approval may not be unreasonably withheld [or delayed]][72] [, provided that the covenants relating to the last year of the Term are not to apply where the Tenant has redecorated the Premises less than *(state period, eg 18 months)* before the end of the Term].

70   The draftsman should discuss with the landlord and his property advisers whether he wishes to have the flexibility of the first option or the certainty of the second.
71   The restricted nature of the demise should be borne in mind when considering the scope of this covenant: see clause 1.40 [733] 'THE PREMISES'.
72   The tenant may amend to provide for the landlord's approval to tints etc to apply only in the last year of the term.

[755]

3.5   Waste and alterations

3.5.1   *Waste, additions and alterations*[73]

The Tenant must not commit any waste, make any addition to the Premises, unite the Premises with any adjoining premises, or make any alteration to the Premises save as permitted by the provisions of this clause 3.5.

73   As to control of alterations see vol 22(1) (2003 Reissue) LANDLORD AND TENANT (BUSINESS TENANCIES) Paragraph 186 [911] et seq.

3.5.2   *Pre-conditions for alterations*

The Tenant must not make any [internal non-structural] alterations to the Premises unless he first —

3.5.2.1   obtains and complies with the necessary consents of the competent authorities and pays their charges for them,

3.5.2.2   makes an application to the Landlord for consent, supported by drawings and where appropriate a specification in duplicate [prepared by an architect[, or a member of some other appropriate profession,] who must supervise the work throughout to completion],

3.5.2.3   pays the fees of the Landlord, any head landlord, any mortgagee and their respective professional advisers,

3.5.2.4   enters into any covenants the Landlord requires as to the execution and reinstatement of the alterations, and

3.5.2.5   obtains the consent of the Landlord, whose consent may not be unreasonably withheld [or delayed].

[In the case of any works of a substantial nature, the Landlord may require the Tenant to provide, before starting the works, adequate security in the form of a deposit of money or the provision of a bond, as assurance to the Landlord that any works he permits from time to time will be fully completed].

[756]

3.5.3   *Removal of alterations*[74]

At the end of the Term, if so requested by the Landlord, the Tenant must remove any additional buildings, additions, alterations or improvements made to the Premises and must make good any part or parts of the Premises that may be damaged by their removal.

74   This clause has probably come to be inserted because landlords hope that it will defeat the effect of the compensation provisions of the Landlord and Tenant Act 1927 Pt I (ss 1–17) (23 Halsbury's Statutes (4th Edn) LANDLORD AND TENANT) — as to which see vol 22(1) (2003 Reissue) LANDLORD AND TENANT (BUSINESS TENANCIES) Paragraph 192 [923] et seq — ie because, if the improvement has been removed, it will not be an improvement to the holding at the time of quitting the premises. In fact, the clause might not achieve this effect, because the Landlord and Tenant Act 1927 s 9 as amended by the Landlord and Tenant Act 1954 s 49 prohibits contracting out. Also, the clause may be void under the Landlord and Tenant Act 1927 s 19(2) so far as it applies to improvements on the grounds that it purports to fetter the court in deciding what is reasonable. The tenant should not, however, rely on the application of these statutory provisions and should seek to strike out the clause.

3.5.4   *Connection to the Conduits*

The Tenant must not make any connection with the Conduits except in accordance with plans and specifications approved by the Landlord[, whose approval may not be unreasonably withheld [or delayed]], and subject to consent to make the connection having previously been obtained from the competent authority, undertaker or supplier.

3.6   Aerials, signs and advertisements

3.6.1   *Masts and wires*

The Tenant must not erect any pole or mast on the Premises [or install any cable or wire on them], whether in connection with telecommunications or otherwise.

3.6.2   *Advertisements*[75]

The Tenant must not, without the consent of the Landlord, fix to or exhibit on the outside of the Building or fix to or exhibit through any window of the Building, or display anywhere on the Premises or the Building any placard, sign, notice, fascia board or advertisement.

75   See the Town and Country Planning (Control of Advertisements) Regulations 1992, SI 1992/666 as amended. In the absence of a covenant such as this and subject to those Regulations, the tenant may exhibit advertisements etc on the premises, whether or not they are connected with his business: see *Clapman v Edwards* [1938] 2 All ER 507.

[757]

3.7   Statutory obligations

3.7.1   *General provision*[76]

The Tenant must comply in all respects with the requirements of any statutes, and any other obligations imposed by law or by any byelaws, applicable to the Premises or the trade or business for the time being carried on there.

76   As to the covenant to comply with statutes see vol 22(1) (2003 Reissue) LANDLORD AND TENANT (BUSINESS TENANCIES) Paragraph 182 [905]. For a provision requiring the landlord to pay compensation for works above a certain value see vol 22(3) (1997 Reissue) LANDLORD AND TENANT (BUSINESS TENANCIES) Form 169 [6693].

3.7.2   *Particular obligations*

3.7.2.1   **Works required by statute, department or authority**

Without prejudice to the generality of clause 3.7.1, the Tenant must execute all works and provide and maintain all arrangements upon or in respect of the Premises or the use to which the Premises are being put that are required in order to comply with the requirements of any statute already or in the future to be passed, or the requirements of any government department, local authority or other public or competent authority or court of competent jurisdiction regardless of whether such requirements are imposed on the owner, the occupier, or any other person.

3.7.2.2   **Acts causing losses**

Without prejudice to the generality of clause 3.7.1, the Tenant must not do in or near the Premises anything by reason of which the Landlord may incur any losses under any statute.

3.7.2.3   Construction (Design and Management) Regulations

Without prejudice to the generality of clause 3.7.1, the Tenant must comply with the provisions of the Construction (Design and Management) Regulations 1994 ('the CDM Regulations'), be the only client, as defined in the provisions of the CDM Regulations, fulfil in relation to all and any works all the obligations of the client as set out in or reasonably to be inferred from the CDM Regulations, and make a declaration to that effect[77] to the Health and Safety Executive in accordance with the Approved Code of Practice published from time to time by the Health and Safety Executive in relation to the CDM Regulations. The provisions of clause 5.7.3 FIRE-FIGHTING EQUIPMENT are to have effect in any circumstances to which these obligations apply.

3.7.2.4   Delivery of health and safety files

At the end of the Term, the Tenant must forthwith deliver to the Landlord any and all health and safety files relating to the Premises in accordance with the CDM Regulations.

---

77   If the works are being carried out for the tenant, the landlord will not want to accept the liabilities that are placed on a client under the Construction (Design and Management) Regulations 1994, SI 1994/ 3140 and the Health and Safety Executive Approved Code of Practice. The landlord will need to ensure that the tenant actually makes the declaration required, and that he obtains the notification served on the tenant by the Health and Safety Executive.

[758]

3.8   Entry to inspect and notice to repair

3.8.1   *Entry and notice*

The Tenant must permit the Landlord[78] [on reasonable notice during normal business hours except in emergency][79] —

3.8.1.1   to enter the Premises to ascertain whether or not the covenants and conditions of this Lease have been observed and performed,

3.8.1.2   to view the state of repair and condition of the Premises, and to open up floors and other parts of the Premises where that is necessary in order to do so, and

3.8.1.3   to give to the Tenant, or notwithstanding clause 8.7 NOTICES leave on the Premises, a notice ('a notice to repair') specifying the works required to remedy any breach of the Tenant's obligations as to the repair and condition of the Premises in this Lease.

provided that any opening-up must be made good by and at the cost of the Landlord if it reveals no breach of the terms of this Lease.

---

78   The provisions of clause 1.42 [735] REFERENCES TO RIGHTS OF ACCESS should be noted.
79   The tenant should add the words in square brackets.

3.8.2   *Works to be carried out*

The Tenant must carry out the works specified in a notice to repair immediately, including making good any opening up that revealed a breach of the terms of this Lease.

[3.8.3   *Landlord's power in default*[80]

If within *(state period, eg 1 month)* of the service of a notice to repair the Tenant has not started to execute the work referred to in that notice or is not proceeding diligently with it, or if the Tenant fails to finish the work within *(state period, eg 2 months)*[81][, or if in the [Landlord's *(or as required)* Surveyor's] [reasonable] opinion the Tenant is unlikely to finish the work within that period], the Tenant must permit the Landlord to enter the

Premises to execute the outstanding work, and must within *(state period, eg 14 days)* of a written demand pay to the Landlord the cost of so doing and all expenses incurred by the Landlord, including legal costs and surveyor's fees.]

80   The advantages for the landlord of this clause must be weighed against the potential liability that it creates under the Defective Premises Act 1972 s 4(4) (31 Halsbury's Statutes (4th Edn) NEGLIGENCE): see *McAuley v Bristol City Council* [1992] QB 134, [1992] 1 All ER 749, CA.

        It has been held that a claim by the landlord for recovery of costs under such a clause is a claim for recovery of a debt, and therefore can be enforced without requiring leave of the court under the Leasehold Property (Repairs) Act 1938: see *Jervis v Harris* [1996] Ch 195, [1996] 1 All ER 303, CA.

        However, even where a landlord has been granted a right of this nature the court does not compel the tenant to allow the landlord the right to enter and carry out repairs where these would be of no benefit and where no loss is being caused to the landlord: see *Hammersmith London Borough Council v Creska (No 2)* [2000] L & TR 288.

81   The tenant would prefer to be given 'a reasonable period' to do the work required to remedy the breaches because it may take longer than the specified number of months.

[759]–[780]

3.9   Alienation[82]

3.9.1   *Alienation prohibited*

The Tenant must not hold the Premises on trust for another. The Tenant must not part with possession of the Premises or any part of the Premises or permit another to occupy them or any part of them except pursuant to a transaction permitted by and effected in accordance with the provisions of this Lease.

82   As to alienation see vol 22(1) (2003 Reissue) LANDLORD AND TENANT (BUSINESS TENANCIES) Paragraph 156 [801] et seq. Where the lease is registrable, this prohibition or restriction on dealings will be reflected in an entry on the register excepting from the effects of registration all estates, rights, interests, powers and remedies arising on or by reason of any dealing made in breach of the prohibition or restriction: see the Land Registration Rules 2003, SI 2003/1417 r 6(2).

3.9.2   *Assignment, subletting and charging of part*[83]

(version 1)

[The Tenant must not assign, sublet or charge part only of the Premises.] *(where assignment, subletting or charging of the whole is allowed)*

(version 2)

[The Tenant must not assign or charge part only of the Premises and must not sublet the whole or any part of the Premises.] *(where assignment or charging of the whole is permitted, but subletting is not allowed at all)*

83   Whether subletting should be permitted is a commercial matter. Some landlords consider that the fact that they cannot unreasonably refuse consent to an assignment gives the tenant all the protection he requires and are not prepared to permit subletting. An advantage to the tenant of the ability to sublet is that he has an element of control over a subtenant but not over an assignee, for whom he may retain liability under an authorised guarantee agreement. Further, with stringent assignment tests or in a bad market, subletting may be the only option open to the tenant.

[781]

3.9.3   *Assignment of the whole*

Subject to clauses 3.9.4 CIRCUMSTANCES and 3.9.5 CONDITIONS, the Tenant must not assign the whole of the Premises without the consent of the Landlord, whose consent may not be unreasonably withheld [or delayed][84].

---

84   This residual discretion is the old test of reasonableness under the Landlord and Tenant Act 1927 s 19(1). Thus the tenant and the proposed assignee may satisfy the circumstances and conditions specified for the purposes of the Landlord and Tenant Act 1927 s 19(1A) as inserted by the Landlord and Tenant (Covenants) Act 1995 s 22 (as to which see clause 3.9.4 [782] CIRCUMSTANCES and clause 3.9.5 [784] CONDITIONS), but the landlord may still refuse consent on reasonable grounds: see vol 22(1) (2003 Reissue) LANDLORD AND TENANT (BUSINESS TENANCIES) Paragraph 159 [812] et seq.

3.9.4   *Circumstances*

If any of the following circumstances[85] — which are specified for the purposes of the Landlord and Tenant Act 1927 Section 19(1A)[86] — applies either at the date when application for consent to assign is made to the Landlord, or after that date but before the Landlord's consent is given, the Landlord may withhold his consent and if, after the Landlord's consent has been given but before the assignment has taken place, any such circumstances apply, the Landlord may revoke his consent[87], whether his consent is expressly subject to a condition as referred to in clause 3.9.5.4 CONDITIONS or not. The circumstances are —

3.9.4.1   that any sum due from the Tenant under this Lease remains unpaid[88],

3.9.4.2   that in the Landlord's reasonable[89] opinion the assignee is not a person who is likely to be able to comply with the tenant covenants of this Lease and to continue to be able to comply with them following the assignment,

[3.9.4.3   that without prejudice to clause 3.9.4.2, in the case of an assignment to a company in the same group as the Tenant[90] within the meaning of the 1954 Act Section 42, in the Landlord's reasonable opinion the assignee is a person who is, or may become, less likely to be able to comply with the tenant covenants of this Lease than the Tenant requesting consent to assign, which likelihood is adjudged by reference in particular to the financial strength of that Tenant aggregated with that of any guarantor of the obligations of that Tenant and the value of any other security for the performance of the tenant covenants of this Lease when assessed at the date of grant or — where that Tenant is not *(name of original tenant)* — the date of the assignment of this Lease to that Tenant[91],] or

3.9.4.4   that the assignee or any guarantor for the assignee, other than any guarantor under an authorised guarantee agreement, is a corporation registered — or otherwise resident — in a jurisdiction in which the order of a court obtained in England and Wales will not necessarily be enforced against the assignee or guarantor without any consideration of the merits of the case.

(for examples of circumstances for use in unusual cases see vol 22(3) (1997 Reissue) LANDLORD AND TENANT (BUSINESS TENANCIES) *Form 117 [6501])*

[782]

85   The Landlord and Tenant Act 1927 s 19(1A) as inserted by the Landlord and Tenant (Covenants) Act 1995 s 22 enables the landlord and tenant to a post-1995 lease to agree in advance the terms upon which an assignment may be permitted. It distinguishes between on the one hand circumstances, the existence of which entitles the landlord to refuse consent to assignment, and on the other hand conditions that may be imposed on his consent. This clause and clause 3.9.5 [784] CONDITIONS are drafted on the assumption that this is a valid approach and seek to draw a clear distinction between circumstances and conditions.

It should be noted that provisions that are overly restrictive may have an adverse impact at any rent review. It should also be noted that it is recommended 'best practice' that unless the particular circumstances of the letting justify greater control, the only restriction on assignment of the whole should be obtaining the landlord's consent, which is not to be unreasonably withheld: see vol 22(1) (2003 Reissue) LANDLORD AND TENANT (BUSINESS TENANCIES) Paragraph 85 [401] and 'A code of practice for commercial leases in England and Wales (2nd edition)' which can be found in vol 22(1) (2003 Reissue) LANDLORD AND TENANT (BUSINESS TENANCIES) as Form 1 [4501].

Each letting must be looked at in the light of its own particular facts and circumstances but it is considered that the provisions of this clause do, in the ordinary course, strike a reasonable balance between the landlord's desire for control and the tenant's ability to dispose of his interest without undue restriction. For a less restrictive approach see vol 22(1) (2003 Reissue) LANDLORD AND TENANT (BUSINESS TENANCIES) Form 7 clause 5.2 [5538].

86   The Landlord and Tenant Act 1927 s 19(1A) as inserted by the Landlord and Tenant (Covenants) Act 1995 s 22 seems to require the alienation clause to state that the circumstances it mentions are specified for the purposes of that subsection.

87   The landlord may require that certain circumstances are absent not only before consent has been given to the assignment, but also up to the date on which the assignment takes place — when the die is cast and the lease covenants bind the assignee. For example, the landlord may require the rent to be paid up to date not only before the application for consent is made, but also at the date when consent is given and the possibly later date when the lease is actually assigned.

88   The tenant may want to limit this to the rent, as it may be thought that a dispute is more likely to arise over the insurance rent or other payments. If the tenant has retained any right of set-off, it should also be referred to here.

89   Circumstances and conditions must be either factual or, if they contain an element of discretion, that discretion must have to be exercised reasonably (see the Landlord and Tenant Act 1927 s 19(1C)(a) as inserted by the Landlord and Tenant (Covenants) Act 1995 s 22) or the tenant must have a right of appeal to an expert (see the Landlord and Tenant Act 1927 s 19(1C)(b) as inserted by the Landlord and Tenant (Covenants) Act 1995 s 22). If the discretion is to be exercised reasonably, as suggested by this provision, the tenant can take any dispute about its exercise to the court. The court will consider whether *this* landlord has acted within the range of reasonable decisions, not whether a reasonable landlord would have reached the same decision nor whether the test is itself reasonable. For a clause where an expert is used see vol 22(3) (1997 Reissue) LANDLORD AND TENANT (BUSINESS TENANCIES) Form 117 [6501].

90   There have been suggestions that intra-group assignments should be banned completely. However, this is considered to be too draconian and would prevent legitimate corporate restructuring needed for reasons other than avoidance of liability under the Landlord and Tenant (Covenants) Act 1995. The landlord's concern is that a strong tenant may assign to a weak group company; the assignment is acceptable because the assignor gives an authorised guarantee agreement for the assignee. The second group company may then itself assign outside the group; the landlord will lose the authorised guarantee agreement of the strong first group company and have only the possibly worthless authorised guarantee agreement of the second group company. The possibilities for exploitation of this scenario are obvious and it is therefore felt that this is the one situation in which measuring the financial strength of the assignee in relation to that of the assignor is justified. Equivalence tests are not generally thought to be appropriate, because a strong first covenant may make the lease almost unassignable, adversely affecting the rent at review.

91   Consider whether the time at which the tenant's financial status is measured should be when he acquired the lease, when his status was acceptable to the landlord, or at the date of the application for consent to assign, when it may have deteriorated sharply. On the other hand, the outgoing tenant may be a better covenant now than when he acquired the lease: the wily landlord may wish to leave himself free to pick whichever of the two dates gives the better picture.

[783]

3.9.5   *Conditions*

The Landlord may impose any or all of the following conditions[92] — which are specified for the purposes of the Landlord and Tenant Act 1927 Section 19(1A)[93] — on giving any consent for an assignment by the Tenant, and any such consent is to be treated as being subject to each of the following conditions —

3.9.5.1   a condition that on or before any assignment and before giving occupation to the assignee, the Tenant requesting consent to assign, together with any former tenant who by virtue of the 1995 Act Section 11 was not released on an earlier assignment of this Lease[94], must enter into an authorised guarantee agreement[95] in favour of the Landlord in the terms set out in schedule 7 THE AUTHORISED GUARANTEE AGREEMENT,

3.9.5.2   a condition that if reasonably so required by the Landlord on an assignment to a limited company, the assignee must ensure that at least *(state number, eg 2)* directors of the company, or some other guarantor or guarantors [reasonably] acceptable to the Landlord, enter into direct covenants with the Landlord in the form of the guarantor's covenants contained in clause 6 GUARANTEE PROVISIONS with 'the Assignee' substituted for 'the Tenant',

3.9.5.3   a condition that upon or before any assignment, the Tenant making the request for consent to assign must give to the Landlord a copy of the health and safety file required to be maintained under the Construction (Design and Management) Regulations 1994 containing full details of all works undertaken to the Premises by that Tenant, and

3.9.5.4   a condition that if, at any time before the assignment, the circumstances specified in clause 3.9.4, or any of them, apply, the Landlord may revoke the consent by written notice to the Tenant.

[784]

---

92   The Landlord and Tenant Act 1927 s 19(1A) as inserted by the Landlord and Tenant (Covenants) Act 1995 s 22 enables the landlord and tenant to a post-1995 lease to agree in advance the terms upon which an assignment may be permitted. It distinguishes between on the one hand circumstances, the existence of which entitles the landlord to refuse consent to assignment, and on the other hand conditions that may be imposed on his consent. This clause and clause 3.9.4 [782] CIRCUMSTANCES are drafted on the assumption that this a valid approach and seek to draw a clear distinction between circumstances and conditions.

It should be noted that provisions that are overly restrictive may have an adverse impact at any rent review. It should also be noted that it is recommended 'best practice' that unless the particular circumstances of the letting justify greater control, the only restriction on assignment of the whole should be obtaining the landlord's consent, which is not to be unreasonably withheld: see vol 22(1) (2003 Reissue) LANDLORD AND TENANT (BUSINESS TENANCIES) Paragraph 85 [401] and 'A code of practice for commercial leases in England and Wales (2nd edition)' which can be found in vol 22(1) (2003 Reissue) LANDLORD AND TENANT (BUSINESS TENANCIES) as Form 1 [4501].

Each letting must be looked at in the light of its own particular facts and circumstances but it is considered that the provisions of this clause do, in the ordinary course, strike a reasonable balance between the landlord's desire for control and the tenant's ability to dispose of his interest without undue restriction.

93   The Landlord and Tenant Act 1927 s 19(1A) as inserted by the Landlord and Tenant (Covenants) Act 1995 s22 seems to require the alienation clause to state that the conditions it mentions are specified for the purposes of that subsection.

94   See the Landlord and Tenant (Covenants) Act 1995 ss 11(2), 16(6).

95   As to authorised guarantee agreements see vol 22(1) (2003 Reissue) LANDLORD AND TENANT (BUSINESS TENANCIES) Paragraph 54 [247]. It should be noted that 'A code of practice for commercial leases in England and Wales (2nd edition)' urges landlords to consider requiring authorised guarantee agreements only where the assignee is of lower financial standing than the assignor at the date of the assignment.

[785]

3.9.6   Charging of the whole

The Tenant must not charge the whole of the Premises without the consent of the Landlord, whose consent may not be unreasonably withheld [or delayed][96].

96   As to unreasonable withholding of consent under the Landlord and Tenant Act 1927 see vol 22(1) (2003 Reissue) LANDLORD AND TENANT (BUSINESS TENANCIES) Paragraph 158.2 [806] and as to unreasonable delay under the Landlord and Tenant Act 1988 (23 Halsbury's Statutes (4th Edn) LANDLORD AND TENANT) see vol 22(1) (2003 Reissue) LANDLORD AND TENANT (BUSINESS TENANCIES) Paragraph 158.3 [808].

[3.9.7   Subletting

The Tenant must not sublet[97] the whole of the Premises without the consent of the Landlord, whose consent may not be unreasonably withheld [or delayed]][98]. *(omit if subletting is prohibited)*

97   See note 83 to clause 3.9.2 [781] ASSIGNMENT, SUBLETTING AND CHARGING OF PART.
98   As to unreasonable withholding of consent under the Landlord and Tenant Act 1927 see vol 22(1) (2003 Reissue) LANDLORD AND TENANT (BUSINESS TENANCIES) Paragraph 158.2 [806] and as to unreasonable delay under the Landlord and Tenant Act 1988 see vol 22(1) (2003 Reissue) LANDLORD AND TENANT (BUSINESS TENANCIES) Paragraph 158.3 [808].

[786]

[3.9.8   Terms of a permitted sublease[99]

Every permitted sublease must be granted, without a fine or premium, at a rent not less than whichever is the greater of the then open market rent payable in respect of the Premises [— to be approved by the Landlord prior to the sublease is granted [and to be determined by the Surveyor, acting as an expert and not as an arbitrator]—] and the Rent[100], to be payable in advance on the days on which the Rent is payable under this Lease. Every permitted sublease must contain provisions approved by the Landlord —

3.9.8.1   for the upwards only review of the rent reserved by it, on the basis set out in schedule 3 THE RENT AND RENT REVIEW and on the Review Dates[101],

3.9.8.2   prohibiting the subtenant from doing or allowing anything in relation to the Premises inconsistent with or in breach of the provisions of this Lease,

3.9.8.3   for re-entry by the sublandlord on breach of any covenant by the subtenant,

3.9.8.4   imposing an absolute prohibition against all dealings with the Premises other than assignment[, subletting] [or charging] of the whole,

3.9.8.5   prohibiting assignment[, subletting][102] [or charging] of the whole of the Premises without the consent of the Landlord under this Lease,

3.9.8.6   requiring the assignee on any assignment of the sublease to enter into direct covenants with the Landlord to the same effect as those contained in clause 3.9.9 SUBTENANT'S DIRECT COVENANTS,

3.9.8.7   requiring on each assignment of the sublease that the assignor enters into an authorised guarantee agreement[104] in favour of the Landlord in the terms set out in schedule 7 THE AUTHORISED GUARANTEE AGREEMENT but adapted to suit the circumstances in which the guarantee is given,

3.9.8.8   prohibiting the subtenant from holding on trust for another or permitting another to share or occupy the whole or any part of the Premises,

3.9.8.9   imposing in relation to any permitted assignment[, subletting] [or charge] the same obligations for registration with the Landlord as are contained in this Lease in relation to dispositions by the Tenant,

[3.9.8.10   imposing in relation to any permitted subletting the same obligations as are contained in this clause 3.9.8 and in clause 3.9.9 SUBTENANT'S DIRECT COVENANTS[, clause 3.9.11 ENFORCEMENT OF THE SUBLEASE and clause 3.9.12 SUBLEASE RENT REVIEW],] and

3.9.8.11   excluding the provisions of Sections 24–28 of the 1954 Act from the letting created by the sublease.] *(omit if subletting is prohibited)*

[787]

99   As to the validity of provisions of this nature see vol 22(1) (2003 Reissue) LANDLORD AND TENANT (BUSINESS TENANCIES) Paragraph 161 [817].

100   It will not be in the landlord's interest for the premises to be sublet at a rent less than that payable under the headlease. This could allow into the premises a subtenant of doubtful financial status, with whom the landlord may in the future have to deal direct, eg on the grant of a new lease under the Landlord and Tenant Act 1954 Pt II (ss 23–46). Also a low rent could be used as a 'comparable' in arriving at the open market rent on rent reviews or lease renewals. On the other hand following the decision in *Allied Dunbar Assurance plc v Homebase Ltd* [2002] EWCA Civ 666, [2003] 1 P & CR 75, [2002] 2 EGLR 23 a provision of this kind may effectively render the lease inalienable and being a potentially onerous restriction on disposition (as to which see vol 22(1) (2003 Reissue) LANDLORD AND TENANT (BUSINESS TENANCIES) Paragraph 348.2 [1440]) have an adverse impact at rent review from a landlord's perspective.

101   Alternatively the landlord might prefer the sublease rents to be reviewed just before the review dates in the headlease. As to recommended 'best practice' in relation to the basis of rent review in leases of business premises see vol 22(1) (2003 Reissue) LANDLORD AND TENANT (BUSINESS TENANCIES) Paragraph 85 [401] and 'A code of practice for commercial leases in England and Wales (2nd edition)' which can be found in vol 22(1) (2003 Reissue) LANDLORD AND TENANT (BUSINESS TENANCIES) as Form 1 [4501].

102   The landlord may well wish to prohibit any further subletting by requiring an absolute covenant against subletting to be inserted in any sublease.

103   By virtue of the Landlord and Tenant (Covenants) Act 1995 s 16(3)(a), where a head landlord's consent is needed to the assignment of a sublease, the head landlord can require the assignor of the sublease to enter into an authorised guarantee agreement. It should be noted that 'A code of practice for commercial leases in England and Wales (2nd edition)' urges landlords to consider requiring authorised guarantee agreements only where the assignee is of lower financial standing than the assignor at the date of the assignment.

[788]

[3.9.9   *Subtenant's direct covenants*[104]

Before any permitted subletting, the Tenant must ensure that the subtenant enters into a direct covenant with the Landlord that while he is bound by the tenant covenants of the sublease[105] and while the subtenant is bound by an authorised guarantee agreement the subtenant will observe and perform the tenant covenants contained in this Lease — except the covenant to pay the rent reserved by this Lease — and in that sublease.] *(omit if subletting is prohibited)*

104   See note 99 to clause 3.9.8 [788] TERMS OF A PERMITTED SUBLEASE.

105   The liability of the subtenant should be expressed to last while he is bound by the tenant covenants of the sublease, rather than while the sublease is vested in him, to take account of the possibility of an excluded assignment being made and the subtenant remaining liable. An excluded assignment means that the subtenant is precluded from tenant release under the Landlord and Tenant (Covenants) Act 1995.

[3.9.10   *Requirement for 1954 Act exclusion*[106]

The Tenant must not grant the sublease or permit the subtenant to occupy the Premises unless an effective agreement has been made to exclude the operation of Sections 24 to 28 of the 1954 Act pursuant to Section 38A of the 1954 Act.] *(omit if subletting is prohibited)*

106   As to contracting out of the security of tenure provisions of the Landlord and Tenant Act 1954 see vol 22(1) (2003 Reissue) LANDLORD AND TENANT (BUSINESS TENANCIES) Paragraph 431 [2035].

[3.9.11   *Enforcement of the sublease*

In relation to any permitted sublease, the Tenant must enforce the performance and observance by every subtenant of the provisions of the sublease, and must not at any time either expressly or by implication waive any breach of the covenants or conditions on the part of any subtenant or assignee of any sublease, or — without the consent of the Landlord, whose consent may not be unreasonably withheld or delayed — vary the terms or accept a surrender of any permitted sublease.] *(omit if subletting is prohibited)*

[789]

[3.9.12   *Sublease rent review*

In relation to any permitted sublease —

3.9.12.1   the Tenant must ensure that the rent is reviewed in accordance with the terms of the sublease,

3.9.12.2   the Tenant must not agree the reviewed rent with the subtenant without the approval of the Landlord,

3.9.12.3   where the sublease provides such an option, the Tenant must not, without the approval of the Landlord, agree whether the third party determining the revised rent in default of agreement should act as an arbitrator or as an expert,

3.9.12.4   the Tenant must not, without the approval of the Landlord, agree any appointment of a person to act as the third party determining the revised rent,

3.9.12.5   the Tenant must incorporate as part of his representations to that third party representations [reasonably] required[107] by the Landlord, and

3.9.12.6   the Tenant must give notice to the Landlord of the details of the determination of every rent review within *(state period, eg 28 days)*,

provided that the Landlord's approvals specified above may not be unreasonably withheld [or delayed].] *(omit if subletting is prohibited)*

107   This seems preferable to providing, as is sometimes done, that the head landlord's representations have to be brought to the attention of the expert or arbitrator because it would appear that he can refuse to have regard to them, the head landlord not being a party to the lease with which he is concerned.

[790]

3.9.13   *Registration of permitted dealings*

Within *(state period, eg 28 days)* of any assignment, charge, [sublease, or subunderlease,] or any transmission or other devolution relating to the Premises, the Tenant must produce a certified copy[108] of any relevant document for registration with the Landlord's solicitor, and must pay the Landlord's solicitor's [reasonable] charges for registration of at least £...

108   There seems to be no reason why the tenant should part with the original. However, under the Land Registration Rules 2003, SI 2003/1417 r 203, it is open to the applicant for registration to ask for the transfer, charge, sublease or subunderlease giving effect to the disposition to be returned for retention by the applicant, provided a certified copy of the instrument is lodged with the application. Accordingly, in such cases, applicants should use this facility if they wish to be able to lodge the lease with the landlord after its return by the registrar. If there is a time limit specified in the lease, then the registrar should be told about this, so that he is aware of the need to return the instrument within the required period.

[3.9.14   *Sharing with a group company*

Notwithstanding clause 3.9.1 ALIENATION PROHIBITED, the Tenant may share the occupation of the whole or any part of the Premises with a company that is a member of the same group as the Tenant within the meaning of the 1954 Act Section 42, for so long as both companies remain members of that group and otherwise than in a manner that transfers or creates a legal estate.] *(omit if sharing with a group company is not to be permitted)*

3.10   Nuisance and residential restrictions

3.10.1   *Nuisance*[109]

The Tenant must not do anything on the Premises, or allow anything to remain on them that may be or become a nuisance, or cause annoyance, disturbance, inconvenience, injury or damage to the Landlord or his tenants or the owners or occupiers of any adjoining property of the Landlord or any other adjacent or neighbouring premises.

109   'Nuisance' is a term to be construed according to 'plain and sober and simple notions among the English people': *Walter v Selfe* (1851) 4 De G & Sm 315 at 322 per Knight-Bruce V-C. 'I have no doubt that what is a nuisance or annoyance will continue to be determined by the courts according to robust and commonsense standards': *Hampstead and Suburban Properties Ltd v Diomedous* [1969] 1 Ch 248 at 258, [1968] 3 All ER 545 at 550 per Megarry J. But a tenant can only be said to have permitted a nuisance if the landlord can show that the tenant has failed to take reasonable steps to prevent the nuisance: see *Commercial General Administration Ltd v Thomsett* [1979] 1 EGLR 62, CA.

[791]

3.10.2   *Auctions, trades and immoral purposes*

The Tenant must not use the Premises for any auction sale, any dangerous, noxious, noisy or offensive[110] trade, business, manufacture or occupation, or any illegal or immoral act or purpose.

110   As to the meaning of 'offensive' see *Re Koumoudouros and Marathon Realty Co Ltd* (1978) 89 DLR (3d) 551 where it was held that the word 'offensive' did not have a definite legal meaning and that it should be read in the context of the lease. Surrounding circumstances can affect whether a particular trade is offensive: see *Nussey v Provincial Bill Posting Co and Eddison* [1909] 1 Ch 734, CA; *Dunraven Securities Ltd v Holloway* [1982] 2 EGLR 47, CA.

3.10.3   *Residential use, sleeping and animals*

The Tenant must not use the Premises as sleeping accommodation or for residential purposes, or keep any animal, bird or reptile on them.

3.11   Costs of applications, notices and recovery of arrears[111]

The Tenant must pay to the Landlord on an indemnity basis all costs, fees, charges, disbursements and expenses — including, without prejudice to the generality of the above, those payable to counsel, solicitors, surveyors and bailiffs — [properly and reasonably] incurred by the Landlord in relation to or incidental to —

3.11.1   every application made by the Tenant for a consent or licence required by the provisions of this Lease, whether it is granted, refused or offered subject to any [lawful] qualification or condition, or the application is withdrawn[, unless the refusal, qualification or condition is unlawful whether because it is unreasonable or otherwise],

3.11.2   the contemplation, preparation and service of a notice under the Law of Property Act 1925 Section 146 or by reason or the contemplation of proceedings under Sections 146 or 147 of that Act, even if forfeiture is avoided otherwise than by relief granted by the court[112],

3.11.3   the recovery or attempted recovery of arrears of rent or other sums due under this Lease, and

3.11.4   any steps taken in [contemplation of or in] [direct] connection with the preparation and service of a schedule of dilapidations during or after the end of the Term[113].

111   As to payment of VAT on legal costs by a person other than the solicitor's own client see the Information Binder: Property [1]: VAT and Property.
112   As to forfeiture see vol 22(1) (2003 Reissue) LANDLORD AND TENANT (BUSINESS TENANCIES) Paragraph 283 [1171] et seq.
113   The landlord should not be tempted to extend this provision to costs etc incurred by him in consequence of serving a notice under the Landlord and Tenant Act 1954 s 25 because that is void: see *Stevenson and Rush (Holdings) Ltd v Langdon* (1978) 38 P & CR 208, CA.

[792]–[800]

3.12   Planning and development

3.12.1   *Compliance with the Planning Acts*

The Tenant must observe and comply with the provisions and requirements of the Planning Acts affecting the Premises and their use, and must indemnify the Landlord and keep him indemnified, both during the Term and following the end of it, against all losses in respect of any contravention of those Acts.

3.12.2   *Consent for applications*

The Tenant must not make any application for planning permission without the consent of the Landlord[, whose consent may not be unreasonably withheld [or delayed] [in any case where the application for and implementation of the planning permission will not create or give rise to any tax liability for the Landlord or where the Tenant indemnifies the Landlord against such liability][114].

114   These words were devised when development land tax — abolished by the Finance Act 1985 s 93 — applied. The provision may, however, still be relevant should similar taxation be introduced in the future.

3.12.3   *Permissions and notices*

The Tenant must at his expense obtain any planning permissions and serve any notices that may be required to carry out any development on or at the Premises.

3.12.4   *Charges and levies*

Subject only to any statutory direction to the contrary, the Tenant must pay and satisfy any charge or levy that may subsequently be imposed under the Planning Acts in respect of the carrying out or maintenance of any development on or at the Premises.

[801]

3.12.5   *Pre-conditions for development*

Notwithstanding any consent that may be granted by the Landlord under this Lease, the Tenant must not carry out any development on or at the Premises until all necessary notices under the Planning Acts have been served and copies produced to the Landlord, all necessary permissions under the Planning Acts have been obtained and produced to the Landlord, and the Landlord has acknowledged that every necessary planning permission is acceptable to him[, such acknowledgement not to be unreasonably withheld]. The Landlord may refuse to acknowledge his acceptance of a planning permission on the grounds that any condition contained in it or anything omitted from it or the period referred to in it would[, in the [reasonable] opinion of the Surveyor,] be, or be likely to be, prejudicial to the Landlord or to his reversionary interest in the Premises or any adjoining property of the Landlord whether during the Term or following the end of it.

3.12.6   *Completion of development*

Where a condition of any planning permission granted for development begun before the end of the Term[115] requires works to be carried out to the Premises by a date after the end of the Term, the Tenant must, unless the Landlord directs otherwise, finish those works before the end of the Term.

---

115   The provisions of clause 1.25 [714] INTERPRETATION OF 'THE LAST YEAR OF THE TERM' AND 'THE END OF THE TERM' should be noted.

3.12.7   *Security for compliance with conditions*

In any case where a planning permission is granted subject to conditions, and if the Landlord [reasonably] so requires, the Tenant must provide sufficient security for his compliance with the conditions and must not implement the planning permission until the security has been provided.

[3.12.8   *Appeal against refusal or conditions*[116]

If [reasonably] required by the Landlord to do so, but[, where reasonable,] at his own cost, the Tenant must appeal against any refusal of planning permission or the imposition of any conditions on a planning permission relating to the Premises following an application for planning permission by the Tenant.]

---

116   The tenant should not accept this clause because it could impose on him the cost of a planning appeal. He should strike it out, leaving planning appeals to be a matter for discussion as and when the situation arises during the term, or at least insist that he should bear the cost only where reasonable.

[802]

3.13   Plans, documents and information

3.13.1   *Evidence of compliance with this Lease*

If so requested, the Tenant must produce to the Landlord or the Surveyor any plans, documents and other evidence the Landlord [reasonably] requires to satisfy himself that the provisions of this Lease have been complied with.

3.13.2   *Information for renewal or rent review*

If so requested, the Tenant must produce to the Landlord, the Surveyor or any person acting as the third party determining the Rent in default of agreement between the Landlord and the Tenant under any provisions for rent review contained in this Lease, any information [reasonably] requested in writing in relation to any pending or intended step under the 1954 Act or the implementation of any provisions for rent review.

3.14   Indemnities[117]

The Tenant must keep the Landlord fully indemnified against all losses arising directly or indirectly out of any act, omission or negligence of the Tenant or any persons at the Estate expressly or impliedly[118] with his authority [and under his control][119], or any breach or non-observance by the Tenant of the covenants, conditions or other provisions of this Lease or any of the matters to which this demise is subject.

---

117 The tenant should seek to delete all *general* indemnity provisions on the basis that his remedies for breach of covenant and in tort adequately protect the landlord. The tenant should argue that an indemnity unreasonably extends his liability. If, however, this clause is omitted, it should be replaced by a covenant to observe and perform restrictions etc to which the demise is subject, possibly coupled with a *specific* indemnity in respect of any breach.

118 The expression 'impliedly' is intended to include a caller, such as a tradesman, where there has been no express invitation but the person cannot be classed as a trespasser.

119 The tenant should add the words in square brackets.

[803]

3.15   Reletting boards and viewing

[Unless [a valid court application under the 1954 Act Section 24 has been made or][120] the Tenant is [otherwise] entitled to remain in occupation or to a new tenancy of the Premises, at any time during *(or as required)* At any time during] the *(state period, eg last 6 months)* of the [Contractual][121] Term and at any time thereafter, [and whenever the Lease Rents or any part of them are in arrear and unpaid for longer than *(state period, eg 14 days)*,] the Tenant must permit the Landlord to enter the Premises and fix and retain anywhere on them a board advertising them for reletting. While any such board is on the Premises the Tenant must permit viewing of the Premises at reasonable times of the day.

---

120 This phrase and the word 'otherwise' should be omitted if the operation of the security of tenure provisions in the Landlord and Tenant Act 1954 ss 24–28 is to be excluded in relation to the lease.

121 This defined term will require amendment where the operation of the security of tenure provisions in the Landlord and Tenant Act 1954 ss 24–28 is to be excluded in relation to the lease: see note 7 to clause 1.7 [709] 'THE [CONTRACTUAL] TERM'.

3.16   Obstruction and encroachment

3.16.1   *Obstruction of windows*

The Tenant must not stop up, darken or obstruct any windows or light belonging to the Premises.

3.16.2   *Encroachments*

The Tenant must take all [reasonable] steps to prevent the construction of any new window, light, opening, doorway, path, passage, pipe or the making of any encroachment or the acquisition of any easement in relation to the Premises, and must notify the Landlord immediately if any such thing is constructed, encroachment is made or easement acquired, or if any attempt is made to construct such a thing, to encroach or acquire an easement. At the request of the Landlord the Tenant must adopt such means as are [reasonably] required to prevent the construction of such a thing, the making of any encroachment or the acquisition of any easement[122].

---

122   For a shorter clause see vol 22(3) (1997 Reissue) LANDLORD AND TENANT (BUSINESS TENANCIES) Form 172 [6696].

[804]

3.17   Yielding up

At the end of the Term[123] the Tenant must yield up the Premises with vacant possession, decorated and repaired in accordance with and in the condition required by the provisions of this Lease, give up all keys of the Premises to the Landlord, remove tenant's fixtures and fittings [if requested to do so by the Landlord], and remove all signs erected by the Tenant or any of his predecessors in title in, on or near the Premises, immediately making good any damage caused by their removal.

---

123   The provisions of clause 1.25 [714] INTERPRETATION OF 'THE LAST YEAR OF THE TERM' AND 'THE END OF THE TERM' should be noted.

3.18   Interest on arrears[124]

The Tenant must pay interest on any of the Lease Rents[125] or other sums due under this Lease that are not paid [within *(state period, eg 14 days)* of the date due], whether formally demanded or not, [the interest to be recoverable as rent][126]. Nothing in this clause is to entitle the Tenant to withhold or delay any payment of the Rent or any other sum due under this Lease or affect the rights of the Landlord in relation to any non-payment.

---

124   As to the covenant to pay interest see vol 22(1) (2003 Reissue) LANDLORD AND TENANT (BUSINESS TENANCIES) Paragraph 154 [767].

125   As to the definition of 'the Lease Rents' see clause 1.44 [735] 'THE RENT'.

126   These words seek to attach to any interest the rights associated with rent. As to the reasons for this see vol 22(1) (2003 Reissue) LANDLORD AND TENANT (BUSINESS TENANCIES) Paragraph 151 [761]. However, this clause applies to interest on arrears both of rents and other sums payable under the lease that are not rent, and it might be felt inappropriate for interest to be deemed to be rent where the payment on which the interest is due is not itself rent.

3.19 Statutory notices

The Tenant must give full particulars to the Landlord of any notice, direction, order or proposal relating to the Premises made, given or issued to the Tenant by any government department or local, public, regulatory or other authority or court within *(state period, eg 7 days)* of receipt, and if so requested by the Landlord must produce it to the Landlord. The Tenant must without delay take all necessary steps to comply with the notice, direction or order. At the request of the Landlord, but at his own cost, the Tenant must make or join with the Landlord in making such objection or representation the Landlord deems expedient against or in respect of any notice, direction, order or proposal.

[805]

3.20 Keyholders

The Tenant must ensure that at all times [the Landlord has *(or as required)* the Landlord and the local police force have] written notice of the name, home address and home telephone number of at least *(state number, eg 2)* keyholders of the Premises.

3.21 Viewing on sale of reversion

The Tenant must[, on reasonable notice,] at any time during the Term, permit prospective purchasers of the Landlord's reversion or any other interest superior to the Term, or agents instructed in connection with the sale of the reversion or such an interest, to view the Premises without interruption, provided they have the prior written authority of the Landlord or his agents.

3.22 Defective premises

The Tenant must give notice to the Landlord of any defect in the Premises that might give rise to an obligation on the Landlord to do or refrain from doing anything in order to comply with the provisions of this Lease or the duty of care imposed on the Landlord, whether pursuant to the Defective Premises Act 1972 or otherwise, and must at all times display and maintain any notices the Landlord from time to time [reasonably] requires him to display at the Premises.

3.23 Replacement guarantor[127]

3.23.1 *Guarantor replacement events*

In this clause 3.23 references to a 'guarantor replacement event' are references, in the case of an individual, to death, bankruptcy, having a receiving order made against him or having a receiver appointed under the Mental Health Act 1983 or entering into a voluntary arrangement, and, in the case of a company, to passing a resolution to wind up, entering into liquidation, a voluntary arrangement or administration or having a receiver appointed.

127   As to guarantors see vol 22(1) (2003 Reissue) LANDLORD AND TENANT (BUSINESS TENANCIES) Paragraph 71 [278] et seq. The tenant should propose that, on the execution of a guarantee by a new guarantor, the original guarantor or his estate should be released.

3.23.2 *Action on occurrence of a guarantor replacement event*

Where during the relevant Liability Period a guarantor replacement event occurs to the Guarantor or any person who has entered into an authorised guarantee agreement, the Tenant must give notice of the event to the Landlord within *(state period, eg 14 days)* of his becoming aware of it. If so required by the Landlord, the Tenant must within *(state period, eg 28 days)* obtain some other person [reasonably] acceptable to the Landlord to execute a guarantee in the form of the Guarantor's covenants in clause 6 GUARANTEE PROVISIONS or the authorised guarantee agreement in schedule 7 THE AUTHORISED GUARANTEE AGREEMENT, as the case may be, for the residue of the relevant Liability Period.

3.24   Exercise of the Landlord's rights[128]

The Tenant must permit the Landlord to exercise any of the rights granted to him by virtue of the provisions of this Lease at all times during the Term without interruption or interference.

128   The provisions of clause 1.42 [735] REFERENCES TO RIGHTS OF ACCESS should be noted.

[806]

3.25   The Industrial Covenants

The Tenant must observe and perform the Industrial Covenants.

3.26   The Services

The Tenant must observe and perform his obligations contained in schedule 6 THE SERVICE CHARGE.

3.27   Costs of grant of this Lease[129]

[The Tenant must pay the fees and disbursements of the Landlord's solicitors, agents and surveyors and all other costs and expenses incurred by the Landlord in relation to the negotiation, preparation, execution and grant of this Lease *(or as required)* On the grant of this Lease the Tenant must pay the sum of £... as a contribution to the Landlord's solicitors' charges for the negotiation, execution and completion of this Lease].

129   As to covenants to pay the landlord's legal fees see vol 22(1) (2003 Reissue) LANDLORD AND TENANT (BUSINESS TENANCIES) Paragraph 155 [769]. As to payment of VAT on legal costs by a person other than the solicitor's own client see the Information Binder: Property [1]: VAT and Property.

3.28   Consent to the Landlord's release[130]

The Tenant must not unreasonably withhold consent to a request made by the Landlord under the 1995 Act Section 8 for a release from all or any of the landlord covenants of this Lease.

130   By virtue of the Landlord and Tenant (Covenants) Act 1995 each successive landlord remains bound by the landlord covenants of the lease unless released under the machinery provided in the Act — as to which see vol 22(1) (2003 Reissue) LANDLORD AND TENANT (BUSINESS TENANCIES) Paragraph 57 [252] et seq — or by a specific release given otherwise (see the Landlord and Tenant (Covenants) Act 1995 s 26(1)(a)). Bald statements limiting the landlord's liability, such as those in use before the commencement of the Act, will not withstand the wide anti-avoidance provisions of the Landlord and Tenant (Covenants) Act 1995 s 25, and covenants by the tenant to give consent to release are unlikely to fall within the exception of s 26. None of the ingenious schemes for limiting the landlord's liability, eg making all covenants personal, suggested in the early days of the 1995 Act has stood up to critical scrutiny, although none has yet been tested by the courts. Thus landlords look instead to the alternative of a right of redress if the tenant makes an unreasonable objection to release. This covenant is modelled on the provisions of the Landlord and Tenant Act 1988, which gives tenants a right of action for loss caused by landlords who unreasonably withhold or delay consent to assignment (see the Landlord and Tenant Act 1988 s 4). In view of the strict time limits under the Landlord and Tenant (Covenants) Act 1995 and the fact that failure to respond to the landlord's request for release is deemed to be consent, it is not thought necessary to extend this covenant to unreasonable delay in replying to such a request.

[807]–[820]

4   THE LANDLORD'S COVENANTS

The Landlord covenants with the Tenant to observe and perform the requirements of this clause 4.

4.1   Quiet enjoyment[131]

The Landlord must permit the Tenant peaceably and quietly to hold and enjoy the Premises without any interruption or disturbance from or by the Landlord or any person claiming under or in trust for him[132] [or by title paramount][133].

131   As to the landlord's covenant for quiet enjoyment see vol 22(1) (2003 Reissue) LANDLORD AND TENANT (BUSINESS TENANCIES) Paragraph 168 [856]. As to covenants for quiet enjoyment generally see 23 Halsbury's Laws (4th Edn Reissue) LANDLORD AND TENANT.
        The words 'the Tenant paying the rents reserved by and observing and performing the covenants on its part and the conditions contained in this lease' are frequently included in a covenant for quiet enjoyment, but they have no practical effect and do not make payment of the rent and performance of the covenants into conditions precedent to the operation of the covenant for quiet enjoyment: see *Edge v Boileau* (1885) 16 QBD 117; *Dawson v Dyer* (1833) 5 B & Ad 584; *Yorkbrook Investments Ltd v Batten* (1985) 52 P & CR 51, [1985] 2 EGLR 100, CA.
132   The covenant is frequently expressed to apply to 'lawful' interruption or by persons 'rightfully' claiming under the landlord, but it seems that the addition of these words has no practical effect: see *Williams v Gabriel* [1906] 1 KB 155 at 157.
133   Without the reference to title paramount the landlord is liable only for the acts of persons so far as they are his successors in title or have authority from him to do the acts complained of: *Harrison Ainslie & Co v Muncaster* [1891] 2 QB 680, CA; *Matania v National Provincial Bank Ltd and Elevenist Syndicate Ltd* [1936] 2 All ER 633, CA; *Miller v Emcer Products Ltd* [1956] Ch 304, [1956] 1 All ER 237, CA. If a subtenant holds under a lease containing a qualified covenant on the part of his landlord — ie one where there is no reference to title paramount — and the head landlord evicts the subtenant because the head rent has not been paid, this is not a breach of the covenant for quiet enjoyment (see *Spencer v Marriott* (1823) 1 B & C 457; *Dennett v Atherton* (1872) LR 7 QB 316, Ex Ch), but it is a breach if the sublandlord submits to judgment in an action by a person with no title to sue, and the subtenant is in consequence evicted (*Cohen v Tannar* [1900] 2 QB 609, CA). Actionable interruptions under this covenant are not confined to interference with title or possession, but may extend to interference with the ordinary and lawful enjoyment of the premises: *Sanderson v Berwick-upon-Tweed Corpn* (1884) 13 QBD 547 at 551, CA. As to persons claiming 'under' the landlord see *Celsteel Ltd v Alton House Holdings Ltd (No 2)* [1987] 2 All ER 240, [1987] 1 WLR 291, CA.

[821]

4.2   The Services[134]

4.2.1   *Provision of the Services*

If the Tenant pays the Service Charge and observes his obligations under this Lease[135], the Landlord must use his best endeavours to provide the Services.

134   As the landlord remains liable on his covenants until he is released under the Landlord and Tenant (Covenants) Act 1995, given the character of the landlord's covenants contained in this lease, the landlord may prefer to avoid liability altogether by including a management company as a party to the lease. The management company then covenants to perform those obligations that would have fallen to the landlord.
135   As to payment as a condition precedent see vol 22(1) (2003 Reissue) LANDLORD AND TENANT (BUSINESS TENANCIES) Paragraph 255 [1093].

4.2.2   *Relief from liability*[136]

The Landlord is not to be liable to the Tenant for any breach of his obligations under clause 4.2.1 where the breach was caused by something beyond his control, provided he uses reasonable endeavours to remedy the breach, except to the extent that the breach —

4.2.2.1   could have been prevented, or

4.2.2.2   its consequences could have been lessened, or

4.2.2.3   the time during which its consequences were experienced could have been shortened,

by the exercise of reasonable skill by the Landlord or those undertaking the obligation on his behalf.

---

136   This clause is likely to be viewed as an exclusion clause if the Unfair Contract Terms Act 1977 (11 Halsbury's Statutes (4th Edn) CONTRACT) applies to the service provisions contained in a lease: see vol 22(1) (2003 Reissue) LANDLORD AND TENANT (BUSINESS TENANCIES) Paragraph 254 notes 4 and 5 [1092].

4.2.3   *Variation and withholding of the Services*

The Landlord may add to, withhold or vary the Services if[, acting reasonably,] he considers the addition, withholding or variation to be necessary or desirable [for the comfort or convenience of the tenants of the Estate] even if it increases the Landlord's Expenses [so long as the Tenant's enjoyment of the Premises is not materially impaired], or if he is required to do so by a competent authority.

4.2.4   *Special services*

Any services rendered to the Tenant by staff employed by the Landlord, other than services referred to in paragraph 6-3 THE SERVICES, are to be deemed to be special services for which, and for the consequences of which, the Tenant will be entirely responsible. The Tenant is not to be entitled to any services from such staff that may in any way whatever interfere with the performance of their duties to the Landlord.

[822]

5   INSURANCE[137]

5.1   Warranty as to convictions[138]

The Tenant warrants that before the execution of this document he has disclosed to the Landlord in writing any conviction, judgment or finding of any court or tribunal relating to the Tenant[, or any director, other officer or major shareholder of the Tenant,] of such a nature as to be likely to affect the decision of any insurer or underwriter to grant or to continue insurance of any of the Insured Risks.

---

137   As to insurance see vol 22(1) (2003 Reissue) LANDLORD AND TENANT (BUSINESS TENANCIES) Paragraph 227 [1021] et seq.

138   A contract of insurance is one uberrimae fidei. The insured must disclose to the insurers all material facts that are within his actual or presumed knowledge, whether there is a formal proposal form or not. A fact is material if non-disclosure of it would influence a prudent and reasonable insurer. This warranty is designed to rebut any suggestion by the landlord's insurers that the landlord had knowledge of the matters concerned. By inserting this clause in the lease, and thus specifically bringing the point to the tenant's attention, the landlord can argue that he has done all that is practical to establish the existence of any such matters. The absence of any written disclosure pursuant to this clause is strong evidence that the landlord has no actual or presumed knowledge of such matters. Further, the landlord has a right of action against the tenant for any breach of the warranty. As to non-disclosure and misrepresentation in contracts of non-marine insurance see 22 Halsbury's Laws (4th Edn Reissue) INSURANCE.

5.2   Covenant to insure

The Landlord covenants with the Tenant to insure the Estate unless the insurance is vitiated by any act of the Tenant or by anyone at the Estate expressly or by implication[139] with the Tenant's authority [and under his control][140].

139   The expression 'by implication' is intended to include a caller, such as a tradesman, where there has been no express invitation but the person cannot be classed as a trespasser.
140   The tenant should add the words in square brackets.

[823]

5.3   Details of the insurance

5.3.1   *Office, underwriters and agency*

Insurance is to be effected in such [substantial and reputable] insurance office, or with such underwriters[141], and through such agency as the Landlord from time to time decides.

141   The expression 'insurance office' would probably not include Lloyd's underwriters. The landlord's right to nominate the office and agency is absolute, with no implied restrictions: *Berrycroft Management Co Ltd v Sinclair Gardens Investments (Kensington) Ltd* (1996) 75 P & CR 210, [1997] 1 EGLR 47, CA.

5.3.2   *Insurance cover*[142]

Insurance must be effected for the following amounts —

5.3.2.1   the sum that the Landlord is from time to time advised [by the Surveyor] is the full cost of rebuilding and reinstating the Estate, including [VAT[143],] architects', surveyors', engineers', solicitors' and all other professional persons' fees, the fees payable on any applications for planning permission or other permits or consents that may be required in relation to rebuilding or reinstating the Estate, the cost of preparation of the site including shoring-up, debris removal, demolition, site clearance and any works that may be required by statute, and incidental expenses, and

5.3.2.2   loss of rental [and service charge] income from the Estate, taking account of any rent reviews that may be due, for *(state period, eg 3 years)* or such longer period as the Landlord from time to time [reasonably] requires for planning and carrying out the rebuilding or reinstatement.

142   As to the sum insured see vol 22(1) (2003 Reissue) LANDLORD AND TENANT (BUSINESS TENANCIES) Paragraph 231 [1028] et seq.
           It should be noted that it is recommended 'best practice' that, where the landlord has arranged insurance, the terms should be made known to the tenant and any material change in the insurance should be notified to the tenant: see Recommendation 14 of 'A code of practice for commercial leases in England and Wales (2nd edition)' which can be found in vol 22(1) (2003 Reissue) LANDLORD AND TENANT (BUSINESS TENANCIES) at Form 1 [4501].
143   As to VAT and the level of insurance cover see the Information Binder: Property [1]: VAT and Property. The expense of insuring against the VAT payable on reinstatement costs is not justified where the landlord may not opt to tax and is able to recover the VAT. There is a theoretical possibility that a future landlord may not opt to tax and that the sum insured may then be too low. It is also possible that a landlord may wish to preserve the 'exempt' status of a property. Normally, however, the cost of reinstatement need not expressly mention VAT, although the cashflow implications of having to pay VAT on construction works need to be remembered.

5.3.3   *Risks insured*[144]

Insurance must be effected against damage or destruction by any of the Insured Risks to the extent that such insurance may ordinarily be arranged [with a substantial and reputable insurer] for properties such as the Estate, subject to such excesses, exclusions or limitations as the insurer requires.

144   As to risks to be insured against see vol 22(1) (2003 Reissue) LANDLORD AND TENANT (BUSINESS TENANCIES) Paragraph 235 [1033].
        It should be noted that it is recommended 'best practice' that, where the landlord has arranged insurance, the terms should be made known to the tenant and any material change in the insurance should be notified to the tenant: see Recommendation 14 of 'A code of practice for commercial leases in England and Wales (2nd edition)' which can be found in vol 22(1) (2003 Reissue) LANDLORD AND TENANT (BUSINESS TENANCIES) at Form 1 [4501].

[824]

5.4   Payment of the Insurance Rent

The Tenant covenants to pay the Insurance Rent for the period starting on the Rent Commencement Date and ending on the day before the next policy renewal date on the date of this document, and subsequently to pay the Insurance Rent on demand and, if so demanded, in advance of the policy renewal date[, but not more than *(state period, eg ... months)* in advance].

5.5   Suspension of the Rent[145]

5.5.1   *Events giving rise to suspension*

If and whenever the Estate or any part of it is damaged or destroyed by one or more of the Insured Risks[146] [— except one against which insurance may not ordinarily be arranged [with a substantial and reputable insurer] for properties such as the Estate unless the Landlord has in fact insured against that risk —] so that the Premises or any part of them are unfit for occupation or use, and payment of the insurance money is not wholly or partly refused because of any act or default of the Tenant or anyone at the Estate expressly or by implication[147] with his authority [and under his control][148], then the provisions of clause 5.5.2 SUSPENDING THE RENT are to have effect.

145   As to suspension of rent see vol 22(1) (2003 Reissue) LANDLORD AND TENANT (BUSINESS TENANCIES) Paragraph 241 [1044] et seq.
146   It should be noted that it is recommended 'best practice' that if premises are so damaged by an uninsured risk as to prevent occupation, the tenant should be allowed to terminate the lease unless the landlord agrees to reinstate at his own cost: see vol 22(1) (2003 Reissue) LANDLORD AND TENANT (BUSINESS TENANCIES) Paragraph 85 [402] and 'A code of practice for commercial leases in England and Wales (2nd edition)' which can be found in vol 22(1) (2003 Reissue) LANDLORD AND TENANT (BUSINESS TENANCIES) at Form 1 [4501]. If adopted, this recommendation involves rent suspension also becoming operative in the event of the premises becoming unusable because of uninsured risks.
147   The expression 'by implication' is intended to include a caller, such as a tradesman, where there has been no express invitation but the person cannot be classed as a trespasser.
148   The tenant should add the words in square brackets.

[825]

5.5.2   *Suspending the Rent*

In the circumstances mentioned in clause 5.5.1 EVENTS GIVING RISE TO SUSPENSION the Rent [and the Service Charge][149], or a fair proportion of the Rent [and the Service Charge] according to the nature and the extent of the damage sustained, is to cease to be payable until the Estate has been rebuilt or reinstated so as to render the Premises, or the affected part, fit for occupation and use, [or until the end of *(state period, eg 3 years)* from the destruction or damage whichever period is the shorter,][150] [the proportion of the Rent [and the Service Charge] suspended and the period of the suspension to be determined by the Surveyor acting as an expert and not as an arbitrator *(or as required)* any dispute as to the proportion of the Rent [and the Service Charge] suspended or the period of the suspension to be determined in accordance with the Arbitration Act 1996 by an arbitrator to be appointed by agreement between the Landlord and the Tenant or in default by the President or other proper officer for the time being of the Royal Institution of Chartered Surveyors upon the application of either the Landlord or the Tenant].

149   As to the nature of the payments to be covered see vol 22(1) (2003 Reissue) LANDLORD AND TENANT (BUSINESS TENANCIES) Paragraph 242 [1045].
150   As to the length of the suspension and the tenant's concerns see vol 22(1) (2003 Reissue) LANDLORD AND TENANT (BUSINESS TENANCIES) Paragraph 244 [1048]. For a provision extending suspension of the rent where reinstatement is delayed see vol 22(3) (1997 Reissue) LANDLORD AND TENANT (BUSINESS TENANCIES) Form 111 [6495].

5.6   Reinstatement and termination[151]

5.6.1   *Obligation to obtain permissions*

If and whenever the Estate or any part of it is damaged or destroyed by one or more of the Insured Risks [— except one against which insurance may not ordinarily be arranged [with a substantial and reputable insurer] for properties such as the Estate, unless the Landlord has in fact insured against that risk —] and payment of the insurance money is not wholly or partly refused because of any act or default of the Tenant or anyone at the Estate expressly or by implication with his authority[152] [and under his control][153], then the Landlord must use his best endeavours[154] to obtain any planning permissions or other permits and consents ('permissions') that are required under the Planning Acts or otherwise to enable him to rebuild and reinstate the Estate.

[826]

151   It has been held that, in the absence of an express covenant to reinstate, where the landlord must keep the premises adequately insured against comprehensive risks and the insurance is effected at the tenant's expense, the obligation is one intended to enure for the benefit of both parties: *Mumford Hotels Ltd v Wheler* [1964] Ch 117, [1963] 3 All ER 250; see also *Mark Rowlands Ltd v Berni Inns Ltd* [1986] QB 211, [1985] 3 All ER 473, CA; *Lonsdale & Thompson Ltd v Black Arrow Group plc* [1993] Ch 361, [1993] 3 All ER 648. This is not, however, a general principle of law and the tenant should therefore always require a specific covenant to reinstate.
      These provisions are restricted to circumstances where damage or destruction is caused by an insured risk. It should be noted that it is recommended 'best practice' that if premises are so damaged by an uninsured risk as to prevent occupation, the tenant should be allowed to terminate the lease unless the landlord agrees to reinstate at his own cost: see vol 22(1) (2003 Reissue) LANDLORD AND TENANT (BUSINESS TENANCIES) Paragraph 85 [401] and 'A code of practice for commercial leases in England and Wales (2nd edition)' which can be found in vol 22(1) (2003 Reissue) LANDLORD AND TENANT (BUSINESS TENANCIES) at Form 1 [4501].
      As to termination where reinstatement is not possible see vol 22(1) (2003 Reissue) LANDLORD AND TENANT (BUSINESS TENANCIES) Paragraph 237 [1037]. For a provision for termination or surrender on destruction or substantial damage see vol 22(3) (1997 Reissue) LANDLORD AND TENANT (BUSINESS TENANCIES) Form 107 [6483].

152   The expression 'by implication' is intended to include a caller, such as a tradesman, where there has been no express invitation but the person cannot be classed as a trespasser.
153   The tenant should add the words in square brackets.
154   The extent of the duty to use best endeavours depends upon the facts in each case: see *Monkland v Jack Barclay Ltd* [1951] 2 KB 252, [1951] 1 All ER 714, CA; *Terrell v Mabie Todd & Co Ltd* [1952] 2 TLR 574; *NW Investments (Erdington) Ltd v Swani* (1970) 214 Estates Gazette 1115. In the light of *IBM United Kingdom Ltd v Rockware Glass Ltd* [1980] FSR 335, CA, it may be that there is little practical difference between a covenant to use best endeavours, a covenant to use reasonable endeavours and a covenant to take all reasonable steps.

[827]

5.6.2   *Obligation to reinstate*

Subject to the provisions of clause 5.6.3 RELIEF FROM THE OBLIGATION TO REINSTATE, and, if any permissions are required, after they have been obtained, the Landlord must as soon as reasonably practicable apply all money received in respect of the insurance effected by the Landlord pursuant to this Lease, except sums in respect of loss of the Rent [and the Service Charge][155], in rebuilding or reinstating the parts of the Estate destroyed or damaged[, making up any difference between the cost of rebuilding and reinstating and the money received out of his own money][156].

155   See note 149 to clause 5.5.2 [827] SUSPENDING THE RENT.
156   Where the landlord's covenant is 'to apply all money received in respect of the insurance in rebuilding or reinstating' rather than simply 'to reinstate', it seems that the landlord does not have to complete the work out of his own money if the insurance money is insufficient because he has complied with his covenant by laying out all the insurance money received. The situation is different if the tenant can establish that the landlord was in breach of his covenant to insure for the full cost of reinstatement and that this has caused the shortfall: see *Mumford Hotels Ltd v Wheler* [1964] Ch 117, [1963] 3 All ER 250. The tenant should, therefore, require a specific covenant from the landlord to make up any shortfall, to prevent a situation in which the landlord refuses to complete the rebuilding. This is of particular concern if the suspension of rent proviso is expressed to operate for a limited period, because on the expiry of that period the tenant becomes liable for rent unless he can satisfy the court that the lease has been frustrated.
   It should be noted that it is recommended 'best practice' that if premises are so damaged by an uninsured risk as to prevent occupation, the tenant should be allowed to terminate the lease unless the landlord agrees to reinstate at his own cost: see vol 22(1) (2003 Reissue) LANDLORD AND TENANT (BUSINESS TENANCIES) Paragraph 85 [401] and 'A code of practice for commercial leases in England and Wales (2nd edition)'which can be found in vol 22(1) (2003 Reissue) LANDLORD AND TENANT (BUSINESS TENANCIES) at Form 1 [4501]. If this recommendation is adopted and the landlord merely covenants to apply insurance money received, the principle should be extended to damage or destruction resulting from insured risks in circumstances where the insurance money is insufficient to enable reinstatement to be completed.
   For a proviso relieving from the obligation to reinstate in the same form see vol 22(3) (1997 Reissue) LANDLORD AND TENANT (BUSINESS TENANCIES) Form 106 [6482].

[828]

5.6.3   *Relief from the obligation to reinstate*[157]

The Landlord need not rebuild or reinstate the Estate if and for so long as rebuilding or reinstating is prevented because —

5.6.3.1   the Landlord, despite using his best endeavours[158], cannot obtain a necessary permission,

5.6.3.2   any permission is granted subject to a lawful condition with which [it is impossible for *(or as required)* in all the circumstances it is unreasonable to expect] the Landlord to comply,

5.6.3.3   there is some defect or deficiency in the site on which the rebuilding or reinstatement is to take place that [renders it impossible *(or as required)* means it can only be undertaken at a cost that is unreasonable in all the circumstances],

5.6.3.4   the Landlord is unable to obtain access to the site to rebuild or reinstate,

5.6.3.5   the rebuilding or reinstating is prevented by war, act of God, government action[, strike or lock-out], or

because of the occurrence of any other circumstances beyond the Landlord's control.

157   As to the need for a right to terminate where reinstatement is not possible see vol 22(1) (2003 Reissue) LANDLORD AND TENANT (BUSINESS TENANCIES) Paragraph 226 [998].

158   The extent of the duty to use best endeavours depends upon the facts in each case: see *Monkland v Jack Barclay Ltd* [1951] 2 KB 252, [1951] 1 All ER 714, CA; *Terrell v Mabie Todd & Co Ltd* [1952] 2 TLR 574; *NW Investments (Erdington) Ltd v Swani* (1970) 214 Estates Gazette 1115. In the light of *IBM United Kingdom Ltd v Rockware Glass Ltd* [1980] FSR 335, CA, it may be that there is little practical difference between a covenant to use best endeavours, a covenant to use reasonable endeavours and a covenant to take all reasonable steps.

[829]

5.6.4   *Notice to terminate*[159]

If at the end of a period[160] of *(state period, eg 3 years)* starting on the date of the damage or destruction the Premises are still not fit for the Tenant's occupation and use, either the Landlord or the Tenant may by notice served at any time within *(state period, eg 6 months)* of the end of that period ('a notice to terminate following failure to reinstate') implement the provisions of clause 5.6.5 TERMINATION FOLLOWING FAILURE TO REINSTATE[161].

159   For alternative provisions where the landlord's right to terminate is limited to specified circumstances see vol 22(3) (1997 Reissue) LANDLORD AND TENANT (BUSINESS TENANCIES) Form 109 [6492].

160   The period to be inserted must be carefully considered. Particular regard should be had to the terms of any rent suspension provision and the extent of insurance cover for loss of rent.

161   As to the effect of the Landlord and Tenant Act 1954 see vol 22(1) (2003 Reissue) LANDLORD AND TENANT (BUSINESS TENANCIES) Paragraph 226 [998].

5.6.5   *Termination following failure to reinstate*

On service of a notice to terminate following failure to reinstate, the Term is to cease absolutely — but without prejudice to any rights or remedies that may have accrued[162]— and all money received in respect of the insurance effected by the Landlord pursuant to this Lease is to belong to the Landlord absolutely[163].

162   The effect of this clause is that the right to terminate arises after the end of the appropriate period, whatever the reason for the delay, but the tenant still has a right of action against the landlord if the landlord is in breach of his covenant to reinstate.

163   In the absence of provision for ownership of the insurance money the position is uncertain. In *Re King, Robinson v Gray* [1963] Ch 459, [1963] 1 All ER 781, CA it was held that the insurance money belongs to the party who paid the premiums even if the insurance was placed in the joint names of the landlord and the tenant. The dissenting view of Denning MR that insurance in joint names envisages that each party should be insured as to his insurable interest and that the insurance money should therefore be divided in proportion to their interests in the property should, however, be noted. In *Beacon Carpets Ltd v Kirby* [1985] QB 755, [1984] 2 All ER 726, CA the court adhered to this view and held that the proportion payable depended on the parties' interests in the premises at the time of the destruction. The landlord will prefer the lease to provide expressly for the insurance money to be retained by him in full if reinstatement proves impossible. The tenant ought perhaps to accept that it would be unrealistic to amend this to provide for the insurance money to belong to the tenant, but should suggest that a provision be inserted under which the money is to be divided in accordance with their respective interests in the premises at the time when the insurance money became due. For an alternative provision for ownership of the insurance money etc see vol 22(3) (1997 Reissue) LANDLORD AND TENANT (BUSINESS TENANCIES) Form 108 [6491].

[830]

5.7   Tenant's further insurance covenants[164]

The Tenant covenants with the Landlord to observe and perform the requirements of this clause 5.7.

164   In order to comply with many of these covenants, the tenant will need to be supplied with details of the landlord's insurance policy. In any event, it should be noted that it is recommended 'best practice' that where the landlord has arranged insurance, the terms should be made known to the tenant and any material change in the insurance should be notified to the tenant: see Recommendation 14 of 'A code of practice for commercial leases in England and Wales (2nd edition)' which can be found in vol 22(1) (2003 Reissue) LANDLORD AND TENANT (BUSINESS TENANCIES) at Form 1 [4501].

5.7.1   *Requirements of insurers*

The Tenant must comply with all the requirements and recommendations of the insurers.

5.7.2   *Policy avoidance and additional premiums*

The Tenant must not do or omit anything that could cause any insurance policy on or in relation to the Estate to become wholly or partly void or voidable, or do or omit anything by which additional insurance premiums may become payable unless he has previously notified the Landlord and has agreed to pay the increased premium.

5.7.3   *Fire-fighting equipment*

The Tenant must keep the Premises supplied with such fire fighting equipment [as the insurers and the fire authority require and must maintain the equipment to their satisfaction *(or as required)* as the Landlord reasonably requires and must maintain the equipment to the reasonable satisfaction of the insurers and the fire authority] and in efficient working order. At least once in every *(state period, eg 6 months)* the Tenant must have any sprinkler system and other fire fighting equipment inspected by a competent person.

5.7.4   *Combustible materials*

The Tenant must not store on the Premises or bring onto them anything of a specially combustible, inflammable or explosive nature, and must comply with the requirements and recommendations of the fire authority [and the [reasonable] requirements of the Landlord] as to fire precautions relating to the Estate.

5.7.5   *Fire escapes, equipment and doors*

The Tenant must not obstruct the access to any fire equipment or the means of escape from the Premises or any part of the Estate or lock any fire door while the Premises are occupied.

[831]

5.7.6   *Notice of events affecting the policy*

The Tenant must give immediate notice to the Landlord of any event that might affect any insurance policy on or relating to the Estate and any event against which the Landlord may have insured under this Lease.

5.7.7   *Notice of convictions*

The Tenant must give immediate notice to the Landlord of any conviction, judgment or finding of any court or tribunal relating to the Tenant, or any director other officer or major shareholder of the Tenant, of such a nature as to be likely to affect the decision of any insurer or underwriter to grant or to continue any insurance[165].

165   This clause provides a continuation of the warranty given by the tenant in clause 5.1 [823] WARRANTY AS TO CONVICTIONS. As to non-disclosure and misrepresentation in contracts of non-marine insurance see 22 Halsbury's Laws (4th Edn Reissue) INSURANCE.

5.7.8   *Other insurance*

If at any time the Tenant is entitled to the benefit of any insurance of the Premises that is not effected or maintained in pursuance of any obligation contained in this Lease, the Tenant must apply all money received by virtue of such insurance in making good the loss or damage in respect of which the money is received[166].

166   An insurance policy frequently provides that if there is any other insurance effected by or on behalf of the insured, covering the premises that are the subject of the policy, the insurers are liable only for a rateable proportion of the damage. Such provisions extend to a case where one of the policies is in the joint names of the persons interested in the premises and the other is in the name of one only of those persons: *Halifax Building Society v Keighley* [1931] 2 KB 248. Therefore, at least when the insurance is in joint names and, ideally, even where it is not, the landlord should ensure that the tenant will use all money received under any policy he has effected to reinstate the premises.

[832]

5.8   Increase or decrease of the Estate

5.8.1   *Variation of the Insurance Rent Percentage*

If the size of the Estate is permanently increased or decreased, the Insurance Rent Percentage may be varied, if the Landlord [acting reasonably] so requires, with effect from the date of any consequent alteration in the Insurance Rent.

5.8.2   *Determination of the variation*[167]

The amount by which the Insurance Rent Percentage is varied is to be agreed by the Landlord and the Tenant or, in default of agreement within *(state period, eg 3 months)* of the first proposal for variation made by the Landlord, is to be the amount the Surveyor, acting as an expert and not as an arbitrator, determines to be fair and reasonable.

167   Without a clause such as this the landlord cannot vary the insurance rent percentage without the consent of all the tenants, and if he subsequently extends the development he would be unable to combine the administration.

[5.9   Landlord's further insurance covenants[168]

The Landlord covenants with the Tenant to observe and perform the requirements set out in this clause 5.9 in relation to the insurance policy effected by the Landlord pursuant to his obligations contained in this Lease.

168   Unless insurance is to be in the joint names of the landlord and the tenant (which is unlikely in the circumstances assumed by this lease), the tenant should seek covenants such as these from the landlord.

5.9.1   Copy policy

The Landlord must produce to the Tenant on demand [a copy of the policy and the last premium renewal receipt (*or as required*) reasonable evidence of the terms of the policy and the fact that the last premium has been paid][169].

169   The landlord can reasonably insist on the second alternative. If the premises are insured under a block policy, it would be inappropriate for the landlord to have to disclose to the tenant information about his other properties.

It should be noted that it is recommended 'best practice' that where the landlord has arranged insurance, the terms should be made known to the tenant and any material change in the insurance should be notified to the tenant: see Recommendation 14 of 'A code of practice for commercial leases in England and Wales (2nd edition)' which can be found in vol 22(1) (2003 Reissue) LANDLORD AND TENANT (BUSINESS TENANCIES) at Form 1 [4501].

[833]

5.9.2   Noting of the Tenant's interest

The Landlord must ensure that the interest of the Tenant is noted or endorsed on the policy[170].

170   Where insurance in the joint names of the landlord and the tenant is not practical, the tenant should insist that a note of his interest is endorsed on the policy. This protects the tenant because the insurers should give notice to him of any lapse in the policy and, where it can be shown that the tenant is responsible for the insurance premium under the terms of the lease, it is likely — but not certain — that the insurers would not exercise subrogation rights against the tenant.

It is recommended 'best practice' that where the landlord has arranged insurance, any interest of the tenant should be covered by the policy: see Recommendation 14 of 'A code of practice for commercial leases in England and Wales (2nd edition)' which can be found in vol 22(1) (2003 Reissue) LANDLORD AND TENANT (BUSINESS TENANCIES) at Form 1 [4501].

5.9.3   Change of risks

The Landlord must notify the Tenant of any [material] change in the risks covered by the policy from time to time[171].

171   It is recommended 'best practice' that where the landlord has arranged insurance, any interest of the tenant should be covered by the policy: see Recommendation 14 of 'A code of practice for commercial leases in England and Wales (2nd edition)' which can be found in vol 22(1) (2003 Reissue) LANDLORD AND TENANT (BUSINESS TENANCIES) at Form 1 [4501].

[5.9.4   Waiver of subrogation[172]

The Landlord must produce to the Tenant on demand written confirmation from the insurers that they have agreed to waive all rights of subrogation against the Tenant.]]

172   Generally an insurer who has paid out under a policy stands in the shoes of the insured with regard to any claim the latter may have had against any third party. If the insurance is in joint names, the tenant is an insured party and there can be no subrogation against him. It would seem, also, that where the tenant covenants to reimburse the landlord for sums expended by the landlord in insuring the premises, the landlord's insurers cannot make a subrogated claim against the tenant where the premises are destroyed by the tenant's negligence: *Mark Rowlands Ltd v Berni Inns Ltd* [1986] QB 211, [1985] 3 All ER 473, CA. The tenant may still, however, wish to obtain a specific waiver of subrogation if possible.

[834]–[850]

6   GUARANTEE PROVISIONS

6.1   The Guarantor's covenants[173]

6.1.1   *Nature and duration*

The Guarantor's covenants with the Landlord are given as sole or principal debtor or covenantor, with the landlord for the time being and with all his successors in title[174] without the need for any express assignment, and the Guarantor's obligations to the Landlord will last throughout the Liability Period.

173   The covenants in this clause should *not* be omitted where no guarantor is a party to the lease, because they may be required under clause 3.9.5.2 [784] CONDITIONS. If it is felt undesirable to have covenants in a lease and no party, at least initially, to enter into them, ie where there is no guarantor for the original tenant, the contents of this clause could alternatively be included in a schedule.

174   The new provisions governing the transmission of the benefit and burden of covenants (see the Landlord and Tenant (Covenants) Act 1995 s 3) only apply to landlord and tenant covenants. The law in force before 1 January 1996 remains unchanged for guarantor covenants, so that the benefit passes with the landlord's reversion. This occurs, not under the Law of Property Act 1925 s 141(1), which has been repealed for post-1995 tenancies by the 1995 Act, but under common law. The guarantee covenant touches and concerns the legal estate vested in the new reversioner: see *P & A Swift Investments v Combined English Stores Group plc* [1989] AC 632, [1988] 2 All ER 885, HL.

[851]

6.1.2   *The covenants*

The Guarantor covenants with the Landlord to observe and perform the requirements of this clause 6.1.2.

6.1.2.1   **Payment of rent and performance of the Lease**

The Tenant must pay the Lease Rents[175] and VAT charged on them punctually and observe and perform the covenants and other terms of this Lease, and if, at any time during the Liability Period while the Tenant is bound by the tenant covenants of this Lease[176], the Tenant defaults in paying the Lease Rents or in observing or performing any of the covenants or other terms of this Lease, then the Guarantor must pay the Lease Rents and observe or perform the covenants or terms in respect of which the Tenant is in default and make good to the Landlord on demand, and indemnify the Landlord against, all losses resulting from such non-payment, non-performance or non-observance notwithstanding —

(a)   any time or indulgence granted by the Landlord to the Tenant, any neglect or forbearance of the Landlord in enforcing the payment of the Lease Rents or the observance or performance of the covenants or other terms of this Lease, or any refusal by the Landlord to accept rent tendered by or on behalf of the Tenant at a time when the Landlord is entitled — or will after the service of a notice under the Law of Property Act 1925 Section 146 be entitled — to re-enter the Premises[177],

(b)   that the terms of this Lease may have been varied by agreement between the Landlord and the Tenant[, provided that no variation is to bind the Guarantor to the extent that it is materially prejudicial to him][178],

(c)   that the Tenant has surrendered part of the Premises — in which event the liability of the Guarantor under this Lease is to continue in respect of the part of the Premises not surrendered after making any necessary apportionments under the Law of Property Act 1925 Section 140[179], and

(d)   anything else (other than a release by deed) by which, but for this clause 6.1.2.1, the Guarantor would be released.

[852]

175   As to the definition of 'the Lease Rents' see clause 1.44 [735] 'THE RENT'.

176   This obligation lasts while the lease is vested in the tenant and for any period of extended liability following an excluded assignment. It is not appropriate once the tenant has entered into an authorised guarantee agreement, when the contractual guarantor's obligations are at one remove: see vol 22(1) (2003 Reissue) LANDLORD AND TENANT (BUSINESS TENANCIES) Paragraph 74 [284] and clause 6.1.2.4 [855] GUARANTEE OF THE TENANT'S LIABILITIES UNDER AN AUTHORISED GUARANTEE AGREEMENT.

177   If a creditor 'gives time' to the debtor in a binding manner, this releases the guarantor: see *Swire v Redman* (1876) 1 QBD 536; *Holme v Brunskill* (1877) 3 QBD 495, CA. The guarantee should, therefore, be expressed to apply notwithstanding any time or indulgence granted by the landlord to the tenant, or neglect or forbearance on the part of the landlord in enforcing the payment of rent and the other covenants in the lease. It has been suggested, however, that such wording does not protect a landlord who refuses to accept rent so as not to waive a breach of covenant by the tenant. This is unresolved but to avoid any doubt the point should be expressly dealt with. It appears that any provision in a guarantor's covenant that purports to exonerate the landlord from the consequences of his own negligence must satisfy the reasonableness test of the Unfair Contract Terms Act 1977.

178   Any variation of the terms of the contract between the creditor and the debtor will discharge the guarantor (*Holme v Brunskill* (1877) 3 QBD 495, CA), unless the guarantor consents, although it has been suggested that an immaterial variation that was not prejudicial to the guarantor might not release him. No guarantor should accept a provision by which the guarantee is to continue notwithstanding any variation, but on the other hand it seems unfair on the landlord for the guarantor to escape his liability merely because a minor change has been agreed between the landlord and the tenant. A provision that the guarantee is to continue to apply notwithstanding an immaterial variation not prejudicial to the guarantor seems a fair compromise. It should be noted that the Landlord and Tenant (Covenants) Act 1995 s 18 does not apply to the guarantor of the current tenant.

It should also be noted that it is recommended 'best practice' that landlords and tenants should seek the agreement of any guarantors to proposed material changes to the terms of the lease, or even minor changes which could increase the guarantor's liability: see Recommendation 15 of 'A code of practice for commercial leases in England and Wales (2nd edition)' which can be found in vol 22(1) (2003 Reissue) LANDLORD AND TENANT (BUSINESS TENANCIES) at Form 1 [4501].

179   In the light of *Holme v Brunskill* (1877) 3 QBD 495, CA, the position on surrender of part of the premises should be dealt with expressly.

[853]

6.1.2.2   New lease following disclaimer[180]

If, at any time during the Liability Period while the Tenant is bound by the tenant covenants of this Lease[181], any trustee in bankruptcy or liquidator of the Tenant disclaims this Lease, the Guarantor must, if so required by notice served by the Landlord within *(state period, eg 60 days)* of the Landlord's becoming aware of the disclaimer, take from the Landlord forthwith a lease of the Premises for the residue of the [Contractual][182] Term as at the date of the disclaimer, at the Rent then payable under this Lease and subject to the same covenants and terms as in this Lease — except that the Guarantor need not ensure that any other person is made a party to that lease as guarantor — the new lease to commence on the date of the disclaimer. The Guarantor must pay the costs of the new lease and VAT charged thereon, except where such VAT is recoverable or available for set-off by the Landlord as input tax[183], and execute and deliver to the Landlord a counterpart of the new lease.

180   This put option should be included because on disclaimer of a lease the lease ceases to exist, although it is deemed to continue for the purpose of determining the liability to the landlord of persons, including guarantors, other than the tenant whose liquidator or trustee has disclaimed: see *Hindcastle Ltd v Barbara Attenborough Associates Ltd* [1997] AC 70, [1996] 1 All ER 737, HL.

181   This obligation lasts while the lease is vested in the tenant and for any period of extended liability following an excluded assignment. It is not appropriate once the tenant has entered into an authorised guarantee agreement when the tenant's — ie the former tenant's — liquidator or trustee in bankruptcy will not be in a position to disclaim the lease because it is no longer be vested in the former tenant.

182   This defined term will require amendment where the operation of the security of tenure provisions in the Landlord and Tenant Act 1954 ss 24–28 is to be excluded in relation to the lease: see note 7 to clause 1.7 [709] 'THE [CONTRACTUAL] TERM'.

183   As to payment of VAT on legal costs by a person other than the solicitor's own client see the Information Binder: Property [1]: VAT and Property.

[854]

6.1.2.3   Payments following disclaimer[184]

If this Lease is disclaimed and the Landlord does not require the Guarantor to accept a new lease of the Premises in accordance with clause 6.1.2.2 NEW LEASE FOLLOWING DISCLAIMER, the Guarantor must pay to the Landlord on demand an amount equal to [the difference between any money received by the Landlord for the use or occupation of the Premises and] the Lease Rents [in both cases] for the period commencing with the date of the disclaimer and ending on whichever is the earlier of the date *(state period, eg 6 months)* after the disclaimer, the date, if any, upon which the Premises are relet, and the end of the [Contractual][185] Term.

184   This clause could be a useful alternative for a landlord, who may not be unhappy to regain possession of the premises but would like some rental income before reletting etc. For a covenant by the tenant to assign to the guarantor see vol 22(3) (1997 Reissue) LANDLORD AND TENANT (BUSINESS TENANCIES) Form 159 [6666].

185   This defined term will require amendment where the operation of the security of tenure provisions in the Landlord and Tenant Act 1954 ss 24–28 is to be excluded in relation to the lease: see note 7 to clause 1.7 [709] 'THE [CONTRACTUAL] TERM'.

6.1.2.4   Guarantee of the Tenant's liabilities under an authorised guarantee agreement

If, at any time during the Liability Period while the Tenant is bound by an authorised guarantee agreement, the Tenant defaults in his obligations under that agreement, the Guarantor must make good to the Landlord on demand, and indemnify the Landlord against, all losses resulting from that default notwithstanding —

(a)   any time or indulgence granted by the Landlord to the Tenant, or neglect or forbearance of the Landlord in enforcing the payment of any sum or the observance or performance of the covenants of the authorised guarantee agreement[186],

(b)   that the terms of the authorised guarantee agreement may have been varied by agreement between the Landlord and the Tenant [provided that no variation is to bind the Guarantor to the extent that it is materially prejudicial to him][187], or

(c)   anything else (other than a release by deed) by which, but for this clause 6.1.2.4, the Guarantor would be released.

186   See note 177 to clause 6.1.2.1 [853] PAYMENT OF RENT AND PERFORMANCE OF THE LEASE.
187   See note 178 to clause 6.1.2.1 [853] PAYMENT OF RENT AND PERFORMANCE OF THE LEASE.

[855]

6.1.3   *Severance*

6.1.3.1   Severance of void provisions

Any provision of this clause 6 rendered void by virtue of the 1995 Act Section 25 is to be severed from all remaining provisions, and the remaining provisions are to be preserved.

6.1.3.2   Limitation of provisions

If any provision in this clause 6 extends beyond the limits permitted by the 1995 Act Section 25, that provision is to be varied so as not to extend beyond those limits.

[6.2   The Landlord's covenant[188]

The Landlord covenants with the Guarantor that he will not attempt to recover from the Guarantor payment of any amount, determined by a court or in binding arbitration or agreed between the Landlord and the Tenant, payable in respect of a breach of covenant by the Tenant, unless he has served on the Guarantor, within 6 months of the payment being determined or agreed, a notice in the form prescribed by Section 27 of the 1995 Act as if the payment were a fixed charge under that Act.]

188   This clause is a tenant's amendment. It provides for a notice equivalent to a default notice under the Landlord and Tenant (Covenants) Act 1995 to be served. It protects the interests of existing and future contractual guarantors. As to service of default notices see vol 22(1) (2003 Reissue) LANDLORD AND TENANT (BUSINESS TENANCIES) Paragraph 61 [260].

[856]–[870]

7   FORFEITURE[189]

If and whenever during the Term —

7.1   the Lease Rents[190], or any of them or any part of them, or any VAT payable on them, are outstanding for *(state period, eg 14 days)* after becoming due, whether formally demanded or not[191], or

7.2   the Tenant [or the Guarantor] breaches any covenant or other term of this Lease, or

7.3   the Tenant [or the Guarantor][192], being an individual, becomes subject to a bankruptcy order[193] [or has an interim receiver appointed to his property][194], or

7.4   the Tenant [or the Guarantor][195], being a company, enters into liquidation[196] whether compulsory or voluntary — but not if the liquidation is for amalgamation or reconstruction of a solvent company — [or enters into administration][197] [or has a receiver appointed over all or any part of its assets][198], or

7.5   the Tenant [or the Guarantor][199] enters into or makes a proposal to enter into any voluntary arrangement pursuant to the Insolvency Act 1986[200] or any other arrangement or composition for the benefit of his creditors, or

7.6   the Tenant has any distress, sequestration or execution levied on his goods,

and, where the Tenant [or the Guarantor] is more than one person, if and whenever any of the events referred to in this clause happens to any one or more of them, the Landlord may at any time re-enter the Premises, or any part of them in the name of the whole — even if any previous right of re-entry has been waived[201] — and thereupon the Term is to cease absolutely but without prejudice to any rights or remedies that may have accrued to the Landlord against the Tenant or the Guarantor [or to the Tenant against the Landlord] in respect of any breach of covenant or other term of this Lease, including the breach in respect of which the re-entry is made.

[871]

189   As to forfeiture generally see vol 22(1) (2003 Reissue) LANDLORD AND TENANT (BUSINESS TENANCIES) Paragraph 283 [1171] et seq.
        The precise range of insolvency-related circumstances that will trigger the proviso should be carefully considered. Tenants should note that their inclusion, in practice, means that the lease cannot be used as security for a loan. Landlords generally seek to have the ability to forfeit in the widest range of circumstances. It should, however, be noted that, in certain circumstances, leave of the court or of the insolvency practitioner administering the procedure may be required before any contractual right can be exercised: see eg, in respect of administration, the Insolvency Act 1986 Sch 1B para 43(4), (6) as inserted by the Enterprise Act 2002 s 248 (4 Halsbury's Statutes (4th Edn) BANKRUPTCY AND INSOLVENCY).

190   As to the definition of 'the Lease Rents' see clause 1.44 [735] 'THE RENT'.
191   The words 'whether formally demanded or not' should be used to avoid the common law requirement that an actual demand has to be made.
192   The lease may provide for a right of re-entry on insolvency of the guarantor or a tenant's covenant to find an acceptable replacement (see clause 3.23 [806] REPLACEMENT GUARANTOR) or both.
193   As to bankruptcy generally see the Insolvency Act 1986 Pt IX (ss 264–371).
194   As to interim receivers see the Insolvency Act 1986 s 286.
195   See note 192 above.
196   As to liquidation generally see the Insolvency Act 1986 Pts IV–VI (ss 73–246).
197   As to administration generally see the Insolvency Act 1986 Pt II as substituted by the Enterprise Act 2002 s 248. The tenant may seek to argue that if the administrator pays rent and if there are no other material breaches of the lease the landlord should not be entitled to forfeit the lease on this ground.
198   The tenant may seek to argue that if the receiver pays rent and if there are no other material breaches of the lease the landlord should not be entitled to forfeit the lease on this ground.
199   See note 192 above.
200   As to company voluntary arrangements see the Insolvency Act 1986 Pt I (ss 1–7B) as amended by the Insolvency Act 2000. As to individual voluntary arrangements see the Insolvency Act 1986 Pt VIII (ss 252–263G) as amended by the Enterprise Act 2002 s 264.
201   The landlord has the option whether to take advantage of a right of forfeiture or not. If he elects not to do so, the forfeiture is waived. The election may be express or implied, eg if the landlord does any act by which he recognises that the relationship of landlord and tenant is still continuing after the cause of forfeiture has come to his knowledge.

[872]

8   MISCELLANEOUS

8.1   Exclusion of warranty as to use

Nothing in this Lease or in any consent granted by the Landlord under this Lease is to imply or warrant that the Premises may lawfully be used under the Planning Acts for the Permitted Use[202].

202   See *Laurence v Lexcourt Holdings Ltd* [1978] 2 All ER 810, [1978] 1 WLR 1128; *Collins v Howell-Jones* [1981] 2 EGLR 108, 259 Estates Gazette 331, CA and the comments of Eveleigh LJ on estate agents' particulars relating to use in *Bovis Group Pension Fund Ltd v GC Flooring & Furnishing Ltd* (1984) 269 Estates Gazette 1252 at 1253, CA.

8.2   Exclusion of third party rights

Nothing in this Lease is intended to confer any benefit on any person who is not a party to it[203].

203   By virtue of the Contracts (Rights of Third Parties) Act 1999 (11 Halsbury's Statutes (4th Edn) CONTRACT) third-party rights may be conferred where they are not clearly excluded. This being so, it is advisable to incorporate a specific exclusion except where the parties actually intend to confer rights of action on a third party. In the standard letting situation it is unlikely that the parties will wish to extend liability in this manner. As to the Contracts (Rights of Third Parties) Act 1999 generally see vol 4(3) (2001 Reissue) BOILERPLATE CLAUSES.

8.3   Representations

The Tenant acknowledges that this Lease has not been entered into wholly or partly in reliance on any statement or representation made by or on behalf of the Landlord except any such statement or representation that is expressly set out in this Lease[204] [or was made by the Landlord's solicitors in any written response to enquiries raised by the Tenant's solicitors in connection with the grant of this Lease].

204   See the comments of Eveleigh LJ on estate agents' particulars relating to use in *Bovis Group Pension Fund Ltd v GC Flooring & Furnishing Ltd* (1984) 269 Estates Gazette 1252 at 1253, CA. For an alternative provision see vol 22(4) (1997 Reissue) LANDLORD AND TENANT (BUSINESS TENANCIES) Form 400 clauses 7.1 [7520], 7.2 [7521].

[873]

8.4   Documents under hand

While the Landlord is a limited company or other corporation, any licence, consent, approval or notice required to be given by the Landlord is to be sufficiently given if given under the hand of a director, the secretary or other duly authorised officer of the Landlord [or by the Surveyor on behalf of the Landlord].

8.5   Tenant's property

If, after the Tenant has vacated the Premises at the end of the Term any property of his remains in or on the Premises and he fails to remove it within *(state period, eg 7 days)* after a written request from the Landlord to do so, or, if the Landlord is unable to make such a request to the Tenant, within *(state period, eg 14 days)* from the first attempt to make it, then the Landlord may, as the agent of the Tenant, sell that property. The Tenant must indemnify the Landlord against any liability incurred by the Landlord to any third party whose property is sold by him in the mistaken belief held in good faith — which is to be presumed unless the contrary is proved — that the property belonged to the Tenant. If, having made reasonable efforts to do so, the Landlord is unable to locate the Tenant, then the Landlord may retain the proceeds of sale absolutely unless the Tenant claims them within *(state period, eg 6 months)* of the date upon which he vacated the Premises. The Tenant must indemnify the Landlord against any damage occasioned to the Premises and any losses caused by or related to the presence of the property in or on the Premises.

8.6   Compensation on vacating excluded

Any statutory right of the Tenant to claim compensation from the Landlord on vacating the Premises is excluded to the extent that the law allows[205].

205   As to compensation where an order for a new tenancy is precluded on certain grounds see the Landlord and Tenant Act 1954 s 37 as amended by the Local Government and Housing Act 1989 s 149, Sch 7 and by SI 2003/3096.

As to the effectiveness of provisions of this nature see vol 22(1) (2003 Reissue) LANDLORD AND TENANT (BUSINESS TENANCIES) Paragraph 468 [3079].

[874]

8.7   Notices

8.7.1   *Form and service of notices*

A notice under this Lease must be in writing and, unless the receiving party or his authorised agent acknowledges receipt, is valid if, and only if[206] —

8.7.1.1   it is given by hand, sent by registered post or recorded delivery, or sent by fax[207] provided a confirmatory copy is given by hand or sent by registered post or recorded delivery on the same day, and

8.7.1.2   it is served —

(a)   where the receiving party is a company incorporated within Great Britain, at the registered office,

(b)   where the receiving party is the Tenant and the Tenant is not such a company, at the Premises, and

(c)   where the receiving party is the Landlord [or the Guarantor] and [the Landlord *(or as required)* that party] is not such a company, at [the Landlord's *(or as required)* that party's] address shown in this Lease or at any address specified in a notice given by [the Landlord to the Tenant *(or as required)* that party to the other parties].

206   Notice clauses are either mandatory or permissive. The words 'and only if' are inserted to make it clear that this clause is mandatory.

207   As to service by fax see *Hastie and Jenkerson v McMahon* [1991] 1 All ER 255, [1990] 1 WLR 1575, CA.

8.7.2   *Deemed delivery*[208]

8.7.2.1   By registered post or recorded delivery

Unless it is returned through the Royal Mail undelivered, a notice sent by registered post or recorded delivery is to be treated as served on the third working day after posting whenever, and whether or not, it is received.

8.7.2.2   By fax

A notice sent by fax is to be treated as served on the day upon which it is sent, or the next working day where the fax is sent after 1600 hours or on a day that is not a working day, whenever and whether or not it or the confirmatory copy is received unless the confirmatory copy is returned through the Royal Mail undelivered.

8.7.2.3   'A working day'

References to 'a working day' are references to a day when the United Kingdom clearing banks are open for business in the City of London.

208   It is a fundamental aspect of any notice clause to specify the circumstances in which the server, provided he has complied with the requirements of the clause, has for the purposes of the document served a notice, even if the recipient claims that he never received it.

8.7.3   *Joint recipients*

If the receiving party consists of more than one person, a notice to one of them is notice to all.

[875]

8.8   Rights and easements[209]

The operation of the Law of Property Act 1925 Section 62 is excluded from this Lease. The only rights granted to the Tenant are those expressly set out in this Lease and the Tenant is not to be entitled to any other rights affecting any adjoining property of the Landlord.

209   Where the Law of Property Act 1925 s 62 may operate, it is sensible to define in the lease those rights that are included, and then specifically exclude the operation of that section.

8.9   Covenants relating to adjoining property

The Tenant is not to be entitled to the benefit of, or the right [to enforce or][210] to prevent the release or modification of, any covenant agreement or condition entered into by any tenant of the Landlord in respect of any adjoining property of the Landlord.

210   As to when tenants would be able to enforce covenants against each other see vol 22(1) (2003 Reissue) LANDLORD AND TENANT (BUSINESS TENANCIES) Paragraph 48 [235]. Where this might arise, 'to enforce or' should be deleted by the tenant.

8.10   Disputes with adjoining occupiers

If any dispute arises between the Tenant and the tenants or occupiers of any of adjoining property of the Landlord in connection with the Premises and any of that adjoining property, it is to be decided [by the Landlord or in such manner as the Landlord directs *(or as required)* by the Surveyor acting as an expert and not as an arbitrator][211].

211   Such a provision is binding on the landlord and the tenant, but binds a tenant of the landlord's adjoining property only if there is a similar provision in his lease.

8.11   Effect of waiver

Each of the Tenant's covenants is to remain in full force both at law and in equity even if the Landlord has waived or released that covenant, or waived or released any similar covenant affecting any adjoining property of the Landlord[212].

212   But as to waiver of a right of forfeiture see vol 22(1) (2003 Reissue) LANDLORD AND TENANT (BUSINESS TENANCIES) Paragraph 284 [1173].

[876]

[8.12   The perpetuity period[213]

The perpetuity period applicable to this Lease is *(state period, eg 80 years)* from the commencement of the [Contractual][214] Term, and whenever in this Lease any party is granted a future interest it must vest within that period or be void for remoteness.]

213   As to the rule against perpetuities see vol 22(1) (2003 Reissue) LANDLORD AND TENANT (BUSINESS TENANCIES) Paragraph 132 [664]. This clause should be included if the term exceeds 21 years because this lease contains grants of future interests.
214   This defined term will require amendment where the operation of the security of tenure provisions in the Landlord and Tenant Act 1954 ss 24–28 is to be excluded in relation to the lease (see note 7 to clause 1.7 [709] 'THE [CONTRACTUAL] TERM') although this is probably unlikely in connection with the grant of such a long lease.

[8.13   Party walls

Any walls dividing the Premises from the other buildings are to be party walls within the meaning of the Law of Property Act 1925 Section 38 and must be maintained at the equally shared expense of the Tenant and the other party.[215]] *(omit if not required in the circumstances)*

215   Internal non-loadbearing and loadbearing walls between the premises and other premises are covered in the description of the premises. It is therefore unlikely that as between the tenant and the landlord or other tenants there can be any party walls.

8.14   Exclusion of liability

The Landlord is not to be responsible to the Tenant or to anyone at the Premises or the Estate expressly or by implication with the Tenant's authority for any accident happening or injury suffered or for any damage to or loss of any chattel sustained in the Premises or on the Estate[216].

216   As to exclusion clauses see vol 22(1) (2003 Reissue) LANDLORD AND TENANT (BUSINESS TENANCIES) Paragraph 140 [679].

8.15   [New *(or)* Old] lease

[This Lease [is *(or as appropriate)* is not] a new tenancy for the purposes of the 1995 Act Section 1. *(or as appropriate)* This Lease is granted under the 1995 Act Section 19 and [is *(or as appropriate)* is not] a new tenancy for the purposes of Section 1 of that Act][217].

217   A tenancy granted on or after 1 January 1996 that is an overriding lease is not a 'new' tenancy where the tenancy being overridden is one granted before that date: see the Landlord and Tenant (Covenants) Act 1995 ss 1(4), 20(1). Where the lease being granted is an overriding lease, the lease must include a statement that it is an overriding lease and indicate whether the overriding lease is or is not a 'new' tenancy: see the Landlord and Tenant (Covenants) Act 1995 s 20(2). In these circumstances the second alternative should be used.

[877]

[8.16   Capacity of tenants

It is declared that the persons comprising the Tenant hold the Premises as [joint tenants *(or as required)* tenants in common].]

[8.17   Exclusion of the 1954 Act Sections 24–28[218]

8.17.1   *Notice and declaration*

On *(date)* the Landlord served notice on the Tenant pursuant to the provisions of the 1954 Act Section 38A(3) as inserted by the Regulatory Reform (Business Tenancies) (England and Wales) Order 2003 and on *(date)* the Tenant made a [simple *(or as appropriate)* statutory] declaration pursuant to schedule 2 of the Regulatory Reform (Business Tenancies) (England and Wales) Order 2003.

8.17.2   *Agreement to exclude*

Pursuant to the provisions of the 1954 Act Section 38A(1) as inserted by the Regulatory Reform (Business Tenancies) (England and Wales) Order 2003, the parties agree that the provisions of the 1954 Act Sections 24–28 inclusive are to be excluded in relation to the tenancy created by this Lease.]

218   As to contracting out of the Landlord and Tenant Act 1954 and the requirements that need to be complied with see vol 22(1) (2003 Reissue) LANDLORD AND TENANT (BUSINESS TENANCIES) Paragraph 431 [2035].

(include other clauses as required: eg, break clauses and options (see vol 22(3) (1997 Reissue) LANDLORD AND TENANT *(BUSINESS TENANCIES) Forms 136 [6544]–142 [6569]) or a proviso as to termination on rent review (see vol 22(3) (1997 Reissue)* LANDLORD AND TENANT *(BUSINESS TENANCIES) Form 143 [6570]))*

IN WITNESS etc *(see vol 12(2) (2003 Reissue) DEEDS, AGREEMENTS ETC)*

[878]

SCHEDULE 1: THE RIGHTS GRANTED[219]

1-1   Rights of way

The right, subject to [temporary] interruption for repair, alteration, rebuilding or replacement, for the Tenant and all persons expressly or by implication authorised by him[220] — in common with the Landlord and all other persons having a like right — to pass and repass[221] to and from the Premises over and along the Estate Roads [at all times *(or as required)* at any time between *(state time, eg 0700 hours)* on Monday and *(state time, eg 1800 hours)* on Friday in each week, except public holidays][222] for all purposes connected with the use and enjoyment of the Premises but not otherwise[223], [with or without vehicles of any description *(or as required)* with vehicles not exceeding ... metres in length or ... kilograms unladen weight][224].

219   As to rights granted see vol 22(1) (2003 Reissue) LANDLORD AND TENANT (BUSINESS TENANCIES) Paragraph 123 [647] et seq.
220   The term 'the Tenant and all persons expressly or by implication authorised by him' is an updated version of 'the Tenant and his successors in title the owners and occupiers for the time being of the Premises and his or their respective servants and licensees': see *Baxendale v North Lambeth Liberal and Radical Club Ltd* [1902] 2 Ch 427 at 429 per Swinfen Eady J; *Hammond v Prentice Bros Ltd* [1920] 1 Ch 201.

221   There is an implied right to stop for a reasonable time for loading and unloading, but there is no right
       to park unless one is specifically granted: see *Bulstrode v Lambert* [1953] 2 All ER 728, [1953] 1 WLR
       1064; *McIlraith v Grady* [1968] 1 QB 468, [1967] 3 All ER 625, CA; *VT Engineering Ltd v Richard
       Barland & Co Ltd* (1968) 19 P & CR 890.
222   Limitation of the right of way to specified hours is justifiable only where there are problems of access,
       security or services.
223   See *Callard v Beeney* [1930] 1 KB 353 at 357 per Talbot J.
224   The landlord may reasonably wish to limit the size and weight of vehicles using the estate roads.

[879]

1-2   Right to use the Common Parts

The right, subject to [temporary] interruption for repair, alteration, rebuilding or
replacement, for the Tenant and all persons expressly or by implication authorised by
him — in common with the Landlord and all other persons having a like right — to use
all appropriate areas of the Common Parts for all proper purposes in connection with the
use and enjoyment of the Premises.

1-3   Passage and running through Adjoining Conduits

The right, subject to temporary interruption for repair, alteration or replacement, to the
free passage and running of all services to and from the Premises through the appropriate
Adjoining Conduits, in common with the Landlord and all other persons having a like
right.

1-4   Support and protection

The right of support and protection for the benefit of the Premises that is now enjoyed
from all other parts of the Estate.

[880]

SCHEDULE 2: THE RIGHTS RESERVED[225]

2-1   Passage and running through the Conduits

The right to the free and uninterrupted passage and running of all appropriate services
and supplies from and to other parts of the Estate or any other adjoining property of the
Landlord in and through the appropriate Conduits and through any structures of a similar
use or nature that may at any time be constructed in, on, over or under the Premises as
permitted by paragraph 2-2 RIGHT TO CONSTRUCT CONDUITS.

225   As to rights reserved see vol 22(1) (2003 Reissue) LANDLORD AND TENANT (BUSINESS TENANCIES)
       Paragraph 124 [648] et seq.

2-2   Right to construct conduits[226]

The right to construct[227] and to maintain at any time during the Term any pipes, sewers,
drains, mains, ducts, conduits, gutters, watercourses, wires, cables, [laser optical fibres,
data or impulse transmission, communication or reception systems,] channels, flues and
all other conducting media for the provision of services or supplies — including any
fixings, louvres, cowls and any other ancillary apparatus — for the benefit of any part of
the Estate or any other adjoining property of the Landlord[, making good any damage
caused by the exercise of the right].

226   If the term of the lease exceeds 21 years a perpetuity provision — see clause 8.12 [877] THE
       PERPETUITY PERIOD — is required in the lease because this is a grant of a future interest.
227   For a covenant to make good after exercising rights of access see vol 22(3) (1997 Reissue) LANDLORD
       AND TENANT (BUSINESS TENANCIES) Form 79 [6453].

[881]

2–3   Access

2–3.1   *Access to inspect etc*[228]

The right to enter, or in emergency to break into and enter, the Premises [at any time during the Term *(or as required)* at reasonable times and on reasonable notice except in emergency] —

2–3.1.1   to inspect the condition and state of repair of the Premises,

2–3.1.2   to inspect, clean, connect to, lay, repair, remove, replace with others, alter or execute any works whatever to or in connection with the conduits, easements, supplies or services referred to in paragraphs 2–1 PASSAGE AND RUNNING THROUGH THE CONDUITS and 2–2 RIGHT TO CONSTRUCT CONDUITS,

2–3.1.3   to view the state and condition of, and repair and maintain and carry out work of any other kind to, the Building and any other buildings where such viewing or work would not otherwise be [reasonably] practicable,

2–3.1.4   to carry out work or do anything whatever that the Landlord is obliged to do under this Lease,

2–3.1.5   to take schedules or inventories of fixtures and other items to be yielded up at the end of the Term, and

2–3.1.6   to exercise any of the rights granted to the Landlord by this Lease.

228   For a covenant to make good after exercising rights of access see vol 22(3) (1997 Reissue) LANDLORD AND TENANT (BUSINESS TENANCIES) Form 79 [6453].

2–3.2   *Access on renewal or rent review*

[The right to enter the Premises with the Surveyor and any third party determining the Rent under any provisions for rent review contained in this Lease, at [any time *(or as required)* convenient hours and on reasonable prior notice], to inspect [and measure] the Premises for all purposes connected with any pending or intended step under the 1954 Act or the implementation of the provisions for rent review. *(or as required in view of the rent review provisions used: see, eg, vol 22(3) (1997 Reissue) LANDLORD AND TENANT (BUSINESS TENANCIES) Forms 180 [6711]–194 [6987])*]

[882]

2–4   Right to erect scaffolding

The right [temporarily] to erect scaffolding for [any purpose connected with or related to the Building *(or as required)* the purpose of inspecting, repairing or cleaning the Building] or any other buildings [even if it restricts *(or as required)* provided it does not materially adversely restrict] the access to or use and enjoyment of the Premises [but not so as to prevent such access, use and enjoyment][229].

229   See *Owen v Gadd* [1956] 2 QB 99, [1956] 2 All ER 28, CA.

2–5   Rights of support and shelter

The rights of light, air, support, shelter, protection and all other easements and rights at the date of this Lease belonging to or enjoyed by other parts of the Building, any other buildings or any other adjoining property of the Landlord.

2-6   Right to erect new buildings[230]

Full right and liberty at any time —

2-6.1   to alter, raise the height of or rebuild the other parts of the Building or any other buildings, and

2-6.2   to erect any new buildings of any height on the Estate or on any other adjoining property of the Landlord

in any manner the Landlord thinks fit, even if doing so may obstruct, affect or interfere with the amenity of or access to the Premises or the passage of light and air to the Premises[and even if they *(or as required)* but provided they do not] materially affect the Premises or the use and enjoyment of the Premises.

230   As to reservation of the right to develop other land see vol 22(1) (2003 Reissue) LANDLORD AND TENANT (BUSINESS TENANCIES) Paragraphs 130 [660], 131 [662].

[883]

SCHEDULE 3: THE RENT AND RENT REVIEW

(insert rent review provisions as required: see vol 22(3) (1997 Reissue) LANDLORD AND TENANT *(BUSINESS TENANCIES)* Forms 180 [6711]–194 [6987])*

SCHEDULE 4: THE INDUSTRIAL COVENANTS

4-1   Use

4-1.1   *Permitted Use*

The Tenant must use the Premises for the Permitted Use only.

4-1.2   *Cesser of business*

The Tenant must not [cease carrying on business in the Premises or] leave the Premises [continuously] unoccupied for more than *(state period, eg 1 month)* [without notifying the Landlord, and providing such caretaking or security arrangements for the protection of the Premises as the Landlord [reasonably] requires and the insurers or underwriters require].

4-2   Smoke abatement

4-2.1   *Furnace construction*

The Tenant must ensure that every furnace boiler or heater at the Premises is constructed and used so as substantially to consume or burn the smoke arising from it.

4-2.2   *Noxious emissions*

The Tenant must not cause or permit any gritty, noxious or offensive emissions from any engine, furnace, chimney or other apparatus on the Premises without using [the best possible *(or as required)* all reasonable] means for preventing or counteracting the emissions.

4-2.3   *Statutory controls*

The Tenant must comply with the provisions of the Clean Air Act 1993 and with the requirements of any notice served under it by the relevant authority or body.

[884]

4-3   Environmental protection[231]

4-3.1   *Discharge of dangerous substances*

4-3.1.1   Damage to the Conduits and environment

The Tenant must not permit any oil or grease or any deleterious, objectionable, dangerous, poisonous or explosive matter or substance to be discharged into any of the Conduits, and must take all [reasonable] measures to ensure that any effluent discharged into the Conduits does not harm the environment, or corrode or otherwise harm the Conduits or cause any obstruction or deposit in them.

4-3.1.2   Poisons and pollutants

The Tenant must not permit the discharge into any of the Conduits of any fluid of a poisonous or noxious nature or of a kind likely to sicken or injure the fish, or that does in fact destroy them, or likely to contaminate or pollute the water of any stream or river.

231   It may be advisable for the landlord and tenant to commission a soil survey before the lease is entered into. The results could be annexed to the lease. A further survey could then be carried out towards the end of the term ascertaining whether or not contamination has in fact occurred. The tenant's obligations regarding restriction or clean-up or both will then be clear. If the original soil survey reveals contamination, then thought should be given to including provisions in the lease making it clear whose responsibility the contamination is and whether or not the tenant is obliged to resolve it or clean it up.

4-3.2   *Spillages and contamination*

The Tenant must take all practicable precautions to ensure that no noxious substances are spilled or deposited on the Premises and that contamination does not occur.

[885]

4-3.3   *Controlled, special or radioactive waste*

The Tenant must not deposit on the Premises any controlled or special waste as defined in the Environmental Protection Act 1990, or radioactive waste as defined in the Radioactive Substances Act 1993 Section 18, or any other substance that may produce concentrations or accumulations of noxious gasses or noxious liquids that may cause pollution of the environment or harm to human health.

4-3.4   *Notice of spillages and inspection*

Within 14 days of the spilling or deposit on the Premises of any noxious substance in a quantity that may cause serious damage to or pollution of the environment or serious damage to property or serious harm to human health, the Tenant must inform the Landlord of this and permit him to enter and inspect the Premises.

4-3.5   *Indemnity for damage and pollution*

The Tenant must indemnify the Landlord, and keep him indemnified, against any losses in respect of damage to, or pollution of, the environment or damage to property or harm to human health caused by the Premises or any substance on them whether in liquid or solid form or in the form of gas or vapour.

4-4   Roof and floor loading

4-4.1   *Heavy items*

The Tenant must not bring into or permit to remain in any building on the Premises any safes, machinery, goods or other articles that will or may strain or damage the building or any part of it.

4-4.2   *Protection of the roof*

The Tenant must not, without the consent of the Landlord, suspend any weight from the [portal frames, stanchions or roof purlins *(or as the case may be)*] of any building on the Premises or use them for the storage of goods or place any weight on them.

4-4.3   *Expert advice*

If the Tenant applies for the Landlord's consent under paragraph 4-4.2 PROTECTION OF THE ROOF the Landlord may consult any engineer or other person in relation to the roof or floor loading proposed by the Tenant, and the Tenant must repay the fees of the engineer or other person to the Landlord on demand.

[886]

4-5   Machinery

4-5.1   *Maintenance of machinery*

The Tenant must keep all plant, apparatus and machinery, including any boilers and furnaces on the Premises, ('the Machinery') properly maintained and in good working order, and for that purpose must employ reputable contractors [to be approved by the Landlord[, whose approval may not be unreasonably withheld [or delayed],]] ('the Contractors') to carry out regular periodic inspection and maintenance of the Machinery.

4-5.2   *Renewal of parts*

The Tenant must renew all working and other parts of the Machinery as and when necessary or when recommended by the Contractors.

4-5.3   *Operation*

The Tenant must ensure by directions to his staff and otherwise that the Machinery is properly operated.

4-5.4   *Damage from the Machinery*

The Tenant must avoid damage to the Premises by vibration or otherwise.

4-6   Signs

The Tenant must at all times display and maintain, at a point on the Premises to be specified in writing by the Landlord, a suitable sign, of a size and kind first approved by the Landlord, showing the Tenant's trading name and business.

4-7   Unloading and parking

4-7.1   *Approved entrances for unloading*

The Tenant must not unload any goods or materials from vehicles and convey them into the Premises except through the approved entrances provided for the purpose, and must not cause congestion of adjoining parking areas or inconvenience to any other user of them.

4-7.2   *Parking restrictions*

The Tenant must not permit any vehicles belonging to him or to any persons calling on the Premises expressly or by implication with his authority[232] to stand on the Estate Roads [so as to cause an obstruction][233] or on the pavements, and must use his best endeavours to ensure that such persons do not permit any vehicle to stand on any of the Estate Roads or pavements.

232   The reference to persons calling 'expressly or by implication with his authority' is an updated version of 'the Tenant and his successors in title the owners and occupiers for the time being of the Premises and his or their respective servants and licensees': see *Baxendale v North Lambeth Liberal and Radical Club Ltd* [1902] 2 Ch 427 at 429 per Swinfen Eady J; *Hammond v Prentice Bros Ltd* [1920] 1 Ch 201.

233   If these words are included, the inference is that cars may be parked on the road provided they do not cause an obstruction. Without specific provision, parking rights are not included in a right of way.

[887]

4-8   Selling in the Common Parts

The Tenant must not place any goods or things whatever, or expose them for sale, on the Common Parts or the Estate Roads or their pavements.

4-9   Regulations

The Tenant must comply with all regulations made by the Landlord from time to time for the management of the Estate [and notified to the Tenant in writing][, provided that nothing in the regulations may purport to amend the terms of this Lease, and in the event of any inconsistency between the terms of this Lease and the regulations the terms of this Lease are to prevail][234].

234   Almost every lease such as this includes this provision, but only rarely are any regulations made. The tenant should strike out the provision on the basis that he is being asked to accept some unknown commitment. Failing this the tenant should —

(i)   if the expression 'regulations and restrictions', which seems to be wider than 'regulations', is used strike out 'and restrictions',

(ii)   insist that he is formally notified in writing of any regulations that may be made, and

(iii)   provide that the regulations must always remain subservient to the lease.

SCHEDULE 5: THE SUBJECTIONS

(insert details)

[888]

SCHEDULE 6: THE SERVICE CHARGE[235]

6-1   Definitions

In this schedule the terms defined below have the meanings given in this paragraph.

235   As to service charges see vol 22(1) (2003 Reissue) LANDLORD AND TENANT (BUSINESS
        TENANCIES) Paragraph 247 [1081] et seq. For alternative service charge provisions see vol 22(3) (1997
        Reissue) LANDLORD AND TENANT (BUSINESS TENANCIES) Forms 149 [6581]–153 [6649].

6-1.1   'A financial year'

References to 'a financial year' are references to the period commencing on *(insert date,
eg 1 January)* in any year and ending on *(insert date, eg 31 December)* in the same year or
such other annual period as the Landlord in his discretion determines as being that for
which his accounts, either generally or in respect of the Estate, are to be made up.

6-1.2   'The Initial Provisional Service Charge'

'The Initial Provisional Service Charge means the sum of £... a year.

6-1.3   'The Management Premises'

'The Management Premises' means all the administrative and control offices, storage
areas, staff rooms and other areas maintained by the Landlord for the purpose of
managing the Estate and performing the Landlord's obligations under this Lease together
with any living accommodation provided by the Landlord for security guards, caretakers
or other staff employed by him for purposes connected with the Estate.

6-1.4   'Other lettable premises'

References to 'other lettable premises' are references to premises in the Estate that are
let, or are from time to time allocated for letting, by the Landlord, other than the
Premises, and respectively include and exclude, where applicable, the equivalent parts of
the Estate included in and excluded from the Premises as described in clause 1.40 THE
PREMISES'.

6-1.5   'The Plant'

'The Plant' means all the electrical, mechanical and other plant, machinery, equipment,
furnishings, furniture, fixtures and fittings of ornament or utility in use for common
benefit from time to time on, in or at the Estate, including, without prejudice to the
generality of the foregoing, goods and passenger lifts, lift shafts, escalators, passenger
conveyors, heating, cooling, lighting and ventilation equipment, cleaning equipment,
internal and public telephones, public address systems, fire precaution equipment, fire
and burglar alarm systems, closed circuit television, refuse compactors and all other such
equipment, including stand-by and emergency systems.

6-1.6   'The Retained Parts'

'The Retained Parts' means the parts of the Estate that are not let or constructed or
adapted for letting, including, without prejudice to the generality of the foregoing, the
Common Parts and any parts of the main structure, walls, foundations and roofs of the
Building or any other buildings that are not included in the Premises and would not be
included in premises demised by leases of other units on the Estate if let on the same
terms as this Lease, and also including office accommodation for the estate manager and
any ancillary staff.

6-2   Service charge provisions

6-2.1   *Certificate of the Landlord's Expenses*

As soon as reasonably practicable[236] after each financial year the Landlord must ensure that the Accountant issues a certificate containing a summary of the Landlord's Expenses for that financial year, and a summary of any expenditure that formed part of the Landlord's Expenses in respect of a previous financial year but has not been taken into account in the certificate for any previous financial year. A copy of the certificate must be supplied by the Landlord to the Tenant.

236   Time is not normally of the essence in relation to the preparation of the service charge account: see vol 22(1) (2003 Reissue) LANDLORD AND TENANT (BUSINESS TENANCIES) Paragraph 271 [1125]. As to certification of expenses see vol 22(1) (2003 Reissue) LANDLORD AND TENANT (BUSINESS TENANCIES) Paragraph 274 [1129].

6-2.2   *Omissions from the certificate*

Omission by the Accountant from a certificate of the Landlord's Expenses of any expenditure incurred in the financial year to which the certificate relates is not to preclude the inclusion of that expenditure in any subsequent certificate.

6-2.3   *Deemed Landlord's Expenses*

In any financial year the Landlord's Expenses are to be deemed to include not only the costs and expenses actually paid or incurred by the Landlord during that year, but also —

6-2.3.1   such fair and reasonable part of all costs and expenditure in respect of or incidental to all or any of the recurring services and other matters referred to in paragraph 6-3 THE SERVICES, whenever paid or incurred, whether before or during the Term — including reasonable provision for anticipated expenditure[237] — as the Surveyor in his reasonable discretion allocates to that financial year as being fair and reasonable, and

6-2.3.2   an amount equal to the fair annual rental value of the Management Premises, as certified by the Surveyor acting reasonably[, whose decision is to be conclusive],

and if the Landlord or a person connected with the Landlord or employed by the Landlord attends to (1) the supervision and management of the provision of services for the Estate[238], and/or (2) the preparation of statements or certificates of the Landlord's Expenses, and/or (3) the auditing of the Landlord's Expenses, and/or (4) the collection of rents from the Estate, then an expense is to be deemed to be paid or incurred by the Landlord, being a reasonable fee not exceeding that which independent agents might properly have charged for the same work.

237   As to sinking funds see vol 22(1) (2003 Reissue) LANDLORD AND TENANT (BUSINESS TENANCIES) Paragraphs 280 [1138], 282 [1140].
238   As to recovery of management costs see vol 22(1) (2003 Reissue) LANDLORD AND TENANT (BUSINESS TENANCIES) Paragraph 263 [1107].

6-2.4   *Certificates conclusive*[239]

Any certificate of the Landlord's Expenses, and any certificate given by the Surveyor or Accountant in connection with the Landlord's Expenses, is to be conclusive as to the matters it purports to certify.

239   As to conclusivity of certificates see vol 22(1) (2003 Reissue) LANDLORD AND TENANT (BUSINESS TENANCIES) Paragraph 275 [1131].

6-2.5   *Payment*

For each financial year the Tenant must pay the Service Charge Percentage of the Landlord's Expenses.

6-2.6   *Variation of the Service Charge Percentage*

The Service Charge Percentage may be varied to the extent that the Surveyor fairly and reasonably considers appropriate.

6-2.7   *Landlord's contribution*

The Landlord is to have no liability to contribute to the Landlord's Expenses except in relation to any other lettable premises for which no contribution is payable by an occupier or other person.

6-2.8   *Payment on account*[240]

For each financial year the Tenant must pay to the Landlord on account of the Service Charge such a sum as the Surveyor certifies to be fair and reasonable having regard to the likely amount of the Service Charge. That sum must be paid in advance, without deduction or set off, by equal instalments on the usual quarter days, the first instalment to be paid on the quarter day immediately before the commencement of the financial year in question. During any financial year the Surveyor may revise the contribution on account of the Service Charge for that financial year so as to take into account any actual or expected increase in expenditure, and as soon as reasonably practicable after such revision the Surveyor must certify the amount of the revised contribution.

240   As to payment on account see vol 22(1) (2003 Reissue) LANDLORD AND TENANT (BUSINESS TENANCIES) Paragraph 272 [1126].

6-2.9   *Service charge for the first financial year*

The sum payable for the financial year current at the date of this document is to be the Initial Provisional Service Charge, of which the Tenant must on the date of this document pay to the Landlord a due proportion calculated from day to day in respect of the period from [the Rent Commencement Date *(or as required)*] to the next quarter day after the date of this document.

6-2.10   *Final account and adjustments*[241]

As soon as reasonably practicable after the end of each financial year, the Landlord must furnish the Tenant with an account of the Service Charge payable by him for that financial year, credit being given for payments made on account. Within *(state period, eg 7 days)* of the furnishing of such an account, the Tenant must pay the Service Charge, or any balance of it payable, to the Landlord. The Landlord must allow to the Tenant any amount overpaid by him against future payments of the Service Charge, whether on account or not. At the end of the financial year current at the end of the Term the Landlord must repay to the Tenant any outstanding overpayment of the Service Charge.

241   As to the tenant's concerns on adjustments see vol 22(1) (2003 Reissue) LANDLORD AND TENANT (BUSINESS TENANCIES) Paragraph 272 [1126].

6-3   The Services[242]

The Services are —

6-3.1   repairing[243] — and, whenever the Landlord, acting reasonably, regards it as necessary in order to repair, replacing or renewing — and decorating the Retained Parts,

6-3.2   operating, maintaining, repairing and, whenever the Landlord, acting reasonably, considers it appropriate, renewing, replacing or modifying the Plant,

6-3.3   placing and running maintenance contracts for the Estate,

6-3.4   providing the Plant[244] that the Landlord, acting reasonably, considers necessary or desirable, or that is required by law or by any government department or local, public or regulatory or other authority or court to be supplied and maintained, including the initial capital expenditure and expenditure on replacement of any machinery — including motor vehicles — articles and materials for, for example, refuse collection and fire fighting,

6-3.5   providing suitable facilities for disposing of refuse, compacting it or removing it from the Estate,

6-3.6   supplying hot and cold water to the lavatory facilities in the Common Parts during normal business hours, and providing towels, soap, toilet paper and other appropriate supplies, [and staffing the lavatory facilities,]

6-3.7   providing reasonable lighting in the Common Parts,

[6-3.8   providing reasonable central heating [and air conditioning] to the Premises and the Common Parts[245],]

6-3.9   cleaning the windows and other glass of the Retained Parts,

6-3.10   supplying, maintaining, servicing and keeping in good condition and, wherever the Landlord considers it appropriate, renewing and replacing all fixtures, fittings, furnishings, bins, receptacles, tools, appliances, equipment, door furniture, floor coverings and any other things the Landlord may consider desirable for performing the Services or for the appearance or upkeep of the Retained Parts,

6-3.11   carrying out any inspections and tests of the Retained Parts, including the Plant, that the Landlord from time to time considers necessary or desirable,

[892]

6-3.12   planting, tidying, tending and landscaping any appropriate part of the Common Parts in such manner as the Landlord from time to time considers appropriate,

6-3.13   providing, replacing and renewing trees, shrubs, flowers, grass and other plants, flags, decorative lights and other decorations, decorative or drinking fountains or other amenities that the Landlord from time to time thinks fit to provide or maintain on the Estate, and providing, maintaining, replacing and renewing seats or benches in the Common Parts,

6-3.14   employing such persons as the Landlord, acting reasonably, considers necessary or desirable from time to time in connection with providing any of the Services, providing caretaking, porterage, security, administration, management and supervision, performing the Landlord's other obligations in this Lease and collecting rents accruing to the Landlord from the Estate, with all incidental expenditure including, but without limiting the generality of the foregoing, remuneration, payment of statutory contributions and such other health, pension, welfare, redundancy and similar or ancillary payments and any other payments the Landlord, acting reasonably, thinks desirable or necessary, and providing uniforms, work or protective clothing[246],

6-3.15   discharging any amounts the Landlord may be liable to pay towards the expense of making, repairing, maintaining, rebuilding and cleaning anything — for example ways, roads, pavements, sewers, drains, pipes, watercourses, party walls, party structures, party fences and other conveniences — that are appurtenant to the Estate or used for the Estate in common with any other adjoining property of the Landlord,

6-3.16   erecting, providing, maintaining, renewing and replacing such notice boards, notices and other signs and directions on the Estate as the Landlord, acting reasonably, from time to time considers appropriate,

6-3.17   administering and managing the Estate[247], performing the Services, performing the Landlord's other obligations in this Lease and preparing statements or certificates of and auditing the Landlord's Expenses,

6-3.18   providing and carrying out all services of any kind whatsoever that the Landlord, acting reasonably, from time to time provides, and all additional or substitute services that the Landlord provides pursuant to clause 4.2.3 VARIATION AND WITHHOLDING OF THE SERVICES[248],

[893]

6-3.19   discharging all existing or future taxes, rates, charges, duties, assessments, impositions and outgoings whatsoever in respect of the Retained Parts, including, without prejudice to the generality of the above, those for water, electricity, gas and telecommunications,

6-3.20   policing the Estate, controlling traffic and pedestrians and providing such security staff as the Landlord, acting reasonably, from time to time thinks fit and proper, and providing, maintaining, replacing and renewing security equipment on the Estate,

6-3.21   paying any interest on any loan or overdraft raised for the purpose of defraying the Landlord's Expenses[249],

6-3.22   taking any steps the Landlord, acting reasonably, from time to time considers appropriate for complying with, making representations against, or otherwise contesting or dealing with any statutory or other obligation affecting or alleged to affect the Estate, including any notice, regulation or order of any government department, local, public, regulatory or other authority or court, compliance with which is not the direct liability of the Tenant or any tenant of any part of the Estate[250],

6-3.23   promoting the Estate including, without prejudice to the generality of the foregoing, advertising in any form of media, sponsorship, staging or organising of events promoting the Estate and other activities designed to promote the Estate and the interests of its occupants, and employing advertising agents and other consultants,

6-3.24   discharging the reasonable and proper cost of any service or matter the Landlord, acting reasonably, thinks proper for the better and more efficient management and use of the Estate and the comfort and convenience of its occupants[251],

6-3.25   renting any item used for carrying out any of the matters referred to in this schedule,

6-3.26   keeping the Building and the Estate open to the general public during normal business hours[252],

6-3.27   keeping appropriate areas of the Common Parts open for servicing the Premises and other units in the Building from *(time)* to *(time)*, and

6-3.28   abating any nuisance affecting the Estate, except to the extent that abating the nuisance is the liability of any tenant of the Estate[253].

[894]

242   This is a comprehensive list of services. Not all may be appropriate to the particular building concerned. The draftsman should tailor the list to reflect the nature of the building, the manner in which it is being divided and the proposed occupancy arrangements.
    As to the standard of performance see vol 22(1) (2003 Reissue) LANDLORD AND TENANT (BUSINESS TENANCIES) Paragraph 256 [1095].
243   As to the position regarding inherent defects see vol 22(1) (2003 Reissue) LANDLORD AND TENANT (BUSINESS TENANCIES) Paragraph 258 [1099].
244   As to plant and machinery see vol 22(1) (2003 Reissue) LANDLORD AND TENANT (BUSINESS TENANCIES) Paragraph 261 [1103].
245   As to the provision of hot water and heating see vol 22(1) (2003 Reissue) LANDLORD AND TENANT (BUSINESS TENANCIES) Paragraph 260 [1102].
246   The landlord performs the services either by means of third parties whose fee he pays and has reimbursed by the tenants, or by his own staff. In the latter case the landlord needs to be able to include the cost of employing the staff as part of the service charge. If there are managing agents, the landlord may also welcome the flexibility of being able to charge a fee for any services that they perform 'in-house' where this is more practical than charging the cost of employing the relevant individuals. As to the description of the duties of staff see vol 22(1) (2003 Reissue) LANDLORD AND TENANT (BUSINESS TENANCIES) Paragraph 262 [1105].
247   If administration and management costs are to be recovered, there must be express references in the lease: see vol 22(1) (2003 Reissue) LANDLORD AND TENANT (BUSINESS TENANCIES) Paragraph 263 [1107].
248   As to 'sweeping-up' clauses and the tenant's concerns see vol 22(1) (2003 Reissue) LANDLORD AND TENANT (BUSINESS TENANCIES) Paragraph 267 [1113].
249   As to recovery of interest payments see vol 22(1) (2003 Reissue) LANDLORD AND TENANT (BUSINESS TENANCIES) Paragraph 265 [1111].
250   The tenant should ensure that any clause entitling the landlord to be reimbursed for the cost of complying with, making representations against or contesting the provisions of any regulation or other provisions that apply to the premises is qualified so that he must act reasonably.
251   As to 'sweeping-up' clauses and the tenant's concerns see vol 22(1) (2003 Reissue) LANDLORD AND TENANT (BUSINESS TENANCIES) Paragraph 267 [1113].
252   As to restrictions on hours of use see vol 22(1) (2003 Reissue) LANDLORD AND TENANT (BUSINESS TENANCIES) Paragraph 174 [870].
253   The tenant should consider restricting this to nuisances affecting parts of the estate including the premises or items used by the tenant.

[895]

SCHEDULE 7: THE AUTHORISED GUARANTEE AGREEMENT

(insert the form of authorised guarantee agreement: see, eg vol 22(3) (1997 Reissue) LANDLORD AND TENANT *(BUSINESS TENANCIES)* Form 217 *[7053])*

(signature (or common seal) of landlord: lease)
(signature (or common seal) of tenant (and guarantor): counterpart)
(signatures of witnesses)
[896]–[950]

2: SHOPS

8

Lease of a shop, with or without a yard, where the landlord does not own adjoining property[1]

CONTENTS

(NB: numbers in [ ] below refer to this volume and should be altered to suit the page or reference numbers actually used)

1 DEFINITIONS AND INTERPRETATION

1.1 'The Conduits' . . . . [957]
1.2 'The [Contractual] Term' . . . . [957]
1.3 'Development' . . . . [958]
[1.4 'The Exterior Decorating Years' . . . . [958]]
1.5 Gender and number . . . . [958]
1.6 Headings . . . . [958]
[1.7 'The Initial Rent' . . . . [958]]
1.8 'The Insurance Rent' . . . . [959]
1.9 'The Insured Risks' . . . . [959]
1.10 'Interest' . . . . [960]
[951]
1.11 'The Interest Rate' . . . . [960]
[1.12 'The Interior Decorating Years' . . . . [961]]
1.13 Interpretation of 'consent' and 'approved' . . . . [961]
1.14 Interpretation of 'the Guarantor' . . . . [961]
1.15 Interpretation of 'the Landlord' . . . . [962]
1.16 Interpretation of 'the last year of the Term' and 'the end of the Term' . . . . [962]
1.17 Interpretation of 'the Tenant' . . . . [962]
1.18 Interpretation of 'this Lease' . . . . [962]
1.19 Joint and several liability . . . . [962]
1.20 'The Liability Period' . . . . [963]
1.21 'Losses' . . . . [964]
1.22 'The 1954 Act' . . . . [964]
1.23 'The 1995 Act' . . . . [964]
1.24 Obligation not to permit or suffer . . . . [964]
1.25 'The Permitted Use' . . . . [965]
1.26 'The Plan' . . . . [965]
1.27 'The Planning Acts' . . . . [965]
1.28 'The Premises' . . . . [966]
1.29 References to clauses and schedules . . . . [967]
1.30 References to rights of access . . . . [967]
1.31 References to statutes . . . . [967]
1.32 'The Rent' . . . . [967]
1.33 'The Rent Commencement Date' . . . . [968]
[1.34 'The Review Dates' . . . . [968]]
1.35 'The Shop Covenants' . . . . [968]
1.36 'The Surveyor' . . . . [969]
[1.37 'The Term' . . . . [969]]
1.38 Terms from the 1995 Act . . . . [969]
1.39 'VAT' . . . . [969]

2 DEMISE . . . . [981]

3 THE TENANT'S COVENANTS
3.1 Rent . . . . [982]
3.2 Outgoings and VAT . . . . [983]
[3.3 Cost of services consumed . . . . [983]]
3.4 Repair, cleaning and decoration . . . . [984]
3.5 Waste and alterations . . . . [986]
3.6 Aerials, signs and advertisements . . . . [987]
3.7 Statutory obligations . . . . [988]
3.8 Entry to inspect and notice to repair . . . . [989]
3.9 Alienation . . . . [1001]
3.10 Nuisance and residential restrictions . . . . [1011]
3.11 Costs of applications, notices and recovery of arrears . . . . [1012]
3.12 Planning and development . . . . [1013]
3.13 Plans, documents and information . . . . [1015]
3.14 Indemnities . . . . [1015]
3.15 Reletting boards and viewing . . . . [1016]
3.16 Obstruction and encroachment . . . . [1016]
3.17 Yielding up . . . . [1017]
3.18 Interest on arrears . . . . [1017]
3.19 Statutory notices . . . . [1017]
3.20 Keyholders . . . . [1017]
3.21 Viewing on sale of reversion . . . . [1018]
3.22 Defective premises . . . . [1018]
3.23 Replacement guarantor . . . . [1018]
3.24 Exercise of the Landlord's rights . . . . [1019]
3.25 The Shop Covenants . . . . [1019]
3.26 Costs of grant of this Lease . . . . [1019]
3.27 Consent to the Landlord's release . . . . [1019]

4 QUIET ENJOYMENT . . . . [1031]
                                                                       [952]

5 INSURANCE
5.1 Warranty as to convictions . . . . [1032]
5.2 Covenant to insure . . . . [1032]
5.3 Details of the insurance . . . . [1033]
5.4 Payment of the Insurance Rent . . . . [1034]
5.5 Suspension of the Rent . . . . [1034]
5.6 Reinstatement and termination . . . . [1035]
5.7 Tenant's further insurance covenants . . . . [1040]
[5.8 The Landlord's insurance covenants . . . . [1042]]

6 GUARANTEE PROVISIONS
6.1 The Guarantor's covenants . . . . [1051]
[6.2 The Landlord's covenant . . . . [1056]]

7 FORFEITURE . . . . [1057]

8 MISCELLANEOUS
8.1 Exclusion of warranty as to use . . . . [1059]
8.2 Exclusion of third party rights . . . . [1059]
8.3 Representations . . . . [1059]

8.4 Documents under hand . . . . [1060]
8.5 Tenant's property . . . . [1060]
8.6 Compensation on vacating excluded . . . . [1060]
8.7 Notices . . . . [1061]
8.8 [New (or) Old] lease . . . . [1062]
[8.9 Capacity of tenants . . . . [1063]]
[8.10 Exclusion of the 1954 Act Sections 24–28 . . . . [1063]]

SCHEDULE 1: THE RIGHTS RESERVED

1-1 Right of entry to inspect . . . . [1064]
1-2 Access on renewal or rent review . . . . [1064]

SCHEDULE 2: THE RENT AND RENT REVIEW

SCHEDULE 3: THE SHOP COVENANTS

3-1 Use . . . . [1065]
3-2 Hours of trading . . . . [1066]
3-3 Window dressing and displays . . . . [1067]
3-4 Ceiling and floor loading . . . . [1068]
3-5 Plate glass . . . . [1068]
[3-6 Fitting out . . . . [1068]]

SCHEDULE 4: THE SUBJECTIONS

SCHEDULE 5: THE AUTHORISED GUARANTEE AGREEMENT

[953]

AGREEMENT

[HM LAND REGISTRY

LAND REGISTRATION ACT 2002

Administrative area	*(insert details)*
Title number out of which lease is granted	*(title number)*
Property let	*(postal address or description)*]

THIS LEASE is made the .... day of .... BETWEEN:

[954]

(1)   *(name of landlord)* [of *(address)* *(or as appropriate)* the registered office of which is at *(address)*] [Company Registration no ...][2] ('the Landlord') [and]

(2)   *(name of tenant)* [of *(address)* *(or as appropriate)* being a company registered in [England and Wales *(or)* Scotland][3] the registered office of which is at *(address)*] [Company Registration no ...] ('the Tenant') [and

(3)   *(name of guarantor)* [of *(address)* *(or as appropriate)* the registered office of which is at *(address)*] [Company Registration no ...] ('the Guarantor')]

[955]

1   As to stamp duty land tax see the Information Binder: Stamp Duty Land Tax [1].

As to Land Registry Fees see the Information Binder: Property [1]: Property Fees.

On the grant out of an unregistered freehold estate in land of a lease for a term of more than seven years from the date of the grant, application must be made to register the title to the leasehold interest granted: see the Land Registration Act 2002 s 4(1)(c) (37 Halsbury's Statutes (4th Edn) REAL PROPERTY). The tenant must obtain an epitome of title to the freehold reversion, investigate it, and mark it as examined, otherwise he will not be able to be registered with an absolute title: see vol 25(1) (2003 Reissue) LAND REGISTRATION Paragraph 21.1 [132].

If the freehold reversion is registered, the grant of a lease for a term of more than seven years from the date of the grant must be completed by registration: see the Land Registration Act 2002 s 27(2)(b)(i).

As to the form and contents of leases see vol 22(1) (2003 Reissue) LANDLORD AND TENANT (BUSINESS TENANCIES) Paragraph 104 [601] et seq. As to registered land generally see vol 25(1) (2003 Reissue) LAND REGISTRATION. As to registration of title to leases see vol 25(1) (2003 Reissue) LAND REGISTRATION Paragraph 143 [601] et seq.

This is a lease of premises consisting of a lock-up shop, with optional clauses if any land that is not built on, eg a yard at the rear, is to be included. The landlord owns no adjoining premises and no rights are granted or services provided. The tenant is responsible for the repair of the premises and the decoration of both the exterior and the interior. The landlord insures the premises and the tenant refunds the cost of the premiums. There is provision for the rent to be reviewed. There is also a provision for a guarantor. This Form may be adapted to include a covenant by the tenant to fit out the shop at the commencement of the term.

2   If any party is a company it is desirable to include the company registration number. This avoids any problems arising when a company has been wound up and a new company formed with the same name, or when the name of a company is changed, or if companies swap names, eg on a reconstruction of a group of companies. In addition, where a company applies to be registered as proprietor of a registered estate or registered charge, the application must state the company's registration number: see the Land Registration Rules 2003, SI 2003/1417 r 181.

3   Where the tenant is a company registered in England and Wales or Scotland, and the lease is registrable, an application for first registration of the lease (where the landlord's title is unregistered), or registration of the lease as a registrable disposition (where the landlord's title is registered), and the tenant as proprietor of the leasehold title, must state the company's registered number: see SI 2003/1417 r 181(1). There seems to be no reason why the certificate and statement should not be contained in the disposition in favour of the proprietor, where convenient.

[956]

NOW THIS DEED WITNESSES as follows:

1   DEFINITIONS AND INTERPRETATION

For all purposes of this Lease[4] the terms defined in this clause have the meanings specified.

4   One view would add 'unless the context otherwise requires' or 'where the context so admits' and in fact this may be implied (see *Meux v Jacobs* (1875) LR 7 HL 481 at 493; *Law Society v United Service Bureau Ltd* [1934] 1 KB 343, DC) but the better course is to use defined terms in such a way that there are no circumstances where the defined meaning does not apply.

1.1   'The Conduits'

'The Conduits' means the pipes, sewers, drains, mains, ducts, conduits, gutters, watercourses, wires, cables, [laser optical fibres, data or impulse transmission, communication or reception systems,] channels, flues and all other conducting media — including any fixings, louvres, cowls, covers and any other ancillary apparatus — that are in, on, over or under the Premises.

1.2   'The [Contractual] Term'[5]

'The [Contractual][6] Term' means *(insert number)* years commencing on and including *(date of commencement of the term)*[7].

5   As to the commencement of the term see vol 22(1) (2003 Reissue) LANDLORD AND TENANT (BUSINESS TENANCIES) Paragraph 135 [670].

As to registration see note 1 above. Where the landlord's title is unregistered, the grantee must apply for registration within a period of two months from the date of the disposition if the lease is granted for a term of more than seven years. If no such application is made the disposition becomes void as regards any transfer, grant or creation of a legal estate: see the Land Registration Act 2002 s 6. Where the landlord's title is registered and the lease is for a term of more than seven years, the tenant should protect the intended lease by applying for an official search, and an application to register the lease should be made before expiry of the search, otherwise the lease will be susceptible to loss of priority: see the Land Registration Act 2002 s 27.

6   The demise in this lease is for 'the Contractual Term', which is defined as a fixed term of years. The expression 'the Term', as defined in clause 1.37 [969] 'THE TERM', is used in covenants so that they continue to apply during any period of holding over or continuance or extension of the contractual term. Some difficulties arise if this structure is used in a draft lease where security of tenure is to be excluded under the Landlord and Tenant Act 1954 s 38A(1) as inserted by SI 2003/3096 (23 Halsbury's Statutes (4th Edn) LANDLORD AND TENANT). The demise is for the contractual term and the inclusion of the definition of 'the Term' does not prevent the lease being 'for a term of years certain' as required by the Landlord and Tenant Act 1954 s 38A(1). However, reference to continuance of the contractual term by statute is inappropriate where the operation of the security of tenure provisions in the Landlord and Tenant Act 1954 ss 24–28 is to be excluded. If a lease is contracted out of the Landlord and Tenant Act 1954 there can be no statutory extension, and if the tenant remains in occupation at the end of the contractual term he is holding over unlawfully unless there is an express agreement to extend the contractual term operating as a surrender and re-grant so that the original lease— and the agreement under the Landlord and Tenant Act 1954 s 38A(1) — has no further effect. It is suggested that in these circumstances the drafting should be simplified to include a single term (defined simply as 'the Term') by reference to the period of the contractual term. This can be achieved by amending this clause in the manner suggested and substituting it for clause 1.37 [969] 'THE TERM'.

7   For estate management reasons it is usually desirable to insert a quarter day here — or a rent day when rent is due on days other than quarter days — ie generally the one preceding the earlier of the date of possession and the date of execution.

[957]

1.3   'Development'

References to 'development' are references to development as defined by the Town and Country Planning Act 1990 Section 55.

[1.4   'The Exterior Decorating Years'

'The Exterior Decorating Years' means *(specify years).*] *(omit if not required, eg if the first alternative in clause 3.4.6 [985] DECORATION is used)*

1.5   Gender and number

Words importing one gender include all other genders; words importing the singular include the plural and vice versa[8].

8   See the Law of Property Act 1925 s 61 (37 Halsbury's Statutes (4th Edn) REAL PROPERTY).

1.6   Headings[9]

The clause, paragraph and schedule headings and the table of contents do not form part of this document and are not to be taken into account in its construction or interpretation. *(amend if marginal notes are used)*

9   Headings and marginal notes require the draftsman to provide a word or two to describe every clause in the lease. This is not always easy and there are times when the draftsman will have to settle for something less than perfection, the only alternative being a heading or note that would be inappropriately long. It would be quite wrong for that title, which its author might admit was not totally apposite but was the best that he could do in a few words, to be used in construing the clause in question.

[958]

[1.7   'The Initial Rent'

'The Initial Rent' means [the sum of £... a year *(or as required by the rent and review provisions to be used)*].] *(this definition is not required if the rent is not reviewable)*

1.8   'The Insurance Rent'[10]

'The Insurance Rent' means the [gross sums including any commission *(or as required)* sums net of any commission] that the Landlord from time to time pays —

1.8.1   by way of premium for insuring the Premises, including insuring for loss of rent, in accordance with his obligations contained in this Lease,

1.8.2   by way of premium for insuring in such amount and on such terms as [the Landlord acting reasonably considers appropriate *(or as required)* is reasonable] against all liability of the Landlord to third parties arising out of or in connection with any matter including or relating to the Premises, and

1.8.3   for insurance valuations.

10   As to reimbursement of insurance premiums see vol 22(1) (2003 Reissue) LANDLORD AND TENANT (BUSINESS TENANCIES) Paragraph 230 [1026].

1.9   'The Insured Risks'

'The Insured Risks' means the risks of loss or damage by fire[, storm, tempest, earthquake, lightning, explosion, riot, civil commotion, malicious damage, [terrorism,] impact by vehicles and by aircraft and articles dropped from aircraft — other than war risks — flood damage and bursting and overflowing of water pipes and tanks,] and such other risks, whether or not in the nature of the foregoing, as the Landlord [acting reasonably] from time to time decides to insure against[11].

11   As to the risks to be insured and the tenant's concerns see vol 22(1) (2003 Reissue) LANDLORD AND TENANT (BUSINESS TENANCIES) Paragraph 235 [1033].

[959]

1.10   'Interest'

References to 'interest' are references to interest payable during the period from the date on which the payment is due to the date of payment, both before and after any judgment, at the Interest Rate then prevailing [*(where the interest rate is defined by reference to a bank base rate)* or, should the base rate referred to in clause 1.11 'THE INTEREST RATE' cease to exist[12], at another rate of interest closely comparable with the Interest Rate [to be agreed between the parties or in default of agreement to be determined by [the Surveyor, acting as an expert and not as an arbitrator *(or as required)* a chartered accountant appointed by agreement between the parties or in default of agreement nominated by the President of the Institute of Chartered Accountants in England and Wales, acting as an expert and not as an arbitrator][13] *(or as required)* decided on by the Landlord acting reasonably]].

12   If basic rates are referred to, the possibility of their ceasing to exist should be provided for. Alternatively, the Law Society's interest rate may be specified.

13   This provision may be expanded to provide for deeming the parties to have disagreed after a certain time, deputy appointors etc.

1.11   'The Interest Rate'

'The Interest Rate'[14] means the rate of ...% a year above[15] [the base lending rate of *(specify bank)* or such other bank [being a member of the British Bankers Association] as the Landlord from time to time nominates in writing[16] *(or as required)* the Law Society's interest rate[17]].

14   As to the covenant to pay interest see vol 22(1) (2003 Reissue) LANDLORD AND TENANT (BUSINESS TENANCIES) Paragraph 154 [767].
15   Words such as 'with a minimum of ...%' should not be used because, if interest rates drop during the term to such an extent that the minimum rate specified represents significantly more than a few percent over the basic borrowing rate, the provision might be void as a penalty. As to what amounts to a penalty see *Dunlop Pneumatic Tyre Co Ltd v New Garage and Motor Co Ltd* [1915] AC 79, HL; *Cellulose Acetate Silk Co Ltd v Widnes Foundry (1925) Ltd* [1933] AC 20, HL. In view of this, landlords would be unwise to provide for a rate of more than a few percent over base rate, and even this is in fact a penalty rate and should be resisted by the tenant.
16   The chance to change the bank may be useful, especially on a sale of the reversion, so that the landlord can always provide for his bank for the time being to be specified. The tenant should try to limit the choice to major clearing banks.
17   The Law Society's interest rate is published weekly in the Law Society's Gazette.

[960]

[1.12   'The Interior Decorating Years'

'The Interior Decorating Years' means *(specify years)*.] *(omit if not required, eg if the first alternative in clause 3.4.6 [985] DECORATION is used)*

1.13   Interpretation of 'consent' and 'approved'

1.13.1   *Prior written consent or approval*

References to 'consent of the Landlord' or words to similar effect are references to a prior written consent signed by or on behalf of the Landlord and references to the need for anything to be 'approved by the Landlord' or words to similar effect are references to the need for a prior written approval by or on behalf of the Landlord.

1.13.2   *Consent or approval of mortgagee or head landlord*

Any provisions in this Lease referring to the consent or approval of the Landlord are to be construed as also requiring the consent or approval of any mortgagee of the Premises and any head landlord where that consent is required [under a mortgage or headlease in existence at the date of this document][18]. Nothing in this Lease is to be construed as imposing any obligation on a mortgagee or head landlord not to refuse any such consent or approval unreasonably.

18   The tenant should include these words, so that the clause applies *only* where the consent of the mortgagee or head landlord is in fact required under the terms of an *existing* mortgage or headlease. The tenant should request a copy of the document concerned to establish the rights of the mortgagee or head landlord in relation to any consents that he may seek. The risk to the tenant of the clause without these words is that, by subsequently creating a mortgage or headlease, the landlord, innocently or deliberately, might bring about a situation where his consent may be refused in circumstances in which it would otherwise have been unreasonable to do so. In particular, the effect on the tenant's ability to assign or sublet could be serious.

1.14   Interpretation of 'the Guarantor'[19]

The expression 'the Guarantor' includes [*(where there is a guarantor for the original tenant)* not only the person named above as the Guarantor, but also][20] any person who enters into covenants with the Landlord pursuant to clause 3.9.5.2 CONDITIONS or clause 3.23 REPLACEMENT GUARANTOR.

19   As to guarantors see vol 22(1) (2003 Reissue) LANDLORD AND TENANT (BUSINESS TENANCIES) Paragraphs 40 [201], 71 [278] et seq.
20   Where there is no guarantor for the original tenant, if it is felt undesirable to have covenants in a lease and no party, at least initially, to enter into them, the guarantor's covenants could be included in a schedule.

[961]

1.15   Interpretation of 'the Landlord'

The expression 'the Landlord' includes the person or persons from time to time entitled to possession of the Premises when this Lease comes to an end.

1.16   Interpretation of 'the last year of the Term' and 'the end of the Term'

References to 'the last year of the Term' are references to the actual last year of the Term howsoever it determines, and references to the 'end of the Term' are references to the end of the Term whensoever and howsoever it determines.

1.17   Interpretation of 'the Tenant'

'The Tenant' includes any person who is for the time being bound by the tenant covenants of this Lease except where the name of *(name of original tenant)* appears.

1.18   Interpretation of 'this Lease'

Unless expressly stated to the contrary, the expression 'this Lease' includes any document supplemental to or collateral with this document or entered into in accordance with this document.

1.19   Joint and several liability

Where any party to this Lease for the time being comprises two or more persons, obligations expressed or implied to be made by or with that party are deemed to be made by or with the persons comprising that party jointly and severally.

[962]

1.20   'The Liability Period'[21]

'The Liability Period' means —

[1.20.1   in the case of *(name of guarantor for the original tenant)*, the period during which *(name of original tenant)* is bound by the tenant covenants of this Lease together with any additional period during which *(name of original tenant)* is liable under an authorised guarantee agreement,] *(omit if there is no guarantor for the original tenant)*

1.20.2   in the case of any guarantor required pursuant to clause 3.9.5.2 CONDITIONS, the period during which the relevant assignee is bound by the tenant covenants of this Lease together with any additional period during which that assignee is liable under an authorised guarantee agreement,

1.20.3   in the case of any guarantor under an authorised guarantee agreement, the period during which the relevant assignee is bound by the tenant covenants of this Lease, and

1.20.4   in the case of any guarantor required pursuant to clause 3.9.8.7 TERMS OF A PERMITTED SUBLEASE, the period during which the relevant assignee of the sublease is bound by the tenant covenants of that sublease.

21   The liability of the guarantor should be expressed to last while the original tenant, or as the case may be the assignee, is bound by the tenant covenants in the lease — or in the case of clause 1.20.4 the sublease — rather than while the lease is vested in that person, to take account of the possibility of an excluded assignment being made and the tenant — or subtenant — remaining liable. An excluded assignment means that the tenant — or subtenant — is precluded from tenant release under the Landlord and Tenant (Covenants) Act 1995 (23 Halsbury's Statutes (4th Edn) LANDLORD AND TENANT).

      The Landlord and Tenant (Covenants) Act 1995 does not clearly indicate whether the liability of a contractual guarantor can be expressed to extend to any period during which the tenant is bound by an authorised guarantee agreement, but the better view is that it is possible. The policy of the Act certainly suggests that this should be the case.

[963]

1.21 'Losses'

References to 'losses' are references to liabilities, damages or losses, awards of damages or compensation, penalties, costs, disbursements and expenses arising from any claim, demand, action or proceedings.

1.22 'The 1954 Act'

'The 1954 Act' means the Landlord and Tenant Act 1954 [and all statutes, regulations and orders included by virtue of clause 1.31 REFERENCES TO STATUTES][22].

22   The words in square brackets are strictly speaking not required because they merely state what would be the case anyway by virtue of clause 1.31 [....] REFERENCES TO STATUTES. Nevertheless, as much could turn on the point (see *Brett v Brett Essex Golf Club Ltd* (1986) 52 P & CR 330, [1986] 1 EGLR 154, CA), the parties may prefer to deal expressly with the point.

1.23 'The 1995 Act'

'The 1995 Act' means the Landlord and Tenant (Covenants) Act 1995 [and all statutes, regulations and orders included by virtue of clause 1.31 REFERENCES TO STATUTES][23].

23   See note 22 to clause 1.22 [964] 'THE 1954 ACT'.

1.24 Obligation not to permit or suffer

Any covenant by the Tenant not to do anything includes an obligation [to use reasonable endeavours] not to permit or suffer[24] that thing to be done by another person [where the Tenant is aware that the thing is being done].

24   'Permit' may have a different meaning from 'suffer': see *Barton v Reed* [1932] 1 Ch 362 at 375 per Luxmore J. A covenant not to 'permit' activity is broken if the covenantor himself carries it on: see *Oceanic Village Ltd v United Attractions Ltd* [2000] Ch 234, [2000] 1 All ER 975.

[964]

1.25 'The Permitted Use'[25]

'The Permitted Use' means [use for the sale of *(specify goods to be sold)* or any other use falling within Class *(specify class, eg A1)* of the Schedule to the Town and Country Planning (Use Classes) Order 1987, notwithstanding any amendment or revocation of that Order[26] as the Landlord from time to time approves [, such approval not to be unreasonably withheld [or delayed]] *(or if the landlord does not require control over the specific goods to be sold)* any use that falls within Class *(specify class, eg A1)* of the Schedule to the Town and Country Planning (Use Classes) Order 1987, notwithstanding any amendment or revocation of that Order].

25   As to use see vol 22(1) (2003 Reissue) LANDLORD AND TENANT (BUSINESS TENANCIES) Paragraph 170 [861] et seq.

26   As use classes orders change frequently, it is important to make clear which class is intended to apply, the class in existence at the date of the lease or the class as amended during the term of the lease.

1.26 'The Plan'[27]

'The Plan' means the plan annexed to this Lease.

27   As to the use and role of plans see vol 22(1) (2003 Reissue) LANDLORD AND TENANT (BUSINESS TENANCIES) Paragraphs 117 [636], 118 [638]. A plan may not always be required, eg a demise of all the land within a registered title. If the lease is registrable, a plan 'for identification purposes only' or where there is some other disclaimer as to the extent to which it can be relied on for conveyancing purposes is not sufficient if part of the land in a registered title is being dealt with.

1.27 'The Planning Acts'

'The Planning Acts' means the Town and Country Planning Act 1990, the Planning (Listed Buildings and Conservation Areas) Act 1990, the Planning (Consequential Provisions) Act 1990, the Planning (Hazardous Substances) Act 1990, the Planning and Compensation Act 1991, the Planning and Compulsory Purchase Act 2004 [and all statutes, regulations and orders included by virtue of clause 1.31 REFERENCE TO STATUTES][28].

28   See note 22 to clause 1.22 [964] 'THE 1954 ACT'.

[965]

1.28 'The Premises'[29]

1.28.1 *Definition of 'the Premises'*

'The Premises' means the land and building known as *(insert postal address)* [shown [for the purpose of identification only] edged *(state colour, eg red)* on the Plan].

29   As to parcels generally see vol 22(1) (2003 Reissue) LANDLORD AND TENANT (BUSINESS TENANCIES) Paragraph 116 [634].

1.28.2 *Interpretation of 'the Premises'*[30]

The expression 'the Premises' includes —

1.28.2.1   all buildings, erections, structures, fixtures[31], fittings and appurtenances on the Premises from time to time,

1.28.2.2   all additions, alterations and improvements carried out during the Term, and

1.28.2.3   the Conduits,

but excludes [the air space above[32] and] any fixtures installed by the Tenant [or any predecessors in title] that can be removed from the Premises without defacing the Premises. Unless the contrary is expressly stated, 'the Premises' includes any part or parts of the Premises.

30   As to implied grants and reservations see vol 22(1) (2003 Reissue) LANDLORD AND TENANT (BUSINESS TENANCIES) Paragraph 125 [650].

31   As to fixtures see vol 22(1) (2003 Reissue) LANDLORD AND TENANT (BUSINESS TENANCIES) Paragraph 121 [644].

32   As to air space, subsoil, cellars and footings see vol 22(1) (2003 Reissue) LANDLORD AND TENANT (BUSINESS TENANCIES) Paragraph 119 [640]. Strictly speaking, this exclusion means that the tenant may not go onto the roof to inspect or repair it unless he is held to have an easement of necessity to do so. As to easements of necessity generally see 13 Halsbury's Laws (4th Edn Reissue) EASEMENTS AND PROFITS À PRENDRE. If the landlord requires the upper limit of the demised premises to be defined, the tenant, in the case of a full repairing lease, should require a right to enter the landlord's air space above the demised premises to inspect or repair the upper limit of the premises. For a form that may be modified for this purpose see vol 22(3) (1997 Reissue) LANDLORD AND TENANT (BUSINESS TENANCIES) Form 77 [6451].

[966]

1.29   References to clauses and schedules

Any reference in this document to a clause, paragraph or schedule without further designation is to be construed as a reference to the clause, paragraph or schedule of this document so numbered.

1.30   References to rights of access

References to any right of the Landlord to have access to the Premises are to be construed as extending to any head landlord and any mortgagee of the Premises [— where the headlease or mortgage grants such rights of access to the head landlord or mortgagee —] and to all persons authorised in writing by the Landlord and any head landlord or mortgagee, including agents, professional advisers, contractors, workmen and others.

1.31   References to statutes

Unless expressly stated to the contrary, any reference to a specific statute includes any statutory extension or modification, amendment or re-enactment of that statute and any regulations or orders made under it, and any general reference to a statute includes any regulations or orders made under it[33].

33   Unfortunately the Interpretation Act 1978 ss 17, 23(3) (41 Halsbury's Statutes (4th Edn) STATUTES) does not quite go far enough to enable this clause to be dispensed with altogether, particularly where a statute is modified.

1.32   'The Rent'[34]

[Until the First Review Date 'the Rent' means the Initial Rent. Thereafter 'the Rent' means the sum ascertained in accordance with schedule 2 THE RENT AND RENT REVIEW. 'The Rent' does not include the Insurance Rent[35], but the term 'the Lease Rents' means both the Rent and the Insurance Rent. *(or as required by the rent and review provisions used)*]

34   This clause assumes that the rent is reviewable. If the rent is not reviewable clause 1.7 [958] 'THE INITIAL RENT' should be omitted and this clause amended as appropriate.

35   Because of this exclusion the insurance rent is not suspended under clause 5.5 [1034] SUSPENSION OF THE RENT.

[967]

1.33   'The Rent Commencement Date'

'The Rent Commencement Date' means *(insert the date on which payment of rent is to start)*[36].

36   This provision may be used to provide for a rent-free period, or for the situation where the tenant had possession before the execution of the lease on the basis that rent should be paid from the date of possession. If either the date of execution of the lease or the date of commencement of the term is to be the date for commencement of rent, that date should be inserted here.

[1.34   'The Review Dates'[37]

'The First Review Date' means *(date)*. 'The Review Dates' means the First Review Date and every *(insert ordinal, eg 3rd)* anniversary of that date during the [Contractual] Term [*(if appropriate for the review provisions used)* — and any other date from time to time specified under *(insert the relevant provision: see eg vol 22(3) (1997 Reissue)* LANDLORD AND TENANT (BUSINESS TENANCIES) *Form 180 paragraph {2}-4 [6728]* EFFECT OF COUNTER-INFLATION PROVISIONS)]. References to 'a review date' are references to any one of the Review Dates.] *(omit if not required by the review provisions to be used, or if the rent is not reviewable)*

37   As to rent review dates and intervals see vol 22(1) (2003 Reissue) LANDLORD AND TENANT (BUSINESS TENANCIES) Paragraph 302 [1333] et seq. Where there might be a statutory continuation of the lease, the landlord may wish to ensure that there is a review date shortly before the end of the contractual term to obviate the need to apply for an interim rent. The tenant may wish to insist on the word 'contractual' remaining so that the rent review provisions do not apply during any period of lawful holding over or extension or continuance of the contractual term. In circumstances where there is no prospect of statutory continuation the word 'contractual' should be omitted in any event: see note 6 to clause 1.2 [957] 'THE [CONTRACTUAL] TERM'.

1.35   'The Shop Covenants'

'The Shop Covenants' means the covenants set out in schedule 3 THE SHOP COVENANTS.

[968]

1.36   'The Surveyor'[38]

'The Surveyor' means *(name)* or any person or firm appointed by the Landlord in his place. The Surveyor may be an employee of the Landlord or a company that is a member of the same group as the Landlord within the meaning of the 1954 Act Section 42. The expression 'the Surveyor' includes the person or firm appointed by the Landlord to collect the Lease Rents[39].

38   For a provision that the landlord's surveyor must be a member of a relevant professional body see vol 22(3) (1997 Reissue) LANDLORD AND TENANT (BUSINESS TENANCIES) Form 152 [6648].
39   As to the definition of 'the Lease Rents' see clause 1.32 [967] 'THE RENT'.

[1.37   'The Term'

'The Term' means the Contractual Term and any period of holding-over or extension or continuance of the Contractual Term by statute or common law[40].] *(omit if the lease is to be contracted out of the Landlord and Tenant Act 1954)*[41]

40   The demise in this lease is for 'the Contractual Term', which is defined as a fixed term of years. The expression 'the Term' is used in covenants so that they continue to apply during any period of holding over or continuance or extension of the contractual term. As to the liability of a guarantor during a period of statutory continuation see vol 22(1) (2003 Reissue) LANDLORD AND TENANT (BUSINESS TENANCIES) Paragraph 73 [282].

41   Some difficulties arise if the structure referred to in note 40 above is used in a draft lease where security of tenure is to be excluded under the Landlord and Tenant Act 1954 s 38A(1) as inserted by SI 2003/3096. The demise is for the contractual term and the inclusion of the definition of 'the Term' does not prevent the lease being 'for a term of years certain' as required by the Landlord and Tenant Act 1954 s 38A(1). However, reference to continuance of the contractual term by statute is inappropriate where the operation of the security of tenure provisions in the Landlord and Tenant Act 1954 ss 24–28 is to be excluded. If a lease is contracted out of the Landlord and Tenant Act 1954 there can be no statutory extension, and if the tenant remains in occupation at the end of the contractual term he is holding over unlawfully unless there is an express agreement to extend the contractual term operating as a surrender and re-grant so that the original lease — and the agreement under the Landlord and Tenant Act 1954 s 38A(1) — has no further effect. It is suggested that in these circumstances the drafting should be simplified to include a single term (defined simply as 'the Term') by reference to the period of the contractual term. This can be achieved by amending clause 1.2 [957] 'THE [CONTRACTUAL] TERM' as suggested and substituting it for this clause.

1.38   Terms from the 1995 Act

Where the expressions 'landlord covenants', 'tenant covenants', or 'authorised guarantee agreement' are used in this Lease they are to have the same meaning as is given by the 1995 Act Section 28(1).

1.39   'VAT'[42]

'VAT' means value added tax or any other tax of a similar nature and unless otherwise expressly stated all references to rents or other sums payable by the Tenant are exclusive of VAT.

42   As to VAT generally see the Information Binder: Property [1]: VAT and Property.

                                                    [969]–[980]

2   DEMISE

The Landlord lets[43] the Premises to the Tenant [with [full *(or)* limited] title guarantee], excepting and reserving to the Landlord the rights specified in schedule 1 THE RIGHTS RESERVED, to hold the Premises to the Tenant for the [Contractual][44] Term, subject to [all rights, easements, privileges, restrictions, covenants and stipulations of whatever nature affecting the Premises including any matters contained or referred to in schedule 4 THE SUBJECTIONS *(or as required)* the rights, easements, privileges, restrictions, covenants and stipulations affecting the Premises contained or referred to in schedule 4 THE SUBJECTIONS][45], yielding and paying[46] to the Landlord —

2.1   the Rent, without any deduction or set off[47], by equal quarterly payments in advance[48] on the usual quarter days[49] in every year and proportionately for any period of less than a year, the first such payment, being a proportionate sum in respect of the period from and including the Rent Commencement Date to and including the day before the quarter day next after the Rent Commencement Date, to be paid on the date of this document[50], and

2.2   by way of further rent, the Insurance Rent[51], payable on demand in accordance with clause 5.4 PAYMENT OF THE INSURANCE RENT.

43   Traditionally, the operative word in a lease executed as a deed was 'demises' but any words sufficient to show the parties' intention may be used.
44   See note 41 to clause 1.37 [969] 'THE TERM'.
45   The tenant should argue for the second version, making the schedule comprehensive rather than illustrative.
46   The words 'yielding and paying' imply a covenant to pay rent: see *Vyvyan v Arthur* (1823) 1 B & C 410. An express covenant is now invariably included, because further procedural matters are contained in it.
47   As to deductions and set off see vol 22(1) (2003 Reissue) LANDLORD AND TENANT (BUSINESS TENANCIES) Paragraph 147 [753].
48   In the absence of an express provision, rent is payable in arrears.
49   The usual quarter days are 25 March, 24 June, 29 September and 25 December. A reference to 'the usual quarter days' is all that is necessary when rent is to be paid on these days.
50   If the first payment is not a complete instalment, the lease must provide for the date on which it is to be paid, the amount, and the period it is to cover.
51   As to the advantages of reserving the insurance rent as rent see vol 22(1) (2003 Reissue) LANDLORD AND TENANT (BUSINESS TENANCIES) Paragraph 151 [761].

[981]

3   THE TENANT'S COVENANTS

The Tenant covenants with the Landlord to observe and perform the requirements of this clause 3.

3.1   Rent

3.1.1   *Payment of the Lease Rents*

The Tenant must pay the Lease Rents[52] on the days and in the manner set out in this Lease, and must not exercise or seek to exercise any right or claim to withhold rent, or any right or claim to legal or equitable set-off[53] [except that referred to in *(give details of any provisions granting an express right of set-off)*][54].

52   As to the definition of 'the Lease Rents' see clause 1.32 [967] 'THE RENT'.
53   See, eg, *British Anzani (Felixstowe) Ltd v International Marine Management (UK) Ltd* [1980] QB 137, [1979] 2 All ER 1063; *Lee-Parker v Izzet* [1971] 3 All ER 1099, [1971] 1 WLR 1688. As to deductions and set-off see vol 22(1) (2003 Reissue) LANDLORD AND TENANT (BUSINESS TENANCIES) Paragraphs 147 [753], 148 [755].
54   If any express right of set-off is granted to the tenant, reference to the provision concerned should be included here to avoid inconsistency.

3.1.2   *Payment by banker's order*[55]

If so required in writing by the Landlord, the Tenant must pay the Lease Rents[56] by banker's order or credit transfer to any bank and account [in the United Kingdom] that the Landlord nominates from time to time.

55   This is a clause with dangers for both parties. If the existence of a breach of covenant is known to the landlord he must instruct his bank to refuse to accept the rent, otherwise his right of forfeiture is lost. As to implied waiver of the right of forfeiture see vol 22(1) (2003 Reissue) LANDLORD AND TENANT (BUSINESS TENANCIES) Paragraph 284 [1173]. The tenant may feel that he requires more control over the payment of rent. In any event, the financial systems operated by many companies prevent payments being made in this way.
56   As to the definition of 'the Lease Rents' see clause 1.32 [967] 'THE RENT'.

[982]

3.2   Outgoings and VAT

The Tenant must pay, and must indemnify the Landlord against —

3.2.1   all rates, taxes[57], assessments, duties, charges, impositions and outgoings that are now or may at any time during the Term be charged, assessed or imposed upon the Premises or on the owner or occupier of them[, excluding any payable by the Landlord occasioned by receipt of the Lease Rents[58] or by any disposition of or dealing with this Lease, or ownership of any interest reversionary to the interest created by it][59] [— provided that if the Landlord suffers any loss of rating relief that may be applicable to empty premises after the end of the Term because the relief has been allowed to the Tenant in respect of any period before the end of the Term, then the Tenant must make good such loss to the Landlord],

3.2.2   all VAT that may from time to time be charged on the Lease Rents or other sums payable by the Tenant under this Lease[60], and

3.2.3   all VAT incurred in relation to any costs that the Tenant is obliged to pay or in respect of which he is required to indemnify the Landlord under the terms of this Lease, save where such VAT is recoverable or available for set-off by the Landlord as input tax[61].

57   As to covenants to pay rates and taxes see vol 22(1) (2003 Reissue) LANDLORD AND TENANT (BUSINESS TENANCIES) Paragraph 153 [765].
58   As to the definition of 'the Lease Rents' see clause 1.32 [967] 'THE RENT'.
59   The tenant should add the words in square brackets to make it clear that he is not paying the landlord's taxes.
60   As to VAT on rent, service charges and insurance premiums see the Information Binder: Property [1]: VAT and Property.
61   As to payment of VAT on legal costs paid by a person other than the solicitor's own client see the Information Binder: Property [1]: VAT and Property.

[3.3   Cost of services consumed[62]

The Tenant must pay to the suppliers, and indemnify the Landlord against, all charges for electricity, water, gas, telecommunications and other services consumed or used at or in relation to the Premises, including meter rents and standing charges, and must comply with the lawful requirements and regulations of their respective suppliers.] *(omit if the premises have independent supplies of all services)*

62   Where the premises comprise a separate building, a separate supply is usually provided and the tenant makes his own arrangements with the suppliers. In that case this clause is unnecessary.

[983]

3.4   Repair, cleaning and decoration

3.4.1   *Repair of the Premises*[63]

The Tenant must repair the Premises and keep them in good condition and repair, except for damage caused by one or more of the Insured Risks save to the extent that the insurance money is irrecoverable due to any act or default of the Tenant or anyone at the Premises expressly or by implication[64] with his authority [and under his control][65].

63   As to repair see vol 22(1) (2003 Reissue) LANDLORD AND TENANT (BUSINESS TENANCIES) Paragraph 196 [931] et seq. For a covenant to repair, rebuild and renew see vol 22(3) (1997 Reissue) LANDLORD AND TENANT (BUSINESS TENANCIES) Form 85 [6460]. For provisos excluding, eg, work that is prevented etc see vol 22(3) (1997 Reissue) LANDLORD AND TENANT (BUSINESS TENANCIES) Forms 87 [6462], 88 [6463].

If a landlord is unable to obtain full insurance cover without excess, it should be made clear whether the tenant is to be liable to pay the excess where damage is caused by an insured risk. For a covenant limiting the tenant's repairing obligations by reference to uninsurable as well as insured risks see vol 22(3) (1997 Reissue) LANDLORD AND TENANT (BUSINESS TENANCIES) Form 90 [6465]. It should be noted that it is now recommended 'best practice' that if the premises are so damaged by an uninsured risk as to prevent occupation, the tenant should be allowed to terminate the lease unless the landlord agrees to reinstate at his own cost: see vol 22(1) (2003 Reissue) LANDLORD AND TENANT (BUSINESS TENANCIES) Paragraph 85 [402]. If adopted, this recommendation involves damage preventing occupation caused by uninsured or uninsurable risks being excluded from the ambit of the tenant's repairing covenant.

64   The expression 'by implication' is intended to include a caller on the premises, such as a tradesman, where there has been no express invitation but the person cannot be classed as a trespasser.

65   The tenant should add the words in square brackets.

3.4.2   *Replacement of landlord's fixtures*

The Tenant must replace from time to time any landlord's fixtures and fittings in the Premises that are beyond repair at any time during or at the end of the Term.

3.4.3   *Cleaning and tidying*

The Tenant must keep the Premises clean and tidy and clear of all rubbish.

[984]

[3.4.4   *The Open Land*

3.4.4.1   **Care of the Open Land**

The Tenant must keep any part of the Premises that is not built on ('the Open Land') adequately surfaced, in good condition and free from weeds [and must keep all landscaped areas properly cultivated].

3.4.4.2   **Storage on the Open Land**

The Tenant must not store anything on the Open Land or bring anything onto it [that is or might become untidy, unclean, unsightly or in any way detrimental to the Premises or the area generally].

3.4.4.3   **Rubbish on the Open Land**

The Tenant must not deposit any waste, rubbish or refuse on the Open Land[, or place any receptacle for them, on it].

3.4.4.4   **Vehicles on the Open Land**

The Tenant must not keep or store any [(*if the land cannot be used for parking*) vehicle,] caravan or movable dwelling on the Open Land.] (*adapt clause 3.4.4 as required in the circumstances, or omit if no open land is included*)

3.4.5   *Care of abutting land*

The Tenant must not cause any land, roads or pavements abutting the Premises to be untidy or dirty and in particular, but without prejudice to the generality of the foregoing, must not deposit refuse or other materials on them.

3.4.6   *Decoration*

[The Tenant must redecorate the outside and inside of the Premises, as often as is necessary in the [reasonable] opinion of the Surveyor in order to maintain a high standard of decorative finish and attractiveness and to preserve the Premises and in the last year of the Term, *(or as required)* The Tenant must redecorate the outside of the Premises in each of the External Decorating Years and the last year of the Term and must redecorate the inside of the Premises in each of the Interior Decorating Years and the last year of the Term, in all instances][66] in a good and workmanlike manner, with appropriate materials of good quality[, to the [reasonable] satisfaction of the Surveyor], any change in the tints, colours and patterns of the decoration to be approved by the Landlord[67][, whose approval may not be unreasonably withheld [or delayed]] [, provided that the covenants relating to the last year of the Term are not to apply where the Tenant has performed the obligation in question less than *(state period, eg 18 months)* before the end of the Term].

66   The draftsman should discuss with the landlord and his property advisers whether he wishes to have the flexibility of the first option or the certainty of the second.
67   The tenant may amend to provide for the landlord's approval to tints etc to apply only in the last year of the term.

[985]

3.4.7   *Shared facilities*

Where the use of any of the Conduits or any boundary structures or other things is common to the Premises and other property, the Tenant must be responsible for, and indemnify the Landlord against, all sums due from the owner, tenant or occupier of the Premises in relation to those Conduits, boundary structures or other things and must undertake all work in relation to them that is his responsibility.

3.5   **Waste and alterations**

3.5.1   *Waste, additions and alterations*[68]

The Tenant must not commit any waste, make any addition to the Premises, unite the Premises with any adjoining premises, or make any alteration to the Premises except as permitted by the provisions of this clause 3.5.

68   As to alterations see vol 22(1) (2003 Reissue) LANDLORD AND TENANT (BUSINESS TENANCIES) Paragraph 186 [911] et seq.

3.5.2   *Pre-conditions for alterations*

The Tenant must not make any [internal non-structural] alterations to the Premises unless he first —

3.5.2.1   obtains and complies with the necessary consents of the competent authorities and pays their charges for them,

3.5.2.2   makes an application to the Landlord for consent, supported by drawings and where appropriate a specification in duplicate [prepared by an architect[, or a member of some other appropriate profession,] who must supervise the work throughout to completion],

3.5.2.3   pays the fees of the Landlord, any head landlord, any mortgagee and their respective professional advisers,

3.5.2.4   enters into any covenants the Landlord requires as to the execution and reinstatement of the alterations, and

3.5.2.5   obtains the consent of the Landlord, whose consent may not be unreasonably withheld [or delayed].

[In the case of any works of a substantial nature, the Landlord may require the Tenant to provide, before starting the works, adequate security in the form of a deposit of money or the provision of a bond, as assurance to the Landlord that any works he permits from time to time will be fully completed.]

                                                                            [986]

3.5.3   *Removal of alterations*[69]

At the end of the Term, if so requested by the Landlord, the Tenant must remove any additional buildings, additions, alterations or improvements made to the Premises, and must make good any part of the Premises damaged by their removal.

69   This clause has probably come to be inserted because landlords hope that it will defeat the effect of the compensation provisions of the Landlord and Tenant Act 1927 Pt I (ss 1–17) (23 Halsbury's Statutes (4th Edn) LANDLORD AND TENANT) — as to which see vol 22(1) (2003 Reissue) LANDLORD AND TENANT (BUSINESS TENANCIES) Paragraph 192 [923] et seq — because, if the improvement has been removed, it will not be an improvement to the holding at the time of quitting the premises. In fact, the clause might not achieve this effect, because the Landlord and Tenant Act 1927 s 9 as amended by the Landlord and Tenant Act 1954 s 49 prohibits contracting out. Also, the clause may be void under the Landlord and Tenant Act 1927 s 19(2), so far as it applies to improvements, on the grounds that it purports to fetter the court in deciding what is reasonable. The tenant should not, however, rely on the application of these statutory provisions and should seek to strike the clause out.

3.5.4   *Connection to the Conduits*

The Tenant must not make any connection with the Conduits except in accordance with plans and specifications approved by the Landlord[, whose approval may not be unreasonably withheld [or delayed]], and subject to consent to make the connection having previously been obtained from the competent authority, undertaker or supplier.

3.6   Aerials, signs and advertisements

3.6.1   *Masts and wires*

The Tenant must not erect any pole or mast [or install any wire or cable] on the Premises, whether in connection with telecommunications or otherwise.

3.6.2   *Advertisements*[70]

The Tenant must not, without the consent of the Landlord, fix to or exhibit on the outside of the Premises, or fix to or exhibit through any window of the Premises, or display anywhere on the Premises, any placard, sign, notice, fascia board or advertisement.

70   See the Town and Country Planning (Control of Advertisements) Regulations 1992, SI 1992/666 as amended. In the absence of a covenant such as this and subject to those Regulations, the tenant may exhibit advertisements etc on the premises, whether or not they are connected with his business: see *Clapman v Edwards* [1938] 2 All ER 507.

                                                                            [987]

3.7 Statutory obligations

3.7.1 *General provision*[71]

The Tenant must comply in all respects with the requirements of any statutes, and any other obligations so applicable imposed by law or by any byelaws, applicable to the Premises or the trade or business for the time being carried on there.

71 As to the covenant to comply with statutes see vol 22(1) (2003 Reissue) LANDLORD AND TENANT (BUSINESS TENANCIES) Paragraph 182 [905]. For a provision requiring the landlord to pay compensation for works above a certain value see vol 22(3) (1997 Reissue) LANDLORD AND TENANT (BUSINESS TENANCIES) Form 169 [6693].

3.7.2 *Particular obligations*

3.7.2.1 Works required by statute, department or authority

Without prejudice to the generality of clause 3.7.1, the Tenant must execute all works and provide and maintain all arrangements on or in respect of the Premises or the use to which they are being put that are required in order to comply with the requirements of any statute already or in the future to be passed, or the requirements of any government department, local authority or other public or competent authority or court of competent jurisdiction, regardless of whether the requirements are imposed on the owner, the occupier, or any other person.

3.7.2.2 Acts causing losses

Without prejudice to the generality of clause 3.7.1, the Tenant must not do in or near the Premises anything by reason of which the Landlord may incur any losses under any statute.

3.7.2.3 Construction (Design and Management) Regulations

Without prejudice to the generality of clause 3.7.1, the Tenant must comply with the provisions of the Construction (Design and Management) Regulations 1994 ('the CDM Regulations'), be the only client as defined in the provisions of the CDM Regulations, fulfil, in relation to all and any works, all the obligations of the client as set out in or reasonably to be inferred from the CDM Regulations, and make a declaration to that effect[72] to the Health and Safety Executive in accordance with the Approved Code of Practice published from time to time by the Health and Safety Executive in relation to the CDM Regulations. The provisions of clause 5.7.3 FIRE-FIGHTING EQUIPMENT are to have effect in any circumstances to which these obligations apply.

3.7.2.4 Delivery of health and safety files

At the end of the Term, the Tenant must forthwith deliver to the Landlord any and all health and safety files relating to the Premises in accordance with the CDM Regulations.

72 If the works are being carried out for the tenant, the landlord will not want to accept the liabilities that are placed on a client under the Construction (Design and Management) Regulations 1994, SI 1994/3140 and the Health and Safety Executive Approved Code of Practice. The landlord will need to ensure that the tenant actually makes the declaration required, and that he obtains the notification served on the tenant by the Health and Safety Executive.

3.8   Entry to inspect and notice to repair

3.8.1   *Entry and notice*

The Tenant must permit the Landlord[73] [on reasonable notice during normal business hours except in emergency][74] —

3.8.1.1   to enter the Premises to ascertain whether or not the covenants and conditions of this Lease have been observed and performed,

3.8.1.2   to view the state of repair and condition of the Premises, and to open up floors and other parts of the Premises where that is necessary in order to do so, and

3.8.1.3   to give to the Tenant, or notwithstanding clause 8.7 NOTICES leave on the Premises, a notice ('a notice to repair') specifying the works required to remedy any breach of the Tenant's obligations in this Lease as to the repair and condition of the Premises,

provided that any opening-up must be made good by and at the cost of the Landlord if it reveals no breach of the terms of this Lease.

73   The provisions of clause 1.30 [967] REFERENCES TO RIGHTS OF ACCESS should be noted.
74   The tenant should add the words in square brackets.

3.8.2   *Works to be carried out*

The Tenant must carry out the works specified in a notice to repair immediately, including making good any opening up that revealed a breach of the terms of this Lease.

[3.8.3   *Landlord's power in default*[75]

If within *(state period, eg 1 month)* of the service of a notice to repair the Tenant has not started to execute the work referred to in that notice or is not proceeding diligently with it, or if the Tenant fails to finish the work within *(state period, eg 2 months)*[76][, or if in the [Landlord's *(or as required)* Surveyor's] [reasonable] opinion the Tenant is unlikely to finish the work within that period], the Tenant must permit the Landlord to enter the Premises to execute the outstanding work, and must within *(state period, eg 14 days)* of a written demand pay to the Landlord the cost of so doing and all expenses incurred by the Landlord, including legal costs and surveyor's fees.]

75   The advantages of this clause for the landlord must be weighed against the potential liability that it creates under the Defective Premises Act 1972 s 4(4) (31 Halsbury's Statutes (4th Edn) NEGLIGENCE): see *McAuley v Bristol City Council* [1992] QB 134, [1992] 1 All ER 749, CA.
        It has been held that a claim by the landlord for recovery of costs under such a clause is a claim for recovery of a debt, and can therefore be enforced without requiring leave of the court under the Leasehold Property (Repairs) Act 1938 (23 Halsbury's Statutes (4th Edn) LANDLORD AND TENANT): see *Jervis v Harris* [1996] Ch 195, [1996] 1 All ER 303, CA.
        However, even where a landlord has been granted a right of this nature the court does not compel the tenant to allow the landlord the right to enter and carry out repairs where these would be of no benefit and where no loss is being caused to the landlord: see *Hammersmith London Borough Council v Creska (No 2)* [2000] L & TR 288.
76   The tenant would prefer to be given 'a reasonable period' to do the work required to remedy the breaches because it may take longer than the specified number of months.

[989]–[1000]

3.9   Alienation[77]

3.9.1   *Alienation prohibited*

The Tenant must not hold the Premises on trust for another. The Tenant must not part with possession of the Premises or any part of the Premises or permit another to occupy them or any part of them except pursuant to a transaction permitted by and effected in accordance with the provisions of this Lease.

> 77   As to alienation see vol 22(1) (2003 Reissue) LANDLORD AND TENANT (BUSINESS TENANCIES) Paragraph 156 [801] et seq. Where the lease is registrable, this prohibition or restriction on dealings will be reflected in an entry on the register excepting from the effects of registration all estates, rights, interests, powers and remedies arising on or by reason of any dealing made in breach of the prohibition or restriction: see the Land Registration Rules 2003, SI 2003/1417 r 6(2).

3.9.2   *Assignment, subletting and charging of part*[78]

(version 1)

[The Tenant must not assign, sublet or charge part only of the Premises.] *(where assignment, subletting or charging of the whole is allowed)*

(version 2)

[The Tenant must not assign or charge part only of the Premises and must not sublet the whole or any part of the Premises.] *(where assignment or charging of the whole is permitted, but subletting is not allowed at all)*

> 78   Whether subletting should be permitted is a commercial matter. Some landlords consider that the fact that they cannot unreasonably refuse consent to an assignment gives the tenant all the protection he requires and are not prepared to permit subletting. An advantage to the tenant of the ability to sublet is that he has an element of control over a subtenant but not over an assignee, for whom he may retain liability under an authorised guarantee agreement. Further, with stringent assignment tests or in a bad market, subletting may be the only option open to the tenant.

[1001]

3.9.3   *Assignment of the whole*

Subject to clauses 3.9.4 CIRCUMSTANCES and 3.9.5 CONDITIONS, the Tenant must not assign the whole of the Premises without the consent of the Landlord, whose consent may not be unreasonably withheld [or delayed][79].

> 79   This residual discretion is the old test of reasonableness under the Landlord and Tenant Act 1927 s 19(1). Thus the tenant and the proposed assignee may satisfy the circumstances and conditions specified for the purposes of the Landlord and Tenant Act 1927 s 19(1A) as inserted by the Landlord and Tenant (Covenants) Act 1995 s 22 (as to which see clause 3.9.4 [1002] CIRCUMSTANCES and clause 3.9.5 [1004] CONDITIONS), but the landlord may still refuse consent on reasonable grounds: see vol 22(1) (2003 Reissue) LANDLORD AND TENANT (BUSINESS TENANCIES) Paragraph 159 [812] et seq.

3.9.4   *Circumstances*

If any of the following circumstances[80] — which are specified for the purposes of the Landlord and Tenant Act 1927 Section 19(1A)[81] — applies either at the date when application for consent to assign is made to the Landlord, or after that date but before the Landlord's consent is given, the Landlord may withhold his consent and if, after the Landlord's consent has been given but before the assignment has taken place, any such circumstances apply, the Landlord may revoke his consent[82], whether his consent is expressly subject to a condition as referred to in clause 3.9.5.4 CONDITIONS or not. The circumstances are —

3.9.4.1   that any sum due from the Tenant under this Lease remains unpaid[83],

3.9.4.2   that in the Landlord's reasonable[84] opinion the assignee is not a person who is likely to be able to comply with the tenant covenants of this Lease and to continue to be able to comply with them following the assignment,

[3.9.4.3   that without prejudice to clause 3.9.4.2, in the case of an assignment to a company in the same group as the Tenant[85] within the meaning of the 1954 Act Section 42 in the Landlord's reasonable opinion the assignee is a person who is, or may become, less likely to be able to comply with the tenant covenants of this Lease than the Tenant requesting consent to assign, which likelihood is adjudged by reference in particular to the financial strength of that Tenant aggregated with that of any guarantor of the obligations of that Tenant and the value of any other security for the performance of the tenant covenants of this Lease when assessed at the date of grant or — where that Tenant is not *(name of original tenant)* — the date of the assignment of this Lease to that Tenant[86]] or

3.9.4.4   that the assignee or any guarantor for the assignee, other than any guarantor under an authorised guarantee agreement, is a corporation registered — or otherwise resident — in a jurisdiction in which the order of a court obtained in England and Wales will not necessarily be enforced against the assignee or guarantor without any consideration of the merits of the case.

(for examples of circumstances for use in unusual cases, see vol 22(3) (1997 Reissue) LANDLORD AND TENANT (BUSINESS TENANCIES) *Form 117 [6501])*

[1002]

80   The Landlord and Tenant Act 1927 s 19(1A) as inserted by the Landlord and Tenant (Covenants) Act 1995 s 22 enables the landlord and tenant to a post-1995 lease to agree in advance the terms upon which an assignment may be permitted. It distinguishes between on the one hand circumstances, the existence of which entitles the landlord to refuse consent to assignment, and on the other hand conditions that may be imposed on the grant of his consent. This clause and clause 3.9.5 [1004] CONDITIONS are drafted on the assumption that this is a valid approach and seek to draw a clear distinction between circumstances and conditions.

     It should be noted that provisions that are overly restrictive may have an adverse impact at any rent review. It should also be noted that it is recommended 'best practice' that unless the particular circumstances of the letting justify greater control, the only restriction on assignment of the whole should be obtaining the landlord's consent, which is not to be unreasonably withheld: see vol 22(1) (2003 Reissue) LANDLORD AND TENANT (BUSINESS TENANCIES) Paragraph 85 [401] and 'A code of practice for commercial leases in England and Wales (2nd edition)' which can be found in vol 22(1) (2003 Reissue) LANDLORD AND TENANT (BUSINESS TENANCIES) as Form 1 [4501].

     Each letting must be looked at in the light of its own particular facts and circumstances but it is considered that the provisions of this clause do, in the ordinary course, strike a reasonable balance between the landlord's desire for control and the tenant's ability to dispose of his interest without undue restriction. For a less restrictive approach see vol 22(1) (2003 Reissue) LANDLORD AND TENANT (BUSINESS TENANCIES) Form 7 clause 5.2 [5538].

81   The Landlord and Tenant Act 1927 s 19(1A) as inserted by the Landlord and Tenant (Covenants) Act 1995 s 22 seems to require the alienation clause to state that the circumstances it mentions are specified for the purposes of that subsection.

82   The landlord may require that certain circumstances are absent not only before consent has been given to the assignment, but also up to the date on which the assignment takes place — when the die is cast and the lease covenants bind the assignee. For example, the landlord may require the rent to be paid up to date not only before the application for consent is made, but also at the date when consent is given and the possibly later date when the lease is actually assigned.

83   The tenant may want to limit this to the rent, as it may be thought that a dispute is more likely to arise over the insurance rent or other payments. If the tenant has retained any right of set-off, it should also be referred to here.

84   Circumstances and conditions must either be factual or, if they contain an element of discretion, require
        that discretion to be exercised reasonably (see the Landlord and Tenant Act 1927 s 19(1C)(a) as inserted
        by the Landlord and Tenant (Covenants) Act 1995 s 22), or must give the tenant a right of appeal to
        an expert (see the Landlord and Tenant Act 1927 s 19(1C)(b) as inserted by the Landlord and Tenant
        (Covenants) Act 1995 s 22). If the discretion is to be exercised reasonably, as suggested by this
        provision, the tenant can take any dispute about its exercise to the court. The court will consider
        whether *this* landlord has acted within the range of reasonable decisions, not whether a reasonable
        landlord would have reached the same decision or whether the test is itself reasonable. For a clause
        where an expert is used see vol 22(3) (1997 Reissue) LANDLORD AND TENANT (BUSINESS
        TENANCIES) Form 117 [6501].

85   There have been suggestions that intra-group assignments should be banned completely. However, this
        is considered to be too draconian and would prevent legitimate corporate restructuring needed for
        reasons other than avoidance of liability under the Landlord and Tenant (Covenants) Act 1995. The
        landlord's concern is that a strong tenant may assign to a weak group company; the assignment is
        acceptable because the assignor gives an authorised guarantee agreement for the assignee. The second
        group company may then itself assign outside the group; the landlord will lose the authorised guarantee
        agreement of the strong first group company and have only the possibly worthless authorised guarantee
        agreement of the second group company. The possibilities for exploitation of this scenario are obvious
        and it is therefore felt that this is the one situation in which measuring the financial strength of the
        assignee in relation to that of the assignor is justified. Equivalence tests are not generally thought to be
        appropriate, because a strong first covenant may make the lease almost unassignable, adversely affecting
        the rent at review.

86   Consider whether the time at which the tenant's financial status is measured should be when he
        acquired the lease, when his status was acceptable to the landlord, or at the date of the application for
        consent to assign, when it may have deteriorated sharply. On the other hand, the outgoing tenant may
        be a better covenant now than when he acquired the lease: the wily landlord may wish to leave himself
        free to pick whichever of the two dates gives the better picture.

[1003]

3.9.5   *Conditions*

The Landlord may impose any or all of the following conditions[87] — which are specified
for the purposes of the Landlord and Tenant Act 1927 Section 19(1A)[88] — on giving any
consent for an assignment by the Tenant, and any such consent is to be treated as being
subject to each of the following conditions —

3.9.5.1   a condition that on or before any assignment and before giving occupation
           to the assignee, the Tenant requesting consent to assign, together with any
           former tenant who by virtue of the 1995 Act Section 11 was not released on
           an earlier assignment of this Lease[89], must enter into an authorised guarantee
           agreement[90] in favour of the Landlord in the terms set out in schedule 5 THE
           AUTHORISED GUARANTEE AGREEMENT,

3.9.5.2   a condition that if reasonably so required by the Landlord on an assignment
           to a limited company, the assignee must ensure that at least *(state number, eg
           2)* directors of the company, or some other guarantor or guarantors
           [reasonably] acceptable to the Landlord, enter into direct covenants with the
           Landlord in the form of the guarantor's covenants contained in clause 6
           GUARANTEE PROVISIONS with 'the Assignee' substituted for 'the Tenant',

3.9.5.3   a condition that upon or before any assignment, the Tenant making the
           request for consent to assign must give to the Landlord a copy of the health
           and safety file required to be maintained under the Construction (Design
           and Management) Regulations 1994 containing full details of all works
           undertaken to the Premises by that Tenant, and

3.9.5.4   a condition that if, at any time before the assignment, the circumstances
           specified in clause 3.9.4, or any of them, apply, the Landlord may revoke the
           consent by written notice to the Tenant.

[1004]

87   The Landlord and Tenant Act 1927 s 19(1A) as inserted by the Landlord and Tenant (Covenants) Act 1995 s 22 enables the landlord and tenant to a post-1995 lease to agree in advance the terms upon which an assignment may be permitted. It distinguishes between on the one hand circumstances, the existence of which entitles the landlord to refuse consent to assignment, and on the other hand conditions that may be imposed on the grant of his consent. This clause and clause 3.9.4 [1002] CIRCUMSTANCES are drafted on the assumption that this a valid approach and seek to draw a clear distinction between circumstances and conditions.

It should be noted that provisions that are overly restrictive may have an adverse impact at any rent review. It should also be noted that it is recommended 'best practice' that unless the particular circumstances of the letting justify greater control, the only restriction on assignment of the whole should be obtaining the landlord's consent, which is not to be unreasonably withheld: see vol 22(1) (2003 Reissue) LANDLORD AND TENANT (BUSINESS TENANCIES) Paragraph 85 [401] and 'A code of practice for commercial leases in England and Wales (2nd edition)' which can be found in vol 22(1) (2003 Reissue) LANDLORD AND TENANT (BUSINESS TENANCIES) as Form 1 [4501].

Each letting must be looked at in the light of its own particular facts and circumstances but it is considered that the provisions of this clause do, in the ordinary course, strike a reasonable balance between the landlord's desire for control and the tenant's ability to dispose of his interest without undue restriction.

88   The Landlord and Tenant Act 1927 s 19(1A) as inserted by the Landlord and Tenant (Covenants) Act 1995 s22 seems to require the alienation clause to state that the conditions it mentions are specified for the purposes of that subsection.

89   See the Landlord and Tenant (Covenants) Act 1995 ss 11(2), 16(6).

90   As to authorised guarantee agreements see vol 22(1) (2003 Reissue) LANDLORD AND TENANT (BUSINESS TENANCIES) Paragraph 54 [247]. It should be noted that 'A code of practice for commercial leases in England and Wales (2nd edition)' urges landlords to consider requiring authorised guarantee agreements only where the assignee is of lower financial standing than the assignor at the date of the assignment.

[1005]

3.9.6   *Charging of the whole*

The Tenant must not charge the whole of the Premises without the consent of the Landlord, whose consent may not be unreasonably withheld [or delayed][91].

91   As to unreasonable withholding of consent under the Landlord and Tenant Act 1927 see vol 22(1) (2003 Reissue) LANDLORD AND TENANT (BUSINESS TENANCIES) Paragraph 158.2 [806] and as to unreasonable delay under the Landlord and Tenant Act 1988 (23 Halsbury's Statutes (4th Edn) LANDLORD AND TENANT) see vol 22(1) (2003 Reissue) LANDLORD AND TENANT (BUSINESS TENANCIES) Paragraph 158.3 [808].

[3.9.7   *Subletting*

The Tenant must not sublet[92] the whole of the Premises without the consent of the Landlord, whose consent may not be unreasonably withheld [or delayed]][93]. *(omit if subletting is prohibited)*

92   See note 78 to clause 3.9.2 [1001] ASSIGNMENT, SUBLETTING AND CHARGING OF PART.
93   As to unreasonable withholding of consent under the Landlord and Tenant Act 1927 see vol 22(1) (2003 Reissue) LANDLORD AND TENANT (BUSINESS TENANCIES) Paragraph 158.2 [806] and as to unreasonable delay under the Landlord and Tenant Act 1988 see vol 22(1) (2003 Reissue) LANDLORD AND TENANT (BUSINESS TENANCIES) Paragraph 158.3 [808].

[3.9.8   *Terms of a permitted sublease*[94]

Every permitted sublease must be granted, without a fine or premium, at a rent not less than whichever is the greater of the then open market rent payable in respect of the Premises [— to be approved by the Landlord before the sublease is granted [and to be determined by the Surveyor, acting as an expert and not as an arbitrator]—] and the Rent[95], to be payable in advance on the days on which the Rent is payable under this Lease. Every permitted sublease must contain provisions approved by the Landlord —

[1006]

3.9.8.1   for the upwards only review of the rent reserved by it, on the basis set out in schedule 2 THE RENT AND RENT REVIEW and on the Review Dates[96],

3.9.8.2   prohibiting the subtenant from doing or allowing anything in relation to the Premises inconsistent with or in breach of the provisions of this Lease,

3.9.8.3   for re-entry by the sublandlord on breach of any covenant by the subtenant,

3.9.8.4   imposing an absolute prohibition against all dealings with the Premises other than assignment[, subletting] [or charging] of the whole,

3.9.8.5   prohibiting assignment[, subletting][97] [or charging] of the whole of the Premises without the consent of the Landlord under this Lease,

3.9.8.6   requiring the assignee on any assignment of the sublease to enter into direct covenants with the Landlord to the same effect as those contained in clause 3.9.9 SUBTENANT'S DIRECT COVENANTS,

3.9.8.7   requiring on each assignment of the sublease that the assignor enters into an authorised guarantee agreement[98] in favour of the Landlord in the terms set out in schedule 5 THE AUTHORISED GUARANTEE AGREEMENT but adapted to suit the circumstances in which the guarantee is given,

3.9.8.8   prohibiting the subtenant from holding on trust for another or permitting another to share or occupy the whole or any part of the Premises,

3.9.8.9   imposing in relation to any permitted assignment[, subletting] [or charge] the same obligations for registration with the Landlord as are contained in this Lease in relation to dispositions by the Tenant,

[3.9.8.10   imposing in relation to any permitted subletting the same obligations as are contained in this clause 3.9.8 and in clause 3.9.9 SUBTENANT'S DIRECT COVENANTS[, clause 3.9.11 ENFORCEMENT OF THE SUBLEASE and clause 3.9.12 SUBLEASE RENT REVIEW],] and

3.9.8.11   excluding the provisions of Sections 24–28 of the 1954 Act from the letting created by the sublease.] *(omit if subletting is prohibited)*

[1007]

94   As to the validity of provisions of this nature see vol 22(1) (2003 Reissue) LANDLORD AND TENANT (BUSINESS TENANCIES) Paragraph 161 [817].

95   It will not be in the landlord's interest for the premises to be sublet at a rent less than that payable under the headlease, because it could allow into the premises a subtenant of doubtful financial status, with whom the landlord may in the future have to deal direct, eg on the grant of a new lease under the Landlord and Tenant Act 1954 Pt II (ss 23–46). Also a low rent could be used as a 'comparable' in arriving at the open market rent on rent reviews or lease renewals. On the other hand following the decision in *Allied Dunbar Assurance plc v Homebase Ltd* [2002] EWCA Civ 666, [2003] 1 P & CR 75, [2002] 2 EGLR 23 a provision of this kind may effectively render the lease inalienable and being a potentially onerous restriction on disposition (as to which see vol 22(1) (2003 Reissue) LANDLORD AND TENANT (BUSINESS TENANCIES) Paragraph 348.2 [1440]) have an adverse impact at rent review from a landlord's perspective.

96   Alternatively the landlord might prefer the sublease rents to be reviewed just before the review dates in the headlease. As to recommended 'best practice' in relation to the basis of rent review in leases of business premises see vol 22(1) (2003 Reissue) LANDLORD AND TENANT (BUSINESS TENANCIES) Paragraph 85 [401] and 'A code of practice for commercial leases in England and Wales (2nd edition)' which can be found in vol 22(1) (2003 Reissue) LANDLORD AND TENANT (BUSINESS TENANCIES) as Form 1 [4501].

97   The landlord may well wish to prohibit any further subletting by requiring an absolute covenant against subletting to be inserted in any sublease.

98   By virtue of the Landlord and Tenant (Covenants) Act 1995 s 16(3)(a), where a head landlord's consent is needed to the assignment of a sublease, the head landlord can require the assignor of the sublease to enter into an authorised guarantee agreement. It should be noted that 'A code of practice for commercial leases in England and Wales (2nd edition)' urges landlords to consider requiring authorised guarantee agreements only where the assignee is of lower financial standing than the assignor at the date of the assignment.

[1008]

[3.9.9   *Subtenant's direct covenants*[99]

Before any permitted subletting, the Tenant must ensure that the subtenant enters into a direct covenant with the Landlord that while the subtenant is bound by the tenant covenants of the sublease[100] and while the subtenant is bound by an authorised guarantee agreement the subtenant will observe and perform the tenant covenants contained in this Lease — except the covenant to pay the rent reserved by this Lease — and in that sublease.] *(omit if subletting is prohibited)*

99   See note 94 to clause 3.9.8 [1008] TERMS OF A PERMITTED SUBLEASE.

100   The liability of the subtenant should be expressed to last while he is bound by the tenant covenants of the sublease, rather than while the sublease is vested in him, to take account of the possibility of an excluded assignment being made and the subtenant remaining liable. An excluded assignment means that the subtenant is precluded from tenant release under the Landlord and Tenant (Covenants) Act 1995.

[3.9.10   *Requirement for 1954 Act exclusion*[101]

The Tenant must not grant a sublease or permit a subtenant to occupy the Premises unless an effective agreement has been made to exclude the operation of Sections 24 to 28 of the 1954 Act pursuant to Section 38A of the 1954 Act.] *(omit if subletting is prohibited)*

101   As to contracting out of the security of tenure provisions of the Landlord and Tenant Act 1954 see vol 22(1) (2003 Reissue) LANDLORD AND TENANT (BUSINESS TENANCIES) Paragraph 431 [2035].

[3.9.11   *Enforcement, waiver and variation of subleases*

In relation to any permitted sublease, the Tenant must enforce the performance and observance by every subtenant of the provisions of the sublease, and must not at any time either expressly or by implication waive any breach of the covenants or conditions on the part of any subtenant or assignee of any sublease, or — without the consent of the Landlord, whose consent may not be unreasonably withheld or delayed — vary the terms or accept a surrender of any permitted sublease.] *(omit if subletting is prohibited)*

[1009]

[3.9.12   *Sublease rent review*

In relation to any permitted sublease —

3.9.12.1   the Tenant must ensure that the rent is reviewed in accordance with the terms of the sublease,

3.9.12.2   the Tenant must not agree the reviewed rent with the subtenant without the approval of the Landlord,

3.9.12.3   where the sublease provides such an option, the Tenant must not, without the approval of the Landlord, agree whether the third party determining the revised rent in default of agreement should act as an arbitrator or as an expert,

3.9.12.4   the Tenant must not, without the approval of the Landlord, agree any appointment of a person to act as the third party determining the revised rent,

3.9.12.5   the Tenant must incorporate as part of his representations to that third party representations [reasonably] required[102] by the Landlord, and

3.9.12.6   the Tenant must give notice to the Landlord of the details of the determination of every rent review within *(state period, eg 28 days)*,

provided that the Landlord's approvals specified above may not be unreasonably withheld [or delayed].] *(omit if subletting is prohibited)*

102   This seems preferable to providing, as is sometimes done, that the head landlord's representations have to be brought to the attention of the expert or arbitrator because it would appear that he can refuse to have regard to them, the head landlord not being a party to the lease with which he is concerned.

3.9.13   *Registration of permitted dealings*

Within *(state period, eg 28 days)* of any assignment, charge, [sublease, or subunderlease,] or any transmission or other devolution relating to the Premises, the Tenant must produce a certified copy[103] of any relevant document for registration with the Landlord's solicitor, and must pay the Landlord's solicitor's [reasonable] charges for registration of at least £...

103   There seems to be no reason why the tenant should part with the original. However, under the Land Registration Rules 2003, SI 2003/1417 r 203, it is open to the applicant for registration to ask for the transfer, charge, sublease or subunderlease giving effect to the disposition to be returned for retention by the applicant, provided a certified copy of the instrument is lodged with the application. Accordingly, in such cases, applicants should use this facility if they wish to be able to lodge the lease with the landlord after its return by the registrar. If there is a time limit specified in the lease, then the registrar should be told about this, so that he is aware of the need to return the instrument within the required period.

[3.9.14   *Sharing with a group company*

Notwithstanding clause 3.9.1 ALIENATION PROHIBITED, the Tenant may share the occupation of the whole or any part of the Premises with a company that is a member of the same group as the Tenant within the meaning of the 1954 Act Section 42, for so long as both companies remain members of that group and otherwise than in a manner that transfers or creates a legal estate.] *(omit if sharing with a group company is not to be permitted)*

[1010]

3.10   Nuisance and residential restrictions

3.10.1   *Nuisance*[104]

The Tenant must not do anything on the Premises, or allow anything to remain on them that may be or become or cause a nuisance, or annoyance, disturbance, inconvenience, injury or damage to the Landlord or his tenants or the owners or occupiers of adjacent or neighbouring premises.

104   'Nuisance' is a term to be construed according to 'plain and sober and simple notions among the English people': *Walter v Selfe* (1851) 4 De G & Sm 315 at 322 per Knight-Bruce V-C. 'I have no doubt that what is a nuisance or annoyance will continue to be determined by the courts according to robust and commonsense standards': *Hampstead and Suburban Properties Ltd v Diomedous* [1969] 1 Ch 248 at 258, [1968] 3 All ER 545 at 550 per Megarry J. But a tenant can only be said to have permitted a nuisance if the landlord can show that the tenant has failed to take reasonable steps to prevent the nuisance: see *Commercial General Administration Ltd v Thomsett* [1979] 1 EGLR 62, CA.

3.10.2   *Auctions, trades and immoral purposes*

The Tenant must not use the Premises for any auction sale, any dangerous, noxious, noisy or offensive[105] trade, business, manufacture or occupation, or any illegal or immoral act or purpose.

105   As to the meaning of 'offensive' see *Re Koumoudouros and Marathon Realty Co Ltd* (1978) 89 DLR (3d) 551 where it was held that the word did not have a definite legal meaning and should be read in the context of the lease. Surrounding circumstances can affect whether a particular trade is offensive: see *Nussey v Provincial Bill Posting Co and Eddison* [1909] 1 Ch 734; *Dunraven Securities Ltd v Holloway* [1982] 2 EGLR 47, CA.

3.10.3   *Residential use, sleeping and animals*

The Tenant must not use the Premises as sleeping accommodation or for residential purposes, or keep any animal, bird or reptile on them.

[1011]

3.11   Costs of applications, notices and recovery of arrears[106]

The Tenant must pay to the Landlord on an indemnity basis all costs, fees, charges, disbursements and expenses — including, without prejudice to the generality of the above, those payable to counsel, solicitors, surveyors and bailiffs — [properly and reasonably] incurred by the Landlord in relation to or incidental to —

3.11.1   every application made by the Tenant for a consent or licence required by the provisions of this Lease, whether it is granted, refused or offered subject to any [lawful] qualification or condition or the application is withdrawn [unless the refusal, qualification or condition is unlawful, whether because it is unreasonable or otherwise],

3.11.2   the contemplation, preparation and service of a notice under the Law of Property Act 1925 Section 146, or by reason or the contemplation or taking of proceedings under Sections 146 or 147 of that Act, even if forfeiture is avoided otherwise than by relief granted by the court[107],

3.11.3   the recovery or attempted recovery of arrears of rent or other sums due under this Lease, and

3.11.4   any steps taken in [contemplation of or in] [direct] connection with the preparation and service of a schedule of dilapidations during or after the end of the Term[108].

106   As to payment of VAT on legal costs by a person other than the solicitor's own client see the Information Binder: Property [1]: VAT and Property.

107   As to forfeiture see vol 22(1) (2003 Reissue) LANDLORD AND TENANT (BUSINESS TENANCIES) Paragraph 283 [1171] et seq.

108   The landlord should not be tempted to extend this provision to costs etc incurred by him in consequence of serving a notice under the Landlord and Tenant Act 1954 s 25 because that is void: see *Stevenson and Rush (Holdings) Ltd v Langdon* (1978) 38 P & CR 208, CA.

[1012]

3.12   Planning and development

3.12.1   *Compliance with the Planning Acts*

The Tenant must observe and comply with the provisions and requirements of the Planning Acts affecting the Premises and their use, and must indemnify the Landlord, and keep him indemnified, both during the Term and following the end of it, against all losses in respect of any contravention of those Acts.

3.12.2   *Consent for applications*

The Tenant must not make any application for planning permission without the consent of the Landlord[, whose consent may not be unreasonably withheld [or delayed] [in any case where application for and implementation of the planning permission will not create or give rise to any tax liability for the Landlord or where the Tenant indemnifies the Landlord against such liability][109]].

109   These words were devised when development land tax — abolished by the Finance Act 1985 s 93 — applied. The provision may, however, still be relevant should similar taxation be introduced in the future.

3.12.3   *Permissions and notices*

The Tenant must at his expense obtain any planning permissions and serve any notices that may be required to carry out any development on or at the Premises.

3.12.4   *Charges and levies*

Subject only to any statutory direction to the contrary, the Tenant must pay and satisfy any charge or levy that may subsequently be imposed under the Planning Acts in respect of the carrying out or maintenance of any development on or at the Premises.

3.12.5   *Pre-conditions for development*

Notwithstanding any consent that may be granted by the Landlord under this Lease, the Tenant must not carry out any development on or at the Premises until all necessary notices under the Planning Acts have been served and copies produced to the Landlord, all necessary permissions under the Planning Acts have been obtained and produced to the Landlord, and the Landlord has acknowledged that every necessary planning permission is acceptable to him[, such acknowledgement not to be unreasonably withheld]. The Landlord may refuse to acknowledge his acceptance of a planning permission on the grounds that any condition contained in it or anything omitted from it or the period referred to in it would[, in the [reasonable] opinion of the Surveyor,] be, or be likely to be, prejudicial to the Landlord or his reversionary interest in the Premises whether during or following the end of the Term.

[1013]

3.12.6   *Completion of development*

Where a condition of any planning permission granted for development begun before the end of the Term[110] requires works to be carried out to the Premises by a date after the end of the Term, the Tenant must, unless the Landlord directs otherwise, finish those works before the end of the Term.

110   The provisions of clause 1.16 [962] INTERPRETATION OF 'THE LAST YEAR OF THE TERM' AND 'THE END OF THE TERM' should be noted.

3.12.7   *Security for compliance with conditions*

In any case where a planning permission is granted subject to conditions, and if the Landlord [reasonably] so requires, the Tenant must provide sufficient security for his compliance with the conditions and must not implement the planning permission until the security has been provided.

[3.12.8   *Appeal against refusal or conditions*[111]

If [reasonably] required by the Landlord to do so, but[, where reasonable,] at his own cost, the Tenant must appeal against any refusal of planning permission or the imposition of any conditions on a planning permission relating to the Premises following an application for planning permission by the Tenant.]

111   The tenant should not accept this clause because it could impose on him the cost of a planning appeal. He should strike it out, leaving planning appeals to be a matter for discussion as and when the situation arises during the term, or at least insist that he should bear the cost only where reasonable.

[1014]

3.13   Plans, documents and information

3.13.1   *Evidence of compliance with this Lease*

If so requested, the Tenant must produce to the Landlord or the Surveyor any plans, documents and other evidence the Landlord [reasonably] requires to satisfy himself that the provisions of this Lease have been complied with.

3.13.2   *Information for renewal or rent review*

If so requested, the Tenant must produce to the Landlord, the Surveyor or any person acting as the third party determining the Rent in default of agreement between the Landlord and the Tenant under any provisions for rent review contained in this Lease, any information [reasonably] requested in writing in relation to any pending or intended step under the 1954 Act or the implementation of any provisions for rent review.

3.14   Indemnities[112]

The Tenant must keep the Landlord fully indemnified against all losses arising directly or indirectly out of any act, omission or negligence of the Tenant, or any persons at the Premises expressly or impliedly[113] with his authority [and under his control][114], or any breach or non-observance by the Tenant of the covenants, conditions or other provisions of this Lease or any of the matters to which this demise is subject.

112   The tenant should seek to delete all *general* indemnity provisions on the basis that his remedies for breach of covenant and in tort adequately protect the landlord. The tenant should argue that an indemnity unreasonably extends his liability. If this clause is omitted, however, it should be replaced by a covenant to observe and perform the restrictions etc to which the demise is subject, possibly coupled with a *specific* indemnity in respect of any breach.

113   The expression 'impliedly' is intended to include a caller on the premises, such as a tradesman, where there has been no express invitation but the person cannot be classed as a trespasser.

114   The tenant should add the words in square brackets.

[1015]

3.15   Reletting boards and viewing

[Unless [a valid court application under the 1954 Act Section 24 has been made or][115] the tenant is [otherwise] entitled to remain in occupation or to a new tenancy of the Premises, at any time during *(or as required)* At any time during] the *(state period, eg last 6 months)* of the [Contractual] Term[116] and at any time thereafter, [and whenever the Lease Rents or any part of them are in arrear and unpaid for longer than *(state period, eg 14 days),*] the Tenant must permit the Landlord to enter the Premises and fix and retain anywhere on them a board advertising them for reletting. While any such board is on the Premises the Tenant must permit viewing of the Premises at reasonable times of the day.

115   This phrase and the word 'otherwise' should be omitted if the operation of the security of tenure provisions in the Landlord and Tenant Act 1954 ss 24–28 is to be excluded in relation to the lease.

116   This defined term will require amendment where the operation of the security of tenure provisions in the Landlord and Tenant Act 1954 ss 24–28 is to be excluded in relation to the lease: see note 6 to clause 1.2 [957] 'THE [CONTRACTUAL] TERM'.

3.16   Obstruction and encroachment

3.16.1   *Obstruction of windows*

The Tenant must not stop up, darken or obstruct any window or light belonging to the Premises.

3.16.2   *Encroachments*

The Tenant must take all [reasonable] steps to prevent the construction of any new window, light, opening, doorway, path, passage, pipe or the making of any encroachment or the acquisition of any easement in relation to the Premises and must notify the Landlord immediately if any such thing is constructed, encroachment is made or easement acquired, or if any attempt is made to construct such a thing, encroach or acquire an easement. At the request of the Landlord the Tenant must adopt such means as are [reasonably] required to prevent the construction of such a thing, the making of any encroachment or the acquisition of any easement[117].

117   For a shorter clause see vol 22(3) (1997 Reissue) LANDLORD AND TENANT (BUSINESS TENANCIES) Form 172 [6696].

[1016]

3.17   Yielding up

At the end of the Term[118] the Tenant must yield up the Premises with vacant possession, decorated and repaired in accordance with and in the condition required by the provisions of this Lease, give up all keys of the Premises to the Landlord, remove tenant's fixtures and fittings [if requested to do so by the Landlord] and remove any signs erected by the Tenant or any of his predecessors in title in, on or near the Premises, immediately making good any damage caused by their removal.

118   The provisions of clause 1.16 [962] INTERPRETATION OF 'THE LAST YEAR OF THE TERM' AND 'THE END OF THE TERM' should be noted.

3.18   Interest on arrears[119]

The Tenant must pay interest on any of the Lease Rents[120] or other sums due under this Lease that are not paid [within *(state period, eg 14 days)* of the date due], whether formally demanded or not[, the interest to be recoverable as rent][121]. Nothing in this clause entitles the Tenant to withhold or delay any payment of the Lease Rents or any other sum due under this Lease or affects the rights of the Landlord in relation to any non-payment.

119   As to the covenant to pay interest see vol 22(1) (2003 Reissue) LANDLORD AND TENANT (BUSINESS TENANCIES) Paragraph 154 [767].
120   As to the definition of 'the Lease Rents' see clause 1.32 [967] 'THE RENT'.
121   These words seek to attach to interest the rights associated with rent. As to the reasons for this see vol 22(1) (2003 Reissue) LANDLORD AND TENANT (BUSINESS TENANCIES) Paragraph 151 [761]. However, this clause applies to interest on arrears of other sums payable under the lease that are not rent as well as to rent itself, and it might be felt inappropriate for interest to be deemed to be rent where the payment on which the interest is due is not rent.

3.19   Statutory notices

The Tenant must give full particulars to the Landlord of any notice, direction, order or proposal relating to the Premises made, given or issued to the Tenant by any government department or local, public, regulatory or other authority or court within *(state period, eg 7 days)* of receipt, and if so requested by the Landlord must produce it to the Landlord.

The Tenant must without delay take all necessary steps to comply with the notice, direction or order. At the request of the Landlord, but at his own cost, the Tenant must make or join with the Landlord in making any objection or representation the Landlord deems expedient against or in respect of any notice, direction, order or proposal.

3.20   Keyholders

The Tenant must ensure that at all times [the Landlord has *(or as required)* the Landlord and the local police force have] written notice of the name, home address and home telephone number of at least *(state number, eg 2)* keyholders of the Premises.

[1017]

3.21   Viewing on sale of reversion

The Tenant must[, on reasonable notice,] at any time during the Term, permit prospective purchasers of the Landlord's reversion or any other interest superior to the Term, or agents instructed in connection with the sale of the reversion or such an interest, to view the Premises without interruption provided they have the prior written authority of the Landlord or his agents.

3.22   Defective premises

The Tenant must give notice to the Landlord of any defect in the Premises that might give rise to an obligation on the Landlord to do or refrain from doing anything in order to comply with the provisions of this Lease or the duty of care imposed on the Landlord, whether pursuant to the Defective Premises Act 1972 or otherwise, and must at all times display and maintain any notices the Landlord from time to time [reasonably] requires him to display at the Premises.

3.23   Replacement guarantor[122]

3.23.1   *Guarantor replacement events*

In this clause 3.23 references to a 'guarantor replacement event' are references, in the case of an individual, to death, bankruptcy, having a receiving order made against him, having a receiver appointed under the Mental Health Act 1983 or entering into a voluntary arrangement and, in the case of a company, to passing a resolution to wind up, entering into liquidation, a voluntary arrangement or administration or having a receiver appointed.

---

122   As to guarantors see vol 22(1) (2003 Reissue) LANDLORD AND TENANT (BUSINESS TENANCIES) Paragraph 71 [278] et seq. The tenant should propose that, on the execution of a guarantee by a new guarantor, the original guarantor or his estate should be released.

3.23.2   *Action on occurrence of a guarantor replacement event*

Where during the relevant Liability Period a guarantor replacement event occurs to the Guarantor or any person who has entered into an authorised guarantee agreement, the Tenant must give notice of the event to the Landlord within *(state period, eg 14 days)* of his becoming aware of it. If so required by the Landlord, the Tenant must within *(state period, eg 28 days)* obtain some other person [reasonably] acceptable to the Landlord to execute a guarantee in the form of the Guarantor's covenants in clause 6 GUARANTEE PROVISIONS or the authorised guarantee agreement in schedule 5 THE AUTHORISED GUARANTEE AGREEMENT, as the case may be, for the residue of the relevant Liability Period.

[1018]

3.24   Exercise of the Landlord's rights[123]

The Tenant must permit the Landlord to exercise any of the rights granted to him by virtue of the provisions of this Lease at all times during the Term without interruption or interference.

123   The provisions of clause 1.30 [967] REFERENCES TO RIGHTS OF ACCESS should be noted.

3.25   The Shop Covenants

The Tenant must observe and perform the Shop Covenants.

3.26   Costs of grant of this Lease[124]

[The Tenant must pay the fees and disbursements of the Landlord's solicitors, agents and surveyors and all other costs and expenses incurred by the Landlord in relation to the negotiation, preparation, execution and grant of this Lease. *(or as required)* On the grant of this lease, the Tenant must pay the sum of £... as a contribution to the Landlord's solicitors' charges for the negotiation, execution and completion of this Lease].

124   As to covenants to pay the landlord's legal fees see vol 22(1) (2003 Reissue) LANDLORD AND TENANT (BUSINESS TENANCIES) Paragraph 155 [769]. As to payment of VAT on legal costs by a person other than the solicitor's own client see the Information Binder: Property [1]: VAT and Property.

3.27   Consent to the Landlord's release[125]

The Tenant must not unreasonably withhold consent to a request made by the Landlord under the 1995 Act Section 8 for a release from all or any of the landlord covenants of this Lease.

125   By virtue of the Landlord and Tenant (Covenants) Act 1995 each successive landlord remains bound by the landlord covenants of the lease unless released under the machinery provided in the Act — as to which see vol 22(1) (2003 Reissue) LANDLORD AND TENANT (BUSINESS TENANCIES) Paragraph 57 [252] et seq — or by a specific release given otherwise (see the Landlord and Tenant (Covenants) Act 1995 s 26(1)(a)). Bald statements limiting the landlord's liability, such as those in use before the commencement of the Act, will not withstand the wide anti-avoidance provisions of the Landlord and Tenant (Covenants) Act 1995 s 25, and covenants by the tenant to give consent to release are unlikely to fall within the exception of s 26. None of the ingenious schemes for limiting the landlord's liability, eg making all covenants personal, suggested in the early days of the 1995 Act has stood up to critical scrutiny, although none has yet been tested by the courts. Thus landlords look instead to the alternative of a right of redress if the tenant makes an unreasonable objection to release. This covenant is modelled on the provisions of the Landlord and Tenant Act 1988, which gives tenants a right of action for loss caused by landlords who unreasonably withhold or delay consent to assignment (see the Landlord and Tenant Act 1988 s 4). In view of the strict time limits under the Landlord and Tenant (Covenants) Act 1995 and the fact that failure to respond to the landlord's request for release is deemed to be consent, it is not thought necessary to extend this covenant to unreasonable delay in replying to such a request.

[1019]–[1030]

4   QUIET ENJOYMENT[126]

The Landlord covenants with the Tenant to permit the Tenant peaceably and quietly to hold and enjoy the Premises without any interruption or disturbance from or by the Landlord or any person claiming under or in trust for him[127] [or by title paramount][128].

126   As to the landlord's covenant for quiet enjoyment see vol 22(1) (2003 Reissue) LANDLORD AND TENANT (BUSINESS TENANCIES) Paragraph 168 [856]. As to covenants for quiet enjoyment generally see 23 Halsbury's Laws (4th Edn Reissue) LANDLORD AND TENANT.
          The words 'the Tenant paying the rents reserved by and observing and performing the covenants on his part and the conditions contained in this lease' are frequently included in a covenant for quiet enjoyment, but they have no practical effect and do not make payment of the rent and performance of the covenants into conditions precedent to the operation of the covenant: see *Edge v Boileau* (1885) 16 QBD 117; *Dawson v Dyer* (1833) 5 B & Ad 584; *Yorkbrook Investments Ltd v Batten* (1985) 52 P & CR 51, [1985] 2 EGLR 100, CA.

127   The covenant is frequently expressed to apply to 'lawful interruption' by persons 'rightfully claiming' under the landlord, but it seems that the addition of these words has no practical effect: see *Williams v Gabriel* [1906] 1 KB 155 at 157.

128   Without the reference to title paramount the landlord is liable only for the acts of persons so far as they are his successors in title or have authority from him to do the acts complained of: *Harrison Ainslie & Co v Muncaster* [1891] 2 QB 680, CA; *Matania v National Provincial Bank Ltd and Elevenist Syndicate Ltd* [1936] 2 All ER 633, CA; *Miller v Emcer Products Ltd* [1956] Ch 304, [1956] 1 All ER 237, CA. If a subtenant holds under a lease containing a qualified covenant on the part of his landlord — ie one where there is no reference to title paramount — and the head landlord evicts the subtenant because the head rent has not been paid, this is not a breach of the covenant for quiet enjoyment (see *Spencer v Marriott* (1823) 1 B & C 457; *Dennett v Atherton* (1872) LR 7 QB 316, Ex Ch), but it is a breach if the sublandlord submits to judgment in an action by a person with no title to sue, and the subtenant is in consequence evicted (*Cohen v Tannar* [1900] 2 QB 609, CA). Actionable interruptions under this covenant are not confined to interference with title or possession, but may extend to interference with the ordinary and lawful enjoyment of the premises: *Sanderson v Berwick-upon-Tweed Corpn* (1884) 13 QBD 547 at 551, CA. As to persons claiming 'under' the landlord see *Celsteel Ltd v Alton House Holdings Ltd (No 2)* [1987] 2 All ER 240, [1987] 1 WLR 291, CA.

[1031]

5   INSURANCE[129]

5.1   Warranty as to convictions[130]

The Tenant warrants that before the execution of this document he has disclosed to the Landlord in writing any conviction, judgment or finding of any court or tribunal relating to the Tenant[, or any director, other officer or major shareholder of the Tenant,] of such a nature as to be likely to affect the decision of any insurer or underwriter to grant or to continue insurance of any of the Insured Risks.

129   As to insurance see vol 22(1) (2003 Reissue) LANDLORD AND TENANT (BUSINESS TENANCIES) Paragraph 227 [1021] et seq.

130   A contract of insurance is one uberrimae fidei. The insured must disclose to the insurers all material facts that are within his actual or presumed knowledge, whether there is a formal proposal form or not. A fact is material if non-disclosure of it would influence a prudent and reasonable insurer. This warranty is designed to rebut any suggestion by the landlord's insurers that the landlord had knowledge of the matters concerned. By inserting this clause in the lease, and thus specifically bringing the point to the tenant's attention, the landlord can argue that he has done all that is practical to establish the existence of any such matters. The absence of any written disclosure pursuant to this clause is strong evidence that the landlord has no actual or presumed knowledge of such matters. Further, the landlord has a right of action against the tenant for any breach of the warranty. As to non-disclosure and misrepresentation in contracts of non-marine insurance see 22 Halsbury's Laws (4th Edn Reissue) INSURANCE.

5.2   Covenant to insure

The Landlord covenants with the Tenant to insure the Premises [in the joint names of the Landlord and the Tenant[131] [and any other person the Landlord [reasonably] requires][132] unless the insurance is vitiated by any act of the Tenant or by anyone at the Premises expressly or by implication[133] with his authority [and under his control][134].

131   As to insurance in joint names see vol 22(1) (2003 Reissue) LANDLORD AND TENANT (BUSINESS TENANCIES) Paragraph 229 [1024].
132   Unless some expression such as this is included, a covenant to insure in specified names is broken by insurance in those and other names: see *Penniall v Harborne* (1848) 11 QB 368.
133   The expression 'by implication' is intended to include a caller on the premises, such as a tradesman, where there has been no express invitation but the person cannot be classed as a trespasser.
134   The tenant should add the words in square brackets.

[1032]

5.3   Details of the insurance

5.3.1   *Office, underwriters and agency*

Insurance is to be effected in such [substantial and reputable] insurance office, or with such underwriters[135], and through such agency as the Landlord from time to time decides[136].

135   The expression 'insurance office' would probably not include Lloyd's underwriters. The landlord's right to nominate the office and agency is absolute, with no implied restrictions: *Berrycroft Management Co Ltd v Sinclair Gardens Investments (Kensington) Ltd* (1996) 75 P & CR 210, [1997] 1 EGLR 47, CA.
136   It should be noted that it is recommended 'best practice' in circumstances where the building is let to one tenant and the landlord insures that, in appropriate cases, the tenant should be given the opportunity to influence the choice of insurer: see vol 22(1) (2003 Reissue) LANDLORD AND TENANT (BUSINESS TENANCIES) Paragraph 85 [401] and 'A code of practice for commercial leases in England and Wales (2nd edition)' which can be found in vol 22(1) (2003 Reissue) LANDLORD AND TENANT (BUSINESS TENANCIES) at Form 1 [4501].

5.3.2   *Insurance cover*[137]

Insurance must be effected for the following amounts —

5.3.2.1   the sum that the Landlord is from time to time advised [by the Surveyor] is the full cost of rebuilding and reinstating the Premises, including [VAT[138],] architects', surveyors', engineers', solicitors' and all other professional persons' fees, the fees payable on any applications for planning permission or other permits or consents that may be required in relation to rebuilding or reinstating the Premises, the cost of preparation of the site including shoring-up, debris removal, demolition, site clearance and any works that may be required by statute, and incidental expenses, and

5.3.2.2   loss of the Rent, taking account of any rent review that may be due, for *(state period, eg 3 years)* or such longer period as the Landlord from time to time [reasonably] requires for planning and carrying out the rebuilding or reinstatement.

137   As to the sum insured see vol 22(1) (2003 Reissue) LANDLORD AND TENANT (BUSINESS TENANCIES) Paragraph 231 [1028] et seq.
        It should be noted that it is recommended 'best practice' that, where the landlord has arranged insurance, the terms should be made known to the tenant and any material change in the insurance should be notified to the tenant: see Recommendation 14 of 'A code of practice for commercial leases in England and Wales (2nd edition)' which can be found in vol 22(1) (2003 Reissue) LANDLORD AND TENANT (BUSINESS TENANCIES) at Form 1 [4501].

138   As to VAT and the level of insurance cover see the Information Binder: Property [1]: VAT and
Property. The expense of insuring against the VAT payable on reinstatement costs is not justified where
the landlord has opted to tax and will be able to recover the VAT. There is a theoretical possibility that
a future landlord may not opt to tax and that the sum insured may then be too low. It is also possible
that a landlord may wish to preserve the 'exempt' status of a property. Normally, however, the cost of
reinstatement need not expressly mention VAT, although the cashflow implications of having to pay
VAT on construction works need to be remembered.

5.3.3   *Risks insured*[139]

Insurance must be effected against damage or destruction by any of the Insured Risks to
the extent that such insurance may ordinarily be arranged [with a substantial and
reputable insurer], for properties such as the Premises subject to such excesses, exclusions
or limitations as the insurer requires.

139   As to risks to be insured against see vol 22(1) (2003 Reissue) LANDLORD AND TENANT (BUSINESS
TENANCIES) Paragraph 235 [1033].
    It should be noted that it is recommended 'best practice' that, where the landlord has arranged
insurance, the terms should be made known to the tenant and any material change in the insurance
should be notified to the tenant: see Recommendation 14 of 'A code of practice for commercial leases
in England and Wales (2nd edition)' which can be found in vol 22(1) (2003 Reissue) LANDLORD AND
TENANT (BUSINESS TENANCIES) at Form 1 [4501].

[1033]

5.4   Payment of the Insurance Rent

The Tenant covenants to pay the Insurance Rent for the period commencing on the
Rent Commencement Date and ending on the day before the next policy renewal date
on the date of this Lease, and subsequently to pay the Insurance Rent on demand and,
if so demanded, in advance of the policy renewal date[, but not more than *(state period,
eg … months)* in advance].

5.5   Suspension of the Rent[140]

5.5.1   *Events giving rise to suspension*

If and whenever the Premises or any part of them are damaged or destroyed by one or
more of the Insured Risks[141] [— except one against which insurance may not ordinarily
be arranged [with a substantial and reputable insurer] for properties such as the Premises
unless the Landlord has in fact insured against that risk —] so that the Premises or any
part of them are unfit for occupation or use, and payment of the insurance money is not
refused in whole or in part by reason of any act or default of the Tenant or anyone at the
Premises expressly or by implication[142] with his authority [and under his control][143], then
the provisions of clause 5.5.2 SUSPENDING THE RENT are to have effect.

140   As to suspension of rent see vol 22(1) (2003 Reissue) LANDLORD AND TENANT (BUSINESS
TENANCIES) Paragraph 241 [1044] et seq.
141   It should be noted that it is recommended 'best practice' that if premises are so damaged by an
uninsured risk as to prevent occupation, the tenant should be allowed to terminate the lease unless the
landlord agrees to reinstate at his own cost: see vol 22(1) (2003 Reissue) LANDLORD AND TENANT
(BUSINESS TENANCIES) Paragraph 85 [402] and 'A code of practice for commercial leases in England
and Wales (2nd edition)' which can be found in vol 22(1) (2003 Reissue) LANDLORD AND TENANT
(BUSINESS TENANCIES) at Form 1 [4501]. If adopted, this recommendation involves rent suspension
also becoming operative in the event of the premises becoming unusable because of uninsured risks.
142   The expression 'by implication' is intended to include a caller on the premises, such as a tradesman,
where there has been no express invitation but the person cannot be classed as a trespasser.
143   The tenant should add the words in square brackets.

[1034]

5.5.2   *Suspending the Rent*

In the circumstances mentioned in clause 5.5.1 EVENTS GIVING RISE TO SUSPENSION the Rent, or a fair proportion of it according to the nature and the extent of the damage sustained, is to cease to be payable until the Premises, or the affected part, have been rebuilt or reinstated so as to render the Premises, or the affected part, fit for occupation and use, [or until the end of *(state period, eg 3 years)* from the destruction or damage, whichever period is the shorter,][144] [the proportion of the Rent suspended and the period of the suspension to be determined by the Surveyor acting as an expert and not as an arbitrator *(or as required)* any dispute as to the proportion of the Rent suspended or the period of the suspension to be determined in accordance with the Arbitration Act 1996 by an arbitrator to be appointed by agreement between the Landlord and the Tenant or in default by the President or other proper officer for the time being of the Royal Institution of Chartered Surveyors on the application of either the Landlord or the Tenant].

144   As to the length of the suspension and the tenant's concerns see vol 22(1) (2003 Reissue) LANDLORD AND TENANT (BUSINESS TENANCIES) Paragraph 244 [1048]. For a provision extending suspension of the rent where reinstatement is delayed see vol 22(3) (1997 Reissue) LANDLORD AND TENANT (BUSINESS TENANCIES) Form 111 [6495].

5.6   **Reinstatement and termination**[145]

5.6.1   *Obligation to obtain permissions*

If and whenever the Premises or any part of them are damaged or destroyed by one or more of the Insured Risks [— except one against which insurance may not ordinarily be arranged [with a substantial and reputable insurer] for properties such as the Premises, unless the Landlord has in fact insured against that risk —] and payment of the insurance money is not wholly or partly refused because of any act or default of the Tenant or anyone at the Premises expressly or by implication[146] with his authority [and under his control][147], the Landlord must use his best endeavours[148] to obtain all the planning permissions or other permits and consents ('permissions') that are required under the Planning Acts or otherwise to enable him to rebuild and reinstate the Premises.

[1035]

145   It has been held that, in the absence of an express covenant to reinstate, where the landlord must keep the premises adequately insured against comprehensive risks and the insurance is effected at the tenant's expense, the obligation is one intended to enure for the benefit of both parties: *Mumford Hotels Ltd v Wheler* [1964] Ch 117, [1963] 3 All ER 250; see also *Mark Rowlands Ltd v Berni Inns Ltd* [1986] QB 211, [1985] 3 All ER 473, CA; *Lonsdale & Thompson Ltd v Black Arrow Group plc* [1993] Ch 361, [1993] 3 All ER 648. This is not, however, a general principle of law and the tenant should therefore always require a specific covenant to reinstate.

These provisions are restricted to circumstances where damage or destruction is caused by an insured risk. It should be noted that it is recommended 'best practice' that if premises are so damaged by an uninsured risk as to prevent occupation, the tenant should be allowed to terminate the lease unless the landlord agrees to reinstate at his own cost: see vol 22(1) (2003 Reissue) LANDLORD AND TENANT (BUSINESS TENANCIES) Paragraph 85 [401] and 'A code of practice for commercial leases in England and Wales (2nd edition)' which can be found in vol 22(1) (2003 Reissue) LANDLORD AND TENANT (BUSINESS TENANCIES) at Form 1 [4501].

As to reinstatement and termination where reinstatement is not possible see vol 22(1) (2003 Reissue) LANDLORD AND TENANT (BUSINESS TENANCIES) Paragraph 237 [1037] et seq. For a provision for termination or surrender on destruction or substantial damage see vol 22(3) (1997 Reissue) LANDLORD AND TENANT (BUSINESS TENANCIES) Form 107 [6483].

146   The expression 'by implication' is intended to include a caller on the premises, such as a tradesman, where there has been no express invitation but the person cannot be classed as a trespasser.

147   The tenant should add the words in square brackets.

148   The extent of the duty to use best endeavours depends upon the facts in each case: see *Monkland v Jack Barclay Ltd* [1951] 2 KB 252, [1951] 1 All ER 714, CA; *Terrell v Mabie Todd & Co Ltd* [1952] 2 TLR 574; *NW Investments (Erdington) Ltd v Swani* (1970) 214 Estates Gazette 1115. In the light of *IBM United Kingdom Ltd v Rockware Glass Ltd* [1980] FSR 335, CA, it may be that there is little practical difference between a covenant to use best endeavours, a covenant to use reasonable endeavours and a covenant to take all reasonable steps.

[1036]

5.6.2   *Obligation to reinstate*

Subject to the provisions of clause 5.6.3 RELIEF FROM THE OBLIGATION TO REINSTATE, and, if any permissions are required, after they have been obtained, the Landlord must as soon as reasonably practicable apply all money received in respect of the insurance effected by the Landlord pursuant to this Lease, except sums in respect of loss of the Rent, in rebuilding or reinstating the Premises[, making up any difference between the cost of rebuilding and reinstating and the money received out of his own money][149].

149   Where the landlord's covenant is 'to apply all money received in respect of the insurance in rebuilding or reinstating' rather than simply 'to reinstate', it seems that the landlord does not have to complete the work out of his own money if the insurance money is insufficient because he has complied with his covenant by laying out all the insurance money received. The situation is different if the tenant can establish that the landlord was in breach of his covenant to insure for the full cost of reinstatement and that this has caused the shortfall: see *Mumford Hotels Ltd v Wheler* [1964] Ch 117, [1963] 3 All ER 250. The tenant should, therefore, require a specific covenant from the landlord to make up any shortfall, to prevent a situation in which the landlord refuses to complete the rebuilding. This is of particular concern if the suspension of rent proviso is expressed to operate for a limited period, because on the expiry of that period the tenant becomes liable for rent unless he can satisfy the court that the lease has been frustrated.
        It should be noted that it is recommended 'best practice' that if premises are so damaged by an uninsured risk as to prevent occupation, the tenant should be allowed to terminate the lease unless the landlord agrees to reinstate at his own cost: see vol 22(1) (2003 Reissue) LANDLORD AND TENANT (BUSINESS TENANCIES) Paragraph 85 [401] and 'A code of practice for commercial leases in England and Wales (2nd edition)'which can be found in vol 22(1) (2003 Reissue) LANDLORD AND TENANT (BUSINESS TENANCIES) at Form 1 [4501]. If this recommendation is adopted and the landlord merely covenants to apply insurance money received, the principle should be extended to damage or destruction resulting from insured risks in circumstances where the insurance money is insufficient to enable reinstatement to be completed.
        For a proviso relieving from the obligation to reinstate in the same form see vol 22(3) (1997 Reissue) LANDLORD AND TENANT (BUSINESS TENANCIES) Form 106 [6482].

[1037]

5.6.3   *Relief from the obligation to reinstate*[150]

The Landlord need not rebuild or reinstate the Premises if and for so long as rebuilding or reinstatement is prevented because —

5.6.3.1   the Landlord, despite using his best endeavours[151], cannot obtain any necessary permission,

5.6.3.2   any permission is granted subject to a lawful condition with which [it is impossible for *(or as required)* in all the circumstances it is unreasonable to expect] the Landlord to comply,

5.6.3.3   there is some defect or deficiency in the site on which the rebuilding or reinstatement is to take place that [renders it impossible *(or as required)* means it can only be undertaken at a cost that is unreasonable in all the circumstances],

5.6.3.4   the Landlord is unable to obtain access to the site to rebuild or reinstate,

5.6.3.5   the rebuilding or reinstating is prevented by war, act of God, government action[, strike or lock-out], or

because of the occurrence of any other circumstances beyond the Landlord's control.

150   As to the need for a right to terminate where reinstatement is not possible see vol 22(1) (2003 Reissue)
       LANDLORD AND TENANT (BUSINESS TENANCIES) Paragraph 226 [998].

151   The extent of the duty to use best endeavours depends upon the facts in each case: see *Monkland v Jack
       Barclay Ltd* [1951] 2 KB 252, [1951] 1 All ER 714, CA; *Terrell v Mabie Todd & Co Ltd* [1952] 2 TLR
       574; *NW Investments (Erdington) Ltd v Swani* (1970) 214 Estates Gazette 1115. In the light of *IBM United
       Kingdom Ltd v Rockware Glass Ltd* [1980] FSR 335, CA, it may be that there is little practical difference
       between a covenant to use best endeavours, a covenant to use reasonable endeavours and a covenant
       to take all reasonable steps.

[1038]

5.6.4   *Notice to terminate*[152]

If at the end of the period[153] of *(state period, eg 3 years)* starting on the date of the damage
or destruction the Premises are still not fit for the Tenant's occupation and use, either
the Landlord or the Tenant may by notice served at any time within *(state period, eg 6
months)* of the end of that period ('a notice to terminate following failure to reinstate')
implement the provisions of clause 5.6.5 TERMINATION FOLLOWING FAILURE TO
REINSTATE[154].

152   For alternative provisions where the landlord's right to terminate is limited to specified circumstances
       see vol 22(3) (1997 Reissue) LANDLORD AND TENANT (BUSINESS TENANCIES) Form 109 [6492].

153   The period to be inserted must be carefully considered. Particular regard should be had to the terms of
       any rent suspension provision and the extent of insurance cover for loss of rent.

154   As to the effect of the Landlord and Tenant Act 1954 see vol 22(1) (2003 Reissue) LANDLORD AND
       TENANT (BUSINESS TENANCIES) Paragraph 226 [998].

5.6.5   *Termination following failure to reinstate*

On service of a notice to terminate following failure to reinstate, the Term is to cease
absolutely — but without prejudice to any rights or remedies that may have accrued[155]—
and all money received in respect of the insurance effected by the Landlord pursuant to
this Lease is to belong to the Landlord absolutely[156].

155   The effect of this clause is that the right to terminate arises after the end of the appropriate period,
       whatever the reason for the delay, but the tenant still has a right of action against the landlord if the
       landlord is in breach of his covenant to reinstate.

156   In the absence of provision for ownership of the insurance money the position is uncertain. In *Re King,
       Robinson v Gray* [1963] Ch 459, [1963] 1 All ER 781, CA it was held that the insurance money belongs
       to the party who paid the premiums even if the insurance was placed in the joint names of the landlord
       and the tenant. The dissenting view of Denning MR that insurance in joint names envisages that each
       party should be insured as to his insurable interest and that the insurance money should therefore be
       divided in proportion to their interests in the property should, however, be noted. In *Beacon Carpets
       Ltd v Kirby* [1985] QB 755, [1984] 2 All ER 726, CA the court adhered to this view and held that the
       proportion payable depended on the parties' interests in the premises at the time of the destruction.
       The landlord will prefer an express provision in the lease for the insurance money to be retained by
       him in full if reinstatement proves impossible. The tenant ought perhaps to accept that it would be
       unrealistic to amend this to provide for the insurance money to belong to the tenant, but should suggest
       that a provision be inserted under which the money is to be divided in accordance with their respective
       interests in the premises at the time when the insurance money became due. For an alternative
       provision for ownership of the insurance money etc, see vol 22(3) (1997 Reissue) LANDLORD AND
       TENANT (BUSINESS TENANCIES) Form 108 [6491].

[1039]

5.7   Tenant's further insurance covenants[157]

The Tenant covenants with the Landlord to observe and perform the requirements contained in this clause 5.7.

157   In order to comply with many of these covenants, the tenant will need to be supplied with details of the landlord's insurance policy. In any event, it should be noted that it is recommended 'best practice' that where the landlord has arranged insurance, the terms should be made known to the tenant and any material change in the insurance should be notified to the tenant: see Recommendation 14 of 'A code of practice for commercial leases in England and Wales (2nd edition)' which can be found in vol 22(1) (2003 Reissue) LANDLORD AND TENANT (BUSINESS TENANCIES) at Form 1 [4501].

5.7.1   *Requirements of insurers*

The Tenant must comply with all the requirements and recommendations of the insurers.

5.7.2   *Policy avoidance and additional premiums*

The Tenant must not do or omit anything that could cause any insurance policy on or in relation to the Premises to become wholly or partly void or voidable, or do or omit anything by which additional insurance premiums may become payable unless he has previously notified the Landlord and has agreed to pay the increased premium.

5.7.3   *Fire-fighting equipment*

The Tenant must keep the Premises supplied with such fire fighting equipment [as the insurers and the fire authority require and must maintain the equipment to their satisfaction *(or as required)* as the Landlord reasonably requires and must maintain the equipment to the reasonable satisfaction of the insurers and the fire authority] and in efficient working order. At least once in every *(state period, eg 6 months)* the Tenant must cause any sprinkler system and other fire fighting equipment to be inspected by a competent person.

5.7.4   *Combustible materials*

The Tenant must not store on the Premises or bring onto them anything of a specially combustible, inflammable or explosive nature, and must comply with the requirements and recommendations of the fire authority [and the [reasonable] requirements of the Landlord] as to fire precautions relating to the Premises.

[1040]

5.7.5   *Fire escapes, equipment and doors*

The Tenant must not obstruct the access to any fire equipment or the means of escape from the Premises, or lock any fire door while the Premises are occupied.

5.7.6   *Notice of events affecting the policy*

The Tenant must give immediate notice to the Landlord of any event that might affect any insurance policy on or relating to the Premises, and any event against which the Landlord may have insured under this Lease.

5.7.7   *Notice of convictions*

The Tenant must give immediate notice to the Landlord of any conviction, judgment or finding of any court or tribunal relating to the Tenant, or any director other officer or major shareholder of the Tenant, of such a nature as to be likely to affect the decision of any insurer or underwriter to grant or to continue any insurance[158].

158   This clause provides a continuation of the warranty given by the tenant in clause 5.1 [1032] WARRANTY AS TO CONVICTIONS. As to non-disclosure and misrepresentation in contracts of non-marine insurance see 22 Halsbury's Laws (4th Edn Reissue) INSURANCE.

5.7.8   *Other insurance*

If at any time the Tenant is entitled to the benefit of any insurance of the Premises that is not effected or maintained in pursuance of any obligation contained in this Lease, the Tenant must apply all money received by virtue of that insurance in making good the loss or damage in respect of which the money is received[159].

159   An insurance policy frequently provides that if there is any other insurance effected by or on behalf of the insured, covering the premises that are the subject of the policy, the insurers are liable only for a rateable proportion of the damage. Such provisions extend to a case where one of the policies is in the joint names of the persons interested in the premises and the other is in the name of one only of those persons: *Halifax Building Society v Keighley* [1931] 2 KB 248. Therefore, at least when the insurance is in joint names, the landlord must ensure that the tenant will use all money received under any policy he has effected to reinstate the premises.

[1041]

[5.7.9   *Reinstatement on refusal of money through default*

If at any time the Premises or any part of them are damaged or destroyed by one or more of the Insured Risks and the insurance money under the policy of insurance effected by the Landlord pursuant to his obligations contained in this Lease is wholly or partly irrecoverable because of any act or default of the Tenant or of anyone at the Premises expressly or by implication[160] with his authority [and under his control][161], the Tenant must immediately, at the option of the Landlord, either rebuild and reinstate the Premises or the part of them destroyed or damaged, to the reasonable satisfaction and under the supervision of the Surveyor — in which case, on completion of the rebuilding and refurbishment, the Landlord must pay to the Tenant the amount that the Landlord has actually received under the insurance policy in respect of the destruction or damage — or pay to the Landlord on demand [with interest] the amount of the insurance money so irrecoverable — in which case the provisions of clauses 5.5 SUSPENSION OF THE RENT and 5.6 REINSTATEMENT AND TERMINATION are to apply.]

160   The expression 'by implication' is intended to include a caller on the premises, such as a tradesman, where there has been no express invitation but the person cannot be classed as a trespasser.
161   The tenant should add the words in square brackets.

[5.8   Landlord's further insurance covenants[162]

The Landlord covenants with the Tenant to observe and perform the requirements set out in this clause 5.8 in relation to the insurance policy he has effected pursuant to his obligations contained in this Lease.

162   Unless insurance is to be in the joint names of the landlord and the tenant, the tenant should seek covenants such as these from the landlord.

5.8.1   Copy policy

The Landlord must produce to the Tenant on demand [a copy of the policy and the last premium renewal receipt *(or as required)* reasonable evidence of the terms of the policy and the fact that the last premium has been paid][163].

> 163   The landlord can reasonably insist on the second alternative. If the premises are insured under a block policy, it would be inappropriate for him to have to disclose to the tenant information about his other properties.
>
> It should be noted that it is recommended 'best practice' that where the landlord has arranged insurance, the terms should be made known to the tenant and any material change in the insurance should be notified to the tenant: see Recommendation 14 of 'A code of practice for commercial leases in England and Wales (2nd edition)' which can be found in vol 22(1) (2003 Reissue) LANDLORD AND TENANT (BUSINESS TENANCIES) at Form 1 [4501].
>
> **[1042]**

5.8.2   Noting of the Tenant's interest

The Landlord must ensure that the interest of the Tenant is noted or endorsed on the policy[164].

> 164   Where insurance in the joint names of the landlord and the tenant is not practical, the tenant should insist that a note of his interest is endorsed on the policy. This protects the tenant because the insurers should give notice to him of any lapse in the policy and, where it can be shown that the tenant is responsible for the insurance premium under the terms of the lease, it is likely — but not certain — that the insurers would not exercise subrogation rights against the tenant.
>
> It is recommended 'best practice' that where the landlord has arranged insurance, any interest of the tenant should be covered by the policy: see Recommendation 14 of 'A code of practice for commercial leases in England and Wales (2nd edition)' which can be found in vol 22(1) (2003 Reissue) LANDLORD AND TENANT (BUSINESS TENANCIES) at Form 1 [4501].

5.8.3   Change of risks

The Landlord must notify the Tenant of any [material] change in the risks covered by the policy from time to time[165].

> 165   It should be noted that it is recommended 'best practice' that where the landlord has arranged insurance, the terms should be made known to the tenant and any material change in the insurance should be notified to the tenant: see Recommendation 14 of 'A code of practice for commercial leases in England and Wales (2nd edition)' which can be found in vol 22(1) (2003 Reissue) LANDLORD AND TENANT (BUSINESS TENANCIES) at Form 1 [4501].

[5.8.4   Waiver of subrogation[166]

The Landlord must produce to the Tenant on demand written confirmation from the insurers that they have agreed to waive all rights of subrogation against the Tenant.]]

> 166   Generally an insurer who has paid out under a policy stands in the shoes of the insured with regard to any claim the latter may have had against any third party. If the insurance is in joint names, the tenant is an insured party and there can be no subrogation against him. It would seem, also, that where the tenant covenants to reimburse the landlord for sums expended by the landlord in insuring the premises, the landlord's insurers cannot make a subrogated claim against the tenant where the premises are destroyed by the tenant's negligence: *Mark Rowlands Ltd v Berni Inns Ltd* [1986] QB 211, [1985] 3 All ER 473, CA. The tenant may still, however, wish to obtain a specific waiver of subrogation if possible.
>
> **[1043]–[1050]**

6   GUARANTEE PROVISIONS

6.1   The Guarantor's covenants[167]

6.1.1   *Nature and duration*

The Guarantor's covenants with the Landlord are given as sole or principal debtor or covenantor, with the landlord for the time being and with all his successors in title[168] without the need for any express assignment, and the Guarantor's obligations to the Landlord will last throughout the Liability Period.

167   The covenants in this clause should *not* be omitted where no guarantor is a party to the lease, because they may be required under clause 3.9.5.2 [1004] CONDITIONS. If it is felt undesirable to have covenants in a lease and no party, at least initially, to enter into them, ie where there is no guarantor for the original tenant, the contents of this clause could alternatively be included in a schedule.

168   The new provisions governing the transmission of the benefit and burden of covenants (see the Landlord and Tenant (Covenants) Act 1995 s 3) only apply to landlord and tenant covenants. The law in force before 1 January 1996 remains unchanged for guarantor covenants, so that the benefit passes with the landlord's reversion. This occurs, not under the Law of Property Act 1925 s 141(1), which has been repealed for post-1995 tenancies by the 1995 Act, but under common law. The guarantee covenant touches and concerns the legal estate vested in the new reversioner: see *P & A Swift Investments v Combined English Stores Group plc* [1989] AC 632, [1988] 2 All ER 885, HL.

[1051]

6.1.2   *The covenants*

The Guarantor covenants with the Landlord to observe and perform the requirements of this clause 6.1.2.

6.1.2.1   **Payment of rent and performance of the Lease**

The Tenant must pay the Lease Rents[169] and VAT charged on them punctually and observe and perform the covenants and other terms of this Lease, and if, at any time during the Liability Period while the Tenant is bound by the tenant covenants of this Lease[170], the Tenant defaults in paying the Lease Rents or in observing or performing any of the covenants or other terms of this Lease, then the Guarantor must pay the Lease Rents and observe or perform the covenants or terms in respect of which the Tenant is in default and make good to the Landlord on demand, and indemnify the Landlord against, all losses resulting from such non-payment, non-performance or non-observance notwithstanding —

(a)   any time or indulgence granted by the Landlord to the Tenant, any neglect or forbearance of the Landlord in enforcing the payment of the Lease Rents or the observance or performance of the covenants or other terms of this Lease, or any refusal by the Landlord to accept rent tendered by or on behalf of the Tenant at a time when the Landlord is entitled — or will after the service of a notice under the Law of Property Act 1925 Section 146 be entitled — to re-enter the Premises[171],

(b)   that the terms of this Lease may have been varied by agreement between the Landlord and the Tenant[, provided that no variation is to bind the Guarantor to the extent that it is materially prejudicial to him][172],

(c)   that the Tenant has surrendered part of the Premises — in which event the liability of the Guarantor under this Lease is to continue in respect of the part of the Premises not surrendered after making any necessary apportionments under the Law of Property Act 1925 Section 140[173], and

(d)   anything else (other than a release by deed) by which, but for this clause 6.1.2.1, the Guarantor would be released.

[1052]

169 As to the definition of 'the Lease Rents' see clause 1.32 [967] 'THE RENT'.

170 This obligation lasts while the lease is vested in the tenant and for any period of extended liability following an excluded assignment. It is not appropriate once the tenant has entered into an authorised guarantee agreement, when the contractual guarantor's obligations are at one remove. As to the guaranteeing of obligations under an authorised guarantee agreement: see vol 22(1) (2003 Reissue) LANDLORD AND TENANT (BUSINESS TENANCIES) Paragraph 74 [284] and clause 6.1.2.4 [1055] GUARANTEE OF THE TENANT'S LIABILITIES UNDER AN AUTHORISED GUARANTEE AGREEMENT.

171 If a creditor 'gives time' to the debtor in a binding manner, this releases the guarantor: see *Swire v Redman* (1876) 1 QBD 536; *Holme v Brunskill* (1877) 3 QBD 495, CA. The guarantee should, therefore, be expressed to apply notwithstanding any time or indulgence granted by the landlord to the tenant, or neglect or forbearance on the part of the landlord in enforcing the payment of rent and the other covenants in the lease. It has been suggested, however, that such wording does not protect a landlord who refuses to accept rent so as not to waive a breach of covenant by the tenant. This is unresolved but to avoid any doubt the point should be expressly dealt with. It appears that any provision in a guarantor's covenant that purports to exonerate the landlord from the consequences of his own negligence must satisfy the reasonableness test of the Unfair Contract Terms Act 1977 (11 Halsbury's Statutes (4th Edn) CONTRACT).

172 Any variation of the terms of the contract between the creditor and the debtor will discharge the guarantor (*Holme v Brunskill* (1877) 3 QBD 495, CA), unless the guarantor consents, although it has been suggested that an immaterial variation that was not prejudicial to the guarantor might not release him. No guarantor should accept a provision by which the guarantee is to continue notwithstanding any variation, but on the other hand it seems unfair on the landlord for the guarantor to escape his liability merely because a minor change has been agreed between the landlord and the tenant. A provision that the guarantee is to continue to apply notwithstanding an immaterial variation not prejudicial to the guarantor seems a fair compromise. It should be noted that the Landlord and Tenant (Covenants) Act 1995 s 18 does not apply to the guarantor of the current tenant.

It should also be noted that it is recommended 'best practice' that landlords and tenants should seek the agreement of any guarantors to proposed material changes to the terms of the lease, or even minor changes which could increase the guarantor's liability: see Recommendation 15 of 'A code of practice for commercial leases in England and Wales (2nd edition)' which can be found in vol 22(1) (2003 Reissue) LANDLORD AND TENANT (BUSINESS TENANCIES) at Form 1 [4501].

173 In the light of *Holme v Brunskill* (1877) 3 QBD 495, CA, the position on surrender of part of the premises should be dealt with expressly.

[1053]

6.1.2.2   New lease following disclaimer[174]

If, at any time during the Liability Period while the Tenant is bound by the tenant covenants of this Lease[175], any trustee in bankruptcy or liquidator of the Tenant disclaims this Lease, the Guarantor must, if so required by notice served by the Landlord within *(state period, eg 60 days)* of the Landlord's becoming aware of the disclaimer, take from the Landlord forthwith a lease of the Premises for the residue of the [Contractual][176] Term as at the date of the disclaimer, at the Rent then payable under this Lease and subject to the same covenants and terms as in this Lease — except that the Guarantor need not ensure that any other person is made a party to that lease as guarantor — the new lease to commence on the date of the disclaimer. The Guarantor must pay the costs of the new lease and VAT charged thereon, save where such VAT is recoverable or available for set-off by the Landlord as input tax[177], and execute and deliver to the Landlord a counterpart of the new lease.

174 This put option should be included because on disclaimer of a lease the lease ceases to exist, although it is deemed to continue for the purpose of determining the liability to the landlord of persons, including guarantors, other than the tenant whose liquidator or trustee has disclaimed: see *Hindcastle Ltd v Barbara Attenborough Associates Ltd* [1997] AC 70, [1996] 1 All ER 737, HL.

175 This obligation lasts while the lease is vested in the tenant and for any period of extended liability following an excluded assignment. It is not appropriate once the tenant has entered into an authorised guarantee agreement when the tenant's — ie the former tenant's — liquidator or trustee in bankruptcy will not be in a position to disclaim the lease because it will no longer be vested in the former tenant.

176 This defined term will require amendment where the operation of the security of tenure provisions in the Landlord and Tenant Act 1954 ss 24–28 is to be excluded in relation to the lease: see note 6 to clause 1.2 [957] 'THE [CONTRACTUAL] TERM'.

177 As to payment of VAT on legal costs by a person other than the solicitor's own client see the Information Binder: Property [1]: VAT and Property.

[1054]

6.1.2.3   Payments following disclaimer[178]

If this Lease is disclaimed and the Landlord does not require the Guarantor to accept a new lease of the Premises in accordance with clause 6.1.2.2 NEW LEASE FOLLOWING DISCLAIMER, the Guarantor must pay to the Landlord on demand an amount equal to [the difference between any money received by the Landlord for the use or occupation of the Premises and] the Lease Rents [in both cases] for the period commencing with the date of the disclaimer and ending on whichever is the earlier of the date *(state period, eg 6 months)* after the disclaimer, the date, if any, upon which the Premises are relet, and the end of the [Contractual][179] Term.

178   This clause could be a useful alternative for a landlord, who may not be unhappy to regain possession of the premises but would like some rental income before reletting etc. For a covenant by the tenant to assign to the guarantor see vol 22(3) (1997 Reissue) LANDLORD AND TENANT (BUSINESS TENANCIES) Form 159 [6666].

179   This defined term will require amendment where the operation of the security of tenure provisions in the Landlord and Tenant Act 1954 ss 24–28 is to be excluded in relation to the lease: see note 6 to clause 1.2 [957] 'THE [CONTRACTUAL] TERM'.

6.1.2.4   Guarantee of the Tenant's liabilities under an authorised guarantee agreement

If, at any time during the Liability Period while the Tenant is bound by an authorised guarantee agreement, the Tenant makes any default in his obligations under that agreement, the Guarantor must make good to the Landlord on demand, and indemnify the Landlord against, all losses resulting from that default notwithstanding —

(a)   any time or indulgence granted by the Landlord to the Tenant, or neglect or forbearance of the Landlord in enforcing the payment of any sum or the observance or performance of the covenants of the authorised guarantee agreement[180],

(b)   that the terms of the authorised guarantee agreement may have been varied by agreement between the Landlord and the Tenant [provided that no variation is to bind the Guarantor to the extent that it is materially prejudicial to him][181], or

(c)   anything else (other than a release by deed) by which, but for this clause 6.1.2.4, the Guarantor would be released.

180   See note 171 to clause 6.1.2.1 [1053] PAYMENT OF RENT AND PERFORMANCE OF THE LEASE.
181   See note 172 to clause 6.1.2.1 [1053] PAYMENT OF RENT AND PERFORMANCE OF THE LEASE.

[1055]

6.1.3 *Severance*

6.1.3.1   Severance of void provisions

Any provision of this clause 6 rendered void by virtue of the 1995 Act Section 25 is to be severed from all remaining provisions, and the remaining provisions are to be preserved.

6.1.3.2   Limitation of provisions

If any provision in this clause 6 extends beyond the limits permitted by the 1995 Act Section 25, that provision is to be varied so as not to extend beyond those limits.

[6.2   The Landlord's covenant[182]

The Landlord covenants with the Guarantor that he will not attempt to recover from the Guarantor payment of any amount, determined by a court or in binding arbitration or agreed between the Landlord and the Tenant, payable in respect of a breach of covenant by the Tenant, unless he has served on the Guarantor, within 6 months of the payment being determined or agreed, a notice in the form prescribed by Section 27 of the 1995 Act as if the payment were a fixed charge under that Act.]

182   This clause is a tenant's amendment. It provides for a notice equivalent to a default notice under the Landlord and Tenant (Covenants) Act 1995 to be served. It protects the interests of existing and future contractual guarantors. As to service of default notices see vol 22(1) (2003 Reissue) LANDLORD AND TENANT (BUSINESS TENANCIES) Paragraph 61 [260].

[1056]

7   FORFEITURE[183]

If and whenever during the Term —

7.1   the Lease Rents[184], or any of them or any part of them, or any VAT payable on them, are outstanding for *(state period, eg 14 days)* after becoming due, whether formally demanded or not[185], or

7.2   the Tenant [or the Guarantor] breaches any covenant or other term of this Lease, or

7.3   the Tenant [or the Guarantor][186], being an individual, becomes subject to a bankruptcy order[187] [or has an interim receiver appointed to his property][188], or

7.4   the Tenant [or the Guarantor][189], being a company, enters into liquidation[190] whether compulsory or voluntary — but not if the liquidation is for amalgamation or reconstruction of a solvent company — [or enters into administration][191] [or has a receiver appointed over all or any part of its assets][192], or

7.5   the Tenant [or the Guarantor][193] enters into or makes a proposal to enter into any voluntary arrangement pursuant to the Insolvency Act 1986[194] or any other arrangement or composition for the benefit of his creditors , or

7.6   the Tenant has any distress, sequestration or execution levied on his goods,

and, where the Tenant [or the Guarantor] is more than one person, if and whenever any of the events referred to in this clause happens to any one or more of them, the Landlord may at any time re-enter the Premises or any part of them in the name of the whole — even if any previous right of re-entry has been waived[195] — and thereupon the Term is to cease absolutely but without prejudice to any rights or remedies that may have accrued to the Landlord against the Tenant or the Guarantor [or to the Tenant against the Landlord] in respect of any breach of covenant or other term of this Lease, including the breach in respect of which the re-entry is made.

[1057]

183   As to forfeiture generally see vol 22(1) (2003 Reissue) LANDLORD AND TENANT (BUSINESS TENANCIES) Paragraph 283 [1171] et seq.
       The precise range of insolvency-related circumstances that will trigger the proviso should be carefully considered. Tenants should note that their inclusion, in practice, means that the lease cannot be used as security for a loan. Landlords generally seek to have the ability to forfeit in the widest range of circumstances. It should, however, be noted that, in certain circumstances, leave of the court or of the insolvency practitioner administering the procedure may be required before any contractual right can be exercised: see eg, in respect of administration, the Insolvency Act 1986 Sch 1B para 43(4), (6) as inserted by the Enterprise Act 2002 s 248 (4 Halsbury's Statutes (4th Edn) BANKRUPTCY AND INSOLVENCY).

184   As to the definition of 'the Lease Rents' see clause 1.32 [967] 'THE RENT'.
185   The words 'whether formally demanded or not' should be used to avoid the common law requirement that an actual demand has to be made.
186   The lease may provide for a right of re-entry on insolvency of the guarantor or a tenant's covenant to find an acceptable replacement (see clause 3.23 [1018] REPLACEMENT GUARANTOR) or both.
187   As to bankruptcy generally see the Insolvency Act 1986 Pt IX (ss 264–371).
188   As to interim receivers see the Insolvency Act 1986 s 286.
189   See note 186 above.
190   As to liquidation generally see the Insolvency Act 1986 Pts IV–VI (ss 73–246).
191   As to administration generally see the Insolvency Act 1986 Pt II as substituted by the Enterprise Act 2002 s 248. The tenant may seek to argue that if the administrator pays rent and if there are no other material breaches of the lease the landlord should not be entitled to forfeit the lease on this ground.
192   The tenant may seek to argue that if the receiver pays rent and if there are no other material breaches of the lease the landlord should not be entitled to forfeit the lease on this ground.
193   See note 186 above.
194   As to company voluntary arrangements see the Insolvency Act 1986 Pt I (ss 1–7B) as amended by the Insolvency Act 2000. As to individual voluntary arrangements see the Insolvency Act 1986 Pt VIII (ss 252–263G) as amended by the Enterprise Act 2002 s 264.
195   The landlord has the option whether to take advantage of a right of forfeiture or not. If he elects not to do so , the forfeiture is waived. The election may be express or implied, eg if the landlord does any act by which he recognises that the relationship of landlord and tenant is still continuing after the event of forfeiture has come to his knowledge.

[1058]

8   MISCELLANEOUS

8.1   Exclusion of warranty as to use

Nothing in this Lease or in any consent granted by the Landlord under this Lease is to imply or warrant that the Premises may lawfully be used under the Planning Acts for the Permitted Use[196].

196   See *Laurence v Lexcourt Holdings Ltd* [1978] 2 All ER 810, [1978] 1 WLR 1128; *Collins v Howell-Jones* [1981] 2 EGLR 108, 259 Estates Gazette 331, CA and the comments of Eveleigh LJ on estate agents' particulars relating to use in *Bovis Group Pension Fund Ltd v GC Flooring & Furnishing Ltd* (1984) 269 Estates Gazette 1252 at 1253, CA.

8.2   Exclusion of third party rights

Nothing in this Lease is intended to confer any benefit on any person who is not a party to it[197].

197   By virtue of the Contracts (Rights of Third Parties) Act 1999 (11 Halsbury's Statutes (4th Edn) CONTRACT) third-party rights may be conferred where they are not clearly excluded. This being so, it is advisable to incorporate a specific exclusion except where the parties actually intend to confer rights of action on a third party. In the standard letting situation it is unlikely that the parties will wish to extend liability in this manner. As to the Contracts (Rights of Third Parties) Act 1999 generally see vol 4(3) (2001 Reissue) BOILERPLATE CLAUSES.

8.3   Representations

The Tenant acknowledges that this Lease has not been entered into in reliance wholly or partly on any statement or representation made by or on behalf of the Landlord, except any such statement or representation expressly set out in this Lease[198] [or made by the Landlord's solicitors in any written response to enquiries raised by the Tenant's solicitors in connection with the grant of this Lease].

198   See the comments of Eveleigh LJ on estate agents' particulars relating to use in *Bovis Group Pension Fund Ltd v GC Flooring & Furnishing Ltd* (1984) 269 Estates Gazette 1252 at 1253, CA. For an alternative provision see vol 22(4) (1997 Reissue) LANDLORD AND TENANT (BUSINESS TENANCIES) Form 400 clauses 7.1 [7520], 7.2 [7521].

[1059]

8.4   Documents under hand

While the Landlord is a limited company or other corporation, any licence, consent, approval or notice required to be given by the Landlord is to be sufficiently given if given under the hand of a director, the secretary or other duly authorised officer of the Landlord [or by the Surveyor on behalf of the Landlord].

8.5   Tenant's property

If, after the Tenant has vacated the Premises at the end of the Term, any property of his remains in or on the Premises and he fails to remove it within *(state period, eg 7 days)* after a written request from the Landlord to do so, or, if the Landlord is unable to make such a request to the Tenant, within *(state period, eg 14 days)* from the first attempt to make it, then the Landlord may, as the agent of the Tenant, sell that property. The Tenant must indemnify the Landlord against any liability incurred by the Landlord to any third party whose property is sold by him in the mistaken belief held in good faith — which is to be presumed unless the contrary is proved — that the property belonged to the Tenant. If, having made reasonable efforts to do so, the Landlord is unable to locate the Tenant, then the Landlord may retain the proceeds of sale absolutely unless the Tenant claims them within *(state period, eg 6 months)* of the date upon which he vacated the Premises. The Tenant must indemnify the Landlord against any damage occasioned to the Premises and any losses caused by or related to the presence of the property in or on the Premises.

8.6   Compensation on vacating excluded

Any statutory right of the Tenant to claim compensation from the Landlord on vacating the Premises is excluded to the extent that the law allows[199].

199   As to compensation where an order for a new tenancy is precluded on certain grounds see the Landlord and Tenant Act 1954 s 37 as amended by the Local Government and Housing Act 1989 s 149, Sch 7 and by SI 2003/3096.
      As to the effectiveness of provisions of this nature see vol 22(1) (2003 Reissue) LANDLORD AND TENANT (BUSINESS TENANCIES) Paragraph 468 [3079].

[1060]

8.7   Notices

8.7.1   *Form and service of notices*

A notice under this Lease must be in writing and, unless the receiving party or his authorised agent acknowledges receipt, is valid if, and only if[200] —

8.7.1.1   it is given by hand, sent by registered post or recorded delivery, or sent by fax[201] provided that a confirmatory copy is given by hand or sent by registered post or recorded delivery on the same day, and

8.7.1.2   it is served —
    (a)   where the receiving party is a company incorporated within Great Britain, at the registered office,
    (b)   where the receiving party is the Tenant and the Tenant is not such a company, at the Premises, and

(c)   where the receiving party is the Landlord [or the Guarantor] and [the Landlord *(or as required)* that party] is not such a company, at [the Landlord's *(or as required)* that party's] address shown in this Lease or at any address specified in a notice given by [the Landlord to the Tenant *(or as required)* that party to the other parties].

200   Notice clauses are either mandatory or permissive. The words 'and only if' are inserted to make it clear that this clause is mandatory.

201   As to service by fax see *Hastie and Jenkerson v McMahon* [1991] 1 All ER 255, [1990] 1 WLR 1575, CA.

8.7.2   *Deemed delivery*²⁰²

8.7.2.1   **By registered post or recorded delivery**

Unless it is returned through the Royal Mail undelivered, a notice sent by registered post or recorded delivery is to be treated as served on the third working day after posting whenever and whether or not it is received.

[1061]

8.7.2.2   **By fax**

A notice sent by fax is to be treated as served on the day upon which it is sent, or the next working day where the fax is sent after 1600 hours or on a day that is not a working day, whenever and whether or not it or the confirmatory copy is received unless the confirmatory copy is returned through the Royal Mail undelivered.

8.7.2.3   **'A working day'**

References to 'a working day' are references to a day when the United Kingdom clearing banks are open for business in the City of London.

202   It is a fundamental aspect of any notice clause to specify the circumstances in which the server, provided he has complied with the requirements of the clause, has for the purposes of the document served a notice, even if the recipient claims that he never received it.

8.7.3   *Joint recipients*

If the receiving party consists of more than one person, a notice to one of them is notice to all.

8.8   **[New *(or)* Old] lease**

[This Lease [is *(or as appropriate)* is not] a new tenancy for the purposes of the 1995 Act Section 1. *(or as appropriate)* This Lease is granted under the 1995 Act section 19 and [is *(or as appropriate)* is not] a new tenancy for the purposes of Section 1 of that Act]²⁰³.

203   A tenancy granted on or after 1 January 1996 that is an overriding lease is not a 'new' tenancy where the tenancy being overridden is one granted before that date: see the Landlord and Tenant (Covenants) Act 1995 ss 1(4), 20(1). Where the lease being granted is an overriding lease, the lease must include a statement that it is an overriding lease and indicate whether the overriding lease is or is not a 'new' tenancy: see the Landlord and Tenant (Covenants) Act 1995 s 20(2). In these circumstances the second alternative should be used.

[1062]

[8.9   Capacity of tenants

It is declared that the persons comprising the Tenant hold the Premises as [joint tenants *(or as required)* tenants in common].]

[8.10   Exclusion of the 1954 Act Sections 24–28²⁰⁴

8.10.1   *Notice and declaration*

On *(date)* the Landlord served notice on the Tenant pursuant to the provisions of the 1954 Act Section 38A(3) as inserted by the Regulatory Reform (Business Tenancies) (England and Wales) Order 2003 and on *(date)* the Tenant made a [simple *(or as appropriate)* statutory] declaration pursuant to schedule 2 of the Regulatory Reform (Business Tenancies) (England and Wales) Order 2003.

8.10.2   *Agreement to exclude*

Pursuant to the provisions of the 1954 Act Section 38A(1) as inserted by the Regulatory Reform (Business Tenancies) (England and Wales) Order 2003, the parties agree that the provisions of the 1954 Act Sections 24–28 inclusive are to be excluded in relation to the tenancy created by this Lease.]

204   As to contracting out of the Landlord and Tenant Act 1954 and the requirements that need to be complied with see vol 22(1) (2003 Reissue) LANDLORD AND TENANT (BUSINESS TENANCIES) Paragraph 431 [2035].

(include other clauses as required: eg, break clauses and options (see vol 22(3) (1997 Reissue) LANDLORD AND TENANT (BUSINESS TENANCIES) Forms 136 [6544]–142 [6569]) or a proviso as to termination on rent review (see vol 22(3) (1997 Reissue) LANDLORD AND TENANT (BUSINESS TENANCIES) Form 143 [6575]))

IN WITNESS etc *(see vol 12(2) (2003 Reissue) DEEDS, AGREEMENTS ETC)*

[1063]

SCHEDULE 1: THE RIGHTS RESERVED

1-1   Right of entry to inspect

The right to enter²⁰⁵, or in emergency to break into and enter, the Premises at any time during the Term [at reasonable times and on reasonable notice except in emergency] to inspect them, to take schedules or inventories of fixtures and other items to be yielded up at the end of the Term, and to exercise any of the rights granted to the Landlord elsewhere in this Lease.

205   For a covenant by the landlord to make good damage so caused see vol 22(3) (1997 Reissue) LANDLORD AND TENANT (BUSINESS TENANCIES) Form 79 [6453].

1-2   Access on renewal or rent review

[The right to enter the Premises with the Surveyor and the third party determining the Rent under any provisions for rent review contained in this Lease at [any time *(or as required)* convenient hours and on reasonable prior notice] to inspect [and measure] the Premises for all purposes connected with any pending or intended step under the 1954 Act or the implementation of the provisions for rent review. *(or as required in view of the rent review provisions used: see vol 22(3) (1997 Reissue) LANDLORD AND TENANT (BUSINESS TENANCIES) Forms 180 [7611]–194 [6987])]*

SCHEDULE 2: THE RENT AND RENT REVIEW

(insert rent review provisions as required: see vol 22(3) (1997 Reissue) LANDLORD AND TENANT *(BUSINESS TENANCIES) Forms 180 [7611]–194 [6987])*

[1064]

SCHEDULE 3: THE SHOP COVENANTS

(the parties must consider how far the restrictions suggested in this schedule are appropriate to the letting concerned)

3–1   Use

3–1.1   *Permitted Use*

The Tenant must use the Premises for the Permitted Use only.

3–1.2   *External displays*

The Tenant must not stand, place, deposit or expose any goods, materials, articles or things whatsoever for display or sale or for any other purpose outside any part of any building on the Premises.

3–1.3   *Noxious discharges*

The Tenant must not discharge into any of the Conduits any noxious or deleterious matter or any substance that might cause an obstruction in or danger or injury to the Conduits or be or become a source of obstruction, danger or injury, and in the event of any such obstruction, danger or injury the Tenant must forthwith make good any damage to the satisfaction of the Surveyor.

3–1.4   *Noisy machinery*

The Tenant must not install in or use on the Premises any machinery or apparatus causing noise or vibration that can be heard or felt in nearby premises or outside the Premises or that may cause damage.

3–1.5   *Sound audible outside*

The Tenant must not play or use on the Premises any musical instrument, audio or other equipment or apparatus producing sound that can be heard outside the Premises [if the Landlord [in his absolute discretion *(or as required)* reasonably] considers such sounds to be undesirable and gives notice to the Tenant to that effect].

3–1.6   *Flashing lights*

The Tenant must not display any flashing lights in the Premises that can be seen from outside the Premises[, or display any other lighting arrangement that can be seen from outside the Premises if the Landlord [in his absolute discretion *(or as required)* reasonably] considers such lighting to be undesirable and gives notice to the Tenant to that effect].

3–1.7   *Exterior lights and awnings*

The Tenant must not install or erect any exterior lighting, shade or awning at the Premises.

3–1.8   *Window cleaning*

The Tenant must clean both sides of all windows and window frames in any building on the Premises at least once every month.

[1065]

3-2   Hours of trading

During normal trading hours[206] for the locality the Tenant must keep the Premises open for business[207] and properly cared for, and must trade actively throughout substantially the whole of the Premises except —

3-2.1   in so far as he is prevented from doing so by destruction or damage to the Premises caused by one or more of the Insured Risks[208],

3-2.2   when non-trading is necessary to allow any major repairs, alterations or additions to the Premises to be carried out with all reasonable speed[209],

3-2.3   where non-trading is necessary to allow a permitted assignment [or subletting] of this Lease to be completed, or

3-2.4   in so far as to do so would be in breach of any other provision of this Lease.

206   A covenant to keep open during 'normal business hours' does not require the tenant to open the shop on Sundays: see the Sunday Trading Act 1994 s 3 (19 Halsbury's Statutes (4th Edn) HEALTH AND SAFETY AT WORK).

207   The landlord should give careful consideration to the inclusion of an obligation of this nature: see vol 22(1) (2003 Reissue) LANDLORD AND TENANT (BUSINESS TENANCIES) Paragraph 177 [876].

208   It should be noted that it is now recommended 'best practice' that if the premises are so damaged by an uninsured risk as to prevent occupation, the tenant should be allowed to terminate the lease unless the landlord agrees to reinstate at his own cost: see vol 22(1) (2003 Reissue) LANDLORD AND TENANT (BUSINESS TENANCIES) Paragraph 85 [402]. It follows that if this recommendation is adopted, this exception also needs to be extended to include damage or destruction caused by both insured and uninsured risks.

209   A tenant may wish to have this provision extended to include periods for stocktaking and, particularly in long leases, to authorise shop fittings.

[1066]

3-3   Window dressing and displays

3-3.1   *Window dressing*

The Tenant must keep the shop windows attractively dressed in a manner [suitable to a high class shopping area *(or as required)* appropriate to the neighbourhood].

3-3.2   *Interior layout*

The Tenant must keep all those parts of the interior of the Premises that are visible from outside the Premises attractively laid out and furnished and with goods well displayed and must keep any showcases in the Premises clean and attractively dressed at all times.

3-3.3   *Posters, placards and signs*

The Tenant must not place or display on the outside of the Premises or on the windows or inside the Premises so as to be visible from outside the Premises any name, writing, notice, sign, placard, poster, sticker or advertisement other than —

3-3.3.1   normal price tickets attached and relating to goods sold in the display area inside the Premises, provided these are not placed on the window glass, [and]

3-3.3.2   the sign referred to in paragraph 3-3.4 APPROVED SIGN OR FASCIA[, and

3-3.3.3   trade placards, posters or advertisements of a temporary and not excessive nature and necessary or usual for the Permitted Use [provided that not more than *(state proportion, eg 25%)* of the surface of the shop window of the Premises may be obscured by the placards, posters or advertisements]].

3-3.4 *Approved sign or fascia*

The Tenant must maintain on the outside of the Premises a [sign *(or as appropriate)* fascia] of a type, size and design approved by the Landlord, whose approval may not be unreasonably withheld or delayed, showing the Tenant's name and business.

[1067]

3-4   Ceiling and floor loading

3-4.1   Heavy items

The Tenant must not bring onto, or permit to remain on, the Premises any safes, machinery, goods or other articles that will or may strain or damage the Premises or any part of them.

3-4.2   Protection of the roof

The Tenant must not, without the consent of the Landlord, suspend anything from any ceiling of the Premises [or store any heavy items in the roof space].

3-4.3   Expert advice

If the Tenant applies for the Landlord's consent under paragraph 3-4.2 PROTECTION OF THE ROOF, the Landlord may consult any engineer or other person in relation to the loading proposed by the Tenant, and the Tenant must repay the fees of the engineer or other person to the Landlord on demand.

3-5   Plate glass

3-5.1   Insurance of plate glass

The Tenant must insure any plate glass against breakage or damage, in a reputable insurance office, for its full reinstatement cost from time to time, and whenever reasonably so required must produce to the Landlord particulars of the insurance policy and evidence of payment of the current year's premium.

3-5.2   Reinstatement of plate glass

Notwithstanding anything to the contrary contained elsewhere in this Lease[210], whenever the whole or any part of the plate glass is broken or damaged the Tenant must as quickly as possible lay out all money received in respect of the insurance of it in reinstating it with new glass of at least the same quality and thickness, and must make good any deficiency in such money.

210   The reference here is to the landlord's obligations under clause 5.6 [1035] REINSTATEMENT AND
      TERMINATION and the intention is to make clear that the landlord's general obligation to make good
      does not apply to the plate glass.

[3-6   Fitting out

(consideration should be given to the fitting out works, if any, to be carried out by the tenant: these may be included here or, more appropriately, dealt with in an agreement for lease (see eg, vol 22(4) (1997 Reissue) LANDLORD AND TENANT (BUSINESS TENANCIES) *Form 400 [7510]) or a licence for alterations (see vol 22(3) (1997 Reissue)* LANDLORD AND TENANT (BUSINESS TENANCIES) *Forms 241 [7203] and 242 [7204]. For examples of fitting out covenants see vol 22(3) (1997 Reissue)* LANDLORD AND TENANT (BUSINESS TENANCIES) *Forms 173 [6697], 174 [6698])]*

[1068]

SCHEDULE 4: THE SUBJECTIONS

(insert details)

SCHEDULE 5: THE AUTHORISED GUARANTEE AGREEMENT

(insert the form of authorised guarantee agreement: see, eg vol 22(3) (1997 Reissue) LANDLORD
AND TENANT (BUSINESS TENANCIES) *Form 217 [7053])*

(signature (or common seal) of landlord: lease)
(signature (or common seal) of tenant (and guarantor): counterpart)
(signatures of witnesses)
[1069]–[1100]

9

Lease of a shop and maisonette forming part of a parade[1]

CONTENTS
*(NB: numbers in [ ] below refer to this volume and should be altered to suit the page or reference
numbers actually used)*

1 DEFINITIONS AND INTERPRETATION
1.1 'The Adjoining Conduits' . . . . [1109]
1.2 'Adjoining property of the Landlord' . . . . [1109]
1.3 'The Common Parts' . . . . [1109]
1.4 'The Conduits' . . . . [1109]
1.5 'The [Contractual] Term' . . . . [1110]
[1.6 'The Decorating Years' . . . . [1111]]
1.7 'Development' . . . . [1111]
1.8 Gender and number . . . . [1111]
1.9 Headings . . . . [1111]
                                                                        [1101]
[1.10 'The Initial Rent' . . . . [1111]]
1.11 'The Insurance Rent' . . . . [1112]
1.12 'The Insured Risks' . . . . [1112]
1.13 'Interest' . . . . [1113]
1.14 'The Interest Rate' . . . . [1113]
1.15 Interpretation of 'consent' and 'approved' . . . . [1114]
1.16 Interpretation of 'the Guarantor' . . . . [1114]
1.17 Interpretation of 'the Landlord' . . . . [1115]
1.18 Interpretation of 'the last year of the Term' and 'the end of the Term' . . [1115]
1.19 Interpretation of 'the Tenant' . . . . [1115]
1.20 Interpretation of 'this Lease' . . . . [1115]
1.21 Joint and several liability . . . . [1115]
1.22 'The Liability Period' . . . . [1116]
1.23 'Losses' . . . . [1117]
1.24 'The 1954 Act' . . . . [1117]
1.25 'The 1995 Act' . . . . [1117]
1.26 Obligation not to permit or suffer . . . . [1117]

1.27 'Other buildings' . . . . [1118]
1.28 'The Parade' . . . . [1118]
1.29 'The Passageway' . . . . [1118]
1.30 'The Permitted Use' . . . . [1118]
1.31 'The Plan' . . . . [1119]
1.32 'The Planning Acts' . . . . [1119]
1.33 'The Premises' . . . . [1119]
1.34 References to clauses and schedules . . . . [1121]
1.35 References to rights of access . . . . [1121]
1.36 References to statutes . . . . [1121]
1.37 'The Rent' . . . . [1121]
1.38 'The Rent Commencement Date' . . . . [1122]
[1.39 'The Review Dates' . . . . [1122]]
1.40 'The Road' . . . . [1122]
1.41 'The Shop and Maisonette Covenants' . . . . [1122]
1.42 'The Staircase' . . . . [1122]
1.43 'The Surveyor' . . . . [1123]
[1.44 'The Term' . . . . [1123]]
1.45 Terms from the 1995 Act . . . . [1123]
1.46 'VAT' . . . . [1123]
           [1102]

2 DEMISE . . . . [1131]

3 THE TENANT'S COVENANTS
3.1 Rent . . . . [1132
3.2 Outgoings and VAT . . . . [1133]
[3.3 Cost of services consumed . . . . [1134]]
3.4 Repair, cleaning and decoration . . . . [1134]
3.5 Waste and alterations . . . . [1137]
3.6 Aerials, signs and advertisements . . . . [1138]
3.7 Statutory obligations . . . . [1139]
3.8 Entry to inspect and notice to repair . . . . [1140]
3.9 Alienation . . . . [1141]
3.10 Nuisance and residential restrictions . . . . [1160]
3.11 Costs of applications, notices and recovery of arrears . . . . [1161]
3.12 Planning and development . . . . [1171]
3.13 Plans, documents and information . . . . [1173]
3.14 Indemnities . . . . [1173]
3.15 Reletting boards and viewing . . . . [1174]
3.16 Obstruction and encroachment . . . . [1174]
3.17 Yielding up . . . . [1175]
3.18 Interest on arrears . . . . [1175]
3.19 Statutory notices . . . . [1176]
3.20 Keyholders . . . . [1176]
3.21 Viewing on sale of reversion . . . . [1176]
3.22 Defective premises . . . . [1176]
3.23 Replacement guarantor . . . . [1176]
3.24 Exercise of the Landlord's rights . . . . [1177]
3.25 The Shop and Maisonette Covenants . . . . [1177]
3.26 Costs of grant of this Lease . . . . [1177]
3.27 Consent to the Landlord's release . . . . [1178]

4 THE LANDLORD'S COVENANTS

4.1 Quiet enjoyment . . . . [1191]
4.2 Maintenance and decoration of the Parade . . . . [1192]
4.3 Prohibition of competing trades . . . . [1192]
[1103]

5 INSURANCE

5.1 Warranty as to convictions . . . . [1193]
5.2 Covenant to insure . . . . [1193]
5.3 Details of the insurance . . . . [1194]
5.4 Payment of the Insurance Rent . . . . [1195]
5.5 Suspension of the Rent . . . . [1196]
5.6 Reinstatement and termination . . . . [1197]
5.7 Tenant's further insurance covenants . . . . [1201]
[5.8 Landlord's further insurance covenants . . . . [1203]]

6 GUARANTEE PROVISIONS

6.1 The Guarantor's covenants . . . . [1221]
[6.2 The Landlord's covenant . . . . [1226]]

7 FORFEITURE . . . . [1231]

8 MISCELLANEOUS

8.1 Exclusion of warranty as to use . . . . [1233]
8.2 Exclusion of third party rights . . . . [1233]
8.3 Representations . . . . [1233]
8.4 Documents under hand . . . . [1234]
8.5 Tenant's property . . . . [1234]
8.6 Compensation on vacating excluded . . . . [1234]
8.7 Notices . . . . [1235]
8.8 Rights and easements . . . . [1236]
8.9 Covenants relating to adjoining property . . . . [1236]
8.10 Disputes with adjoining occupiers . . . . [1236]
8.11 Effect of waiver . . . . [1237]
[8.12 The perpetuity period . . . . [1237]]
[8.13 Party walls . . . . [1237]]
8.14 Exclusion of liability . . . . [1237]
8.15 [New (or) Old] lease . . . . [1238]
[8.16 Capacity of tenants . . . . [1238]]
[8.17 Exclusion of the 1954 Act Sections 24–28 . . . . [1238]]

SCHEDULE 1: THE RIGHTS GRANTED

1-1 Rights of way . . . . [1239]
1-2 Right to use the Common Parts . . . . [1239]
1-3 Passage and running through Adjoining Conduits . . . . [1239]
1-4 Support and protection . . . . [1239]
[1104]

SCHEDULE 2: THE RIGHTS RESERVED

2-1 Passage and running through the Conduits . . . . [1240]
2-2 Right to construct conduits . . . . [1240]
2-3 Access . . . . [1241]
2-4 Right to erect scaffolding . . . . [1242]
2-5 Rights of support and shelter . . . . [1242]
2-6 Right to erect new buildings . . . . [1242]

SCHEDULE 3: THE RENT AND RENT REVIEW

SCHEDULE 4: THE SHOP AND MAISONETTE COVENANTS

4-1 Use . . . . [1243]
4-2 Damage precautions . . . . [1245]
4-3 Care of the Common Parts . . . . [1245]
4-4 Landlord's expenditure . . . . [1245]
4-5 Hours of trading . . . . [1246]
4-6 Window dressing and displays . . . . [1247]
4-7 Ceiling and floor loading . . . . [1248]
4-8 Plate glass . . . . [1248]
4-9 Loading and unloading . . . . [1249]
[4-10 Fitting out . . . . [1249]]

SCHEDULE 5: THE SUBJECTIONS

SCHEDULE 6: PROVISIONAL PAYMENTS

6-1 Service of a provisional charge notice . . . . [1250]
6-2 Payment of the Provisional Charge . . . . [1250]
6-3 The Final Notice . . . . [1250]
6-4 Excess or shortfall . . . . [1250]

SCHEDULE 7: THE AUTHORISED GUARANTEE AGREEMENT

[1105]

AGREEMENT

[HM LAND REGISTRY

LAND REGISTRATION ACT 2002

Administrative area	*(insert details)*
Title number out of which lease is granted	*(title number)*
Property let	*(postal address or description)*]

[1106]

THIS LEASE is made the .... day of .... BETWEEN:

(1)   *(name of landlord)* [of *(address)* *(or as appropriate)* the registered office of which is at *(address)*] [Company Registration no ...][2] ('the Landlord') [and]

(2)   *(name of tenant)* [of *(address)* *(or as appropriate)* being a company registered in [England and Wales *(or)* Scotland][3] the registered office of which is at *(address)*] [Company Registration no ...] ('the Tenant') [and

(3)   *(name of guarantor)* [of *(address)* *(or as appropriate)* the registered office of which is at *(address)*] [Company Registration no ...] ('the Guarantor')]

[1107]

1   As to stamp duty land tax see the Information Binder: Stamp Duty Land Tax [1].

As to Land Registry Fees see the Information Binder: Property [1]: Property Fees.

On the grant out of an unregistered freehold estate in land of a lease for a term of more than seven years from the date of the grant, application must be made to register the title to the leasehold interest granted: see the Land Registration Act 2002 s 4(1)(c) (37 Halsbury's Statutes (4th Edn) REAL PROPERTY). The tenant must obtain an epitome of title to the freehold reversion, investigate it, and mark it as examined, otherwise he will not be able to be registered with an absolute title: see vol 25(1) (2003 Reissue) LAND REGISTRATION Paragraph 21.1 [132].

If the freehold reversion is registered, the grant of a lease for a term of more than seven years from the date of the grant must be completed by registration: see the Land Registration Act 2002 s 27(2)(b)(i).

As to the form and contents of leases see vol 22(1) (2003 Reissue) LANDLORD AND TENANT (BUSINESS TENANCIES) Paragraph 104 [601] et seq. As to registered land generally see vol 25(1) (2003 Reissue) LAND REGISTRATION. As to registration of title to leases see vol 25(1) (2003 Reissue) LAND REGISTRATION Paragraph 143 [601] et seq.

This is a lease of premises comprising a shop and maisonette that form part of a suburban parade. Access to the maisonette is through both the shop and a private road at the rear with a staircase and passageway providing entry to the maisonette at first floor level. Rights are granted over land adjoining the premises. The tenant is responsible for the repair and decoration of the interior of the premises. The landlord covenants to decorate the exterior of the parade and to repair and maintain the structure of the parade, including the foundations, roof and common parts. The tenant covenants to pay the landlord a fair proportion of sums incurred by the landlord in the performance of these obligations, and there are provisions by which the landlord can require payment in advance when major work is contemplated. The landlord insures the parade and the tenant refunds a proportion of the premium. The landlord covenants not to permit a competing business to be carried on at other premises within the parade. There is provision for the rent to be reviewed and for a guarantor.

The tenant should ensure that the landlord deduces title to the land affected by the rights he is granted, especially where the lease is registrable, because if title is not shown and any consents, eg of any chargee or landlord of the adjoining land, obtained, the rights may be excluded from the title.

2   If any party is a company it is desirable to include the company registration number. This avoids any problems arising when a company has been wound up and a new company formed with the same name, or when the name of a company is changed, or if companies swap names, eg on a reconstruction of a group of companies. In addition, where a company applies to be registered as proprietor of a registered estate or registered charge, the application must state the company's registration number: see the Land Registration Rules 2003, SI 2003/1417 r 181.

3   Where the tenant is a company registered in England and Wales or Scotland, and the lease is registrable, an application for first registration of the lease (where the landlord's title is unregistered), or registration of the lease as a registrable disposition (where the landlord's title is registered), and the tenant as proprietor of the leasehold title, must state the company's registered number: see SI 2003/1417 r 181(1). There seems to be no reason why the certificate and statement should not be contained in the disposition in favour of the proprietor, where convenient.

[1108]

NOW THIS DEED WITNESSES as follows:

1   DEFINITIONS AND INTERPRETATION

For all purposes of this Lease[4] the terms defined in this clause have the meanings specified.

4   One view would add 'unless the context otherwise requires' or 'where the context so admits' and in fact this may be implied (see *Meux v Jacobs* (1875) LR 7 HL 481 at 493; *Law Society v United Service Bureau Ltd* [1934] 1 KB 343, DC) but the better course is to use defined terms in such a way that there are no circumstances where the defined meaning does not apply.

1.1   'The Adjoining Conduits'

'The Adjoining Conduits' means the pipes, sewers, drains, mains, ducts, conduits, gutters, watercourses, wires, cables, [laser optical fibres, data or impulse transmission, communication or reception systems,] channels, flues and all other conducting media — including any fixings, louvres, cowls, covers and other ancillary apparatus — that are in, on, over or under any adjoining property of the Landlord that serve the Premises.

1.2   'Adjoining property of the Landlord'

References to 'adjoining property of the Landlord' are references to each and every part of any neighbouring or adjoining land, including the rest of the Parade, in which the Landlord, or a company that is a member of the same group as the Landlord within the meaning of the 1954 Act Section 42, has or during the Term acquires an interest or estate.

1.3   'The Common Parts'

'The Common Parts' means the Road, the Staircase, the Passageway and all other areas from time to time used in common with the other tenants and occupiers of the Parade and those authorised by them.

1.4   'The Conduits'

'The Conduits' means the pipes, sewers, drains, mains, ducts, conduits, gutters, watercourses, wires, cables, [laser optical fibres, data or impulse transmission, communication or reception systems,] channels, flues and all other conducting media — including any fixings, louvres, cowls, covers and any other ancillary apparatus — that are in, on, over or under the Premises.

[1109]

1.5   'The [Contractual] Term'[5]

'The [Contractual][6] Term' means *(insert number)* years commencing on and including *(insert date of commencement of the term)*[7].

5   As to the commencement of the term see vol 22(1) (2003 Reissue) LANDLORD AND TENANT (BUSINESS TENANCIES) Paragraph 135 [670].
    As to registration see note 1 above. Where the landlord's title is unregistered, the grantee must apply for registration within a period of two months from the date of the disposition if the lease is granted for a term of more than seven years. If no such application is made the disposition becomes void as regards any transfer, grant or creation of a legal estate: see the Land Registration Act 2002 s 6 (37 Halsbury's Statutes (4th Edn) REAL PROPERTY). Where the landlord's title is registered and the lease is for a term of more than seven years, the tenant should protect the intended lease by applying for an official search, and an application to register the lease should be made before expiry of the search, otherwise the lease will be susceptible to loss of priority: see the Land Registration Act 2002 s 27.
6   The demise in this lease is for 'the Contractual Term', which is defined as a fixed term of years. The expression 'the Term', as defined in clause 1.44 [1123] 'THE TERM', is used in covenants so that they continue to apply during any period of holding over or continuance or extension of the contractual term. Some difficulties arise if this structure is used in a draft lease where security of tenure is to be excluded under the Landlord and Tenant Act 1954 s 38A(1) as inserted by SI 2003/3096 (23 Halsbury's Statutes (4th Edn) LANDLORD AND TENANT). The demise is for the contractual term and the inclusion of the definition of 'the Term' does not prevent the lease being 'for a term of years certain' as required by the Landlord and Tenant Act 1954 s 38A(1). However, reference to continuance of the contractual term by statute is inappropriate where the operation of the security of tenure provisions in the Landlord and Tenant Act 1954 ss 24–28 is to be excluded. If a lease is contracted out of the Landlord and Tenant Act 1954 there can be no statutory extension, and if the tenant remains in occupation at the end of the contractual term he is holding over unlawfully unless there is an express agreement to extend the contractual term operating as a surrender and re-grant so that the original lease— and the agreement under the Landlord and Tenant Act 1954 s 38A(1) — has no further effect. It is suggested that in these circumstances the drafting should be simplified to include a single term (defined simply as 'the Term') by reference to the period of the contractual term. This can be achieved by amending this clause in the manner suggested and substituting it for clause 1.44 [1123] 'THE TERM'.
7   For estate management reasons it is usually desirable to insert a quarter day here — or a rent day when rent is due on days other than quarter days — ie generally the one preceding the earlier of the date of possession and the date of execution.

[1110]

[1.6   'The Decorating Years'

'The Decorating Years' means *(specify years).*] *(omit if not required, eg if the first alternative in clause 3.4.6 [1136] DECORATION is used)*

1.7   'Development'

References to 'development' are references to development as defined by the Town and Country Planning Act 1990 Section 55.

1.8   Gender and number

Words importing one gender include all other genders; words importing the singular include the plural and vice versa[8].

8   See the Law of Property Act 1925 s 61 (37 Halsbury's Statutes (4th Edn) REAL PROPERTY).

1.9   Headings[9]

The clause, paragraph and schedule headings and the table of contents do not form part of this document and must not be taken into account in its construction or interpretation. *(amend if marginal notes are used instead of headings)*

9   Headings and marginal notes require the draftsman to provide a word or two to describe every clause in the lease. This is not always easy and there are times when the draftsman will have to settle for something less than perfection, the only alternative being a heading or note that would be inappropriately long. It would be quite wrong for that title, which its author might admit was not totally apposite but was the best that he could do in a few words, to be used in construing the clause in question.

[1.10 'The Initial Rent'

'The Initial Rent' means [the sum of £... a year *(or as required by the rent and review provisions to be used)*].] *(this definition is not required if the rent is not reviewable)*

[1111]

1.11   'The Insurance Rent'[10]

'The Insurance Rent' means a fair proportion reasonably attributable to the Premises of the [gross sums including any commission *(or as required)* sums net of any commission] that the Landlord is from time to time liable to pay —

1.11.1   by way of premium for insuring the Parade, including insuring for loss of rent, in accordance with his obligations contained in this Lease,

1.11.2   by way of premium for insuring in such a manner and on such terms as [the Landlord acting reasonably considers appropriate *(or as required)* is reasonable] against all liability of the Landlord to third parties arising out of or in connection with any matter including or relating to the Parade, and

1.11.3   for insurance valuations,

and all of any increased premium payable because of any act or omission of the Tenant.

10   As to reimbursement of insurance premiums see vol 22(1) (2003 Reissue) LANDLORD AND TENANT (BUSINESS TENANCIES) Paragraph 230 [1026].

1.12 'The Insured Risks'

'The Insured Risks' means the risks of loss or damage by fire[, storm, tempest, earthquake, lightning, explosion, riot, civil commotion, malicious damage, [terrorism,] impact by vehicles and by aircraft and articles dropped from aircraft — other than war risks — flood damage and bursting and overflowing of water pipes and tanks,] and such other risks, whether or not in the nature of the foregoing, as the Landlord [acting reasonably] from time to time decides to insure against[11].

11   As to the risks to be insured and the tenant's concerns see vol 22(1) (2003 Reissue) LANDLORD AND
      TENANT (BUSINESS TENANCIES) Paragraph 235 [1033].

[1112]

1.13 'Interest'

References to 'interest' are references to interest payable during the period from the date on which the payment is due to the date of payment, both before and after any judgment, at the Interest Rate then prevailing [*(where the interest rate is defined by reference to a bank base rate)* or, should the base rate referred to in clause 1.14 'THE INTEREST RATE' cease to exist[12] at another rate of interest closely comparable with the Interest Rate [to be agreed between the parties or in default of agreement to be determined by [the Surveyor, acting as an expert and not as an arbitrator *(or as required)* a chartered accountant appointed by agreement between the parties or in default of agreement nominated by the President of the Institute of Chartered Accountants in England and Wales, acting as an expert and not as an arbitrator][13] *(or as required)* decided on by the Landlord acting reasonably]].

12   If base rates are referred to, the possibility of their ceasing to exist should be provided for. Alternatively,
      the Law Society's interest rate may be specified.
13   This provision may be expanded to provide for deeming the parties to have disagreed after a certain
      time, deputy appointors etc.

1.14 'The Interest Rate'

'The Interest Rate'[14] means the rate of ...% a year[15] above [the base lending rate of *(specify bank)* or such other bank [being a member of the British Bankers Association] as the Landlord from time to time nominates in writing[16] *(or as required)* the Law Society's interest rate[17]].

14   As to the covenant to pay interest see vol 22(1) (2003 Reissue) LANDLORD AND TENANT (BUSINESS
      TENANCIES) Paragraph 154 [767].
15   Words such as 'with a minimum of ...%' should not be used because, if interest rates drop during the
      term to such an extent that the minimum rate specified represents significantly more than a few percent
      over the basic borrowing rate the provision might be void as a penalty. As to what amounts to a penalty
      see *Dunlop Pneumatic Tyre Co Ltd v New Garage and Motor Co Ltd* [1915] AC 79, HL; *Cellulose Acetate
      Silk Co Ltd v Widnes Foundry (1925) Ltd* [1933] AC 20, HL. In view of this, landlords would be unwise
      to provide for more than a few percent over base rate, and even this is in fact a penalty and should be
      resisted by the tenant.
16   The chance to change the bank may be useful, especially on a sale of the reversion, so that the landlord
      can always provide for his bank for the time being to be specified. The tenant should try to limit the
      choice to major clearing banks.
17   The Law Society's interest rate is published weekly in the Law Society's Gazette.

[1113]

1.15   Interpretation of 'consent' and 'approved'

1.15.1   *Prior written consent or approval*

References to 'consent of the Landlord' or words to similar effect are references to a prior written consent signed by or on behalf of the Landlord and references to the need for anything to be 'approved by the Landlord' or words to similar effect are references to the need for a prior written approval by or on behalf of the Landlord.

1.15.2   *Consent or approval of mortgagee or head landlord*

Any provisions in this Lease referring to the consent or approval of the Landlord are to be construed as also requiring the consent or approval of any mortgagee of the Premises and any head landlord, where that consent is required [under a mortgage or headlease in existence at the date of this lease][18]. Nothing in this Lease is to be construed as imposing any obligation on a mortgagee or head landlord not to refuse any such consent or approval unreasonably.

18   The tenant should include these words so that the clause applies *only* where the consent of the mortgagee or head landlord is in fact required under the terms of an *existing* mortgage or headlease. The tenant should request a copy of the document concerned to establish the rights of the mortgagee or head landlord in relation to any consents that he may seek. The risk to the tenant of the clause without these words is that, by subsequently creating a mortgage or headlease, the landlord could, innocently or deliberately, bring about a situation where his consent may be refused in circumstances in which it would otherwise have been unreasonable to do so. In particular, the effect on the tenant's ability to assign or sublet could be serious.

1.16   Interpretation of 'the Guarantor'[19]

The expression 'the Guarantor' includes [*(where there is a guarantor for the original tenant)* not only the person named above as the Guarantor, but also][20] any person who enters into covenants with the Landlord pursuant to clause 3.9.5.2 CONDITIONS or clause 3.23 REPLACEMENT GUARANTOR.

19   As to guarantors see vol 22(1) (2003 Reissue) LANDLORD AND TENANT (BUSINESS TENANCIES) Paragraphs 40 [201], 71 [278] et seq.
20   Where there is no guarantor for the original tenant, if it is felt undesirable to have covenants in a lease and no party, at least initially, to enter into them, the guarantor's covenants could be included in a schedule.

[1114]

1.17   Interpretation of 'the Landlord'

The expression 'the Landlord' includes the person or persons from time to time entitled to possession of the Premises when this Lease comes to an end.

1.18   Interpretation of 'the last year of the Term' and 'the end of the Term'

References to 'the last year of the Term' are references to the actual last year of the Term howsoever it determines, and references to the 'end of the Term' are references to the end of the Term whensoever and howsoever it determines.

1.19   Interpretation of 'the Tenant'

'The Tenant' includes any person who is for the time being bound by the tenant covenants of this Lease except where the name of *(name of original tenant)* appears.

1.20 Interpretation of 'this Lease'

Unless expressly stated to the contrary, the expression 'this Lease' includes any document supplemental to or collateral with this document or entered into in accordance with this document.

1.21 Joint and several liability

Where any party to this Lease for the time being comprises two or more persons, obligations expressed or implied to be made by or with that party are deemed to be made by or with the persons comprising that party jointly and severally.

[1115]

1.22 'The Liability Period'[21]

'The Liability Period' means —

[1.22.1   in the case of *(name of guarantor for the original tenant)*, the period during which *(name of original tenant)* is bound by the tenant covenants of this Lease together with any additional period during which *(name of original tenant)* is liable under an authorised guarantee agreement,] *(omit where there is no guarantor for the original tenant)*

1.22.2   in the case of any guarantor required pursuant to clause 3.9.5.2 CONDITIONS, the period during which the relevant assignee is bound by the tenant covenants of this Lease together with any additional period during which that assignee is liable under an authorised guarantee agreement,

1.22.3   in the case of any guarantor under an authorised guarantee agreement, the period during which the relevant assignee is bound by the tenant covenants of this Lease, and

1.22.4   in the case of any guarantor required pursuant to clause 3.9.8.7 TERMS OF A PERMITTED SUBLEASE, the period during which the relevant assignee of the sublease is bound by the tenant covenants of that sublease.

21   The liability of the guarantor should be expressed to last while the original tenant, or as the case may be the assignee, is bound by the tenant covenants in the lease — or in the case of clause 1.22.4 the sublease — rather than while the lease is vested in that person, to take account of the possibility of an excluded assignment being made and the tenant — or subtenant — remaining liable. An excluded assignment means that the tenant — or subtenant — is precluded from tenant release under the Landlord and Tenant (Covenants) Act 1995 (23 Halsbury's Statutes (4th Edn) LANDLORD AND TENANT).
       The Landlord and Tenant (Covenants) Act 1995 does not clearly indicate whether the liability of a contractual guarantor can be expressed to extend to any period during which the tenant is bound by an authorised guarantee agreement, but the better view is that it is possible. The policy of the Act certainly suggests that this should be the case.

[1116]

1.23 'Losses'

References to 'losses' are references to liabilities, damages or losses, awards of damages or compensation, penalties, costs, disbursements or expenses arising from any claim, demand, action or proceedings.

1.24 'The 1954 Act'

'The 1954 Act' means the Landlord and Tenant Act 1954 [and all statutes, regulations and orders included by virtue of clause 1.36 REFERENCES TO STATUTES][22].

22   The words in square brackets are strictly speaking not required because they merely state what would be the case anyway by virtue of clause 1.36 [1121] REFERENCES TO STATUTES. Nevertheless, as much could turn on the point (see *Brett v Brett Essex Golf Club Ltd* (1986) 52 P & CR 330, [1986] 1 EGLR 154, CA), the parties may prefer to deal expressly with the point.

1.25 'The 1995 Act'

'The 1995 Act' means the Landlord and Tenant (Covenants) Act 1995 [and all statutes, regulations and orders included by virtue of clause 1.36 REFERENCES TO STATUTES][23].

23   See note 22 to clause 1.24 [1117] 'THE 1954 ACT'.

1.26 Obligation not to permit or suffer

Any covenant by the Tenant not to do anything includes an obligation [to use reasonable endeavours] not to permit or suffer[24] that thing to be done by another person [where the Tenant is aware that the thing is being done].

24   'Permit' may have a different meaning from 'suffer': see *Barton v Reed* [1932] 1 Ch 362 at 375 per Luxmore J. A covenant not to 'permit' activity is broken if the covenantor himself carries it on: see *Oceanic Village Ltd v United Attractions Ltd* [2000] Ch 234, [2000] 1 All ER 975.

[1117]

1.27 'Other buildings'

References to 'other buildings' are references to all the buildings other than the Parade now or at any time during the Term erected on any adjoining property of the Landlord.

1.28 'The Parade'

'The Parade' means the *(describe the parade)* shown [for the purpose of identification only] edged *(state colour, eg blue)* on the Plan.

1.29 'The Passageway'

'The Passageway' means the passageway shown coloured *(state colour, eg green)* on the Plan.

1.30 'The Permitted Use'[25]

'The Permitted Use' means [use for the sale of *(specify goods)* or any other use falling within Class *(specify class, eg A1)* of the Schedule to the Town and Country Planning (Use Classes) Order 1987, notwithstanding any amendment or revocation of that Order[26] as the Landlord from time to time approves[, such approval not to be unreasonably withheld [or delayed]] *(or if the landlord does not require control over the specific goods to be sold)* any use that falls within Class *(specify class, eg A1)* of the Schedule to the Town and Country Planning (Use Classes) Order 1987, notwithstanding any amendment or revocation of that Order].

25   As to use see vol 22(1) (2003 Reissue) LANDLORD AND TENANT (BUSINESS TENANCIES) Paragraph 170 [861] et seq.
26   As use classes orders change frequently, it is important to make clear which class is intended to apply, the class in existence at the date of the lease or the class as amended during the term of the lease.

[1118]

1.31 'The Plan'[27]

'The Plan' means the plan annexed to this Lease.

27   As to the use and role of plans see vol 22(1) (2003 Reissue) LANDLORD AND TENANT (BUSINESS TENANCIES) Paragraphs 117 [636], 118 [638]. Although a plan is necessary in the circumstances assumed by this lease, a plan may not always be required, eg a demise of all the land within a registered title. If the lease is registrable, a plan 'for identification purposes only' or where there is some other disclaimer as to the extent to which it can be relied on for conveyancing purposes is not sufficient if part of the land in a registered title is being dealt with.

1.32 'The Planning Acts'

'The Planning Acts' means the Town and Country Planning Act 1990, the Planning (Listed Buildings and Conservation Areas) Act 1990, the Planning (Consequential Provisions) Act 1990, the Planning (Hazardous Substances) Act 1990, the Planning and Compensation Act 1991, the Planning and Compulsory Purchase Act 2004 [and all statutes, regulations and orders included by virtue of clause 1.36 REFERENCES TO STATUTES][28].

28   See note 22 to clause 1.24 [1117] 'THE 1954 ACT'.

1.33 'The Premises'[29]

1.33.1   *Definition of 'the Premises'*

'The Premises' means Number ... of the Parade shown [for the purpose of identification only] edged *(state colour, eg red)* on the Plan.

29   As to parcels generally see vol 22(1) (2003 Reissue) LANDLORD AND TENANT (BUSINESS TENANCIES) Paragraph 116 [634]. As to the property definition in leases of part of a building see vol 22(1) (2003 Reissue) LANDLORD AND TENANT (BUSINESS TENANCIES) Paragraph 120 [642].

[1119]

1.33.2   *Interpretation of 'the Premises'[30]*

The expression 'the Premises' includes —

[1.33.2.1   the floor and ceiling finishes, but not any other part, of the floor slabs and ceiling slabs that bound the Premises,

1.33.2.2   the inner half severed medially of the internal non-loadbearing walls that divide the Premises from any other premises,

1.33.2.3   the interior plaster and decorative finishes of all walls bounding the Premises,

1.33.2.4   the whole of the shop front,

1.33.2.5   the doors and windows and door and window frames at the Premises,

1.33.2.6   all additions and improvements to the Premises,

1.33.2.7   all the Landlord's fixtures and fittings and fixtures of every kind that are from time to time in or on the Premises, whether originally fixed or fastened to or on the Premises or otherwise, except any fixtures installed by the Tenant [or any predecessors in title] that can be removed from the Premises without defacing them[31], and

1.33.2.8   the Conduits exclusively serving the Premises,

but excludes the roof and the roof space, the foundations, all external, structural or loadbearing walls, columns, beams and supports, and any of the Conduits that do not exclusively serve the Premises *(or as required in the circumstances, according to the construction methods used)*][32]. Unless the contrary is expressly stated 'the Premises' includes any part or parts of the Premises.

30   As to implied grants and reservations see vol 22(1) (2003 Reissue) LANDLORD AND TENANT (BUSINESS TENANCIES) Paragraph 125 [650].
31   As to fixtures see vol 22(1) (2003 Reissue) LANDLORD AND TENANT (BUSINESS TENANCIES) Paragraph 121 [644].

32   It is very dangerous for the draftsman to rely on one set of general words that he hopes will apply to the division of all buildings. These 'standard words' may prove totally unsuitable for a particular building having regard to its nature, configuration and the methods of construction used and also having regard to the nature and extent of any surrounding land included within the demise. Surveyors and engineers must be involved and each building must be looked at individually. There can be no uniform answer as to who should repair which parts of the premises. This clause may need amendment according to the view taken. As to the allocation of legal and financial responsibility for repairs see vol 22(1) (2003 Reissue) LANDLORD AND TENANT (BUSINESS TENANCIES) Paragraph 199 [936].

[1120]

1.34   References to clauses and schedules

Any reference in this document to a clause, paragraph or schedule without further designation is to be construed as a reference to the clause, paragraph or schedule of this document so numbered.

1.35   References to rights of access

References to any right of the Landlord to have access to the Premises are to be construed as extending to any head landlord and any mortgagee of the Premises [— where the headlease or mortgage grants such rights of access to the head landlord or mortgagee —] and to all persons authorised in writing by the Landlord and any head landlord or mortgagee, including agents, professional advisers, contractors, workmen and others.

1.36   References to statutes

Unless expressly stated to the contrary any references to a specific statute include any statutory extension or modification, amendment or re-enactment of that statute and any regulations or orders made under that statute, and any general reference to a statute includes any regulations or orders made under that statute[33].

33   Unfortunately the Interpretation Act 1978 ss 17, 23(3) (41 Halsbury's Statutes (4th Edn) STATUTES) does not quite go far enough to enable this clause to be dispensed with altogether, particularly where a statute is modified.

1.37   'The Rent'[34]

[Until the First Review Date 'the Rent' means the Initial Rent. Thereafter 'the Rent' means the sum ascertained in accordance with schedule 3 THE RENT AND RENT REVIEW. 'The Rent' does not include the Insurance Rent[35], but the term 'the Lease Rents' means both the Rent and the Insurance Rent[36] *(or as required by the rent and review provisions used)*].

34   This clause assumes that the rent is reviewable. If the rent is not reviewable clause 1.10 [1111] 'THE INITIAL RENT' should be omitted and this clause amended as appropriate.
35   Because of this exclusion the insurance rent is not suspended under clause 5.5 [1196] SUSPENSION OF THE RENT.
36   The tenant's obligation to contribute to the landlord's expenditure in relation to the maintenance and decoration of the parade could also be incorporated in the definition of 'Lease Rents'. However, unless regular substantial expenditure is anticipated, this is probably not necessary.

[1121]

1.38   'The Rent Commencement Date'

'The Rent Commencement Date' means *(insert the date on which payment of the rent is to start)*[37].

37   This provision may be used to provide for a rent-free period, or for the situation where the tenant has had possession before the execution of the lease on the basis that rent should be paid from the date of possession. If either the date of execution of the lease, or the date of commencement of the term, is to be the date of commencement of rent, that date should be inserted here.

[1.39   'The Review Dates'[38]

'The First Review Date' means *(date)*. 'The Review Dates' means the First Review Date and every *(insert ordinal, eg 3rd)* anniversary of that date during the [Contractual] Term [*(if appropriate for the review provisions used)* — and any other date from time to time specified under *(insert the relevant provision: see eg vol 22(3) (1997 Reissue) LANDLORD AND TENANT (BUSINESS TENANCIES) Form 180 paragraph {2}-4 [6728] EFFECT OF COUNTER-INFLATION PROVISIONS]*. References to 'a review date' are references to any one of the Review Dates.] *(omit if not required by the review provisions to be used, or if the rent is not reviewable)*

38   As to rent review dates and intervals see vol 22(1) (2003 Reissue) LANDLORD AND TENANT (BUSINESS TENANCIES) Paragraph 302 [1333] et seq. Where there might be a statutory continuation of the lease, the landlord may wish to ensure that there is a review date shortly before the end of the contractual term to obviate the need to apply for an interim rent. The tenant may wish to insist on the word 'contractual' remaining so that the rent review provisions do not apply during any period of lawful holding over or extension or continuance of the contractual term.

1.40   'The Road'

'The Road' means the road coloured *(state colour, eg brown)* on the Plan.

1.41   'The Shop and Maisonette Covenants'

'The Shop and Maisonette Covenants' means the covenants set out in schedule 4 THE SHOP AND MAISONETTE COVENANTS.

1.42   'The Staircase'

'The Staircase' means the staircase between the ground floor and the [first] floor at the rear of the Parade, shown coloured *(state colour, eg yellow)* on the Plan.

[1122]

1.43   'The Surveyor'[39]

'The Surveyor' means *(name)* or any person or firm appointed by the Landlord in his place. The Surveyor may be an employee of the Landlord or a company that is a member of the same group as the Landlord within the meaning of the 1954 Act Section 42. The expression 'the Surveyor' includes the person or firm appointed by the Landlord to collect the Lease Rents.

39   For a provision that the landlord's surveyor must be a member of a relevant professional body see vol 22(3) (1997 Reissue) LANDLORD AND TENANT (BUSINESS TENANCIES) Form 152 [6648].

[1.44 'The Term'

'The Term' means the Contractual Term and any period of holding-over or extension or continuance of the Contractual Term by statute or common law[40].] *(omit if the lease is to be contracted out of the Landlord and Tenant Act 1954)*[41]

40   The demise in this lease is for 'the Contractual Term', which is defined as a fixed term of years. The expression 'the Term' is used in covenants so that they continue to apply during any period of holding over or continuance or extension of the contractual term. As to the liability of a guarantor during a period of statutory continuation see vol 22(1) (2003 Reissue) LANDLORD AND TENANT (BUSINESS TENANCIES) Paragraph 73 [282].

41   Some difficulties arise if the structure referred to in note 40 above is used in a draft lease where security of tenure is to be excluded under the Landlord and Tenant Act 1954 s 38A(1) as inserted by SI 2003/3096. The demise is for the contractual term and the inclusion of the definition of 'the Term' does not prevent the lease being 'for a term of years certain' as required by the Landlord and Tenant Act 1954 s 38A(1). However, reference to continuance of the contractual term by statute is inappropriate where the operation of the security of tenure provisions in the Landlord and Tenant Act 1954 ss 24–28 is to be excluded. If a lease is contracted out of the Landlord and Tenant Act 1954 there can be no statutory extension, and if the tenant remains in occupation at the end of the contractual term he is holding over unlawfully unless there is an express agreement to extend the contractual term operating as a surrender and re-grant so that the original lease — and the agreement under the Landlord and Tenant Act 1954 s 38A(1) — has no further effect. It is suggested that in these circumstances the drafting should be simplified to include a single term (defined simply as 'the Term') by reference to the period of the contractual term. This can be achieved by amending clause 1.5 [1110] 'THE [CONTRACTUAL] TERM' as suggested and substituting it for this clause.

1.45   Terms from the 1995 Act

Where the expressions 'landlord covenants', 'tenant covenants', or 'authorised guarantee agreement' are used in this Lease they are to have the same meaning as is given by the 1995 Act Section 28(1).

1.46   'VAT'[42]

'VAT' means value added tax or any other tax of a similar nature and unless otherwise expressly stated all references to rents or other sums payable by the Tenant are exclusive of VAT.

42   As to VAT generally see the Information Binder: Property [1]: VAT and Property.

[1123]–[1130]

2   DEMISE

The Landlord lets[43] the Premises to the Tenant [with [full *(or)* limited] title guarantee], together with the rights specified in schedule 1 THE RIGHTS GRANTED but excepting and reserving to the Landlord the rights specified in schedule 2 THE RIGHTS RESERVED, to hold the Premises to the Tenant for the [Contractual][44] Term, subject to [all rights, easements, privileges, restrictions, covenants and stipulations of whatever nature affecting the Premises including any matters contained or referred to in schedule 5 THE SUBJECTIONS *(or as required)* the rights, easements, privileges, restrictions, covenants and stipulations affecting the Premises contained or referred to in schedule 5 THE SUBJECTIONS][45], yielding and paying[46] to the Landlord —

2.1   the Rent without any deduction or set off[47] by equal quarterly payments in advance[48] on the usual quarter days[49] in every year and proportionately for any period of less than a year, the first such payment, being a proportionate sum in respect of the period from and including the Rent Commencement Date to and including the day before the quarter day next after the Rent Commencement Date, to be paid on the date of this document[50], and

2.2   by way of further rent the Insurance Rent[51] payable on demand in accordance with clause 5.4 PAYMENT OF THE INSURANCE RENT.

43   Traditionally, the operative word in a lease executed as a deed was 'demises' but any words sufficient to show the parties' intention may be used.

44   See note 41 to clause 1.44 [1123] 'THE TERM'.

45   The tenant should argue for the second version, making the schedule comprehensive rather than illustrative.

46   The words 'yielding and paying' imply a covenant to pay rent: see *Vyvyan v Arthur* (1823) 1 B & C 410. An express covenant is now invariably included because further procedural matters are contained in it.

47   As to deductions and set off see vol 22(1) (2003 Reissue) LANDLORD AND TENANT (BUSINESS TENANCIES) Paragraph 147 [753].

48   In the absence of an express provision, rent is payable in arrears.

49   The usual quarter days are 25 March, 24 June, 29 September and 25 December. A reference to 'the usual quarter days' is all that is necessary when rent is to be paid on these days.

50   If the first payment is not a complete instalment, the lease must provide for the date on which it is to be paid, the amount, and the period it is to cover.

51   As to the advantages of reserving the insurance rent as rent see vol 22(1) (2003 Reissue) LANDLORD AND TENANT (BUSINESS TENANCIES) Paragraph 151 [761]. The tenant's obligation to contribute to the landlord's expenditure in relation to the maintenance and decoration of the parade could also be incorporated in this clause. However, unless regular expenditure of substance is anticipated, it is considered to be more appropriate, if required, simply to refer to the payment as 'additional rent' in the operative provision: see paragraph 4-4.1 [1245] PAYMENT OF PROPORTION OF COSTS.

[1131]

3   THE TENANT'S COVENANTS

The Tenant covenants with the Landlord to observe and perform the requirements of this clause 3.

3.1   Rent

3.1.1   *Payment of the Lease Rents*

The Tenant must pay the Lease Rents[52] on the days and in the manner set out in this Lease, and must not exercise or seek to exercise any right or claim to withhold rent, or any right or claim to legal or equitable set-off[53] [except that referred to in *(give details of any provisions granting an express right of set-off)*][54].

52   As to the definition of 'the Lease Rents' see clause 1.37 [1121] 'THE RENT'.

53   See, eg, *British Anzani (Felixstowe) Ltd v International Marine Management (UK) Ltd* [1980] QB 137, [1979] 2 All ER 1063; *Lee-Parker v Izzet* [1971] 3 All ER 1099, [1971] 1 WLR 1688. As to deductions and set-off see vol 22(1) (2003 Reissue) LANDLORD AND TENANT (BUSINESS TENANCIES) Paragraphs 147 [753], 148 [755].

54   If any express right of set-off is granted to the tenant, reference to the provision concerned should be included here to avoid inconsistency.

3.1.2   *Payment by banker's order*[55]

If so required in writing by the Landlord, the Tenant must pay the Lease Rents[56] by banker's order or credit transfer to any bank and account [in the United Kingdom] that the Landlord nominates from time to time.

55   This is a clause with dangers for both parties. If the existence of a breach of covenant is known to the landlord he must instruct his bank to refuse to accept the rent, otherwise his right of forfeiture is lost. As to implied waiver of the right of forfeiture see vol 22(1) (2003 Reissue) LANDLORD AND TENANT (BUSINESS TENANCIES) Paragraph 284 [1173]. The tenant may feel that he requires more control over the payment of rent. In any event, the financial systems operated by many companies prevent payments being made in this way.

56   As to the definition of 'the Lease Rents' see clause 1.37 [1121] 'THE RENT'.

[1132]

3.2   Outgoings and VAT

3.2.1   *Outgoings exclusive to the Premises*

The Tenant must pay, and must indemnify the Landlord against —

3.2.1.1   all rates, taxes[57], assessments, duties, charges, impositions and outgoings that are now or may at any time during the Term be charged, assessed or imposed upon the Premises or upon the owner or occupier of them[, excluding any payable by the Landlord occasioned by receipt of the Lease Rents[58] or by any disposition of or dealing with this Lease or ownership of any interest reversionary to the interest created by it][59] [— provided that if the Landlord suffers any loss of rating relief that may be applicable to empty premises after the end of the Term because the relief has been allowed to the Tenant in respect of any period before the end of the Term then the Tenant must make good such loss to the Landlord],

3.2.1.2   all VAT that may from time to time be charged on the Lease Rents or other sums payable by the Tenant under this Lease[60], and

3.2.1.3   all VAT incurred in relation to any costs that the Tenant is obliged to pay or in respect of which he is required to indemnify the Landlord under the terms of this Lease, save where such VAT is recoverable or available for set-off by the Landlord as input tax[61].

57   As to covenants to pay rates and taxes see vol 22(1) (2003 Reissue) LANDLORD AND TENANT (BUSINESS TENANCIES) Paragraph 153 [765].
58   As to the definition of 'the Lease Rents' see clause 1.37 [1121] 'THE RENT'.
59   The tenant should add the words in square brackets to make it clear that he is not paying the landlord's taxes.
60   As to VAT on rent, service charges and insurance premiums see the Information Binder: Property [1]: VAT and Property.
61   As to payment of VAT on legal costs paid by a person other than the solicitor's own client see the Information Binder: Property [1]: VAT and Property.

3.2.2   *Outgoings assessed on the Premises and other property*

The Tenant must pay, and must indemnify the Landlord against, the proportion reasonably attributable to the Premises — to be determined from time to time by the Surveyor, acting as an expert and not as an arbitrator[62] — of all rates, taxes, assessments, duties, charges, impositions and outgoings that are now or at any time during the Term may be charged, assessed or imposed on the Premises and any other premises, including any adjoining property of the Landlord, or on their owners or occupiers.

62   As to the distinction between an expert and an arbitrator see vol 22(1) (2003 Reissue) LANDLORD AND TENANT (BUSINESS TENANCIES) Paragraph 364 [1523].

[1133]

[3.3   Cost of services consumed[63]

The Tenant must pay to the suppliers, and indemnify the Landlord against, all charges for electricity, water, gas, telecommunications and other services consumed or used at or in relation to the Premises, including meter rents and standing charges, and must comply with the lawful requirements and regulations of their respective suppliers.] *(omit if the premises have independent supplies of all services)*

63   Where the premises comprise a separate building, a separate supply is usually provided and the tenant makes his own arrangements with the suppliers. In that case this clause is unnecessary.

3.4   Repair, cleaning and decoration

3.4.1   *Repair of the Premises*[64]

The Tenant must repair the Premises and keep them in good condition and repair, except for damage caused by one or more of the Insured Risks save to the extent that the insurance money is irrecoverable due to any act or default of the Tenant or anyone at the Premises expressly or by implication[65] with his authority [and under his control][66].

64   As to repair see vol 22(1) (2003 Reissue) LANDLORD AND TENANT (BUSINESS TENANCIES) Paragraph 196 [931] et seq. For a covenant to repair, rebuild and renew see vol 22(3) (1997 Reissue) LANDLORD AND TENANT (BUSINESS TENANCIES) Form 85 [6460]. For provisos excluding, eg, work that is prevented etc see vol 22(3) (1997 Reissue) LANDLORD AND TENANT (BUSINESS TENANCIES) Forms 87 [6462], 88 [6463].

     If a landlord is unable to obtain full insurance cover without excess, it should be made clear whether the tenant is to be liable to pay the excess where damage is caused by an insured risk. For a covenant limiting the tenant's repairing obligations by reference to uninsurable as well as insured risks see vol 22(3) (1997 Reissue) LANDLORD AND TENANT (BUSINESS TENANCIES) Form 90 [6465]. It should be noted that it is now recommended 'best practice' that if the premises are so damaged by an uninsured risk as to prevent occupation, the tenant should be allowed to terminate the lease unless the landlord agrees to reinstate at his own cost: see vol 22(1) (2003 Reissue) LANDLORD AND TENANT (BUSINESS TENANCIES) Paragraph 85 [402]. If adopted, this recommendation involves damage preventing occupation caused by uninsured or uninsurable risks being excluded from the ambit of the tenant's repairing covenant.

65   The expression 'by implication' is intended to include a caller on the premises, such as a tradesman, where there has been no express invitation but the person cannot be classed as a trespasser.

66   The tenant should add the words in square brackets.

[1134]

3.4.2   *Replacement of landlord's fixtures*

The Tenant must replace any landlord's fixtures and fittings in the Premises that are beyond repair at any time during or at the end of the Term.

3.4.3   *Cleaning and tidying*

The Tenant must keep the Premises clean and tidy and clear of all rubbish.

[3.4.4   *The Open Land*

3.4.4.1   Care of the Open Land

The Tenant must keep any part of the Premises that is not built on ('the Open Land') adequately surfaced, in good condition and free from weeds [and keep all landscaped areas properly cultivated].

3.4.4.2   Storage on the Open Land

The Tenant must not store anything on the Open Land or bring anything onto it [that is or might become untidy, unclean, unsightly or in any way detrimental to the Premises or the area generally].

3.4.4.3   Rubbish on the Open Land

The Tenant must not deposit any waste, rubbish or refuse on the Open Land, [or place any receptacle for them on it].

3.4.4.4   Vehicles on the Open Land

The Tenant must not keep or store any [*(if the land cannot be used for parking)* vehicle] caravan or movable dwelling on the Open Land.] *(adapt clause 3.4.4 as required or omit if no open land is included)*

3.4.5   Care of abutting land

The Tenant must not cause any adjoining property of the Landlord or any other land, roads or pavements abutting the Premises to be untidy or dirty, and in particular, but without prejudice to the generality of the foregoing, must not deposit refuse or other materials on them.

[1135]

3.4.6   Decoration

[As often as may in the [reasonable] opinion of the Surveyor be necessary in order to maintain a high standard of decorative finish and attractiveness and to preserve the Premises *(or as required)* In each of the Decorating Years][67] and in the last year of the Term the Tenant must redecorate the Premises[68] in a good and workmanlike manner, with appropriate materials of good quality[to the [reasonable] satisfaction of the Surveyor], any change in the tints, colours and patterns of the decoration to be approved by the Landlord[, whose approval may not be unreasonably withheld [or delayed]][69] [, provided that the covenants relating to the last year of the Term are not to apply where the Tenant has redecorated the Premises less than *(state period, eg 18 months)* before the end of the Term].

67   The draftsman should discuss with the landlord and his property advisers whether the landlord wishes to have the flexibility of the first option in square brackets or the certainty of the second.
68   The restricted nature of the demise should be borne in mind when considering the scope of this covenant: see clause 1.33 [1119] 'THE PREMISES'.
69   The tenant may amend to provide for the landlord's approval to tints etc to apply only in the last year of the term.

3.4.7   Shared facilities

Where the use of any of the Conduits or any boundary structures or other things is common to the Premises and any adjoining or neighbouring premises, other than any adjoining property of the Landlord, the Tenant must be responsible for, and indemnify the Landlord against, all sums due from the owner, tenant or occupier of the Premises in relation to those Conduits, boundary structures or other things and must undertake all work in relation to them that is his responsibility[70].

70   This covenant applies to items common to the demised premises and property other than that retained by the landlord. Its effect is to impose on the tenant all liability attaching to the owner or occupier of the demised premises in relation to such items.

[1136]

3.5   Waste and alterations

3.5.1   *Waste, additions and alterations*[71]

The Tenant must not commit any waste, make any addition to the Premises, unite the Premises with any adjoining premises, or make any alteration to the Premises save as permitted by the provisions of this clause 3.5.

71   As to control of alterations see vol 22(1) (2003 Reissue) LANDLORD AND TENANT (BUSINESS TENANCIES) Paragraph 186 [911] et seq.

3.5.2   *Preconditions for alterations*

The Tenant must not make any [internal non-structural] alterations to the Premises unless he first —

3.5.2.1   obtains and complies with the necessary consents of the competent authorities and pays their charges for them,

3.5.2.2   makes an application to the Landlord for consent, supported by drawings and where appropriate a specification in duplicate [prepared by an architect[, or a member of some other appropriate profession,] who must supervise the work throughout to completion],

3.5.2.3   pays the fees of the Landlord, any head landlord, any mortgagee and their respective professional advisers,

3.5.2.4   enters into any covenants the Landlord requires as to the execution and reinstatement of the alterations, and

3.5.2.5   obtains the consent of the Landlord, whose consent may not be unreasonably withheld [or delayed].

[In the case of any works of a substantial nature, the Landlord may require the Tenant to provide, before starting the works, adequate security in the form of a deposit of money or the provision of a bond, as assurance to the Landlord that any works he permits from time to time will be fully completed].

[1137]

3.5.3   *Removal of alterations*[72]

At the end of the Term, if so requested by the Landlord, the Tenant must remove any additional buildings, additions, alterations or improvements made to the Premises, and must make good any part or parts of the Premises that may be damaged by their removal.

72   This clause has probably come to be inserted because landlords hope that it will defeat the effect of the compensation provisions of the Landlord and Tenant Act 1927 Pt I (ss 1–17) (23 Halsbury's Statutes (4th Edn) LANDLORD AND TENANT) — as to which see vol 22(1) (2003 Reissue) LANDLORD AND TENANT (BUSINESS TENANCIES) Paragraph 192 [923] et seq — ie because, if the improvement has been removed, it will not be an improvement to the holding at the time of quitting the premises. In fact, the clause might not achieve this effect, because the Landlord and Tenant Act 1927 s 9 as amended by the Landlord and Tenant Act 1954 s 49 prohibits contracting out. Also the clause may be void under the Landlord and Tenant Act 1927 s 19(2), so far as it applies to improvements, on the grounds that it purports to fetter the court in deciding what is reasonable. The tenant should not, however, rely on the application of these statutory provisions and should seek to strike out the clause.

3.5.4   *Connection to the Conduits*

The Tenant must not make any connection with the Conduits except in accordance with plans and specifications approved by the Landlord[, whose approval may not be unreasonably withheld [or delayed]], and subject to consent to make the connection having previously been obtained from the competent authority, undertaker or supplier.

3.6   Aerials, signs and advertisements

3.6.1   *Masts and wires*

The Tenant must not erect any pole or mast on the Premises [or install any wire or cable on them], whether in connection with telecommunications or otherwise.

3.6.2   *Advertisements*[73]

The Tenant must not, without the consent of the Landlord, fix to or exhibit on the outside of the Premises, or fix to or exhibit through any window of the Premises, or display anywhere on the Premises, any placard, sign, notice, fascia board or advertisement.

73   See the Town and Country Planning (Control of Advertisements) Regulations 1992, SI 1992/666 as amended. In the absence of a covenant such as this and subject to those Regulations, the tenant may exhibit advertisements etc on the premises, whether or not they are connected with his business: see *Clapman v Edwards* [1938] 2 All ER 507.

[1138]

3.7   Statutory obligations

3.7.1   *General provision*[74]

The Tenant must comply in all respects with the requirements of any statutes, and any other obligations imposed by law or by any byelaws, applicable to the Premises or the trade or business for the time being carried on there.

74   As to the covenant to comply with statutes see vol 22(1) (2003 Reissue) LANDLORD AND TENANT (BUSINESS TENANCIES) Paragraph 182 [905]. For a provision requiring the landlord to pay compensation for works above a certain value see vol 22(3) (1997 Reissue) LANDLORD AND TENANT (BUSINESS TENANCIES) Form 169 [6693].

3.7.2   *Particular obligations*

3.7.2.1   **Works required by statute, department or authority**

Without prejudice to the generality of clause 3.7.1, the Tenant must execute all works and provide and maintain all arrangements on or in respect of the Premises or the use to which they are being put that are required in order to comply with the requirements of any statute already or in the future to be passed, or the requirements of any government department, local authority or other public or competent authority or court of competent jurisdiction, regardless of whether the requirements are imposed on the owner, the occupier, or any other person.

3.7.2.2   **Acts causing losses**

Without prejudice to the generality of clause 3.7.1, the Tenant must not do in or near the Premises anything by reason of which the Landlord may incur any losses under any statute.

3.7.2.3   **Construction (Design and Management) Regulations**

Without prejudice to the generality of clause 3.7.1, the Tenant must comply with the provisions of the Construction (Design and Management) Regulations 1994 ('the CDM Regulations'), be the only client as defined in the provisions of the CDM Regulations, fulfil, in relation to all and any works, all the obligations of the client as set out in or reasonably to be inferred from the CDM Regulations, and make a declaration to that effect[75] to the Health and Safety Executive in accordance with the Approved Code of Practice published from time to time by the Health and Safety Executive in relation to the CDM Regulations. The provisions of clause 5.3.3 FIRE-FIGHTING EQUIPMENT are to have effect in any circumstances to which these obligations apply.

3.7.2.4   Delivery of health and safety files

At the end of the Term, the Tenant must forthwith deliver to the Landlord any and all health and safety files relating to the premises in accordance with the CDM Regulations.

75   If works are being carried out for the tenant, the landlord will not want to accept the liabilities that are placed on a client under the Construction (Design and Management) Regulations 1994, SI 1994/3140 and the Health and Safety Executive Approved Code of Practice. The landlord will need to ensure that the tenant actually makes the declaration required, and that he obtains the notification served on the tenant by the Health and Safety Executive.

[1139]

3.8   Entry to inspect and notice to repair

3.8.1   *Entry and notice*

The Tenant must permit the Landlord[76] [on reasonable notice during normal business hours except in emergency][77] —

3.8.1.1   to enter the Premises to ascertain whether or not the covenants and conditions of this Lease have been observed and performed,

3.8.1.2   to view the state of repair and condition of the Premises, and to open up floors and other parts of the Premises where that is necessary in order to do so, and

3.8.1.3   to give to the Tenant, or notwithstanding clause 8.7 NOTICES leave on the Premises, a notice ('a notice to repair') specifying the works required to remedy any breach of the Tenant's obligations as to the repair and condition of the Premises in this Lease,

provided that any opening-up must be made good by and at the cost of the Landlord if it reveals no breach of the terms of this Lease.

76   The provisions of clause 1.35 [1121] REFERENCES TO RIGHTS OF ACCESS should be noted.
77   The tenant should add the words in square brackets.

3.8.2   *Works to be carried out*

The Tenant must carry out the works specified in a notice to repair immediately, including making good any opening up that revealed a breach of the terms of this Lease.

[3.8.3   *Landlord's power in default*[78]

If within *(state period, eg 1 month)* of the service of a notice to repair the Tenant has not started to execute the work referred to in that notice or is not proceeding diligently with it, or if the Tenant fails to finish the work within *(state period, eg 2 months)*[79][, or if in the [Landlord's *(or as required)* Surveyor's] [reasonable] opinion the Tenant is unlikely to finish the work within that period], the Tenant must permit the Landlord to enter the Premises to execute the outstanding work, and must within *(state period, eg 14 days)* of a written demand pay to the Landlord the cost of so doing and all expenses incurred by the Landlord, including legal costs and surveyor's fees.]

78   The advantages of this clause for the landlord must be weighed against the potential liability that it creates under the Defective Premises Act 1972 s 4(4) (31 Halsbury's Statutes (4th Edn) NEGLIGENCE): see *McAuley v Bristol City Council* [1992] QB 134, [1992] 1 All ER 749, CA.

It has been held that a claim by the landlord for recovery of costs under such a clause is a claim for recovery of a debt, and can therefore be enforced without requiring leave of the court under the Leasehold Property (Repairs) Act 1938 (23 Halsbury's Statutes (4th Edn) LANDLORD AND TENANT): see *Jervis v Harris* [1996] Ch 195, [1996] 1 All ER 303, CA.

However, even where a landlord has been granted a right of this nature the court does not compel the tenant to allow the landlord the right to enter and carry out repairs where these would be of no benefit and where no loss is being caused to the landlord: see *Hammersmith London Borough Council v Creska (No 2)* [2000] L & TR 288.

79   The tenant would prefer to be given 'a reasonable period' to do the work required to remedy the breaches because it may take longer than the specified number of months.

[1140]

3.9   Alienation[80]

3.9.1   *Alienation prohibited*

The Tenant must not hold the Premises on trust for another. The Tenant must not part with the possession of the Premises or any part of the Premises or permit another to occupy them or any part of them except pursuant to a transaction permitted by and effected in accordance with the provisions of this Lease.

80   As to alienation see vol 22(1) (2003 Reissue) LANDLORD AND TENANT (BUSINESS TENANCIES) Paragraph 156 [801] et seq. Where the lease is registrable, this prohibition or restriction on dealings will be reflected in an entry on the register excepting from the effects of registration all estates, rights, interests, powers and remedies arising on or by reason of any dealing made in breach of the prohibition or restriction: see the Land Registration Rules 2003, SI 2003/1417 r 6(2).

3.9.2   *Assignment, subletting and charging of part*[81]

(version 1)

[The Tenant must not assign, sublet or charge part only of the Premises.] *(where assignment, subletting or charging of the whole is allowed)*

(version 2)

[The Tenant must not assign or charge part only of the Premises and must not sublet the whole or any part of them.] *(where assignment or charging of the whole is permitted, but subletting is not allowed at all)*

81   Whether subletting should be permitted is a commercial matter. Some landlords consider that the fact that they cannot unreasonably refuse consent to an assignment gives the tenant all the protection he requires and are not prepared to permit subletting. An advantage to the tenant of the ability to sublet is that he has an element of control over a subtenant but not over an assignee, for whom he may retain liability under an authorised guarantee agreement. Further, with stringent assignment tests or in a bad market, subletting may be the only option open to the tenant.

3.9.3   *Assignment of the whole*

Subject to clauses 3.9.4 CIRCUMSTANCES and 3.9.5 CONDITIONS, the Tenant must not assign the whole of the Premises without the consent of the Landlord, whose consent may not be unreasonably withheld [or delayed][82].

82   This residual discretion is the old test of reasonableness under the Landlord and Tenant Act 1927 s 19(1). Thus the tenant and the proposed assignee may satisfy the circumstances and conditions specified for the purposes of the Landlord and Tenant Act 1927 s 19(1A) as inserted by the Landlord and Tenant (Covenants) Act 1995 s 22 (as to which see clause 3.9.4 [1151] CIRCUMSTANCES and clause 3.9.5 [1153] CONDITIONS), but the landlord may still refuse consent on reasonable grounds: see vol 22(1) (2003 Reissue) LANDLORD AND TENANT (BUSINESS TENANCIES) Paragraph 159 [812] et seq.

[1141]–[1150]

3.9.4   *Circumstances*

If any of the following circumstances[83] — which are specified for the purposes of the Landlord and Tenant Act 1927 Section 19(1A)[84] — applies either at the date when application for consent to assign is made to the Landlord, or after that date but before the Landlord's consent is given, the Landlord may withhold his consent and if, after the Landlord's consent has been given but before the assignment has taken place, any such circumstances apply, the Landlord may revoke his consent[85], whether his consent is expressly subject to a condition as referred to in clause 3.9.5.4 CONDITIONS or not. The circumstances are —

3.9.4.1   that any sum due from the Tenant under this Lease remains unpaid[86],

3.9.4.2   that in the Landlord's reasonable[87] opinion the assignee is not a person who is likely to be able to comply with the tenant covenants of this Lease and to continue to be able to comply with them following the assignment,

[3.9.4.3   that without prejudice to clause 3.9.4.2, in the case of an assignment to a company in the same group as the Tenant[88] within the meaning of the 1954 Act Section 42 in the Landlord's reasonable opinion the assignee is a person who is, or may become, less likely to be able to comply with the tenant covenants of this Lease than the Tenant requesting consent to assign, which likelihood is adjudged by reference in particular to the financial strength of that Tenant aggregated with that of any guarantor of the obligations of that Tenant and the value of any other security for the performance of the tenant covenants of this Lease when assessed at the date of grant or — where that Tenant is not *(name of original tenant)* — the date of the assignment of this Lease to that Tenant[89],] or

3.9.4.4   that the assignee or any guarantor for the assignee, other than any guarantor under an authorised guarantee agreement, is a corporation registered — or otherwise resident — in a jurisdiction in which the order of a court obtained in England and Wales will not necessarily be enforced against the assignee or guarantor without any consideration of the merits of the case.

(for examples of circumstances for use in unusual cases, see vol 22(3) (1997 Reissue) LANDLORD AND TENANT (BUSINESS TENANCIES) Form 117 [6501])

[1151]

---

83   The Landlord and Tenant Act 1927 s 19(1A) as inserted by the Landlord and Tenant (Covenants) Act 1995 s 22 enables the landlord and tenant to a post-1995 lease to agree in advance the terms upon which an assignment may be permitted. It distinguishes between on the one hand circumstances, the existence of which entitles the landlord to refuse consent to assignment, and on the other hand conditions that may be imposed on his consent. This clause and clause 3.9.5 [1153] CONDITIONS are drafted on the assumption that this is a valid approach and seek to draw a clear distinction between circumstances and conditions.

It should be noted that provisions that are overly restrictive may have an adverse impact at any rent review. It should also be noted that it is recommended 'best practice' that unless the particular circumstances of the letting justify greater control, the only restriction on assignment of the whole should be obtaining the landlord's consent, which is not to be unreasonably withheld: see vol 22(1) (2003 Reissue) LANDLORD AND TENANT (BUSINESS TENANCIES) Paragraph 85 [401] and 'A code of practice for commercial leases in England and Wales (2nd edition)' which can be found in vol 22(1) (2003 Reissue) LANDLORD AND TENANT (BUSINESS TENANCIES) as Form 1 [4501].

Each letting must be looked at in the light of its own particular facts and circumstances but it is considered that the provisions of this clause do, in the ordinary course, strike a reasonable balance between the landlord's desire for control and the tenant's ability to dispose of his interest without undue restriction. For a less restrictive approach see vol 22(1) (2003 Reissue) LANDLORD AND TENANT (BUSINESS TENANCIES) Form 7 clause 5.2 [5538].

84   The Landlord and Tenant Act 1927 s 19(1A) as inserted by the Landlord and Tenant (Covenants) Act 1995 s 22 seems to require the alienation clause to state that the circumstances it mentions are specified for the purposes of that subsection.

85   The landlord may require that certain circumstances are absent not only before consent has been given to the assignment, but also up to the date on which the assignment takes place — when the die is cast and the lease covenants bind the assignee. For example, the landlord may require the rent to be paid up to date not only before the application for consent is made, but also at the date when consent is given and the possibly later date when the lease is actually assigned.

86   The tenant may want to limit this to the rent, as it may be thought that a dispute is more likely to arise over the insurance rent or other payments. If the tenant has retained any right of set-off, it should also be referred to here.

87   Circumstances and conditions must either be factual or, if they contain an element of discretion, require that discretion to be exercised reasonably (see the Landlord and Tenant Act 1927 s 19(1C)(a) as inserted by the Landlord and Tenant (Covenants) Act 1995 s 22), or must give the tenant a right of appeal to an expert (see the Landlord and Tenant Act 1927 s 19(1C)(b) as inserted by the Landlord and Tenant (Covenants) Act 1995 s 22). If the discretion is to be exercised reasonably, as suggested by this provision, the tenant can take any dispute about its exercise to the court. The court will consider whether *this* landlord has acted within the range of reasonable decisions, not whether a reasonable landlord would have reached the same decision or whether the test is itself reasonable. For a clause where an expert is used see vol 22(3) (1997 Reissue) LANDLORD AND TENANT (BUSINESS TENANCIES) Form 117 [6501].

88   There have been suggestions that intra-group assignments should be banned completely. However, this is considered to be too draconian and would prevent legitimate corporate restructuring needed for reasons other than avoidance of liability under the Landlord and Tenant (Covenants) Act 1995. The landlord's concern is that a strong tenant may assign to a weak group company; the assignment is acceptable because the assignor gives an authorised guarantee agreement for the assignee. The second group company may then itself assign outside the group; the landlord will lose the authorised guarantee agreement of the strong first group company and have only the possibly worthless authorised guarantee agreement of the second group company. The possibilities for exploitation of this scenario are obvious and it is therefore felt that this is the one situation in which measuring the financial strength of the assignee in relation to that of the assignor is justified. Equivalence tests are not generally thought to be appropriate, because a strong first covenant may make the lease almost unassignable, adversely affecting the rent at review.

89   Consider whether the time at which the tenant's financial status is measured should be when he acquired the lease, when his status was acceptable to the landlord, or at the date of the application for consent to assign, when it may have deteriorated sharply. On the other hand, the outgoing tenant may be a better covenant now than when he acquired the lease: the wily landlord may wish to leave himself free to pick whichever of the two dates gives the better picture.

[1152]

3.9.5   *Conditions*

The Landlord may impose any or all of the following conditions[90] — which are specified for the purposes of the Landlord and Tenant Act 1927 Section 19(1A)[91] — on giving any consent for an assignment by the Tenant, and any such consent is to be treated as being subject to each of the following conditions —

3.9.5.1   a condition that upon or before any assignment and before giving occupation to the assignee, the Tenant requesting consent to assign, together with any former tenant who by virtue of the 1995 Act Section 11 was not released on an earlier assignment of this Lease[92], must enter into an authorised guarantee agreement[93] in favour of the Landlord in the terms set out in schedule 7 THE AUTHORISED GUARANTEE AGREEMENT,

3.9.5.2   a condition that if reasonably so required by the Landlord on an assignment to a limited company, the assignee must ensure that at least *(state number, eg 2)* directors of the company, or some other guarantor or guarantors [reasonably] acceptable to the Landlord, enter into direct covenants with the Landlord in the form of the guarantor's covenants contained in clause 6 GUARANTEE PROVISIONS with 'the Assignee' substituted for 'the Tenant',

3.9.5.3   a condition that upon or before any assignment, the Tenant making the request for consent to assign must give to the Landlord a copy of the health and safety file required to be maintained under the Construction (Design and Management) Regulations 1994 containing full details of all works undertaken to the Premises by that Tenant, and

3.9.5.4   a condition that if, at any time before the assignment, the circumstances specified in clause 3.9.4 CIRCUMSTANCES, or any of them, apply, the Landlord may revoke the consent by written notice to the Tenant.

[1153]

90   The Landlord and Tenant Act 1927 s 19(1A) as inserted by the Landlord and Tenant (Covenants) Act 1995 s 22 enables the landlord and tenant to a post-1995 lease to agree in advance the terms upon which an assignment may be permitted. It distinguishes between on the one hand circumstances, the existence of which entitles the landlord to refuse consent to assignment, and on the other hand conditions that may be imposed on his consent. This clause and clause 3.9.4 [1151] CIRCUMSTANCES are drafted on the assumption that this a valid approach and seek to draw a clear distinction between circumstances and conditions.

It should be noted that provisions that are overly restrictive may have an adverse impact at any rent review. It should also be noted that it is recommended 'best practice' that unless the particular circumstances of the letting justify greater control, the only restriction on assignment of the whole should be obtaining the landlord's consent, which is not to be unreasonably withheld: see vol 22(1) (2003 Reissue) LANDLORD AND TENANT (BUSINESS TENANCIES) Paragraph 85 [401] and 'A code of practice for commercial leases in England and Wales (2nd edition)' which can be found in vol 22(1) (2003 Reissue) LANDLORD AND TENANT (BUSINESS TENANCIES) as Form 1 [4501].

Each letting must be looked at in the light of its own particular facts and circumstances but it is considered that the provisions of this clause do, in the ordinary course, strike a reasonable balance between the landlord's desire for control and the tenant's ability to dispose of his interest without undue restriction.

91   The Landlord and Tenant Act 1927 s 19(1A) as inserted by the Landlord and Tenant (Covenants) Act 1995 s 22 seems to require the alienation clause to state that the conditions it mentions are specified for the purposes of that subsection.

92   See the Landlord and Tenant (Covenants) Act 1995 ss 11(2), 16(6).

93   As to authorised guarantee agreements see vol 22(1) (2003 Reissue) LANDLORD AND TENANT (BUSINESS TENANCIES) Paragraph 54 [247]. It should be noted that 'A code of practice for commercial leases in England and Wales (2nd edition)' urges landlords to consider requiring authorised guarantee agreements only where the assignee is of lower financial standing than the assignor at the date of the assignment.

[1154]

3.9.6   *Charging of the whole*

The Tenant must not charge the whole of the Premises without the consent of the Landlord, whose consent may not be unreasonably withheld [or delayed][94].

94   As to unreasonable withholding of consent under the Landlord and Tenant Act 1927 see vol 22(1) (2003 Reissue) LANDLORD AND TENANT (BUSINESS TENANCIES) Paragraph 158.2 [806] and as to unreasonable delay under the Landlord and Tenant Act 1988 (23 Halsbury's Statutes (4th Edn) LANDLORD AND TENANT) see vol 22(1) (2003 Reissue) LANDLORD AND TENANT (BUSINESS TENANCIES) Paragraph 158.3 [808].

[3.9.7   *Subletting*

The Tenant must not sublet[95] the whole of the Premises without the consent of the Landlord, whose consent may not be unreasonably withheld [or delayed]][96]. *(omit if subletting is prohibited)*

95   See note 81 to clause 3.9.2 [1141] ASSIGNMENT, SUBLETTING AND CHARGING OF PART.

96   As to unreasonable withholding of consent under the Landlord and Tenant Act 1927 see vol 22(1) (2003 Reissue) LANDLORD AND TENANT (BUSINESS TENANCIES) Paragraph 158.2 [806] and as to unreasonable delay under the Landlord and Tenant Act 1988 see vol 22(1) (2003 Reissue) LANDLORD AND TENANT (BUSINESS TENANCIES) Paragraph 158.3 [808].

[1155]

[3.9.8   *Terms of a permitted sublease*[97]

Every permitted sublease must be granted, without a fine or premium, at a rent not less than whichever is the greater of the then open market rent payable in respect of the Premises [— to be approved by the Landlord before the sublease is granted [and to be determined by the Surveyor, acting as an expert and not as an arbitrator]—] and the Rent[98], to be payable in advance on the days on which the Rent is payable under this Lease. Every permitted sublease must contain provisions approved by the Landlord —

3.9.8.1   for the upwards only review of the rent reserved by it, on the basis set out in schedule 3 THE RENT AND RENT REVIEW and on the Review Dates[99],

3.9.8.2   prohibiting the subtenant from doing or allowing anything in relation to the Premises inconsistent with or in breach of the provisions of this Lease,

3.9.8.3   for re-entry by the sublandlord on breach of any covenant by the subtenant,

3.9.8.4   imposing an absolute prohibition against all dealings with the Premises other than assignment[, subletting] [or charging] of the whole,

3.9.8.5   prohibiting assignment[, subletting][100] [or charging] of the whole of the Premises without the consent of the Landlord under this Lease,

3.9.8.6   requiring the assignee on any assignment of the sublease to enter into direct covenants with the Landlord to the same effect as those contained in clause 3.9.9 SUBTENANT'S DIRECT COVENANTS,

3.9.8.7   requiring on each assignment of the sublease that the assignor enters into an authorised guarantee agreement[101] in favour of the Landlord in the terms set out in schedule 7 THE AUTHORISED GUARANTEE AGREEMENT but adapted to suit the circumstances in which the guarantee is given,

3.9.8.8   prohibiting the subtenant from holding on trust for another or permitting another to share or occupy the whole or any part of the Premises,

3.9.8.9   imposing in relation to any permitted assignment[, subletting] [or charge] the same obligations for registration with the Landlord as are contained in this Lease in relation to dispositions by the Tenant,

[3.9.8.10   imposing in relation to any permitted subletting the same obligations as are contained in this clause 3.9.8 and in clause 3.9.9 SUBTENANT'S DIRECT COVENANTS[, clause 3.9.11 ENFORCEMENT OF THE SUBLEASE and clause 3.9.12 SUBLEASE RENT REVIEW],] and

3.9.8.11   excluding the provisions of Sections 24–28 of the 1954 Act from the letting created by the sublease.] *(omit if subletting is prohibited)*

[1156]

---

97   As to the validity of provisions of this nature see vol 22(1) (2003 Reissue) LANDLORD AND TENANT (BUSINESS TENANCIES) Paragraph 161 [817].

98   It will not be in the landlord's interest for the premises to be sublet at a rent less than that payable under the headlease, because it could allow into the premises a subtenant of doubtful financial status, with whom the landlord may in the future have to deal direct, eg on the grant of a new lease under the Landlord and Tenant Act 1954 Pt II (ss 23–46). Also a low rent could be used as a 'comparable' in arriving at the open market rent on rent reviews or lease renewals. On the other hand following the decision in *Allied Dunbar Assurance plc v Homebase Ltd* [2002] EWCA Civ 666, [2003] 1 P & CR 75, [2002] 2 EGLR 23 a provision of this kind may effectively render the lease inalienable and being a potentially onerous restriction on disposition (as to which see vol 22(1) (2003 Reissue) LANDLORD AND TENANT (BUSINESS TENANCIES) Paragraph 348.2 [1440]) have an adverse impact at rent review from a landlord's perspective.

99   Alternatively the landlord might prefer the sublease rents to be reviewed just before the review dates in the headlease. As to recommended 'best practice' in relation to the basis of rent review in leases of business premises see vol 22(1) (2003 Reissue) LANDLORD AND TENANT (BUSINESS TENANCIES) Paragraph 85 [401] and 'A code of practice for commercial leases in England and Wales (2nd edition)' which can be found in vol 22(1) (2003 Reissue) LANDLORD AND TENANT (BUSINESS TENANCIES) as Form 1 [4501].

100   The landlord may well wish to prohibit any further subletting by requiring an absolute covenant against subletting to be inserted in any sublease.

101   By virtue of the Landlord and Tenant (Covenants) Act 1995 s 16(3)(a), where a head landlord's consent is needed to the assignment of a sublease, the head landlord can require the assignor of the sublease to enter into an authorised guarantee agreement. It should be noted that 'A code of practice for commercial leases in England and Wales (2nd edition)' urges landlords to consider requiring authorised guarantee agreements only where the assignee is of lower financial standing than the assignor at the date of the assignment.

[1157]

[3.9.9   *Subtenant's direct covenants*[102]

Before any permitted subletting, the Tenant must ensure that the subtenant enters into a direct covenant with the Landlord that while the subtenant is bound by the tenant covenants of the sublease[103] and while the subtenant is bound by an authorised guarantee agreement the subtenant will observe and perform the tenant covenants contained in this Lease — except the covenant to pay the rent reserved by this Lease — and in that sublease.] *(omit if subletting is prohibited)*

102   See note 97 to clause 3.9.8 [1157] TERMS OF A PERMITTED SUBLEASE.

103   The liability of the subtenant should be expressed to last while he is bound by the tenant covenants of the sublease, rather than while the sublease is vested in him, to take account of the possibility of an excluded assignment being made and the subtenant remaining liable. An excluded assignment means that the subtenant is precluded from tenant release under the Landlord and Tenant (Covenants) Act 1995.

[3.9.10   *Requirement for 1954 Act exclusion*[104]

The Tenant must not grant a sublease or permit a subtenant to occupy the Premises unless an effective agreement has been made to exclude the operation of Sections 24 to 28 of the 1954 Act pursuant to Section 38A of the 1954 Act.] *(omit if subletting is prohibited)*

104   As to contracting out of the security of tenure provisions of the Landlord and Tenant Act 1954 see vol 22(1) (2003 Reissue) LANDLORD AND TENANT (BUSINESS TENANCIES) Paragraph 431 [2035].

[3.9.11   *Enforcement, waiver and variation of subleases*

In relation to any permitted sublease, the Tenant must enforce the performance and observance by every subtenant of the provisions of the sublease, and must not at any time either expressly or by implication waive any breach of the covenants or conditions on the part of any subtenant or assignee of any sublease, or — without the consent of the Landlord, whose consent may not be unreasonably withheld or delayed — vary the terms or accept a surrender of any permitted sublease.] *(omit if subletting is prohibited)*

[1158]

[3.9.12   *Sublease rent review*

In relation to any permitted sublease —

3.9.12.1   the Tenant must ensure that the rent is reviewed in accordance with the terms of the sublease,

3.9.12.2   the Tenant must not agree the reviewed rent with the subtenant without the approval of the Landlord,

3.9.12.3   where the sublease provides such an option, the Tenant must not, without the approval of the Landlord, agree whether the third party determining the revised rent in default of agreement should act as an arbitrator or as an expert,

3.9.12.4   the Tenant must not, without the approval of the Landlord, agree any appointment of a person to act as the third party determining the revised rent,

3.9.12.5   the Tenant must incorporate as part of his representations to that third party representations [reasonably] required[105] by the Landlord, and

3.9.12.6   the Tenant must give notice to the Landlord of the details of the determination of every rent review within *(state period, eg 28 days)*,

provided that the Landlord's approvals specified above may not be unreasonably withheld [or delayed].] *(omit if subletting is prohibited)*

---

105   This seems preferable to providing, as is sometimes done, that the head landlord's representations have to be brought to the attention of the expert or arbitrator because it would appear that he can refuse to have regard to them, the head landlord not being a party to the lease with which he is concerned.

3.9.13   *Registration of permitted dealings*

Within *(state period, eg 28 days)* of any assignment, charge, [sublease, or subunderlease,] or any transmission or other devolution relating to the Premises, the Tenant must produce a certified copy[106] of any relevant document for registration with the Landlord's solicitor, and must pay the Landlord's solicitor's [reasonable] charges for registration of at least £...

---

106   There seems to be no reason why the tenant should part with the original. However, under the Land Registration Rules 2003, SI 2003/1417 r 203, it is open to the applicant for registration to ask for the transfer, charge, sublease or subunderlease giving effect to the disposition to be returned for retention by the applicant, provided a certified copy of the instrument is lodged with the application. Accordingly, in such cases, applicants should use this facility if they wish to be able to lodge the lease with the landlord after its return by the registrar. If there is a time limit specified in the lease, then the registrar should be told about this, so that he is aware of the need to return the instrument within the required period.

[3.9.14   *Sharing with a group company*

Notwithstanding clause 3.9.1 ALIENATION PROHIBITED, the Tenant may share the occupation of the whole or any part of the Premises with a company that is a member of the same group as the Tenant within the meaning of the 1954 Act Section 42, for so long as both companies remain members of that group and otherwise than in a manner that transfers or creates a legal estate.] *(omit if sharing with a group company is not to be permitted)*

3.10   Nuisance and residential restrictions

3.10.1   *Nuisance*[107]

The Tenant must not do anything on the Premises, or allow anything to remain on them, that may be or become a nuisance, or cause annoyance, disturbance, inconvenience, injury or damage to the Landlord or his tenants or the owners or occupiers of any adjoining property of the Landlord or any other adjacent or neighbouring premises.

107   'Nuisance' is a term to be construed according to 'plain and sober and simple notions among the English people': *Walter v Selfe* (1851) 4 De G & Sm 315 at 322 per Knight-Bruce V-C. 'I have no doubt that what is a nuisance or annoyance will continue to be determined by the courts according to robust and commonsense standards': *Hampstead and Suburban Properties Ltd v Diomedous* [1969] 1 Ch 248 at 258, [1968] 3 All ER 545 at 550 per Megarry J. But a tenant can only be said to have permitted a nuisance if the landlord can show that the tenant has failed to take reasonable steps to prevent the nuisance: see *Commercial General Administration Ltd v Thomsett* [1979] 1 EGLR 62, CA.

3.10.2   *Auctions, trades and immoral purposes*

The Tenant must not use the Premises for any auction sale, any dangerous, noxious, noisy or offensive[108] trade, business, manufacture or occupation, or any illegal or immoral act or purpose.

108   As to the meaning of 'offensive' see *Re Koumoudouros and Marathon Realty Co Ltd* (1978) 89 DLR (3d) 551 where it was held that the word 'offensive' did not have a definite legal meaning and that it should be read in the context of the lease. Surrounding circumstances can affect whether a particular trade is offensive: see *Nussey v Provincial Bill Posting Co and Eddison* [1909] 1 Ch 734, CA; *Dunraven Securities Ltd v Holloway* [1982] 2 EGLR 47, CA.

[1160]

3.10.3   *Residential use, sleeping and animals*

The Tenant must not use the ground floor of the Premises as sleeping accommodation or for residential purposes, or keep any animal, bird or reptile anywhere on the Premises [other than a normal domestic pet].

3.11   Costs of applications, notices and recovery of arrears[109]

The Tenant must pay to the Landlord on an indemnity basis all costs, fees, charges, disbursements and expenses — including, without prejudice to the generality of the above, those payable to counsel, solicitors, surveyors and bailiffs — [properly and reasonably] incurred by the Landlord in relation to or incidental to —

3.11.1   every application made by the Tenant for a consent or licence required by the provisions of this Lease, whether it is granted, refused or offered subject to any [lawful] qualification or condition or the application is withdrawn[, unless the refusal, qualification or condition is unlawful whether because it is unreasonable or otherwise],

3.11.2   the contemplation, preparation and service of a notice under the Law of Property Act 1925 Section 146, or by reason or the contemplation of proceedings under Sections 146 or 147 of that Act, even if forfeiture is avoided otherwise than by relief granted by the court[110],

3.11.3   the recovery or attempted recovery of arrears of rent or other sums due under this Lease, and

3.11.4   any steps taken in [contemplation of or in] [direct] connection with the preparation and service of a schedule of dilapidations during or after the end of the Term[111].

109   As to payment of VAT on legal costs by a person other than the solicitor's own client see the Information Binder: Property [1]: VAT and Property.
110   As to forfeiture see vol 22(1) (2003 Reissue) LANDLORD AND TENANT (BUSINESS TENANCIES) Paragraph 283 [1171] et seq.
111   The landlord should not be tempted to extend this provision to costs etc incurred by him in consequence of serving a notice under the Landlord and Tenant Act 1954 s 25 because that is void: see *Stevenson and Rush (Holdings) Ltd v Langdon* (1978) 38 P & CR 208, CA.

[1161]–[1170]

3.12   Planning and development

3.12.1   *Compliance with the Planning Acts*

The Tenant must observe and comply with the provisions and requirements of the Planning Acts affecting the Premises and their use, and must indemnify the Landlord, and keep him indemnified, both during the Term and following the end of it, against all losses in respect of any contravention of those Acts.

3.12.2   *Consent for applications*

The Tenant must not make any application for planning permission without the consent of the Landlord[, whose consent may not be unreasonably withheld [or delayed] [in any case where application for and implementation of the planning permission will not create or give rise to any tax liability for the Landlord or where the Tenant indemnifies the Landlord against such liability][112]].

112   The words in square brackets were devised when development land tax — abolished by the Finance Act 1985 s 93 — applied. The provision may, however, still be relevant should similar taxation be introduced in the future.

3.12.3   *Permissions and notices*

The Tenant must at his expense obtain any planning permissions and serve any notices that may be required for the carrying out of any development on or at the Premises.

3.12.4   *Charges and levies*

Subject only to any statutory direction to the contrary, the Tenant must pay and satisfy any charge or levy that may subsequently be imposed under the Planning Acts in respect of the carrying out or maintenance of any development on or at the Premises.

[1171]

3.12.5   *Pre-conditions for development*

Notwithstanding any consent that may be granted by the Landlord under this Lease, the Tenant must not carry out any development on or at the Premises until all necessary notices under the Planning Acts have been served and copies produced to the Landlord, all necessary permissions under the Planning Acts have been obtained and produced to the Landlord, and the Landlord has acknowledged that every necessary planning permission is acceptable to him[, such acknowledgement not to be unreasonably withheld]. The Landlord may refuse to acknowledge his acceptance of a planning permission on the grounds that any condition contained in it or anything omitted from it or the period referred to in it would[, in the [reasonable] opinion of the Surveyor,] be, or be likely to be, prejudicial to the Landlord or to his reversionary interest in the Premises or any of his adjoining property whether during the Term or following the end of it.

3.12.6   *Completion of development*

Where a condition of any planning permission granted for development begun before the end of the Term[113] requires works to be carried out to the Premises by a date after the end of the Term, the Tenant must, unless the Landlord directs otherwise, finish those works before the end of the Term.

113   The provisions of clause 1.18 [1115] INTERPRETATION OF 'THE LAST YEAR OF THE TERM' AND 'THE END OF THE TERM' should be noted.

3.12.7   *Security for compliance with conditions*

In any case where a planning permission is granted subject to conditions, and if the Landlord [reasonably] so requires, the Tenant must provide sufficient security for his compliance with the conditions and must not implement the planning permission until that security has been provided.

[3.12.8   *Appeal against refusal or conditions*[114]

If [reasonably] required by the Landlord to do so, but[, where reasonable,] at his own cost, the Tenant must appeal against any refusal of planning permission or the imposition of any conditions on a planning permission relating to the Premises following an application for planning permission by the Tenant.]

114   The tenant should not accept this clause because it could impose on him the cost of a planning appeal. He should strike it out, leaving planning appeals to be a matter for discussion as and when the situation arises during the term, or at least insist that he should bear the cost only where reasonable.

[1172]

3.13   Plans, documents and information

3.13.1   *Evidence of compliance with this Lease*

If so requested, the Tenant must produce to the Landlord or the Surveyor any plans, documents and other evidence the Landlord [reasonably] requires to satisfy himself that the provisions of this Lease have been complied with.

3.13.2   *Information for renewal or rent review*

If so requested, the Tenant must produce to the Landlord, the Surveyor or any person acting as the third party determining the Rent in default of agreement between the Landlord and the Tenant under any provisions for rent review contained in this Lease, any information [reasonably] requested in writing in relation to any pending or intended step under the 1954 Act or the implementation of any provisions for rent review.

3.14   Indemnities[115]

The Tenant must keep the Landlord fully indemnified against all losses arising directly or indirectly out of any act, omission or negligence of the Tenant, or any persons at the Parade expressly or impliedly[116] with his authority [and under his control][117], or any breach or non-observance by the Tenant of the covenants, conditions or other provisions of this Lease or any of the matters to which this demise is subject.

115   The tenant should seek to delete all *general* indemnity provisions on the basis that his remedies for breach of covenant and in tort adequately protect the landlord. The tenant should argue that an indemnity unreasonably extends his liability. If, however, this clause is omitted, it should be replaced by a covenant to observe and perform restrictions etc to which the demise is subject, possibly coupled with a *specific* indemnity in respect of any breach.
116   The expression 'impliedly' is intended to include a caller on the premises, such as a tradesman, where there has been no express invitation but the person cannot be classed as a trespasser.
117   The tenant should add the words in square brackets.

[1173]

3.15   Reletting boards and viewing

[Unless [a valid court application under the 1954 Act Section 24 has been made or][118] the Tenant is [otherwise] entitled to remain in occupation or to a new tenancy of the Premises, at any time during *(or as required)* At any time during] the *(state period, eg last 6 months)* of the [Contractual][119] Term and at any time thereafter, [and whenever the Lease Rents or any part of them are in arrear and unpaid for longer than *(state period, eg 14 days)*,] the Tenant must permit the Landlord to enter the Premises and fix and retain anywhere on them a board advertising them for reletting. While any such board is on the Premises the Tenant must permit viewing of the Premises at reasonable times of the day.

118   This phrase and the word 'otherwise' should be omitted if the operation of the security of tenure provisions in the Landlord and Tenant Act 1954 ss 24–28 is to be excluded in relation to the lease.

119   This defined term will require amendment where the operation of the security of tenure provisions in the Landlord and Tenant Act 1954 ss 24–28 is to be excluded in relation to the lease: see note 6 to clause 1.5 [1110] 'THE [CONTRACTUAL] TERM'.

3.16   Obstruction and encroachment

3.16.1   *Obstruction of windows*

The Tenant must not stop up, darken or obstruct any window or light belonging to the Premises.

3.16.2   *Encroachments*

The Tenant must take all [reasonable] steps to prevent the construction of any new window, light, opening, doorway, path, passage, pipe or the making of any encroachment or the acquisition of any easement in relation to the Premises and must notify the Landlord immediately if any such thing is constructed, encroachment is made or easement acquired, or if any attempt is made to construct such a thing, to encroach or acquire an easement. At the request of the Landlord the Tenant must adopt such means as are [reasonably] required to prevent the construction of such a thing, the making of any encroachment or the acquisition of any easement[120].

120   For a shorter clause see vol 22(3) (1997 Reissue) LANDLORD AND TENANT (BUSINESS TENANCIES) Form 172 [6696].

[1174]

3.17   Yielding up

At the end of the Term[121] the Tenant must yield up the Premises with vacant possession, decorated and repaired in accordance with and in the condition required by the provisions of this Lease, give up all keys of the Premises to the Landlord, remove tenant's fixtures and fittings [if requested to do so by the Landlord], and remove all signs erected by the Tenant or any of his predecessors in title in upon or near the Premises immediately making good any damage caused by their removal.

121   The provisions of clause 1.18 [1115] INTERPRETATION OF 'THE LAST YEAR OF THE TERM' AND 'THE END OF THE TERM' should be noted.

3.18   Interest on arrears[122]

The Tenant must pay interest on any of the Lease Rents[123] or other sums due under this Lease that are not paid [within *(state period, eg 14 days)* of the date due], whether formally demanded or not [, the interest to be recoverable as rent][124]. Nothing in this clause entitles the Tenant to withhold or delay any payment of the Rent or any other sum due under this Lease or affects the rights of the Landlord in relation to any non-payment.

122   As to the covenant to pay interest see vol 22(1) (2003 Reissue) LANDLORD AND TENANT (BUSINESS TENANCIES) Paragraph 154 [767].
123   As to the definition of 'the Lease Rents' see clause 1.37 [1121] 'THE RENT'.
124   These words seek to attach to interest the rights associated with rent. As to the reasons for this see vol 22(1) (2003 Reissue) LANDLORD AND TENANT (BUSINESS TENANCIES) Paragraph 151 [761]. However, this clause applies to interest on arrears of other sums payable under the lease that are not rent as well as to rent itself, and it might be felt inappropriate for interest to be deemed to be rent where the payment on which the interest is due is not itself rent.

[1175]

3.19   Statutory notices

The Tenant must give full particulars to the Landlord of any notice, direction, order or proposal relating to the Premises made, given or issued to the Tenant by any government department or local, public, regulatory or other authority or court within *(state period, eg 7 days)* of receipt, and if so requested by the Landlord must produce it to the Landlord. The Tenant must without delay take all necessary steps to comply with the notice, direction or order. At the request of the Landlord, but at his own cost, the Tenant must make or join with the Landlord in making any objection or representation the Landlord deems expedient against or in respect of any notice, direction, order or proposal.

3.20   Keyholders

The Tenant must ensure that at all times [the Landlord has *(or as required)* the Landlord and the local police force have] written notice of the name, home address and home telephone number of at least *(state number, eg 2)* keyholders of the Premises.

3.21   Viewing on sale of reversion

The Tenant must[, on reasonable notice,] at any time during the Term, permit prospective purchasers of the Landlord's reversion or any other interest superior to the Term, or agents instructed in connection with the sale of the reversion or such an interest, to view the Premises without interruption provided they have the prior written authority of the Landlord or his agents.

3.22   Defective premises

The Tenant must give notice to the Landlord of any defect in the Premises that might give rise to an obligation on the Landlord to do or refrain from doing anything in order to comply with the provisions of this Lease or the duty of care imposed on the Landlord, whether pursuant to the Defective Premises Act 1972 or otherwise, and must at all times display and maintain any notices the Landlord from time to time [reasonably] requires him to display at the Premises.

3.23   Replacement guarantor[125]

3.23.1   *Guarantor replacement events*

In this clause 3.23 references to a 'guarantor replacement event' are references, in the case of an individual, to death, bankruptcy, having a receiving order made against him or having a receiver appointed under the Mental Health Act 1983 or entering into a voluntary arrangement and, in the case of a company, to passing a resolution to wind up, entering into liquidation, a voluntary arrangement or administration or having a receiver appointed.

125   As to guarantors see vol 22(1) (2003 Reissue) LANDLORD AND TENANT (BUSINESS TENANCIES) Paragraph 71 [278] et seq. The tenant should propose that, on the execution of a guarantee by a new guarantor, the original guarantor or his estate should be released.

[1176]

3.23.2   *Action on occurrence of a guarantor replacement event*

Where during the relevant Liability Period a guarantor replacement event occurs to the Guarantor or any person who has entered into an authorised guarantee agreement, the Tenant must give notice of the event to the Landlord within *(state period, eg 14 days)* of his becoming aware of it. If so required by the Landlord, the Tenant must within *(state period, eg 28 days)* obtain some other person [reasonably] acceptable to the Landlord to execute a guarantee in the form of the Guarantor's covenants in clause 6 GUARANTEE PROVISIONS or the authorised guarantee agreement in schedule 7 THE AUTHORISED GUARANTEE AGREEMENT, as the case may be, for the residue of the relevant Liability Period.

3.24   Exercise of the Landlord's rights[126]

The Tenant must permit the Landlord at all times during the Term to exercise any of the rights granted to him by virtue of the provisions of this Lease without interruption or interference.

126   The provisions of clause 1.35 [1121] REFERENCES TO RIGHTS OF ACCESS should be noted.

3.25   The Shop and Maisonette Covenants

The Tenant must observe and perform the Shop and Maisonette Covenants.

3.26   Costs of grant of this Lease[127]

[The Tenant must pay the fees and disbursements of the Landlord's solicitors, agents and surveyors and all other costs and expenses incurred by the Landlord in relation to the negotiation, preparation, execution and grant of this Lease. *(or as required)* On the grant of this Lease the Tenant must pay the sum of £... as a contribution to the Landlord's solicitors' charges for the negotiation, execution and completion of this Lease].

127   As to covenants to pay the landlord's legal fees see vol 22(1) (2003 Reissue) LANDLORD AND TENANT (BUSINESS TENANCIES) Paragraph 155 [769]. As to payment of VAT on legal costs by a person other than the solicitor's own client see the Information Binder: Property [1]: VAT and Property.

[1177]

3.27   Consent to the Landlord's release[128]

The Tenant must not unreasonably withhold consent to a request made by the Landlord under the 1995 Act Section 8 for a release from all or any of the landlord covenants of this Lease.

128   By virtue of the Landlord and Tenant (Covenants) Act 1995 each successive landlord remains bound by the landlord covenants of the lease unless released under the machinery provided in the Act — as to which see vol 22(1) (2003 Reissue) LANDLORD AND TENANT (BUSINESS TENANCIES) Paragraph 57 [252] et seq — or by a specific release given otherwise (see the Landlord and Tenant (Covenants) Act 1995 s 26(1)(a)). Bald statements limiting the landlord's liability, such as those in use before the commencement of the Act, will not withstand the wide anti-avoidance provisions of the Landlord and Tenant (Covenants) Act 1995 s 25, and covenants by the tenant to give consent to release are unlikely to fall within the exception of s 26. None of the ingenious schemes for limiting the landlord's liability, eg making all covenants personal, suggested in the early days of the 1995 Act has stood up to critical scrutiny, although none has yet been tested by the courts. Thus landlords look instead to the alternative of a right of redress if the tenant makes an unreasonable objection to release. This covenant is modelled on the provisions of the Landlord and Tenant Act 1988, which gives tenants a right of action for loss caused by landlords who unreasonably withhold or delay consent to assignment (see the Landlord and Tenant Act 1988 s 4). In view of the strict time limits under the Landlord and Tenant (Covenants) Act 1995 and the fact that failure to respond to the landlord's request for release is deemed to be consent, it is not thought necessary to extend this covenant to unreasonable delay in replying to such a request.

[1178]–[1190]

4   THE LANDLORD'S COVENANTS

The Landlord covenants with the Tenant to observe and perform the requirements of this clause 4.

4.1   Quiet enjoyment[129]

The Landlord must permit the Tenant peaceably and quietly to hold and enjoy the Premises without any interruption or disturbance from or by the Landlord or any person claiming under or in trust for him[130] [or by title paramount][131].

129   As to the landlord's covenant for quiet enjoyment see vol 22(1) (2003 Reissue) LANDLORD AND TENANT (BUSINESS TENANCIES) Paragraph 168 [856]. As to covenants for quiet enjoyment generally see 23 Halsbury's Laws (4th Edn Reissue) LANDLORD AND TENANT.
        The words 'the Tenant paying the rents reserved by and observing and performing the covenants on his part and the conditions contained in this lease' are frequently included in a covenant for quiet enjoyment, but they have no practical effect and do not make payment of the rent and performance of the covenants into conditions precedent to the operation of the covenant for quiet enjoyment: see *Edge v Boileau* (1885) 16 QBD 117; *Dawson v Dyer* (1833) 5 B & Ad 584; *Yorkbrook Investments Ltd v Batten* (1985) 52 P & CR 51, [1985] 2 EGLR 100, CA.
130   The covenant is frequently expressed to apply to 'lawful' interruption by persons 'rightfully' claiming under the landlord, but it seems that the addition of these words has no practical effect: see *Williams v Gabriel* [1906] 1 KB 155 at 157.
131   Without the reference to title paramount, the landlord is liable only for the acts of persons so far as they are his successors in title or have authority from him to do the acts complained of: *Harrison Ainslie & Co v Muncaster* [1891] 2 QB 680, CA; *Matania v National Provincial Bank Ltd and Elevenist Syndicate Ltd* [1936] 2 All ER 633, CA; *Miller v Emcer Products Ltd* [1956] Ch 304, [1956] 1 All ER 237, CA. If a subtenant holds under a lease containing a qualified covenant on the part of his landlord — ie one where there is no reference to title paramount — and the head landlord evicts the subtenant because the head rent has not been paid, this is not a breach of the covenant for quiet enjoyment (see *Spencer v Marriott* (1823) 1 B & C 457; *Dennett v Atherton* (1872) LR 7 QB 316, Ex Ch), but it is a breach if the sublandlord submits to judgment in an action by a person with no title to sue, and the subtenant is in consequence evicted (*Cohen v Tannar* [1900] 2 QB 609, CA). Actionable interruptions under this covenant are not confined to interference with title or possession, but may extend to interference with the ordinary and lawful enjoyment of the premises: *Sanderson v Berwick-upon-Tweed Corpn* (1884) 13 QBD 547 at 551, CA. As to persons claiming 'under' the landlord see *Celsteel Ltd v Alton House Holdings Ltd (No 2)* [1987] 2 All ER 240, [1987] 1 WLR 291, CA.

[1191]

4.2   Maintenance and decoration of the Parade

4.2.1   *Maintenance*

The Landlord must repair and keep in good repair and condition all parts of the Parade for which neither the Tenant nor any other tenant is wholly responsible[132] including, but without prejudice to the generality of the foregoing —

4.2.1.1   the foundations of the Parade,

4.2.1.2   the external, structural or loadbearing walls, columns, beams and supports, but excluding the interior plaster and decorative finishes of the external walls, the floorboards and the internal non-loadbearing walls of the Parade[133],

4.2.1.3   the roof of the Parade,

4.2.1.4   the Common Parts and the Adjoining Conduits, and

4.2.1.5   the exterior walls of the Parade[134]

provided that this covenant does not require the Landlord to carry out any works required as a result of (1) the Tenant's negligence, (2) breach of any of the tenant's covenants in this Lease or in any other lease of any part of the Parade, (3) any alteration or addition to the Premises not made by the Landlord, or (4) the installation of any item on the Premises otherwise than by the Landlord.

132   This is an attempt to remove doubts as to whether or not certain parts of the parade fall within the landlord's or the tenant's respective responsibilities.
133   Ie because, under this Form as drafted, these are the responsibility of the tenant.
134   The comments regarding the dangers of reliance upon standard wording to define the respective responsibilities of landlord and tenant contained in note 32 to clause 1.33.2 [1120] INTERPRETATION OF 'THE PREMISES' should be noted.

4.2.2   *Decoration*

The Landlord must decorate the exterior of the Parade and such of the Common Parts as he reasonably considers appropriate to a reasonable standard.

4.2.3   *Relief where the Provisional Charge is unpaid*

Notwithstanding the provisions of clauses 4.2.1 MAINTENANCE and 4.2.2 DECORATION, where a provisional charge notice has been served in accordance with schedule 6 PROVISIONAL PAYMENTS the Landlord need not carry out any works if the Tenant [or if any tenant of any other part of the Parade][135] has failed to pay the Provisional Charge as therein defined.

135   The words in square brackets should be resisted by the tenant — why should he suffer because of non-payment by other tenants in the parade?

4.3   Prohibition of competing trades[136]

The Landlord must not carry on the Permitted Use or allow it to be carried on in any other part of the Parade during the Term. This covenant is to bind each and every part of the Parade other than the Premises[137].

136   As to landlords' covenants not to let or use for particular purposes see vol 22(1) (2003 Reissue) LANDLORD AND TENANT (BUSINESS TENANCIES) Paragraph 179 [881].
137   The tenant should satisfy himself that the landlord owns the rest of the parade and is therefore in a position to covenant to bind the whole of it.

5   INSURANCE[138]

5.1   Warranty as to convictions[139]

The Tenant warrants that before the execution of this document he has disclosed to the Landlord in writing any conviction, judgment or finding of any court or tribunal relating to the Tenant[, or any director, other officer or major shareholder of the Tenant,] of such a nature as to be likely to affect the decision of any insurer or underwriter to grant or to continue insurance of any of the Insured Risks.

138   As to insurance see vol 22(1) (2003 Reissue) LANDLORD AND TENANT (BUSINESS TENANCIES) Paragraph 227 [1021] et seq.
139   A contract of insurance is one uberrimae fidei. The insured must disclose to the insurers all material facts that are within his actual or presumed knowledge, whether there is a formal proposal form or not. A fact is material if non-disclosure of it would influence a prudent and reasonable insurer. This warranty is designed to rebut any suggestion by the landlord's insurers that the landlord had knowledge of the matters concerned. By inserting this clause in the lease, and thus specifically bringing the point to the tenant's attention, the landlord can argue that he has done all that is practical to establish the existence of any such matters. The absence of any written disclosure pursuant to this clause is strong evidence that the landlord has no actual or presumed knowledge of such matters. Further, the landlord has a right of action against the tenant for any breach of the warranty. As to non-disclosure and misrepresentation in contracts of non-marine insurance see 22 Halsbury's Laws (4th Edn Reissue) INSURANCE.

5.2   Covenant to insure

The Landlord covenants with the Tenant to insure the Parade unless the insurance is vitiated by any act of the Tenant or by anyone at the Parade expressly or by implication[140] with his authority [and under his control][141].

140   The expression 'by implication' is intended to include a caller, such as a tradesman, where there has been no express invitation but the person cannot be classed as a trespasser.
141   The tenant should add the words in square brackets.

[1193]

5.3   Details of the insurance

5.3.1   *Office, underwriters and agency*

Insurance is to be effected in such [substantial and reputable] insurance office, or with such underwriters[142], and through such agency as the Landlord from time to time decides.

142   The expression 'insurance office' would probably not include Lloyd's underwriters. The landlord's right to nominate the office and agency is absolute, with no implied restrictions: *Berrycroft Management Co Ltd v Sinclair Gardens Investments (Kensington) Ltd* (1996) 75 P & CR 210, [1997] 1 EGLR 47, CA.

5.3.2   *Insurance cover*[143]

Insurance must be effected for the following amounts —

5.3.2.1   the sum that the Landlord is from time to time advised [by the Surveyor] is the full cost of rebuilding and reinstating the Parade, including [VAT[144],] architects', surveyors', engineers', solicitors' and all other professional persons' fees, the fees payable on any applications for planning permission or other permits or consents that may be required in relation to rebuilding or reinstating the Parade, the cost of preparation of the site including shoring-up, debris removal, demolition, site clearance and any works that may be required by statute, and incidental expenses, and

5.3.2.2   loss of rental income from the Parade, taking account of any rent reviews that
            may be due, for *(state period, eg 3 years)* or such longer period as the Landlord
            from time to time [reasonably] requires for planning and carrying out the
            rebuilding or reinstatement.

143   As to the sum insured see vol 22(1) (2003 Reissue) LANDLORD AND TENANT (BUSINESS
        TENANCIES) Paragraph 231 [1028] et seq.
            It should be noted that it is recommended 'best practice' that, where the landlord has arranged
        insurance, the terms should be made known to the tenant and any material change in the insurance
        should be notified to the tenant: see Recommendation 14 of 'A code of practice for commercial leases
        in England and Wales (2nd edition)' which can be found in vol 22(1) (2003 Reissue) LANDLORD AND
        TENANT (BUSINESS TENANCIES) at Form 1 [4501].
144   As to VAT and the level of insurance cover see the Information Binder: Property [1]: VAT and
        Property. The expense of insuring against the VAT payable on reinstatement costs is not justified where
        the landlord has opted to tax and is able to recover the VAT. There is a theoretical possibility that a
        future landlord may not opt to tax and that the sum insured may then be too low. It is also possible that
        a landlord may wish to preserve the 'exempt' status of a property. Normally, however, the cost of
        reinstatement need not expressly mention VAT, although the cashflow implications of having to pay
        VAT on construction works need to be remembered.

[1194]

5.3.3   Risks insured[145]

Insurance must be effected against damage or destruction by any of the Insured Risks to
the extent that such insurance may ordinarily be arranged [with a substantial and
reputable insurer] for properties such as the Parade subject to such excesses, exclusions
or limitations as the insurer requires.

145   As to risks to be insured against see vol 22(1) (2003 Reissue) LANDLORD AND TENANT (BUSINESS
        TENANCIES) Paragraph 235 [1033].
            It should be noted that it is recommended 'best practice' that, where the landlord has arranged
        insurance, the terms should be made known to the tenant and any material change in the insurance
        should be notified to the tenant: see Recommendation 14 of 'A code of practice for commercial leases
        in England and Wales (2nd edition)' which can be found in vol 22(1) (2003 Reissue) LANDLORD AND
        TENANT (BUSINESS TENANCIES) at Form 1 [4501].

5.4   Payment of the Insurance Rent

The Tenant covenants to pay the Insurance Rent for the period starting on the Rent
Commencement Date and ending on the day before the next policy renewal date on the
date of this document, and subsequently to pay the Insurance Rent on demand and, if
so demanded, in advance of the policy renewal date[, but not more than *(state period, eg
... months)* in advance].

[1195]

5.5   Suspension of the Rent[146]

5.5.1   Events giving rise to suspension

If and whenever the Parade or any part of it is damaged or destroyed by one or more of
the Insured Risks[147] [— except one against which insurance may not ordinarily be
arranged [with a substantial and reputable insurer] for properties such as the Parade unless
the Landlord has in fact insured against that risk —] so that the Premises or any part of
them are unfit for occupation or use, and payment of the insurance money is not wholly
or partly refused because of any act or default of the Tenant or anyone at the Parade
expressly or by implication[148] with his authority [and under his control][149], then the
provisions of clause 5.5.2 SUSPENDING THE RENT are to have effect.

146   As to suspension of rent see vol 22(1) (2003 Reissue) LANDLORD AND TENANT (BUSINESS
       TENANCIES) Paragraph 241 [1044] et seq.
147   It should be noted that it is recommended 'best practice' that if premises are so damaged by an
       uninsured risk as to prevent occupation, the tenant should be allowed to terminate the lease unless the
       landlord agrees to reinstate at his own cost: see vol 22(1) (2003 Reissue) LANDLORD AND TENANT
       (BUSINESS TENANCIES) Paragraph 85 [402] and 'A code of practice for commercial leases in England
       and Wales (2nd edition)' which can be found in vol 22(1) (2003 Reissue) LANDLORD AND TENANT
       (BUSINESS TENANCIES) at Form 1 [4501]. If adopted, this recommendation involves rent suspension
       also becoming operative in the event of the premises becoming unusable because of uninsured risks.
148   The expression 'by implication' is intended to include a caller, such as a tradesman, where there has
       been no express invitation but the person cannot be classed as a trespasser.
149   The tenant should add the words in square brackets.

5.5.2   *Suspending the Rent*

In the circumstances mentioned in clause 5.5.1 EVENTS GIVING RISE TO SUSPENSION, the
Rent, or a fair proportion of it according to the nature and the extent of the damage
sustained, is to cease to be payable until the Parade has been rebuilt or reinstated so as to
render the Premises or the affected part, fit for occupation and use, [or until the end of
(state period, eg 3 years) from the destruction or damage, whichever period is the
shorter,][150] [the proportion of the Rent suspended and the period of the suspension to
be determined by the Surveyor acting as an expert and not as an arbitrator *(or as required)*
any dispute as to the proportion of the Rent suspended or the period of the suspension
to be determined in accordance with the Arbitration Act 1996 by an arbitrator to be
appointed by agreement between the Landlord and the Tenant or in default by the
President or other proper officer for the time being of the Royal Institution of Chartered
Surveyors on the application of either the Landlord or the Tenant].

150   As to the length of the suspension and the tenant's concerns see vol 22(1) (2003 Reissue) LANDLORD
       AND TENANT (BUSINESS TENANCIES) Paragraph 244 [1048]. For a provision extending suspension
       of the rent where reinstatement is delayed see vol 22(3) (1997 Reissue) LANDLORD AND TENANT
       (BUSINESS TENANCIES) Form 111 [6495].

[1196]

5.6   Reinstatement and termination[151]

5.6.1   *Obligation to obtain permissions*

If and whenever the Parade or any part of it is damaged or destroyed by one or more of
the Insured Risks [— except one against which insurance may not ordinarily be arranged
[with a substantial and reputable insurer] for properties such as the Parade unless the
Landlord has in fact insured against that risk —], and payment of the insurance money
is not wholly or partly refused because of any act or default of the Tenant or anyone at
the Parade expressly or by implication with his authority[152] [and under his control][153],
then the Landlord must use his best endeavours[154] to obtain the planning permissions or
other permits and consents ('permissions') that are required under the Planning Acts or
otherwise to enable him to rebuild and reinstate the Parade.

151   It has been held that, in the absence of an express covenant to reinstate, where the landlord must keep
       the premises adequately insured against comprehensive risks and the insurance is effected at the tenant's
       expense, the obligation is one intended to enure for the benefit of both parties: *Mumford Hotels Ltd v
       Wheler* [1964] Ch 117, [1963] 3 All ER 250; see also *Mark Rowlands Ltd v Berni Inns Ltd* [1986] QB
       211, [1985] 3 All ER 473, CA; *Lonsdale & Thompson Ltd v Black Arrow Group plc* [1993] Ch 361, [1993]
       3 All ER 648. This is not, however, a general principle of law and the tenant should therefore always
       require a specific covenant to reinstate.

These provisions are restricted to circumstances where damage or destruction is caused by an insured risk. It should be noted that it is recommended 'best practice' that if premises are so damaged by an uninsured risk as to prevent occupation, the tenant should be allowed to terminate the lease unless the landlord agrees to reinstate at his own cost: see vol 22(1) (2003 Reissue) LANDLORD AND TENANT (BUSINESS TENANCIES) Paragraph 85 [401] and 'A code of practice for commercial leases in England and Wales (2nd edition)' which can be found in vol 22(1) (2003 Reissue) LANDLORD AND TENANT (BUSINESS TENANCIES) at Form 1 [4501].

As to termination where reinstatement is not possible see vol 22(1) (2003 Reissue) LANDLORD AND TENANT (BUSINESS TENANCIES) Paragraph 237 [1037]. For a provision for termination or surrender on destruction or substantial damage see vol 22(3) (1997 Reissue) LANDLORD AND TENANT (BUSINESS TENANCIES) Form 107 [6483].

152   The expression 'by implication' is intended to include a caller, such as a tradesman, where there has been no express invitation but the person cannot be classed as a trespasser.

153   The tenant should add the words in square brackets.

154   The extent of the duty to use best endeavours depends upon the facts in each case: see *Monkland v Jack Barclay Ltd* [1951] 2 KB 252, [1951] 1 All ER 714, CA; *Terrell v Mabie Todd & Co Ltd* [1952] 2 TLR 574; *NW Investments (Erdington) Ltd v Swani* (1970) 214 Estates Gazette 1115. In the light of *IBM United Kingdom Ltd v Rockware Glass Ltd* [1980] FSR 335, CA, it may be that there is little practical difference between a covenant to use best endeavours, a covenant to use reasonable endeavours and a covenant to take all reasonable steps.

[1197]

5.6.2   *Obligation to reinstate*

Subject to the provisions of clause 5.6.3 RELIEF FROM THE OBLIGATION TO REINSTATE, and, if any permissions are required, after they have been obtained the Landlord must as soon as reasonably practicable apply all money received in respect of the insurance effected by the Landlord pursuant to this Lease, except sums in respect of loss of the Rent, in rebuilding or reinstating the parts of the Parade destroyed or damaged [making up any difference between the cost of rebuilding and reinstating and the money received out of his own money][155].

155   Where the landlord's covenant is 'to apply all money received in respect of the insurance in rebuilding or reinstating' rather than simply 'to reinstate', it seems that the landlord does not have to complete the work out of his own money if the insurance money is insufficient because he has complied with his covenant by laying out all the insurance money received. The situation is different if the tenant can establish that the landlord was in breach of his covenant to insure for the full cost of reinstatement and that this has caused the shortfall: see *Mumford Hotels Ltd v Wheler* [1964] Ch 117, [1963] 3 All ER 250. The tenant should, therefore, require a specific covenant from the landlord to make up any shortfall, to prevent a situation in which the landlord refuses to complete the rebuilding. This is of particular concern if the suspension of rent proviso is expressed to operate for a limited period, because on the expiry of that period the tenant becomes liable for rent unless he can satisfy the court that the lease has been frustrated.

It should be noted that it is recommended 'best practice' that if premises are so damaged by an uninsured risk as to prevent occupation, the tenant should be allowed to terminate the lease unless the landlord agrees to reinstate at his own cost: see vol 22(1) (2003 Reissue) LANDLORD AND TENANT (BUSINESS TENANCIES) Paragraph 85 [401] and 'A code of practice for commercial leases in England and Wales (2nd edition)' which can be found in vol 22(1) (2003 Reissue) LANDLORD AND TENANT (BUSINESS TENANCIES) at Form 1 [4501]. If this recommendation is adopted and the landlord merely covenants to apply insurance money received, the principle should be extended to damage or destruction resulting from insured risks in circumstances where the insurance money is insufficient to enable reinstatement to be completed.

For a proviso relieving from the obligation to reinstate in the same form see vol 22(3) (1997 Reissue) LANDLORD AND TENANT (BUSINESS TENANCIES) Form 106 [6482].

[1198]

5.6.3   *Relief from the obligation to reinstate*[156]

The Landlord need not rebuild or reinstate the Parade if and for so long as rebuilding or reinstatement is prevented because —

5.6.3.1   the Landlord, despite using his best endeavours[157], cannot obtain any necessary permission,

5.6.3.2   any Permission is granted subject to a lawful condition with which [it is impossible for *(or as required)* in all the circumstances it is unreasonable to expect] the Landlord to comply,

5.6.3.3   there is some defect or deficiency in the site upon which the rebuilding or reinstatement is to take place [that renders it impossible *(or as required)* that means it can only be undertaken at a cost that is unreasonable in all the circumstances],

5.6.3.4   the Landlord is unable to obtain access to the site to rebuild or reinstate,

5.6.3.5   the rebuilding or reinstating is prevented by war, act of God, government action[, strike or lock-out], or

because of the occurrence of any other circumstances beyond the Landlord's control.

156   As to the need for a right to terminate where reinstatement is not possible see vol 22(1) (2003 Reissue) LANDLORD AND TENANT (BUSINESS TENANCIES) Paragraph 226 [998].

157   The extent of the duty to use best endeavours depends upon the facts in each case: see *Monkland v Jack Barclay Ltd* [1951] 2 KB 252, [1951] 1 All ER 714, CA; *Terrell v Mabie Todd & Co Ltd* [1952] 2 TLR 574; *NW Investments (Erdington) Ltd v Swani* (1970) 214 Estates Gazette 1115. In the light of *IBM United Kingdom Ltd v Rockware Glass Ltd* [1980] FSR 335, CA, it may be that there is little practical difference between a covenant to use best endeavours, a covenant to use reasonable endeavours and a covenant to take all reasonable steps.

[1199]

5.6.4   *Notice to terminate*[158]

If at the end of a period[159] of *(state period, eg 3 years)* starting on the date of the damage or destruction the Premises are still not fit for the Tenant's occupation and use, either the Landlord or the Tenant may by notice served at any time within *(state period, eg 6 months)* of the end of that period ('a notice to terminate following failure to reinstate') implement the provisions of clause 5.6.5 TERMINATION FOLLOWING FAILURE TO REINSTATE[160].

158   For alternative provisions where the landlord's right to terminate is limited to specified circumstances see vol 22(3) (1997 Reissue) LANDLORD AND TENANT (BUSINESS TENANCIES) Form 109 [6492].

159   The period to be inserted must be carefully considered. Particular regard should be had to the terms of any rent suspension provision and the extent of insurance cover for loss of rent.

160   As to the effect of the Landlord and Tenant Act 1954 see vol 22(1) (2003 Reissue) LANDLORD AND TENANT (BUSINESS TENANCIES) Paragraph 226 [998].

5.6.5   *Termination following failure to reinstate*

On service of a notice to terminate following failure to reinstate, the Term is to cease absolutely — but without prejudice to any rights or remedies that may have accrued[161]— and all money received in respect of the insurance effected by the Landlord pursuant to this Lease is to belong to the Landlord absolutely[162].

161   The effect of this clause is that the right to terminate arises after the end of the appropriate period, whatever the reason for the delay, but the tenant still has a right of action against the landlord if the landlord is in breach of his covenant to reinstate.

162   In the absence of provision for ownership of the insurance money the position is uncertain. In *Re King, Robinson v Gray* [1963] Ch 459, [1963] 1 All ER 781, CA it was held that the insurance money belongs to the party who paid the premiums even if the insurance was placed in the joint names of the landlord and the tenant. The dissenting view of Denning MR that insurance in joint names envisages that each party should be insured as to his insurable interest and that the insurance money should therefore be divided in proportion to their interests in the property should, however, be noted. In *Beacon Carpets Ltd v Kirby* [1985] QB 755, [1984] 2 All ER 726, CA the court adhered to this view and held that the proportion payable depended on the parties' interests in the premises at the time of the destruction. The landlord will prefer the lease to provide expressly for the insurance money to be retained by him in full if reinstatement proves impossible. The tenant ought perhaps to accept that it would be unrealistic to amend this to provide for the insurance money to belong to the tenant, but should suggest that a provision be inserted under which the money is to be divided in accordance with their respective interests in the premises at the time when the insurance money became due. For an alternative provision for ownership of the insurance money etc see vol 22(3) (1997 Reissue) LANDLORD AND TENANT (BUSINESS TENANCIES) Form 108 [6491].

[1200]

5.7   Tenant's further insurance covenants[163]

The Tenant covenants with the Landlord to observe and perform the requirements of this clause 5.4.

163   In order to comply with many of these covenants, the tenant will need to be supplied with details of the landlord's insurance policy. In any event, it should be noted that it is recommended 'best practice' that where the landlord has arranged insurance, the terms should be made known to the tenant and any material change in the insurance should be notified to the tenant: see Recommendation 14 of 'A code of practice for commercial leases in England and Wales (2nd edition)' which can be found in vol 22(1) (2003 Reissue) LANDLORD AND TENANT (BUSINESS TENANCIES) at Form 1 [4501].

5.7.1   *Requirements of insurers*

The Tenant must comply with all the requirements and recommendations of the insurers.

5.7.2   *Policy avoidance and additional premiums*

The Tenant must not do or omit anything that could cause any insurance policy on or in relation to the Parade to become wholly or partly void or voidable, or do or omit anything by which additional insurance premiums may become payable unless he has previously notified the Landlord and has agreed to pay the increased premium.

5.7.3   *Fire-fighting equipment*

The Tenant must keep the Premises supplied with such fire fighting equipment [as the insurers and the fire authority require and must maintain the equipment to their satisfaction *(or as required)* as the Landlord reasonably requires and must maintain the equipment to the reasonable satisfaction of the insurers and the fire authority] and in efficient working order. At least once in every *(state period, eg 6 months)* the Tenant must have any sprinkler system and other fire fighting equipment to be inspected by a competent person.

5.7.4   *Combustible materials*

The Tenant must not store on the Premises or bring onto them anything of a specially combustible, inflammable or explosive nature, and must comply with the requirements and recommendations of the fire authority [and the [reasonable] requirements of the Landlord] as to fire precautions relating to the Parade.

[1201]

5.7.5   *Fire escapes, equipment and doors*

The Tenant must not obstruct the access to any fire equipment or the means of escape from the Premises or any part of the Parade or lock any fire door while the Premises are occupied.

5.7.6   *Notice of events affecting the policy*

The Tenant must give immediate notice to the Landlord of any event that might affect any insurance policy on or relating to the Parade, and any event against which the Landlord may have insured under this Lease.

5.7.7   *Notice of convictions*

The Tenant must give immediate notice to the Landlord of any conviction, judgment or finding of any court or tribunal relating to the Tenant, or any director other officer or major shareholder of the Tenant, of such a nature as to be likely to affect the decision of any insurer or underwriter to grant or to continue any insurance[164].

164   This clause provides a continuation of the warranty given by the tenant in clause 5.1 [1193] WARRANTY AS TO CONVICTIONS. As to non-disclosure and misrepresentation in contracts of non-marine insurance see 22 Halsbury's Laws (4th Edn Reissue) INSURANCE.

5.7.8   *Other insurance*

If at any time the Tenant is entitled to the benefit of any insurance of the Premises that is not effected or maintained in pursuance of any obligation contained in this Lease, the Tenant must apply all money received by virtue of that insurance in making good the loss or damage in respect of which the money is received[165].

165   An insurance policy frequently provides that if there is any other insurance effected by or on behalf of the insured, covering the premises that are the subject of the policy, the insurers are liable only for a rateable proportion of the damage. Such provisions extend to a case where one of the policies is in the joint names of the persons interested in the premises and the other is in the name of one only of those persons: *Halifax Building Society v Keighley* [1931] 2 KB 248. Therefore, at least when the insurance is in joint names and, ideally, even where it is not, the landlord should ensure that the tenant will use all money received under any policy he has effected to reinstate the premises.

[1202]

[5.7.9   *Reinstatement on refusal of money through default*

If at any time the Parade or any part of it is damaged or destroyed by one or more of the Insured Risks and the insurance money under the policy of insurance effected by the Landlord pursuant to his obligations contained in this Lease is wholly or partly irrecoverable because of any act or default of the Tenant or of anyone at the Parade expressly or by implication[166] with his authority [and under his control][167], the Tenant must immediately, at the option of the Landlord, either rebuild and reinstate the Parade or the part of it destroyed or damaged to the reasonable satisfaction and under the supervision of the Surveyor — in which case, on completion of the rebuilding and refurbishment, the Landlord must pay to the Tenant the amount that the Landlord has actually received under the insurance policy in respect of the destruction or damage — or pay to the Landlord on demand [with interest] the amount of the insurance money so irrecoverable — in which case the provisions of clauses 5.5 SUSPENSION OF THE RENT and 5.6 REINSTATEMENT AND TERMINATION are to apply.] *(omit if considered impracticable in the circumstances)*

166   The expression 'by implication' is intended to include a caller, such as a tradesman, where there has been no express invitation but the person cannot be classed as a trespasser.
167   The tenant should add the words in square brackets.

[5.8   Landlord's further insurance covenants[168]

The Landlord covenants with the Tenant to observe and perform the requirements set out in this clause 5.8 in relation to the insurance policy effected by the Landlord pursuant to his obligations contained in this Lease.

168   Unless insurance is to be in the joint names of the landlord and the tenant (which is unlikely in the circumstances assumed by this lease), the tenant should seek covenants such as these from the landlord.

5.8.1   *Copy policy*

The Landlord must produce to the Tenant on demand [a copy of the policy and the last premium renewal receipt *(or as required)* reasonable evidence of the terms of the policy and the fact that the last premium has been paid][169].

169   The landlord can reasonably insist on the second alternative. If the premises are insured under a block policy, it would be inappropriate for him to have to disclose to the tenant information about his other properties.
        It should be noted that it is recommended 'best practice' that where the landlord has arranged insurance, the terms should be made known to the tenant and any material change in the insurance should be notified to the tenant: see Recommendation 14 of 'A code of practice for commercial leases in England and Wales (2nd edition)' which can be found in vol 22(1) (2003 Reissue) LANDLORD AND TENANT (BUSINESS TENANCIES) at Form 1 [4501].

[1203]

5.8.2   *Noting of the Tenant's interest*

The Landlord must ensure that the interest of the Tenant is noted or endorsed on the policy[170].

170   Where insurance in the joint names of the landlord and the tenant is not practical, the tenant should insist that a note of his interest is endorsed on the policy. This protects the tenant because the insurers should give notice to him of any lapse in the policy and, where it can be shown that the tenant is responsible for the insurance premium under the terms of the lease, it is likely — but not certain — that the insurers would not exercise subrogation rights against the tenant.
        It is recommended 'best practice' that where the landlord has arranged insurance, any interest of the tenant should be covered by the policy: see Recommendation 14 of 'A code of practice for commercial leases in England and Wales (2nd edition)' which can be found in vol 22(1) (2003 Reissue) LANDLORD AND TENANT (BUSINESS TENANCIES) at Form 1 [4501].

5.8.3   *Change of risks*

The Landlord must notify the Tenant of any [material] change in the risks covered by the policy from time to time[171].

171   It is recommended 'best practice' that where the landlord has arranged insurance, any interest of the tenant should be covered by the policy: see Recommendation 14 of 'A code of practice for commercial leases in England and Wales (2nd edition)' which can be found in vol 22(1) (2003 Reissue) LANDLORD AND TENANT (BUSINESS TENANCIES) at Form 1 [4501].

[5.8.4   *Waiver of subrogation*[172]

The Landlord must produce to the Tenant on demand written confirmation from the insurers that they have agreed to waive all rights of subrogation against the Tenant.]]

172   Generally an insurer who has paid out under a policy stands in the shoes of the insured with regard to any claim the latter may have had against any third party. If the insurance is in joint names, the tenant is an insured party and there can be no subrogation against him. It would seem, also, that where the tenant covenants to reimburse the landlord for sums expended by the landlord in insuring the premises, the landlord's insurers cannot make a subrogated claim against the tenant where the premises are destroyed by the tenant's negligence: *Mark Rowlands Ltd v Berni Inns Ltd* [1986] QB 211, [1985] 3 All ER 473, CA. The tenant may still, however, wish to obtain a specific waiver of subrogation if possible.

[1204]–[1220]

6   GUARANTEE PROVISIONS

6.1   The Guarantor's covenants[173]

6.1.1   *Nature and duration*

The Guarantor's covenants with the Landlord are given as sole or principal debtor or covenantor, with the landlord for the time being and with all his successors in title[174] without the need for any express assignment, and the Guarantor's obligations to the Landlord will last throughout the Liability Period.

173   The covenants in this clause should *not* be omitted where no guarantor is a party to the lease, because they may be required under clause 3.9.5.2 [1153] CONDITIONS. If it is felt undesirable to have covenants in a lease and no party, at least initially, to enter into them, ie where there is no guarantor for the original tenant, the contents of this clause could alternatively be included in a schedule.

174   The new provisions governing the transmission of the benefit and burden of covenants (see the Landlord and Tenant (Covenants) Act 1995 s 3) only apply to landlord and tenant covenants. The law in force before 1 January 1996 remains unchanged for guarantor covenants, so that the benefit passes with the landlord's reversion. This occurs, not under the Law of Property Act 1925 s 141(1), which has been repealed for post-1995 tenancies by the 1995 Act, but under common law. The guarantee covenant touches and concerns the legal estate vested in the new reversioner: see *P & A Swift Investments v Combined English Stores Group plc* [1989] AC 632, [1988] 2 All ER 885, HL.

[1221]

6.1.2   *The covenants*

The Guarantor covenants with the Landlord to observe and perform the requirements of this clause 6.1.2.

6.1.2.1   **Payment of rent and performance of the Lease**

The Tenant must pay the Lease Rents[175] and VAT charged on them punctually and observe and perform the covenants and other terms of this Lease, and if, at any time during the Liability Period while the Tenant is bound by the tenant covenants of this Lease[176], the Tenant defaults in paying the Lease Rents or in observing or performing any of the covenants or other terms of this Lease, then the Guarantor must pay the Lease Rents and observe or perform the covenants or terms in respect of which the Tenant is in default and make good to the Landlord on demand, and indemnify the Landlord against, all losses resulting from such non-payment, non-performance or non-observance notwithstanding —

(a)   any time or indulgence granted by the Landlord to the Tenant, any neglect or forbearance of the Landlord in enforcing the payment of the Lease Rents or the observance or performance of the covenants or other terms of this Lease, or any refusal by the Landlord to accept rent tendered by or on behalf of the Tenant at a time when the Landlord is entitled — or will after the service of a notice under the Law of Property Act 1925 Section 146 be entitled — to re-enter the Premises[177],

(b)   that the terms of this Lease may have been varied by agreement between the Landlord and the Tenant[, provided that no variation is to bind the Guarantor to the extent that it is materially prejudicial to him][178],

(c)   that the Tenant has surrendered part of the Premises — in which event the liability of the Guarantor under this Lease is to continue in respect of the part of the Premises not surrendered after making any necessary apportionments under the Law of Property Act 1925 Section 140[179], and

(d)   anything else (other than a release by deed) by which, but for this clause 6.1.2.1, the Guarantor would be released.

[1222]

175   As to the definition of 'the Lease Rents' see clause 1.37 [1121] 'THE RENT'.

176   This obligation lasts while the lease is vested in the tenant and for any period of extended liability following an excluded assignment. It is not appropriate once the tenant has entered into an authorised guarantee agreement, when the contractual guarantor's obligations are at one remove: see vol 22(1) (2003 Reissue) LANDLORD AND TENANT (BUSINESS TENANCIES) Paragraph 74 [284] and clause 6.1.2.4 [1225] GUARANTEE OF THE TENANT'S LIABILITIES UNDER AN AUTHORISED GUARANTEE AGREEMENT.

177   If a creditor 'gives time' to the debtor in a binding manner, this releases the guarantor: see *Swire v Redman* (1876) 1 QBD 536; *Holme v Brunskill* (1877) 3 QBD 495, CA. The guarantee should, therefore, be expressed to apply notwithstanding any time or indulgence granted by the landlord to the tenant, or neglect or forbearance on the part of the landlord in enforcing the payment of rent and the other covenants in the lease. It has been suggested, however, that such wording does not protect a landlord who refuses to accept rent so as not to waive a breach of covenant by the tenant. This is unresolved but to avoid any doubt the point should be expressly dealt with. It appears that any provision in a guarantor's covenant that purports to exonerate the landlord from the consequences of his own negligence must satisfy the reasonableness test of the Unfair Contract Terms Act 1977 (11 Halsbury's Statutes (4th Edn) CONTRACT).

178   Any variation of the terms of the contract between the creditor and the debtor will discharge the guarantor (*Holme v Brunskill* (1877) 3 QBD 495, CA), unless the guarantor consents, although it has been suggested that an immaterial variation that was not prejudicial to the guarantor might not release him. No guarantor should accept a provision by which the guarantee is to continue notwithstanding any variation, but on the other hand it seems unfair on the landlord for the guarantor to escape his liability merely because a minor change has been agreed between the landlord and the tenant. A provision that the guarantee is to continue to apply notwithstanding an immaterial variation not prejudicial to the guarantor seems a fair compromise. It should be noted that the Landlord and Tenant (Covenants) Act 1995 s 18 does not apply to the guarantor of the current tenant.

It should also be noted that it is recommended 'best practice' that landlords and tenants should seek the agreement of any guarantors to proposed material changes to the terms of the lease, or even minor changes which could increase the guarantor's liability: see Recommendation 15 of 'A code of practice for commercial leases in England and Wales (2nd edition)' which can be found in vol 22(1) (2003 Reissue) LANDLORD AND TENANT (BUSINESS TENANCIES) at Form 1 [4501].

179   In the light of *Holme v Brunskill* (1877) 3 QBD 495, CA, the position on surrender of part of the premises should be dealt with expressly.

[1223]

6.1.2.2   New lease following disclaimer[180]

If, at any time during the Liability Period while the Tenant is bound by the tenant covenants of this Lease[181], any trustee in bankruptcy or liquidator of the Tenant disclaims this Lease, the Guarantor must, if so required by notice served by the Landlord within *(state period, eg 60 days)* of the Landlord's becoming aware of the disclaimer, take from the Landlord forthwith a lease of the Premises for the residue of the [Contractual][182] Term as at the date of the disclaimer, at the Rent then payable under this Lease and subject to the same covenants and terms as in this Lease — except that the Guarantor need not ensure that any other person is made a party to that lease as guarantor — the new lease to commence on the date of the disclaimer. The Guarantor must pay the costs of the new lease and VAT charged thereon, save where such VAT is recoverable or available for set-off by the Landlord as input tax[183], and execute and deliver to the Landlord a counterpart of the new lease.

180   This put option should be included because on disclaimer of a lease the lease ceases to exist, although it is deemed to continue for the purpose of determining the liability to the landlord of persons, including guarantors, other than the tenant whose liquidator or trustee has disclaimed: see *Hindcastle Ltd v Barbara Attenborough Associates Ltd* [1997] AC 70, [1996] 1 All ER 737, HL.

181   This obligation lasts while the lease is vested in the tenant and for any period of extended liability following an excluded assignment. It is not appropriate once the tenant has entered into an authorised guarantee agreement when the tenant's — ie the former tenant's — liquidator or trustee in bankruptcy will not be in a position to disclaim the lease because it will no longer be vested in the former tenant.

182   This defined term will require amendment where the operation of the security of tenure provisions in the Landlord and Tenant Act 1954 ss 24–28 is to be excluded in relation to the lease: see note 6 to clause 1.5 [1110] 'THE [CONTRACTUAL] TERM'.

183   As to payment of VAT on legal costs by a person other than the solicitor's own client see the Information Binder: Property [1]: VAT and Property.

[1224]

6.1.2.3   Payments following disclaimer[184]

If this Lease is disclaimed and the Landlord does not require the Guarantor to accept a new lease of the Premises in accordance with clause 6.1.2.2 NEW LEASE FOLLOWING DISCLAIMER, the Guarantor must pay to the Landlord on demand an amount equal to [the difference between any money received by the Landlord for the use or occupation of the Premises and] the Lease Rents [in both cases] for the period commencing with the date of the disclaimer and ending on whichever is the earlier of the date *(state period, eg 6 months)* after the disclaimer, the date, if any, upon which the Premises are relet, and the end of the [Contractual][185] Term.

---

184   This clause could be a useful alternative for a landlord, who may not be unhappy to regain possession of the premises but would like some rental income before reletting etc. For a covenant by the tenant to assign to the guarantor see vol 22(3) (1997 Reissue) LANDLORD AND TENANT (BUSINESS TENANCIES) Form 159 [6666].

185   This defined term will require amendment where the operation of the security of tenure provisions in the Landlord and Tenant Act 1954 ss 24–28 is to be excluded in relation to the lease: see note 6 to clause 1.5 [1110] 'THE [CONTRACTUAL] TERM'.

6.1.2.4   Guarantee of the Tenant's liabilities under an authorised guarantee agreement

If, at any time during the Liability Period while the Tenant is bound by an authorised guarantee agreement, the Tenant defaults in his obligations under that agreement, the Guarantor must make good to the Landlord on demand, and indemnify the Landlord against, all losses resulting from that default notwithstanding —

(a)   any time or indulgence granted by the Landlord to the Tenant, or neglect or forbearance of the Landlord in enforcing the payment of any sum or the observance or performance of the covenants of the authorised guarantee agreement[186],

(b)   that the terms of the authorised guarantee agreement may have been varied by agreement between the Landlord and the Tenant [provided that no variation is to bind the Guarantor to the extent that it is materially prejudicial to him][187], or

(c)   anything else (other than a release by deed) by which, but for this clause 6.1.2.4, the Guarantor would be released.

---

186   See note 177 to clause 6.1.2.1 [1223] PAYMENT OF RENT AND PERFORMANCE OF THE LEASE.

187   See note 178 to clause 6.1.2.1 [1223] PAYMENT OF RENT AND PERFORMANCE OF THE LEASE.

[1225]

6.1.3   *Severance*

6.1.3.1   Severance of void provisions

Any provision of this clause 6 rendered void by virtue of the 1995 Act Section 25 is to be severed from all remaining provisions, and the remaining provisions are to be preserved.

6.1.3.2   Limitation of provisions

If any provision in this clause 6 extends beyond the limits permitted by the 1995 Act Section 25, that provision is to be varied so as not to extend beyond those limits.

[6.2 The Landlord's covenant[188]

The Landlord covenants with the Guarantor that he will not attempt to recover from the Guarantor payment of any amount, determined by a court or in binding arbitration or agreed between the Landlord and the Tenant, payable in respect of a breach of covenant by the Tenant, unless he has served on the Guarantor, within 6 months of the payment being determined or agreed, a notice in the form prescribed by Section 27 of the 1995 Act as if the payment were a fixed charge under that Act.]

188   This clause is a tenant's amendment. It provides for a notice equivalent to a default notice under the Landlord and Tenant (Covenants) Act 1995 to be served. It protects the interests of existing and future contractual guarantors. As to service of default notices see vol 22(1) (2003 Reissue) LANDLORD AND TENANT (BUSINESS TENANCIES) Paragraph 61 [260].

[1226]–[1230]

7   FORFEITURE[189]

If and whenever during the Term —

7.1   the Lease Rents[190], or any of them or any part of them, or any VAT payable on them, are outstanding for *(state period, eg 14 days)* after becoming due, whether formally demanded or not[191] or

7.2   the Tenant [or the Guarantor] breaches any covenant or other term of this Lease, or

7.3   the Tenant [or the Guarantor][192], being an individual, becomes subject to a bankruptcy order[193] [or has an interim receiver appointed to his property][194], or

7.4   the Tenant [or the Guarantor][195], being a company, enters into liquidation[196] whether compulsory or voluntary — but not if the liquidation is for amalgamation or reconstruction of a solvent company — [or enters into administration][197] [or has a receiver appointed over all or any part of its assets][198], or

7.5   the Tenant [or the Guarantor][199] enters into or makes a proposal to enter into any voluntary arrangement pursuant to the Insolvency Act 1986[200] or any other arrangement or composition for the benefit of his creditors, or

7.6   the Tenant has any distress, sequestration or execution levied on his goods,

and, where the Tenant [or the Guarantor] is more than one person, if and whenever any of the events referred to in this clause happens to any one or more of them, the Landlord may at any time re-enter the Premises or any part of them in the name of the whole — even if any previous right of re-entry has been waived[201] — and thereupon the Term is to cease absolutely but without prejudice to any rights or remedies that may have accrued to the Landlord against the Tenant or the Guarantor [or to the Tenant against the Landlord] in respect of any breach of covenant or other term of this Lease, including the breach in respect of which the re-entry is made.

[1231]

189   As to forfeiture generally see vol 22(1) (2003 Reissue) LANDLORD AND TENANT (BUSINESS TENANCIES) Paragraph 283 [1171] et seq.
      The precise range of insolvency-related circumstances that will trigger the proviso should be carefully considered. Tenants should note that their inclusion, in practice, means that the lease cannot be used as security for a loan. Landlords generally seek to have the ability to forfeit in the widest range of circumstances. It should, however, be noted that, in certain circumstances, leave of the court or of the insolvency practitioner administering the procedure may be required before any contractual right can be exercised: see eg, in respect of administration, the Insolvency Act 1986 Sch 1B para 43(4), (6) as inserted by the Enterprise Act 2002 s 248 (4 Halsbury's Statutes (4th Edn) BANKRUPTCY AND INSOLVENCY).

109   As to the definition of 'the Lease Rents' see clause 1.37 [1121] 'THE RENT'.
191   The words 'whether formally demanded or not' should be used to avoid the common law requirement that an actual demand has to be made.
192   The lease may provide for a right of re-entry on insolvency of the guarantor or a tenant's covenant to find an acceptable replacement (see clause 3.23 [1176] REPLACEMENT GUARANTOR) or both.
193   As to bankruptcy generally see the Insolvency Act 1986 Pt IX (ss 264–371).
194   As to interim receivers see the Insolvency Act 1986 s 286.
195   See note 192 above.
196   As to liquidation generally see the Insolvency Act 1986 Pts IV–VI (ss 73–246).
197   As to administration generally see the Insolvency Act 1986 Pt II as substituted by the Enterprise Act 2002 s 248. The tenant may seek to argue that if the administrator pays rent and if there are no other material breaches of the lease the landlord should not be entitled to forfeit the lease on this ground.
198   The tenant may seek to argue that if the receiver pays rent and if there are no other material breaches of the lease the landlord should not be entitled to forfeit the lease on this ground.
199   See note 192 above.
200   As to company voluntary arrangements see the Insolvency Act 1986 Pt I (ss 1–7B) as amended by the Insolvency Act 2000. As to individual voluntary arrangements see the Insolvency Act 1986 Pt VIII (ss 252–263G) as amended by the Enterprise Act 2002 s 264.
201   The landlord has the option whether to take advantage of a right of forfeiture or not. If he elects not to do so, the forfeiture is waived. The election may be express or implied, eg if the landlord does any act by which he recognises that the relationship of landlord and tenant is still continuing after the cause of forfeiture has come to his knowledge.

[1232]

8   MISCELLANEOUS

8.1   Exclusion of warranty as to use

Nothing in this Lease or in any consent granted by the Landlord under this Lease is to imply or warrant that the Premises may lawfully be used under the Planning Acts for the Permitted Use[202].

202   See *Laurence v Lexcourt Holdings Ltd* [1978] 2 All ER 810, [1978] 1 WLR 1128; *Collins v Howell-Jones* [1981] 2 EGLR 108, 259 Estates Gazette 331, CA and the comments of Eveleigh LJ on estate agents' particulars relating to use in *Bovis Group Pension Fund Ltd v GC Flooring & Furnishing Ltd* (1984) 269 Estates Gazette 1252 at 1253, CA.

8.2   Exclusion of third party rights

Nothing in this Lease is intended to confer any benefit on any person who is not a party to it[203].

203   By virtue of the Contracts (Rights of Third Parties) Act 1999 (11 Halsbury's Statutes (4th Edn) CONTRACT) third-party rights may be conferred where they are not clearly excluded. This being so, it is advisable to incorporate a specific exclusion except where the parties actually intend to confer rights of action on a third party. In the standard letting situation it is unlikely that the parties will wish to extend liability in this manner. As to the Contracts (Rights of Third Parties) Act 1999 generally see vol 4(3) (2001 Reissue) BOILERPLATE CLAUSES.

8.3   Representations

The Tenant acknowledges that this Lease has not been entered into wholly or partly in reliance on any statement or representation made by or on behalf of the Landlord except any such statement or representation that is expressly set out in this Lease[204] [or was made by the Landlord's solicitors in any written response to enquiries raised by the Tenant's solicitors in connection with the grant of this Lease].

204   See the comments of Eveleigh LJ on estate agents' particulars relating to use in *Bovis Group Pension Fund Ltd v GC Flooring & Furnishing Ltd* (1984) 269 Estates Gazette 1252 at 1253, CA. For an alternative provision see vol 22(4) (1997 Reissue) LANDLORD AND TENANT (BUSINESS TENANCIES) Form 400 clauses 7.1 [7520], 7.2 [7521].

[1233]

8.4   Documents under hand

While the Landlord is a limited company or other corporation, any licence, consent, approval or notice required to be given by the Landlord is to be sufficiently given if given under the hand of a director, the secretary or other duly authorised officer of the Landlord [or by the Surveyor on behalf of the Landlord].

8.5   Tenant's property

If, after the Tenant has vacated the Premises at the end of the Term any property of his remains in or on the Premises and he fails to remove it within *(state period, eg 7 days)* after a written request from the Landlord to do so, or, if the Landlord is unable to make such a request to the Tenant, within *(state period, eg 14 days)* from the first attempt to make it, then the Landlord may, as the agent of the Tenant, sell that property. The Tenant must indemnify the Landlord against any liability incurred by the Landlord to any third party whose property is sold by him in the mistaken belief held in good faith — which is to be presumed unless the contrary is proved — that the property belonged to the Tenant. If, having made reasonable efforts to do so, the Landlord is unable to locate the Tenant, then the Landlord may retain the proceeds of sale absolutely unless the Tenant claims them within *(state period, eg 6 months)* of the date upon which he vacated the Premises. The Tenant must indemnify the Landlord against any damage occasioned to the Premises and any losses caused by or related to the presence of the property in or on the Premises.

8.6   Compensation on vacating excluded

Any statutory right of the Tenant to claim compensation from the Landlord on vacating the Premises is excluded to the extent that the law allows[205].

---

205   As to compensation where an order for a new tenancy is precluded on certain grounds see the Landlord and Tenant Act 1954 s 37 as amended by the Local Government and Housing Act 1989 s 149, Sch 7 and by SI 2003/3096.

   As to the effectiveness of provisions of this nature see vol 22(1) (2003 Reissue) LANDLORD AND TENANT (BUSINESS TENANCIES) Paragraph 468 [3079].

[1234]

8.7   Notices

8.7.1   *Form and service of notices*

A notice under this Lease must be in writing and, unless the receiving party or his authorised agent acknowledges receipt, is valid if, and only if[206] —

8.7.1.1   it is given by hand, sent by registered post or recorded delivery, or sent by fax[207] provided a confirmatory copy is given by hand or sent by registered post or recorded delivery on the same day, and

8.7.1.2   it is served —

    (a)   where the receiving party is a company incorporated within Great Britain, at the registered office,

    (b)   where the receiving party is the Tenant and the Tenant is not such a company, at the Premises, and

    (c)   where the receiving party is the Landlord [or the Guarantor] and [the Landlord *(or as required)* that party] is not such a company, at [the Landlord's *(or as required)* that party's] address shown in this Lease or at any address specified in a notice given by [the Landlord to the Tenant *(or as required)* that party to the other parties].

---

206   Notice clauses are either mandatory or permissive. The words 'and only if' are inserted to make it clear that this clause is mandatory.

207   As to service by fax see *Hastie and Jenkerson v McMahon* [1991] 1 All ER 255, [1990] 1 WLR 1575, CA.

8.7.2   *Deemed delivery*[208]

8.7.2.1   **By registered post or recorded delivery**

Unless it is returned through the Royal Mail undelivered, a notice sent by registered post or recorded delivery is to be treated as served on the third working day after posting whenever, and whether or not, it is received.

8.7.2.2   **By fax**

A notice sent by fax is to be treated as served on the day upon which it is sent, or the next working day where the fax is sent after 1600 hours or on a day that is not a working day, whenever and whether or not it or the confirmatory copy is received unless the confirmatory copy is returned through the Royal Mail undelivered.

8.7.2.3   **'A working day'**

References to 'a working day' are references to a day when the United Kingdom clearing banks are open for business in the City of London.

208   It is a fundamental aspect of any notice clause to specify the circumstances in which the server, provided he has complied with the requirements of the clause, has for the purposes of the document served a notice, even if the recipient claims that he never received it.

[1235]

8.7.3   *Joint recipients*

If the receiving party consists of more than one person, a notice to one of them is notice to all.

8.8   **Rights and easements**[209]

The operation of the Law of Property Act 1925 Section 62 is excluded from this Lease. The only rights granted to the Tenant are those expressly set out in this Lease and the Tenant is not to be entitled to any other rights affecting any adjoining property of the Landlord.

209   Where the Law of Property Act 1925 s 62 may operate, it is sensible to define in the lease those rights that are included, and then specifically exclude the operation of that section.

8.9   **Covenants relating to adjoining property**

The Tenant is not to be entitled to the benefit of or the right [to enforce or][210] to prevent the release or modification of any covenant agreement or condition entered into by any tenant of the Landlord in respect of any adjoining property of the Landlord.

210   As to when tenants would be able to enforce covenants against each other see vol 22(1) (2003 Reissue) LANDLORD AND TENANT (BUSINESS TENANCIES) Paragraph 48 [235]. Where this might arise, 'to enforce or' should be deleted by the tenant.

8.10   **Disputes with adjoining occupiers**

If any dispute arises between the Tenant and the tenants or occupiers of any adjoining property of the Landlord in connection with the Premises and any of that adjoining property, it is to be decided [by the Landlord or in such manner as the Landlord directs *(or as required)* by the Surveyor acting as an expert and not as an arbitrator][211].

211   Such a provision is binding on the landlord and the tenant, but binds a tenant of the landlord's adjoining property only if there is a similar provision in his lease.

[1236]

8.11   Effect of waiver

Each of the Tenant's covenants is to remain in full force both at law and in equity even if the Landlord has waived or released that covenant, or waived or released any similar covenant affecting any adjoining property of the Landlord[212].

212   But as to waiver of a right of forfeiture see vol 22(1) (2003 Reissue) LANDLORD AND TENANT (BUSINESS TENANCIES) Paragraph 284 [1173].

[8.12   The perpetuity period[213]

The perpetuity period applicable to this Lease is *(state period, eg 80 years)* from the commencement of the [Contractual][214] Term, and whenever in this Lease any party is granted a future interest it must vest within that period or be void for remoteness.]

213   As to the rule against perpetuities see vol 22(1) (2003 Reissue) LANDLORD AND TENANT (BUSINESS TENANCIES) Paragraph 132 [664]. This clause should be included if the term exceeds 21 years because this lease contains grants of future interests.
214   This defined term will require amendment where the operation of the security of tenure provisions in the Landlord and Tenant Act 1954 ss 24–28 is to be excluded in relation to the lease (see note 6 to clause 1.5 [1110] 'THE [CONTRACTUAL] TERM') although this is probably unlikely in connection with the grant of such a long lease.

[8.13   Party walls

Any walls dividing the Premises from the other buildings are to be party walls within the meaning of the Law of Property Act 1925 Section 38 and must be maintained at the equally shared expense of the Tenant and the other party[215].] *(omit if not required in the circumstances)*

215   Internal non-loadbearing and loadbearing walls between the premises and other premises are covered in the description of the premises. It is therefore unlikely that as between the tenant and the landlord or other tenants there can be any party walls.

8.14   Exclusion of liability

The Landlord is not to be responsible to the Tenant or to anyone at the Premises or the Parade expressly or by implication with the Tenant's authority for any accident happening or injury suffered or for any damage to or loss of any chattel sustained in the Premises or on the Parade[216].

216   As to exclusion clauses see vol 22(1) (2003 Reissue) LANDLORD AND TENANT (BUSINESS TENANCIES) Paragraph 140 [679].

[1237]

8.15   [New *(or)* Old] lease

[This Lease [is *(or as appropriate)* is not] a new tenancy for the purposes of the 1995 Act Section 1. *(or as appropriate)* This Lease is granted under the 1995 Act Section 19 and [is *(or as appropriate)* is not] a new tenancy for the purposes of Section 1 of that Act][217].

217   A tenancy granted on or after 1 January 1996 that is an overriding lease is not a 'new' tenancy where the tenancy being overridden is one granted before that date: see the Landlord and Tenant (Covenants) Act 1995 ss 1(4), 20(1). Where the lease being granted is an overriding lease, the lease must include a statement that it is an overriding lease and indicate whether the overriding lease is or is not a 'new' tenancy: see the Landlord and Tenant (Covenants) Act 1995 s 20(2). In these circumstances the second alternative should be used.

[8.16   Capacity of tenants

It is declared that the persons comprising the Tenant hold the Premises as [joint tenants *(or as required)* tenants in common].]

[8.17   Exclusion of the 1954 Act Sections 24–28[218]

8.17.1   *Notice and declaration*

On *(date)* the Landlord served notice on the Tenant pursuant to the provisions of the 1954 Act Section 38A(3) as inserted by the Regulatory Reform (Business Tenancies) (England and Wales) Order 2003 and on *(date)* the Tenant made a [simple *(or as appropriate)* statutory] declaration pursuant to schedule 2 of the Regulatory Reform (Business Tenancies) (England and Wales) Order 2003.

8.17.2   *Agreement to exclude*

Pursuant to the provisions of the 1954 Act Section 38A(1) as inserted by the Regulatory Reform (Business Tenancies) (England and Wales) Order 2003, the parties agree that the provisions of the 1954 Act Sections 24–28 inclusive are to be excluded in relation to the tenancy created by this Lease.]

218   As to contracting out of the Landlord and Tenant Act 1954 and the requirements that need to be complied with see vol 22(1) (2003 Reissue) LANDLORD AND TENANT (BUSINESS TENANCIES) Paragraph 431 [2035].

(include other clauses as required: eg, break clauses and options (see vol 22(3) (1997 Reissue) LANDLORD AND TENANT (BUSINESS TENANCIES) Forms 136 [6544]–142 [6569]) or a proviso as to termination on rent review (see vol 22(3) (1997 Reissue) LANDLORD AND TENANT (BUSINESS TENANCIES) Form 143 [6570]))

IN WITNESS etc *(see vol 12(2) (2003 Reissue) DEEDS, AGREEMENTS ETC)*

[1238]

SCHEDULE 1: THE RIGHTS GRANTED[219]

1-1   Rights of way

The right, subject to temporary interruption for repair, alteration or replacement, for the Tenant and all persons expressly or by implication authorised by him[220] — in common with the Landlord and all other persons having a like right — to pass and repass[221] to and from the Premises at all times, for all purposes connected with the use and enjoyment of the Premises but not otherwise[222], [with or without vehicles of any description *(or as required)* with vehicles not exceeding ... metres in length or ... kilograms unladen weight over and along the Road][223], and on foot only over and along the Staircase and the Passageway.

219   As to rights granted see vol 22(1) (2003 Reissue) LANDLORD AND TENANT (BUSINESS TENANCIES) Paragraph 123 [647] et seq.
220   The term 'the Tenant and all persons expressly or by implication authorised by him' is an updated version of 'the Tenant and his successors in title the owners and occupiers for the time being of the Premises and his or their respective servants and licensees': see *Baxendale v North Lambeth Liberal and Radical Club Ltd* [1902] 2 Ch 427 at 429 per Swinfen Eady J; *Hammond v Prentice Bros Ltd* [1920] 1 Ch 201.
221   There is an implied right to stop for a reasonable time for loading and unloading, but there is no right to park unless one is specifically granted: see *Bulstrode v Lambert* [1953] 2 All ER 728, [1953] 1 WLR 1064; *McIlraith v Grady* [1968] 1 QB 468, [1967] 3 All ER 625, CA; *VT Engineering Ltd v Richard Barland & Co Ltd* (1968) 19 P & CR 890.
222   See *Callard v Beeney* [1930] 1 KB 353 at 357 per Talbot J.
223   The landlord may reasonably wish to limit the size and weight of vehicles using the road.

1-2   Right to use the Common Parts

The right, subject to [temporary] interruption for repair, alteration or replacement, for the Tenant and all persons expressly or by implication authorised by him — in common with the Landlord and all other persons having a like right and in so far as such right has not been granted in paragraph 1-1 RIGHTS OF WAY — to use all appropriate areas of the Common Parts for all proper purposes in connection with the use and enjoyment of the Premises.

1-3   Passage and running through the Adjoining Conduits

The right, subject to temporary interruption for repair, alteration or replacement, to the free passage and running of all services to and from the Premises through the appropriate Adjoining Conduits, in common with the Landlord and all other persons having a like right.

1-4   Support and protection

The right of support and protection for the benefit of the Premises that is now enjoyed from all other parts of the Parade.

[1239]

SCHEDULE 2: THE RIGHTS RESERVED[224]

2-1   Passage and running through the Conduits

The right to the free and uninterrupted passage and running of all appropriate services and supplies from and to other parts of the Parade or any other adjoining property of the Landlord in and through the appropriate Conduits and through any structures of a similar use or nature that may at any time be constructed in, on, over or under the Premises as permitted by paragraph 2-2 RIGHT TO CONSTRUCT CONDUITS.

224   As to rights reserved see vol 22(1) (2003 Reissue) LANDLORD AND TENANT (BUSINESS TENANCIES) Paragraph 124 [648] et seq.

2-2   Right to construct conduits[225]

The right to construct[226] and to maintain at any time during the Term any pipes, sewers, drains, mains, ducts, conduits, gutters, watercourses, wires, cables, [laser optical fibres, data or impulse transmission, communication or reception systems,] channels, flues and all other conducting media for the provision of services or supplies — including any fixings, louvres, cowls and any other ancillary apparatus — for the benefit of any part of the Parade or any other adjoining property of the Landlord[, making good any damage caused by the exercise of the right]

225   If the term of the lease exceeds 21 years a perpetuity provision — see clause 8.12 [1237] THE PERPETUITY PERIOD — is required in the lease because this is a grant of a future interest.
226   For a covenant to make good after exercising rights of access see vol 22(3) (1997 Reissue) LANDLORD AND TENANT (BUSINESS TENANCIES) Form 79 [6453].

[1240]

2-3   Access

2-3.1   *Access to inspect*[227]

The right to enter, or in emergency to break into and enter, the Premises [at any time during the Term *(or as required)* at reasonable times and on reasonable notice except in emergency] —

2-3.1.1   to inspect, clean, connect to, lay, repair, remove, replace with others, alter or execute any works whatever to or in connection with the conduits, easements, supplies or services referred to in paragraphs 2-1 PASSAGE AND RUNNING THROUGH THE CONDUITS and 2-2 RIGHT TO CONSTRUCT CONDUITS,

2-3.1.2   to view the state and condition of, and repair and maintain and carry out work of any other kind to, the Premises, the Parade, the Common Parts and any other buildings where such viewing or work would not otherwise be reasonably practicable,

2-3.1.3   to carry out work, or do anything whatever, comprised within the Landlord's obligations in this Lease whether or not the Tenant is liable to make a contribution,

2-3.1.4   to take schedules or inventories of fixtures and other items to be yielded up at the end of the Term, and

2-3.1.5   to exercise any of the rights granted to the Landlord in this Lease.

227   For a covenant to make good after exercising rights of access see vol 22(3) (1997 Reissue) LANDLORD AND TENANT (BUSINESS TENANCIES) Form 79 [6453].

2-3.2   *Access on renewal or rent review*

[The right to enter the Premises with the Surveyor and the third party determining the Rent under any provisions for rent review contained in this Lease at [any time *(or as required)* convenient hours and on reasonable prior notice], to inspect [and measure] the Premises for all purposes connected with any pending or intended step under the 1954 Act or the implementation of the provisions for rent review. *(or as required in view of the rent review provisions used: see, eg, vol 22(3) (1997 Reissue) LANDLORD AND TENANT (BUSINESS TENANCIES) Forms 180 [6711]–194 [6987])*]

[1241]

2-4   Right to erect scaffolding

The right [temporarily] to erect scaffolding for [any purpose connected with or related to the Parade *(or as required)* the purpose of inspecting, repairing or cleaning the Parade] or any other buildings [even if it restricts *(or as required)* provided it does not materially adversely restrict] the access to or use and enjoyment of the Premises [but not so as to prevent such access, use and enjoyment][228].

228   See *Owen v Gadd* [1956] 2 QB 99, [1956] 2 All ER 28, CA.

2-5   Rights of support and shelter

The right of light, air, support, protection, shelter and all other easements and rights at the date of this Lease belonging to or enjoyed by other parts of the Parade and any other buildings.

2-6   Right to erect new buildings[229]

Full right and liberty at any time —

2-6.1   to alter, raise the height of, or rebuild the Parade or any other buildings, and

2-6.2   to erect any new buildings of any height on the Parade or on any other adjoining property of the Landlord

in such manner as the Landlord thinks fit, even if doing so may obstruct, affect, or interfere with the amenity of or access to the Premises or the passage of light and air to the Premises[and even if they *(or as required)* but provided they do not] materially affect the Premises or the use and enjoyment of the Premises.

229   As to reservation of the right to develop other land see vol 22(1) (2003 Reissue) LANDLORD AND TENANT (BUSINESS TENANCIES) Paragraphs 130 [660], 131 [662].

SCHEDULE 3: THE RENT AND RENT REVIEW

(insert rent review provisions as required: see vol 22(3) (1997 Reissue) LANDLORD AND TENANT (BUSINESS TENANCIES) Forms 180 [6711]–194 [6987])

[1242]

SCHEDULE 4: THE SHOP AND MAISONETTE COVENANTS

(the parties must consider how far the restrictions suggested in this schedule are appropriate to the letting concerned — if the landlord requires further restrictions see Form 10 schedule 4 THE SHOP COVENANTS [1495])

4-1   Use

4-1.1   *The Shop*

The Tenant must use the ground floor of the Premises ('the Shop') for the Permitted Use only.

4-1.2   *The Maisonette*

The Tenant must not use the first and second floors of the Premises ('the Maisonette') for any purpose other than as a private residence for either —

4-1.2.1   the Tenant and his family, where the Tenant is an individual, or

4-1.2.2   an employee of the Tenant, where the Tenant is a company, who is employed on a permanent basis by the Tenant in the Shop [and his family] provided that—

4-1.2.2.1   such use is by virtue of a service occupancy not affording any security of tenure to the employee [and his family][230], and

4-1.2.2.2   the Tenant gives to the Landlord full particulars of any proposed occupancy, including the name of the employee, the nature of his employment and a copy of any documents entered into between the Tenant and the employee relating to such occupancy.

230   As to occupation by employees see vol 22(1) (2003 Reissue) LANDLORD AND TENANT (BUSINESS TENANCIES) Paragraph 8 [15].

4-1.3   *Use restrictions for the Maisonette*

The Tenant must not take lodgers or paying guests into the Maisonette, or use it for any trade, profession or business.

[1243]

4-1.4   *External displays*

The Tenant must not stand, place, deposit or expose any goods, materials, articles or things whatsoever for display or sale or for any other purpose outside any part of the Premises.

4-1.5   *Noxious discharges*

The Tenant must not discharge into any of the Conduits or the Adjoining Conduits any noxious or deleterious matter or any substance that might cause an obstruction in or danger or injury to the Conduits or the Adjoining Conduits or be or become a source of obstruction, danger or injury, and in the event of any such obstruction, danger or injury the Tenant must forthwith make good any damage to the satisfaction of the Surveyor.

4-1.6   *Noisy machinery*

The Tenant must not install in or use on the Premises any machinery or apparatus causing noise or vibration that can be heard or felt in nearby premises in nearby premises or outside the Premises or that may cause damage.

4-1.7   *Sound audible outside*

The Tenant must not play or use on the Premises any musical instrument, audio or other equipment or apparatus producing sound that can be heard outside the Premises [if the Landlord [in his absolute discretion *(or as required)* reasonably] considers such sounds to be undesirable and gives notice to the Tenant to that effect].

4-1.8   *Flashing lights*

The Tenant must not display any flashing lights in the Premises that can be seen from outside the Premises[, or display any other lighting arrangement that can be seen from outside the Premises if the Landlord [in his absolute discretion *(or as required)* reasonably] considers such lighting to be undesirable and gives written notice to the Tenant to that effect].

4-1.9   *Exterior lights and awnings*

The Tenant must not install or erect any exterior lighting, shade or awning at the Premises.

4-1.10   *Window cleaning*

The Tenant must clean both sides of all windows and window frames at the Premises at least once every month.

[1244]

4-2   Damage precautions

4-2.1   *Frost precautions*

The Tenant must take all necessary precautions against frost damage to the Conduits.

4-2.2   *Water damage*

The Tenant must take all necessary care and precautions to avoid water damage to any other part of the Parade caused by the bursting or overflowing of any pipe or water apparatus in the Premises.

4-3   Care of the Common Parts

The Tenant must not cause the Common Parts to become untidy or dirty, and must at all times keep them free from deposits of materials and refuse.

4-4   Landlord's expenditure[231]

4-4.1   *Payment of proportion of costs*[232]

Subject to the provisions of schedule 6 PROVISIONAL PAYMENTS, the Tenant must pay to the Landlord on demand as additional rent[233] a fair proportion to be determined by the Surveyor, acting as an expert and not as an arbitrator, of all sums that the Landlord may be liable to pay in connection with the performance of his covenants contained in clause 4.2 MAINTENANCE AND DECORATION OF THE PARADE [provided that where any costs that the Landlord becomes liable to pay in or incidental to the performance of those covenants are incurred only in relation to one or more of the units in the Parade but not all of those units — the Premises being regarded for this purpose as one of those units — then the determination of the proportion by the Surveyor must be made in respect only of the units that are benefited or affected by the works in respect of which the costs were incurred, in exoneration of the units that are not so benefited or affected][234].

231   As to methods of apportionment for reimbursement of landlord's expenditure see vol 22(1) (2003 Reissue) LANDLORD AND TENANT (BUSINESS TENANCIES) Paragraph 268 [1115].
232   If regular substantial expenditure is anticipated, this obligation should be included in the definition of 'Lease Rents': see note 36 [1121] to clause 1.37 'THE RENT'.
233   See note 51 [1131] to clause 2 DEMISE.
234   In order to avoid disputes as to whether or not the premises are benefited or affected by any particular works and the extent of such benefit or effect, it may be advisable to add to this proviso a provision for arbitration eg vol 22(3) (1997 Reissue) LANDLORD AND TENANT (BUSINESS TENANCIES) Form 168 [6691].

4-4.2 *Provisional payments*

The Tenant must observe and perform the obligations on his part set out in schedule 6 PROVISIONAL PAYMENTS.

[1245]

4-5   Hours of trading

During normal trading hours[235] for the locality the Tenant must keep the Premises open for business[236] and properly cared for, and must trade actively throughout substantially the whole of the Premises except —

4-5.1   in so far as he is prevented from doing so by destruction or damage to the Premises caused by one or more of the Insured Risks[237],

4-5.2   when non-trading is necessary to allow any major repairs, alterations or additions to the Premises to be carried out with all reasonable speed[238],

4-5.3   where non-trading is necessary to allow a permitted assignment [or subletting] of this Lease to be completed, or

4-5.4   in so far as to do so would be in breach of any other provision of this Lease.

235   A covenant to keep open during 'normal business hours' does not require the tenant to open the shop on Sundays: see the Sunday Trading Act 1994 s 3 (19 Halsbury's Statutes (4th Edn) HEALTH AND SAFETY AT WORK).
236   The landlord should give careful consideration to the inclusion of an obligation of this nature: see vol 22(1) (2003 Reissue) LANDLORD AND TENANT (BUSINESS TENANCIES) Paragraph 177 [876].

237   It should be noted that it is now recommended 'best practice' that if the premises are so damaged by an uninsured risk as to prevent occupation, the tenant should be allowed to terminate the lease unless the landlord agrees to reinstate at his own cost: see vol 22(1) (2003 Reissue) LANDLORD AND TENANT (BUSINESS TENANCIES) Paragraph 85 [402]. It follows that if this recommendation is adopted, this exception also needs to be extended to include damage or destruction caused by both insured and uninsured risks.

238   A tenant may wish to have this provision extended to include periods for stocktaking and, particularly in long leases, to authorise shop fittings.

[1246]

4-6   Window dressing and displays

4-6.1   *Window dressing*

The Tenant must keep the shop windows attractively dressed in a manner [suitable to a high class shopping area *(or as required)* appropriate to the neighbourhood].

4-6.2   *Interior layout*

The Tenant must keep all those parts of the interior of the Premises that are visible from outside the Premises attractively laid out and furnished and with goods well displayed and must keep any showcases in the Premises clean and attractively dressed at all times [to the reasonable satisfaction of the Landlord].

4-6.3   *Posters, placards and signs*

The Tenant must not place or display on the outside of the Premises or on the windows or inside the Premises so as to be visible from outside the Premises any name, writing, notice, sign, placard, poster, sticker or advertisement other than —

4-6.3.1   normal price tickets attached and relating to goods sold in the display area inside the Premises, provided these are not placed on the window glass, [and]

4-6.3.2   the sign referred to in paragraph 4-6.4 APPROVED SIGN OR FASCIA[, and

4-6.3.3   trade placards, posters or advertisements of a temporary and not excessive nature and necessary or usual for the Permitted Use [provided that not more than *(state proportion, eg 25%)* of the surface area of the shop window of the Premises may be obscured by the placards, posters or advertisements]].

4-6.4   *Approved sign or fascia*

The Tenant must maintain on the outside of the Premises a [sign *(or as appropriate)* fascia] of a type, size and design approved by the Landlord, whose approval may not be unreasonably withheld or delayed, showing the Tenant's name and business.

[1247]

4-7   Ceiling and floor loading

4-7.1   *Heavy items*

The Tenant must not bring onto, or permit to remain on, the Premises any safes, machinery, goods or other articles that will or may strain or damage the Premises or any part of them.

4-7.2   *Protection of the roof*

The Tenant must not, without the consent of the Landlord, suspend anything from any ceiling of the Premises [or store any heavy items in the roof space].

4-7.3   *Expert advice*

If the Tenant applies for the Landlord's consent under paragraph 4-7.2 PROTECTION OF THE ROOF, the Landlord may consult any engineer or other person in relation to the loading proposed by the Tenant, and the Tenant must repay the fees of the engineer or other person to the Landlord on demand.

4-8   Plate glass

4-8.1   *Insurance of plate glass*

The Tenant must insure any plate glass against breakage or damage, in a reputable insurance office, for its full reinstatement cost from time to time, and whenever reasonably so required must produce to the Landlord particulars of the insurance policy and evidence of payment of the current year's premium.

4-8.2   *Reinstatement of plate glass*

Notwithstanding anything to the contrary contained elsewhere in this Lease[239], whenever the whole or any part of the plate glass is broken or damaged the Tenant must as quickly as possible lay out all money received in respect of the insurance of it in reinstating it with new glass of at least the same quality and thickness, and must make good any deficiency in such money.

239   The reference here is to the landlord's obligations under clause 5.6 [1197] REINSTATEMENT AND TERMINATION and the intention is to make clear that the landlord's general obligation to make good does not apply to the plate glass.

[1248]

4-9   Loading and unloading

4-9.1   *Parking for loading and unloading only*

Except when loading or unloading goods and materials, the Tenant must not permit any vehicles belonging to him or to any persons calling on the Premises expressly or by implication with his authority to stand on the Road, and must use his best endeavours to ensure that persons calling on the Premises do not permit any vehicle to stand on the Road or the pavement.

4-9.2   *Use of rear entrance*

The Tenant must not convey any goods or materials to or from the Premises except through the rear entrance provided for the purpose.

[4-10   Fitting out

(consideration should be given to the fitting out works (if any) to be carried out by the tenant: these may be included here or, more appropriately dealt with in an agreement for lease (see, eg, vol 22(4) (1997 Reissue) LANDLORD AND TENANT (BUSINESS TENANCIES) Form 400 [7510]) or a licence for alterations (see vol 22(3) (1997 Reissue) LANDLORD AND TENANT (BUSINESS TENANCIES) Forms 241 [7203] and 242 [7204]), for examples of fitting out covenants see vol 22(3) (1997 Reissue) LANDLORD AND TENANT (BUSINESS TENANCIES) Forms 173 [6697], 174 [6698])]

SCHEDULE 5: THE SUBJECTIONS

(insert details)

[1249]

SCHEDULE 6: PROVISIONAL PAYMENTS[240]

6-1   Service of a provisional charge notice

If and whenever the Landlord believes or is advised that work should be carried out pursuant to clause 4.2 MAINTENANCE AND DECORATION OF THE PARADE the Landlord may— but need not — serve on the Tenant a notice ('a provisional charge notice') indicating —

6-1.1   the nature of the work,

6-1.2   the estimated cost of the work, and

6-1.3   the proportion of the cost of the work that the Surveyor has provisionally determined[241] is payable by the Tenant in accordance with paragraph 4-4 LANDLORD'S EXPENDITURE ('the Provisional Charge').

240   Notwithstanding all the rights and remedies of the landlord, it can, as a practical matter, prove difficult to collect sums due from a tenant under 'reimbursement of Landlord's expenditure' clauses. As most of them are drafted, the collection process can begin only after the work has been done and thus the expenditure incurred. This schedule 'borrows' from a lease containing a full service charge clause, and in effect provides for payment on account.

241   Such wording gives the Surveyor the flexibility to change the share after the work has been done perhaps, eg, as a result of information that came to light only during the carrying out of the work.

6-2   Payment of the Provisional Charge

The Tenant must pay the Provisional Charge to the Landlord within *(state period, eg 14 days)* of the service of a provisional charge notice.

6-3   The Final Notice

[As soon as convenient after *(or as required)* After] the work has been carried out the Landlord must give to the Tenant a notice ('a final notice') setting out —

6-3.1   the actual cost of the work,

6-3.2   the proportion of the cost of the work that the Surveyor has determined is payable by the Tenant in accordance with paragraph 4-4 LANDLORD'S EXPENDITURE ('the Actual Charge'), and

6-3.3   the difference between the Provisional Charge and the Actual Charge.

6-4   Excess or shortfall

If the Provisional Charge exceeds the Actual Charge, the Landlord must refund the excess to the Tenant, and if the Actual Charge exceeds the Provisional Charge the shortfall must be paid to the Landlord by the Tenant, in either case within *(state period, eg 14 days)* of the service of the final notice.

[1250]

SCHEDULE 7: THE AUTHORISED GUARANTEE AGREEMENT

(insert the form of authorised guarantee agreement: see, eg, vol 22(3) (1997 Reissue) LANDLORD AND TENANT (BUSINESS TENANCIES) *Form 217 [7053])*

(signature (or common seal) of landlord: lease)
(signature (or common seal) of tenant (and guarantor): counterpart)
(signatures of witnesses
[1251]–[1300]

10

Lease of a shop in a shopping centre[1]

CONTENTS

(NB: numbers in [ ] below refer to this volume and should be altered to suit the page or reference numbers actually used)

1 DEFINITIONS AND INTERPRETATION

1.1 'The Accountant' . . . . [1308]
1.2 'The Adjoining Conduits' . . . . [1308]
1.3 'Adjoining property of the Landlord' . . . . [1309]
1.4 'The Centre' . . . . [1309]
1.5 'The Common Parts' . . . . [1309]
1.6 'The Conduits' . . . . [1309]
1.7 'The [Contractual] Term' . . . . [1310]
[1.8 'The Decorating Years' . . . . [1311]]
1.9 'Development' . . . . [1311]
                                                                             [1301]
1.10 Gender and number . . . . [1311]
1.11 Headings . . . . [1311]
[1.12 'The Initial Rent' . . . . [1312]]
1.13 'The Insurance Rent' . . . . [1312]
1.14 'The Insurance Rent Percentage' . . . . [1312]
1.15 'The Insured Risks' . . . . [1312]
1.16 'Interest' . . . . [1313]
1.17 'The Interest Rate' . . . . [1313]
1.18 Interpretation of 'the Centre' . . . . [1321]
1.19 Interpretation of 'consent' and 'approved' . . . . [1321]
1.20 Interpretation of 'external parts' . . . . [1321]
1.21 Interpretation of 'the Guarantor' . . . . [1322]
1.22 Interpretation of 'the Landlord' . . . . [1322]
1.23 Interpretation of 'the last year of the Term' and 'the end of the Term' . . . [1322]
1.24 Interpretation of 'the Tenant' . . . . [1322]
1.25 Interpretation of 'this Lease' . . . . [1322]
1.26 Joint and several liability . . . . [1322]
1.27 'The Landlord's Expenses' . . . . [1322]
1.28 'The Liability Period' . . . . [1323]
1.29 'Losses' . . . . [1324]
1.30 'The 1954 Act' . . . . [1324]
1.31 'The 1995 Act' . . . . [1324]
1.32 Obligation not to permit or suffer . . . . [1324]
1.33 'Other buildings' . . . . [1325]
1.34 'The Permitted Use' . . . . [1325]
1.35 'The Plan' . . . . [1325]
1.36 'The Planning Acts' . . . . [1325]
1.37 'The Premises' . . . . [1326]
1.38 'The Prohibited Uses' . . . . [1327]
1.39 References to clauses and schedules . . . . [1327]
1.40 References to rights of access . . . . [1327]

1.41 References to statutes . . . . [1327]
1.42 'The Rent' . . . . [1341]
1.43 'The Rent Commencement Date' . . . . [1341]
[1.44 'The Review Dates' . . . . [1341]]
1.45 'The Service Charge' . . . . [1342]
1.46 'The Service Charge Percentage' . . . . [1342
1.47 'The Services' . . . . [1342]
1.48 'The Shop Covenants' . . . . [1342]
1.49 'The Shop Opening Hours' . . . . [1342]
1.5 'The Surveyor' . . . . [1342]
[1.51 'The Term' . . . . [1343]]
1.52 Terms from the 1995 Act . . . . [1343]
1.53 'VAT' . . . . [1343]

2 DEMISE . . . . [1361]
                                                                          [1302]

3 THE TENANT'S COVENANTS

3.1 Rent . . . . [1362]
3.2 Outgoings and VAT . . . . [1363]
[3.3 Cost of services consumed . . . . [1363]]
3.4 Repair, cleaning and decoration . . . . [1365]
3.5 Waste and alterations . . . . [1367]
3.6 Aerials, signs and advertisements . . . . [1368]
3.7 Statutory obligations . . . . [1369]
3.8 Entry to inspect and notice to repair . . . . [1370]
3.9 Alienation . . . . [1381]
3.10 Nuisance and residential restrictions . . . . [1391]
3.11 Costs of applications, notices and recovery of arrears . . . . [1392]
3.12 Planning and development . . . . [1401]
3.13 Plans, documents and information . . . . [1403]
3.14 Indemnities . . . . [1403]
3.15 Reletting boards and viewing . . . . [1404]
3.16 Obstruction and encroachment . . . . [1404]
3.17 Yielding up . . . . [1405]
3.18 Interest on arrears . . . . [1405]
3.19 Statutory notices . . . . [1405]
3.20 Keyholders . . . . [1406]
3.21 Viewing on sale of reversion . . . . [1406]
3.22 Defective premises . . . . [1406]
3.23 Replacement guarantor . . . . [1406]
3.24 Exercise of the Landlord's rights . . . . [1407]
3.25 The Shop Covenants . . . . [1407]
3.26 The Services . . . . [1407]
3.27 Costs of grant of this Lease . . . . [1407]
3.28 Consent to the Landlord's release . . . . [1408]

4 THE LANDLORD'S COVENANTS

4.1 Quiet enjoyment . . . . [1421]
4.2 The Services . . . . [1422]

5 INSURANCE

5.1 Warranty as to convictions . . . . [1423]
5.2 Covenant to insure . . . . [1423]
5.3 Details of the insurance . . . . [1424]
5.4 Payment of the Insurance Rent . . . . [1425]
5.5 Suspension of the Rent . . . . [1425]
5.6 Reinstatement and termination . . . . [1427]
5.7 Tenant's further insurance covenants . . . . [1431]
5.8 Increase or decrease of the Centre . . . . [1433]
[5.9 Landlord's further insurance covenants . . . . [1433]]
                                                                          [1303]

6 GUARANTEE PROVISIONS

6.1 The Guarantor's covenants . . . . [1451]
[6.2 The Landlord's covenant . . . . [1456]]

7 FORFEITURE . . . . [1457]

8 MISCELLANEOUS

8.1 Exclusion of warranty as to use . . . . [1471]
8.2 Exclusion of third party rights . . . . [1471]
8.3 Representations . . . . [1471]
8.4 Documents under hand . . . . [1472]
8.5 Tenant's property . . . . [1472]
8.6 Compensation on vacating excluded . . . . [1472]
8.7 Notices . . . . [1473]
8.8 Rights and easements . . . . [1474]
8.9 Covenants relating to adjoining property . . . . [1474]
8.10 Disputes with adjoining occupiers . . . . [1474]
8.11 Effect of waiver . . . . [1474]
[8.12 The perpetuity period . . . . [1475]]
[8.13 Party walls . . . . [1475]]
8.14 Exclusion of liability . . . . [1475]
8.15 [New (or) Old] lease . . . . [1476]
[8.16 Capacity of tenants . . . . [1476]]
[8.17 Exclusion of the 1954 Act Sections 24–28 . . . . [1476]]

SCHEDULE 1: THE RIGHTS GRANTED

1-1 Right to use the Common Parts . . . . [1491]
1-2 Passage and running through the Adjoining Conduits . . . . [1491]
1-3 Support and protection . . . . [1491]

SCHEDULE 2: THE RIGHTS RESERVED

2-1 Passage and running through the Conduits . . . . [1492]
2-2 Right to construct conduits . . . . [1492]
2-3 Access . . . . [1493]
2-4 Right to erect scaffolding . . . . [1494]
2-5 Rights of support and shelter . . . . [1494]
2-6 Right to erect new buildings . . . . [1494]

SCHEDULE 3: THE RENT AND RENT REVIEW

SCHEDULE 4: THE SHOP COVENANTS

4-1 Use . . . . [1495]
4-2 Damage precautions . . . . [1496]
4-3 Hours of trading . . . . [1497]
4-4 Window dressing and displays . . . . [1498]
4-5 Cleaning and tidying . . . . [1499]
4-6 Ceiling and floor loading . . . . [1500]
4-7 Loading and unloading . . . . [1500]
4-8 Security, fire alarms and sprinkler . . . . [1501]
4-9 Heating, cooling and ventilation . . . . [1502]
4-10 Plate glass . . . . [1502]
4-11 Regulations . . . . [1502]
[4-12 Fitting out . . . . [1502]]

SCHEDULE 5: THE SUBJECTIONS

SCHEDULE 6: THE SERVICE CHARGE

6-1 Definitions . . . . [1503]
6-2 Service charge provisions . . . . [1504]
6-3 The Services . . . . [1508]

SCHEDULE 7: THE AUTHORISED GUARANTEE AGREEMENT

[1304]

AGREEMENT

[HM LAND REGISTRY

LAND REGISTRATION ACT 2002

Administrative area	*(insert details)*
Title number out of which lease is granted	*(title number)*
Property let	*(postal address or description)*]

[1305]

THIS LEASE is made the .... day of .... BETWEEN:

(1)   *(name of landlord)* [of *(address)* *(or as appropriate)* the registered office of which is at *(address)*] [Company Registration no ...][2] ('the Landlord') [and]

(2)   *(name of tenant)* [of *(address)* *(or as appropriate)* being a company registered in [England and Wales *(or)* Scotland][3] the registered office of which is at *(address)*] [Company Registration no ...] ('the Tenant') [and

(3)   *(name of guarantor)* [of *(address)* *(or as appropriate)* the registered office of which is at *(address)*] [Company Registration no ...] ('the Guarantor')]

[1306]

1   As to stamp duty land tax see the Information Binder: Stamp Duty Land Tax [1].
        As to Land Registry Fees see the Information Binder: Property [1]: Property Fees.
        On the grant out of an unregistered freehold estate in land of a lease for a term of more than seven
        years from the date of the grant, application must be made to register the title to the leasehold interest
        granted: see the Land Registration Act 2002 s 4(1)(c) (37 Halsbury's Statutes (4th Edn) REAL
        PROPERTY). The tenant must obtain an epitome of title to the freehold reversion, investigate it, and
        mark it as examined, otherwise he will not be able to be registered with an absolute title: see vol 25(1)
        (2003 Reissue) LAND REGISTRATION Paragraph 21.1 [132].
        If the freehold reversion is registered, the grant of a lease for a term of more than seven years from
        the date of the grant must be completed by registration: see the Land Registration Act 2002
        s 27(2)(b)(i).
        As to the form and contents of leases see vol 22(1) (2003 Reissue) LANDLORD AND TENANT
        (BUSINESS TENANCIES) Paragraph 104 [601] et seq. As to registered land generally see vol 25(1)
        (2003 Reissue) LAND REGISTRATION. As to registration of title to leases see vol 25(1) (2003 Reissue)
        LAND REGISTRATION Paragraph 143 [601] et seq.
        This is a lease of premises comprising a unit in a shopping centre. Public access to the shops is
        through pedestrian malls forming part of the centre, while trade deliveries are made through the
        centre's service areas. No part of the structure of the centre is included in the unit, the demise being
        limited to the floor and ceiling finishes and the inner half of the non-structural walls that divide the unit
        from its neighbours. The tenant's repairing covenant is similarly limited. Rights are granted over land
        adjoining the premises. The landlord covenants to provide services, including the operation of the
        centre and the repair and maintenance of those parts of the centre not intended for letting, such as the
        common parts, structure, roof and foundations of the centre. The landlord is to be fully reimbursed by
        means of a service charge, the tenant paying a fixed percentage of the costs of providing the services
        and any other sums incurred by the landlord in relation to the centre. The landlord insures the centre
        and the tenant refunds a proportion of the premium. There is provision for the rent to be reviewed,
        and for a guarantor.
        The tenant should ensure that the landlord deduces title to the land affected by the rights he is
        granted, especially where the lease is registrable, because if title is not shown and any consents, eg of
        any chargee or landlord of the adjoining land, obtained, the rights may be excluded from the title.
2   If any party is a company it is desirable to include the company registration number. This avoids any
        problems arising when a company has been wound up and a new company formed with the same
        name, or when the name of a company is changed, or if companies swap names, eg on a reconstruction
        of a group of companies. In addition, where a company applies to be registered as proprietor of a
        registered estate or registered charge, the application must state the company's registration number: see
        the Land Registration Rules 2003, SI 2003/1417 r 181.
3   Where the tenant is a company registered in England and Wales or Scotland, and the lease is registrable,
        an application for first registration of the lease (where the landlord's title is unregistered), or registration
        of the lease as a registrable disposition (where the landlord's title is registered), and the tenant as
        proprietor of the leasehold title, must state the company's registered number: see SI 2003/1417
        r 181(1). There seems to be no reason why the certificate and statement should not be contained in the
        disposition in favour of the proprietor, where convenient.

                                                                                                        [1307]

NOW THIS DEED WITNESSES as follows:

1   DEFINITIONS AND INTERPRETATION

For all purposes of this Lease[4] the terms defined in this clause have the meanings
specified.

4   One view would add 'unless the context otherwise requires' or 'where the context so admits' and in
        fact this may be implied (see *Meux v Jacobs* (1875) LR 7 HL 481 at 493; *Law Society v United Service
        Bureau Ltd* [1934] 1 KB 343, DC) but the better course is to use defined terms in such a way that there
        are no circumstances where the defined meaning does not apply.

1.1   'The Accountant'[5]

'The Accountant' means *(name)* or any qualified accountant or firm of accountants
appointed by the Landlord in his place. The Accountant may be an employee of the
Landlord or a company that is a member of the same group of the Landlord within the
meaning of the 1954 Act Section 42.

5   For a provision that a surveyor or accountant must be a member of a relevant professional body see vol
        22(3) (1997 Reissue) LANDLORD AND TENANT (BUSINESS TENANCIES) Form 152 [6648].

1.2   'The Adjoining Conduits'

'The Adjoining Conduits' means all the pipes, sewers, drains, mains, ducts, conduits, gutters, watercourses, wires, cables, [laser optical fibres, data or impulse transmission, communication or reception systems,] channels, flues and all other conducting media — including any fixings, louvres, cowls, covers and other ancillary apparatus — that are in, on, over or under the Centre that serve the Premises.

[1308]

1.3   'Adjoining property of the Landlord'

References to 'adjoining property of the Landlord' are references to each and every part of any neighbouring or adjoining land, including the Centre, in which the Landlord, or a company that is a member of the same group as the Landlord within the meaning of the 1954 Act Section 42, has or during the Term acquires an interest or estate.

1.4   'The Centre'

'The Centre' means all that *(describe the shopping centre)* shown [for the purpose of identification only] edged *(state colour, eg blue)* on the Plan.

1.5   'The Common Parts'

'The Common Parts' means the areas and amenities in the Centre made available from time to time by the Landlord for use in common by the tenants and occupiers of the Centre and visitors to the Centre or any of them, including the pedestrian malls, circulation areas, entrances, concourses, balconies, service courtyards, service areas, common loading areas, forecourts, access ramps or service roads, staircases, escalators, lifts, fire escapes, landscaped areas, landscaped courtyards, lavatories, store accommodation and areas designated for the keeping and collecting of refuse but not limited to them.

1.6   'The Conduits'

'The Conduits' means the pipes, sewers, drains, mains, ducts, conduits, gutters, watercourses, wires, cables, [laser optical fibres, data or impulse transmission, communication or reception systems,] channels, flues and all other conducting media — including any fixings, louvres, cowls, covers and any other ancillary apparatus — that are in, on, over or under the Premises.

[1309]

1.7   'The [Contractual] Term'[6]

'The [Contractual][7] Term' means *(insert number)* years commencing on and including *(date of commencement of term)*[8].

6   As to commencement of the term see vol 22(1) (2003 Reissue) LANDLORD AND TENANT (BUSINESS TENANCIES) Paragraph 135 [670].
        As to registration see note 1 above. Where the landlord's title is unregistered, the grantee must apply for registration within a period of two months from the date of the disposition if the lease is granted for a term of more than seven years. If no such application is made the disposition becomes void as regards any transfer, grant or creation of a legal estate: see the Land Registration Act 2002 s 6 (37 Halsbury's Statutes (4th Edn) REAL PROPERTY). Where the landlord's title is registered and the lease is for a term of more than seven years, the tenant should protect the intended lease by applying for an official search, and an application to register the lease should be made before expiry of the search, otherwise the lease will be susceptible to loss of priority: see the Land Registration Act 2002 s 27.
7   The demise in this lease is for 'the Contractual Term', which is defined as a fixed term of years. The expression 'the Term', as defined in clause 1.51 [1343] 'THE TERM', is used in covenants so that they continue to apply during any period of holding over or continuance or extension of the contractual term. Some difficulties arise if this structure is used in a draft lease where security of tenure is to be excluded under the Landlord and Tenant Act 1954 s 38A(1) as inserted by SI 2003/3096 (23 Halsbury's Statutes (4th Edn) LANDLORD AND TENANT). The demise is for the contractual term and the inclusion of the definition of 'the Term' does not prevent the lease being 'for a term of years certain'

as required by the Landlord and Tenant Act 1954 s 38A(1). However, reference to continuance of the contractual term by statute is inappropriate where the operation of the security of tenure provisions in the Landlord and Tenant Act 1954 ss 24–28 is to be excluded. If a lease is contracted out of the Landlord and Tenant Act 1954 there can be no statutory extension, and if the tenant remains in occupation at the end of the contractual term he is holding over unlawfully unless there is an express agreement to extend the contractual term operating as a surrender and re-grant so that the original lease— and the agreement under the Landlord and Tenant Act 1954 s 38A(1) — has no further effect. It is suggested that in these circumstances the drafting should be simplified to include a single term (defined simply as 'the Term') by reference to the period of the contractual term. This can be achieved by amending this clause in the manner suggested and substituting it for clause 1.50 [1343] 'THE TERM'.

8   For estate management reasons it is usually desirable to insert a quarter day here — or a rent day when rent is due on days other than quarter days — ie generally the one preceding the earlier of the date of possession and the date of execution.

[1310]

[1.8   'The Decorating Years'

'The Decorating Years' means *(specify years).*] *(omit if not required, eg if the first alternative in clause 3.4.5 [1366] DECORATION is used)*

1.9   'Development'

References to 'development' are references to development as defined by the Town and Country Planning Act 1990 Section 55.

1.10   Gender and number

Words importing one gender include all other genders; words importing the singular include the plural and vice versa[9].

9   See the Law of Property Act 1925 s 61 (37 Halsbury's Statutes (4th Edn) REAL PROPERTY).

1.11   Headings[10]

The clause, paragraph and schedule headings and the table of contents do not form part of this document and are not to be taken into account in its construction or interpretation. *(amend if marginal notes are used instead of headings)*

10   Headings and marginal notes require the draftsman to provide a word or two to describe every clause in the lease. This is not always easy and there are times when the draftsman will have to settle for something less than perfection, the only alternative being a heading or note that would be inappropriately long. It would be quite wrong for that title, which its author might admit was not totally apposite but was the best that he could do in a few words, to be used in construing the clause in question.

[1311]

[1.12   'The Initial Rent'

'The Initial Rent' means [the sum of £... a year *(or as required by the rent and review provisions to be used)*].] *(this definition is not required if the rent is not reviewable)*

1.13   'The Insurance Rent'[11]

'The Insurance Rent' means the Insurance Rent Percentage of the [gross sums including any commission *(or as required)* sums net of any commission] that the Landlord is from time to time liable to pay —

1.13.1   by way of premium for insuring the Centre, including insuring for loss of rent, in accordance with his obligations contained in this Lease[— or, where the insurance includes the Centre and other property[12], the proportion of such sums [reasonably] attributable to the Centre, such proportion to be determined from time to time by the Surveyor acting as an expert and not as an arbitrator],

1.13.2   by way of premium for insuring in such amount and on such terms as [the Landlord acting reasonably considers appropriate *(or as required)* is reasonable] against all liability of the Landlord to third parties arising out of or in connection with any matter involving or relating to the Centre, and

1.13.3   for insurance valuations,

and all of any increased premium payable by reason of any act or omission of the Tenant.

11   As to reimbursement of insurance premiums see vol 22(1) (2003 Reissue) LANDLORD AND TENANT (BUSINESS TENANCIES) Paragraph 230 [1026].
12   The centre may be insured with other property under a block policy.

1.14   'The Insurance Rent Percentage'

'The Insurance Rent Percentage' means ...%.

1.15   'The Insured Risks'

'The Insured Risks' means the risks of loss or damage by fire[, storm, tempest, earthquake, lightning, explosion, riot, civil commotion, malicious damage, [terrorism,] impact by vehicles and by aircraft and articles dropped from aircraft — other than war risks — flood damage and bursting and overflowing of water pipes and tanks,] and such other risks, whether or not in the nature of the foregoing, as the Landlord [acting reasonably] from time to time decides to insure against[13].

13   As to the risks to be insured and the tenant's concerns see vol 22(1) (2003 Reissue) LANDLORD AND TENANT (BUSINESS TENANCIES) Paragraph 235 [1033].

[1312]

1.16   'Interest'

References to 'interest' are references to interest payable during the period from the date on which the payment is due to the date of payment, both before and after any judgment, at the Interest Rate then prevailing [*(where the interest rate is defined by reference to a bank base rate)* or, should the base rate referred to in clause 1.17 'THE INTEREST RATE' cease to exist[14], at another rate of interest closely comparable with the Interest Rate [to be agreed between the parties or in default of agreement to be determined by the Accountant[15], acting as an expert and not as an arbitrator *(or as required)* determined upon by the Landlord acting reasonably]].

14   If base rates are referred to, the possibility of their ceasing to exist should be provided for. Alternatively, the Law Society interest rate may be specified.
15   Where the structure of the lease is such that an accountant is required in the operation of its terms he is a more appropriate person than the surveyor to determine this issue.

1.17   'The Interest Rate'

'The Interest Rate'[16] means the rate of ...% a year[17] above [the base lending rate of *(specify bank)* or such other bank [being a member of the British Bankers Association] as the Landlord from time to time nominates in writing[18] *(or as required)* the Law Society's interest rate[19]].

16   As to the covenant to pay interest see vol 22(1) (2003 Reissue) LANDLORD AND TENANT (BUSINESS TENANCIES) Paragraph 154 [767].
17   Words such as 'with a minimum of ...%' should not be used because, if interest rates drop during the term to such an extent that the minimum rate specified represents significantly more than a few percent over the basic borrowing rate, the provision might be void as a penalty. As to what amounts to a penalty

see *Dunlop Pneumatic Tyre Co Ltd v New Garage and Motor Co Ltd* [1915] AC 79, HL; *Cellulose Acetate Silk Co Ltd v Widnes Foundry (1925) Ltd* [1933] AC 20, HL. In view of this, landlords would be unwise to provide for more than a few percent over base rate, and even this is in fact a penalty and should be resisted by the tenant.

18   The chance to change the bank may be useful, especially on a sale of the reversion, so that the landlord can always provide for his bank for the time being to be specified. The tenant should try to limit the choice to major clearing banks.

19   The Law Society's interest rate is published weekly in the Law Society's Gazette.

[1313]–[1320]

1.18   Interpretation of 'the Centre'

The expression 'the Centre', where the context so admits, includes any other adjoining property of the Landlord constructed or adapted to form [an integral] part of the Centre[20].

20   As to problems that may arise when additional land is acquired see vol 22(1) (2003 Reissue) LANDLORD AND TENANT (BUSINESS TENANCIES) Paragraph 269.1 [1117].

1.19   Interpretation of 'consent' and 'approved'

1.19.1   *Prior written consent or approval*

References to 'consent of the Landlord' or words to similar effect are references to a prior written consent signed by or on behalf of the Landlord and references to the need for anything to be 'approved by the Landlord' or words to similar effect are references to the need for a prior written approval by or on behalf of the Landlord.

1.19.2   *Consent or approval of mortgagee or head landlord*

Any provisions in this Lease referring to the consent or approval of the Landlord are to be construed as also requiring the consent or approval of any mortgagee of the Premises and any head landlord, where that consent is required [under a mortgage or headlease in existence at the date of this document][21]. Nothing in this Lease is to be construed as imposing any obligation on a mortgagee or head landlord not to refuse any such consent or approval unreasonably.

21   The tenant should include these words so that the clause applies *only* where the consent of the mortgagee or head landlord is in fact required under the terms of an *existing* mortgage or headlease. The tenant should then request a copy of the document concerned to establish the rights of the mortgagee or head landlord in relation to any consents that he may seek. The risk to the tenant of the clause without these words is that, by subsequently creating a mortgage or headlease, the landlord could, innocently or deliberately, bring about a situation where his consent may be refused in circumstances in which it would otherwise have been unreasonable to do so. In particular, the effect on the tenant's ability to assign or sublet could be serious.

1.20   Interpretation of 'external parts'

Any part of the Premises facing onto any of the Common Parts is to be regarded as an external part of the Premises, even if that area of the Common Parts is covered in, and 'exterior', 'external' and other words to similar effect are to be construed accordingly.

[1321]

1.21   Interpretation of 'the Guarantor'[22]

The expression 'the Guarantor' includes [*(where there is a guarantor for the original tenant)* not only the person named above as the Guarantor, but also][23] any person who enters into covenants with the Landlord pursuant to clause 3.9.5.2 CONDITIONS or clause 3.23 REPLACEMENT GUARANTOR.

22   As to guarantors see vol 22(1) (2003 Reissue) LANDLORD AND TENANT (BUSINESS TENANCIES) Paragraphs 40 [201], 71 [278] et seq.
23   Where there is no guarantor for the original tenant, if it is felt undesirable to have covenants in a lease and no party, at least initially, to enter into them, the guarantor's covenants could be included in a schedule.

1.22   Interpretation of 'the Landlord'

The expression 'the Landlord' includes the person or persons from time to time entitled to possession of the Premises when this Lease comes to an end.

1.23   Interpretation of 'the last year of the Term' and 'the end of the Term'

References to 'the last year of the Term' are references to the actual last year of the Term howsoever it determines, and references to the 'end of the Term' are references to the end of the Term whensoever and howsoever it determines.

1.24   Interpretation of 'the Tenant'

'The Tenant' includes any person who is for the time being bound by the tenant covenants in this Lease except where the name of *(name of original tenant)* appears.

1.25   Interpretation of 'this Lease'

Unless expressly stated to the contrary the expression 'this Lease' includes any document supplemental to or collateral with this document or entered into in accordance with this document.

1.26   Joint and several liability

Where any party to this Lease for the time being comprises two or more persons, obligations expressed or implied to be made by or with that party are deemed to be made by or with the persons comprising that party jointly and severally.

1.27   'The Landlord's Expenses'

'The Landlord's Expenses' means the costs and expenditure — including all charges, commissions, premiums, fees and interest — paid or incurred, or deemed in accordance with the provisions of paragraph 6-2.3 DEEMED LANDLORD'S EXPENSES to be paid or incurred, by the Landlord in respect of or incidental to all or any of the Services or otherwise required to be taken into account for the purpose of calculating the Service Charge, except those recovered from any insurance policy effected by the Landlord pursuant to clause 5.2 COVENANT TO INSURE.

1.28 'The Liability Period'[24]

'The Liability Period' means —

[1.28.1   in the case of *(name of guarantor for the original tenant)*, the period during which *(name of original tenant)* is bound by the tenant covenants of this Lease together with any additional period during which *(name of original tenant)* is liable under an authorised guarantee agreement,] *(omit if there is no guarantor for the original tenant)*

1.28.2   in the case of any guarantor required pursuant to clause 3.9.5.2 of CONDITIONS, the period during which the relevant assignee is bound by the tenant covenants of this Lease together with any additional period during which that assignee is liable under an authorised guarantee agreement,

1.28.3   in the case of any guarantor under an authorised guarantee agreement, the period during which the relevant assignee is bound by the tenant covenants of this Lease, and

1.28.4   in the case of any guarantor required pursuant to clause 3.9.8.7 TERMS OF A PERMITTED SUBLEASE, the period during which the relevant assignee of the sublease is bound by the tenant covenants of that sublease.

24   The liability of the guarantor should be expressed to last while the original tenant, or as the case may be the assignee, is bound by the tenant covenants in the lease — or in the case of clause 1.28.4 the sublease — rather than while the lease is vested in that person, to take account of the possibility of an excluded assignment being made and the tenant — or subtenant — remaining liable. An excluded assignment means that the tenant — or subtenant — is precluded from tenant release under the Landlord and Tenant (Covenants) Act 1995 (23 Halsbury's Statutes (4th Edn) LANDLORD AND TENANT).
        The Landlord and Tenant (Covenants) Act 1995 does not clearly indicate whether the liability of a contractual guarantor can be expressed to extend to any period during which the tenant is bound by an authorised guarantee agreement, but the better view is that it is possible. The policy of the Act certainly suggests that this should be the case.

[1323]

1.29 'Losses'

References to 'losses' are references to liabilities, damages or losses, awards of damages or compensation, penalties, costs, disbursements or expenses arising from any claim, demand, action or proceedings.

1.30 'The 1954 Act'

'The 1954 Act' means the Landlord and Tenant Act 1954 [and all statutes, regulations and orders included by virtue of clause 1.40 REFERENCES TO STATUTES][25].

25   The words in square brackets are strictly speaking not required because they merely state what would be the case anyway by virtue of clause 1.40 [1327] REFERENCES TO STATUTES. Nevertheless, as much could turn on the point (see *Brett v Brett Essex Golf Club Ltd* (1986) 52 P & CR 330, [1986] 1 EGLR 154, CA), the parties may prefer to deal expressly with the point.

1.31 'The 1995 Act'

'The 1995 Act' means the Landlord and Tenant (Covenants) Act 1995 [and all statutes, regulations and orders included by virtue of clause 1.40 REFERENCES TO STATUTES][26].

26   See note 25 to clause 1.30 [1324] 'THE 1954 ACT'.

1.32   Obligation not to permit or suffer

Any covenant by the Tenant not to do an act or thing includes an obligation [to use reasonable endeavours] not to permit or suffer[27] that act or thing to be done by another person [where the Tenant is aware that the act or thing is being done].

27   'Permit' may have a different meaning from 'suffer': see *Barton v Reed* [1932] 1 Ch 362 at 375 per Luxmore J. A covenant not to 'permit' activity is broken if the covenantor himself carries it on: see *Oceanic Village Ltd v United Attractions Ltd* [2000] Ch 234, [2000] 1 All ER 975.

[1324]

1.33   'Other buildings'

References to 'other buildings' are references to all the buildings other than the Centre now or at any time during the Term erected on any adjoining property of the Landlord.

1.34   'The Permitted Use'[28]

'The Permitted Use' means [use [for the sale of *(specify goods)*][29] or any other use, not being one of the Prohibited Uses, falling within Class *(specify class, eg A1)* of the Schedule to the Town and Country Planning (Use Classes) Order 1987, notwithstanding any amendment or revocation of that Order[30], as the Landlord from time to time approves[, such approval not to be unreasonably withheld [or delayed]] *(or where the landlord does not require control over the specific trade)* any use, not being one of the Prohibited Uses, that falls within Class *(specify class, eg A1)* of the Schedule to the Town and Country Planning (Use Classes) Order 1987, notwithstanding any amendment or revocation of that Order].

28   As to use see vol 22(1) (2003 Reissue) LANDLORD AND TENANT (BUSINESS TENANCIES) Paragraph 170 [861] et seq.
29   Where the landlord requires control over the specific trade to be carried on — as is likely in the case of a shop in a shopping centre — that trade should be specified here.
30   As use classes orders change frequently, it is important to make clear which class is intended to apply, the class in existence at the date of the lease or the class as amended during the term of the lease.

1.35   'The Plan'[31]

'The Plan' means the plan annexed to this Lease.

31   As to the use and role of plans see vol 22(1) (2003 Reissue) LANDLORD AND TENANT (BUSINESS TENANCIES) Paragraphs 117 [636], 118 [638]. Although a plan is necessary in the circumstances assumed by this lease, a plan may not always be required, eg in a case where there is a demise of all the land within a registered title. If the lease is registrable, a plan 'for identification purposes only' or where there is some other disclaimer as to the extent to which it can be relied on for conveyancing purposes is not sufficient if part of the land in a registered title is being dealt with.

1.36   'The Planning Acts'

'The Planning Acts' means the Town and Country Planning Act 1990, the Planning (Listed Buildings and Conservation Areas) Act 1990, the Planning (Consequential Provisions) Act 1990, the Planning (Hazardous Substances) Act 1990, the Planning and Compensation Act 1991, the Planning and Compulsory Purchase Act 2004 [and all statutes, regulations and orders included by virtue of clause 1.42 REFERENCE TO STATUTES][32].

32   See note 25 to clause 1.30 [1324] 'THE 1954 ACT'.

[1325]

1.37 'The Premises'[33]

1.37.1 *Definition of 'the Premises'*

'The Premises' means Unit *(number of unit)* of the Building shown [for the purpose of identification only] edged *(state colour, eg red)* on the Plan.

33   As to parcels generally see vol 22(1) (2003 Reissue) LANDLORD AND TENANT (BUSINESS TENANCIES) Paragraph 116 [634]. As to the property definition in leases of part of a building see vol 22(1) (2003 Reissue) LANDLORD AND TENANT (BUSINESS TENANCIES) Paragraph 120 [642].

1.37.2 Interpretation of 'the Premises'[34]

The expression 'the Premises' includes —

[1.37.2.1   the floor and ceiling finishes, but not any other part of the floor slabs and ceiling slabs that bound the Premises,

1.37.2.2   the inner half severed medially of the internal non-loadbearing walls that divide the Premises from any other premises,

1.37.2.3   the interior plaster and decorative finishes of all walls bounding the Premises,

1.37.2.4   the whole of the shop front,

1.37.2.5   the doors and windows and door and window frames at the Premises,

1.37.2.6   all additions and improvements to the Premises,

1.37.2.7   all the landlord's fixtures and fittings and fixtures of every kind that are from time to time in or on the Premises, whether originally fixed or fastened to or on the Premises or otherwise, except any fixtures installed by the Tenant [or any predecessors in title] that can be removed from the Premises without defacing them[35], and

1.37.2.8   the Conduits exclusively serving the Premises,

but excludes the air space above the Premises, the foundations, all external or structural or loadbearing walls, columns, beams and supports, and any of the Conduits that do not exclusively serve the Premises *(or as required in the circumstances according to the construction methods used)*][36]. Unless the contrary is expressly stated 'the Premises' includes any part or parts of the Premises.

34   As to implied grants and reservations see vol 22(1) (2003 Reissue) LANDLORD AND TENANT (BUSINESS TENANCIES) Paragraph 125 [650].

35   As to fixtures see vol 22(1) (2003 Reissue) LANDLORD AND TENANT (BUSINESS TENANCIES) Paragraph 121 [644].

36   It is very dangerous for the draftsman to rely on one set of general words that he hopes will apply to the division of all buildings. These 'standard words' may prove totally unsuitable for a particular building having regard to its nature, configuration and the methods of construction used and also having regard to the nature and extent of any surrounding land included within the demise. Surveyors and engineers must be involved and each building must be looked at individually. There can be no uniform answer as to who should repair which parts of the premises. This clause may need amendment according to the view taken. As to the allocation of legal and financial responsibility for repairs see vol 22(1) (2003 Reissue) LANDLORD AND TENANT (BUSINESS TENANCIES) Paragraph 199 [936].

1.38   'The Prohibited Uses'

'The Prohibited Uses' means *(specify prohibited uses)*.

1.39   References to clauses and schedules

Any reference in this document to a clause, paragraph or schedule without further designation is to be construed as a reference to the clause, paragraph or schedule of this document so numbered.

1.40   References to rights of access

References to any right of the Landlord to have access to the Premises are to be construed as extending to any head landlord and any mortgagee of the Premises [—where the headlease or mortgage grants such rights of access to the head landlord or mortgagee —] and to all persons authorised in writing by the Landlord and any head landlord or mortgagee, including agents, professional advisers, contractors, workmen and others.

1.41   References to statutes

Unless expressly stated to the contrary any references to a specific statute include any statutory extension or modification, amendment or re-enactment of that statute and any regulations or orders made under that statute, and any general reference to a statute includes any regulations or orders made under that statute[37].

37   Unfortunately the Interpretation Act 1978 ss 17, 23(3) (41 Halsbury's Statutes (4th Edn) STATUTES) does not quite go far enough to enable this clause to be dispensed with altogether, particularly where a statute is modified.

[1327]–[1340]

1.42   'The Rent'[38]

[Until the First Review Date 'the Rent' means the Initial Rent. Thereafter 'the Rent' means the sum ascertained in accordance with schedule 3 THE RENT AND RENT REVIEW. 'The Rent' does not include the Insurance Rent and the Service Charge[39], but the term 'the Lease Rents' means both the Rent and the Insurance Rent and the Service Charge. *(or as required by the rent and review provisions used)*]

38   This clause assumes that the rent is reviewable. If the rent is not reviewable clause 1.12 [1312] 'THE INITIAL RENT' should be omitted and this clause amended as appropriate.

39   Because of this exclusion the insurance rent and service charge are not suspended under clause 5.5 [1425] SUSPENSION OF THE RENT.

1.43   'The Rent Commencement Date'

'The Rent Commencement Date' means *(insert date on which payment of the rent is to start)*[40].

40   This provision may be used to provide for a rent-free period, or for the situation where the tenant has had possession before the execution of the lease on the basis that rent should be paid from the date of possession. If either the date of execution of the lease, or the date of commencement of the term, is to be the date of commencement of rent, that date should be inserted here.

[1.44 'The Review Dates'[41]

'The First Review Date' means *(date)*. 'The Review Dates' means the First Review Date and every *(insert ordinal, eg 3rd)* anniversary of that date during the [Contractual] Term [*(if appropriate for the review provisions used)* — and any other date from time to time specified under *(insert the relevant provision: see eg vol 22(3) (1997 Reissue)* LANDLORD AND TENANT *(BUSINESS TENANCIES)* Form 180 paragraph {2}-4 [6728] *EFFECT OF COUNTER-INFLATION PROVISIONS)*]. References to 'a review date' are references to any one of the Review Dates.] *(omit if not required by the review provisions to be used, or if the rent is not reviewable)*

41   As to rent review dates and intervals see vol 22(1) (2003 Reissue) LANDLORD AND TENANT (BUSINESS TENANCIES) Paragraph 302 [1333] et seq. Where there might be a statutory continuation of the lease the landlord may wish to ensure that there is a review date shortly before the end of the contractual term to obviate the need to apply for an interim rent. The tenant may wish to insist on the word 'contractual' remaining so that the rent review provisions do not apply during any period of lawful holding over or extension or continuance of the contractual term.

[1341]

1.45   'The Service Charge'

'The Service Charge' means the Service Charge Percentage of the Landlord's Expenses.

1.46   'The Service Charge Percentage'

'The Service Charge Percentage' means ...% subject to the provisions for variation contained in paragraph 6-2.6 VARIATION OF THE SERVICE CHARGE PERCENTAGE. *(this definition may not be required if, eg, the tenant's proportion is determined by reference to net internal areas: see, eg, vol 22(3) (1997 Reissue)* LANDLORD AND TENANT (BUSINESS TENANCIES) *Form 150 [6626])*

1.47   'The Services'

'The Services' means the services, facilities and amenities specified in paragraph 6-3 THE SERVICES.

1.48   'The Shop Covenants'

'The Shop Covenants' means the covenants set out in schedule 4 THE SHOP COVENANTS.

1.49   'The Shop Opening Hours'

'The Shop Opening Hours'[42] means *(specify hours)* on Mondays to Saturdays (inclusive) [and *(specify hours)* on Sundays] other than Christmas Day, Good Friday and any other statutory bank, public, or local, holiday.

42   As to normal trading hours see vol 22(1) (2003 Reissue) LANDLORD AND TENANT (BUSINESS TENANCIES) Paragraph 174 [870].

1.50   'The Surveyor'[43]

'The Surveyor' means *(name)* or any person or firm appointed by the Landlord in his place. The Surveyor may be an employee of the landlord or a company that is a member of the same group as the Landlord within the meaning of the 1954 Act Section 42. The expression 'the Surveyor' includes the person or firm appointed by the Landlord to collect the Lease Rents.

43   For a provision that the landlord's surveyor must be a member of a relevant professional body see vol 22(3) (1997 Reissue) LANDLORD AND TENANT (BUSINESS TENANCIES) Form 152 [6648].

[1342]

[1.51 'The Term'

'The Term' means the Contractual Term and any period of holding-over or extension or continuance of the Contractual Term by statute or common law[44].] *(omit if the lease is to be contracted out of the Landlord and Tenant Act 1954)*[45]

44   The demise in this lease is for 'the Contractual Term', which is defined as a fixed term of years. The expression 'the Term' is used in covenants so that they continue to apply during any period of holding over or continuance or extension of the contractual term. As to the liability of a guarantor during a period of statutory continuation see vol 22(1) (2003 Reissue) LANDLORD AND TENANT (BUSINESS TENANCIES) Paragraph 73 [282].

45   Some difficulties arise if the structure referred to in note 44 above is used in a draft lease where security of tenure is to be excluded under the Landlord and Tenant Act 1954 s 38A(1) as inserted by SI 2003/3096. The demise is for the contractual term and the inclusion of the definition of 'the Term' does not prevent the lease being 'for a term of years certain' as required by the Landlord and Tenant Act 1954 s 38A(1). However, reference to continuance of the contractual term by statute is inappropriate where the operation of the security of tenure provisions in the Landlord and Tenant Act 1954 ss 24–28 is to be excluded. If a lease is contracted out of the Landlord and Tenant Act 1954 there can be no statutory extension, and if the tenant remains in occupation at the end of the contractual term he is holding over unlawfully unless there is an express agreement to extend the contractual term operating as a surrender and re-grant so that the original lease — and the agreement under the Landlord and Tenant Act 1954 s 38A(1) — has no further effect. It is suggested that in these circumstances the drafting should be simplified to include a single term (defined simply as 'the Term') by reference to the period of the contractual term. This can be achieved by amending clause 1.7 [1310] 'THE [CONTRACTUAL] TERM' as suggested and substituting it for this clause.

1.52   Terms from the 1995 Act

Where the expressions 'landlord covenants', 'tenant covenants', or 'authorised guarantee agreement' are used in this Lease they are to have the same meaning as is given by the 1995 Act Section 28(1).

1.53   'VAT'[46]

'VAT' means value added tax or any other tax of a similar nature and unless otherwise expressly stated all references to rents or other sums payable by the Tenant are exclusive of VAT.

46   As to VAT generally see the Information Binder: Property [1]: VAT and Property.

[1343]–[1360]

2   DEMISE

The Landlord lets[47] the Premises to the Tenant [with [full *(or)* limited] title guarantee], together with the rights specified in schedule 1 THE RIGHTS GRANTED but excepting and reserving to the Landlord the rights specified in schedule 2 THE RIGHTS RESERVED, to hold the Premises to the Tenant for the [Contractual][48] Term, subject to [all rights, easements, privileges, restrictions, covenants and stipulations of whatever nature affecting the Premises including any matters contained or referred to in schedule 5 THE SUBJECTIONS *(or as required)* the rights, easements, privileges, restrictions, covenants and stipulations affecting the Premises contained or referred to in schedule 5 THE SUBJECTIONS][49] yielding and paying[50] to the Landlord —

2.1   the Rent, without any deduction or set off[51], by equal quarterly payments in advance[52] on the usual quarter days[53] in every year and proportionately for any period of less than a year, the first such payment, being a proportionate sum in respect of the period from and including the Rent Commencement Date to and including the day before the quarter day next after the Rent Commencement Date, to be paid on the date of this document[54], and

2.2   by way of further rent the Insurance Rent[55] payable on demand in accordance with clause 5.4 PAYMENT OF THE INSURANCE RENT, and

2.3   by way of further rent the Service Charge[56] payable in accordance with schedule 6 THE SERVICE CHARGE.

47   Traditionally, the operative word in a lease executed as a deed was 'demises' but any words sufficient to show the parties' intention may be used.

48   See note 45 to clause 1.51 [1343] 'THE TERM'.

49   The tenant should argue for the second version, making the schedule comprehensive rather than illustrative.

50   The words 'yielding and paying' imply a covenant to pay rent: see *Vyvyan v Arthur* (1823) 1 B & C 410. An express covenant is now invariably included because further procedural matters are contained in it.

51   As to deductions and set off see vol 22(1) (2003 Reissue) LANDLORD AND TENANT (BUSINESS TENANCIES) Paragraph 147 [753].

52   In the absence of an express provision, rent is payable in arrears.

53   The usual quarter days are 25 March, 24 June, 29 September and 25 December. A reference to 'the usual quarter days' is all that is necessary when rent is to be paid on these days.

54   If the first payment is not a complete instalment, the lease must provide for the date on which it is to be paid, the amount, and the period it is to cover.

55   As to the advantages of reserving the insurance rent as rent see vol 22(1) (2003 Reissue) LANDLORD AND TENANT (BUSINESS TENANCIES) Paragraph 151 [761].

56   As to the advantages of reserving the service charge as rent see vol 22(1) (2003 Reissue) LANDLORD AND TENANT (BUSINESS TENANCIES) Paragraph 151 [761].

[1361]

3   THE TENANT'S COVENANTS

The Tenant covenants with the Landlord to observe and perform the requirements of this clause 3.

3.1   Rent

3.1.1   *Payment of the Lease Rents*

The Tenant must pay the Lease Rents[57] on the days and in the manner set out in this Lease, and must not exercise or seek to exercise any right or claim to withhold rent, or any right or claim to legal or equitable set-off[58] [except that referred to in *(give details of any provisions granting an express right of set-off)*][59].

57   As to the definition of 'the Lease Rents' see clause 1.42 [1341] 'THE RENT'.

58   See eg *British Anzani (Felixstowe) Ltd v International Marine Management (UK) Ltd* [1980] QB 137, [1979] 2 All ER 1063; *Lee-Parker v Izzet* [1971] 3 All ER 1099, [1971] 1 WLR 1688. As to deductions and set-off see vol 22(1) (2003 Reissue) LANDLORD AND TENANT (BUSINESS TENANCIES) Paragraphs 147 [753], 148 [755].

59   If any express right of set-off is granted to the tenant, reference to the provision concerned should be included here to avoid inconsistency.

3.1.2   *Payment by banker's order*[60]

If so required in writing by the Landlord, the Tenant must pay the Lease Rents[61] by banker's order or credit transfer to any bank and account [in the United Kingdom] that the Landlord nominates from time to time.

60   This is a clause with dangers for both parties. If the existence of a breach of covenant is known to the landlord he must instruct his bank to refuse to accept the rent, otherwise his right of forfeiture is lost. As to implied waiver of the right of forfeiture see vol 22(1) (2003 Reissue) LANDLORD AND TENANT (BUSINESS TENANCIES) Paragraph 284 [1173]. The tenant may feel that he requires more control over the payment of rent. In any event, the financial systems operated by many companies prevent payments being made in this way.

61   As to the definition of 'the Lease Rents' see clause 1.42 [1341] 'THE RENT'.

[1362]

3.2   Outgoings and VAT

3.2.1   *Outgoings exclusive to the Premises*

The Tenant must pay, and must indemnify the Landlord against —

3.2.1.1   all rates, taxes[62], assessments, duties, charges, impositions and outgoings that are now or may at any time during the Term be charged, assessed or imposed upon the Premises or on the owner or occupier of them[, excluding any payable by the Landlord occasioned by receipt of the Lease Rents[63] or by any disposition of or dealing with this Lease or ownership of any interest reversionary to the interest created by it][64] [— provided that if the Landlord suffers any loss of rating relief that may be applicable to empty premises after the end of the Term because the relief has been allowed to the Tenant in respect of any period before the end of the Term then the Tenant must make good such loss to the Landlord],

3.2.1.2   all VAT that may from time to time be charged on the Lease Rents or other sums payable by the Tenant under this Lease[65], and

3.2.1.3   all VAT incurred in relation to any costs that the Tenant is obliged to pay or in respect of which he is required to indemnify the Landlord under the terms of this Lease, save where such VAT is recoverable or available for set-off by the Landlord as input tax[66].

62   As to covenants to pay rates and taxes see vol 22(1) (2003 Reissue) LANDLORD AND TENANT (BUSINESS TENANCIES) Paragraph 153 [765].
63   As to the definition of 'the Lease Rents' see clause 1.42 [1341] 'THE RENT'.
64   The tenant should add the words in square brackets to make it clear that he is not paying the landlord's taxes.
65   As to VAT on rent, service charges and insurance premiums see the Information Binder: Property [1]: VAT and Property.
66   As to payment of VAT on legal costs paid by a person other than the solicitor's own client see the Information Binder: Property [1]: VAT and Property.

[1363]

3.2.2   *Outgoings assessed on the Premises and other property*

The Tenant must pay, and must indemnify the Landlord against, the proportion reasonably attributable to the Premises — to be determined from time to time by the Surveyor, acting as an expert and not as an arbitrator[67] — of all rates, taxes, assessments, duties, charges, impositions and outgoings that are now or at any time during the Term may be charged, assessed or imposed on the Premises and any other property, including any adjoining property of the Landlord, or on their owners or occupiers.

67   As to the distinction between an expert and an arbitrator see vol 22(1) (2003 Reissue) LANDLORD AND TENANT (BUSINESS TENANCIES) Paragraph 364 [1523].

[3.3   Cost of services consumed[68]

The Tenant must pay to the suppliers, and indemnify the Landlord against, all charges for electricity, water, gas, telecommunications and other services consumed or used at or in relation to the Premises, including meter rents and standing charges, and must comply with the lawful requirements and regulations of their respective suppliers.] *(omit if the premises have independent supplies of all services)*

68   Premises comprising only part of a building may not have separate supplies of all services and, in these circumstances, this clause should be included.

[1364]

3.4   Repair, cleaning and decoration

3.4.1   *Repair of the Premises*[69]

The Tenant must repair the Premises and keep them in good condition and repair, except for damage caused by one or more of the Insured Risks save to the extent that the insurance money is irrecoverable due to any act or default of the Tenant or anyone at the Premises expressly or by implication[70] with his authority [and under his control][71].

69   As to repair see vol 22(1) (2003 Reissue) LANDLORD AND TENANT (BUSINESS TENANCIES) Paragraph 196 [931] et seq. For a covenant to repair, rebuild and renew see vol 22(3) (1997 Reissue) LANDLORD AND TENANT (BUSINESS TENANCIES) Form 85 [6460]. For provisos excluding, eg, work that is prevented etc see vol 22(3) (1997 Reissue) LANDLORD AND TENANT (BUSINESS TENANCIES) Forms 87 [6462], 88 [6463].
         If a landlord is unable to obtain full insurance cover without excess, it should be made clear whether the tenant is to be liable to pay the excess where damage is caused by an insured risk. For a covenant limiting the tenant's repairing obligations by reference to uninsurable as well as insured risks see vol 22(3) (1997 Reissue) LANDLORD AND TENANT (BUSINESS TENANCIES) Form 90 [6465]. It should be noted that it is now recommended 'best practice' that if the premises are so damaged by an uninsured risk as to prevent occupation, the tenant should be allowed to terminate the lease unless the landlord agrees to reinstate at his own cost: see vol 22(1) (2003 Reissue) LANDLORD AND TENANT (BUSINESS TENANCIES) Paragraph 85 [402]. If adopted, this recommendation involves damage preventing occupation caused by uninsured or uninsurable risks being excluded from the ambit of the tenant's repairing covenant.
70   The expression 'by implication' is intended to include a caller on the premises, such as a tradesman, where there has been no express invitation but the person cannot be classed as a trespasser.
71   The tenant should add the words in square brackets.

3.4.2   *Replacement of landlord's fixtures*

The Tenant must replace from time to time any landlord's fixtures and fittings in the Premises that may be or become beyond repair at any time during or at the end of the Term.

[1365]

3.4.3   *Cleaning and tidying*

The Tenant must keep the Premises clean and tidy and clear of all rubbish.

(if any land that is not built on is included in the premises eg parking bays, appropriate obligations should be included: see, eg, Form 12 clause 3.4.4 [1847])

3.4.4   *Care of abutting land*

The Tenant must not cause any land, roads or pavements abutting the Premises to be untidy or dirty and in particular, but without prejudice to the generality of the foregoing, must not deposit refuse or other materials on them.

3.4.5   *Decoration*

[As often as may in the [reasonable] opinion of the Surveyor be necessary in order to maintain a high standard of decorative finish and attractiveness and to preserve the Premises *(or as required)* In each of the Decorating Years][72] and in the last year of the Term the Tenant must redecorate the Premises[73] in a good and workmanlike manner, with appropriate materials of good quality[, to the [reasonable] satisfaction of the Surveyor], any change in the tints, colours and patterns of the decoration to be approved by the Landlord [, whose approval may not be unreasonably withheld [or delayed]][74] [, provided that the covenants relating to the last year of the Term are not to apply where the Tenant has redecorated the Premises less than *(state period, eg 18 months)* before the end of the Term].

72   The draftsman should discuss with the landlord and his property advisers whether he wishes to have the flexibility of the first option or the certainty of the second.

73   The restricted nature of the demise should be borne in mind when considering the scope of this covenant: see clause 1.37 [1326] 'THE PREMISES'.

74   The tenant may amend to provide for the landlord's approval to tints etc to apply only in the last year of the term.

[1366]

3.5   Waste and alterations

3.5.1   *Waste, additions and alterations*[75]

The Tenant must not commit any waste, make any addition to the Premises, unite the Premises with any adjoining premises, or make any alteration to the Premises except as permitted by the provisions of this clause 3.5.

75   As to control of alterations see vol 22(1) (2003 Reissue) LANDLORD AND TENANT (BUSINESS TENANCIES) Paragraph 186 [911] et seq.

3.5.2   *Preconditions for alterations*

The Tenant must not make any [internal non-structural] alterations to the Premises unless he first —

3.5.2.1   obtains and complies with the necessary consents of the competent authorities and pays their charges for them,

3.5.2.2   makes an application to the Landlord for consent, supported by drawings and where appropriate a specification in duplicate [prepared by an architect[, or a member of some other appropriate profession,] who must supervise the work throughout to completion],

3.5.2.3   pays the fees of the Landlord, any head landlord, any mortgagee and their respective professional advisers,

3.5.2.4   enters into any covenants the Landlord requires as to the execution and reinstatement of the alterations, and

3.5.2.5   obtains the consent of the Landlord, whose consent may not be unreasonably withheld [or delayed].

[In the case of any works of a substantial nature, the Landlord may require the Tenant to provide, before starting the works, adequate security in the form of a deposit of money or the provision of a bond, as assurance to the Landlord that any works he permits from time to time will be fully completed.]

[1367]

3.5.3   *Removal of alterations*[76]

At the end of the Term, if so requested by the Landlord, the Tenant must remove any additional buildings, additions, alterations or improvements made to the Premises, and must make good any part of the Premises damaged by their removal.

76   This clause has probably come to be inserted because landlords hope that it will defeat the effect of the compensation provisions of the Landlord and Tenant Act 1927 Pt I (ss 1–17) (23 Halsbury's Statutes (4th Edn) LANDLORD AND TENANT) — as to which see vol 22(1) (2003 Reissue) LANDLORD AND TENANT (BUSINESS TENANCIES) Paragraph 192 [923] et seq — ie because, if the improvement has been removed, it will not be an improvement to the holding at the time of quitting the premises. In fact, the clause might not achieve this effect, because the Landlord and Tenant Act 1927 s 9 as amended by the Landlord and Tenant Act 1954 s 49 prohibits contracting out. Also, the clause may be void under the Landlord and Tenant Act 1927 s 19(2), so far as it applies to improvements, on the grounds that it purports to fetter the court in deciding what is reasonable. The tenant should not, however, rely on the application of these statutory provisions and should seek to strike out the clause.

3.5.4   *Connection to the Conduits*

The Tenant must not make any connection with the Conduits except in accordance with plans and specifications approved by the Landlord[, whose approval may not be unreasonably withheld [or delayed]], and subject to consent to make the connection having previously been obtained from the competent authority, undertaker or supplier.

3.6   Aerials, signs and advertisements

3.6.1   *Masts and wires*

The Tenant must not [erect any pole or mast or] install any cable or wire on the Premises, whether in connection with telecommunications or otherwise.

3.6.2   *Advertisements*[77]

The Tenant must not, without the consent of the Landlord, fix to or exhibit on the outside of the Premises, or fix to or exhibit through any window of the Premises, or display anywhere on the Premises, any placard, sign, notice, fascia board or advertisement.

77   See the Town and Country Planning (Control of Advertisements) Regulations 1992, SI 1992/666 as amended. In the absence of a covenant such as this and subject to those Regulations, the tenant is entitled to exhibit advertisements etc on the premises, whether or not they are connected with his business: see *Clapman v Edwards* [1938] 2 All ER 507.

[1368]

3.7   Statutory obligations

3.7.1   *General provision*[78]

The Tenant must comply in all respects with the requirements of any statutes, and any other obligations imposed by law or by any byelaws, applicable to the Premises or the trade or business for the time being carried on there.

78   As to the covenant to comply with statutes see vol 22(1) (2003 Reissue) LANDLORD AND TENANT (BUSINESS TENANCIES) Paragraph 182 [905]. For a provision requiring the landlord to pay compensation for works above a certain value see vol 22(3) (1997 Reissue) LANDLORD AND TENANT (BUSINESS TENANCIES) Form 169 [6693].

3.7.2   *Particular obligations*

3.7.2.1   **Works required by statute, department or authority**

Without prejudice to the generality of clause 3.7.1, the Tenant must execute all works and provide and maintain all arrangements upon or in respect of the Premises or the use to which the Premises are being put that are required in order to comply with the requirements of any statute already or in the future to be passed, or the requirements of any government department, local authority or other public or competent authority or court of competent jurisdiction, regardless of whether such requirements are imposed on the owner, the occupier, or any other person.

3.7.2.2   **Acts causing losses**

Without prejudice to the generality of clause 3.7.1, the Tenant must not do in or near the Premises anything by reason of which the Landlord may incur any losses under any statute.

3.7.2.3   Construction (Design and Management) Regulations

Without prejudice to the generality of clause 3.7.1, the Tenant must comply with the provisions of the Construction (Design and Management) Regulations 1994 ('the CDM Regulations'), be the only client as defined in the provisions of the CDM Regulations, fulfil, in relation to all and any works, all the obligations of the client as set out in or reasonably to be inferred from the CDM Regulations, and make a declaration to that effect[79] to the Health and Safety Executive in accordance with the Approved Code of Practice published from time to time by the Health and Safety Executive in relation to the CDM Regulations. The provisions of clause 5.7.3 FIRE-FIGHTING EQUIPMENT are to have effect in any circumstances to which these obligations apply.

3.7.2.4   Delivery of health and safety files

At the end of the Term, the Tenant must forthwith deliver to the Landlord any and all health and safety files relating to the premises in accordance with the CDM Regulations.

79   If works are being carried out for the tenant, the landlord will not want to accept the liabilities that are placed on a client under the Construction (Design and Management) Regulations 1994, SI 1994/3140 and the Health and Safety Executive Approved Code of Practice. The landlord will need to ensure that the tenant actually makes the declaration required, and that he obtains the notification served on the tenant by the Health and Safety Executive.

[1369]

3.8   Entry to inspect and notice to repair

3.8.1   *Entry and notice*

The Tenant must permit the Landlord[80] [on reasonable notice during normal business hours except in emergency][81] —

3.8.1.1   to enter the Premises to ascertain whether or not the covenants and conditions of this Lease have been observed and performed,

3.8.1.2   to view the state of repair and condition of the Premises, and to open up floors and other parts of the Premises where that is necessary in order to do so, and

3.8.1.3   to give to the Tenant, or notwithstanding clause 8.7 NOTICES leave on the Premises, a notice ('a notice to repair') specifying the works required to remedy any breach of the Tenant's obligations as to the repair and condition of the Premises in this Lease,

provided that any opening-up must be made good by and at the cost of the Landlord if it reveals no breach of the terms of this Lease.

80   The provisions of clause 1.40 [1327] REFERENCES TO RIGHTS OF ACCESS should be noted.
81   The tenant should add the words in square brackets.

3.8.2   *Works to be carried out*

The Tenant must carry out the works specified in a notice to repair immediately, including making good any opening up that revealed a breach of the terms of this Lease.

[3.8.3   *Landlord's power in default*[82]

If within *(state period, eg 1 month)* of the service of a notice to repair the Tenant has not started to execute the work referred to in that notice or is not proceeding diligently with it, or if the Tenant fails to finish the work within *(state period, eg 2 months)*[83][, or if in the [Landlord's *(or as required)* Surveyor's] [reasonable] opinion the Tenant is unlikely to have finished the work within that period], the Tenant must permit the Landlord to enter the Premises to execute the outstanding work, and must within *(state period, eg 14 days)* of a written demand pay to the Landlord the cost of so doing and all expenses incurred by the Landlord, including legal costs and surveyor's fees.]

82   The advantages of this clause for the landlord must be weighed against the potential liability that it creates under the Defective Premises Act 1972 s 4(4) (31 Halsbury's Statutes (4th Edn) NEGLIGENCE): see *McAuley v Bristol City Council* [1992] QB 134, [1992] 1 All ER 749, CA.
      It has been held that a claim by the landlord for recovery of costs under such a clause is a claim for recovery of a debt, and therefore can be enforced without requiring leave of the court under the Leasehold Property (Repairs) Act 1938: see *Jervis v Harris* [1996] Ch 195, [1996] 1 All ER 303, CA.
      However, even where a landlord has been granted a right of this nature the court does not compel the tenant to allow the landlord the right to enter and carry out repairs where these would be of no benefit and where no loss is being caused to the landlord: see *Hammersmith London Borough Council v Creska (No 2)* [2000] L & TR 288.
83   The tenant would prefer to be given 'a reasonable period' to do the work required to remedy the breaches because it may take longer than the specified number of months.

[1370]–[1380]

3.9   Alienation[84]

3.9.1   *Alienation prohibited*

The Tenant must not hold the Premises on trust for another. The Tenant must not part with possession of the Premises or any part of the Premises or permit another to occupy them or any part of them except pursuant to a transaction permitted by and effected in accordance with the provisions of this Lease.

84   As to alienation see vol 22(1) (2003 Reissue) LANDLORD AND TENANT (BUSINESS TENANCIES) Paragraph 156 [801] et seq. Where the lease is registrable, this prohibition or restriction on dealings will be reflected in an entry on the register excepting from the effects of registration all estates, rights, interests, powers and remedies arising on or by reason of any dealing made in breach of the prohibition or restriction: see the Land Registration Rules 2003, SI 2003/1417 r 6(2).

3.9.2   *Assignment, subletting and charging of part*[85]

(version 1)

[The Tenant must not assign, sublet or charge part only of the Premises.] *(where assignment, subletting or charging of the whole is allowed)*

(version 2)

[The Tenant must not assign or charge part only of the Premises and must not sublet the whole or any part of the Premises.] *(where assignment or charging of the whole is permitted, but subletting is not allowed at all)*

85   Whether subletting should be permitted is a commercial matter. Some landlords consider that the fact that they cannot unreasonably refuse consent to an assignment gives the tenant all the protection he requires and are not prepared to permit subletting. An advantage to the tenant of the ability to sublet is that he has an element of control over a subtenant but not over an assignee, for whom he may retain liability under an authorised guarantee agreement. Further, with stringent assignment tests or in a bad market, subletting may be the only option open to the tenant.

[1381]

3.9.3   *Assignment of the whole*

Subject to clauses 3.9.4 CIRCUMSTANCES and 3.9.5 CONDITIONS, the Tenant must not assign the whole of the Premises without the consent of the Landlord, whose consent may not be unreasonably withheld [or delayed][86].

86   This residual discretion is the old test of reasonableness under the Landlord and Tenant Act 1927 s 19(1). Thus the tenant and the proposed assignee may satisfy the circumstances and conditions specified for the purposes of the Landlord and Tenant Act 1927 s 19(1A) as inserted by the Landlord and Tenant (Covenants) Act 1995 s 22 (as to which see clause 3.9.4 [1382] CIRCUMSTANCES and clause 3.9.5 [1384] CONDITIONS), but the landlord may still refuse consent on reasonable grounds: see vol 22(1) (2003 Reissue) LANDLORD AND TENANT (BUSINESS TENANCIES) Paragraph 159 [812] et seq.

3.9.4   *Circumstances*

If any of the following circumstances[87] — which are specified for the purposes of the Landlord and Tenant Act 1927 Section 19(1A)[88] — applies either at the date when application for consent to assign is made to the Landlord, or after that date but before the Landlord's consent is given, the Landlord may withhold his consent and if, after the Landlord's consent has been given but before the assignment has taken place, any such circumstances apply, the Landlord may revoke his consent[89], whether his consent is expressly subject to a condition as referred to in clause 3.9.5.4 CONDITIONS or not. The circumstances are —

3.9.4.1   that any sum due from the Tenant under this Lease remains unpaid[90],

3.9.4.2   that in the Landlord's reasonable[91] opinion the assignee is not a person who is likely to be able to comply with the tenant covenants of this Lease and to continue to be able to comply with them following the assignment,

[3.9.4.3   that without prejudice to clause 3.9.4.2, in the case of an assignment to a company in the same group as the Tenant[92] within the meaning of the 1954 Act Section 42, in the Landlord's reasonable opinion the assignee is a person who is, or may become, less likely to be able to comply with the tenant covenants of this Lease than the Tenant requesting consent to assign, which likelihood is adjudged by reference in particular to the financial strength of that Tenant aggregated with that of any guarantor of the obligations of that Tenant and the value of any other security for the performance of the tenant covenants of this Lease when assessed at the date of grant or — where that Tenant is not *(name of original tenant)* — the date of the assignment of this Lease to that Tenant[93],] or

3.9.4.4   that the assignee or any guarantor for the assignee, other than any guarantor under an authorised guarantee agreement, is a corporation registered — or otherwise resident — in a jurisdiction in which the order of a court obtained in England and Wales will not necessarily be enforced against the assignee or guarantor without any consideration of the merits of the case.

(for examples of circumstances for use in unusual case, see vol 22(3) (1997 Reissue) LANDLORD AND TENANT (BUSINESS TENANCIES) Form 117 [6501])

[1382]

87   The Landlord and Tenant Act 1927 s 19(1A) as inserted by the Landlord and Tenant (Covenants) Act 1995 s 22 enables the landlord and tenant to a post-1995 lease to agree in advance the terms upon which an assignment may be permitted. It distinguishes between on the one hand circumstances, the existence of which entitles the landlord to refuse consent to assignment, and on the other hand conditions that may be imposed on his consent. This clause and clause 3.9.5 [1384] CONDITIONS are drafted on the assumption that this is a valid approach and seek to draw a clear distinction between circumstances and conditions.

It should be noted that provisions that are overly restrictive may have an adverse impact at any rent review. It should also be noted that it is recommended 'best practice' that unless the particular circumstances of the letting justify greater control, the only restriction on assignment of the whole should be obtaining the landlord's consent, which is not to be unreasonably withheld: see vol 22(1) (2003 Reissue) LANDLORD AND TENANT (BUSINESS TENANCIES) Paragraph 85 [401] and 'A code of practice for commercial leases in England and Wales (2nd edition)' which can be found in vol 22(1) (2003 Reissue) LANDLORD AND TENANT (BUSINESS TENANCIES) as Form 1 [4501].

Each letting must be looked at in the light of its own particular facts and circumstances but it is considered that the provisions of this clause do, in the ordinary course, strike a reasonable balance between the landlord's desire for control and the tenant's ability to dispose of his interest without undue restriction. For a less restrictive approach see vol 22(1) (2003 Reissue) LANDLORD AND TENANT (BUSINESS TENANCIES) Form 7 clause 5.2 [5538].

88   The Landlord and Tenant Act 1927 s 19(1A) as inserted by the Landlord and Tenant (Covenants) Act 1995 s 22 seems to require the alienation clause to state that the circumstances it mentions are specified for the purposes of that subsection.

89   The landlord may require that certain circumstances are absent not only before consent has been given to the assignment, but also up to the date on which the assignment takes place — when the die is cast and the lease covenants bind the assignee. For example, the landlord may require the rent to be paid up to date not only before the application for consent is made, but also at the date when consent is given and the possibly later date when the lease is actually assigned.

90   The tenant may want to limit this to the rent, as it may be thought that a dispute is more likely to arise over the insurance rent or other payments. If the tenant has retained any right of set-off, it should also be referred to here.

91   Circumstances and conditions must be either factual or, if they contain an element of discretion, that discretion must have to be exercised reasonably (see the Landlord and Tenant Act 1927 s 19(1C)(a) as inserted by the Landlord and Tenant (Covenants) Act 1995 s 22) or the Tenant must have a right of appeal to an expert (see the Landlord and Tenant Act 1927 s 19(1C)(b) as inserted by the Landlord and Tenant (Covenants) Act 1995 s 22). If the discretion is to be exercised reasonably, as suggested by this provision, the Tenant can take any dispute about its exercise to the court. The court will consider whether *this* Landlord has acted within the range of reasonable decisions, not whether a reasonable landlord would have reached the same decision nor whether the test is itself reasonable. For a clause where an expert is used see vol 22(3) (1997 Reissue) LANDLORD AND TENANT (BUSINESS TENANCIES) Form 117 [6501].

92   There have been suggestions that intra-group assignments should be banned completely. However, this is considered to be too draconian and would prevent legitimate corporate restructuring needed for reasons other than avoidance of liability under the Landlord and Tenant (Covenants) Act 1995. The landlord's concern is that a strong tenant may assign to a weak group company; the assignment is acceptable because the assignor gives an authorised guarantee agreement for the assignee. The second group company may then itself assign outside the group; the landlord will lose the authorised guarantee agreement of the strong first group company and have only the possibly worthless authorised guarantee agreement of the second group company. The possibilities for exploitation of this scenario are obvious and it is therefore felt that this is the one situation in which measuring the financial strength of the assignee in relation to that of the assignor is justified. Equivalence tests are not generally thought to be appropriate, because a strong first covenant may make the lease almost unassignable, adversely affecting the rent at review.

93   Consider whether the time at which the tenant's financial status is measured should be when he acquired the lease, when his status was acceptable to the landlord, or at the date of the application for consent to assign, when it may have deteriorated sharply. On the other hand, the outgoing tenant may be a better covenant now than when he acquired the lease: the wily landlord may wish to leave himself free to pick whichever of the two dates gives the better picture.

[1383]

3.9.5   *Conditions*

The Landlord may impose any or all of the following conditions[94] — which are specified for the purposes of the Landlord and Tenant Act 1927 Section 19(1A)[95] — on giving any consent for an assignment by the Tenant, and any such consent is to be treated as being subject to each of the following conditions —

3.9.5.1   a condition that on or before any assignment and before giving occupation to the assignee, the Tenant requesting consent to assign, together with any former tenant who by virtue of the 1995 Act Section 11 was not released on an earlier assignment of this Lease[96], must enter into an authorised guarantee agreement[97] in favour of the Landlord in the terms set out in schedule 7 THE AUTHORISED GUARANTEE AGREEMENT,

3.9.5.2   a condition that if reasonably so required by the Landlord on an assignment to a limited company, the assignee must ensure that at least *(state number, eg 2)* directors of the company, or some other guarantor or guarantors [reasonably] acceptable to the Landlord, enter into direct covenants with the Landlord in the form of the guarantor's covenants contained in clause 6 GUARANTEE PROVISIONS with 'the Assignee' substituted for 'the Tenant',

3.9.5.3   a condition that on or before any assignment, the Tenant making the request for consent to assign must give to the Landlord a copy of the health and safety file required to be maintained under the Construction (Design and Management) Regulations 1994 containing full details of all works undertaken to the Premises by that Tenant, and

3.9.5.4   a condition that if, at any time before the assignment, the circumstances specified in clause 3.9.4, or any of them, apply, the Landlord may revoke the consent by written notice to the Tenant.

[1384]

94   The Landlord and Tenant Act 1927 s 19(1A) as inserted by the Landlord and Tenant (Covenants) Act 1995 s 22 enables the landlord and tenant to a post-1995 lease to agree in advance the terms upon which an assignment may be permitted. It distinguishes between on the one hand circumstances, the existence of which entitles the landlord to refuse consent to assignment, and on the other hand conditions that may be imposed on his consent. This clause and clause 3.9.4 [1382] CIRCUMSTANCES are drafted on the assumption that this a valid approach and seek to draw a clear distinction between circumstances and conditions.

It should be noted that provisions that are overly restrictive may have an adverse impact at any rent review. It should also be noted that it is recommended 'best practice' that unless the particular circumstances of the letting justify greater control, the only restriction on assignment of the whole should be obtaining the landlord's consent, which is not to be unreasonably withheld: see vol 22(1) (2003 Reissue) LANDLORD AND TENANT (BUSINESS TENANCIES) Paragraph 85 [401] and 'A code of practice for commercial leases in England and Wales (2nd edition)' which can be found in vol 22(1) (2003 Reissue) LANDLORD AND TENANT (BUSINESS TENANCIES) as Form 1 [4501].

Each letting must be looked at in the light of its own particular facts and circumstances but it is considered that the provisions of this clause do, in the ordinary course, strike a reasonable balance between the landlord's desire for control and the tenant's ability to dispose of his interest without undue restriction.

95   The Landlord and Tenant Act 1927 s 19(1A) as inserted by the Landlord and Tenant (Covenants) Act 1995 s 22 seems to require the alienation clause to state that the conditions it mentions are specified for the purposes of that subsection.

96   See the Landlord and Tenant (Covenants) Act 1995 ss 11(2), 16(6).

97   As to authorised guarantee agreements see vol 22(1) (2003 Reissue) LANDLORD AND TENANT (BUSINESS TENANCIES) Paragraph 54 [247]. It should be noted that 'A code of practice for commercial leases in England and Wales (2nd edition)' urges landlords to consider requiring authorised guarantee agreements only where the assignee is of lower financial standing than the assignor at the date of the assignment.

[1385]

3.9.6   *Charging of the whole*

The Tenant must not charge the whole of the Premises without the consent of the Landlord, whose consent may not be unreasonably withheld [or delayed][98].

98   As to unreasonable withholding of consent under the Landlord and Tenant Act 1927 see vol 22(1) (2003 Reissue) LANDLORD AND TENANT (BUSINESS TENANCIES) Paragraph 158.2 [806] and as to unreasonable delay under the Landlord and Tenant Act 1988 (23 Halsbury's Statutes (4th Edn) LANDLORD AND TENANT) see vol 22(1) (2003 Reissue) LANDLORD AND TENANT (BUSINESS TENANCIES) Paragraph 158.3 [808].

[3.9.7   *Subletting*

The Tenant must not sublet[99] the whole of the Premises without the consent of the Landlord, whose consent may not be unreasonably withheld [or delayed]][100]. *(omit if subletting is prohibited)*

99   See note 85 to clause 3.9.2 [1381] ASSIGNMENT, SUBLETTING AND CHARGING OF PART.
100   As to unreasonable witholding of consent under the Landlord and Tenant Act 1927 see vol 22(1) (2003 Reissue) LANDLORD AND TENANT (BUSINESS TENANCIES) Paragraph 158.2 [806] and as to unreasonable delay under the Landlord and Tenant Act 1988 see vol 22(1) (2003 Reissue) LANDLORD AND TENANT (BUSINESS TENANCIES) Paragraph 158.3 [808].

[1386]

[3.9.8   *Terms of a permitted sublease*[101]

Every permitted sublease must be granted, without a fine or premium, at a rent not less than whichever is the greater of the then open market rent payable in respect of the Premises [— to be approved by the Landlord prior to the sublease is granted [and to be determined by the Surveyor, acting as an expert and not as an arbitrator]—]and the Rent[102], to be payable in advance on the days on which the Rent is payable under this Lease. Every permitted sublease must contain provisions approved by the Landlord —

3.9.8.1   for the upwards only review of the rent reserved by it, on the basis set out in schedule 3 THE RENT AND RENT REVIEW and on the Review Dates[103],

3.9.8.2   prohibiting the subtenant from doing or allowing anything in relation to the Premises inconsistent with or in breach of the provisions of this Lease,

3.9.8.3   for re-entry by the sublandlord on breach of any covenant by the subtenant,

3.9.8.4   imposing an absolute prohibition against all dealings with the Premises other than an assignment[, subletting] [or charging] of the whole,

3.9.8.5   prohibiting assignment[, subletting][104] [or charging] of the whole of the Premises without the consent of the Landlord under this Lease,

3.9.8.6   requiring the assignee on any assignment of the sublease to enter into direct covenants with the Landlord to the same effect as those contained in clause 3.9.9 SUBTENANT'S DIRECT COVENANTS,

3.9.8.7   requiring on each assignment of the sublease that the assignor enters into an authorised guarantee agreement[105] in favour of the Landlord in the terms set out in schedule 7 THE AUTHORISED GUARANTEE AGREEMENT but adapted to suit the circumstances in which the guarantee is given,

3.9.8.8   prohibiting the subtenant from holding on trust for another or permitting another to share or occupy the whole or any part of the Premises,

3.9.8.9   imposing in relation to any permitted assignment[, subletting] [or charge] the same obligations for registration with the Landlord as are contained in this Lease in relation to dispositions by the Tenant,

[3.9.8.10   imposing in relation to any permitted subletting the same obligations as are contained in this clause 3.9.8 and in clause 3.9.9 SUBTENANT'S DIRECT COVENANTS[, clause 3.9.11 ENFORCEMENT OF THE SUBLEASE and clause 3.9.12 SUBLEASE RENT REVIEW],] and

3.9.8.11   excluding the provisions of Sections 24–28 of the 1954 Act from the letting created by the sublease.] *(omit if subletting is prohibited)*

[1387]

101   As to the validity of provisions of this nature see vol 22(1) (2003 Reissue) LANDLORD AND TENANT
         (BUSINESS TENANCIES) Paragraph 161 [817].
102   It will not be in the landlord's interest for the premises to be sublet at a rent less than that payable under
         the headlease. This could allow into the premises a subtenant of doubtful financial status, with whom
         the landlord may in the future have to deal direct, eg on the grant of a new lease under the Landlord
         and Tenant Act 1954 Pt II (ss 23–46). Also a low rent could be used as a 'comparable' in arriving at the
         open market rent on rent reviews or lease renewals. On the other hand following the decision in *Allied
         Dunbar Assurance plc v Homebase Ltd* [2002] EWCA Civ 666, [2003] 1 P & CR 75, [2002] 2 EGLR 23
         a provision of this kind may effectively render the lease inalienable and being a potentially onerous
         restriction on disposition (as to which see vol 22(1) (2003 Reissue) LANDLORD AND TENANT
         (BUSINESS TENANCIES) Paragraph 348.2 [1440]) have an adverse impact at rent review from a
         landlord's perspective.
103   Alternatively the landlord might prefer the sublease rents to be reviewed just before the review dates
         in the headlease. As to recommended 'best practice' in relation to the basis of rent review in leases of
         business premises see vol 22(1) (2003 Reissue) LANDLORD AND TENANT (BUSINESS TENANCIES)
         Paragraph 85 [401] and 'A code of practice for commercial leases in England and Wales (2nd edition)'
         which can be found in vol 22(1) (2003 Reissue) LANDLORD AND TENANT (BUSINESS TENANCIES)
         as Form 1 [4501].
104   The landlord may well wish to prohibit any further subletting by requiring an absolute covenant against
         subletting to be inserted in any sublease.
105   By virtue of the Landlord and Tenant (Covenants) Act 1995 s 16(3)(a), where a head landlord's consent
         is needed to the assignment of a sublease, the head landlord can require the assignor of the sublease to
         enter into an authorised guarantee agreement. It should be noted that 'A code of practice for
         commercial leases in England and Wales (2nd edition)' urges landlords to consider requiring authorised
         guarantee agreements only where the assignee is of lower financial standing than the assignor at the date
         of the assignment.

[1388]

[3.9.9   *Subtenant's direct covenants*[106]

Before any permitted subletting, the Tenant must ensure that the subtenant enters into
a direct covenant with the Landlord that while he is bound by the tenant covenants of
the sublease[107] and while the subtenant is bound by an authorised guarantee agreement,
the subtenant will observe and perform the tenant covenants contained in this Lease —
except the covenant to pay the rent reserved by this Lease — and in that sublease.] *(omit
if subletting is prohibited)*

106   See note 101 to clause 3.9.8 [1388] TERMS OF A PERMITTED SUBLEASE.
107   The liability of the subtenant should be expressed to last while he is bound by the tenant covenants of
         the sublease, rather than while the sublease is vested in him, to take account of the possibility of an
         excluded assignment being made and the subtenant remaining liable. An excluded assignment means that
         the subtenant is precluded from tenant release under the Landlord and Tenant (Covenants) Act 1995.

[3.9.10   *Requirement for 1954 Act exclusion*[108]

The Tenant must not grant a sublease or permit a subtenant to occupy the Premises unless
an effective agreement has been made to exclude the operation of Sections 24 to 28 of
the 1954 Act pursuant to Section 38A of the 1954 Act.] *(omit if subletting is prohibited)*

108   As to contracting out of the security of tenure provisions of the Landlord and Tenant Act 1954 see vol
         22(1) (2003 Reissue) LANDLORD AND TENANT (BUSINESS TENANCIES) Paragraph 431 [2035].

[3.9.11   *Enforcement of the sublease*

In relation to any permitted sublease, the Tenant must enforce the performance and
observance by every subtenant of the provisions of the sublease, and must not at any time
either expressly or by implication waive any breach of the covenants or conditions on
the part of any subtenant or assignee of any sublease, or — without the consent of the
Landlord, whose consent may not be unreasonably withheld or delayed — vary the terms
or accept a surrender of any permitted sublease.] *(omit if subletting is prohibited)*

[1389]

[3.9.12   *Sublease rent review*

In relation to any permitted sublease —

3.9.12.1   the Tenant must ensure that the rent is reviewed in accordance with the terms of the sublease,

3.9.12.2   the Tenant must not agree the reviewed rent with the subtenant without the approval of the Landlord,

3.9.12.3   where the sublease provides such an option, the Tenant must not, without the approval of the Landlord, agree whether the third party determining the revised rent in default of agreement should act as an arbitrator or as an expert,

3.9.12.4   the Tenant must not, without the approval of the Landlord, agree any appointment of a person to act as the third party determining the revised rent,

3.9.12.5   the Tenant must incorporate as part of his representations to that third party representations [reasonably] required[109] by the Landlord, and

3.9.12.6   the Tenant must give notice to the Landlord of the details of the determination of every rent review within *(state period, eg 28 days)*,

provided that the Landlord's approvals specified above may not be unreasonably withheld [or delayed].] *(omit if subletting is prohibited)*

109   This seems preferable to providing, as is sometimes done, that the head landlord's representations have to be brought to the attention of the expert or arbitrator because it would appear that he can refuse to have regard to them, the head landlord not being a party to the lease with which he is concerned.

3.9.13   *Registration of permitted dealings*

Within *(state period, eg 28 days)* of any assignment, charge, [sublease, or subunderlease,] or any transmission or other devolution relating to the Premises, the Tenant must produce a certified copy[110] of any relevant document for registration with the Landlord's solicitor, and must pay the Landlord's solicitor's [reasonable] charges for registration of at least £...

110   There seems to be no reason why the tenant should part with the original. However, under the Land Registration Rules 2003, SI 2003/1417 r 203, it is open to the applicant for registration to ask for the transfer, charge, sublease or subunderlease giving effect to the disposition to be returned for retention by the applicant, provided a certified copy of the instrument is lodged with the application. Accordingly, in such cases, applicants should use this facility if they wish to be able to lodge the lease with the landlord after its return by the registrar. If there is a time limit specified in the lease, then the registrar should be told about this, so that he is aware of the need to return the instrument within the required period.

[1390]

[3.9.14   *Sharing with a group company*

Notwithstanding clause 3.9.1 ALIENATION PROHIBITED, the Tenant may share the occupation of the whole or any part of the Premises with a company that is a member of the same group as the Tenant within the meaning of the 1954 Act Section 42, for so long as both companies remain members of that group and otherwise than in a manner that transfers or creates a legal estate.] *(omit if sharing with a group company is not to be permitted)*

3.10   Nuisance and residential restrictions

3.10.1   *Nuisance*[111]

The Tenant must not do anything on the Premises, or allow anything to remain on them that may be or become a nuisance, or cause annoyance, disturbance, inconvenience, injury or damage to the Landlord or his tenants or the owners or occupiers of any adjoining property of the Landlord or any other adjacent or neighbouring premises.

111   'Nuisance' is a term to be construed according to 'plain and sober and simple notions among the English people': *Walter v Selfe* (1851) 4 De G & Sm 315 at 322 per Knight-Bruce V-C. 'I have no doubt that what is a nuisance or annoyance will continue to be determined by the courts according to robust and commonsense standards': *Hampstead and Suburban Properties Ltd v Diomedous* [1969] 1 Ch 248 at 258, [1968] 3 All ER 545 at 550 per Megarry J. But a tenant can only be said to have permitted a nuisance if the landlord can show that the tenant has failed to take reasonable steps to prevent the nuisance: see *Commercial General Administration Ltd v Thomsett* [1979] 1 EGLR 62, CA.

3.10.2   *Auctions, trades and immoral purposes*

The Tenant must not use the Premises for any auction sale, any dangerous, noxious, noisy or offensive[112] trade, business, manufacture or occupation, or any illegal or immoral act or purpose.

112   As to the meaning of 'offensive' see *Re Koumoudouros and Marathon Realty Co Ltd* (1978) 89 DLR (3d) 551 where it was held that the word 'offensive' did not have a definite legal meaning and that it should be read in the context of the lease. Surrounding circumstances can affect whether a particular trade is offensive: see *Nussey v Provincial Bill Posting Co and Eddison* [1909] 1 Ch 734, CA; *Dunraven Securities Ltd v Holloway* [1982] 2 EGLR 47, CA.

[1391]

3.10.3   *Residential use, sleeping and animals*

The Tenant must not use the Premises as sleeping accommodation or for residential purposes, or keep any animal, bird or reptile on them.

3.11   Costs of applications, notices and recovery of arrears[113]

The Tenant must pay to the Landlord on an indemnity basis all costs, fees, charges, disbursements and expenses — including, without prejudice to the generality of the above, those payable to counsel, solicitors, surveyors and bailiffs — [properly and reasonably] incurred by the Landlord in relation to or incidental to —

3.11.1   every application made by the Tenant for a consent or licence required by the provisions of this Lease, whether it is granted, refused or offered subject to any [lawful] qualification or condition or the application is withdrawn[unless the refusal, qualification or condition is unlawful, whether because it is unreasonable or otherwise],

3.11.2   the contemplation, preparation and service of a notice under the Law of Property Act 1925 Section 146 or by reason or the contemplation of proceedings under Sections 146 or 147 of that Act, even if forfeiture is avoided otherwise than by relief granted by the court[114],

3.11.3   the recovery or attempted recovery of arrears of rent or other sums due under this Lease, and

3.11.4   any steps taken in [contemplation of or in] [direct] connection with the preparation and service of a schedule of dilapidations during or after the end of the Term[115].

113   As to payment of VAT on legal costs by a person other than the solicitor's own client see the Information Binder: Property [1]: VAT and Property.

114   As to forfeiture see vol 22(1) (2003 Reissue) LANDLORD AND TENANT (BUSINESS TENANCIES) Paragraph 283 [1171] et seq.

115   The landlord should not be tempted to extend this provision to costs etc incurred by him in consequence of serving a notice under the Landlord and Tenant Act 1954 s 25 because that is void: see *Stevenson and Rush (Holdings) Ltd v Langdon* (1978) 38 P & CR 208, CA.

[1392]–[1400]

3.12   Planning and development

3.12.1   *Compliance with the Planning Acts*

The Tenant must observe and comply with the provisions and requirements of the Planning Acts affecting the Premises and their use, and must indemnify the Landlord, and keep him indemnified, both during and following the end of the Term, against all losses in respect of any contravention of those Acts.

3.12.2   *Consent for applications*

The Tenant must not make any application for planning permission without the consent of the Landlord[, whose consent may not be unreasonably withheld [or delayed] [in any case where application for and implementation of the planning permission will not create or give rise to any tax liability for the Landlord or where the Tenant indemnifies the Landlord against such liability][116]].

116   The words in square brackets were devised when development land tax — abolished by the Finance Act 1985 s 93 — applied. The provision may, however, still be relevant should similar taxation be introduced in the future.

3.12.3   *Permissions and notices*

The Tenant must at his expense obtain any planning permissions and serve any notices that may be required for the carrying out of any development on or at the Premises.

3.12.4   *Charges and levies*

Subject only to any statutory direction to the contrary, the Tenant must pay and satisfy any charge or levy that may subsequently be imposed under the Planning Acts in respect of the carrying out or maintenance of any development on or at the Premises.

[1401]

3.12.5   *Pre-conditions for development*

Notwithstanding any consent that may be granted by the Landlord under this Lease, the Tenant must not carry out any development on or at the Premises until all necessary notices under the Planning Acts have been served and copies produced to the Landlord, all necessary permissions under the Planning Acts have been obtained and produced to the Landlord, and the Landlord has acknowledged that every necessary planning permission is acceptable to him[, such acknowledgement not to be unreasonably withheld]. The Landlord may refuse to acknowledge his acceptance of a planning permission on the grounds that any condition contained in it or anything omitted from it or the period referred to in it would[, in the [reasonable] opinion of the Surveyor,] be, or be likely to be, prejudicial to the Landlord or to his reversionary interest in the Premises, the Centre or any other of his adjoining property whether during the Term or following the end of it.

3.12.6   *Completion of development*

Where a condition of any planning permission granted for development begun before the end of the Term[117] requires works to be carried out to the Premises by a date after the end of the Term, the Tenant must, unless the Landlord directs otherwise, finish those works before the end of the Term.

117   The provisions of clause 1.23 [1322] INTERPRETATION OF 'THE LAST YEAR OF THE TERM' AND 'THE END OF THE TERM' should be noted.

3.12.7   *Security for compliance with conditions*

In any case where a planning permission is granted subject to conditions, and if the Landlord [reasonably] so requires, the Tenant must provide sufficient security for his compliance with the conditions and must not implement the planning permission until the security has been provided.

[3.12.8   *Appeal against refusal or conditions*[118]

If [reasonably] required by the Landlord to do so, but[, where reasonable,] at his own cost, the Tenant must appeal against any refusal of planning permission or the imposition of any conditions on a planning permission relating to the Premises following an application for planning permission by the Tenant.]

118   The tenant should not accept this clause because it could impose on him the cost of a planning appeal. He should strike it out, leaving planning appeals to be a matter for discussion as and when the situation arises during the term, or at least insist that he should bear the cost only where reasonable.

[1402]

3.13   Plans, documents and information

3.13.1   *Evidence of compliance with this Lease*

If so requested, the Tenant must produce to the Landlord or the Surveyor any plans, documents and other evidence the Landlord [reasonably] requires to satisfy himself that the provisions of this Lease have been complied with.

3.13.2   *Information for renewal or rent review*

If so requested, the Tenant must produce to the Landlord, the Surveyor or any person acting as the third party determining the Rent in default of agreement between the Landlord and the Tenant under any provisions for rent review contained in this Lease, any information [reasonably] requested in writing in relation to any pending or intended step under the 1954 Act or the implementation of any provisions for rent review.

3.14   Indemnities[119]

The Tenant must keep the Landlord fully indemnified against all losses arising directly or indirectly out of any act, omission or negligence of the Tenant, or any persons at the Centre expressly or impliedly[120] with his authority [and under his control][121], or any breach or non-observance by the Tenant of the covenants, conditions or other provisions of this Lease or any of the matters to which this demise is subject.

119   The tenant should seek to delete all *general* indemnity provisions on the basis that his remedies for breach of covenant and in tort adequately protect the landlord. The tenant should argue that an indemnity unreasonably extends his liability. If this clause is omitted, however, it should be replaced by a covenant to observe and perform the restrictions etc to which the demise is subject, possibly coupled with a *specific* indemnity in respect of any breach.
120   The expression 'impliedly' is intended to include a caller, such as a tradesman, where there has been no express invitation but the person cannot be classed as a trespasser.
121   The tenant should add the words in square brackets.

[1403]

3.15 Reletting boards and viewing

[Unless [a valid court application under the 1954 Act Section 24 has been made or][122] the Tenant is [otherwise] entitled to remain in occupation or to a new tenancy of the Premises, at any time during *(or as required)* At any time during] the *(state period, eg last 6 months)* of the [Contractual][123] Term and at any time thereafter, [and whenever the Lease Rents or any part of them are in arrear and unpaid for longer than *(state period, eg 14 days)*,] the Tenant must permit the Landlord to enter the Premises and fix and retain anywhere on them a board advertising them for reletting. While any such board is on the Premises the Tenant must permit viewing of the Premises at reasonable times of the day.

122   This phrase and the word 'otherwise' should be omitted if the operation of the security of tenure provisions in the Landlord and Tenant Act 1954 ss 24–28 is to be excluded in relation to the lease.
123   This defined term will require amendment where the operation of the security of tenure provisions in the Landlord and Tenant Act 1954 ss 24–28 is to be excluded in relation to the lease: see note 7 to clause 1.7 [1310] 'THE [CONTRACTUAL] TERM'.

3.16 Obstruction and encroachment

3.16.1 *Obstruction of windows*

The Tenant must not stop up, darken or obstruct any window or light belonging to the Premises.

3.16.2 *Encroachments*

The Tenant must take all [reasonable] steps to prevent the construction of any new window, light, opening, doorway, path, passage, pipe or the making of any encroachment or the acquisition of any easement in relation to the Premises and must notify the Landlord immediately if any such thing is constructed, encroachment is made or easement acquired, or if any attempt is made to construct such a thing, to encroach or acquire an easement. At the request of the Landlord the Tenant must adopt such means as are [reasonably] required to prevent the construction of such a thing, the making of any encroachment or the acquisition of any easement[124].

124   For a shorter clause see vol 22(3) (1997 Reissue) LANDLORD AND TENANT (BUSINESS TENANCIES) Form 172 [6696].

[1404]

3.17 Yielding up

At the end of the Term[125] the Tenant must yield up the Premises with vacant possession, decorated and repaired in accordance with and in the condition required by the provisions of this Lease, give up all keys of the Premises to the Landlord, remove tenant's fixtures and fittings [if requested to do so by the Landlord], and remove all signs erected by the Tenant or any of his predecessors in title in, on or near the Premises, immediately making good any damage caused by their removal.

125   The provisions of clause 1.23 [1322] INTERPRETATION OF 'THE LAST YEAR OF THE TERM' AND 'THE END OF THE TERM' should be noted.

3.18   Interest on arrears[126]

The Tenant must pay interest on any of the Lease Rents[127] or other sums due under this Lease that are not paid [within *(state period, eg 14 days)* of the date due], whether formally demanded or not, [the interest to be recoverable as rent][128]. Nothing in this clause is to entitle the Tenant to withhold or delay any payment of the Rent or any other sum due under this Lease or affect the rights of the Landlord in relation to any non-payment.

126   As to the covenant to pay interest see vol 22(1) (2003 Reissue) LANDLORD AND TENANT (BUSINESS TENANCIES) Paragraph 154 [767].

127   As to the definition of 'the Lease Rents' see clause 1.42 [1341] 'THE RENT'.

128   These words seek to attach to any interest the rights associated with rent. As to the reasons for this see vol 22(1) (2003 Reissue) LANDLORD AND TENANT (BUSINESS TENANCIES) Paragraph 151 [761]. However, this clause applies to interest on arrears both of rents and other sums payable under the lease that are not rent, and it might be felt inappropriate for interest to be deemed to be rent where the payment on which the interest is due is not itself rent.

3.19   Statutory notices

The Tenant must give full particulars to the Landlord of any notice, direction, order or proposal relating to the Premises made, given or issued to the Tenant by any government department or local, public, regulatory or other authority or court within *(state period, eg 7 days)* of receipt, and if so requested by the Landlord must produce it to the Landlord. The Tenant must without delay take all necessary steps to comply with the notice, direction or order. At the request of the Landlord, but at the cost of the Tenant, the Tenant must make or join with the Landlord in making any objection or representation the Landlord deems expedient against or in respect of any notice, direction, order or proposal.

[1405]

3.20   Keyholders

The Tenant must ensure that at all times [the Landlord has *(or as required)* the Landlord and the local police force have] written notice of the name, home address and home telephone number of at least *(state number, eg 2)* keyholders of the Premises.

3.21   Viewing on sale of reversion

The Tenant must[, on reasonable notice,] at any time during the Term, permit prospective purchasers of the Landlord's reversion or any other interest superior to the Term, or agents instructed in connection with the sale of the reversion or such an interest, to view the Premises without interruption, provided they have the prior written authority of the Landlord or his agents.

3.22   Defective premises

The Tenant must give notice to the Landlord of any defect in the Premises that might give rise to an obligation on the Landlord to do or refrain from doing anything in order to comply with the provisions of this Lease or the duty of care imposed on the Landlord, whether pursuant to the Defective Premises Act 1972 or otherwise, and must at all times display and maintain any notices the Landlord from time to time [reasonably] requires him to display at the Premises.

3.23   Replacement guarantor[129]

3.23.1   *Guarantor replacement events*

In this clause 3.23 references to a 'guarantor replacement event' are references, in the case of an individual, to death, bankruptcy, having a receiving order made against him or having a receiver appointed under the Mental Health Act 1983 or entering into a voluntary arrangement, and, in the case of a company, to passing a resolution to wind up, entering into liquidation, a voluntary arrangement or administration or having a receiver appointed.

129   As to guarantors see vol 22(1) (2003 Reissue) LANDLORD AND TENANT (BUSINESS TENANCIES) Paragraph 71 [278] et seq. The tenant should propose that, on the execution of a guarantee by a new guarantor, the original guarantor or his estate should be released.

3.23.2   *Action on occurrence of a guarantor replacement event*

Where during the relevant Liability Period a guarantor replacement event occurs to the Guarantor or any person who has entered into an authorised guarantee agreement, the Tenant must give notice of the event to the Landlord within *(state period, eg 14 days)* of his becoming aware of it. If so required by the Landlord, the Tenant must within *(state period, eg 28 days)* obtain some other person [reasonably] acceptable to the Landlord to execute a guarantee in the form of the Guarantor's covenants in clause 6 GUARANTEE PROVISIONS or the authorised guarantee agreement in schedule 7 THE AUTHORISED GUARANTEE AGREEMENT, as the case may be, for the residue of the relevant Liability Period.

[1406]

3.24   Exercise of the Landlord's rights[130]

The Tenant must permit the Landlord to exercise any of the rights granted to him by virtue of the provisions of this Lease at all times during the Term without interruption or interference.

130   The provisions of clause 1.40 [1327] REFERENCES TO RIGHTS OF ACCESS should be noted.

3.25   The Shop Covenants

The Tenant must observe and perform the Shop Covenants.

3.26   The Services

The Tenant must observe and perform his obligations contained in schedule 6 THE SERVICE CHARGE.

3.27   Costs of grant of this Lease[131]

[The Tenant must pay the fees and disbursements of the Landlord's solicitors, agents and surveyors and all other costs and expenses incurred by the Landlord in relation to the negotiation, preparation, execution and grant of this Lease *(or as required)* On the grant of this Lease the Tenant must pay the sum of £... as a contribution to the Landlord's solicitors' charges for the negotiation, execution and completion of this Lease].

131   As to covenants to pay the landlord's legal fees see vol 22(1) (2003 Reissue) LANDLORD AND TENANT (BUSINESS TENANCIES) Paragraph 155 [769]. As to payment of VAT on legal costs by a person other than the solicitor's own client see the Information Binder: Property [1]: VAT and Property.

[1407]

3.28   Consent to the Landlord's release[132]

The Tenant must not unreasonably withhold consent to a request made by the Landlord under the 1995 Act Section 8 for a release from all or any of the landlord covenants of this Lease.

132   By virtue of the Landlord and Tenant (Covenants) Act 1995 each successive landlord remains bound by the landlord covenants of the lease unless released under the machinery provided in the Act — as to which see vol 22(1) (2003 Reissue) LANDLORD AND TENANT (BUSINESS TENANCIES) Paragraph 57 [252] et seq — or by a specific release given otherwise (see the Landlord and Tenant (Covenants) Act 1995 s 26(1)(a)). Bald statements limiting the landlord's liability, such as those in use before the commencement of the Act, will not withstand the wide anti-avoidance provisions of the Landlord and Tenant (Covenants) Act 1995 s 25, and covenants by the tenant to give consent to release are unlikely to fall within the exception of s 26. None of the ingenious schemes for limiting the landlord's liability, eg making all covenants personal, suggested in the early days of the 1995 Act has stood up to critical scrutiny, although none has yet been tested by the courts. Thus landlords look instead to the alternative of a right of redress if the tenant makes an unreasonable objection to release. This covenant is modelled on the provisions of the Landlord and Tenant Act 1988, which gives tenants a right of action for loss caused by landlords who unreasonably withhold or delay consent to assignment (see the Landlord and Tenant Act 1988 s 4). In view of the strict time limits under the Landlord and Tenant (Covenants) Act 1995 and the fact that failure to respond to the landlord's request for release is deemed to be consent, it is not thought necessary to extend this covenant to unreasonable delay in replying to such a request.

[1408]–[1420]

4   THE LANDLORD'S COVENANTS

The Landlord covenants with the Tenant to observe and perform the requirements of this clause 4.

4.1   Quiet enjoyment[133]

The Landlord must permit the Tenant peaceably and quietly to hold and enjoy the Premises without any interruption or disturbance from or by the Landlord or any person claiming under or in trust for him[134] [or by title paramount][135].

133   As to the landlord's covenant for quiet enjoyment see vol 22(1) (2003 Reissue) LANDLORD AND TENANT (BUSINESS TENANCIES) Paragraph 168 [856]. As to covenants for quiet enjoyment generally see 23 Halsbury's Laws (4th Edn Reissue) LANDLORD AND TENANT.
       The words 'the Tenant paying the rents reserved by and observing and performing the covenants on his part and the conditions contained in this lease' are frequently included in a covenant for quiet enjoyment, but they have no practical effect and do not make payment of the rent and performance of the covenants into conditions precedent to the operation of the covenant for quiet enjoyment: see *Edge v Boileau* (1885) 16 QBD 117; *Dawson v Dyer* (1833) 5 B & Ad 584; *Yorkbrook Investments Ltd v Batten* (1985) 52 P & CR 51, [1985] 2 EGLR 100, CA.
134   The covenant is frequently expressed to apply to 'lawful' interruption by persons 'rightfully' claiming under the landlord, but it seems that the addition of these words has no practical effect: see *Williams v Gabriel* [1906] 1 KB 155 at 157.
135   Without the reference to title paramount the landlord is liable only for the acts of persons so far as they are his successors in title or have authority from him to do the acts complained of: *Harrison Ainslie & Co v Muncaster* [1891] 2 QB 680, CA; *Matania v National Provincial Bank Ltd and Elevenist Syndicate Ltd* [1936] 2 All ER 633, CA; *Miller v Emcer Products Ltd* [1956] Ch 304, [1956] 1 All ER 237, CA. If a subtenant holds under a lease containing a qualified covenant on the part of his landlord — ie one where there is no reference to title paramount — and the head landlord evicts the subtenant because the head rent has not been paid, this is not a breach of the covenant for quiet enjoyment (see *Spencer v Marriott* (1823) 1 B & C 457; *Dennett v Atherton* (1872) LR 7 QB 316, Ex Ch), but it is a breach if the sublandlord submits to judgment in an action by a person with no title to sue, and the subtenant is in consequence evicted (*Cohen v Tannar* [1900] 2 QB 609, CA). Actionable interruptions under this covenant are not confined to interference with title or possession, but may extend to interference with the ordinary and lawful enjoyment of the premises: *Sanderson v Berwick-upon-Tweed Corpn* (1884) 13 QBD 547 at 551, CA. As to persons claiming 'under' the landlord see *Celsteel Ltd v Alton House Holdings Ltd (No 2)* [1987] 2 All ER 240, [1987] 1 WLR 291, CA.

[1421]

4.2   The Services[136]

4.2.1   *Provision of the Services*

If the Tenant pays the Service Charge and observes his obligations under this Lease[137], the Landlord must use his best endeavours to provide the Services.

136   As the Landlord remains liable on his covenants until he is released under the Landlord and Tenant
      (Covenants) Act 1995, given the character of the landlord's covenants contained in this lease, the
      landlord may prefer to avoid liability altogether by including a management company as a party to the
      lease. The management company then covenants to perform those obligations that would have fallen
      to the landlord.
137   As to payment as a condition precedent see vol 22(1) (2003 Reissue) LANDLORD AND TENANT
      (BUSINESS TENANCIES) Paragraph 255 [1093].

4.2.2   *Relief from liability*[138]

The Landlord is not to be liable to the Tenant for any breach of his obligations under clause 4.2.1 where the breach was caused by something beyond his control, provided he uses reasonable endeavours to remedy the breach, except to the extent that the breach —

4.2.2.1   could have been prevented, or

4.2.2.2   its consequences could have been lessened, or

4.2.2.3   the time during which its consequences were experienced could have been shortened,

by the exercise of reasonable skill by the Landlord or those undertaking the obligation on his behalf.

138   This clause is likely to be viewed as an exclusion clause if the Unfair Contract Terms Act 1977 (11
      Halsbury's Statutes (4th Edn) CONTRACT) applies to the service provisions contained in a lease: see
      vol 22(1) (2003 Reissue) LANDLORD AND TENANT (BUSINESS TENANCIES) Paragraph 254 notes 4
      and 5 [1092].

4.2.3   *Variation and withholding of the Services*

The Landlord may add to, withhold or vary the Services if[, acting reasonably,] he considers the addition, withholding or variation to be necessary or desirable [for the comfort or convenience of the tenants in the Centre] even if it increases the Landlord's Expenses [so long as the Tenant's enjoyment of the Premises is not materially impaired], or if he is required to do so by a competent authority.

4.2.4   *Special services*

Any services rendered to the Tenant by staff employed by the Landlord, other than services referred to in paragraph 6-3 THE SERVICES, are to be deemed to be special services for which, and for the consequences of which, the Tenant will be entirely responsible. The Tenant is not to be entitled to any services from such staff that may in any way whatever interfere with the performance of their duties to the Landlord.

5   INSURANCE[139]

5.1   Warranty as to convictions[140]

The Tenant warrants that before the execution of this document he has disclosed to the Landlord in writing any conviction, judgment or finding of any court or tribunal relating to the Tenant[, or any director, other officer or major shareholder of the Tenant,] of such a nature as to be likely to affect the decision of any insurer or underwriter to grant or to continue insurance of any of the Insured Risks.

139   As to insurance see vol 22(1) (2003 Reissue) LANDLORD AND TENANT (BUSINESS TENANCIES) Paragraph 227 [1021] et seq.
140   A contract of insurance is one uberrimae fidei. The insured must disclose to the insurers all material facts that are within his actual or presumed knowledge, whether there is a formal proposal form or not. A fact is material if non-disclosure of it would influence a prudent and reasonable insurer. This warranty is designed to rebut any suggestion by the landlord's insurers that the landlord had knowledge of the matters concerned. By inserting this clause in the lease, and thus specifically bringing the point to the tenant's attention, the landlord can argue that he has done all that is practical to establish the existence of any such matters. The absence of any written disclosure pursuant to this clause is strong evidence that the landlord has no actual or presumed knowledge of such matters. Further, the landlord has a right of action against the tenant for any breach of the warranty. As to non-disclosure and misrepresentation in contracts of non-marine insurance see 22 Halsbury's Laws (4th Edn Reissue) INSURANCE.

5.2   Covenant to insure

The Landlord covenants with the Tenant to insure the Centre unless the insurance is vitiated by any act of the Tenant or by anyone at the Centre expressly or by implication[141] with his authority [and under his control][142].

141   The expression 'by implication' is intended to include a caller, such as a tradesman, where there has been no express invitation but the person cannot be classed as a trespasser.
142   The tenant should add the words in square brackets.

[1423]

5.3   Details of the insurance

5.3.1   *Office, underwriters and agency*

Insurance is to be effected in such [substantial and reputable] insurance office, or with such underwriters[143], and through such agency as the Landlord from time to time decides.

143   The expression 'insurance office' would probably not include Lloyd's underwriters. The landlord's right to nominate the office and agency is absolute, with no implied restrictions: *Berrycroft Management Co Ltd v Sinclair Gardens Investments (Kensington) Ltd* (1996) 75 P & CR 210, [1997] 1 EGLR 47, CA.

5.3.2   *Insurance cover*[144]

Insurance must be effected for the following amounts —

5.3.2.1   the sum that the Landlord is from time to time advised [by the Surveyor] is the full cost of rebuilding and reinstating the Centre, including [VAT[145],] architects', surveyors', engineers', solicitors' and all other professional persons' fees, the fees payable on any applications for planning permission or other permits or consents that may be required in relation to rebuilding or reinstating the Centre, the cost of preparation of the site including shoring-up, debris removal, demolition, site clearance and any works that may be required by statute, and incidental expenses, and

5.3.2.2   loss of rental [and service charge] income from the Centre, taking account of any rent review that may be due, for *(state period, eg 3 years)* or such longer period as the Landlord from time to time [reasonably] requires for planning and carrying out the rebuilding or reinstatement.

144   As to the sum insured see vol 22(1) (2003 Reissue) LANDLORD AND TENANT (BUSINESS TENANCIES) Paragraph 231 [1028] et seq.

It should be noted that it is recommended 'best practice' that, where the landlord has arranged insurance, the terms should be made known to the tenant and any material change in the insurance should be notified to the tenant: see Recommendation 14 of 'A code of practice for commercial leases in England and Wales (2nd edition)' which can be found in vol 22(1) (2003 Reissue) LANDLORD AND TENANT (BUSINESS TENANCIES) at Form 1 [4501].

145   As to VAT and the level of insurance cover see the Information Binder: Property [1]: VAT and Property. The expense of insuring against the VAT payable on reinstatement costs is not justified where the landlord has opted to tax and is able to recover the VAT. There is a theoretical possibility that a future landlord may not opt to tax and that the sum insured may then be too low. It is also possible that a landlord may wish to preserve the 'exempt' status of a property. Normally, however, the cost of reinstatement need not expressly mention VAT, although the cashflow implications of having to pay VAT on construction works need to be remembered.

5.3.3   *Risks insured*[146]

Insurance must be effected against damage or destruction by any of the Insured Risks to the extent that such insurance may ordinarily be arranged [with a substantial and reputable insurer] for properties such as the Centre, and subject to such excesses, exclusions or limitations as the insurer requires.

146   As to risks to be insured against see vol 22(1) (2003 Reissue) LANDLORD AND TENANT (BUSINESS TENANCIES) Paragraph 235 [1033].

It should be noted that it is recommended 'best practice' that, where the landlord has arranged insurance, the terms should be made known to the tenant and any material change in the insurance should be notified to the tenant: see Recommendation 14 of 'A code of practice for commercial leases in England and Wales (2nd edition)' which can be found in vol 22(1) (2003 Reissue) LANDLORD AND TENANT (BUSINESS TENANCIES) at Form 1 [4501].

[1424]

5.4   Payment of the Insurance Rent

The Tenant covenants to pay the Insurance Rent for the period starting on the Rent Commencement Date and ending on the day before the next policy renewal date on the date of this document, and subsequently to pay the Insurance Rent on demand and, if so demanded, in advance of the policy renewal date[, but not more than *(state period, eg ... months)* in advance].

5.5   Suspension of the Rent[147]

5.5.1   *Events giving rise to suspension*

If and whenever the Centre or any part of it is damaged or destroyed by one or more of the Insured Risks[148] [—except one against which insurance may not ordinarily be arranged [with a substantial and reputable insurer] for properties such as the Centre unless the Landlord has in fact insured against that risk —] so that the Premises or any part of them are unfit for occupation or use, and payment of the insurance money is not wholly or partly refused because of any act or default of the Tenant or anyone at the Centre expressly or by implication[149] with his authority [and under his control][150], then the provisions of clause 5.5.2 SUSPENDING THE RENT are to have effect.

147   As to suspension of rent see vol 22(1) (2003 Reissue) LANDLORD AND TENANT (BUSINESS TENANCIES) Paragraph 241 [1044] et seq.

148   It should be noted that it is recommended 'best practice' that if premises are so damaged by an uninsured risk as to prevent occupation, the tenant should be allowed to terminate the lease unless the landlord agrees to reinstate at his own cost: see vol 22(1) (2003 Reissue) LANDLORD AND TENANT (BUSINESS TENANCIES) Paragraph 85 [402] and 'A code of practice for commercial leases in England and Wales (2nd edition)' which can be found in vol 22(1) (2003 Reissue) LANDLORD AND TENANT (BUSINESS TENANCIES) at Form 1 [4501]. If adopted, this recommendation involves rent suspension also becoming operative in the event of the premises becoming unusable because of uninsured risks.

149   The expression 'by implication' is intended to include a caller, such as a tradesman, where there has been no express invitation but the person cannot be classed as a trespasser.

150   The tenant should add the words in square brackets.

[1425]

5.5.2 *Suspending the Rent*

In the circumstances mentioned in clause 5.5.1 EVENTS GIVING RISE TO SUSPENSION, the Rent [and the Service Charge][151], or a fair proportion of the Rent [and the Service Charge] according to the nature and the extent of the damage sustained, [is *(or as required)* are] to cease to be payable until the Centre has been rebuilt or reinstated so as to render the Premises, or the affected part, fit for occupation and use, [or until the end of *(state period, eg 3 years)* from the destruction or damage whichever period is the shorter,][152] [the proportion of the Rent [and the Service Charge] suspended and the period of the suspension to be determined by the Surveyor acting as an expert and not as an arbitrator *(or as required)* any dispute as to the proportion of the Rent [and the Service Charge] suspended and the period of the suspension to be determined in accordance with the Arbitration Act 1996 by an arbitrator to be appointed by agreement between the Landlord and the Tenant or in default by the President or other proper officer for the time being of the Royal Institution of Chartered Surveyors upon the application of either the Landlord or the Tenant].

151   As to the nature of the payments to be covered see vol 22(1) (2003 Reissue) LANDLORD AND TENANT (BUSINESS TENANCIES) Paragraph 242 [1045].

152   As to the length of the suspension and the tenant's concerns see vol 22(1) (2003 Reissue) LANDLORD AND TENANT (BUSINESS TENANCIES) Paragraph 244 [1048]. For a provision extending suspension of the rent where reinstatement is delayed see vol 22(3) (1997 Reissue) LANDLORD AND TENANT (BUSINESS TENANCIES) Form 111 [6495].

[1426]

5.6   Reinstatement and termination[153]

5.6.1   *Obligation to obtain permissions*

If and whenever the Centre or any part of it is damaged or destroyed by one or more of the Insured Risks [— except one against which insurance may not ordinarily be arranged with [a substantial and reputable insurer] for properties such as the Centre, unless the Landlord has in fact insured against that risk —] and payment of the insurance money is not wholly or partly refused because of any act or default of the Tenant or anyone at the Centre expressly or by implication with his authority[154] [and under his control][155], then the Landlord must use his best endeavours[156] to obtain any planning permissions or other permits and consents ('permissions') that are required under the Planning Acts or otherwise to enable him to rebuild and reinstate.

153   It has been held that, in the absence of an express covenant to reinstate, where the landlord must keep the premises adequately insured against comprehensive risks and the insurance is effected at the tenant's expense, the obligation is one intended to enure for the benefit of both parties: *Mumford Hotels Ltd v Wheler* [1964] Ch 117, [1963] 3 All ER 250; see also *Mark Rowlands Ltd v Berni Inns Ltd* [1986] QB 211, [1985] 3 All ER 473, CA; *Lonsdale & Thompson Ltd v Black Arrow Group plc* [1993] Ch 361, [1993] 3 All ER 648. This is not, however, a general principle of law and the tenant should therefore always require a specific covenant to reinstate.

These provisions are restricted to circumstances where damage or destruction is caused by an insured risk. It should be noted that it is recommended 'best practice' that if premises are so damaged by an uninsured risk as to prevent occupation, the tenant should be allowed to terminate the lease unless the landlord agrees to reinstate at his own cost: see vol 22(1) (2003 Reissue) LANDLORD AND TENANT (BUSINESS TENANCIES) Paragraph 85 [401] and 'A code of practice for commercial leases in England and Wales (2nd edition)' which can be found in vol 22(1) (2003 Reissue) LANDLORD AND TENANT (BUSINESS TENANCIES) at Form 1 [4501].

As to termination where reinstatement is not possible see vol 22(1) (2003 Reissue) LANDLORD AND TENANT (BUSINESS TENANCIES) Paragraph 237 [1037]. For a provision for termination or surrender on destruction or substantial damage see vol 22(3) (1997 Reissue) LANDLORD AND TENANT (BUSINESS TENANCIES) Form 107 [6483].

154   The expression 'by implication' is intended to include a caller, such as a tradesman, where there has been no express invitation but the person cannot be classed as a trespasser.

155   The tenant should add the words in square brackets.

156   The extent of the duty to use best endeavours depends upon the facts in each case: see *Monkland v Jack Barclay Ltd* [1951] 2 KB 252, [1951] 1 All ER 714, CA; *Terrell v Mabie Todd & Co Ltd* [1952] 2 TLR 574; *NW Investments (Erdington) Ltd v Swani* (1970) 214 Estates Gazette 1115. In the light of *IBM United Kingdom Ltd v Rockware Glass Ltd* [1980] FSR 335, CA, it may be that there is little practical difference between a covenant to use best endeavours, a covenant to use reasonable endeavours and a covenant to take all reasonable steps.

[1427]

5.6.2   *Obligation to reinstate*

Subject to the provisions of clause 5.6.3 RELIEF FROM THE OBLIGATION TO REINSTATE, and, if any permissions are required, after they have been obtained, the Landlord must as soon as reasonably practicable apply all money received in respect of the insurance effected by the Landlord pursuant to this Lease, except sums in respect of loss of the Rent [and Service Charge][157], in rebuilding or reinstating the parts of the Centre destroyed or damaged [and must make up out of his own money any difference between the cost of rebuilding and reinstating and the money received][158].

157   See note 151 to clause 5.5.2 [1426] SUSPENDING THE RENT.

158   Where the landlord's covenant is 'to apply all money received in respect of the insurance in rebuilding or reinstating' rather than simply 'to reinstate', it seems that the landlord does not have to complete the work out of his own money if the insurance money is insufficient because he has complied with his covenant by laying out all the insurance money received. The situation is different if the tenant can establish that the landlord was in breach of his covenant to insure for the full cost of reinstatement and that this has caused the shortfall: see *Mumford Hotels Ltd v Wheler* [1964] Ch 117, [1963] 3 All ER 250. The tenant should, therefore, require a specific covenant from the landlord to make up any shortfall, to prevent a situation in which the landlord refuses to complete the rebuilding. This is of particular concern if the suspension of rent proviso is expressed to operate for a limited period, because on the expiry of that period the tenant becomes liable for rent unless he can satisfy the court that the lease has been frustrated.

It should be noted that it is recommended 'best practice' that if premises are so damaged by an uninsured risk as to prevent occupation, the tenant should be allowed to terminate the lease unless the landlord agrees to reinstate at his own cost: see vol 22(1) (2003 Reissue) LANDLORD AND TENANT (BUSINESS TENANCIES) Paragraph 85 [401] and 'A code of practice for commercial leases in England and Wales (2nd edition)'which can be found in vol 22(1) (2003 Reissue) LANDLORD AND TENANT (BUSINESS TENANCIES) at Form 1 [4501]. If this recommendation is adopted and the landlord merely covenants to apply insurance money received, the principle should be extended to damage or destruction resulting from insured risks in circumstances where the insurance money is insufficient to enable reinstatement to be completed.

For a proviso relieving from the obligation to reinstate in the same form see vol 22(3) (1997 Reissue) LANDLORD AND TENANT (BUSINESS TENANCIES) Form 106 [6482].

[1428]

5.6.3 *Relief from the obligation to reinstate*[159]

The Landlord need not rebuild or reinstate the Centre if and for so long as the rebuilding or reinstating is prevented because —

5.6.3.1   the Landlord, despite using his best endeavours[160], cannot obtain a necessary permission,

5.6.3.2   any permission is granted subject to a lawful condition with which [it is impossible for *(or as required)* in all the circumstances it is unreasonable to expect] the Landlord to comply,

5.6.3.3   there is some defect or deficiency in the site on which the rebuilding or reinstatement is to take place [that renders it impossible *(or as required)* that means it can only be undertaken at a cost that is unreasonable in all the circumstances],

5.6.3.4   the Landlord is unable to obtain access to the site to rebuild or reinstate,

5.6.3.5   the rebuilding or reinstating is prevented by war, act of God, government action[, strike or lock-out], or

because of the occurrence of any other circumstances beyond the Landlord's control.

159   As to the need for a right to terminate where reinstatement is not possible see vol 22(1) (2003 Reissue) LANDLORD AND TENANT (BUSINESS TENANCIES) Paragraph 226 [998].
160   The extent of the duty to use best endeavours depends upon the facts in each case: see *Monkland v Jack Barclay Ltd* [1951] 2 KB 252, [1951] 1 All ER 714, CA; *Terrell v Mabie Todd & Co Ltd* [1952] 2 TLR 574; *NW Investments (Erdington) Ltd v Swani* (1970) 214 Estates Gazette 1115. In the light of *IBM United Kingdom Ltd v Rockware Glass Ltd* [1980] FSR 335, CA, it may be that there is little practical difference between a covenant to use best endeavours, a covenant to use reasonable endeavours and a covenant to take all reasonable steps.

[1429]

5.6.4   *Notice to terminate*[161]

If at the end of a period[162] of *(state period, eg 3 years)* starting on the date of the damage or destruction the Premises are still not fit for the Tenant's occupation and use, either the Landlord or the Tenant may by notice served at any time within *(state period, eg 6 months)* of the end of that period ('a notice to terminate following failure to reinstate') implement the provisions of clause 5.6.5 TERMINATION FOLLOWING FAILURE TO REINSTATE[163].

161   For alternative provisions where the landlord's right to terminate is limited to specified circumstances see vol 22(3) (1997 Reissue) LANDLORD AND TENANT (BUSINESS TENANCIES) Form 109 [6492].
162   The period to be inserted must be carefully considered. Particular regard should be had to the terms of any rent suspension provision and the extent of insurance cover for loss of rent.
163   As to the effect of the Landlord and Tenant Act 1954 see vol 22(1) (2003 Reissue) LANDLORD AND TENANT (BUSINESS TENANCIES) Paragraph 226 [998].

5.6.5   *Termination following failure to reinstate*

On service of a notice to terminate following failure to reinstate, the Term is to cease absolutely — but without prejudice to any rights or remedies that may have accrued[164]— and all money received in respect of the insurance effected by the Landlord pursuant to this Lease is to belong to the Landlord absolutely[165].

164   The effect of this clause is that the right to terminate arises after the end of the appropriate period, whatever the reason for the delay, but the tenant still has a right of action against the landlord if the landlord is in breach of his covenant to reinstate.

165   In the absence of provision for ownership of the insurance money the position is uncertain. In *Re King, Robinson v Gary* [1963] Ch 459, [1963] 1 All ER 781, CA it was held that the insurance money belongs to the party who paid the premiums even if the insurance was placed in the joint names of the landlord and the tenant. The dissenting view of Denning MR that insurance in joint names envisages that each party should be insured as to his insurable interest and that the insurance money should therefore be divided in proportion to their interests in the property should, however, be noted. In *Beacon Carpets Ltd v Kirby* [1985] QB 755, [1984] 2 All ER 726, CA the court adhered to this view and held that the proportion payable depended on the parties' interests in the premises at the time of the destruction. The landlord will prefer the lease to provide expressly for the insurance money to be retained by him in full if reinstatement proves impossible. The tenant ought perhaps to accept that it would be unrealistic to amend this to provide for the insurance money to belong to the tenant, but should suggest that a provision be inserted under which the money is to be divided in accordance with their respective interests in the premises at the time when the insurance money became due. For an alternative provision for ownership of the insurance money etc see vol 22(3) (1997 Reissue) LANDLORD AND TENANT (BUSINESS TENANCIES) Form 108 [6491].

[1430]

5.7   Tenant's further insurance covenants[166]

The Tenant covenants with the Landlord to observe and perform the requirements of this clause 5.7.

166   In order to comply with many of these covenants, the tenant will need to be supplied with details of the landlord's insurance policy. In any event, it should be noted that it is recommended 'best practice' that where the landlord has arranged insurance, the terms should be made known to the tenant and any material change in the insurance should be notified to the tenant: see Recommendation 14 of 'A code of practice for commercial leases in England and Wales (2nd edition)' which can be found in vol 22(1) (2003 Reissue) LANDLORD AND TENANT (BUSINESS TENANCIES) at Form 1 [4501].

5.7.1   *Requirements of insurers*

The Tenant must comply with all the requirements and recommendations of the insurers.

5.7.2   *Policy avoidance and additional premiums*

The Tenant must not do or omit anything that could cause any insurance policy on or in relation to the Centre to become wholly or partly void or voidable, or do or omit anything by which additional insurance premiums may become payable unless he has previously notified the Landlord and has agreed to pay the increased premium.

5.7.3   *Fire-fighting equipment*

The Tenant must keep the Premises supplied with such fire fighting equipment [as the insurers and the fire authority require and must maintain the equipment to their satisfaction *(or as required)* as the Landlord reasonably requires and must maintain the equipment to the reasonable satisfaction of the insurers and the fire authority] and in efficient working order. At least once in every *(state period, eg 6 months)* the Tenant must have the sprinkler system and other fire fighting equipment inspected by a competent person.

5.7.4   *Combustible materials*

The Tenant must not store on the Premises or bring onto them anything of a specially combustible, inflammable or explosive nature, and must comply with the requirements and recommendations of the fire authority [and the [reasonable] requirements of the Landlord] as to fire precautions relating to the Centre.

[1431]

5.7.5   *Fire escapes, equipment and doors*

The Tenant must not obstruct the access to any fire equipment or the means of escape from the Premises or any part of the Centre or lock any fire door while the Premises are occupied.

5.7.6   *Notice of events affecting the policy*

The Tenant must give immediate notice to the Landlord of any event that might affect any insurance policy on or relating to the Centre, and of any event against which the Landlord may have insured under this Lease.

5.7.7   *Notice of convictions*

The Tenant must give immediate notice to the Landlord of any conviction, judgment or finding of any court or tribunal relating to the Tenant, or any director other officer or major shareholder of the Tenant, of such a nature as to be likely to affect the decision of any insurer or underwriter to grant or to continue any insurance[167].

167   This clause provides a continuation of the warranty given by the tenant in clause 5.1 [1423] WARRANTY AS TO CONVICTIONS. As to non-disclosure and misrepresentation in contracts of non-marine insurance see 22 Halsbury's Laws (4th Edn Reissue) INSURANCE.

5.7.8   *Other insurance*

If at any time the Tenant is entitled to the benefit of any insurance of the Premises that is not effected or maintained in pursuance of any obligation contained in this Lease, the Tenant must apply all money received by virtue of such insurance in making good the loss or damage in respect of which the money is received[168].

168   An insurance policy frequently provides that if there is any other insurance effected by or on behalf of the insured, covering the premises that are the subject of the policy, the insurers are liable only for a rateable proportion of the damage. Such provisions extend to a case where one of the policies is in the joint names of the persons interested in the premises and the other is in the name of one only of those persons: *Halifax Building Society v Keighley* [1931] 2 KB 248. Therefore, at least when the insurance is in joint names and, ideally, even where it is not, the landlord should ensure that the tenant will use all money received under any policy he has effected to reinstate the premises.

[1432]

5.8   Increase or decrease of the Centre

5.8.1   *Variation of the Insurance Rent Percentage*

If the size of the Centre is permanently increased or decreased, the Insurance Rent Percentage may be varied, if the Landlord [acting reasonably] so requires, with effect from the date of any consequent alteration in the Insurance Rent.

5.8.2   *Determination of the variation*[169]

The amount by which the Insurance Rent Percentage is varied is to be agreed by the Landlord and the Tenant or, in default of agreement within *(state period, eg 3 months)* of the first proposal for variation made by the Landlord, is to be the amount the Surveyor, acting as an expert and not as an arbitrator, determines to be fair and reasonable.

169   Without a clause such as this the landlord cannot vary the insurance rent percentage without the consent of all the tenants, and if he subsequently extends the development he would be unable to combine the administration.

[5.9   Landlord's further insurance covenants[170]

The Landlord covenants with the Tenant to observe and perform the requirements set out in this clause 5.9 in relation to the insurance policy effected by the Landlord pursuant to his obligations contained in this Lease.

170   Unless insurance is to be in the joint names of the landlord and the tenant (which is unlikely in the circumstances assumed by this lease), the tenant should seek covenants such as these from the landlord.

5.9.1   *Copy policy*

The Landlord must produce to the Tenant on demand [a copy of the policy and the last premium renewal receipt *(or as required)* reasonable evidence of the terms of the policy and the fact that the last premium has been paid][171].

171   The landlord can reasonably insist on the second alternative. If the premises are insured under a block policy, it would be inappropriate for him to have to disclose to the tenant information about his other properties.
       It should be noted that it is recommended 'best practice' that where the landlord has arranged insurance, the terms should be made known to the tenant and any material change in the insurance should be notified to the tenant: see Recommendation 14 of 'A code of practice for commercial leases in England and Wales (2nd edition)' which can be found in vol 22(1) (2003 Reissue) LANDLORD AND TENANT (BUSINESS TENANCIES) at Form 1 [4501].

[1433]

5.9.2   *Noting of the Tenant's interest*

The Landlord must ensure that the interest of the Tenant is noted or endorsed on the policy[172].

172   Where insurance in the joint names of the landlord and the tenant is not practical, the tenant should insist that a note of his interest is endorsed on the policy. This protects the tenant because the insurers should give notice to him of any lapse in the policy and, where it can be shown that the tenant is responsible for the insurance premium under the terms of the lease, it is likely — but not certain — that the insurers would not exercise subrogation rights against the tenant.
       It is recommended 'best practice' that where the landlord has arranged insurance, any interest of the tenant should be covered by the policy: see Recommendation 14 of 'A code of practice for commercial leases in England and Wales (2nd edition)' which can be found in vol 22(1) (2003 Reissue) LANDLORD AND TENANT (BUSINESS TENANCIES) at Form 1 [4501].

5.9.3   *Change of risks*

The Landlord must notify the Tenant of any [material] change in the risks covered by the policy from time to time[173].

173   It is recommended 'best practice' that where the landlord has arranged insurance, any interest of the tenant should be covered by the policy: see Recommendation 14 of 'A code of practice for commercial leases in England and Wales (2nd edition)' which can be found in vol 22(1) (2003 Reissue) LANDLORD AND TENANT (BUSINESS TENANCIES) at Form 1 [4501].

[5.9.4   *Waiver of subrogation*[174]

The Landlord must produce to the Tenant on demand written confirmation from the insurers that they have agreed to waive all rights of subrogation against the Tenant.]]

174   Generally an insurer who has paid out under a policy stands in the shoes of the insured with regard to any claim the latter may have had against any third party. If the insurance is in joint names, the tenant is an insured party and there can be no subrogation against him. It would seem, also, that where the tenant covenants to reimburse the landlord for sums expended by the landlord in insuring the premises, the landlord's insurers cannot make a subrogated claim against the tenant where the premises are destroyed by the tenant's negligence: *Mark Rowlands Ltd v Berni Inns Ltd* [1986] QB 211, [1985] 3 All ER 473, CA. The tenant may still, however, wish to obtain a specific waiver of subrogation if possible.

[1434]–[1450]

6   GUARANTEE PROVISIONS

6.1   The Guarantor's covenants[175]

6.1.1   *Nature and duration*

The Guarantor's covenants with the Landlord are given as sole or principal debtor or covenantor, with the landlord for the time being and with all his successors in title[176] without the need for any express assignment, and the Guarantor's obligations to the Landlord will last throughout the Liability Period.

175   The covenants in this clause should *not* be omitted where no guarantor is a party to the lease, because they may be required under clause 3.9.5.2 [1384] CONDITIONS. If it is felt undesirable to have covenants in a lease and no party, at least initially, to enter into them, ie where there is no guarantor for the original tenant, the contents of this clause could alternatively be included in a schedule.

176   The new provisions governing the transmission of the benefit and burden of covenants (see the Landlord and Tenant (Covenants) Act 1995 s 3) only apply to landlord and tenant covenants. The law in force before 1 January 1996 remains unchanged for guarantor covenants, so that the benefit passes with the landlord's reversion. This occurs, not under the Law of Property Act 1925 s 141(1), which has been repealed for post-1995 tenancies by the 1995 Act, but under common law. The guarantee covenant touches and concerns the legal estate vested in the new reversioner: see *P & A Swift Investments v Combined English Stores Group plc* [1989] AC 632, [1988] 2 All ER 885, HL.

[1451]

6.1.2   *The covenants*

The Guarantor covenants with the Landlord to observe and perform the requirements of this clause 6.1.2.

6.1.2.1   **Payment of rent and performance of the Lease**

The Tenant must pay the Lease Rents[177] and VAT charged on them punctually and observe and perform the covenants and other terms of this Lease, and if, at any time during the Liability Period while the Tenant is bound by the tenant covenants of this Lease[178], the Tenant defaults in paying the Lease Rents or in observing or performing any of the covenants or other terms of this Lease, then the Guarantor must pay the Lease Rents and observe or perform the covenants or terms in respect of which the Tenant is in default and make good to the Landlord on demand, and indemnify the Landlord against, all losses resulting from such non-payment, non-performance or non-observance notwithstanding —

(a)   any time or indulgence granted by the Landlord to the Tenant, any neglect or forbearance of the Landlord in enforcing the payment of the Lease Rents or the observance or performance of the covenants or other terms of this Lease, or any refusal by the Landlord to accept rent tendered by or on behalf of the Tenant at a time when the Landlord is entitled — or will after the service of a notice under the Law of Property Act 1925 Section 146 be entitled — to re-enter the Premises[179],

(b)   that the terms of this Lease may have been varied by agreement between the Landlord and the Tenant[, provided that no variation is to bind the Guarantor to the extent that it is materially prejudicial to him][180],

(c)   that the Tenant has surrendered part of the Premises — in which event the liability of the Guarantor under this Lease is to continue in respect of the part of the Premises not surrendered after making any necessary apportionments under the Law of Property Act 1925 Section 140[181], and

(d)   anything else (other than a release by deed) by which, but for this clause 6.1.2.1, the Guarantor would be released.

[1452]

177   As to the definition of 'the Lease Rents' see clause 1.42 [1341] 'THE RENT'.

178   This obligation lasts while the lease is vested in the tenant and for any period of extended liability following an excluded assignment. It is not appropriate once the tenant has entered into an authorised guarantee agreement, when the contractual guarantor's obligations are at one remove: see vol 22(1) (2003 Reissue) LANDLORD AND TENANT (BUSINESS TENANCIES) Paragraph 74 [284] and clause 6.1.2.4 [1455] GUARANTEE OF THE TENANT'S LIABILITIES UNDER AN AUTHORISED GUARANTEE AGREEMENT.

179   If a creditor 'gives time' to the debtor in a binding manner, this releases the guarantor: see *Swire v Redman* (1876) 1 QBD 536; *Holme v Brunskill* (1877) 3 QBD 495, CA. The guarantee should, therefore, be expressed to apply notwithstanding any time or indulgence granted by the landlord to the tenant, or neglect or forbearance on the part of the landlord in enforcing the payment of rent and the other covenants in the lease. It has been suggested, however, that such wording does not protect a landlord who refuses to accept rent so as not to waive a breach of covenant by the tenant. This is unresolved but to avoid any doubt the point should be expressly dealt with. It appears that any provision in a guarantor's covenant that purports to exonerate the landlord from the consequences of his own negligence must satisfy the reasonableness test of the Unfair Contract Terms Act 1977.

180   Any variation of the terms of the contract between the creditor and the debtor will discharge the guarantor (*Holme v Brunskill* (1877) 3 QBD 495, CA), unless the guarantor consents, although it has been suggested that an immaterial variation that was not prejudicial to the guarantor might not release him. No guarantor should accept a provision by which the guarantee is to continue notwithstanding any variation, but on the other hand it seems unfair on the landlord for the guarantor to escape his liability merely because a minor change has been agreed between the landlord and the tenant. A provision that the guarantee is to continue to apply notwithstanding an immaterial variation not prejudicial to the guarantor seems a fair compromise. It should be noted that the Landlord and Tenant (Covenants) Act 1995 s 18 does not apply to the guarantor of the current tenant.

It should also be noted that it is recommended 'best practice' that landlords and tenants should seek the agreement of any guarantors to proposed material changes to the terms of the lease, or even minor changes which could increase the guarantor's liability: see Recommendation 15 of 'A code of practice for commercial leases in England and Wales (2nd edition)' which can be found in vol 22(1) (2003 Reissue) LANDLORD AND TENANT (BUSINESS TENANCIES) at Form 1 [4501].

181   In the light of *Holme v Brunskill* (1877) 3 QBD 495, CA, the position on surrender of part of the premises should be dealt with expressly.

[1453]

6.1.2.2   New lease following disclaimer[182]

If, at any time during the Liability Period while the Tenant is bound by the tenant covenants of this Lease[183], any trustee in bankruptcy or liquidator of the Tenant disclaims this Lease, the Guarantor must, if so required by notice served by the Landlord within *(state period, eg 60 days)* of the Landlord's becoming aware of the disclaimer, take from the Landlord forthwith a lease of the Premises for the residue of the [Contractual][184] Term as at the date of the disclaimer, at the Rent then payable under this Lease and subject to the same covenants and terms as in this Lease — except that the Guarantor need not ensure that any other person is made a party to that lease as guarantor — the new lease to commence on the date of the disclaimer. The Guarantor must pay the costs of the new lease and VAT charged thereon, save where such VAT is recoverable or available for set-off by the Landlord as input tax[185], and execute and deliver to the Landlord a counterpart of the new lease.

182   This put option should be included because on disclaimer of a lease the lease ceases to exist, although it is deemed to continue for the purpose of determining the liability to the landlord of persons, including guarantors, other than the tenant whose liquidator or trustee has disclaimed: see *Hindcastle Ltd v Barbara Attenborough Associates Ltd* [1997] AC 70, [1996] 1 All ER 737, HL.

183   This obligation lasts while the lease is vested in the tenant and for any period of extended liability following an excluded assignment. It is not appropriate once the tenant has entered into an authorised guarantee agreement when the tenant's — ie the former tenant's — liquidator or trustee in bankruptcy will not be in a position to disclaim the lease because it will no longer be vested in the former tenant.

184   This defined term will require amendment where the operation of the security of tenure provisions in the Landlord and Tenant Act 1954 ss 24–28 is to be excluded in relation to the lease: see note 7 to clause 1.7 [1310] 'THE [CONTRACTUAL] TERM'.

185   As to payment of VAT on legal costs by a person other than the solicitor's own client see the Information Binder: Property [1]: VAT and Property.

[1454]

6.1.2.3   Payments following disclaimer[186]

If this Lease is disclaimed and the Landlord does not require the Guarantor to accept a new lease of the Premises in accordance with clause 6.1.2.2 NEW LEASE FOLLOWING DISCLAIMER, the Guarantor must pay to the Landlord on demand an amount equal to [the difference between any money received by the Landlord for the use or occupation of the Premises and] the Lease Rents [in both cases] for the period commencing with the date of the disclaimer and ending on whichever is the earlier of the date *(state period, eg 6 months)* after the disclaimer, the date, if any, upon which the Premises are relet, and the end of the [Contractual][187] Term.

186   This clause could be a useful alternative for a landlord, who may not be unhappy to regain possession of the premises but would like some rental income before reletting etc. For a covenant by the tenant to assign to the guarantor see vol 22(3) (1997 Reissue) LANDLORD AND TENANT (BUSINESS TENANCIES) Form 159 [6666].

187   This defined term will require amendment where the operation of the security of tenure provisions in the Landlord and Tenant Act 1954 ss 24–28 is to be excluded in relation to the lease: see note 7 to clause 1.7 [1310] 'THE [CONTRACTUAL] TERM'.

6.1.2.4   Guarantee of the Tenant's liabilities under an authorised guarantee agreement

If, at any time during the Liability Period while the Tenant is bound by an authorised guarantee agreement, the Tenant defaults in his obligations under that agreement, the Guarantor must make good to the Landlord on demand, and indemnify the Landlord against, all losses resulting from that default notwithstanding —

(a)   any time or indulgence granted by the Landlord to the Tenant, or neglect or forbearance of the Landlord in enforcing the payment of any sum or the observance or performance of the covenants of the authorised guarantee agreement[188],

(b)   that the terms of the authorised guarantee agreement may have been varied by agreement between the Landlord and the Tenant [provided that no variation is to bind the Guarantor to the extent that it is materially prejudicial to him][189], or

(c)   anything else (other than a release by deed) by which, but for this clause 6.1.2.4, the Guarantor would be released.

188   See note 179 to clause 6.1.2.1 [1453] PAYMENT OF RENT AND PERFORMANCE OF THE LEASE.
189   See note 180 to clause 6.1.2.1 [1453] PAYMENT OF RENT AND PERFORMANCE OF THE LEASE.

[1455]

6.1.3   *Severance*

6.1.3.1   Severance of void provisions

Any provision of this clause 6 rendered void by virtue of the 1995 Act Section 25 is to be severed from all remaining provisions, and the remaining provisions are to be preserved.

6.1.3.2   Limitation of provisions

If any provision in this clause 6 extends beyond the limits permitted by the 1995 Act Section 25, that provision is to be varied so as not to extend beyond those limits.

[6.2   The Landlord's covenant[190]

The Landlord covenants with the Guarantor that he will not attempt to recover from the Guarantor payment of any amount, determined by a court or in binding arbitration or agreed between the Landlord and the Tenant, payable in respect of a breach of covenant by the Tenant, unless he has served on the Guarantor, within 6 months of the payment being determined or agreed, a notice in the form prescribed by Section 27 of the 1995 Act as if the payment were a fixed charge under that Act.]

190   This clause is a tenant's amendment. It provides for a notice equivalent to a default notice under the Landlord and Tenant (Covenants) Act 1995 to be served. It protects the interests of existing and future contractual guarantors. As to service of default notices see vol 22(1) (2003 Reissue) LANDLORD AND TENANT (BUSINESS TENANCIES) Paragraph 61 [260].

[1456]

7   FORFEITURE[191]

If and whenever during the Term —

7.1   the Lease Rents[192], or any of them or any part of them, or any VAT payable on them, are outstanding for *(state period, eg 14 days)* after becoming due, whether formally demanded or not[193], or

7.2   the Tenant [or the Guarantor] breaches any covenant or other term of this Lease, or

7.3   the Tenant [or the Guarantor][194], being an individual, becomes subject to a bankruptcy order[195] [or has an interim receiver appointed to his property][196], or

7.4   the Tenant [or the Guarantor][197], being a company, enters into liquidation[198] whether compulsory or voluntary — but not if the liquidation is for amalgamation or reconstruction of a solvent company — [or enters into administration][199] [or has a receiver appointed over all or any part of its assets][200], or

7.5   the Tenant [or the Guarantor][201] enters into or makes a proposal to enter into any voluntary arrangement pursuant to the Insolvency Act 1986[202] or any other arrangement or composition for the benefit of his creditors, or

7.6   the Tenant has any distress, sequestration or execution levied on his goods,

and, where the Tenant [or the Guarantor] is more than one person, if and whenever any of the events referred to in this clause happens to any one or more of them, the Landlord may at any time re-enter the Premises or any part of them in the name of the whole — even if any previous right of re-entry has been waived[203] — and thereupon the Term is to cease absolutely but without prejudice to any rights or remedies that may have accrued to the Landlord against the Tenant or the Guarantor [or to the Tenant against the Landlord] in respect of any breach of covenant or other term of this Lease, including the breach in respect of which the re-entry is made.

[1457]

191   As to forfeiture generally see vol 22(1) (2003 Reissue) LANDLORD AND TENANT (BUSINESS TENANCIES) Paragraph 283 [1171] et seq.
      The precise range of insolvency-related circumstances that will trigger the proviso should be carefully considered. Tenants should note that their inclusion, in practice, means that the lease cannot be used as security for a loan. Landlords generally seek to have the ability to forfeit in the widest range of circumstances. It should, however, be noted that, in certain circumstances, leave of the court or of the insolvency practitioner administering the procedure may be required before any contractual right can be exercised: see eg, in respect of administration, the Insolvency Act 1986 Sch 1B para 43(4), (6) as inserted by the Enterprise Act 2002 s 248 (4 Halsbury's Statutes (4th Edn) BANKRUPTCY AND INSOLVENCY).

192   As to the definition of 'the Lease Rents' see clause 1.42 [1341] 'THE RENT'.
193   The words 'whether formally demanded or not' should be used to avoid the common law requirement that an actual demand has to be made.
194   The lease may provide for a right of re-entry on insolvency of the guarantor or a tenant's covenant to find an acceptable replacement (see clause 3.23 [1406] REPLACEMENT GUARANTOR) or both.
195   As to bankruptcy generally see the Insolvency Act 1986 Pt IX (ss 264–371).
196   As to interim receivers see the Insolvency Act 1986 s 286.
197   See note 194 above.
198   As to liquidation generally see the Insolvency Act 1986 Pts IV–VI (ss 73–246).
199   As to administration generally see the Insolvency Act 1986 Pt II as substituted by the Enterprise Act 2002 s 248. The tenant may seek to argue that if the administrator pays rent and if there are no other material breaches of the lease the landlord should not be entitled to forfeit the lease on this ground.
200   The tenant may seek to argue that if the receiver pays rent and if there are no other material breaches of the lease the landlord should not be entitled to forfeit the lease on this ground.
201   See note 194 above.
202   As to company voluntary arrangements see the Insolvency Act 1986 Pt I (ss 1–7B) as amended by the Insolvency Act 2000. As to individual voluntary arrangements see the Insolvency Act 1986 Pt VIII (ss 252–263G) as amended by the Enterprise Act 2002 s 264.
203   The landlord has the option whether to take advantage of a right of forfeiture or not. If he elects not to do so, the forfeiture is waived. The election may be express or implied, eg if the landlord does any act by which he recognises that the relationship of landlord and tenant is still continuing after the cause of forfeiture has come to his knowledge.

[1458]–[1470]

8   MISCELLANEOUS

8.1   Exclusion of warranty as to use

Nothing in this Lease or in any consent granted by the Landlord under this Lease is to imply or warrant that the Premises may lawfully be used under the Planning Acts for the Permitted Use[204].

204   See *Laurence v Lexcourt Holdings Ltd* [1978] 2 All ER 810, [1978] 1 WLR 1128; *Collins v Howell-Jones* [1981] 2 EGLR 108, 259 Estates Gazette 331, CA and the comments of Eveleigh LJ on estate agents' particulars relating to use in *Bovis Group Pension Fund Ltd v GC Flooring & Furnishing Ltd* (1984) 269 Estates Gazette 1252 at 1253, CA.

8.2   Exclusion of third party rights

Nothing in this Lease is intended to confer any benefit on any person who is not a party to it[205].

205   By virtue of the Contracts (Rights of Third Parties) Act 1999 (11 Halsbury's Statutes (4th Edn) CONTRACT) third-party rights may be conferred where they are not clearly excluded. This being so, it is advisable to incorporate a specific exclusion except where the parties actually intend to confer rights of action on a third party. In the standard letting situation it is unlikely that the parties will wish to extend liability in this manner. As to the Contracts (Rights of Third Parties) Act 1999 generally see vol 4(3) (2001 Reissue) BOILERPLATE CLAUSES.

8.3   Representations

The Tenant acknowledges that this Lease has not been entered into wholly or partly in reliance on any statement or representation made by or on behalf of the Landlord except any such statement or representation that is expressly set out in this Lease[206] [or was made by the Landlord's solicitors in any written response to enquiries raised by the Tenant's solicitors in connection with the grant of this Lease].

206   See the comments of Eveleigh LJ on estate agents' particulars relating to use in *Bovis Group Pension Fund Ltd v GC Flooring & Furnishing Ltd* (1984) 269 Estates Gazette 1252 at 1253, CA. For an alternative provision see vol 22(4) (1997 Reissue) LANDLORD AND TENANT (BUSINESS TENANCIES) Form 400 clauses 7.1 [7520], 7.2 [7521].

[1471]

8.4   Documents under hand

While the Landlord is a limited company or other corporation, any licence, consent, approval or notice required to be given by the Landlord is to be sufficiently given if given under the hand of a director, the secretary or other duly authorised officer of the Landlord [or by the Surveyor on behalf of the Landlord].

8.5   Tenant's property

If, after the Tenant has vacated the Premises at the end of the Term any property of his remains in or on the Premises and he fails to remove it within *(state period, eg 7 days)* after a written request from the Landlord to do so or, if the Landlord is unable to make such a request to the Tenant, within *(state period, eg 14 days)* from the first attempt to make it, then the Landlord may, as the agent of the Tenant, sell that property . The Tenant must indemnify the Landlord against any liability incurred by the Landlord to any third party whose property is sold by him in the mistaken belief held in good faith — which is to be presumed unless the contrary is proved — that the property belonged to the Tenant. If, having made reasonable efforts to do so, the Landlord is unable to locate the Tenant, then the Landlord may retain the proceeds of sale absolutely unless the Tenant claims them within *(state period, eg 6 months)* of the date upon which he vacated the Premises. The Tenant must indemnify the Landlord against any damage occasioned to the Premises and any losses caused by or related to the presence of the property in or on the Premises.

8.6   Compensation on vacating excluded

Any statutory right of the Tenant to claim compensation from the Landlord on vacating the Premises is excluded to the extent that the law allows[207].

207   As to compensation where an order for a new tenancy is precluded on certain grounds see the Landlord and Tenant Act 1954 s 37 as amended by the Local Government and Housing Act 1989 s 149, Sch 7 and by SI 2003/3096.

       As to the effectiveness of provisions of this nature see vol 22(1) (2003 Reissue) LANDLORD AND TENANT (BUSINESS TENANCIES) Paragraph 468 [3079].

[1472]

8.7   Notices

8.7.1   *Form and service of notices*

Any notice under this Lease must be in writing and, unless the receiving party or his authorised agent acknowledges receipt, is valid if, and only if[208] —

8.7.1.1   it is given by hand, sent by registered post or recorded delivery, or sent by fax[209] provided a confirmatory copy is given by hand or sent by registered post or recorded delivery on the same day, and

8.7.1.2   it is served —

        (a)   where the receiving party is a company incorporated within Great Britain, at the registered office,

        (b)   where the receiving party is the Tenant and the Tenant is not such a company, at the Premises, and

        (c)   where the receiving party is the Landlord [or the Guarantor] and [the Landlord *(or as required)* that party] is not such a company, at [the Landlord's *(or as required)* that party's] address shown in this Lease or at any address specified in a notice given by [the Landlord to the Tenant *(or as required)* that party to the other parties].

208   Notice clauses are either mandatory or permissive. The words 'and only if' are inserted to make it clear that this clause is mandatory.

209   As to service by fax see *Hastie and Jenkerson v McMahon* [1991] 1 All ER 255, [1990] 1 WLR 1575.

8.7.2 *Deemed delivery*[210]

8.7.2.1 By registered post or recorded delivery

Unless it is returned through the Royal Mail undelivered, a notice sent by registered post or recorded delivery is to be treated as served on the third working day after posting whenever, and whether or not, it is received.

8.7.2.2 By fax

A notice sent by fax is to be treated as served on the day on which it is sent, or the next working day where the fax is sent after 1600 hours or on a day that is not a working day, whenever and whether or not it or the confirmatory copy is received unless the confirmatory copy is returned through the Royal Mail undelivered.

8.7.2.3 'A working day'

References to 'a working day' are references to a day when the United Kingdom clearing banks are open for business in the City of London.

210   It is a fundamental aspect of any notice clause to specify the circumstances in which the server, provided he has complied with the requirements of the clause, has for the purposes of the document served a notice, even if the recipient claims that he never received it.

[1473]

8.7.3 *Joint recipients*

If the receiving party consists of more than one person, a notice to one of them is notice to all.

8.8 Rights and easements[211]

The operation of the Law of Property Act 1925 Section 62 is excluded from this Lease and the only rights granted to the Tenant are those expressly set out in this Lease and the Tenant is not to be entitled to any other rights affecting any adjoining property of the Landlord.

211   Where the Law of Property Act 1925 s 62 may operate, it is sensible to define in the lease those rights that are included, and then specifically exclude the operation of that section.

8.9 Covenants relating to adjoining property

The Tenant is not to be entitled to the benefit of or the right [to enforce or][212] to prevent the release or modification of any covenant agreement or condition entered into by any tenant of the Landlord in respect of any adjoining property of the Landlord.

212   As to when tenants would be able to enforce covenants against each other see vol 22(1) (2003 Reissue) LANDLORD AND TENANT (BUSINESS TENANCIES) Paragraph 48 [235]. Where this might arise, 'to enforce or' should be deleted by the tenant.

8.10 Disputes with adjoining occupiers

If any dispute arises between the Tenant and the tenants or occupiers of any adjoining property of the Landlord in connection with the Premises and any of that adjoining property, it is to be decided [by the Landlord or in such manner as the Landlord directs *(or as required)* by the Surveyor acting as an expert and not as an arbitrator][213].

213   Such a provision is binding on the landlord and the tenant, but binds a tenant of the landlord's adjoining property only if there is a similar provision in his lease.

8.11   Effect of waiver

Each of the Tenant's covenants is to remain in full force both at law and in equity even if the Landlord has waived or released that covenant, or waived or released any similar covenant affecting any of his adjoining property of the Landlord[214].

214   But as to waiver of a right of forfeiture see vol 22(1) (2003 Reissue) LANDLORD AND TENANT (BUSINESS TENANCIES) Paragraph 284 [1173].

[1474]

[8.12   The perpetuity period[215]

The perpetuity period applicable to this Lease is *(state period, eg 80 years)* from the commencement of the [Contractual][216] Term, and whenever in this Lease any party is granted a future interest it must vest within that period or be void for remoteness.]

215   As to the rule against perpetuities see vol 22(1) (2003 Reissue) LANDLORD AND TENANT (BUSINESS TENANCIES) Paragraph 132 [664]. This clause should be included if the term exceeds 21 years because the lease contains grants of future interests.
216   This defined term will require amendment where the operation of the security of tenure provisions in the Landlord and Tenant Act 1954 ss 24–28 is to be excluded in relation to the lease (see note 7 to clause 1.7 [1310] 'THE [CONTRACTUAL] TERM') although this is probably unlikely in connection with the grant of such a long lease.

[8.13   Party walls

Any walls dividing the Premises from the other buildings are to be party walls within the meaning of the Law of Property Act 1925 Section 38 and must be maintained at the equally shared expense of the Tenant and the other party.][217] *(omit if not required in the circumstances)*

217   Internal non-loadbearing and loadbearing walls between the premises and other premises are covered in the description of the premises. It is therefore unlikely that as between the tenant and the landlord or other tenants there can be any party walls.

8.14   Exclusion of liability

The Landlord is not to be responsible to the Tenant or to anyone at the Premises or the Centre expressly or by implication with the Tenant's authority for any accident happening or injury suffered or for any damage to or loss of any chattel sustained in the Premises or on the Centre[218].

218   As to exclusion clauses see vol 22(1) (2003 Reissue) LANDLORD AND TENANT (BUSINESS TENANCIES) Paragraph 140 [679].

[1475]

8.15   [New *(or)* Old] lease

[This Lease [is *(or as appropriate)* is not] a new tenancy for the purposes of the 1995 Act Section 1. *(or as appropriate)* This Lease is granted under the 1995 Act Section 19 and [is *(or as appropriate)* is not] a new tenancy for the purposes of Section 1 of that Act.][219]

219   A tenancy granted on or after 1 January 1996 that is an overriding lease is not a 'new' tenancy where the tenancy being overridden is one granted before that date: see the Landlord and Tenant (Covenants) Act 1995 ss 1(4), 20(1). Where the lease being granted is an overriding lease, the lease must include a statement that it is an overriding lease and indicate whether the overriding lease is or is not a 'new' tenancy: see the Landlord and Tenant (Covenants) Act 1995 s 20(2). In these circumstances the second alternative should be used.

[8.16   Capacity of tenants

It is declared that the persons comprising the Tenant hold the Premises as [joint tenants *(or as required)* tenants in common].]

[8.17   Exclusion of the 1954 Act Sections 24–28[220]

8.17.1   *Notice and declaration*

On *(date)* the Landlord served notice on the Tenant pursuant to the provisions of the 1954 Act Section 38A(3) as inserted by the Regulatory Reform (Business Tenancies) (England and Wales) Order 2003 and on *(date)* the Tenant made a [simple *(or as appropriate)* statutory] declaration pursuant to schedule 2 of the Regulatory Reform (Business Tenancies) (England and Wales) Order 2003.

8.17.2   *Agreement to exclude*

Pursuant to the provisions of the 1954 Act Section 38A(1) as inserted by the Regulatory Reform (Business Tenancies) (England and Wales) Order 2003, the parties agree that the provisions of the 1954 Act Sections 24–28 inclusive are to be excluded in relation to the tenancy created by this Lease.]

220   As to contracting out of the Landlord and Tenant Act 1954 and the requirements that need to be complied with see vol 22(1) (2003 Reissue) LANDLORD AND TENANT (BUSINESS TENANCIES) Paragraph 431 [2035].

(include other clauses as required: eg, break clauses and options (see vol 22(3) (1997 Reissue) LANDLORD AND TENANT (BUSINESS TENANCIES) *Forms 136 [6544]–142 [6569]) or a proviso as to termination on rent review (see vol 22(3) (1997 Reissue)* LANDLORD AND TENANT (BUSINESS TENANCIES) *Form 143 [6570]))*

IN WITNESS etc *(see vol 12(2) (2003 Reissue) DEEDS, AGREEMENTS ETC)*
[1476]–[1490]

SCHEDULE 1: THE RIGHTS GRANTED[221]

1–1   Right to use the Common Parts

The right, subject to [temporary] interruption for repair, alteration, rebuilding or replacement, for the Tenant and all persons expressly or by implication authorised by him[222] — in common with the Landlord and all other persons having a like right — to use all appropriate areas of the Common Parts for all proper purposes in connection with the use and enjoyment of the Premises at such times as they are open in accordance with the Landlord's obligations in this Lease.

221   As to rights granted see vol 22(1) (2003 Reissue) LANDLORD AND TENANT (BUSINESS TENANCIES) Paragraph 123 [647] et seq.
222   The term 'the Tenant and all persons expressly or by implication authorised by him' is an updated version of 'the Tenant and his successors in title the owners and occupiers for the time being of the Premises and his or their respective servants and licensees': see *Baxendale v North Lambeth Liberal and Radical Club Ltd* [1902] 2 Ch 427 at 429 per Swinfen Eady J; *Hammond v Prentice Bros Ltd* [1920] 1 Ch 201.

1-2   Passage and running through the Adjoining Conduits

The right, subject to temporary interruption for repair, alteration or replacement, to the free passage and running of all services to and from the Premises through the appropriate Adjoining Conduits, in common with the Landlord and all other persons having a like right.

1-3   Support and protection

The right of support and protection for the benefit of the Premises that is now enjoyed from all other parts of the Centre.

[1491]

SCHEDULE 2: THE RIGHTS RESERVED[223]

2-1   Passage and running through the Conduits

The right to the free and uninterrupted passage and running of all appropriate services and supplies from and to other parts of the Centre or any other adjoining property of the Landlord in and through the appropriate Conduits and through any structures of a similar use or nature that may at any time be constructed in, on, over or under the Premises as permitted by paragraph 2-2 RIGHT TO CONSTRUCT CONDUITS.

223   As to rights reserved see vol 22(1) (2003 Reissue) LANDLORD AND TENANT (BUSINESS TENANCIES) Paragraph 124 [648] et seq.

2-2   Right to construct conduits[224]

The right to construct[225] and to maintain at any time during the Term any pipes, sewers, drains, mains, ducts, conduits, gutters, watercourses, wires, cables, [laser optical fibres, data or impulse transmission, communication or reception systems,] channels, flues and other necessary conducting media for the provision of services or supplies— including any fixings, louvres, cowls and any other ancillary apparatus — for the benefit of any part of the Centre or any other adjoining property of the Landlord [, making good any damage caused by the exercise of the right].

224   If the term of the lease exceeds 21 years a perpetuity provision — see clause 8.12 [1475] THE PERPETUITY PERIOD — is required in the lease because this is a grant of a future interest.
225   For a covenant to make good after exercising rights of access see vol 22(3) (1997 Reissue) LANDLORD AND TENANT (BUSINESS TENANCIES) Form 79 [6453].

[1492]

2-3   Access

2-3.1   *Access to inspect etc*[226]

The right to enter, or in emergency to break into and enter, the Premises [at any time during the Term *(or as required)* at reasonable times and on reasonable notice except in emergency] —

2-3.1.1   to inspect the condition and the state of repair of the Premises,

2-3.1.2   to inspect, clean, connect to, lay, repair, remove, replace with others, alter or execute any works whatever to or in connection with the conduits, easements, supplies or services referred to in paragraphs 2-1 PASSAGE AND RUNNING THROUGH THE CONDUITS and 2-2 RIGHT TO CONSTRUCT CONDUITS,

2-3.1.3   to view the state and condition of and repair and maintain and carry out work of any other kind to, the Centre and any other buildings where such viewing or work would not otherwise be [reasonably] practicable,

2-3.1.4   to carry out work or do anything whatever that the Landlord is obliged to do under this Lease,

2-3.1.5   to take schedules or inventories of fixtures and other items to be yielded up at the end of the Term, and

2-3.1.6   to exercise any of the rights granted to the Landlord by this Lease.

226   For a covenant to make good after exercising rights of access see vol 22(3) (1997 Reissue) LANDLORD AND TENANT (BUSINESS TENANCIES) Form 79 [6453].

2-3.2   *Access on renewal or rent review*

The right to enter the Premises with the Surveyor and any third party determining the Rent under any provisions for rent review contained in this Lease at [any time *(or as required)* convenient hours and on reasonable prior notice], to inspect [and measure] the Premises for all purposes connected with any pending or intended step under the 1954 Act or the implementation of the provisions for rent review. *(or as required in view of the rent review provisions used: see, eg, vol 22(3) (1997 Reissue) LANDLORD AND TENANT (BUSINESS TENANCIES) Forms 180 [6711]–194 [6987])*

[1493]

2-4   Right to erect scaffolding

The right [temporarily] to erect scaffolding for [any purpose connected with or related to the Centre *(or as required)* the purpose of inspecting, repairing or cleaning the Centre] or any buildings [even if it restricts *(or as required)* provided it does not materially adversely restrict] access to or the use and enjoyment of the Premises [but not so as to prevent such access, use and enjoyment][227].

227   See *Owen v Gadd* [1956] 2 QB 99, [1956] 2 All ER 28, CA.

2-5   Rights of support and shelter

The rights of light, air, support, shelter, protection and all other easements and rights at the date of this Lease belonging to or enjoyed by other parts of the Centre or any other adjoining property of the Landlord.

2-6   Right to erect new buildings[228]

Full right and liberty at any time —

2-6.1   to alter, raise the height of, or rebuild the Centre or any other building, and

2-6.2   to erect any new buildings of any height on any adjoining property of the Landlord

in such manner as the Landlord thinks fit, even if doing so may obstruct, affect, or interfere with the amenity of or access to the Premises or the passage of light and air to the Premises, [and even if they *(or as required)* but provided they do not] materially affect the Premises or the use and enjoyment of the Premises.

228   As to reservation of the right to develop other land see vol 22(1) (2003 Reissue) LANDLORD AND TENANT (BUSINESS TENANCIES) Paragraphs 130 [660], 131 [662].

SCHEDULE 3: THE RENT AND RENT REVIEW

(insert rent review provisions as required: see vol 22(3) (1997 Reissue) LANDLORD AND TENANT *(BUSINESS TENANCIES) Forms 180 [6711]–194 [6987])*

[1494]

SCHEDULE 4: THE SHOP COVENANTS

(landlords of shopping centres tend to impose stringent requirements on their tenants on the basis that this is required by the principles of good estate management. A balance must, however, be found because restrictions that place unreasonable burdens on the traders may even persuade some not to take a lease in that centre)

4-1   Use

4-1.1   *Permitted Use*

The Tenant must use the Premises for the Permitted Use only.

4-1.2   *External displays*

The Tenant must not stand, place, deposit or expose any goods, materials, articles or things whatsoever for display or sale or for any other purpose outside any part of the Premises.

4-1.3   *Noxious discharges*

The Tenant must not discharge into any of the Conduits or the Adjoining Conduits any noxious or deleterious matter or any other substance that might cause an obstruction in or danger or injury to the Conduits or the Adjoining Conduits or be or become a source of obstruction, danger or injury, and in the event of any such obstruction, danger or injury the Tenant must forthwith make good all damage to the satisfaction of the Surveyor.

4-1.4   *Noisy machinery*

The Tenant must not install or use in or on the Premises any machinery or apparatus causing noise or vibration that can be heard or felt in nearby premises or outside the Premises or that may cause damage.

4-1.5   *Sound audible outside*

The Tenant must not play or use on the Premises any musical instrument, audio or other equipment or apparatus producing sound that can be heard outside the Premises [if the Landlord [in his absolute discretion *(or as required)* reasonably] considers such sounds to be undesirable and gives notice to the Tenant to that effect].

[1495]

4-1.6   *Flashing lights*

The Tenant must not display any flashing lights in the Premises that can be seen from outside the Premises [or display any other lighting arrangement that can be seen from outside the Premises if the Landlord [in his absolute discretion *(or as required)* reasonably] considers such lighting to be undesirable and gives notice to the Tenant to that effect].

4-1.7   *Exterior lights and awnings*

The Tenant must not install or erect any exterior lighting, shade or awning at the Premises.

4-1.8   *Cooking*

The Tenant must not cook or heat any food in the Premises other than for the purpose of making of hot drinks.

4-2   Damage precautions

4-2.1   *Frost precautions*

The Tenant must take all necessary precautions against frost damage to the Conduits.

4-2.2   *Water damage*

The Tenant must take all necessary care and precautions to avoid water damage to any other part of the Centre by reason of the bursting or overflowing of any pipe or water apparatus in the Premises.

[1496]

4-3   Hours of trading

4-3.1   *Trading during Shop Opening Hours*

During the Shop Opening Hours the Tenant must keep the Premises open for business[229] and properly cared for, and must trade actively throughout substantially the whole of the Premises except —

4-3.1.1   in so far as he is prevented from doing so by destruction or damage to the Premises caused by one or more of the Insured Risks[230],

4-3.1.2   when non-trading is necessary to allow any major repairs, alterations or additions to the Premises to be carried out with all reasonable speed[231],

4-3.1.3   where non-trading is necessary to allow a permitted assignment [or subletting] of this Lease to be completed, or

4-3.1.4   in so far as to do so would be in breach of any other provision of this Lease.

229   A covenant to keep open during 'normal business hours' does not require the tenant to open the shop on Sundays: see the Sunday Trading Act 1994 s 3 (19 Halsbury's Statutes (4th Edn) HEALTH AND SAFETY AT WORK). The landlord should give careful consideration to the inclusion of an obligation of this nature: see vol 22(1) (2003 Reissue) LANDLORD AND TENANT (BUSINESS TENANCIES) Paragraph 177 [876].

230   It should be noted that it is now recommended 'best practice' that if the premises are so damaged by an uninsured risk as to prevent occupation, the tenant should be allowed to terminate the lease unless the landlord agrees to reinstate at his own cost: see vol 22(1) (2003 Reissue) LANDLORD AND TENANT (BUSINESS TENANCIES) Paragraph 85 [402]. It follows that if this recommendation is adopted, this exception also needs to be extended to include damage or destruction caused by both insured and uninsured risks.

231   A tenant may wish to have this provision extended to include periods for stocktaking and, particularly in long leases, to authorise shop fittings.

[4-3.2   *Trading outside Shop Opening Hours*

The Tenant must not open the Premises for business outside the Shop Opening Hours][232].

232   As to covenants not to trade outside normal trading hours see vol 22(1) (2003 Reissue) LANDLORD AND TENANT (BUSINESS TENANCIES) Paragraph 174 [870].

[1497]

4-4   Window dressing and displays

4-4.1   *Window dressing*

The Tenant must keep the shop windows attractively dressed in a manner suitable to a high class shopping centre.

4-4.2   *Interior layout*

The Tenant must keep all those parts of the interior of the Premises that are visible from outside the Premises attractively laid out and furnished, with goods well displayed, and must keep any showcases in the Premises clean and attractively dressed at all times [to the reasonable satisfaction of the Landlord].

4-4.3   *Posters, placards and signs*

The Tenant must not place or display on the outside of the Premises or on the windows or inside the Premises so as to be visible from outside the Premises any name, writing, notice, sign, placard, poster, sticker or advertisement other than —

4-4.3.1   normal price tickets attached and relating to goods sold in the display area inside the Premises, provided these are not placed on the window glass, [and]

4-4.3.2   the sign referred to in paragraph 4-4.4 APPROVED SIGN OR FASCIA [, and

4-4.3.3   trade placards, posters or advertisements of a temporary and not excessive nature and necessary or usual for the Permitted Use [provided that not more than *(state proportion, eg 25%)* of the surface area of the shop window of the Premises may be obscured by such placards, posters or advertisements]].

4-4.4   *Approved sign or fascia*

The Tenant must maintain on the exterior of the Premises a [sign *(or as appropriate)* fascia] of a type, size and design approved by the Landlord, whose approval may not be unreasonably withheld or delayed, showing the Tenant's name and business.

[1498]

4-4.5   *Display lighting*

Unless prevented by any regulation or requirement of a competent government department or local, public, regulatory or other authority or court, or by any interruption by the supplier in the supply of electricity, the Tenant must keep all display windows and showcases of the Premises well lit during such hours as the Surveyor from time to time determines or, in the absence of such determination, during the Shop Opening Hours and the *(state period, eg 30 minutes)* immediately preceding those hours and the *(state period, eg 30 minutes)* immediately following those hours. This obligation is not to apply during the periods specified in paragraphs 4-3.1.1–4-3.1.4, but during those periods the Tenant must take such steps as the Surveyor [reasonably] requires to ensure that [a reasonably *(or as required)* an] attractive external appearance to the Premises is maintained.

4-5   Cleaning and tidying

4-5.1   *Care of the Common Parts*

The Tenant must not cause the Common Parts to become untidy or dirty and must keep them free from deposits of materials and refuse.

4-5.2   *Shop front and windows*

The Tenant must clean both sides of the shop front [and the doors and windows and door and window frames] of the Premises [at least *(state frequency, eg once every week) (or as required)* as often as is [reasonably] necessary].

[1499]

4-6   Ceiling and floor loading

4-6.1   *Heavy items*

The Tenant must not bring onto, or permit to remain on, the Premises any safes, machinery, goods or other articles that will or may strain or damage the Premises or any part of them[233].

233   A more specific clause could be drafted that sets out the maximum permitted weight in terms of kilograms per square metre.

4-6.2   *Protection of the ceiling*

The Tenant must not, without the consent of the Landlord, suspend anything from the ceiling of the Premises.

4-6.3   *Expert advice*

If the Tenant applies for the Landlord's consent under paragraph 4-6.2 PROTECTION OF THE CEILING, the Landlord may consult any engineer or other person in relation to the loading proposed by the Tenant, and the Tenant must repay the fees of the engineer or other person to the Landlord on demand.

4-7   Loading and unloading

4-7.1   *Loading bays to be used*

The Tenant must not load or unload any goods or materials from any vehicle unless the vehicle is parked in the loading bay coloured *(state colour, eg brown)* on the Plan, and must not cause congestion of that or any adjoining loading bays or inconvenience to any other user of it or them[234].

234   Landlords of shopping centres frequently insist that deliveries are made through the service areas and not through the shop.

[1500]

4-7.2   *Standing vehicles*

The Tenant must not permit any vehicles belonging to him or any persons calling on the Premises expressly or by implication with his authority to stand on the service roads [or any pavements] or, except when and for so long as they are actually loading or unloading goods and materials, on the loading bays, and must [use his best endeavours to] ensure that such persons do not permit any vehicle so to stand.

4-7.3   *Use of goods entrances required*

The Tenant must not convey any goods or materials to or from the Premises except through the entrances and service areas provided for the purpose, and, without prejudice to the generality of the above, must not convey goods or materials through the shopping malls.

4-8   Security, fire alarms and sprinkler

4-8.1   *Entry for servicing and maintenance*

The Tenant must permit persons authorised by the Landlord to enter the Premises upon reasonable notice during the Shop Opening Hours [accompanied by an employee of the Tenant] to service and maintain any security, fire alarm and sprinkler systems in the Centre [provided that the Landlord must cause as little disturbance as possible and must make good any damage caused by such entry].

4-8.2   *Access on security alarm call*

The Tenant must permit persons authorised by the Landlord to have such access to the Premises as may be required in the event of an security alarm call.

4-8.3   *Repair of alarms etc*

The Tenant must maintain, repair and when necessary renew any security, fire alarm, sprinkler and ancillary equipment installed in the Premises.

4-8.4   *Incompatible apparatus*

The Tenant must not install or maintain in the Premises any equipment or apparatus that may adversely affect the performance of any security, fire alarm or sprinkler systems.

4-8.5   *Unauthorised connections*

The Tenant must not make any connection to any security, fire alarm or sprinkler systems without the consent of the Landlord[, whose consent may not be unreasonably withheld [or delayed]].

[4-8.6   *Telephones*

The Tenant must install and maintain a telephone in the Premises.]

[1501]

4-9   Heating, cooling and ventilation

4-9.1   *Interference and additional loading*

The Tenant must not do anything that interferes with the [heating, cooling or ventilation *(or as required)* air conditioning] of the Common Parts or that imposes an additional load on the [heating, cooling or ventilation *(or as required)* air conditioning] plant and equipment.

[4-9.2   *Operation of systems*

During the Shop Opening Hours the Tenant must operate the ventilation equipment in the Premises, which comprises part of the system for the air conditioning of the Centre, in accordance with the [reasonable] regulations made by the Landlord from time to time for that purpose.]

4-10   Plate glass

4-10.1   *Insurance of plate glass*

The Tenant must insure any plate glass against breakage or damage, in a reputable insurance office, for its full reinstatement cost from time to time, and whenever reasonably so required must produce to the Landlord particulars of the policy of insurance and evidence of payment of the current year's premium.

4-10.2   *Reinstatement of plate glass*

Notwithstanding anything to the contrary contained elsewhere in this Lease[235], whenever the whole or any part of the plate glass is broken or damaged the Tenant must as quickly as possible lay out all money received in respect of the insurance of it in reinstating it with new glass of at least the same quality and thickness, and must make good any deficiency in such money.

235   The reference here is to the landlord's obligations under clause 5.6 [1427] REINSTATEMENT AND TERMINATION and the intention is to make clear that the landlord's general obligation to make good does not apply to the plate glass.

4-11   Regulations

The Tenant must comply with all [reasonable] regulations made by the Landlord from time to time for the management of the Centre [and notified to the Tenant in writing][, provided that nothing in the regulations may purport to amend the terms of this Lease and, in the event of any inconsistency between the terms of this Lease and the regulations, the terms of this Lease are to prevail][236].

236   Almost every lease such as this one includes this provision, but only rarely are any regulations made. The tenant should strike out the provision on the basis that he is being asked to accept some unknown commitment. Failing this the tenant should —
        (i)   if the expression 'regulations and restrictions', which seems to be wider than 'regulations' is used, strike out 'and restrictions',
        (ii)   insist that he is formally notified in writing of any regulations that may be made, and
        (iii)   provide that the regulations must always remain subservient to the lease.

[4-12   Fitting out

(consideration should be given to the fitting out works (if any) to be carried out by the tenant: these may be included here or, more appropriately, dealt with in an agreement for lease (see, eg, vol 22(4) (1997 Reissue) LANDLORD AND TENANT (BUSINESS TENANCIES) *Form 400 [7510]) or a licence for alterations (see vol 22(3) (1997 Reissue)* LANDLORD AND TENANT (BUSINESS TENANCIES) *Forms 241 [7203] and 242 [7204]), for examples of fitting out covenants, see vol 22(3) (1997 Reissue)* LANDLORD AND TENANT (BUSINESS TENANCIES) *Forms 173 [6697], 174 [6698])]*

SCHEDULE 5: THE SUBJECTIONS

(insert details)

[1502]

SCHEDULE 6: THE SERVICE CHARGE[237]

6-1   Definitions

In this schedule the terms defined below have the meanings given in this paragraph.

237   As to service charges see vol 22(1) (2003 Reissue) LANDLORD AND TENANT (BUSINESS TENANCIES) Paragraph 247 [1081] et seq. For alternative service charge provisions see vol 22(3) (1997 Reissue) LANDLORD AND TENANT (BUSINESS TENANCIES) Forms 149 [6581]–153 [6649].

6-1.1   *'A financial year'*

References to 'a financial year' are references to the period commencing on *(insert date, eg 1 January)* in any year and ending on *(insert date, eg 31 December)* in the same year or such other annual period as the Landlord in his discretion determines as being that for which his accounts, either generally or in respect of the Centre, are to be made up.

6-1.2   'The Initial Provisional Service Charge'

'The Initial Provisional Service Charge means the sum of £... a year.

6-1.3   'The Management Premises'

'The Management Premises' means all the administrative and control offices and storage areas, staff rooms and other areas maintained by the Landlord for the purpose of managing the Centre and performing the Landlord's obligations under this Lease together with any living accommodation provided by the Landlord for security guards, caretakers or other staff employed by him for purposes connected with the Centre.

6-1.4   'Other lettable premises'

References to 'other lettable premises' are references to premises in the Centre that are let, or are from time to time allocated for letting, by the Landlord, other than the Premises, and respectively include and exclude, where applicable, the equivalent parts of the Centre included in and excluded from the Premises as described in clause 1.37 THE PREMISES.

[1503]

6-1.5   'The Plant'

'The Plant' means all the electrical, mechanical and other plant, machinery, equipment, furnishings, furniture, fixtures and fittings of ornament or utility in use for common benefit from time to time on, in or at the Centre, including, without prejudice to the generality of the foregoing, goods and passenger lifts, lift shafts, escalators, passenger conveyors, [heating, cooling, lighting and ventilation *(or as required)* air conditioning] equipment, cleaning equipment, internal and public telephones, public address systems, fire precaution equipment, fire and burglar alarm systems, closed circuit television, refuse compactors and all other such equipment, including stand-by and emergency systems.

6-1.6   'The Retained Parts'

'The Retained Parts' means the parts of the Centre that are not let, or constructed or adapted for letting, including, but without prejudice to the generality of the foregoing, the Common Parts and such parts of the main structure, walls, foundations and roofs of the Centre as are not included in the Premises and would not be included in premises demised by leases of the other units in the Centre if let on the same terms as this Lease, and also including office accommodation for the Centre manager and any ancillary staff.

6-2   Service charge provisions

6-2.1   Certificate of the Landlord's Expenses

As soon as reasonably practicable[238] after each financial year the Landlord must ensure that the Accountant issues a certificate containing a summary of the Landlord's Expenses for that financial year, and a summary of any expenditure that formed part of the Landlord's Expenses in respect of a previous financial year but has not been taken into account in the certificate for any previous financial year. A copy of the certificate must be supplied by the Landlord to the Tenant.

---

238   Time is not normally of the essence in relation to the preparation of the service charge account: see vol 22(1) (2003 Reissue) LANDLORD AND TENANT (BUSINESS TENANCIES) Paragraph 271 [1125]. As to certification of expenses see vol 22(1) (2003 Reissue) LANDLORD AND TENANT (BUSINESS TENANCIES) Paragraph 274 [1129].

[1504]

6-2.2   *Omissions from the certificate*

Omission by the Accountant to include in a certificate of the Landlord's Expenses any expenditure incurred in the financial year to which the certificate relates is not to preclude the inclusion of that expenditure in any subsequent certificate.

6-2.3   *Deemed Landlord's Expenses*

In any financial year the Landlord's Expenses are to be deemed to include not only the costs and expenses actually paid or incurred by the Landlord during that year, but also —

6-2.3.1   such fair and reasonable part of all costs and expenditure in respect of or incidental to all or any of the recurring services and other matters referred to in paragraph 6-3, whenever paid or incurred whether before or during the Term — including reasonable provision for anticipated expenditure[239] — as the Surveyor in his reasonable discretion allocates to that financial year as being fair and reasonable, and

6-2.3.2   an amount equal to the fair annual rental value of the Management Premises, as certified by the Surveyor acting reasonably[, whose decision is to be conclusive],

and if the Landlord or a person connected with the Landlord or employed by the Landlord attends to (1) the supervision and management of the provision of services for the Centre[240], and/or (2) the preparation of statements or certificates of the Landlord's Expenses, and/or (3) the auditing of the Landlord's Expenses, and/or (4) the collection of rents from the Centre, then an expense is to be deemed to be paid or a cost incurred by the Landlord, being a reasonable fee not exceeding that which independent agents might properly have charged for the same work.

239   As to sinking funds see vol 22(1) (2003 Reissue) LANDLORD AND TENANT (BUSINESS TENANCIES) Paragraphs 280 [1138], 282 [1140].

240   As to recovery of management costs see vol 22(1) (2003 Reissue) LANDLORD AND TENANT (BUSINESS TENANCIES) Paragraph 263 [1107].

[1505]

6-2.4   *Certificates conclusive*[241]

Any certificate of the Landlord's Expenses, and any certificate given by the Surveyor or Accountant in connection with the Landlord's Expenses, is to be conclusive as to the matters it purports to certify.

241   As to conclusivity of certificates see vol 22(1) (2003 Reissue) LANDLORD AND TENANT (BUSINESS TENANCIES) Paragraph 275 [1131].

6-2.5   *Payment*

For each financial year the Tenant must pay the Service Charge Percentage of the Landlord's Expenses.

6-2.6   *Variation of the Service Charge Percentage*

The Service Charge Percentage may be varied to the extent that the Surveyor fairly and reasonably considers appropriate.

6-2.7   *Landlord's contribution*

The Landlord is to have no liability to contribute to the Landlord's Expenses except in relation to any other lettable premises for which no contribution is payable by an occupier or other person.

[1506]

6-2.8   *Payment on account*²⁴²

For each financial year the Tenant must pay to the Landlord on account of the Service Charge such a sum as the Surveyor certifies to be fair and reasonable having regard to the likely amount of the Service Charge. That sum must be paid in advance, without deduction or set off, by equal instalments on the usual quarter days, the first instalment to be paid on the quarter day immediately before the commencement of the financial year in question. During any financial year the Surveyor may revise the contribution on account of the Service Charge for that financial year so as to take into account any actual or expected increase in expenditure, and as soon as reasonably practicable after such revision the Surveyor must certify the amount of the revised contribution.

242   As to payment on account see vol 22(1) (2003 Reissue) LANDLORD AND TENANT (BUSINESS TENANCIES) Paragraph 272 [1126].

6-2.9   *Service charge for the first financial year*

The sum payable for the financial year current at the date of this document is to be the Initial Provisional Service Charge, of which the Tenant must, on the date of this document, pay to the Landlord a due proportion calculated from day to day in respect of the period from [the Rent Commencement Date *(or as required)*] to the next quarter day after the date of this document.

6-2.10   *Final account and adjustments*²⁴³

As soon as reasonably practicable after the end of each financial year, the Landlord must furnish the Tenant with an account of the Service Charge payable by him for that financial year, credit being given for payments made by the Tenant on account. Within *(state period, eg 7 days)* of the furnishing of such an account, the Tenant must pay the Service Charge, or any balance of it payable, to the Landlord. The Landlord must allow any amount overpaid by the Tenant to him against future payments of the Service Charge, whether on account or not. At the end of the financial year current at the end of the Term the Landlord must repay to the Tenant any outstanding overpayment of the Service Charge.

243   As to the tenant's concerns on adjustments see vol 22(1) (2003 Reissue) LANDLORD AND TENANT (BUSINESS TENANCIES) Paragraph 272 [1126].

[1507]

6-3   The Services²⁴⁴

The Services are —

6-3.1   repairing²⁴⁵ — and, whenever the Landlord, acting reasonably, regards it as necessary in order to repair, replacing or renewing — and decorating the Retained Parts,

6-3.2   operating, maintaining, repairing and, whenever the Landlord, acting reasonably, considers it appropriate, renewing, replacing or modifying the Plant²⁴⁶,

6-3.3   placing and running maintenance contracts for the Centre,

6-3.4   providing the Plant that the Landlord, acting reasonably, considers necessary or desirable, or that is required by law or by any government department or local, public or regulatory or other authority or court to be supplied and maintained, including the initial capital expenditure and expenditure on replacement of any machinery — including motor vehicles — articles and materials for, for example, refuse collection and fire fighting,

6-3.5   providing suitable facilities for disposing of rubbish, compacting it or removing it from the Centre,

6-3.6   supplying hot and cold water to the lavatory facilities in the Common Parts during normal business hours, and providing towels, soap, toilet paper and other appropriate supplies, [and staffing the lavatory facilities,]

6-3.7   providing reasonable lighting in the Common Parts,

6-3.8   providing reasonable central heating [and air conditioning] to the Premises and the Common Parts[247] during the Shop Opening Hours and the *(state period, eg 30 minutes)* immediately preceding and the *(state period, eg 30 minutes)* immediately following the Shop Opening Hours,

6-3.9   cleaning the windows and other glass of the Common Parts,

[1508]

6-3.10   supplying, maintaining, servicing and keeping in good condition and, wherever the Landlord considers it appropriate, renewing and replacing all fixtures, fittings, furnishings, bins, receptacles, tools, appliances, equipment, door furniture, floor coverings and any other things the Landlord may consider desirable for performing the Services or for the appearance or upkeep of the Retained Parts,

6-3.11   carrying out inspections and tests of the Retained Parts, including the Plant, that the Landlord from time to time considers necessary or desirable,

6-3.12   planting, tidying, tending and landscaping any appropriate part of the Common Parts in such manner as the Landlord from time to time considers appropriate,

6-3.13   providing, replacing and renewing trees, shrubs, flowers, grass and other plants, flags, decorative lights and other decorations, decorative or drinking fountains or other amenities that the Landlord from time to time thinks fit to provide or maintain in the Centre, and providing, maintaining, replacing and renewing seats or benches in the Common Parts,

6-3.14   employing such persons as the Landlord, acting reasonably, considers necessary or desirable from time to time in connection with providing any of the Services, providing caretaking, porterage, security, administration, management and supervision, performing the Landlord's other obligations in this Lease and collecting rents accruing to the Landlord from the Centre, with all incidental expenditure including, but without limiting the generality of the above, remuneration, payment of statutory contributions and such other health, pension, welfare, redundancy and similar or ancillary payments and any other payments the Landlord, acting reasonably, thinks desirable or necessary, and providing work clothing[248],

6-3.15   discharging any amounts the Landlord may be liable to pay towards the expense of making, repairing, maintaining, rebuilding and cleaning anything— for example ways, roads, pavements, sewers, drains, pipes, watercourses, party walls, party structures, party fences and other conveniences — that are appurtenant to the Centre or are used for the Centre in common with any other adjoining property of the Landlord,

6-3.16   erecting, providing, maintaining, renewing and replacing such notice boards, notices and other signs and directions in the Centre as the Landlord, acting reasonably, from time to time considers appropriate,

6-3.17   administering and managing the Centre[249], performing the Services, performing the Landlord's other obligations in this Lease and preparing statements or certificates of and auditing the Landlord's Expenses,

[1509]

6-3.18   providing and performing all services of any kind whatsoever that the Landlord, acting reasonably, from time to time provides and all additional or substitute services that the Landlord provides pursuant to clause 4.2.3 VARIATION AND WITHHOLDING OF THE SERVICES[250],

6-3.19   discharging all existing or future taxes, rates, charges, duties, assessments, impositions and outgoings whatsoever in respect of the Retained Parts, including, without prejudice to the generality of the above, those for water, electricity, gas and telecommunications,

6-3.20   policing the Centre, controlling traffic and pedestrians and providing such security staff as the Landlord, acting reasonably, from time to time thinks fit and proper, and providing, maintaining, replacing and renewing security equipment in the Centre,

6-3.21   paying any interest on any loan or overdraft raised for the purpose of defraying the Landlord's Expenses[251],

6-3.22   taking any steps the Landlord, acting reasonably, from time to time considers appropriate for complying with, making representations against, or otherwise contesting or dealing with any statutory or other obligation affecting or alleged to affect the Centre, including any notice, regulation or order of any government department, local, public, regulatory or other authority or court, compliance with which is not the direct liability of the Tenant or any tenant of any part of the Centre[252],

6-3.23   promoting the Centre including, without prejudice to the generality of the foregoing, advertising in any form of media, sponsorship, staging or organising of events promoting the Centre and other activities designed to promote the Centre and the interests of its occupants, and employing advertising agents and other consultants,

6-3.24   discharging the reasonable and proper cost of any service or matter the Landlord, acting reasonably, thinks proper for the better and more efficient management and use of the Centre and the comfort and convenience of its occupants[253],

6-3.25   renting any item used for carrying out any of the matters referred to in this schedule,

6-3.26   keeping the malls and other public pedestrian ways of the Centre open to the general public during the Shop Opening Hours and the *(state period, eg 30 minutes)* immediately preceding and the *(state period, eg 30 minutes)* immediately following the Shop Opening Hours[254],

6-3.27   keeping appropriate areas of the Common Parts open for servicing the Premises and other units in the Centre from *(time)* to *(time)*, and

6-3.28   abating any nuisance affecting the Centre, except to the extent that abating the nuisance is the liability of any tenant of the Centre[255].

[1510]

244   This is a comprehensive list of services. Not all may be appropriate to the particular building concerned. The draftsman should tailor the list to reflect the nature of the building, the manner in which it is being divided and the proposed occupancy arrangements.

   As to the standard of performance see vol 22(1) (2003 Reissue) LANDLORD AND TENANT (BUSINESS TENANCIES) Paragraph 256 [1095].

245   As to the position regarding inherent defects see vol 22(1) (2003 Reissue) LANDLORD AND TENANT (BUSINESS TENANCIES) Paragraph 258 [1099].

246   As to plant and machinery see vol 22(1) (2003 Reissue) LANDLORD AND TENANT (BUSINESS TENANCIES) Paragraph 261 [1103].

247   As to the provision of hot water and heating see vol 22(1) (2003 Reissue) LANDLORD AND TENANT (BUSINESS TENANCIES) Paragraph 260 [1102].

248   The landlord performs the services either by means of third parties whose fee he pays and has reimbursed by the tenants, or by his own staff. In the latter case the landlord needs to be able to include the cost of employing the staff as part of the service charge. If there are managing agents, the landlord may also welcome the flexibility of being able to charge a fee for any services that they perform 'in-house' where this is more practical than charging the cost of employing the relevant individuals. As to the description of the duties of staff see vol 22(1) (2003 Reissue) LANDLORD AND TENANT (BUSINESS TENANCIES) Paragraph 262 [1105].

249   If management and administration costs are to be recovered, there must be express references in the lease: see vol 22(1) (2003 Reissue) LANDLORD AND TENANT (BUSINESS TENANCIES) Paragraph 263 [1107].

250   As to 'sweeping-up' clauses and the tenant's concerns see vol 22(1) (2003 Reissue) LANDLORD AND TENANT (BUSINESS TENANCIES) Paragraph 267 [1113].

251   As to recovery of interest payments see vol 22(1) (2003 Reissue) LANDLORD AND TENANT (BUSINESS TENANCIES) Paragraph 265 [1111].

252   The tenant should ensure that any clause entitling the landlord to be reimbursed for the cost of complying with, making representations against or contesting the provisions of any regulation or other provisions that apply to the premises is qualified so that he must act reasonably.

253   As to 'sweeping-up' clauses and the tenant's concerns see vol 22(1) (2003 Reissue) LANDLORD AND TENANT (BUSINESS TENANCIES) Paragraph 267 [1113].

254   As to restrictions on hours of use see vol 22(1) (2003 Reissue) LANDLORD AND TENANT (BUSINESS TENANCIES) Paragraph 174 [870].

255   The tenant should consider restricting this to nuisances affecting parts of the centre including the premises or items used by the tenant.

[1511]

SCHEDULE 7: THE AUTHORISED GUARANTEE AGREEMENT

(insert the form of authorised guarantee agreement: see, eg vol 22(3) (1997 Reissue) LANDLORD AND TENANT (BUSINESS TENANCIES) *Form 217 [7053])*

(signature (or common seal) of landlord: lease)
(signature (or common seal) of tenant (and guarantor): counterpart)
(signatures of witnesses)
[1512]–[1600]

3: OFFICES

11

Lease of the whole of an office building, with or without land, where the landlord does not own adjoining property[1]

CONTENTS

(NB: numbers in [ ] below refer to this volume and should be altered to suit the page or reference numbers actually used)

1 DEFINITIONS AND INTERPRETATION

1.1 'The Conduits' . . . . [1608]
1.2 'The [Contractual] Term' . . . . [1609]
1.3 'Development' . . . . [1610]
[1.4 'The Exterior Decorating Years' . . . . [1610]]
1.5 Gender and number . . . . [1610]
1.6 Headings . . . . [1610]
[1.7 'The Initial Rent' . . . . [1610]]
1.8 'The Insurance Rent' . . . . [1611]
1.9 'The Insured Risks' . . . . [1611]
1.10 'Interest' . . . . [1612]
1.11 'The Interest Rate' . . . . [1612]
[1.12 'The Interior Decorating Years' . . . . [1612]]
1.13 Interpretation of 'consent' and 'approved' . . . . [1612]
1.14 Interpretation of 'the Guarantor' . . . . [1613]
                                                                         [1601]
1.15 Interpretation of 'the Landlord' . . . . [1613]
1.16 Interpretation of 'the last year of the Term' and 'the end of the Term' . . . [1613]
1.17 Interpretation of 'the Tenant' . . . . [1613]
1.18 Interpretation of 'this Lease' . . . . [1614]
1.19 Joint and several liability . . . . [1614]
1.20 'The Liability Period' . . . . [1614]
1.21 'Losses' . . . . [1615]
1.22 'The 1954 Act' . . . . [1615]
1.23 'The 1995 Act' . . . . [1615]
1.24 Obligation not to permit or suffer . . . . [1615]
1.25 'The Office Covenants' . . . . [1616]
1.26 'The Permitted Use' . . . . [1616]
1.27 'The Plan' . . . . [1616]
1.28 'The Planning Acts' . . . . [1616]
1.29 'The Premises' . . . . [1617]
1.30 References to clauses and schedules . . . . [1618]
1.31 References to rights of access . . . . [1618]
1.32 References to statutes . . . . [1618]
1.33 'The Rent' . . . . [1618]
1.34 'The Rent Commencement Date' . . . . [1618]
[1.35 'The Review Dates' . . . . [1619]]
1.36 'The Surveyor' . . . . [1619]

[1.37 'The Term' . . . . [1620]]
1.38 Terms from the 1995 Act . . . . [1620]
1.39 'VAT' . . . . [1620

2 DEMISE . . . . [1641]

[1602]

3 THE TENANT'S COVENANTS

3.1 Rent . . . . [1642]
3.2 Outgoings and VAT . . . . [1643]
[3.3 Cost of services consumed . . . . [1643]]
3.4 Repair, cleaning and decoration . . . . [1644
3.5 Waste and alterations . . . . [1647]
3.6 Aerials, signs and advertisements . . . . [1648]
3.7 Statutory obligations . . . . [1649]
3.8 Entry to inspect and notice to repair . . . . [1650]
3.9 Alienation . . . . [1671]
3.10 Nuisance and residential restrictions . . . . [1682]
3.11 Costs of applications, notices and recovery of arrears . . . . [1683]
3.12 Planning and development . . . . [1684]
3.13 Plans, documents and . . . . [1686]
3.14 Indemnities . . . . [1686]
3.15 Reletting boards and viewing . . . . [1687]
3.16 Obstruction and encroachment . . . . [1687]
3.17 Yielding up . . . . [1688]
3.18 Interest on arrears . . . . [1688]
3.19 Statutory notices . . . . [1688]
3.20 Keyholders . . . . [1689]
3.21 Viewing on sale of reversion . . . . [1689]
3.22 Defective premises . . . . [1689]
3.23 Replacement guarantor . . . . [1689]
3.24 Exercise of the Landlord's rights . . . . [1690]
3.25 The Office Covenants . . . . [1690]
3.26 Costs of grant of this Lease . . . . [1690]
3.27 Consent to the Landlord's release . . . . [1691]

4 QUIET ENJOYMENT . . . . [1701]

5 INSURANCE

5.1 Warranty as to convictions . . . . [1702]
5.2 Covenant to insure . . . . [1703]
5.3 Details of the insurance . . . . [1703]
5.4 Payment of the Insurance Rent . . . . [1705]
5.5 Suspension of the Rent . . . . [1706]
5.6 Reinstatement and termination . . . . [1708]
5.7 Tenant's further insurance covenants . . . . [1712]
[5.8 Landlord's further insurance covenants . . . . [1715]]

[1603]

6 GUARANTEE PROVISIONS
6.1 The Guarantor's covenants . . . . [1731]
[6.2 The Landlord's covenant . . . . [1736]]

7 FORFEITURE . . . . [1737]

8 MISCELLANEOUS
8.1 Exclusion of warranty as to use . . . . [1739]
8.2 Exclusion of third party rights . . . . [1739]
8.3 Representations . . . . [1739]
8.4 Documents under hand . . . . [1740]
8.5 Tenant's property . . . . [1740]
8.6 Compensation on vacating excluded . . . . [1740]
8.7 Notices . . . . [1741]
8.8 [New (or) Old] lease . . . . [1743]
[8.9 Capacity of tenants . . . . [1743]]
[8.10 Exclusion of the 1954 Act Sections 24–28 . . . . [1743]]

SCHEDULE 1: THE RIGHTS RESERVED
1-1 Right of entry to inspect . . . . [1761]
1-2 Access on renewal or rent review . . . . [1761]

SCHEDULE 2: THE RENT AND RENT REVIEW

SCHEDULE 3: THE OFFICE COVENANTS
3-1 Use . . . . [1762]
3-2 Ceiling and floor loading . . . . [1763]
3-3 Machinery . . . . [1763]
3-4 Signs . . . . [1763]

SCHEDULE 4: THE SUBJECTIONS

SCHEDULE 5: THE AUTHORISED GUARANTEE AGREEMENT

[1604]

AGREEMENT

[HM LAND REGISTRY

LAND REGISTRATION ACT 2002

Administrative area	*(insert details)*
Title number out of which lease is granted	*(title number)*
Property let	*(postal address or description)*]

[1605]

THIS LEASE is made the .... day of .... BETWEEN:

(1)   *(name of landlord)* [of *(address)* *(or as appropriate)* the registered office of which is at *(address)*] [Company Registration no ...]² ('the Landlord') [and]

(2)   *(name of tenant)* [of *(address)* *(or as appropriate)* being a company registered in [England and Wales *(or)* Scotland]³ the registered office of which is at *(address)*] [Company Registration no ...] ('the Tenant') [and

(3)   *(name of guarantor)* [of *(address)* *(or as appropriate)* the registered office of which is at *(address)*] [Company Registration no ...] ('the Guarantor')]

[1606]

1   As to stamp duty land tax see the Information Binder: Stamp Duty Land Tax [1].

As to Land Registry Fees see the Information Binder: Property [1]: Property Fees.

On the grant out of an unregistered freehold estate in land of a lease for a term of more than seven years from the date of the grant, application must be made to register the title to the leasehold interest granted: see the Land Registration Act 2002 s 4(1)(c) (37 Halsbury's Statutes (4th Edn) REAL PROPERTY). The tenant must obtain an epitome of title to the freehold reversion, investigate it, and mark it as examined, otherwise he will not be able to be registered with an absolute title: see vol 25(1) (2003 Reissue) LAND REGISTRATION Paragraph 21.1 [132].

If the freehold reversion is registered, the grant of a lease for a term of more than seven years from the date of the grant must be completed by registration: see the Land Registration Act 2002 s 27(2)(b)(i).

As to the form and contents of leases see vol 22(1) (2003 Reissue) LANDLORD AND TENANT (BUSINESS TENANCIES) Paragraph 104 [601] et seq. As to registered land generally see vol 25(1) (2003 Reissue) LAND REGISTRATION. As to registration of title to leases see vol 25(1) (2003 Reissue) LAND REGISTRATION Paragraph 143 [601] et seq.

This is a lease of premises comprising the whole of an office building, with optional clauses for use if any unbuilt-on land is included in the demise. The landlord owns no adjoining premises and no rights are granted or services provided. The tenant is responsible for the repair of the premises and the decoration of both the exterior and the interior. The landlord insures the premises and the tenant refunds the cost of the premiums. There is provision for rent review, and also for a guarantor.

2   If any party is a company it is desirable to include the company registration number. This avoids any problems arising when a company has been wound up and a new company formed with the same name, or when the name of a company is changed, or if companies swap names, eg on a reconstruction of a group of companies. In addition, where a company applies to be registered as proprietor of a registered estate or registered charge, the application must state the company's registration number: see the Land Registration Rules 2003, SI 2003/1417 r 181.

3   Where the tenant is a company registered in England and Wales or Scotland, and the lease is registrable, an application for first registration of the lease (where the landlord's title is unregistered), or registration of the lease as a registrable disposition (where the landlord's title is registered), and the tenant as proprietor of the leasehold title, must state the company's registered number: see SI 2003/1417 r 181(1). There seems to be no reason why the certificate and statement should not be contained in the disposition in favour of the proprietor, where convenient.

[1607]

NOW THIS DEED WITNESSES as follows:

1   DEFINITIONS AND INTERPRETATION

For all purposes of this Lease[4] the terms defined in this clause have the meanings specified.

4   One view would add 'unless the context otherwise requires' or 'where the context so admits' and in fact this may be implied (see *Meux v Jacobs* (1875) LR 7 HL 481 at 493; *Law Society v United Service Bureau Ltd* [1934] 1 KB 343, DC) but the better course is to use defined terms in such a way that there are no circumstances where the defined meaning does not apply.

1.1   'The Conduits'

'The Conduits' means the pipes, sewers, drains, mains, ducts, conduits, gutters, watercourses, wires, cables, [laser optical fibres, data or impulse transmission, communication or reception systems,] channels, flues and all other conducting media — including any fixings, louvres, cowls, covers and any other ancillary apparatus — that are in, on, over or under the Premises.

[1608]

1.2   'The [Contractual] Term'[5]

'The [Contractual][6] Term' means *(insert number)* years commencing on and including *(date of commencement of term)*[7].

5   As to the commencement of the term see vol 22(1) (2003 Reissue) LANDLORD AND TENANT (BUSINESS TENANCIES) Paragraph 135 [670].
    As to registration see note 1 above. Where the landlord's title is unregistered, the grantee must apply for registration within a period of two months from the date of the disposition if the lease is granted for a term of more than seven years. If no such application is made the disposition becomes void as regards any transfer, grant or creation of a legal estate: see the Land Registration Act 2002 s 6. Where the landlord's title is registered and the lease is for a term of more than seven years, the tenant should protect the intended lease by applying for an official search, and an application to register the lease should be made before expiry of the search, otherwise the lease will be susceptible to loss of priority: see the Land Registration Act 2002 s 27.

6   The demise in this lease is for 'the Contractual Term', which is defined as a fixed term of years. The expression 'the Term', as defined in clause 1.37 [1620] 'THE TERM', is used in covenants so that they continue to apply during any period of holding over or continuance or extension of the contractual term. Some difficulties arise if this structure is used in a draft lease where security of tenure is to be excluded under the Landlord and Tenant Act 1954 s 38A(1) as inserted by SI 2003/3096 (23 Halsbury's Statutes (4th Edn) LANDLORD AND TENANT). The demise is for the contractual term and the inclusion of the definition of 'the Term' does not prevent the lease being 'for a term of years certain' as required by the Landlord and Tenant Act 1954 s 38A(1). However, reference to continuance of the contractual term by statute is inappropriate where the operation of the security of tenure provisions in the Landlord and Tenant Act 1954 ss 24–28 is to be excluded. If a lease is contracted out of the Landlord and Tenant Act 1954 there can be no statutory extension, and if the tenant remains in occupation at the end of the contractual term he is holding over unlawfully unless there is an express agreement to extend the contractual term operating as a surrender and re-grant so that the original lease— and the agreement under the Landlord and Tenant Act 1954 s 38A(1) — has no further effect. It is suggested that in these circumstances the drafting should be simplified to include a single term (defined simply as 'the Term') by reference to the period of the contractual term. This can be achieved by amending this clause in the manner suggested and substituting it for clause 1.37 [1620] 'THE TERM'.

7   For estate management reasons it is usually desirable to insert a quarter day here — or a rent day when rent is due on days other than quarter days — ie generally the one preceding the earlier of the date of possession and the date of execution.

[1609]

1.3   'Development'

References to 'development' are references to development as defined by the Town and Country Planning Act 1990 Section 55.

[1.4   'The Exterior Decorating Years'

'The Exterior Decorating Years' means *(specify years)*.] *(omit if not required, eg if the first alternative in clause 3.4.6 [1646] DECORATION is used)*

1.5   Gender and number

Words importing one gender include all other genders; words importing the singular include the plural and vice versa[8].

8   See the Law of Property Act 1925 s 61 (37 Halsbury's Statutes (4th Edn) REAL PROPERTY).

1.6   Headings[9]

The clause, paragraph and schedule headings and the table of contents do not form part of this document and are not to be taken into account in its construction or interpretation. *(amend if marginal notes are used)*

9   Headings and marginal notes require the draftsman to provide a word or two to describe every clause in the lease. This is not always easy and there are times when the draftsman will have to settle for something less than perfection, the only alternative being a heading or note that would be inappropriately long. It would be quite wrong for that title, which its author might admit was not totally apposite but was the best that he could do in a few words, to be used in construing the clause in question.

[1.7   'The Initial Rent'

'The Initial Rent' means [the sum of £... a year *(or as required by the rent and review provisions to be used)*].] *(this definition is not required if the rent is not reviewable)*

[1610]

1.8   'The Insurance Rent'[10]

'The Insurance Rent' means the [gross sums including any commission *(or as required)* sums net of any commission] that the Landlord from time to time pays —

1.8.1   by way of premium for insuring the Premises, including insuring for loss of rent, in accordance with his obligations contained in this Lease,

1.8.2   by way of premium for insuring in such amount and on such terms as [the Landlord acting reasonably considers appropriate *(or as required)* is reasonable] against all liability of the Landlord to third parties arising out of or in connection with any matter including or relating to the Premises, and

1.8.3   for insurance valuations.

10   As to reimbursement of insurance premiums see vol 22(1) (2003 Reissue) LANDLORD AND TENANT (BUSINESS TENANCIES) Paragraph 230 [1026].

1.9   'The Insured Risks'

'The Insured Risks' means the risks of loss or damage by fire[, storm, tempest, earthquake, lightning, explosion, riot, civil commotion, malicious damage, [terrorism,] impact by vehicles and by aircraft and articles dropped from aircraft—other than war risks — flood damage and bursting and overflowing of water pipes and tanks,] and such other risks, whether or not in the nature of the foregoing, as the Landlord [acting reasonably] from time to time decides to insure against[11].

11   As to the risks to be insured and the tenant's concerns see vol 22(1) (2003 Reissue) LANDLORD AND TENANT (BUSINESS TENANCIES) Paragraph 235 [1033].

[1611]

1.10   'Interest'

• References to 'interest' are references to interest payable during the period from the date on which the payment is due to the date of payment, both before and after any judgment, at the Interest Rate then prevailing [*(where the interest rate is defined by reference to a bank base rate)* or, should the base rate referred to in clause 1.11 'THE INTEREST RATE' cease to exist[12], at another rate of interest closely comparable with the Interest Rate [to be agreed between the parties or in default of agreement to be determined by [the Surveyor, acting as an expert and not as an arbitrator *(or as required)* a chartered accountant appointed by agreement between the parties or in default of agreement nominated by the President of the Institute of Chartered Accountants in England and Wales, acting as an expert and not as an arbitrator][13] *(or as required)* decided on by the Landlord acting reasonably]].

12   If base rates are referred to, the possibility of their ceasing to exist should be provided for. Alternatively, the Law Society's interest rate may be specified.

13   This provision may be expanded to provide for deeming the parties to have disagreed after a certain time, deputy appointors etc.

1.11   'The Interest Rate'

'The Interest Rate'[14] means the rate of ...% a year[15] above [the base lending rate of *(specify bank)* or such other bank [being a member of the British Bankers Association] as the Landlord from time to time nominates in writing[16] *(or as required)* the Law Society's interest rate[17]].

14   As to the covenant to pay interest see vol 22(1) (2003 Reissue) LANDLORD AND TENANT (BUSINESS TENANCIES) Paragraph 154 [767].
15   Words such as 'with a minimum of ...%' should not be used because, if interest rates drop during the term to such an extent that the minimum rate specified represents significantly more than a few percent over the basic borrowing rate, the provision might be void as a penalty. As to what amounts to a penalty see *Dunlop Pneumatic Tyre Co Ltd v New Garage and Motor Co Ltd* [1915] AC 79, HL; *Cellulose Acetate Silk Co Ltd v Widnes Foundry (1925) Ltd* [1933] AC 20, HL. In view of this, landlords would be unwise to provide for a rate of more than a few percent over base rate, and even this is in fact a penalty rate and should be resisted by the tenant.
16   The chance to change the bank may be useful, especially on a sale of the reversion, so that the landlord can always provide for his bank for the time being to be specified. The tenant should try to limit the choice to major clearing banks.
17   The Law Society's interest rate is published weekly in the Law Society's Gazette.

[1.12   'The Interior Decorating Years'

'The Interior Decorating Years' means *(specify years).*] *(omit if not required, eg if the first alternative in clause 3.4.6 [1646] DECORATION is used)*

1.13   Interpretation of 'consent' and 'approved'

1.13.1   *Prior written consent or approval*

References to 'consent of the Landlord' or words to similar effect are references to a prior written consent signed by or on behalf of the Landlord and references to the need for anything to be 'approved by the Landlord' or words to similar effect are references to the need for a prior written approval by or on behalf of the Landlord.

[1612]

1.13.2   *Consent or approval of mortgagee or head landlord*

Any provisions in this Lease referring to the consent or approval of the Landlord are to be construed as also requiring the consent or approval of any mortgagee of the Premises and any head landlord, where that consent is required [under a mortgage or headlease in existence at the date of this document][18]. Nothing in this Lease is to be construed as imposing any obligation on a mortgagee or head landlord not to refuse any such consent or approval unreasonably.

18   The tenant should include these words so that the clause applies *only* where the consent of the mortgagee or head landlord is in fact required under the terms of an *existing* mortgage or headlease. The tenant should request a copy of the document concerned to establish the rights of the mortgagee or head landlord in relation to any consents that he may seek. The risk to the tenant of the clause without these words is that, by subsequently creating a mortgage or headlease, the landlord could, innocently or deliberately, bring about a situation where his consent may be refused in circumstances in which it would otherwise have been unreasonable to do so. In particular, the effect on the tenant's ability to assign or sublet could be serious.

1.14   Interpretation of 'the Guarantor'[19]

The expression 'the Guarantor' includes [*(where there is a guarantor for the original tenant)* not only the person named above as the Guarantor, but also][20] any person who enters into covenants with the Landlord pursuant to clause 3.9.5.2 CONDITIONS or clause 3.23 REPLACEMENT GUARANTOR.

19   As to guarantors see vol 22(1) (2003 Reissue) LANDLORD AND TENANT (BUSINESS TENANCIES) Paragraphs 40 [201], 71 [278] et seq.
20   Where there is no guarantor for the original tenant, if it is felt undesirable to have covenants in a lease and no party, at least initially, to enter into them, the guarantor's covenants could be included in a schedule.

1.15   Interpretation of 'the Landlord'

The expression 'the Landlord' includes the person or persons from time to time entitled to possession of the Premises when this Lease comes to an end.

1.16   Interpretation of 'the last year of the Term' and 'the end of the Term'

References to 'the last year of the Term' are references to the actual last year of the Term howsoever it determines, and references to the 'end of the Term' are references to the end of the Term whensoever and howsoever it determines.

1.17   Interpretation of 'the Tenant'

'The Tenant' includes any person who is for the time being bound by the tenant covenants of this Lease except where the name of *(name of original tenant)* appears.

[1613]

1.18   Interpretation of 'this Lease'

Unless expressly stated to the contrary, the expression 'this Lease' includes any document supplemental to or collateral with this document or entered into in accordance with this document.

1.19   Joint and several liability

Where any party to this Lease for the time being comprises two or more persons, obligations expressed or implied to be made by or with that party are deemed to be made by or with the persons comprising that party jointly and severally.

1.20   'The Liability Period'[21]

'The Liability Period' means —

[1.20.1   in the case of *(name of guarantor for the original tenant)*, the period during which *(name of original tenant)* is bound by the tenant covenants of this Lease together with any additional period during which *(name of original tenant)* is liable under an authorised guarantee agreement,] *(omit if there is no guarantor for the original tenant)*

1.20.2   in the case of any guarantor required pursuant to clause 3.9.5.2 CONDITIONS, the period during which the relevant assignee is bound by the tenant covenants of this Lease together with any additional period during which that assignee is liable under an authorised guarantee agreement,

1.20.3   in the case of any guarantor under an authorised guarantee agreement, the period during which the relevant assignee is bound by the tenant covenants of this Lease, and

1.20.4   in the case of any guarantor required pursuant to clause 3.9.8.7 TERMS OF A PERMITTED SUBLEASE, the period during which the relevant assignee of the sublease is bound by the tenant covenants of that sublease.

21   The liability of the guarantor should be expressed to last while the original tenant, or as the case may be the assignee, is bound by the tenant covenants in the lease — or in the case of clause 1.20.4 the sublease — rather than while the lease is vested in that person, to take account of the possibility of an excluded assignment being made and the tenant — or subtenant — remaining liable. An excluded assignment means that the tenant — or subtenant — is precluded from tenant release under the Landlord and Tenant (Covenants) Act 1995 (23 Halsbury's Statutes (4th Edn) LANDLORD AND TENANT).

    The Landlord and Tenant (Covenants) Act 1995 does not clearly indicate whether the liability of a contractual guarantor can be expressed to extend to any period during which the tenant is bound by an authorised guarantee agreement, but the better view is that it is possible. The policy of the Act certainly suggests that this should be the case.

[1614]

1.21 'Losses'

References to 'losses' are references to liabilities, damages or losses, awards of damages or compensation, penalties, costs, disbursements and expenses arising from any claim, demand, action or proceedings.

1.22 'The 1954 Act'

'The 1954 Act' means the Landlord and Tenant Act 1954 [and all statutes, regulations and orders included by virtue of clause 1.32 REFERENCES TO STATUTES][22].

22   The words in square brackets are strictly speaking not required because they merely state what would be the case anyway by virtue of clause 1.32 [1618] REFERENCES TO STATUTES. Nevertheless, as much could turn on the point (see *Brett v Brett Essex Golf Club Ltd* (1986) 52 P & CR 330, [1986] 1 EGLR 154, CA), the parties may prefer to deal expressly with the point.

1.23 'The 1995 Act'

'The 1995 Act' means the Landlord and Tenant (Covenants) Act 1995 [and all statutes, regulations and orders included by virtue of clause 1.32 REFERENCES TO STATUTES][23].

23   See note 22 to clause 1.22 [1615] 'THE 1954 ACT'.

1.24 Obligation not to permit or suffer

Any covenant by the Tenant not to do anything includes an obligation [to use reasonable endeavours] not to permit or suffer[24] that thing to be done by another person [where the Tenant is aware that the thing is being done].

24   'Permit' may have a different meaning from 'suffer': see *Barton v Reed* [1932] 1 Ch 362 at 375 per Luxmore J. A covenant not to 'permit' activity is broken if the covenantor himself carries it on: see *Oceanic Village Ltd v United Attractions Ltd* [2000] Ch 234, [2002] 1 All ER 975.

[1615]

1.25 'The Office Covenants'

'The Office Covenants' mean the covenants set out in schedule 3 THE OFFICE COVENANTS.

1.26 'The Permitted Use'

'The Permitted Use' means use as offices[25].

25   As to use see vol 22(1) (2003 Reissue) LANDLORD AND TENANT (BUSINESS TENANCIES)
      Paragraph 170 [861] et seq.
          In appropriate cases, the landlord may require control over the specific business to be carried on,
      in which case the formula adopted in Form 4 clause 1.26 [167] THE PERMITTED USE should be used,
      amended as appropriate. Valuation advice should be sought regarding the impact on rent review of any
      limitation imposed.

1.27 'The Plan'[26]

'The Plan' means the plan annexed to this Lease.

26   As to the use and role of plans see vol 22(1) (2003 Reissue) LANDLORD AND TENANT (BUSINESS
      TENANCIES) Paragraphs 117 [636], 118 [638]. A plan may not always be required, eg a demise of all
      the land within a registered title. If the lease is registrable, a plan 'for identification purposes only' or
      where there is some other disclaimer as to the extent to which it can be relied on for conveyancing
      purposes is not sufficient if part of the land in a registered title is being dealt with.

1.28 'The Planning Acts'

'The Planning Acts' means the Town and Country Planning Act 1990, the Planning
(Listed Buildings and Conservation Areas) Act 1990, the Planning (Consequential
Provisions) Act 1990, the Planning (Hazardous Substances) Act 1990, the Planning and
Compensation Act 1991, the Planning and Compulsory Purchase Act 2004 [and all
statutes, regulations and orders included by virtue of clause 1.32 REFERENCES TO
STATUTES][27].

27   See note 22 to clause 1.22 [1615] 'THE 1954 ACT'.

[1616]

1.29 'The Premises'[28]

1.29.1 *Definition of 'the Premises'*

'The Premises' means the land and building known as *(insert postal address)* [shown [for
the purpose of identification only] edged *(state colour, eg red)* on the Plan].

28   As to parcels generally see vol 22(1) (2003 Reissue) LANDLORD AND TENANT (BUSINESS
      TENANCIES) Paragraph 116 [634].

1.29.2 *Interpretation of 'the Premises'*[29]

The expression 'the Premises' includes —

1.29.1   all buildings, erections, structures, fixtures[30], fittings and appurtenances on the
          Premises from time to time,

1.29.2   all additions, alterations and improvements carried out during the Term, and

1.29.3   the Conduits,

but excludes [the air space above[31] and] any fixtures installed by the Tenant [or any
predecessors in title] that can be removed from the Premises without defacing the
Premises. Unless the contrary is expressly stated, 'the Premises' includes any part or parts
of the Premises.

29   As to implied grants and reservations see vol 22(1) (2003 Reissue) LANDLORD AND TENANT (BUSINESS TENANCIES) Paragraph 125 [650].

30   As to fixtures see vol 22(1) (2003 Reissue) LANDLORD AND TENANT (BUSINESS TENANCIES) Paragraph 121 [644].

31   As to air space, subsoil, cellars and footings see vol 22(1) (2003 Reissue) LANDLORD AND TENANT (BUSINESS TENANCIES) Paragraph 119 [640]. Strictly speaking, this exclusion means that the tenant may not go onto the roof to inspect or repair it unless he is held to have an easement of necessity to do so. As to easements of necessity generally see 13 Halsbury's Laws (4th Edn Reissue) EASEMENTS AND PROFITS À PRENDRE. If the landlord requires the upper limit of the demised premises to be defined, the tenant, in the case of a full repairing lease, should require a right to enter the landlord's air space above the demised premises to inspect or repair the upper limit of the premises. For a form that may be modified for this purpose see vol 22(3) (1997 Reissue) LANDLORD AND TENANT (BUSINESS TENANCIES) Form 77 [6452].

[1617]

1.30   References to clauses and schedules

Any reference in this document to a clause, paragraph or schedule without further designation is to be construed as a reference to the clause, paragraph or schedule of this document so numbered.

1.31   References to rights of access

References to any right of the Landlord to have access to the Premises are to be construed as extending to any head landlord and any mortgagee of the Premises [— where the headlease or mortgage grants such rights of access to the head landlord or mortgagee —] and to all persons authorised in writing by the Landlord and any head landlord or mortgagee, including agents, professional advisers, contractors, workmen and others.

1.32   References to statutes

Unless expressly stated to the contrary, any reference to a specific statute includes any statutory extension or modification, amendment or re-enactment of that statute and any regulations or orders made under it, and any general reference to a statute includes any regulations or orders made under that statute[32].

32   Unfortunately the Interpretation Act 1978 ss 17, 23(3) (41 Halsbury's Statutes (4th Edn) STATUTES) does not quite go far enough to enable this clause to be dispensed with altogether, particularly where a statute is modified.

1.33   'The Rent'[33]

[Until the First Review Date 'the Rent' means the Initial Rent. Thereafter 'the Rent' means the sum ascertained in accordance with schedule 2 THE RENT AND RENT REVIEW. 'The Rent' does not include the Insurance Rent[34], but the term 'the Lease Rents' means both the Rent and the Insurance Rent. *(or as required by the rent and review provisions used)*]

33   This clause assumes that the rent is reviewable. If the rent is not reviewable clause 1.7 [1610] 'THE INITIAL RENT' should be omitted and this clause amended as appropriate.

34   Because of this exclusion the insurance rent is not suspended under clause 5.5 [1706] SUSPENSION OF THE RENT.

1.34   'The Rent Commencement Date'

'The Rent Commencement Date' means *(insert the date on which payment of rent is to start)*[35].

35   This provision may be used to provide for a rent-free period, or for the situation where the tenant had possession before the execution of the lease on the basis that rent should be paid from the date of possession. If either the date of execution of the lease or the date of commencement of the term is to be the date for commencement of rent, that date should be inserted here.

[1618]

[1.35 'The Review Dates'[36]

'The First Review Date' means *(date)*. 'The Review Dates' means the First Review Date and every *(insert ordinal, eg 3rd)* anniversary of that date during the [Contractual] Term [*(if appropriate for the review provisions used)* — and any other date from time to time specified under *(insert the relevant provision: see eg vol 22(3) (1997 Reissue)* LANDLORD AND TENANT (BUSINESS TENANCIES) *Form 180 paragraph {2}-4 [6728]* EFFECT OF COUNTER-INFLATION PROVISIONS)]. References to 'a review date' are references to any one of the Review Dates.] *(omit if not required by the review provisions to be used, or if the rent is not reviewable*

36   As to rent review dates and intervals see vol 22(1) (2003 Reissue) LANDLORD AND TENANT (BUSINESS TENANCIES) Paragraph 302 [1333] et seq. Where there might be a statutory continuation of the lease the landlord may wish to ensure that there is a review date shortly before the end of the contractual term to obviate the need to apply for an interim rent. The tenant may wish to insist on the word 'contractual' remaining so that the rent review provisions do not apply during any period of lawful holding over or extension or continuance of the contractual term. In circumstances where there is no prospect of statutory continuation the word 'contractual' should be omitted in any event: see note 6 to clause 1.2 [1609 'THE [CONTRACTUAL] TERM'.

1.36 'The Surveyor'[37]

'The Surveyor' means *(name)* or any person or firm appointed by the Landlord in his place. The Surveyor may be an employee of the Landlord or a company that is a member of the same group as the Landlord within the meaning of the 1954 Act Section 42. The expression 'the Surveyor' includes the person or firm appointed by the Landlord to collect the Lease Rents[38].

37   For a provision that the landlord's surveyor must be a member of a relevant professional body see vol 22(3) (1997 Reissue) LANDLORD AND TENANT (BUSINESS TENANCIES) Form 152 [6648].
38   As to the definition of 'the Lease Rents' see clause 1.33 [1618] 'THE RENT'.

[1619]

[1.37 'The Term'

'The Term' means the Contractual Term and any period of holding-over or extension or continuance of the Contractual Term by statute or common law[39]] *(omit if the lease is to be contracted out of the Landlord and Tenant Act 1954)*[40]

39   The demise in this lease is for 'the Contractual Term', which is defined as a fixed term of years. The expression 'the Term' is used in covenants so that they continue to apply during any period of holding over or continuance or extension of the contractual term. As to the liability of a guarantor during a period of statutory continuation see vol 22(1) (2003 Reissue) LANDLORD AND TENANT (BUSINESS TENANCIES) Paragraph 73 [282].
40   Some difficulties arise if the structure referred to in note 39 above is used in a draft lease where security of tenure is to be excluded under the Landlord and Tenant Act 1954 s 38A(1) as inserted by SI 2003/3096. The demise is for the contractual term and the inclusion of the definition of 'the Term' does not prevent the lease being 'for a term of years certain' as required by the Landlord and Tenant Act 1954 s 38A(1). However, reference to continuance of the contractual term by statute is inappropriate where the operation of the security of tenure provisions in the Landlord and Tenant Act 1954 ss 24–28 is to be excluded. If a lease is contracted out of the Landlord and Tenant Act 1954 there can be no statutory extension, and if the tenant remains in occupation at the end of the contractual term he is holding over unlawfully unless there is an express agreement to extend the contractual term operating as a surrender and re-grant so that the original lease — and the agreement under the Landlord and Tenant Act 1954 s 38A(1) — has no further effect. It is suggested that in these circumstances the drafting should be simplified to include a single term (defined simply as 'the Term') by reference to the period of the contractual term. This can be achieved by amending clause 1.2 [1609] 'THE [CONTRACTUAL] TERM' as suggested and substituting it for this clause.

1.38   Terms from the 1995 Act

Where the expressions 'landlord covenants', 'tenant covenants', or 'authorised guarantee agreement' are used in this Lease they are to have the same meaning as is given by the 1995 Act Section 28(1).

1.39   'VAT'[41]

'VAT' means value added tax or any other tax of a similar nature and, unless otherwise expressly stated, all references to rents or other sums payable by the Tenant are exclusive of VAT.

---

41   As to VAT generally see the Information Binder: Property [1]: VAT and Property.

[1620]–[1640]

2   DEMISE

The Landlord lets[42] the Premises to the Tenant [with [full (or) limited] title guarantee], excepting and reserving to the Landlord the rights specified in schedule 1 THE RIGHTS RESERVED, to hold the Premises to the Tenant for the [Contractual][43] Term, subject to [all rights, easements, privileges, restrictions, covenants and stipulations of whatever nature affecting the Premises including any matters contained or referred to in schedule 4 THE SUBJECTIONS (or as required) the rights, easements, privileges, restrictions, covenants and stipulations affecting the Premises contained or referred to in schedule 4 THE SUBJECTIONS][44], yielding and paying[45] to the Landlord —

2.1   the Rent, without any deduction or set off[46], by equal quarterly payments in advance[47] on the usual quarter days[48] in every year and proportionately for any period of less than a year, the first such payment, being a proportionate sum in respect of the period from and including the Rent Commencement Date to and including the day before the quarter day next after the Rent Commencement Date, to be paid on the date of this document[49], and

2.2   by way of further rent, the Insurance Rent[50], payable on demand in accordance with clause 5.4 PAYMENT OF THE INSURANCE RENT.

---

42   Traditionally, the operative word in a lease executed as a deed was 'demises' but any words sufficient to show the parties' intention may be used.

43   See note 40 to clause 1.37 [1620] 'THE TERM'.

44   The tenant should argue for the second version, making the schedule comprehensive rather than illustrative.

45   The words 'yielding and paying' imply a covenant to pay rent: see *Vyvyan v Arthur* (1823) 1 B & C 410. An express covenant is now invariably included, because further procedural matters are contained in it.

46   As to deductions and set off see vol 22(1) (2003 Reissue) LANDLORD AND TENANT (BUSINESS TENANCIES) Paragraph 147 [753].

47   In the absence of an express provision, rent is payable in arrears.

48   The usual quarter days are 25 March, 24 June, 29 September and 25 December. A reference to 'the usual quarter days' is all that is necessary when rent is to be paid on these days.

49   If the first payment is not a complete instalment, the lease must provide for the date on which it is to be paid, the amount, and the period it is to cover.

50   As to the advantages of reserving the insurance rent as rent see vol 22(1) (2003 Reissue) LANDLORD AND TENANT (BUSINESS TENANCIES) Paragraph 151 [761].

[1641]

3 THE TENANT'S COVENANTS

The Tenant covenants with the Landlord to observe and perform the requirements of this clause 3.

3.1 Rent

3.1.1 *Payment of the Lease Rents*

The Tenant must pay the Lease Rents[51] on the days and in the manner set out in this Lease, and must not exercise or seek to exercise any right or claim to withhold rent, or any right or claim to legal or equitable set-off[52] [except that referred to in *(give details of any provisions granting an express right of set-off)*][53].

51 As to the definition of 'the Lease Rents' see clause 1.33 [1618] 'THE RENT'.
52 See, eg, *British Anzani (Felixstowe) Ltd v International Marine Management (UK) Ltd* [1980] QB 137, [1979] 2 All ER 1063; *Lee-Parker v Izzet* [1971] 3 All ER 1099, [1971] 1 WLR 1688. As to deductions and set-off see vol 22(1) (2003 Reissue) LANDLORD AND TENANT (BUSINESS TENANCIES) Paragraphs 147 [753], 148 [755].
53 If any express right of set-off is granted to the tenant, reference to the provision concerned should be included here to avoid inconsistency.

3.1.2 *Payment by banker's order*[54]

If so required in writing by the Landlord, the Tenant must pay the Lease Rents[55] by banker's order or credit transfer to any bank and account [in the United Kingdom] that the Landlord nominates from time to time.

54 This is a clause with dangers for both parties. If the existence of a breach of covenant is known to the landlord he must instruct his bank to refuse to accept the rent, otherwise his right of forfeiture is lost. As to implied waiver of the right of forfeiture see vol 22(1) (2003 Reissue) LANDLORD AND TENANT (BUSINESS TENANCIES) Paragraph 284 [1173]. The tenant may feel that he requires more control over the payment of rent. In any event, the financial systems operated by many companies prevent payments being made in this way.
55 As to the definition of 'the Lease Rents' see clause 1.33 [1618] 'THE RENT'.

[1642]

3.2 Outgoings and VAT

The Tenant must pay, and must indemnify the Landlord against —

3.2.1 all rates, taxes[56], assessments, duties, charges, impositions and outgoings that are now or may at any time during the Term be charged, assessed or imposed upon the Premises or on the owner or occupier of them[, excluding any payable by the Landlord occasioned by receipt of the Lease Rents[57] or by any disposition of or dealing with this Lease or ownership of any interest reversionary to the interest created by it][58] [— provided that if the Landlord suffers any loss of rating relief that may be applicable to empty premises after the end of the Term because the relief has been allowed to the Tenant in respect of any period before the end of the Term then the Tenant must make good such loss to the Landlord],

3.2.2 all VAT that may from time to time be charged on the Lease Rents or other sums payable by the Tenant under this Lease[59], and

3.2.3 all VAT incurred in relation to any costs that the Tenant is obliged to pay or in respect of which he is required to indemnify the Landlord under the terms of this Lease, save where such VAT is recoverable or available for set-off by the Landlord as input tax[60].

56   As to covenants to pay rates and taxes see vol 22(1) (2003 Reissue) LANDLORD AND TENANT (BUSINESS TENANCIES) Paragraph 153 [765].

57   As to the definition of 'the Lease Rents' see clause 1.33 [1618] 'THE RENT'.

58   The tenant should add the words in square brackets to make it clear that he is not paying the landlord's taxes.

59   As to VAT on rent, service charges and insurance premiums see the Information Binder: Property [1]: VAT and Property.

60   As to payment of VAT on legal costs paid by a person other than the solicitor's own client see the Information Binder: Property [1]: VAT and Property.

[3.3   Cost of services consumed[61]

The Tenant must pay to the suppliers, and indemnify the Landlord against, all charges for electricity, water, gas, telecommunications and other services consumed or used at or in relation to the Premises, including meter rents and standing charges, and must comply with the lawful requirements and regulations of their respective suppliers.] *(omit if the premises have independent supplies of all services)*

61   Where the premises comprise a separate building, a separate supply is usually provided and the tenant makes his own arrangements with the suppliers. In that case this clause is unnecessary.

[1643]

3.4   Repair, cleaning and decoration

3.4.1   *Repair of the Premises*[62]

The Tenant must repair the Premises and keep them in good condition and repair, except for damage caused by one or more of the Insured Risks save to the extent that the insurance money is irrecoverable due to any act or default of the Tenant or anyone at the Premises expressly or by implication[63] with the Tenant's authority [and under his control][64].

62   As to repair see vol 22(1) (2003 Reissue) LANDLORD AND TENANT (BUSINESS TENANCIES) Paragraph 196 [931] et seq. For a covenant to repair, rebuild and renew see vol 22(3) (1997 Reissue) LANDLORD AND TENANT (BUSINESS TENANCIES) Form 85 [6460]. For provisos excluding, eg, work that is prevented etc see vol 22(3) (1997 Reissue) LANDLORD AND TENANT (BUSINESS TENANCIES) Forms 87 [6462], 88 [6463].

      If a landlord is unable to obtain full insurance cover without excess, it should be made clear whether the tenant is to be liable to pay the excess where damage is caused by an insured risk. For a covenant limiting the tenant's repairing obligations by reference to uninsurable as well as insured risks see vol 22(3) (1997 Reissue) LANDLORD AND TENANT (BUSINESS TENANCIES) Form 90 [6465]. It should be noted that it is now recommended 'best practice' that if the premises are so damaged by an uninsured risk as to prevent occupation, the tenant should be allowed to terminate the lease unless the landlord agrees to reinstate at his own cost: see vol 22(1) (2003 Reissue) LANDLORD AND TENANT (BUSINESS TENANCIES) Paragraph 85 [402]. If adopted, this recommendation involves damage preventing occupation caused by uninsured or uninsurable risks being excluded from the ambit of the tenant's repairing covenant.

63   The expression 'by implication' is intended to include a caller on the premises, such as a tradesman, where there has been no express invitation but the person cannot be classed as a trespasser.

64   The tenant should add the words in square brackets.

3.4.2   *Replacement of landlord's fixtures*

The Tenant must replace from time to time any landlord's fixtures and fittings in the Premises that are beyond repair at any time during or at the end of the Term.

3.4.3   *Cleaning and tidying*

The Tenant must keep the Premises clean and tidy and clear of all rubbish.

[1644]

[3.4.4   *The Open Land*

3.4.4.1   Care of the Open Land

The Tenant must keep any part of the Premises that is not built on ('the Open Land') adequately surfaced, in good condition and free from weeds [and must keep all landscaped areas properly cultivated].

3.4.4.2   Storage on the Open Land

The Tenant must not store anything on the Open Land [or bring anything onto it] [that is or might become untidy, unclean, unsightly or in any way detrimental to the Premises or the area generally].

3.4.4.3   Rubbish on the Open Land

The Tenant must not deposit any waste, rubbish or refuse on the Open Land[, or place any receptacle for them, on it].

3.4.4.4   Vehicles on the Open Land

The Tenant must not keep or store any [*(if the land cannot be used for parking)* vehicle,] caravan or movable dwelling on the Open Land.] *(adapt clause 3.4.4 as required in the circumstances, or omit if no open land is included)*

3.4.5   *Care of abutting land*

The Tenant must not cause any land, roads or pavements abutting the Premises to be untidy or dirty and in particular, but without prejudice to the generality of the foregoing, must not deposit refuse or other materials on them.

[1645]

3.4.6   *Decoration*

[The Tenant must redecorate the outside and inside of the Premises, as often as is necessary in the [reasonable] opinion of the Surveyor in order to maintain a high standard of decorative finish and attractiveness and to preserve the Premises and in the last year of the Term, *(or as required)* The Tenant must redecorate the outside of the Premises in each of the External Decorating Years and the last year of the Term and must redecorate the inside of the Premises in each of the Interior Decorating Years and the last year of the Term, in all instances][65] in a good and workmanlike manner, with appropriate materials of good quality[, to the [reasonable] satisfaction of the Surveyor], any change in the tints, colours and patterns of the decoration to be approved by the Landlord[66][, whose approval may not be unreasonably withheld [or delayed]] [, provided that the covenants relating to the last year of the Term are not to apply where the Tenant has performed the obligation in question less than *(state period, eg 18 months)* before the end of the Term].

65   The draftsman should discuss with the landlord and his property advisers whether he wishes to have the flexibility of the first option or the certainty of the second.

66   The tenant may amend to provide for the landlord's approval to tints etc to apply only in the last year of the term.

3.4.7   *Shared facilities*

Where the use of any of the Conduits or any boundary structures or other things is common to the Premises and other property, the Tenant must be responsible for, and indemnify the Landlord against, all sums due from the owner, tenant or occupier of the Premises in relation to those Conduits, boundary structures or other things, and must undertake all work in relation to them that is his responsibility.

[1646]

3.5   Waste and alterations

3.5.1   *Waste, additions and alterations*[67]

The Tenant must not commit any waste, make any addition to the Premises, unite the Premises with any adjoining premises, or make any alteration to the Premises except as permitted by the provisions of this clause 3.5.

67   As to alterations see vol 22(1) (2003 Reissue) LANDLORD AND TENANT (BUSINESS TENANCIES) Paragraph 186 [911] et seq.

3.5.2   *Pre-conditions for alterations*

The Tenant must not make any [internal non-structural] alterations to the Premises unless he first —

3.5.2.1   obtains and complies with the necessary consents of the competent authorities and pays their charges for them,

3.5.2.2   makes an application to the Landlord for consent, supported by drawings and where appropriate a specification in duplicate [prepared by an architect[, or a member of some other appropriate profession,] who must supervise the work throughout to completion],

3.5.2.3   pays the fees of the Landlord, any head landlord, any mortgagee and their respective professional advisers,

3.5.2.4   enters into any covenants the Landlord requires as to the execution and reinstatement of the alterations, and

3.5.2.5   obtains the consent of the Landlord, whose consent may not be unreasonably withheld [or delayed].

[In the case of any works of a substantial nature, the Landlord may require the Tenant to provide, before starting the works, adequate security in the form of a deposit of money or the provision of a bond, as assurance to the Landlord that any works he permits from time to time will be fully completed.]

3.5.3   *Internal partitions*

Without prejudice to the provisions of this clause 3.5, the Tenant may install and remove internal demountable partitions if he gives notice of the works and supplies a plan and specification to the Landlord within one month of completion of the works, consults a qualified services consultant before commencement of the works, and ensures that there is no disruption of the services and supplies in, to and through the Premises.

[1647]

3.5.4   *Removal of alterations*[68]

At the end of the Term, if so requested by the Landlord, the Tenant must remove any additional buildings, additions, alterations or improvements made to the Premises, and must make good any part of the Premises damaged by their removal.

68   This clause has probably come to be inserted because landlords hope that it will defeat the effect of the compensation provisions of the Landlord and Tenant Act 1927 Pt I (ss 1–17) (23 Halsbury's Statutes (4th Edn) LANDLORD AND TENANT) — as to which see vol 22(1) (2003 Reissue) LANDLORD AND TENANT (BUSINESS TENANCIES) Paragraph 192 [923] et seq — because, if the improvement has been removed, it will not be an improvement to the holding at the time of quitting the premises. In fact, the clause might not achieve this effect, because the Landlord and Tenant Act 1927 s 9 as amended by the

Landlord and Tenant Act 1954 s 49 prohibits contracting out. Also, the clause may be void under the Landlord and Tenant Act 1927 s 19(2), so far as it applies to improvements, on the grounds that it purports to fetter the court in deciding what is reasonable. The tenant should not, however, rely on the application of these statutory provisions and should seek to strike the clause out.

3.5.5   *Connection to the Conduits*

The Tenant must not make any connection with the Conduits except in accordance with plans and specifications approved by the Landlord[, whose approval may not be unreasonably withheld [or delayed]], and subject to consent to make the connection having previously been obtained from the competent authority, undertaker or supplier.

3.6   Aerials, signs and advertisements

3.6.1   *Masts and wires*

The Tenant must not erect any pole or mast [or install any cable or wire] on the Premises, whether in connection with telecommunications or otherwise.

3.6.2   *Advertisements*[69]

The Tenant must not, without the consent of the Landlord, fix to or exhibit on the outside of the Premises, or fix to or exhibit through any window of the Premises, or display anywhere on the Premises, any placard, sign, notice, fascia board or advertisement.

69   See the Town and Country Planning (Control of Advertisements) Regulations 1992, SI 1992/666 as amended. In the absence of a covenant such as this and subject to those Regulations, the tenant may exhibit advertisements etc on the premises, whether or not they are connected with his business: see *Clapman v Edwards* [1938] 2 All ER 507.

[1648]

3.7   Statutory obligations

3.7.1   *General provision*[70]

The Tenant must comply in all respects with the requirements of any statutes, and any other obligations so applicable imposed by law or by any byelaws, applicable to the Premises or the trade or business for the time being carried on there.

70   As to the covenant to comply with statutes see vol 22(1) (2003 Reissue) LANDLORD AND TENANT (BUSINESS TENANCIES) Paragraph 182 [905]. For a provision requiring the landlord to pay compensation for works above a certain value see vol 22(3) (1997 Reissue) LANDLORD AND TENANT (BUSINESS TENANCIES) Form 169 [6693].

3.7.2   *Particular obligations*

3.7.2.1   **Works required by statute, department or authority**

Without prejudice to the generality of clause 3.7.1, the Tenant must execute all works and provide and maintain all arrangements on or in respect of the Premises or the use to which they are being put that are required in order to comply with the requirements of any statute already or in the future to be passed, or the requirements of any government department, local authority or other public or competent authority or court of competent jurisdiction, regardless of whether such requirements are imposed on the owner, the occupier, or any other person.

3.7.2.2   Acts causing losses

Without prejudice to the generality of clause 3.7.1, the Tenant must not do in or near the Premises anything by reason of which the Landlord may incur any losses under any statute.

3.7.2.3   Construction (Design and Management) Regulations

Without prejudice to the generality of clause 3.7.1, the Tenant must comply with the provisions of the Construction (Design and Management) Regulations 1994 ('the CDM Regulations'), be the only client as defined in the provisions of the CDM Regulations, fulfil, in relation to all and any works, all the obligations of the client as set out in or reasonably to be inferred from the CDM Regulations, and make a declaration to that effect[71] to the Health and Safety Executive in accordance with the Approved Code of Practice published from time to time by the Health and Safety Executive in relation to the CDM Regulations. The provisions of clause 5.7.3 FIRE-FIGHTING EQUIPMENT are to have effect in any circumstances to which these obligations apply.

3.7.2.4   Delivery of health and safety files

At the end of the Term, the Tenant must forthwith deliver to the Landlord any and all health and safety files relating to the Premises in accordance with the CDM Regulations.

71   If works are being carried out for the tenant, the landlord will not want to accept the liabilities that are placed on a client under the Construction (Design and Management) Regulations 1994, SI 1994/3140 and the Health and Safety Executive Approved Code of Practice. The landlord will need to ensure that the tenant actually makes the declaration required, and that he obtains the notification served on the tenant by the Health and Safety Executive.

[1649]

3.8   Entry to inspect and notice to repair

3.8.1   *Entry and notice*

The Tenant must permit the Landlord[72] [on reasonable notice during normal business hours except in emergency][73] —

3.8.1.1   to enter the Premises to ascertain whether or not the covenants and conditions of this Lease have been observed and performed,

3.8.1.2   to view the state of repair and condition of the Premises, and to open up floors and other parts of the Premises where that is necessary in order to do so, and

3.8.1.3   to give to the Tenant, or notwithstanding clause 8.7 NOTICES leave on the Premises, a notice ('a notice to repair') specifying the works required to remedy any breach of the Tenant's obligations in this Lease as to the repair and condition of the Premises,

provided that any opening-up must be made good by and at the cost of the Landlord if it reveals no breach of the terms of this Lease.

72   The provisions of clause 1.31 [1618] REFERENCES TO RIGHTS OF ACCESS should be noted.
73   The tenant should add the words in square brackets.

3.8.2   *Works to be carried out*

The Tenant must carry out the works specified in a notice to repair immediately, including making good any opening up that revealed a breach of the terms of this Lease.

[3.8.3   *Landlord's power in default*[74]

If within *(state period, eg 1 month)* of the service of a notice to repair the Tenant has not started to execute the work referred to in that notice or is not proceeding diligently with it, or if the Tenant fails to finish the work within *(state period, eg 2 months)*[75][, or if in the [Landlord's *(or as required)* Surveyor's] [reasonable] opinion the Tenant is unlikely to finish the work within that period], the Tenant must permit the Landlord to enter the Premises to execute the outstanding work, and must within *(state period, eg 14 days)* of a written demand pay to the Landlord the cost of so doing and all expenses incurred by the Landlord, including legal costs and surveyor's fees.]

74   The advantages of this clause for the landlord must be weighed against the potential liability that it creates under the Defective Premises Act 1972 s 4(4) (31 Halsbury's Statutes (4th Edn) NEGLIGENCE): see *McAuley v Bristol City Council* [1992] QB 134, [1992] 1 All ER 749, CA.
          It has been held that a claim by the landlord for recovery of costs under such a clause is a claim for recovery of a debt, and can therefore be enforced without requiring leave of the court under the Leasehold Property (Repairs) Act 1938: see *Jervis v Harris* [1996] Ch 195, [1996] 1 All ER 303, CA.
          However, even where a landlord has been granted a right of this nature the court does not compel the tenant to allow the landlord the right to enter and carry out repairs where these would be of no benefit and where no loss is being caused to the landlord: see *Hammersmith London Borough Council v Creska (No 2)* [2000] L & TR 288.
75   The tenant would prefer to be given 'a reasonable period' to carry out the work required to remedy the breaches because it may take longer than the specified number of months.

[1650]–[1670]

3.9   Alienation[76]

3.9.1   *Alienation prohibited*

The Tenant must not hold the Premises on trust for another. The Tenant must not part with possession of the Premises or any part of the Premises or permit another to occupy them or any part of them except pursuant to a transaction permitted by and effected in accordance with the provisions of this Lease.

76   As to alienation see vol 22(1) (2003 Reissue) LANDLORD AND TENANT (BUSINESS TENANCIES) Paragraph 156 [801] et seq. Where the lease is registrable, this prohibition or restriction on dealings will be reflected in an entry on the register excepting from the effects of registration all estates, rights, interests, powers and remedies arising on or by reason of any dealing made in breach of the prohibition or restriction: see the Land Registration Rules 2003, SI 2003/1417 r 6(2).

3.9.2   *Assignment, subletting and charging of part*[77]

(version 1)

[The Tenant must not assign, sublet or charge part only of the Premises.] *(where assignment, subletting or charging of the whole is allowed)*

(version 2)

[The Tenant must not assign or charge part only of the Premises and must not sublet the whole or any part of them.] *(where assignment or charging of the whole is permitted, but subletting is not allowed at all)*

77   Whether subletting should be permitted is a commercial matter. Some landlords consider that the fact that they cannot unreasonably refuse consent to an assignment gives the tenant all the protection he requires and are not prepared to permit subletting. An advantage to the tenant of the ability to sublet is that he has an element of control over a subtenant but not over an assignee, for whom he may retain liability under an authorised guarantee agreement. Further, with stringent assignment tests or in a bad market, subletting may be the only option open to the tenant.

[1671]

3.9.3   *Assignment of the whole*

Subject to clauses 3.9.4 CIRCUMSTANCES and 3.9.5 CONDITIONS, the Tenant must not assign the whole of the Premises without the consent of the Landlord, whose consent may not be unreasonably withheld [or delayed][78].

78   This residual discretion is the old test of reasonableness under the Landlord and Tenant Act 1927 s 19(1). Thus the tenant and the proposed assignee may satisfy the circumstances and conditions specified for the purposes of the Landlord and Tenant Act 1927 s 19(1A) as inserted by the Landlord and Tenant (Covenants) Act 1995 s 22 (as to which see clause 3.9.4 [1672] CIRCUMSTANCES and clause 3.9.5 [1675] CONDITIONS), but the landlord may still refuse consent on reasonable grounds: see vol 22(1) (2003 Reissue) LANDLORD AND TENANT (BUSINESS TENANCIES) Paragraph 159 [812] et seq.

3.9.4   *Circumstances*

If any of the following circumstances[79] — which are specified for the purposes of the Landlord and Tenant Act 1927 Section 19(1A)[80] — applies either at the date when application for consent to assign is made to the Landlord, or after that date but before the Landlord's consent is given, the Landlord may withhold his consent and if, after the Landlord's consent has been given but before the assignment has taken place, any such circumstances apply, the Landlord may revoke his consent[81], whether his consent is expressly subject to a condition as referred to in clause 3.9.5.4 CONDITIONS or not. The circumstances are —

3.9.4.1   that any sum due from the Tenant under this Lease remains unpaid[82],

3.9.4.2   that in the Landlord's reasonable[83] opinion the assignee is not a person who is likely to be able to comply with the tenant covenants of this Lease and to continue to be able to comply with them following the assignment,

[3.9.4.3   that without prejudice to clause 3.9.4.2, in the case of an assignment to a company in the same group as the Tenant[84] within the meaning of the 1954 Act Section 42 in the Landlord's reasonable opinion the assignee is a person who is, or may become, less likely to be able to comply with the tenant covenants of this Lease than the Tenant requesting consent to assign, which likelihood is adjudged by reference in particular to the financial strength of that Tenant aggregated with that of any guarantor of the obligations of that Tenant and the value of any other security for the performance of the tenant covenants of this Lease when assessed at the date of grant or — where that Tenant is not *(name of original tenant)* — the date of the assignment of this Lease to that Tenant[85],] or

3.9.4.4   that the assignee or any guarantor for the assignee, other than any guarantor under an authorised guarantee agreement, is a corporation registered — or otherwise resident — in a jurisdiction in which the order of a court obtained in England and Wales will not necessarily be enforced against the assignee or guarantor without any consideration of the merits of the case.

(for examples of circumstances for use in unusual cases, see vol 22(3) (1997 Reissue) LANDLORD AND TENANT (BUSINESS TENANCIES) *Form 117 [6501])*

[1672]

79   The Landlord and Tenant Act 1927 s 19(1A) as inserted by the Landlord and Tenant (Covenants) Act 1995 s 22 enables the landlord and tenant to a post-1995 lease to agree in advance the terms upon which an assignment may be permitted. It distinguishes between on the one hand circumstances, the existence of which entitles the landlord to refuse consent to assignment, and on the other hand conditions that may be imposed on the grant of his consent. This clause and clause 3.9.5 [1675] CONDITIONS are drafted on the assumption that this is a valid approach and seek to draw a clear distinction between circumstances and conditions.

It should be noted that provisions that are overly restrictive may have an adverse impact at any rent review. It should also be noted that it is recommended 'best practice' that unless the particular circumstances of the letting justify greater control, the only restriction on assignment of the whole should be obtaining the landlord's consent, which is not to be unreasonably withheld: see vol 22(1) (2003 Reissue) LANDLORD AND TENANT (BUSINESS TENANCIES) Paragraph 85 [401] and 'A code of practice for commercial leases in England and Wales (2nd edition)' which can be found in vol 22(1) (2003 Reissue) LANDLORD AND TENANT (BUSINESS TENANCIES) as Form 1 [4501].

Each letting must be looked at in the light of its own particular facts and circumstances but it is considered that the provisions of this clause do, in the ordinary course, strike a reasonable balance between the landlord's desire for control and the tenant's ability to dispose of his interest without undue restriction. For a less restrictive approach see vol 22(1) (2003 Reissue) LANDLORD AND TENANT (BUSINESS TENANCIES) Form 7 clause 5.2 [5538].

80   The Landlord and Tenant Act 1927 s 19(1A) as inserted by the Landlord and Tenant (Covenants) Act 1995 s 22 seems to require the alienation clause to state that the circumstances it mentions are specified for the purposes of that subsection.

81   The landlord may require that certain circumstances are absent not only before consent has been given to the assignment, but also up to the date on which the assignment takes place — when the die is cast and the lease covenants bind the assignee. For example, the landlord may require the rent to be paid up to date not only before the application for consent is made, but also at the date when consent is given and the possibly later date when the lease is actually assigned.

82   The tenant may want to limit this to the rent, as it may be thought that a dispute is more likely to arise over the insurance rent or other payments. If the tenant has retained any right of set-off, it should also be referred to here.

[1673]

83   Circumstances and conditions must either be factual or, if they contain an element of discretion, require that discretion to be exercised reasonably (see the Landlord and Tenant Act 1927 s 19(1C)(a) as inserted by the Landlord and Tenant (Covenants) Act 1995 s 22), or must give the tenant a right of appeal to an expert (see the Landlord and Tenant Act 1927 s 19(1C)(b) as inserted by the Landlord and Tenant (Covenants) Act 1995 s 22). If the discretion is to be exercised reasonably, as suggested by this provision, the tenant can take any dispute about its exercise to the court. The court will consider whether *this* landlord has acted within the range of reasonable decisions, not whether a reasonable landlord would have reached the same decision or whether the test is itself reasonable. For a clause where an expert is used see vol 22(3) (1997 Reissue) LANDLORD AND TENANT (BUSINESS TENANCIES) Form 117 [6501].

84   There have been suggestions that intra-group assignments should be banned completely. However, this is considered to be too draconian and would prevent legitimate corporate restructuring needed for reasons other than avoidance of liability under the Landlord and Tenant (Covenants) Act 1995. The landlord's concern is that a strong tenant may assign to a weak group company; the assignment is acceptable because the assignor gives an authorised guarantee agreement for the assignee. The second group company may then itself assign outside the group; the landlord will lose the authorised guarantee agreement of the strong first group company and have only the possibly worthless authorised guarantee agreement of the second group company. The possibilities for exploitation of this scenario are obvious and it is therefore felt that this is the one situation in which measuring the financial strength of the assignee in relation to that of the assignor is justified. Equivalence tests are not generally thought to be appropriate, because a strong first covenant may make the lease almost unassignable, adversely affecting the rent at review.

85   Consider whether the time at which the tenant's financial status is measured should be when he acquired the lease, when his status was acceptable to the landlord, or at the date of the application for consent to assign, when it may have deteriorated sharply. On the other hand, the outgoing tenant may be a better covenant now than when he acquired the lease: the wily landlord may wish to leave himself free to pick whichever of the two dates gives the better picture.

[1674]

3.9.5   *Conditions*

The Landlord may impose any or all of the following conditions[86] — which are specified for the purposes of the Landlord and Tenant Act 1927 Section 19(1A)[87] — on giving any consent for an assignment by the Tenant, and any such consent is to be treated as being subject to each of the following conditions —

3.9.5.1   a condition that on or before any assignment and before giving occupation to the assignee, the Tenant requesting consent to assign, together with any former tenant who by virtue of the 1995 Act Section 11 was not released on an earlier assignment of this Lease[88], must enter into an authorised guarantee agreement[89] in favour of the Landlord in the terms set out in schedule 5 THE AUTHORISED GUARANTEE AGREEMENT,

3.9.5.2   a condition that if reasonably so required by the Landlord on an assignment to a limited company, the assignee must ensure that at least *(state number, eg 2)* directors of the company, or some other guarantor or guarantors [reasonably] acceptable to the Landlord, enter into direct covenants with the Landlord in the form of the guarantor's covenants contained in clause 6 GUARANTEE PROVISIONS with 'the Assignee' substituted for 'the Tenant',

3.9.5.3   a condition that on or before any assignment, the Tenant making the request for consent to assign must give to the Landlord a copy of the health and safety file required to be maintained under the Construction (Design and Management) Regulations 1994 containing full details of all works undertaken to the Premises by that Tenant, and

3.9.5.4   a condition that if, at any time before the assignment, the circumstances specified in clause 3.9.4 CIRCUMSTANCES, or any of them, apply, the Landlord may revoke the consent by written notice to the Tenant.

[1675]

---

86   The Landlord and Tenant Act 1927 s 19(1A) as inserted by the Landlord and Tenant (Covenants) Act 1995 s 22 enables the landlord and tenant to a post-1995 lease to agree in advance the terms upon which an assignment may be permitted. It distinguishes between on the one hand circumstances, the existence of which entitles the landlord to refuse consent to assignment, and on the other hand conditions that may be imposed on the grant of his consent. This clause and clause 3.9.4 [1672] CIRCUMSTANCES are drafted on the assumption that this a valid approach and seek to draw a clear distinction between circumstances and conditions.

It should be noted that provisions that are overly restrictive may have an adverse impact at any rent review. It should also be noted that it is recommended 'best practice' that unless the particular circumstances of the letting justify greater control, the only restriction on assignment of the whole should be obtaining the landlord's consent, which is not to be unreasonably withheld: see vol 22(1) (2003 Reissue) LANDLORD AND TENANT (BUSINESS TENANCIES) Paragraph 85 [401] and 'A code of practice for commercial leases in England and Wales (2nd edition)' which can be found in vol 22(1) (2003 Reissue) LANDLORD AND TENANT (BUSINESS TENANCIES) as Form 1 [4501].

Each letting must be looked at in the light of its own particular facts and circumstances but it is considered that the provisions of this clause do, in the ordinary course, strike a reasonable balance between the landlord's desire for control and the tenant's ability to dispose of his interest without undue restriction.

87   The Landlord and Tenant Act 1927 s 19(1A) as inserted by the Landlord and Tenant (Covenants) Act 1995 s 22 seems to require the alienation clause to state that the conditions it mentions are specified for the purposes of that subsection.

88   See the Landlord and Tenant (Covenants) Act 1995 ss 11(2), 16(6).

89   As to authorised guarantee agreements see vol 22(1) (2003 Reissue) LANDLORD AND TENANT (BUSINESS TENANCIES) Paragraph 54 [247]. It should be noted that 'A code of practice for commercial leases in England and Wales (2nd edition)' urges landlords to consider requiring authorised guarantee agreements only where the assignee is of lower financial standing than the assignor at the date of the assignment.

[1676]

3.9.6   *Charging of the whole*

The Tenant must not charge the whole of the Premises without the consent of the Landlord, whose consent may not be unreasonably withheld [or delayed][90].

90   As to unreasonable withholding of consent under the Landlord and Tenant Act 1927 see vol 22(1) (2003 Reissue) LANDLORD AND TENANT (BUSINESS TENANCIES) Paragraph 158.2 [806] and as to unreasonable delay under the Landlord and Tenant Act 1988 (23 Halsbury's Statutes (4th Edn) LANDLORD AND TENANT) see vol 22(1) (2003 Reissue) LANDLORD AND TENANT (BUSINESS TENANCIES) Paragraph 158.3 [808].

[3.9.7   *Subletting*

The Tenant must not sublet[91] the whole of the Premises without the consent of the Landlord, whose consent may not be unreasonably withheld [or delayed]][92]. *(omit if subletting is prohibited)*

91   See note 77 to clause 3.9.2 [1671] ASSIGNMENT, SUBLETTING AND CHARGING OF PART.
92   As to unreasonable withholding of consent under the Landlord and Tenant Act 1927 see vol 22(1) (2003 Reissue) LANDLORD AND TENANT (BUSINESS TENANCIES) Paragraph 158.2 [806] and as to unreasonable delay under the Landlord and Tenant Act 1988 see vol 22(1) (2003 Reissue) LANDLORD AND TENANT (BUSINESS TENANCIES) Paragraph 158.3 [808].

[3.9.8   *Terms of a permitted sublease*[93]

Every permitted sublease must be granted, without a fine or premium, at a rent not less than whichever is the greater of the then open market rent payable in respect of the Premises [— to be approved by the Landlord before the sublease is granted [and to be determined by the Surveyor, acting as an expert and not as an arbitrator]—] and the Rent[94], to be payable in advance on the days on which the Rent is payable under this Lease. Every permitted sublease must contain provisions approved by the Landlord —

[1677]

3.9.8.1   for the upwards only review of the rent reserved by it, on the basis set out in schedule 2 THE RENT AND RENT REVIEW and on the Review Dates[95],

3.9.8.2   prohibiting the subtenant from doing or allowing anything in relation to the Premises inconsistent with or in breach of the provisions of this Lease,

3.9.8.3   for re-entry by the sublandlord on breach of any covenant by the subtenant,

3.9.8.4   imposing an absolute prohibition against all dealings with the Premises other than assignment[, subletting] [or charging] of the whole,

3.9.8.5   prohibiting assignment[, subletting][96] [or charging] of the whole of the Premises without the consent of the Landlord under this Lease,

3.9.8.6   requiring the assignee on any assignment of the sublease to enter into direct covenants with the Landlord to the same effect as those contained in clause 3.9.9 SUBTENANT'S DIRECT COVENANTS,

3.9.8.7   requiring on each assignment of the sublease that the assignor enters into an authorised guarantee agreement[97] in favour of the Landlord in the terms set out in schedule 5 THE AUTHORISED GUARANTEE AGREEMENT but adapted to suit the circumstances in which the guarantee is given,

3.9.8.8   prohibiting the subtenant from holding on trust for another or permitting another to share or occupy the whole or any part of the Premises,

3.9.8.9   imposing in relation to any permitted assignment[, subletting] [or charge] the same obligations for registration with the Landlord as are contained in this Lease in relation to dispositions by the Tenant,

[3.9.8.10   imposing in relation to any permitted subletting the same obligations as are contained in this clause 3.9.8 and in clause 3.9.9 SUBTENANT'S DIRECT COVENANTS[, clause 3.9.11 ENFORCEMENT OF THE SUBLEASE and clause 3.9.12 SUBLEASE RENT REVIEW],] and

3.9.8.11   excluding the provisions of Sections 24–28 of the 1954 Act from the letting created by the sublease.] *(omit if subletting is prohibited)*

[1678]

93   As to the validity of provisions of this nature see vol 22(1) (2003 Reissue) LANDLORD AND TENANT (BUSINESS TENANCIES) Paragraph 161 [817].

94   It will not be in the landlord's interest for the premises to be sublet at a rent less than that payable under the headlease, because it could allow into the premises a subtenant of doubtful financial status, with whom the landlord may in the future have to deal direct, eg on the grant of a new lease under the Landlord and Tenant Act 1954 Pt II (ss 23–46). Also a low rent could be used as a 'comparable' in arriving at the open market rent on rent reviews or lease renewals. On the other hand following the decision in *Allied Dunbar Assurance plc v Homebase Ltd* [2002] EWCA Civ 666, [2003] 1 P & CR 75, [2002] 2 EGLR 23 a provision of this kind may effectively render the lease inalienable and being a potentially onerous restriction on disposition (as to which see vol 22(1) (2003 Reissue) LANDLORD AND TENANT (BUSINESS TENANCIES) Paragraph 348.2 [1440]) have an adverse impact at rent review from a landlord's perspective.

95   Alternatively the landlord might prefer the sublease rents to be reviewed just before the review dates in the headlease. As to recommended 'best practice' in relation to the basis of rent review in leases of business premises see vol 22(1) (2003 Reissue) LANDLORD AND TENANT (BUSINESS TENANCIES) Paragraph 85 [401] and 'A code of practice for commercial leases in England and Wales (2nd edition)' which can be found in vol 22(1) (2003 Reissue) LANDLORD AND TENANT (BUSINESS TENANCIES) as Form 1 [4501].

96   The landlord may well wish to prohibit any further subletting by requiring an absolute covenant against subletting to be inserted in any sublease.

97   By virtue of the Landlord and Tenant (Covenants) Act 1995 s 16(3)(a), where a head landlord's consent is needed to the assignment of a sublease, the head landlord can require the assignor of the sublease to enter into an authorised guarantee agreement. It should be noted that 'A code of practice for commercial leases in England and Wales (2nd edition)' urges landlords to consider requiring authorised guarantee agreements only where the assignee is of lower financial standing than the assignor at the date of the assignment.

[1679]

[3.9.9   Subtenant's direct covenants[98]

Before any permitted subletting, the Tenant must ensure that the subtenant enters into a direct covenant with the Landlord that while the subtenant is bound by the tenant covenants of the sublease[99] and while he is bound by an authorised guarantee agreement the subtenant will observe and perform the tenant covenants contained in this Lease — except the covenant to pay the rent reserved by this Lease — and in that sublease.] *(omit if subletting is prohibited)*

98   See note 93 to clause 3.9.8 [1679] TERMS OF A PERMITTED SUBLEASE.

99   The liability of the subtenant should be expressed to last while he is bound by the tenant covenants of the sublease, rather than while the sublease is vested in him, to take account of the possibility of an excluded assignment being made and the subtenant remaining liable. An excluded assignment means that the subtenant is precluded from tenant release under the Landlord and Tenant (Covenants) Act 1995.

[3.9.10   Requirement for 1954 Act exclusion[100]

The Tenant must not grant a sublease or permit a subtenant to occupy the Premises unless an effective agreement has been made to exclude the operation of Sections 24 to 28 of the 1954 Act pursuant to Section 38A of the 1954 Act.] *(omit if subletting is prohibited)*

100   As to contracting out of the security of tenure provisions of the Landlord and Tenant Act 1954 see vol 22(1) (2003 Reissue) LANDLORD AND TENANT (BUSINESS TENANCIES) Paragraph 431 [2035].

[3.9.11   *Enforcement, waiver and variation of subleases*

In relation to any permitted sublease, the Tenant must enforce the performance and observance by every subtenant of the provisions of the sublease, and must not at any time either expressly or by implication waive any breach of the covenants or conditions on the part of any subtenant or assignee of any sublease, or — without the consent of the Landlord, whose consent may not be unreasonably withheld or delayed — vary the terms or accept a surrender of any permitted sublease.] *(omit if subletting is prohibited)*

[1680]

[3.9.12   *Sublease rent review*

In relation to any permitted sublease —

3.9.12.1   the Tenant must ensure that the rent is reviewed in accordance with the terms of the sublease,

3.9.12.2   the Tenant must not agree the reviewed rent with the subtenant without the approval of the Landlord,

3.9.12.3   where the sublease provides such an option, the Tenant must not, without the approval of the Landlord, agree whether the third party determining the revised rent in default of agreement should act as an arbitrator or as an expert,

3.9.12.4   the Tenant must not, without the approval of the Landlord, agree any appointment of a person to act as the third party determining the revised rent,

3.9.12.5   the Tenant must incorporate as part of his representations to that third party representations [reasonably] required[101] by the Landlord, and

3.9.12.6   the Tenant must give notice to the Landlord of the details of the determination of every rent review within *(state period, eg 28 days),*

provided that the Landlord's approvals specified above may not be unreasonably withheld [or delayed].] *(omit if subletting is prohibited)*

---

101   This seems preferable to providing, as is sometimes done, that the head landlord's representations have to be brought to the attention of the expert or arbitrator because it would appear that he can refuse to have regard to them, the head landlord not being a party to the lease with which he is concerned.

3.9.13   *Registration of permitted dealings*

Within *(state period, eg 28 days)* of any assignment, charge, [sublease, or subunderlease,] or any transmission or other devolution relating to the Premises, the Tenant must produce a certified copy[102] of any relevant document for registration with the Landlord's solicitor, and must pay the Landlord's solicitor's [reasonable] charges for registration of at least £...

---

102   There seems to be no reason why the tenant should part with the original. However, under the Land Registration Rules 2003, SI 2003/1417 r 203, it is open to the applicant for registration to ask for the transfer, charge, sublease or subunderlease giving effect to the disposition to be returned for retention by the applicant, provided a certified copy of the instrument is lodged with the application. Accordingly, in such cases, applicants should use this facility if they wish to be able to lodge the lease with the landlord after its return by the registrar. If there is a time limit specified in the lease, then the registrar should be told about this, so that he is aware of the need to return the instrument within the required period.

[1681]

[3.9.14   *Sharing with a group company*

Notwithstanding clause 3.9.1 ALIENATION PROHIBITED, the Tenant may share the occupation of the whole or any part of the Premises with a company that is a member of the same group as the Tenant within the meaning of the 1954 Act Section 42, for so long as both companies remain members of that group and otherwise than in a manner that transfers or creates a legal estate.] *(omit if sharing with a group company is not to be permitted)*

3.10   Nuisance and residential restrictions

3.10.1   *Nuisance*[103]

The Tenant must not do anything on the Premises, or allow anything to remain on them, that may be or become or cause a nuisance, or annoyance, disturbance, inconvenience, injury or damage to the Landlord or his tenants or the owners or occupiers of adjacent or neighbouring premises.

103   'Nuisance' is a term to be construed according to 'plain and sober and simple notions among the English people': *Walter v Selfe* (1851) 4 De G & Sm 315 at 322 per Knight-Bruce V-C. 'I have no doubt that what is a nuisance or annoyance will continue to be determined by the courts according to robust and commonsense standards': *Hampstead and Suburban Properties Ltd v Diomedous* [1969] 1 Ch 248 at 258, [1968] 3 All ER 545 at 550 per Megarry J. But a tenant can only be said to have permitted a nuisance if the landlord can show that the tenant has failed to take reasonable steps to prevent the nuisance: see *Commercial General Administration Ltd v Thomsett* [1979] 1 EGLR 62, CA.

3.10.2   *Auctions, trades and immoral purposes*

The Tenant must not use the Premises for any auction sale, any dangerous, noxious, noisy or offensive[104] trade, business, manufacture or occupation, or any illegal or immoral act or purpose.

104   As to the meaning of 'offensive' see *Re Koumoudouros and Marathon Realty Co Ltd* (1978) 89 DLR (3d) 551 where it was held that the word did not have a definite legal meaning and should be read in the context of the lease. Surrounding circumstances can affect whether a particular trade is offensive: see *Nussey v Provincial Bill Posting Co and Eddison* [1909] 1 Ch 734, CA; *Dunraven Securities Ltd v Holloway* [1982] 2 EGLR 47, CA.

3.10.3   *Residential use, sleeping and animals*

The Tenant must not use the Premises as sleeping accommodation or for residential purposes, or keep any animal, bird or reptile on them.

[1682]

3.11   Costs of applications, notices and recovery of arrears[105]

The Tenant must pay to the Landlord on an indemnity basis all costs, fees, charges, disbursements and expenses — including, without prejudice to the generality of the above, those payable to counsel, solicitors, surveyors and bailiffs — [properly and reasonably] incurred by the Landlord in relation to or incidental to —

3.11.1   every application made by the Tenant for a consent or licence required by the provisions of this Lease, whether it is granted, refused or offered subject to any [lawful] qualification or condition, or the application is withdrawn[, unless the refusal, qualification or condition is unlawful whether because it is unreasonable or otherwise],

3.11.2   the contemplation, preparation and service of a notice under the Law of Property Act 1925 Section 146, or by reason or the contemplation of proceedings under Sections 146 or 147 of that Act, even if forfeiture is avoided otherwise than by relief granted by the court[106],

3.11.3   the recovery or attempted recovery of arrears of rent or other sums due under this Lease, and

3.11.4   any steps taken in [contemplation of or in] [direct] connection with the preparation and service of a schedule of dilapidations during or after the end of the Term[107].

---

105   As to payment of VAT on legal costs by a person other than the solicitor's own client see the Information Binder: Property [1]: VAT and Property.

106   As to forfeiture see vol 22(1) (2003 Reissue) LANDLORD AND TENANT (BUSINESS TENANCIES) Paragraph 283 [1171] et seq.

107   The landlord should not be tempted to extend this provision to costs etc incurred by him in consequence of serving a notice under the Landlord and Tenant Act 1954 s 25 because that is void: see *Stevenson and Rush (Holdings) Ltd v Langdon* (1978) 38 P & CR 208, CA.

[1683]

3.12   Planning and development

3.12.1   *Compliance with the Planning Acts*

The Tenant must observe and comply with the provisions and requirements of the Planning Acts affecting the Premises and their use, and must indemnify the Landlord, and keep him indemnified, both during the Term and following the end of it, against all losses in respect of any contravention of those Acts.

3.12.2   *Consent for applications*

The Tenant must not make any application for planning permission without the consent of the Landlord[, whose consent may not be unreasonably withheld [or delayed] [in any case where application for and implementation of the planning permission will not create or give rise to any tax liability for the Landlord or where the Tenant indemnifies the Landlord against such liability][108]].

---

108   These words were devised when development land tax — abolished by the Finance Act 1985 s 93 — applied. The provision may, however, still be relevant should similar taxation be introduced in the future.

3.12.3   *Permissions and notices*

The Tenant must at his expense obtain any planning permissions and serve any notices that may be required to carry out any development on or at the Premises.

3.12.4   *Charges and levies*

Subject only to any statutory direction to the contrary, the Tenant must pay and satisfy any charge or levy that may subsequently be imposed under the Planning Acts in respect of the carrying out or maintenance of any development on or at the Premises.

3.12.5   *Pre-conditions for development*

Notwithstanding any consent that may be granted by the Landlord under this Lease, the Tenant must not carry out any development on or at the Premises until all necessary notices under the Planning Acts have been served and copies produced to the Landlord, all necessary permissions under the Planning Acts have been obtained and produced to the Landlord, and the Landlord has acknowledged that every necessary planning permission is acceptable to him[, such acknowledgement not to be unreasonably withheld]. The Landlord may refuse to acknowledge his acceptance of a planning permission on the grounds that any condition contained in it or anything omitted from it or the period referred to in it would[, in the [reasonable] opinion of the Surveyor,] be, or be likely to be, prejudicial to the Landlord or to his reversionary interest in the Premises whether during or following the end of the Term.

[1684]

3.12.6   *Completion of development*

Where a condition of any planning permission granted for development begun before the end of the Term[109] requires works to be carried out to the Premises by a date after the end of the Term, the Tenant must, unless the Landlord directs otherwise, finish those works before the end of the Term.

109   The provisions of clause 1.16 [1613] INTERPRETATION OF 'THE LAST YEAR OF THE TERM' AND 'THE END OF THE TERM' should be noted.

3.12.7   *Security for compliance with conditions*

In any case where a planning permission is granted subject to conditions, and if the Landlord [reasonably] so requires, the Tenant must provide sufficient security for his compliance with the conditions and must not implement the planning permission until the security has been provided.

[3.12.8   *Appeal against refusal or conditions*[110]

If [reasonably] required by the Landlord to do so, but[, where reasonable,] at his own cost, the Tenant must appeal against any refusal of planning permission or the imposition of any conditions on a planning permission relating to the Premises following an application for planning permission by the Tenant.]

110   The tenant should not accept this clause because it could impose on him the cost of a planning appeal. He should strike it out, leaving planning appeals to be a matter for discussion as and when the situation arises during the term, or at least insist that he should bear the cost only where reasonable.

[1685]

3.13   Plans, documents and information

3.13.1   *Evidence of compliance with this Lease*

If so requested, the Tenant must produce to the Landlord or the Surveyor any plans, documents and other evidence the Landlord [reasonably] requires to satisfy himself that the provisions of this Lease have been complied with.

3.13.2   *Information for renewal or rent review*

If so requested, the Tenant must produce to the Landlord, the Surveyor, or any person acting as the third party determining the Rent in default of agreement between the Landlord and the Tenant under any provisions for rent review contained in this Lease any information [reasonably] requested in writing in relation to any pending or intended step under the 1954 Act or the implementation of any provisions for rent review.

3.14 Indemnities[111]

The Tenant must keep the Landlord fully indemnified against all losses arising directly or indirectly out of any act, omission or negligence of the Tenant, or any persons at the Premises expressly or impliedly[112] with his authority [and under his control][113], or any breach or non-observance by the Tenant of the covenants, conditions or other provisions of this Lease or any of the matters to which this demise is subject.

111 The tenant should seek to delete all *general* indemnity provisions on the basis that his remedies for breach of covenant and in tort adequately protect the landlord. The tenant should argue that an indemnity unreasonably extends his liability. If this clause is omitted, however, it should be replaced by a covenant to observe and perform the restrictions etc to which the demise is subject, possibly coupled with a *specific* indemnity in respect of any breach.
112 The expression 'impliedly' is intended to include a caller on the premises, such as a tradesman, where there has been no express invitation but the person cannot be classed as a trespasser.
113 The tenant should add the words in square brackets.

[1686]

3.15 Reletting boards and viewing

[Unless [a valid court application under the 1954 Act Section 24 has been made or][114] the Tenant is [otherwise] entitled to remain in occupation or to a new tenancy of the Premises, at any time during *(or as required)* At any time during] the *(state period, eg last 6 months)* of the [Contractual] Term[115] and at any time thereafter, [and whenever the Lease Rents or any part of them are in arrear and unpaid for longer than *(state period, eg 14 days)*,] the Tenant must permit the Landlord to enter the Premises and fix and retain anywhere on them a board advertising them for reletting. While any such board is on the Premises the Tenant must permit viewing of the Premises at reasonable times of the day.

114 This phrase and the word 'otherwise' should be omitted if the operation of the security of tenure provisions in the Landlord and Tenant Act 1954 ss 24–28 is to be excluded in relation to the lease.
115 This defined term will require amendment where the operation of the security of tenure provisions in the Landlord and Tenant Act 1954 ss 24–28 is to be excluded in relation to the lease: see note 6 to clause 1.2 [1609] 'THE [CONTRACTUAL] TERM'.

3.16 Obstruction and encroachment

3.16.1 *Obstruction of windows*

The Tenant must not stop up, darken or obstruct any window or light belonging to the Premises.

3.16.2 *Encroachments*

The Tenant must take all [reasonable] steps to prevent the construction of any new window, light, opening, doorway, path, passage, pipe or the making of any encroachment or the acquisition of any easement in relation to the Premises and must notify the Landlord immediately if any such thing is constructed, encroachment is made or easement acquired, or if any attempt is made to construct such a thing, encroach or acquire an easement. At the request of the Landlord the Tenant must adopt such means as are [reasonably] required to prevent the construction of such a thing, the making of any encroachment or the acquisition of any easement[116].

116 For a shorter clause see vol 22(3) (1997 Reissue) LANDLORD AND TENANT (BUSINESS TENANCIES) Form 172 [6696].

[1687]

3.17   Yielding up

At the end of the Term[117] the Tenant must yield up the Premises with vacant possession, decorated and repaired in accordance with and in the condition required by the provisions of this Lease, give up all keys of the Premises to the Landlord, remove tenant's fixtures and fittings [if requested to do so by the Landlord], and remove any signs erected by the Tenant or any of his predecessors in title in, on or near the Premises, immediately making good any damage caused by their removal.

117   The provisions of clause 1.16 [1613] INTERPRETATION OF 'THE LAST YEAR OF THE TERM' AND 'THE END OF THE TERM' should be noted.

3.18   Interest on arrears[118]

The Tenant must pay interest on any of the Lease Rents[119] or other sums due under this Lease that are not paid [within *(state period, eg 14 days)* of the date due], whether formally demanded or not[, the interest to be recoverable as rent][120]. Nothing in this clause entitles the Tenant to withhold or delay any payment of the Rent or any other sum due under this Lease or affects the rights of the Landlord in relation to any non-payment.

118   As to the covenant to pay interest see vol 22(1) (2003 Reissue) LANDLORD AND TENANT (BUSINESS TENANCIES) Paragraph 154 [767].
119   As to the definition of 'the Lease Rents' see clause 1.33 [1618] 'THE RENT'.
120   These words seek to attach to interest the rights associated with rent. As to the reasons for this see vol 22(1) (2003 Reissue) LANDLORD AND TENANT (BUSINESS TENANCIES) Paragraph 151 [761]. However, this clause applies to interest on arrears of other sums payable under the lease that are not rent as well as to rent itself, and it might be felt inappropriate for interest to be deemed to be rent where the payment on which the interest is due is not itself rent.

3.19   Statutory notices

The Tenant must give to the Landlord full particulars of any notice, direction, order or proposal relating to the Premises made, given or issued to the Tenant by any government department or local, public, regulatory or other authority or court within *(state period, eg 7 days)* of receipt, and if so requested by the Landlord must produce it to the Landlord. The Tenant must without delay take all necessary steps to comply with the notice, direction or order. At the request of the Landlord, but at his own cost, the Tenant must make or join with the Landlord in making any objection or representation the Landlord deems expedient against or in respect of any notice, direction, order or proposal.

[1688]

3.20   Keyholders

The Tenant must ensure that at all times [the Landlord has *(or as required)* the Landlord and the local police force have] written notice of the name, home address and home telephone number of at least *(state number, eg 2)* keyholders of the Premises.

3.21   Viewing on sale of reversion

The Tenant must[, on reasonable notice,] at any time during the Term, permit prospective purchasers of the Landlord's reversion or any other interest superior to the Term, or agents instructed in connection with the sale of the reversion or such an interest, to view the Premises without interruption provided they have the prior written authority of the Landlord or his agents.

3.22   Defective premises

The Tenant must give notice to the Landlord of any defect in the Premises that might give rise to an obligation on the Landlord to do or refrain from doing anything in order to comply with the provisions of this Lease or the duty of care imposed on the Landlord, whether pursuant to the Defective Premises Act 1972 or otherwise, and must at all times display and maintain any notices the Landlord from time to time [reasonably] requires him to display at the Premises.

3.23   Replacement guarantor[121]

3.23.1   *Guarantor replacement events*

In this clause 3.23 references to a 'guarantor replacement event' are references, in the case of an individual, to death, bankruptcy, having a receiving order made against him, having a receiver appointed under the Mental Health Act 1983 or entering into a voluntary arrangement, and, in the case of a company, to passing a resolution to wind up, entering into liquidation, a voluntary arrangement or administration or having a receiver appointed.

121   As to guarantors see vol 22(1) (2003 Reissue) LANDLORD AND TENANT (BUSINESS TENANCIES) Paragraph 71 [278] et seq. The tenant should propose that, on the execution of a guarantee by a new guarantor, the original guarantor or his estate should be released.

[1689]

3.23.2   *Action on occurrence of a guarantor replacement event*

Where during the relevant Liability Period a guarantor replacement event occurs to the Guarantor or any person who has entered into an authorised guarantee agreement, the Tenant must give notice of the event to the Landlord within *(state period, eg 14 days)* of his becoming aware of it. If so required by the Landlord, the Tenant must within *(state period, eg 28 days)* obtain some other person [reasonably] acceptable to the Landlord to execute a guarantee in the form of the Guarantor's covenants in clause 6 GUARANTEE PROVISIONS or the authorised guarantee agreement in schedule 5 THE AUTHORISED GUARANTEE AGREEMENT, as the case may be, for the residue of the relevant Liability Period.

3.24   Exercise of the Landlord's rights[122]

The Tenant must permit the Landlord to exercise any of the rights granted to him by virtue of the provisions of this Lease at all times during the Term without interruption or interference.

122   The provisions of clause 1.31 [1618] REFERENCES TO RIGHTS OF ACCESS should be noted.

3.25   The Office Covenants

The Tenant must observe and perform the Office Covenants.

3.26   Costs of grant of this Lease[123]

[The Tenant must pay the fees and disbursements of the Landlord's solicitors, agents and surveyors and all other costs and expenses incurred by the Landlord in relation to the negotiation, preparation, execution and grant of this Lease. *(or as required)* On the grant of this Lease, the Tenant must pay the sum of £... as a contribution to the Landlord's solicitors' charges for the negotiation, execution and completion of this Lease].

123   As to covenants to pay the landlord's legal fees see vol 22(1) (2003 Reissue) LANDLORD AND TENANT (BUSINESS TENANCIES) Paragraph 155 [769]. As to payment of VAT on legal costs by a person other than the solicitor's own client see the Information Binder: Property [1]: VAT and Property.

[1690]

3.27   Consent to the Landlord's release[124]

The Tenant must not unreasonably withhold consent to a request made by the Landlord under the 1995 Act Section 8 for a release from all or any of the landlord covenants of this Lease.

124   By virtue of the Landlord and Tenant (Covenants) Act 1995 each successive landlord remains bound by the landlord covenants of the lease unless released under the machinery provided in the Act — as to which see vol 22(1) (2003 Reissue) LANDLORD AND TENANT (BUSINESS TENANCIES) Paragraph 57 [252] et seq —or by a specific release given otherwise (see the Landlord and Tenant (Covenants) Act 1995 s 26(1)(a)). Bald statements limiting the landlord's liability, such as those in use before the commencement of the Act, will not withstand the wide anti-avoidance provisions of the Landlord and Tenant (Covenants) Act 1995 s 25, and covenants by the tenant to give consent to release are unlikely to fall within the exception of s 26. None of the ingenious schemes for limiting the landlord's liability, eg making all covenants personal, suggested in the early days of the 1995 Act has stood up to critical scrutiny, although none has yet been tested by the courts. Thus landlords look instead to the alternative of a right of redress if the tenant makes an unreasonable objection to release. This covenant is modelled on the provisions of the Landlord and Tenant Act 1988, which gives tenants a right of action for loss caused by landlords who unreasonably withhold or delay consent to assignment (see the Landlord and Tenant Act 1988 s 4). In view of the strict time limits under the Landlord and Tenant (Covenants) Act 1995 and the fact that failure to respond to the landlord's request for release is deemed to be consent, it is not thought necessary to extend this covenant to unreasonable delay in replying to such a request.

[1691]–[1700]

4   QUIET ENJOYMENT[125]

The Landlord covenants with the Tenant to permit the Tenant peaceably and quietly to hold and enjoy the Premises without any interruption or disturbance from or by the Landlord or any person claiming under or in trust for him[126] [or by title paramount][127].

125   As to the landlord's covenant for quiet enjoyment see vol 22(1) (2003 Reissue) LANDLORD AND TENANT (BUSINESS TENANCIES) Paragraph 168 [856]. As to covenants for quiet enjoyment generally see 23 Halsbury's Laws (4th Edn Reissue) LANDLORD AND TENANT.
        The words 'the Tenant paying the rents reserved by and observing and performing the covenants on his part and the conditions contained in this lease' are frequently included in a covenant for quiet enjoyment, but they have no practical effect and do not make payment of the rent and performance of the covenants into conditions precedent to the operation of the covenant for quiet enjoyment: see *Edge v Boileau* (1885) 16 QBD 117; *Dawson v Dyer* (1833) 5 B & Ad 584; *Yorkbrook Investments Ltd v Batten* (1985) 52 P & CR 51, [1985] 2 EGLR 100, CA.
126   The covenant is frequently expressed to apply to 'lawful interruption' by persons 'rightfully claiming' under the landlord, but it seems that the addition of these words has no practical effect: see *Williams v Gabriel* [1906] 1 KB 155 at 157.
127   Without the reference to title paramount the landlord is liable only for the acts of persons so far as they are his successors in title or have authority from him to do the acts complained of: *Harrison Ainslie & Co v Muncaster* [1891] 2 QB 680, CA; *Matania v National Provincial Bank Ltd and Elevenist Syndicate Ltd* [1936] 2 All ER 633, CA; *Miller v Emcer Products Ltd* [1956] Ch 304, [1956] 1 All ER 237, CA. If a subtenant holds under a lease containing a qualified covenant on the part of his landlord — ie one where there is no reference to title paramount — and the head landlord evicts the subtenant because the head rent has not been paid, this is not a breach of the covenant for quiet enjoyment (see *Spencer v Marriott* (1823) 1 B & C 457; *Dennett v Atherton* (1872) LR 7 QB 316, Ex Ch), but it is a breach if the sublandlord submits to judgment in an action by a person with no title to sue, and the subtenant is in consequence evicted (*Cohen v Tannar* [1900] 2 QB 609, CA). Actionable interruptions under this covenant are not confined to interference with title or possession, but may extend to interference with the ordinary and lawful enjoyment of the premises: *Sanderson v Berwick-upon-Tweed Corpn* (1884) 13 QBD 547 at 551, CA. As to persons claiming 'under' the landlord see *Celsteel Ltd v Alton House Holdings Ltd (No 2)* [1987] 2 All ER 240, [1987] 1 WLR 291, CA.

[1701]

5   INSURANCE[128]

5.1   Warranty as to convictions[129]

The Tenant warrants that before the execution of this document he has disclosed to the Landlord in writing any conviction, judgment or finding of any court or tribunal relating to the Tenant[, or any director, other officer or major shareholder of the Tenant,] of such a nature as to be likely to affect the decision of any insurer or underwriter to grant or to continue insurance of any of the Insured Risks.

128   As to insurance see vol 22(1) (2003 Reissue) LANDLORD AND TENANT (BUSINESS TENANCIES) Paragraph 227 [1021] et seq.

129   A contract of insurance is one uberrimae fidei. The insured must disclose to the insurers all material facts that are within his actual or presumed knowledge, whether there is a formal proposal form or not. A fact is material if non-disclosure of it would influence a prudent and reasonable insurer. This warranty is designed to rebut any suggestion by the landlord's insurers that the landlord had knowledge of the matters concerned. By inserting this clause in the lease, and thus specifically bringing the point to the tenant's attention, the landlord can argue that he has done all that is practical to establish the existence of any such matters. The absence of any written disclosure pursuant to this clause is strong evidence that the landlord has no actual or presumed knowledge of such matters. Further, the landlord has a right of action against the tenant for any breach of the warranty. As to non-disclosure and misrepresentation in contracts of non-marine insurance see 22 Halsbury's Laws (4th Edn Reissue) INSURANCE.

[1702]

5.2   Covenant to insure

The Landlord covenants with the Tenant to insure the Premises [in the joint names of the Landlord and the Tenant[130] [and any other person the Landlord [reasonably] requires][131]] unless the insurance is vitiated by any act of the Tenant or by anyone at the Premises expressly or by implication[132] with his authority [and under his control][133].

130   As to insurance in joint names see vol 22(1) (2003 Reissue) LANDLORD AND TENANT (BUSINESS TENANCIES) Paragraph 229 [1024].

131   Unless some expression such as this is included, a covenant to insure in specified names is broken by insurance in those names and other names: see *Penniall v Harborne* (1848) 11 QB 368.

132   The expression 'by implication' is intended to include a caller on the premises, such as a tradesman, where there has been no express invitation but the person cannot be classed as a trespasser.

133   The tenant should add the words in square brackets.

5.3   Details of the insurance

5.3.1   *Office, underwriters and agency*

Insurance is to be effected in such [substantial and reputable] insurance office, or with such underwriters[134], and through such agency as the Landlord decides from time to time[135].

134   The expression 'insurance office' would probably not include Lloyd's underwriters. The landlord's right to nominate the office and agency is absolute, with no implied restrictions: *Berrycroft Management Co Ltd v Gardens Investments (Kensington) Ltd* (1996) 75 P & CR 210, [1997] 1 EGLR 47, CA.

135   It should be noted that it is recommended 'best practice' in circumstances where the building is let to one tenant and the landlord insures that, in appropriate cases, the tenant should be given the opportunity to influence the choice of insurer: see vol 22(1) (2003 Reissue) LANDLORD AND TENANT (BUSINESS TENANCIES) Paragraph 85 [401] and 'A code of practice for commercial leases in England and Wales (2nd edition)' which can be found in vol 22(1) (2003 Reissue) LANDLORD AND TENANT (BUSINESS TENANCIES) at Form 1 [4501].

[1703]

5.3.2   *Insurance cover*[136]

Insurance must be effected for the following amounts —

5.3.2.1   the sum that the Landlord is from time to time advised [by the Surveyor] is the full cost of rebuilding and reinstating the Premises, including [VAT[137],] architects', surveyors', engineers', solicitors' and all other professional persons' fees, the fees payable on any applications for planning permission or other permits or consents that may be required in relation to rebuilding or reinstating the Premises, the cost of preparation of the site including shoring-up, debris removal, demolition, site clearance and any works that may be required by statute, and incidental expenses, and

5.3.2.2   loss of the Rent, taking account of any rent review that may be due, for *(state period, eg 3 years)* or such longer period as the Landlord from time to time [reasonably] requires for planning and carrying out the rebuilding or reinstatement.

136   As to the sum insured see vol 22(1) (2003 Reissue) LANDLORD AND TENANT (BUSINESS TENANCIES) Paragraph 231 [1028] et seq.
   It should be noted that it is recommended 'best practice' that, where the landlord has arranged insurance, the terms should be made known to the tenant and any material change in the insurance should be notified to the tenant: see Recommendation 14 of 'A code of practice for commercial leases in England and Wales (2nd edition)' which can be found in vol 22(1) (2003 Reissue) LANDLORD AND TENANT (BUSINESS TENANCIES) at Form 1 [4501].

137   As to VAT and the level of insurance cover see the Information Binder: Property [1]: VAT and Property. The expense of insuring against the VAT payable on reinstatement costs is not justified where the landlord has opted to tax and will be able to recover the VAT. There is a theoretical possibility that a future landlord may not opt to tax and that the sum insured may then be too low. It is also possible that a landlord may wish to preserve the 'exempt' status of a property. Normally, however, the cost of reinstatement need not expressly mention VAT, although the cashflow implications of having to pay VAT on construction works need to be remembered.

[1704]

5.3.3   *Risks insured*[138]

Insurance must be effected against damage or destruction by any of the Insured Risks to the extent that such insurance may ordinarily be arranged [with a substantial and reputable insurer] for properties such as the Premises, subject to such excesses, exclusions or limitations as the insurer requires.

138   As to risks to be insured against see vol 22(1) (2003 Reissue) LANDLORD AND TENANT (BUSINESS TENANCIES) Paragraph 235 [1033].
   It should be noted that it is recommended 'best practice' that, where the landlord has arranged insurance, the terms should be made known to the tenant and any material change in the insurance should be notified to the tenant: see Recommendation 14 of 'A code of practice for commercial leases in England and Wales (2nd edition)' which can be found in vol 22(1) (2003 Reissue) LANDLORD AND TENANT (BUSINESS TENANCIES) at Form 1 [4501].

5.4   Payment of the Insurance Rent

The Tenant covenants to pay the Insurance Rent for the period commencing on the Rent Commencement Date and ending on the day before the next policy renewal date on the date of this document, and subsequently to pay the Insurance Rent on demand and, if so demanded, in advance of the policy renewal date[, but not more than *(state period, eg … months)* in advance].

[1705]

5.5   Suspension of the Rent[139]

5.5.1   *Events giving rise to suspension*

If and whenever the Premises or any part of them are damaged or destroyed by one or more of the Insured Risks[140] [— except one against which insurance may not ordinarily be arranged [with a substantial and reputable insurer] for properties such as the Premises unless the Landlord has in fact insured against that risk —] so that the Premises or any part of them are unfit for occupation or use, and payment of the insurance money is not wholly or partly refused because of any act or default of the Tenant or anyone at the Premises expressly or by implication[141] with his authority [and under his control][142], then the provisions of clause 5.5.2 SUSPENDING THE RENT are to have effect.

139   As to suspension of rent see vol 22(1) (2003 Reissue) LANDLORD AND TENANT (BUSINESS TENANCIES) Paragraph 241 [1044] et seq.
140   It should be noted that it is recommended 'best practice' that if premises are so damaged by an uninsured risk as to prevent occupation, the tenant should be allowed to terminate the lease unless the landlord agrees to reinstate at his own cost: see vol 22(1) (2003 Reissue) LANDLORD AND TENANT (BUSINESS TENANCIES) Paragraph 85 [402] and 'A code of practice for commercial leases in England and Wales (2nd edition)' which can be found in vol 22(1) (2003 Reissue) LANDLORD AND TENANT (BUSINESS TENANCIES) at Form 1 [4501]. If adopted, this recommendation involves rent suspension also becoming operative in the event of the premises becoming unusable because of uninsured risks.
141   The expression 'by implication' is intended to include a caller on the premises, such as a tradesman, where there has been no express invitation but the person cannot be classed as a trespasser.
142   The tenant should add the words in square brackets.

[1706]

5.5.2   *Suspending the Rent*

In the circumstances mentioned in clause 5.5.1 EVENTS GIVING RISE TO SUSPENSION the Rent, or a fair proportion of it according to the nature and the extent of the damage sustained, is to cease to be payable until the Premises, or the affected part, have been rebuilt or reinstated so as to render the Premises, or the affected part, fit for occupation and use, [or until the end of *(state period, eg 3 years)* from the destruction or damage, whichever period is the shorter,][143] [the proportion of the Rent suspended and the period of the suspension to be determined by the Surveyor acting as an expert and not as an arbitrator *(or as required)* any dispute as to the proportion of the Rent suspended or the period of the suspension to be determined in accordance with the Arbitration Act 1996 by an arbitrator to be appointed by agreement between the Landlord and the Tenant or in default by the President or other proper officer for the time being of the Royal Institution of Chartered Surveyors on the application of either the Landlord or the Tenant].

143   As to the length of the suspension and the tenant's concerns see vol 22(1) (2003 Reissue) LANDLORD AND TENANT (BUSINESS TENANCIES) Paragraph 244 [1048]. For a provision extending suspension of the rent where reinstatement is delayed, see vol 22(3) (1997 Reissue) LANDLORD AND TENANT (BUSINESS TENANCIES) Form 111 [6495].

[1707]

5.6   Reinstatement and termination[144]

5.6.1   *Requirement to obtain permissions*

If and whenever the Premises or any part of them are damaged or destroyed by one or more of the Insured Risks [— except one against which insurance may not ordinarily be arranged [with a substantial and reputable insurer] for properties such as the Premises, unless the Landlord has in fact insured against that risk —] and payment of the insurance money is not wholly or partly refused because of any act or default of the Tenant or anyone at the Premises expressly or by implication[145] with his authority [and under his control][146], the Landlord must use his best endeavours[147] to obtain all the planning permissions or other permits and consents ('permissions') that are required under the Planning Acts or otherwise to enable him to rebuild and reinstate.

144   It has been held that, in the absence of an express covenant to reinstate, where the landlord must keep the premises adequately insured against comprehensive risks and the insurance is effected at the tenant's expense, the obligation is one intended to enure for the benefit of both parties: *Mumford Hotels Ltd v Wheler* [1964] Ch 117, [1963] 3 All ER 250; see also *Mark Rowlands Ltd v Berni Inns Ltd* [1986] QB 211, [1985] 3 All ER 473, CA; *Lonsdale & Thompson Ltd v Black Arrow Group plc* [1993] Ch 361, [1993] 3 All ER 648. This is not, however, a general principle of law and the tenant should therefore always require a specific covenant to reinstate.

These provisions are restricted to circumstances where damage or destruction is caused by an insured risk. It should be noted that it is recommended 'best practice' that if premises are so damaged by an uninsured risk as to prevent occupation, the tenant should be allowed to terminate the lease unless the landlord agrees to reinstate at his own cost: see vol 22(1) (2003 Reissue) LANDLORD AND TENANT (BUSINESS TENANCIES) Paragraph 85 [401] and 'A code of practice for commercial leases in England and Wales (2nd edition)' which can be found in vol 22(1) (2003 Reissue) LANDLORD AND TENANT (BUSINESS TENANCIES) at Form 1 [4501].

As to reinstatement and termination where reinstatement is not possible see vol 22(1) (2003 Reissue) LANDLORD AND TENANT (BUSINESS TENANCIES) Paragraph 237 [1037] et seq. For a provision for termination or surrender on destruction or substantial damage see vol 22(3) (1997 Reissue) LANDLORD AND TENANT (BUSINESS TENANCIES) Form 107 [6483].

145   The expression 'by implication' is intended to include a caller on the premises, such as a tradesman, where there has been no express invitation but the person cannot be classed as a trespasser.

146   The tenant should add the words in square brackets.

147   The extent of the duty to use best endeavours depends upon the facts in each case: see *Monkland v Jack Barclay Ltd* [1951] 2 KB 252, [1951] 1 All ER 714, CA; *Terrell v Mabie Todd & Co Ltd* [1952] 2 TLR 574; *NW Investments (Erdington) Ltd v Swani* (1970) 214 Estates Gazette 1115. In the light of *IBM United Kingdom Ltd v Rockware Glass Ltd* [1980] FSR 335, CA, it may be that there is little practical difference between a covenant to use best endeavours, a covenant to use reasonable endeavours and a covenant to take all reasonable steps.

[1708]

5.6.2   *Obligation to reinstate*

Subject to the provisions of clause 5.6.3 RELIEF FROM THE OBLIGATION TO REINSTATE, and, if any permissions are required, after they have been obtained, the Landlord must as soon as reasonably practicable apply all money received in respect of the insurance effected by the Landlord pursuant to this Lease, except sums in respect of loss of the Rent, in rebuilding or reinstating the Premises[, making up any difference between the cost of rebuilding and reinstating and the money received out of his own money][148].

148   Where the landlord's covenant is 'to apply all money received in respect of the insurance in rebuilding or reinstating' rather than simply 'to reinstate', it seems that the landlord does not have to complete the work out of his own money if the insurance money is insufficient because he has complied with his covenant by laying out all the insurance money received. The situation is different if the tenant can establish that the landlord was in breach of his covenant to insure for the full cost of reinstatement and that this has caused the shortfall: see *Mumford Hotels Ltd v Wheler* [1964] Ch 117, [1963] 3 All ER 250. The tenant should, therefore, require a specific covenant from the landlord to make up any shortfall, to prevent a situation in which the landlord refuses to complete the rebuilding. This is of particular concern if the suspension of rent proviso is expressed to operate for a limited period, because on the expiry of that period the tenant becomes liable for rent unless he can satisfy the court that the lease has been frustrated.

It should be noted that it is recommended 'best practice' that if premises are so damaged by an uninsured risk as to prevent occupation, the tenant should be allowed to terminate the lease unless the landlord agrees to reinstate at his own cost: see vol 22(1) (2003 Reissue) LANDLORD AND TENANT (BUSINESS TENANCIES) Paragraph 85 [401] and 'A code of practice for commercial leases in England and Wales (2nd edition)'which can be found in vol 22(1) (2003 Reissue) LANDLORD AND TENANT (BUSINESS TENANCIES) at Form 1 [4501]. If this recommendation is adopted and the landlord merely covenants to apply insurance money received, the principle should be extended to damage or destruction resulting from insured risks in circumstances where the insurance money is insufficient to enable reinstatement to be completed.

For a proviso relieving the landlord from the obligation to reinstate the premises in the same form see vol 22(3) (1997 Reissue) LANDLORD AND TENANT (BUSINESS TENANCIES) Form 106 [6482].

[1709]

5.6.3   *Relief from the obligation to reinstate*[149]

The Landlord need not rebuild or reinstate the Premises if and for so long as rebuilding or reinstatement is prevented because —

5.6.3.1   the Landlord, despite using his best endeavours[150], cannot obtain any necessary permission,

5.6.3.2   any permission is granted subject to a lawful condition with which [it is impossible for *(or as required)* in all the circumstances it is unreasonable to expect] the Landlord to comply,

5.6.3.3   there is some defect or deficiency in the site on which the rebuilding or reinstatement is to take place that [renders it impossible *(or as required)* means it can only be undertaken at a cost that is unreasonable in all the circumstances],

5.6.3.4   the Landlord is unable to obtain access to the site to rebuild or reinstate,

5.6.3.5   the rebuilding or reinstating is prevented by war, act of God, government action[, strike or lock-out], or

because of the occurrence of any other circumstances beyond the Landlord's control.

149   As to the need for a right to terminate where reinstatement is not possible see vol 22(1) (2003 Reissue) LANDLORD AND TENANT (BUSINESS TENANCIES) Paragraph 226 [998].

150   The extent of the duty to use best endeavours depends upon the facts in each case: see *Monkland v Jack Barclay Ltd* [1951] 2 KB 252, [1951] 1 All ER 714, CA; *Terrell v Mabie Todd & Co Ltd* [1952] 2 TLR 574; *NW Investments (Erdington) Ltd v Swani* (1970) 214 Estates Gazette 1115. In the light of *IBM United Kingdom Ltd v Rockware Glass Ltd* [1980] FSR 335, CA, it may be that there is little practical difference between a covenant to use best endeavours, a covenant to use reasonable endeavours and a covenant to take all reasonable steps.

[1710]

5.6.4   *Notice to terminate*[151]

If, at the end of the period[152] of *(state period, eg 3 years)* starting on the date of the damage or destruction, the Premises are still not fit for the Tenant's occupation and use, either the Landlord or the Tenant may by notice served at any time within *(state period, eg 6 months)* of the end of that period ('a notice to terminate following failure to reinstate') implement the provisions of clause 5.6.5 TERMINATION FOLLOWING FAILURE TO REINSTATE[153].

151   For alternative provisions where the landlord's right to terminate is limited to specified circumstances see vol 22(3) (1997 Reissue) LANDLORD AND TENANT (BUSINESS TENANCIES) Form 109 [6492].

152   The period to be inserted must be carefully considered. Particular regard should be had to the terms of any rent suspension provision and the extent of insurance cover for loss of rent.

153   As to the effect of the Landlord and Tenant Act 1954 see vol 22(1) (2003 Reissue) LANDLORD AND TENANT (BUSINESS TENANCIES) Paragraph 226 [998].

5.6.5   *Termination following failure to reinstate*

On service of a notice to terminate following failure to reinstate, the Term is to cease absolutely — but without prejudice to any rights or remedies that may have accrued[154]— and all money received in respect of the insurance effected by the Landlord pursuant to this Lease is to belong to the Landlord absolutely[155].

154   The effect of this clause is that the right to terminate arises after the end of the appropriate period, whatever the reason for the delay, but the tenant still has a right of action against the landlord if the landlord is in breach of his covenant to reinstate.

155   In the absence of provision for ownership of the insurance money the position is uncertain. In *Re King, Robinson v Gary* [1963] Ch 459, [1963] 1 All ER 781, CA it was held that the insurance money belongs to the party who paid the premiums even if the insurance was placed in the joint names of the landlord and the tenant. The dissenting view of Denning MR that insurance in joint names envisages that each party should be insured as to his insurable interest and that the insurance money should therefore be

divided in proportion to their interests in the property should, however, be noted. In *Beacon Carpets Ltd v Kirby* [1985] QB 755, [1984] 2 All ER 726, CA the court adhered to this view and held that the proportion payable depended on the parties' interests in the premises at the time of the destruction. The landlord will prefer an express provision in the lease for the insurance money to be retained by him in full if reinstatement proves impossible. The tenant ought perhaps to accept that it would be unrealistic to amend this to provide for the insurance money to belong to the tenant, but should suggest that a provision be inserted under which the money is to be divided in accordance with their respective interests in the premises at the time when the insurance money became due. For an alternative provision for ownership of the insurance money etc see vol 22(3) (1997 Reissue) LANDLORD AND TENANT (BUSINESS TENANCIES) Form 108 [6491].

[1711]

5.7   Tenant's further insurance covenants[156]

The Tenant covenants with the Landlord to observe and perform the requirements of this clause 5.7.

156   In order to comply with many of these covenants, the tenant will need to be supplied with details of the landlord's insurance policy. In any event, it should be noted that it is recommended 'best practice' that where the landlord has arranged insurance, the terms should be made known to the tenant and any material change in the insurance should be notified to the tenant: see Recommendation 14 of 'A code of practice for commercial leases in England and Wales (2nd edition)' which can be found in vol 22(1) (2003 Reissue) LANDLORD AND TENANT (BUSINESS TENANCIES) at Form 1 [4501].

5.7.1   *Requirements of insurers*

The Tenant must comply with all the requirements and recommendations of the insurers.

5.7.2   *Policy avoidance and additional premiums*

The Tenant must not do or omit anything that could cause any insurance policy on or in relation to the Premises to become wholly or partly void or voidable, or do or omit anything by which additional insurance premiums may become payable unless he has previously notified the Landlord and has agreed to pay the increased premium.

5.7.3   *Fire-fighting equipment*

The Tenant must keep the Premises supplied with such fire fighting equipment [as the insurers and the fire authority require and must maintain the equipment to their satisfaction *(or as required)* as the Landlord reasonably requires and must maintain the equipment to the reasonable satisfaction of the insurers and the fire authority] and in efficient working order. At least once in every *(state period, eg 6 months)* the Tenant must cause any sprinkler system and other fire fighting equipment to be inspected by a competent person.

[1712]

5.7.4   *Combustible materials*

The Tenant must not store on the Premises or bring onto them anything of a specially combustible, inflammable or explosive nature, and must comply with the requirements and recommendations of the fire authority [and the [reasonable] requirements of the Landlord] as to fire precautions relating to the Premises.

5.7.5   *Fire escapes, equipment and doors*

The Tenant must not obstruct the access to any fire equipment or the means of escape from the Premises, or lock any fire door while the Premises are occupied.

5.7.6   *Notice of events affecting the policy*

The Tenant must give immediate notice to the Landlord of any event that might affect any insurance policy on or relating to the Premises, and any event against which the Landlord may have insured under this Lease.

5.7.7   *Notice of convictions*

The Tenant must give immediate notice to the Landlord of any conviction, judgment or finding of any court or tribunal relating to the Tenant, or any director other officer or major shareholder of the Tenant, of such a nature as to be likely to affect the decision of any insurer or underwriter to grant or to continue any insurance[157].

157   This clause provides a continuation of the warranty given by the tenant in clause 5.1 [1702] WARRANTY AS TO CONVICTIONS. As to non-disclosure and misrepresentation in contracts of non-marine insurance see 22 Halsbury's Laws (4th Edn Reissue) INSURANCE.

[1713]

5.7.8   *Other insurance*

If at any time the Tenant is entitled to the benefit of any insurance of the Premises that is not effected or maintained in pursuance of any obligation contained in this Lease, the Tenant must apply all money received by virtue of that insurance in making good the loss or damage in respect of which the money is received[158].

158   An insurance policy frequently provides that if there is any other insurance effected by or on behalf of the insured, covering the premises that are the subject of the policy, the insurers are liable only for a rateable proportion of the damage. Such provisions extend to a case where one of the policies is in the joint names of the persons interested in the premises and the other is in the name of one only of those persons: *Halifax Building Society v Keighley* [1931] 2 KB 248. Therefore, at least when the insurance is in joint names, the landlord must ensure that the tenant will use all money received under any policy he has effected to reinstate the premises.

[5.7.9   *Reinstatement on refusal of money through default*

If at any time the Premises or any part of them are damaged or destroyed by one or more of the Insured Risks and the insurance money under the policy of insurance effected by the Landlord pursuant to his obligations contained in this Lease is wholly or partially irrecoverable because of any act or default of the Tenant or of anyone at the Premises expressly or by implication[159] with his authority [and under his control][160], the Tenant must immediately, at the option of the Landlord, either rebuild and reinstate the Premises or the part of them destroyed or damaged to the reasonable satisfaction and under the supervision of the Surveyor — in which case, on completion of the rebuilding and refurbishment, the Landlord must pay to the Tenant the amount that the Landlord has actually received under the insurance policy in respect of the destruction or damage — or pay to the Landlord on demand [with Interest] the amount of the insurance money so irrecoverable — in which case the provisions of clauses 5.5 SUSPENSION OF THE RENT and 5.6 REINSTATEMENT AND TERMINATION are to apply.]

159   The expression 'by implication' is intended to include a caller on the premises, such as a tradesman, where there has been no express invitation but the person cannot be classed as a trespasser.
160   The tenant should add the words in square brackets.

[1714]

[5.8   Landlord's further insurance covenants[161]

The Landlord covenants with the Tenant to observe and perform the requirements set out in this clause 5.8 in relation to the insurance policy he has effected pursuant to his obligations contained in this Lease.

161   Unless insurance is to be in the joint names of the landlord and the tenant, the tenant should seek covenants such as these from the landlord.

5.8.1   *Copy policy*

The Landlord must produce to the Tenant on demand [a copy of the policy and the last premium renewal receipt *(or as required)* reasonable evidence of the terms of the policy and the fact that the last premium has been paid][162].

162   The landlord can reasonably insist on the second alternative in square brackets. If the premises are insured under a block policy, it would be inappropriate for him to have to disclose to the tenant information about his other properties.

It should be noted that it is recommended 'best practice' that where the landlord has arranged insurance, the terms should be made known to the tenant and any material change in the insurance should be notified to the tenant: see Recommendation 14 of 'A code of practice for commercial leases in England and Wales (2nd edition)' which can be found in vol 22(1) (2003 Reissue) LANDLORD AND TENANT (BUSINESS TENANCIES) at Form 1 [4501].

5.8.2   *Noting of the Tenant's interest*

The Landlord must ensure that the interest of the Tenant is noted or endorsed on the policy[163].

163   Where insurance in the joint names of the landlord and the tenant is not practical, the tenant should insist that a note of his interest is endorsed on the policy. This protects the tenant because the insurers should give notice to him of any lapse in the policy and, where it can be shown that the tenant is responsible for the insurance premium under the terms of the lease, it is likely — but not certain — that the insurers would not exercise subrogation rights against the tenant.

It is recommended 'best practice' that where the landlord has arranged insurance, any interest of the tenant should be covered by the policy: see Recommendation 14 of 'A code of practice for commercial leases in England and Wales (2nd edition)' which can be found in vol 22(1) (2003 Reissue) LANDLORD AND TENANT (BUSINESS TENANCIES) at Form 1 [4501].

[1715]

5.8.3   *Change of risks*

The Landlord must notify the Tenant of any [material] change in the risks covered by the policy from time to time[164].

164   It should be noted that it is recommended 'best practice' that where the landlord has arranged insurance, the terms should be made known to the tenant and any material change in the insurance should be notified to the tenant: see Recommendation 14 of 'A code of practice for commercial leases in England and Wales (2nd edition)' which can be found in vol 22(1) (2003 Reissue) LANDLORD AND TENANT (BUSINESS TENANCIES) at Form 1 [4501].

[5.8.4   *Waiver of subrogation*[165]

The Landlord must produce to the Tenant on demand written confirmation from the insurers that they have agreed to waive all rights of subrogation against the Tenant.]]

165   Generally an insurer who has paid out under a policy stands in the shoes of the insured with regard to any claim the latter may have had against any third party. If the insurance is in joint names, the tenant is an insured party and there can be no subrogation against him. It would seem, also, that where the tenant covenants to reimburse the landlord for sums expended by the landlord in insuring the premises, the landlord's insurers cannot make a subrogated claim against the tenant where the premises are destroyed by the tenant's negligence: *Mark Rowlands Ltd v Berni Inns Ltd* [1986] QB 211, [1985] 3 All ER 473, CA. The tenant may still, however, wish to obtain a specific waiver of subrogation if possible.

[1716]–[1730]

6   GUARANTEE PROVISIONS

6.1   The Guarantor's covenants[166]

6.1.1   *Nature and duration*

The Guarantor's covenants with the Landlord are given as sole or principal debtor or covenantor, with the landlord for the time being and with all his successors in title[167] without the need for any express assignment, and the Guarantor's obligations to the Landlord will last throughout the Liability Period.

166   The covenants in this clause should *not* be omitted where no guarantor is a party to the lease, because they may be required under clause 3.9.5.2 [1675] CONDITIONS. If it is felt undesirable to have covenants in a lease and no party, at least initially, to enter into them, ie where there is no guarantor for the original tenant, the contents of this clause could alternatively be included in a schedule.

167   The new provisions governing the transmission of the benefit and burden of covenants (see the Landlord and Tenant (Covenants) Act 1995 s 3) only apply to landlord and tenant covenants. The law in force before 1 January 1996 remains unchanged for guarantor covenants, so that the benefit passes with the landlord's reversion. This occurs, not under the Law of Property Act 1925 s 141(1), which has been repealed for post-1995 tenancies by the 1995 Act, but under common law. The guarantee covenant touches and concerns the legal estate vested in the new reversioner: see *P & A Swift Investments v Combined English Stores Group plc* [1989] AC 632, [1988] 2 All ER 885, HL.

[1731]

6.1.2   *The covenants*

The Guarantor covenants with the Landlord to observe and perform the requirements of this clause 6.1.2.

6.1.2.1   **Payment of rent and performance of the Lease**

The Tenant must pay the Lease Rents[168] and VAT charged on them punctually and observe and perform the covenants and other terms of this Lease, and if, at any time during the Liability Period while the Tenant is bound by the tenant covenants of this Lease[169], the Tenant defaults in paying the Lease Rents or in observing or performing any of the covenants or other terms of this Lease, then the Guarantor must pay the Lease Rents and observe or perform the covenants or terms in respect of which the Tenant is in default and make good to the Landlord on demand, and indemnify the Landlord against, all losses resulting from the non-payment, non-performance or non-observance notwithstanding —

(a)   any time or indulgence granted by the Landlord to the Tenant, any neglect or forbearance of the Landlord in enforcing the payment of the Lease Rents or the observance or performance of the covenants or other terms of this Lease, or any refusal by the Landlord to accept rent tendered by or on behalf of the Tenant at a time when the Landlord is entitled — or will after the service of a notice under the Law of Property Act 1925 Section 146 be entitled — to re-enter the Premises[170],

(b)   that the terms of this Lease may have been varied by agreement between the Landlord and the Tenant[, provided that no variation is to bind the Guarantor to the extent that it is materially prejudicial to him][171],

(c)   that the Tenant has surrendered part of the Premises — in which event the liability of the Guarantor under this Lease is to continue in respect of the part of the Premises not surrendered after making any necessary apportionments under the Law of Property Act 1925 Section 140[172], and

(d)   anything else (other than a release by deed) by which, but for this clause 6.1.2.1, the Guarantor would be released.

[1732]

168   As to the definition of 'the Lease Rents' see clause 1.33 [1618] 'THE RENT'.

169   This obligation lasts while the lease is vested in the tenant and for any period of extended liability following an excluded assignment. It is not appropriate once the tenant has entered into an authorised guarantee agreement, when the contractual guarantor's obligations are at one remove. As to the guaranteeing of obligations under an authorised guarantee agreement: see vol 22(1) (2003 Reissue) LANDLORD AND TENANT (BUSINESS TENANCIES) Paragraph 74 [284] and clause 6.1.2.4 [1735] GUARANTEE OF THE TENANT'S LIABILITIES UNDER AN AUTHORISED GUARANTEE AGREEMENT.

170   If a creditor 'gives time' to the debtor in a binding manner, this releases the guarantor: see *Swire v Redman* (1876) 1 QBD 536; *Holme v Brunskill* (1877) 3 QBD 495, CA. The guarantee should, therefore, be expressed to apply notwithstanding any time or indulgence granted by the landlord to the tenant, or neglect or forbearance on the part of the landlord in enforcing the payment of rent and the other covenants in the lease. It has been suggested, however, that such wording does not protect a landlord who refuses to accept rent so as not to waive a breach of covenant by the tenant. This is unresolved but to avoid any doubt the point should be expressly dealt with. It appears that any provision in a guarantor's covenant that purports to exonerate the landlord from the consequences of his own negligence must satisfy the reasonableness test of the Unfair Contract Terms Act 1977(11 Halsbury's Statutes (4th Edn) CONTRACT).

171   Any variation of the terms of the contract between the creditor and the debtor will discharge the guarantor (*Holme v Brunskill* (1877) 3 QBD 495, CA), unless the guarantor consents, although it has been suggested that an immaterial variation that was not prejudicial to the guarantor might not release him. No guarantor should accept a provision by which the guarantee is to continue notwithstanding any variation, but on the other hand it seems unfair on the landlord for the guarantor to escape his liability merely because a minor change has been agreed between the landlord and the tenant. A provision that the guarantee is to continue to apply notwithstanding an immaterial variation not prejudicial to the guarantor seems a fair compromise. It should be noted that the Landlord and Tenant (Covenants) Act 1995 s 18 does not apply to the guarantor of the current tenant.

    It should also be noted that it is recommended 'best practice' that landlords and tenants should seek the agreement of any guarantors to proposed material changes to the terms of the lease, or even minor changes which could increase the guarantor's liability: see Recommendation 15 of 'A code of practice for commercial leases in England and Wales (2nd edition)' which can be found in vol 22(1) (2003 Reissue) LANDLORD AND TENANT (BUSINESS TENANCIES) at Form 1 [4501].

172   In the light of *Holme v Brunskill* (1877) 3 QBD 495, CA, the position on surrender of part of the premises should be dealt with expressly.

[1733]

6.1.2.2   New lease following disclaimer[173]

If, at any time during the Liability Period while the Tenant is bound by the tenant covenants of this Lease[174], any trustee in bankruptcy or liquidator of the Tenant disclaims this Lease, the Guarantor must, if so required by notice served by the Landlord within *(state period, eg 60 days)* of the Landlord's becoming aware of the disclaimer, take from the Landlord forthwith a lease of the Premises for the residue of the [Contractual] Term[175] as at the date of the disclaimer, at the Rent then payable under this Lease and subject to the same covenants and terms as in this Lease — except that the Guarantor need not ensure that any other person is made a party to that lease as guarantor — the new lease to commence on the date of the disclaimer. The Guarantor must pay the costs of the new lease and VAT charged thereon, save where such VAT is recoverable or available for set-off by the Landlord as input tax[176], and execute and deliver to the Landlord a counterpart of the new lease.

173   This put option should be included because on disclaimer of a lease the lease ceases to exist, although it is deemed to continue for the purpose of determining the liability to the landlord of persons, including guarantors, other than the tenant whose liquidator or trustee has disclaimed: see *Hindcastle Ltd v Barbara Attenborough Associates Ltd* [1997] AC 70, [1996] 1 All ER 737, HL.

174   This obligation lasts while the lease is vested in the tenant and for any period of extended liability following an excluded assignment. It is not appropriate once the tenant has entered into an authorised guarantee agreement when the tenant's — ie the former tenant's — liquidator or trustee in bankruptcy will not be in a position to disclaim the lease because it will no longer be vested in the former tenant.

175   This defined term will require amendment where the operation of the security of tenure provisions in the Landlord and Tenant Act 1954 ss 24–28 is to be excluded in relation to the lease: see note 6 to clause 1.2 [1609] 'THE [CONTRACTUAL] TERM'.

176   As to payment of VAT on legal costs by a person other than the solicitor's own client see the Information Binder: Property [1]: VAT and Property.

[1734]

6.1.2.3   Payments following disclaimer[177]

If this Lease is disclaimed and the Landlord does not require the Guarantor to accept a new lease of the Premises in accordance with clause 6.1.2.2 NEW LEASE FOLLOWING DISCLAIMER, the Guarantor must pay to the Landlord on demand an amount equal to [the difference between any money received by the Landlord for the use or occupation of the Premises and] the Lease Rents [in both cases] for the period commencing with the date of the disclaimer and ending on whichever is the earlier of the date *(state period, eg 6 months)* after the disclaimer, the date, if any, upon which the Premises are relet, and the end of the [Contractual][178] Term.

177   This clause could be a useful alternative for a landlord, who may not be unhappy to regain possession of the premises but would like some rental income before reletting etc. For a covenant by the tenant to assign to the guarantor see vol 22(3) (1997 Reissue) LANDLORD AND TENANT (BUSINESS TENANCIES) Form 159 [6666].

178   This defined term will require amendment where the operation of the security of tenure provisions in the Landlord and Tenant Act 1954 ss 24–28 is to be excluded in relation to the lease: see note 6 to clause 1.2 [1609] 'THE [CONTRACTUAL] TERM'.

6.1.2.4   Guarantee of the Tenant's liabilities under an authorised guarantee agreement

If, at any time during the Liability Period while the Tenant is bound by an authorised guarantee agreement, the Tenant makes any default in his obligations under that agreement, the Guarantor must make good to the Landlord on demand, and indemnify the Landlord against, all losses resulting from that default notwithstanding —

(a)   any time or indulgence granted by the Landlord to the Tenant, or neglect or forbearance of the Landlord in enforcing the payment of any sum or the observance or performance of the covenants of the authorised guarantee agreement[179],

(b)   that the terms of the authorised guarantee agreement may have been varied by agreement between the Landlord and the Tenant [provided that no variation is to bind the Guarantor to the extent that it is materially prejudicial to him][180], or

(c)   anything else (other than a release by deed) by which, but for this clause 6.1.2.4, the Guarantor would be released.

179   See note 170 to clause 6.1.2.1 [1733] PAYMENT OF RENT AND PERFORMANCE OF THE LEASE.
180   See note 171 to clause 6.1.2.1 [1733] PAYMENT OF RENT AND PERFORMANCE OF THE LEASE.

[1735]

6.1.3   *Severance*

6.1.3.1   Severance of void provisions

Any provision of this clause 6 rendered void by virtue of the 1995 Act Section 25 is to be severed from all remaining provisions, and the remaining provisions are to be preserved.

6.1.3.2   Limitation of provisions

If any provision in this clause 6 extends beyond the limits permitted by the 1995 Act Section 25, that provision is to be varied so as not to extend beyond those limits.

[6.2   The Landlord's covenant[181]

The Landlord covenants with the Guarantor that he will not attempt to recover from the Guarantor payment of any amount, determined by a court or in binding arbitration or agreed between the Landlord and the Tenant, payable in respect of a breach of covenant by the Tenant, unless he has served on the Guarantor, within 6 months of the payment being determined or agreed, a notice in the form prescribed by Section 27 of the 1995 Act as if the payment were a fixed charge under that Act.]

181   This clause is a tenant's amendment. It provides for a notice equivalent to a default notice under the Landlord and Tenant (Covenants) Act 1995 to be served. It protects the interests of existing and future contractual guarantors. As to service of default notices see vol 22(1) (2003 Reissue) LANDLORD AND TENANT (BUSINESS TENANCIES) Paragraph 61 [260].

[1736]

7   FORFEITURE[182]

If and whenever during the Term —

7.1   the Lease Rents[183], or any of them or any part of them, or any VAT payable on them, are outstanding for *(state period, eg 14 days)* after becoming due, whether formally demanded or not[184], or

7.2   the Tenant [or the Guarantor] breaches any covenant or other term of this Lease, or

7.3   the Tenant [or the Guarantor][185], being an individual, becomes subject to a bankruptcy order[186] [or has an interim receiver appointed to his property][187], or

7.4   the Tenant [or the Guarantor][188], being a company, enters into liquidation[189] whether compulsory or voluntary — but not if the liquidation is for amalgamation or reconstruction of a solvent company — [or enters into administration][190] [or has a receiver appointed over all or any part of its assets][191], or

7.5   the Tenant [or the Guarantor][192] enters into or makes a proposal to enter into any voluntary arrangement pursuant to the Insolvency Act 1986[193] or any other arrangement or composition for the benefit of his creditors, or

7.6   the Tenant has any distress, sequestration or execution levied on his goods,

and, where the Tenant [or the Guarantor] is more than one person, if and whenever any of the events referred to in this clause happens to any one or more of them, the Landlord may at any time re-enter the Premises or any part of them in the name of the whole — even if any previous right of re-entry has been waived[194] — and thereupon the Term is to cease absolutely but without prejudice to any rights or remedies that may have accrued to the Landlord against the Tenant or the Guarantor [or to the Tenant against the Landlord] in respect of any breach of covenant or other term of this Lease, including the breach in respect of which the re-entry is made.

[1737]

182   As to forfeiture generally see vol 22(1) (2003 Reissue) LANDLORD AND TENANT (BUSINESS TENANCIES) Paragraph 283 [1171] et seq.
    The precise range of insolvency-related circumstances that will trigger the proviso should be carefully considered. Tenants should note that their inclusion, in practice, means that the lease cannot be used as security for a loan. Landlords generally seek to have the ability to forfeit in the widest range of circumstances. It should, however, be noted that, in certain circumstances, leave of the court or of the insolvency practitioner administering the procedure may be required before any contractual right can be exercised: see eg, in respect of administration, the Insolvency Act 1986 Sch 1B para 43(4), (6) as inserted by the Enterprise Act 2002 s 248 (4 Halsbury's Statutes (4th Edn) BANKRUPTCY AND INSOLVENCY).

183   As to the definition of 'the Lease Rents' see clause 1.33 [1618] 'THE RENT'.
184   The words 'whether formally demanded or not' should be used to avoid the common law requirement that an actual demand has to be made.
185   The lease may provide for a right of re-entry on insolvency of the guarantor or a tenant's covenant to find an acceptable replacement (see clause 3.23 [1689] REPLACEMENT GUARANTOR) or both.
186   As to bankruptcy generally see the Insolvency Act 1986 Pt IX (ss 264–371).
187   As to interim receivers see the Insolvency Act 1986 s 286.
188   See note 185 above.
189   As to liquidation generally see the Insolvency Act 1986 Pts IV–VI (ss 73–246).
190   As to administration generally see the Insolvency Act 1986 Pt II as substituted by the Enterprise Act 2002 s 248. The tenant may seek to argue that if the administrator pays rent and if there are no other material breaches of the lease the landlord should not be entitled to forfeit the lease on this ground.
191   The tenant may seek to argue that if the receiver pays rent and if there are no other material breaches of the lease the landlord should not be entitled to forfeit the lease on this ground.
192   See note 185 above.
193   As to company voluntary arrangements see the Insolvency Act 1986 Pt I (ss 1–7B) as amended by the Insolvency Act 2000. As to individual voluntary arrangements see the Insolvency Act 1986 Pt VIII (ss 252–263G) as amended by the Enterprise Act 2002 s 264.
194   The landlord has the option whether to take advantage of a right of forfeiture or not. If he elects not to do so , the forfeiture is waived. The election may be express or implied, eg if the landlord does any act by which he recognises that the relationship of landlord and tenant is still continuing after the event of forfeiture has come to his knowledge.

[1738]

8   MISCELLANEOUS

8.1   Exclusion of warranty as to use

Nothing in this Lease or in any consent granted by the Landlord under this Lease is to imply or warrant that the Premises may lawfully be used under the Planning Acts for the Permitted Use[195].

195   See *Laurence v Lexcourt Holdings Ltd* [1978] 2 All ER 810, [1978] 1 WLR 1128; *Collins v Howell-Jones* [1981] 2 EGLR 108, 259 Estates Gazette 331, CA and the comments of Eveleigh LJ on estate agents' particulars relating to use in *Bovis Group Pension Fund Ltd v GC Flooring & Furnishing Ltd* (1984) 269 Estates Gazette 1252 at 1253, CA.

8.2   Exclusion of third party rights

Nothing in this Lease is intended to confer any benefit on any person who is not a party to it[196].

196   By virtue of the Contracts (Rights of Third Parties) Act 1999 (11 Halsbury's Statutes (4th Edn) CONTRACT) third-party rights may be conferred where they are not clearly excluded. This being so, it is advisable to incorporate a specific exclusion except where the parties actually intend to confer rights of action on a third party. In the standard letting situation it is unlikely that the parties will wish to extend liability in this manner. As to the Contracts (Rights of Third Parties) Act 1999 generally see vol 4(3) (2001 Reissue) BOILERPLATE CLAUSES.

8.3   Representations

The Tenant acknowledges that this Lease has not been entered into in reliance wholly or partly on any statement or representation made by or on behalf of the Landlord except any such statement or representation expressly set out in this Lease[197] [or made by the Landlord's solicitors in any written response to enquiries raised by the Tenant's solicitors in connection with the grant of this Lease].

197   See the comments of Eveleigh LJ on estate agents' particulars relating to use in *Bovis Group Pension Fund Ltd v GC Flooring & Furnishing Ltd* (1984) 269 Estates Gazette 1252 at 1253, CA. For an alternative provision see vol 22(4) (1997 Reissue) LANDLORD AND TENANT (BUSINESS TENANCIES) Form 400 clauses 7.1 [7520], 7.2 [7521].

[1739]

8.4   Documents under hand

While the Landlord is a limited company or other corporation, any licence, consent, approval or notice required to be given by the Landlord is to be sufficiently given if given under the hand of a director, the secretary or other duly authorised officer of the Landlord [or by the Surveyor on behalf of the Landlord].

8.5   Tenant's property

If, after the Tenant has vacated the Premises at the end of the Term, any property of his remains in or on the Premises and he fails to remove it within *(state period, eg 7 days)* after a written request from the Landlord to do so, or, if the Landlord is unable to make such a request to the Tenant, within *(state period, eg 14 days)* from the first attempt to make it, then the Landlord may, as the agent of the Tenant, sell that property. The Tenant must indemnify the Landlord against any liability incurred by the Landlord to any third party whose property is sold by him in the mistaken belief held in good faith — which is to be presumed unless the contrary is proved — that the property belonged to the Tenant. If, having made reasonable efforts to do so, the Landlord is unable to locate the Tenant, then the Landlord may retain the proceeds of sale absolutely unless the Tenant claims them within *(state period, eg 6 months)* of the date upon which he vacated the Premises. The Tenant must indemnify the Landlord against any damage occasioned to the Premises and any losses caused by or related to the presence of the property in or on the Premises.

8.6   Compensation on vacating excluded

Any statutory right of the Tenant to claim compensation from the Landlord on vacating the Premises is excluded to the extent that the law allows[198].

198   As to compensation where an order for a new tenancy is precluded on certain grounds, see the Landlord and Tenant Act 1954 s 37 as amended by the Local Government and Housing Act 1989 s 149, Sch 7 and by SI 2003/3096.

As to the effectiveness of provisions of this nature see vol 22(1) (2003 Reissue) LANDLORD AND TENANT (BUSINESS TENANCIES) Paragraph 468 [3079].

[1740]

8.7   Notices

8.7.1   *Form and service of notices*

A notice under this Lease must be in writing and, unless the receiving party or his authorised agent acknowledges receipt, is valid if, and only if[199] —

8.7.1.1   it is given by hand, sent by registered post or recorded delivery, or sent by fax[200] provided that a confirmatory copy is given by hand or sent by registered post or recorded delivery on the same day, and

8.7.1.2   it is served —

    (a)   where the receiving party is a company incorporated within Great Britain, at the registered office,

    (b)   where the receiving party is the Tenant and the Tenant is not such a company, at the Premises, and

    (c)   where the receiving party is the Landlord [or the Guarantor] and [the Landlord *(or as required)* that party] is not such a company, at [the Landlord's *(or as required)* that party's] address shown in this Lease or at any address specified in a notice given by [the Landlord to the Tenant *(or as required)* that party to the other parties].

199   Notice clauses are either mandatory or permissive. The words 'and only if' are inserted to make it clear that this clause is mandatory.

200   As to service by fax see *Hastie and Jenkerson v McMahon* [1991] 1 All ER 255, [1990] 1 WLR 1575, CA.

[1741]

8.7.2   *Deemed delivery*[201]

8.7.2.1   **By registered post or recorded delivery**

Unless it is returned through the Royal Mail undelivered, a notice sent by registered post or recorded delivery is to be treated as served on the third working day after posting whenever and whether or not it is received.

8.7.2.2   **By fax**

A notice sent by fax is to be treated as served on the day upon which it is sent, or the next working day where the fax is sent after 1600 hours or on a day that is not a working day, whenever and whether or not it or the confirmatory copy is received unless the confirmatory copy is returned through the Royal Mail undelivered.

8.7.2.3   **'A working day'**

References to 'a working day' are references to a day when the United Kingdom clearing banks are open for business in the City of London.

201   It is a fundamental aspect of any notice clause to specify the circumstances in which the server, provided he has complied with the requirements of the clause, has for the purposes of the document served a notice, even if the recipient claims that he never received it.

8.7.3   *Joint recipients*

If the receiving party consists of more than one person, a notice to one of them is notice to all.

                                                                                    [1742]

8.8   **[New *(or)* Old] lease**

[This Lease [is *(or as appropriate)* is not] a new tenancy for the purposes of the 1995 Act Section 1. *(or as appropriate)* This Lease is granted under the 1995 Act Section 19 and [is *(or as appropriate)* is not] a new tenancy for the purposes of Section 1 of that Act][202].

202   A tenancy granted on or after 1 January 1996 that is an overriding lease is not a 'new' tenancy where the tenancy being overridden is one granted before that date: see the Landlord and Tenant (Covenants) Act 1995 ss 1(4), 20(1). Where the lease being granted is an overriding lease, the lease must include a statement that it is an overriding lease and indicate whether the overriding lease is or is not a 'new' tenancy: see the Landlord and Tenant (Covenants) Act 1995 s 20(2). In these circumstances the second alternative should be used.

[8.9   **Capacity of tenants**

It is declared that the persons comprising the Tenant hold the Premises as [joint tenants *(or as required)* tenants in common].]

[8.10   **Exclusion of the 1954 Act Sections 24–28**[203]

8.10.1   *Notice and declaration*

On *(date)* the Landlord served notice on the Tenant pursuant to the provisions of the 1954 Act Section 38A(3) as inserted by the Regulatory Reform (Business Tenancies) (England and Wales) Order 2003 and on *(date)* the Tenant made a [simple *(or as appropriate)* statutory] declaration pursuant to schedule 2 of the Regulatory Reform (Business Tenancies) (England and Wales) Order 2003.

8.10.2   *Agreement to exclude*

Pursuant to the provisions of the 1954 Act Section 38A(1) as inserted by the Regulatory Reform (Business Tenancies) (England and Wales) Order 2003, the parties agree that the provisions of the 1954 Act Sections 24–28 inclusive are to be excluded in relation to the tenancy created by this Lease.]

203   As to contracting out of the Landlord and Tenant Act 1954 and the requirements that need to be complied with see vol 22(1) (2003 Reissue) LANDLORD AND TENANT (BUSINESS TENANCIES) Paragraph 431 [2035].

(include other clauses as required: eg, break clauses and options (see vol 22(3) (1997 Reissue) LANDLORD AND TENANT (BUSINESS TENANCIES) *Forms 136 [6544]–142 [6569]) or a proviso as to termination on rent review (see vol 22(3) (1997 Reissue)* LANDLORD AND TENANT (BUSINESS TENANCIES) *Form 143 [6570]))*

IN WITNESS etc *(see vol 12(2) (2003 Reissue) DEEDS, AGREEMENTS ETC)*

[1743]–[1760]

SCHEDULE 1: THE RIGHTS RESERVED[204]

1-1   Right of entry to inspect

The right to enter[205], or in emergency to break into and enter, the Premises at any time during the Term [at reasonable times and upon reasonable notice except in emergency] to inspect them, to take schedules or inventories of fixtures and other items to be yielded up at the end of the Term, and to exercise any of the rights granted to the Landlord elsewhere in this Lease.

204   As to rights reserved see vol 22(1) (2003 Reissue) LANDLORD AND TENANT (BUSINESS TENANCIES) Paragraph 124 [648] et seq.
205   For a covenant by the landlord to make good damage so caused see vol 22(3) (1997 Reissue) LANDLORD AND TENANT (BUSINESS TENANCIES) Form 79 [6453].

1-2   Access on renewal or rent review

[The right to enter the Premises with the Surveyor and the third party determining the Rent under any provisions for rent review contained in this Lease at [any time *(or as required)* convenient hours and on reasonable prior notice] to inspect [and measure] the Premises for all purposes connected with any pending or intended step under the 1954 Act or the implementation of the provisions for rent review. *(or as required in view of the rent review provisions used: see vol 22(3) (1997 Reissue)* LANDLORD AND TENANT (BUSINESS *TENANCIES) Forms 180 [6711]–194 [6987])*]

SCHEDULE 2: THE RENT AND RENT REVIEW

(insert rent review provisions as required: see vol 22(3) (1997 Reissue) LANDLORD AND TENANT *(BUSINESS TENANCIES) Forms 180 [6711]–194 [6987])*

[1761]

SCHEDULE 3: THE OFFICE COVENANTS

(the draftsman should tailor the covenants contained in this schedule to reflect the nature of the building)

3-1   Use

3-1.1   *Permitted Use*

The Tenant must use the Premises for the Permitted Use only.

3-1.2   *Cesser of business*

The Tenant must not [cease carrying on business in the Premises or] leave the Premises [continuously] unoccupied for more than *(state period, eg 1 month)* [without notifying the Landlord and providing such caretaking or security arrangements for the protection of the Premises as the Landlord [reasonably] requires and the insurers or underwriters require].

3-1.3   *Noxious discharges*

The Tenant must not discharge into any of the Conduits any noxious or deleterious matter or any other substance that might cause an obstruction in or danger or injury to the Conduits or be or become a source of obstruction, danger or injury, and in the event of any such obstruction, danger or injury the Tenant must forthwith make good any damage to the satisfaction of the Surveyor.

3-1.4   *Window cleaning*

The Tenant must clean both sides of all windows and window frames in the building on the Premises at least once every month.

3-1.5   *Sound audible outside*

The Tenant must not play or use in the Premises any musical instrument, audio or other equipment or apparatus that produces sound that may be heard outside the Premises [if the Landlord [in his absolute discretion *(or as required)* reasonably] considers such sounds to be undesirable and gives notice to the Tenant to that effect].

[1762]

3-2   Ceiling and floor loading

3-2.1   *Heavy items*

The Tenant must not bring onto or permit to remain on the Premises any safes, machinery, goods or other articles that will or may strain or damage the Premises or any part of them.

3-2.2   *Protection of the roof*

The Tenant must not without the consent of the Landlord suspend anything from any ceiling on the Premises [or store any heavy items in the roof space].

3-2.3   *Expert advice*

If the Tenant applies for the Landlord's consent under paragraph 3-2.2 PROTECTION OF THE ROOF the Landlord may consult any engineer or other person in relation to the loading proposed by the Tenant, and the Tenant must repay the fees of the engineer or other person to the Landlord on demand.

3-3   Machinery

3-3.1   *Noisy machinery*

The Tenant must not install or use in or upon the Premises any machinery or apparatus [other than usual office machinery] that will cause noise or vibration that can be heard or felt in nearby premises or outside the Premises or that may cause damage.

3-3.2   *Maintenance of machinery*

The Tenant must keep all machinery and equipment on the Premises ('the Machinery') properly maintained and in good working order and for that purpose must employ reputable contractors [to be approved by the Landlord[, whose approval may not be unreasonably refused [or delayed],]] ('the Contractors') to carry out regular periodic inspection and maintenance of the Machinery.

3-3.3   *Renewal of parts*

The Tenant must renew all working and other parts of the Machinery as and when necessary or when recommended by the Contractors.

3-3.4   *Operation*

The Tenant must ensure by directions to his staff and otherwise that the Machinery is properly operated.

3-4   Signs

The Tenant must at all times display and maintain at a point on the outside of the Premises or elsewhere on the Premises to be specified in writing by the Landlord, a suitable sign, of a size and kind first approved by the Landlord, showing the Tenant's trading name and business.

[1763]

SCHEDULE 4: THE SUBJECTIONS

(insert details)

SCHEDULE 5: THE AUTHORISED GUARANTEE AGREEMENT

(insert the form of authorised guarantee agreement: see, eg vol 22(3) (1997 Reissue) LANDLORD AND TENANT (BUSINESS TENANCIES) *Form 217 [7053])*

(signature (or common seal) of landlord: lease)
(signature (or common seal) of tenant (and guarantor): counterpart)
(signatures of witnesses)
[1764]–[1800]

12

Lease of a suite of offices forming part of a building, with parking bays and additional parking rights[1]

CONTENTS

(NB: numbers in [ ] below refer to this volume and should be altered to suit the page or reference numbers actually used)

1 DEFINITIONS AND INTERPRETATION

1.1 'The Accountant' .... [1809]
1.2 'The Adjoining Conduits' .... [1809]
1.3 'Adjoining property of the Landlord' .... [1809]
1.4 'The Building' .... [1809]
1.5 'The Common Parts' .... [1809]
1.6 'The Conduits' .... [1809]
1.7 'The [Contractual] Term' .... [1810]
[1.8 'The Decorating Years' .... [1811]]
1.9 'Development' .... [1811]
                                                              [1801]
1.10 Gender and number .... [1811]
1.11 Headings .... [1811]
[1.12 'The Initial Rent' .... [1811]]
1.13 'The Insurance Rent' .... [1812]
1.14 'The Insurance Rent Percentage' .... [1812]
1.15 'The Insured Risks' .... [1812]
1.16 'Interest' .... [1813]
1.17 'The Interest Rate' .... [1813]
1.18 Interpretation of 'the Building' .... [1814]
1.19 Interpretation of 'consent' and 'approved' .... [1814]
1.20 Interpretation of 'the Guarantor' .... [1815]
1.21 Interpretation of 'the Landlord' .... [1815]
1.22 Interpretation of 'the last year of the Term' and 'the end of the Term' ... [1815]
1.23 Interpretation of 'the Tenant' .... [1815]
1.24 Interpretation of 'this Lease' .... [1815]
1.25 Joint and several liability .... [1815]
1.26 'The Landlord's Expenses' .... [1816]
1.27 'The Liability Period' .... [1816]
1.28 'Losses' .... [1817]
1.29 'The 1954 Act' .... [1817]
1.30 'The 1995 Act' .... [1817]
1.31 Obligation not to permit or suffer .... [1817]
1.32 'The Office Covenants' .... [1817]
1.33 'Other buildings' .... [1818]
1.34 The Parking Bays .... [1818]
1.35 'The Permitted Hours' .... [1818]
1.36 'The Plan' .... [1818]
1.37 'The Planning Acts' .... [1819]
1.38 'The Premises' .... [1819]
1.39 References to clauses and schedules .... [1821]

1.40 References to rights of access . . . . [1821]
1.41 References to statutes . . . . [1821]
1.42 'The Rent' . . . . [1821]
1.43 'The Rent Commencement Date' . . . . [1821]
[1.44 'The Review Dates' . . . . [1822]]
1.45 'The Service Charge' . . . . [1822]
1.46 'The Service Charge Percentage' . . . . [1822]
1.47 'The Services' . . . . [1822]
1.48 'The Surveyor' . . . . [1822]
[1.49 'The Term' . . . . [1823]]
1.50 Terms from the 1995 Act . . . . [1823]
1.51 'VAT' . . . . [1823]
                                              [1802]

2 DEMISE . . . . [1841]

3 THE TENANT'S COVENANTS
3.1 Rent . . . . [1843
3.2 Outgoings and VAT . . . . [1844]
[3.3 Cost of services consumed . . . . [1845]]
3.4 Repair, cleaning and decoration . . . . [1846]
3.5 Waste and alterations . . . . [1848]
3.6 Aerials, signs and advertisements . . . . [1850]
3.7 Statutory obligations . . . . [1850]
3.8 Entry to inspect and notice to repair . . . . [1852]
3.9 Alienation . . . . [1853]
3.10 Nuisance and residential restrictions . . . . [1871
3.11 Costs of applications, notices and recovery of arrears . . . . [1872]
3.12 Planning and development . . . . [1873]
3.13 Plans, documents and information . . . . [1875]
3.14 Indemnities . . . . [1875]
3.15 Reletting boards and viewing . . . . [1876]
3.16 Obstruction and encroachment . . . . [1876]
3.17 Yielding up . . . . [1877]
3.18 Interest on arrears . . . . [1877]
3.19 Statutory notices . . . . [1878]
[3.20 Keyholders . . . . [1878]]
3.21 Viewing on sale of reversion . . . . [1878]
3.22 Defective premises . . . . [1878]
3.23 Replacement guarantor . . . . [1879]
3.24 Exercise of the Landlord's rights . . . . [1879]
3.25 The Office Covenants . . . . [1879]
3.26 The Services . . . . [1879]
3.27 Costs of grant of this Lease . . . . [1880]
3.28 Consent to the Landlord's release . . . . [1880]
                                              [1803]

4 THE LANDLORD'S COVENANTS
4.1 Quiet enjoyment . . . . [1901]
4.2 The Services . . . . [1902]

5 INSURANCE

5.1 Warranty as to convictions .... [1903]
5.2 Covenant to insure .... [1903]
5.3 Details of the insurance .... [1904]
5.4 Payment of the Insurance Rent .... [1905]
5.5 Suspension of the Rent .... [1905]
5.6 Reinstatement and termination .... [1907]
5.7 Tenant's further insurance covenants .... [1912]
5.8 Increase or decrease of the Building .... [1914]
[5.9 Landlord's further insurance covenants .... [1914]]

6 GUARANTEE PROVISIONS

6.1 The Guarantor's covenants .... [1931]
[6.2 The Landlord's covenant .... [1936]]

7 FORFEITURE .... [1937]

8 MISCELLANEOUS

8.1 Exclusion of warranty as to use .... [1951]
8.2 Exclusion of third party rights .... [1951]
8.3 Representations .... [1951]
8.4 Documents under hand .... [1952]
8.5 Tenant's property .... [1952]
8.6 Compensation on vacating excluded .... [1952]
8.7 Notices .... [1953]
8.8 Rights and easements .... [1955]
8.9 Covenants relating to adjoining property .... [1955]
8.10 Disputes with adjoining occupiers .... [1955]
8.11 Effect of waiver .... [1955]
[8.12 The perpetuity period .... [1956]]
[8.13 Party walls .... [1956]]
8.14 Exclusion of liability .... [1956]
8.15 [New (or) Old] lease .... [1957]
[8.16 Capacity of tenants .... [1957]]
[8.17 Exclusion of the 1954 Act Sections 24–28 .... [1957]]
                                                              [1804]

SCHEDULE 1: THE RIGHTS GRANTED

1-1 Right to use the Common Parts .... [1971]
1-2 Passage and running through the Adjoining Conduits .... [1971]
1-3 Support and protection .... [1971]
1-4 Display of nameplates or signs .... [1971]
1-5 Right to use the Additional Parking Bays .... [1971]
1-6 Right to use toilets .... [1971]

SCHEDULE 2: THE RIGHTS RESERVED

2-1 Passage and running through the Conduits .... [1972]
2-2 Right to construct conduits .... [1972]
2-3 Access .... [1973]
2-4 Right to erect scaffolding .... [1974]
2-5 Rights of support and shelter .... [1974]
2-6 Right to erect new buildings .... [1974]

SCHEDULE 3: THE RENT AND RENT REVIEW

SCHEDULE 4: THE OFFICE COVENANTS

4-1 Use . . . . [1975]
4-2 Ceiling and floor loading . . . . [1976]
4-3 Common Parts . . . . [1976
4-4 Machinery . . . . [1977]
4-5 Unloading . . . . [1977]
4-6 Heating, cooling and ventilation. . . . . [1978]
4-7 Regulations . . . . [1978]
4-8 Nameplates or signs . . . . [1978]

SCHEDULE 5: THE SUBJECTIONS

SCHEDULE 6: THE SERVICE CHARGE

6-1 Definitions . . . . [1979]
6-2 Service charge provisions . . . . [1980]
6-3 The Services . . . . [1983]

SCHEDULE 7: THE AUTHORISED GUARANTEE AGREEMENT

[1805]

AGREEMENT

[HM LAND REGISTRY

LAND REGISTRATION ACT 2002

Administrative area	*(insert details)*
Title number out of which lease is granted	*(title number)*
Property let	*(postal address or description)*]

[1806]

THIS LEASE is made the .... day of .... BETWEEN:

(1)   *(name of landlord)* [of *(address)* *(or as appropriate)* the registered office of which is at *(address)*] [Company Registration no ...][2] ('the Landlord') [and]

(2)   *(name of tenant)* [of *(address)* *(or as appropriate)* being a company registered in [England and Wales *(or)* Scotland][3] the registered office of which is at *(address)*] [Company Registration no ...] ('the Tenant') [and

(3)   *(name of guarantor)* [of *(address)* *(or as appropriate)* the registered office of which is at *(address)*] [Company Registration no ...] ('the Guarantor')]

[1807]

---

1   As to stamp duty land tax see the Information Binder: Stamp Duty Land Tax [1].
       As to Land Registry Fees see the Information Binder: Property [1]: Property Fees.
       On the grant out of an unregistered freehold estate in land of a lease for a term of more than seven years from the date of the grant, application must be made to register the title to the leasehold interest granted: see the Land Registration Act 2002 s 4(1)(c) (37 Halsbury's Statutes (4th Edn) REAL PROPERTY). The tenant must obtain an epitome of title to the freehold reversion, investigate it, and mark it as examined, otherwise he will not be able to be registered with an absolute title: see vol 25(1) (2003 Reissue) LAND REGISTRATION Paragraph 21.1 [132].
       If the freehold reversion is registered, the grant of a lease for a term of more than seven years from the date of the grant must be completed by registration: see the Land Registration Act 2002 s 27(2)(b)(i).

As to the form and contents of leases see vol 22(1) (2003 Reissue) LANDLORD AND TENANT (BUSINESS TENANCIES) Paragraph 104 [601] et seq. As to registered land generally see vol 25(1) (2003 Reissue) LAND REGISTRATION. As to registration of title to leases see vol 25(1) (2003 Reissue) LAND REGISTRATION Paragraph 143 [601] et seq.

This is a lease of premises comprising a suite of offices in an office building. The demise includes only the interior of the walls, floors and ceilings and the inner half of any non-structural walls that divide the premises from other parts of the building. The tenant's repairing covenant is similarly limited. Rights are granted over land adjoining the premises. The landlord covenants to provide services that include the repair and maintenance of those parts of the building not intended for letting such as the common parts and the structure, roof and foundations. The landlord is to be fully reimbursed by means of a service charge, the tenant paying a fixed percentage of the cost of providing the services and any other sums incurred by the landlord in relation to the building. The landlord insures the building and the tenant refunds a proportion of the premium. There is provision for the rent to be reviewed, and for a guarantor. The lease includes some parking bays and grants a right to use additional bays.

The tenant should ensure that the landlord deduces title to the land affected by the rights he is granted, especially where the lease is registrable, because if title is not shown and any consents, eg of any chargee or landlord of the adjoining land, obtained, the rights may be excluded from the title.

2   If any party is a company it is desirable to include the company registration number. This avoids any problems arising when a company has been wound up and a new company formed with the same name, or when the name of a company is changed, or if companies swap names, eg on a reconstruction of a group of companies. In addition, where a company applies to be registered as proprietor of a registered estate or registered charge, the application must state the company's registration number: see the Land Registration Rules 2003, SI 2003/1417 r 181.

3   Where the tenant is a company registered in England and Wales or Scotland, and the lease is registrable, an application for first registration of the lease (where the landlord's title is unregistered), or registration of the lease as a registrable disposition (where the landlord's title is registered), and the tenant as proprietor of the leasehold title, must state the company's registered number: see SI 2003/1417 r 181(1). There seems to be no reason why the certificate and statement should not be contained in the disposition in favour of the proprietor, where convenient.

[1808]

NOW THIS DEED WITNESSES as follows:

1   DEFINITIONS AND INTERPRETATION

For all purposes of this Lease[4] the terms defined in this clause have the meanings specified.

4   One view would add 'unless the context otherwise requires' or 'where the context so admits' and in fact this may be implied (see *Meux v Jacobs* (1875) LR 7 HL 481 at 493; *Law Society v United Service Bureau Ltd* [1934] 1 KB 343, DC) but the better course is to use defined terms so that there are no circumstances where the defined meaning does not apply.

1.1   'The Accountant'[5]

'The Accountant' means *(name)* or a qualified accountant or firm of accountants appointed by the Landlord in his place. The Accountant may be an employee of the Landlord or a company that is a member of the same group of the Landlord within the meaning of the 1954 Act Section 42.

5   For a provision that a surveyor or accountant must be a member of a relevant professional body see vol 22(3) (1997 Reissue) LANDLORD AND TENANT (BUSINESS TENANCIES) Form 152 [6648].

1.2   'The Adjoining Conduits'

'The Adjoining Conduits' means all the pipes, sewers, drains, mains, ducts, conduits, gutters, watercourses, wires, cables, [laser optical fibres, data or impulse transmission, communication or reception systems,] channels, flues and all other conducting media — including any fixings, louvres, cowls, covers and other ancillary apparatus — that are in, on, over or under the Building that serve the Premises.

1.3   'Adjoining property of the Landlord'

References to 'adjoining property of the Landlord' are references to each and every part of any neighbouring or adjoining land, including the Building, in which the Landlord, or a company that is a member of the same group as the Landlord within the meaning of the 1954 Act Section 42, has or during the Term acquires an interest or estate.

1.4   'The Building'

'The Building' means all that the *(describe the building)* [and surrounding land] shown [for the purpose of identification only] edged *(state colour, eg blue)* on the Plan.

1.5   'The Common Parts'

'The Common Parts' means the areas and amenities made available from time to time by the Landlord for use in common by the tenants and occupiers of the Building and all persons expressly or by implication authorised by them including the pedestrian ways, forecourts, [car parks,] [loading bays, service roads,] landscaped areas, entrance halls, landings, [lifts, lift-shafts,] staircases, passages and areas designated for the keeping and collecting of refuse, but not limited to them.

1.6   'The Conduits'

'The Conduits' means the pipes, sewers, drains, mains, ducts, conduits, gutters, watercourses, wires, cables, [laser optical fibres, data or impulse transmission, communication or reception systems,] channels, flues and all other conducting media — including any fixings, louvres, cowls, covers and any other ancillary apparatus — that are in, on, over or under the Premises.

[1809]

1.7   'The [Contractual] Term'[6]

'The [Contractual][7] Term' means *(insert number)* years commencing on and including *(insert date of start of the term)*[8].

6   As to commencement of the term see vol 22(1) (2003 Reissue) LANDLORD AND TENANT (BUSINESS TENANCIES) Paragraph 135 [670].
     As to registration see note 1 above. Where the landlord's title is unregistered, the grantee must apply for registration within a period of two months from the date of the disposition if the lease is granted for a term of more than seven years. If no such application is made the disposition becomes void as regards any transfer, grant or creation of a legal estate: see the Land Registration Act 2002 s 6 (37 Halsbury's Statutes (4th Edn) REAL PROPERTY). Where the landlord's title is registered and the lease is for a term of more than seven years, the tenant should protect the intended lease by applying for an official search, and an application to register the lease should be made before expiry of the search, otherwise the lease will be susceptible to loss of priority: see the Land Registration Act 2002 s 27.
7   The demise in this lease is for 'the Contractual Term', which is defined as a fixed term of years. The expression 'the Term', as defined in clause 1.49 [1823] 'THE TERM', is used in covenants so that they continue to apply during any period of holding over or continuance or extension of the contractual term. Some difficulties arise if this structure is used in a draft lease where security of tenure is to be excluded under the Landlord and Tenant Act 1954 s 38A(1) as inserted by SI 2003/3096 (23 Halsbury's Statutes (4th Edn) LANDLORD AND TENANT). The demise is for the contractual term and the inclusion of the definition of 'the Term' does not prevent the lease being 'for a term of years certain' as required by the Landlord and Tenant Act 1954 s 38A(1). However, reference to continuance of the contractual term by statute is inappropriate where the operation of the security of tenure provisions in the Landlord and Tenant Act 1954 ss 24–28 is to be excluded. If a lease is contracted out of the Landlord and Tenant Act 1954 there can be no statutory extension, and if the tenant remains in occupation at the end of the contractual term he is holding over unlawfully unless there is an express agreement to extend the contractual term operating as a surrender and re-grant so that the original lease — and the agreement under the Landlord and Tenant Act 1954 s 38A(1) — has no further effect. It is suggested that in these circumstances the drafting should be simplified to include a single term (defined simply as 'the Term') by reference to the period of the contractual term. This can be achieved by amending this clause in the manner suggested and substituting it for clause 1.49 [1823] 'THE TERM'.
8   For estate management reasons it is usually desirable to insert a quarter day here — or a rent day when rent is due on days other than quarter days — ie generally the one preceding the earlier of the date of possession and the date of execution.

[1810]

[1.8 'The Decorating Years'

'The Decorating Years' means *(specify years).*] *(omit if not required, eg if the first alternative in clause 3.4.5 [1847]* DECORATION *is used)*

1.9 'Development'

References to 'development' are references to development as defined by the Town and Country Planning Act 1990 Section 55.

1.10 Gender and number

Words importing one gender include all other genders; words importing the singular include the plural and vice versa[9].

9   See the Law of Property Act 1925 s 61 (37 Halsbury's Statutes (4th Edn) REAL PROPERTY).

1.11 Headings[10]

The clause, paragraph and schedule headings and the table of contents do not form part of this document and are not to be taken into account in its construction or interpretation. *(amend if marginal notes are used instead of headings)*

10   Headings and marginal notes require the draftsman to provide a word or two to describe every clause in the lease. This is not always easy and there are times when the draftsman will have to settle for something less than perfection, the only alternative being a heading or note that would be inappropriately long. It would be quite wrong for that title, which its author might admit was not totally apposite but was the best that he could do in a few words, to be used in construing the clause in question.

[1.12 'The Initial Rent'

'The Initial Rent' means [the sum of £... a year *(or as required by the rent and review provisions to be used)*].] *(this definition is not required if the rent is not reviewable*

[1811]

1.13 'The Insurance Rent'[11]

'The Insurance Rent' means the Insurance Rent Percentage of the [gross sums including any commission *(or as required)* sums net of any commission] that the Landlord is from time to time liable to pay —

1.13.1   by way of premium for insuring the Building, including insuring for loss of rent, in accordance with his obligations contained in this Lease[— or, where the insurance includes the Building and other property[12], the proportion of those sums [reasonably] attributable to the Building such proportion to be determined from time to time by the Surveyor acting as an expert and not as an arbitrator],

1.13.2   by way of premium for insuring in such amount and on such terms as [the Landlord acting reasonably considers appropriate *(or as required)* is reasonable] against all liability of the Landlord to third parties arising out of or in connection with any matter involving or relating to the Building, and

1.13.3   for insurance valuations,

and all of any increased premium payable by reason of any act or omission of the Tenant.

11   As to reimbursement of insurance premiums see vol 22(1) (2003 Reissue) LANDLORD AND TENANT (BUSINESS TENANCIES) Paragraph 230 [1026].
12   The building may be insured with other property under a block policy.

1.14   'The Insurance Rent Percentage'

'The Insurance Rent Percentage' means ...%.

1.15   'The Insured Risks'

'The Insured Risks' means the risks of loss or damage by fire[, storm, tempest, earthquake, lightning, explosion, riot, civil commotion, malicious damage, [terrorism,] impact by vehicles and by aircraft and by articles dropped from aircraft—other than war risks — flood damage and bursting and overflowing of water pipes and tanks,] and such other risks, whether or not in the nature of the foregoing, as the Landlord [acting reasonably] from time to time decides to insure against[13].

13   As to the risks to be insured and the tenant's concerns see vol 22(1) (2003 Reissue) LANDLORD AND TENANT (BUSINESS TENANCIES) Paragraph 235 [1033].

[1812]

1.16   'Interest'

References to 'interest' are references to interest payable during the period from the date on which the payment is due to the date of payment, both before and after any judgment, at the Interest Rate then prevailing [*(where the interest rate is defined by reference to a bank base rate)* or, should the base rate referred to in clause 1.17 'THE INTEREST RATE' cease to exist[14], at another rate of interest closely comparable with the Interest Rate [to be agreed between the parties or in default of agreement to be determined by the Accountant[15], acting as an expert and not as an arbitrator *(or as required)* determined upon by the Landlord acting reasonably]].

14   If base rates are referred to, the possibility of their ceasing to exist should be provided for. Alternatively, the Law Society's interest rate may be specified.
15   Where the structure of the lease is such that an accountant is required in the operation of its terms he is a more appropriate person than the surveyor to determine this issue.

1.17   'The Interest Rate'

'The Interest Rate'[16] means the rate of ...% a year[17] above [the base lending rate of *(specify bank)* or such other bank [being a member of the British Bankers Association] as the Landlord from time to time nominates in writing[18] *(or as required)* the Law Society's interest rate[19]].

16   As to the covenant to pay interest see vol 22(1) (2003 Reissue) LANDLORD AND TENANT (BUSINESS TENANCIES) Paragraph 154 [767].
17   Words such as 'with a minimum of ...%' should not be used because, if interest rates drop during the term to such an extent that the minimum rate specified represents significantly more than a few percent over the basic borrowing rate, the provision might be void as a penalty. As to what amounts to a penalty see *Dunlop Pneumatic Tyre Co Ltd v New Garage and Motor Co Ltd* [1915] AC 79, HL; *Cellulose Acetate Silk Co Ltd v Widnes Foundry (1925) Ltd* [1933] AC 20, HL. In view of this, landlords would be unwise to provide for more than a few percent over base rate, and even this is in fact a penalty and should be resisted by the tenant.
18   The chance to change the bank may be useful, especially on a sale of the reversion, so that the landlord can always provide for his bank for the time being to be specified. The tenant should try to limit the choice to major clearing banks.
19   The Law Society's interest rate is published weekly in the Law Society's Gazette.

[1813]

1.18   Interpretation of 'the Building'

The expression 'the Building', where the context so admits, includes any other adjoining property of the Landlord constructed or adapted to form [an integral] part of the Building[20].

20   As to problems that may arise when additional land is acquired see vol 22(1) (2003 Reissue) LANDLORD AND TENANT (BUSINESS TENANCIES) Paragraph 269.1 [1117].

1.19   Interpretation of 'consent' and 'approved'

1.19.1   *Prior written consent or approval*

References to 'consent of the Landlord' or words to similar effect are references to a prior written consent signed by or on behalf of the Landlord and references to the need for anything to be 'approved by the Landlord' or words to similar effect are references to the need for a prior written approval by or on behalf of the Landlord.

1.19.2   *Consent or approval of mortgagee or head landlord*

Any provisions in this Lease referring to the consent or approval of the Landlord are to be construed as also requiring the consent or approval of any mortgagee of the Premises and any head landlord, where that consent is required [under the terms of a mortgage or headlease in existence at the date of this document][21]. Nothing in this Lease is to be construed as imposing any obligation on a mortgagee or head landlord not to refuse any consent or approval unreasonably.

21   The tenant should include these words so that the clause applies *only* where the consent of the mortgagee or head landlord is in fact required under the terms of an *existing* mortgage or headlease. The tenant should request a copy of the document concerned to establish the rights of the mortgagee or head landlord in relation to any consents that he may seek. The risk to the tenant of the clause without these words is that, by subsequently creating a mortgage or headlease, the landlord could, innocently or deliberately, bring about a situation where his consent may be refused in circumstances in which it would otherwise have been unreasonable to do so. In particular, the effect on the tenant's ability to assign or sublet could be serious.

[1814]

1.20   Interpretation of 'the Guarantor'[22]

The expression 'the Guarantor' includes [*(where there is a guarantor for the original tenant)* not only the person named above as the Guarantor, but also][23] any person who enters into covenants with the Landlord pursuant to clause 3.9.5.2 CONDITIONS or clause 3.23 REPLACEMENT GUARANTOR.

22   As to guarantors see vol 22(1) (2003 Reissue) LANDLORD AND TENANT (BUSINESS TENANCIES) Paragraphs 40 [201], 71 [278] et seq.
23   Where there is no guarantor for the original tenant, if it is felt undesirable to have covenants in a lease and no party, at least initially, to enter into them, the guarantor's covenants could be included in a schedule.

1.21   Interpretation of 'the Landlord'

The expression 'the Landlord' includes the person or persons from time to time entitled to possession of the Premises when this Lease comes to an end.

1.22   Interpretation of 'the last year of the Term' and 'the end of the Term'

References to 'the last year of the Term' are references to the actual last year of the Term howsoever it determines, and references to the 'end of the Term' are references to the end of the Term whensoever and howsoever it determines.

1.23   Interpretation of 'the Tenant'

'The Tenant' includes any person who is for the time being bound by the tenant covenants of this Lease except where the name of *(name of original tenant)* appears.

1.24   Interpretation of 'this Lease'

Unless expressly stated to the contrary, the expression 'this Lease' includes any document supplemental to or collateral with this document or entered into in accordance with this document.

1.25   Joint and several liability

Where any party to this Lease for the time being comprises two or more persons, obligations expressed or implied to be made by or with that party are deemed to be made by or with the persons comprising that party jointly and severally.

[1815]

1.26   'The Landlord's Expenses'

'The Landlord's Expenses' means the costs and expenditure — including all charges, commissions, premiums, fees and interest — paid or incurred, or deemed in accordance with the provisions of paragraph 6-2.3 DEEMED LANDLORD'S EXPENSES to be paid or incurred, by the Landlord in respect of or incidental to all or any of the Services or otherwise required to be taken into account for the purpose of calculating the Service Charge, except those recovered from any insurance policy effected by the Landlord pursuant to clause 5.2 COVENANT TO INSURE.

1.27   'The Liability Period'[24]

'The Liability Period' means —

[1.27.1   in the case of *(name of guarantor for the original tenant)*, the period during which *(name of original tenant)* is bound by the tenant covenants of this Lease together with any additional period during which *(name of original tenant)* is liable under an authorised guarantee agreement,] *(omit if there is no guarantor for the original tenant)*

1.27.2   in the case of any guarantor required pursuant to clause 3.9.5.2 CONDITIONS, the period during which the relevant assignee is bound by the tenant covenants of this Lease together with any additional period during which that assignee is liable under an authorised guarantee agreement,

1.27.3   in the case of any guarantor under an authorised guarantee agreement, the period during which the relevant assignee is bound by the tenant covenants of this Lease, and

1.27.4   in the case of any guarantor required pursuant to clause 3.9.8.7 TERMS OF A PERMITTED SUBLEASE, the period during which the relevant assignee of the sublease is bound by the tenant covenants of that sublease.

24   The liability of the guarantor should be expressed to last while the original tenant, or as the case may be the assignee, is bound by the tenant covenants in the lease — or in the case of clause 1.27.4 the sublease — rather than while the lease is vested in that person, to take account of the possibility of an excluded assignment being made and the tenant — or subtenant — remaining liable. An excluded assignment means that the tenant — or subtenant — is precluded from tenant release under the Landlord and Tenant (Covenants) Act 1995 (23 Halsbury's Statutes (4th Edn) LANDLORD AND TENANT).
      The Landlord and Tenant (Covenants) Act 1995 does not clearly indicate whether the liability of a contractual guarantor can be expressed to extend to any period during which the tenant is bound by an authorised guarantee agreement, but the better view is that it is possible. The policy of the Act certainly suggests that this should be the case.

[1816]

1.28 'Losses'

References to 'losses' are references to liabilities, damages or losses, awards of damages or compensation, penalties, costs, disbursements or expenses arising from any claim, demand, action or proceedings.

1.29 'The 1954 Act'

'The 1954 Act' means the Landlord and Tenant Act 1954 [and all statutes regulations and orders included by virtue of clause 1.41 REFERENCES TO STATUTES][25].

25   The words in square brackets are strictly speaking not required because they merely state what would be the case anyway by virtue of clause 1.41 [1821] REFERENCES TO STATUTES. Nevertheless, as much could turn on the point (see *Brett v Brett Essex Golf Club Ltd* (1986) 52 P & CR 330, [1986] 1 EGLR 154, CA), the parties may prefer to deal expressly with the point.

1.30 'The 1995 Act'

'The 1995 Act' means the Landlord and Tenant (Covenants) Act 1995 [and all statutes, regulations and orders included by virtue of clause 1.42 REFERENCES TO STATUTES][26].

26   See note 25 to clause 1.29 [1817] 'THE 1954 ACT'.

1.31 Obligation not to permit or suffer

Any covenant by the Tenant not to do anything includes an obligation [to use reasonable endeavours] not to permit or suffer[27] that thing to be done by another person [where the Tenant is aware that the thing is being done].

27   'Permit' may have a different meaning from 'suffer': see *Barton v Reed* [1932] 1 Ch 362 at 375 per Luxmore J. A covenant not to 'permit' activity is broken if the covenantor himself carries it on: see *Oceanic Village Ltd v United Attractions Ltd* [2000] Ch 234, [2000] 1 All ER 975.

1.32 'The Office Covenants'

'The Office Covenants' means the covenants set out in schedule 4 THE OFFICE COVENANTS.

[1817]

1.33 'Other buildings'

References to 'other buildings' are references to all the buildings other than the Building now or at any time during the Term erected on any adjoining property of the Landlord.

1.34 The Parking Bays[28]

1.34.1 *'The Additional Parking Bays'*

'The Additional Parking Bays' means the parking bays numbered ... to ... inclusive in the car park of the Building, shown coloured *(state colour, eg brown)* on the Plan.

28   Car parking is always an emotive issue in the case of an office building in multi-occupation. Where car parking is provided and it is practicable, tenants generally prefer to have 'their' car parking bays actually included as part of the demised premises as this gives the individual tenant control over his own parking. Landlords, however, frequently prefer merely to grant the right to park in a defined number of parking bays in a communal parking area. This can be unsatisfactory for the tenants if 'illegal' parking takes place because they have to rely on the landlord's control. If there is extensive parking, a combination of the two approaches might be appropriate as suggested in this lease, ie some parking bays included within the demise and the right granted to park in other bays.

1.34.2   'The Included Parking Bays'

'The Included Parking Bays' means the parking bays numbered ... to ... inclusive in the car park of the Building, shown coloured *(state colour, eg green)* on the Plan.

1.35   'The Permitted Hours'

'The Permitted Hours' means the period from ... to ... *(insert the hours during which the offices may be used)*

1.36   'The Plan'[29]

'The Plan' means the plan annexed to this Lease.

29   As to the use and role of plans see vol 22(1) (2003 Reissue) LANDLORD AND TENANT (BUSINESS TENANCIES) Paragraphs 117 [636], 118 [638]. Although a plan is necessary in the circumstances assumed by this lease, a plan may not always be required, eg in a case where there is a demise of all the land within a registered title. If the lease is registrable, a plan 'for identification purposes only' or where there is some other disclaimer as to the extent to which it can be relied on for conveyancing purposes is not sufficient if part of the land in a registered title is being dealt with.

[1818]

1.37   'The Planning Acts'

'The Planning Acts' means the Town and Country Planning Act 1990, the Planning (Listed Buildings and Conservation Areas) Act 1990, the Planning (Consequential Provisions) Act 1990, the Planning (Hazardous Substances) Act 1990, the Planning and Compensation Act 1991, the Planning and Compulsory Purchase Act 2004 [and all statutes, regulations and orders included by virtue of clause 1.41 REFERENCES TO STATUTES][30].

30   See note 25 to clause 1.29 [1817] 'THE 1954 ACT'.

1.38   'The Premises'[31]

1.38.1   *Definition of 'the Premises'*

'The Premises means [the first and second floors [and part of the third floor] *(or as the case may be)*][32] of the Building and the Included Parking Bays, shown [for the purpose of identification only] edged *(state colour, eg red)* and coloured *(state colour, eg green)* on the Plan.

31   As to parcels generally see vol 22(1) (2003 Reissue) LANDLORD AND TENANT (BUSINESS TENANCIES) Paragraph 116 [634]. As to the property definition in leases of part of a building see vol 22(1) (2003 Reissue) LANDLORD AND TENANT (BUSINESS TENANCIES) Paragraph 120 [642].
32   Where several floors are involved, more than one plan may be needed to show them and the definition of 'the Plan' should be amended accordingly.

[1819]

1.38.2   *Interpretation of 'the Premises'*[33]

The expression 'the Premises' includes —

[1.38.2.1   the floor and ceiling finishes, but not any other part of the floor slabs and ceiling slabs that bound the Premises,

1.38.2.2   the inner half severed medially of the internal non-loadbearing walls that divide the Premises from any other premises,

1.38.2.3   the interior plaster and decorative finishes of all walls bounding the Premises,

1.38.2.4   the doors and windows and door and window frames at the Premises,

1.38.2.5   all additions and improvements to the Premises,

1.38.2.6   all the landlord's fixtures and fittings and fixtures of every kind that are from time to time in or on the Premises — whether originally fixed or fastened to or on the Premises or otherwise — except any fixtures installed by the Tenant [or any predecessors in title] that can be removed from the Premises without defacing them[34],

1.38.2.7   the Conduits exclusively serving the Premises, and

1.38.2.8   the Included Parking Bays,

but excludes the roof and the roof space, the foundations, and all external, structural or loadbearing walls, columns, beams and supports, and any of the Conduits that do not exclusively serve the Premises *(or as required in the circumstances according to the construction methods used)*][35]. Unless the contrary is expressly stated 'the Premises' includes any part or parts of the Premises.

33   As to implied grants and reservations see vol 22(1) (2003 Reissue) LANDLORD AND TENANT (BUSINESS TENANCIES) Paragraph 125 [650].
34   As to fixtures see vol 22(1) (2003 Reissue) LANDLORD AND TENANT (BUSINESS TENANCIES) Paragraph 121 [644].
35   It is very dangerous for the draftsman to rely on one set of general words that he hopes will apply to the division of all buildings. These 'standard words' may prove totally unsuitable for a particular building having regard to its nature, configuration and the methods of construction used and also having regard to the nature and extent of any surrounding land included within the demise. Surveyors and engineers must be involved and each building must be looked at individually. There can be no uniform answer as to who should repair which parts of the premises. This clause may need amendment according to the view taken. As to the allocation of legal and financial responsibility for repairs see vol 22(1) (2003 Reissue) LANDLORD AND TENANT (BUSINESS TENANCIES) Paragraph 199 [936].

[1820]

1.39   References to clauses and schedules

Any reference in this document to a clause, paragraph or schedule without further designation is to be construed as a reference to the clause, paragraph or schedule to this document so numbered.

1.40   References to rights of access

References to any right of the Landlord to have access to the Premises are to be construed as extending to any head landlord and any mortgagee of the Premises [— where the headlease or mortgage grants such rights of access to the head landlord or mortgagee —] and to all persons authorised in writing by the Landlord and any head landlord or mortgagee, including agents, professional advisers, contractors, workmen and others.

1.41   References to statutes

Unless expressly stated to the contrary any references to a specific statute include any statutory extension or modification, amendment or re-enactment of that statute and any regulations or orders made under that statute, and any general reference to a statute includes any regulations or orders made under that statute[36].

36   Unfortunately the Interpretation Act 1978 ss 17, 23(3) (41 Halsbury's Statutes (4th Edn) STATUTES) does not quite go far enough to enable this clause to be dispensed with altogether, particularly where a statute is modified.

1.42 'The Rent'[37]

[Until the First Review Date 'the Rent' means the Initial Rent. Thereafter 'the Rent' means the sum ascertained in accordance with schedule 3 THE RENT AND RENT REVIEW. 'The Rent' does not include the Insurance Rent and the Service Charge[38], but the term 'the Lease Rents' means both the Rent and the Insurance Rent and the Service Charge. *(or as required by the rent and review provisions used)*]

37   This clause assumes that the rent is reviewable. If the rent is not reviewable clause 1.12 [1811] 'THE INITIAL RENT' should be omitted and this clause amended as appropriate.

38   Because of this exclusion the insurance rent and service charge are not suspended under clause 5.5 [1905] SUSPENSION OF THE RENT.

1.43 'The Rent Commencement Date'

'The Rent Commencement Date' means *(insert the date on which payment of the rent is to start)*[39].

39   This provision may be used to provide for a rent-free period, or for the situation where the tenant has had possession before execution of the lease on the basis that rent should be paid from the date of possession. If either the date of execution of the lease, or the date of commencement of the term, is to be the date for commencement of rent, that date should be inserted here.

[1821]

[1.44 'The Review Dates'[40]

'The First Review Date' means *(date)*. 'The Review Dates' means the First Review Date and every *(insert ordinal, eg 3rd)* anniversary of that date during the [Contractual] Term [*(if appropriate for the review provisions used)* — and any other date from time to time specified under *(insert the relevant provision: see eg vol 22(3) (1997 Reissue) LANDLORD AND TENANT (BUSINESS TENANCIES) Form 180 paragraph {2}-4 [6728] EFFECT OF COUNTER-INFLATION PROVISIONS)*]. References to 'a review date' are reference to any one of the Review Dates.] *(omit if not required by the review provisions to be used, or if the rent is not reviewable)*

40   As to rent review dates and intervals see vol 22(1) (2003 Reissue) LANDLORD AND TENANT (BUSINESS TENANCIES) Paragraph 302 [1333] et seq. Where there might be a statutory continuation of the lease the landlord may wish to ensure that there is a review date shortly before the end of the contractual term to obviate the need to apply for an interim rent. The tenant may wish to insist on the word 'contractual' remaining so that the rent review provisions do not apply during any period of lawful holding over or extension or continuance of the contractual term.

1.45 'The Service Charge'

'The Service Charge' means the Service Charge Percentage of the Landlord's Expenses.

1.46 'The Service Charge Percentage'

'The Service Charge Percentage' means ...% subject to the provisions for variation contained in paragraph 6-2.6 VARIATION OF THE SERVICE CHARGE PERCENTAGE. *(this definition may not be required if, eg, the tenant's proportion is determined by reference to net internal areas: see eg vol 22(3) (1997 Reissue) LANDLORD AND TENANT (BUSINESS TENANCIES) Form 150 [6629])*

1.47 'The Services'

'The Services' means the services, facilities and amenities specified in paragraph 6-3 THE SERVICES.

1.48   'The Surveyor'[41]

'The Surveyor' means *(name)* or any person or firm appointed by the Landlord in his place. The Surveyor may be an employee of the Landlord or a company that is a member of the same group as the Landlord within the meaning of the 1954 Act Section 42. The expression 'the Surveyor' includes the person or firm appointed by the Landlord to collect the Lease Rents.

41   For a provision that the landlord's surveyor must be a member of a relevant professional body see vol 22(3) (1997 Reissue) LANDLORD AND TENANT (BUSINESS TENANCIES) Form 152 [6648].

[1822]

[1.49   'The Term'

'The Term' means the Contractual Term and any period of holding-over or extension or continuance of the Contractual Term by statute or common law[42].] *(omit if the lease is to be contracted out of the Landlord and Tenant Act 1954)*[43]

42   The demise in this lease is for 'the Contractual Term', which is defined as a fixed term of years. The expression 'the Term' is used in covenants so that they continue to apply during any period of holding over or continuance or extension of the contractual term. As to the liability of a guarantor during a period of statutory continuation see vol 22(1) (2003 Reissue) LANDLORD AND TENANT (BUSINESS TENANCIES) Paragraph 73 [282].

43   Some difficulties arise if the structure referred to in note 42 above is used in a draft lease where security of tenure is to be excluded under the Landlord and Tenant Act 1954 s 38A(1) as inserted by SI 2003/3096. The demise is for the contractual term and the inclusion of the definition of 'the Term' does not prevent the lease being 'for a term of years certain' as required by the Landlord and Tenant Act 1954 s 38A(1). However, reference to continuance of the contractual term by statute is inappropriate where the operation of the security of tenure provisions in the Landlord and Tenant Act 1954 ss 24–28 is to be excluded. If a lease is contracted out of the Landlord and Tenant Act 1954 there can be no statutory extension, and if the tenant remains in occupation at the end of the contractual term he is holding over unlawfully unless there is an express agreement to extend the contractual term operating as a surrender and re-grant so that the original lease — and the agreement under the Landlord and Tenant Act 1954 s 38A(1) — has no further effect. It is suggested that in these circumstances the drafting should be simplified to include a single term (defined simply as 'theTerm') by reference to the period of the contractual term. This can be achieved by amending clause 1.7 [1810] 'THE [CONTRACTUAL] TERM' as suggested and substituting it for this clause.

1.50   Terms from the 1995 Act

Where the expressions 'landlord covenants', 'tenant covenants', or 'authorised guarantee agreement' are used in this Lease they are to have the same meaning as is given by the 1995 Act Section 28(1).

1.51   'VAT'[44]

'VAT' means value added tax or any other tax of a similar nature and, unless otherwise expressly stated, all references to rents or other sums payable by the Tenant are exclusive of VAT.

44   As to VAT generally see the Information Binder: Property [1]: VAT and Property.

[1823]–[1840]

2   DEMISE

The Landlord lets[45] the Premises to the Tenant [with [full *(or)* limited] title guarantee], together with the rights specified in schedule 1 THE RIGHTS GRANTED but excepting and reserving to the Landlord the rights specified in schedule 2 THE RIGHTS RESERVED, to hold the Premises to the Tenant for the [Contractual][46] Term subject to [all rights, easements, privileges, restrictions, covenants and stipulations of whatever nature affecting the Premises including any matters contained or referred to in schedule 5 THE SUBJECTIONS *(or as required)* the rights, easements, privileges, restrictions, covenants and stipulations affecting the Premises contained or referred to in schedule 5 THE SUBJECTIONS][47], yielding and paying[48] to the Landlord —

2.1   the Rent, without any deduction or set-off[49], by equal quarterly payments in advance[50] on the usual quarter days[51] in every year and proportionately for any period of less than a year, the first such payment, being a proportionate sum in respect of the period from and including the Rent Commencement Date to and including the day before the quarter day next after the Rent Commencement Date, to be paid on the date of this document[52], and

2.2   by way of further rent the Insurance Rent[53] payable on demand in accordance with clause 5.4 PAYMENT OF THE INSURANCE RENT, and

2.3   by way of further rent the Service Charge[54] payable in accordance with schedule 6 THE SERVICE CHARGE.

[1841]

45   Traditionally, the operative word in a lease executed as a deed was 'demises' but any words sufficient to show the parties' intention may be used.

46   See note 43 to clause 1.49 [1823] 'THE TERM'.

47   The tenant should argue for the second version, making the schedule comprehensive rather than illustrative.

48   The words 'yielding and paying' imply a covenant to pay rent: see *Vyvyan v Arthur* (1823) 1 B & C 410. An express covenant is now invariably included because further procedural matters are contained in it.

49   As to deductions and set off see vol 22(1) (2003 Reissue) LANDLORD AND TENANT (BUSINESS TENANCIES) Paragraph 147 [753].

50   In the absence of an express provision, rent is payable in arrears.

51   The usual quarter days are 25 March, 24 June, 29 September and 25 December. A reference to 'the usual quarter days' is all that is necessary when rent is to be paid on these days.

52   If the first payment is not a complete instalment, the lease must provide for the date on which it is to be paid, the amount, and the period it is to cover.

53   As to the advantages of reserving the insurance rent as rent see vol 22(1) (2003 Reissue) LANDLORD AND TENANT (BUSINESS TENANCIES) Paragraph 151 [761].

54   As to the advantages of reserving the service charge as rent see vol 22(1) (2003 Reissue) LANDLORD AND TENANT (BUSINESS TENANCIES) Paragraph 151 [761].

[1842]

3   THE TENANT'S COVENANTS

The Tenant covenants with the Landlord to observe and perform the requirements of this clause 3.

3.1   Rent

3.1.1   *Payment of the Lease Rents*

The Tenant must pay the Lease Rents[55] on the days and in the manner set out in this Lease, and must not exercise or seek to exercise any right or claim to withhold rent, or any right or claim to legal or equitable set-off[56] [except that referred to in *(give details of any provisions granting an express right of set-off)*][57].

55   As to the definition of 'the Lease Rents' see clause 1.42 [1821] 'THE RENT'.

56   See eg *British Anzani (Felixstowe) Ltd v International Marine Management (UK) Ltd* [1980] QB 137, [1979] 2 All ER 1063; *Lee-Parker v Izzet* [1971] 3 All ER 1099, [1971] 1 WLR 1688. As to deductions and set-off see vol 22(1) (2003 Reissue) LANDLORD AND TENANT (BUSINESS TENANCIES) Paragraphs 147 [753], 148 [755].

57   If any express right of set-off is granted to the tenant, reference to the provision concerned should be included here to avoid inconsistency.

3.1.2   *Payment by banker's order*[58]

If so required in writing by the Landlord, the Tenant must pay the Lease Rents[59] by banker's order or credit transfer to any bank and account [in the United Kingdom] that the Landlord nominates from time to time.

58   This is a clause with dangers for both parties. If the existence of a breach of covenant is known to the landlord he must instruct his bank to refuse to accept the rent, otherwise his right of forfeiture is lost. As to implied waiver of the right of forfeiture see vol 22(1) (2003 Reissue) LANDLORD AND TENANT (BUSINESS TENANCIES) Paragraph 284 [1173]. The tenant may feel that he requires more control over the payment of rent. In any event, the financial systems operated by many companies prevent payments being made in this way.

59   As to the definition of 'the Lease Rents' see clause 1.42 [1821] 'THE RENT'.

[1843]

3.2   Outgoings and VAT

3.2.1   *Outgoings exclusive to the Premises*

The Tenant must pay, and must indemnify the Landlord against —

3.2.1.1   all rates, taxes[60], assessments, duties, charges, impositions and outgoings that are now or may at any time during the Term be charged, assessed or imposed upon the Premises or on the owner or occupier of them[, excluding any payable by the Landlord occasioned by receipt of the Lease Rents[61] or by any disposition of or dealing with this Lease or ownership of any interest reversionary to the interest created by it][62] [— provided that if the Landlord suffers loss of any rating relief applicable to empty premises after the end of the Term because the relief has been allowed to the Tenant in respect of a period before the end of the Term, then the Tenant must make good such loss to the Landlord],

3.2.1.2   all VAT from time to time charged on the Lease Rents or other sums payable by the Tenant under this Lease[63], and

3.2.1.3   all VAT incurred in relation to any costs that the Tenant is obliged to pay or in respect of which he is required to indemnify the Landlord under the terms of this Lease, save where such VAT is recoverable or available for set-off by the Landlord as input tax[64].

60   As to covenants to pay rates and taxes see vol 22(1) (2003 Reissue) LANDLORD AND TENANT (BUSINESS TENANCIES) Paragraph 153 [765].

61   As to the definition of 'the Lease Rents' see clause 1.42 [1821] 'THE RENT'.

62   The tenant should add the words in square brackets to make it clear that he is not paying the landlord's taxes.

63   As to VAT on rent, service charges and insurance premiums see the Information Binder: Property [1]: VAT and Property.

64   As to payment of VAT on legal costs paid by a person other than the solicitor's own client see the Information Binder: Property [1]: VAT and Property.

[1844]

3.2.2 *Outgoings assessed on the Premises and other property*

The Tenant must pay, and must indemnify the Landlord against, the proportion reasonably attributable to the Premises — to be determined from time to time by the Surveyor, acting as an expert and not as an arbitrator[65] — of all rates, taxes, assessments, duties, charges, impositions and outgoings that are now or at any time during the Term may be charged, assessed or imposed on the Premises and any other property, including any adjoining property of the Landlord, or on the owner or occupier of them and it.

65   As to the distinction between an expert and an arbitrator see vol 22(1) (2003 Reissue) LANDLORD AND TENANT (BUSINESS TENANCIES) Paragraph 364 [1523].

[3.3   Cost of services consumed[66]

The Tenant must pay to the suppliers, and indemnify the Landlord against, all charges for electricity, water, gas, telecommunications and other services consumed or used at or in relation to the Premises, including meter rents and standing charges, and must comply with the lawful requirements and regulations of the respective suppliers.] *(omit if the premises have independent supplies of all services)*

66   Premises comprising only part of a building may not have separate supplies of all services and, in these circumstances, this clause should be included.

[1845]

3.4   Repair, cleaning and decoration

3.4.1   *Repair of the Premises*[67]

The Tenant must repair the Premises and keep them in good condition and repair, except for damage caused by one or more of the Insured Risks save to the extent that the insurance money is irrecoverable due to any act or default of the Tenant or anyone at the Premises expressly or by implication[68] with his authority [and under his control][69].

67   As to repair see vol 22(1) (2003 Reissue) LANDLORD AND TENANT (BUSINESS TENANCIES) Paragraph 196 [931] et seq. For a covenant to repair, rebuild and renew see vol 22(3) (1997 Reissue) LANDLORD AND TENANT (BUSINESS TENANCIES) Form 85 [6460]. For provisos excluding, eg, work that is prevented etc see vol 22(3) (1997 Reissue) LANDLORD AND TENANT (BUSINESS TENANCIES) Forms 87 [6462], 88 [6463].
        If a landlord is unable to obtain full insurance cover without excess, it should be made clear whether the tenant is to be liable to pay the excess where damage is caused by an insured risk. For a covenant limiting the tenant's repairing obligations by reference to uninsurable as well as insured risks see vol 22(3) (1997 Reissue) LANDLORD AND TENANT (BUSINESS TENANCIES) Form 90 [6465]. It should be noted that it is now recommended 'best practice' that if the premises are so damaged by an uninsured risk as to prevent occupation, the tenant should be allowed to terminate the lease unless the landlord agrees to reinstate at his own cost: see vol 22(1) (2003 Reissue) LANDLORD AND TENANT (BUSINESS TENANCIES) Paragraph 85 [402]. If adopted, this recommendation involves damage preventing occupation caused by uninsured or uninsurable risks being excluded from the ambit of the tenant's repairing covenant.
68   The expression 'by implication' is intended to include a caller on the premises, such as a tradesman, where there has been no express invitation but the person cannot be classed as a trespasser.
69   The tenant should add the words in square brackets.

3.4.2   *Replacement of landlord's fixtures*

The Tenant must replace from time to time any landlord's fixtures and fittings in the Premises that are beyond repair at any time during or at the end of the Term.

[1846]

3.4.3   *Cleaning and tidying*

The Tenant must keep the Premises clean and tidy and clear of all rubbish.

3.4.4   *The Included Parking Bays*

3.4.4.1   **Care of the Included Parking Bays**

The Tenant must keep the Included Parking Bays adequately marked out, surfaced, in good condition and free from weeds, and must use them for car parking only.

3.4.4.2   **Storage on the Included Parking Bays**

The Tenant must not store anything on the Included Parking Bays [or bring anything onto them] [that is or might become untidy, unclean, unsightly or in any way detrimental to the Building or the area generally].

3.4.4.3   **Rubbish on the Included Parking Bays**

The Tenant must not deposit any waste, rubbish or refuse on the Included Parking Bays [or place any receptacle for waste, rubbish or refuse on them].

3.4.4.4   **Caravans on the Included Parking Bays**

The Tenant must not keep or store any caravan or movable dwelling on the Included Parking Bays.

3.4.5   *Decoration*

[As often as may in the [reasonable] opinion of the Surveyor be necessary in order to maintain a high standard of decorative finish and attractiveness and to preserve the Premises *(or as required)* In each of the Decorating Years][70] and in the last year of the Term the Tenant must redecorate the Premises[71] in a good and workmanlike manner, with appropriate materials of good quality[, to the [reasonable] satisfaction of the Surveyor], any change in the tints, colours and patterns of the decoration to be approved by the Landlord [, whose approval may not be unreasonably withheld [or delayed]]][72] [, provided that the covenants relating to the last year of the Term are not to apply where the Tenant has redecorated the Premises less than *(state period, eg 18 months)* before the end of the Term].

---

70   The draftsman should discuss with the landlord and his property advisers whether he wishes to have the flexibility of the first option or the certainty of the second.

71   The restricted nature of the demise should be borne in mind when considering the scope of this covenant: see clause 1.38 [1819] 'THE PREMISES'.

72   The tenant may amend to provide for the landlord's approval to tints etc to apply only in the last year of the term.

3.5   Waste and alterations

3.5.1   *Waste, additions and alterations*[73]

The Tenant must not commit any waste, make any addition to the Premises, unite the Premises with any adjoining premises, or make any alteration to the Premises except as permitted by the provisions of this clause 3.5.

73   As to control of alterations see vol 22(1) (2003 Reissue) LANDLORD AND TENANT (BUSINESS TENANCIES) Paragraph 186 [911] et seq.

3.5.2   *Pre-conditions for alterations*

The Tenant must not make any [internal non-structural] alterations to the Premises unless he first —

3.5.2.1   obtains and complies with the necessary consents of the competent authorities and pays their charges for them,

3.5.2.2   makes an application to the Landlord for consent, supported by drawings and where appropriate a specification in duplicate [prepared by an architect[, or a member of some other appropriate profession,] who must supervise the work throughout to completion],

3.5.2.3   pays the fees of the Landlord, any head landlord, any mortgagee and their respective professional advisers,

3.5.2.4   enters into any covenants the Landlord requires as to the execution and reinstatement of the alterations, and

3.5.2.5   obtains the consent of the Landlord, whose consent may not be unreasonably withheld [or delayed].

[In the case of any works of a substantial nature, the Landlord may require the Tenant to provide, before starting the works, adequate security in the form of a deposit of money or the provision of a bond as assurance to the Landlord that any works he permits from time to time will be fully completed.]

[1848]

3.5.3   *Internal partitions*

Without prejudice to the provisions of this clause 3.5, the Tenant may install and remove internal demountable partitions if he gives notice of the works and supplies a plan and specification to the Landlord within one month of completion of the works, consults a qualified services consultant before commencement of the works, and ensures that there is no disruption of the services and supplies in, to and through the Premises.

3.5.4   *Removal of alterations*[74]

At the end of the Term, if so requested by the Landlord, the Tenant must remove any additions, alterations or improvements made to the Premises, and must make good any part of the Premises damaged by their removal.

74   This clause has probably come to be inserted because landlords hope that it will defeat the effect of the compensation provisions of the Landlord and Tenant Act 1927 Pt I (ss 1–17) (23 Halsbury's Statutes (4th Edn) LANDLORD AND TENANT) — as to which see vol 22(1) (2003 Reissue) LANDLORD AND TENANT (BUSINESS TENANCIES) Paragraph 192 [923] et seq — ie because, if the improvement has been removed, it will not be an improvement to the holding at the time of quitting the premises. In fact, the clause might not achieve this effect, because the Landlord and Tenant Act 1927 s 9 as amended by the Landlord and Tenant Act 1954 s 49 prohibits contracting out. Also, the clause may be void under the Landlord and Tenant Act 1927 s 19(2), so far as it applies to improvements, on the grounds that it purports to fetter the court in deciding what is reasonable. The tenant should not, however, rely on the application of these statutory provisions and should seek to strike out the clause.

3.5.5   *Connection to the Conduits*

The Tenant must not make any connection with the Conduits except in accordance with plans and specifications approved by the Landlord[, whose approval may not be unreasonably withheld [or delayed]], and subject to consent to make the connection having previously been obtained from the competent authority, undertaker or supplier.

[1849]

3.6   Aerials signs and advertisements

3.6.1   *Masts and wires*

The Tenant must not [erect any pole or mast or] install any cable or wire on the Premises, whether in connection with telecommunications or otherwise.

3.6.2   *Advertisements*[75]

The Tenant must not fix to or exhibit on the outside of the Premises, or fix to or exhibit through any window of the Premises, or display anywhere on the Premises any placard, sign, notice, fascia, board or advertisement, except, with the consent of the Landlord, a sign of the same design, so far as possible, as those the Tenant has the right, by virtue of paragraph 1-4 DISPLAY OF NAMEPLATES OR SIGNS, to have displayed on the outside of the Building and in the reception area of the Building.

75   See the Town and Country Planning (Control of Advertisements) Regulations 1992, SI 1992/666 as amended. In the absence of a covenant such as this and subject to those Regulations, the tenant is entitled to exhibit advertisements etc on the premises, whether or not they are connected with his business: see *Clapman v Edwards* [1938] 2 All ER 507.

3.7   Statutory obligations

3.7.1   *General provision*[76]

The Tenant must comply in all respects with the requirements of any statutes, and any other obligations imposed by law or by any byelaws, applicable to the Premises or the trade or business for the time being carried on there.

76   As to the covenant to comply with statutes see vol 22(1) (2003 Reissue) LANDLORD AND TENANT (BUSINESS TENANCIES) Paragraph 182 [905]. For a provision requiring the landlord to pay compensation for works above a certain value see vol 22(3) (1997 Reissue) LANDLORD AND TENANT (BUSINESS TENANCIES) Form 169 [6693].

[1850]

3.7.2   *Particular obligations*

3.7.2.1   Works required by statute, department or authority

Without prejudice to the generality of clause 3.7.1, the Tenant must execute all works and provide and maintain all arrangements on or in respect of the Premises or the use to which the Premises are being put that are required in order to comply with the requirements of any statute already or in the future to be passed, or the requirements of any government department, local authority or other public or competent authority or court of competent jurisdiction, regardless of whether such requirements are imposed on the owner, the occupier, or any other person.

3.7.2.2   Acts causing losses

Without prejudice to the generality of clause 3.7.1, the Tenant must not do in or near the Premises anything by reason of which the Landlord may incur any losses under any statute.

3.7.2.3   Construction (Design and Management) Regulations

Without prejudice to the generality of clause 3.7.1, the Tenant must comply with the provisions of the Construction (Design and Management) Regulations 1994 ('the CDM Regulations'), be the only client as defined in the provisions of the CDM Regulations, fulfil in relation to all and any works all the obligations of the client as set out in or reasonably to be inferred from the CDM Regulations, and make a declaration to that effect[77] to the Health and Safety Executive in accordance with the Approved Code of Practice published from time to time by the Health and Safety Executive in relation to the CDM Regulations. The provisions of clause 5.7.3 FIRE-FIGHTING EQUIPMENT are to have effect in any circumstances to which these obligations apply.

3.7.2.4   Delivery of health and safety files

At the end of the Term, the Tenant must forthwith deliver to the Landlord any and all health and safety files relating to the premises in accordance with the CDM Regulations.

77   If works are being carried out for the tenant, the landlord will not want to accept the liabilities that are placed on a client under the Construction (Design and Management) Regulations 1994, SI 1994/3140 and the Health and Safety Executive Approved Code of Practice. The landlord will need to ensure that the tenant actually makes the declaration required, and that he obtains the notification served on the tenant by the Health and Safety Executive.

[1851]

3.8   Entry to inspect and notice to repair

3.8.1   *Entry and notice*

The Tenant must permit the Landlord[78] [on reasonable notice during normal business hours except in emergency][79] —

3.8.1.1   to enter the Premises to ascertain whether or not the covenants and conditions of this Lease have been observed and performed,

3.8.1.2   to view the state of repair and condition of the Premises, and to open up floors and other parts of the Premises where that is necessary in order to do so, and

3.8.1.3   to give to the Tenant, or notwithstanding clause 8.7 NOTICES leave on the Premises, a notice ('a notice to repair') specifying the works required to remedy any breach of the Tenant's obligations in this Lease,

provided that any opening-up must be made good by and at the cost of the Landlord if it reveals no breach of the terms of this Lease.

78   The provisions of clause 1.40 [1821] REFERENCES TO RIGHTS OF ACCESS should be noted.
79   The tenant should add the words in square brackets.

3.8.2   *Works to be carried out*

The Tenant must carry out the works specified in a notice to repair immediately, including making good any opening up that revealed a breach of the terms of this Lease.

[1852]

[3.8.3   *Landlord's power in default*[80]

If within *(state period, eg 1 month)* of the service of a notice to repair the Tenant has not started to execute the work referred to in that notice or is not proceeding diligently with it, or if the Tenant fails to finish the work within *(state period, eg 2 months)*[81][, or if in the [Landlord's *(or as required)* Surveyor's] [reasonable] opinion the Tenant is unlikely to have finished the work within that period], the Tenant must permit the Landlord to enter the Premises to execute the outstanding work, and must, within *(state period, eg 14 days)* of a written demand, pay to the Landlord the cost of so doing and all expenses incurred by the Landlord, including legal costs and surveyor's fees.]

80   The advantages of this clause for the landlord must be weighed against the potential liability that it creates under the Defective Premises Act 1972 s 4(4) (31 Halsbury's Statutes (4th Edn) NEGLIGENCE): see *McAuley v Bristol City Council* [1992] QB 134, [1992] 1 All ER 749, CA.
         It has been held that a claim by the landlord for recovery of costs under such a clause is a claim for recovery of a debt, and can therefore be enforced without requiring leave of the court under the Leasehold Property (Repairs) Act 1938: see *Jervis v Harris* [1996] Ch 195, [1996] 1 All ER 303, CA.
         However, even where a landlord has been granted a right of this nature the court does not compel the tenant to allow the landlord the right to enter and carry out repairs where these would be of no benefit and where no loss is being caused to the landlord: see *Hammersmith London Borough Council v Creska (No 2)* [2000] L & TR 288.
81   The tenant would prefer to be given 'a reasonable period' to do the work required to remedy the breaches because it may take longer than the specified number of months.

3.9   Alienation[82]

3.9.1   *Alienation prohibited*

The Tenant must not hold the Premises on trust for another. The Tenant must not part with possession of the Premises or any part of the Premises or permit another to occupy them or any part of them except pursuant to a transaction permitted by and effected in accordance with the provisions of this Lease.

82   As to alienation see vol 22(1) (2003 Reissue) LANDLORD AND TENANT (BUSINESS TENANCIES) Paragraph 156 [801] et seq. Where the lease is registrable, this prohibition or restriction on dealings will be reflected in an entry on the register excepting from the effects of registration all estates, rights, interests, powers and remedies arising on or by reason of any dealing made in breach of the prohibition or restriction: see the Land Registration Rules 2003, SI 2003/1417 r 6(2).

[1853]

3.9.2   *Assignment, subletting and charging of part*[83]

(version 1)

[The Tenant must not assign, sublet or charge part only of the Premises.] *(where assignment, subletting or charging of the whole is allowed)*

(version 2)

[The Tenant must not assign or charge part only of the Premises and must not sublet the whole or any part of the Premises.] *(where assignment or charging of the whole is permitted, but subletting is not allowed at all)*

83   Whether subletting should be permitted is a commercial matter. Some landlords consider that the fact that they cannot unreasonably refuse consent to an assignment gives the tenant all the protection he requires and are not prepared to permit subletting. An advantage to the tenant of the ability to sublet is that he has an element of control over a subtenant but not over an assignee, for whom he may retain liability under an authorised guarantee agreement. Further, with stringent assignment tests or in a bad market, subletting may be the only option open to the tenant.

3.9.3   *Assignment of the whole*

Subject to clauses 3.9.4 CIRCUMSTANCES and 3.9.5 CONDITIONS, the Tenant must not assign the whole of the Premises without the consent of the Landlord, whose consent may not be unreasonably withheld [or delayed][84].

84   This residual discretion is the old test of reasonableness under the Landlord and Tenant Act 1927 s 19(1). Thus the tenant and the proposed assignee may satisfy the circumstances and conditions specified for the purposes of the Landlord and Tenant Act 1927 s 19(1A) as inserted by the Landlord and Tenant (Covenants) Act 1995 s 22 (as to which see clause 3.9.4 [1855] CIRCUMSTANCES and clause 3.9.5 [1858] CONDITIONS), but the landlord may still refuse consent on reasonable grounds: see vol 22(1) (2003 Reissue) LANDLORD AND TENANT (BUSINESS TENANCIES) Paragraph 159 [812] et seq.

[1854]

3.9.4   *Circumstances*

If any of the following circumstances[85] — which are specified for the purposes of the Landlord and Tenant Act 1927 Section 19(1A)[86] — applies either at the date when application for consent to assign is made to the Landlord, or after that date but before the Landlord's consent is given, the Landlord may withhold his consent and if, after the Landlord's consent has been given but before the assignment has taken place, any such circumstances apply, the Landlord may revoke his consent[87], whether his consent is expressly subject to a condition as referred to in clause 3.9.5.4 CONDITIONS or not. The circumstances are —

3.9.4.1   that any sum due from the Tenant under this Lease remains unpaid[88],

3.9.4.2   that in the Landlord's reasonable[89] opinion the assignee is not a person who is likely to be able to comply with the tenant covenants of this Lease and to continue to be able to comply with them following the assignment,

[3.9.4.3   that without prejudice to clause 3.9.4.2, in the case of an assignment to a company in the same group as the Tenant[90] within the meaning of the 1954 Act Section 42, in the Landlord's reasonable opinion the assignee is a person who is, or may become, less likely to be able to comply with the tenant covenants of this Lease than the Tenant requesting consent to assign, which likelihood is adjudged by reference in particular to the financial strength of that Tenant aggregated with that of any guarantor of the obligations of that Tenant and the value of any other security for the performance of the tenant covenants of this Lease when assessed at the date of grant or — where that Tenant is not *(name of original tenant)* — the date of the assignment of this Lease to that Tenant[91],] or

3.9.4.4   that the assignee or any guarantor for the assignee, other than any guarantor under an authorised guarantee agreement, is a corporation registered — or otherwise resident — in a jurisdiction in which the order of a court obtained in England and Wales will not necessarily be enforced against the assignee or guarantor without any consideration of the merits of the case.

(for examples of circumstances for use in unusual cases, see vol 22(3) (1997 Reissue) LANDLORD AND TENANT (BUSINESS TENANCIES) *Form 117 [6501])*

[1855]

85   The Landlord and Tenant Act 1927 s 19(1A) as inserted by the Landlord and Tenant (Covenants) Act 1995 s 22 enables the landlord and tenant to a post-1995 lease to agree in advance the terms upon which an assignment may be permitted. It distinguishes between on the one hand circumstances, the existence of which entitles the landlord to refuse consent to assignment, and on the other hand conditions that may be imposed on his consent. This clause and clause 3.9.5 [1858] CONDITIONS are drafted on the assumption that this is a valid approach and seek to draw a clear distinction between circumstances and conditions.

    It should be noted that provisions that are overly restrictive may have an adverse impact at any rent review. It should also be noted that it is recommended 'best practice' that unless the particular circumstances of the letting justify greater control, the only restriction on assignment of the whole should be obtaining the landlord's consent, which is not to be unreasonably withheld: see vol 22(1) (2003 Reissue) LANDLORD AND TENANT (BUSINESS TENANCIES) Paragraph 85 [401] and 'A code of practice for commercial leases in England and Wales (2nd edition)' which can be found in vol 22(1) (2003 Reissue) LANDLORD AND TENANT (BUSINESS TENANCIES) as Form 1 [4501].

    Each letting must be looked at in the light of its own particular facts and circumstances but it is considered that the provisions of this clause do, in the ordinary course, strike a reasonable balance between the landlord's desire for control and the tenant's ability to dispose of his interest without undue restriction. For a less restrictive approach see vol 22(1) (2003 Reissue) LANDLORD AND TENANT (BUSINESS TENANCIES) Form 7 clause 5.2 [5538].

86   The Landlord and Tenant Act 1927 s 19(1A) as inserted by the Landlord and Tenant (Covenants) Act 1995 s 22 seems to require the alienation clause to state that the circumstances it mentions are specified for the purposes of that subsection.

87   The landlord may require that certain circumstances are absent not only before consent has been given to the assignment, but also up to the date on which the assignment takes place — when the die is cast and the lease covenants bind the assignee. For example, the landlord may require the rent to be paid up to date not only before the application for consent is made, but also at the date when consent is given and the possibly later date when the lease is actually assigned.

[1856]

88   The tenant may want to limit this to the rent, as it may be thought that a dispute is more likely to arise over the insurance rent or other payments. If the tenant has retained any right of set-off, it should also be referred to here.

89   Circumstances and conditions must be either factual or, if they contain an element of discretion, that discretion must have to be exercised reasonably (see the Landlord and Tenant Act 1927 s 19(1C)(a) as inserted by the Landlord and Tenant (Covenants) Act 1995 s 22) or the Tenant must have a right of appeal to an expert (see the Landlord and Tenant Act 1927 s 19(1C)(b) as inserted by the Landlord and Tenant (Covenants) Act 1995 s 22). If the discretion is to be exercised reasonably, as suggested by this provision, the Tenant can take any dispute about its exercise to the court. The court will consider whether *this* Landlord has acted within the range of reasonable decisions, not whether a reasonable landlord would have reached the same decision nor whether the test is itself reasonable. For a clause where an expert is used see vol 22(3) (1997 Reissue) LANDLORD AND TENANT (BUSINESS TENANCIES) Form 117 [6501].

90   There have been suggestions that intra-group assignments should be banned completely. However, this is considered to be too draconian and would prevent legitimate corporate restructuring needed for reasons other than avoidance of liability under the Landlord and Tenant (Covenants) Act 1995. The landlord's concern is that a strong tenant may assign to a weak group company; the assignment is acceptable because the assignor gives an authorised guarantee agreement for the assignee. The second group company may then itself assign outside the group; the landlord will lose the authorised guarantee agreement of the strong first group company and have only the possibly worthless authorised guarantee agreement of the second group company. The possibilities for exploitation of this scenario are obvious and it is therefore felt that this is the one situation in which measuring the financial strength of the assignee in relation to that of the assignor is justified. Equivalence tests are not generally thought to be appropriate, because a strong first covenant may make the lease almost unassignable, adversely affecting the rent at review.

91   Consider whether the time at which the tenant's financial status is measured should be when he acquired the lease, when his status was acceptable to the landlord, or at the date of the application for consent to assign, when it may have deteriorated sharply. On the other hand, the outgoing tenant may be a better covenant now than when he acquired the lease: the wily landlord may wish to leave himself free to pick whichever of the two dates gives the better picture.

[1857]

3.9.5   *Conditions*

The Landlord may impose any or all of the following conditions[92] — which are specified for the purposes of the Landlord and Tenant Act 1927 Section 19(1A)[93] — on giving any consent for an assignment by the Tenant, and any such consent is to be treated as being subject to each of the following conditions —

3.9.5.1   a condition that on or before any assignment and before giving occupation to the assignee, the Tenant requesting consent to assign, together with any former tenant who by virtue of the 1995 Act Section 11 was not released on an earlier assignment of this Lease[94], must enter into an authorised guarantee agreement[95] in favour of the Landlord in the terms set out in schedule 7 THE AUTHORISED GUARANTEE AGREEMENT,

3.9.5.2   a condition that if reasonably so required by the Landlord on an assignment to a limited company, the assignee must ensure that at least *(state number, eg 2)* directors of the company, or some other guarantor or guarantors [reasonably] acceptable to the Landlord, enter into direct covenants with the Landlord in the form of the guarantor's covenants contained in clause 6 GUARANTEE PROVISIONS with 'the Assignee' substituted for 'the Tenant',

3.9.5.3   a condition that upon or before any assignment, the Tenant making the request for consent to assign must give to the Landlord a copy of the health and safety file required to be maintained under the Construction (Design and Management) Regulations 1994 containing full details of all works undertaken to the Premises by that Tenant, and

3.9.5.4   a condition that if, at any time before the assignment, the circumstances specified in clause 3.9.4, or any of them, apply, the Landlord may revoke the consent by written notice to the Tenant.

[1858]

92   The Landlord and Tenant Act 1927 s 19(1A) as inserted by the Landlord and Tenant (Covenants) Act 1995 s 22 enables the landlord and tenant to a post-1995 lease to agree in advance the terms upon which an assignment may be permitted. It distinguishes between on the one hand circumstances, the existence of which entitles the landlord to refuse consent to assignment, and on the other hand conditions that may be imposed on his consent. This clause and clause 3.9.4 [1855] CIRCUMSTANCES are drafted on the assumption that this a valid approach and seek to draw a clear distinction between circumstances and conditions.

It should be noted that provisions that are overly restrictive may have an adverse impact at any rent review. It should also be noted that it is recommended 'best practice' that unless the particular circumstances of the letting justify greater control, the only restriction on assignment of the whole should be obtaining the landlord's consent, which is not to be unreasonably withheld: see vol 22(1) (2003 Reissue) LANDLORD AND TENANT (BUSINESS TENANCIES) Paragraph 85 [401] and 'A code of practice for commercial leases in England and Wales (2nd edition)' which can be found in vol 22(1) (2003 Reissue) LANDLORD AND TENANT (BUSINESS TENANCIES) as Form 1 [4501].

Each letting must be looked at in the light of its own particular facts and circumstances but it is considered that the provisions of this clause do, in the ordinary course, strike a reasonable balance between the landlord's desire for control and the tenant's ability to dispose of his interest without undue restriction.

93   The Landlord and Tenant Act 1927 s 19(1A) as inserted by the Landlord and Tenant (Covenants) Act 1995 s 22 seems to require the alienation clause to state that the conditions it mentions are specified for the purposes of that subsection.

94   See the Landlord and Tenant (Covenants) Act 1995 ss 11(2), 16(6).

95   As to authorised guarantee agreements see vol 22(1) (2003 Reissue) LANDLORD AND TENANT (BUSINESS TENANCIES) Paragraph 54 [247]. It should be noted that 'A code of practice for commercial leases in England and Wales (2nd edition)' urges landlords to consider requiring authorised guarantee agreements only where the assignee is of lower financial standing than the assignor at the date of the assignment.

3.9.6   *Charging of the whole*

The Tenant must not charge the whole of the Premises without the consent of the Landlord, whose consent may not be unreasonably withheld [or delayed][96].

96   As to unreasonable withholding of consent under the Landlord and Tenant Act 1927 see vol 22(1) (2003 Reissue) LANDLORD AND TENANT (BUSINESS TENANCIES) Paragraph 158.2 [806] and as to unreasonable delay under the Landlord and Tenant Act 1988 (23 Halsbury's Statutes (4th Edn) LANDLORD AND TENANT) see vol 22(1) (2003 Reissue) LANDLORD AND TENANT (BUSINESS TENANCIES) Paragraph 158.3 [808].

[3.9.7   *Subletting*

The Tenant must not sublet[97] the whole of the Premises without the consent of the Landlord, whose consent may not be unreasonably withheld [or delayed]][98]. *(omit if subletting is prohibited)*

97   See note 83 to clause 3.9.2 [1854] ASSIGNMENT, SUBLETTING AND CHARGING OF PART.
98   As to unreasonable withholding of consent under the Landlord and Tenant Act 1927 see vol 22(1) (2003 Reissue) LANDLORD AND TENANT (BUSINESS TENANCIES) Paragraph 158.2 [806] and as to unreasonable delay under the Landlord and Tenant Act 1988 see vol 22(1) (2003 Reissue) LANDLORD AND TENANT (BUSINESS TENANCIES) Paragraph 158.3 [808].

[1859]

[3.9.8   *Terms of a permitted sublease*[99]

Every permitted sublease must be granted, without a fine or premium, at a rent not less than whichever is the greater of the then open market rent payable in respect of the Premises [— to be approved by the Landlord before the sublease is granted [and to be determined by the Surveyor, acting as an expert and not as an arbitrator]—]and the Rent[100], to be payable in advance on the days on which the Rent is payable under this Lease. Every permitted sublease must contain provisions approved by the Landlord —

3.9.8.1   for the upwards only review of the rent reserved by it, on the basis set out in schedule 3 THE RENT AND RENT REVIEW and on the Review Dates[101],

3.9.8.2   prohibiting the subtenant from doing or allowing anything in relation to the Premises inconsistent with or in breach of the provisions of this Lease,

3.9.8.3   for re-entry by the sublandlord on breach of any covenant by the subtenant,

3.9.8.4   imposing an absolute prohibition against all dealings with the Premises other than assignment[, subletting] [or charging] of the whole,

3.9.8.5   prohibiting assignment[, subletting][102] [or charging] of the whole of the Premises without the prior consent of the Landlord under this Lease,

3.9.8.6   requiring the assignee on any assignment of the sublease to enter into direct covenants with the Landlord to the same effect as those contained in clause 3.9.9 SUBTENANT'S DIRECT COVENANTS,

3.9.8.7   requiring on each assignment of the sublease that the assignor enters into an authorised guarantee agreement[102] in favour of the Landlord in the terms set out in schedule 7 THE AUTHORISED GUARANTEE AGREEMENT but adapted to suit the circumstances in which the guarantee is given,

3.9.8.8   prohibiting the subtenant from holding on trust for another or permitting another to share or occupy the whole or any part of the Premises,

3.9.8.9   imposing in relation to any permitted assignment[, subletting] [or charge] the same obligations for registration with the Landlord as are contained in this Lease in relation to dispositions by the Tenant,

[3.9.8.10   imposing in relation to any permitted subletting the same obligations as are
contained in this clause 3.9.8 and in clause 3.9.9 SUBTENANT'S DIRECT
COVENANTS[, clause 3.9.11 ENFORCEMENT OF THE SUBLEASE and clause 3.9.12
SUBLEASE RENT REVIEW],] and

3.9.8.11   excluding the provisions of Sections 24–28 of the 1954 Act from the letting
created by the sublease.] *(omit if subletting is prohibited)*

[1860]

99   As to the validity of provisions of this nature see vol 22(1) (2003 Reissue) LANDLORD AND TENANT
(BUSINESS TENANCIES) Paragraph 161 [817].
100   It will not be in the landlord's interest for the premises to be sublet at a rent less than that payable under
the headlease. This could allow into the premises a subtenant of doubtful financial status, with whom
the landlord may in the future have to deal direct, eg on the grant of a new lease under the Landlord
and Tenant Act 1954 Pt II (ss 23–46). Also a low rent could be used as a 'comparable' in arriving at the
open market rent on rent reviews or lease renewals. On the other hand following the decision in *Allied
Dunbar Assurance plc v Homebase Ltd* [2002] EWCA Civ 666, [2003] 1 P & CR 75, [2002] 2 EGLR 23
a provision of this kind may effectively render the lease inalienable and being a potentially onerous
restriction on disposition (as to which see vol 22(1) (2003 Reissue) LANDLORD AND TENANT
(BUSINESS TENANCIES) Paragraph 348.2 [1440]) have an adverse impact at rent review from a
landlord's perspective.
101   Alternatively the landlord might prefer the sublease rents to be reviewed just before the review dates
in the headlease. As to recommended 'best practice' in relation to the basis of rent review in leases of
business premises see vol 22(1) (2003 Reissue) LANDLORD AND TENANT (BUSINESS TENANCIES)
Paragraph 85 [401] and 'A code of practice for commercial leases in England and Wales (2nd edition)'
which can be found in vol 22(1) (2003 Reissue) LANDLORD AND TENANT (BUSINESS TENANCIES)
as Form 1 [4501].
102   The landlord may well wish to prohibit any further subletting by requiring an absolute covenant against
subletting to be inserted in any sublease.
103   By virtue of the Landlord and Tenant (Covenants) Act 1995 s 16(3)(a), where a head landlord's consent
is needed to the assignment of a sublease, the head landlord can require the assignor of the sublease to
enter into an authorised guarantee agreement. It should be noted that 'A code of practice for
commercial leases in England and Wales (2nd edition)' urges landlords to consider requiring authorised
guarantee agreements only where the assignee is of lower financial standing than the assignor at the date
of the assignment.

[1861]

[3.9.9   Subtenant's direct covenants[104]

Before any permitted subletting, the Tenant must ensure that the subtenant enters into
a direct covenant with the Landlord that while the subtenant is bound by the tenant
covenants of the sublease[105] and while he is bound by an authorised guarantee agreement
the subtenant will observe and perform the tenant covenants contained in this Lease —
except the covenant to pay the rent reserved by this Lease — and in that sublease.] *(omit
if subletting is prohibited)*

104   See note 99 to clause 3.9.8 [1861] TERMS OF A PERMITTED SUBLEASE.
105   The liability of the subtenant should be expressed to last while he is bound by the tenant covenants of
the sublease, rather than while the sublease is vested in him, to take account of the possibility of an
excluded assignment being made and the subtenant remaining liable. An excluded assignment means that
the subtenant is precluded from tenant release under the Landlord and Tenant (Covenants) Act 1995.

[3.9.10   Requirement for 1954 Act exclusion[106]

The Tenant must not grant a sublease or permit a subtenant to occupy the Premises unless
an effective agreement has been made to exclude the operation of Sections 24 to 28 of
the 1954 Act pursuant to Section 38A of the 1954 Act.] *(omit if subletting is prohibited)*

106   As to contracting out of the security of tenure provisions of the Landlord and Tenant Act 1954 see vol
22(1) (2003 Reissue) LANDLORD AND TENANT (BUSINESS TENANCIES) Paragraph 431 [2035].

[3.9.11   *Enforcement, waiver and variation of subleases*

In relation to any permitted sublease, the Tenant must enforce the performance and observance by every subtenant of the provisions of the sublease, and must not at any time either expressly or by implication waive any breach of the covenants or conditions on the part of any subtenant or assignee of any sublease, or — without the consent of the Landlord, whose consent may not be unreasonably withheld or delayed — vary the terms or accept a surrender of any permitted sublease.] *(omit if subletting is prohibited)*

[1862]

[3.9.12   *Sublease rent review*

In relation to any permitted sublease —

3.9.12.1   the Tenant must ensure that the rent is reviewed in accordance with the terms of the sublease,

3.9.12.2   the Tenant must not agree the reviewed rent with the subtenant without the approval of the Landlord,

3.9.12.3   where the sublease provides such an option, the Tenant must not, without the approval of the Landlord, agree whether the third party determining the revised rent in default of agreement should act as an arbitrator or as an expert,

3.9.12.4   the Tenant must not, without the approval of the Landlord, agree any appointment of a person to act as the third party determining the revised rent,

3.9.12.5   the Tenant must incorporate as part of his representations to that third party representations [reasonably] required[107] by the Landlord, and

3.9.12.6   the Tenant must give notice to the Landlord of the details of the determination of every rent review within *(state period, eg 28 days)*,

provided that the Landlord's approvals specified above may not be unreasonably withheld [or delayed].] *(omit if subletting is prohibited)*

---

107   This seems preferable to providing, as is sometimes done, that the head landlord's representations have to be brought to the attention of the expert or arbitrator because it would appear that he can refuse to have regard to them, the head landlord not being a party to the lease with which he is concerned.

3.9.13   *Registration of permitted dealings*

Within *(state period, eg 28 days)* of any assignment, charge, [sublease, or subunderlease,] or any transmission or other devolution relating to the Premises, the Tenant must produce a certified copy[108] of any relevant document for registration with the Landlord's solicitor, and must pay the Landlord's solicitor's [reasonable] charges for registration of at least £...

---

108   There seems to be no reason why the tenant should part with the original. However, under the Land Registration Rules 2003, SI 2003/1417 r 203, it is open to the applicant for registration to ask for the transfer, charge, sublease or subunderlease giving effect to the disposition to be returned for retention by the applicant, provided a certified copy of the instrument is lodged with the application. Accordingly, in such cases, applicants should use this facility if they wish to be able to lodge the lease with the landlord after its return by the registrar. If there is a time limit specified in the lease, then the registrar should be told about this, so that he is aware of the need to return the instrument within the required period.

[3.9.14   *Sharing with a Group Company*

Notwithstanding clause 3.9.1 ALIENATION PROHIBITED, the Tenant may share the occupation of the whole or any part of the Premises with a company that is a member of the same group as the Tenant within the meaning of the 1954 Act Section 42, for so long as both companies remain members of that group and otherwise than in a manner that transfers or creates a legal estate.] *(omit if sharing with a group company is not to be permitted)*

[1863]–[1870]

3.10   Nuisance and residential restrictions

3.10.1   *Nuisance*[109]

The Tenant must not do anything on the Premises or allow anything to remain on them that may be or become a nuisance, or cause annoyance, disturbance, inconvenience, injury or damage to the Landlord or his tenants or the owners or occupiers of any adjoining property of the Landlord of or any other adjacent or neighbouring premises.

---

109   'Nuisance' is a term to be construed according to 'plain and sober and simple notions among the English people': *Walter v Selfe* (1851) 4 De G & Sm 315 at 322 per Knight-Bruce V-C. 'I have no doubt that what is a nuisance or annoyance will continue to be determined by the courts according to robust and commonsense standards': *Hampstead and Suburban Properties Ltd v Diomedous* [1969] 1 Ch 248 at 258, [1968] 3 All ER 545 at 550 per Megarry J. But a tenant can only be said to have permitted a nuisance if the landlord can show that the tenant has failed to take reasonable steps to prevent the nuisance: see *Commercial General Administration Ltd v Thomsett* [1979] 1 EGLR 62, CA.

3.10.2   *Auctions, trades and immoral purposes*

The Tenant must not use the Premises for any auction sale, any dangerous, noxious, noisy or offensive[110] trade, business, manufacture or occupation, or any illegal or immoral act or purpose.

---

110   As to the meaning of 'offensive' see *Re Koumoudouros and Marathon Realty Co Ltd* (1978) 89 DLR (3d) 551 where it was held that the word 'offensive' did not have a definite legal meaning and that it should be read in the context of the lease. Surrounding circumstances can affect whether a particular trade is offensive: see *Nussey v Provincial Bill Posting Co and Eddison* [1909] 1 Ch 734, CA; *Dunraven Securities Ltd v Holloway* [1982] 2 EGLR 47, CA.

3.10.3   *Residential use, sleeping and animals*

The Tenant must not use the Premises as sleeping accommodation or for residential purposes, or keep any animal, bird or reptile on them.

[1871]

3.11   Costs of applications, notices and recovery of arrears[111]

The Tenant must pay to the Landlord on an indemnity basis all costs, fees, charges, disbursements and expenses — including without prejudice to the generality of the above those payable to counsel, solicitors, surveyors and bailiffs — [properly and reasonably] incurred by the Landlord in relation to or incidental to —

3.11.1   every application made by the Tenant for a consent or licence required by the provisions of this Lease, whether it is granted, refused or offered subject to any [lawful] qualification or condition, or the application is withdrawn[unless the refusal, qualification or condition is unlawful, whether because it is unreasonable or otherwise],

3.11.2 the contemplation, preparation and service of a notice under the Law of Property Act 1925 Section 146, or by reason or the contemplation of proceedings under Sections 146 or 147 of that Act, even if forfeiture is avoided otherwise than by relief granted by the court[112],

3.11.3 the recovery or attempted recovery of arrears of rent or other sums due under this Lease, and

3.11.4 any steps taken in [contemplation of or in] [direct] connection with the preparation and service of a schedule of dilapidations during or after the end of the Term[113].

111 As to payment of VAT on legal costs by a person other than the solicitor's own client see the Information Binder: Property [1]: VAT and Property.

112 As to forfeiture see vol 22(1) (2003 Reissue) LANDLORD AND TENANT (BUSINESS TENANCIES) Paragraph 283 [1171] et seq.

113 The landlord should not be tempted to extend this provision to costs etc incurred by him in consequence of serving a notice under the Landlord and Tenant Act 1954 s 25 because that is void: see *Stevenson and Rush (Holdings) Ltd v Langdon* (1978) 38 P & CR 208, CA.

[1872]

3.12 Planning and development

3.12.1 *Compliance with the Planning Acts*

The Tenant must observe and comply with the provisions and requirements of the Planning Acts affecting the Premises and their use, and must indemnify the Landlord, and keep him indemnified, both during and following the end of the Term, against all losses in respect of any contravention of those Acts.

3.12.2 *Consent for applications*

The Tenant must not make any application for planning permission without the consent of the Landlord[, whose consent may not be unreasonably withheld [or delayed] [in any case where application for and implementation of the planning permission will not create or give rise to any tax liability for the Landlord or where the Tenant indemnifies the Landlord against such liability][114]].

114 The words in square brackets were devised when development land tax — abolished by the Finance Act 1985 s 93 — applied. The provision may, however, still be relevant should similar taxation be introduced in the future.

3.12.3 *Permissions and notices*

The Tenant must at his expense obtain any planning permissions and serve any notices that may be required for the carrying out of any development on or at the Premises.

3.12.4 *Charges and levies*

Subject only to any statutory direction to the contrary, the Tenant must pay and satisfy any charge or levy that may subsequently be imposed under the Planning Acts in respect of carrying out or maintaining any development on or at the Premises.

[1873]

3.12.5   *Pre-conditions for development*

Notwithstanding any consent that may be granted by the Landlord under this Lease, the Tenant must not carry out any development on or at the Premises until all necessary notices under the Planning Acts have been served and copies produced to the Landlord, all necessary permissions under the Planning Acts have been obtained and produced to the Landlord, and the Landlord has acknowledged that every necessary planning permission is acceptable to him[, such acknowledgement not to be unreasonably withheld]. The Landlord may refuse to acknowledge his acceptance of a planning permission on the grounds that any condition contained in it or anything omitted from it or the period referred to in it would[, in the [reasonable] opinion of the Surveyor,] be, or be likely to be, prejudicial to the Landlord or to his reversionary interest in the Premises, the Building or any other of his adjoining property whether during the Term or following the end of it.

3.12.6   *Completion of development*

Where a condition of any planning permission granted for development begun before the end of the Term[115] requires works to be carried out to the Premises by a date after the end of the Term, the Tenant must, unless the Landlord directs otherwise, finish those works before the end of the Term.

115   The provisions of clause 1.22 [1815] INTERPRETATION OF 'THE LAST YEAR OF THE TERM' AND 'THE END OF THE TERM' should be noted.

3.12.7   *Security for compliance with conditions*

In any case where a planning permission is granted subject to conditions, and if the Landlord [reasonably] so requires, the Tenant must provide sufficient security for his compliance with the conditions and must not implement the planning permission until the security has been provided.

[3.12.8   *Appeal against refusal or conditions*[116]

If [reasonably] required by the Landlord to do so, but[, where reasonable,] at his own cost, the Tenant must appeal against any refusal of planning permission or the imposition of any conditions on a planning permission relating to the Premises following an application for planning permission by the Tenant.]

116   The tenant should not accept this clause because it could impose on him the cost of a planning appeal. He should strike it out, leaving planning appeals to be a matter for discussion as and when the situation arises during the term, or at least insist that he should bear the cost only where reasonable.

[1874]

3.13   Plans, documents and information

3.13.1   *Evidence of compliance with this Lease*

If so requested, the Tenant must produce to the Landlord or the Surveyor any plans, documents and other evidence the Landlord [reasonably] requires to satisfy himself that the provisions of this Lease have been complied with.

3.13.2   *Information for renewal or rent review*

If so requested, the Tenant must produce to the Landlord, the Surveyor or any person acting as the third party determining the Rent in default of agreement between the Landlord and the Tenant under any provisions for rent review contained in this Lease, any information [reasonably] requested in writing in relation to any pending or intended step under the 1954 Act or the implementation of any provisions for rent review.

3.14   Indemnities[117]

The Tenant must keep the Landlord fully indemnified against all losses arising directly or indirectly out of any act, omission or negligence of the Tenant, or any persons at the Building expressly or impliedly[118] with his authority [and under his control][119], or any breach or non-observance by the Tenant of the covenants, conditions or other provisions of this Lease or any of the matters to which this demise is subject.

117   The tenant should seek to delete all *general* indemnity provisions on the basis that his remedies for breach of covenant and in tort adequately protect the landlord. The tenant should argue that an indemnity unreasonably extends his liability. If this clause is omitted, however, it should be replaced by a covenant to observe and perform the restrictions etc to which the demise is subject, possibly coupled with a *specific* indemnity in respect of any breach.
118   The expression 'impliedly' is intended to include a caller, such as a tradesman, where there has been no express invitation but the person cannot be classed as a trespasser.
119   The tenant should add the words in square brackets.

[1875]

3.15   Reletting boards and viewing

[Unless [a valid court application under the 1954 Act Section 24 has been made or][120] the Tenant is [otherwise] entitled to remain in occupation or to a new tenancy of the Premises, at any time during *(or as required)* At any time during] the *(state period, eg last 6 months)* of the [Contractual][121] Term and at any time thereafter, [and whenever the Lease Rents or any part of them are in arrear and unpaid for longer than *(state period, eg 14 days)*,] the Tenant must permit the Landlord to enter the Premises and fix and retain anywhere on them a board advertising them for reletting. While any such board is on the Premises the Tenant must permit viewing of the Premises at reasonable times of the day.

120   This phrase and the word 'otherwise' should be omitted if the operation of the security of tenure provisions in the Landlord and Tenant Act 1954 ss 24–28 is to be excluded in relation to the lease.
121   This defined term will require amendment where the operation of the security of tenure provisions in the Landlord and Tenant Act 1954 ss 24–28 is to be excluded in relation to the lease: see note 6 to clause 1.7 [1810] 'THE [CONTRACTUAL] TERM'.

3.16   Obstruction and encroachment

3.16.1   *Obstruction of windows*

The Tenant must not stop up, darken or obstruct any window or light belonging to the Premises.

3.16.2   *Encroachments*

The Tenant must take all [reasonable] steps to prevent the construction of any new window, light, opening, doorway, path, passage, pipe or the making of any encroachment or the acquisition of any easement in relation to the Premises and must notify the Landlord immediately if any such thing is constructed, encroachment is made or easement acquired, or if any attempt is made to construct such a thing, to encroach or acquire an easement. At the request of the Landlord the Tenant must adopt such means as are [reasonably] required to prevent the construction of such a thing, the making of any encroachment or the acquisition of any easement[122].

122   For a shorter clause see vol 22(3) (1997 Reissue) LANDLORD AND TENANT (BUSINESS TENANCIES) Form 172 [6696].

[1876]

3.17 Yielding up

At the end of the Term[123] the Tenant must yield up the Premises with vacant possession, decorated and repaired in accordance with and in the condition required by the provisions of this Lease, give up all keys of the Premises to the Landlord, remove tenant's fixtures and fittings [if requested to do so by the Landlord], and remove all signs erected by the Tenant or any of his predecessors in title in, on or near the Premises, immediately making good any damage caused by their removal.

123   The provisions of clause 1.22 [1815] INTERPRETATION OF 'THE LAST YEAR OF THE TERM' AND 'THE END OF THE TERM' should be noted.

3.18 Interest on arrears[124]

The Tenant must pay interest on any of the Lease Rents[125] or other sums due under this Lease that are not paid [within *(state period, eg 14 days)* of the date due], whether formally demanded or not, [the interest to be recoverable as rent][126]. Nothing in this clause is to entitle the Tenant to withhold or delay any payment of the Rent or any other sum due under this Lease or affect the rights of the Landlord in relation to any non-payment.

124   As to the covenant to pay interest see vol 22(1) (2003 Reissue) LANDLORD AND TENANT (BUSINESS TENANCIES) Paragraph 154 [767].
125   As to the definition of 'the Lease Rents' see clause 1.42 [1821] 'THE RENT'.
126   These words seek to attach to any interest the rights associated with rent. As to the reasons for this see vol 22(1) (2003 Reissue) LANDLORD AND TENANT (BUSINESS TENANCIES) Paragraph 151 [761]. However, this clause applies to interest on arrears both of rents and other sums payable under the lease that are not rent, and it might be felt inappropriate for interest to be deemed to be rent where the payment on which the interest is due is not itself rent.

[1877]

3.19 Statutory notices

The Tenant must give full particulars to the Landlord of any notice, direction, order or proposal relating to the Premises made, given or issued to the Tenant by any government department or local, public, regulatory or other authority or court within *(state period, eg 7 days)* of receipt, and if so requested by the Landlord must produce it to the Landlord. The Tenant must without delay take all necessary steps to comply with the notice, direction or order. At the request of the Landlord, but at the cost of the Tenant, the Tenant must make or join with the Landlord in making any objection or representation the Landlord deems expedient against or in respect of any notice, direction, order or proposal.

3.20 Keyholders

The Tenant must ensure that at all times [the Landlord has *(or as required)* the Landlord and the local police force have] written notice of the name, home address and home telephone number of at least *(state number, eg 2)* keyholders of the Premises.

3.21 Viewing on sale of reversion

The Tenant must[, on reasonable notice,] at any time during the Term, permit prospective purchasers of the Landlord's reversion or any other interest superior to the Term, or agents instructed in connection with the sale of the reversion or such an interest, to view the Premises without interruption provided they have the prior written authority of the Landlord or his agents.

3.22   Defective premises

The Tenant must give notice to the Landlord of any defect in the Premises that might give rise to an obligation on the Landlord to do or refrain from doing anything in order to comply with the provisions of this Lease or the duty of care imposed on the Landlord, whether pursuant to the Defective Premises Act 1972 or otherwise, and must at all times display and maintain any notices the Landlord from time to time [reasonably] requires him to display at the Premises.

[1878]

3.23   Replacement guarantor[127]

3.23.1   *Guarantor replacement events*

In this clause 3.23 references to a 'guarantor replacement event' are references, in the case of an individual, to death, bankruptcy, having a receiving order made against him or having a receiver appointed under the Mental Health Act 1983 or entering into a voluntary arrangement, and, in the case of a company, to passing a resolution to wind up, entering into liquidation, a voluntary arrangement or administration or having a receiver appointed.

127   As to guarantors see vol 22(1) (2003 Reissue) LANDLORD AND TENANT (BUSINESS TENANCIES) Paragraph 71 [278] et seq. The tenant should propose that, on the execution of a guarantee by a new guarantor, the original guarantor or his estate should be released.

3.23.2   *Action on occurrence of a guarantor replacement event*

Where during the relevant Liability Period a guarantor replacement event occurs to the Guarantor or any person who has entered into an authorised guarantee agreement, the Tenant must give notice of the event to the Landlord within *(state period, eg 14 days)* of his becoming aware of it. If so required by the Landlord, the Tenant must within *(state period, eg 28 days)* obtain some other person [reasonably] acceptable to the Landlord to execute a guarantee in the form of the Guarantor's covenants in clause 6 GUARANTEE PROVISIONS or the authorised guarantee agreement in schedule 7 THE AUTHORISED GUARANTEE AGREEMENT, as the case may be, for the residue of the relevant Liability Period.

3.24   Exercise of the Landlord's rights[128]

The Tenant must permit the Landlord to exercise any of the rights granted to him by virtue of the provisions of this Lease at all times during the Term without interruption or interference.

128   The provisions of clause 1.40 [1821] REFERENCES TO RIGHTS OF ACCESS should be noted.

3.25   The Office Covenants

The Tenant must observe and perform the Office Covenants.

3.26   The Services

The Tenant must observe and perform his obligations contained in schedule 6 THE SERVICE CHARGE .

[1879]

3.27   Costs of grant of this Lease[129]

[The Tenant must pay the fees and disbursements of the Landlord's solicitors, agents and surveyors and all other costs and expenses incurred by the Landlord in relation to the negotiation, preparation, execution and grant of this Lease *(or as required)* On the grant of this Lease the Tenant must pay the sum of £... as a contribution to the Landlord's solicitors' charges for the negotiation, execution and completion of this Lease].

129   As to covenants to pay the landlord's legal fees see vol 22(1) (2003 Reissue) LANDLORD AND TENANT (BUSINESS TENANCIES) Paragraph 155 [769]. As to payment of VAT on legal costs by a person other than the solicitor's own client see the Information Binder: Property [1]: VAT and Property.

3.28   Consent to the Landlord's release[130]

The Tenant must not unreasonably withhold consent to a request made by the Landlord under the 1995 Act Section 8 for a release from all or any of the landlord covenants of this Lease.

130   By virtue of the Landlord and Tenant (Covenants) Act 1995 each successive landlord remains bound by the landlord covenants of the lease unless released under the machinery provided in the Act — as to which see vol 22(1) (2003 Reissue) LANDLORD AND TENANT (BUSINESS TENANCIES) Paragraph 57 [252] et seq — or by a specific release given otherwise (see the Landlord and Tenant (Covenants) Act 1995 s 26(1)(a)). Bald statements limiting the landlord's liability, such as those in use before the commencement of the Act, will not withstand the wide anti-avoidance provisions of the Landlord and Tenant (Covenants) Act 1995 s 25, and covenants by the tenant to give consent to release are unlikely to fall within the exception of s 26. None of the ingenious schemes for limiting the landlord's liability, eg making all covenants personal, suggested in the early days of the 1995 Act has stood up to critical scrutiny, although none has yet been tested by the courts. Thus landlords look instead to the alternative of a right of redress if the tenant makes an unreasonable objection to release. This covenant is modelled on the provisions of the Landlord and Tenant Act 1988, which gives tenants a right of action for loss caused by landlords who unreasonably withhold or delay consent to assignment (see the Landlord and Tenant Act 1988 s 4). In view of the strict time limits under the Landlord and Tenant (Covenants) Act 1995 and the fact that failure to respond to the landlord's request for release is deemed to be consent, it is not thought necessary to extend this covenant to unreasonable delay in replying to such a request.

[1880]–[1900]

4   THE LANDLORD'S COVENANTS

The Landlord covenants with the Tenant to observe and perform the requirements of this clause 4.

4.1   Quiet enjoyment[131]

The Landlord must permit the Tenant peaceably and quietly to hold and enjoy the Premises without any interruption or disturbance from or by the Landlord or any person claiming under or in trust for him[132] [or by title paramount][133].

131   As to the landlord's covenant for quiet enjoyment see vol 22(1) (2003 Reissue) LANDLORD AND TENANT (BUSINESS TENANCIES) Paragraph 168 [856]. As to covenants for quiet enjoyment generally see 23 Halsbury's Laws (4th Edn Reissue) LANDLORD AND TENANT.
    The words 'the Tenant paying the rents reserved by and observing and performing the covenants on his part and the conditions contained in this lease' are frequently included in a covenant for quiet enjoyment, but they have no practical effect and do not make payment of the rent and performance of the covenants into conditions precedent to the operation of the covenant for quiet enjoyment: see *Edge v Boileau* (1885) 16 QBD 117; *Dawson v Dyer* (1833) 5 B & Ad 584; *Yorkbrook Investments Ltd v Batten* (1985) 52 P & CR 51, [1985] 2 EGLR 100, CA.

132   The covenant is frequently expressed to apply to 'lawful' interruption by persons 'rightfully' claiming under the landlord, but it seems that the addition of these words has no practical effect: see *Williams v Gabriel* [1906] 1 KB 155 at 157.

133   Without the reference to title paramount the landlord is liable only for the acts of persons so far as they are his successors in title or have authority from him to do the acts complained of: *Harrison Ainslie & Co v Muncaster* [1891] 2 QB 680, CA; *Matania v National Provincial Bank Ltd and Elevenist Syndicate Ltd* [1936] 2 All ER 633, CA; *Miller v Emcer Products Ltd* [1956] Ch 304, [1956] 1 All ER 237, CA. If a subtenant holds under a lease containing a qualified covenant on the part of his landlord — ie one where there is no reference to title paramount — and the head landlord evicts the subtenant because the head rent has not been paid, this is not a breach of the covenant for quiet enjoyment (see *Spencer v Marriott* (1823) 1 B & C 457; *Dennett v Atherton* (1872) LR 7 QB 316, Ex Ch), but it is a breach if the sublandlord submits to judgment in an action by a person with no title to sue, and the subtenant is in consequence evicted (*Cohen v Tannar* [1900] 2 QB 609, CA). Actionable interruptions under this covenant are not confined to interference with title or possession, but may extend to interference with the ordinary and lawful enjoyment of the premises: *Sanderson v Berwick-upon-Tweed Corpn* (1884) 13 QBD 547 at 551, CA. As to persons claiming 'under' the landlord see *Celsteel Ltd v Alton House Holdings Ltd (No 2)* [1987] 2 All ER 240, [1987] 1 WLR 291, CA.

[1901]

4.2   The Services[134]

4.2.1   *Provision of the Services*

If the Tenant pays the Service Charge and observes his obligations under this Lease[135], the Landlord must use his best endeavours to provide the Services.

134   As the landlord remains liable on his covenants until he is released under the Landlord and Tenant (Covenants) Act 1995, given the character of the landlord's covenants contained in this lease, the landlord may prefer to avoid liability altogether by including a management company as a party to the lease. The management company then covenants to perform those obligations that would have fallen to the landlord.

135   As to payment as a condition precedent see vol 22(1) (2003 Reissue) LANDLORD AND TENANT (BUSINESS TENANCIES) Paragraph 255 [1093].

4.2.2   *Relief from liability*[136]

The Landlord is not to be liable to the Tenant for any breach of his obligations under clause 4.2.1 where the breach is caused by something beyond his control, provided he uses reasonable endeavours to remedy the breach, except to the extent that the breach —

4.2.2.1   could have been prevented, or

4.2.2.2   its consequences could have been lessened, or

4.2.2.3   the time during which its consequences were experienced could have been shortened,

by the exercise of reasonable skill by the Landlord or those undertaking the obligation on his behalf.

136   This clause is likely to be viewed as an exclusion clause, if the Unfair Contract Terms Act 1977 (11 Halsbury's Statutes (4th Edn) CONTRACT) applies to the service provisions contained in a lease: see vol 22(1) (2003 Reissue) LANDLORD AND TENANT (BUSINESS TENANCIES) Paragraph 254 notes 4 and 5 [1092].

4.2.3   *Variation and withholding of the Services*

The Landlord may add to, withhold or vary the Services if[, acting reasonably,] he considers the addition, withholding or variation to be necessary or desirable [for the comfort or convenience of the tenants in the Building] even if it increases the Landlord's Expenses [so long as the Tenant's enjoyment of the Premises is not materially impaired], or if he is required to do so by a competent authority.

4.2.4   *Special services*

Any services rendered to the Tenant by staff employed by the Landlord, other than services referred to in paragraph 6-3 THE SERVICES, are to be deemed to be special services for which, and for the consequences of which, the Tenant will be entirely responsible. The Tenant is not to be entitled to any services from such staff that may in any way whatever interfere with the performance of their duties to the Landlord.

[1902]

5   INSURANCE[137]

5.1   Warranty as to convictions[138]

The Tenant warrants that before the execution of this document he has disclosed to the Landlord in writing any conviction, judgment or finding of any court or tribunal relating to the Tenant[, or any director, other officer or major shareholder of the Tenant,] of such a nature as to be likely to affect the decision of any insurer or underwriter to grant or to continue insurance of any of the Insured Risks.

137   As to insurance see vol 22(1) (2003 Reissue) LANDLORD AND TENANT (BUSINESS TENANCIES) Paragraph 227 [1021] et seq.

138   A contract of insurance is one uberrimae fidei. The insured must disclose to the insurers all material facts that are within his actual or presumed knowledge, whether there is a formal proposal form or not. A fact is material if non-disclosure of it would influence a prudent and reasonable insurer. This warranty is designed to rebut any suggestion by the landlord's insurers that the landlord had knowledge of the matters concerned. By inserting this clause in the lease, and thus specifically bringing the point to the tenant's attention, the landlord can argue that he has done all that is practical to establish the existence of any such matters. The absence of any written disclosure pursuant to this clause is strong evidence that the landlord has no actual or presumed knowledge of such matters. Further, the landlord has a right of action against the tenant for any breach of the warranty. As to non-disclosure and misrepresentation in contracts of non-marine insurance see 22 Halsbury's Laws (4th Edn Reissue) INSURANCE.

5.2   Covenant to insure

The Landlord covenants with the Tenant to insure the Building unless the insurance is vitiated by any act of the Tenant or by anyone at the Building expressly or by implication[139] with his authority [and under his control][140].

139   The expression 'by implication' is intended to include a caller, such as a tradesman, where there has been no express invitation but the person cannot be classed as a trespasser.

140   The tenant should add the words in square brackets.

[1903]

5.3   Details of the insurance

5.3.1   *Office, underwriters and agency*

Insurance is to be effected in such [substantial and reputable] insurance office, or with such underwriters[141], and through such agency as the Landlord from time to time decides.

141   The expression 'insurance office' would probably not include Lloyd's underwriters. The landlord's right to nominate the office and agency is absolute, with no implied restrictions: *Berrycroft Management Co Ltd v Sinclair Gardens Investments (Kensington) Ltd* (1996) 75 P & CR 210, [1997] 1 EGLR 47, CA.

5.3.2   *Insurance cover*[142]

Insurance must be effected for the following amounts —

5.3.2.1   the sum that the Landlord is from time to time advised [by the Surveyor] is the full cost of rebuilding and reinstating the Building, including [VAT[143],] architects', surveyors', engineers', solicitors' and all other professional persons' fees, the fees payable on any applications for planning permission or other permits or consents that may be required in relation to rebuilding or reinstating the Building, the cost of preparation of the site including shoring-up, debris removal, demolition, site clearance and any works that may be required by statute, and incidental expenses, and

5.3.2.2   loss of rental [and service charge] income from the Building, taking account of any rent review that may be due, for *(state period, eg 3 years)* or such longer period as the Landlord from time to time [reasonably] requires for planning and carrying out the rebuilding or reinstatement.

142   As to the sum insured see vol 22(1) (2003 Reissue) LANDLORD AND TENANT (BUSINESS TENANCIES) Paragraph 231 [1028] et seq.
  It should be noted that it is recommended 'best practice' that, where the landlord has arranged insurance, the terms should be made known to the tenant and any material change in the insurance should be notified to the tenant: see Recommendation 14 of 'A code of practice for commercial leases in England and Wales (2nd edition)' which can be found in vol 22(1) (2003 Reissue) LANDLORD AND TENANT (BUSINESS TENANCIES) at Form 1 [4501].
143   As to VAT and the level of insurance cover see the Information Binder: Property [1]: VAT and Property. The expense of insuring against the VAT payable on reinstatement costs is not justified where the landlord has opted to tax and is able to recover the VAT. There is a theoretical possibility that a future landlord may not opt to tax and that the sum insured may then be too low. It is also possible that a landlord may wish to preserve the 'exempt' status of a property. Normally, however, the cost of reinstatement need not expressly mention VAT, although the cashflow implications of having to pay VAT on construction works need to be remembered.

5.3.3   *Risks insured*[144]

Insurance must be effected against damage or destruction by any of the Insured Risks to the extent that such insurance may ordinarily be arranged [with a substantial and reputable insurer] for properties such as the Building, and subject to such excesses, exclusions or limitations as the insurer requires.

144   As to risks to be insured against see vol 22(1) (2003 Reissue) LANDLORD AND TENANT (BUSINESS TENANCIES) Paragraph 235 [1033].
  It should be noted that it is recommended 'best practice' that, where the landlord has arranged insurance, the terms should be made known to the tenant and any material change in the insurance should be notified to the tenant: see Recommendation 14 of 'A code of practice for commercial leases in England and Wales (2nd edition)' which can be found in vol 22(1) (2003 Reissue) LANDLORD AND TENANT (BUSINESS TENANCIES) at Form 1 [4501].

[1904]

5.4   Payment of the Insurance Rent

The Tenant covenants to pay the Insurance Rent for the period starting on the Rent Commencement Date and ending on the day before the next policy renewal date on the date of this document, and subsequently to pay the Insurance Rent on demand and, if so demanded, in advance of the policy renewal date[, but not more than *(state period, eg ... months)* in advance].

5.5   Suspension of the Rent[145]

5.5.1   *Events giving rise to suspension*

If and whenever the Building or any part of it is damaged or destroyed by one or more of the Insured Risks[146] [— except one against which insurance may not ordinarily be arranged [with a substantial and reputable insurer] for properties such as the Building unless the Landlord has in fact insured against that risk —] so that the Premises or any part of them are unfit for occupation or use, and payment of the insurance money is not wholly or partly refused because of any act or default of the Tenant or anyone at the Building expressly or by implication[147] with his authority [and under his control][148], then the provisions of clause 5.5.2 SUSPENDING THE RENT are to have effect.

145   As to suspension of rent see vol 22(1) (2003 Reissue) LANDLORD AND TENANT (BUSINESS
       TENANCIES) Paragraph 241 [1044] et seq.

146   It should be noted that it is recommended 'best practice' that if premises are so damaged by an
       uninsured risk as to prevent occupation, the tenant should be allowed to terminate the lease unless the
       landlord agrees to reinstate at his own cost: see vol 22(1) (2003 Reissue) LANDLORD AND TENANT
       (BUSINESS TENANCIES) Paragraph 85 [402] and 'A code of practice for commercial leases in England
       and Wales (2nd edition)' which can be found in vol 22(1) (2003 Reissue) LANDLORD AND TENANT
       (BUSINESS TENANCIES) at Form 1 [4501]. If adopted, this recommendation involves rent suspension
       also becoming operative in the event of the premises becoming unusable because of uninsured risks.

147   The expression 'by implication' is intended to include a caller, such as a tradesman, where there has
       been no express invitation but the person cannot be classed as a trespasser.

148   The tenant should add the words in square brackets.

[1905]

5.5.2   *Suspending the Rent*

In the circumstances mentioned in clause 5.5.1 EVENTS GIVING RISE TO SUSPENSION, the
Rent [and the Service Charge][149], or a fair proportion of the Rent [and the Service
Charge] according to the nature and the extent of the damage sustained, [is *(or as required)*
are] to cease to be payable until the Building has been rebuilt or reinstated so as to render
the Premises, or the affected part, fit for occupation and use, [or until the end of *(state
period, eg 3 years)* from the destruction or damage whichever period is the shorter,][150] [the
proportion of the Rent [and the Service Charge] suspended and the period of the
suspension to be determined by the Surveyor acting as an expert and not as an arbitrator
(or as required) any dispute as to the proportion of the Rent [and the Service Charge]
suspended and the period of the suspension to be determined in accordance with the
Arbitration Act 1996 by an arbitrator to be appointed by agreement between the
Landlord and the Tenant or in default by the President or other proper officer for the
time being of the Royal Institution of Chartered Surveyors upon the application of
either the Landlord or the Tenant].

149   As to the nature of the payments to be covered see vol 22(1) (2003 Reissue) LANDLORD AND
       TENANT (BUSINESS TENANCIES) Paragraph 242 [1045].

150   As to the length of the suspension and the tenant's concerns see vol 22(1) (2003 Reissue) LANDLORD
       AND TENANT (BUSINESS TENANCIES) Paragraph 244 [1048]. For a provision extending suspension
       of the rent where reinstatement is delayed see vol 22(3) (1997 Reissue) LANDLORD AND TENANT
       (BUSINESS TENANCIES) Form 111 [6495].

[1906]

5.6   Reinstatement and termination[151]

5.6.1   *Obligation to obtain permissions*

If and whenever the Building or any part of it is damaged or destroyed by one or more
of the Insured Risks [— except one against which insurance may not ordinarily be
arranged with [a substantial and reputable insurer] for properties such as the Building
unless the Landlord has in fact insured against that risk —], and payment of the insurance
money is not wholly or partly refused because of any act or default of the Tenant or
anyone at the Building expressly or by implication with his authority[152] [and under his
control][153], then the Landlord must use his best endeavours[154] to obtain any planning
permissions or other permits and consents ('permissions') that are required under the
Planning Acts or otherwise to enable him to rebuild and reinstate.

[1907]

151   It has been held that, in the absence of an express covenant to reinstate, where the landlord must keep the premises adequately insured against comprehensive risks and the insurance is effected at the tenant's expense, the obligation is one intended to enure for the benefit of both parties: *Mumford Hotels Ltd v Wheler* [1964] Ch 117, [1963] 3 All ER 250; see also *Mark Rowlands Ltd v Berni Inns Ltd* [1986] QB 211, [1985] 3 All ER 473, CA; *Lonsdale & Thompson Ltd v Black Arrow Group plc* [1993] Ch 361, [1993] 3 All ER 648. This is not, however, a general principle of law and the tenant should therefore always require a specific covenant to reinstate.

These provisions are restricted to circumstances where damage or destruction is caused by an insured risk. It should be noted that it is recommended 'best practice' that if premises are so damaged by an uninsured risk as to prevent occupation, the tenant should be allowed to terminate the lease unless the landlord agrees to reinstate at his own cost: see vol 22(1) (2003 Reissue) LANDLORD AND TENANT (BUSINESS TENANCIES) Paragraph 85 [401] and 'A code of practice for commercial leases in England and Wales (2nd edition)' which can be found in vol 22(1) (2003 Reissue) LANDLORD AND TENANT (BUSINESS TENANCIES) at Form 1 [4501].

As to termination where reinstatement is not possible see vol 22(1) (2003 Reissue) LANDLORD AND TENANT (BUSINESS TENANCIES) Paragraph 237 [1037]. For a provision for termination or surrender on destruction or substantial damage see vol 22(3) (1997 Reissue) LANDLORD AND TENANT (BUSINESS TENANCIES) Form 107 [6483].

152   The expression 'by implication' is intended to include a caller, such as a tradesman, where there has been no express invitation but the person cannot be classed as a trespasser.

153   The tenant should add the words in square brackets.

154   The extent of the duty to use best endeavours depends upon the facts in each case: see *Monkland v Jack Barclay Ltd* [1951] 2 KB 252, [1951] 1 All ER 714, CA; *Terrell v Mabie Todd & Co Ltd* [1952] 2 TLR 574; *NW Investments (Erdington) Ltd v Swani* (1970) 214 Estates Gazette 1115. In the light of *IBM United Kingdom Ltd v Rockware Glass Ltd* [1980] FSR 335, CA, it may be that there is little practical difference between a covenant to use best endeavours, a covenant to use reasonable endeavours and a covenant to take all reasonable steps.

[1908]

5.6.2   *Obligation to reinstate*

Subject to the provisions of clauses 5.6.3 RELIEF FROM THE OBLIGATION TO REINSTATE, and, if any permissions are required, after they have been obtained, the Landlord must as soon as reasonably practicable apply all money received in respect of the insurance effected by the Landlord pursuant to this Lease, except sums in respect of loss of the Rent [and Service Charge], in rebuilding or reinstating the parts of the Building destroyed or damaged [and must make up out of his own money any difference between the cost of rebuilding and reinstating and the money received][155].

155   Where the landlord's covenant is 'to apply all money received in respect of the insurance in rebuilding or reinstating' rather than simply 'to reinstate', it seems that the landlord does not have to complete the work out of his own money if the insurance money is insufficient because he has complied with his covenant by laying out all the insurance money received. The situation is different if the tenant can establish that the landlord was in breach of his covenant to insure for the full cost of reinstatement and that this has caused the shortfall: see *Mumford Hotels Ltd v Wheler* [1964] Ch 117, [1963] 3 All ER 250. The tenant should, therefore, require a specific covenant from the landlord to make up any shortfall, to prevent a situation in which the landlord refuses to complete the rebuilding. This is of particular concern if the suspension of rent proviso is expressed to operate for a limited period, because on the expiry of that period the tenant becomes liable for rent unless he can satisfy the court that the lease has been frustrated.

It should be noted that it is recommended 'best practice' that if premises are so damaged by an uninsured risk as to prevent occupation, the tenant should be allowed to terminate the lease unless the landlord agrees to reinstate at his own cost: see vol 22(1) (2003 Reissue) LANDLORD AND TENANT (BUSINESS TENANCIES) Paragraph 85 [401] and 'A code of practice for commercial leases in England and Wales (2nd edition)'which can be found in vol 22(1) (2003 Reissue) LANDLORD AND TENANT (BUSINESS TENANCIES) at Form 1 [4501]. If this recommendation is adopted and the landlord merely covenants to apply insurance money received, the principle should be extended to damage or destruction resulting from insured risks in circumstances where the insurance money is insufficient to enable reinstatement to be completed.

For a proviso relieving from the obligation to reinstate in the same form see vol 22(3) (1997 Reissue) LANDLORD AND TENANT (BUSINESS TENANCIES) Form 106 [6482].

[1909]

5.6.3   *Relief from the obligation to reinstate*[156]

The Landlord need not rebuild or reinstate the Building if and for so long as the rebuilding or reinstating is prevented because —

5.6.3.1   the Landlord, despite using his best endeavours[157], cannot obtain a necessary permission,

5.6.3.2   any permission is granted subject to a lawful condition with which [it is impossible for *(or as required)* in all the circumstances it is unreasonable to expect] the Landlord to comply,

5.6.3.3   there is some defect or deficiency in the site on which the rebuilding or reinstatement is to take place [that renders it impossible *(or as required)* that means it can only be undertaken at a cost that is unreasonable in all the circumstances],

5.6.3.4   the Landlord is unable to obtain access to the site to rebuild or reinstate,

5.6.3.5   the rebuilding or reinstating is prevented by war, act of God, government action[, strike or lock-out], or

because of the occurrence of any other circumstances beyond the Landlord's control.

156   As to the need for a right to terminate where reinstatement is not possible see vol 22(1) (2003 Reissue) LANDLORD AND TENANT (BUSINESS TENANCIES) Paragraph 226 [998].
157   The extent of the duty to use best endeavours depends upon the facts in each case: see *Monkland v Jack Barclay Ltd* [1951] 2 KB 252, [1951] 1 All ER 714, CA; *Terrell v Mabie Todd & Co Ltd* [1952] 2 TLR 574; *NW Investments (Erdington) Ltd v Swani* (1970) 214 Estates Gazette 1115. In the light of *IBM United Kingdom Ltd v Rockware Glass Ltd* [1980] FSR 335, CA, it may be that there is little practical difference between a covenant to use best endeavours, a covenant to use reasonable endeavours and a covenant to take all reasonable steps.

[1910]

5.6.4   *Notice to terminate*[158]

If at the end of a period[159] of *(state period, eg 3 years)* starting on the date of the damage or destruction the Premises are still not fit for the Tenant's occupation and use, either the Landlord or the Tenant may by notice served at any time within *(state period, eg 6 months)* of the end of that period ('a notice to terminate following failure to reinstate') implement the provisions of clause 5.6.5 TERMINATION FOLLOWING FAILURE TO REINSTATE[160].

158   For alternative provisions where the landlord's right to terminate is limited to specified circumstances see vol 22(3) (1997 Reissue) LANDLORD AND TENANT (BUSINESS TENANCIES) Form 109 [6492].
159   The period to be inserted must be carefully considered. Particular regard should be had to the terms of any rent suspension provision and the extent of insurance cover for loss of rent.
160   As to the effect of the Landlord and Tenant Act 1954 see vol 22(1) (2003 Reissue) LANDLORD AND TENANT (BUSINESS TENANCIES) Paragraph 226 [998].

5.6.5   *Termination following failure to reinstate*

On service of a notice to terminate following failure to reinstate, the Term is to cease absolutely — but without prejudice to any rights or remedies that may have accrued[161]— and all money received in respect of the insurance effected by the Landlord pursuant to this Lease is to belong to the Landlord absolutely[162].

161   The effect of this clause is that the right to terminate arises after the end of the appropriate period, whatever the reason for the delay, but the tenant still has a right of action against the landlord if the landlord is in breach of his covenant to reinstate.
162   In the absence of provision for ownership of the insurance money the position is uncertain. In *Re King, Robinson v Gary* [1963] Ch 459, [1963] 1 All ER 781, CA it was held that the insurance money belongs to the party who paid the premiums even if the insurance was placed in the joint names of the landlord and the tenant. The dissenting view of Denning MR that insurance in joint names envisages that each party should be insured as to his insurable interest and that the insurance money should therefore be

divided in proportion to their interests in the property should, however, be noted. In *Beacon Carpets Ltd v Kirby* [1985] QB 755, [1984] 2 All ER 726, CA the court adhered to this view and held that the proportion payable depended on the parties' interests in the premises at the time of the destruction. The landlord will prefer the lease to provide expressly for the insurance money to be retained by him in full if reinstatement proves impossible. The tenant ought perhaps to accept that it would be unrealistic to amend this to provide for the insurance money to belong to the tenant, but should suggest that a provision be inserted under which the money is to be divided in accordance with their respective interests in the premises at the time when the insurance money became due. For an alternative provision for ownership of the insurance money etc see vol 22(3) (1997 Reissue) LANDLORD AND TENANT (BUSINESS TENANCIES) Form 108 [6491].

[1911]

5.7   Tenant's further insurance covenants[163]

The Tenant covenants with the Landlord to observe and perform the requirements contained in this clause 5.7.

163   In order to comply with many of these covenants, the tenant will need to be supplied with details of the landlord's insurance policy. In any event, it should be noted that it is recommended 'best practice' that where the landlord has arranged insurance, the terms should be made known to the tenant and any material change in the insurance should be notified to the tenant: see Recommendation 14 of 'A code of practice for commercial leases in England and Wales (2nd edition)' which can be found in vol 22(1) (2003 Reissue) LANDLORD AND TENANT (BUSINESS TENANCIES) at Form 1 [4501].

5.7.1   *Requirements of insurers*

The Tenant must comply with all the requirements and recommendations of the insurers.

5.7.2   *Policy avoidance and additional premiums*

The Tenant must not do or omit anything that could cause any insurance policy on or in relation to the Building to become wholly or partly void or voidable, or do or omit anything by which additional insurance premiums may become payable unless he has previously notified the Landlord and has agreed to pay the increased premium.

5.7.3   *Fire-fighting equipment*

The Tenant must keep the Premises supplied with such fire fighting equipment [as the insurers and the fire authority require and must maintain the equipment to their satisfaction *(or as required)* as the Landlord reasonably requires and must maintain the equipment to the reasonable satisfaction of the insurers and the fire authority] and in efficient working order. At least once in every *(state period, eg 6 months)* the Tenant must have the sprinkler system and other fire fighting equipment inspected by a competent person.

5.7.4   *Combustible materials*

The Tenant must not store on the Premises or bring onto them anything of a specially combustible, inflammable or explosive nature, and must comply with the requirements and recommendations of the fire authority [and the [reasonable] requirements of the Landlord] as to fire precautions relating to the Building.

5.7.5   *Fire escapes, equipment and doors*

The Tenant must not obstruct the access to any fire equipment or the means of escape from the Premises or any part of the Building or lock any fire door while the Premises are occupied.

[1912]

5.7.6   *Notice of events affecting the policy*

The Tenant must give immediate notice to the Landlord of any event that might affect any insurance policy on or relating to the Building, and of any event against which the Landlord may have insured under this Lease.

5.7.7   *Notice of convictions*

The Tenant must give immediate notice to the Landlord of any conviction, judgment or finding of any court or tribunal relating to the Tenant, or any director other officer or major shareholder of the Tenant, of such a nature as to be likely to affect the decision of any insurer or underwriter to grant or to continue any insurance[164].

164   This clause provides a continuation of the warranty given by the tenant in clause 5.1 [1903] WARRANTY AS TO CONVICTIONS. As to non-disclosure and misrepresentation in contracts of non-marine insurance see 22 Halsbury's Laws (4th Edn Reissue) INSURANCE.

5.7.8   *Other insurance*

If at any time the Tenant is entitled to the benefit of any insurance of the Premises that is not effected or maintained in pursuance of any obligation contained in this Lease, the Tenant must apply all money received by virtue of such insurance in making good the loss or damage in respect of which the money is received[165].

165   An insurance policy frequently provides that if there is any other insurance effected by or on behalf of the insured, covering the premises that are the subject of the policy, the insurers are liable only for a rateable proportion of the damage. Such provisions extend to a case where one of the policies is in the joint names of the persons interested in the premises and the other is in the name of one only of those persons: *Halifax Building Society v Keighley* [1931] 2 KB 248. Therefore, at least when the insurance is in joint names and, ideally, even where it is not, the landlord should ensure that the tenant will use all money received under any policy he has effected to reinstate the premises.

[1913]

5.8   Increase or decrease of the Building

5.8.1   *Variation of the Insurance Rent Percentage*

If the size of the Building is permanently increased or decreased, the Insurance Rent Percentage may be varied, if the Landlord [acting reasonably] so requires, with effect from the date of any consequent alteration in the Insurance Rent.

5.8.2   *Determination of the variation*[166]

The amount by which the Insurance Rent Percentage is varied is to be agreed by the Landlord and the Tenant or, in default of agreement within *(state period, eg 3 months)* of the first proposal for variation made by the Landlord, is to be the amount the Surveyor, acting as an expert and not as an arbitrator, determines to be fair and reasonable.

166   Without a clause such as this the landlord cannot vary the insurance rent percentage without the consent of all the tenants, and if he subsequently extends the development he would be unable to combine the administration.

[5.9   Landlord's further insurance covenants[167]

The Landlord covenants with the Tenant to observe and perform the requirements set out in this clause 5.9 in relation to the insurance policy effected by the Landlord pursuant to his obligations contained in this Lease.

167   Unless insurance is to be in the joint names of the landlord and the tenant (which is unlikely in the circumstances assumed by this lease), the tenant should seek covenants such as these from the landlord.

5.9.1   *Copy policy*

The Landlord must produce to the Tenant on demand [a copy of the policy and the last premium renewal receipt *(or as required)* reasonable evidence of the terms of the policy and the fact that the last premium has been paid][168].

168   The landlord can reasonably insist on the second alternative. If the premises are insured under a block policy, it would be inappropriate for him to have to disclose to the tenant information about his other properties.

    It should be noted that it is recommended 'best practice' that where the landlord has arranged insurance, the terms should be made known to the tenant and any material change in the insurance should be notified to the tenant: see Recommendation 14 of 'A code of practice for commercial leases in England and Wales (2nd edition)' which can be found in vol 22(1) (2003 Reissue) LANDLORD AND TENANT (BUSINESS TENANCIES) at Form 1 [4501].

[1914]

5.9.2   *Noting of the Tenant's interest*

The Landlord must ensure that the interest of the Tenant is noted or endorsed on the policy[169].

169   Where insurance in the joint names of the landlord and the tenant is not practical, the tenant should insist that a note of his interest is endorsed on the policy. This protects the tenant because the insurers should give notice to him of any lapse in the policy and, where it can be shown that the tenant is responsible for the insurance premium under the terms of the lease, it is likely — but not certain — that the insurers would not exercise subrogation rights against the tenant.

    It is recommended 'best practice' that where the landlord has arranged insurance, any interest of the tenant should be covered by the policy: see Recommendation 14 of 'A code of practice for commercial leases in England and Wales (2nd edition)' which can be found in vol 22(1) (2003 Reissue) LANDLORD AND TENANT (BUSINESS TENANCIES) at Form 1 [4501].

5.9.3   *Change of risks*

The Landlord must notify the Tenant of any [material] change in the risks covered by the policy from time to time[170].

170   It is recommended 'best practice' that where the landlord has arranged insurance, any interest of the tenant should be covered by the policy: see Recommendation 14 of 'A code of practice for commercial leases in England and Wales (2nd edition)' which can be found in vol 22(1) (2003 Reissue) LANDLORD AND TENANT (BUSINESS TENANCIES) at Form 1 [4501].

[5.9.4   *Waiver of subrogation*[171]

The Landlord must produce to the Tenant on demand written confirmation from the insurers that they have agreed to waive all rights of subrogation against the Tenant.]]

171   Generally an insurer who has paid out under a policy stands in the shoes of the insured with regard to any claim the latter may have had against any third party. If the insurance is in joint names, the tenant is an insured party and there can be no subrogation against him. It would seem, also, that where the tenant covenants to reimburse the landlord for sums expended by the landlord in insuring the premises, the landlord's insurers cannot make a subrogated claim against the tenant where the premises are destroyed by the tenant's negligence: *Mark Rowlands Ltd v Berni Inns Ltd* [1986] QB 211, [1985] 3 All ER 473, CA. The tenant may still, however, wish to obtain a specific waiver of subrogation if possible.

[1915]–[1930]

6   GUARANTEE PROVISIONS

6.1   The Guarantor's covenants[172]

6.1.1   *Nature and duration*

The Guarantor's covenants with the Landlord are given as sole or principal debtor or covenantor, with the landlord for the time being and with all his successors in title[173] without the need for any express assignment, and the Guarantor's obligations to the Landlord will last throughout the Liability Period.

172   The covenants in this clause should *not* be omitted where no guarantor is a party to the lease, because they may be required under clause 3.9.5.2 [1858] CONDITIONS. If it is felt undesirable to have covenants in a lease and no party, at least initially, to enter into them, ie where there is no guarantor for the original tenant, the contents of this clause could alternatively be included in a schedule.

173   The new provisions governing the transmission of the benefit and burden of covenants (see the Landlord and Tenant (Covenants) Act 1995 s 3) only apply to landlord and tenant covenants. The law in force before 1 January 1996 remains unchanged for guarantor covenants, so that the benefit passes with the landlord's reversion. This occurs, not under the Law of Property Act 1925 s 141(1), which has been repealed for post-1995 tenancies by the 1995 Act, but under common law. The guarantee covenant touches and concerns the legal estate vested in the new reversioner: see *P & A Swift Investments v Combined English Stores Group plc* [1989] AC 632, [1988] 2 All ER 885, HL.

[1931]

6.1.2   *The covenants*

The Guarantor covenants with the Landlord to observe and perform the requirements of this clause 6.1.2.

6.1.2.1   Payment of rent and performance of the Lease

The Tenant must pay the Lease Rents[174] and VAT charged on them punctually and observe and perform the covenants and other terms of this Lease, and if, at any time during the Liability Period while the Tenant is bound by the tenant covenants of this Lease[175], the Tenant defaults in paying the Lease Rents or in observing or performing any of the covenants or other terms of this Lease, then the Guarantor must pay the Lease Rents and observe or perform the covenants or terms in respect of which the Tenant is in default and make good to the Landlord on demand, and indemnify the Landlord against, all losses resulting from such non-payment, non-performance or non-observance notwithstanding —

(a)   any time or indulgence granted by the Landlord to the Tenant, any neglect or forbearance of the Landlord in enforcing the payment of the Lease Rents or the observance or performance of the covenants or other terms of this Lease, or any refusal by the Landlord to accept rent tendered by or on behalf of the Tenant at a time when the Landlord is entitled — or will after the service of a notice under the Law of Property Act 1925 Section 146 be entitled — to re-enter the Premises[176],

(b)   that the terms of this Lease may have been varied by agreement between the Landlord and the Tenant[, provided that no variation is to bind the Guarantor to the extent that it is materially prejudicial to him][177],

(c)   that the Tenant has surrendered part of the Premises — in which event the liability of the Guarantor under this Lease is to continue in respect of the part of the Premises not surrendered after making any necessary apportionments under the Law of Property Act 1925 Section 140[178], and

(d)   anything else (other than a release by deed) by which, but for this clause 6.1.2.1, the Guarantor would be released.

[1932]

174   As to the definition of 'the Lease Rents' see clause 1.42 [1821] 'THE RENT'.

175   This obligation lasts while the lease is vested in the tenant and for any period of extended liability following an excluded assignment. It is not appropriate once the tenant has entered into an authorised guarantee agreement, when the contractual guarantor's obligations are at one remove: see vol 22(1) (2003 Reissue) LANDLORD AND TENANT (BUSINESS TENANCIES) Paragraph 74 [284] and clause 6.1.2.4 [1935] GUARANTEE OF THE TENANT'S LIABILITIES UNDER AN AUTHORISED GUARANTEE AGREEMENT.

176   If a creditor 'gives time' to the debtor in a binding manner, this releases the guarantor: see *Swire v Redman* (1876) 1 QBD 536; *Holme v Brunskill* (1877) 3 QBD 495, CA. The guarantee should, therefore, be expressed to apply notwithstanding any time or indulgence granted by the landlord to the tenant, or neglect or forbearance on the part of the landlord in enforcing the payment of rent and the other covenants in the lease. It has been suggested, however, that such wording does not protect a landlord who refuses to accept rent so as not to waive a breach of covenant by the tenant. This is unresolved but to avoid any doubt the point should be expressly dealt with. It appears that any provision in a guarantor's covenant that purports to exonerate the landlord from the consequences of his own negligence must satisfy the reasonableness test of the Unfair Contract Terms Act 1977.

177   Any variation of the terms of the contract between the creditor and the debtor will discharge the guarantor (*Holme v Brunskill* (1877) 3 QBD 495, CA), unless the guarantor consents, although it has been suggested that an immaterial variation that was not prejudicial to the guarantor might not release him. No guarantor should accept a provision by which the guarantee is to continue notwithstanding any variation, but on the other hand it seems unfair on the landlord for the guarantor to escape his liability merely because a minor change has been agreed between the landlord and the tenant. A provision that the guarantee is to continue to apply notwithstanding an immaterial variation not prejudicial to the guarantor seems a fair compromise. It should be noted that the Landlord and Tenant (Covenants) Act 1995 s 18 does not apply to the guarantor of the current tenant.

       It should also be noted that it is recommended 'best practice' that landlords and tenants should seek the agreement of any guarantors to proposed material changes to the terms of the lease, or even minor changes which could increase the guarantor's liability: see Recommendation 15 of 'A code of practice for commercial leases in England and Wales (2nd edition)' which can be found in vol 22(1) (2003 Reissue) LANDLORD AND TENANT (BUSINESS TENANCIES) at Form 1 [4501].

178   In the light of *Holme v Brunskill* (1877) 3 QBD 495, CA, the position on surrender of part of the premises should be dealt with expressly.

[1933]

6.1.2.2   New lease following disclaimer[179]

If, at any time during the Liability Period while the Tenant is bound by the tenant covenants of this Lease[180], any trustee in bankruptcy or liquidator of the Tenant disclaims this Lease, the Guarantor must, if so required by notice served by the Landlord within *(state period, eg 60 days)* of the Landlord's becoming aware of the disclaimer, take from the Landlord forthwith a lease of the Premises for the residue of the [Contractual][181] Term as at the date of the disclaimer, at the Rent then payable under this Lease and subject to the same covenants and terms as in this Lease — except that the Guarantor need not ensure that any other person is made a party to that lease as guarantor — the new lease to commence on the date of the disclaimer. The Guarantor must pay the costs of the new lease and VAT charged thereon, save where such VAT is recoverable or available for set-off by the Landlord as input tax[182], and execute and deliver to the Landlord a counterpart of the new lease.

179   This put option should be included because on disclaimer of a lease the lease ceases to exist, although it is deemed to continue for the purpose of determining the liability to the landlord of persons, including guarantors, other than the tenant whose liquidator or trustee has disclaimed: see *Hindcastle Ltd v Barbara Attenborough Associates Ltd* [1997] AC 70, [1996] 1 All ER 737, HL.

180   This obligation lasts while the lease is vested in the tenant and for any period of extended liability following an excluded assignment. It is not appropriate once the tenant has entered into an authorised guarantee agreement when the tenant's — ie the former tenant's — liquidator or trustee in bankruptcy will not be in a position to disclaim the lease because it will no longer be vested in the former tenant.

181   This defined term will require amendment where the operation of the security of tenure provisions in the Landlord and Tenant Act 1954 ss 24–28 is to be excluded in relation to the lease: see note 7 to clause 1.7 [1810] 'THE [CONTRACTUAL] TERM'.

182   As to payment of VAT on legal costs by a person other than the solicitor's own client see the Information Binder: Property [1]: VAT and Property.

[1934]

6.1.2.3   Payments following disclaimer[183]

If this Lease is disclaimed and the Landlord does not require the Guarantor to accept a new lease of the Premises in accordance with clause 6.1.2.2 NEW LEASE FOLLOWING DISCLAIMER, the Guarantor must pay to the Landlord on demand an amount equal to [the difference between any money received by the Landlord for the use or occupation of the Premises and] the Lease Rents [in both cases] for the period commencing with the date of the disclaimer and ending on whichever is the earlier of the date *(state period, eg 6 months)* after the disclaimer, the date, if any, upon which the Premises are relet, and the end of the [Contractual][184] Term.

183   This clause could be a useful alternative for a landlord, who may not be unhappy to regain possession of the premises but would like some rental income before reletting etc. For a covenant by the tenant to assign to the guarantor see vol 22(3) (1997 Reissue) LANDLORD AND TENANT (BUSINESS TENANCIES) Form 159 [6666].
184   This defined term will require amendment where the operation of the security of tenure provisions in the Landlord and Tenant Act 1954 ss 24–28 is to be excluded in relation to the lease: see note 7 to clause 1.7 [1810] 'THE [CONTRACTUAL] TERM'.

6.1.2.4   Guarantee of the Tenant's liabilities under an authorised guarantee agreement

If, at any time during the Liability Period while the Tenant is bound by an authorised guarantee agreement, the Tenant defaults in his obligations under that agreement, the Guarantor must make good to the Landlord on demand, and indemnify the Landlord against, all losses resulting from that default notwithstanding —

(a)   any time or indulgence granted by the Landlord to the Tenant, or neglect or forbearance of the Landlord in enforcing the payment of any sum or the observance or performance of the covenants of the authorised guarantee agreement[185],

(b)   that the terms of the authorised guarantee agreement may have been varied by agreement between the Landlord and the Tenant [provided that no variation is to bind the Guarantor to the extent that it is materially prejudicial to him][186], or

(c)   anything else (other than a release by deed) by which, but for this clause 6.1.2.4, the Guarantor would be released.

185   See note 176 to clause 6.1.2.1 [1933] PAYMENT OF RENT AND PERFORMANCE OF THE LEASE.
186   See note 177 to clause 6.1.2.1 [1933] PAYMENT OF RENT AND PERFORMANCE OF THE LEASE.

[1935]

6.1.3   *Severance*

6.1.3.1   Severance of void provisions

Any provision of this clause 6 rendered void by virtue of the 1995 Act Section 25 is to be severed from all remaining provisions, and the remaining provisions are to be preserved.

6.1.3.2   Limitation of provisions

If any provision in this clause 6 extends beyond the limits permitted by the 1995 Act Section 25, that provision is to be varied so as not to extend beyond those limits.

[6.2   The Landlord's covenant[187]

The Landlord covenants with the Guarantor that he will not attempt to recover from the Guarantor payment of any amount, determined by a court or in binding arbitration or agreed between the Landlord and the Tenant, payable in respect of a breach of covenant by the Tenant, unless he has served on the Guarantor, within 6 months of the payment being determined or agreed, a notice in the form prescribed by Section 27 of the 1995 Act as if the payment were a fixed charge under that Act.]

187   This clause is a tenant's amendment. It provides for a notice equivalent to a default notice under the Landlord and Tenant (Covenants) Act 1995 to be served. It protects the interests of existing and future contractual guarantors. As to service of default notices see vol 22(1) (2003 Reissue) LANDLORD AND TENANT (BUSINESS TENANCIES) Paragraph 61 [260].

[1936]

7   FORFEITURE[188]

If and whenever during the Term —

7.1   the Lease Rents[189], or any of them or any part of them, or any VAT payable on them, are outstanding for *(state period, eg 14 days)* after becoming due, whether formally demanded or not[190], or

7.2   the Tenant [or the Guarantor] breaches any covenant or other term of this Lease, or

7.3   the Tenant [or the Guarantor][191], being an individual, becomes subject to a bankruptcy order[192] [or has an interim receiver appointed to his property][193], or

7.4   the Tenant [or the Guarantor][194], being a company, enters into liquidation[195] whether compulsory or voluntary — but not if the liquidation is for amalgamation or reconstruction of a solvent company — [or enters into administration][196] [or has a receiver appointed over all or any part of its assets][197], or

7.5   the Tenant [or the Guarantor][198] enters into or makes a proposal to enter into any voluntary arrangement pursuant to the Insolvency Act 1986[199] or any other arrangement or composition for the benefit of his creditors, or

7.6   the Tenant has any distress, sequestration or execution levied on his goods,

and, where the Tenant [or the Guarantor] is more than one person, if and whenever any of the events referred to in this clause happens to any one or more of them, the Landlord may at any time re-enter the Premises or any part of them in the name of the whole — even if any previous right of re-entry has been waived[200] — and thereupon the Term is to cease absolutely but without prejudice to any rights or remedies that may have accrued to the Landlord against the Tenant or the Guarantor [or to the Tenant against the Landlord] in respect of any breach of covenant or other term of this Lease, including the breach in respect of which the re-entry is made.

[1937]

188   As to forfeiture generally see vol 22(1) (2003 Reissue) LANDLORD AND TENANT (BUSINESS TENANCIES) Paragraph 283 [1171] et seq.
       The precise range of insolvency-related circumstances that will trigger the proviso should be carefully considered. Tenants should note that their inclusion, in practice, means that the lease cannot be used as security for a loan. Landlords generally seek to have the ability to forfeit in the widest range of circumstances. It should, however, be noted that, in certain circumstances, leave of the court or of the insolvency practitioner administering the procedure may be required before any contractual right can be exercised: see eg, in respect of administration, the Insolvency Act 1986 Sch 1B para 43(4), (6) as inserted by the Enterprise Act 2002 s 248 (4 Halsbury's Statutes (4th Edn) BANKRUPTCY AND INSOLVENCY).

189   As to the definition of 'the Lease Rents' see clause 1.42 [1821] 'THE RENT'.
190   The words 'whether formally demanded or not' should be used to avoid the common law requirement that an actual demand has to be made.
191   The lease may provide for a right of re-entry on insolvency of the guarantor or a tenant's covenant to find an acceptable replacement (see clause 3.23 [1879] REPLACEMENT GUARANTOR) or both.
192   As to bankruptcy generally see the Insolvency Act 1986 Pt IX (ss 264–371).
193   As to interim receivers see the Insolvency Act 1986 s 286.
194   See note 191 above.
195   As to liquidation generally see the Insolvency Act 1986 Pts IV–VI (ss 73–246).
196   As to administration generally see the Insolvency Act 1986 Pt II as substituted by the Enterprise Act 2002 s 248. The tenant may seek to argue that if the administrator pays rent and if there are no other material breaches of the lease the landlord should not be entitled to forfeit the lease on this ground.
197   The tenant may seek to argue that if the receiver pays rent and if there are no other material breaches of the lease the landlord should not be entitled to forfeit the lease on this ground.
198   See note 191 above.
199   As to company voluntary arrangements see the Insolvency Act 1986 Pt I (ss 1–7B) as amended by the Insolvency Act 2000. As to individual voluntary arrangements see the Insolvency Act 1986 Pt VIII (ss 252–263G) as amended by the Enterprise Act 2002 s 264.
200   The landlord has the option whether to take advantage of a right of forfeiture or not. If he elects not to do so, the forfeiture is waived. The election may be express or implied, eg if the landlord does any act by which he recognises that the relationship of landlord and tenant is still continuing after the cause of forfeiture has come to his knowledge.

[1938]–[1950]

8   MISCELLANEOUS

8.1   Exclusion of warranty as to use

Nothing in this Lease or in any consent granted by the Landlord under this Lease is to imply or warrant that the Premises may lawfully be used under the Planning Acts as offices[201].

201   See *Laurence v Lexcourt Holdings Ltd* [1978] 2 All ER 810, [1978] 1 WLR 1128; *Collins v Howell-Jones* [1981] 2 EGLR 108, 259 Estates Gazette 331, CA and the comments of Eveleigh LJ on estate agents' particulars relating to use in *Bovis Group Pension Fund Ltd v GC Flooring & Furnishing Ltd* (1984) 269 Estates Gazette 1252 at 1253, CA.

8.2   Exclusion of third party rights

Nothing in this Lease is intended to confer any benefit on any person who is not a party to it[202].

202   By virtue of the Contracts (Rights of Third Parties) Act 1999 (11 Halsbury's Statutes (4th Edn) CONTRACT) third-party rights may be conferred where they are not clearly excluded. This being so, it is advisable to incorporate a specific exclusion except where the parties actually intend to confer rights of action on a third party. In the standard letting situation it is unlikely that the parties will wish to extend liability in this manner. As to the Contracts (Rights of Third Parties) Act 1999 generally see vol 4(3) (2001 Reissue) BOILERPLATE CLAUSES.

8.3   Representations

The Tenant acknowledges that this Lease has not been entered into wholly or partly in reliance on any statement or representation made by or on behalf of the Landlord except any such statement or representation expressly set out in this Lease[203] [or made by the Landlord's solicitors in any written response to enquiries raised by the Tenant's solicitors in connection with the grant of this Lease].

203   See the comments of Eveleigh LJ on estate agents' particulars relating to use in *Bovis Group Pension Fund Ltd v GC Flooring & Furnishing Ltd* (1984) 269 Estates Gazette 1252 at 1253, CA. For an alternative provision see vol 22(4) (1997 Reissue) LANDLORD AND TENANT (BUSINESS TENANCIES) Form 400 clauses 7.1 [7520], 7.2 [7521].

[1951]

8.4   Documents under hand

While the Landlord is a limited company or other corporation, any licence, consent, approval or notice required to be given by the Landlord is to be sufficiently given if given under the hand of a director, the secretary or other duly authorised officer of the Landlord [or by the Surveyor on behalf of the Landlord].

8.5   Tenant's property

If, after the Tenant has vacated the Premises at the end of the Term any property of his remains in or on the Premises and he fails to remove it within *(state period, eg 7 days)* after a written request from the Landlord to do so or, if the Landlord is unable to make such a request to the Tenant, within *(state period, eg 14 days)* from the first attempt to make it, then the Landlord may, as the agent of the Tenant, sell that property. The Tenant must indemnify the Landlord against any liability incurred by the Landlord to any third party whose property is sold by him in the mistaken belief held in good faith — which is to be presumed unless the contrary is proved — that the property belonged to the Tenant. If, having made reasonable efforts to do so, the Landlord is unable to locate the Tenant, then the Landlord may retain the proceeds of sale absolutely unless the Tenant claims them within *(state period, eg 6 months)* of the date upon which he vacated the Premises. The Tenant must indemnify the Landlord against any damage occasioned to the Premises and any losses caused by or related to the presence of the property in or on the Premises.

8.6   Compensation on vacating excluded

Any statutory right of the Tenant to claim compensation from the Landlord on vacating the Premises is excluded to the extent that the law allows[204].

204   As to compensation where an order for a new tenancy is precluded on certain grounds, see the Landlord and Tenant Act 1954 s 37 as amended by the Local Government and Housing Act 1989 s 149, Sch 7 and by SI 2003/3096.
        As to the effectiveness of provisions of this nature see vol 22(1) (2003 Reissue) LANDLORD AND TENANT (BUSINESS TENANCIES) Paragraph 468 [3079].

                                                                          [1952]

8.7   Notices

8.7.1   *Form and service of notices*

A notice under this Lease must be in writing and, unless the receiving party or his authorised agent acknowledges receipt, is valid if, and only if[205] —

8.7.1.1   it is given by hand, sent by registered post or recorded delivery, or sent by fax[206] provided a confirmatory copy is given by hand or sent by registered post or recorded delivery on the same day, and

8.7.1.2   it is served —
            (a)   where the receiving party is a company incorporated within Great Britain, at the registered office,
            (b)   where the receiving party is the Tenant and the Tenant is not such a company, at the Premises, and

(c)   where the receiving party is the Landlord [or the Guarantor] and [the Landlord *(or as required)* that party] is not such a company, at [the Landlord's *(or as required)* that party's] address shown in this Lease or at any address specified in a notice given by [the Landlord to the Tenant *(or as required)* that party to the other parties].

205   Notice clauses are either mandatory or permissive. The words 'and only if' are inserted to make it clear that this clause is mandatory.

206   As to service by fax see *Hastie and Jenkerson v McMahon* [1991] 1 All ER 255, [1990] 1 WLR 1575, CA.

[1953]

8.7.2   *Deemed delivery*[207]

8.7.2.1   By registered post or recorded delivery

Unless it is returned through the Royal Mail undelivered, a notice sent by registered post or recorded delivery is to be treated as served on the third working day after posting whenever, and whether or not, it is received.

8.7.2.2   By fax

A notice sent by fax is to be treated as served on the day on which it is sent, or the next working day where the fax is sent after 1600 hours or on a day that is not a working day, whenever and whether or not it or the confirmatory copy is received unless the confirmatory copy is returned through the Royal Mail undelivered.

8.7.2.3   'A working day'

References to 'a working day' are references to a day when the United Kingdom clearing banks are open for business in the City of London.

207   It is a fundamental aspect of any notice clause to specify the circumstances in which the server, provided he has complied with the requirements of the clause, has for the purposes of the document served a notice, even if the recipient claims that he never received it.

8.7.3   *Joint recipients*

If the receiving party consists of more than one person, a notice to one of them is notice to all.

[1954]

8.8   Rights and easements[208]

The operation of the Law of Property Act 1925 Section 62 is excluded from this Lease and the only rights granted to the Tenant are those expressly set out in this Lease and the Tenant is not to be entitled to any other rights affecting any adjoining property of the Landlord.

208   Where the Law of Property Act 1925 s 62 may operate, it is sensible to define in the lease those rights that are included, and then specifically exclude the operation of that section.

8.9   Covenants relating to adjoining property

The Tenant is not to be entitled to the benefit of or the right [to enforce or][209] to prevent the release or modification of any covenant agreement or condition entered into by any tenant of the Landlord in respect of any adjoining property of the Landlord.

209   As to when tenants would be able to enforce covenants against each other see vol 22(1) (2003 Reissue) LANDLORD AND TENANT (BUSINESS TENANCIES) Paragraph 48 [235]. Where this might arise, 'to enforce or' should be deleted by the tenant.

8.10   Disputes with adjoining occupiers

If any dispute arises between the Tenant and the tenants or occupiers of any adjoining property of the Landlord in connection with the Premises and any of that adjoining property, it is to be decided [by the Landlord or in such manner as the Landlord directs *(or as required)* by the Surveyor acting as an expert and not as an arbitrator][210].

210   Such a provision is binding on the landlord and the tenant, but binds a tenant of the landlord's adjoining property only if there is a similar provision in his lease.

8.11   Effect of waiver

Each of the Tenant's covenants is to remain in full force both at law and in equity even if the Landlord has waived or released that covenant, or waived or released any similar covenant affecting any adjoining property of the Landlord[211].

211   But as to waiver of a right of forfeiture vol 22(1) (2003 Reissue) LANDLORD AND TENANT (BUSINESS TENANCIES) Paragraph 284 [1173].

[1955]

[8.12   The perpetuity period[212]

The perpetuity period applicable to this Lease is *(state period, eg 80 years)* from the commencement of the [Contractual][213] Term, and whenever in this Lease any party is granted a future interest it must vest within that period or be void for remoteness].

212   As to the rule against perpetuities see vol 22(1) (2003 Reissue) LANDLORD AND TENANT (BUSINESS TENANCIES) Paragraph 132 [664]. This clause should be included if the term exceeds 21 years because the lease contains grants of future interests.
213   This defined term will require amendment where the operation of the security of tenure provisions in the Landlord and Tenant Act 1954 ss 24–28 is to be excluded in relation to the lease (see note 7 to clause 1.7 [1810] 'THE [CONTRACTUAL] TERM') although this is probably unlikely in connection with the grant of such a long lease.

[8.13   Party walls

Any walls dividing the Premises from the other buildings are to be party walls within the meaning of the Law of Property Act 1925 Section 38 and must be maintained at the equally shared expense of the Tenant and the other part.][214] *(omit if not required in the circumstances)*

214   Internal non-loadbearing and loadbearing walls between the premises and other premises are covered in the description of the premises. It is therefore unlikely that as between the tenant and the landlord or other tenants there can be any party walls.

8.14   Exclusion of liability

The Landlord is not to be responsible to the Tenant or to anyone at the Premises or the Building expressly or by implication with the Tenant's authority for any accident happening or injury suffered or for any damage to or loss of any chattel sustained in the Premises or on the Building[215].

215   As to exclusion clauses see vol 22(1) (2003 Reissue) LANDLORD AND TENANT (BUSINESS TENANCIES) Paragraph 140 [679].

[1956]

8.15   [New (or) Old] lease

[This Lease [is (or as appropriate) is not] a new tenancy for the purposes of the 1995 Act Section 1. (or as appropriate) This Lease is granted under the 1995 Act Section 19 and [is (or as appropriate) is not] a new tenancy for the purposes of Section 1 of that Act.][216]

216   A tenancy granted on or after 1 January 1996 that is an overriding lease is not a 'new' tenancy where the tenancy being overridden is one granted before that date: see the Landlord and Tenant (Covenants) Act 1995 ss 1(4), 20(1). Where the lease being granted is an overriding lease, the lease must include a statement that it is an overriding lease and indicate whether the overriding lease is or is not a 'new' tenancy: see the Landlord and Tenant (Covenants) Act 1995 s 20(2). In these circumstances the second alternative should be used.

[8.16   Capacity of tenants

It is declared that the persons comprising the Tenant hold this Lease as [joint tenants (or as required) tenants in common].]

[8.17   Exclusion of the 1954 Act Sections 24–28[217]

8.17.1   *Notice and declaration*

On (date) the Landlord served notice on the Tenant pursuant to the provisions of the 1954 Act Section 38A(3) as inserted by the Regulatory Reform (Business Tenancies) (England and Wales) Order 2003 and on (date) the Tenant made a [simple (or as appropriate) statutory] declaration pursuant to schedule 2 of the Regulatory Reform (Business Tenancies) (England and Wales) Order 2003.

8.17.2   *Agreement to exclude*

Pursuant to the provisions of the 1954 Act Section 38A(1) as inserted by the Regulatory Reform (Business Tenancies) (England and Wales) Order 2003, the parties agree that the provisions of the 1954 Act Sections 24–28 inclusive are to be excluded in relation to the tenancy created by this Lease.]

217   As to contracting out of the Landlord and Tenant Act 1954 and the requirements that need to be complied with see vol 22(1) (2003 Reissue) LANDLORD AND TENANT (BUSINESS TENANCIES) Paragraph 431 [2035].

(include other clauses as required: eg, break clauses and options (see vol 22(3) (1997 Reissue) LANDLORD AND TENANT (BUSINESS TENANCIES) Forms 136 [6544]–142 [6569]) or a proviso as to termination on rent review (see vol 22(3) (1997 Reissue) LANDLORD AND TENANT (BUSINESS TENANCIES) Form 143 [6570]))

IN WITNESS etc (see vol 12(2) (2003 Reissue) DEEDS, AGREEMENTS ETC)

[1957]–[1970]

SCHEDULE 1: THE RIGHTS GRANTED[218]

1-1 Right to use the Common Parts

The right, subject to [temporary] interruption for repair, alteration, rebuilding or replacement, for the Tenant and all persons expressly or by implication authorised by him[219] — in common with the Landlord and all other persons having a like right — to use appropriate areas of the Common Parts for all proper purposes in connection with the use and enjoyment of the Premises at such times as they are open in accordance with the Landlord's obligations in this Lease.

218   As to rights granted see vol 22(1) (2003 Reissue) LANDLORD AND TENANT (BUSINESS TENANCIES) Paragraph 123 [647] et seq.
219   The term 'the Tenant and all persons expressly or by implication authorised by him' is an updated version of 'the Tenant and his successors in title the owners and occupiers for the time being of the Premises and his or their respective servants and licensees': see *Baxendale v North Lambeth Liberal and Radical Club Ltd* [1902] 2 Ch 427 at 429 per Swinfen Eady J; *Hammond v Prentice Bros Ltd* [1920] 1 Ch 201.

1-2 Passage and running through the Adjoining Conduits

The right, subject to temporary interruption for repair, alteration or replacement, to the free passage and running of all services to and from the Premises through the appropriate Adjoining Conduits, in common with the Landlord and all other persons having a like right.

1-3 Support and protection

The right of support and protection for the benefit of the Premises that is now enjoyed from all other parts of the Building.

1-4 Display of nameplates or signs

The right to have two nameplates or signs displayed in positions on the outside of the Building adjacent to its main entrance and in the reception area of the Building, of sizes to be specified by the Landlord [acting reasonably], showing the Tenant's name and any other details approved by the Landlord[, whose approval may not be unreasonably withheld or delayed].

1-5 Right to use the Additional Parking Bays

The right to use the Additional Parking Bays [or such other *(state number)* car parking bays as the Landlord from time to time designates in writing][220].

220   Whenever the tenant is granted the right to park in certain defined parking bays, the landlord should give himself the flexibility to vary the actual bays involved, provided that the number is not reduced.

1-6 Right to use toilets

The right for the Tenant and all persons expressly or by implication authorised by him, in common with the Landlord and all other persons having a like right, to use such toilets in the Building as are from time to time designated in writing by the Landlord[221].

221   The tenant should require the landlord to grant a specific right to use defined lavatories if there are none in the premises.

[1971]

SCHEDULE 2: THE RIGHTS RESERVED[222]

2-1   Passage and running through the Conduits

The right to the free and uninterrupted passage and running of all appropriate services and supplies from and to other parts of the Building or any other adjoining property of the Landlord in and through the appropriate Conduits and through any structures of a similar use or nature that may at any time be constructed in, on, over or under the Premises as permitted by paragraph 2-2 RIGHT TO CONSTRUCT CONDUITS.

222   As to rights reserved see vol 22(1) (2003 Reissue) LANDLORD AND TENANT (BUSINESS TENANCIES) Paragraph 124 [648] et seq.

2-2   Right to construct conduits[223]

The right to construct[224] and to maintain at any time during the Term any pipes, sewers, drains, mains, ducts, conduits, gutters, watercourses, wires, cables, [laser optical fibres, data or impulse transmission, communication or reception systems,] channels, flues and other necessary conducting media for the provision of services or supplies — including any fixings, louvres, cowls and any other ancillary apparatus — for the benefit of any part of the Building or any other adjoining property of the Landlord[, making good any damage caused by the exercise of the right].

223   If the term of the lease exceeds 21 years a perpetuity provision — see clause 8.12 [1956] THE PERPETUITY PERIOD — is required in the lease because this is a grant of a future interest.
224   For a covenant to make good after exercising rights of access see vol 22(3) (1997 Reissue) LANDLORD AND TENANT (BUSINESS TENANCIES) Form 79 [6453].

[1972]

2-3   Access

2-3.1   *Access to inspect etc*[225]

The right to enter, or in emergency to break into and enter, the Premises [at any time during the Term *(or as required)* at reasonable times and on reasonable notice except in emergency] —

2-3.1.1   to inspect the condition and the state of repair of the Premises,

2-3.1.2   to inspect, clean, connect to, lay, repair, remove, replace with others, alter or execute any works whatever to or in connection with the conduits, easements, supplies or services referred to in paragraphs 2-1 PASSAGE AND RUNNING THROUGH THE CONDUITS and 2-2 RIGHT TO CONSTRUCT CONDUITS,

2-3.1.3   to view the state and condition of and repair and maintain and carry out work of any other kind to, the Building and any other buildings where such viewing or work would not otherwise be [reasonably] practicable,

2-3.1.4   to carry out work or do anything whatever that the Landlord is obliged to do under this Lease,

2-3.1.5   to take schedules or inventories of fixtures and other items to be yielded up at the end of the Term, and

2-3.1.6   to exercise any of the rights granted to the Landlord by this Lease.

225   For a covenant to make good after exercising rights of access see vol 22(3) (1997 Reissue) LANDLORD AND TENANT (BUSINESS TENANCIES) Form 79 [6453].

2-3.2   *Access on renewal or rent review*

The right to enter the Premises with the Surveyor and any third party determining the Rent under any provisions for rent review contained in this Lease at [any time *(or as required)* convenient hours and on reasonable prior notice], to inspect [and measure] the Premises for all purposes connected with any pending or intended step under the 1954 Act or the implementation of the provisions for rent review. *(or as required in view of the rent review provisions used: see, eg, vol 22(3) (1997 Reissue)* LANDLORD AND TENANT *(BUSINESS* TENANCIES) *Forms 180 [6711]–194 [6987])*

[1973]

2-4   Right to erect scaffolding

The right [temporarily] to erect scaffolding for [any purpose connected with or related to the Building *(or as required)* the purpose of inspecting, repairing or cleaning the Building] or any other buildings [even if it restricts *(or as required)* provided it does not materially adversely restrict] access to or the use and enjoyment of the Premises [but not so as to prevent such access, use and enjoyment][226].

226   See *Owen v Gadd* [1956] 2 QB 99, [1956] 2 All ER 28, CA.

2-5   Rights of support and shelter

The rights of light, air, support, shelter, protection and all other easements and rights at the date of this Lease belonging to or enjoyed by other parts of the Building or any other adjoining property of the Landlord.

2-6   Right to erect new buildings[227]

Full right and liberty at any time —

2-6.1   to alter, raise the height of, or rebuild the Building or any other building, and

2-6.2   to erect any new buildings of any height on any adjoining property of the Landlord

in such manner as the Landlord thinks fit even if doing so may obstruct, affect, or interfere with the amenity of or access to the Premises or the passage of light and air to the Premises, [and even if they *(or as required)* but provided they do not] materially affect the Premises or their use and enjoyment.

227   As to reservation of the right to develop other land see vol 22(1) (2003 Reissue) LANDLORD AND TENANT (BUSINESS TENANCIES) Paragraphs 130 [660], 131 [662].

SCHEDULE 3: THE RENT AND RENT REVIEW

(insert rent review provisions as required: see vol 22(3) (1997 Reissue) LANDLORD AND TENANT *(BUSINESS* TENANCIES) *Forms 180 [6711]–194 [6987])*

[1974]

SCHEDULE 4: THE OFFICE COVENANTS

(the draftsman should tailor the covenants contained in this schedule to reflect the nature of the building)

4-1   Use

4-1.1   *Use as offices*

The Tenant must not use the Premises for any purpose other than as offices.

[4-1.2   *Permitted hours*

The Tenant must use and occupy the Premises during the Permitted Hours only[228].]

228   As to restrictions on hours of use see vol 22(1) (2003 Reissue) LANDLORD AND TENANT (BUSINESS TENANCIES) Paragraph 174 [870].

4-1.3   *Cesser of business*

The Tenant must not [cease carrying on business in the Premises or] leave the Premises [continuously] unoccupied for more than *(state period, eg 1 month)* [without notifying the Landlord and providing such caretaking or security arrangements for the protection of the Premises as the Landlord [reasonably] requires and the insurers or underwriters require].

4-1.4   *Noxious discharges*

The Tenant must not discharge into any of the Conduits or the Adjoining Conduits any noxious or deleterious matter or any other substance that might cause an obstruction in or danger or injury to the Conduits or the Adjoining Conduits or be or become a source of obstruction, danger or injury, and in the event of any such obstruction, danger or injury the Tenant must forthwith make good any damage to the satisfaction of the Surveyor.

4-1.5   *Window cleaning*

The Tenant must clean both sides of all windows and window frames in the Premises at least once every month.

4-1.6   *Sound audible outside*

The Tenant must not play or use in the Premises any musical instrument, audio or other equipment or apparatus that produces sound that may be heard outside the Premises [if the Landlord [in his absolute discretion *(or as required)* reasonably] considers such sounds to be undesirable and gives notice to the Tenant to that effect].

[1975]

4-2   Ceiling and floor loading

4-2.1   *Heavy items*

The Tenant must not bring onto or permit to remain on the Premises any safes, machinery, goods or other articles that will or may strain or damage the Premises or any part of them.

4-2.2   *Protection of ceilings*

The Tenant must not without the consent of the Landlord suspend anything from any ceiling on the Premises.

4-2.3   *Expert advice*

If the Tenant applies for the Landlord's consent under paragraph 4-2.2 PROTECTION OF CEILINGS the Landlord may consult any engineer or other person in relation to the ceiling loading proposed by the Tenant, and the Tenant must repay the fees of the engineer or other person to the Landlord on demand.

4-3   Common Parts

4-3.1   *Care of the Common Parts*

The Tenant must not cause the Common Parts [or any [other] land, roads or pavements adjoining the Building] to become untidy or dirty.

4-3.2   *Display of goods outside*

The Tenant must not display or deposit anything whatsoever outside the Premises for display or sale or for any other purpose, or cause any obstruction of the Common Parts.

[1976]

4-4   Machinery

4-4.1   *Noisy machinery*

The Tenant must not install or use in or upon the Premises any machinery or apparatus [other than usual office machinery] that will cause noise or vibration that can be heard or felt in nearby premises or outside the Premises or that may cause damage.

4-4.2   *Maintenance of machinery*

The Tenant must keep all machinery and equipment on the Premises ('the Machinery') properly maintained and in good working order and for that purpose must employ reputable contractors [to be approved by the Landlord[, whose approval may not be unreasonably refused [or delayed],]] ('the Contractors') to carry out regular periodic inspection and maintenance of the Machinery.

4-4.3   *Renewal of parts*

The Tenant must renew all working and other parts of the Machinery as and when necessary or when recommended by the Contractors.

4-4.4   *Operation*

The Tenant must ensure by directions to his staff and otherwise that the Machinery is properly operated.

4-5   Unloading

[4-5.1   *Loading bays to be used*

The Tenant must not load or unload any goods or materials from any vehicle unless the vehicle is parked in the loading bay coloured *(state colour, eg yellow)* on the Plan, and must not cause congestion of that or any adjoining loading bays or inconvenience to any other user of it or them.]

4-5.2   *Standing vehicles*

The Tenant must not permit any vehicles belonging to him or any persons calling on the Premises expressly or by implication with his authority to stand on the [service roads [or any [other] land, roads or pavements adjoining the Building] or, except when and for so long as they are actually loading or unloading goods and materials, on the loading bays *(or as required)* the Common Parts [or any [other] land, roads or pavements adjoining the Building], and must [use his best endeavours to] ensure that such persons do not permit any vehicle so to stand.

[4-5.3   *Use of goods entrances required*

The Tenant must not convey any goods or materials to or from the Premises except through the entrances and service areas provided for the purpose.]

[1977]

4-6   Heating, cooling and ventilation

4-6.1   *Interference and additional loading*

The Tenant must not do anything that interferes with the [heating, cooling or ventilation *(or as required)* air conditioning] of the Common Parts or that imposes an additional load on any [heating, cooling or ventilation *(or as required)* air conditioning] plant and equipment in the Building.

[4-6.2   *Operation of systems*

During the Permitted Hours, the Tenant must operate the ventilation equipment in the Premises, which comprises part of the system for the air conditioning of the Building, in accordance with the [reasonable] regulations made by the Landlord from time to time for that purpose.]

4-7   Regulations

The Tenant must comply with all [reasonable] regulations made by the Landlord from time to time for the management of the Building [and notified to the Tenant in writing][, provided that nothing in the regulations may purport to amend the terms of this Lease and, in the event of any inconsistency between the terms of this Lease and the regulations, the terms of this Lease are to prevail][229].

229   Almost every lease such as this one includes this provision, but only rarely are any regulations made. The tenant should strike out the provision on the basis that he is being asked to accept some unknown commitment. Failing this the tenant should —
   (i)   if the expression 'regulations and restrictions' is used, which seems to be wider than 'regulations', strike out 'and restrictions',
   (ii)   insist that he is formally notified in writing of any regulations that may be made, and
   (iii)   provide that the regulations must always remain subservient to the lease.

4-8   Nameplates or signs

Before occupying the Premises for the purpose of his business at the commencement of the Term and following a permitted assignment [or subletting], the Tenant must provide the Landlord with details of the information that he wishes to have included in the nameplates or signs referred to in paragraph 1-4 DISPLAY OF NAMEPLATES OR SIGNS, and must pay to the Landlord on demand the [reasonable] charges of the Landlord for making and installing every such nameplate or sign.

[1978]

SCHEDULE 5: THE SUBJECTIONS

(insert details)

SCHEDULE 6: THE SERVICE CHARGE[230]

6-1   Definitions

In this schedule the terms defined below have the meanings given in this paragraph.

230   As to service charges see vol 22(1) (2003 Reissue) LANDLORD AND TENANT (BUSINESS
        TENANCIES) Paragraph 247 [1081] et seq. For alternative service charge provisions see vol 22(3)
        (1997 Reissue) LANDLORD AND TENANT (BUSINESS TENANCIES) Forms 149 [6581]–153 [6649].

6-1.1   *'A financial year'*

References to 'a financial year' are references to the period commencing on *(state date, eg 1 January)* in any year and ending on *(state date, eg 31 December)* in the same year or such other annual period as the Landlord in his discretion determines as being that for which his accounts, either generally or in respect of the Building, are to be made up.

6-1.2   *'The Initial Provisional Service Charge'*

'The Initial Provisional Service Charge means the sum of £... a year.

6-1.3   *'The Management Premises'*

'The Management Premises' means all the administrative and control offices and storage areas, staff rooms and other areas maintained by the Landlord for the purpose of managing the Building and performing the Landlord's obligations under this Lease together with any living accommodation provided by the Landlord for security guards, caretakers or other staff employed by him for purposes connected with the Building.

6-1.4   *'Other lettable premises'*

References to 'other lettable premises' are references to premises in the Building that are let, or are from time to time allocated for letting, by the Landlord, other than the Premises, and respectively include and exclude, where applicable, the equivalent parts of the Building included in and excluded from the Premises as described in clause 1.38 THE PREMISES.

[1979]

6-1.5   *'The Plant'*

'The Plant' means all the electrical, mechanical and other plant, machinery, equipment, furnishings, furniture, fixtures and fittings of ornament or utility in use for common benefit from time to time on, in or at the Building, including, without prejudice to the generality of the foregoing, goods and passenger lifts, lift shafts, escalators, passenger conveyors, [heating, cooling, lighting and ventilation *(or as required)* air conditioning] equipment, cleaning equipment, internal and public telephones, public address systems, fire precaution equipment, fire and burglar alarm systems, closed circuit television, refuse compactors and all other such equipment, including stand-by and emergency systems.

6-1.6   'The Retained Parts'

'The Retained Parts' means the parts of the Building that are not let, or constructed or adapted for letting, including, but without prejudice to the generality of the foregoing, the Common Parts and such parts of the main structure, walls, foundations and roofs of the Building as are not included in the Premises and would not be included in premises demised by leases of the other units in the Building if let on the same terms as this Lease, and also including office accommodation for the Building manager and any ancillary staff.

6-2   Service charge provisions

6-2.1   Certificate of the Landlord's Expenses

As soon as reasonably practicable[231] after each financial year the Landlord must ensure that the Accountant issues a certificate containing a summary of the Landlord's Expenses for that financial year, and a summary of any expenditure that formed part of the Landlord's Expenses in respect of a previous financial year but has not been taken into account in the certificate for any previous financial year. A copy of the certificate must be supplied by the Landlord to the Tenant.

---

231   Time is not normally of the essence in relation to the preparation of the service charge account: see vol 22(1) (2003 Reissue) LANDLORD AND TENANT (BUSINESS TENANCIES) Paragraph 271 [1125]. As to certification of expenses see vol 22(1) (2003 Reissue) LANDLORD AND TENANT (BUSINESS TENANCIES) Paragraph 274 [1129].

[1980]

6-2.2   Omissions from the certificate

Omission by the Accountant to include in a certificate of the Landlord's Expenses of any expenditure incurred in the financial year to which the certificate relates is not to preclude the inclusion of that expenditure in any subsequent certificate.

6-2.3   Deemed Landlord's Expenses

In any financial year the Landlord's Expenses are to be deemed to include not only the costs and expenses actually paid or incurred by the Landlord during that year, but also —

6-2.3.1   such fair and reasonable part of all costs and expenditure in respect of or incidental to all or any of the recurring services and other matters referred to in paragraph 6-3, whenever paid or incurred whether before or during the Term — including reasonable provision for anticipated expenditure[232] — as the Surveyor in his reasonable discretion allocates to that financial year as being fair and reasonable, and

6-2.3.2   an amount equal to the fair annual rental value of the Management Premises, as certified by the Surveyor acting reasonably[whose decision is to be conclusive],

and if the Landlord or a person connected with the Landlord or employed by the Landlord attends to (1) the supervision and management of the provision of services for the Building[233], and/or (2) the preparation of statements or certificates of the Landlord's Expenses, and/or (3) the auditing of the Landlord's Expenses, and/or (4) the collection of rents from the Building, then an expense is to be deemed to be paid or a cost incurred by the Landlord, being a reasonable fee not exceeding that which independent agents might properly have charged for the same work.

---

232   As to sinking funds see vol 22(1) (2003 Reissue) LANDLORD AND TENANT (BUSINESS TENANCIES) Paragraphs 280 [1138], 282 [1140].
233   As to recovery of management costs see vol 22(1) (2003 Reissue) LANDLORD AND TENANT (BUSINESS TENANCIES) Paragraph 263 [1107].

6-2.4   Certificates conclusive[234]

Any certificate of the Landlord's Expenses, and any certificate given by the Surveyor or Accountant in connection with the Landlord's Expenses, is to be conclusive as to the matters it purports to certify.

234   As to conclusivity of certificates see vol 22(1) (2003 Reissue) LANDLORD AND TENANT (BUSINESS TENANCIES) Paragraph 275 [1131].

6-2.5   Payment

For each financial year the Tenant must pay the Service Charge Percentage of the Landlord's Expenses.

6-2.6   Variation of the Service Charge Percentage

The Service Charge Percentage may be varied to the extent that the Surveyor fairly and reasonably considers appropriate.

[1981]

6-2.7   Landlord's contribution

The Landlord is to have no liability to contribute to the Landlord's Expenses except in relation to any other lettable premises for which no contribution is payable by an occupier or other person.

6-2.8   Payment on account[235]

For each financial year the Tenant must pay to the Landlord on account of the Service Charge such a sum as the Surveyor certifies to be fair and reasonable having regard to the likely amount of the Service Charge. That sum must be paid in advance, without deduction or set off, by equal instalments on the usual quarter days, the first instalment to be paid on the quarter day immediately before the commencement of the financial year in question. During any financial year the Surveyor may revise the contribution on account of the Service Charge for that financial year so as to take into account any actual or expected increase in expenditure, and as soon as reasonably practicable after a revision the Surveyor must certify the amount of the revised contribution.

235   As to payment on account see vol 22(1) (2003 Reissue) LANDLORD AND TENANT (BUSINESS TENANCIES) Paragraph 272 [1126].

6-2.9   Service charge for the first financial year

The sum payable for the financial year current at the date of this document is to be the Initial Provisional Service Charge, of which the Tenant must, on the date of this document, pay to the Landlord a due proportion calculated from day to day in respect of the period from [the Rent Commencement Date (or as required)] to the next quarter day after the date of this document.

6-2.10   Final account and adjustments[236]

As soon as reasonably practicable after the end of each financial year, the Landlord must furnish the Tenant with an account of the Service Charge payable by him for that financial year, credit being given for payments made by the Tenant on account. Within (state period, eg 7 days) of the furnishing of such an account, the Tenant must pay the Service Charge, or any balance of it payable, to the Landlord. The Landlord must allow any amount overpaid by the Tenant to him against future payments of Service Charge, whether on account or not. At the end of the financial year current at the end of the Term the Landlord must repay to the Tenant any outstanding overpayment of the Service Charge.

236   As to the tenant's concerns on adjustments see vol 22(1) (2003 Reissue) LANDLORD AND TENANT
       (BUSINESS TENANCIES) Paragraph 272 [1126].

[1982]

6-3   The Services[237]

The Services are —

6-3.1   repairing[238] — and, whenever the Landlord, acting reasonably, regards it as necessary in order to repair, replacing or renewing — and decorating the Retained Parts,

6-3.2   operating, maintaining, repairing and, whenever the Landlord, acting reasonably, considers it appropriate, renewing, replacing or modifying the Plant[239],

6-3.3   placing and running maintenance contracts for the Building,

6-3.4   providing the Plant that the Landlord, acting reasonably, considers necessary or desirable, or that is required by law or by any government department or local, public or regulatory or other authority or court to be supplied and maintained, including the initial capital expenditure and expenditure on replacement of any machinery — including motor vehicles — articles and materials for, for example, refuse collection and fire fighting,

6-3.5   providing suitable facilities for disposing of refuse, compacting it or removing it from the Building,

6-3.6   supplying hot and cold water to the lavatory facilities in the Common Parts during normal business hours, and providing towels, soap, toilet paper and other appropriate supplies, [and staffing the lavatory facilities,]

6-3.7   providing reasonable lighting in the Common Parts,

6-3.8   providing reasonable central heating [and air conditioning] to the Premises and the Common Parts[240] during the Permitted Hours,

6-3.9   cleaning the windows and other glass of the Common Parts,

6-3.10   supplying, maintaining, servicing and keeping in good condition and, wherever the Landlord considers it appropriate, renewing and replacing all fixtures, fittings, furnishings, bins, receptacles, tools, appliances, equipment, door furniture, floor coverings and any other things the Landlord may consider desirable for performing the Services or for the appearance or upkeep of the Retained Parts,

[1983]

6-3.11   carrying out inspections and tests of the Retained Parts, including the Plant, that the Landlord from time to time considers necessary or desirable,

6-3.12   planting, tidying, tending and landscaping any appropriate part of the Common Parts in such manner as the Landlord from time to time considers appropriate,

6-3.13   providing, replacing and renewing trees, shrubs, flowers, grass and other plants, flags, decorative lights and other decorations, decorative or drinking fountains or other amenities that the Landlord from time to time thinks fit to provide or maintain in the Building, and providing, maintaining, replacing and renewing seats or benches in the Common Parts,

6-3.14   employing such persons as the Landlord, acting reasonably, considers necessary or desirable from time to time in connection with providing any of the Services, providing caretaking, porterage, security, administration, management and supervision, performing the Landlord's other obligations in this Lease and collecting rents accruing to the Landlord from the Building, with all incidental expenditure including, but without limiting the generality of the above, remuneration, payment of statutory contributions and such other health, pension, welfare, redundancy and similar or ancillary payments and any other payments the Landlord, acting reasonably, thinks desirable or necessary, and providing work clothing[241],

6-3.15   discharging any amounts the Landlord may be liable to pay towards the expense of making, repairing, maintaining, rebuilding and cleaning anything — for example ways, roads, pavements, sewers, drains, pipes, watercourses, party walls, party structures, party fences and other conveniences — that are appurtenant to the Building or are used for the Building in common with any other adjoining property of the Landlord,

6-3.16   erecting, providing, maintaining, renewing and replacing such notice boards, notices and other signs and directions in the Building as the Landlord, acting reasonably, from time to time considers appropriate,

6-3.17   administering and managing the Building[242], performing the Services, performing the Landlord's other obligations in this Lease and preparing statements or certificates of and auditing the Landlord's Expenses,

6-3.18   providing and performing all services of any kind whatsoever that the Landlord, acting reasonably, from time to time provides and all additional or substitute services that the Landlord provides pursuant to clause 4.2.3 VARIATION AND WITHHOLDING OF THE SERVICES[243],

[1984]

6-3.19   discharging all existing or future taxes, rates, charges, duties, assessments, impositions and outgoings whatsoever in respect of the Retained Parts, including, without prejudice to the generality of the above, those for water, electricity, gas and telecommunications,

6-3.20   policing the Building[, controlling traffic and pedestrians] and providing such security staff as the Landlord, acting reasonably, from time to time thinks fit and proper, and providing, maintaining, replacing and renewing security equipment in the Building,

6-3.21   paying any interest on any loan or overdraft raised for the purpose of defraying the Landlord's Expenses[244],

6-3.22   taking any steps the Landlord, acting reasonably, from time to time considers appropriate for complying with, making representations against, or otherwise contesting or dealing with any statutory or other obligation affecting or alleged to affect the Building, including any notice, regulation or order of any government department, local, public, regulatory or other authority or court, compliance with which is not the direct liability of the Tenant or any tenant of any part of the Building[245],

6-3.23   discharging the reasonable and proper cost of any service or matter the Landlord, acting reasonably, thinks proper for the better and more efficient management and use of the Building and the comfort and convenience of its occupants[246],

6-3.24   renting any item used for carrying out any of the matters referred to in this schedule,

6-3.25   keeping appropriate areas of the Common Parts open for servicing the Premises and other units in the Building from *(time)* to *(time)*, and

6-3.26   abating any nuisance affecting the Building, except to the extent that abating it is the liability of any tenant of the Building[247]

[1985]

237   This is a comprehensive list of services. Not all may be appropriate to the particular building concerned. The draftsman should tailor the list to reflect the nature of the building, the manner in which it is being divided and the proposed occupancy arrangements.
        As to the standard of performance see vol 22(1) (2003 Reissue) LANDLORD AND TENANT (BUSINESS TENANCIES) Paragraph 256 [1095].

238   As to the position regarding inherent defects see vol 22(1) (2003 Reissue) LANDLORD AND TENANT (BUSINESS TENANCIES) Paragraph 258 [1099].

239   As to plant and machinery see vol 22(1) (2003 Reissue) LANDLORD AND TENANT (BUSINESS TENANCIES) Paragraph 261 [1103].

240   As to the provision of hot water and heating see vol 22(1) (2003 Reissue) LANDLORD AND TENANT (BUSINESS TENANCIES) Paragraph 260 [1102].

241   The landlord performs the services either by means of third parties whose fee he pays and has reimbursed by the tenants, or by his own staff. In the latter case the landlord needs to be able to include the cost of employing the staff as part of the service charge. If there are managing agents, the landlord may also welcome the flexibility of being able to charge a fee for any services that they perform 'in-house' where this is more practical than charging the cost of employing the relevant individuals. As to the description of the duties of staff see vol 22(1) (2003 Reissue) LANDLORD AND TENANT (BUSINESS TENANCIES) Paragraph 262 [1105].

242   If administration and management costs are to be recovered, there must be express references in the lease: see vol 22(1) (2003 Reissue) LANDLORD AND TENANT (BUSINESS TENANCIES) Paragraph 263 [1107].

243   As to 'sweeping-up' clauses and the tenant's concerns see vol 22(1) (2003 Reissue) LANDLORD AND TENANT (BUSINESS TENANCIES) Paragraph 267 [1113].

244   As to recovery of interest payments see vol 22(1) (2003 Reissue) LANDLORD AND TENANT (BUSINESS TENANCIES) Paragraph 265 [1111].

245   The tenant should ensure that any clause entitling the landlord to be reimbursed for the cost of complying with, making representations against or contesting the provisions of any regulation or other provisions that apply to the premises is qualified so that he must act reasonably.

246   As to 'sweeping-up' clauses and the tenant's concerns see vol 22(1) (2003 Reissue) LANDLORD AND TENANT (BUSINESS TENANCIES) Paragraph 267 [1113].

247   The tenant should consider restricting this to nuisances affecting parts of the building including the premises or items used by the tenant.

SCHEDULE 7: THE AUTHORISED GUARANTEE AGREEMENT

(insert the form of authorised guarantee agreement: see, eg vol 22(3) (1997 Reissue) LANDLORD AND TENANT (BUSINESS TENANCIES) Form 217 [7053])

(signature (or common seal) of landlord: lease)
(signature (or common seal) of tenant (and guarantor): counterpart)
(signatures of witnesses)
[1986]–[2100]

4: HOTELS

13

Lease of a hotel[1]

CONTENTS

(NB: numbers in [ ] below refer to this volume and should be altered to suit the page or reference numbers actually used)

1 DEFINITIONS AND INTERPRETATION
1.1 'The Conduits' . . . . [2108]
1.2 'The [Contractual] Term' . . . . [2108]
1.3 'Development' . . . . [2109]
[1.4 'The Exterior Decorating Years' . . . . [2109]]
1.5 Gender and number . . . . [2109]
1.6 Headings . . . . [2109]
1.7 'The Hotel Covenants' . . . . [2109]
[1.8 'The Initial Rent' . . . . [2109]]
1.9 'The Insurance Rent' . . . . [2110]
1.10 'The Insured Risks' . . . . [2110]
                                                                      [2101]
1.11 'Interest' . . . . [2110]
1.12 'The Interest Rate' . . . . [2111]
[1.13 'The Interior Decorating Years' . . . . [2111]]
1.14 Interpretation of 'consent' and 'approved' . . . . [2112]
1.15 Interpretation of 'the Guarantor' . . . . [2112]
1.16 Interpretation of 'the Landlord' . . . . [2113]
1.17 Interpretation of 'the last year of the Term' and 'the end of the Term' . . . [2113]
1.18 Interpretation of 'the Tenant' . . . . [2113]
1.19 Interpretation of 'this Lease' . . . . [2113]
1.20 Joint and several liability . . . . [2113]
1.21 'The Liability Period' . . . . [2114]
1.22 'Losses' . . . . [2115]
1.23 'The 1954 Act' . . . . [2115]
1.24 'The 1995 Act' . . . . [2115]
1.25 Obligation not to permit or suffer . . . . [2115]
1.26 'The Plan' . . . . [2115]
1.27 'The Planning Acts' . . . . [2115]
1.28 'The Premises' . . . . [2116]
1.29 References to clauses and schedules . . . . [2117]
1.30 References to rights of access . . . . [2117]
1.31 References to statutes . . . . [2117]
1.32 'The Rent' . . . . [2118]
1.33 'The Rent Commencement Date' . . . . [2118]
[1.34 'The Review Dates' . . . . [2119]]
1.35 'The Surveyor' . . . . [2119]
[1.36 'The Term' . . . . [2120]]
1.37 Terms from the 1995 Act . . . . [2120]
1.38 'VAT' . . . . [2120]

2 DEMISE . . . . [2141]
                                                                      [2102]

3 THE TENANT'S COVENANTS

3.1 Rent . . . . [2143]
3.2 Outgoings and VAT . . . . [2144]
[3.3 Cost of services consumed . . . . [2145]]
3.4 Repair, cleaning and decoration . . . . [2145]
3.5 Waste and alterations . . . . [2148]
3.6 Aerials, signs and advertisements . . . . [2149
3.7 Statutory obligations . . . . [2150]
3.8 Entry to inspect and notice to repair . . . . [2152]
3.9 Alienation . . . . [2161]
3.10 Nuisance and residential restrictions . . . . [2173]
3.11 Costs of applications, notices and recovery of arrears . . . . [2174]
3.12 Planning and development . . . . [2175]
3.13 Plans, documents and information . . . . [2177]
3.14 Indemnities . . . . [2177]
3.15 Reletting boards and viewing . . . . [2178]
3.16 Obstruction and encroachment . . . . [2178]
3.17 Yielding up . . . . [2179]
3.18 Interest on arrears . . . . [2179]
3.19 Statutory notices . . . . [2179]
3.20 Keyholders . . . . [2180]
3.21 Viewing on sale of reversion . . . . [2180]
3.22 Defective premises . . . . [2180]
3.23 Replacement guarantor . . . . [2180]
3.24 Exercise of the Landlord's rights . . . . [2181]
3.25 The Hotel Covenants . . . . [2181]
3.26 Costs of grant of this Lease . . . . [2182]
3.27 Consent to the Landlord's release . . . . [2182]

4 QUIET ENJOYMENT . . . . [2183]
[2103]

5 INSURANCE

5.1 Warranty as to convictions . . . . [2191]
5.2 Covenant to insure . . . . [2192]
5.3 Details of the insurance . . . . [2192]
5.4 Payment of the Insurance Rent . . . . [2194]
5.5 Suspension of the Rent . . . . [2194]
5.6 Reinstatement and termination . . . . [2195]
5.7 Tenant's further insurance covenants . . . . [2200]
[5.8 Landlord's further insurance covenants . . . . [2202]]

6 GUARANTEE PROVISIONS

6.1 The Guarantor's covenants . . . . [2204]
[6.2 The Landlord's covenant . . . . [2209]]

7 FORFEITURE . . . . [2210]

8 MISCELLANEOUS

8.1 Exclusion of warranty as to use .... [2212]
8.2 Exclusion of third party rights .... [2212]
8.3 Representations .... [2212]
8.4 Documents under hand .... [2213]
8.5 Tenant's property .... [2213]
8.6 Compensation on vacating excluded .... [2213]
8.7 Notices .... [2214]
8.8 [New (or) Old] lease .... [2215]
[8.9 Capacity of tenants .... [2215]]
[8.10 Exclusion of the 1954 Act Sections 24–28 .... [2215]]

SCHEDULE 1: THE RIGHTS RESERVED

1-1 Right of entry to inspect .... [2216]
1-2 Access on renewal or rent review .... [2216]

SCHEDULE 2: THE RENT AND RENT REVIEW

SCHEDULE 3: THE HOTEL COVENANTS

3-1 Use .... [2217]
3-2 Environmental protection .... [2218]
3-3 Ceiling and floor loading .... [2219]
3-4 Machinery .... [2219]
3-5 Signs and name .... [2220]

SCHEDULE 4: THE SUBJECTIONS

SCHEDULE 5: THE AUTHORISED GUARANTEE AGREEMENT

[2104]

AGREEMENT

[HM LAND REGISTRY

LAND REGISTRATION ACT 2002

Administrative area	*(insert details)*
Title number out of which lease is granted	*(title number)*
Property let	*(postal address or description)*]

[2105]

THIS LEASE is made the .... day of .... BETWEEN:

(1)   *(name of landlord)* [of *(address)* *(or as appropriate)* the registered office of which is at *(address)*] [Company Registration no ...][2] ('the Landlord') [and]

(2)   *(name of tenant)* [of *(address)* *(or as appropriate)* being a company registered in [England and Wales *(or)* Scotland][3] the registered office of which is at *(address)*] [Company Registration no ...] ('the Tenant') [and

(3)   *(name of guarantor)* [of *(address)* *(or as appropriate)* the registered office of which is at *(address)*] [Company Registration no ...] ('the Guarantor')]

[2106]

1   As to stamp duty land tax see the Information Binder: Stamp Duty Land Tax [1].

As to Land Registry Fees see the Information Binder: Property [1]: Property Fees.

On the grant out of an unregistered freehold estate in land of a lease for a term of more than seven years from the date of the grant, application must be made to register the title to the leasehold interest granted: see the Land Registration Act 2002 s 4(1)(c) (37 Halsbury's Statutes (4th Edn) REAL PROPERTY). The tenant must obtain an epitome of title to the freehold reversion, investigate it, and mark it as examined, otherwise he will not be able to be registered with an absolute title: see vol 25(1) (2003 Reissue) LAND REGISTRATION Paragraph 21.1 [132].

If the freehold reversion is registered, the grant of a lease for a term of more than seven years from the date of the grant must be completed by registration: see the Land Registration Act 2002 s 27(2)(b)(i).

As to the form and contents of leases see vol 22(1) (2003 Reissue) LANDLORD AND TENANT (BUSINESS TENANCIES) Paragraph 104 [601] et seq. As to registered land generally see vol 25(1) (2003 Reissue) LAND REGISTRATION. As to registration of title to leases see vol 25(1) (2003 Reissue) LAND REGISTRATION Paragraph 143 [601] et seq. For a form of lease to be used in connection with a public house see vol 24(2) (2002 Reissue) Form 56.

This lease relates to premises comprising a hotel standing in its own grounds. The landlord owns no adjoining premises and no rights are granted or services provided. The tenant is responsible for the repair of the premises and the decoration of both the exterior and the interior. The landlord insures the premises and the tenant refunds the cost of the premiums. There is provision for rent review, and also for a guarantor.

2   If any party is a company it is desirable to include the company registration number. This avoids any problems arising when a company has been wound up and a new company formed with the same name, or when the name of a company is changed, or if companies swap names, eg on a reconstruction of a group of companies. In addition, where a company applies to be registered as proprietor of a registered estate or registered charge, the application must state the company's registration number: see the Land Registration Rules 2003, SI 2003/1417 r 181.

3   Where the tenant is a company registered in England and Wales or Scotland, and the lease is registrable, an application for first registration of the lease (where the landlord's title is unregistered), or registration of the lease as a registrable disposition (where the landlord's title is registered), and the tenant as proprietor of the leasehold title, must state the company's registered number: see SI 2003/1417 r 181(1). There seems to be no reason why the certificate and statement should not be contained in the disposition in favour of the proprietor, where convenient.

[2107]

NOW THIS DEED WITNESSES as follows:

1   DEFINITIONS AND INTERPRETATION

For all purposes of this Lease[4] the terms defined in this clause have the meanings specified.

4   One view would add 'unless the context otherwise requires' or 'where the context so admits' and in fact this may be implied (see *Meux v Jacobs* (1875) LR 7 HL 481 at 493; *Law Society v United Service Bureau Ltd* [1934] 1 KB 343, DC) but the better course is to use defined terms in such a way that there are no circumstances where the defined meaning does not apply.

1.1   'The Conduits'

'The Conduits' means the pipes, sewers, drains, mains, ducts, conduits, gutters, watercourses, wires, cables, [laser optical fibres, data or impulse transmission, communication or reception systems,] channels, flues and all other conducting media — including any fixings, louvres, cowls, covers and any other ancillary apparatus — that are in, on, over or under the Premises.

1.2   'The [Contractual] Term'[5]

'The [Contractual][6] Term' means *(insert number)* years commencing on and including *(date of start of term)*[7].

5   As to the commencement of the term see vol 22(1) (2003 Reissue) LANDLORD AND TENANT (BUSINESS TENANCIES) Paragraph 135 [670].
    As to registration see note 1 above. Where the landlord's title is unregistered, the grantee must apply for registration within a period of two months from the date of the disposition if the lease is granted for a term of more than seven years. If no such application is made the disposition becomes void as regards any transfer, grant or creation of a legal estate: see the Land Registration Act 2002 s 6. Where the landlord's title is registered and the lease is for a term of more than seven years, the tenant should protect the intended lease by applying for an official search, and an application to register the lease should be made before expiry of the search, otherwise the lease will be susceptible to loss of priority: see the Land Registration Act 2002 s 27.

6   The demise in this lease is for 'the Contractual Term', which is defined as a fixed term of years. The expression 'the Term', as defined in clause 1.36 [2120] 'THE TERM', is used in covenants so that they continue to apply during any period of holding over or continuance or extension of the contractual term. Some difficulties arise if this structure is used in a draft lease where security of tenure is to be excluded under the Landlord and Tenant Act 1954 s 38A(1) as inserted by SI 2003/3096 (23 Halsbury's Statutes (4th Edn) LANDLORD AND TENANT). The demise is for the contractual term and the inclusion of the definition of 'the Term' does not prevent the lease being 'for a term of years certain' as required by the Landlord and Tenant Act 1954 s 38A(1). However, reference to continuance of the contractual term by statute is inappropriate where the operation of the security of tenure provisions in the Landlord and Tenant Act 1954 ss 24–28 is to be excluded. If a lease is contracted out of the Landlord and Tenant Act 1954 there can be no statutory extension, and if the tenant remains in occupation at the end of the contractual term he is holding over unlawfully unless there is an express agreement to extend the contractual term operating as a surrender and re-grant so that the original lease— and the agreement under the Landlord and Tenant Act 1954 s 38A(1) — has no further effect. It is suggested that in these circumstances the drafting should be simplified to include a single term (defined simply as 'the Term') by reference to the period of the contractual term. This can be achieved by amending this clause in the manner suggested and substituting it for clause 1.36 [2120] 'THE TERM'.

7   For estate management reasons it is usually desirable to insert a quarter day here — or a rent day when rent is due on days other than quarter days — ie generally the one preceding the earlier of the date of possession and the date of execution.

[2108]

1.3   'Development'

References to 'development' are references to development as defined by the Town and Country Planning Act 1990 Section 55.

[1.4   'The Exterior Decorating Years'

'The Exterior Decorating Years' means (specify years).] *(omit if not required, eg if the first alternative in clause 3.4.6 [2147] DECORATION is used)*

1.5   Gender and number

Words importing one gender include all other genders; words importing the singular include the plural and vice versa[8].

8   See the Law of Property Act 1925 s 61 (37 Halsbury's Statutes (4th Edn) REAL PROPERTY).

1.6   Headings[9]

The clause, paragraph and schedule headings and the table of contents do not form part of this document and are not to be taken into account in its construction or interpretation. *(amend if marginal notes are used instead of headings)*

9   Headings and marginal notes require the draftsman to provide a word or two to describe every clause in the lease. This is not always easy and there are times when the draftsman will have to settle for something less than perfection, the only alternative being a heading or note that would be inappropriately long. It would be quite wrong for that title, which its author might admit was not totally apposite but was the best that he could do in a few words, to be used in construing the clause in question.

1.7   'The Hotel Covenants'

'The Hotel Covenants' means the covenants set out in schedule 3 THE HOTEL COVENANTS.

[1.8   'The Initial Rent'

'The Initial Rent' means [the sum of £... a year. *(or as required by the rent and review provisions to be used)*].] *(this definition is not required if the rent is not reviewable)*

[2109]

1.9   'The Insurance Rent'[10]

'The Insurance Rent' means the [gross sums including any commission *(or as required)* sums net of any commission] that the Landlord from time to time pays —

1.9.1   by way of premium for insuring the Premises, including insuring for loss of rent, in accordance with his obligations contained in this Lease,

1.9.2   by way of premium for insuring in such amount and on such terms as [the Landlord acting reasonably considers appropriate *(or as required)* is reasonable] against all liability of the Landlord to third parties arising out of or in connection with any matter including or relating to the Premises, and

1.9.3   for insurance valuations.

10   As to reimbursement of insurance premiums see vol 22(1) (2003 Reissue) LANDLORD AND TENANT (BUSINESS TENANCIES) Paragraph 230 [1026].

1.10   'The Insured Risks'

'The Insured Risks' means the risks of loss or damage by fire[, storm, tempest, earthquake, lightning, explosion, riot, civil commotion, malicious damage, [terrorism,] impact by vehicles and by aircraft and articles dropped from aircraft — other than war risks — flood damage and bursting and overflowing of water pipes and tanks,] and such other risks, whether or not in the nature of the foregoing, as the Landlord [acting reasonably] from time to time decides to insure against[11].

11   As to the risks to be insured and the tenant's concerns see vol 22(1) (2003 Reissue) LANDLORD AND TENANT (BUSINESS TENANCIES) Paragraph 235 [1033].

1.11   'Interest'

References to 'interest' are references to interest payable during the period from the date on which the payment is due to the date of payment, both before and after any judgment, at the Interest Rate then prevailing [*(where the interest rate is defined by reference to a bank base rate)* or, should the base rate referred to in clause 1.12 'THE INTEREST RATE' cease to exist[12], at another rate of interest closely comparable with the Interest Rate [to be agreed between the parties or in default of agreement to be determined by [the Surveyor, acting as an expert and not as an arbitrator *(or as required)* a chartered accountant appointed by agreement between the parties or in default of agreement nominated by the President of the Institute of Chartered Accountants in England and Wales, acting as an expert and not as an arbitrator[13]] *(or as required)* decided upon by the Landlord acting reasonably]]].

12   If base rates are referred to the possibility of their ceasing to exist should be provided for. Alternatively, the Law Society's interest rate may be specified.
13   This provision may be expanded to provide for deeming the parties to have disagreed after a certain time, deputy appointors etc.

[2110]

1.12   'The Interest Rate'

'The Interest Rate'[14] means the rate of ...% a year[15] above [the base lending rate of *(specify bank)* or such other bank [being a member of the British Bankers Association] as the Landlord may from time to time nominate in writing[16] *(or as required)* the Law Society's interest rate[17]].

14   As to the covenant to pay interest see vol 22(1) (2003 Reissue) LANDLORD AND TENANT (BUSINESS TENANCIES) Paragraph 154 [767].

15   Words such as 'with a minimum of ...%' should not be used because, if interest rates drop during the term to such an extent that the minimum rate specified represents significantly more than a few percent over the basic borrowing rate, the provision might be void as a penalty. As to what amounts to a penalty see *Dunlop Pneumatic Tyre Co Ltd v New Garage and Motor Co Ltd* [1915] AC 79, HL; *Cellulose Acetate Silk Co Ltd v Widnes Foundry (1925) Ltd* [1933] AC 20, HL. In view of this, landlords would be unwise to provide for a rate of more than a few percent over base rate, and even this is in fact a penalty rate and should be resisted by the tenant.

16   The chance to change the bank may be useful, especially on a sale of the reversion, so that the landlord can always provide for his bank for the time being to be specified. The tenant should try to limit the choice to major clearing banks.

17   The Law Society's interest rate is published weekly in the Law Society's Gazette.

[1.13   'The Interior Decorating Years'

'The Interior Decorating Years' means *(specify years).*] *(omit if not required, eg if the first alternative in clause 3.4.6 [2147] DECORATION is used)*

[2111]

1.14   Interpretation of 'consent' and 'approved'

1.14.1   *Prior written consent or approval*

References to 'consent of the Landlord' or words to similar effect are references to a prior written consent signed by or on behalf of the Landlord and references to the need for anything to be 'approved by the Landlord' or words to similar effect are references to the need for a prior written approval by or on behalf of the Landlord.

1.14.2   *Consent or approval of mortgagee or head landlord*

Any provisions in this Lease referring to the consent or approval of the Landlord are to be construed as also requiring the consent or approval of any mortgagee of the Premises and any head landlord where that consent is required [under a mortgage or headlease in existence at the date of this document][18]. Nothing in this Lease is to be construed as imposing any obligation on a mortgagee or head landlord not to refuse any such consent or approval unreasonably.

18   The tenant should these words so that the clause applies *only* where the consent of the mortgagee or head landlord is in fact required under the terms of an *existing* mortgage or headlease. The tenant should request a copy of the document concerned to establish the rights of the mortgagee or head landlord in relation to any consents that he may seek. The risk to the tenant of the clause without these words is that, by subsequently creating a mortgage or headlease, the landlord could, innocently or deliberately, bring about a situation where a consent may be refused in circumstances in which it would otherwise have been unreasonable to do so. In particular, the effect on the tenant's ability to assign or sublet could be serious.

1.15   Interpretation of 'the Guarantor'[19]

The expression 'the Guarantor' includes [*(where there is a guarantor for the original tenant)* not only the person named above as the Guarantor, but also][20] any person who enters into covenants with the Landlord pursuant to clause 3.9.5.2 CONDITIONS or clause 3.23 REPLACEMENT GUARANTOR.

19   As to guarantors see vol 22(1) (2003 Reissue) LANDLORD AND TENANT (BUSINESS TENANCIES) Paragraphs 40 [201], 71 [278] et seq.
20   Where there is no guarantor for the original tenant, if it is felt undesirable to have covenants in a lease and no party, at least initially, to enter into them, the guarantor's covenants could be included in a schedule.

[2112]

1.16   Interpretation of 'the Landlord'

The expression 'the Landlord' includes the person or persons from time to time entitled to possession of the Premises when this Lease comes to an end.

1.17   Interpretation of 'the last year of the Term' and 'the end of the Term'

References to 'the last year of the Term' are references to the actual last year of the Term howsoever it determines, and references to the 'end of the Term' are references to the end of the Term whensoever and howsoever it determines.

1.18   Interpretation of 'the Tenant'

'The Tenant' includes any person who is for the time being bound by the tenant covenants of this Lease except where the name of *(name of original tenant)* appears.

1.19   Interpretation of 'this Lease'

Unless expressly stated to the contrary, the expression 'this Lease' includes any document supplemental to or collateral with this document or entered into in accordance with this document.

1.20   Joint and several liability

Where any party to this Lease for the time being comprises two or more persons, obligations expressed or implied to be made by or with that party are deemed to be made by or with the persons comprising that party jointly and severally.

[2113]

1.21   'The Liability Period'[21]

'The Liability Period' means —

[1.21.1   in the case of *(name of guarantor for the original tenant)*, the period during which *(name of original tenant)* is bound by the tenant covenants of this Lease together with any additional period during which *(name of original tenant)* is liable under an authorised guarantee agreement,] *(omit where there is no guarantor for the original tenant)*

1.21.2   in the case of any guarantor required pursuant to clause 3.9.5.2 CONDITIONS, the period during which the relevant assignee is bound by the tenant covenants of this Lease together with any additional period during which that assignee is liable under an authorised guarantee agreement,

1.21.3   in the case of any guarantor under an authorised guarantee agreement, the period during which the relevant assignee is bound by the tenant covenants of this Lease, and

1.21.4   in the case of any guarantor required pursuant to clause 3.9.8.7 TERMS OF A PERMITTED SUBLEASE, the period during which the relevant assignee of the sublease is bound by the tenant covenants of that sublease.

21   The liability of the guarantor should be expressed to last while the original tenant, or as the case may be the assignee, is bound by the tenant covenants in the lease — or in the case of clause 1.21.4 the sublease — rather than while the lease is vested in that person, to take account of the possibility of an excluded assignment being made and the tenant — or subtenant — remaining liable. An excluded assignment means that the tenant — or subtenant — is precluded from tenant release under the Landlord and Tenant (Covenants) Act 1995 (23 Halsbury's Statutes (4th Edn) LANDLORD AND TENANT).

      The Landlord and Tenant (Covenants) Act 1995 does not clearly indicate whether the liability of a contractual guarantor can be expressed to extend to any period during which the tenant is bound by an authorised guarantee agreement, but the better view is that it is possible. The policy of the Act certainly suggests that this should be the case.

                                                                 [2114]

1.22 'Losses'

References to 'losses' are references to liabilities, damages or losses, awards of damages or compensation, penalties, costs, disbursements and expenses arising from any claim, demand, action or proceedings.

1.23 'The 1954 Act'

'The 1954 Act' means the Landlord and Tenant Act 1954 [and all statutes, regulations and orders included by virtue of clause 1.31 REFERENCES TO STATUTES][22].

22   The words in square brackets are strictly speaking not required because they merely state what would be the case anyway by virtue of clause 1.31 [2117] REFERENCES TO STATUTES. Nevertheless, as much could turn on the point (see *Brett v Brett Essex Golf Club Ltd* (1986) 52 P & CR 330, [1986] 1 EGLR 154, CA), the parties may prefer to deal expressly with the point.

1.24 'The 1995 Act'

'The 1995 Act' means the Landlord and Tenant (Covenants) Act 1995 [and all statutes, regulations and orders include by virtue of clause 1.31 REFERENCES TO STATUTES][23].

23   See note 22 to clause 1.23 [2115] 'THE 1954 ACT'.

1.25 Obligation not to permit or suffer

Any covenant by the Tenant not to do anything includes an obligation [to use reasonable endeavours] not to permit or suffer[24] that thing to be done by another person [where the Tenant is aware that the thing is being done].

24   'Permit' may have a different meaning from 'suffer': see *Barton v Reed* [1932] 1 Ch 362 at 375 per Luxmore J. A covenant not to 'permit' activity is broken if the covenantor himself carries it on: see *Oceanic Village Ltd v United Attractions Ltd* [2000] Ch 234, [2000] 1 All ER 975.

1.26   'The Plan'[25]

'The Plan' means the plan annexed to this Lease.

25   As to the use and role of plans see vol 22(1) (2003 Reissue) LANDLORD AND TENANT (BUSINESS
      TENANCIES) Paragraphs 117 [636], 118 [638]. A plan may not always be required, eg a demise of all
      the land within a registered title. If the lease is registrable, a plan 'for identification purposes only' or
      where there is some other disclaimer as to the extent to which it can be relied on for conveyancing
      purposes is not sufficient if part of the land in a registered title is being dealt with.

1.27   'The Planning Acts'

'The Planning Acts' means the Town and Country Planning Act 1990, the Planning
(Listed Buildings and Conservation Areas) Act 1990, the Planning (Consequential
Provisions) Act 1990, the Planning (Hazardous Substances) Act 1990, the Planning and
Compensation Act 1991, the Planning and Compulsory Purchase Act 2004 [and all
statutes, regulations and orders included by virtue of clause 1.31 REFERENCES TO
STATUTES][26].

26   See note 22 to clause 1.23 [2115] 'THE 1954 ACT'.

                                                                                              [2115]

1.28   'The Premises'[27]

1.28.1   *Definition of 'the Premises'*

'The Premises' means the land and building known as *(insert postal address)* [shown [for
the purpose of identification only] edged *(state colour, eg red)* on the Plan].

27   As to parcels generally see vol 22(1) (2003 Reissue) LANDLORD AND TENANT (BUSINESS
      TENANCIES) Paragraph 116 [634].

1.28.2   *Interpretation of 'the Premises'*[28]

The expression 'the Premises' includes —

1.28.2.1   all buildings, erections, structures, fixtures[29], fittings and appurtenances on the
            Premises from time to time,

1.28.2.2   all additions, alterations and improvements carried out during the Term, and

1.28.2.3   the Conduits,

but excludes [the air space above[30] and] any fixtures installed by the Tenant [or any
predecessors in title] that can be removed from the Premises without defacing the
Premises. Unless the contrary is expressly stated, 'the Premises' includes any part or parts
of the Premises.

28   As to implied grants and reservations see vol 22(1) (2003 Reissue) LANDLORD AND TENANT
      (BUSINESS TENANCIES) Paragraph 125 [650].
29   As to fixtures see vol 22(1) (2003 Reissue) LANDLORD AND TENANT (BUSINESS TENANCIES)
      Paragraph 121 [644].
30   As to air space, subsoil, cellars and footings see vol 22(1) (2003 Reissue) LANDLORD AND TENANT
      (BUSINESS TENANCIES) Paragraph 119 [640]. Strictly speaking, this exclusion means that the tenant
      may not go onto the roof to inspect or repair it unless he is held to have an easement of necessity to do
      so. As to easements of necessity generally see 13 Halsbury's Laws (4th Edn Reissue) EASEMENTS AND
      PROFITS À PRENDRE. If the landlord requires the upper limit of the demised premises to be defined,
      the tenant, in the case of a full repairing lease, should require a right to enter the landlord's air space
      above the demised premises to inspect or repair the upper limit of the premises. For a form that may
      be modified for this purpose see vol 22(3) (1997 Reissue) LANDLORD AND TENANT (BUSINESS
      TENANCIES) Form 77 [6451].

                                                                                              [2116]

1.29   References to clauses and schedules

Any reference in this document to a clause, paragraph or schedule without further designation is to be construed as a reference to the clause, paragraph or schedule of this document so numbered.

1.30   References to rights of access

References to any right of the Landlord to have access to the Premises are to be construed as extending to any head landlord and any mortgagee of the Premises [— where the headlease or mortgage grants such rights of access to the head landlord or mortgagee —] and to all persons authorised in writing by the Landlord and any head landlord or mortgagee, including agents, professional advisers, contractors, workmen and others.

1.31   References to statutes

Unless expressly stated to the contrary, any reference to a specific statute includes any statutory extension or modification, amendment or re-enactment of that statute and any regulations or orders made under it, and any general reference to a statute includes any regulations or orders made under that statute[31].

31   Unfortunately the Interpretation Act 1978 ss 17, 23(3) (41 Halsbury's Statutes (4th Edn) STATUTES) does not quite go far enough to enable this clause to be dispensed with altogether, particularly where a statute is modified.

[2117]

1.32   'The Rent'[32]

[Until the First Review Date 'the Rent' means, the Initial Rent. Thereafter 'the Rent' means the sum ascertained in accordance with schedule 2 THE RENT AND RENT REVIEW. 'The Rent' does not include the Insurance Rent[33], but the term 'the Lease Rents' means both the Rent and the Insurance Rent. *(or as required by the rent and review provisions used)*]

32   This clause assumes that the rent is reviewable. If the rent is not reviewable clause 1.8 [2109] 'THE INITIAL RENT' should be omitted and this clause amended as appropriate. In the case of a hotel it may be appropriate to gear an element of the rent to turnover. For an example of a provision linking rent to turnover see vol 22(3) (1997 Reissue) LANDLORD AND TENANT (BUSINESS TENANCIES). It may also be appropriate to include an assumption as to the existence of any necessary licences. For an example of a provision of this nature in relation to a public house see vol 24(2) (2002 Reissue) Form 56.
33   Because of this exclusion the insurance rent would not be suspended under clause 5.5 [2194] SUSPENSION OF THE RENT.

1.33   'The Rent Commencement Date'

'The Rent Commencement Date' means *(insert the date on which payment of rent is to start)*[34].

34   This provision may be used to provide for a rent-free period, or for the situation where the tenant had possession before the execution of the lease on the basis that rent should be paid from the date of possession. If either the date of execution of the lease or the date of commencement of the term is to be the date for commencement of rent, that date should be inserted here.

[2118]

[1.34 'The Review Dates'[35]

'The First Review Date' means *(date)*. 'The Review Dates' means the First Review Date and every *(insert ordinal, eg 3rd)* anniversary of that date during the [Contractual] Term [*(if appropriate for the review provisions used)* — and any other date from time to time specified under *(insert the relevant provision see eg vol 22(3) (1997 Reissue)* LANDLORD AND TENANT (BUSINESS TENANCIES) *Form 180 paragraph {2}-4 [6728]* EFFECT OF COUNTER-INFLATION PROVISIONS)]. References to 'a review date' are references to any one of the Review Dates.] *(omit if not required by the review provisions to be used, or if the rent is not reviewable)*

35   As to rent review dates and intervals see vol 22(1) (2003 Reissue) LANDLORD AND TENANT (BUSINESS TENANCIES) Paragraph 302 [1333] et seq. Where there might be a statutory continuation of the lease the landlord may wish to ensure that there is a review date shortly before the end of the contractual term to obviate the need to apply for an interim rent. The tenant may wish to insist on the word 'contractual' remaining so that the rent review provisions do not apply during any period of lawful holding over or extension or continuance of the contractual term. In circumstances where there is no prospect of statutory continuation the word 'contractual' should be omitted in any event: see note 6 to clause 1.2 [2108] 'THE [CONTRACTUAL] TERM'.

1.35   'The Surveyor'[36]

'The Surveyor' means *(name)* or any person or firm appointed by the Landlord in his place. The Surveyor may be an employee of the Landlord or a company that is a member of the same group as the Landlord within the meaning of the 1954 Act Section 42. The expression 'the Surveyor' includes the person or firm appointed by the Landlord to collect the Lease Rents[37].

36   For a provision that the landlord's surveyor must be a member of a relevant professional body, see vol 22(3) (1997 Reissue) LANDLORD AND TENANT (BUSINESS TENANCIES) Form 152 [6648].
37   As to the definition of 'the Lease Rents' see clause 1.32 [2118] 'THE RENT'.

[2119]

[1.36 'The Term'

'The Term' means the Contractual Term and any period of holding–over or extension or continuance of the Contractual Term by statute or common law[38].] *(omit if the lease is to be contracted out of the Landlord and Tenant Act 1954)*[39]

38   The demise in this lease is for 'the Contractual Term', which is defined as a fixed term of years. The expression 'the Term' is used in covenants so that they continue to apply during any period of holding over or continuance or extension of the contractual term. As to the liability of a guarantor during a period of statutory continuation see vol 22(1) (2003 Reissue) LANDLORD AND TENANT (BUSINESS TENANCIES) Paragraph 73 [282].
39   Some difficulties arise if the structure referred to in note 38 above is used in a draft lease where security of tenure is to be excluded under the Landlord and Tenant Act 1954 s 38A(1) as inserted by SI 2003/3096. The demise is for the contractual term and the inclusion of the definition of 'the Term' does not prevent the lease being 'for a term of years certain' as required by the Landlord and Tenant Act 1954 s 38A(1). However, reference to continuance of the contractual term by statute is inappropriate where the operation of the security of tenure provisions in the Landlord and Tenant Act 1954 ss 24–28 is to be excluded. If a lease is contracted out of the Landlord and Tenant Act 1954 there can be no statutory extension, and if the tenant remains in occupation at the end of the contractual term he is holding over unlawfully unless there is an express agreement to extend the contractual term operating as a surrender and re-grant so that the original lease — and the agreement under the Landlord and Tenant Act 1954 s 38A(1) — has no further effect. It is suggested that in these circumstances the drafting should be simplified to include a single term (defined simply as 'the Term') by reference to the period of the contractual term. This can be achieved by amending clause 1.2 [2108] 'THE [CONTRACTUAL] TERM' as suggested and substituting it for this clause.

1.37   Terms from the 1995 Act

Where the expressions 'landlord covenants', 'tenant covenants', or 'authorised guarantee agreement' are used in this Lease they are to have the same meaning as is given by the 1995 Act Section 28(1).

1.38   'VAT'[40]

'VAT' means value added tax or any other tax of a similar nature and unless otherwise expressly stated all references to rents or other sums payable by the Tenant are exclusive of VAT.

40   As to VAT generally see the Information Binder: Property [1]: VAT and Property.

[2120]–[2140]

2   DEMISE

The Landlord lets[41] the Premises to the Tenant [with [full *(or)* limited] title guarantee], excepting and reserving to the Landlord the rights specified in schedule 1 THE RIGHTS RESERVED, to hold the Premises to the Tenant for the [Contractual][42] Term, subject to [all rights, easements, privileges, restrictions, covenants and stipulations of whatever nature affecting the Premises including any matters contained or referred to in schedule 4 THE SUBJECTIONS *(or as required)* the rights, easements, privileges, restrictions, covenants and stipulations affecting the Premises contained or referred to in schedule 4 THE SUBJECTIONS][43], yielding and paying[44] to the Landlord —

2.1   the Rent, without any deduction or set-off[45], by equal quarterly payments in advance[46] on the usual quarter days[47] in every year and proportionately for any period of less than a year, the first such payment, being a proportionate sum in respect of the period from and including the Rent Commencement Date to and including the day before the quarter day next after the Rent Commencement Date, to be paid on the date of this document[48], and

2.2   by way of further rent, the Insurance Rent[49], payable on demand in accordance with clause 5.4 PAYMENT OF THE INSURANCE RENT.

[2141]

41   Traditionally, the operative word in a lease executed as a deed was 'demises' but any words sufficient to show the parties' intention may be used.
42   See note 39 to clause 1.36 [2120] 'THE TERM'.
43   The tenant should argue for the second version, making the schedule comprehensive rather than illustrative.
44   The words 'yielding and paying' imply a covenant to pay rent: see *Vyvyan v Arthur* (1823) 1 B & C 410. An express covenant is now invariably included, because further procedural matters are contained in it.
45   As to deductions and set off see vol 22(1) (2003 Reissue) LANDLORD AND TENANT (BUSINESS TENANCIES) Paragraph 147 [753].
46   In the absence of an express provision, rent is payable in arrears.
47   The usual quarter days are 25 March, 24 June, 29 September and 25 December. A reference to 'the usual quarter days' is all that is necessary when rent is to be paid on these days.
48   If the first payment is not a complete instalment, the lease must provide for the date on which it is to be paid, the amount, and the period it is to cover.
49   As to the advantages of reserving the insurance rent as rent see vol 22(1) (2003 Reissue) LANDLORD AND TENANT (BUSINESS TENANCIES) Paragraph 151 [761].

[2142]

3   THE TENANT'S COVENANTS

The Tenant covenants with the Landlord to observe and perform the requirements of this clause 3.

3.1   Rent

3.1.1   *Payment of the Lease Rents*

The Tenant must pay the Lease Rents[50] on the days and in the manner set out in this Lease, and must not exercise or seek to exercise any right or claim to withhold rent, or any right or claim to legal or equitable set-off[51] [except that referred to in *(give details of any provisions granting an express right of set-off)*][52].

50   As to the definition of 'the Lease Rents' see clause 1.32 [2118] 'THE RENT'.
51   See, eg, *British Anzani (Felixstowe) Ltd v International Marine Management (UK) Ltd* [1980] QB 137, [1979] 2 All ER 1063; *Lee-Parker v Izzet* [1971] 3 All ER 1099, [1971] 1 WLR 1688. As to deductions and set-off see vol 22(1) (2003 Reissue) LANDLORD AND TENANT (BUSINESS TENANCIES) Paragraphs 147 [753], 148 [755].
52   If any express right of set-off is granted to the tenant, reference to the provision concerned should be included here to avoid inconsistency.

3.1.2   *Payment by banker's order*[53]

If so required in writing by the Landlord, the Tenant must pay the Lease Rents[54] by banker's order or credit transfer to any bank and account [in the United Kingdom] that the Landlord nominates from time to time.

53   This is a clause with dangers for both parties. If the existence of a breach of covenant is known to the landlord he must instruct his bank to refuse to accept the rent, otherwise his right of forfeiture is lost. As to implied waiver of the right of forfeiture see vol 22(1) (2003 Reissue) LANDLORD AND TENANT (BUSINESS TENANCIES) Paragraph 284 [1173]. The tenant may feel that he requires more control over the payment of rent. In any event, the financial systems operated by many companies prevent payments being made in this way.
54   As to the definition of 'the Lease Rents' see clause 1.32 [2118] 'THE RENT'.

[2143]

3.2   Outgoings and VAT

The Tenant must pay, and must indemnify the Landlord against —

3.2.1   all rates, taxes[55], assessments, duties, charges, impositions and outgoings that are now or may at any time during the Term be charged, assessed or imposed upon the Premises or upon the owner or occupier of them[, excluding any payable by the Landlord occasioned by receipt of the Lease Rents[56] or by any disposition of or dealing with this Lease or ownership of any interest reversionary to the interest created by it][57] [— provided that if the Landlord suffers any loss of rating relief that may be applicable to empty premises after the end of the Term because the relief has been allowed to the Tenant in respect of any period before the end of the Term then the Tenant must make good such loss to the Landlord],

3.2.2   all VAT that may from time to time be charged on the Lease Rents or other sums payable by the Tenant under this Lease[58], and

3.2.3   all VAT incurred in relation to any costs that the Tenant is obliged to pay or in respect of which he is required to indemnify the Landlord under the terms of this Lease, save where such VAT is recoverable or available for set-off by the Landlord as input tax[59].

55   As to covenants to pay rates and taxes see vol 22(1) (2003 Reissue) LANDLORD AND TENANT (BUSINESS TENANCIES) Paragraph 153 [765].
56   As to the definition of 'the Lease Rents' see clause 1.32 [2118] 'THE RENT'.
57   The tenant should add the words in square brackets to make it clear that he is not paying the landlord's taxes.
58   As to VAT on rent, service charges and insurance premiums see the Information Binder: Property [1]: VAT and Property.
59   As to payment of VAT on legal costs paid by a person other than the solicitor's own client see the Information Binder: Property [1]: VAT and Property.

[2144]

[3.3   Cost of services consumed[60]

The Tenant must pay to the suppliers, and indemnify the Landlord against, all charges for electricity, water, gas, telecommunications and other services consumed or used at or in relation to the Premises, including meter rents and standing charges, and must comply with the lawful requirements and regulations of their respective suppliers.] *(omit if the premises have independent supplies of all services)*

60   Where the premises comprise a separate building, a separate supply is usually provided and the tenant makes his own arrangements with the suppliers. In that case this clause is unnecessary.

3.4   Repair, cleaning and decoration

3.4.1   *Repair of the Premises*[61]

The Tenant must repair the Premises and keep them in good condition and repair, except for damage caused by one or more of the Insured Risks save to the extent that the insurance money is irrecoverable due to any act or default of the Tenant or anyone at the Premises expressly or by implication[62] with his authority [and under his control][63].

61   As to repair see vol 22(1) (2003 Reissue) LANDLORD AND TENANT (BUSINESS TENANCIES) Paragraph 196 [931] et seq. For a covenant to repair, rebuild and renew see vol 22(3) (1997 Reissue) LANDLORD AND TENANT (BUSINESS TENANCIES) Form 85 [6460]. For provisos excluding, eg, work that is prevented etc see vol 22(3) (1997 Reissue) LANDLORD AND TENANT (BUSINESS TENANCIES) Forms 87 [6462], 88 [6463].
       If a landlord is unable to obtain full insurance cover without excess, it should be made clear whether the tenant is to be liable to pay the excess where damage is caused by an insured risk. For a covenant limiting the tenant's repairing obligations by reference to uninsurable as well as insured risks see vol 22(3) (1997 Reissue) LANDLORD AND TENANT (BUSINESS TENANCIES) Form 90 [6465]. It should be noted that it is now recommended 'best practice' that if the premises are so damaged by an uninsured risk as to prevent occupation, the tenant should be allowed to terminate the lease unless the landlord agrees to reinstate at his own cost: see vol 22(1) (2003 Reissue) LANDLORD AND TENANT (BUSINESS TENANCIES) Paragraph 85 [402]. If adopted, this recommendation involves damage preventing occupation caused by uninsured or uninsurable risks being excluded from the ambit of the tenant's repairing covenant.
62   The expression 'by implication' is intended to include a caller on the premises, such as a tradesman, where there has been no express invitation but the person cannot be classed as a trespasser.
63   The tenant should add the words in square brackets.

[2145]

3.4.2   *Replacement of landlord's fixtures*

The Tenant must replace from time to time any landlord's fixtures and fittings in the Premises that are beyond repair at any time during or at the end of the Term.

3.4.3   *Cleaning and tidying*

The Tenant must keep the Premises clean and tidy and clear of all rubbish.

3.4.4   *The Open Land*

3.4.4.1   Care of the Open Land

The Tenant must keep any part of the Premises that is not built on ('the Open Land') adequately surfaced, in good condition and free from weeds [and must keep all landscaped areas properly cultivated].

3.4.4.2   Storage on the Open Land

The Tenant must not store anything on the Open Land [or bring anything onto it] [that is or might become untidy, unclean, unsightly or in any way detrimental to the Premises or the area generally].

3.4.4.3   Rubbish on the Open Land

The Tenant must not deposit any waste, rubbish or refuse on the Open Land[, or place any receptacle for them, on it].

3.4.4.4   Vehicles on the Open Land

The Tenant must not keep or store any caravan or movable dwelling on the Open Land. *(adapt clause 3.4.4 as required in the circumstances)*

3.4.5   *Care of abutting land*

The Tenant must not cause any land, roads or pavements abutting the Premises to be untidy or dirty and in particular, but without prejudice to the generality of the above, must not deposit refuse or other materials on them.

[2146]

3.4.6   *Decoration*

[The Tenant must redecorate the outside and inside of the Premises, as often as is necessary in the [reasonable] opinion of the Surveyor in order to maintain a high standard of decorative finish and attractiveness and to preserve the Premises and in the last year of the Term, *(or as required)* The Tenant must redecorate the outside of the Premises in each of the External Decorating Years and the last year of the Term and must redecorate the inside of the Premises in each of the Interior Decorating Years and the last year of the Term, in all instances][64] in a good and workmanlike manner, with appropriate materials of good quality, [to the [reasonable] satisfaction of the Surveyor,] any change in the tints, colours and patterns of the decoration to be approved by the Landlord[65][, whose approval may not be unreasonably withheld [or delayed]] [, provided that the covenants relating to the last year of the Term are not to apply where the Tenant has performed the obligation in question less than *(state period, eg 18 months)* before the end of the Term].

---

64   The draftsman should discuss with the landlord and his property advisers whether he wishes to have the flexibility of the first option or the certainty of the second.

65   The tenant may amend to provide for the landlord's approval to tints etc to apply only in the last year of the term.

3.4.7   *Shared facilities*

Where the use of any of the Conduits or any boundary structures or other things is common to the Premises and other property, the Tenant must be responsible for, and indemnify the Landlord against, all sums due from the owner, tenant or occupier of the Premises in relation to those Conduits, boundary structures or other things, and must undertake all work in relation to them that is his responsibility.

[2147]

3.5   Waste and alterations

3.5.1   *Waste, additions and alterations*[66]

The Tenant must not commit any waste, make any addition to the Premises, unite the Premises with any adjoining premises, or make any alteration to the Premises except as permitted by the provisions of this clause 3.5.

66   As to alterations see vol 22(1) (2003 Reissue) LANDLORD AND TENANT (BUSINESS TENANCIES) Paragraph 186 [911] et seq.

3.5.2   *Pre-conditions for alterations*

The Tenant must not make any [internal non-structural] alterations to the Premises unless he first —

3.5.2.1   obtains and complies with the necessary consents of the competent authorities and pays their charges for them,

3.5.2.2   makes an application to the Landlord for consent, supported by drawings and where appropriate a specification in duplicate [prepared by an architect[, or a member of some other appropriate profession,] who must supervise the work throughout to completion],

3.5.2.3   pays the fees of the Landlord, any head landlord, any mortgagee and their respective professional advisers,

3.5.2.4   enters into any covenants the Landlord requires as to the execution and reinstatement of the alterations, and

3.5.2.5   obtains the consent of the Landlord, whose consent may not be unreasonably withheld [or delayed].

[In the case of any works of a substantial nature, the Landlord may require the Tenant to provide, before starting the works, adequate security in the form of a deposit of money or the provision of a bond, as assurance to the Landlord that any works he permits from time to time will be fully completed].

[2148]

3.5.3   *Removal of alterations*[67]

At the end of the Term, if so requested by the Landlord, the Tenant must remove any additional buildings, additions, alterations or improvements made to the Premises and must make good any part of the Premises that is damaged by the removal.

67   This clause has probably come to be inserted because landlords hope that it will defeat the effect of the compensation provisions of the Landlord and Tenant Act 1927 Pt I (ss 1–17) (23 Halsbury's Statutes (4th Edn) LANDLORD AND TENANT) — as to which see vol 22(1) (2003 Reissue) LANDLORD AND TENANT (BUSINESS TENANCIES) Paragraph 192 [923] et seq ˉ because, if the improvement has been removed, it will not be an improvement to the holding at the time of quitting the premises. In fact, the

clause might not achieve this effect, because the Landlord and Tenant Act 1927 s 9 as amended by the Landlord and Tenant Act 1954 s 49 prohibits contracting out. Also, the clause may be void under the Landlord and Tenant Act 1927 s 19(2), so far as that applies to improvements, on the grounds that it purports to fetter the court in deciding what is reasonable. The tenant should not, however, rely on the application of these statutory provisions and should seek to strike out the clause.

3.5.4   *Connection to the Conduits*

The Tenant must not make any connection with the Conduits except in accordance with plans and specifications approved by the Landlord[, whose approval may not be unreasonably withheld [or delayed]], and subject to consent to make the connection having previously been obtained from the competent authority, undertaker or supplier.

3.6   Aerials, signs and advertisements

3.6.1   *Masts and wires*

The Tenant must not erect any pole or mast [or install any cable or wire] on the Premises, whether in connection with telecommunications or otherwise.

3.6.2   *Advertisements*[68]

The Tenant must not, without the consent of the Landlord, fix to or exhibit on the outside of the Premises, or fix to or exhibit through any window of the Premises, or display anywhere on the Premises, any placard, sign, notice, fascia board or advertisement.

68   See the Town and Country Planning (Control of Advertisements) Regulations 1992, SI 1992/666 as amended. In the absence of a covenant such as this and subject to those Regulations, the tenant may exhibit advertisements etc on the premises, whether or not they are connected with his business: see *Clapman v Edwards* [1938] 2 All ER 507.

[2149]

3.7   Statutory obligations

3.7.1   *General provision*[69]

The Tenant must comply in all respects with the requirements of any statutes, and any other obligations so applicable imposed by law or by any byelaws, applicable to the Premises or the trade or business for the time being carried on there.

69   As to the covenant to comply with statutes see vol 22(1) (2003 Reissue) LANDLORD AND TENANT (BUSINESS TENANCIES) Paragraph 182 [905]. For a provision requiring the landlord to pay compensation for works above a certain value see vol 22(3) (1997 Reissue) LANDLORD AND TENANT (BUSINESS TENANCIES) Form 169 [6693].

3.7.2   *Particular obligations*

3.7.2.1   **Works required by statute, department or authority**

Without prejudice to the generality of clause 3.7.1, the Tenant must execute all works and provide and maintain all arrangements on or in respect of the Premises or the use to which they are being put that are required in order to comply with the requirements of any statute already or in the future to be passed, or the requirements of any government department, local authority or other public or competent authority or court of competent jurisdiction, regardless of whether the requirements are imposed on the owner, the occupier, or any other person.

[2150]

3.7.2.2   Acts causing losses

Without prejudice to the generality of clause 3.7.1, the Tenant must not do in or near the Premises anything by reason of which the Landlord may incur any losses under any statute.

3.7.2.3   Construction (Design and Management) Regulations

Without prejudice to the generality of clause 3.7.1, the Tenant must comply with the provisions of the Construction (Design and Management) Regulations 1994 ('the CDM Regulations'), be the only client, as defined in the provisions of the CDM Regulations, fulfil, in relation to all and any works, all the obligations of the client as set out in or reasonably to be inferred from the CDM Regulations, and make a declaration to that effect[70] to the Health and Safety Executive in accordance with the Approved Code of Practice published from time to time by the Health and Safety Executive in relation to the CDM Regulations. The provisions of clause 5.7.3 FIRE-FIGHTING EQUIPMENT are to have effect in any circumstances to which these obligations apply.

3.7.2.4   Delivery of health and safety files

At the end of the Term, the Tenant must forthwith deliver to the Landlord any and all health and safety files relating to the premises in accordance with the CDM Regulations.

70   If works are being carried out for the tenant, the landlord will not want to accept the liabilities that are placed on a client under the Construction (Design and Management) Regulations 1994, SI 1994/3140 and the Health and Safety Executive Approved Code of Practice. The landlord will need to ensure that the tenant actually makes the declaration required, and that he obtains the notification served on the tenant by the Health and Safety Executive.

[2151]

3.8   Entry to inspect and notice to repair

3.8.1   *Entry and notice*

The Tenant must permit the Landlord[71] [on reasonable notice during normal business hours except in emergency][72] —

3.8.1.1   to enter the Premises to ascertain whether or not the covenants and conditions of this Lease have been observed and performed,

3.8.1.2   to view the state of repair and condition of the Premises, and to open up floors and other parts of the Premises where that is necessary in order to do so, and

3.8.1.3   to give to the Tenant, or notwithstanding clause 8.7 NOTICES leave on the Premises, a notice ('a notice to repair') specifying the works required to remedy any breach of the Tenant's obligations in this Lease as to the repair and condition of the Premises,

provided that any opening-up must be made good by and at the cost of the Landlord if it reveals no breach of the terms of this Lease.

71   The provisions of clause 1.30 [2117] REFERENCES TO RIGHTS OF ACCESS should be noted.
72   The tenant should add the words in square brackets.

3.8.2   *Works to be carried out*

The Tenant must carry out the works specified in a notice to repair immediately, including making good any opening up that revealed a breach of the terms of this Lease.

[3.8.3   *Landlord's power in default*[73]

If within *(state period, eg 1 month)* of the service of a notice to repair the Tenant has not started to execute the work referred to in that notice or is not proceeding diligently with it, or if the Tenant fails to finish the work within *(state period, eg 2 months)*[74][, or if in the [Landlord's *(or as required)* Surveyor's] [reasonable] opinion the Tenant is unlikely to finish the work within that period], the Tenant must permit the Landlord to enter the Premises to execute the outstanding work, and must within *(state period, eg 14 days)* of a written demand pay to the Landlord the cost of so doing and all expenses incurred by the Landlord, including legal costs and surveyor's fees.]

73   The advantages of this clause for the landlord must be weighed against the potential liability that it creates under the Defective Premises Act 1972 s 4(4) (31 Halsbury's Statutes (4th Edn) NEGLIGENCE): see *McAuley v Bristol City Council* [1992] QB 134, [1992] 1 All ER 749, CA.
       It has been held that a claim by the landlord for recovery of costs under such a clause is a claim for recovery of a debt, and can therefore be enforced without requiring leave of the court under the Leasehold Property (Repairs) Act 1938(23 Halsbury's Statutes (4th Edn) LANDLORD AND TENANT): see *Jervis v Harris* [1996] Ch 195, [1996] 1 All ER 303, CA.
       However, even where a landlord has been granted a right of this nature the court does not compel the tenant to allow the landlord the right to enter and carry out repairs where these would be of no benefit and where no loss is being caused to the landlord: see *Hammersmith London Borough Council v Creska (No 2)* [2000] L & TR 288.
74   The tenant would prefer to be given 'a reasonable period' to do the work required to remedy the breaches because it may take longer than the specified number of months.

[2152]–[2160]

3.9   Alienation[75]

3.9.1   *Alienation prohibited*

The Tenant must not hold the Premises on trust for another. The Tenant must not part with possession of the Premises or any part of the Premises or permit another to occupy them or any part of them except pursuant to a transaction permitted by and effected in accordance with the provisions of this Lease.

75   As to alienation see vol 22(1) (2003 Reissue) LANDLORD AND TENANT (BUSINESS TENANCIES) Paragraph 156 [801] et seq. Where the lease is registrable, this prohibition or restriction on dealings will be reflected in an entry on the register excepting from the effects of registration all estates, rights, interests, powers and remedies arising on or by reason of any dealing made in breach of the prohibition or restriction: see the Land Registration Rules 2003, SI 2003/1417 r 6(2).
       The identity and character of the tenant may be of particular importance to the landlord in a lease such as this. For example, if the tenant is a famous chef, an assignee may have the financial resources and the experience to run the business but may lack the cachet and, therefore, be unacceptable to the landlord. In these circumstances, the draftsman may wish to consider including a provision that seeks to force the tenant to offer the lease back to the landlord before alienation. For examples of provisions of this nature see vol 22(3) (1997 Reissue) LANDLORD AND TENANT (BUSINESS TENANCIES). If the identity and character of the tenant are crucial, the inclusion of provisions should also be considered to prevent changes in those who control a tenant company without consent (see vol 24(2) (2002 Reissue) Form 56) and to provide for forfeiture if the ownership profile of the company changes (see vol 22(3) (1997 Reissue) LANDLORD AND TENANT (BUSINESS TENANCIES)).

[2161]

3.9.2 *Assignment and charging of part, and subletting*[76]

(version 1)

[The Tenant must not assign, sublet or charge part only of the Premises.] *(where assignment, subletting or charging of the whole is allowed)*

(version 2)

[The Tenant must not assign or charge part only of the Premises and must not sublet the whole or any part of the Premises.] *(where assignment or charging of the whole is permitted, but subletting is not allowed at all)*

76   Although subletting may not often be appropriate in relation to a hotel, whether it should be permitted is, ultimately, a commercial matter. In general terms, some landlords consider that the fact that they cannot unreasonably refuse consent to an assignment gives the tenant all the protection he requires and are not prepared to permit subletting in any circumstances. An advantage to the tenant of the ability to sublet is that he has an element of control over a subtenant but not over an assignee, for whom he may retain liability under an authorised guarantee agreement. It should also be remembered that, with stringent assignment tests or in a bad market, subletting may be the only option open to the tenant.

3.9.3 *Assignment of the whole*

Subject to clauses 3.9.4 CIRCUMSTANCES and 3.9.5 CONDITIONS, the Tenant must not assign the whole of the Premises without the consent of the Landlord, whose consent may not be unreasonably withheld [or delayed][77].

77   This residual discretion is the old test of reasonableness under the Landlord and Tenant Act 1927 s 19(1). Thus the tenant and the proposed assignee may satisfy the circumstances and conditions specified for the purposes of the Landlord and Tenant Act 1927 s 19(1A) as inserted by the Landlord and Tenant (Covenants) Act 1995 s 22 (as to which see clause 3.9.4 [2163] CIRCUMSTANCES and clause 3.9.5 [2166] CONDITIONS), but the landlord may still refuse consent on reasonable grounds: see vol 22(1) (2003 Reissue) LANDLORD AND TENANT (BUSINESS TENANCIES) Paragraph 159 [812] et seq.

[2162]

3.9.4 *Circumstances*

If any of the following circumstances[78] — which are specified for the purposes of the Landlord and Tenant Act 1927 Section 19(1A)[79] — applies either at the date when application for consent to assign is made to the Landlord, or after that date but before the Landlord's consent is given, the Landlord may withhold his consent and if, after the Landlord's consent has been given but before the assignment has taken place, any such circumstances apply, the Landlord may revoke his consent[80], whether his consent is expressly subject to a condition as referred to in clause 3.9.5.4 CONDITIONS or not. The circumstances are —

3.9.4.1   that any sum due from the Tenant under this Lease remains unpaid[81],

3.9.4.2   that in the Landlord's reasonable[82] opinion the assignee is not a person who is likely to be able to comply with the tenant covenants of this Lease and to continue to be able to comply with them following the assignment,

[3.9.4.3   that without prejudice to clause 3.9.4.2, in the case of an assignment to a company in the same group as the Tenant[83] within the meaning of the 1954 Act Section 42 in the Landlord's reasonable opinion the assignee is a person who is, or may become, less likely to be able to comply with the tenant covenants of this Lease than the Tenant requesting consent to assign, which likelihood is adjudged by reference in particular to the financial strength of that Tenant aggregated with that of any guarantor of the obligations of that

Tenant and the value of any other security for the performance of the tenant covenants of this Lease when assessed at the date of grant or — where that Tenant is not *(name of original tenant)* — the date of the assignment of this Lease to that Tenant[84],] or

3.9.4.4   that the assignee or any guarantor for the assignee, other than any guarantor under an authorised guarantee agreement, is a corporation registered — or otherwise resident — in a jurisdiction in which the order of a court obtained in England and Wales will not necessarily be enforced against the assignee or guarantor without any consideration of the merits of the case.

(for examples of circumstances for use in unusual cases, see vol 22(3) (1997 Reissue) LANDLORD AND TENANT (BUSINESS TENANCIES) *Form 117 [6501])*

[2163]

78   The Landlord and Tenant Act 1927 s 19(1A) as inserted by the Landlord and Tenant (Covenants) Act 1995 s 22 enables the landlord and tenant to a post-1995 lease to agree in advance the terms upon which an assignment may be permitted. It distinguishes between on the one hand circumstances, the existence of which entitles the landlord to refuse consent to assignment, and on the other hand conditions that may be imposed on the grant of his consent. This clause and clause 3.9.5 [2166] CONDITIONS are drafted on the assumption that this is a valid approach and seek to draw a clear distinction between circumstances and conditions.

It should be noted that provisions that are overly restrictive may have an adverse impact at any rent review. It should also be noted that it is recommended 'best practice' that unless the particular circumstances of the letting justify greater control, the only restriction on assignment of the whole should be obtaining the landlord's consent, which is not to be unreasonably withheld: see vol 22(1) (2003 Reissue) LANDLORD AND TENANT (BUSINESS TENANCIES) Paragraph 85 [401] and 'A code of practice for commercial leases in England and Wales (2nd edition)' which can be found in vol 22(1) (2003 Reissue) LANDLORD AND TENANT (BUSINESS TENANCIES) as Form 1 [4501].

Each letting must be looked at in the light of its own particular facts and circumstances but it is considered that the provisions of this clause do, in the ordinary course, strike a reasonable balance between the landlord's desire for control and the tenant's ability to dispose of his interest without undue restriction. For a less restrictive approach see vol 22(1) (2003 Reissue) LANDLORD AND TENANT (BUSINESS TENANCIES) Form 7 clause 5.2 [5538]. For additional circumstances that may be relevant in relation to licensed premises see vol 24(2) (2002 Reissue) Form 56.

79   The Landlord and Tenant Act 1927 s 19(1A) as inserted by the Landlord and Tenant (Covenants) Act 1995 s 22 seems to require the alienation clause to state that the circumstances it mentions are specified for the purposes of that subsection.

[2164]

80   The landlord may require that certain circumstances are absent not only before consent has been given to the assignment, but also up to the date on which the assignment takes place — when the die is cast and the lease covenants bind the assignee. For example, the landlord may require the rent to be paid up to date not only before the application for consent is made, but also at the date when consent is given and the possibly later date when the lease is actually assigned.

81   The tenant may want to limit this to the rent, as it may be thought that a dispute is more likely to arise over the insurance rent or other payments. If the tenant has retained any right of set-off, it should also be referred to here.

82   Circumstances and conditions must either be factual or, if they contain an element of discretion, require that discretion to be exercised reasonably (see the Landlord and Tenant Act 1927 s 19(1C)(a) as inserted by the Landlord and Tenant (Covenants) Act 1995 s 22), or must give the tenant a right of appeal to an expert (see the Landlord and Tenant Act 1927 s 19(1C)(b) as inserted by the Landlord and Tenant (Covenants) Act 1995 s 22). If the discretion is to be exercised reasonably, as suggested by this provision, the tenant can take any dispute about its exercise to the court. The court will consider whether *this* landlord has acted within the range of reasonable decisions, not whether a reasonable landlord would have reached the same decision or whether the test is itself reasonable. For a clause where an expert is used see vol 22(3) (1997 Reissue) LANDLORD AND TENANT (BUSINESS TENANCIES) Form 117 [6501].

83   There have been suggestions that intra-group assignments should be banned completely. However, this is considered to be too draconian and would prevent legitimate corporate restructuring needed for reasons other than avoidance of liability under the Landlord and Tenant (Covenants) Act 1995. The landlord's concern is that a strong tenant may assign to a weak group company; the assignment is

acceptable because the assignor gives an authorised guarantee agreement for the assignee. The second group company may then itself assign outside the group; the landlord will lose the authorised guarantee agreement of the strong first group company and have only the possibly worthless authorised guarantee agreement of the second group company. The possibilities for exploitation of this scenario are obvious and it is therefore felt that this is the one situation in which measuring the financial strength of the assignee in relation to that of the assignor is justified. Equivalence tests are not generally thought to be appropriate, because a strong first covenant may make the lease almost unassignable, adversely affecting the rent at review.

84   Consider whether the time at which the tenant's financial status is measured should be when he acquired the lease, when his status was acceptable to the landlord, or at the date of the application for consent to assign, when it may have deteriorated sharply. On the other hand, the outgoing tenant may be a better covenant now than when he acquired the lease: the wily landlord may wish to leave himself free to pick whichever of the two dates gives the better picture.

[2165]

3.9.5   *Conditions*

The Landlord may impose any or all of the following conditions[85] — which are specified for the purposes of the Landlord and Tenant Act 1927 Section 19(1A)[86] — on giving any consent for an assignment by the Tenant, and any such consent is to be treated as being subject to each of the following conditions —

3.9.5.1   a condition that on or before any assignment and before giving occupation to the assignee, the Tenant requesting consent to assign, together with any former tenant who by virtue of the 1995 Act Section 11 was not released on an earlier assignment of this Lease[87], must enter into an authorised guarantee agreement[88] in favour of the Landlord in the terms set out in schedule 5 THE AUTHORISED GUARANTEE AGREEMENT,

3.9.5.2   a condition that if reasonably so required by the Landlord on an assignment to a limited company, the assignee must ensure that at least *(state number, eg 2)* directors of the company, or some other guarantor or guarantors [reasonably] acceptable to the Landlord, enter into direct covenants with the Landlord in the form of the guarantor's covenants contained in clause 6 GUARANTEE PROVISIONS with 'the Assignee' substituted for 'the Tenant',

3.9.5.3   a condition that upon or before any assignment, the Tenant making the request for consent to assign must give to the Landlord a copy of the health and safety file required to be maintained under the Construction (Design and Management) Regulations 1994 containing full details of all works undertaken to the Premises by that Tenant, and

3.9.5.4   a condition that if, at any time before the assignment, the circumstances specified in clause 3.9.4 CIRCUMSTANCES, or any of them, apply, the Landlord may revoke the consent by written notice to the Tenant.

[2166]

85   The Landlord and Tenant Act 1927 s 19(1A) as inserted by the Landlord and Tenant (Covenants) Act 1995 s 22 enables the landlord and tenant to a post-1995 lease to agree in advance the terms upon which an assignment may be permitted. It distinguishes between on the one hand circumstances, the existence of which entitles the landlord to refuse consent to assignment, and on the other hand conditions that may be imposed on the grant of his consent. This clause and clause 3.9.4 [2163] CIRCUMSTANCES are drafted on the assumption that this a valid approach and seek to draw a clear distinction between circumstances and conditions.

    It should be noted that provisions that are overly restrictive may have an adverse impact at any rent review. It should also be noted that it is recommended 'best practice' that unless the particular circumstances of the letting justify greater control, the only restriction on assignment of the whole should be obtaining the landlord's consent, which is not to be unreasonably withheld: see vol 22(1) (2003 Reissue) LANDLORD AND TENANT (BUSINESS TENANCIES) Paragraph 85 [401] and 'A code of practice for commercial leases in England and Wales (2nd edition)' which can be found in vol 22(1) (2003 Reissue) LANDLORD AND TENANT (BUSINESS TENANCIES) as Form 1 [4501].

Each letting must be looked at in the light of its own particular facts and circumstances but it is considered that the provisions of this clause do, in the ordinary course, strike a reasonable balance between the landlord's desire for control and the tenant's ability to dispose of his interest without undue restriction. For additional conditions that may be relevant in relation to licensed premises see vol 24(2) (2002 Reissue) Form 56.

86   The Landlord and Tenant Act 1927 s 19(1A) as inserted by the Landlord and Tenant (Covenants) Act 1995 s 22 seems to require the alienation clause to state that the conditions it mentions are specified for the purposes of that subsection.

87   See the Landlord and Tenant (Covenants) Act 1995 ss 11(2), 16(6).

88   As to authorised guarantee agreements see vol 22(1) (2003 Reissue) LANDLORD AND TENANT (BUSINESS TENANCIES) Paragraph 54 [247]. It should be noted that 'A code of practice for commercial leases in England and Wales (2nd edition)' urges landlords to consider requiring authorised guarantee agreements only where the assignee is of lower financial standing than the assignor at the date of the assignment.

[2167]

3.9.6   Charging of the whole

The Tenant must not charge the whole of the Premises without the consent of the Landlord, whose consent may not be unreasonably withheld [or delayed][89].

89   As to unreasonable withholding of consent under the Landlord and Tenant Act 1927 see vol 22(1) (2003 Reissue) LANDLORD AND TENANT (BUSINESS TENANCIES) Paragraph 158.2 [806] and as to unreasonable delay under the Landlord and Tenant Act 1988 (23 Halsbury's Statutes (4th Edn) LANDLORD AND TENANT) see vol 22(1) (2003 Reissue) LANDLORD AND TENANT (BUSINESS TENANCIES) Paragraph 158.3 [808].

[3.9.7   Subletting

The Tenant must not sublet[90] the whole of the Premises without the consent of the Landlord, whose consent may not be unreasonably withheld [or delayed]][91]. *(omit if subletting is prohibited)*

90   See note 76 to clause 3.9.2 [2162] ASSIGNMENT, SUBLETTING AND CHARGING OF PART.

91   As to unreasonable withholding of consent under the Landlord and Tenant Act 1927 see vol 22(1) (2003 Reissue) LANDLORD AND TENANT (BUSINESS TENANCIES) Paragraph 158.2 [806] and as to unreasonable delay under the Landlord and Tenant Act 1988 see vol 22(1) (2003 Reissue) LANDLORD AND TENANT (BUSINESS TENANCIES) Paragraph 158.3 [808].

[2168]

[3.9.8   Terms of a permitted sublease[92]

Every permitted sublease must be granted, without a fine or premium, at a rent not less than whichever is the greater of the then open market rent payable in respect of the Premises [— to be approved by the Landlord before the sublease is granted [and to be determined by the Surveyor, acting as an expert and not as an arbitrator]—] and the Rent[93], to be payable in advance on the days on which the Rent is payable under this Lease. Every permitted sublease must contain provisions approved by the Landlord —

3.9.8.1   for the upwards only review of the rent reserved by it, on the basis set out in schedule 2 THE RENT AND RENT REVIEW and on the Review Dates[94],

3.9.8.2   prohibiting the subtenant from doing or allowing anything in relation to the Premises inconsistent with or in breach of the provisions of this Lease,

3.9.8.3   for re-entry by the sublandlord on breach of any covenant by the subtenant,

3.9.8.4   imposing an absolute prohibition against all dealings with the Premises other than assignment[, subletting] [or charging] of the whole,

3.9.8.5   prohibiting assignment[, subletting][95] [or charging] of the whole of the Premises without the consent of the Landlord under this Lease,

3.9.8.6   requiring the assignee on any assignment of the sublease to enter into direct covenants with the Landlord to the same effect as those contained in clause 3.9.9 SUBTENANT'S DIRECT COVENANTS,

3.9.8.7   requiring on each assignment of the sublease that the assignor enters into an authorised guarantee agreement[96] in favour of the Landlord in the terms set out in schedule 5 THE AUTHORISED GUARANTEE AGREEMENT but adapted to suit the circumstances in which the guarantee is given,

3.9.8.8   prohibiting the subtenant from holding on trust for another or permitting another to share or occupy the whole or any part of the Premises,

3.9.8.9   imposing in relation to any permitted assignment[, subletting] [or charge] the same obligations for registration with the Landlord as are contained in this Lease in relation to dispositions by the Tenant,

[3.9.8.10   imposing in relation to any permitted subletting the same obligations as are contained in this clause 3.9.8 and in clause 3.9.9 SUBTENANT'S DIRECT COVENANTS[, clause 3.9.11 ENFORCEMENT OF THE SUBLEASE and clause 3.9.12 SUBLEASE RENT REVIEW],] and

3.9.8.11   excluding the provisions of Sections 24–28 of the 1954 Act from the letting created by the sublease.] *(omit if subletting is prohibited)*

[2169]

92   As to the validity of provisions of this nature see vol 22(1) (2003 Reissue) LANDLORD AND TENANT (BUSINESS TENANCIES) Paragraph 161 [817].

93   It will not be in the landlord's interest for the premises to be sublet at a rent less than that payable under the headlease, because it could allow into the premises a subtenant of doubtful financial status, with whom the landlord may in the future have to deal direct, eg on the grant of a new lease under the Landlord and Tenant Act 1954 Pt II (ss 23–46). Also a low rent could be used as a 'comparable' in arriving at the open market rent on rent reviews or lease renewals. On the other hand following the decision in *Allied Dunbar Assurance plc v Homebase Ltd* [2002] EWCA Civ 666, [2003] 1 P & CR 75, [2002] 2 EGLR 23 a provision of this kind may effectively render the lease inalienable and being a potentially onerous restriction on disposition (as to which see vol 22(1) (2003 Reissue) LANDLORD AND TENANT (BUSINESS TENANCIES) Paragraph 348.2 [1440]) have an adverse impact at rent review from a landlord's perspective.

94   Alternatively the landlord might prefer the sublease rents to be reviewed just before the review dates in the headlease. As to recommended 'best practice' in relation to the basis of rent review in leases of business premises see vol 22(1) (2003 Reissue) LANDLORD AND TENANT (BUSINESS TENANCIES) Paragraph 85 [401] and 'A code of practice for commercial leases in England and Wales (2nd edition)' which can be found in vol 22(1) (2003 Reissue) LANDLORD AND TENANT (BUSINESS TENANCIES) as Form 1 [4501].

95   The landlord may well wish to prohibit any further subletting by requiring an absolute covenant against subletting to be inserted in any sublease.

96   By virtue of the Landlord and Tenant (Covenants) Act 1995 s 16(3)(a), where a head landlord's consent is needed to the assignment of a sublease, the head landlord can require the assignor of the sublease to enter into an authorised guarantee agreement. It should be noted that 'A code of practice for commercial leases in England and Wales (2nd edition)' urges landlords to consider requiring authorised guarantee agreements only where the assignee is of lower financial standing than the assignor at the date of the assignment.

[2170]

[3.9.9   *Subtenant's direct covenants*[97]

Before any permitted subletting, the Tenant must ensure that the subtenant enters into a direct covenant with the Landlord that while he is bound by the tenant covenants of the sublease[98] and while the subtenant is bound by an authorised guarantee agreement the subtenant will observe and perform the tenant covenants contained in this Lease — except the covenant to pay the rent reserved by this Lease — and in that sublease.] *(omit if subletting is prohibited)*

97   See note 92 to clause 3.9.8 [2170] TERMS OF A PERMITTED SUBLEASE.
98   The liability of the subtenant should be expressed to last while he is bound by the tenant covenants of the sublease, rather than while the sublease is vested in him, to take account of the possibility of an excluded assignment being made and the subtenant remaining liable. An excluded assignment means that the subtenant is precluded from tenant release under the Landlord and Tenant (Covenants) Act 1995.

[3.9.10   *Requirement for 1954 Act exclusion*[99]

The Tenant must not grant a sublease or permit a subtenant to occupy the Premises unless an effective agreement has been made to exclude the operation of Sections 24 to 28 of the 1954 Act pursuant to Section 38A of the 1954 Act.] *(omit if subletting is prohibited)*

99   As to contracting out of the security of tenure provisions of the Landlord and Tenant Act 1954 see vol 22(1) (2003 Reissue) LANDLORD AND TENANT (BUSINESS TENANCIES) Paragraph 431 [2035].

[3.9.11   *Enforcement, waiver and variation of subleases*

In relation to any permitted sublease, the Tenant must enforce the performance and observance by every subtenant of the provisions of the sublease, and must not at any time either expressly or by implication waive any breach of the covenants or conditions on the part of any subtenant or assignee of any sublease, or — without the consent of the Landlord, whose consent may not be unreasonably withheld or delayed — vary the terms or accept a surrender of any permitted sublease.] *(omit if subletting is prohibited)*

[2171]

[3.9.12   *Sublease rent review*

In relation to any permitted sublease —

3.9.12.1   the Tenant must ensure that the rent is reviewed in accordance with the terms of the sublease,

3.9.12.2   the Tenant must not agree the reviewed rent with the subtenant without the approval of the Landlord,

3.9.12.3   where the sublease provides such an option, the Tenant must not, without the approval of the Landlord, agree whether the third party determining the revised rent in default of agreement should act as an arbitrator or as an expert,

3.9.12.4   the Tenant must not, without the approval of the Landlord, agree any appointment of a person to act as the third party determining the revised rent,

3.9.12.5   the Tenant must incorporate as part of his representations to that third party representations [reasonably] required[100] by the Landlord, and

3.9.12.6   the Tenant must give notice to the Landlord of the details of the determination of every rent review within *(state period, eg 28 days),*

provided that the Landlord's approvals specified above may not be unreasonably withheld [or delayed].] *(omit if subletting is prohibited)*

---

100   This seems preferable to providing, as is sometimes done, that the head landlord's representations have to be brought to the attention of the expert or arbitrator because it would appear that he can refuse to have regard to them, the head landlord not being a party to the lease with which he is concerned.

3.9.13   *Registration of permitted dealings*

Within *(state period, eg 28 days)* of any assignment, charge, [sublease, or subunderlease,] or any transmission or other devolution relating to the Premises, the Tenant must produce a certified copy[101] of any relevant document for registration with the Landlord's solicitor, and must pay the Landlord's solicitor's [reasonable] charges for registration of at least £...

---

101   There seems to be no reason why the tenant should part with the original. However, under the Land Registration Rules 2003, SI 2003/1417 r 203, it is open to the applicant for registration to ask for the transfer, charge, sublease or subunderlease giving effect to the disposition to be returned for retention by the applicant, provided a certified copy of the instrument is lodged with the application. Accordingly, in such cases, applicants should use this facility if they wish to be able to lodge the lease with the landlord after its return by the registrar. If there is a time limit specified in the lease, then the registrar should be told about this, so that he is aware of the need to return the instrument within the required period.

[3.9.14   *Sharing with a group company*

Notwithstanding clause 3.9.1 ALIENATION PROHIBITED, the Tenant may share the occupation of the whole or any part of the Premises with a company that is a member of the same group as the Tenant within the meaning of the 1954 Act Section 42, for so long as both companies remain members of that group and otherwise than in a manner that transfers or creates a legal estate.] *(omit if sharing with a group company is not permitted)*

[2172]

3.10   **Nuisance and residential restrictions**

3.10.1   *Nuisance*[102]

The Tenant must not do anything on the Premises, or allow anything to remain on them that may be or become or cause a nuisance, or annoyance, disturbance, inconvenience, injury or damage to the Landlord or his tenants or the owners or occupiers of adjacent or neighbouring premises.

---

102   'Nuisance' is a term to be construed according to 'plain and sober and simple notions among the English people': *Walter v Selfe* (1851) 4 De G & Sm 315 at 322 per Knight-Bruce V-C. 'I have no doubt that what is a nuisance or annoyance will continue to be determined by the courts according to robust and commonsense standards': *Hampstead and Suburban Properties Ltd v Diomedous* [1969] 1 Ch 248 at 258, [1968] 3 All ER 545 at 550 per Megarry J. But a tenant can only be said to have permitted a nuisance if the landlord can show that the tenant has failed to take reasonable steps to prevent the nuisance: see *Commercial General Administration Ltd v Thomsett* [1979] 1 EGLR 62, CA.

3.10.2   *Auctions, trades and immoral purposes*

The Tenant must not use the Premises for any auction sale, any dangerous, noxious, noisy or offensive[103] trade, business, manufacture or occupation, or any illegal or immoral act or purpose.

103   As to the meaning of 'offensive' see *Re Koumoudouros and Marathon Realty Co Ltd* (1978) 89 DLR (3d) 551 where it was held that the word did not have a definite legal meaning and should be read in the context of the lease. Surrounding circumstances can affect whether a particular trade is offensive: see *Nussey v Provincial Bill Posting Co and Eddison* [1909] 1 Ch 734, CA; *Dunraven Securities Ltd v Holloway* [1982] 2 EGLR 47, CA.

[2173]

3.11   Costs of applications, notices and recovery of arrears[104]

The Tenant must pay to the Landlord on an indemnity basis all costs, fees, charges, disbursements and expenses — including, without prejudice to the generality of the above, those payable to counsel, solicitors, surveyors and bailiffs — [properly and reasonably] incurred by the Landlord in relation to or incidental to —

3.11.1   every application made by the Tenant for a consent or licence required by the provisions of this Lease, whether it is granted, refused, offered subject to any [lawful] qualification or condition, or the application is withdrawn[, unless the refusal, qualification or condition is unlawful whether because it is unreasonable or otherwise],

3.11.2   the contemplation, preparation and service of a notice under the Law of Property Act 1925 Section 146, or by reason or the contemplation of proceedings under Sections 146 or 147 of that Act, even if forfeiture is avoided otherwise than by relief granted by the court[105],

3.11.3   the recovery or attempted recovery of arrears of rent or other sums due under this Lease, and

3.11.4   any steps taken in [contemplation of or in] [direct] connection with the preparation and service of a schedule of dilapidations during or after the end of the Term[106].

104   As to payment of VAT on legal costs by a person other than the solicitor's own client see the Information Binder: Property [1]: VAT and Property.
105   As to forfeiture see vol 22(1) (2003 Reissue) LANDLORD AND TENANT (BUSINESS TENANCIES) Paragraph 283 [1171] et seq.
106   The landlord should not be tempted to extend this provision to costs etc incurred by him in consequence of serving a notice under the Landlord and Tenant Act 1954 s 25 because that is void: see *Stevenson and Rush (Holdings) Ltd v Langdon* (1978) 38 P & CR 208, CA.

[2174]

3.12   Planning and development

3.12.1   *Compliance with the Planning Acts*

The Tenant must observe and comply with the provisions and requirements of the Planning Acts affecting the Premises and their use, and must indemnify the Landlord, and keep him indemnified, both during the Term and following the end of it, against all losses in respect of any contravention of those Acts.

3.12.2   *Consent for applications*

The Tenant must not make any application for planning permission without the consent of the Landlord[, whose consent may not be unreasonably withheld [or delayed] [in any case where application for and implementation of the planning permission will not create or give rise to any tax liability for the Landlord or where the Tenant indemnifies the Landlord against such liability][107]].

107   These words were devised when development land tax — abolished by the Finance Act 1985 s 93 — applied. The provision may, however, still be relevant should similar taxation be introduced in the future.

3.12.3   *Permissions and notices*

The Tenant must at his expense obtain any planning permissions and serve any notices that may be required to carry out any development on or at the Premises.

3.12.4   *Charges and levies*

Subject only to any statutory direction to the contrary, the Tenant must pay and satisfy any charge or levy that may subsequently be imposed under the Planning Acts in respect of the carrying out or maintenance of any development on or at the Premises.

3.12.5   *Pre-conditions for development*

Notwithstanding any consent that may be granted by the Landlord under this Lease, the Tenant must not carry out any development on or at the Premises until all necessary notices under the Planning Acts have been served and copies produced to the Landlord, all necessary permissions under the Planning Acts have been obtained and produced to the Landlord, and the Landlord has acknowledged that every necessary planning permission is acceptable to him[, such acknowledgement not to be unreasonably withheld]. The Landlord may refuse to acknowledge his acceptance of a planning permission on the grounds that any condition contained in it or anything omitted from it or the period referred to in it would[, in the [reasonable] opinion of the Surveyor,] be, or be likely to be, prejudicial to the Landlord or to his reversionary interest in the Premises whether during or following the end of the Term.

[2175]

3.12.6   *Completion of development*

Where a condition of any planning permission granted for development begun before the end of the Term[108] requires works to be carried out to the Premises by a date after the end of the Term, the Tenant must, unless the Landlord directs otherwise, finish those works before the end of the Term.

108   The provisions of clause 1.17 [2113] INTERPRETATION OF 'THE LAST YEAR OF THE TERM' AND 'THE END OF THE TERM' should be noted.

3.12.7   *Security for compliance with conditions*

In any case where a planning permission is granted subject to conditions, and if the Landlord [reasonably] so requires, the Tenant must provide sufficient security for his compliance with the conditions and must not implement the planning permission until that security has been provided.

[3.12.8   *Appeal against refusal or conditions*[109]

If [reasonably] required by the Landlord to do so, but[, where reasonable,] at his own cost, the Tenant must appeal against any refusal of planning permission or the imposition of any conditions on a planning permission relating to the Premises following an application for planning permission by the Tenant.]

109   The tenant should not accept this clause because it could impose on him the cost of a planning appeal. He should strike it out, leaving planning appeals to be a matter for discussion as and when the situation arises during the term, or at least insist that he should bear the cost only where reasonable.

[2176]

3.13   Plans, documents and information

3.13.1   *Evidence of compliance with this Lease*

If so requested, the Tenant must produce to the Landlord or the Surveyor any plans, documents and other evidence the Landlord [reasonably] requires to satisfy himself that the provisions of this Lease have been complied with.

3.13.2   *Information for renewal or rent review*

If so requested, the Tenant must produce to the Landlord, the Surveyor, or any person acting as the third party determining the Rent in default of agreement between the Landlord and the Tenant under any provisions for rent review contained in this Lease, any information [reasonably] requested in writing in relation to any pending or intended step under the 1954 Act or the implementation of any provisions for rent review.

3.14   Indemnities[110]

The Tenant must keep the Landlord fully indemnified against all losses arising directly or indirectly out of any act, omission or negligence of the Tenant, or any persons at the Premises expressly or impliedly[111] with his authority [and under his control][112], or any breach or non-observance by the Tenant of the covenants, conditions or other provisions of this Lease or any of the matters to which this demise is subject.

110   The tenant should seek to delete all *general* indemnity provisions on the basis that his remedies for breach of covenant and in tort adequately protect the landlord. The tenant should argue that an indemnity unreasonably extends his liability. If this clause is omitted, however, it should be replaced by a covenant to observe and perform the restrictions etc to which the demise is subject, possibly coupled with a *specific* indemnity in respect of any breach.
111   The expression 'impliedly' is intended to include a caller on the premises, such as a tradesman, where there has been no express invitation but the person cannot be classed as a trespasser.
112   The tenant should add the words in square brackets.

[2177]

3.15   Reletting boards and viewing

[Unless [a valid court application under the 1954 Act Section 24 has been made or][113] the Tenant is [otherwise] entitled to remain in occupation or to a new tenancy of the Premises, at any time during *(or as required)* At any time during] the *(state period, eg 6 months)* of the [Contractual][114] Term and at any time thereafter [and whenever the Lease Rents or any part of them are in arrear and unpaid for longer than *(state period, eg 14 days)*] the Tenant must permit the Landlord to enter the Premises and fix and retain anywhere on them a board advertising them for reletting. While such a board is on the Premises the Tenant must permit viewing of the Premises at reasonable times of the day.

113   This phrase and the word 'otherwise' should be omitted if the operation of the security of tenure
       provisions in the Landlord and Tenant Act 1954 ss 24–28 is to be excluded in relation to the lease.

114   This defined term will require amendment where the operation of the security of tenure provisions in
       the Landlord and Tenant Act 1954 ss 24–28 is to be excluded in relation to the lease: see note 6 to
       clause 1.2 [2108] 'THE [CONTRACTUAL] TERM'.

3.16   Obstruction and encroachment

3.16.1   *Obstruction of windows*

The Tenant must not stop up, darken or obstruct any window or light belonging to the
Premises.

3.16.2   *Encroachments*

The Tenant must take all [reasonable] steps to prevent the construction of any new
window, light, opening, doorway, path, passage, pipe or the making of any
encroachment or the acquisition of any easement in relation to the Premises and must
notify the Landlord immediately if any such thing is constructed, encroachment is made
or easement acquired, or if any attempt is made to construct such a thing, encroach or
acquire an easement. At the request of the Landlord the Tenant must adopt such means
as are [reasonably] required to prevent the construction of such a thing, the making of
any encroachment or the acquisition of any easement[115].

115   For a shorter clause see vol 22(3) (1997 Reissue) LANDLORD AND TENANT (BUSINESS TENANCIES)
       Form 172 [6696].

[2178]

3.17   Yielding up

At the end of the Term[116] the Tenant must yield up the Premises with vacant possession,
decorated and repaired in accordance with and in the condition required by the
provisions of this Lease, give up all keys of the Premises to the Landlord, remove tenant's
fixtures and fittings [if requested to do so by the Landlord], and remove all signs erected
by the Tenant or any of his predecessors in title in, on or near the Premises, immediately
making good any damage caused by their removal.

116   The provisions of clause 1.17 [2113] INTERPRETATION OF 'THE LAST YEAR OF THE TERM' AND
       'THE END OF THE TERM' should be noted.

3.18   Interest on arrears[117]

The Tenant must pay interest on any of the Lease Rents[118] or other sums due under this
Lease that are not paid [within *(state period, eg 14 days)* of the date due], whether formally
demanded or not[, the interest to be recoverable as rent][119]. Nothing in this clause
entitles the Tenant to withhold or delay any payment of the Lease Rents or any other
sum due under this Lease or affects the rights of the Landlord in relation to any non-
payment.

117   As to the covenant to pay interest see vol 22(1) (2003 Reissue) LANDLORD AND TENANT (BUSINESS
       TENANCIES) Paragraph 154 [767].

118   As to the definition of 'the Lease Rents' see clause 1.32 [2118] 'THE RENT'.

119   These words seek to attach to interest the rights associated with rent. As to the reasons for this see vol
       22(1) (2003 Reissue) LANDLORD AND TENANT (BUSINESS TENANCIES) Paragraph 151 [761].
       However, this clause applies to interest on arrears of other sums payable under the lease that are not
       rent as well as to rent itself, and it might be felt inappropriate for interest to be deemed to be rent where
       the payment on which the interest is due is not itself rent.

3.19   Statutory notices

The Tenant must give to the Landlord full particulars of any notice, direction, order or proposal relating to the Premises made, given or issued to the Tenant by any government department or local, public, regulatory or other authority or court within *(state period, eg 7 days)* of receipt, and if so requested by the Landlord must produce it to the Landlord. The Tenant must without delay take all necessary steps to comply with the notice, direction or order. At the request of the Landlord, but at his own cost, the Tenant must make or join with the Landlord in making any objection or representation the Landlord deems expedient against or in respect of any notice, direction, order or proposal.

[2179]

[3.20   Keyholders

The Tenant must ensure that at all times **[the Landlord has *(or as required)* the Landlord and the local police force have]** written notice of the name, home address and home telephone number of at least *(state number, eg 2)* keyholders of the Premises.] *(omit if not required in the circumstances)*

3.21   Viewing on sale of reversion

The Tenant must**[, on reasonable notice,]** at any time during the Term, permit prospective purchasers of the Landlord's reversion or any other interest superior to the Term, or agents instructed in connection with the sale of the reversion or such an interest, to view the Premises without interruption provided they have the prior written authority of the Landlord or his agents.

3.22   Defective premises

The Tenant must give notice to the Landlord of any defect in the Premises that might give rise to an obligation on the Landlord to do or refrain from doing anything in order to comply with the provisions of this Lease or the duty of care imposed on the Landlord, whether pursuant to the Defective Premises Act 1972 or otherwise, and must at all times display and maintain any notices the Landlord from time to time **[reasonably]** requires him to display at the Premises.

3.23   Replacement guarantor[120]

3.23.1   *Guarantor replacement events*

In this clause 3.23 references to a 'guarantor replacement event' are references, in the case of an individual, to death, bankruptcy, having a receiving order made against him or having a receiver appointed under the Mental Health Act 1983 or entering into a voluntary arrangement and, in the case of a company, to passing a resolution to wind up, entering into liquidation, a voluntary arrangement or administration or having a receiver appointed.

---

120   As to guarantors see vol 22(1) (2003 Reissue) LANDLORD AND TENANT (BUSINESS TENANCIES) Paragraph 71 [278] et seq. The tenant should propose that, on the execution of a guarantee by a new guarantor, the original guarantor or his estate should be released.

[2180]

3.23.2   *Action on occurrence of a guarantor replacement event*

Where during the relevant Liability Period a guarantor replacement event occurs to the Guarantor or any person who has entered into an authorised guarantee agreement, the Tenant must give notice of the event to the Landlord within *(state period, eg 14 days)* of his becoming aware of it. If so required by the Landlord, the Tenant must within *(state period, eg 28 days)* obtain some other person [reasonably] acceptable to the Landlord to execute a guarantee in the form of the Guarantor's covenants in clause 6 GUARANTEE PROVISIONS or the authorised guarantee agreement in schedule 5 THE AUTHORISED GUARANTEE AGREEMENT, as the case may be, for the residue of the relevant Liability Period.

3.24   Exercise of the Landlord's rights[121]

The Tenant must permit the Landlord to exercise any of the rights granted to him by virtue of the provisions of this Lease at all times during the Term without interruption or interference.

121   The provisions of clause 1.30 [2117] REFERENCES TO RIGHTS OF ACCESS should be noted.

3.25   The Hotel Covenants

The Tenant must observe and perform the Hotel Covenants.

[2181]

3.26   Costs of grant of this Lease[122]

[The Tenant must pay the fees and disbursements of the Landlord's solicitors, agents and surveyors and all other costs and expenses incurred by the Landlord in relation to the negotiation, preparation, execution and grant of this Lease. *(or as required)* On the grant of this Lease the Tenant must pay the sum of £... as a contribution to the Landlord's solicitors' charges for the negotiation, execution and completion of this Lease].

122   As to covenants to pay the landlord's legal fees see vol 22(1) (2003 Reissue) LANDLORD AND TENANT (BUSINESS TENANCIES) Paragraph 155 [769]. As to payment of VAT on legal costs by a person other than the solicitor's own client see the Information Binder: Property [1]: VAT and Property.

3.27   Consent to the Landlord's release[123]

The Tenant must not unreasonably withhold consent to a request made by the Landlord under the 1995 Act Section 8 for a release from all or any of the landlord covenants of this Lease.

123   By virtue of the Landlord and Tenant (Covenants) Act 1995 each successive landlord remains bound by the landlord covenants of the lease unless released under the machinery provided in the Act — as to which see vol 22(1) (2003 Reissue) LANDLORD AND TENANT (BUSINESS TENANCIES) Paragraph 57 [252] et seq — or by a specific release given otherwise (see the Landlord and Tenant (Covenants) Act 1995 s 26(1)(a)). Bald statements limiting the landlord's liability, such as those in use before the commencement of the Act, will not withstand the wide anti-avoidance provisions of the Landlord and Tenant (Covenants) Act 1995 s 25, and covenants by the tenant to give consent to release are unlikely to fall within the exception of s 26. None of the ingenious schemes for limiting the landlord's liability, eg making all covenants personal, suggested in the early days of the 1995 Act has stood up to critical scrutiny, although none has yet been tested by the courts. Thus landlords look instead to the alternative of a right of redress if the tenant makes an unreasonable objection to release. This covenant is modelled on the provisions of the Landlord and Tenant Act 1988, which gives tenants a right of action for loss caused by landlords who unreasonably withhold or delay consent to assignment (see the Landlord and Tenant Act 1988 s 4). In view of the strict time limits under the Landlord and Tenant (Covenants) Act 1995 and the fact that failure to respond to the landlord's request for release is deemed to be consent, it is not thought necessary to extend this covenant to unreasonable delay in replying to such a request.

[2182]

4   QUIET ENJOYMENT[124]

The Landlord covenants with the Tenant to permit the Tenant peaceably and quietly to hold and enjoy the Premises without any interruption or disturbance from or by the Landlord or any person claiming under or in trust for him[125] [or by title paramount][126].

124   As to the landlord's covenant for quiet enjoyment see vol 22(1) (2003 Reissue) LANDLORD AND TENANT (BUSINESS TENANCIES) Paragraph 168 [856]. As to covenants for quiet enjoyment generally see 23 Halsbury's Laws (4th Edn Reissue) LANDLORD AND TENANT.
          The words 'the Tenant paying the rents reserved by and observing and performing the covenants on his part and the conditions contained in this lease' are frequently included in a covenant for quiet enjoyment, but they have no practical effect and do not make payment of the rent and performance of the covenants into conditions precedent to the operation of the covenant for quiet enjoyment: see *Edge v Boileau* (1885) 16 QBD 117; *Dawson v Dyer* (1833) 5 B & Ad 584; *Yorkbrook Investments Ltd v Batten* (1985) 52 P & CR 51, [1985] 2 EGLR 100, CA.
125   The covenant is frequently expressed to apply to 'lawful' interruption by persons 'rightfully' claiming under the landlord, but it seems that the addition of these words has no practical effect: see *Williams v Gabriel* [1906] 1 KB 155 at 157.
126   Without the reference to title paramount the landlord is liable only for the acts of persons so far as they are his successors in title or have authority from him to do the acts complained of: *Harrison Ainslie & Co v Muncaster* [1891] 2 QB 680, CA; *Matania v National Provincial Bank Ltd and Elevenist Syndicate Ltd* [1936] 2 All ER 633, CA; *Miller v Emcer Products Ltd* [1956] Ch 304, [1956] 1 All ER 237, CA. If a subtenant holds under a lease containing a qualified covenant on the part of his landlord — ie one where there is no reference to title paramount — and the head landlord evicts the subtenant because the head rent has not been paid, this is not a breach of the covenant for quiet enjoyment (see *Spencer v Marriott* (1823) 1 B & C 457; *Dennett v Atherton* (1872) LR 7 QB 316, Ex Ch), but it is a breach if the sublandlord submits to judgment in an action by a person with no title to sue, and the subtenant is in consequence evicted (*Cohen v Tannar* [1900] 2 QB 609, CA). Actionable interruptions under this covenant are not confined to interference with title or possession, but may extend to interference with the ordinary and lawful enjoyment of the premises: *Sanderson v Berwick-upon-Tweed Corpn* (1884) 13 QBD 547 at 551. As to persons claiming 'under' the landlord see *Celsteel Ltd v Alton House Holdings Ltd (No 2)* [1987] 2 All ER 240, [1987] 1 WLR 291, CA.

[2183]–[2190]

5   INSURANCE[127]

5.1   Warranty as to convictions[128]

The Tenant warrants that before the execution of this document he has disclosed to the Landlord in writing any conviction, judgment or finding of any court or tribunal relating to the Tenant[, or any director, other officer or major shareholder of the Tenant,] of such a nature as to be likely to affect the decision of any insurer or underwriter to grant or to continue insurance of any of the Insured Risks.

127   As to insurance see vol 22(1) (2003 Reissue) LANDLORD AND TENANT (BUSINESS TENANCIES) Paragraph 227 [1021] et seq.
128   A contract of insurance is one uberrimae fidei. The insured must disclose to the insurers all material facts that are within his actual or presumed knowledge, whether there is a formal proposal form or not. A fact is material if non-disclosure of it would influence a prudent and reasonable insurer. This warranty is designed to rebut any suggestion by the landlord's insurers that the landlord had knowledge of the matters concerned. By inserting this clause in the lease, and thus specifically bringing the point to the tenant's attention, the landlord can argue that he has done all that is practical to establish the existence of any such matters. The absence of any written disclosure pursuant to this clause is strong evidence that the landlord has no actual or presumed knowledge of such matters. Further, the landlord has a right of action against the tenant for any breach of the warranty. As to non-disclosure and misrepresentation in contracts of non-marine insurance see 22 Halsbury's Laws (4th Edn Reissue) INSURANCE.

[2191]

5.2   Covenant to insure

The Landlord covenants with the Tenant to insure the Premises [in the joint names of the Landlord and the Tenant[129] [and any other person the Landlord [reasonably] requires][130]] unless the insurance is vitiated by any act of the Tenant or by anyone at the Premises expressly or by implication[131] with his authority [and under his control][132].

129   As to insurance in joint names see vol 22(1) (2003 Reissue) LANDLORD AND TENANT (BUSINESS TENANCIES) Paragraph 229 [1024].
130   Unless some expression such as this is included, a covenant to insure in specified names is broken by insurance in those and other names: see *Penniall v Harborne* (1848) 11 QB 368.
131   The expression 'by implication' is intended to include a caller on the premises, such as a tradesman, where there has been no express invitation but the person cannot be classed as a trespasser.
132   The tenant should add the words in square brackets.

5.3   Details of the insurance

5.3.1   *Office, underwriters and agency*

Insurance is to be effected in such [substantial and reputable] insurance office, or with such underwriters[133], and through such agency as the Landlord from time to time decides[134].

133   The expression 'insurance office' would probably not include Lloyd's underwriters. The landlord's right to nominate the office and agency is absolute, with no implied restrictions: *Berrycroft Management Co Ltd v Sinclair Gardens Investments (Kensington) Ltd* (1996) 75 P & CR 210, [1997] 1 EGLR 47, CA.
134   It should be noted that it is recommended 'best practice' in circumstances where the building is let to one tenant and the landlord insures that, in appropriate cases, the tenant should be given the opportunity to influence the choice of insurer: see vol 22(1) (2003 Reissue) LANDLORD AND TENANT (BUSINESS TENANCIES) Paragraph 85 [401] and 'A code of practice for commercial leases in England and Wales (2nd edition)' which can be found in vol 22(1) (2003 Reissue) LANDLORD AND TENANT (BUSINESS TENANCIES) at Form 1 [4501].

[2192]

5.3.2   *Insurance cover*[135]

Insurance must be effected for the following amounts —

5.3.2.1   the sum that the Landlord is from time to time advised [by the Surveyor] is the full cost of rebuilding and reinstating the Premises, including [VAT[136],] architects', surveyors', engineers', solicitors' and all other professional persons' fees, the fees payable on any applications for planning permission or other permits or consents that may be required in relation to rebuilding or reinstating the Premises, the cost of preparation of the site including shoring-up, debris removal, demolition, site clearance and any works that may be required by statute, and incidental expenses, and

5.3.2.2   loss of the Rent, taking account of any rent review that may be due, for *(state period, eg 3 years)* or such longer period as the Landlord from time to time [reasonably] requires for planning and carrying out the rebuilding or reinstatement.

135   As to the sum insured see vol 22(1) (2003 Reissue) LANDLORD AND TENANT (BUSINESS TENANCIES) Paragraph 231 [1028] et seq.
        It should be noted that it is recommended 'best practice' that, where the landlord has arranged insurance, the terms should be made known to the tenant and any material change in the insurance should be notified to the tenant: see Recommendation 14 of 'A code of practice for commercial leases in England and Wales (2nd edition)' which can be found in vol 22(1) (2003 Reissue) LANDLORD AND TENANT (BUSINESS TENANCIES) at Form 1 [4501].

136   As to VAT and the level of insurance cover see the Information Binder: Property [1]: VAT and Property. The expense of insuring against the VAT payable on reinstatement costs is not justified where the landlord has opted to tax and will be able to recover the VAT. There is a theoretical possibility that a future landlord may not opt to tax and that the sum insured may then be too low. It is also possible that a landlord may wish to preserve the 'exempt' status of a property. Normally, however, the cost of reinstatement need not expressly mention VAT, although the cashflow implications of having to pay VAT on construction works need to be remembered.

5.3.3   *Risks insured*[137]

Insurance must be effected against damage or destruction by any of the Insured Risks to the extent that such insurance may ordinarily be arranged [with a substantial and reputable insurer] for properties such as the Premises, subject to such excesses, exclusions or limitations as the insurer requires.

137   As to risks to be insured against see vol 22(1) (2003 Reissue) LANDLORD AND TENANT (BUSINESS TENANCIES) Paragraph 235 [1033].
       It should be noted that it is recommended 'best practice' that, where the landlord has arranged insurance, the terms should be made known to the tenant and any material change in the insurance should be notified to the tenant: see Recommendation 14 of 'A code of practice for commercial leases in England and Wales (2nd edition)' which can be found in vol 22(1) (2003 Reissue) LANDLORD AND TENANT (BUSINESS TENANCIES) at Form 1 [4501].

[2193]

5.4   Payment of the Insurance Rent

The Tenant covenants to pay the Insurance Rent for the period commencing on the Rent Commencement Date and ending on the day before the next policy renewal date on the date of this document, and subsequently to pay the Insurance Rent on demand and, if so demanded, in advance of the policy renewal date[, but not more than *(state period, eg ... months)* in advance].

5.5   Suspension of the Rent[138]

5.5.1   *Events giving rise to suspension*

If and whenever the Premises or any part of them are damaged or destroyed by one or more of the Insured Risks[139] [— except one against which insurance may not ordinarily be arranged [with a substantial and reputable insurer] for properties such as the Premises unless the Landlord has in fact insured against that risk —] so that the Premises or any part of them are unfit for occupation or use, and payment of the insurance money is not wholly or partly refused because of any act or default of the Tenant or anyone at the Premises expressly or by implication[140] with his authority [and under his control][141], then the provisions of clause 5.5.2 SUSPENDING THE RENT are to have effect.

138   As to suspension of rent see vol 22(1) (2003 Reissue) LANDLORD AND TENANT (BUSINESS TENANCIES) Paragraph 241 [1044] et seq.
139   It should be noted that it is recommended 'best practice' that if premises are so damaged by an uninsured risk as to prevent occupation, the tenant should be allowed to terminate the lease unless the landlord agrees to reinstate at his own cost: see vol 22(1) (2003 Reissue) LANDLORD AND TENANT (BUSINESS TENANCIES) Paragraph 85 [402] and 'A code of practice for commercial leases in England and Wales (2nd edition)' which can be found in vol 22(1) (2003 Reissue) LANDLORD AND TENANT (BUSINESS TENANCIES) at Form 1 [4501]. If adopted, this recommendation involves rent suspension also becoming operative in the event of the premises becoming unusable because of uninsured risks.
140   The expression 'by implication' is intended to include a caller on the premises, such as a tradesman, where there has been no express invitation but the person cannot be classed as a trespasser.
141   The tenant should add the words in square brackets.

[2194]

5.5.2   Suspending the Rent

In the circumstances mentioned in clause 5.5.1 EVENTS GIVING RISE TO SUSPENSION, the Rent, or a fair proportion of it according to the nature and the extent of the damage sustained, is to cease to be payable until the Premises, or the affected part, have been rebuilt or reinstated so as to render the Premises, or the affected part, fit for occupation and use, [or until the end of *(state period, eg 3 years)* from the destruction or damage, whichever period is the shorter,][142] [the proportion of the Rent suspended and the period of the suspension to be determined by the Surveyor acting as an expert and not as an arbitrator *(or as required)* any dispute as to the proportion of the Rent suspended or the period of the suspension to be determined in accordance with the Arbitration Act 1996 by an arbitrator to be appointed by agreement between the Landlord and the Tenant or in default by the President or other proper officer for the time being of the Royal Institution of Chartered Surveyors on the application of either the Landlord or the Tenant].

142   As to the length of the suspension and the tenant's concerns see vol 22(1) (2003 Reissue) LANDLORD AND TENANT (BUSINESS TENANCIES) Paragraph 244 [1048]. For a provision extending suspension of the rent where reinstatement is delayed see vol 22(3) (1997 Reissue) LANDLORD AND TENANT (BUSINESS TENANCIES) Form 111 [6495].

5.6   Reinstatement and termination[143]

5.6.1   *Obligation to obtain permissions*

If and whenever the Premises or any part of them are damaged or destroyed by one or more of the Insured Risks [— except one against which insurance may not ordinarily be arranged [with a substantial and reputable insurer] for properties such as the Premises, unless the Landlord has in fact insured against that risk —] and payment of the insurance money is not wholly or partly refused because of any act or default of the Tenant or anyone at the Premises expressly or by implication[144] with his authority [and under his control][145], the Landlord must use his best endeavours[146] to obtain the planning permissions or other permits and consents ('permissions') that are required under the Planning Acts or otherwise to enable him to rebuild and reinstate the Premises.

[2195]

143   It has been held that, in the absence of an express covenant to reinstate, where the landlord must keep the premises adequately insured against comprehensive risks and the insurance is effected at the tenant's expense, the obligation is one intended to enure for the benefit of both parties: *Mumford Hotels Ltd v Wheler* [1964] Ch 117, [1963] 3 All ER 250; see also *Mark Rowlands Ltd v Berni Inns Ltd* [1986] QB 211, [1985] 3 All ER 473, CA; *Lonsdale & Thompson Ltd v Black Arrow Group plc* [1993] Ch 361, [1993] 3 All ER 648. This is not, however, a general principle of law and the tenant should therefore always require a specific covenant to reinstate.

    These provisions are restricted to circumstances where damage or destruction is caused by an insured risk. It should be noted that it is recommended 'best practice' that if premises are so damaged by an uninsured risk as to prevent occupation, the tenant should be allowed to terminate the lease unless the landlord agrees to reinstate at his own cost: see vol 22(1) (2003 Reissue) LANDLORD AND TENANT (BUSINESS TENANCIES) Paragraph 85 [401] and 'A code of practice for commercial leases in England and Wales (2nd edition)' which can be found in vol 22(1) (2003 Reissue) LANDLORD AND TENANT (BUSINESS TENANCIES) at Form 1 [4501].

    As to reinstatement and termination where reinstatement is not possible see vol 22(1) (2003 Reissue) LANDLORD AND TENANT (BUSINESS TENANCIES) Paragraph 237 [1037] et seq. For a provision for termination or surrender on destruction or substantial damage see vol 22(3) (1997 Reissue) LANDLORD AND TENANT (BUSINESS TENANCIES) Form 107 [6483].

144   The expression 'by implication' is intended to include a caller on the premises, such as a tradesman, where there has been no express invitation but the person cannot be classed as a trespasser.

145   The tenant should add the words in square brackets.

146   The extent of the duty to use best endeavours depends upon the facts in each case: see *Monkland v Jack Barclay Ltd* [1951] 2 KB 252, [1951] 1 All ER 714, CA; *Terrell v Mabie Todd & Co Ltd* [1952] 2 TLR 574; *NW Investments (Erdington) Ltd v Swani* (1970) 214 Estates Gazette 1115. In the light of *IBM United Kingdom Ltd v Rockware Glass Ltd* [1980] FSR 335, CA, it may be that there is little practical difference between a covenant to use best endeavours, a covenant to use reasonable endeavours and a covenant to take all reasonable steps.

[2196]

5.6.2   *Obligation to reinstate*

Subject to the provisions of clause 5.6.3 RELIEF FROM THE OBLIGATION TO REINSTATE, and, if any permissions are required, after they have been obtained, the Landlord must as soon as reasonably practicable apply all money received in respect of the insurance effected by the Landlord pursuant to this Lease, except sums in respect of loss of the Rent, in rebuilding or reinstating the Premises[, making up any difference between the cost of rebuilding and reinstating and the money received out of his own money][147].

147   Where the landlord's covenant is 'to apply all money received in respect of the insurance in rebuilding or reinstating' rather than simply 'to reinstate', it seems that the landlord does not have to complete the work out of his own money if the insurance money is insufficient because he has complied with his covenant by laying out all the insurance money received. The situation is different if the tenant can establish that the landlord was in breach of his covenant to insure for the full cost of reinstatement and that this has caused the shortfall: see *Mumford Hotels Ltd v Wheler* [1964] Ch 117, [1963] 3 All ER 250. The tenant should, therefore, require a specific covenant from the landlord to make up any shortfall, to prevent a situation in which the landlord refuses to complete the rebuilding. This is of particular concern if the suspension of rent proviso is expressed to operate for a limited period, because on the expiry of that period the tenant becomes liable for rent unless he can satisfy the court that the lease has been frustrated.

It should be noted that it is recommended 'best practice' that if premises are so damaged by an uninsured risk as to prevent occupation, the tenant should be allowed to terminate the lease unless the landlord agrees to reinstate at his own cost: see vol 22(1) (2003 Reissue) LANDLORD AND TENANT (BUSINESS TENANCIES) Paragraph 85 [401] and 'A code of practice for commercial leases in England and Wales (2nd edition)'which can be found in vol 22(1) (2003 Reissue) LANDLORD AND TENANT (BUSINESS TENANCIES) at Form 1 [4501]. If this recommendation is adopted and the landlord merely covenants to apply insurance money received, the principle should be extended to damage or destruction resulting from insured risks in circumstances where the insurance money is insufficient to enable reinstatement to be completed.

For a proviso relieving the landlord from the obligation to reinstate the premises in the same form see vol 22(3) (1997 Reissue) LANDLORD AND TENANT (BUSINESS TENANCIES) Form 106 [6482].

[2197]

5.6.3   *Relief from the obligation to reinstate*[148]

The Landlord need not rebuild or reinstate the Premises if and for so long as rebuilding or reinstatement is prevented because —

5.6.3.1   the Landlord, despite using his best endeavours[149], cannot obtain any necessary permission,

5.6.3.2   any permission is granted subject to a lawful condition with which [it is impossible for *(or as required)* in all the circumstances it is unreasonable to expect] the Landlord to comply,

5.6.3.3   there is some defect or deficiency in the site on which the rebuilding or reinstatement is to take place that [renders it impossible *(or as required)* means it can only be undertaken at a cost that is unreasonable in all the circumstances],

5.6.3.4   the Landlord is unable to obtain access to the site to rebuild or reinstate,

5.6.3.5   the rebuilding or reinstating is prevented by war, act of God, government action[, strike or lock-out], or

because of the occurrence of any other circumstances beyond the Landlord's control.

148   As to the need for a right to terminate where reinstatement is not possible see vol 22(1) (2003 Reissue) LANDLORD AND TENANT (BUSINESS TENANCIES) Paragraph 226 [998].

149   The extent of the duty to use best endeavours depends upon the facts in each case: see *Monkland v Jack Barclay Ltd* [1951] 2 KB 252, [1951] 1 All ER 714, CA; *Terrell v Mabie Todd & Co Ltd* [1952] 2 TLR 574; *NW Investments (Erdington) Ltd v Swani* (1970) 214 Estates Gazette 1115. In the light of *IBM United Kingdom Ltd v Rockware Glass Ltd* [1980] FSR 335, CA, it may be that there is little practical difference between a covenant to use best endeavours, a covenant to use reasonable endeavours and a covenant to take all reasonable steps.

[2198]

5.6.4   *Notice to terminate*[150]

If, at the end of the period[151] of *(state period, eg 3 years)* starting on the date of the damage or destruction, the Premises are still not fit for the Tenant's occupation and use, either the Landlord or the Tenant may by notice served at any time within *(state period, eg 6 months)* of the end of that period ('a notice to terminate following failure to reinstate') implement the provisions of clause 5.6.5 TERMINATION FOLLOWING FAILURE TO REINSTATE[152].

150   For alternative provisions where the landlord's right to terminate is limited to specified circumstances see vol 22(3) (1997 Reissue) LANDLORD AND TENANT (BUSINESS TENANCIES) Form 109 [6492].

151   The period to be inserted must be carefully considered. Particular regard should be had to the terms of any rent suspension provision and the extent of insurance cover for loss of rent.

152   As to the effect of the Landlord and Tenant Act 1954 see vol 22(1) (2003 Reissue) LANDLORD AND TENANT (BUSINESS TENANCIES) Paragraph 226 [998].

5.6.5   *Termination following failure to reinstate*

On service of a notice to terminate following failure to reinstate, the Term is to cease absolutely — but without prejudice to any rights or remedies that may have accrued[153]— and all money received in respect of the insurance effected by the Landlord pursuant to this Lease is to belong to the Landlord absolutely[154].

153   The effect of this clause is that the right to terminate arises after the end of the appropriate period, whatever the reason for the delay, but the tenant still has a right of action against the landlord if the landlord is in breach of his covenant to reinstate.

154   In the absence of provision for ownership of the insurance money the position is uncertain. In *Re King, Robinson v Gray* [1963] Ch 459, [1963] 1 All ER 781, CA it was held that the insurance money belongs to the party who paid the premiums even if the insurance was placed in the joint names of the landlord and the tenant. The dissenting view of Denning MR that insurance in joint names envisages that each party should be insured as to his insurable interest and that the insurance money should therefore be divided in proportion to their interests in the property should, however, be noted. In *Beacon Carpets Ltd v Kirby* [1985] QB 755, [1984] 2 All ER 726, CA the court adhered to this view and held that the proportion payable depended on the parties' interests in the premises at the time of the destruction. The landlord will prefer an express provision in the lease for the insurance money to be retained by him in full if reinstatement proves impossible. The tenant ought perhaps to accept that it would be unrealistic to amend this to provide for the insurance money to belong to the tenant, but should suggest that a provision be inserted under which the money is to be divided in accordance with their respective interests in the premises at the time when the insurance money became due. For an alternative provision for ownership of the insurance money etc see vol 22(3) (1997 Reissue) LANDLORD AND TENANT (BUSINESS TENANCIES) Form 108 [6491].

[2199]

5.7   Tenant's further insurance covenants[155]

The Tenant covenants with the Landlord to observe and perform the requirements of this clause 5.7.

155   In order to comply with many of these covenants, the tenant will need to be supplied with details of the landlord's insurance policy. In any event, it should be noted that it is recommended 'best practice' that where the landlord has arranged insurance, the terms should be made known to the tenant and any material change in the insurance should be notified to the tenant: see Recommendation 14 of 'A code of practice for commercial leases in England and Wales (2nd edition)' which can be found in vol 22(1) (2003 Reissue) LANDLORD AND TENANT (BUSINESS TENANCIES) at Form 1 [4501].

5.7.1   *Requirements of insurers*

The Tenant must comply with all the requirements and recommendations of the insurers.

5.7.2   *Policy avoidance and additional premiums*

The Tenant must not do or omit anything that could cause any insurance policy on or in relation to the Premises to become wholly or partly void or voidable, or do or omit anything by which additional insurance premiums may become payable unless he has previously notified the Landlord and has agreed to pay the increased premium.

5.7.3   *Fire-fighting equipment*

The Tenant must keep the Premises supplied with such fire fighting equipment [as the insurers and the fire authority require and must maintain the equipment to their satisfaction *(or as required)* as the Landlord reasonably requires and must maintain the equipment to the reasonable satisfaction of the insurers and the fire authority] and in efficient working order. At least once in every *(state period, eg 6 months)* the Tenant must cause any sprinkler system and other fire fighting equipment to be inspected by a competent person.

5.7.4   *Combustible materials*

The Tenant must not store on the Premises or bring onto them anything of a specially combustible, inflammable or explosive nature, and must comply with the requirements and recommendations of the fire authority [and the [reasonable] requirements of the Landlord] as to fire precautions relating to the Premises.

[2200]

5.7.5   *Fire escapes, equipment and doors*

The Tenant must not obstruct the access to any fire equipment or the means of escape from the Premises, or lock any fire door while the Premises are occupied.

5.7.6   *Notice of events affecting the policy*

The Tenant must give immediate notice to the Landlord of any event that might affect any insurance policy on or relating to the Premises, and any event against which the Landlord may have insured under this Lease.

5.7.7   *Notice of convictions*

The Tenant must give immediate notice to the Landlord of any conviction, judgment or finding of any court or tribunal relating to the Tenant, or any director other officer or major shareholder of the Tenant, of such a nature as to be likely to affect the decision of any insurer or underwriter to grant or to continue any such insurance[156].

156   This clause provides a continuation of the warranty given by the tenant in clause 5.1 [2191] WARRANTY AS TO CONVICTIONS. As to non-disclosure and misrepresentation in contracts of non-marine insurance see 22 Halsbury's Laws (4th Edn Reissue) INSURANCE.

5.7.8   *Other insurance*

If at any time the Tenant is entitled to the benefit of any insurance of the Premises that is not effected or maintained in pursuance of any obligation contained in this Lease, the Tenant must apply all money received by virtue of that insurance in making good the loss or damage in respect of which the money is received[157].

157   An insurance policy frequently provides that if there is any other insurance effected by or on behalf of the insured, covering the premises that are the subject of the policy, the insurers are liable only for a rateable proportion of the damage. Such provisions extend to a case where one of the policies is in the joint names of the persons interested in the premises and the other is in the name of one only of those persons: *Halifax Building Society v Keighley* [1931] 2 KB 248. Therefore, at least when the insurance is in joint names, the landlord must ensure that the tenant will use all money received under any policy he has effected to reinstate the premises.

[2201]

[5.7.9   *Reinstatement on refusal of money through default*

If at any time the Premises or any part of them are damaged or destroyed by one or more of the Insured Risks and the insurance money under the policy of insurance effected by the Landlord pursuant to his obligations contained in this Lease is wholly or partly irrecoverable because of any act or default of the Tenant or of anyone at the Premises expressly or by implication[158] with his authority [and under his control][159], the Tenant must immediately, at the option of the Landlord, either rebuild and reinstate the Premises or the part of them destroyed or damaged, to the reasonable satisfaction and under the supervision of the Surveyor — in which case, on completion of the rebuilding and refurbishment, the Landlord must pay to the Tenant the amount that the Landlord has actually received under the insurance policy in respect of the destruction or damage — or pay to the Landlord on demand [with Interest] the amount of the insurance money so irrecoverable — in which case the provisions of clauses 5.5 SUSPENSION OF THE RENT and 5.6 REINSTATEMENT AND TERMINATION are to apply.]

158   The expression 'by implication' is intended to include a caller on the premises, such as a tradesman, where there has been no express invitation but the person cannot be classed as a trespasser.
159   The tenant should add the words in square brackets.

[5.8   **Landlord's further insurance covenants**[160]

The Landlord covenants with the Tenant to observe and perform the requirements set out in this clause 5.8 in relation to the insurance policy effected by the Landlord pursuant to his obligations contained in this Lease.

160   Unless insurance is to be in the joint names of the landlord and the tenant, the tenant should seek covenants such as these from the landlord.

5.8.1   *Copy policy*

The Landlord must produce to the Tenant on demand [a copy of the policy and the last premium renewal receipt *(or as required)* reasonable evidence of the terms of the policy and the fact that the last premium has been paid][161].

161   The landlord can reasonably insist on the second alternative. If the premises are insured under a block policy, it would be inappropriate for him to have to disclose to the tenant information about his other properties.

It should be noted that it is recommended 'best practice' that where the landlord has arranged insurance, the terms should be made known to the tenant and any material change in the insurance should be notified to the tenant: see Recommendation 14 of 'A code of practice for commercial leases in England and Wales (2nd edition)' which can be found in vol 22(1) (2003 Reissue) LANDLORD AND TENANT (BUSINESS TENANCIES) at Form 1 [4501].

[2202]

5.8.2   *Noting of the Tenant's interest*

The Landlord must ensure that the interest of the Tenant is noted or endorsed on the policy[162].

162   Where insurance in the joint names of the landlord and the tenant is not practical, the tenant should insist that a note of his interest is endorsed on the policy. This protects the tenant because the insurers should give notice to him of any lapse in the policy and, where it can be shown that the tenant is responsible for the insurance premium under the terms of the lease, it is likely — but not certain — that the insurers would not exercise subrogation rights against the tenant.

It is recommended 'best practice' that where the landlord has arranged insurance, any interest of the tenant should be covered by the policy: see Recommendation 14 of 'A code of practice for commercial leases in England and Wales (2nd edition)' which can be found in vol 22(1) (2003 Reissue) LANDLORD AND TENANT (BUSINESS TENANCIES) at Form 1 [4501].

5.8.3   *Change of risks*

The Landlord must notify the Tenant of any [material] change in the risks covered by the policy from time to time[163].

163   It should be noted that it is recommended 'best practice' that where the landlord has arranged insurance, the terms should be made known to the tenant and any material change in the insurance should be notified to the tenant: see Recommendation 14 of 'A code of practice for commercial leases in England and Wales (2nd edition)' which can be found in vol 22(1) (2003 Reissue) LANDLORD AND TENANT (BUSINESS TENANCIES) at Form 1 [4501].

[5.8.4   *Waiver of subrogation*[164]

The Landlord must produce to the Tenant on demand written confirmation from the insurers that they have agreed to waive all rights of subrogation against the Tenant.]]

164   Generally an insurer who has paid out under a policy stands in the shoes of the insured with regard to any claim the latter may have had against any third party. If the insurance is in joint names, the tenant is an insured party and there can be no subrogation against him. It would seem, also, that where the tenant covenants to reimburse the landlord for sums expended by the landlord in insuring the premises, the landlord's insurers cannot make a subrogated claim against the tenant where the premises are destroyed by the tenant's negligence: *Mark Rowlands Ltd v Berni Inns Ltd* [1986] QB 211, [1985] 3 All ER 473, CA. The tenant may still, however, wish to obtain a specific waiver of subrogation if possible.

[2203]

6   GUARANTEE PROVISIONS

6.1   The Guarantor's covenants[165]

6.1.1 *Nature and duration*

The Guarantor's covenants with the Landlord are given as sole or principal debtor or covenantor, with the landlord for the time being and with all his successors in title[166] without the need for any express assignment, and the Guarantor's obligations to the Landlord will last throughout the Liability Period.

165   The covenants in this clause should *not* be omitted where no guarantor is a party to the lease, because they may be required under clause 3.9.5.2 [2166] CONDITIONS. If it is felt undesirable to have covenants in a lease and no party, at least initially, to enter into them, ie where there is no guarantor for the original tenant, the contents of this clause could alternatively be included in a schedule.

166   The new provisions governing the transmission of the benefit and burden of covenants (see the Landlord and Tenant (Covenants) Act 1995 s 3) only apply to landlord and tenant covenants. The law in force before 1 January 1996 remains unchanged for guarantor covenants, so that the benefit passes with the landlord's reversion. This occurs, not under the Law of Property Act 1925 s 141(1), which has been repealed for post-1995 tenancies by the 1995 Act, but under common law. The guarantee covenant touches and concerns the legal estate vested in the new reversioner: see *P & A Swift Investments v Combined English Stores Group plc* [1989] AC 632, [1988] 2 All ER 885, HL.

6.1.2   *The covenants*

The Guarantor covenants with the Landlord to observe and perform the requirements of this clause 6.1.2.

[2204]

6.1.2.1   **Payment of rent and performance of the Lease**

The Tenant must pay the Lease Rents[167] and VAT charged on them punctually and observe and perform the covenants and other terms of this Lease, and if, at any time during the Liability Period while the Tenant is bound by the tenant covenants of this Lease[168], the Tenant defaults in paying the Lease Rents or in observing or performing any of the covenants or other terms of this Lease, then the Guarantor must pay the Lease Rents and observe or perform the covenants or terms in respect of which the Tenant is in default and make good to the Landlord on demand, and indemnify the Landlord against, all losses resulting from such non-payment, non-performance or non-observance notwithstanding —

(a)   any time or indulgence granted by the Landlord to the Tenant, any neglect or forbearance of the Landlord in enforcing the payment of the Lease Rents or the observance or performance of the covenants or other terms of this Lease, or any refusal by the Landlord to accept rent tendered by or on behalf of the Tenant at a time when the Landlord is entitled — or will after the service of a notice under the Law of Property Act 1925 Section 146 be entitled — to re-enter the Premises[169],

(b)   that the terms of this Lease may have been varied by agreement between the Landlord and the Tenant[, provided that no variation is to bind the Guarantor to the extent that it is materially prejudicial to him][170],

(c)   that the Tenant has surrendered part of the Premises — in which event the liability of the Guarantor under this Lease is to continue in respect of the part of the Premises not surrendered after making any necessary apportionments under the Law of Property Act 1925 Section 140[171], and

(d)   anything else (other than a release by deed) by which, but for this clause 6.1.2.1, the Guarantor would be released.

[2205]

167   As to the definition of 'the Lease Rents' see clause 1.32 [2118] 'THE RENT'.

168   This obligation lasts while the lease is vested in the tenant and for any period of extended liability following an excluded assignment. It is not appropriate once the tenant has entered into an authorised guarantee agreement, when the contractual guarantor's obligations are at one remove. . As to the guaranteeing of obligations under an authorised guarantee agreement: see vol 22(1) (2003 Reissue) LANDLORD AND TENANT (BUSINESS TENANCIES) Paragraph 74 [284] and clause 6.1.2.4 [2208] GUARANTEE OF THE TENANT'S LIABILITIES UNDER AN AUTHORISED GUARANTEE AGREEMENT.

169   If a creditor 'gives time' to the debtor in a binding manner, this releases the guarantor: see *Swire v Redman* (1876) 1 QBD 536; *Holme v Brunskill* (1877) 3 QBD 495, CA. The guarantee should, therefore, be expressed to apply notwithstanding any time or indulgence granted by the landlord to the tenant, or neglect or forbearance on the part of the landlord in enforcing the payment of rent and the other covenants in the lease. It has been suggested, however, that such wording does not protect a landlord who refuses to accept rent so as not to waive a breach of covenant by the tenant. This is unresolved but to avoid any doubt the point should be expressly dealt with. It appears that any provision in a guarantor's covenant that purports to exonerate the landlord from the consequences of his own negligence must satisfy the reasonableness test of the Unfair Contract Terms Act 1977 (11 Halsbury's Statutes (4th Edn) CONTRACT).

170   Any variation of the terms of the contract between the creditor and the debtor will discharge the guarantor (*Holme v Brunskill* (1877) 3 QBD 495, CA), unless the guarantor consents, although it has been suggested that an immaterial variation that was not prejudicial to the guarantor might not release him. No guarantor should accept a provision by which the guarantee is to continue notwithstanding any variation, but on the other hand it seems unfair on the landlord for the guarantor to escape his liability merely because a minor change has been agreed between the landlord and the tenant. A provision that the guarantee is to continue to apply notwithstanding an immaterial variation not prejudicial to the guarantor seems a fair compromise. It should be noted that the Landlord and Tenant (Covenants) Act 1995 s 18 does not apply to the guarantor of the current tenant.

        It should also be noted that it is recommended 'best practice' that landlords and tenants should seek the agreement of any guarantors to proposed material changes to the terms of the lease, or even minor changes which could increase the guarantor's liability: see Recommendation 15 of 'A code of practice for commercial leases in England and Wales (2nd edition)' which can be found in vol 22(1) (2003 Reissue) LANDLORD AND TENANT (BUSINESS TENANCIES) at Form 1 [4501].

171   In the light of *Holme v Brunskill* (1877) 3 QBD 495, CA, the position on surrender of part of the premises should be dealt with expressly.

[2206]

6.1.2.2   New lease following disclaimer[172]

If, at any time during the Liability Period while the Tenant is bound by the tenant covenants of this Lease[173], any trustee in bankruptcy or liquidator of the Tenant disclaims this Lease, the Guarantor must, if so required by notice served by the Landlord within *(state period, eg 60 days)* of the Landlord's becoming aware of the disclaimer, take from the Landlord forthwith a lease of the Premises for the residue of the [Contractual][174] Term as at the date of the disclaimer, at the Rent then payable under this Lease and subject to the same covenants and terms as in this Lease — except that the Guarantor need not ensure that any other person is made a party to that lease as guarantor — the new lease to commence on the date of the disclaimer. The Guarantor must pay the costs of the new lease and VAT charged thereon, save where such VAT is recoverable or available for set-off by the Landlord as input tax[175], and execute and deliver to the Landlord a counterpart of the new lease.

172   This put option should be included because on disclaimer of a lease the lease ceases to exist, although it is deemed to continue for the purpose of determining the liability to the landlord of persons, including guarantors, other than the tenant whose liquidator or trustee has disclaimed: see *Hindcastle Ltd v Barbara Attenborough Associates Ltd* [1997] AC 70, [1996] 1 All ER 737, HL.

173   This obligation lasts while the lease is vested in the tenant and for any period of extended liability following an excluded assignment. It is not appropriate once the tenant has entered into an authorised guarantee agreement when the tenant's — ie the former tenant's — liquidator or trustee in bankruptcy will not be in a position to disclaim the lease because it will no longer be vested in the former tenant.

174   This defined term will require amendment where the operation of the security of tenure provisions in the Landlord and Tenant Act 1954 ss 24–28 is to be excluded in relation to the lease: see note 6 to clause 1.2 [2108] 'THE [CONTRACTUAL] TERM'.

175   As to payment of VAT on legal costs by a person other than the solicitor's own client see the Information Binder: Property [1]: VAT and Property.

[2207]

6.1.2.3   Payments following disclaimer[176]

If this Lease is disclaimed and the Landlord does not require the Guarantor to accept a new lease of the Premises in accordance with clause 6.1.2.2 NEW LEASE FOLLOWING DISCLAIMER, the Guarantor must pay to the Landlord on demand an amount equal to [the difference between any money received by the Landlord for the use or occupation of the Premises and] the Lease Rents [in both cases] for the period commencing with the date of the disclaimer and ending on whichever is the earlier of the date *(state period, eg 6 months)* after the disclaimer, the date, if any, upon which the Premises are relet, and the end of the [Contractual][177] Term.

176   This clause could be a useful alternative for a landlord who may not be unhappy to regain possession of the premises but would like some rental income before reletting etc. For a covenant by the tenant to assign to the guarantor see vol 22(3) (1997 Reissue) LANDLORD AND TENANT (BUSINESS TENANCIES) Form 159 [6666].

177   This defined term will require amendment where the operation of the security of tenure provisions in the Landlord and Tenant Act 1954 ss 24–28 is to be excluded in relation to the lease: see note 6 to clause 1.2 [2108] 'THE [CONTRACTUAL] TERM'.

6.1.2.4   Guarantee of the Tenant's liabilities under an authorised guarantee agreement

If, at any time during the Liability Period while the Tenant is bound by an authorised guarantee agreement, the Tenant defaults in his obligations under that agreement, the Guarantor must make good to the Landlord on demand, and indemnify the Landlord against, all losses resulting from that default notwithstanding —

(a)   any time or indulgence granted by the Landlord to the Tenant, or neglect or forbearance of the Landlord in enforcing the payment of any sum or the observance or performance of the covenants of the authorised guarantee agreement[178],

(b)   that the terms of the authorised guarantee agreement may have been varied by agreement between the Landlord and the Tenant [provided that no variation is to bind the Guarantor to the extent that it is materially prejudicial to him][179], or

(c)   anything else (other than a release by deed) by which, but for this clause 6.1.2.4, the Guarantor would be released.

178   See note 169 to clause 6.1.2.1 [2206] PAYMENT OF RENT AND PERFORMANCE OF THE LEASE.

179   See note 170 to clause 6.1.2.1 [2206] PAYMENT OF RENT AND PERFORMANCE OF THE LEASE.

[2208]

6.1.3   *Severance*

6.1.3.1   **Severance of void provisions**

Any provision of this clause 6 rendered void by virtue of the 1995 Act Section 25 is to be severed from all remaining provisions, and the remaining provisions are to be preserved.

6.1.3.2   **Limitation of provisions**

If any provision in this clause 6 extends beyond the limits permitted by the 1995 Act Section 25, that provision is to be varied so as not to extend beyond those limits.

[6.2   The Landlord's covenant[180]

The Landlord covenants with the Guarantor that he will not attempt to recover from the Guarantor payment of any amount, determined by a court or in binding arbitration or agreed between the Landlord and the Tenant, payable in respect of a breach of covenant by the Tenant, unless he has served on the Guarantor, within 6 months of the payment being determined or agreed, a notice in the form prescribed by Section 27 of the 1995 Act as if the payment were a fixed charge under that Act.]

180   This clause is a tenant's amendment. It provides for a notice equivalent to a default notice under the Landlord and Tenant (Covenants) Act 1995 to be served. It protects the interests of existing and future contractual guarantors. As to service of default notices see vol 22(1) (2003 Reissue) LANDLORD AND TENANT (BUSINESS TENANCIES) Paragraph 61 [260].

[2209]

7   FORFEITURE[181]

If and whenever during the Term —

7.1   the Lease Rents[182], or any of them or any part of them, or any VAT payable on them, are outstanding for *(state period, eg 14 days)* after becoming due, whether formally demanded or not[183], or

7.2   the Tenant [or the Guarantor] breaches any covenant or other term of this Lease, or

7.3   the Tenant [or the Guarantor][184], being an individual, becomes subject to a bankruptcy order[185] [or has an interim receiver appointed to his property][186], or

7.4   the Tenant [or the Guarantor][187], being a company, enters into liquidation[188] whether compulsory or voluntary — but not if the liquidation is for amalgamation or reconstruction of a solvent company — [or enters into administration][189] [or has a receiver appointed over all or any part of its assets][190], or

7.5   the Tenant [or the Guarantor][191] enters into or makes a proposal to enter into any voluntary arrangement pursuant to the Insolvency Act 1986[192] or any other arrangement or composition for the benefit of his creditors, or

7.6   the Tenant has any distress, sequestration or execution levied on his goods

and, where the Tenant [or the Guarantor] is more than one person, if and whenever any of the events referred to in this clause happens to any one or more of them, the Landlord may at any time re-enter the Premises or any part of them in the name of the whole — even if any previous right of re-entry has been waived[193] — and thereupon the Term is to cease absolutely but without prejudice to any rights or remedies that may have accrued to the Landlord against the Tenant or the Guarantor [or to the Tenant against the Landlord] in respect of any breach of covenant or other term of this Lease, including the breach in respect of which the re-entry is made.

[2210]

181   As to forfeiture generally see vol 22(1) (2003 Reissue) LANDLORD AND TENANT (BUSINESS TENANCIES) Paragraph 283 [1171] et seq.

       The precise range of insolvency-related circumstances that will trigger the proviso should be carefully considered. Tenants should note that their inclusion, in practice, means that the lease cannot be used as security for a loan. Landlords generally seek to have the ability to forfeit in the widest range of circumstances. It should, however, be noted that, in certain circumstances, leave of the court or of the insolvency practitioner administering the procedure may be required before any contractual right can be exercised: see eg, in respect of administration, the Insolvency Act 1986 Sch 1B para 43(4), (6) as inserted by the Enterprise Act 2002 s 248 (4 Halsbury's Statutes (4th Edn) BANKRUPTCY AND INSOLVENCY).

       The identity and character of the tenant may be of particular importance to the landlord in a lease such as this. In these circumstances, the draftsman may wish to consider including a provision providing for forfeiture if changes are made in the ownership profile of a tenant company. For an example of a provision of this nature see vol 22(3) (1997 Reissue) LANDLORD AND TENANT (BUSINESS TENANCIES. If the identity and character of the tenant are crucial, the draftsman may also wish to consider seeking to force the tenant to offer the lease back to the landlord before alienation and requiring consent to any change in control of a tenant company: see note 75 to clause 3.9.1 [2161] ALIENATION PROHIBITED.

       For a provision triggering forfeiture in the event of the existence of any licences for the sale of alcohol etc being compromised or potentially compromised see vol 24(2) (2002 Reissue) Form 56.

182   As to the definition of 'the Lease Rents' see clause 1.32 [2118] 'THE RENT'.

183   The words 'whether formally demanded or not' should be used to avoid the common law requirement that an actual demand has to be made.

184   The lease may provide for a right of re-entry on insolvency of the guarantor or a tenant's covenant to find an acceptable replacement (see clause 3.23 [2180] REPLACEMENT GUARANTOR) or both.

185   As to bankruptcy generally see the Insolvency Act 1986 Pt IX (ss 264–371).

186   As to interim receivers see the Insolvency Act 1986 s 286.

187   See note 184 above.

188   As to liquidation generally see the Insolvency Act 1986 Pts IV–VI (ss 73–246).

189   As to administration generally see the Insolvency Act 1986 Pt II as substituted by the Enterprise Act 2002 s 248. The tenant may seek to argue that if the administrator pays rent and if there are no other material breaches of the lease the landlord should not be entitled to forfeit the lease on this ground.

190   The tenant may seek to argue that if the receiver pays rent and if there are no other material breaches of the lease the landlord should not be entitled to forfeit the lease on this ground.

191   See note 184 above.

192   As to company voluntary arrangements see the Insolvency Act 1986 Pt I (ss 1–7B) as amended by the Insolvency Act 2000. As to individual voluntary arrangements see the Insolvency Act 1986 Pt VIII (ss 252–263G) as amended by the Enterprise Act 2002 s 264.

193   The landlord has the option whether to take advantage of a right of forfeiture or not. If he elects not to do so , the forfeiture is waived. The election may be express or implied, eg if the landlord does any act by which he recognises that the relationship of landlord and tenant is still continuing after the event of forfeiture has come to his knowledge.

[2211]

8   MISCELLANEOUS

8.1   Exclusion of warranty as to use

Nothing in this Lease or in any consent granted by the Landlord under this Lease is to imply or warrant that the Premises may lawfully be used under the Planning Acts as a hotel[194].

194   See *Laurence v Lexcourt Holdings Ltd* [1978] 2 All ER 810, [1978] 1 WLR 1128; *Collins v Howell-Jones* [1981] 2 EGLR 108, 259 Estates Gazette 331, CA and the comments of Eveleigh LJ on estate agents' particulars relating to use in *Bovis Group Pension Fund Ltd v GC Flooring & Furnishing Ltd* (1984) 269 Estates Gazette 1252 at 1253, CA.

8.2   Exclusion of third party rights

Nothing in this Lease is intended to confer any benefit on any person who is not a party to it[195].

195   By virtue of the Contracts (Rights of Third Parties) Act 1999 (11 Halsbury's Statutes (4th Edn) CONTRACT) third-party rights may be conferred where they are not clearly excluded. This being so, it is advisable to incorporate a specific exclusion except where the parties actually intend to confer rights of action on a third party. In the standard letting situation it is unlikely that the parties will wish to extend liability in this manner. As to the Contracts (Rights of Third Parties) Act 1999 generally see vol 4(3) (2001 Reissue) BOILERPLATE CLAUSES.

8.3   Representations

The Tenant acknowledges that this Lease has not been entered into in reliance wholly or partly on any statement or representation made by or on behalf of the Landlord except any such statement or representation expressly set out in this Lease[196] [or made by the Landlord's solicitors in any written response to enquiries raised by the Tenant's solicitors in connection with the grant of this Lease].

196   See the comments of Eveleigh LJ on estate agents' particulars relating to use in *Bovis Group Pension Fund Ltd v GC Flooring & Furnishing Ltd* (1984) 269 Estates Gazette 1252 at 1253, CA. For an alternative provision see vol 22(4) (1997 Reissue) LANDLORD AND TENANT (BUSINESS TENANCIES) Form 400 clauses 7.1 [7520], 7.2 [7521].

[2212]

8.4   Documents under hand

While the Landlord is a limited company or other corporation, any licence, consent, approval or notice required to be given by the Landlord is to be sufficiently given if given under the hand of a director, the secretary or other duly authorised officer of the Landlord [or by the Surveyor on behalf of the Landlord].

8.5   Tenant's property

If, after the Tenant has vacated the Premises at the end of the Term, any property of his remains in or on the Premises and he fails to remove it within *(state period, eg 7 days)* after a written request from the Landlord to do so, or, if the Landlord is unable to make such a request to the Tenant, within *(state period, eg 14 days)* from the first attempt to make it, then the Landlord may, as the agent of the Tenant, sell that property. The Tenant must indemnify the Landlord against any liability incurred by the Landlord to any third party whose property is sold by him in the mistaken belief held in good faith — which is to be presumed unless the contrary is proved — that the property belonged to the Tenant. If, having made reasonable efforts to do so, the Landlord is unable to locate the Tenant, then the Landlord may retain the proceeds of sale absolutely unless the Tenant claims them within *(state period, eg 6 months)* of the date upon which he vacated the Premises. The Tenant must indemnify the Landlord against any damage occasioned to the Premises and any losses caused by or related to the presence of the property in or on the Premises.

8.6   Compensation on vacating excluded

Any statutory right of the Tenant to claim compensation from the Landlord on vacating the Premises is excluded to the extent that the law allows[197].

197   As to compensation where an order for a new tenancy is precluded on certain grounds see the Landlord and Tenant Act 1954 s 37 as amended by the Local Government and Housing Act 1989 s 149, Sch 7 and by SI 2003/3096.
        As to the effectiveness of provisions of this nature see vol 22(1) (2003 Reissue) LANDLORD AND TENANT (BUSINESS TENANCIES) Paragraph 468 [3079].

[2213]

8.7   Notices

8.7.1   *Form and service of notices*

A notice under this Lease must be in writing and, unless the receiving party or his authorised agent acknowledges receipt, is valid if, and only if[198] —

8.7.1.1   it is given by hand, sent by registered post or recorded delivery, or sent by fax[199] provided that a confirmatory copy is given by hand or sent by registered post or recorded delivery on the same day, and

8.7.1.2   it is served —

(a)   where the receiving party is a company incorporated within Great Britain, at the registered office,

(b)   where the receiving party is the Tenant and the Tenant is not such a company, at the Premises, and

(c)   where the receiving party is the Landlord [or the Guarantor] and [the Landlord *(or as required)* that party] is not such a company, at [the Landlord's *(or as required)* that party's] address shown in this Lease or at any address specified in a notice given by [the Landlord to the Tenant *(or as required)* that party to the other parties].

---

198   Notice clauses are either mandatory or permissive. The words 'and only if' are inserted to make it clear that this clause is mandatory.

197   As to service by fax see *Hastie and Jenkerson v McMahon* [1991] 1 All ER 255, [1990] 1 WLR 1575, CA.

8.7.2   *Deemed delivery*[200]

8.7.2.1   **By registered post or recorded delivery**

Unless it is returned through the Royal Mail undelivered, a notice sent by registered post or recorded delivery is to be treated as served on the third working day after posting whenever and whether or not it is received.

8.7.2.2   **By fax**

A notice sent by fax is to be treated as served on the day upon which it is sent, or the next working day where the fax is sent after 1600 hours or on a day that is not a working day, whenever and whether or not it or the confirmatory copy is received unless the confirmatory copy is returned through the Royal Mail undelivered.

8.7.2.3   **'A working day'**

References to 'a working day' are references to a day when the United Kingdom clearing banks are open for business in the City of London.

---

200   It is a fundamental aspect of any notice clause to specify the circumstances in which the server, provided he has complied with the requirements of the clause, has for the purposes of the document served a notice, even if the recipient claims that he never received it.

8.7.3   *Joint recipients*

If the receiving party consists of more than one person, a notice to one of them is notice to all.

[2214]

8.8   [New *(or)* Old] lease

[This Lease [is *(or as appropriate)* is not] a new tenancy for the purposes of the 1995 Act Section 1. *(or as appropriate)* This Lease is granted under the 1995 Act Section 19 and [is *(or as appropriate)* is not] a new tenancy for the purposes of Section 1 of that Act]²⁰¹.

200   A tenancy granted on or after 1 January 1996 that is an overriding lease is not a 'new' tenancy where the tenancy being overridden is one granted before that date: see the Landlord and Tenant (Covenants) Act 1995 ss 1(4), 20(1). Where the lease being granted is an overriding lease, the lease must include a statement that it is an overriding lease and indicate whether the overriding lease is or is not a 'new' tenancy: see the Landlord and Tenant (Covenants) Act 1995 s 20(2). In these circumstances the second alternative should be used.

[8.9   Capacity of tenants

It is declared that the persons comprising the Tenant hold the Premises as [joint tenants *(or as required)* tenants in common].]

[8.10   Exclusion of the 1954 Act Sections 24–28²⁰²

8.10.1   *Notice and declaration*

On *(date)* the Landlord served notice on the Tenant pursuant to the provisions of the 1954 Act Section 38A(3) as inserted by the Regulatory Reform (Business Tenancies) (England and Wales) Order 2003 and on *(date)* the Tenant made a [simple *(or as appropriate)* statutory] declaration pursuant to schedule 2 of the Regulatory Reform (Business Tenancies) (England and Wales) Order 2003.

8.10.2   *Agreement to exclude*

Pursuant to the provisions of the 1954 Act Section 38A(1) as inserted by the Regulatory Reform (Business Tenancies) (England and Wales) Order 2003, the parties agree that the provisions of the 1954 Act Sections 24–28 inclusive are to be excluded in relation to the tenancy created by this Lease.]

202   As to contracting out of the Landlord and Tenant Act 1954 and the requirements that need to be complied with see vol 22(1) (2003 Reissue) LANDLORD AND TENANT (BUSINESS TENANCIES) Paragraph 431 [2035].

(include other clauses as required: eg, break clauses and options (see vol 22(3) (1997 Reissue) LANDLORD AND TENANT (BUSINESS TENANCIES) Forms 136 [6544]–142 [6569]) or a proviso as to termination on rent review (see vol 22(3) (1997 Reissue) LANDLORD AND TENANT (BUSINESS TENANCIES) Form 143 [6570]))

IN WITNESS etc *(see vol 12(2) (2003 Reissue) DEEDS, AGREEMENTS ETC)*

[2215]

SCHEDULE 1: THE RIGHTS RESERVED[203]

1-1   Right of entry to inspect

The right to enter[204], or in emergency to break into and enter, the Premises at any time during the Term [at reasonable times and upon reasonable notice except in emergency] to inspect them, to take schedules or inventories of fixtures and other items to be yielded up at the end of the Term, and to exercise any of the rights granted to the Landlord elsewhere in this Lease.

---

203   As to rights reserved see vol 22(1) (2003 Reissue) LANDLORD AND TENANT (BUSINESS TENANCIES) Paragraph 124 [648] et seq.
204   For a covenant by the landlord to make good damage so caused see vol 22(3) (1997 Reissue) LANDLORD AND TENANT (BUSINESS TENANCIES) Form 79 [6453].

1-2   Access on renewal or rent review

[The right to enter the Premises with the Surveyor and the third party determining the Rent under any provisions for rent review contained in this Lease at [any time *(or as required)* convenient hours and on reasonable prior notice] to inspect [and measure] the Premises for all purposes connected with any pending or intended step under the 1954 Act or the implementation of the provisions for rent review. *(or as required in view of the rent review provisions used: see vol 22(3) (1997 Reissue) LANDLORD AND TENANT (BUSINESS TENANCIES) Forms 180 [6711]–194 [6987])*]

SCHEDULE 2: THE RENT AND RENT REVIEW

(insert rent review provisions as required: see vol 22(3) (1997 Reissue) LANDLORD AND TENANT (BUSINESS TENANCIES) Forms 180 [6711]–194 [6987])

[2216]

SCHEDULE 3: THE HOTEL COVENANTS

3-1   Use

3-1.1   *Hotel use*

The Tenant must not use the Premises otherwise than as a high class hotel.

3-1.2   *Opening period*

The Tenant must keep the Premises open for business [at least during the months of *(state months, eg April to October inclusive)* in every year].

3-1.3   *Sleeping accommodation*

While the Premises are open for business, the Tenant must offer sleeping accommodation consisting wholly or mainly of bedrooms available to the public generally.

3-1.4   *Restriction on stay*

The Tenant must not permit any person, except staff employed in the Premises, to occupy any bedroom for more than *(state period, eg 1 month)*.

3-1.5   *Services*

The Tenant must provide services for guests, including providing breakfast and an evening meal, making beds and cleaning rooms.

[2217]

3-1.6   *Application for justices licence*[205]

The Tenant must apply to the licensing justices for, and use his best endeavours to obtain, the grant or renewal of any justices' licence necessary for the Premises to be used as a fully licensed hotel ('the Licence'), and must pay all fees and duties in relation to it.

205   For alternative provisions regarding licences that could be adapted for use with this form see vol 24(2) (2002 Reissue) Form 56.

3-1.7   *Protection of the Licence*

The Tenant must not do or omit to do on the Premises anything as a result of which the Licence may be forfeit, suspended or otherwise imperilled.

3-1.8   *Maintenance and renewal of the Licence*

The Tenant must do everything necessary to maintain and from time to time renew the Licence, and must not do anything that might prejudice the future grant or renewal of the Licence, whether to the Tenant or any future occupier of the Premises, and must comply with all requirements and recommendations of the licensing justices.

3-1.9   *Justices consent to alterations*

The Tenant must not make any alteration to the Premises without the consent — when required — of the licensing justices.

3-1.10   *Gardens*

The Tenant must cultivate and maintain the gardens and grounds forming part of the Premises and keep them properly planted with healthy plants.

3-1.11   *Car park*

The Tenant must keep the car park of the Premises adequately surfaced, free from weeds and in good condition, and must not place upon it any materials, equipment, receptacle for refuse or waste or any other item that is unsightly.

3-2   Environmental protection

The Tenant must not permit any oil or grease or any deleterious, objectionable, dangerous, poisonous or explosive matter or substance to be discharged into any of the Conduits, and must take all [reasonable] measures to ensure that any effluent discharged into the Conduits does not harm the environment or corrode or otherwise harm the Conduits or cause obstruction or deposit in them. [The Tenant must comply with the provisions of the Clean Air Act 1993 and with the requirements of any notice served under it by the relevant authority or body].

[2218]

3-3   Ceiling and floor loading

3-3.1   *Heavy items*

The Tenant must not bring into or permit to remain in any building on the Premises any safes, machinery, goods or other articles that will or may strain or damage the building or any part of it.

3-3.2   *Suspension from ceiling*

The Tenant must not, without the consent of the Landlord, suspend anything from any ceiling of any building on the Premises.

3-3.3   *Expert advice*

If the Tenant applies for the Landlord's consent under paragraph 3-3.2 SUSPENSION FROM CEILING the Landlord may consult any engineer or other person in relation to the ceiling loading proposed by the Tenant, and the Tenant must repay the fees of the engineer or other person to the Landlord on demand.

3-4   Machinery

3-4.1   *Noisy machinery*

The Tenant must not install or use in or on the Premises any machinery or apparatus [other than usual hotel machinery] that causes noise or vibration that can be heard or felt in nearby premises or outside the Premises or that may cause structural damage.

3-4.2   *Maintenance and use of machinery*

3-4.2.1   **Maintenance of machinery**

The Tenant must keep all machinery and equipment on the Premises ('the Machinery') properly maintained and in good working order, and for that purpose must employ reputable contractors [to be approved by the Landlord[, whose approval may not be unreasonably refused [or delayed],]] ('the Contractors') to carry out regular, periodic inspection and maintenance of the Machinery.

3-4.2.2   **Renewal of parts**

The Tenant must renew all working and other parts of the Machinery as and when necessary or when recommended by the Contractors.

3-4.2.3   **Operation**

The Tenant must ensure by directions to his staff and otherwise that the Machinery is properly operated.

[2219]

3-5   Signs and name

3-5.1   *Signs*

The Tenant must at all times display and maintain at a point to be approved by the Landlord[, whose approval may not be unreasonably withheld [or delayed]], a suitable sign, of a size and kind first approved by the Landlord, showing the name of the hotel.

3-5.2   *Hotel name*

The Tenant must call the hotel only by a name that has been approved by the Landlord[, whose approval may not be unreasonably withheld [or delayed]].

SCHEDULE 4: THE SUBJECTIONS

(insert details)

SCHEDULE 5: THE AUTHORISED GUARANTEE AGREEMENT

(insert the form of authorised guarantee agreement: see, eg vol 22(3) (1997 Reissue) LANDLORD AND TENANT (BUSINESS TENANCIES) Form 217 [7053])

(signature (or common seal) of landlord: lease)
(signature (or common seal) of tenant (and guarantor): counterpart)
(signatures of witnesses)
[2220]–[2300]

5: CAR PARKS

14

Lease of land for use as a commercial car park[1]

CONTENTS

(NB: numbers in [ ] below refer to this volume and should be altered to suit the page or reference numbers actually used)

1 DEFINITIONS AND INTERPRETATION
1.1 'The [Contractual] Term' .... [2308]
1.2 'Development' .... [2309]
1.3 Gender and number .... [2309]
1.4 Headings .... [2309]
1.5 'Interest' .... [2309]
1.6 'The Interest Rate' .... [2310]
1.7 Interpretation of 'consent' and 'approved' .... [2310]
1.8 Interpretation of 'the Landlord' .... [2311]
[2301]

1.9 Interpretation of 'the last year of the Term' and 'the end of the Term' . . . . [2311]
1.10 Interpretation of 'the Tenant' . . . . [2311]
1.11 Interpretation of 'this Lease' . . . . [2311]
1.12 Joint and several liability . . . . [2311]
1.13 'The Liability Period' . . . . [2312]
1.14 'Losses' . . . . [2313]
1.15 'The 1954 Act' . . . . [2313]
1.16 'The 1995 Act' . . . . [2313]
1.17 Obligation not to permit or suffer . . . . [2313]
1.18 'The Plan' . . . . [2313]
1.19 'The Planning Acts' . . . . [2313]
1.20 'The Premises' . . . . [2314]
1.21 References to clauses and schedules . . . . [2314]
1.22 References to rights of access . . . . [2314]
1.23 References to statutes . . . . [2314]
1.24 'The Rent' . . . . [2314]
1.25 'The Surveyor'. . . . . [2315]
[1.26 'The Term' . . . . [2315]]
1.27 Terms from the 1995 Act . . . . [2315]
1.28 'VAT' . . . . [2315]

2 DEMISE . . . . [2331]
                                                                              [2302]

3 THE TENANT'S COVENANTS

3.1 Rent . . . . [2332]
[3.2 Outgoings and VAT . . . . [2333]]
3.3 Repair and cleaning . . . . [2334]
3.4 Waste and alterations . . . . [2335]
3.5 Aerials, signs and advertisements . . . . [2336]
3.6 Statutory obligations . . . . [2336]
3.7 Use . . . . [2337]
3.8 Entry to inspect and notice to repair . . . . [2338]
3.9 Alienation . . . . [2340]
3.10 Costs of applications, notices and recovery of arrears . . . . [2347]
3.11 Planning . . . . [2347]
3.12 Indemnities . . . . [2348]
3.13 Reletting boards and viewing . . . . [2348]
3.14 Encroachments . . . . [2349]
3.15 Yielding up . . . . [2349]
3.16 Interest on arrears . . . . [2349]
3.17 Statutory notices . . . . [2350]
[3.18 Keyholders . . . . [2350]]
3.19 Viewing on sale of reversion . . . . [2350]
3.20 Defective premises . . . . [2350]
3.21 Exercise of the Landlord's rights . . . . [2350]
3.22 Costs of grant of this Lease . . . . [2351]
3.23 Consent to the Landlord's release . . . . [2351]

4 QUIET ENJOYMENT . . . . [2361]
                                                                              [2303]

5 INSURANCE

5.1 Definitions . . . . [2362]
5.2 Covenant to insure . . . . [2363]
5.3 Tenant's further insurance covenants . . . . [2364]
5.4 Reinstatement . . . . [2365]

6 FORFEITURE . . . . [2366]

7 MISCELLANEOUS

7.1 Exclusion of warranty as to use . . . . [2368]
7.2 Exclusion of third party rights . . . . [2368]
7.3 Representations . . . . [2368]
7.4 Documents under hand . . . . [2369]
7.5 Tenant's property . . . . [2369]
7.6 Compensation on vacating excluded . . . . [2369]
7.7 Notices . . . . [2370]
7.8 [New (or) Old] lease . . . . [2371]
[7.9 Capacity of tenants . . . . [2371]]
[7.10 Exclusion of the 1954 Act Sections 24–28 . . . . [2371]]

SCHEDULE 1: THE AUTHORISED GUARANTEE AGREEMENT

SCHEDULE 2: THE GUARANTEE PROVISIONS

[2304]

AGREEMENT

[HM LAND REGISTRY

LAND REGISTRATION ACT 2002

Administrative area	*(insert details)*
Title number out of which lease is granted	*(title number)*
Property let	*(postal address or description)*]

[2305]

THIS LEASE is made the .... day of .... BETWEEN:

(1)   *(name of landlord)* [of *(address etc)* *(or as appropriate)* the registered office of which is at *(address)*] [Company Registration no ...][2] ('the Landlord') and

(2)   *(name of tenant)* [of *(address etc)* *(or as appropriate)* being a company registered in [England and Wales *(or)* Scotland][3] the registered office of which is at *(address)*] [Company Registration no ...] ('the Tenant')

[2306]

1   As to stamp duty land tax see the Information Binder: Stamp Duty Land Tax [1].

    As to Land Registry Fees see the Information Binder: Property [1]: Property Fees.

    On the grant out of an unregistered freehold estate in land of a lease for a term of more than seven years from the date of the grant, application must be made to register the title to the leasehold interest granted: see the Land Registration Act 2002 s 4(1)(c) (37 Halsbury's Statutes (4th Edn) REAL PROPERTY). The tenant must obtain an epitome of title to the freehold reversion, investigate it, and mark it as examined, otherwise he will not be able to be registered with an absolute title: see vol 25(1) (2003 Reissue) LAND REGISTRATION Paragraph 21.1 [132].

    If the freehold reversion is registered, the grant of a lease for a term of more than seven years from the date of the grant must be completed by registration: see the Land Registration Act 2002 s 27(2)(b)(i).

    As to the form and contents of leases see vol 22(1) (2003 Reissue) LANDLORD AND TENANT (BUSINESS TENANCIES) Paragraph 104 [601] et seq. As to registered land generally see vol 25(1) (2003 Reissue) LAND REGISTRATION. As to registration of title to leases see vol 25(1) (2003 Reissue) LAND REGISTRATION Paragraph 143 [601] et seq.

    This is a lease of premises comprising a car park with no buildings erected on it although the tenant is obliged to erect a hut or shed for the use of his attendants. The tenant is to insure. There are no provisions for a rent review or a guarantor. It is assumed that the demised premises directly abut the public highway and that the tenant requires no right of way. If the tenant requires a right of way see Form 5 paragraph 1-1 [501] RIGHT OF WAY. If the landlord owns adjoining property the demise should be amended and rights should be reserved: see Form 5 [351].

2   If any party is a company it is desirable to include the company registration number. This avoids any problems arising when a company has been wound up and a new company formed with the same name, or when the name of a company is changed, or if companies swap names, eg on a reconstruction of a group of companies. In addition, where a company applies to be registered as proprietor of a registered estate or registered charge, the application must state the company's registration number: see the Land Registration Rules 2003, SI 2003/1417 r 181.

3   Where the tenant is a company registered in England and Wales or Scotland, and the lease is registrable, an application for first registration of the lease (where the landlord's title is unregistered), or registration of the lease as a registrable disposition (where the landlord's title is registered), and the tenant as proprietor of the leasehold title, must state the company's registered number: see SI 2003/1417 r 181(1). There seems to be no reason why the certificate and statement should not be contained in the disposition in favour of the proprietor, where convenient.

[2307]

NOW THIS DEED WITNESSES as follows:

1   DEFINITIONS AND INTERPRETATION

For all purposes of this Lease[4] the terms defined in this clause have the meanings specified.

4   One view would add 'unless the context otherwise requires' or 'where the context so admits' and in fact this may be implied (see *Meux v Jacobs* (1875) LR 7 HL 481 at 493; *Law Society v United Service Bureau Ltd* [1934] 1 KB 343, DC) but the better course is to use defined terms in such a way that there are no circumstances where the defined meaning does not apply.

1.1   'The [Contractual] Term'[5]

'The [Contractual][6] Term' means *(insert number)* years commencing on and including *(date of commencement of term)*[7].

5   As to the commencement of the term see vol 22(1) (2003 Reissue) LANDLORD AND TENANT (BUSINESS TENANCIES) Paragraph 135 [670].

    As to registration see note 1 above. Where the landlord's title is unregistered, the grantee must apply for registration within a period of two months from the date of the disposition if the lease is granted for a term of more than seven years. If no such application is made the disposition becomes void as regards any transfer, grant or creation of a legal estate: see the Land Registration Act 2002 s 6. Where the landlord's title is registered and the lease is for a term of more than seven years, the tenant should protect the intended lease by applying for an official search, and an application to register the lease should be made before expiry of the search, otherwise the lease will be susceptible to loss of priority: see the Land Registration Act 2002 s 27.

6   The demise in this lease is for 'the Contractual Term', which is defined as a fixed term of years. The expression 'the Term', as defined in clause 1.26 [2315] 'THE TERM', is used in covenants so that they continue to apply during any period of holding over or continuance or extension of the contractual term. Some difficulties arise if this structure is used in a draft lease where security of tenure is to be excluded under the Landlord and Tenant Act 1954 s 38A(1) as inserted by SI 2003/3096 (23 Halsbury's Statutes (4th Edn) LANDLORD AND TENANT). The demise is for the contractual term and the inclusion of the definition of 'the Term' does not prevent the lease being 'for a term of years certain' as required by the Landlord and Tenant Act 1954 s 38A(1). However, reference to continuance of the contractual term by statute is inappropriate where the operation of the security of tenure provisions in the Landlord and Tenant Act 1954 ss 24–28 is to be excluded. If a lease is contracted out of the Landlord and Tenant Act 1954 there can be no statutory extension, and if the tenant remains in occupation at the end of the contractual term he is holding over unlawfully unless there is an express agreement to extend the contractual term operating as a surrender and re-grant so that the original lease — and the agreement under the Landlord and Tenant Act 1954 s 38A(1) — has no further effect. It is suggested that in these circumstances the drafting should be simplified to include a single term (defined simply as 'the Term') by reference to the period of the contractual term. This can be achieved by amending this clause in the manner suggested and substituting it for clause 1.26 [2315] 'THE TERM'.

7   For estate management reasons it is usually desirable to insert a quarter day here — or a rent day when rent is due on days other than quarter days — ie generally the one preceding the earlier of the date of possession and the date of execution.

[2308]

1.2 'Development'

References to 'development' are references to development as defined by the Town and Country Planning Act 1990 Section 55.

1.3 Gender and number

Words importing one gender include all other genders; words importing the singular include the plural and vice versa[8].

8   See the Law of Property Act 1925 s 61 (37 Halsbury's Statutes (4th Edn) REAL PROPERTY).

1.4 Headings[9]

The clause, paragraph and schedule headings and the table of contents do not form part of this document and are not to be taken into account in its construction or interpretation. *(amend if marginal notes are used instead of headings)*

9   Headings and marginal notes require the draftsman to provide a word or two to describe every clause in the lease. This is not always easy and there are times when the draftsman will have to settle for something less than perfection, the only alternative being a heading or note that would be inappropriately long. It would be quite wrong for that title, which its author might admit was not totally apposite but was the best that he could do in a few words, to be used in construing the clause in question.

1.5 'Interest'

References to 'interest' are references to interest payable during the period from the date on which the payment is due to the date of payment, both before and after any judgment, at the Interest Rate then prevailing [*(where the interest rate is defined by reference to a bank base rate)* or, should the base rate referred to in clause 1.6 'THE INTEREST RATE' cease to exist[10], at another rate of interest closely comparable with the Interest Rate [to be agreed between the parties or in default of agreement to be determined by [the Surveyor, acting as an expert and not as an arbitrator *(or as required)* a chartered accountant appointed by agreement between the parties or in default of agreement nominated by the President of the Institute of Chartered Accountants in England and Wales, acting as an expert and not as an arbitrator][11] *(or as required)* decided on by the Landlord acting reasonably]].

10   If base rates are referred to, the possibility of their ceasing to exist should be provided for. Alternatively, the Law Society's interest rate may be specified.

11   This provision may be expanded to provide for deeming the parties to have disagreed after a certain time, deputy appointors etc.

[2309]

1.6 'The Interest Rate'

'The Interest Rate'[12] means the rate of ...% a year[13] above [the base lending rate of *(specify bank)* or such other bank [being a member of the British Bankers Association] as the Landlord may from time to time nominate in writing[14] *(or as required)* the Law Society's interest rate[15]].

12   As to the covenant to pay interest see vol 22(1) (2003 Reissue) LANDLORD AND TENANT (BUSINESS TENANCIES) Paragraph 154 [767].

13   Words such as 'with a minimum of ...%' should not be used because if interest rates drop during the term to such an extent that the minimum rate specified represents significantly more than a few percent over the basic borrowing rate, the provision might be void as a penalty. As to what amounts to a penalty see *Dunlop Pneumatic Tyre Co Ltd v New Garage and Motor Co Ltd* [1915] AC 79, HL; *Cellulose Acetate Silk Co Ltd v Widnes Foundry (1925) Ltd* [1933] AC 20, HL. In view of this, landlords would be unwise to provide for a rate of more than a few percent over base rate, and even this is in fact a penalty and should be resisted by the tenant.

14   The chance to change the bank may be useful, especially on a sale of the reversion, so that the landlord can always provide for his bank for the time being to be specified, but the tenant should try to limit the choice to major clearing banks.

15   The Law Society's interest rate is published weekly in the Law Society's Gazette.

1.7 Interpretation of 'consent' and 'approved'

1.7.1 *Prior written consent or approval*

References to 'consent of the Landlord' or words to similar effect are references to a prior written consent signed by or on behalf of the Landlord and references to the need for anything to be 'approved by the Landlord' or words to similar effect are references to the need for a prior written approval by or on behalf of the Landlord.

1.7.2 *Consent or approval of mortgagee or head landlord*

Any provisions in this Lease referring to the consent or approval of the Landlord are to be construed as also requiring the consent or approval of any mortgagee of the Premises and any head landlord, where that consent is required [under a mortgage or headlease in existence at the date of this lease][16]. Nothing in this Lease is to be construed as imposing any obligation on a mortgagee or head landlord not to refuse any such consent or approval unreasonably.

16   The tenant should include these words so that the clause applies *only* where the consent of the mortgagee or head landlord is in fact required under the terms of an *existing* mortgage or headlease. The tenant should request a copy of the document concerned to establish the rights of the mortgagee or head landlord in relation to any consents that he may seek. The risk to the tenant of the clause as drafted is that, by subsequently creating a mortgage or headlease, the landlord could, innocently or deliberately, bring about a situation where a consent may be refused in circumstances in which it would otherwise have been unreasonable to do so. In particular, the effect on the tenant's ability to assign or sublet could be serious.

[2310]

1.8 Interpretation of 'the Landlord'

The expression 'the Landlord' includes the person or persons from time to time entitled to possession of the Premises when this Lease comes to an end.

1.9 Interpretation of 'the last year of the Term' and 'the end of the Term'

References to 'the last year of the Term' are references to the actual last year of the Term howsoever it determines, and references to the 'end of the Term' are references to the end of the Term whensoever and howsoever it determines.

1.10   Interpretation of 'the Tenant'

'The Tenant' includes any person who is for the time being bound by the tenant covenants of this Lease except where the name of *(name of original tenant)* appears.

1.11   Interpretation of 'this Lease'

Unless expressly stated to the contrary, the expression 'this Lease' includes any document supplemental to or collateral with this document or entered into in accordance with this document.

1.12   Joint and several liability

Where any party to this Lease for the time being comprises two or more persons, obligations expressed or implied to be made by or with that party are deemed to be made by or with the persons comprising that party jointly and severally.

[2311]

1.13   'The Liability Period'[17]

'The Liability Period' means —

[1.13.1   in the case of *(name of guarantor for the original tenant)*, the period during which *(name of original tenant)* is bound by the tenant covenants of this Lease together with any additional period during which *(name of original tenant)* is liable under an authorised guarantee agreement,] *(omit if there is no guarantor for the original tenant)*

1.13.2   in the case of any guarantor required pursuant to clause 3.9.5.2 CONDITIONS, the period during which the relevant assignee is bound by the tenant covenants of this Lease together with any additional period during which that assignee is liable under an authorised guarantee agreement, and

1.13.3   in the case of any guarantor under an authorised guarantee agreement, the period during which the relevant assignee is bound by the tenant covenants of this Lease.

---

17   The liability of the guarantor should be expressed to last while the original tenant, or as the case may be the assignee, is bound by the tenant covenants in the lease rather than while the lease is vested in that person, to take account of the possibility of an excluded assignment being made and the tenant remaining liable. An excluded assignment means that the tenant is precluded from tenant release under the Landlord and Tenant (Covenants) Act 1995 (23 Halsbury's Statutes (4th Edn) LANDLORD AND TENANT).

The Landlord and Tenant (Covenants) Act 1995 does not clearly indicate whether the liability of a contractual guarantor can be expressed to extend to any period during which the tenant is bound by an authorised guarantee agreement, but the better view is that it is possible. The policy of the Act certainly suggests that this should be the case.

1.14   'Losses'

References to 'losses' are references to liabilities, damages or losses, awards of damages or compensation, penalties, costs, disbursements and expenses arising from any claim, demand, action or proceedings.

[2312]

1.15 'The 1954 Act'

'The 1954 Act' means the Landlord and Tenant Act 1954 [and all statutes, regulations and orders included by virtue of clause 1.23 REFERENCES TO STATUTES][18].

18   The words in square brackets are strictly speaking not required because they merely state what would be the case anyway by virtue of clause 1.23 [2314] REFERENCES TO STATUTES. Nevertheless, as much could turn on the point (see *Brett v Brett Essex Golf Club Ltd* (1986) 52 P & CR 330, [1986] 1 EGLR 154, CA), the parties may prefer to deal expressly with the point.

1.16 'The 1995 Act'

'The 1995 Act' means the Landlord and Tenant (Covenants) Act 1995 [and all statutes, regulations and orders include by virtue of clause 1.23 REFERENCES TO STATUTES][19].

19   See note 18 to clause 1.15 [2313] 'THE 1954 ACT'.

1.17   Obligation not to permit or suffer

Any covenant by the Tenant not to do anything includes an obligation [to use reasonable endeavours] not to permit or suffer[20] that thing to be done by another person [where the Tenant is aware that the thing is being done].

20   'Permit' may have a different meaning from 'suffer': see *Barton v Reed* [1932] 1 Ch 362 at 375 per Luxmore J. A covenant not to 'permit' activity is broken if the covenantor himself carries it on: see *Oceanic Village Ltd v United Attractions Ltd* [2000] Ch 234, [2000] 1 All ER 975.

1.18   'The Plan'[21]

'The Plan' means the plan annexed to this Lease.

21   As to the use and role of plans see vol 22(1) (2003 Reissue) LANDLORD AND TENANT (BUSINESS TENANCIES) Paragraphs 117 [636], 118 [638]. A plan may not always be required, eg a demise of all the land within a registered title. If the lease is registrable, a plan 'for identification purposes only' or where there is some other disclaimer as to the extent to which it can be relied on for conveyancing purposes is not sufficient if part of the land in a registered title is being dealt with.

1.19   'The Planning Acts'

'The Planning Acts' means the Town and Country Planning Act 1990, the Planning (Listed Buildings and Conservation Areas) Act 1990, the Planning (Consequential Provisions) Act 1990, the Planning (Hazardous Substances) Act 1990, the Planning and Compensation Act 1991, the Planning and Compulsory Purchase Act 2004 [and all statutes, regulations and orders included by virtue of clause 1.23 REFERENCES TO STATUTES][22].

22   See note 18 to clause 1.15 [2313] 'THE 1954 ACT'.

[2313]

1.20   'The Premises'[23]

'The Premises' means the land known as *(insert name or brief description)* [shown [for the purposes of identification only] edged *(state colour, eg red)* on the Plan.

23   As to parcels generally see vol 22(1) (2003 Reissue) LANDLORD AND TENANT (BUSINESS TENANCIES) Paragraph 116 [634].

1.21   References to clauses and schedules

Any reference in this document to a clause, paragraph or schedule without further designation is to be construed as a reference to the clause, paragraph or schedule of this document so numbered.

1.22 References to rights of access

References to any right of the Landlord to have access to the Premises are to be construed as extending to any head landlord and any mortgagee of the Premises [— where the headlease or mortgage grants such rights of access to the head landlord or mortgagee —] and to all persons authorised in writing by the Landlord and any head landlord or mortgagee, including agents, professional advisers, contractors, workmen and others.

1.23 References to statutes

Unless expressly stated to the contrary any reference to a specific statute includes any statutory extension or modification, amendment or re-enactment of that statute and any regulations or orders made under that statute, and any general reference to a statute includes any regulations or orders made under that statute[24].

24 Unfortunately the Interpretation Act 1978 ss 17, 23(3) (41 Halsbury's Statutes (4th Edn) STATUTES) does not quite go far enough to enable this clause to be dispensed with altogether, particularly where a statute is modified.

1.24 'The Rent'

'The Rent' means the rent of £... a year [together with VAT].

[2314]

1.25 'The Surveyor'[25]

'The Surveyor' means *(name)* or any person or firm appointed by the Landlord in his place. The Surveyor may be an employee of the Landlord or a company that is a member of the same group as the Landlord within the meaning of the 1954 Act Section 42. The expression 'the Surveyor' includes the person or firm appointed by the Landlord to collect the Rent.

25 For a provision that the landlord's surveyor must be a member of a relevant professional body, see vol 22(3) (1997 Reissue) LANDLORD AND TENANT (BUSINESS TENANCIES) Form 152 [6648].

[1.26 'The Term'

'The Term' includes the Contractual Term and any period of holding-over or extension or continuance of the Contractual Term by statute or common law[26].] *(omit if the lease is to be contracted out of the Landlord and Tenant Act 1954)*[27]

26 The demise in this lease is for 'the Contractual Term', which is defined as a fixed term of years. The expression 'the Term' is used in covenants so that they continue to apply during any period of holding-over or continuance or extension of the contractual term.

27 Some difficulties arise if the structure referred to in note 26 above is used in a draft lease where security of tenure is to be excluded under the Landlord and Tenant Act 1954 s 38A(1) as inserted by SI 2003/3096. The demise is for the contractual term and the inclusion of the definition of 'the Term' does not prevent the lease being 'for a term of years certain' as required by the Landlord and Tenant Act 1954 s 38A(1). However, reference to continuance of the contractual term by statute is inappropriate where the operation of the security of tenure provisions in the Landlord and Tenant Act 1954 ss 24–28 is to be excluded. If a lease is contracted out of the Landlord and Tenant Act 1954 there can be no statutory extension, and if the tenant remains in occupation at the end of the contractual term he is holding over unlawfully unless there is an express agreement to extend the contractual term operating as a surrender and re-grant so that the original lease — and the agreement under the Landlord and Tenant Act 1954 s 38A(1) — has no further effect. It is suggested that in these circumstances the drafting should be simplified to include a single term (defined simply as 'the Term') by reference to the period of the contractual term. This can be achieved by amending clause 1.1 [2308] 'THE [CONTRACTUAL] TERM' as suggested and substituting it for this clause.

1.27   Terms from the 1995 Act

Where the expressions 'landlord covenants', 'tenant covenants', or 'authorised guarantee agreement' are used in this Lease they are to have the same meaning as is given by the 1995 Act Section 28(1).

1.28   'VAT'[28]

'VAT' means value added tax or any other tax of a similar nature and unless otherwise expressly stated all references to rents or other sums payable by the Tenant are exclusive of VAT.

28   As to VAT generally see the Information Binder: Property [1]: VAT and Property.

                                                                                       [2315]–[2330]

2   DEMISE

The Landlord lets[29] the Premises to the Tenant [with [full *(or)* limited] title guarantee], to hold the Premises to the Tenant for the [Contractual][30] Term, yielding and paying[31] to the Landlord the Rent payable without any deduction or set-off[32] by equal quarterly payments in advance[33] on the usual quarter days[34] in every year and proportionately for any period of less than a year, the first such payment, being a proportionate sum in respect of the period commencing on *(date)* to and including the day before the next quarter day after that date, to be paid on the date of this document[35].

29   Traditionally, the operative word in a lease executed as a deed was 'demises' but any words sufficient
      to show the parties' intention may be used.
30   See note 27 to clause 1.26 [2315] 'THE TERM'.
31   The words 'yielding and paying' imply a covenant to pay rent: see *Vyvyan v Arthur* (1823) 1 B & C
      410. An express covenant is now invariably included, because further procedural matters are contained
      in it.
32   As to deductions and set off see vol 22(1) (2003 Reissue) LANDLORD AND TENANT (BUSINESS
      TENANCIES) Paragraph 147 [753].
33   In the absence of an express provision, rent is payable in arrears.
34   The usual quarter days are 25 March, 24 June, 29 September and 25 December. A reference to 'the
      usual quarter days' is all that is necessary when rent is to be paid on these days.
35   If the first payment is not a complete instalment, the lease must provide for the date on which it is to
      be paid, the amount, and the period it is to cover.

                                                                                       [2331]

3   THE TENANT'S COVENANTS

The Tenant covenants with the Landlord to observe and perform the requirements of this clause 3.

3.1   Rent

3.1.1   *Payment of the Rent*

The Tenant must pay the Rent on the days and in the manner set out in this Lease and must not exercise or seek to exercise any right or claim to withhold rent or any right or claim to legal or equitable set-off[36] [except that referred to in *(give details of any provisions granting an express right of set-off)*][37].

36   See, eg, *British Anzani (Felixstowe) Ltd v International Marine Management (UK) Ltd* [1980] QB 137,
      [1979] 2 All ER 1063; *Lee-Parker v Izzet* [1971] 3 All ER 1099, [1971] 1 WLR 1688. As to deductions
      and set-off see vol 22(1) (2003 Reissue) LANDLORD AND TENANT (BUSINESS TENANCIES)
      Paragraphs 147 [753], 148 [755].
37   If any express right of set-off is granted to the tenant the point should also be dealt with here to avoid
      inconsistency.

3.1.2   *Payment by banker's order*[38]

If so required in writing by the Landlord, the Tenant must pay the Rent by banker's order or credit transfer to any bank and account [in the United Kingdom] that the Landlord nominates from time to time.

38   This is a clause with dangers for both parties. If the existence of a breach of covenant is known to the landlord he must instruct his bank to refuse to accept the rent, otherwise his right of forfeiture is lost. As to implied waiver of the right of forfeiture see vol 22(1) (2003 Reissue) LANDLORD AND TENANT (BUSINESS TENANCIES) Paragraph 284 [1173]. The tenant may feel that he requires more control over the payment of rent. In any event, the financial systems operated by many companies prevent payments being made in this way.

[2332]

[3.2   Outgoings and VAT[39]

The Tenant must pay, and must indemnify the Landlord against —

3.2.1   all rates, taxes[40], assessments, duties, charges, impositions and outgoings that are now or may at any time during the Term be charged, assessed or imposed upon the Premises or on the owner or occupier of them[, excluding any payable by the Landlord occasioned by receipt of the Rent or by any disposition of or dealing with this Lease or ownership of any interest reversionary to the interest created by it][41] [— provided that if the Landlord suffers any loss of rating relief that may be applicable to empty premises after the end of the Term because the relief has been allowed to the Tenant in respect of any period before the end of the Term then the Tenant must make good such loss to the Landlord],

3.2.2   all VAT that may from time to time be charged on the Rent or other sums payable by the Tenant under this Lease[42], and

3.2.3   all VAT incurred in relation to any costs that the Tenant is obliged to pay or in respect of which he is required to indemnify the Landlord under the terms of this Lease, save where such VAT is recoverable or available for set-off by the Landlord as input tax[43].]

39   If the hut or shed to be erected on the car park (as to which see clause 3.4.4 [2335] ATTENDANT'S HUT) is to be supplied with mains electricity or gas, for light or heat, or with a lavatory, the landlord may want to include a tenant's obligation to pay outgoings.
40   As to covenants to pay rates and taxes see vol 22(1) (2003 Reissue) LANDLORD AND TENANT (BUSINESS TENANCIES) Paragraph 153 [765].
41   The tenant should add the words in square brackets to make it clear that he is not paying the landlord's taxes.
42   As to VAT on rent, service charges and insurance premiums see the Information Binder: Property [1]: VAT and Property.
43   As to payment of VAT on legal costs paid by a person other than the solicitor's own client see the Information Binder: Property [1]: VAT and Property.

[2333]

3.3   Repair and cleaning

3.3.1   *Repair of the Premises*[44]

The Tenant must repair the Premises and keep them in good repair.

44   As to repair see vol 22(1) (2003 Reissue) LANDLORD AND TENANT (BUSINESS TENANCIES) Paragraph 196 [931] et seq. For provisos excluding, eg, work that is prevented see vol 22(3) (1997 Reissue) LANDLORD AND TENANT (BUSINESS TENANCIES) Form 87 [6462], 88 [6463].
        It should be noted that it is now recommended 'best practice' that if the premises are so damaged by an uninsured risk as to prevent occupation, the tenant should be allowed to terminate the lease unless the landlord agrees to reinstate at his own cost: see vol 22(1) (2003 Reissue) LANDLORD AND TENANT (BUSINESS TENANCIES) Paragraph 85 [402]. If adopted, this recommendation involves damage preventing occupation caused by uninsured or uninsurable risks being excluded from the ambit of the tenant's repairing covenant.

3.3.2   *Replacement of landlord's fixtures*

The Tenant must replace from time to time any landlord's fixtures and fittings in the Premises that are beyond repair at any time during or at the end of the Term.

3.3.3   *Cleaning and tidying*

The Tenant must keep the Premises clean and tidy and clear of all rubbish.

3.3.4   *The Open Land*

3.3.4.1   **Care of the Open Land**

The Tenant must keep any part of the Premises that is not built on ('the Open Land') adequately surfaced, in good condition and free from weeds [and keep all landscaped areas properly cultivated].

3.3.4.2   **Storage on the Open Land**

The Tenant must not store anything upon the Open Land [or bring anything onto it] [that is or might become untidy, unclean, unsightly or in any way detrimental to the Premises or the area generally].

3.3.4.3   **Rubbish on the Open Land**

The Tenant must not deposit any waste, rubbish or refuse on the Open Land[, or place any receptacle for them, on it].

3.3.4.4   **Vehicles on the Open Land**

The Tenant must not keep or store any caravan or movable dwelling on the Open Land. *(adapt clause 3.3.4 as required in the circumstances)*

[2334]

3.3.5   *Care of abutting land*

The Tenant must not cause any land, roads or pavements abutting the Premises to be untidy or dirty and in particular, but without prejudice to the generality of the above, must not deposit refuse or other materials on them.

3.3.6   *Shared facilities*

Where the use of any of the Conduits or any boundary structures or other things is common to the Premises and other property, the Tenant must be responsible for, and indemnify the Landlord against, all sums due from the owner, tenant or occupier of the Premises in relation to those Conduits, boundary structures or other things, and must undertake all work in relation to them that is his responsibility.

3.4   **Waste and alterations**

3.4.1   *Waste, additions and alterations*[45]

The Tenant must not commit any waste, make any addition to the Premises, unite the Premises with any adjoining premises, or make any alteration to the Premises except as required by clauses 3.4.3 FENCING and 3.4.4 ATTENDANT'S HUT.

---

45   As to alterations see vol 22(1) (2003 Reissue) LANDLORD AND TENANT (BUSINESS TENANCIES) Paragraph 186 [911] et seq

3.4.2   *Connection to conduits*

The Tenant must not make any connection with the Conduits except in accordance with plans and specifications approved by the Landlord[, whose approval may not be unreasonably withheld [or delayed]], and subject to consent to make the connection having previously been obtained from the competent authority, undertaker or supplier.

3.4.3   *Fencing*

The Tenant must immediately erect and subsequently keep in repair a close-boarded fence along the boundaries of the Premises.

3.4.4   *Attendant's hut*

The Tenant must erect on the Premises a hut or shed, for the use only of the attendants supervising the car parking, in accordance with plans first submitted to and approved by the Landlord[, whose approval may not be unreasonably withheld [or delayed]] and subsequently must repair it and keep it in repair.

[2335]

3.5   Aerials, signs and advertisements

3.5.1   *Masts and wires*

The Tenant must not erect any pole or mast [or install any cable or wire] on the Premises, whether in connection with telecommunications or otherwise.

3.5.2   *Advertisements*[46]

The Tenant must not, without the consent of the Landlord, fix to or exhibit or display anywhere on the Premises, any placard, sign, notice, fascia board or advertisement.

46   See the Town and Country Planning (Control of Advertisements) Regulations 1992, SI 1992/666 as amended. In the absence of a covenant such as this and subject to those Regulations, the tenant may exhibit advertisements etc on the premises, whether or not they are connected with his business: see *Clapman v Edwards* [1938] 2 All ER 507.

3.6   Statutory obligations

3.6.1   *General provision*[47]

The Tenant must comply in all respects with the requirements of any statutes, and any other obligations so applicable imposed by law or by any byelaws, applicable to the Premises or the trade or business for the time being carried on there.

47   As to the covenant to comply with statutes see vol 22(1) (2003 Reissue) LANDLORD AND TENANT (BUSINESS TENANCIES) Paragraph 182 [905]. For a provision requiring the landlord to pay compensation for works above a certain value see vol 22(3) (1997 Reissue) LANDLORD AND TENANT (BUSINESS TENANCIES) Form 169 [6693].

3.6.2   *Particular obligations*

3.6.2.1   **Works required by statute, department or authority**

Without prejudice to the generality of clause 3.6.1, the Tenant must execute all works and provide and maintain all arrangements on or in respect of the Premises or the use to which they are being put that are required in order to comply with the requirements of any statute already or in the future to be passed, or the requirements of any government department, local authority or other public or competent authority or court of competent jurisdiction, regardless of whether such requirements are imposed on the owner, the occupier, or any other person.

3.6.2.2   **Acts causing losses**

Without prejudice to the generality of clause 3.6.1, the Tenant must not do in or near the Premises anything by reason of which the Landlord may incur any losses under any statute.

[2336]

3.7   **Use**

3.7.1   *Car park*

The Tenant must not use the Premises for any purpose other than as a car park for motor cars, motor cycles and light commercial vehicles not exceeding ... tonnes unladen weight only.

3.7.2   *Nuisance*[48]

The Tenant must not do anything on the Premises, or allow anything to remain on them, that may be or become or cause a nuisance, or annoyance, disturbance, inconvenience, injury or damage to the Landlord or his tenants or the owners or occupiers of adjacent or neighbouring premises.

48   'Nuisance' is a term to be construed according to 'plain and sober and simple notions among the English people': *Walter v Selfe* (1851) 4 De G & Sm 315 at 322 per Knight-Bruce V-C. 'I have no doubt that what is a nuisance or annoyance will continue to be determined by the courts according to robust and commonsense standards': *Hampstead and Suburban Properties Ltd v Diomedous* [1969] 1 Ch 248 at 258, [1968] 3 All ER 545 at 550 per Megarry J. But a tenant can only be said to have permitted a nuisance if the landlord can show that the tenant has failed to take reasonable steps to prevent the nuisance: see *Commercial General Administration Ltd v Thomsett* [1979] 1 EGLR 62, CA.

3.7.3   *Auctions, trades and immoral purposes*

The Tenant must not use the Premises for any auction sale, any dangerous, noxious, noisy or offensive[49] trade, business, manufacture or occupation, or for any illegal or immoral act or purpose.

49   As to the meaning of 'offensive' see *Re Koumoudouros and Marathon Realty Co Ltd* (1978) 89 DLR (3d) 551 where it was held that the word did not have a definite legal meaning and should be read in the context of the lease. Surrounding circumstances can affect whether a particular trade is offensive: see *Nussey v Provincial Bill Posting Co and Eddison* [1909] 1 Ch 734, CA; *Dunraven Securities Ltd v Holloway* [1982] 2 EGLR 47, CA.

[2337]

3.7.4   *Residential use, sleeping and animals*

The Tenant must not use the Premises as sleeping accommodation or for residential purposes, or keep any animal, bird or reptile on them.

3.7.5   *Attendants*

The Tenant must provide attendants adequate to supervise the parking at all times that the Premises are open for parking.

3.8   Entry to inspect and notice to repair

3.8.1   *Entry and notice*

The Tenant must permit the Landlord[50] [on reasonable notice during normal business hours except in emergency][51] —

3.8.1.1   to enter the Premises to ascertaining whether or not the covenants and conditions of this Lease have been observed and performed,

3.8.1.2   to view the state of repair and condition of the Premises, and

3.8.1.3   to give to the Tenant, or, notwithstanding clause 7.7 NOTICES leave on the Premises, a notice ('a notice to repair') specifying the works required to remedy any breach of the Tenant's obligations in this Lease as to the repair and condition of the Premises.

50   The provisions of clause 1.22 [2314] REFERENCES TO RIGHTS OF ACCESS should be noted.
51   The tenant should add the words in square brackets.

[2338]

3.8.2   *Works to be carried out*

The Tenant must immediately carry out the works specified in a notice to repair.

[3.8.3   *Landlord's power in default*[52]

If within *(state period, eg 1 month)* of the service of a notice to repair the Tenant has not started to execute the work referred to in the notice or is not proceeding diligently with it, or if the Tenant fails to finish the work within *(state period, eg 2 months)*[53][, or if in the [Landlord's *(or as required)* Surveyor's] [reasonable] opinion the Tenant is unlikely to finish the work within that period], the Tenant must permit the Landlord to enter the Premises to execute the outstanding work and must within *(state period, eg 14 days)* of a written demand pay to the Landlord the cost of so doing and all expenses incurred by the Landlord, including legal costs and surveyor's fees.]

52   The advantages for the landlord of this clause must be weighed against the potential liability that it creates under the Defective Premises Act 1972 s 4(4) (31 Halsbury's Statutes (4th Edn) NEGLIGENCE): see *McAuley v Bristol City Council* [1992] QB 134, [1992] 1 All ER 749, CA.
         It has been held that a claim by the landlord for recovery of costs under such a clause is a claim for recovery of a debt, and can therefore be enforced without requiring leave of the court under the Leasehold Property (Repairs) Act 1938 (23 Halsbury's Statutes (4th Edn) LANDLORD AND TENANT): see *Jervis v Harris* [1996] Ch 195, [1996] 1 All ER 303, CA.
         However, even where a landlord has been granted a right of this nature the court does not compel the tenant to allow the landlord the right to enter and carry out repairs where these would be of no benefit and where no loss is being caused to the landlord: see *Hammersmith London Borough Council v Creska (No 2)* [2000] L & TR 288.
53   The tenant would prefer to be given 'a reasonable period' to do the work required to remedy the breaches because it may take longer than the specified number of months.

[2339]

3.9   Alienation[54]

3.9.1   *Alienation prohibited*

The Tenant must not hold the Premises on trust for another. The Tenant must not part with possession of the whole or any part of the Premises or permit another to occupy them or any part of them except pursuant to a transaction permitted by and effected in accordance with the provisions of this Lease.

54   As to alienation see vol 22(1) (2003 Reissue) LANDLORD AND TENANT (BUSINESS TENANCIES) Paragraph 156 [801] et seq. Where the lease is registrable, this prohibition or restriction on dealings will be reflected in an entry on the register excepting from the effects of registration all estates, rights, interests, powers and remedies arising on or by reason of any dealing made in breach of the prohibition or restriction: see the Land Registration Rules 2003, SI 2003/1417 r 6(2).

3.9.2   *Assignment and charging of part, and subletting*

The Tenant must not assign, sublet or charge part only of the Premises and must not sublet the whole or any part of them[55].

55   In view of the nature of the demise, this Form assumes that subletting is to be entirely prohibited. In general terms, whether subletting should be permitted is a commercial matter. Some landlords consider that the fact that they cannot unreasonably refuse consent to an assignment gives the tenant all the protection he requires and are not prepared to permit subletting. An advantage to the tenant of the ability to sublet is that he has an element of control over a subtenant but not over an assignee, for whom he may retain liability under an authorised guarantee agreement. The tenant should also bear in mind that with stringent assignment tests or in a bad market, subletting may be the only option open to him.

[2340]

3.9.3   *Assignment of the whole*

Subject to clauses 3.9.4 CIRCUMSTANCES and 3.9.5 CONDITIONS, the Tenant must not assign the whole of the Premises without the consent of the Landlord, whose consent may not be unreasonably withheld [or delayed][56].

56   This residual discretion is the old test of reasonableness under the Landlord and Tenant Act 1927 s 19(1). Thus the tenant and the proposed assignee may satisfy the circumstances and conditions specified for the purposes of the Landlord and Tenant Act 1927 s 19(1A) as inserted by the Landlord and Tenant (Covenants) Act 1995 s 22 (as to which see clause 3.9.4 [2341] CIRCUMSTANCES and clause 3.9.5 [2344] CONDITIONS), but the landlord may still refuse consent on reasonable grounds: see vol 22(1) (2003 Reissue) LANDLORD AND TENANT (BUSINESS TENANCIES) Paragraph 159 [812] et seq.

3.9.4   *Circumstances*

If any of the following circumstances[57] — which are specified for the purposes of the Landlord and Tenant Act 1927 Section 19(1A)[58] — applies either at the date when application for consent to assign is made to the Landlord, or after that date but before the Landlord's consent is given, the Landlord may withhold his consent and if, after the Landlord's consent has been given but before the assignment has taken place, any such circumstances apply, the Landlord may revoke his consent[59], whether his consent is expressly subject to a condition as referred to in clause 3.9.5.4 CONDITIONS or not. The circumstances are —

3.9.4.1   that any sum due from the Tenant under this Lease remains unpaid[60],

3.9.4.2   that in the Landlord's reasonable[61] opinion the assignee is not a person who is likely to be able to comply with the tenant covenants of this Lease and to continue to be able to comply with them following the assignment,

[3.9.4.3   that without prejudice to clause 3.9.4.2, in the case of an assignment to a company in the same group as the Tenant[62] within the meaning of the 1954 Act Section 42 in the Landlord's reasonable opinion the assignee is a person who is, or may become, less likely to be able to comply with the tenant covenants of this Lease than the Tenant requesting consent to assign, which likelihood is adjudged by reference in particular to the financial strength of that Tenant aggregated with that of any guarantor of the obligations of that Tenant and the value of any other security for the performance of the tenant covenants of this Lease when assessed at the date of grant or — where that Tenant is not *(name of original tenant)* — the date of the assignment of this Lease to that Tenant[63],] or

3.9.4.4   that the assignee or any guarantor for the assignee, other than any guarantor under an authorised guarantee agreement, is a corporation registered — or otherwise resident — in a jurisdiction in which the order of a court obtained in England and Wales will not necessarily be enforced against the assignee or guarantor without any consideration of the merits of the case.

[2341]

57   The Landlord and Tenant Act 1927 s 19(1A) as inserted by the Landlord and Tenant (Covenants) Act 1995 s 22 enables the landlord and tenant to a post-1995 lease to agree in advance the terms upon which an assignment may be permitted. It distinguishes between on the one hand circumstances, the existence of which entitles the landlord to refuse consent to assignment, and on the other hand conditions that may be imposed on the grant of his consent. This clause and clause 3.9.5 [2344] CONDITIONS are drafted on the assumption that this is a valid approach and seek to draw a clear distinction between circumstances and conditions.

It should be noted that provisions that are overly restrictive may have an adverse impact at any rent review. It should also be noted that it is recommended 'best practice' that unless the particular circumstances of the letting justify greater control, the only restriction on assignment of the whole should be obtaining the landlord's consent, which is not to be unreasonably withheld: see vol 22(1) (2003 Reissue) LANDLORD AND TENANT (BUSINESS TENANCIES) Paragraph 85 [401] and 'A code of practice for commercial leases in England and Wales (2nd edition)' which can be found in vol 22(1) (2003 Reissue) LANDLORD AND TENANT (BUSINESS TENANCIES) as Form 1 [4501].

Each letting must be looked at in the light of its own particular facts and circumstances but it is considered that the provisions of this clause do, in the ordinary course, strike a reasonable balance between the landlord's desire for control and the tenant's ability to dispose of his interest without undue restriction. For a less restrictive approach see vol 22(1) (2003 Reissue) LANDLORD AND TENANT (BUSINESS TENANCIES) Form 7 clause 5.2 [5538].

58   The Landlord and Tenant Act 1927 s 19(1A) as inserted by the Landlord and Tenant (Covenants) Act 1995 s 22 seems to require the alienation clause to state that the circumstances it mentions are specified for the purposes of that subsection.

59   The landlord may require that certain circumstances are absent not only before consent has been given to the assignment, but also up to the date on which the assignment takes place — when the die is cast and the lease covenants bind the assignee. For example, the landlord may require the rent to be paid up to date not only before the application for consent is made, but also at the date when consent is given and the possibly later date when the lease is actually assigned.

60   The tenant may want to limit this to the rent, as it may be thought that a dispute is more likely to arise over the insurance rent or other payments. If the tenant has retained any right of set-off, it should also be referred to here.

[2342]

61   Circumstances and conditions must either be factual or, if they contain an element of discretion, require that discretion to be exercised reasonably (see the Landlord and Tenant Act 1927 s 19(1C)(a) as inserted by the Landlord and Tenant (Covenants) Act 1995 s 22), or must give the tenant a right of appeal to an expert (see the Landlord and Tenant Act 1927 s 19(1C)(b) as inserted by the Landlord and Tenant (Covenants) Act 1995 s 22). If the discretion is to be exercised reasonably, as suggested by this provision, the tenant can take any dispute about its exercise to the court. The court will consider whether *this* landlord has acted within the range of reasonable decisions, not whether a reasonable landlord would have reached the same decision or whether the test is itself reasonable. For a clause where an expert is used see vol 22(3) (1997 Reissue) LANDLORD AND TENANT (BUSINESS TENANCIES) Form 117 [6501].

62   There have been suggestions that intra-group assignments should be banned completely. However, this is considered to be too draconian and would prevent legitimate corporate restructuring needed for reasons other than avoidance of liability under the Landlord and Tenant (Covenants) Act 1995. The landlord's concern is that a strong tenant may assign to a weak group company; the assignment is acceptable because the assignor gives an authorised guarantee agreement for the assignee. The second group company may then itself assign outside the group; the landlord will lose the authorised guarantee agreement of the strong first group company and have only the possibly worthless authorised guarantee agreement of the second group company. The possibilities for exploitation of this scenario are obvious and it is therefore felt that this is the one situation in which measuring the financial strength of the assignee in relation to that of the assignor is justified. Equivalence tests are not generally thought to be appropriate, because a strong first covenant may make the lease almost unassignable, adversely affecting the rent at review.

63   Consider whether the time at which the tenant's financial status is measured should be when he acquired the lease, when his status was acceptable to the landlord, or at the date of the application for consent to assign, when it may have deteriorated sharply. On the other hand, the outgoing tenant may be a better covenant now than when he acquired the lease: the wily landlord may wish to leave himself free to pick whichever of the two dates gives the better picture.

[2343]

3.9.5   *Conditions*

The Landlord may impose any or all of the following conditions[64] — which are specified for the purposes of the Landlord and Tenant Act 1927 Section 19(1A)[65] — on giving any consent for an assignment by the Tenant, and any such consent is to be treated as being subject to each of the following conditions —

3.9.5.1   a condition that on or before any assignment and before giving occupation to the assignee, the Tenant requesting consent to assign, together with any former tenant who by virtue of the 1995 Act Section 11 was not released on an earlier assignment of this Lease[66], must enter into an authorised guarantee agreement[67] in favour of the Landlord in the terms set out in schedule 1 THE AUTHORISED GUARANTEE AGREEMENT,

3.9.5.2   a condition that, if reasonably so required by the Landlord, on an assignment to a limited company, the assignee must ensure that at least *(state number, eg 2)* directors of the company, or some other guarantor or guarantors [reasonably] acceptable to the Landlord, enter into direct covenants with the Landlord in the form of the guarantor's covenants contained in schedule 2 THE GUARANTEE PROVISIONS, and

3.9.5.3   a condition that if, at any time before the assignment, the circumstances specified in clause 3.9.4 CIRCUMSTANCES, or any of them, apply, the Landlord may revoke the consent by notice to the Tenant.

[2344]

64   The Landlord and Tenant Act 1927 s 19(1A) as inserted by the Landlord and Tenant (Covenants) Act 1995 s 22 enables the landlord and tenant to a post-1995 lease to agree in advance the terms upon which an assignment may be permitted. It distinguishes between on the one hand circumstances, the existence of which entitles the landlord to refuse consent to assignment, and on the other hand conditions that may be imposed on the grant of his consent. This clause and clause 3.9.4 [2341] CIRCUMSTANCES are drafted on the assumption that this a valid approach and seek to draw a clear distinction between circumstances and conditions.

It should be noted that provisions that are overly restrictive may have an adverse impact at any rent review. It should also be noted that it is recommended 'best practice' that unless the particular circumstances of the letting justify greater control, the only restriction on assignment of the whole should be obtaining the landlord's consent, which is not to be unreasonably withheld: see vol 22(1) (2003 Reissue) LANDLORD AND TENANT (BUSINESS TENANCIES) Paragraph 85 [401] and 'A code of practice for commercial leases in England and Wales (2nd edition)' which can be found in vol 22(1) (2003 Reissue) LANDLORD AND TENANT (BUSINESS TENANCIES) as Form 1 [4501].

Each letting must be looked at in the light of its own particular facts and circumstances but it is considered that the provisions of this clause do, in the ordinary course, strike a reasonable balance between the landlord's desire for control and the tenant's ability to dispose of his interest without undue restriction.

65   The Landlord and Tenant Act 1927 s 19(1A) as inserted by the Landlord and Tenant (Covenants) Act 1995 s 22 seems to require the alienation clause to state that the conditions it mentions are specified for the purposes of that subsection.
66   See the Landlord and Tenant (Covenants) Act 1995 ss 11(2), 16(6).
67   As to authorised guarantee agreements see vol 22(1) (2003 Reissue) LANDLORD AND TENANT (BUSINESS TENANCIES) Paragraph 54 [247]. It should be noted that 'A code of practice for commercial leases in England and Wales (2nd edition)' urges landlords to consider requiring authorised guarantee agreements only where the assignee is of lower financial standing than the assignor at the date of the assignment.

[2345]

3.9.6   *Charging of the whole*

The Tenant must not charge the whole of the Premises without the consent of the Landlord, whose consent may not be unreasonably withheld [or delayed][68].

68   As to unreasonable withholding of consent under the Landlord and Tenant Act 1927 see vol 22(1) (2003 Reissue) LANDLORD AND TENANT (BUSINESS TENANCIES) Paragraph 158.2 [806] and as to unreasonable delay under the Landlord and Tenant Act 1988 (23 Halsbury's Statutes (4th Edn) LANDLORD AND TENANT) see vol 22(1) (2003 Reissue) LANDLORD AND TENANT (BUSINESS TENANCIES) Paragraph 158.3 [808].

3.9.7   *Registration of permitted dealings*

Within *(state period, eg 28 days)* of any assignment or charge or any transmission or other devolution relating to the Premises the Tenant must produce a certified copy[69] of any relevant document for registration with the Landlord's solicitor, and must pay the Landlord's solicitor's [reasonable] charges for registration of at least £...

69   There seems to be no reason why the tenant should part with the original. However, under the Land Registration Rules 2003, SI 2003/1417 r 203, it is open to the applicant for registration to ask for the transfer, charge, sublease or subunderlease giving effect to the disposition to be returned for retention by the applicant, provided a certified copy of the instrument is lodged with the application. Accordingly, in such cases, applicants should use this facility if they wish to be able to lodge the lease with the landlord after its return by the registrar. If there is a time limit specified in the lease, then the registrar should be told about this, so that he is aware of the need to return the instrument within the required period.

[3.9.8   *Sharing with a group company*

Notwithstanding clause 3.9.1 ALIENATION PROHIBITED, the Tenant may share the occupation of the whole or any part of the Premises with a company that is a member of the same group as the Tenant within the meaning of the 1954 Act Section 42, for so long as both companies remain members of that group and otherwise than in a manner that transfers or creates a legal estate.] *(omit if sharing with a group company is not to be permitted)*

[2346]

3.10   Costs of applications, notices and recovery of arrears[69]

The Tenant must pay to the Landlord on an indemnity basis all costs, fees, charges, disbursements and expenses — including, without prejudice to the generality of the above, those payable to counsel, solicitors, surveyors and bailiffs — [properly and reasonably] incurred by the Landlord in relation to or incidental to —

3.10.1   every application made by the Tenant for a consent or licence required by the provisions of this Lease, whether it is granted, refused or offered subject to any [lawful] qualification or condition, or the application is withdrawn[, unless the refusal, qualification or condition is unlawful, whether because it is unreasonable or otherwise],

3.10.2   the contemplation, preparation and service of a notice under the Law of Property Act 1925 Section 146, or by reason or the contemplation of proceedings under Sections 146 or 147 of that Act, even if forfeiture is avoided otherwise than by relief granted by the court[71],

3.10.3   the recovery or attempted recovery of arrears of rent or other sums due under this Lease, and

3.10.4   any steps taken in [contemplation of or in] [direct] connection with the preparation and service of a schedule of dilapidations during or after the end of the Term[72].

70   As to payment of VAT on legal costs by a person other than the solicitor's own client see the Information Binder: Property [1]: VAT and Property.
71   As to forfeiture see vol 22(1) (2003 Reissue) LANDLORD AND TENANT (BUSINESS TENANCIES) Paragraph 283 [1171] et seq.
72   The landlord should not be tempted to extend this provision to costs etc incurred by him in consequence of serving a notice under the Landlord and Tenant Act 1954 s 25 because that is void: see *Stevenson and Rush (Holdings) Ltd v Langdon* (1978) 38 P & CR 208, CA.

3.11   Planning

3.11.1   *Compliance with the Planning Acts*

The Tenant must observe and comply with the provisions and requirements of the Planning Acts affecting the Premises and their use, and must indemnify the Landlord, and keep him indemnified, both during the Term and following the end of it, against all losses in respect of any contravention of those Acts.

3.11.2   *Planning applications prohibited*

The Tenant must not make any application for planning permission relating to the Premises[73].

73   In view of the nature of the demise, the prohibition is absolute rather than qualified.

[2347]

3.12   Indemnities[74]

The Tenant must keep the Landlord fully indemnified against all losses arising directly or indirectly out of any act, omission or negligence of the Tenant, or any persons at the Premises expressly or impliedly[75] with his authority [and under his control][76], or any breach or non-observance by the Tenant of the covenants, conditions or other provisions of this Lease or any of the matters to which this demise is subject.

74   The tenant should seek to delete all *general* indemnity provisions on the basis that his remedies for breach of covenant and in tort adequately protect the landlord. The tenant should argue that an indemnity unreasonably extends his liability. If this clause is omitted, however, it should be replaced by a covenant to observe and perform the restrictions etc to which the demise is subject, possibly coupled with a *specific* indemnity in respect of any breach.
75   The expression 'impliedly' is intended to include a caller on the premises, such as a tradesman, where there has been no express invitation but the person cannot be classed as a trespasser.
76   The tenant should add the words in square brackets.

3.13   Reletting boards and viewing

[Unless [a valid court application under the 1954 Act Section 24 has been made or][77] the Tenant is [otherwise] entitled to remain in occupation or to a new tenancy of the Premises, at any time during *(or as required)* At any time during] the *(state period, eg last 6 months)* of the [Contractual] Term[78] and at any time thereafter, [and whenever the Lease Rents or any part of them are in arrear and unpaid for longer than *(state period, eg 14 days)*,] the Tenant must permit the Landlord to enter the Premises and fix and retain anywhere on them a board advertising them for reletting. While any such board is on the Premises the Tenant must permit viewing of the Premises at reasonable times of the day.

77   This phrase and the word 'otherwise' should be omitted if the operation of the security of tenure provisions in the Landlord and Tenant Act 1954 ss 24–28 is to be excluded in relation to the lease.

78   This defined term will require amendment where the operation of the security of tenure provisions in the Landlord and Tenant Act 1954 ss 24–28 is to be excluded in relation to the lease: see note 6 to clause 1.1 [2308] 'THE [CONTRACTUAL] TERM'.

[2348]

3.14   Encroachments

The Tenant must take all [reasonable] steps to prevent the construction of any new window, light, opening, doorway, path, passage, pipe or the making of any encroachment or the acquisition of any easement in relation to the Premises and must notify the Landlord immediately if any such thing is constructed, encroachment is made or easement acquired, or if any attempt is made to construct such a thing, encroach or acquire an easement. At the request of the Landlord the Tenant must adopt such means as are [reasonably] required to prevent the construction of such a thing, the making of any encroachment or the acquisition of any easement[79].

79   For a shorter clause see vol 22(3) (1997 Reissue) LANDLORD AND TENANT (BUSINESS TENANCIES) Form 172 [6696].

3.15   Yielding up

At the end of the Term[80] the Tenant must yield up the Premises with vacant possession, repaired in accordance with and in the condition required by the provisions of this Lease, [give up all keys of the Premises to the Landlord,] remove tenant's fixtures and fittings [if requested to do so by the Landlord], and remove all signs erected by the Tenant or any of his predecessors in title in, on or near the Premises, immediately making good any damage caused by their removal.

80   The provisions of clause 1.9 [2311] INTERPRETATION OF 'THE LAST YEAR OF THE TERM' AND 'THE END OF THE TERM' should be noted.

3.16   Interest on arrears[81]

The Tenant must pay interest on the Rent or any other sums due under this Lease that are not paid [within *(state period, eg 14 days)* of the date due], whether formally demanded or not, [the interest to be recoverable as rent][82]. Nothing in this clause entitles the Tenant to withhold or delay any payment of the Rent or any other sum due under this Lease or affects the rights of the Landlord in relation to any non-payment.

81   As to the covenant to pay interest see vol 22(1) (2003 Reissue) LANDLORD AND TENANT (BUSINESS TENANCIES) Paragraph 154 [767].

82   These words seek to attach to interest the rights associated with rent. As to the reasons for this see vol 22(1) (2003 Reissue) LANDLORD AND TENANT (BUSINESS TENANCIES) Paragraph 151 [761]. However, this clause applies to interest on arrears of other sums payable under the lease that are not rent as well as to rent itself, and it might be felt inappropriate for interest to be deemed to be rent where the payment on which the interest is due is not itself rent.

[2349]

3.17   Statutory notices

The Tenant must give full particulars to the Landlord of any notice, direction, order or proposal relating to the Premises made, given or issued to the Tenant by any government department or local, public, regulatory or other authority or court within *(state period, eg 7 days)* of receipt, and if so requested by the Landlord must produce it to the Landlord. The Tenant must without delay take all necessary steps to comply with the notice, direction or order. At the request of the Landlord, but at his own cost, the Tenant must make or join with the Landlord in making any objection or representation the Landlord deems expedient against or in respect of any notice, direction, order or proposal.

[3.18   Keyholders

The Tenant must ensure that at all times [the Landlord has *(or as required)* the Landlord and the local police force have] written notice of the name, home address and home telephone number of at least *(state number, eg 2)* keyholders of the Premises.] *(omit if not required)*

3.19   Viewing on sale of reversion

The Tenant must[, on reasonable notice,] at any time during the Term, permit prospective purchasers of the Landlord's reversion or any other interest superior to the Term, or agents instructed in connection with the sale of the reversion or such an interest, to view the Premises without interruption provided they have the prior written authority of the Landlord or his agents.

3.20   Defective premises

The Tenant must give notice to the Landlord of any defect in the Premises that might give rise to an obligation on the Landlord to do or refrain from doing anything in order to comply with the provisions of this Lease or the duty of care imposed on the Landlord, whether pursuant to the Defective Premises Act 1972 or otherwise, and must at all times display and maintain any notices the Landlord from time to time [reasonably] requires him to display at the Premises.

3.21   Exercise of the Landlord's rights[83]

The Tenant must permit the Landlord to exercise any of the rights granted to him by virtue of the provisions of this Lease at all times during the Term without interruption or interference.

83   The provisions of clause 1.22 [2314] REFERENCES TO RIGHTS OF ACCESS should be noted.

[2350]

3.22   Costs of grant of this Lease[84]

[The Tenant must pay the fees and disbursements of the Landlord's solicitors, agents and surveyors and all other costs and expenses incurred by the Landlord in relation to the negotiation, preparation, execution and grant of this Lease. *(or as required)* On the grant of this Lease, the Tenant must pay the sum of £... as a contribution to the Landlord's solicitors' charges for the negotiation, execution and completion of this Lease].

84   As to covenants to pay the landlord's legal fees see vol 22(1) (2003 Reissue) LANDLORD AND TENANT (BUSINESS TENANCIES) Paragraph 155 [769]. As to payment of VAT on legal costs by a person other than the solicitor's own client see the Information Binder: Property [1]: VAT and Property.

3.23   Consent to the Landlord's release[85]

The Tenant must not unreasonably withhold consent to a request made by the Landlord under the 1995 Act Section 8 for a release from all or any of the landlord covenants of this Lease.

85   By virtue of the Landlord and Tenant (Covenants) Act 1995 each successive landlord remains bound by the landlord covenants of the lease unless released under the machinery provided in the Act — as to which see vol 22(1) (2003 Reissue) LANDLORD AND TENANT (BUSINESS TENANCIES) Paragraph 57 [252] et seq — or by a specific release given otherwise (see the Landlord and Tenant (Covenants) Act 1995 s 26(1)(a)). Bald statements limiting the landlord's liability, such as those in use before the commencement of the Act, will not withstand the wide anti-avoidance provisions of the Landlord and Tenant (Covenants) Act 1995 s 25, and covenants by the tenant to give consent to release are unlikely to fall within the exception of s 26. None of the ingenious schemes for limiting the landlord's liability, eg making all covenants personal, suggested in the early days of the 1995 Act has stood up to critical scrutiny, although none has yet been tested by the courts. Thus landlords look instead to the alternative of a right of redress if the tenant makes an unreasonable objection to release. This covenant is modelled on the provisions of the Landlord and Tenant Act 1988, which gives tenants a right of action for loss caused by landlords who unreasonably withhold or delay consent to assignment (see the Landlord and Tenant Act 1988 s 4). In view of the strict time limits under the Landlord and Tenant (Covenants) Act 1995 and the fact that failure to respond to the landlord's request for release is deemed to be consent, it is not thought necessary to extend this covenant to unreasonable delay in replying to such a request.

[2351]–[2360]

4   QUIET ENJOYMENT[86]

The Landlord covenants with the Tenant to permit the Tenant peaceably and quietly to hold and enjoy the Premises without any interruption or disturbance from or by the Landlord or any person claiming under or in trust for him[87] [or by title paramount][88].

86   As to the landlord's covenant for quiet enjoyment see vol 22(1) (2003 Reissue) LANDLORD AND TENANT (BUSINESS TENANCIES) Paragraph 168 [856]. As to covenants for quiet enjoyment generally see 23 Halsbury's Laws (4th Edn Reissue) LANDLORD AND TENANT.
       The words 'the Tenant paying the rents reserved by and observing and performing the covenants on his part and the conditions contained in this lease' are frequently included in a covenant for quiet enjoyment, but they have no practical effect and do not make payment of the rent and performance of the covenants into conditions precedent to the operation of the covenant for quiet enjoyment: see *Edge v Boileau* (1885) 16 QBD 117; *Dawson v Dyer* (1833) 5 B & Ad 584; *Yorkbrook Investments Ltd v Batten* (1985) 52 P & CR 51, [1985] 2 EGLR 100, CA.
87   The covenant is frequently expressed to apply to 'lawful' interruption or by persons 'rightfully' claiming under the landlord, but it seems that the addition of these words has no practical effect: see *Williams v Gabriel* [1906] 1 KB 155 at 157.
88   Without the reference to title paramount the landlord is liable only for the acts of persons so far as they are his successors in title or have authority from him to do the acts complained of: *Harrison Ainslie & Co v Muncaster* [1891] 2 QB 680, CA; *Matania v National Provincial Bank Ltd and Elevenist Syndicate Ltd* [1936] 2 All ER 633, CA; *Miller v Emcer Products Ltd* [1956] Ch 304, [1956] 1 All ER 237, CA. If a subtenant holds under a lease containing a qualified covenant on the part of his landlord — ie one

where there is no reference to title paramount — and the head landlord evicts the subtenant because the head rent has not been paid, this is not a breach of the covenant for quiet enjoyment (see *Spencer v Marriott* (1823) 1 B & C 457; *Dennett v Atherton* (1872) LR 7 QB 316), but it is a breach if the sublandlord submits to judgment in an action by a person with no title to sue, and the subtenant is in consequence evicted (*Cohen v Tannar* [1900] 2 QB 609, CA). Actionable interruptions under this covenant, are not confined to interference with title or possession, but may extend to interference with the ordinary and lawful enjoyment of the premises: *Sanderson v Berwick-upon-Tweed Corpn* (1884) 13 QBD 547 at 551, CA. As to persons claiming 'under' the landlord see *Celsteel Ltd v Alton House Holdings Ltd (No 2)* [1987] 2 All ER 240, [1987] 1 WLR 291, CA.

[2361]

5   INSURANCE[89]

5.1   Definitions

In this clause 5 the terms defined in this clause 5.1 have the meanings specified.

89   In view of the nature of this particular demise, it is assumed the tenant is to insure. As to insurance by the tenant generally see vol 22(1) (2003 Reissue) LANDLORD AND TENANT (BUSINESS TENANCIES) Paragraphs 245 [1050], 246 [1052].

5.1.1   *'The Insured Risks'*

'The Insured Risks' means the risks of loss or damage by fire[, storm, tempest, earthquake, lightning, explosion, riot, civil commotion, malicious damage, [terrorism,] impact by vehicles and by aircraft and articles dropped from aircraft — other than war risks — flood damage and bursting and overflowing of water pipes and tanks,] and such other risks, whether or not in the nature of the foregoing, as the Landlord from time to time by notice to the Tenant [reasonably] requires the Tenant to insure against.

5.1.2   *'Permissions'*

References to 'permissions' are references to all the planning permissions and other permits and consents that may be required under the Planning Acts or other statutes for the time being in force to enable the Premises to be rebuilt and reinstated lawfully in the event of any damage or destruction.

[2362]

5.2   Covenant to insure

5.2.1   *Insurance of the Premises*

The Tenant covenants with the Landlord to insure the Premises, and keep them insured, against damage or destruction by any of the Insured Risks, in the joint names of the Landlord and the Tenant and of any other persons the Landlord from time to time by notice to the Tenant [reasonably] requires, in an amount equal to the full cost of rebuilding and reinstating the Premises as new in the event of their total destruction including [VAT[90],] architects', surveyors', engineers', solicitors' and all other professional persons', the fees payable on applications for any permissions, the cost of preparation of the site including debris removal, demolition, site clearance and any works that may be required by statute, and incidental expenses.

90   As to VAT and the level of insurance cover see the Information Binder: Property [1]: VAT and Property. The expense of insuring against the VAT payable on reinstatement costs is not justified where the landlord has opted to tax and will be able to recover the VAT. There is a theoretical possibility that a future landlord may not opt to tax and that the sum insured may then be too low. It is also possible that a landlord may wish to preserve the 'exempt' status of a property. Normally, however, the cost of reinstatement need not expressly mention VAT, although the cashflow implications of having to pay VAT on construction works need to be remembered.

5.2.2   *Liability insurance*

The Tenant covenants with the Landlord to effect and maintain such insurance, in such amount, as the Landlord from time to time by notice to the Tenant requires in respect of the Tenant's liability to indemnify the Landlord against losses arising from the Tenant's acts, omissions or negligence and all liability of the Landlord to third parties arising out of or in connection with any matter involving or relating to the Premises.

5.2.3   *Office, underwriters and agency*

All insurance must be effected in a substantial and reputable insurance office, or with such underwriters, and through such agency as the Landlord from time to time [by notice to the Tenant [reasonably] requires *(or as required)* approves[, such approval not to be unreasonably withheld [or delayed]]][91].

91   The expression 'insurance office' would probably not include Lloyd's underwriters.

[2363]

5.3   Tenant's further insurance covenants

The Tenant covenants with the Landlord to observe and perform the requirements of this clause 5.3.

5.3.1   *Requirements of insurers*

The Tenant must comply with all requirements and recommendations of the insurers.

5.3.2   *Policy avoidance*

The Tenant must not do or omit anything that could cause any insurance policy effected in accordance with this Lease to become wholly or partly void or voidable.

5.3.3   *Fire authority requirements*

The Tenant must comply with all requirements and recommendations of the fire authority as to fire precautions relating to the Premises.

5.3.4   *Notice of events and damage*

The Tenant must give immediate notice to the Landlord of any event that might affect any insurance policy effected in accordance with this Lease, and of any destruction of or damage to the Premises, whether or not caused by one or more of the Insured Risks.

5.3.5   *Production of the policy*

The Tenant must produce to the Landlord on demand every insurance policy effected in accordance with this Lease and the receipt for the then current year's premium, and if so required must supply the Landlord with a copy of every such policy.

[2364]

5.4   Reinstatement

If and whenever during the Term the Premises are damaged or destroyed by one or more of the Insured Risks, then —

5.4.1   all money received under any insurance policy effected in accordance with this Lease must be placed in an account in the joint names of the Landlord and the Tenant at a bank designated by the Landlord [acting reasonably], and must subsequently be released to the Tenant from that account by instalments, against architect's certificates or other evidence acceptable to the Landlord, whose acceptance may not be unreasonably withheld, of expenditure actually incurred by the Tenant in rebuilding and reinstating the Premises, and

5.4.2   the Tenant must with all convenient speed obtain the permissions, and as soon as they have been obtained rebuild and reinstate the Premises in accordance with them, making up out of his own money any difference between the cost of rebuilding and reinstatement and the money received from the insurance policy[92].

92   As to the tenant's covenant to reinstate see vol 22(1) (2003 Reissue) LANDLORD AND TENANT (BUSINESS TENANCIES) Paragraph 246 [1052]. In strict terms, if the provisions of the tenant's repairing covenant are unqualified, an express covenant to reinstate is unnecessary although the draftsman may wish to see one included for the avoidance of doubt.

It should be noted that it is recommended 'best practice' that if premises are so damaged by an uninsured risk as to prevent occupation, the tenant should be allowed to terminate the lease unless the landlord agrees to reinstate at his own cost: see vol 22(1) (2003 Reissue) LANDLORD AND TENANT (BUSINESS TENANCIES) Paragraph 85 [401] and 'A code of practice for commercial leases in England and Wales (2nd edition)' which can be found in vol 22(1) (2003 Reissue) LANDLORD AND TENANT (BUSINESS TENANCIES) at Form 1 [4501].

[2365]

6   FORFEITURE[93]

If and whenever during the Term —

6.1   the Rent, or any of it, or any VAT payable on it, is outstanding for *(state period, eg 14 days)* after becoming due whether formally demanded or not[94], or

6.2   the Tenant breaches any covenant or other term of this Lease, or

6.3   the Tenant, being an individual, becomes subject to a bankruptcy order[95] [or has an interim receiver appointed to his property][96], or

6.4   the Tenant, being a company, enters into liquidation[97] whether compulsory or voluntary — but not if the liquidation is for amalgamation or reconstruction of a solvent company — [or enters into administration][98] [or has a receiver appointed over all or any part of its assets][99], or

6.5   the Tenant enters into or makes a proposal to enter into any voluntary arrangement pursuant to the Insolvency Act 1986[100] or any other arrangement or composition for the benefit of his creditors, or

6.6   the Tenant has any distress, sequestration or execution levied on his goods,

and, where the Tenant is more than one person, if and whenever any of the events referred to in this clause happens to any one or more of them, the Landlord may at any time re-enter the Premises or any part of them in the name of the whole — even if any previous right of re-entry has been waived[101] — and thereupon the Term is to cease absolutely but without prejudice to any rights or remedies that may have accrued to the Landlord against the Tenant [or to the Tenant against the Landlord] in respect of any breach of covenant or other term of this Lease, including the breach in respect of which the re-entry is made.

[2366]

93   As to forfeiture generally see vol 22(1) (2003 Reissue) LANDLORD AND TENANT (BUSINESS TENANCIES) Paragraph 283 [1171] et seq.

The precise range of insolvency-related circumstances that will trigger the proviso should be carefully considered. Tenants should note that their inclusion, in practice, means that the lease cannot be used as security for a loan. Landlords generally seek to have the ability to forfeit in the widest range of circumstances. It should, however, be noted that, in certain circumstances, leave of the court or of the insolvency practitioner administering the procedure may be required before any contractual right can be exercised: see eg, in respect of administration, the Insolvency Act 1986 Sch 1B para 43(4), (6) as inserted by the Enterprise Act 2002 s 248 (4 Halsbury's Statutes (4th Edn) BANKRUPTCY AND INSOLVENCY).

94   The words 'whether formally demanded or not' should be used to avoid the common law requirement that an actual demand has to be made.

95   As to bankruptcy generally see the Insolvency Act 1986 Pt IX (ss 264–371).

96   As to interim receivers see the Insolvency Act 1986 s 286.

97   As to liquidation generally see the Insolvency Act 1986 Pts IV–VI (ss 73–246).

98   As to administration generally see the Insolvency Act 1986 Pt II as substituted by the Enterprise Act 2002 s 248. The tenant may seek to argue that if the administrator pays rent and if there are no other material breaches of the lease the landlord should not be entitled to forfeit the lease on this ground.

99   The tenant may seek to argue that if the receiver pays rent and if there are no other material breaches of the lease the landlord should not be entitled to forfeit the lease on this ground.

100   As to company voluntary arrangements see the Insolvency Act 1986 Pt I (ss 1–7B) as amended by the Insolvency Act 2000. As to individual voluntary arrangements see the Insolvency Act 1986 Pt VIII (ss 252–263G) as amended by the Enterprise Act 2002 s 264.

101   The landlord has the option whether to take advantage of a right of forfeiture or not. If he elects not to do so , the forfeiture is waived. The election may be express or implied, eg if the landlord does any act by which he recognises that the relationship of landlord and tenant is still continuing after the event of forfeiture has come to his knowledge.

[2367]

7   MISCELLANEOUS

7.1   Exclusion of warranty as to use

Nothing in this Lease or in any consent granted by the Landlord under this Lease is to imply or warrants that the Premises may lawfully be used under the Planning Acts for the use permitted by this Lease[102].

102   See *Laurence v Lexcourt Holdings Ltd* [1978] 2 All ER 810, [1978] 1 WLR 1128; *Collins v Howell-Jones* [1981] 2 EGLR 108, 259 Estates Gazette 331, CA and the comments of Eveleigh LJ on estate agents' particulars relating to use in *Bovis Group Pension Fund Ltd v GC Flooring & Furnishing Ltd* (1984) 269 Estates Gazette 1252 at 1253, CA.

7.2   Exclusion of third party rights

Nothing in this Lease is intended to confer any benefit on any person who is not a party to it[103].

103   By virtue of the Contracts (Rights of Third Parties) Act 1999 (11 Halsbury's Statutes (4th Edn) CONTRACT) third-party rights may be conferred where they are not clearly excluded. This being so, it is advisable to incorporate a specific exclusion except where the parties actually intend to confer rights of action on a third party. In the standard letting situation it is unlikely that the parties will wish to extend liability in this manner. As to the Contracts (Rights of Third Parties) Act 1999 generally see vol 4(3) (2001 Reissue) BOILERPLATE CLAUSES.

7.3   Representations

The Tenant acknowledges that this Lease has not been entered into in reliance wholly or partly on any statement or representation made by or on behalf of the Landlord, except any such statement or representation expressly set out in this Lease[104] [or made by the Landlord's solicitors in any written response to enquiries raised by the Tenant's solicitors in connection with the grant of this Lease].

104   See the comments of Eveleigh LJ on estate agents' particulars relating to use in *Bovis Group Pension Fund Ltd v GC Flooring & Furnishing Ltd* (1984) 269 Estates Gazette 1252 at 1253, CA. For an alternative provision see vol 22(4) (1997 Reissue) LANDLORD AND TENANT (BUSINESS TENANCIES) Form 400 clauses 7.1 [7520], 7.2 [7521].

[2368]

7.4   Documents under hand

While the Landlord is a limited company or other corporation, any licence, consent, approval or notice required to be given by the Landlord is to be sufficiently given if given under the hand of a director, the secretary or other duly authorised officer of the Landlord [or by the Surveyor on behalf of the Landlord].

7.5   Tenant's property

If, after the Tenant has vacated the Premises at the end of the Term, any property of his remains in or on the Premises and he fails to remove it within *(state period, eg 7 days)* after a written requested from the Landlord to do so, or, if the Landlord is unable to make such a request to the Tenant, within *(state period, eg 14 days)* from the first attempt to make it, then the Landlord may, as the agent of the Tenant, sell that property. The Tenant must indemnify the Landlord against any liability incurred by the Landlord to any third party whose property is sold by him in the mistaken belief held in good faith — which is to be presumed unless the contrary is proved — that the property belonged to the Tenant. If, having made reasonable efforts to do so, the Landlord is unable to locate the Tenant, then the Landlord may retain the proceeds of sale absolutely unless the Tenant claims them within *(state period, eg 6 months)* of the date on which he vacated the Premises. The Tenant must indemnify the Landlord against any damage occasioned to the Premises and any losses caused by or related to the presence of the property in or on the Premises.

7.6   Compensation on vacating excluded

Any statutory right of the Tenant to claim compensation from the Landlord on vacating the Premises is excluded to the extent that the law allows[105].

105   As to compensation where an order for a new tenancy is precluded on certain grounds see the Landlord and Tenant Act 1954 s 37 as amended by the Local Government and Housing Act 1989 s 149, Sch 7 and by SI 2003/3096.
      As to the effectiveness of provisions of this nature see vol 22(1) (2003 Reissue) LANDLORD AND TENANT (BUSINESS TENANCIES) Paragraph 468 [3079].

[2369]

7.7   Notices

7.7.1   *Form and service of notices*

A notice under this Lease must be in writing and, unless the receiving party or his authorised agent acknowledges receipt, is valid if, and only if[106] —

7.7.1.1   it is given by hand, sent by registered post or recorded delivery, or sent by fax[107] provided a confirmatory copy is given by hand or sent by registered post or recorded delivery on the same day, and

7.7.1.2   it is served —

(a)   where the receiving party is a company incorporated within Great Britain, at the registered office, or

(b)   where the receiving party is the Tenant, and the Tenant is not such a company, at the Premises, or

(c)   where the receiving party is the Landlord and the Landlord is not such a company, at the Landlord's address shown in this Lease or at any address specified in a notice given by the Landlord to the Tenant.

---

106   Notice clauses are either mandatory or permissive. The words 'and only if' are inserted to make it clear that this clause is mandatory.

107   As to service by fax see *Hastie and Jenkerson v McMahon* [1991] 1 All ER 255, [1990] 1 WLR 1575, CA.

7.7.2   *Deemed delivery*[108]

7.7.2.1   **By registered post or recorded delivery**

Unless it is returned through the Royal Mail undelivered, a notice sent by registered post or recorded delivery is to be treated as served on the third working day after posting whenever and whether or not it is received.

7.7.2.2   **By fax**

A notice sent by fax is to be treated as served on the day upon which it is sent or the next working day where the fax is sent after 1600 hours or on a day that is not a working day, whenever and whether or not it or the confirmatory copy is received unless the confirmatory copy is returned through the Royal Mail undelivered.

7.7.2.3   **'A working day'**

References to 'a working day' are references to a day when the United Kingdom clearing banks are open for business in the City of London.

---

108   It is a fundamental aspect of any notice clause to provide the circumstances in which the server, provided he has complied with the requirements of the clause, has for the purposes of the document served a notice, even if the recipient claims that he never received it.

7.7.3   *Joint recipients*

If the receiving party consists of more than one person a notice to one of them is notice to all.

7.8   [New *(or)* Old] lease

[This Lease [is *(or as appropriate)* is not] a new tenancy for the purposes of the 1995 Act Section 1. *(or as appropriate)* This Lease is granted under the 1995 Act Section 19 and [is *(or as appropriate)* is not] a new tenancy for the purposes of Section 1 of that Act][109].

109   A tenancy granted on or after 1 January 1996 that is an overriding lease is not a 'new' tenancy where the tenancy being overridden is one granted before that date: see the Landlord and Tenant (Covenants) Act 1995 ss 1(4), 20(1). Where the lease being granted is an overriding lease, the lease must include a statement that it is an overriding lease and indicate whether the overriding lease is or is not a 'new' tenancy: see the Landlord and Tenant (Covenants) Act 1995 s 20(2). In these circumstances the second alternative should be used.

[7.9   Capacity of tenants

It is declared that the persons comprising the Tenant hold the Premises as [joint tenants *(or as required)* tenants in common].]

[7.10   Exclusion of the 1954 Act Sections 24–28[110]

7.10.1   *Notice and declaration*

On *(date)* the Landlord served notice on the Tenant pursuant to the provisions of the 1954 Act Section 38A(3) as inserted by the Regulatory Reform (Business Tenancies) (England and Wales) Order 2003 and on *(date)* the Tenant made a [simple *(or as appropriate)* statutory] declaration pursuant to schedule 2 of the Regulatory Reform (Business Tenancies) (England and Wales) Order 2003.

7.10.2   *Agreement to exclude*

Pursuant to the provisions of the 1954 Act Section 38A(1) as inserted by the Regulatory Reform (Business Tenancies) (England and Wales) Order 2003, the parties agree that the provisions of the 1954 Act Sections 24–28 inclusive are to be excluded in relation to the tenancy created by this Lease.]

110   As to contracting out of the Landlord and Tenant Act 1954 and the requirements that need to be complied with see vol 22(1) (2003 Reissue) LANDLORD AND TENANT (BUSINESS TENANCIES) Paragraph 431 [2035].

IN WITNESS etc *(see vol 12(2) (2003 Reissue) DEEDS, AGREEMENTS ETC)*

SCHEDULE 1: THE AUTHORISED GUARANTEE AGREEMENT

(insert the form of authorised guarantee agreement: see, eg vol 22(3) (1997 Reissue) LANDLORD AND TENANT (BUSINESS TENANCIES) Form 217 [7053])

SCHEDULE 2: THE GUARANTEE PROVISIONS

(insert the guarantee provisions: see, eg Form 4 clause 6 [281])

(signature (or common seal) of landlord: lease)
(signature (or common seal) of tenant: counterpart)
(signatures of witnesses)
[2371]–[2995]

INDEX

References are to the numbers in square brackets which appear on the right hand side of the text

BUSINESS LEASE

car park, land for use as. *See* CAR PARK

hotel, of. *See* HOTEL

light industrial premises, of. *See* LIGHT INDUSTRIAL AND WAREHOUSE PREMISES

office, of. See OFFICE

shop, of. *See* SHOP

warehouse, of. *See* LIGHT INDUSTRIAL AND WAREHOUSE PREMISES

CAR PARK

lease of land for use as—
  meaning, [2311]
  1954 Act—
    meaning, [2313]
    exclusion of provisions, [2371]
  1995 Act—
    meaning, [2313]
    terms from, [2315]
  advertisements, fixing, [2336]
  alienation—
    assignment of whole, [2341]
    assignment, subletting and charging of part, [2340]
    charging of whole, [2346]
    circumstances for assignment, [2341]
    conditions of assignment, [2344]
    group company, sharing with, [2346]
    permitted dealings, registration of, [2346]
    prohibition of, [2340]
    subletting of whole, [2340]
  alterations, prohibition, [2335]
  approval—
    mortgagee or head landlord, of, [2310]
    prior written, [2310]

CAR PARK—*Cont*

lease of land for use as—*Cont*
  assignment—
    circumstances for, [2341]
    conditions of, [2344]
    consent for, [2341]
    part, of, [2340]
    whole, of, [2341]
  attendant's hut, [2335]
  attendants, provision of, [2338]
  auctions, trades and immoral purposes, use of premises for, [2337]
  charging—
    part, of, [2340]
    whole, of, [2346]
  clauses and schedules, references to, [2314]
  compensation on vacating, exclusion of, [2369]
  conduits, connection to, [2335]
  consent—
    mortgagee or head landlord, of, [2310]
    prior written, [2310]
  contractual term, [2308]
  costs of grant, [2351]
  definitions and interpretation, [2308]–[2315]
  demise, [2331]
  development, *meaning*, [2309]
  documents under hand, [2369]
  encroachments, [2349]
  end of term, *meaning*, [2311]
  fencing, [2335]
  forfeiture, [2366]
  gender and number, [2309]
  group company, sharing with, [2346]
  headings, [2309]

CAR PARK—*Cont*
  lease of land for use as—*Cont*
    insurance—
      covenant to insure, [2363]
      definitions, [2362]
      events affecting policy, notice
        of, [2364]
      fire authority requirements,
        [2364]
      liability, [2363]
      office, underwriters and
        agency, [2363]
      policy avoidance, [2364]
      premises of, [2363]
      production of policy, [2364]
      requirements of insurers,
        [2364]
      tenant's covenants, [2364]
    interest—
      meaning, [2309]
      rate, [2310]
    joint and several liability, [2311]
    keyholders, [2350]
    landlord—
      meaning, [2311]
      covenants, [2361]
      release, consent to, [2351]
    last year of term, *meaning*, [2311]
    liability period, *meaning*, [2312]
    losses, *meaning*, [2312]
    masts and wires, erection of,
      [2336]
    new or old, [2371]
    notices, [2370]
    nuisance, [2337]
    parties, [2306]
    plan, *meaning*, [2313]
    planning—
      applications, prohibited,
        [2347]
      Planning Acts, compliance
        with, [2347]
    Planning Acts—
      meaning, [2313]
      compliance with, [2347]
    premises—
      meaning, [2314]
      auctions, trades and immoral
        purposes, use for, [2337]
      defect, notice of, [2350]
      reinstatement, [2365]
      residential use, sleeping and
        keeping of animals on, [2338]

CAR PARK—*Cont*
  lease of land for use as—*Cont*
    quiet enjoyment, [2361]
    reinstatement of premises, [2365]
    rent—
      meaning, [2314]
      arrears, interest on, [2349]
      banker's order, payment by,
        [2332]
      payment of, [2332]
    repair—
      entry to inspect and notice to
        repair, [2338]
      landlord's power in default,
        [2339]
      tenant's covenants, [2333]
        [2334]
      works, carrying out, [2339]
    representations, [2368]
    rights of access, references to,
      [2314]
    statutes, references to, [2314]
    statutory notices, [2350]
    statutory obligations of tenant—
      general provisions, [2335]
      particular, [2336]
    tenant—
      meaning, [2311]
      capacity, [2371]
      property remaining in
        premises, [2369]
    tenant's covenants—
      abutting land, care of, [2335]
      aerials, signs and
        advertisements, [2336]
      alienation, [2340]–[2346]
      cleaning and tidying, [2334]
      costs of applications, notices
        and recovery of arrears,
        payment of, [2347]
      costs of grant, [2351]
      defective premises, [2350]
      encroachments, [2349]
      entry to inspect and notice to
        repair, [2338] [2339]
      fixtures, replacement of,
        [2334]
      indemnities, [2348]
      interest on arrears, payment of,
        [2349]
      keyholders, [2350]

CAR PARK—*Cont*
    lease of land for use as—*Cont*
        tenant's covenants—*Cont*
            landlord's release, consent to,
                [2351]
            nuisance and use restrictions,
                [2337] [2338]
            open land, as to, [2334]
            outgoings and VAT, payment
                of, [2333]
            planning and development,
                [2347]
            reletting boards and viewing,
                [2348]
            rent, [2332]
            repair, [2333]
            shared facilities, [2335]
            statutory notices, [2350]
            statutory obligations, [2336]
            use, [2337]
            viewing on sale of reversion,
                [2350]
            waste and alterations, [2335]
            yielding up, [2349]
        term, *meaning*, [2315]
        third party rights, exclusion of,
            [2368]
        VAT, *meaning*, [2315]
        warranty as to use, exclusion of,
            [2368]
        waste, [2335]
HOTEL
    lease—
        meaning, [2113]
        1954 Act—
            meaning, [2115]
            exclusion of provisions, [2215]
        1995 Act—
            meaning, [2115]
            terms from, [2120]
        advertisements, fixing, [2149]
        alienation—
            assignment of whole, [2162]
            assignment, subletting and
                charging of part, [2162]
            charging of whole, [2168]
            circumstances for assignment,
                [2163]
            conditions of assignment,
                [2166]
            enforcement, waiver and
                variation of subleases, [2171]

HOTEL—*Cont*
    lease—*Cont*
        alienation—*Cont*
            exclusion agreement,
                requirement for, [2171]
            group company, sharing with,
                [2172]
            permitted dealings, registration
                of, [2172]
            permitted sublease, terms of,
                [2169]
            prohibition of, [2161]
            sublease rent review, [2172]
            subletting of whole, [2168]
            subtenant's direct covenants,
                [2171]
        alterations—
            pre-conditions, [2148]
            prohibition, [2148]
            removal, [2149]
        approval—
            mortgagee or head landlord,
                of, [2112]
            prior written, [2112]
        assignment—
            circumstances for, [2163]
            conditions of, [2166]
            consent for, [2162]
            part, of, [2162]
            whole, of, [2162]
        auctions, trades and immoral
            purposes, use of premises for,
            [2173]
        charging—
            part, of, [2162]
            whole, of, [2168]
        clauses and schedules, references
            to, [2117]
        compensation on vacating,
            exclusion of, [2213]
        compliance with, evidence of,
            [2177]
        conduits—
            meaning, [2108]
            connection to, [2149]
        consent—
            mortgagee or head landlord,
                of, [2112]
            prior written, [2112]
        contractual term, [2108]
        costs of grant, [2182]

HOTEL—*Cont*
  lease—*Cont*
    definitions and interpretation,
      [2108]–[2120]
    demise, [2141]
    development, *meaning*, [2109]
    disclaimer—
      new lease following, [2207]
      payments following, [2208]
    documents under hand, [2213]
    encroachments, [2178]
    end of term, *meaning*, [2113]
    exterior decorating years, *meaning*,
      [2109]
    forfeiture, [2210]
    gender and number, [2109]
    group company, sharing with,
      [2172]
    guarantor—
      meaning, [2112]
      authorised guarantee
        agreement, liabilities under,
        [2208]
      covenants, [2204]–[2209]
      landlord's covenants, [2209]
      replacement, [2180] [2181]
      severance of provisions, [2209]
    headings, [2109]
    hotel covenants—
      meaning, [2109]
      ceiling and floor loading,
        [2219]
      environmental protection,
        [2218]
      machinery, [2219]
      observance of, [2181]
      signs and name, [2220]
      use, [2217] [218]
    insurance—
      application of moneys, [2201]
      change of risks, [2203]
      conviction, notice of, [2201]
      copy policy, [2202]
      covenant to insure, [2192]
      cover, [2193]
      events affecting policy, notice
        of, [2201]
      insured risks, [2110] [2193]
      landlord's covenants, [2202]
        [2203]
      office, underwriters and
        agency, [2192]

HOTEL—*Cont*
  lease—*Cont*
    insurance——*Cont*
      policy avoidance and
        additional premiums, [2200]
      rent, [2110]
        payment of, [2194]
      requirements of insurers,
        [2200]
      subrogation, waiver of, [2203]
      tenant's covenants, [2200]
        [2201]
      tenant's interest, noting, [2203]
      warranty as to convictions,
        [2191]
    interest—
      meaning, [2110]
      rate, [2111]
    interior decorating years, *meaning*,
      [2111]
    joint and several liability, [2113]
    keyholders, [2180]
    landlord—
      meaning, [2113]
      covenants, [2183]
      guarantor, covenants with,
        [2209]
      release, consent to, [2182]
      rights, exercise of, [2181]
    last year of term, *meaning*, [2113]
    liability period, *meaning*, [2114]
    losses, *meaning*, [2115]
    masts and wires, erection of,
      [2149]
    new or old, [2215]
    notices—
      deemed delivery, [2214]
      form and service of, [2214]
      joint recipients, [2214]
    nuisance, [2173]
    obstruction of windows, [2178]
    parties, [2106]
    plan, *meaning*, [2115]
    planning—
      appeals, [2176]
      charges and levies, [2175]
      completion of development,
        [2176]
      compliance with conditions,
        security for, [2176]

HOTEL—*Cont*
  lease—*Cont*
    planning—*Cont*
      consent for applications,
        [2175]
      permissions and notices,
        [2175]
      Planning Acts, compliance
        with, [2175]
      pre-conditions for
        development, [2175]
    Planning Acts—
      meaning, [2115]
      compliance with, [2175]
    premises—
      auctions, trades and immoral
        purposes, use for, [2173]
      combustible materials on,
        [2200]
      defect, notice of, [2180]
      definition, [2116]
      fire escapes, equipment and
        doors, [2201]
      fire-fighting equipment,
        provision of, [2200]
      interpretation, [2116]
      reinstatement, [2195]–[2199]
    quiet enjoyment, [2183]
    reinstatement of premises—
      notice to terminate, [2199]
      obligation of, [2197]
      permissions, obligation to
        obtain, [2195]
      refusal of money through
        default, on, [2202]
      relief from obligation, [2198]
      termination following failure
        of, [2199]
    renewal, information for, [2177]
    rent—
      meaning, [2118]
      arrears, interest on, [2179]
      banker's order, payment by,
        [2143]
      commencement date, [2118]
      guarantor's covenants, [2205]
      initial, [2109]
      insurance, [2110] [2194]
      payment of, [2143]
      suspension, [2194] [2195]

HOTEL—*Cont*
  lease—*Cont*
    rent review—
      dates, [2119]
      information for, [2177]
      right of access for, [2216]
      sublease, [2172]
    repair—
      entry to inspect and notice to
        repair, [2152]
      landlord's power in default,
        [2152]
      tenant's covenants, [2145]–
        [2147]
      works, carrying out, [2152]
    representations, [2212]
    rights of access, references to,
      [2117]
    rights reserved—
      entry to inspect, [2216]
      renewal or rent review, access
        on, [2216]
    statutes, references to, [2117]
    statutory notices, [2179]
    statutory obligations of tenant—
      general provisions, [2150]
      particular, [2150] [2151]
    sublease—
      consent to, [2168]
      enforcement, waiver and
        variation, [2171]
      exclusion agreement,
        requirement for, [2171]
      part, of, [2162]
      rent review, [2172]
      subtenant's direct covenants,
        [2171]
      terms of, [2169]
    surveyor, *meaning*, [2119]
    tenant—
      meaning, [2113]
      capacity, [2215]
      property remaining in
        premises, [2213]
    tenant's covenants—
      abutting land, care of, [2146]
      aerials, signs and
        advertisements, [2149]
      alienation, [2161]–[2172]
      cleaning and tidying, [2146]

HOTEL—*Cont*
  lease—*Cont*
    tenant's covenants—*Cont*
      costs of applications, notices
        and recovery of arrears,
        payment of, [2174]
      costs of grant, [2182]
      decoration, [2147]
      defective premises, [2180]
      entry to inspect and notice to
        repair, [2152]
      exercise of landlord's rights,
        permitting, [2181]
      fixtures, replacement of,
        [2146]
      hotel, observance of, [2181]
      indemnities, [2177]
      interest on arrears, payment of,
        [2179]
      keyholders, [2180]
      landlord's release, consent to,
        [2182]
      nuisance and residential
        restrictions, [2173] [2174]
      obstruction and
        encroachment, [2178]
      open land, as to, [2146]
      outgoings and VAT, payment
        of, [2144]
      planning and development,
        [2175] [2176]
      plans, documents and
        information, [2177]
      reletting boards and viewing,
        [2178]
      rent, [2143]
      repair, [2145]
      replacement guarantor, [2180]
        [2181]
      services, cost of, [2145]
      shared facilities, [2147]
      statutory notices, [2179]
      statutory obligations, [2150]
        [2151]
      viewing on sale of reversion,
        [2180]
      waste and alterations, [2148]
        [2149]
      yielding up, [2179]
    term, *meaning*, [2120]
    third party rights, exclusion of,
      [2212]

HOTEL—*Cont*
  lease—*Cont*
    VAT, *meaning*, [2120]
    warranty as to use, exclusion of,
      [2212]
    waste, [2148]

LIGHT INDUSTRIAL AND
WAREHOUSE PREMISES
  access via private road across adjoining
    property, lease with—
    meaning, [372]
    1954 Act—
      meaning, [374]
      exclusion of provisions, [496]
    1995 Act—
      meaning, [374]
      terms from, [379]
  access, rights of, [503]
  adjoining property, *meaning*, [358]
  advertisements, fixing, [398]
  alienation—
    assignment of whole, [402]
    assignment, subletting and
      charging of part, [402]
    charging of whole, [407]
    circumstances for assignment,
      [403]
    conditions of assignment,
      [405]
    enforcement, waiver and
      variation of subleases, [410]
    exclusion order, requirement
      for, [410]
    group company, sharing with,
      [412]
    part, of, [402]
    permitted dealings, registration
      of, [412]
    permitted sublease, terms of,
      [408]
    prohibition of, [402]
    sublease rent review, [411]
    subletting of whole, [407]–
      [410]
    subtenant's direct covenants,
      [410]
  alterations—
    pre-conditions for, [397]
    prohibited, [02621]
    removal of, [398]

LIGHT INDUSTRIAL AND WAREHOUSE PREMISES
access via private road across adjoining property, lease with—*Cont*
approval—
mortgagee or head landlord, of, [371]
prior written, [371]
assignment—
circumstances for, [403]
conditions of, [405]
consent for, [403]
part, of, [402]
whole, of, [402]
auctions, trades and immoral purposes, use of premises for, [413]
authorised guarantee agreement, guarantee of tenant's liabilities under, [465]
charging—
part, of, [402]
whole, of, [407]
clauses and schedules, references to, [377]
compensation on vacating, exclusion of, [492]
compliance with, evidence of, [416]
conduits—
meaning, [358]
adjoining, [358]
passage and running through, [501]
use of, [504]
connection to, [398]
passage and running through, [502]
right to construct, [502]
consent—
mortgagee or head landlord, of, [371]
prior written, [371]
contractual term, [359]
definitions and interpretation, [358]–[379]
demise, [380]
development, *meaning*, [360]
disclaimer—
new lease following, [464]
payments following, [465]
documents under hand, [491]

LIGHT INDUSTRIAL AND WAREHOUSE PREMISES
access via private road across adjoining property, lease with—*Cont*
encroachments, [417]
end of term, *meaning*, [372]
exterior decorating years, *meaning*, [360]
forfeiture, [467]
gender and number, [360]
guarantor—
meaning, [372]
guarantor's covenants, [461]–[466]
landlord's covenants with, [466]
replacement, [419] [420]
severance of provisions, [466]
headings, [360]
industrial covenants—
meaning, [360]
environmental protection, [506]
machinery, [507]
observance and performance of, [420]
road and adjoining conduits, use of, [504]
roof and floor loading, [507]
signs, [507]
smoke abatement, [505]
use, [505]
insurance—
application of moneys, [442]
change of risks, [445]
convictions, notice of, [442]
copy policy, [444]
covenant to insure, [432]
cover, [433]
events affecting policy, notice of, [442]
insured risks, [361] [434]
landlord's covenants, [443]–[445]
office, underwriters and agency, [433]
policy avoidance and additional premiums, [441]
rent, [361]
payment of, [434]
requirements of insurers, [441]
subrogation, waiver of, [445]

LIGHT INDUSTRIAL AND
WAREHOUSE PREMISES
  access via private road across adjoining
    property, lease with—*Cont*
    insurance—*Cont*
      tenant's covenants, [441]–[443]
      tenant's interest, noting, [444]
      warranty as to convictions,
        [432]
    interest—
      meaning, [362]
      rate, [362]
    interior decorating years, *meaning*,
      [370]
    joint and several liability, [373]
    landlord—
      meaning, [372]
      covenants, [431]
      guarantor, covenants with,
        [466]
      release, consent to, [421]
      reserved rights, [502] [503]
      rights, exercise of, [420]
    last year of term, *meaning*, [372]
    liability period, *meaning*, [373]
    losses, *meaning*, [374]
    masts and wires, erection of, [398]
    new buildings, right to erect, [503]
    new or old, [495]
    notices—
      deemed delivery, [494]
      form and service of, [493]
    nuisance, [412]
    obstruction of windows, [417]
    open land, care of, [395] [396]
    other buildings, *meaning*, [374]
    parties, [356]
    party walls, [495]
    permitted use, [374]
    perpetuity period, [495]
    plan, *meaning*, [375]
    planning—
      appeals, [415]
      charges and levies, [414]
      completion of development,
        [415]
      compliance with conditions,
        security for, [415]
      consent for applications, [414]
      permissions and notices, [414]
      pre-conditions for
        development, [415]

LIGHT INDUSTRIAL AND
WAREHOUSE PREMISES
  access via private road across adjoining
    property, lease with—*Cont*
    Planning Acts—
      meaning, [375]
      compliance with, [414]
    premises—
      additions to, [397]
      defect, notice of, [419]
      definition, [376]
      interpretation, [376]
      use of, [505]
    quiet enjoyment, [431]
    reinstatement of premises—
      notice to terminate, [440]
      obligation of, [438]
      permissions, obligation to
        obtain, [437]
      refusal of money through
        default, on, [443]
      relief from obligation, [439]
      termination following failure
        of, [440]
    rent—
      meaning, [378]
      arrears, interest on, [418]
      banker's order, payment by,
        [391]
      commencement date, [378]
      initial, [360]
      insurance, [361] [434]
      payment of, [391]
      suspension, [435] [436]
    rent review—
      access on, [503]
      dates, [378]
      information for, [416]
      sublease, [411]
    repair—
      entry to inspect and notice to
        repair, [400]
      landlord's covenants, [431]
      landlord's power in default,
        [401]
      tenant's covenants, [395]
      works, carrying out, [400]
    representations, [491]
    rights granted—
      passage and running though
        adjoining conduits, [501]
      right of way, [501]

LIGHT INDUSTRIAL AND
WAREHOUSE PREMISES
  access via private road across adjoining
    property, lease with—*Cont*
    rights of access, references to,
      [377]
    rights reserved, [502] [503]
    road, *meaning*, [378]
    statutes, references to, [377]
    statutory obligations of tenant—
      general provisions, [399]
      particular, [399]
    sublease—
      consent for, [407]
      enforcement, waiver and
        variation, [410]
      exclusion order, requirement
        for, [410]
      rent review, [411]
      subtenant's direct covenants,
        [410]
      terms of, [408]
    surveyor, *meaning*, [379]
    tenant—
      meaning, [372]
      capacity, [496]
      property remaining in
        premises, [492]
    tenant's covenants—
      adjoining property and
        abutting land, care of, [396]
      aerials, signs and
        advertisements, [398]
      alienation, [402]–[412]
      auctions, trades and immoral
        purposes, use for, [413]
      cleaning and tidying, [395]
      costs of applications, notices
        and recovery of arrears,
        payment of, [413]
      costs of grant, payment of,
        [420]
      decoration, [396]
      defective premises, [419]
      entry to inspect and notice to
        repair, [400] [401]
      fixtures, replacement of, [395]
      indemnities, [416]
      industrial, observance of, [420]
      interest on arrears, payment of,
        [418]

LIGHT INDUSTRIAL AND
WAREHOUSE PREMISES
  access via private road across adjoining
    property, lease with—*Cont*
    tenant's covenants—*Cont*
      keyholders, [419]
      landlord's release, consent to,
        [421]
      landlord's rights, exercise of,
        [420]
      nuisance and residential
        restrictions, [412] [413]
      obligation not to permit or
        suffer, [374]
      obstruction and
        encroachment, [417]
      open land, as to, [395] [396]
      outgoings and VAT, payment
        of, [391] [392]
      Planning Acts, compliance
        with, [414]
      planning and development,
        [414] [415]
      plans, documents and
        information, [416]
      reletting boards and viewing,
        [417]
      rent, [391]
      repair, [395]
      replacement guarantor, [419]
        [420]
      residential use, sleeping and
        keeping of animals on, [413]
      services, cost of, [393]
      shared facilities, as to, [396]
      statutory notices, [419]
      statutory obligations, [399]
      viewing on sale of reversion,
        [419]
      waste and alterations, [397]
        [398]
      works, carrying out, [400]
      yielding up, [418]
    term, *meaning*, [379]
    third party rights, exclusion, [491]
    VAT, *meaning*, [379]
    warranty as to use, exclusion of,
      [491]
    waste, [397]

**LIGHT INDUSTRIAL AND
  WAREHOUSE PREMISES**—*Cont*
  premises where landlord not owning
  adjoining property, lease of—
  meaning, [164]
  1954 Act—
    meaning, [166]
    exclusion of provisions, [315]
  1995 Act—
    meaning, [166]
    terms from, [172]
  advertisements, fixing, [198]
  alienation—
    assignment of whole, [212]
    assignment, subletting and
      charging of part, [211]
    charging of whole, [216]
    circumstances for assignment,
      [212]
    conditions of assignment, [214]
    enforcement, waiver and
      variation of subleases, [220]
    exclusion order, requirement
      for, [219]
    group company, sharing with,
      [221]
    permitted dealings, registration
      of, [221]
    permitted sublease, terms of,
      [217]
    prohibition of, [211]
    sublease rent review, [220]
    subletting of whole, [216]
    subtenant's direct covenants,
      [219]
  alterations—
    pre-conditions for, [196]
    prohibited, [196]
    removal of, [197]
  approval—
    mortgagee or head landlord,
      of, [163]
    prior written, [163]
  assignment—
    circumstances for, [212]
    conditions of, [214]
    consent for, [212]–[214]
    part, of, [211]
    whole, of, [212]
  auctions, trades and immoral
    purposes, use of premises for,
    [222]

**LIGHT INDUSTRIAL AND
  WAREHOUSE PREMISES**—*Cont*
  premises where landlord not owning
  adjoining property, lease of—*Cont*
  authorised guarantee agreement,
    tenant's liabilities under, [285]
  charging—
    part, of, [211]
    whole, of, [216]
  clauses and schedules, references
    to, [169]
  compensation on vacating,
    exclusion of, [312]
  compliance with, evidence of,
    [234]
  conduits—
    meaning, [158]
    connection to, [197]
  consent—
    mortgagee or head landlord,
      of, [163]
    prior written, [163]
  contractual term, [159]
  costs of grant, [239]
  definitions and interpretation,
    [158]–[172]
  demise, [181]
  development, *meaning*, [160]
  disclaimer—
    new lease following, [284]
    payments following, [285]
  documents under hand, [312]
  encroachments, [236]
  end of term, *meaning*, [164]
  exterior decorating years, *meaning*,
    [160]
  forfeiture, [301]
  gender and number, [160]
  guarantor—
    meaning, [164]
    covenants, [281]–[286]
    landlord's covenants with,
      [286]
    replacement, [238]
    severance of provisions, [286]
  headings, [160]
  industrial covenants—
    meaning, [161]
    environmental protection,
      [323] [324]
    machinery, [325]

LIGHT INDUSTRIAL AND
  WAREHOUSE PREMISES—*Cont*
  premises where landlord not owning
    adjoining property, lease of—*Cont*
    industrial covenants—*Cont*
      observance and performance
        of, [239]
      roof and floor loading, [325]
      signs, [325]
      smoke abatement, [322]
      use, [322]
    insurance—
      application of moneys, [263]
      change of risks, [265]
      convictions, notice of, [263]
      copy policy, [264]
      covenant to insure, [253]
      cover, [254]
      events affecting policy, notice
        of, [263]
      insured risks, [161] [255]
      landlord's covenants, [264]
        [265]
      office, underwriters and
        agency, [253]
      policy avoidance and
        additional premiums, [262]
      rent, [161]
        payment of, [255]
      requirements of insurers, [262]
      subrogation, waiver of, [265]
      tenant's covenants, [262] [263]
      tenant's interest, noting, [264]
      warranty as to convictions,
        [252]
    interest—
      meaning, [162]
      rate, [162]
    interior decorating years, *meaning*,
      [163]
    joint and several liability, [165]
    landlord—
      meaning, [164]
      guarantor, covenants with,
        [286]
      release, consent to, [239]
      reserved rights, [321]
      rights, exercise of, [238]
    last year of term, *meaning*, [164]
    liability period, *meaning*, [165]
    losses, *meaning*, [166]
    masts and wires, erection of, [198]

LIGHT INDUSTRIAL AND
  WAREHOUSE PREMISES—*Cont*
  premises where landlord not owning
    adjoining property, lease of—*Cont*
    new or old, [314]
    notices—
      deemed delivery, [314]
      form and service of, [313]
    nuisance, [222]
    obstruction of windows, [236]
    parties, [156]
    permitted use, [167]
    plan, *meaning*, [167]
    planning—
      appeals, [234]
      charges and levies, [231]
      completion of development,
        [233]
      compliance with conditions,
        security for, [233]
      consent for applications, [231]
      permissions and notices, [231]
      Planning Acts, compliance
        with, [232]
      pre-conditions for
        development, [233]
    Planning Acts—
      meaning, [168]
      compliance with, [232]
    premises—
      additions to, [196]
      auctions, trades and immoral
        purposes, use for, [222]
      combustible materials on,
        [262]
      defect, notice of, [237]
      definition, [168]
      fire escapes, equipment and
        doors, [262]
      fire-fighting equipment,
        provision of, [262]
      interpretation, [168]
      reinstatement, [259]–[261]
      residential use, sleeping and
        keeping of animals on, [231]
    quiet enjoyment, [251]
    reinstatement of premises—
      notice to terminate, [261]
      obligation of, [259]
      permissions, obligation to
        obtain, [257]
      refusal of money through
        default, on, [263]

LIGHT INDUSTRIAL AND
  WAREHOUSE PREMISES—*Cont*
  premises where landlord not owning
    adjoining property, lease of—*Cont*
    reinstatement of premises—*Cont*
      relief from obligation, [260]
      termination following failure
        of, [261]
    renewal, information for, [234]
    rent—
      meaning, [170]
      arrears, interest on, [237]
      banker's order, payment by,
        [191]
      commencement date, [170]
      guarantor's covenants, [280]
      initial, [161]
      insurance, [161]
      insurance, [255]
      payment of, [191]
      suspension, [256] [257]
    rent review—
      access on, [321]
      dates, [171]
      information for, [234]
      sublease, [220]
    repair—
      entry to inspect and notice to
        repair, [200]
      landlord's power in default,
        [201]
      tenant's covenants, [193]
      works, carrying out, [200]
        [201]
    representations, [311]
    rights of access, references to,
      [169]
    statutes, references to, [169]
    statutory obligations of tenant—
      general provisions, [198]
      particular, [199]
    sublease—
      consent for, [216]
      enforcement, waiver and
        variation, [220]
      exclusion order, requirement
        for, [219]
      part, of, [211]
      rent review, [220]
      subtenant's direct covenants,
        [219]
      terms of, [217]
    surveyor, *meaning*, [171]

LIGHT INDUSTRIAL AND
  WAREHOUSE PREMISES—*Cont*
  premises where landlord not owning
    adjoining property, lease of—*Cont*
    tenant—
      meaning, [164]
      capacity, [315]
      property remaining in
        premises, [312]
    tenant's covenants—
      abutting land, care of, [195]
      aerials, signs and
        advertisements, [3268]
      alienation, [211]–[221]
      cleaning and tidying, [194]
      costs of applications, notices
        and recovery of arrears,
        payment of, [231]
      costs of grant, payment of,
        [239]
      decoration, [195]
      defective premises, [237]
      entry to inspect and notice to
        repair, [200] [201]
      fixtures, replacement of, [194]
      indemnities, [235]
      industrial, observance of, [239]
      interest on arrears, payment of,
        [237]
      keyholders, [237]
      landlord's release, consent to,
        [239]
      landlord's rights, exercise of,
        [238]
      nuisance and residential
        restrictions, [222] [231]
      obstruction and
        encroachment, [236]
      open land, as to, [194]
      outgoings and VAT, payment
        of, [192]
      planning and development,
        [232]–[234]
      plans, documents and
        information, [234]
      reletting boards and viewing,
        [235]
      rent, [191]
      repair, [193]
      replacement guarantor, [238]
      services, cost of, [192]
      shared facilities, as to, [195]

LIGHT INDUSTRIAL AND
  WAREHOUSE PREMISES—*Cont*
  premises where landlord not owning
    adjoining property, lease of—*Cont*
    tenant's covenants—*Cont*
      statutory notices, [237]
      statutory obligations, [198]
        [199]
      viewing on sale of reversion,
        [237]
      waste and alterations, [196]
        [197]
      yielding up, [236]
    term, *meaning*, [172]
    third party rights, exclusion, [311]
    VAT, *meaning*, [172]
    warranty as to use, exclusion of,
      [311]
    waste, [196]
  small estate, lease on—
    meaning, [564]
    1954 Act—
      meaning, [566]
      exclusion of provisions, [659]
    1995 Act—
      meaning, [566]
      terms from, [571]
    access, rights of, [673]
    adjoining occupiers, disputes with,
      [657]
    adjoining property—
      meaning, [558]
      care of, [587]
      covenants relating to, [657]
    advertisements, fixing, [590]
    alienation—
      assignment of whole, [594]
      assignment, subletting and
        charging of part, [594]
      charging of whole, [600]
      circumstances for assignment,
        [595]
      conditions of assignment,
        [598]
      enforcement, waiver and
        variation of subleases, [603]
      exclusion order, requirement
        for, [603]
      group company, sharing with,
        [604]
      permitted dealings, registration
        of, [604]

LIGHT INDUSTRIAL AND
  WAREHOUSE PREMISES—*Cont*
  small estate, lease on—*Cont*
    alienation—*Cont*
      permitted sublease, terms of,
        [601]
      prohibition of, [593]
      sublease rent review, [604]
      subletting of whole, [600]
      subtenant's direct covenants,
        [603]
    alterations—
      pre-conditions for, [589]
      prohibited, [589]
      removal of, [590]
    approval—
      mortgagee or head landlord,
        of, [563]
      prior written, [563]
    assignment—
      circumstances for, [595]
      conditions of, [598]
      consent for, [595]
      part, of, [594]
      whole, of, [594]
    auctions, trades and immoral
      purposes, use of premises for,
      [605]
    charging—
      part, of, [594]
      whole, of, [600]
    clauses and schedules, references
      to, [569]
    compensation on vacating,
      exclusion of, [654]
    compliance with, evidence of,
      [608]
    conduits—
      meaning, [558]
      adjoining, [558]
        passage and running
          through, [671]
        repair of, [621]
      connection to, [590]
      passage and running through,
        [672]
      right to construct, [672]
    consent—
      mortgagee or head landlord,
        of, [563]
      prior written, [563]

LIGHT INDUSTRIAL AND
WAREHOUSE PREMISES—*Cont*
small estate, lease on—*Cont*
contractual term, [559]
definitions and interpretation,
[558]–[571]
demise, [581]
development, *meaning*, [560]
disclaimer—
new lease following, [644]
payments following, [645]
documents under hand, [654]
encroachments, [610]
end of term, *meaning*, [564]
estate, *meaning*, [560]
estate roads—
meaning, [560]
repairs, [621]
exterior decorating years, *meaning*,
[560]
forfeiture, [651]
gender and number, [560]
guarantor—
meaning, [564]
covenants, [641]–[646]
landlord's covenants with,
[646]
replacement, [612] [613]
severance of provisions, [646]
headings, [560]
industrial covenants—
meaning, [561]
environmental protection,
[675] [676]
machinery, [677]
observance and performance
of, [613]
parking, [678]
regulations, [678]
roof and floor loading, [676]
service charge, [677]
signs, [677]
smoke abatement, [674]
use, [674]
insurance—
application of moneys, [632]
change of risks, [634]
convictions, notice of, [632]
copy policy, [633]
covenant to insure, [623]
cover, [624]

LIGHT INDUSTRIAL AND
WAREHOUSE PREMISES—*Cont*
small estate, lease on—*Cont*
insurance—*Cont*
events affecting policy, notice
of, [632]
insured risks, [561] [624]
landlord's covenants, [633]
[634]
office, underwriters and
agency, [623]
policy avoidance and
additional premiums, [631]
rent, [561]
payment of, [625]
requirements of insurers, [631]
subrogation, waiver of, [634]
tenant's covenants, [631] [632]
tenant's interest, noting, [633]
warranty as to convictions,
[622]
interest—
meaning, [562]
rate, [562]
interior decorating years, *meaning*,
[563]
joint and several liability, [564]
landlord—
meaning, [564]
covenants, [621]
guarantor, covenants with,
[646]
release, consent to, [614]
reserved rights, [672] [673]
rights, exercise of, [613]
last year of term, *meaning*, [564]
liability period, *meaning*, [565]
losses, *meaning*, [566]
masts and wires, erection of, [590]
new buildings, right to erect, [673]
new or old, [658]
notices—
deemed delivery, [656]
form and service of, [655]
nuisance, [605]
obstruction of windows, [610]
other buildings, *meaning*, [566]
parties, [556]
party walls, [658]
permitted use, [567]
perpetuity period, [657]

LIGHT INDUSTRIAL AND
    WAREHOUSE PREMISES—*Cont*
  premises where landlord not owning
    adjoining property, lease of—*Cont*
    plan, *meaning*, [567]
    planning—
        appeals, [608]
        charges and levies, [608]
        completion of development,
            [608]
        compliance with conditions,
            security for, [608]
        consent for applications, [607]
        permissions and notices, [607]
        Planning Acts, compliance
            with, [607]
        pre-conditions for
            development, [608]
    Planning Acts—
        meaning, [567]
        compliance with, [607]
    premises—
        additions to, [589]
        auctions, trades and immoral
            purposes, use for, [605]
        combustible materials on,
            [631]
        defect, notice of, [612]
        definition, [568]
        fire escapes, equipment and
            doors, [631]
        fire-fighting equipment,
            provision of, [631]
        interpretation, [568]
        reinstatement, [626]–[630]
        residential use, sleeping and
            keeping of animals on, [605]
    quiet enjoyment, [621]
    reinstatement of premises—
        notice to terminate, [629]
        obligation of, [628]
        permissions, obligation to
            obtain, [626]
        refusal of money through
            default, on, [632]
        relief from obligation, [629]
        termination following failure
            of, [630]
    rent—
        meaning, [569]
        arrears, interest on, [611]
        banker's order, payment by,
            [583]

LIGHT INDUSTRIAL AND
    WAREHOUSE PREMISES—*Cont*
  premises where landlord not owning
    adjoining property, lease of—*Cont*
    rent—*Cont*
        commencement date, [570]
        guarantor's covenants, [642]
        initial, [561]
        insurance, [561]
        insurance, [625]
        payment of, [583]
        suspension, [625] [626]
    rent review—
        access on, [673]
        dates, [570]
        information for, [609]
        sublease, [604]
    repair—
        entry to inspect and notice to
            repair, [592]
        landlord's covenants, [621]
        landlord's power in default,
            [593]
        tenant's covenants, [586]
        works, carrying out, [592]
    representations, [653]
    rights and easements, [657]
    rights granted—
        passage and running though
            adjoining conduits, [672]
        right of way, [671]
    rights of access, references to,
        [569]
    rights reserved, [672] [673]
    statutes, references to, [569]
    statutory obligations of tenant—
        general provisions, [591]
        particular, [591]
    sublease—
        consent for, [600]
        enforcement, waiver and
            variation, [603]
        exclusion order, requirement
            for, [603]
        part, of, [594]
        rent review, [604]
        subtenant's direct covenants,
            [603]
        terms of, [601]
    surveyor, *meaning*, [570]

LIGHT INDUSTRIAL AND
  WAREHOUSE PREMISES—*Cont*
  premises where landlord not owning
    adjoining property, lease of—*Cont*
    tenant—
      meaning, [564]
      capacity, [658]
      property remaining in
        premises, [654]
    tenant's covenants—
      adjoining property and
        abutting land, care of, [587]
      aerials, signs and
        advertisements, [590]
      alienation, [593]–[604]
      cleaning and tidying, [587]
      costs of applications, notices
        and recovery of arrears,
        payment of, [606]
      costs of grant, payment of,
        [613]
      decoration, [588]
      defective premises, [612]
      entry to inspect and notice to
        repair, [592] [593]
      fixtures, replacement of, [587]
      indemnities, [609]
      industrial, observance and
        performance of, [613]
      interest on arrears, payment of,
        [611]
      keyholders, [612]
      landlord's release, consent to,
        [614]
      landlord's rights, exercise of,
        [613]
      nuisance and residential
        restrictions, [605]
      obstruction and
        encroachment, [610]
      open land, as to, [587]
      outgoings and VAT, payment
        of, [584] [585]
      planning and development,
        [607] [608]
      plans, documents and
        information, [609]
      reletting boards and viewing,
        [610]
      rent, [583]
      repair, [586]

LIGHT INDUSTRIAL AND
  WAREHOUSE PREMISES—*Cont*
  premises where landlord not owning
    adjoining property, lease of—*Cont*
    tenant's covenants—*Cont*
      replacement guarantor, [612]
        [613]
      services, cost of, [585]
      shared facilities, as to, [588]
      statutory notices, [611]
      statutory obligations, [591]
      viewing on sale of reversion,
        [612]
      waste and alterations, [589]
        [590]
      yielding up, [611]
    term, *meaning*, [571]
    third party rights, exclusion of,
      [653]
    VAT, *meaning*, [571]
    waiver of covenants, effect of,
      [657]
    warranty as to use, exclusion of,
      [653]
    waste, [589]
  unit forming part of building on
    estate, lease of—
    meaning, [714]
    1954 Act—
      meaning, [732]
      exclusion of provisions, [878]
    1995 Act—
      meaning, [732]
      terms from, [737]
    accountant, *meaning*, [708]
    adjoining occupiers, disputes with,
      [876]
    adjoining property—
      meaning, [708]
      care of, [755]
      covenants relating to, [876]
    advertisements, fixing, [757]
    alienation—
      assignment of whole, [782]
      assignment, subletting and
        charging of part, [781]
      charging of whole, [786]
      circumstances for assignment,
        [782]
      conditions of assignment,
        [784]

LIGHT INDUSTRIAL AND
   WAREHOUSE PREMISES—*Cont*
   unit forming part of building on
   estate, lease of—*Cont*
      alienation—*Cont*
         enforcement, waiver and
            variation of subleases, [789]
         exclusion order, requirement
            for, [789]
         group company, sharing with,
            [791]
         permitted dealings, registration
            of, [791]
         permitted sublease, terms of,
            [787]
         prohibition of, [781]
         sublease rent review, [790]
         subletting of whole, [786]
         subtenant's direct covenants,
            [789]
      approval—
         mortgagee or head landlord,
            of, [713]
         prior written, [713]
      assignment—
         circumstances for, [782]
         conditions of, [784]
         consent for, [784]
         part, of, [781]
         whole, of, [782]
      auctions, trades and immoral
         purposes, use of premises for,
         [792]
      building, *meaning*, [708]
      charging—
         part, of, [781]
         whole, of, [786]
      clauses and schedules, references
         to, [735]
      common parts—
         meaning, [708]
         right to use, [880]
         selling in, [888]
      compensation on vacating,
         exclusion of, [874]
      compliance with, evidence of,
         [803]
      conduits—
         meaning, [709]
         adjoining, [708]
            passage and running
               through, [880]
         connection to, [757]

LIGHT INDUSTRIAL AND
   WAREHOUSE PREMISES—*Cont*
   unit forming part of building on
   estate, lease of—*Cont*
      conduits—*Cont*
         construction of, [881]
         passage and running through,
            [881]
      consent—
         mortgagee or head landlord,
            of, [713]
         prior written, [713]
      contractual term, [709]
      costs of grant, [807]
      decorating years, *meaning*, [710]
      definitions and interpretation,
         [708]–[737]
      demise, [738]
      development, *meaning*, [710]
      disclaimer—
         new lease following, [854]
         payments following, [855]
      documents under hand, [874]
      encroachments, [804]
      end of term, *meaning*, [714]
      estate—
         meaning, [710] [713]
         increase or decrease of, [833]
      estate roads, *meaning*, [710]
      exclusion of liability, [877]
      forfeiture, [871]
      gender and number, [710]
      group company, sharing with,
         [791]
      guarantor—
         meaning, [713]
         covenants, [851]–[856]
         landlord's covenants with,
            [856]
         replacement, [806]
         severance of provisions, [856]
      headings, [710]
      industrial covenants—
         meaning, [710]
         common parts, selling in, [888]
         environmental protection,
            [885] [886]
         machinery, [887]
         observation and performance
            of, [807]
         regulations, [888]
         roof and floor loading, [886]
         signs, [887]

LIGHT INDUSTRIAL AND
  WAREHOUSE PREMISES—*Cont*
  unit forming part of building on
  estate, lease of—*Cont*
    industrial covenants—*Cont*
      smoke abatement, [884]
      unloading and parking, [887]
      use, [884]
    insurance—
      application of moneys, [832]
      change of risks, [834]
      convictions, notice of, [832]
      copy policy, [833]
      covenant to insure, [823]
      cover, [824]
      events affecting policy, notice
        of, [832]
      insured risks, [711] [824]
      landlord's covenants, [833]
      office, underwriters and
        agency, [824]
      policy avoidance and
        additional premiums, [831]
      rent, [711]
        payment of, [825]
      rent percentage—
        meaning, [711]
        variation of, [833]
      requirements of insurers, [831]
      subrogation, waiver of, [834]
      tenant's covenants, [831] [832]
      tenant's interest, noting, [834]
      warranty as to convictions,
        [823]
    interest—
      meaning, [712]
      rate, [712]
    joint and several liability, [714]
    keyholders, [806]
    landlord—
      meaning, [714]
      covenants, [821] [822]
      expenses, *meaning*, [714]
      guarantor, covenants with,
        [856]
      release, consent to, [807]
      rights, exercise of, [806]
      services, provision of, [822]
    last year of term, *meaning*, [714]
    liability period, *meaning*, [731]
    losses, *meaning*, [732]
    masts and wires, erection of, [757]

LIGHT INDUSTRIAL AND
  WAREHOUSE PREMISES—*Cont*
  unit forming part of building on
  estate, lease of—*Cont*
    new or old, [877]
    notices—
      deemed delivery, [875]
      form and service of, [875]
      joint recipients, [875]
    nuisance, [791]
    obstruction of windows, [804]
    parking bays, tenant's covenants,
      [755]
    parties, [706]
    party walls, [877]
    permitted use, [733]
    perpetuity period, [877]
    plan, *meaning*, [733]
    planning—
      appeals, [802]
      charges and levies, [801]
      completion of development,
        [802]
      compliance with conditions,
        security for, [802]
      consent for applications, [801]
      permissions and notices, [801]
      Planning Acts, compliance
        with, [801]
      pre-conditions for
        development, [802]
    Planning Acts—
      meaning, [733]
      compliance with, [801]
    premises—
      auctions, trades and immoral
        purposes, use for, [792]
      combustible materials on,
        [831]
      defect, notice of, [806]
      definition, [733]
      fire escapes, equipment and
        doors, [831]
      fire-fighting equipment,
        provision of, [831]
      interpretation, [734]
      reinstatement, [826]–[831]
      residential use, sleeping and
        keeping of animals on, [792]
    quiet enjoyment, [821]

LIGHT INDUSTRIAL AND
  WAREHOUSE PREMISES—*Cont*
  unit forming part of building on
  estate, lease of—*Cont*
    reinstatement of premises—
      notice to terminate, [830]
      obligation of, [828]
      permissions, obligation to
        obtain, [826]
      relief from obligation, [829]
      termination following failure
        of, [830]
    renewal, information for, [803]
    rent—
      meaning, [735]
      arrears, interest on, [805]
      banker's order, payment by,
        [752]
      commencement date, [735]
      guarantor's covenants, [852]
      initial, [711]
      insurance, [711]
      insurance, [825]
      payment of, [752]
      suspension, [825] [826]
    rent review—
      dates, [736]
      information for, [803]
      sublease, [790]
    repair—
      entry to inspect and notice to
        repair, [759]
      landlord's power in default,
        [759]
      tenant's covenants, [754] [755]
      works, carrying out, [759]
    representations, [873]
    rights and easements, [876]
    rights granted—
      adjoining conduits, passage
        and running through, [880]
      common parts, use of, [880]
      right of way, [879]
      support and protection, [880]
    rights of access, references to,
      [735]
    rights reserved—
      conduits, passage and running
        through, [881]
      construction of conduits, [881]
      entry on renewal or rent
        review, [882]

LIGHT INDUSTRIAL AND
  WAREHOUSE PREMISES—*Cont*
  unit forming part of building on
  estate, lease of—*Cont*
    rights reserved—*Cont*
      entry to inspect, [882]
      new buildings, erection of,
        [883]
      scaffolding, right to erect,
        [883]
      support and shelter, of, [883]
    service charge—
      meaning, [736]
      deemed expenses, [890]
      definitions, [889]
      final account and adjustments,
        [891]
      first financial year, for, [891]
      landlord's contribution, [891]
      landlord's expenses, certificate
        of, [890]
      payment on account, [891]
      payment, [891]
      percentage—
        meaning, [736]
        variation of, [891]
      services, [892]–[894]
    services—
      meaning, [736]
      list of, [892]–[894]
      provision of, [822]
      relief from liability, [822]
      special, [822]
      variation and withholding,
        [822]
    smoke abatement, [884]
    statutes, references to, [735]
    statutory obligations of tenant—
      general provisions, [758]
      particular, [758]
    subjections, [888]
    sublease—
      consent for, [786]
      enforcement, waiver and
        variation, [789]
      exclusion order, requirement
        for, [789]
      part, of, [781]
      rent review, [790]
      subtenant's direct covenants,
        [789]
      terms of, [787]

LIGHT INDUSTRIAL AND WAREHOUSE PREMISES—*Cont*

unit forming part of building on estate, lease of—*Cont*

surveyor, *meaning*, [737]

tenant—

  meaning, [714]

  capacity, [878]

  property remaining in premises, [874]

tenant's covenants—

  adjoining property and abutting land, care of, [755]

  aerials, signs and advertisements, [757]

  alienation, [781]–[791]

  cleaning and tidying, [755]

  costs of applications, notices and recovery of arrears, payment of, [792]

  costs of grant, [807]

  decoration, [755]

  defective premises, [806]

  entry to inspect and notice to repair, [759]

  exercise of landlord's rights, permitting, [806]

  fixtures, replacement of, [755]

  indemnities, [803]

  interest on arrears, payment of, [805]

  keyholders, [806]

  landlord's release, consent to, [807]

  nuisance and residential restrictions, [791] [792]

  obstruction and encroachment, [804]

  outgoings and VAT, payment of, [753]

  parking bays, as to, [755]

  planning and development, [801] [802]

  plans, documents and information, [803]

  reletting boards and viewing, [804]

  rent, [752]

  repair, [754]

  replacement guarantor, [806]

  services, cost of, [754]

  statutory notices, [805]

LIGHT INDUSTRIAL AND WAREHOUSE PREMISES—*Cont*

unit forming part of building on estate, lease of—*Cont*

tenant's covenants—*Cont*

  statutory obligations, [758]

  viewing on sale of reversion, [806]

  waste and alterations, [756] [757]

  yielding up, [805]

term, *meaning*, [737]

third party rights, exclusion of, [873]

VAT, *meaning*, [737]

waiver of covenants, effect of, [876]

warranty as to use, exclusion of, [873]

waste, [756]

LICENCE

occupy, to—

accessways—

  meaning, [5]

  undertaking not to obstruct, [12]

assignment, prohibition of, [15]

building, *meaning*, [5]

car park, *meaning*, [5]

clauses, reference to, [7]

definitions and interpretation, [5]–[7]

designated hours, *meaning*, [5]

designated parking space—

  meaning, [6]

  nuisance, undertaking not to cause, [13]

  registration numbers, notification of, [13]

designated space—

  meaning, [6]

  nuisance, undertaking not to cause, [13]

determination, [15]

headings, [6]

liability, exclusion of, [16]

licence fee—

  meaning, [7]

  undertaking to pay, [11]

licence, generally, [11]

licence period, *meaning*, [7]

LICENCE—*Cont*
  occupy, to—*Cont*
    licensee's undertakings—
      accessways, not obstructing, [12]
      chattels, consent for, [12]
      deposit, payment of, [12]
      goods, display of, [12]
      indemnity, [13]
      licence fee and outgoings, payment of, [11]
      nuisance, not to cause, [13]
      owner's costs, as to, [14]
      owner's rights, as to, [14]
      property, condition of, [12]
      registration numbers, notification of, [13]
      restrictions of owner's lease, observation of, [14]
      rules and regulations, observing, [13]
      signs and notices, display of, [12]
      statutory requirements, not breaching, [13]
    notices, [16]
    parties, [3]
    premises, *meaning*, [7]
    VAT, *meaning*, [7]
    warranty, exclusion of, [16]

OFFICE
  suite, lease of—
    meaning, [1815]
    1954 Act—
      meaning, [1817]
      exclusion of provisions, [1957]
    1995 Act—
      meaning, [1817]
      terms from, [1823]
    accountant, *meaning*, [1809]
    adjoining owners, disputes with, [1955]
    adjoining property—
      meaning, [1809]
      covenants relating to, [1955]
    advertisements, fixing, [1850]
    alienation—
      assignment of whole, [1854]
      assignment, subletting and charging of part, [1854]
      charging of whole, [1859]

OFFICE—*Cont*
  suite, lease of—*Cont*
    alienation—*Cont*
      circumstances for assignment, [1855]
      conditions of assignment, [1858]
      enforcement, waiver and variation of subleases, [1862]
      exclusion order, requirement for, [1862]
      group company, sharing with, [1863]
      permitted dealings, registration of, [1863]
      permitted sublease, terms of, [1860]
      prohibition of, [1853]
      sublease rent review, [1863]
      subletting of whole, [1859]
      subtenant's direct covenants, [1862]
    alterations—
      internal partitions, [1849]
      pre-conditions, [1848]
      prohibition, [1848]
      removal, [1849]
    approval—
      mortgagee or head landlord, of, [1814]
      prior written, [1814]
    assignment—
      circumstances for, [1855]
      conditions of, [1858]
      consent for, [1854]
      part, of, [1854]
      whole, of, [1854]
    auctions, trades and immoral purposes, use of premises for, [1871]
    building, *meaning*, [1809] [1814]
    charging—
      part, of, [1854]
      whole, of, [1859]
    clauses and schedules, references to, [1821]
    common parts—
      meaning, [1809]
      office covenants, [1976]
      right to use, [1971]
    compensation on vacating, exclusion of, [1952]

OFFICE—*Cont*
   suite, lease of—*Cont*
     compliance with, evidence of,
      [1875]
     conduits—
      meaning, [1809]
      adjoining—
       meaning, [1809]
       passage and running
        through, [1971]
      connection to, [1849]
      construction of, [1972]
      passage and running through,
       [1972]
     consent—
      mortgagee or head landlord,
       of, [1814]
      prior written, [1814]
     contractual term, [1810]
     costs of grant, [1880]
     decorating years, *meaning*, [1811]
     definitions and interpretation,
      [1809]–[1823]
     demise, [1841]
     development, *meaning*, [1811]
     disclaimer—
      new lease following, [1934]
      payments following, [1935]
     documents under hand, [1952]
     encroachments, [1876]
     end of term, *meaning*, [1815]
     exclusion of liability, [1956]
     forfeiture, [1937]
     gender and number, [1811]
     group company, sharing with,
      [1863]
     guarantor—
      meaning, [1815]
      authorised guarantee
       agreement, liabilities under,
       [1935]
      covenants, [1930]–[1936]
      landlord's covenants with,
       [1936]
      replacement, [1879]
      severance of provisions, [1936]
     headings, [1811]
     insurance—
      application of moneys, [1913]
      change of risks, [1915]
      convictions, notice of, [1913]
      copy policy, [1914]

OFFICE—*Cont*
   suite, lease of—*Cont*
     insurance—*Cont*
      covenant to insure, [1903]
      cover, [1904]
      events affecting policy, notice
       of, [1913]
      insured risks, [1812] [1904]
      landlord's covenants, [1914]
       [1915]
      office, underwriters and
       agency, [1904]
      policy avoidance and
       additional premiums, [1912]
      rent percentage, [1812]
       variation of, [1914]
      rent, [1812]
       payment of, [1905]
      requirements of insurers,
       [1912]
      subrogation, waiver of, [1915]
      tenant's covenants, [1912]
       [1913]
      tenant's interest, noting, [1915]
      warranty as to convictions,
       [1903]
     interest—
      meaning, [1813]
      rate, [1813]
     joint and several liability, [1815]
     keyholders, [1878]
     landlord—
      meaning, [1815]
      covenants, [1901] [1902]
      expenses, *meaning*, [1816]
      guarantor, covenants with,
       [1936]
      release, consent to, [1880]
      rights, exercise of, [1879]
      services, provision of, [1902]
     last year of term, *meaning*, [1815]
     liability period, *meaning*, [1816]
     losses, *meaning*, [1817]
     masts and wires, erection of,
      [1850]
     new or old, [1957]
     notices—
      deemed delivery, [1954]
      form and service of, [1953]
      joint recipients, [1954]
     nuisance, [1871]

OFFICE—*Cont*
  suite, lease of—*Cont*
    obstruction of windows, [1876]
    office covenants—
      meaning, [1817]
      ceiling and floor loading,
        [1976]
      cesser of business, [1975]
      common parts, [1976]
      heating, cooling and
        ventilation, [1978]
      machinery, [1977]
      nameplates or signs, [1978]
      noxious discharges, [1975]
      observance of, [1879]
      permitted hours, [1975]
      regulations, compliance with,
        [1978]
      sound audible outside, [1975]
      unloading, [1977]
      use, [1975]
      window cleaning, [1975]
    other buildings, *meaning*, [1818]
    parking bays—
      additional, [1818]
        right to use, [1971]
      included, [1818]
        covenants, [1847]
    parties, [1807]
    party walls, [1956]
    permitted hours, [1818]
    perpetuity period, [1956]
    plan, *meaning*, [1818]
    planning—
      appeals, [1874]
      charges and levies, [1873]
      completion of development,
        [1874]
      compliance with conditions,
        security for, [1874]
      consent for applications,
        [1873]
      permissions and notices,
        [1873]
      Planning Acts, compliance
        with, [1873]
      pre-conditions for
        development, [1874]
    Planning Acts—
      meaning, [1819]
      compliance with, [1873]

OFFICE—*Cont*
  suite, lease of—*Cont*
    premises—
      auctions, trades and immoral
        purposes, use for, [1871]
      combustible materials on,
        [1912]
      defect, notice of, [1878]
      definition, [1819]
      fire escapes, equipment and
        doors, [1912]
      fire-fighting equipment,
        provision of, [1912]
      interpretation, [1820]
      reinstatement, [1907]–[1911]
      residential use, sleeping and
        keeping of animals on, [1871]
    quiet enjoyment, [1901]
    reinstatement of premises—
      notice to terminate, [1911]
      obligation of, [1909]
      permissions, obligation to
        obtain, [1907]
      relief from obligation, [1910]
      termination following failure
        of, [1911]
    renewal, information for, [1875]
    rent—
      meaning, [1821]
      arrears, interest on, [1877]
      banker's order, payment by,
        [1843]
      commencement date, [1821]
      guarantor's covenants, [1932]
      initial, [1811]
      insurance, [1812] [1905]
      payment of, [1843]
      suspension, [1905] [1906]
    rent review—
      access on, [1973]
      dates, [1822]
      information for, [1875]
      sublease, [1863]
    repair—
      entry to inspect and notice to
        repair, [1852]
      landlord's power in default,
        [1853]
      tenant's covenants, [1846]
      works, carrying out, [1852]
    representations, [1951]
    right and easements, [1955]

OFFICE—*Cont*
suite, lease of—*Cont*
rights granted—
additional parking bays, use of, [1971]
adjoining conduits, passage and running through, [1971]
common parts, use of, [1971]
nameplates or signs, display of, [1971]
support and protection, [1971]
toilets, use of, [1971]
rights of access, references to, [1821]
rights reserved—
conduits, passage and running through, [1972]
construction of conduits, [1972]
new buildings, erection of, [1974]
renewal or rent review, access on, [1973]
right of access to inspect, [1973]
scaffolding, erection of, [1974]
support, [1974]
service charge—
meaning, [1822]
certificate of expenses, [1980] [1981]
deemed expenses, [1981]
definitions, [1979] [1980]
final account and adjustments, [1982]
first financial year, for, [1982]
landlord's contribution, [1982]
payment on account, [1982]
payment, [1981]
percentage, [1822]
variation of, [1981]
services, [1983]–[1985]
services—
meaning, [1822]
list of, [1983]–[1985]
obligations, performance of, [1879]
provision of, [1902]
relief from liability, [1902]
special, [1902]
variation and withholding, [1902]

OFFICE—*Cont*
suite, lease of—*Cont*
statutes, references to, [1821]
statutory notices, [1878]
statutory obligations of tenant—
general provisions, [1850]
particular, [1851]
sublease—
consent for, [1859]
enforcement, waiver and variation, [1862]
exclusion order, requirement for, [1862]
part, of, [1854]
rent review, [1863]
subtenant's direct covenants, [1862]
terms of, [1860]
surveyor, *meaning*, [1822]
tenant—
meaning, [1815]
capacity, [1957]
obligation not to permit or suffer, [1817]
property remaining in premises, [1952]
works, carrying out, [1852]
tenant's covenants—
aerials, signs and advertisements, [1850]
alienation, [1853]–[1863]
cleaning and tidying, [1847]
costs of applications, notices and recovery of arrears, payment of, [1872]
costs of grant, [1880]
decoration, [1847]
defective premises, [1878]
entry to inspect and notice to repair, [1852] [1853]
exercise of landlord's rights, permitting, [1879]
fixtures, replacement of, [1847]
included parking bays, as to, [1847]
indemnities, [1875]
interest on arrears, payment of, [1877]
keyholders, [1878]
landlord's release, consent to, [1880]
nuisance and residential restrictions, [1871]

OFFICE—*Cont*
  suite, lease of—*Cont*
    tenant's covenants—*Cont*
      obstruction and
        encroachment, [1876]
      office, observance of, [1879]
      outgoings and VAT, payment
        of, [1844] [1845]
      planning and development,
        [1873] [1874]
      plans, documents and
        information, [1875]
      reletting boards and viewing,
        [1876]
      rent, [1843]
      repair, [1846] [1847]
      replacement guarantor, [1879]
      service obligations,
        performance of, [1879]
      services, cost of, [1845]
      statutory notices, [1878]
      statutory obligations, [1850]
        [1851]
      viewing on sale of reversion,
        [1878]
      waiver, effect of, [1955]
      waste and alterations, [1848]
        [1849]
      yielding up, [1877]
    term, *meaning*, [1823]
    third party rights, exclusion of,
      [1951]
    VAT, *meaning*, [1823]
    warranty as to use, exclusion of,
      [1951]
    waste, [1848]
  whole building, lease of—
    meaning, [1614]
    1954 Act—
      meaning, [1615]
      exclusion of provisions, [1743]
    1995 Act—
      meaning, [1615]
      terms from, [1620]
    advertisements, fixing, [1648]
    alienation—
      assignment of whole, [1672]
      assignment, subletting and
        charging of part, [1671]
      charging of whole, [1677]
      circumstances for assignment,
        [1672]

OFFICE—*Cont*
  whole building, lease of—*Cont*
    alienation—*Cont*
      conditions for assignment,
        [1675]
      enforcement, waiver and
        variation of subleases, [1680]
      exclusion agreement,
        requirement for, [1680]
      group company, sharing with,
        [1682]
      permitted dealings, registration
        of, [1681]
      permitted sublease, terms of,
        [1677] [1678]
      prohibition of, [1671]
      sublease rent review, [1681]
      subletting of whole, [1677]
      subtenant's direct covenants,
        [1680]
    alterations—
      internal partitions, [1647]
      pre-conditions, [1647]
      prohibition, [1647]
      removal, [1648]
    approval—
      mortgagee or head landlord,
        of, [1613]
      prior written, [1612]
    assignment—
      circumstances for, [1672]
      conditions of, [1675]
      consent for, [1672]
      part, of, [1671]
      whole, of, [1672]
    auctions, trades and immoral
      purposes, use of premises for,
      [1682]
    charging—
      part, of, [1671]
      whole, of, [1677]
    clauses and schedules, references
      to, [1618]
    compensation on vacating,
      exclusion of, [1740]
    compliance with, evidence of,
      [1686]
    conduits—
      meaning, [1608]
      connection to, [1648]

OFFICE—*Cont*
  whole building, lease of—*Cont*
    consent—
      mortgagee or head landlord,
        of, [1613]
      prior written, [1612]
    contractual term, [1609]
    costs of grant, [1690]
    definitions and interpretation,
      [1608]–[1620]
    demise, [1641]
    development, *meaning*, [1610]
    disclaimer—
      new lease following, [1734]
      payments following, [1735]
    documents under hand, [1740]
    encroachments, [1687]
    end of term, *meaning*, [1613]
    exterior decorating years, *meaning*,
      [1610]
    forfeiture, [1737]
    gender and number, [1610]
    group company, sharing with,
      [1682]
    guarantor—
      meaning, [1613]
      authorised guarantee
       agreement, liabilities under,
       [1735]
      covenants, [1731]–[1736]
      landlord's covenants, [1736]
      replacement, [1689] [1690]
      severance of provisions, [1736]
    headings, [1610]
    insurance—
      application of moneys, [1714]
      change of risks, [1716]
      convictions, notice of, [1713]
      copy policy, [1715]
      covenant to insure, [1703]
      cover, [1704]
      events affecting policy, notice
       of, [1713]
      insured risks, [1611] [1705]
      landlord's covenants, [1715]
       [1716]
      office, underwriters and
       agency, [1703]
      policy avoidance and
       additional premiums, [1712]
      rent, [1611]
        payment of, [1705]

OFFICE—*Cont*
  whole building, lease of—*Cont*
    insurance—*Cont*
      requirements of insurers,
       [1712]
      subrogation, waiver of, [1716]
      tenant's covenants, [1712]–
       [1714]
      tenant's interest, noting, [1715]
      warranty as to convictions,
       [1702]
    interest—
      meaning, [1612]
      rate, [1612]
    interior decorating years, *meaning*,
      [1612]
    joint and several liability, [1614]
    keyholders, [1689]
    landlord—
      meaning, [1613]
      covenants, [1701]
      guarantor, covenants with,
       [1736]
      release, consent to, [1691]
      rights, exercise of, [1690]
    last year of term, *meaning*, [1613]
    liability period, *meaning*, [1614]
    losses, *meaning*, [1615]
    masts and wires, erection of,
      [1648]
    new or old, [1743]
    notices—
      deemed delivery, [1742]
      form and service of, [1741]
      joint recipients, [1742]
    nuisance, [1682]
    obstruction of windows, [1687]
    office covenants—
      meaning, [1616]
      ceiling and floor loading,
       [1763]
      cesser of business, [1762]
      machinery, [1763]
      noxious discharges, [1762]
      observance of, [1690]
      signs, [1763]
      sound audible outside, [1762]
      use, [1762]
      window cleaning, [1762]
    parties, [1606]
    permitted use, [1616]

OFFICE—*Cont*
  whole building, lease of—*Cont*
  plan, *meaning*, [1616]
  planning—
      appeals, [1685]
      charges and levies, [1684]
      completion of development,
        [1685]
      compliance with conditions,
        security for, [1685]
      consent for applications,
        [1684]
      permissions and notices,
        [1684]
      Planning Acts, compliance
        with, [1684]
      pre-conditions for
        development, [1684]
  Planning Acts—
      meaning, [1616]
      compliance with, [1684]
  premises—
      auctions, trades and immoral
        purposes, use for, [1682]
      combustible materials on,
        [1713]
      defect, notice of, [1689]
      definition, [1617]
      fire escapes, equipment and
        doors, [1713]
      fire-fighting equipment,
        provision of, [1712]
      interpretation, [1617]
      reinstatement, [1708]–[1711]
      residential use, sleeping and
        keeping of animals on, [1682]
  quiet enjoyment, [1701]
  reinstatement of premises—
      notice to terminate, [1711]
      obligation of, [1709]
      permissions, obligation to
        obtain, [1708]
      refusal of money through
        default on, [1714]
      relief from obligation, [1710]
      termination following failure
        of, [1711]
  renewal, information for, [1686]
  rent—
      meaning, [1618]
      arrears, interest on, [1688]
      banker's order, payment by,
        [1642]

OFFICE—*Cont*
  whole building, lease of—*Cont*
  rent—*Cont*
      commencement date, [1618]
      guarantor's covenants, [1732]
      initial, [1610]
      insurance, [1611] [1705]
      payment of, [1642]
      suspension, [1706] [1707]
  rent review—
      access on, [1761]
      dates, [1619]
      information for, [1686]
      sublease, [1681]
  repair—
      entry to inspect and notice to
        repair, [1650]
      landlord's power in default,
        [1650]
      tenant's covenants, [1644]
      works, carrying out, [1650]
  representations, [1739]
  rights of access, references to,
    [1618]
  rights reserved—
      access, [1761]
      right of entry to inspect, [1761]
  statutes, references to, [1618]
  statutory notices, [1688]
  statutory obligations of tenant—
      general provisions, [1649]
      particular, [1649]
  sublease—
      consent for, [1677]
      enforcement, waiver and
        variation, [1680]
      exclusion agreement,
        requirement for, [1680]
      part, of, [1671]
      rent review, [1681]
      subtenant's direct covenants,
        [1680]
      terms of, [1677] [1678]
  surveyor, *meaning*, [1619]
  tenant—
      meaning, [1613]
      capacity, [1743]
      property remaining in
        premises, [1740]
  tenant's covenants—
      abutting land, care of, [1645]
      aerials, signs and
        advertisements, [1648]

OFFICE—*Cont*
  whole building, lease of—*Cont*
    tenant's covenants—*Cont*
      alienation, [1671]–[1682]
      cleaning and tidying, [1645]
      costs of applications, notices
        and recovery of arrears,
        payment of, [1683]
      costs of grant, [1690]
      decoration, [1646]
      defective premises, [1689]
      entry to inspect and notice to
        repair, [1650]
      exercise of landlord's rights,
        permitting, [1690]
      fixtures, replacement of,
        [1645]
      indemnities, [1686]
      interest on arrears, payment of,
        [1688]
      keyholders, [1689]
      landlord's release, consent to,
        [1691]
      nuisance and residential
        restrictions, [1682]
      obstruction and
        encroachment, [1687]
      office, observance of, [1690]
      open land, as to, [1645]
      outgoings and VAT, payment
        of, [1643]
      planning and development,
        [1684] [1685]
      plans, documents and
        information, [1686]
      reletting boards and viewing,
        [1687]
      rent, [1642]
      repair, [1644]–[1646]
      replacement guarantor, [1689]
        [1690]
      services, cost of, [1643]
      shared facilities, [1646]
      statutory notices, [1688]
      statutory obligations, [1649]
      viewing on sale of reversion,
        [1689]
      waste and alterations, [1647]
        [1648]
      yielding up, [1688]
    term, *meaning*, [1620]
    third party rights, exclusion of,
      [1739]

OFFICE—*Cont*
  whole building, lease of—*Cont*
    VAT, *meaning*, [1620]
    warranty as to use, exclusion of,
      [1739]
    waste, [1647]

RENT REVIEW
  hotel, lease of. *See* HOTEL
  office, lease of. *See* OFFICE
  shop, lease of. *See* SHOP
  warehouse, lease of. *See* LIGHT
    INDUSTRIAL AND WAREHOUSE PREMISES

SHOP
  forming part of parade, lease with
  maisonette—
    meaning, [1115]
    1954 Act—
      meaning, [1117]
      exclusion of provisions, [1238]
    1995 Act—
      meaning, [1117]
      terms from, [1123]
    adjoining occupiers, disputes with,
      [1236]
    adjoining property—
      meaning, [1109]
      covenants relating to, [1236]
    advertisements, fixing, [1138]
    alienation—
      assignment of whole, [1151]
      assignment, subletting and
        charging of part, [1141]
      charging of whole, [1155]
      circumstances for assignment,
        [1151]
      conditions of assignment,
        [1153]
      enforcement, waiver and
        variation of subleases, [1158]
      exclusion order, requirement
        for, [1158]
      group company, sharing with,
        [1159]
      permitted dealings, registration
        of, [1159]
      permitted sublease, terms of,
        [1156]
      prohibition of, [1141]
      sublease rent review, [1159]
      subletting of whole, [1155]
      subtenant's direct covenants,
        [1158]

SHOP—*Cont*
  forming part of parade, lease with
    maisonette—*Cont*
    alterations—
      preconditions, [1137]
      prohibition, [1137]
      removal, [1138]
    approval—
      mortgagee or head landlord,
        of, [1114]
      prior written, [1114]
    assignment—
      circumstances for, [1151]
      conditions of, [1153]
      consent for, [1151]
      part, of, [1141]
      whole, of, [1151]
    auctions, trades and immoral
     purposes, use of premises for,
     [1160]
    charging—
      part, of, [1141]
      whole, of, [1155]
    clauses and schedules, references
     to, [1121]
    common parts—
      meaning, [1109]
      care of, [1245]
    compensation on vacating,
     exclusion of, [1234]
    competing trades, prohibition of,
     [1192]
    compliance with, evidence of,
     [1173]
    conduits—
      meaning, [1109]
      adjoining, [1109]
        passage and running
         through, [1239]
      connection to, [1138]
      passage and running through,
       [1240]
      right to construct, [1240]
    consent—
      mortgagee or head landlord,
        of, [1114]
      prior written, [1114]
    contractual term, [1110]
    costs of grant, [1177]
    decorating years, *meaning*, [1111]
    definitions and interpretation,
     [1109]–[1123]

SHOP—*Cont*
  forming part of parade, lease with
    maisonette—*Cont*
    demise, [1131]
    development, *meaning*, [1111]
    disclaimer—
      new lease following, [1224]
      payments following, [1225]
    documents under hand, [1234]
    encroachments, [1174]
    end of term, *meaning*, [1115]
    exclusion of liability, [1237]
    forfeiture, [1231]
    gender and number, [1111]
    group company, sharing with,
     [1159]
    guarantor—
      meaning, [1114]
      authorised guarantee
        agreement, liabilities under,
        [1225]
      covenants, [1221]–[1226]
      landlord's, covenants with,
        [1226]
      replacement, [1176] [1177]
      severance of provisions, [1226]
  headings, [1111]
  insurance—
    application of moneys, [1202]
    change of risks, [1204]
    convictions, notice of, [1202]
    copy policy, [1203]
    covenant to insure, [1193]
    cover, [1194]
    events affecting policy, notice
     of, [1202]
    insured risks, [1112] [1195]
    landlord's covenants, [1203]
     [1204]
    office, underwriters and
     agency, [1194]
    policy avoidance and
     additional premiums, [1201]
    rent, [1112]
      payment of, [1195]
    requirements of insurers,
     [1201]
    subrogation, waiver of, [1204]
    tenant's covenants, [1201]–
     [1203]
    tenant's interest, noting, [1204]
    warranty as to convictions,
     [1193]

SHOP—*Cont*
  forming part of parade, lease with
    maisonette—*Cont*
      interest—
        meaning, [1113]
        rate, [1113]
      joint and several liability, [1115]
      keyholders, [1176]
      landlord—
        meaning, [1115]
        covenants, [1191] [1192]
        guarantor, covenants with,
          [1226]
        release, consent to, [1178]
        rights, exercise of, [1177]
      last year of term, *meaning*, [1115]
      liability period, *meaning*, [1116]
      losses, *meaning*, [1117]
      masts and wires, erection of,
        [1138]
      new or old, [1238]
      notices—
        deemed delivery, [1235]
        form and service of, [1235]
        joint recipients, [1236]
      nuisance, [1160]
      obstruction of windows, [1174]
      other buildings, *meaning*, [1118]
      parade—
        meaning, [1118]
        decoration, [1192]
        maintenance of, [1192]
      parties, [1107]
      party walls, [1237]
      passageway, *meaning*, [1118]
      permitted use, [1118]
      perpetuity period, [1237]
      plan, *meaning*, [1119]
      planning—
        appeals, [1172]
        charges and levies, [1171]
        completion of development,
          [1172]
        compliance with conditions,
          security for, [1172]
        consent for applications,
          [1171]
        permissions and notices,
          [1171]
        Planning Acts, compliance
          with, [1171]
        pre-conditions for
          development, [1172]

SHOP—*Cont*
  forming part of parade, lease with
    maisonette—*Cont*
      Planning Acts—
        meaning, [1119]
        compliance with, [1171]
      premises—
        auctions, trades and immoral
          purposes, use for, [1160]
        combustible materials on,
          [1201]
        defect, notice of, [1176]
        definition, [1119]
        fire escapes, equipment and
          doors, [1202]
        fire-fighting equipment,
          provision of, [1201]
        interpretation, [1120]
        reinstatement, [1197]–[1200]
        residential use, sleeping and
          keeping of animals on,
          [1161]
      provisional charge—
        excess or shortfall, [1250]
        final notice, [1250]
        notice, service of, [1250]
        payment of, [1250]
        unpaid, [1192]
      quiet enjoyment, [1191]
      reinstatement of premises—
        notice to terminate, [1200]
        obligation of, [1198]
        permissions, obligation to
          obtain, [1197]
        refusal of money through
          default on, [1203]
        relief from obligation, [1199]
        termination following failure
          of, [1200]
      renewal, information for, [1173]
      rent—
        meaning, [1121]
        arrears, interest on, [1175]
        banker's order, payment by,
          [1132]
        commencement date, [1122]
        guarantor's covenants, [1222]
        initial, [1111]
        insurance, [1112] [1195]
        payment of, [1132]
        suspension, [1196]

SHOP—*Cont*
 forming part of parade, lease with
  maisonette—*Cont*
  rent review—
   access on, [1241]
   dates, [1122]
   information for, [1173]
   sublease, [1159]
  repair—
   entry to inspect and notice to
    repair, [1140]
   landlord's power in default,
    [1140]
   tenant's covenants, [1134]
   works, carrying out, [1140]
  representations, [1233]
  rights and easements, [1236]
  rights granted—
   adjoining conduits, passage
    and running through, [1239]
   common parts, right to use,
    [1239]
   rights of way, [1239]
   support, [1239]
  rights of access, references to,
   [1121]
  rights reserved—
   access, [1241]
   conduits, passage and running
    through, [1240]
   construction of conduits,
    [1240]
   new buildings, right to erect,
    [1242]
   scaffolding, erection of, [1242]
   support and shelter, [1242]
  road, *meaning*, [1122]
  shop and maisonette covenants—
   meaning, [1122]
   ceiling and floor loading,
    [1248]
   common parts, care of, [1245]
   damage precautions, [1245]
   exterior lights and awnings,
    [1244]
   external displays, [1244]
   fitting out, [1249]
   flashing lights, [1244]
   hours of trading, [1246]
   landlord's expenditure, [1245]
   loading and unloading, [1249]
   noisy machinery, [1244]

SHOP—*Cont*
 forming part of parade, lease with
  maisonette—*Cont*
  shop and maisonette covenants—
   Cont
   noxious discharges, [1244]
   plate glass, [1248]
   sound audible outside, [1244]
   use, [1243] [1244]
   window cleaning, [1244]
   window dressing and displays,
    [1247]
  staircase, *meaning*, [1122]
  statutes, references to, [1121]
  statutory notices, [1176]
  statutory obligations of tenant—
   general provisions, [1139]
   particular, [1139]
  sublease—
   consent for, [1155]
   enforcement, waiver and
    variation, [1158]
   exclusion order, requirement
    for, [1158]
   part, of, [1141]
   rent review, [1159]
   subtenant's direct covenants,
    [1158]
   terms of, [1156]
  surveyor, *meaning*, [1123]
  tenant—
   meaning, [1115]
   capacity, [1238]
   property remaining in
    premises, [1234]
  tenant's covenants—
   abutting land, care of, [1135]
   aerials, signs and
    advertisements, [1138]
   alienation, [1141]–[1159]
   cleaning and tidying, [1135]
   costs of applications, notices
    and recovery of arrears,
    payment of, [1161]
   costs of grant, [1177]
   decoration, [1136]
   defective premises, [1176]
   entry to inspect and notice to
    repair, [1140]
   exercise of landlord's rights,
    permitting, [1177]

SHOP—*Cont*
   forming part of parade, lease with
      maisonette—*Cont*
      tenant's covenants—*Cont*
         fixtures, replacement of,
            [1135]
         indemnities, [1173]
         interest on arrears, payment of,
            [1175]
         keyholders, [1176]
         landlord's release, consent to,
            [1178]
         nuisance and residential
            restrictions, [1160] [1161]
         obstruction and
            encroachment, [1174]
         open land, as to, [1135]
         outgoings and VAT, payment
            of, [1133]
         planning and development,
            [1171] [1172]
         plans, documents and
            information, [1173]
         reletting boards and viewing,
            [1174]
         rent, [1132]
         repair, [1134]
         replacement guarantor, [1176]
            [1177]
         services, cost of, [1134]
         shared facilities, [1136]
         statutory notices, [1176]
         statutory obligations, [1139]
         viewing on sale of reversion,
            [1176]
         waste and alterations, [1137]
            [1138]
         yielding up, [1175]
      term, *meaning*, [1123]
      third party rights, exclusion of,
         [1233]
      VAT, *meaning*, [1123]
      waiver of covenants, effect of,
         [1237]
      warranty as to use, exclusion of,
         [1233]
      waste, [1137]
   lease with or without yard, landlord
      not owning adjoining property—
      meaning, [962]
      1954 Act—
         meaning, [964]
         exclusion of provisions, [1063]

SHOP—*Cont*
   lease with or without yard, landlord
      not owning adjoining property—
      Cont
      1995 Act—
         meaning, [964]
         terms from, [969]
      advertisements, fixing, [987]
      alienation—
         assignment of whole, [1002]
         assignment, subletting and
            charging of part, [1001]
         charging of whole, [1006]
         circumstances for assignment,
            [1002]
         conditions of assignment,
            [1004]
         enforcement, waiver and
            variation of subleases, [1009]
         exclusion order, requirement
            for, [1009]
         group company, sharing with,
            [1010]
         permitted dealings, registration
            of, [1010]
         permitted sublease, terms of,
            [1006] [1007]
         prohibition of, [1001]
         sublease rent review, [1010]
         subletting, [1006]
         subtenant's direct covenants,
            [1009]
      alterations—
         pre-conditions, [986]
         prohibition, [986]
         removal, [987]
      approval—
         mortgagee or head landlord,
            of, [961]
         prior written, [961]
      assignment—
         circumstances for, [1002]
         conditions of, [1004]
         consent for, [1002]
         part, of, [1001]
         whole, of, [1002]
      auctions, trades and immoral
         purposes, use of premises for,
         [1011]
      charging—
         part, of, [1001]
         whole, of, [1006]

SHOP—*Cont*
  lease with or without yard, landlord
  not owning adjoining property—
  Cont
    clauses and schedules, references
      to, [967]
    compensation on vacating,
      exclusion of, [1060]
    compliance with, evidence of,
      [1015]
    conduits—
      meaning, [957]
      connection to, [987]
    consent—
      mortgagee or head landlord,
        of, [961]
      prior written, [961]
    contractual term, [957]
    costs of grant, [1019]
    definitions and interpretation,
      [957]–[969]
    demise, [981]
    development, *meaning*, [958]
    disclaimer—
      new lease following, [1054]
      payments following, [1055]
    documents under hand, [1060]
    encroachments, [1016]
    end of term, *meaning*, [962]
    exterior decorating years, *meaning*,
      [958]
    forfeiture, [1057]
    gender and number, [958]
    group company, sharing with,
      [1010]
    guarantor—
      meaning, [961]
      authorised guarantee
        agreement, guarantee of
        liabilities under, [1055]
      covenants, [1051]–[1056]
      landlord's covenants with,
        [1056]
      replacement, [1018]
      severance of provisions, [1056]
    headings, [958]
    insurance—
      application of moneys, [1041]
      change of risks, [1043]
      convictions, notice of, [1041]
      copy policy, [1042]
      covenant to insure, [1032]

SHOP—*Cont*
  lease with or without yard, landlord
  not owning adjoining property—
  Cont
    insurance—*Cont*
      cover, [1033]
      events affecting policy, notice
        of, [1041]
      insured risks, [959] [1033]
      landlord's covenants, [1042]
        [1043]
      office, underwriters and
        agency, [1033]
      policy avoidance and
        additional premiums, [1040]
      rent, [959]
        payment of, [1034]
      requirements of insurers,
        [1040]
      subrogation, waiver of, [1043]
      tenant's covenants, [1040]
        [1041]
      tenant's interest, noting, [1043]
      warranty as to convictions,
        [1032]
    interest—
      meaning, [960]
      rate, [960]
    interior decorating years, *meaning*,
      [961]
    joint and several liability, [962]
    keyholders, [1017]
    landlord—
      meaning, [962]
      covenants, [1031]
      guarantor, covenants with,
        [1056]
      release, consent to, [1019]
      rights, exercise of, [1019]
    last year of term, *meaning*, [962]
    liability period, *meaning*, [963]
    losses, *meaning*, [964]
    masts and wires, erection of, [987]
    new or old, [1062]
    notices—
      deemed delivery, [1061] [1062]
      form and service of, [1061]
      joint recipients, [1062]
    nuisance, [1011]
    obstruction of windows, [1016]

SHOP—*Cont*
　　lease with or without yard, landlord
　　not owning adjoining property—
　　Cont
　　　parties, [955]
　　　permitted use, [965]
　　　plan, *meaning*, [965]
　　　planning—
　　　　appeals, [1014]
　　　　charges and levies, [1013]
　　　　completion of development,
　　　　　[1014]
　　　　compliance with conditions,
　　　　　security for, [1014]
　　　　consent for applications,
　　　　　[1013]
　　　　permissions and notices,
　　　　　[1013]
　　　　Planning Acts, compliance
　　　　　with, [1013]
　　　　pre-conditions for
　　　　　development, [1013]
　　　Planning Acts—
　　　　meaning, [965]
　　　　compliance with, [1013]
　　　premises—
　　　　auctions, trades and immoral
　　　　　purposes, use for, [1011]
　　　　combustible materials on,
　　　　　[1040]
　　　　defect, notice of, [1018]
　　　　definition, [966]
　　　　fire escapes, equipment and
　　　　　doors, [1041]
　　　　fire-fighting equipment,
　　　　　provision of, [1040]
　　　　interpretation, [966]
　　　　reinstatement, [1035]–[1039]
　　　　residential use, sleeping and
　　　　　keeping of animals on, [1011]
　　　quiet enjoyment, [1031]
　　　reinstatement of premises—
　　　　notice to terminate, [1039]
　　　　obligation of, [1037]
　　　　permissions, obligation to
　　　　　obtain, [1035]
　　　　refusal of money through
　　　　　default on, [1042]
　　　　relief from obligation, [1038]
　　　　termination following failure
　　　　　of, [1039]
　　　renewal, information for, [1015]

SHOP—*Cont*
　　lease with or without yard, landlord
　　not owning adjoining property—
　　Cont
　　　rent—
　　　　meaning, [967]
　　　　arrears, interest on, [1017]
　　　　banker's order, payment by,
　　　　　[982]
　　　　commencement date, [968]
　　　　guarantor's covenants, [1052]
　　　　initial, [958]
　　　　insurance, [959] [1034]
　　　　payment of, [982]
　　　　suspension, [1034] [1035]
　　　rent review—
　　　　access on, [1064]
　　　　dates, [968]
　　　　information for, [1015]
　　　　sublease, [1010]
　　　repair—
　　　　entry to inspect and notice to
　　　　　repair, [989]
　　　　landlord's power in default,
　　　　　[989]
　　　　tenant's covenants, [984]
　　　　works, carrying out, [989]
　　　representations, [1059]
　　　rights of access, references to,
　　　　[967]
　　　rights reserved—
　　　　access, [1064]
　　　　right of entry to inspect,
　　　　　[1064]
　　　shop covenants—
　　　　meaning, [968]
　　　　ceiling and floor loading,
　　　　　[1068]
　　　　exterior lights and awnings,
　　　　　[1065]
　　　　external displays, [1065]
　　　　fitting out, [1068]
　　　　flashing lights, [1065]
　　　　hours of trading, [1066]
　　　　noisy machinery, [1065]
　　　　noxious discharges, [1065]
　　　　observance of, [1019]
　　　　plate glass, [1068]
　　　　sound audible outside, [1065]
　　　　use, [1065]
　　　　window cleaning, [1065]
　　　　window dressing and displays,
　　　　　[1067]

SHOP—*Cont*
  lease with or without yard, landlord
    not owning adjoining property—
    Cont
    statutes, references to, [967]
    statutory notices, [1017]
    statutory obligations of tenant—
      general provisions, [988]
      particular, [988]
    sublease—
      consent for, [1006]
      enforcement, waiver and
        variation, [1009]
      exclusion order, requirement
        for, [1009]
      part, of, [1001]
      rent review, [1010]
      subtenant's direct covenants,
        [1009]
      terms of, [1006] [1007]
    surveyor, *meaning*, [969]
    tenant—
      meaning, [962]
      capacity, [1063]
      property remaining in
        premises, [1060]
    tenant's covenants—
      abutting land, care of, [985]
      aerials, signs and
        advertisements, [987]
      alienation, [1001]–[1010]
      cleaning and tidying, [984]
      costs of applications, notices
        and recovery of arrears,
        payment of, [1012]
      costs of grant, [1019]
      decoration, [985]
      defective premises, [1018]
      entry to inspect and notice to
        repair, [989]
      exercise of landlord's rights,
        permitting, [1019]
      fixtures, replacement of, [984]
      indemnities, [1015]
      interest on arrears, payment of,
        [1017]
      keyholders, [1017]
      landlord's release, consent to,
        [1019]
      nuisance and residential
        restrictions, [1011]
      obstruction and
        encroachment, [1016]

SHOP—*Cont*
  lease with or without yard, landlord
    not owning adjoining property—
    Cont
    tenant's covenants—*Cont*
      open land, as to, [985]
      outgoings and VAT, payment
        of, [983]
      planning and development,
        [1013] [1014]
      plans, documents and
        information, [1015]
      reletting boards and viewing,
        [1016]
      rent, [982]
      repair, [984]–[986]
      replacement guarantor, [1018]
      services, cost of, [983]
      shared facilities, [986]
      shop, observance of, [1019]
      statutory notices, [1017]
      statutory obligations, [988]
      viewing on sale of reversion,
        [1018]
      waste and alterations, [986]
        [987]
      yielding up, [1017]
    term, *meaning*, [969]
    third party rights, exclusion of,
      [1059]
    VAT, *meaning*, [969]
    warranty as to use, exclusion of,
      [1059]
    waste, [986]
  shopping centre, lease in—
    meaning, [1322]
    1954 Act—
      meaning, [1324]
      exclusion of provisions, [1476]
    1995 Act—
      meaning, [1324]
      terms from, [1343]
    accountant, *meaning*, [1308]
    adjoining occupiers, disputes with,
      [1474]
    adjoining property—
      meaning, [1309]
      covenants relating to, [1474]
    advertisements, fixing, [1368]
    alienation—
      assignment of whole, [1382]
      assignment, subletting and
        charging of part, [1381]

SHOP—*Cont*
  shopping centre, lease in—*Cont*
    alienation—*Cont*
      charging of whole, [1386]
      circumstances for assignment,
        [1382]
      conditions of assignment,
        [1384]
      enforcement, waiver and
        variation of subleases, [1389]
      exclusion agreement,
        requirement for, [1389]
      group company, sharing with,
        [1391]
      permitted dealings, registration
        of, [1390]
      permitted sublease, terms of,
        [1387]
      prohibition of, [1381]
      sublease rent review, [1390]
      subletting, [1386]
      subtenant's direct covenants,
        [1389]
    alterations—
      preconditions, [1367]
      prohibition, [1367]
      removal, [1368]
    approval—
      mortgagee or head landlord,
        of, [1321]
      prior written, [1321]
    assignment—
      circumstances for, [1382]
      conditions of, [1384]
      consent for, [1382]
      part, of, [1381]
      whole, of, [1382]
    auctions, trades and immoral
      purposes, use of premises for,
      [1391]
    centre—
      meaning, [1309]
      interpretation, [1321]
    charging—
      part, of, [1381]
      whole, of, [1386]
    clauses and schedules, references
      to, [1327]
    common parts—
      meaning, [1309]
      care of, [1499]
      right to use, [1491]

SHOP—*Cont*
  shopping centre, lease in—*Cont*
    compensation on vacating,
      exclusion of, [1472]
    compliance with, evidence of,
      [1402]
    conduits—
      meaning, [1309]
      adjoining, [1308]
        passage and running
          through, [1491]
      connection to, [1368]
      passage and running through,
        [1492]
      right to construct, [1492]
    consent—
      mortgagee or head landlord,
        of, [1321]
      prior written, [1321]
    contractual term, [1310]
    costs of grant, [1407]
    decorating years, *meaning*, [1311]
    definitions and interpretation,
      [1308]–[1343]
    demise, [1361]
    development, *meaning*, [1311]
    disclaimer—
      new lease following, [1454]
      payments following, [1455]
    documents under hand, [1472]
    encroachments, [1404]
    end of term, *meaning*, [1322]
    external parts, *meaning*, [1321]
    forfeiture, [1457]
    gender and number, [1311]
    group company, sharing with,
      [1391]
    guarantor—
      meaning, [1322]
      authorised guarantee
        agreement, liabilities under,
        [1455]
      covenants, [1441]–[1456]
      landlord's covenants, [1456]
      replacement, [1406]
      severance of provisions, [1456]
    headings, [1311]
    insurance—
      application of moneys, [1432]
      change of risks, [1434]
      convictions, notice of, [1432]
      copy policy, [1433]

SHOP—*Cont*
  shopping centre, lease in—*Cont*
    insurance—*Cont*
      covenant to insure, [1423]
      cover, [1424]
      events affecting policy, notice
        of, [1432]
      insured risks, [1312] [1424]
      landlord's covenants, [1433]
        [1434]
      office, underwriters and
        agency, [1424]
      policy avoidance and
        additional premiums, [1431]
      rent percentage, [1312]
        variation of, [1433]
      rent, [1312]
        payment of, [1425]
      requirements of insurers,
        [1431]
      subrogation, waiver of, [1434]
      tenant's covenants, [1431]
        [1432]
      tenant's interest, noting, [1434]
      warranty as to convictions,
        [1423]
    interest—
      meaning, [1313]
      rate, [1313]
    joint and several liability, [1322]
    keyholders, [1406]
    landlord—
      meaning, [1322]
      covenants, [1421] [1422]
      exclusion of liability, [1475]
      expenses, [1322]
      guarantor, covenants with,
        [1456]
      release, consent to, [1408]
      rights, exercise of, [1407]
      services, provision of, [1422]
    last year of term, *meaning*, [1322]
    liability period, *meaning*, [1323]
    losses, *meaning*, [1324]
    masts and wires, erection of,
      [1368]
    new or old, [1476]
    notices—
      deemed delivery, [1473]
      form and service of, [1473]
      joint recipients, [1474]

SHOP—*Cont*
  shopping centre, lease in—*Cont*
    nuisance, [1391]
    obstruction of windows, [1404]
    parties, [1306]
    party walls, [1475]
    permitted use, [1325]
    perpetuity period, [1475]
    plan, *meaning*, [1325]
    planning—
      appeals, [1402]
      charges and levies, [1401]
      completion of development,
        [1402]
      compliance with conditions,
        security for, [1402]
      consent for applications,
        [1401]
      permissions and notices,
        [1401]
      Planning Acts, compliance
        with, [1401]
      pre-conditions for
        development, [1402]
    Planning Acts—
      meaning, [1325]
      compliance with, [1401]
    premises—
      meaning, [1326]
      auctions, trades and immoral
        purposes, use for, [1391]
      combustible materials on,
        [1431]
      defect, notice of, [1406]
      fire escapes, equipment and
        doors, [1432]
      fire-fighting equipment,
        provision of, [1431]
      reinstatement, [1427]–[1430]
      residential use, sleeping and
        keeping of animals on, [1392]
    prohibited uses, [1327]
    quiet enjoyment, [1421]
    reinstatement of premises—
      notice to terminate, [1430]
      obligation of, [1428]
      permissions, obligation to
        obtain, [1427]
      relief from obligation, [1429]
      termination following failure
        of, [1430]
    renewal, information for, [1403]

SHOP—*Cont*
  shopping centre, lease in—*Cont*
    rent—
      meaning, [1341]
      arrears, interest on, [1405]
      banker's order, payment by,
        [1362]
      commencement date, [1341]
      guarantor's covenants, [1452]
      initial, [1312]
      insurance, [1312]
        payment of, [1425]
      payment of, [1362]
      suspension, [1425] [1426]
    rent review—
      access on, [1493]
      dates, [1341]
      information for, [1403]
      sublease, [1390]
    repair—
      entry to inspect and notice to
        repair, [1370]
      landlord's power in default,
        [1370]
      tenant's covenants, [1365]
        [1366]
      works, carrying out, [1370]
    representations, [1471]
    rights and easements, [1474]
    rights granted—
      adjoining conduits, passage
        and running through, [1491]
      common parts, right to use,
        [1491]
      support and protection, [1491]
    rights of access, references to,
      [1327]
    rights reserved—
      access, [1493]
      conduits, passage and running
        through, [1492]
      construction of conduits,
        [1492]
      new buildings, right to erect,
        [1494]
      scaffolding, erection of, [1494]
      support and shelter, [1494]
    service charge—
      meaning, [1342]
      certificate of expenses, [1504]–
        [1506]
      deemed expenses, [1505]

SHOP—*Cont*
  shopping centre, lease in—*Cont*
    service charge—*Cont*
      definitions, [1503] [1504]
      final account and adjustments,
        [1507]
      first financial year, in, [1507]
      landlord's contribution, [1506]
      payment, [1506]
      payment on account, [1507]
      percentage, [1342]
        variation of, [1506]
      services, [1508]–[1510]
    services—
      meaning, [1342]
      list of, [1508]–[1510]
      provision of, [1422]
      relief from liability, [1422]
      special, [1422]
      tenant's obligations, [1407]
      variation and withholding,
        [1422]
    shop covenants—
      meaning, [1342]
      ceiling and floor loading,
        [1500]
      cleaning and tidying, [1499]
      cooking, [1496]
      damage precautions, [1496]
      exterior lights and awnings,
        [1496]
      external displays, [1495]
      fitting out, [1502]
      flashing lights, [1496]
      heating, cooling and
        ventilation, [1502]
      hours of opening, [1497]
      loading and unloading, [1500]
        [1501]
      noisy machinery, [1495]
      noxious discharges, [1495]
      observance of, [1407]
      plate glass, [1502]
      regulations, compliance with,
        [1502]
      security, fire alarms and
        sprinkler, [1501]
      sound audible outside, [1495]
      use, [1495] [1496]
      window dressing and displays,
        [1498] [1499]

SHOP—*Cont*
  shopping centre, lease in—*Cont*
  shop opening hours, *meaning*,
    [1342]
  statutes, references to, [1327]
  statutory notices, [1405]
  statutory obligations of tenant—
    general provisions, [1369]
    particular, [1369]
  sublease—
    consent for, [1386]
    enforcement, waiver and
      variation, [1389]
    exclusion agreement,
      requirement for, [1389]
    part, of, [1381]
    rent review, [1390]
    subtenant's direct covenants,
      [1389]
    terms of, [1387]
  surveyor, *meaning*, [1342]
  tenant—
    meaning, [1322]
    capacity, [1476]
    property remaining in
      premises, [1472]
  tenant's covenants—
    abutting land, care of, [1366]
    aerials, signs and
      advertisements, [1368]
    alienation, [1381]–[1391]
    cleaning and tidying, [1366]
    costs of applications, notices
      and recovery of arrears,
      payment of, [1392]
    costs of grant, [1407]
    decoration, [1366]
    defective premises, [1406]
    entry to inspect and notice to
      repair, [1370]
    exercise of landlord's rights,
      permitting, [1407]
    fixtures, replacement of,
      [1365]
    indemnities, [1403]
    interest on arrears, payment of,
      [1405]
    keyholders, [1406]
    landlord's release, consent to,
      [1408]
    nuisance and residential
      restrictions, [1391] [1392]

SHOP—*Cont*
  shopping centre, lease in—*Cont*
  tenant's covenants—*Cont*
    obstruction and
      encroachment, [1404]
    outgoings and VAT, payment
      of, [1363] [1364]
    planning and development,
      [1401] [1402]
    plans, documents and
      information, [1403]
    reletting boards and viewing,
      [1404]
    rent, [1362]
    repair, [1365]
    replacement guarantor, [1406]
    services, as to, [1407]
    services, cost of, [1364]
    shop, observance of, [1407]
    statutory notices, [1405]
    statutory obligations, [1369]
    viewing on sale of reversion,
      [1406]
    waste and alterations, [1367]
      [1368]
    yielding up, [1405]
  term, *meaning*, [1343]
  third party rights, exclusion of,
    [1471]
  VAT, *meaning*, [1343]
  waiver of covenants, effect of,
    [1474]
  warranty as to use, exclusion of,
    [1471]
  waste, [1367]

TENANCY AT WILL
  meaning, [54]
  agreement—
    clauses, reference to, [56]
    costs, [64]
    declarations, [64]
    definitions and interpretation,
      [55]–[56]
    determination, [64]
    gender and number, [55]
    headings, [55]
    indemnity, [64]
    interior, *meaning*, [55]
    joint and several liability, [56]
    parties, [53]
    periodic tenancy, exclusion of,
      [62]

TENANCY AT WILL—*Cont*
  agreement—*Cont*
    permitted use, [56]
    premises, *meaning*, [56]
    recitals, [61]
    rent—
      meaning, [56]
      payment of, [62]
      refund on termination, [62]
      tenant's obligations, [62]
    tenancy, [61]
      meaning, [56]
    tenant's obligations—
      alterations, [63]
      disposal of premises, [63]
      entry, [63]
      nuisance, [63]
      occupation, [63]
      outgoings, payment of, [62]
      rent, payment of, [62]
      repair, [63]
      return of premises, [63]
      use, [63]
    use, exclusion of warranty, [64]
    VAT, *meaning*, [56]
  excluded lease, on termination of—
    clauses, reference to, [106]
    costs, [115]
    declarations, [114]
    definitions and interpretation,
      [105] [106]
    determination, [114]
    gender and number, [105]
    headings, [105]
    indemnity, [114]
    joint and several liability, [106]
    parties, [103]
    periodic tenancy, exclusion of,
      [112]
    premises, *meaning*, [106]
    recitals, [111]
    rent—
      meaning, [106]
      payment of, [112]
      refund on termination, [112]
      tenant's obligations, [112]
    tenancy, [106] [111]
    tenant's obligations—
      alterations, [113]
      disposal of premises, [113]
      entry, [113]
      nuisance, [113]

TENANCY AT WILL—*Cont*
  excluded lease, on termination of—
    Cont
    tenant's obligations—*Cont*
      occupation, [113]
      outgoings, payment of, [113]
      rent, payment of, [113]
      return of premises, [113]
      terms of lease, compliance
        with, [112112]
    use, exclusion of warranty, [115]
    VAT, *meaning*, [106]